S0-ARB-371

The Design and Implementation of the

FreeBSD® Operating System

Second Edition

The Design and Implementation of the

FreeBSD® Operating System

Second Edition

Marshall Kirk McKusick

George V. Neville-Neil

Robert N.M. Watson

Addison-Wesley

Upper Saddle River, NJ • Boston • Indianapolis • San Francisco
New York • Toronto • Montreal • London • Munich • Paris • Madrid
Capetown • Sydney • Tokyo • Singapore • Mexico City

For information about buying this title in bulk quantities, or for special sales opportunities (which may include electronic versions; custom cover designs; and content particular to your business, training goals, marketing focus, or branding interests), please contact our corporate sales department at corpsales@pearsoned.com or (800) 382-3419.

For government sales inquiries, please contact governmentsales@pearsoned.com.

For questions about sales outside the United States, please contact international@pearsoned.com

Visit us on the Web: informit.com/aw

Library of Congress Cataloging-in-Publication Data

McKusick, Marshall Kirk.
The design and implementation of the FreeBSD operating system / Marshall Kirk McKusick, George V. Neville-Neil, Robert N. M. Watson.
pages cm
Includes bibliographical references and index.
ISBN-13: 978-0-321-96897-5 (hardcover : alk. paper)
ISBN-10: 0-321-96897-2 (hardcover : alk. paper)
1. FreeBSD. 2. Free computer software. 3. Operating systems (Computers) I. Neville-Neil, George V. II. Watson, Robert N. M. III. Title.
QA76.774.F74M35 2014
005.4'32—dc23 2014020072

ISBN-13: 978-0-321-96897-5
ISBN-10: 0-321-96897-2
Text printed on recycled and acid-free paper at Courier in Westford, Massachusetts.
First Printing, September 2014

Dedication

This book is dedicated to the BSD community.
Without the contributions of that community's members,
there would be nothing about which to write.

Dedication

[illegible]

Contents

Preface

This book follows the earlier authoritative and full-length descriptions of the design and implementation of the 4.3BSD and 4.4BSD versions of the UNIX system developed at the University of California at Berkeley. Since the final Berkeley release in 1994, several groups have continued development of BSD. This book details FreeBSD, the system with the largest set of developers and the most widely distributed releases. Although the FreeBSD distribution includes nearly 1000 utility programs in its base system and nearly 25,000 optional utilities in its ports collection, this book concentrates almost exclusively on the kernel.

UNIX-like Systems

UNIX-like systems include the traditional vendor systems such as Solaris and HP-UX; the Linux-based distributions such as Red Hat, Debian, Suse, and Slackware; and the BSD-based distributions such as FreeBSD, NetBSD, OpenBSD, and Darwin. They run on computers ranging from smart phones to the largest supercomputers. They are the operating system of choice for most multiprocessor, graphics, and vector-processing systems, and are widely used for the original purpose of timesharing. The most common platform for providing network services (from FTP to WWW) on the Internet, they are collectively the most portable operating system ever developed. This portability is due partly to their implementation language, C [Kernighan & Ritchie, 1989] (which is itself a widely ported language), and partly to the elegant design of the system.

Since its inception in 1969 [Ritchie & Thompson, 1978], the UNIX system has developed in several divergent and rejoining streams. The original developers continued to advance the state of the art with their Ninth and Tenth Edition UNIX inside AT&T Bell Laboratories, and then their Plan 9 successor to UNIX. Meanwhile, AT&T licensed UNIX System V as a product before merging it with Sun Microsystem's BSD-based SunOS to produce Solaris. Ninth Edition UNIX, System V, and Solaris were all strongly influenced by the Berkeley Software

Distributions produced by the Computer Systems Research Group (CSRG) of the University of California at Berkeley. The Linux operating system, although developed independently of the other UNIX variants, implements the UNIX interface. Thus, applications developed to run on other UNIX-based platforms can be easily ported to run on Linux.

Berkeley Software Distributions

The distributions from Berkeley were the first UNIX-based systems to introduce many important features including the following:

- Demand-paged virtual-memory support
- Automatic configuration of the hardware and I/O system
- A fast and recoverable filesystem
- The socket-based interprocess-communication (IPC) primitives
- The reference implementation of TCP/IP

The Berkeley releases found their way into the UNIX systems of many vendors and were used internally by the development groups of many other vendors. The implementation of the TCP/IP networking protocol suite in 4.2BSD and 4.3BSD, and the availability of those systems, played a key role in making the TCP/IP networking protocol suite a world standard. Even the non-UNIX vendors such as Microsoft have adopted the Berkeley socket design in their Winsock IPC interface.

The BSD releases have also been a strong influence on the POSIX (IEEE Std 1003.1) operating-system interface standard, and on related standards. Several features—such as reliable signals, job control, multiple access groups per process, and the routines for directory operations—have been adapted from BSD for POSIX.

Early BSD releases contained licensed UNIX code, thus requiring recipients to have an AT&T source license to be able to obtain and use BSD. In 1988, Berkeley separated its distribution into AT&T-licensed and freely redistributable code. The freely redistributable code was licensed separately and could be obtained, used, and redistributed by anyone. The final freely redistributable 4.4BSD-Lite2 release from Berkeley in 1994 contained nearly the entire kernel and all the important libraries and utilities.

Two groups, NetBSD and FreeBSD, sprang up in 1993 to begin supporting and distributing systems built from the freely redistributable releases being done by Berkeley. The NetBSD group emphasized portability and the minimalist approach, porting the systems to nearly 60 platforms and they were determined to keep the system lean to aid embedded applications. The FreeBSD group emphasized maximal support for the PC architecture and pushed to ease installation for, and market their system to, as wide an audience as possible.

In 1995, the OpenBSD group split from the NetBSD group to develop a distribution that emphasized security. In 2003, the Dragonfly group split from the FreeBSD group to develop a distribution that used a significantly lighter-weight mechanism to support multiprocessing. Over the years, there has been a healthy competition among the BSD distributions, with many ideas and much code flowing between them.

Material Covered in this Book

This book is about the internal structure of the FreeBSD 11 kernel and about the concepts, data structures, and algorithms used in implementing FreeBSD's system facilities. The book covers FreeBSD from the system-call level down—from the interface to the kernel to the hardware itself. The kernel includes system facilities, such as process management, security, virtual memory, the I/O system, filesystems, the *socket* IPC mechanism, and network protocol implementations. Material above the system-call level—such as libraries, shells, commands, programming languages, and other user interfaces—is excluded, except for some material related to the terminal interface and to system startup. Following the organization first established by Organick's book about Multics [Organick, 1975], this book is an in-depth study of a contemporary operating system.

Where particular hardware is relevant, the book refers to the Intel 32-bit architecture and the similar AMD 64-bit architecture. Because FreeBSD has emphasized development on these architectures, they are the architectures with the most complete support and so provide a convenient point of reference.

Use by Computer Professionals

FreeBSD is widely used to support the core infrastructure of many companies worldwide. Because it can be built with a small footprint, it is also seeing increased use in embedded applications. The licensing terms of FreeBSD do not require the distribution of changes and enhancements to the system. The licensing terms of Linux require that all changes and enhancements to the kernel be made available in source form at minimal cost. Thus, companies that need to control the distribution of their intellectual property build their products using FreeBSD.

This book is of direct use to the professionals who work with FreeBSD systems. Individuals involved in technical and sales support can learn the capabilities and limitations of the system; applications developers can learn how to interface with the system effectively and efficiently; system administrators without direct experience with the FreeBSD kernel can learn how to maintain, tune, and configure the system; and systems programmers can learn how to extend, enhance, and interface with the system.

Readers who will benefit from this book include operating-system implementors, system programmers, UNIX application developers, administrators, and curious users. The book can be read as a companion to the source code of the system, falling as it does between the manual pages and the code in its level of detail. But this book is neither exclusively a UNIX programming manual nor a user tutorial. Familiarity with the use of some version of the UNIX system (see, for example, Stevens [1992]) and with the C programming language (see, for example, Kernighan & Ritchie [1989]) would be extremely useful. The FreeBSD Handbook gives a comprehensive introduction to the setting up, operation, and programming of FreeBSD [FreeBSD Mall, 2004; FreeBSD.org, 2014]. FreeBSD packaging, designed to be easy to install and use for both desktop and laptop users, is available in the PC-BSD distribution [Lavigne, 2010; PC-BSD.org, 2014].

Use in Courses on Operating Systems

This book is suitable for use as a reference text to provide background for a primary textbook in a first-level course on operating systems. It is not intended for use as an introductory operating-system textbook; the reader should have already encountered terminology such as "memory management," "process scheduling," and "I/O systems" [Silberschatz et al., 2012]. Familiarity with the concepts of network protocols [Comer, 2000; Stallings, 2000; Tanenbaum, 2010] will be useful for understanding some of the later chapters.

This book can be used in combination with a copy of the FreeBSD system for more advanced operating-systems courses. Students' assignments can include changes to, or replacements of, key system components such as the scheduler, the paging daemon, the filesystems, thread signalling, various networking layers, and I/O management. The ability to load, replace, and unload modules from a running kernel allows students to experiment without the need to compile and reboot the system. By working with a real operating system, students can directly measure and experience the effects of their changes. Because of the intense peer review and insistence on well-defined coding standards throughout its 35-year lifetime, the FreeBSD kernel is considerably cleaner, more modular, and thus easier to understand and modify than most software projects of its size and age. Sample course material is available at www.teachbsd.com (see description following the index).

Exercises are provided at the end of each chapter. The exercises are graded into three categories indicated by zero, one, or two asterisks. The answers to exercises that carry no asterisks can be found in the text. Exercises with a single asterisk require a step of reasoning, critical thinking, or intuition beyond a concept presented in the text. Exercises with two asterisks present major design projects or open research questions.

Organization

This text discusses both philosophical and design issues, as well as details of the system's actual implementation. Often, the discussion starts at the system-call level and descends into the kernel. Tables and figures are used to clarify data structures and control flow. Pseudocode similar to the C language displays algorithms. A bold font identifies program names and filesystem pathnames. A bold and italic font introduces glossary terms. An italic font identifies the names of system calls, variables, routines, and structure names. Routine names (other than system calls) are further identified by the name followed by parentheses (e.g., *malloc*() is the name of a routine, whereas *argv* is the name of a variable).

The book is divided into five parts, organized as follows:

- **Part I, Overview** Three introductory chapters provide the context for the complete operating system and for the rest of the book. Chapter 1, History and Goals, sketches the historical development of the system, emphasizing the system's research orientation. Chapter 2, Design Overview of FreeBSD, describes the services offered by the system and outlines the internal organization of the kernel. It also discusses the design decisions that were made as the system was developed. Sections 2.3 through 2.15 in Chapter 2 give an overview of their corresponding chapters. Chapter 3, Kernel Services, explains how system calls are performed and describes in detail several of the basic services of the kernel.

- **Part II, Processes** The first chapter in this part—Chapter 4, Process Management—lays the foundation for later chapters by describing the structure of a process, the algorithms used for scheduling the execution of the threads that make up a process, and the synchronization mechanisms used by the system to ensure consistent access to kernel-resident data structures. Chapter 5, Security, explains the security framework used throughout the kernel. It also details the security facilities that are available to control process access to the resources on the system and to each other. In Chapter 6, Memory Management, the virtual-memory-management system is discussed in detail.
- **Part III, I/O System** First, Chapter 7, I/O System Overview, explains the system interface to I/O and describes the structure of the facilities that support this interface. Following this introduction are four chapters that give the details of the main parts of the I/O system. Chapter 8, Devices, gives a description of the I/O architecture of the Intel and AMD systems, and describes how the I/O subsystem is managed and how the kernel initially maps out and later manages the arrival and departure of connected devices. Chapter 9, The Fast Filesystem, details the data structures and algorithms that implement the original local filesystem as seen by application programs, as well as how local filesystems are interfaced with the device interface described in Chapter 8. Chapter 10, The Zettabyte Filesystem, describes the filesystem most recently added to FreeBSD from the OpenSolaris operating system. Chapter 11, The Network Filesystem, explains the latest version 4.2 network filesystem from both the server and client perspectives.
- **Part IV, Interprocess Communication** Chapter 12, Interprocess Communication, describes the mechanism for providing communication between related or unrelated processes. Chapters 13 and 14, Network-Layer Protocols and Transport-Layer Protocols, are closely related because the facilities explained in the former are used by the protocols, such as the UDP, TCP, and SCTP, explained in the latter.
- **Part V, System Operation** Chapter 15, System Startup and Shutdown, explains system initialization at the process level from kernel initialization to user login.

The book is intended to be read in the order that the chapters are presented, but the parts other than Part I are independent of one another and can be read separately. Chapter 15 should be read after all the others, but knowledgeable readers may find it useful independently.

At the end of the book are a glossary with brief definitions of major terms and an index. Each chapter contains a Reference section with citations of related material.

Getting BSD

All the BSD distributions are available either for downloading from the net or on removable media such as CD-ROM or DVD. Information on obtaining source and binaries for FreeBSD can be obtained from http://www.FreeBSD.org. The NetBSD distribution is compiled and ready to run on most workstation architectures. For more information, contact the NetBSD Project at http://www.NetBSD.org/. The OpenBSD distribution is compiled and ready to run on a wide variety of workstation architectures and has been extensively vetted for security and reliability. For more information, visit the OpenBSD project's Web site at http://www.OpenBSD.org/.

You diehards that read to the end of the preface are rewarded by finding out that you can get a 32-hour introductory video course based on this book, a 40-hour advanced video course based on the FreeBSD 5 source code, a 2.5-hour video lecture on the history of BSD, and a 4-CD set containing all the releases and the source-control history of BSD from Berkeley. These items are described in the advertisements that follow the index.

Acknowledgments

We extend special thanks to Matt Ahrens (Delphix) who provided invaluable insight on the workings of the ZFS filesystem including countless e-mails answering our questions about how it works and why specific design decisions were made.

We also thank the following people who provided extensive review of areas of the kernel in which they have deep knowledge: John Baldwin (The FreeBSD Project) on locking, scheduling, and virtual memory; Alan Cox (Rice University) on virtual memory; Jeffrey Roberson (EMC) on the ULE scheduler; and Randall Stewart (Adara Networks) on the SCTP implementation.

We thank the following people, all of whom read and commented on early drafts of various chapters of the book: Jonathan Anderson (Memorial University of Newfoundland); David Chisnall (University of Cambridge); Paul Dagnelie (Delphix); Brooks Davis (SRI International); Paweł Jakub Dawidek (Wheel Systems); Peter Grehan (The FreeBSD Project); Scott Long (Netflix); Jake Luck; Rick Macklem (The FreeBSD Project); Ilias Marinos (University of Cambridge); Roger Pau Monné (Citrex); Mark Robert Vaughan Murray; Edward Tomasz Napierała (The FreeBSD Project); Peter G. Neumann (SRI International); Rui Paolo; Luigi Rizzo (Universitá di Pisa, Italy); Margo Seltzer (Harvard University); Keith Sklower (University of California, Berkeley); Lawrence Stewart (Swinburne University of Technology); Michael Tuexen (Muenster University of Applied Sciences); Bryan Venteicher (NetApp); Erez Zadok (Stony Brook University); and Bjoern A. Zeeb (The FreeBSD Project).

We are grateful to our now-retired editor of 25 years, Peter Gordon, who had faith in our ability to get the book written despite several years of delays on our part. We are equally grateful to our new editor, Debra Williams, who saw this project to completion and who accelerated the production when we finally had a completed manuscript. We thank all the professional people at Addison-Wesley and Pearson Education who helped us bring the book to completion: managing editor John Fuller; production editor Mary Kesel Wilson; cover designer Chuti Prasertsith; copy editor Deborah Thompson; and proofreader Melissa Panagos. Finally we acknowledge the contributions of Jaap Akkerhuis, who designed the troff macros for the BSD books.

This book was produced using James Clark's implementations of **pic**, **tbl**, **eqn**, and **groff**. The index was generated by **awk** scripts derived from indexing programs written by Jon Bentley and Brian Kernighan [Bentley & Kernighan, 1986]. Most of the art was created with **xfig**. Figure placement and widow elimination were handled by the **groff** macros, but orphan elimination and production of even page bottoms had to be done by hand.

We encourage readers to send us suggested improvements or comments about typographical or other errors found in the book; please send electronic mail to **FreeBSDbook-bugs@McKusick.COM**.

References

Bentley & Kernighan, 1986.
J. Bentley & B. Kernighan, "Tools for Printing Indexes," Computing Science Technical Report 128, AT&T Bell Laboratories, Murray Hill, NJ, October 1986.

Comer, 2000.
D. Comer, *Internetworking with TCP/IP Volume 1, 4th ed.,* Prentice-Hall, Upper Saddle River, NJ, 2000.

FreeBSD Mall, 2004.
FreeBSD Mall, *The FreeBSD Handbook,* available from http://www.freebsdmall.com, March 2004.

FreeBSD.org, 2014.
FreeBSD.org, *The Online FreeBSD Handbook,* available from http://www.freebsd.org/doc/en_US.ISO8859-1/books/handbook, March 2014.

Kernighan & Ritchie, 1989.
B. W. Kernighan & D. M. Ritchie, *The C Programming Language,* 2nd ed., Prentice-Hall, Englewood Cliffs, NJ, 1989.

Lavigne, 2010.
D. Lavigne, *The Definitive Guide to PC-BSD,* Apress / Springer-Verlag, March 2010.

Organick, 1975.
E. I. Organick, *The Multics System: An Examination of Its Structure,* MIT Press, Cambridge, MA, 1975.

PC-BSD.org, 2014.
PC-BSD.org, *The PC-BSD Users Handbook,* available from http://wiki.pcbsd.org, June 2014.

Ritchie & Thompson, 1978.
D. M. Ritchie & K. Thompson, "The UNIX Time-Sharing System," *Bell System Technical Journal*, vol. 57, no. 6, Part 2, pp. 78–90, July–August

1978. The original version [*Comm. ACM vol. 7, no. 7*, pp. 365–375 (July 1974)] described the 6th edition; this citation describes the 7th edition.

Silberschatz et al., 2012.

A. Silberschatz, P. Galvin, & G. Gagne, *Operating System Concepts, 9th ed.,* John Wiley and Sons, Hoboken, NJ, 2012.

Stallings, 2000.

R. Stallings, *Data and Computer Communications, 6th ed.,* Prentice Hall, Hoboken, NJ, 2000.

Stevens, 1992.

W. Stevens, *Advanced Programming in the UNIX Environment,* Addison-Wesley, Reading, MA, 1992.

Tanenbaum, 2010.

A. S. Tanenbaum, *Computer Networks,* 5th ed., Prentice-Hall, Englewood Cliffs, NJ, 2010.

About the Authors

left to right
Marshall Kirk McKusick, Robert N.M. Watson, and George V. Neville-Neil

Marshall Kirk McKusick writes books and articles, consults, and teaches classes on UNIX- and BSD-related subjects. While at the University of California at Berkeley, he implemented the 4.2BSD fast filesystem and was the Research Computer Scientist at the Berkeley Computer Systems Research Group (CSRG), overseeing the development and release of 4.3BSD and 4.4BSD. His particular areas of interest are the virtual-memory system and the filesystem. He earned his undergraduate degree in electrical engineering from Cornell University and did his graduate work at the University of California at Berkeley, where he received master's degrees in computer science and business administration, and a doctoral degree in computer science. He has twice been president of the board of the Usenix Association, is currently a member of the FreeBSD Foundation Board of Directors, a member of the editorial board of ACM's *Queue* magazine, a senior member of the IEEE, and a member of the Usenix Association, ACM, and AAAS. In his spare time, he enjoys swimming, scuba diving, and wine collecting. The wine is stored in a specially constructed wine cellar (accessible from the Web at http://www.McKusick.com/cgi-bin/readhouse) in the basement of the house that he shares with Eric Allman, his partner of 35-and-some-odd years and husband since 2013.

George V. Neville-Neil hacks, writes, teaches, and consults in the areas of Security, Networking, and Operating Systems. Other areas of interest include embedded and real-time systems, network time protocols, and code spelunking. In 2007, he helped start the AsiaBSDCon series of conferences in Tokyo, Japan, and has served on the program committee every year since then. He is a member of the FreeBSD Foundation Board of Directors, and was a member of the FreeBSD Core Team for 4 years. Contributing broadly to open source, he is the lead developer on the Precision Time Protocol project (http://ptpd.sf.net) and the developer of the Packet Construction Set (http://pcs.sf.net). Since 2004, he has written a monthly column, "Kode Vicious," that appears both in ACM's *Queue* and *Communications of the ACM*. He serves on the editorial board of ACM's *Queue* magazine, is vice-chair of ACM's *Practitioner Board*, and is a member of the Usenix Association, ACM, IEEE, and AAAS. He earned his bachelor's degree in computer science at Northeastern University in Boston, Massachusetts. He is an avid bicyclist, hiker, and traveler who has lived in Amsterdam, The Netherlands, and Tokyo, Japan. He is currently based in Brooklyn, New York, where he lives with his husband, Kaz Senju.

Robert N.M. Watson is a University Lecturer in Systems, Security, and Architecture in the Security Research Group at the University of Cambridge Computer Laboratory. He supervises doctoral students and postdoctoral researchers in cross-layer research projects spanning computer architecture, compilers, program analysis, program transformation, operating systems, networking, and security. Dr. Watson is a member of the FreeBSD Foundation Board of Directors, was a member of the FreeBSD Core Team for 10 years, and has been a FreeBSD committer for 15 years. His open-source contributions include work on FreeBSD networking, security, and multiprocessing. Having grown up in Washington, D. C., he earned his undergraduate degree in Logic and Computation, with a double major in Computer Science, at Carnegie Mellon University in Pittsburgh, Pennsylvania, and then worked at a series of industrial research labs investigating computer security. He earned his doctoral degree at the University of Cambridge, where his graduate research was in extensible operating-system access control. Dr. Watson and his wife Dr. Leigh Denault have lived in Cambridge, England, for 10 years.

PART I

Overview

CHAPTER 1

History and Goals

1.1 History of the UNIX System

The UNIX system has been in wide use for over 40 years and has helped to define many areas of computing. Although numerous individuals and organizations have contributed (and still contribute) to the development of the UNIX system, this book primarily concentrates on the BSD thread of development:

- Bell Laboratories, which invented UNIX
- The Computer Systems Research Group (CSRG) at the University of California at Berkeley, which gave UNIX virtual memory and the reference implementation of TCP/IP
- The FreeBSD project, the NetBSD project, the OpenBSD project, and the Dragonfly project, which continue the work started by the CSRG
- The Darwin operating system at the core of Apple's OS X (Darwin is based on FreeBSD)

Origins

The first version of the UNIX system was developed at Bell Laboratories in 1969 by Ken Thompson as a private research project to use an otherwise idle PDP-7. Thompson was joined shortly thereafter by Dennis Ritchie, who not only contributed to the design and implementation of the system, but also invented the C programming language. The system was completely rewritten into C, leaving almost no assembly language. The original elegant design of the system [Ritchie, 1978] and developments of the first 15 years [Ritchie, 1984a; Compton, 1985] have made the UNIX system an important and powerful operating system [Ritchie, 1987].

Ritchie, Thompson, and other early UNIX developers at Bell Laboratories had worked previously on the Multics project [Peirce, 1985; Organick, 1975], which had a strong influence on the newer operating system. Even the name *UNIX* is merely a pun on *Multics*; in areas where Multics attempted to do many tasks, UNIX tried to do only one task but do it well. The basic organization of the UNIX filesystem, the idea of using a user process for the command interpreter, the general organization of the filesystem interface, and many other system characteristics come directly from Multics.

Ideas from various other operating systems, such as the Massachusetts Institute of Technology's (MIT's) CTSS, also have been incorporated. The *fork* operation to create new processes comes from Berkeley's GENIE (SDS-940, later XDS-940) operating system. Allowing a user to create processes inexpensively led to using one process per command rather than commands being run as procedure calls, as is done in Multics.

Research UNIX

The first major editions of UNIX were the Research systems from Bell Laboratories. In addition to the earliest versions of the system, these systems include the UNIX Time-Sharing System, Sixth Edition, commonly known as V6, which in 1976 was the first version widely available outside of Bell Laboratories. Systems are identified by the edition numbers of the *UNIX Programmer's Manual* that were current when the distributions were made.

The UNIX system was distinguished from other operating systems in three important ways:

1. It was written in a high-level language.
2. It was distributed in source form.
3. It provided powerful primitives normally found in only those operating systems that ran on much more expensive hardware.

Most of the system source code was written in C rather than in assembly language. The prevailing belief at the time was that an operating system had to be written in assembly language to provide reasonable efficiency and to get access to the hardware. The C language itself was at a sufficiently high level to allow it to be compiled easily for a wide range of computer hardware, without it being so complex or restrictive that systems programmers had to revert to assembly language to get reasonable efficiency or functionality. Access to the hardware was provided through assembly-language stubs for the 3 percent of the operating-system functions—such as context switching—that needed them. Although the success of UNIX does not stem solely from its being written in a high-level language, the use of C was a critical first step [Kernighan & Ritchie, 1978; Kernighan & Ritchie, 1989; Ritchie et al., 1978]. Ritchie's C language is descended [Rosler, 1984] from Thompson's B language, which was itself descended from BCPL [Richards & Whitby-Strevens, 1980]. C continues to evolve [Tuthill, 1985; ISO, 2011].

The second important distinction of UNIX was its early release from Bell Laboratories to other research environments in source form. By providing source, the system's founders ensured that other organizations would be able not only to use the system, but also to tinker with its inner workings. The ease with which new ideas could be adopted into the system always has been key to the changes that have been made to it. Whenever a new system that tried to upstage UNIX came along, somebody would dissect the newcomer and clone its central ideas into UNIX. The unique ability to use a small, comprehensible system, written in a high-level language, in an environment swimming in new ideas led to a UNIX system that evolved far beyond its humble beginnings. Though recipients of the source code had to be licensed, campus-wide licenses were cheaply available to universities. Thus, many people became versed in the way that UNIX worked, setting the stage for the open-source world that would follow.

The third important distinction of UNIX was that it provided individual users with the ability to run multiple processes concurrently and to connect these processes into pipelines of commands. At the time, only operating systems running on large and expensive machines had the ability to run multiple processes, and the number of concurrent processes usually was controlled tightly by a system administrator.

Most early UNIX systems ran on the PDP-11, which was inexpensive and powerful for its time. Nonetheless, there was at least one early port of Sixth Edition UNIX to a machine with a different architecture: the Interdata 7/32 [Miller, 1978]. The PDP-11 also had an inconveniently small address space. The introduction of machines with 32-bit address spaces, especially the VAX-11/780, provided an opportunity for UNIX to expand its services to include virtual memory and networking. Earlier experiments by the Research group in providing UNIX-like facilities on different hardware had led to the conclusion that it was as easy to move the entire operating system as it was to duplicate UNIX's services under another operating system. The first UNIX system with portability as a specific goal was UNIX Time-Sharing System, Seventh Edition (V7), which ran on the PDP-11 and the Interdata 8/32 and had a VAX variety called UNIX/32V Time-Sharing, System Version 1.0 (32V). The Research group at Bell Laboratories has also developed UNIX Time-Sharing System, Eighth Edition (V8); UNIX Time-Sharing System, Ninth Edition (V9); and UNIX Time-Sharing System, Tenth Edition (V10). Their 1996 system is Plan 9. Regrettably, Bell Laboratories was disbanded after the release of Plan 9.

AT&T UNIX System III and System V

After the distribution of Seventh Edition in 1978, the Research group turned over external distributions to the UNIX Support Group (USG). USG had previously distributed such systems internally as the UNIX Programmer's Work Bench (PWB), and had sometimes distributed them externally as well [Mohr, 1985].

USG's first external distribution after Seventh Edition was UNIX System III (System III) in 1982, which incorporated features of Seventh Edition, of 32V, and also of several UNIX systems developed by groups other than the Research group.

Features of UNIX/RT (a real-time UNIX system) were included, as were many features from PWB. USG released UNIX System V (System V) in 1983; that system is largely derived from System III. The court-ordered divestiture of the Bell Operating Companies from AT&T permitted AT&T to market System V aggressively [Bach, 1986; Wilson, 1985].

USG metamorphosed into the UNIX System Development Laboratory (USDL), which released UNIX System V, Release 2 in 1984. System V, Release 2, Version 4 introduced paging [Jung, 1985; Miller, 1984], including copy-on-write and shared memory, to System V. The System V implementation was not based on the Berkeley paging system. USDL was succeeded by AT&T Information Systems (ATTIS), which distributed UNIX System V, Release 3, in 1987. That system included STREAMS, an IPC mechanism adopted from V8 [Presotto & Ritchie, 1985]. Shortly after the release of UNIX System V as a product, AT&T and Sun Microsystems worked together to merge it with Sun Microsystem's BSD-based SunOS to produce Solaris. Solaris and its open-source variant Open Solaris are the primary System V variants of UNIX still in use today.

Berkeley Software Distributions

The most influential of the non-Bell Laboratories and non-AT&T UNIX development groups was the University of California at Berkeley [DiBona et al., 1999]. Software from Berkeley was released in Berkeley Software Distributions (BSD)—for example, as 4.4BSD. Berkeley was the source of the BSD name, and its distributions were the first distinct identity for the BSD operating system. The first Berkeley VAX UNIX work was the addition to 32V of virtual memory, demand paging, and page replacement in 1979 by William Joy and Ozalp Babaoğlu, to produce 3BSD [Babaoğlu & Joy, 1981]. The reason for the large virtual-memory space of 3BSD was the development of what at the time were large programs, such as Berkeley's *Franz* LISP. This memory-management work convinced the Defense Advanced Research Projects Agency (DARPA) to fund the Berkeley team for the later development of a standard system (4BSD) for DARPA's contractors to use.

A goal of the 4BSD project was to provide support for the DARPA Internet networking protocols, TCP/IP [Comer, 2000]. The networking implementation was general enough to communicate among diverse network facilities, ranging from local networks, such as Ethernets and token rings, to long-haul networks, such as DARPA's ARPANET.

We refer to all the Berkeley VAX UNIX systems following 3BSD as 4BSD, although there were really several releases: 4.0BSD, 4.1BSD, 4.2BSD, 4.3BSD, 4.3BSD Tahoe, and 4.3BSD Reno. 4BSD was the UNIX operating system of choice for VAXes from the time that the VAX first became available in 1977 until the release of System V in 1983. Most organizations would purchase a 32V license but would order 4BSD from Berkeley. Many installations inside the Bell System ran 4.1BSD (and replaced it with 4.3BSD when the latter became available). A new virtual-memory system was released with 4.4BSD. The VAX was reaching the end of its useful lifetime, so 4.4BSD was not ported to that machine. Instead, 4.4BSD ran on the newer 68000, SPARC, MIPS, and Intel PC architectures.

The 4BSD work for DARPA was guided by a steering committee that included many notable people from both commercial and academic institutions. The culmination of the original Berkeley DARPA UNIX project was the release of 4.2BSD in 1983; further research at Berkeley produced 4.3BSD in mid-1986. The next releases included the 4.3BSD Tahoe release of June 1988 and the 4.3BSD Reno release of June 1990. These releases were primarily ports to the Computer Consoles Incorporated hardware platform. Interleaved with these releases were two unencumbered networking releases: the 4.3BSD Net1 release of March 1989 and the 4.3BSD Net2 release of June 1991. These releases extracted nonproprietary code from 4.3BSD; they could be redistributed freely in source and binary form to companies and individuals not covered by a UNIX source license. The final CSRG release requiring an AT&T source license was 4.4BSD in June 1993. Following a year of litigation (see Section 1.3), the free-redistributable 4.4BSD-Lite was released in April 1994. The final CSRG release was 4.4BSD-Lite Release 2 in June 1995.

UNIX in the World

The UNIX system is also a fertile field for academic endeavor. Thompson and Ritchie were given the Association for Computing Machinery Turing award for the design of the system [Ritchie, 1984b]. The UNIX system and related, specially designed teaching systems—such as Tunis [Ewens et al., 1985; Holt, 1983], XINU [Comer, 1984], and MINIX [Tanenbaum, 1987]—are widely used in courses on operating systems. Linus Torvalds reimplemented the UNIX interface in his freely redistributable Linux operating system. The UNIX system is ubiquitous in universities and research facilities throughout the world, and is ever more widely used in industry and commerce.

1.2 BSD and Other Systems

The CSRG incorporated features from not only UNIX systems but from other operating systems. Many of the features of the 4BSD terminal drivers are from TENEX/TOPS-20. Job control (in concept—not in implementation) is derived from TOPS-20 and from the MIT Incompatible Timesharing System (ITS). The virtual-memory interface first proposed for 4.2BSD, and finally implemented in 4.4BSD, was based on the file-mapping and page-level interfaces that first appeared in TENEX/TOPS-20. The current FreeBSD virtual-memory system (see Chapter 6) was adapted from Mach, which was itself an offshoot of 4.3BSD. Multics has often been a reference point in the design of new facilities.

The quest for efficiency was a major factor in much of the CSRG's work. Some efficiency improvements were made because of comparisons with the proprietary VMS operating system for the VAX [Joy, 1980; Kashtan, 1980].

Other UNIX variants have adopted many 4BSD features. AT&T UNIX System V [AT&T, 1987], the IEEE POSIX.1 standard [P1003.1, 1988], and the related National Bureau of Standards (NBS) Federal Information Processing Standard (FIPS) have adopted the following:

- Job control (Chapter 2)
- Reliable signals (Chapter 4)
- Multiple file-access permission groups (Chapter 5)
- Filesystem interfaces (Chapter 9)

The X/OPEN Group (originally consisting of only European vendors but now including most US UNIX vendors) produced the X/OPEN *Portability Guide*[X/OPEN, and, more recently, the *Spec 1170 Guide*. These documents specify both the kernel interface and many of the utility programs available to UNIX system users. When Novell purchased UNIX from AT&T in 1993, it transferred exclusive ownership of the UNIX name to X/OPEN. Thus, all systems that want to brand themselves as UNIX must meet the X/OPEN interface specifications. To date, no BSD system has ever been put through the X/OPEN interface-specification tests, so none of them can be called UNIX. The X/OPEN guides have adopted many of the POSIX facilities. The POSIX.1 standard is also an ISO International Standard, named SC22 WG15. Thus, the POSIX facilities have been accepted in most UNIX-like systems worldwide.

The 4BSD *socket* interprocess-communication mechanism (see Chapter 12) was designed for portability and was immediately ported to AT&T System III, although it was never distributed with that system. The 4BSD implementation of the TCP/IP networking protocol suite (see Chapter 14) is widely used as the basis for further implementations on systems ranging from AT&T 3B machines running System V to VMS to embedded operating systems such as VxWorks.

The CSRG cooperated closely with vendors whose systems are based on 4.2BSD and 4.3BSD. This simultaneous development contributed to the ease of further ports of 4.3BSD and to ongoing development of the system.

The Influence of the User Community

Much of the Berkeley development work was done in response to the user community. Ideas and expectations came not only from DARPA, the principal direct-funding organization, but also from users of the system at companies and universities worldwide.

The Berkeley researchers accepted not only ideas from the user community but also actual software. Contributions to 4BSD came from universities and other organizations in Australia, Canada, Europe, Japan, and the United States. These contributions included major features, such as autoconfiguration and disk quotas. A few ideas, such as the *fcntl* system call, were taken from System V, although licensing and pricing considerations prevented the use of any code from

System III or System V in 4BSD. In addition to contributions that were included in the distributions proper, the CSRG also distributed a set of user-contributed software.

An example of a community-developed facility is the public-domain time-zone-handling package that was adopted with the 4.3BSD Tahoe release. It was designed and implemented by an international group, including Arthur Olson, Robert Elz, and Guy Harris, partly because of discussions in the USENET newsgroup **comp.std.unix**. This package takes time-zone-conversion rules completely out of the C library, putting them in files that require no system-code changes to change time-zone rules; this change is especially useful with binary-only distributions of UNIX. The method also allows individual processes to choose rules rather than keeping one ruleset specification systemwide. The distribution includes a large database of rules used in many areas throughout the world, from China to Australia to Europe. Distributions are thus simplified because it is not necessary to have the software set up differently for different destinations, as long as the whole database is included. The adoption of the time-zone package into BSD brought the technology to the attention of commercial vendors, such as Sun Microsystems, causing them to incorporate it into their systems. This time-zone framework is still in use 30 years later.

1.3 The Transition of BSD to Open Source

Up through the release of 4.3BSD Tahoe, all recipients of BSD had to first get an AT&T source license. That was because the BSD systems were never released by Berkeley in a binary-only format; the distributions always contained the complete source to every part of the system. The history of the UNIX system, and the BSD system in particular, had shown the power of making the source available to the users. Instead of passively using the system, they actively worked to fix bugs, improve performance and functionality, and even add completely new features.

With the increasing cost of the AT&T source licenses, vendors that wanted to build stand-alone TCP/IP-based networking products for the PC market using the BSD code found the per-binary costs prohibitive. So they requested that Berkeley break out the networking code and utilities, and provide them under licensing terms that did not require an AT&T source license. The TCP/IP networking code clearly did not exist in 32/V and thus had been developed entirely by Berkeley and its contributors. The BSD-originated networking code and supporting utilities were released in June 1989 as Networking Release 1, the first freely redistributable code from Berkeley.

The licensing terms were liberal. A licensee could release the code modified or unmodified in source or binary form with no accounting or royalties to Berkeley. The only requirements were that the copyright notices in the source file be left intact and that products that incorporated the code include in their documentation that the product contained code from the University of California and its contributors. Although Berkeley charged a $1000 fee to get a tape, anyone was free to get a copy from somebody who already had it. Indeed, several large sites put it up for anonymous FTP shortly after it was released. Though the code was freely available, several hundred organizations purchased tapes, which helped to fund the CSRG and encouraged further development.

Networking Release 2

With the success of the first open-source release, the CSRG decided to see how much more of BSD they could spring free. Keith Bostic led the charge by soliciting people to rewrite the UNIX utilities from scratch based solely on their published descriptions. Their only compensation would be to have their name listed among the Berkeley contributors next to the name of the utility that they rewrote. The contributions started slowly and were mostly for the trivial utilities. But as the list of completed utilities grew, and Bostic continued to hold forth for contributions at public events such as Usenix, the rate of contributions continued to grow. Soon the list crossed 100 utilities, and within 18 months nearly all the important utilities and libraries had been rewritten.

The kernel proved to be a bigger task because it could not easily be rewritten from scratch. The entire kernel was reviewed, file by file, removing code that had originated in the 32/V release. When the review was completed, there were only six remaining kernel files that were still contaminated and that could not be trivially rewritten. While consideration was given to rewriting those six files so that a complete kernel could be released, the CSRG decided to release just the less-controversial set. The CSRG sought permission for the expanded release from folks higher up in the university administration. After much internal debate and verification of the methods used for detecting proprietary code, the CSRG was given permission to do the release.

The initial thought was to come up with a new name for the second freely redistributable release. However, getting a new license written and approved by the university lawyers would have taken many months. So, the new release was named Networking Release 2, since that could be done with just a revision of the approved Networking Release 1 license agreement. This second, greatly expanded, freely redistributable release began shipping in June 1991. The redistribution terms and cost were the same as the terms and cost of the first networking release. As before, several hundred individuals and organizations paid the $1000 fee to get the distribution from Berkeley.

Closing the gap from the Networking Release 2 distribution to a fully functioning system did not take long. Within 6 months of the release, Bill Jolitz had written replacements for the six missing files. He promptly released a fully compiled and bootable system for the 386-based PC architecture in January 1992, which he called 386/BSD. Jolitz's 386/BSD distribution was done almost entirely on the net. He simply put it up for anonymous FTP and let anyone who wanted it download it for free. Within weeks he had a huge following.

Unfortunately, the demands of keeping a full-time job meant that Jolitz could not devote the time needed to keep up with the flood of incoming bug fixes and enhancements to 386/BSD. So within a few months of the release of 386/BSD, a group of avid 386/BSD users formed the NetBSD group to pool their collective resources to help maintain and later enhance the system. By early 1993, they were doing releases that became known as the NetBSD distribution. The NetBSD group chose to emphasize the support of as many platforms as possible and continued the research-style development done by the CSRG. Until 1998, their distribution was done solely over the net with no distribution media available. Their group continues to target primarily the hard-core technical users.

The FreeBSD group was formed a few months after the NetBSD group with a charter to support just the PC architecture and to go after a larger and less technically advanced audience, much as Linux had done. They built elaborate installation scripts and began shipping their system on a low-cost CD-ROM in December 1993. The combination of ease-of-installation and heavy promotion on the net and at major trade shows, such as Comdex, led to a large, rapid growth curve. FreeBSD quickly rose to have the largest installed base of all the Networking Release 2-derived systems.

FreeBSD also rode the wave of Linux popularity by adding a Linux emulation mode that allows Linux binaries to run on the FreeBSD platform. This feature allows FreeBSD users to use the ever growing set of applications available for Linux while getting the robustness, reliability, and performance of the FreeBSD system.

In 1995, OpenBSD spun off from the NetBSD group. Their technical focus was aimed at improving the security of the system. Their marketing focus was to make the system easier to use and more widely available. Thus, they began producing and selling CD-ROMs, with many of the ease of installation ideas from the FreeBSD distribution.

The Lawsuit

In addition to the groups organized to freely redistribute systems originating from the Networking Release 2 tape, a company, Berkeley Software Design Incorporated (BSDI), was formed to develop and distribute a commercially supported version of the code. Like the other groups, it started by adding the six missing files that Bill Jolitz had written for his 386/BSD release. BSDI began selling its system, including both source and binaries, in January 1992 for $995. It began running advertisements touting its 99 percent discount over the price charged for System V source plus binary systems. Interested readers were told to call 1-800-ITS-UNIX.

Shortly after BSDI began its sales campaign, it received a letter from UNIX System Laboratory (USL) (a mostly owned subsidiary of AT&T spun off to develop and sell UNIX) [Ritchie, 2004]. The letter demanded that BSDI stop promoting its product as UNIX and, in particular, that it stop using the deceptive phone number. Although the phone number was promptly dropped and the advertisements changed to explain that the product was not UNIX, USL was still unhappy and filed suit to enjoin BSDI from selling its product. The suit alleged that the BSDI product contained USL proprietary code and trade secrets. USL sought to get an injunction to halt BSDI's sales until the lawsuit was resolved claiming that it would suffer irreparable harm from the loss of its trade secrets if the BSDI distributions continued.

At the preliminary hearing for the injunction, BSDI contended that it was simply using the sources being freely distributed by the University of California plus six additional files. BSDI was willing to discuss the content of any of the six added files but did not believe it should be held responsible for the files being distributed by the University of California. The judge agreed with BSDI's argument and told USL that it would have to restate its complaint based solely on the six files or the case would be dismissed. Recognizing that it would have a hard time making a case from just the six files, USL decided to refile the suit against both BSDI and the University of California. As before, USL requested an injunction on the shipping of Networking Release 2 from the university and of the BSDI products.

With the impending injunction hearing just a few short weeks away, preparation began in earnest. All the members of the CSRG were deposed, as was nearly everyone employed by BSDI. Briefs, counterbriefs, and counter-counterbriefs flew back and forth between the lawyers. The staff of the CSRG turned from writing code to writing several hundred pages of material that found its way into various briefs.

In December 1992, Dickinson R. Debevoise, a United States District Judge in New Jersey, heard the arguments for the injunction. Although judges usually rule on injunction requests immediately, he decided to take it under advisement. On a Friday about 6 weeks later, he issued a 40-page opinion in which he denied the injunction and threw out all but two of the complaints [Debevoise, 1993]. The remaining two complaints were narrowed to recent copyrights and the possibility of the loss of trade secrets. He also suggested that the matter should be heard in a state court system before being heard in federal court.

The University of California took the hint and rushed to California state court the following Monday morning with a countersuit against USL. By filing first in California, the university had established the locale of any further state court action. Constitutional law requires all state filings to be done in a single state to prevent litigants with deep pockets from bleeding opponents dry by filing 50 cases against them, one in each state. The result was that if USL wanted to take any action against the university in state courts, it would be forced to do so in California rather than in its home state of New Jersey.

The university's suit claimed that USL had failed in its obligation to provide due credit to the university for the use of BSD code in System V as required by the license that it had signed with the university [Linzner & MacDonald, 1993]. If the claim were found to be valid, the university asked that USL be forced to reprint all its documentation with the appropriate due credit added, to notify all its licensees of its oversight, and to run full-page advertisements in major publications such as the *Wall Street Journal* and *Fortune* magazine, notifying the business world of its inadvertent oversight.

Soon after the filing in state court, USL was bought from AT&T by Novell. The CEO of Novell, Ray Noorda, stated publicly that he would rather compete in the marketplace than in court. By the summer of 1993, settlement talks had started. Unfortunately, the two sides had dug in so deep that the talks proceeded very slowly. With some further prodding by Ray Noorda on the USL side, many of the sticking points were removed, and a settlement was finally reached in January 1994. The result was that three files were removed from the 18,000 that made up Networking Release 2, and a few minor changes were made to other files. In addition, the university agreed to add USL copyrights to about 70 files, although those files continued to be freely redistributed.

4.4BSD

The newly blessed release was called 4.4BSD-Lite and was released in June 1994 under terms identical to those used for the Networking releases. Specifically, the terms allow free redistribution in source and binary form, subject only to the constraint that the university copyrights remain intact and that the university receive credit when others use the code. Simultaneously, the complete system was released as 4.4BSD-Encumbered, which still required recipients to have a USL source license.

The lawsuit settlement also stipulated that USL would not sue any organization using 4.4BSD-Lite as the base for its system. So all the extant BSD groups—BSDI, NetBSD, and FreeBSD—had to restart their code base with the 4.4BSD-Lite sources into which they then merged their enhancements and improvements. While this reintegration caused a short-term delay in the development of the various BSD systems, it was a blessing in disguise, since it forced all the divergent groups to resynchronize with the 3 years of development that had occurred at the CSRG since the release of Networking Release 2.

4.4BSD-Lite Release 2

The money received from the 4.4BSD-Encumbered and 4.4BSD-Lite releases was used to fund a part-time effort to integrate bug fixes and enhancements. These changes continued for 2 years until the rate of bug reports and feature enhancements had died down to a trickle. The final set of changes was released as 4.4BSD-Lite Release 2 in June 1995. Most of the changes incorporated into 4.4BSD-Lite Release 2 eventually made it into the other systems' source bases.

Though the license term requiring that due credit be given to the university had been extremely helpful in the lawsuit, the university agreed to drop it following the final release. As many people began using the BSD-style copyrights for their own code, the proliferation of due-credit clauses in open-source software became difficult to determine and unmanageably large. By agreeing to drop the due-credit clause, the university hoped to set an example for others using its license. Over time, and with much effort from the BSD community, the due-credit clause has been dropped from many of the open-source programs that use the BSD-style license.

Following the release of 4.4BSD-Lite Release 2, the CSRG was disbanded. After 15 years of piloting the BSD ship, it was time to let others with fresh ideas and boundless enthusiasm take over. While it might seem best to have a single centralized authority overseeing the system development, the idea of having several groups with different charters ensures that many different approaches will be tried and that there is no single point of failure. Because the system is released in source form, the best ideas can easily be picked up by other groups. Indeed, cross-pollination of ideas between open-source projects is common.

1.4 The FreeBSD Development Model

Running an open-source project is different from running traditional software development. In traditional development, the staff are paid, so it is possible to have managers and a system architect that set schedules and direct the programmers' activities. With open source, the developers are volunteers. They tend to be transient, usually doing a project or two before finding some other activity on which they prefer to spend their free time. They cannot be directed because they only work on what interests them. Because their jobs, families, and social lives often take precedence over their work on the project, it is impossible to put together schedules. Finally, there is no paid staff to fill the management role of traditional development. Thus, a successful open-source-development project must be self-organizing and set up to gracefully handle a high turnover of its active developers.

The development model used by FreeBSD (as well as NetBSD and OpenBSD) was first set in motion by the CSRG [McKusick et al., 1989]. The CSRG was always a small group of software developers. This resource limitation required careful software-engineering management. Careful coordination was needed not only of the CSRG personnel but also of members of the general community who contributed to the development of the system. Certain outside developers had permission to modify the master copy of the system source directly. People given access to the master sources were carefully screened beforehand but were not closely supervised. Everyone committing changes to the system source received notification of all changes, allowing everyone to be aware of changes going into the system. Everyone was required to have any nontrivial changes reviewed by at least one other person before committing them to the tree. This model allowed many lines of development to proceed concurrently while still keeping the project coherent.

The FreeBSD project is organized in much the same way as the CSRG. The entire FreeBSD project, including all the source code, documentation, bug reports, mailing-list archives, and even administrative data, is maintained in a publicly readable source-code-control system. Anyone may view the source code and existing bug reports, track progress on fixing bugs, and post bug reports. Anyone may join and participate in the numerous FreeBSD mailing lists. There are three groups of people that directly work on FreeBSD: developers, committers, and the core team.

There are 5000 to 6000 developers, each of whom works on some part of the system such as maintaining the FreeBSD kernel, continuing development of the

1000 core FreeBSD utilities, writing FreeBSD documentation, and updating other open-source software in the FreeBSD ports collection. Developers are able to access the source-code repository, but they are not permitted to change it. Instead, they must work with a committer or file a problem report to get their changes added to the system.

There are currently 300 to 400 committers. Like the developers, most of them specialize in some part of the system. Unlike the developers, they are permitted to make changes to those parts of the source-code repository in which they have been authorized to work. All nontrivial changes should be reviewed by one or more other committers before being checked into the source tree. Most committers are doing work of their own as well as reviewing and committing the work of several developers.

Nomination for advancement from developer to committer is done by the existing committers. Most commonly a developer will be nominated by the committer with whom he has been working. The nomination, along with a description and evaluation of past work and an initial scope of new work, is sent to the core team for approval.

At the center of the project is the core team. The core team is composed of nine people who are elected every 2 years. The candidates for the core team come from the committers and the committers elect the core team. The core team acts as the final gatekeepers of the source code. They monitor what is being committed and resolve conflicts if two or more committers cannot agree on how to solve a particular problem. The core team also approves the advancement of developers to committers and (in rare circumstances) temporarily or permanently evicts someone from the committer group. The usual reason for departure from the committer group is inactivity (making no changes to the system for more than a year).

The development structure of the FreeBSD project is directly derived from the one that we had established at the CSRG. Both the CSRG and FreeBSD use a central source-code-controlled repository. The FreeBSD core team is analogous to the CSRG staff. The FreeBSD committers are much like the people to whom Berkeley gave accounts on the CSRG development machine that allowed them to commit changes to the CSRG sources. And the FreeBSD developers are similar to the people that contributed to Berkeley, but they did not have accounts on the CSRG development machine.

The FreeBSD project has made some important improvements. First, its members recognize that even the most dedicated programmer will eventually burn out, lose interest, or otherwise decide to move on. There must be some way to let these people gracefully step aside rather than letting their inattention create a void at a critical point in the project. So unlike the CSRG model of having staff that were dictators for life, FreeBSD went to an elected core that is answerable to the committers. A core member who is burned out can decide (or be persuaded) not to run for reelection when his or her term ends. Core members who are not serving the interest of the committers will not be reelected. Equally important, active and energetic people have plenty of opportunity to move up through the ranks. Because the core team is elected, people rise into that rank because their peers who are actively working on the project feel that they should have the job. This approach works better than advancing because you are good buddies with somebody at the top. It also ensures that the core team is made up of those who are good at communicating with others, an important skill to have in that position.

Another significant improvement made by the FreeBSD project is to automate many tasks and set up remote mirrors of the source-code repository, Web site, and bug reports. These changes have allowed the project to support many more contributors than would have been possible under the CSRG model. The FreeBSD project has also managed to become much less US–centric by welcoming developers from around the world, including active people in Japan, Australia, Russia, South Africa, Ukraine, Hungary, India, Denmark, France, Germany, and the United Kingdom, to name just a few of the countries with active FreeBSD development.

The CSRG used to release new versions of the system about every 2 years. Changes to these distributions were rare, typically only small and critical security- or stability-related changes. Between versions, the CSRG would do test releases to gain experience with the new features that were being developed.

The FreeBSD project has greatly expanded on the CSRG distribution scheme. At any point in time there are at least two FreeBSD distributions. The first is the "stable" release that is intended to be used in production environments. The second is the "current" release that represents the current state of the FreeBSD system and is intended for use by developers and users needing the latest features.

The stable release changes slowly, and the changes are limited to fixing bugs, improving performance, and adding incremental hardware support. The stable system is released three to four times per year, although users wishing to upgrade more often can download and install the latest stable code as frequently as they need to do so (for example, after a major security patch has been made). The stable version of FreeBSD is analogous to the CSRG major-version releases except that they are more actively updated and are made available to the users. Like the stable release, snapshots of the current release are created every few months. However, most users of the current release update much more frequently (daily updates are common). By having mirrored copies of the stable and current distributions available throughout the world, the FreeBSD project allows its worldwide user base to stay up to date much more easily than was possible with the CSRG distributions.

About every 2 years, the current branch is forked to create a new stable release. Once the new stable branch has proven to be reliable enough for production use, work largely ceases on the old stable branch and production users switch over to the new stable release. The mainline development continues on the current branch. Nearly all changes are made first to the current branch. Only after a change has been tested in the current branch and proven to work in that environment is it merged-from-current (MFC-ed) to the stable release.

One advantage that the CSRG long had over the FreeBSD project was that the CSRG was part of the University of California at Berkeley. Since the university is a nonprofit organization, contributions made to the CSRG were tax-deductible to the contributor. Some people at the FreeBSD project had long felt that they should find a way to let contributors to the project get a tax deduction. In 2000, they set up the FreeBSD Foundation, which after 3 years of good nonprofit work, was granted 501(c)3 status by the United States taxing authorities. This certification means that contributions made to the FreeBSD Foundation can be deducted from United States federal and state taxes in the same way as a contribution made to the university can be deducted. The ability to get a tax deduction has markedly increased the volume of monetary contributions to the FreeBSD project, which has enabled them to fund development of parts of the system that are tedious to create but necessary and important.

Over the past 20 years, the FreeBSD project has grown at a steady but sustainable pace. Although Linux has attracted a mass following, FreeBSD continues to hold its place in the high-performance-server space. Indeed, Linux has helped to evangelize the viability of open source to the corporate marketplace, and FreeBSD has ridden on its coattails. It is far easier to convince your management to switch from Linux to FreeBSD than it is to convince them to move from Microsoft's Windows to FreeBSD. Linux has also supplied a steady stream of developers for FreeBSD. Until recently, Linux had no central source-code repository, so to contribute you had to work for a Linux distributor or you had to get the ear of a member of the small set of people who could get changes put into the system. The much more egalitarian and merit-based organization of the FreeBSD project has provided a steady influx of high-quality developers. The typical new committer to the FreeBSD project is in his or her mid- to late 20s and has been programming Linux or other open-source projects for a decade. These people have enough experience and maturity that they are quickly able to become effective contributors to the project. And the mentoring inherent in the progression of developer to committer ensures that by the time someone has the right to directly commit code to the FreeBSD tree, they understand the style and code-clarity guidelines that are critically important to preserving the quality, robustness, and maintainability of FreeBSD.

The goal of the FreeBSD project is to provide software that may be used for any purpose and without strings attached. Many of the developers have a significant investment in the code (and project) and certainly do not mind a little financial compensation occasionally, but they certainly do not insist on it. They believe that their first and foremost mission is to provide code to any and all comers, for whatever purpose, so that the code gets the widest possible use and provides the greatest possible benefit [Hubbard, 2014].

References

AT&T, 1987.

AT&T, *The System V Interface Definition (SVID)*, Issue 2, American Telephone and Telegraph, Murray Hill, NJ, January 1987.

Babaoğlu & Joy, 1981.

Ö. Babaoğlu & W. N. Joy, "Converting a Swap-Based System to Do Paging in an Architecture Lacking Page-Referenced Bits," *Proceedings of the Eighth Symposium on Operating Systems Principles*, pp. 78–86, December 1981.

Bach, 1986.
M. J. Bach, *The Design of the UNIX Operating System,* Prentice-Hall, Englewood Cliffs, NJ, 1986.

Comer, 1984.
D. Comer, *Operating System Design: The Xinu Approach,* Prentice-Hall, Englewood Cliffs, NJ, 1984.

Comer, 2000.
D. Comer, *Internetworking with TCP/IP Volume 1, 4th ed.,* Prentice-Hall, Upper Saddle River, NJ, 2000.

Compton, 1985.
M. Compton, editor, "The Evolution of UNIX," *UNIX Review*, vol. 3, no. 1, January 1985.

Debevoise, 1993.
D. Debevoise, *Civ. No. 92-1667, UNIX System Laboratories Inc. vs. Berkeley Software Design Inc.,* available from http://sco.tuxrocks.com/Docs/USL/Doc-92.html, March 3, 1993.

DiBona et al., 1999.
C. DiBona, S. Ockman, & M. Stone, *Open Sources: Voices from the Open Source Revolution,* pp. 31–46, Chapter 2—Twenty Years of Berkeley UNIX: From AT&T-Owned to Freely Redistributable, available from http://www.oreilly.com/ catalog/ opensources/ book/ kirkmck.html, ISBN 1-56592-582-3, O'Reilly & Associates, Inc., Sebastopol, CA, 1999.

Ewens et al., 1985.
P. Ewens, D. R. Blythe, M. Funkenhauser, & R. C. Holt, "Tunis: A Distributed Multiprocessor Operating System," *USENIX Association Conference Proceedings*, pp. 247–254, June 1985.

Holt, 1983.
R. C. Holt, *Concurrent Euclid, the UNIX System, and Tunis,* Addison-Wesley, Reading, MA, 1983.

Hubbard, 2014.
J. Hubbard, "A Brief History of FreeBSD," FreeBSD Handbook, section 1.3.1, available from http://www.freebsd.org/doc/en_US.ISO8859-1/books/handbook/history.html, March 2014.

ISO, 2011.
ISO, "ISO/IEC 9899:2011 Programming Language C Standard," ISO 9899:2011, available from http://www.iso.org, December, 2011.

Joy, 1980.
W. N. Joy, "Comments on the Performance of UNIX on the VAX," Technical Report, University of California Computer System Research Group, Berkeley, CA, April 1980.

Jung, 1985.
R. S. Jung, "Porting the AT&T Demand Paged UNIX Implementation

to Microcomputers," *USENIX Association Conference Proceedings*, pp. 361–370, June 1985.

Kashtan, 1980.
D. L. Kashtan, "UNIX and VMS: Some Performance Comparisons," Technical Report, SRI International, Menlo Park, CA, February 1980.

Kernighan & Ritchie, 1978.
B. W. Kernighan & D. M. Ritchie, *The C Programming Language,* Prentice-Hall, Englewood Cliffs, NJ, 1978.

Kernighan & Ritchie, 1989.
B. W. Kernighan & D. M. Ritchie, *The C Programming Language,* 2nd ed., Prentice-Hall, Englewood Cliffs, NJ, 1989.

Linzner & MacDonald, 1993.
J. Linzner & M. MacDonald, *University of California at Berkeley versus UNIX System Laboratories Inc.,* available from http://cm.bell-labs.com/cm/cs/who/dmr/ bsdi/930610.ucb_complaint.txt, June 1993.

McKusick et al., 1989.
M. K. McKusick, M. Karels, & K. Bostic, "The Release Engineering of 4.3BSD," *Proceedings of the New Orleans USENIX Workshop on Software Management*, pp. 95–100, April 1989.

Miller, 1978.
R. Miller, "UNIX—A Portable Operating System," *ACM Operating System Review*, vol. 12, no. 3, pp. 32–37, July 1978.

Miller, 1984.
R. Miller, "A Demand Paging Virtual Memory Manager for System V," *USENIX Association Conference Proceedings*, pp. 178–182, June 1984.

Mohr, 1985.
A. Mohr, "The Genesis Story," *UNIX Review*, vol. 3, no. 1, p. 18, January 1985.

Organick, 1975.
E. I. Organick, *The Multics System: An Examination of Its Structure,* MIT Press, Cambridge, MA, 1975.

P1003.1, 1988.
P1003.1, *IEEE P1003.1 Portable Operating System Interface for Computer Environments (POSIX),* Institute of Electrical and Electronic Engineers, Piscataway, NJ, 1988.

Peirce, 1985.
N. Peirce, "Putting UNIX in Perspective: An Interview with Victor Vyssotsky," *UNIX Review*, vol. 3, no. 1, p. 58, January 1985.

Presotto & Ritchie, 1985.
D. L. Presotto & D. M. Ritchie, "Interprocess Communication in the Eighth Edition UNIX System," *USENIX Association Conference Proceedings*, pp. 309–316, June 1985.

Richards & Whitby-Strevens, 1980.
M. Richards & C. Whitby-Strevens, *BCPL: The Language and Its Compiler,* Cambridge University Press, Cambridge, U.K., 1980.

Ritchie, 1978.

D. M. Ritchie, "A Retrospective," *Bell System Technical Journal*, vol. 57, no. 6, pp. 1947–1969, July–August 1978.

Ritchie, 1984a.

D. M. Ritchie, "The Evolution of the UNIX Time-Sharing System," *AT&T Bell Laboratories Technical Journal*, vol. 63, no. 8, pp. 1577–1593, October 1984.

Ritchie, 1984b.

D. M. Ritchie, "Reflections on Software Research," *Comm ACM*, vol. 27, no. 8, pp. 758–760, August 1984.

Ritchie, 1987.

D. M. Ritchie, "UNIX: A Dialectic," *USENIX Association Conference Proceedings*, pp. 29–34, January 1987.

Ritchie, 2004.

D. M. Ritchie, *Documents on UNIX System Laboratories Inc. versus Berkeley Software Design Inc.,* available from http://cm.bell-labs.com/cm/cs/who/dmr/bsdi/bsdisuit.html, March 2004.

Ritchie et al., 1978.

D. M. Ritchie, S. C. Johnson, M. E. Lesk, & B. W. Kernighan, "The C Programming Language," *Bell System Technical Journal*, vol. 57, no. 6, pp. 1991–2019, July–August 1978.

Rosler, 1984.

L. Rosler, "The Evolution of C—Past and Future," *AT&T Bell Laboratories Technical Journal*, vol. 63, no. 8, pp. 1685–1699, October 1984.

Tanenbaum, 1987.

A. S. Tanenbaum, *Operating Systems: Design and Implementation,* Prentice-Hall, Englewood Cliffs, NJ, 1987.

Tuthill, 1985.

B. Tuthill, "The Evolution of C: Heresy and Prophecy," *UNIX Review*, vol. 3, no. 1, p. 80, January 1985.

Wilson, 1985.

O. Wilson, "The Business Evolution of the UNIX System," *UNIX Review*, vol. 3, no. 1, p. 46, January 1985.

X/OPEN, 1987.

X/OPEN, *The X/OPEN Portability Guide (XPG),* Issue 2, Elsevier Science, Amsterdam, Netherlands, 1987.

CHAPTER 2

Design Overview of FreeBSD

2.1 FreeBSD Facilities and the Kernel

The FreeBSD kernel provides four basic facilities: processes, filesystems, communications, and system startup. This section outlines where each of these four basic services is described in this book:

1. A process is composed of an address space with one or more threads of control running within it. Mechanisms for creating, terminating, and otherwise controlling processes are discussed in Chapter 4. The system multiplexes separate virtual-address spaces for each process. This memory management is discussed in Chapter 6.
2. The user interfaces to the filesystem and devices are similar; common aspects are discussed in Chapter 7. The organization and management of the devices in the I/O subsystem is described in Chapter 8. The filesystem provides operations to manipulate a set of named files, organized in a tree-structured hierarchy of directories. The filesystem must organize the storage of these files and directories on physical media, such as disks. The role of the traditional fast filesystem in doing these tasks is presented in Chapter 9; the role of the Zettabyte filesystem in doing these tasks is presented in Chapter 10. Access to files on remote machines is the subject of Chapter 11.
3. Communication mechanisms provided by traditional UNIX systems include simplex reliable byte streams between related processes (see pipes, Section 7.1), and notification of exceptional events (see Signals, Section 4.7). FreeBSD also has a general interprocess-communication facility. This facility, described in Chapter 12, uses access mechanisms distinct from those of the filesystem, but once a connection is set up, a process can access it as though it were a pipe. There is a general networking framework, discussed in

Chapter 13, that is normally used as a layer underlying the IPC facility. Chapter 14 describes particular networking implementations in detail.

4. Any real operating system has operational issues, such as how to start it running. Startup and operational issues are described in Chapter 15.

Sections 2.3 through 2.15 present introductory material related to Chapters 3 through 15. We define terms, examine basic system calls, and explore historical developments. Finally, we give the reasons for many major design decisions.

The Kernel

The ***kernel*** is the part of the system that runs in protected mode and mediates access by all user programs to the underlying hardware (e.g., CPU, keyboard, monitor, disks, network links) and software constructs (e.g., filesystem, network protocols). The kernel provides the basic system facilities; it creates and manages processes and provides functions to access the filesystem and communication facilities. These functions, called ***system calls***, appear to user processes as library subroutines. These system calls are the only interface that processes have to these facilities. Details of the system-call mechanism are given in Chapter 3, as are descriptions of several kernel mechanisms that do not execute as the direct result of a process doing a system call.

A kernel, in traditional operating-system terminology, is a small nucleus of software that provides only the minimal facilities necessary for implementing additional operating-system services. Through much of the 1980s, research operating systems—such as Tunis [Ewens et al., 1985], Chorus [Rozier et al., 1988], Mach [Accetta et al., 1986], and the V Kernel [Cheriton, 1988]—attempted to make this division of functionality into more than just a logical one. Services such as filesystems and networking protocols were implemented as client application processes of the nucleus or kernel. These micro-kernels largely failed because of the high overhead of transitioning between kernel processes.

The FreeBSD kernel is not partitioned into multiple processes. This basic design decision was made in the earliest versions of UNIX. The first two implementations by Ken Thompson had no memory mapping and thus made no hardware-enforced distinction between user and kernel space [Ritchie, 1988]. A message-passing system could have been implemented as readily as the actually implemented model of kernel and user processes. The monolithic kernel was chosen for simplicity and performance. And the early kernels were small; the inclusion of facilities such as networking into the kernel has increased its size, although the kernel is still small compared to many of the applications that run on it.

Users ordinarily interact with the system through a command-language interpreter, called a ***shell***, and through additional user application programs. Such programs and the shell are implemented with processes rather than being part of the kernel. Details of such programs are beyond the scope of this book, which instead concentrates almost exclusively on the kernel.

Sections 2.3 and 2.4 describe the services provided by the FreeBSD kernel and give an overview of the latter's design. Later chapters describe the detailed design and implementation of these services as they appear in FreeBSD.

2.2 Kernel Organization

In this section, we view the organization of the FreeBSD kernel in two ways:

1. As a static body of software, categorized by the functionality offered by the modules that make up the kernel
2. By its dynamic operation, categorized according to the services provided to users

The largest part of the kernel implements the system services that applications access through system calls. In FreeBSD, this software has been organized according to the following:

- Basic kernel facilities: timer and system-clock handling, descriptor management, and process management
- Security features: conventional UNIX model, but also sandboxing, virtualization, event auditing, and cryptographic services
- Memory-management support: paging and swapping
- Generic system interfaces: the I/O, control, and multiplexing operations performed on descriptors
- Filesystems: files, directories, pathname translation, file locking, and I/O buffer management
- Terminal-handling support: the pseudo-terminal interface and terminal line disciplines
- Interprocess-communication facilities: sockets
- Support for network communication: communication protocols and generic network facilities, such as routing

Most of the software in these categories is machine independent and is portable across different hardware architectures.

The machine-dependent aspects of the kernel are isolated from the mainstream code. In particular, none of the machine-independent code contains conditional code for specific architectures. When an architecture-dependent action is needed, the machine-independent code calls an architecture-dependent function that is located in the machine-dependent code. The software that is machine dependent includes the following:

Table 2.1 Machine-independent software in the FreeBSD kernel.

Category	Lines of Code	Percentage of Kernel
headers	59,070	3.8%
initialization	1,438	0.1%
kernel facilities	136,277	8.6%
generic interfaces	6,522	0.4%
interprocess communication	24,791	1.6%
terminal handling	19,163	1.2%
virtual memory	34,484	2.2%
vnode management	29,664	1.9%
fast filesystem	45,788	2.9%
Zettabyte filesystem	256,125	16.2%
miscellaneous filesystems (17)	71,468	4.5%
network filesystem	51,127	3.2%
network communication	73,260	4.6%
netgraph	88,447	5.6%
Internet V4 protocols	142,033	9.0%
Internet V6 protocols	40,480	2.6%
wireless	51,489	3.3%
packet filter	37,330	2.4%
IPsec	18,746	1.2%
cryptographic support	17,908	1.1%
security support	48,516	3.1%
GEOM layer	87,711	5.6%
CAM layer	96,238	6.1%
PCI bus	26,604	1.7%
virtualization	21,479	1.4%
kernel debugging	8,707	0.6%
Linux compatibility	20,839	1.3%
total machine independent	1,515,704	96.2%

Key: GEOM—geometry; CAM—Common Access Method; PCI—Peripheral Component Interconnect.

- Low-level system-startup actions
- Trap and fault handling
- Low-level manipulation of the run-time context of a process

Table 2.2 Machine-dependent software for the PC in the FreeBSD kernel.

Category	Lines of Code	Percentage of Kernel
machine dependent headers	7,927	0.5%
PCI bus	755	0.1%
virtual memory	16,637	1.1%
other machine dependent	15,489	1.0%
routines in assembly language	3,737	0.2%
Linux compatibility	13,532	0.9%
total machine dependent	58,077	3.8%

Key: PCI—Peripheral Component Interconnect.

- Configuration and initialization of hardware devices
- Run-time support for I/O devices

Table 2.1 summarizes the machine-independent software that constitutes the FreeBSD kernel for the 64-bit AMD architecture. The numbers in column 2 are for lines of C source code, header files, and assembly language. Virtually all the software in the kernel is written in the C programming language; a mere 0.6 percent is written in assembly language. As the statistics in Table 2.2 show, the machine-dependent software, excluding device support, accounts for a minuscule 3.8 percent of the kernel. Not shown are the 2,814,900 lines of code for the hundreds of supported devices, only a few of which will be loaded into any particular kernel.

In the 10 years since the previous edition of this book, the total size of the kernel has grown from 798,140 to 1,573,780 lines. The merger of ZFS into FreeBSD represents about a third of this growth. The machine-independent code has grown from 689,794 lines (86.4%) to 1,515,700 lines (96.2%). The machine-dependent code has shrunk from 108,346 lines (13.6%) to 58,077 lines (3.8%). These statistics do not include the device driver code that has grown from 846,525 lines to 2,814,900 lines.

Only a small part of the kernel is devoted to initializing the system. This code is used when the system is ***bootstrapped*** into operation and is responsible for setting up the kernel hardware and software environment (see Chapter 15). Some operating systems (especially those with limited physical memory) discard or ***overlay*** the software that performs these functions after that software has been executed. The FreeBSD kernel does not reclaim the memory used by the startup code because that memory space is barely 0.2 percent of the kernel resources used on a typical machine. Also, the startup code does not appear in one place in the kernel—it is scattered throughout, and it usually appears in places logically associated with what is being initialized.

2.3 Kernel Services

The boundary between the kernel- and user-level code is enforced by hardware-protection facilities provided by the underlying hardware. The kernel operates in a separate address space that is inaccessible to user processes. Privileged operations—such as starting I/O and halting the central processing unit (CPU)—are available to only the kernel. Applications request services from the kernel with system calls. System calls are used to cause the kernel to execute complicated operations, such as writing data to secondary storage, and simple operations, such as returning the current time of day. All system calls appear ***synchronous*** to applications: An application does not run while the kernel performs the actions associated with a system call. The kernel may finish some operations associated with a system call after it has returned. For example, a *write* system call will copy the data to be written from the user process to a kernel buffer while the process waits, but it will usually return from the system call before the kernel buffer is written to the disk.

A system call usually is implemented as a hardware trap that changes the CPU's execution mode and the current address-space mapping. Parameters supplied by users in system calls are validated by the kernel before being used. Such checking ensures the integrity of the system. All parameters passed into the kernel are copied into the kernel's address space to ensure that validated parameters are not changed as a side effect of the system call. System-call results are returned by the kernel, either in hardware registers or by their values being copied to user-specified memory addresses. Like parameters passed into the kernel, addresses used for the return of results must be validated to ensure that they are part of an application's address space. If the kernel encounters an error while processing a system call, it returns an error code to the user. For the C programming language, this error code is stored in the global variable ***errno***, and the function that executed the system call returns the value −1.

User applications and the kernel operate independently of each other. FreeBSD does not store I/O control blocks or other operating-system-related data structures in the application's address space. Each user-level application is provided an independent address space in which it executes. The kernel makes most state changes—such as suspending a process while another is running—invisible to the processes involved.

2.4 Process Management

FreeBSD supports a multitasking environment. Each task or thread of execution is termed a ***process***. In FreeBSD, the ***process context*** consists of user-level state, including the contents of its address space and the run-time environment, and kernel-level state, which includes scheduling parameters, resource controls, and identification information. The context includes everything used by the kernel in providing services for the process. Users can create processes, control the processes' execution, and receive notification when the processes' execution status changes. Every process is assigned a unique value, termed a ***process identifier*** (***PID***). This value is used by the kernel to identify a process when reporting status changes to a user, and by a user when referencing a process in a system call.

The kernel creates a process by duplicating the context of another process. The new process is termed a ***child process*** of the original ***parent process***. The context duplicated in process creation includes both the user-level execution state of the process and the process's system state managed by the kernel. Important components of the kernel state are described in Chapter 4.

The process lifecycle is depicted in Figure 2.1. A process may create a new process that is a copy of the original by using the *fork* system call. The *fork* call returns twice: once in the parent process, where the return value is the process identifier of the child, and once in the child process, where the return value is 0. The parent–child relationship induces a hierarchical structure on the set of processes in the system. The new process shares all its parent's resources, such as file descriptors, signal-handling status, and memory layout.

Although there are occasions when the new process is intended to be a copy of the parent, the loading and execution of a different program is a more useful and typical action. A process can overlay itself with the memory image of another program, passing to the newly created image a set of parameters, using the system call *execve*. One parameter is the name of a file whose contents are in a format recognized by the system—either a binary-executable file or a file that causes the execution of a specified interpreter program to interpret its contents.

A process may terminate by executing an *exit* system call, sending 8 bits of exit status to its parent. If a process wants to communicate more than a single byte of information with its parent, it must either set up an interprocess-communication channel using pipes or sockets, or use an intermediate file. Interprocess communication is discussed extensively in Chapter 12.

A process can suspend execution until any of its child processes terminate using the *wait* system call, which returns the PID and exit status of the terminated child process. A parent process can arrange to be notified by a signal when a child process exits or terminates abnormally. Using the *wait4* system call, the parent can retrieve information about the event that caused termination of the child

Figure 2.1 Process-management system calls.

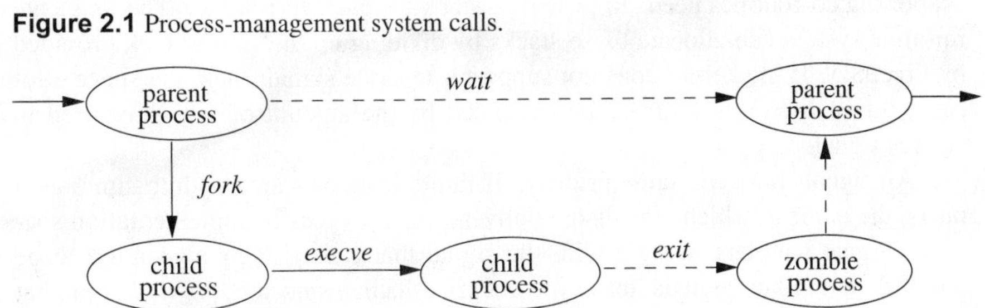

process and about resources consumed by the process during its lifetime. If a process is orphaned because its parent exits before it is finished, then the kernel arranges for the child's exit status to be passed back to a special system process, **init** (see Sections 3.1 and 15.5). The details of how the kernel creates and destroys processes are given in Chapter 6.

Processes are scheduled for execution according to a ***process-priority*** parameter. Under the default timesharing scheduler, this priority is managed by a kernel-based scheduling algorithm. Users can influence the scheduling of a process by specifying a parameter (***nice***) that weights the overall scheduling priority but are still obligated to share the underlying CPU resources according to the kernel's scheduling policy. FreeBSD also has a real-time scheduler. Processes running under the real-time scheduler manage their own priority, which is not changed by the kernel. The kernel will run the highest priority real-time process to the exclusion of all other processes. Thus, real-time processes are not obliged to share the underlying CPU resources.

Signals

The system defines a set of ***signals*** that may be delivered to a process. Signals in FreeBSD are modeled after hardware interrupts. A process may specify a user-level subroutine to be a ***handler*** to which a signal should be delivered. When a signal is generated, it is blocked from further occurrence while it is being ***caught*** by the handler. Catching a signal involves saving the current process context and building a new one in which to run the handler. The signal is then delivered to the handler, which can either abort the process or return to the executing process (perhaps after setting a global variable). If the handler returns, the signal is unblocked and can be generated (and caught) again.

Alternatively, a process may specify that a signal is to be ignored or that a default action, as determined by the kernel, is to be taken. The default action of certain signals is to terminate the process. This termination may be accompanied by creation of a ***core file*** that contains the current memory image of the process for use in postmortem debugging.

Some signals cannot be caught or ignored. These signals include SIGKILL, which kills runaway processes, and the job-control signal SIGSTOP.

A process may choose to have signals delivered on a special stack so that sophisticated software stack manipulations are possible. For example, a language supporting co-routines needs to provide a stack for each co-routine. The language run-time system can allocate these stacks by dividing up the single stack provided by FreeBSD. If the kernel does not support a separate signal stack, the space allocated for each co-routine must be expanded by the amount of space required to catch a signal.

All signals have the same priority. If multiple signals are pending simultaneously, the order in which signals are delivered to a process is implementation specific. Signal handlers execute with the signal that caused their invocation to be blocked, but other signals may yet occur. Mechanisms are provided so that processes can protect critical sections of code against the occurrence of specified signals.

The design and implementation of signals are described in Section 4.7.

Process Groups and Sessions

Processes are organized into ***process groups***. Process groups are used to control access to terminals and to provide a means of distributing signals to collections of related processes. A process inherits its process group from its parent process. Mechanisms are provided by the kernel to allow a process to alter its process group or the process group of its descendants. Creating a new process group is easy; the value of a new process group is ordinarily the process identifier of the creating process.

The group of processes in a process group is sometimes referred to as a ***job*** and is manipulated by high-level system software, such as the shell. A common kind of job created by a shell is a ***pipeline*** of several processes connected by pipes, such that the output of the first process is the input of the second, the output of the second is the input of the third, and so forth. The shell creates such a job by forking a process for each stage of the pipeline, and then putting all those processes into a separate process group.

A user process can send a signal to each process in a process group as well as to a single process. A process in a specific process group may receive software interrupts affecting the group, causing the group to suspend or resume execution, or to be interrupted or terminated.

A terminal (or more commonly a software emulation of a terminal called a pseudo-terminal) has a process-group identifier assigned to it. This identifier is normally set to the identifier of a process group associated with the terminal. A job-control shell may create several process groups associated with the same terminal; the terminal is the ***controlling terminal*** for each process in these groups. A process may read from a descriptor for its controlling terminal only if the terminal's process-group identifier matches that of the process. If the identifiers do not match, the process will be blocked if it attempts to read from the terminal. By changing the process-group identifier of the terminal, a shell can arbitrate a terminal among several different jobs. This arbitration is called ***job control*** and is described, with process groups, in Section 4.8.

Just as a set of related processes can be collected into a process group, a set of process groups can be collected into a ***session***. The main uses for sessions are to create an isolated environment for a daemon process and its children, and to collect a user's login shell and the jobs that that shell spawns.

2.5 Security

The FreeBSD security model has been developed over 40 years of evolving application needs. The key insight is that security must be part of system design; it cannot be successfully added later. The model addresses many different goals:

- Support authenticated local and remote access by multiple users, as well as integration with distributed authentication and directory services
- Allow users to define permissions/access control lists to control use of their files by other users and groups
- Support application authors in implementing compartmentalization for the purposes of intra-application policy and vulnerability mitigation
- Implement efficient lightweight virtualization allowing administrators to delegate safe subsets of root access to guest operating-system instances
- Allow the system administrator to control interactions between multiple users subject to various mandatory policies including information flow
- Permit fine-grained logging of security events in the system such as filesystem operations or network accesses
- Support and implement higher-level cryptographic services such as IPSec, **ssh**, transport-layer security (TLS), and full-disk encryption (GELI)

Application developers and system administrators can build on these features in a broad variety of ways. Software authors can implement features such as application-level sandboxing, cryptographic protocols such as https and PGP, or intrusion detection and security monitoring tools. System administrators and integrators can build systems or appliances providing Virtual Private Networks (VPNs), multiuser file servers, or virtual hosting platforms. These concrete goals in turn imply several design principles and elements for the kernel and core operating-system components themselves:

- A self-protecting Trusted Computing Base (TCB) guarantees enough system integrity to implement features such as multiple users and key storage
- Strong process isolation using virtual memory ensures that the kernel is protected from user code, and that user processes are protected from one another
- Identification and instrumentation of security-relevant operations throughout the kernel to implement access control, resource limits, and event auditing
- A coherent privilege model, internal to the kernel, that allows exceptional operations (such as system administration, device-driver implementations) to occur in a structured way despite being outside the regular access-control model
- Design abstractions that facilitate future security models, as well as security localization in downstream products; for example, clean separation of policy and mechanism, object-oriented structure (subject to the limitations of C), and a userspace capability-system model providing protection, rather than policy, as the primitive for application compartmentalization

- Cryptographic primitives, such as secure random number generation and a library of encryption and signature functions, that can support many different higher-level operating-system features and applications

Process Credentials

The kernel associates a set of ***process credentials*** with each process, which contain its various UNIX user identifiers (UIDs), group identifiers (GIDs), resource limits, audit properties, mandatory access control labels, capability-mode state, etc. Security-relevant operations throughout the kernel check these credentials, known as the subject, along with object properties (such as file permissions and ownership), before allowing the operation to proceed. Credential contents are protected by virtue of being in the kernel address space: they can be modified only using system calls that impose rules preventing circumvention of security policies.

FreeBSD implements the UNIX set-user-identity (setuid) and set-group-identity (setgid) permissions that allow programs executed by one user to operate with the privileges of another user or group. When the kernel detects an execution of such a binary, the process's credentials are modified to have a user or group ID reflecting the file's own IDs.

When the file is owned by the root user, it allows elevated privileges to be acquired—but only for the purposes of running the program in question. The program can then implement specific functions, such as modifying the system password file to change the user's password, but not the password of any other user. However, the technique is not limited to the root user: several users and groups serve to own common directories or devices, such as printers or terminals, which can be accessed by normal users only through specific binaries.

Privilege Model

Privilege refers to the necessary "safety valves" that exist in operating-system design to describe exceptions to normal access-control rules; for example:

- configuring network interfaces and network filtering;
- mounting, unmounting, and exporting filesystems;
- accessing or modifying kernel data and modules;
- overriding ACLs as a system administrator or for backups; or
- debugging system processes.

Historically, UNIX implemented a simple privilege model: processes with UID 0 (the ***root user***) were able to bypass almost all protections in the system. BSD, and later FreeBSD, have gradually refined this approach through the introduction of securelevels, jails, and mandatory access control.

The privilege model has required a change from a single in-kernel function, *suser*(), that simply checks to see if the current thread has root credentials, to a more complex in-kernel interface named *priv_check*(). Although the user-visible policy remains roughly similar to the UNIX root model, internal subdivision into roughly 200 named privileges allows a variety of refinements, such as subsetting of rights allowed in jails versus the remainder of the OS, as well as allowing MAC policies to have controlled interactions with the privilege model. These changes have also proven valuable in meeting the goal of supporting downstream consumers: product localizations frequently seek to extend the privilege model, and the privilege space itself is extensible.

Discretionary Access Control

Another area of refinement of the original UNIX security model is through the more flexible and fine-grained ***discretionary access control***, the specification of protections properties for other users by object owners. UNIX allowed read, write, and execute permission controls for the file owner, the file group, and everyone else. FreeBSD added access-control lists, in which the set of permissions is expanded to read, write, execute, lookup, and administration. These expanded permissions can be applied to a list of users each with their own permissions, a list of groups each with their own permissions, and access granted for everyone else. This model permits full backward compatibility with historical implementations while also providing vastly finer-grain control.

Capability Model

The Capsicum security framework is a new feature added in FreeBSD 9 to provide sandboxing of libraries or modules, either because the code is of untrustworthy origin, or because it is suspected that the code might experience vulnerabilities when acting on data of unknown or dubious provenance. Capsicum allows the creation of processes that execute with only the system rights that they have been explicitly delegated.

A process running in capability mode can only work with the set of file descriptors that it was explicitly granted at creation time, or later delegated via IPC. The creator can further limit the set of operations that may be performed on the granted descriptors. For example, it may allow I/O on a descriptor, but not the right to change file modes or test for events using *select*, *poll*, or *kqueue*. The process is denied access to the system's global namespaces such as process identifiers or the filesystem. Thus the *open* system call will fail but the *openat* system call will work if given an appropriately privileged descriptor open on a directory from which to start.

Jail Lightweight Virtualization

While FreeBSD operates well under several full-machine virtualization technologies such as Xen and its own bhyve hypervisor, FreeBSD jails provide lighter-weight ***virtual machines*** at a much lower resource commitment. Each jail creates a group of processes with their own root-administered environment giving the illusion that it is running on its own dedicated hardware. Unlike a full virtual machine emulator that can run any operating system, a jail can only provide a FreeBSD kernel environment. However, it can provide that environment much more efficiently than a full virtual machine emulator: a single physical machine is typically limited to dozens or hundreds of concurrent full virtual machines, while it can support thousands of jails simultaneously.

Three techniques underly the jail implementation:

- access control, which prevents operations such as inter-jail process debugging;
- resource subsetting, which limits jails to a specific subset of the hierarchical filesystem namespace (via *chroot*); and
- true virtualization, in which jails are each presented a unique instance of global system namespaces.

Access control and resource subsetting come at little cost, whereas full virtualization can incur substantial kernel-memory overhead. Virtualization is therefore configurable: jails may be granted access to a subset of system IP addresses within the global network-stack instance, or optional full network-stack virtualization can be configured.

In a typical configuration, each jail has an independent FreeBSD userspace installation in a jail-specific filesystem tree—or for stronger resource isolation at greater resource commitment, its own filesystem instance. Each jail will be delegated its own subset of system IP addresses. Processes will operate as normal, but will be limited to those addresses; for example, an ISP might grant each virtual-domain customer its own virtual FreeBSD installation, with its own user account database, and each of which contains a webserver instance binding only the jail's IP addresses. Most operations are permitted within a jail including:

- running or signalling processes within the jail;
- changing files within the jail;
- binding low port numbers on the jail's IP addresses; and
- optionally managing ZFS data sets within a larger volume delegated to the jail.

Processes running within a jail are not permitted to perform operations that would allow them to see or affect anything running outside their jail. This restriction is implemented in large part by masking the set of named system privileges available to root processes running within a jail. Constrained privileges include:

- getting information on processes outside the jail;
- changing kernel variables;

- mounting or unmounting filesystems;
- modifying physical network interfaces or configurations; and
- rebooting the system.

Mandatory Access Control

Mandatory access control (***MAC***) describes a broad class of security policies that allow the system administrator (or system integrator) to control systemic behaviors such as information flow (for example, ***multilevel security*** (***MLS***)), or fine-grained system-scale rules (such as type enforcement (TE)). As there remains significant disagreement about which mandatory policies best solve particular practical security problems, FreeBSD implements a framework for kernel access-control extensibility, the MAC framework.

The framework allows policies compiled into the kernel or kernel modules to instrument kernel security decisions, but also provides common infrastructure required by many policies such as object label storage, policy-agnostic APIs for security management, and tracing/debugging features. Kernel subsystems invoke MAC framework entry points at strategic points in kernel operation—creation and destruction of objects, before access to operations on objects, and system security events such as privilege checks. The framework in turn invokes different policy modules, composing their results.

Security policies are able to control access to a broad set of security-relevant system objects and services including filesystem objects such as files/directories, IPC objects such as pipes, and access to network sockets. They can also limit interprocess operations such as execution, visibility, signalling, and tracing.

Many policies use security labels to tag processes and objects with additional security metadata to be used during access control checks; for example, labels might contain per-object or per-process confidentiality information for MLS to use in blocking illegitimate information flow, or domain and type information that will be checked against Type Enforcement rules controlling their interactions.

The MAC framework requires maintaining labels not just on userspace-visible objects acted on directly by system calls, but also internal objects such as in-flight network data stored in mbuf chains. A key design concern in the framework is performance proportionality: more intrusive policies, such as labelled MAC policies, may incur greater expense for labelling, but policies using only existing security information, such as process-credential UIDs and file ownership, should not.

FreeBSD includes several sample policy modules such as confidentiality and integrity models, but downstream consumers of FreeBSD have used the framework to implement many other policies including Apple's sandboxing models for Mac OS X and iOS, and application sandboxing in Juniper's Junos router operating system.

Event Auditing

The original UNIX accounting and the added FreeBSD tracing have been expanded to include full auditing to provide accountability and intrusion detection. It is based on Open Basic Security Module. When enabled, it generates records for kernel events involving access control, authentication, security management, audit management, and user-level audit reports. For each event, it records the user credentials that can be augmented with an audit identifier that holds terminal and session information to be added to each audit record.

The volume of the audit trail is controllable using a global audit preselection policy with an optional audit mask to subset the global policy. Audit records can be further thinned using the **auditreduce** utility.

Cryptography and Random-Number Generators

Contemporary operating systems depend on a variety of cryptographic services:

- one-way hashes protect user passwords;
- digital signatures protect software updates and user data from tampering; and
- symmetric and asymmetric encryption protect user data on disk and the network.

All these functions require strong cryptographic foundations. The FreeBSD kernel includes a strong cryptographic random number generator, and libraries of encryption, integrity checking, and hashing algorithms. These libraries are used by kernel services such as GELI disk encryption and IPSec virtual private networks, but also userspace applications such as **ssh**, GPG, and Kerberos.

FreeBSD employs the Yarrow cryptographic pseudorandom number generator to implement both sources of in-kernel randomness and **/dev/random**. Yarrow reuses existing cryptographic primitives such as cryptographic hashes and counter-mode block encryption. The key to making the output of Yarrow unguessable is having a good source of truly random seeds; Yarrow is able to combine multiple sources of entropy, and tolerate compromise of a subset of sources.

Many CPUs now implement built-in hardware random number generators using oscillator loops to generate difficult-to-predict output. The first of these built-in hardware random number generators was the VIA generator used since FreeBSD 5.3. More recently, Intel introduced a random number generator that is accessed using the `rdrand` instruction, supported since FreeBSD 9.2. Since 10.1, FreeBSD feeds the output of hardware entropy sources through Yarrow as it is hard to determine whether these sources are operating correctly, or have perhaps been compromised. With FreeBSD 11, Yarrow was replaced by Fortuna, which automates the estimation of how and when to use alternate entropy sources.

FreeBSD makes use of cryptographic services within the kernel such as for providing full-disk encryption. These cryptographic services may be implemented in software or by hardware accelerators—historically they were found in add-on boards, but increasingly, they are implemented via instruction-set extensions. Access to hardware encryption is also exported to processes that need to provide large streams of encrypted data.

These security components combine to meet the requirements of the diverse systems that run FreeBSD, ranging across hand-held computing devices, network devices, storage appliances, and Internet service providers' large-scale hosting environments.

2.6 Memory Management

Each process has its own private address space. The address space is initially divided into three logical ***segments***: ***text***, ***data***, and ***stack***. The text segment is read-only and contains the machine instructions of a program. The data and stack segments are both readable and writable. The data segment contains the initialized and uninitialized data portions of a program, whereas the stack segment holds the application's run-time stack. The stack segment is extended automatically by the kernel as the process executes. A process can expand or contract its data segment by making a system call, whereas a process can change the size of its text segment only when the segment's contents are overlaid with data from the filesystem or when debugging takes place. The initial contents of the segments of a child process are duplicates of the segments of a parent process.

The entire contents of a process address space do not need to be resident for a process to execute. If a process references a part of its address space that is not resident in main memory, the system ***pages*** the necessary information into memory. When system resources are scarce, the system uses a two-level approach to maintain available resources. If a modest amount of memory is available, the system will take memory resources away from processes if these resources have not been used recently. Should there be a severe resource shortage, the system will resort to ***swapping*** the entire context of a process to secondary storage. The ***demand paging*** and ***swapping*** done by the system are effectively transparent to processes. A process may, however, advise the system about expected future memory utilization as a performance aid.

BSD Memory-Management Design Decisions

The support of large, sparse address spaces, mapped files, and shared memory was a requirement for 4.2BSD. An interface was specified, called *mmap*(), that allowed unrelated processes to request a shared mapping of a file into their address spaces. If multiple processes mapped the same file into their address spaces, changes to the file's portion of an address space by one process would be reflected in the area mapped by the other processes, as well as in the file itself. Ultimately, 4.2BSD was shipped without the *mmap*() interface, because of pressure to make other features, such as networking, available.

Further development of the *mmap*() interface continued during the work on 4.3BSD. Over 40 companies and research groups participated in the discussions leading to the revised architecture that was described in the Berkeley Software Architecture Manual [McKusick et al., 1994]. The first UNIX implementation of the interface was done by Sun Microsystems [Gingell et al., 1987].

Once again, time pressure prevented 4.3BSD from providing an implementation of the interface. Although the latter could have been built into the existing 4.3BSD virtual-memory system, the developers decided not to put it in because that implementation was nearly 10 years old. Furthermore, the original virtual-memory design was based on the assumption that computer memories were small and expensive, whereas disks were locally connected, fast, large, and inexpensive. Thus, the virtual-memory system was designed to be frugal with its use of memory at the expense of generating extra disk traffic. In addition, the 4.3BSD implementation was riddled with VAX memory-management hardware dependencies that impeded its portability to other computer architectures. Finally, the virtual-memory system was not designed to support the tightly coupled multiprocessors that were becoming increasingly common and important.

Attempts to improve the old implementation incrementally seemed doomed to failure. A completely new design, on the other hand, could take advantage of large memories, conserve disk transfers, and have the potential to run on multiprocessors. Consequently, the virtual-memory system was completely replaced in 4.4BSD. The 4.4BSD virtual-memory system was based on the Mach 2.0 virtual-memory system [Tevanian, 1987], with updates from Mach 2.5 and Mach 3.0.

The FreeBSD virtual-memory system is an extensively tuned version of the virtual-memory implementation in 4.4BSD. It features efficient support for sharing, a clean separation of machine-independent and machine-dependent features, as well as multiprocessor support. Processes can map files anywhere in their address space. They can share parts of their address space by doing a shared mapping of the same file. Changes made by one process are visible in the address space of the other process and also are written back to the file itself. Processes can also request private mappings of a file, which prevents any changes that they make from being visible to other processes mapping the file or being written back to the file itself.

Another issue with the virtual-memory system is the way that information is passed into the kernel when a *read* or *write* system call is made. For these system calls, FreeBSD always copies data from the process address space into a buffer in the kernel. The copy is done for several reasons:

- Often, the user data are not page aligned and are not a multiple of the hardware page length.
- If the page is taken away from the process, it will no longer be able to reference that page. Some programs depend on the data remaining in the buffer even after those data have been written.
- If the process is allowed to keep a copy of the page (as it is in current FreeBSD semantics), the page must be made ***copy-on-write***. A copy-on-write page is one

that is protected against being written by being made read-only. If the process attempts to modify the page, the kernel gets a write fault. The kernel then makes a copy of the page that the process can modify. Unfortunately, the typical process will immediately try to write new data to its output buffer, forcing the data to be copied anyway.

- When pages are remapped to new virtual-memory addresses, most memory-management hardware requires that the hardware address-translation cache be purged selectively. The cache purges are often slow. The net effect is that remapping is slower than copying for blocks of data less than 4 to 8 Kbyte.

For read or write operations that are transferring large quantities of data, doing the copy can be time consuming. An alternative to doing the copying is to remap the process memory into the kernel. The biggest incentives for memory mapping are the needs for accessing big files and for passing large quantities of data between processes. The *mmap*() interface provides a way for both of these tasks to be done without copying.

The *mmap* system call is not supported between processes running on different machines. Such processes must communicate using sockets connected across the network. Thus, sending the contents of a file across the network is another common operation where it is desirable to avoid copying. Historically, the sending of a file was done by reading the file into an application buffer, and then writing that buffer to a socket. This approach required two copies of the data: first from the kernel to the application buffer, and then from the application buffer back into the kernel to send on the socket. FreeBSD pioneered the *sendfile* system call that sends data from a file down a socket without doing any copying.

Memory Management Inside the Kernel

The kernel often does allocations of memory that are needed for only the duration of a single system call. In a user process, such short-term memory would be allocated on the run-time stack. Because the kernel has a limited run-time stack, it is not feasible to allocate even moderate-size blocks of memory on it. Consequently, such memory must be allocated through a more dynamic mechanism. For example, when the system must translate a pathname, it must allocate a 1-Kbyte buffer to hold the name. Other blocks of memory must be more persistent than a single system call, and thus could not be allocated on the stack even if there were space. An example is protocol-control blocks that remain throughout the duration of a network connection.

Demands for dynamic memory allocation in the kernel have increased as more services have been added. A generalized memory allocator reduces the complexity of writing code inside the kernel. Thus, the FreeBSD kernel has a general memory allocator that can be used by any part of the system. It has an interface similar to the C library routines *malloc*() and *free*() that provide memory allocation to application programs [McKusick & Karels, 1988]. Like the C library interface, the allocation routine takes a parameter specifying the size of memory that is needed. The range of sizes for memory requests is not constrained; however, physical memory is allocated and is not paged. The free routine takes a pointer to the storage being freed, but it does not require the size of the piece of memory being freed.

Some large and persistent allocations, such as the structure that tracks information about a process during its lifetime, are not well handled by the general memory allocator. The kernel provides a zone allocator for these types of allocations. Each memory type is given its own zone from which all its allocations are made. Memory allocated in one zone cannot be used by any other zone or by the general memory allocator. The semantics of the interface are similar to the general-memory allocator; memory is allocated from a zone with the *zalloc*() routine and freed with the *zfree*() routine.

2.7 I/O System Overview

The basic model of the UNIX I/O system is a sequence of bytes that can be accessed either randomly or sequentially. There are no access methods and no control blocks in a typical UNIX user process.

Different programs expect various levels of structure, but the kernel does not impose structure on I/O. For instance, the convention for text files is lines of ASCII characters separated by a single newline character (the ASCII line-feed character), but the kernel knows nothing about this convention. For the purposes of most programs, the model is further simplified to just a stream of data bytes, or an ***I/O stream***. It is this single common data form that makes the characteristic UNIX tool-based approach work [Kernighan & Pike, 1984]. An I/O stream from one program can be fed as input to almost any other program.

Descriptors and I/O

UNIX processes use ***descriptors*** to reference I/O streams. Descriptors are small unsigned integers obtained from the *open* and *socket* system calls. The *open* system call takes as arguments the name of a file and a permission mode to specify whether the file should be open for reading or for writing, or for both. This system call also can be used to create a new, empty file. A *read* or *write* system call can be applied to a descriptor to transfer data. The *close* system call can be used to deallocate any descriptor.

Descriptors represent underlying objects supported by the kernel and are created by system calls specific to the type of object. In FreeBSD, seven kinds of objects can be represented by descriptors—files, pipes, fifos, sockets, POSIX IPC, event queues, and processes:

1. A ***file*** is a linear array of bytes with at least one name. A file exists until all of its names are deleted explicitly and no process holds a descriptor for it. A process acquires a descriptor for a file by opening that file's name with the *open* system call. Most I/O devices are accessed as files.

2. A ***pipe*** is a linear array of bytes, as is a file, but it is used solely as an I/O stream, and it is unidirectional. It also has no name and thus cannot be opened with *open*. Instead, it is created by the *pipe* system call, which returns two descriptors, one of which accepts input that is sent to the other descriptor reliably, without duplication, and in order.

3. A ***fifo*** is often referred to as a named pipe. A fifo has properties identical to a pipe, except that it appears in the filesystem; thus, it can be opened using the *open* system call. Two processes that wish to communicate each open the fifo: one opens it for reading, the other for writing.

4. A ***socket*** is a transient object that is used for interprocess communication; it exists only as long as some process holds a descriptor referring to it. A socket is created by the *socket* system call, which returns a descriptor for it. There are different kinds of sockets that support various communication semantics, such as reliable delivery of data, preservation of message ordering, and preservation of message boundaries.

5. POSIX IPC includes message queues, shared memory, and semaphores. Each type of IPC has its own set of system calls that are described in Section 7.2.

6. An event queue is a descriptor for which an application registers notification requests for a wide set of events. The events include arrival of data for a descriptor, availability of space for output on a descriptor, completion of asynchronous I/O, various timer-based events, and change in status of a set of its processes. An event queue is created by the *kqueue* system call, which returns a descriptor for it.

7. A process descriptor is used by the Capsicum capability model to control the set of processes to which a sandboxed process can have access. A process descriptor is created by specifying the RFPROCDESC flag to the *rfork* system call. Capsicum and its use of process descriptors is described in Section 5.8.

In systems before 4.2BSD, pipes were implemented using the filesystem; when sockets were introduced in 4.2BSD, pipes were reimplemented as sockets. For performance reasons, FreeBSD no longer uses sockets to implement pipes and fifos. Rather, it uses a separate implementation optimized for local communication.

The kernel keeps a ***descriptor table*** for each process, which is a table that the kernel uses to translate the external representation of a descriptor into an internal representation. (The descriptor is merely an index into this table.) The descriptor table of a process is inherited from that process's parent, and thus access to the objects to which the descriptors refer also is inherited. The main ways that a process can obtain a descriptor are

1. by opening or creating an object, or

2. by inheriting from the parent process.

In addition, socket IPC allows passing descriptors in messages between unrelated processes on the same machine.

Every valid descriptor has an associated ***file offset*** in bytes from the beginning of the object. Read and write operations start at this offset, which is updated after each data transfer. For objects that permit random access, the file offset also may be set with the *lseek* system call. Ordinary files permit random access, and some devices do, too. The remaining descriptor types including pipes, fifos, and sockets do not.

When a process terminates, the kernel reclaims all the descriptors that were in use by that process. If the process was holding the final reference to an object, the object's manager is notified so that it can do any necessary cleanup actions, such as final deletion of a file or deallocation of a socket.

Descriptor Management

Most processes expect three descriptors to be open already when they start running. These descriptors are 0, 1, and 2, more commonly known as ***standard input***, ***standard output***, and ***standard error***, respectively. Usually, all three are associated with the user's terminal by the login process (see Section 15.4) and are inherited through *fork* and *exec* by processes run by the user. Thus, a program can read what the user types by reading standard input, and the program can send output to the user's screen by writing to standard output. The standard error descriptor also is open for writing and is used for error output, whereas standard output is used for ordinary output.

These (and other) descriptors can be mapped to objects other than the terminal; such mapping is called ***I/O redirection***, and all the standard shells permit users to do it. The shell can direct the output of a program to a file by closing descriptor 1 (standard output) and opening the desired output file to produce a new descriptor 1. It can similarly redirect standard input to come from a file by closing descriptor 0 and opening the file.

Pipes allow the output of one program to be input to another program without rewriting or even relinking of either program. Instead of descriptor 1 (standard output) of the source program being set up to write to the terminal, it is set up to be the input descriptor of a pipe. Similarly, descriptor 0 (standard input) of the sink program is set up to reference the output of the pipe instead of the terminal keyboard. The resulting set of two processes and the connecting pipe is known as a ***pipeline***. Pipelines can be arbitrarily long series of processes connected by pipes.

The *open*, *pipe*, and *socket* system calls produce new descriptors with the lowest unused number usable for a descriptor. For pipelines to work, some mechanism must be provided to map such descriptors into 0 and 1. The *dup* system call creates a copy of a descriptor that points to the same file-table entry. The new descriptor is also the lowest unused one, but if the desired descriptor is closed first, *dup* can be used to do the desired mapping. Care is required, however: If descriptor 1 is desired, and descriptor 0 happens also to have been closed, descriptor 0 will be the result. To avoid this problem, the system provides the *dup2* system call; it is like *dup*, but it takes an additional argument specifying the number of the desired descriptor (if the desired descriptor was already open, *dup2* closes it before reusing it).

Devices

Hardware devices have filenames and may be accessed by the user via the same system calls used for regular files. The kernel can distinguish a ***device special file*** or ***special file***, and it can determine to what device it refers, but most processes do not need to make this determination. Terminals, printers, and tape drives are all accessed as though they were streams of bytes, like FreeBSD disk files. Thus, device dependencies and peculiarities are kept in the kernel as much as possible, and even in the kernel most of them are segregated in the device drivers.

Processes typically access devices through special files in the filesystem. I/O operations to these files are handled by kernel-resident software modules termed ***device drivers***. Most network-communication hardware devices are accessible through only the interprocess-communication facilities and do not have special files in the filesystem namespace, because the ***raw-socket*** interface provides a more natural interface than does a special file.

Device special files are created in the **/dev** filesystem by their device driver when the hardware is first found. The *ioctl* system call manipulates the underlying device parameters of special files. The operations that can be done differ for each device. This system call allows the special characteristics of devices to be accessed, rather than overloading the semantics of other system calls. For example, there is an *ioctl* on a sound card to set the audio-encoding format instead of there being a special or modified version of *write*.

Socket IPC

The 4.2BSD kernel introduced an IPC mechanism more flexible than pipes, based on sockets. A socket is an endpoint of communication referred to by a descriptor, just like a file or a pipe. Two processes can each create a socket and then connect those two endpoints to produce a reliable byte stream. Once connected, the descriptors for the sockets can be read or written by processes, just as the latter would do with a pipe. The transparency of sockets allows the kernel to redirect the output of one process to the input of another process residing on another machine. A major difference between pipes and sockets is that pipes require a common parent process to set up the communications channel. A connection between sockets can be set up by two unrelated processes, possibly residing on different machines.

Fifos appear as an object in the filesystem that unrelated processes can open and send data through in the same way as they would communicate through a pair of sockets. Thus, fifos do not require a common parent to set them up; they can be connected after a pair of processes are up and running. Unlike sockets, fifos can be used on only a local machine; they cannot be used to communicate between processes on different machines.

The socket mechanism requires extensions to the traditional UNIX I/O system calls to provide the associated naming and connection semantics. Rather than overloading the existing interface, the developers used the existing interfaces to the extent that the latter worked without being changed and designed new interfaces to handle the added semantics. The *read* and *write* system calls were used for byte-stream-type connections, but six new system calls were added to allow sending and receiving addressed messages such as network datagrams. The system calls for writing messages include *send*, *sendto*, and *sendmsg*. The system calls for reading messages include *recv*, *recvfrom*, and *recvmsg*. In retrospect, the first two in each class are special cases of the others; *recvfrom* and *sendto* probably should have been added as library interfaces to *recvmsg* and *sendmsg*, respectively.

Scatter-Gather I/O

In addition to the traditional *read* and *write* system calls, 4.2BSD introduced the ability to do ***scatter-gather I/O***. Scatter input uses the *readv* system call to allow a single read to be placed in several different buffers. Conversely, the *writev* system call allows several different buffers to be written in a single atomic write. Instead of passing a single buffer and length parameter, as is done with *read* and *write*, the process passes in a pointer to an array of buffers and lengths, along with a count describing the size of the array.

This facility allows buffers in different parts of a process address space to be written atomically, without the need to copy them to a single contiguous buffer. Atomic writes are necessary in the case where the underlying abstraction is record based, such as datagrams that output a single message on each write request. It is also convenient to be able to read a single request into several different buffers (such as a record header into one place and the data into another). Although an application can simulate the ability to scatter data by reading the data into a large buffer and then copying the pieces to their intended destinations, the cost of memory-to-memory copying in such cases often would more than double the running time of the affected application.

Just as *send* and *recv* could have been implemented as library interfaces to *sendto* and *recvfrom*, it also would have been possible to simulate *read* using *readv* and *write* using *writev*. However, *read* and *write* are used so much more frequently that the added cost of simulating them would not have been worthwhile.

Multiple Filesystem Support

With the expansion of network computing, it became desirable to support both local and remote filesystems. To simplify the support of multiple filesystems, the developers added a new virtual node or ***vnode*** interface to the kernel. The set of operations exported from the vnode interface appear much like the filesystem operations previously supported by the local filesystem. However, they may be supported by a wide range of filesystem types:

- Local disk-based filesystems
- Files imported using a variety of remote filesystem protocols
- Read-only CD-ROM filesystems
- Filesystems providing special-purpose interfaces, for example, the **/dev** filesystem

By using loadable kernel modules (see Section 15.3), FreeBSD allows filesystems to be loaded dynamically when the filesystems are first referenced by the *mount* system call. The vnode interface is described in Section 7.3; its ancillary support routines are described in Section 7.4; several of the special-purpose filesystems are described in Section 7.5.

2.8 Devices

Historically, the device interface was static and simple. Devices were discovered as the system was booted and did not change thereafter. A typical disk driver could be written in a few hundred lines of code. As the system has evolved, the complexity of the I/O system has increased, with the addition of new functionality. Devices may appear and later disappear while the system is running. With increasing complexity and types of I/O buses, the routing of I/O requests has become complex. In a multiprocessor, for example, device interrupts must be routed to the most appropriate processor, which may not be the same one that previously handled the device. An overview of the PC architecture is given in Section 8.1.

Devices are described by character device drivers. Sections 8.2 through 8.6 introduce the structure of device drivers and then detail device drivers for disks, network interfaces, and terminals.

Logical disks may no longer refer to a partition on a single physical disk but instead may combine several slices and/or partitions to create a virtual partition on which to build a filesystem that spans several disks. The aggregation of physical disk partitions into a virtual partition in these ways is referred to as volume management. Rather than building all this functionality into all the filesystems or disk drivers, it has been abstracted out into the GEOM (geometry) layer. The operation of the GEOM layer is described in Section 8.7. The management of the disk subsystem in FreeBSD is described in Section 8.8.

Autoconfiguration is the procedure carried out by the system to recognize and enable the hardware devices present in a system. Historically, autoconfiguration was done just once when the system was booted. In current machines, particularly portable machines such as laptop computers, devices routinely come and go while the machine is operating. Thus, the kernel must be prepared to configure, initialize, and make available hardware when it arrives and to drop operations with hardware that has departed. FreeBSD uses a device-driver infrastructure called ***newbus*** to manage the devices on the system. The newbus architecture is described in Section 8.9.

2.9 The Fast Filesystem

A regular file is a linear array of bytes and can be read and written starting at any byte in the file. The kernel distinguishes no record boundaries in regular files, although many programs recognize line-feed characters as distinguishing the ends of lines, and other programs may impose other structure. No system-related information about a file is kept in the file itself, but the filesystem stores a small amount of ownership, protection, and usage information with each file.

A ***filename*** component is a string of up to 255 characters. These filenames are stored in a type of file called a ***directory***. The information in a directory about a file is called a ***directory entry*** and includes, in addition to the filename, a pointer to the file itself. Directory entries may refer to other directories, as well as to plain files. A hierarchy of directories and files is thus formed, called a ***filesystem***; a small one is shown in Figure 2.2. Directories may contain subdirectories, and there is no inherent limitation to the depth with which directory nesting may occur. To protect the consistency of the filesystem, the kernel does not permit processes to write directly into directories. A filesystem may include not only plain files and directories but also references to other objects, such as sockets and fifos.

The filesystem forms a tree, the beginning of which is the ***root directory***, sometimes referred to by the name **slash**, spelled with a single solidus character (**/**). The root directory contains files; in our example in Figure 2.2, it contains **kernel**, a copy of the kernel-executable object file. It also contains directories; in this example, it contains the **usr** directory. Within the **usr** directory is the **bin** directory, which mostly contains executable object code of programs, such as the files **ls** and **vi**.

Figure 2.2 A small filesystem tree.

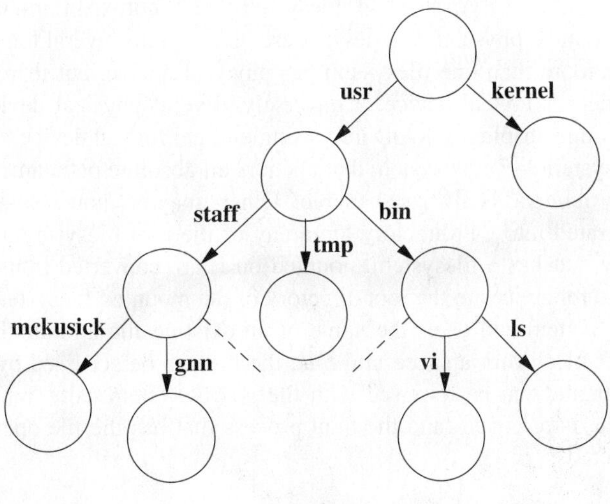

A process identifies a file by specifying that file's ***pathname***, which is a string composed of zero or more filenames separated by slash (/) characters. The kernel associates two directories with each process for use in interpreting pathnames. A process's root directory is the topmost point in the filesystem that the process can access; it is ordinarily set to the root directory of the entire filesystem. A pathname beginning with a slash is called an ***absolute pathname*** and is interpreted by the kernel starting with the process's root directory.

A pathname that does not begin with a slash is called a ***relative pathname*** and is interpreted relative to the ***current working directory*** of the process. (This directory also is known by the shorter names *current directory* or ***working directory***.) The current directory itself may be referred to directly by the name **dot**, spelled with a single period (**.**). The filename **dot-dot** (**..**) refers to a directory's parent directory. The root directory is its own parent.

A process may set its root directory with the *chroot* system call and its current directory with the *chdir* system call. Any process may do *chdir* at any time, but *chroot* is permitted only a process with superuser privileges. *Chroot* is normally used to set up restricted access to the system.

Using the filesystem shown in Figure 2.2, if a process has the root of the filesystem as its root directory and has **/usr** as its current directory, it can refer to the file **vi** either from the root with the absolute pathname **/usr/bin/vi** or from its current directory with the relative pathname **bin/vi**.

System utilities and databases are kept in certain well-known directories. Part of the well-defined hierarchy includes a directory that contains the ***home directory*** for each user—for example, **/usr/staff/mckusick** and **/usr/staff/gnn** in Figure 2.2. When users log in, the current working directory of their shell is set to the home directory. Within their home directories, users can create directories as easily as they can regular files. Thus, a user can build arbitrarily complex subhierarchies.

The user usually knows of only one filesystem, but the system may know that this one virtual filesystem is really composed of several physical filesystems, each on a different device. A physical filesystem may not span multiple logical devices. Since most physical disk devices are divided into several logical devices, there may be more than one filesystem per physical device, but there will be no more than one per logical device. Conversely, several physical devices may be combined through striping or RAID into a single larger logical device.

One filesystem—the filesystem that anchors all absolute pathnames—is called the ***root filesystem*** and is always available. Others may be mounted—that is, they may be integrated into the directory hierarchy of the root filesystem. References to a directory that has a filesystem mounted on it are converted transparently by the kernel into references to the root directory of the mounted filesystem.

The *link* system call takes the name of an existing file and another name to create for that file. After a successful *link*, the file can be accessed by either filename. A filename can be removed with the *unlink* system call. When the final name for a file is removed (and the final process that has the file open closes it), the file is deleted.

Files are organized hierarchically in directories . A directory is a type of file, but, in contrast to regular files, a directory has a structure imposed on it by the system. A process can read a directory as it would an ordinary file, but only the kernel is permitted to modify a directory. Directories are created by the *mkdir* system call and are removed by the *rmdir* system call. Before 4.2BSD, the *mkdir* and *rmdir* system calls were implemented by a series of *link* and *unlink* system calls being performed. There were three reasons for adding system calls explicitly to create and delete directories:

1. The operation could be made atomic. If the system crashed, the directory would not be left half-constructed, as could happen when a series of link operations were used.

2. When a networked filesystem is being run, the creation and deletion of files and directories need to be specified atomically so that they can be serialized.

3. When supporting non-UNIX filesystems, such as an NTFS filesystem, on another partition of the disk, the other filesystem may not support link operations. Although other filesystems might support the concept of directories, they probably would not create and delete the directories with links, as the UNIX filesystem does. Consequently, they could create and delete directories only if explicit directory create and delete requests were presented.

The *chown* system call sets the owner and group of a file, and *chmod* changes protection attributes. *Stat* applied to a filename can be used to read back such properties of a file. The *fchown*, *fchmod*, and *fstat* system calls are applied to a descriptor instead of to a filename to do the same set of operations. The *rename* system call can be used to give a file a new name in the filesystem, replacing one of the file's old names. Like the directory-creation and directory-deletion operations, the *rename* system call was added to 4.2BSD to provide atomicity to name changes in the local filesystem. Later, it proved useful explicitly to export renaming operations to foreign filesystems and over the network.

The *truncate* system call was added to 4.2BSD to allow files to be set to an arbitrary size. Thus, *truncate* is poorly named because it may be used to both shorten and lengthen a file. Files may have ***holes*** in them. Holes are void areas in the linear extent of the file where data have never been written. A process can create these holes by positioning the pointer past the current end-of-file and writing. Alternatively, a hole may be added to the end of a file by using the *truncate* system call to increase its length. When read, holes are treated by the system as zero-valued bytes.

Once the filesystem had the ability to shorten files, the kernel took advantage of that ability to shorten large, empty directories. The advantage of shortening empty directories is that it reduces the time spent in the kernel searching them when names are being created or deleted.

Newly created files are assigned the user identifier of the process that created them and the group identifier of the directory in which they were created. A three-level access-control mechanism is provided for the protection of files. The following three levels specify the accessibility of a file:

1. To the user who owns the file
2. To the group that owns the file
3. To everybody else

Each level of access has separate indicators for read permission, write permission, and execute permission. If finer granularity access control is needed, FreeBSD 5 also provides ACLs (access control lists) to allow specification of read, write, execute, and administrative permission on a per-user or per-group level.

Files are created with zero length and may grow when they are written. While a file is open, the system maintains a pointer into the file showing the current location in the file associated with the descriptor. This pointer can be moved about in the file in a random-access fashion. Processes sharing a file descriptor through a *fork* or *dup* system call share the current location pointer. Descriptors created by separate *open* system calls have separate current location pointers.

Filestores

The user-visible part of the filesystem is its hierarchical naming, locking, quotas, attribute management, and protection. But the bulk of the filesystem implementation involves the organization and management of the data on the storage media. Laying out the contents of files on the storage media is the responsibility of the filestore. By default, FreeBSD uses the traditional Berkeley fast filesystem format. The disk is organized into groups of contiguous blocks called ***cylinder groups***. Files that are likely to be accessed together, based on their locations in the filesystem hierarchy, are stored in the same cylinder group. Files that are not expected to be accessed together are moved into different cylinder groups.

A key responsibility of the filestore is to ensure that the filesystem is always kept in a state in which it can be recovered after a hardware or software failure. While recoverability can be maintained by using synchronous writes to the disk, the performance of a filesystem using this technique would be unacceptably slow. FreeBSD uses a technique called ***soft updates*** (see Sections 9.6 and 9.8) to ensure recoverability while still delivering good performance and fast restart after a system crash.

Another useful feature of the FreeBSD filestore is the ability to take a filesystem ***snapshot*** quickly. Snapshots can be taken every few hours and mounted in a well-known location so that users can recover inadvertently deleted files that they created or wrote earlier in the day. Snapshots can also be used to allow the creation of consistent archives of filesystems that are in continuous active use. Snapshots are described in Section 9.7.

2.10 The Zettabyte Filesystem

The Zettabyte filesystem (ZFS) is in a class of filesystems that never overwrite existing data. This type of filesystem design was pioneered at Berkeley and a production-capable implementation was released as the log-structured filesystem in 4.4BSD.

The idea of a non-overwriting filesystem is sound and was picked up and greatly enhanced by Sun Microsystems, which released it as the Zettabye filesystem in OpenSolaris. The FreeBSD Project replaced the little-used log-structured filesystem with ZFS in 2007. Within a few years, ZFS became the filesystem of choice for FreeBSD installations with large storage components.

The design of ZFS provides many benefits:

- Creation of snapshots (read-only) and clones (writable) is easy and cheap. Many of them can be created with no performance hit.
- The on-disk filesystem state is never inconsistent. A ZFS filesystem moves from one consistent state to the next without ever passing through an inconsistent state.
- All the disks on the machine can be pooled together and the pool of space is then shared among all the filesystems. Allocation of the pool space can be controlled through the use of several types of quotas and reservations.
- Massive scale supports petabyte-size storage pools with data structures that allow scalability to zettabytes.
- Provides for fast remote replication and backups.
- Strong data integrity is provided by checksums and disk-level redundancy through mirroring and single, double, and triple parity RAID.
- Supports a hybrid storage pool by using fast devices such as solid-state disks (SSDs) to cache reads and non-volatile memory (NVRAM) to accelerate synchronous writes.

ZFS was designed to easily manage and operate enormous filesystems, which it does well. Its design assumed that it would have many fast 64-bit CPUs with large amounts of memory to support these enormous filesystems. When these resources are available, it works extremely well. However, it is neither designed for nor is it well suited to run on resource-constrained systems using 32-bit CPUs with less than 8 Gbytes of memory and one small, nearly full disk typical of many embedded systems. Thus, the fast filesystem continues to be the filesystem of choice for these smaller systems.

2.11 The Network Filesystem

Initially, networking was used to transfer data from one machine to another. Later, it evolved to allowing users to log in remotely to another machine. The next logical step was to bring the data to the user, instead of having the user go to the data—and network filesystems were born. Users working locally do not experience the network delays on each keystroke, so they have a more responsive environment.

Bringing the filesystem to a local machine was among the first of the major client–server applications. The server is the remote machine that exports one or more of its filesystems. The client is the local machine that imports those filesystems. From the local client's point of view, a remotely mounted filesystem appears in the file-tree namespace just like any other locally mounted filesystem. Users and programs running on clients can change into directories on the remote filesystem and can read, write, and execute binaries within that remote filesystem identically to the way they can do these operations on a local filesystem.

When the client performs an operation on a remote filesystem, the request is packaged and sent to the server. The server performs the requested operation and returns either the requested information or an error explaining why the request was denied. To get reasonable performance, the client must cache frequently accessed data. The complexity of remote filesystems lies in maintaining cache consistency between the server and its many clients.

Although many remote-filesystem protocols have been developed over the years, the most pervasive one in use among UNIX systems is the Network Filesystem (NFS), whose protocol and most widely used implementation were done by Sun Microsystems. The FreeBSD kernel supports the NFS protocol, although the implementation was done independently from the protocol specification [Macklem, 1994]. The continued success of NFS has resulted in a significant update of the protocol in version 4. The new protocol has little in common with its predecessors other than its name and its goal of giving a set of clients shared access to a single store of files. It adds several new features including integrated security, better caching, and enhanced file and byte-range locking. Both of the currently used NFS protocols, NFSv3 and NFSv4 are described in Chapter 11.

2.12 Interprocess Communication

Interprocess communication in FreeBSD is organized in ***communication domains***. The most important domains currently supported include the ***local domain***, for communication between processes executing on the same machine; the ***IPv4 domain***, for communication between processes using the TCP/IP protocol suite (version 4); and the ***IPv6 domain***, which is the newest version of the Internet protocols.

Within a domain, communication takes place between communication endpoints known as sockets. As mentioned in Section 2.7, the *socket* system call creates a socket and returns a descriptor; other IPC system calls are described in Chapter 12. Each socket has a type that defines its communications semantics; these semantics include properties such as reliability, ordering, and prevention of the duplication of messages.

Each socket has associated with it a ***communication protocol***. This protocol provides the semantics required by the socket according to the latter's type. Applications may request a specific protocol when creating a socket or may allow the system to select a protocol that is appropriate for the type of socket being created.

Sockets may have addresses bound to them. The form and meaning of socket addresses are dependent on the communication domain in which the socket is created. Binding a name to a socket in the local domain causes a file to be created in the filesystem, while binding an IP address to a socket only updates an entry in the socket structure.

Normal data transmitted and received through sockets are untyped. Data-representation issues are the responsibility of libraries built on top of the interprocess-communication facilities.

Networking implementations on UNIX before 4.2BSD usually worked by overloading the character-device interfaces. One goal of the socket interface was for naive programs to be able to work without change on stream-style connections. Such programs can work only if the *read* and *write* system calls are unchanged. Consequently, the original interfaces were left intact and were made to work on stream-type sockets. A new interface was added for datagram sockets, where a destination address must be presented with each *send* call.

Implementations of the sockets API exist for pretty much every modern operating system, including several that differ greatly from UNIX.

FreeBSD also supports several local IPC mechanisms not related to networking, including ***semaphores***, ***message queues***, and ***shared memory***. These mechanisms are covered in Section 7.2.

The increasing power of computer systems has lead to the virtualization of many kernel services, including those related to IPC. A recent feature of FreeBSD is a virtualized network stack in which elements such as sockets, network addresses, and network routing tables may not be global across the entire system, but contained within a single network stack instance. The purpose of these virtualization features is to allow a system administrator to configure a single system to serve several separate networks as might be common at an ISP.

2.13 Network-Layer Protocols

Most of the communication domains supported by the socket IPC mechanism provide access to network protocols. These protocols are implemented as a separate software layer logically below the socket software in the kernel. The kernel provides many ancillary services, such as buffer management, message routing, standardized interfaces to the protocols, and interfaces to the network interface drivers for the use of the various network protocols.

Network layer protocols are layered just above or close to the network-interface software that manages the networking hardware. The Internet protocols IPv4 and IPv6 are two examples of a network layer protocol. FreeBSD has supported multiple protocols since 4.2BSD, providing interoperability and resource sharing among the diverse set of machines that exist in the Internet. Multiple-protocol support also provides for future changes. Today's protocols designed for 1- and 10-Gbit Ethernets are likely to be inadequate for tomorrow's 40- to 100-Gbit networks. Consequently, the network-communication layer is designed to support multiple protocols. New protocols are added to the kernel without the support for older protocols being affected. Older applications can continue to operate using the old protocol over the same physical network as is used by newer applications running with a newer network protocol.

The original Internet protocols were not designed with security in mind. Protocols for securing the Internet have been added at multiple layers of the network stack, including the network layer itself. The IPSec suite of protocols introduces a framework for authenticating packet data and making them private at the network layer of the system.

Network firewalls such as PF and IPFW that need to modify network data as they pass through a system are also implemented at the network layer of the kernel software. The FreeBSD kernel has several packet-processing frameworks that manipulate network data as they pass through the system and that are outside the normal processing of incoming or outgoing network traffic. Other packet-processing frameworks exist for protocol experimentation and to give applications high-speed access to raw network packets without any network or transport layer protocol processing.

2.14 Transport-Layer Protocols

Transport layer protocols are responsible for end-to-end connectivity in a network. The Transmission Control Protocol (TCP) remains by far the most commonly used end-to-end transport protocol. However, key Internet services, such as the Domain Name System, allow users to look up systems by name using the User Datagram Protocol (UDP). The popularity of TCP has lead to a continuous set of improvements to the protocol that enhances stability and improves performance. FreeBSD includes a framework specific to TCP that allows the tuning of certain performance and stability features. Newer transport protocols such as SCTP have added features for security and failover across communication paths. The UDP, TCP, and SCTP implementations are described in detail in Chapter 14.

2.15 System Startup and Shutdown

Bootstrapping (or "booting") the operating system is a complex multistep process that begins with the hardware platform's BIOS or firmware loading an escalating series of operating-system vendor boot loaders, which in turn load a kernel and modules. Once loaded, the kernel begins execution and after initialization it starts the first user process, **init**. The **init** process is responsible for starting the userspace boot process. The startup details vary by hardware platform: higher-end servers and workstations will, on the path to kernel load, run a series of smaller boot loaders that ultimately start **/boot/loader**, a scriptable loader environment supporting interactive selection of kernels, and network booting via NFS. By contrast, lower-end embedded systems often have a kernel that will be loaded directly by firmware without any intervening stages.

The kernel starts by initializing a variety of internal subsystems such as the kernel memory allocator and scheduler. It uses platform-specific hardware enumeration methods to identify available hardware resources and attach drivers. Different techniques reflect different operational models: some hardware buses are self-enumerating (e.g., PCI), whereas other require manual description (e.g., many system-on-chip buses). On desktop/server systems, one kernel will frequently be used on a variety of machine types from many different vendors. By contrast, embedded installations usually have a kernel configured for each target device. On the PC, this enumeration is normally done via ACPI, which allows the BIOS to describe the processor configuration, bus topology, and directly attached hardware devices. On embedded systems, device enumeration is done via systems such as Flattened Device Trees (FDT) that provide a static description of directly attached resources. Unlike ACPI, whose hardware descriptors are almost always shipped with the hardware itself, FDT hardware descriptions are usually embedded in the kernel. Buses such as PCI can do further dynamic enumeration by discovering attached devices such as Ethernet NICs, and bridges to further buses to enumerate.

The in-kernel boot process is controlled by a system known as SYSINIT, which takes advantage of a compiler/linker feature called linker sets. Linker sets allow symbols for data structures and functions to be tagged for inclusion in a particular part of the kernel. Subsystem initializers are tagged for inclusion in the kernel initialization section along with information on the order in which they should be done. When the kernel and its modules are linked, the kernel linker iterates through various tagged functions, sorting and then invoking them to start those kernel subsystems. A similar SYSUNINIT mechanism exists to perform ordered shutdown of modules before unloading them and in preparation for kernel shutdown or reboot.

The kernel starts by initializing its own data structures, such as its virtual-memory structures that describe physical memory. Next, it starts a set of kernel threads that implement services such as timers. Devices are enumerated, and device drivers attached. The network stack may perform not only per-protocol initialization, but also per-device initialization such as address generation and router discovery. The GEOM subsystem will identify storage devices and configure transforms such as RAID or encryption via GELI. Encryption services may require the user to have entered a passphrase in the boot loader. Eventually, a storage device suitable to use as the root filesystem will be discovered and its filesystem then mounted. Additional processors are enumerated and their schedulers likewise started. The final kernel-bootstrap step is to create the first user process with PID 1, to execute the **/sbin/init** binary. The **init** process is responsible for executing the startup scripts that perform filesystem checks, configure network interfaces, start accounting and quotas, start system daemons such as **inetd** and **sshd**, and bring the system up to full multiuser operation.

In multiuser operation, the system may act as a general timesharing system, supporting direct or network-based logins by users who then start processes running on their behalf. FreeBSD often acts as a server, providing file services and serving Web requests to network clients. All these network-based services can be started automatically at boot time. When used as a server, there is typically just one human user logged into the system (the administrator).

Exercises

2.1 How does a user process request a service from the kernel?

2.2 How are data transferred between a process and the kernel? What alternatives are available?

2.3 How does a process access an I/O stream? List three types of I/O streams.

2.4 What are the four steps in the lifecycle of a process?

2.5 Why are process groups provided in FreeBSD?

2.6 Describe four machine-dependent functions of the kernel.

2.7 Describe the difference between an absolute and a relative pathname.

2.8 Give three reasons why the *mkdir* system call was added to 4.2BSD.

2.9 Define ***scatter-gather I/O***. Why is it useful?

2.10 What is the difference between a pipe and a socket?

2.11 Describe how to create a group of processes in a pipeline.

*2.12 List the three system calls that were required to create a new directory **foo** in the current directory before the addition of the *mkdir* system call.

*2.13 Explain the difference between interprocess communication and networking.

References

Accetta et al., 1986.
M. Accetta, R. Baron, W. Bolosky, D. Golub, R. Rashid, A. Tevanian, & M. Young, "Mach: A New Kernel Foundation for UNIX Development," *USENIX Association Conference Proceedings*, pp. 93–113, June 1986.

Cheriton, 1988.
D. R. Cheriton, "The V Distributed System," *Comm ACM*, vol. 31, no. 3, pp. 314–333, March 1988.

Ewens et al., 1985.
P. Ewens, D. R. Blythe, M. Funkenhauser, & R. C. Holt, "Tunis: A Distributed Multiprocessor Operating System," *USENIX Association Conference Proceedings*, pp. 247–254, June 1985.

Gingell et al., 1987.
R. Gingell, J. Moran, & W. Shannon, "Virtual Memory Architecture in SunOS," *USENIX Association Conference Proceedings*, pp. 81–94, June 1987.

Kernighan & Pike, 1984.
B. W. Kernighan & R. Pike, *The UNIX Programming Environment,* Prentice-Hall, Englewood Cliffs, NJ, 1984.

Macklem, 1994.
R. Macklem, "The 4.4BSD NFS Implementation," in *4.4BSD System Manager's Manual*, pp. 6:1–14, O'Reilly & Associates, Inc., Sebastopol, CA, 1994.

McKusick & Karels, 1988.
M. K. McKusick & M. Karels, "Design of a General Purpose Memory Allocator for the 4.3BSD UNIX Kernel," *USENIX Association Conference Proceedings*, pp. 295–304, June 1988.

McKusick et al., 1994.
M. K. McKusick, M. Karels, S. J. Leffler, W. N. Joy, & R. S. Fabry, "Berkeley Software Architecture Manual, 4.4BSD Edition," in *4.4BSD Programmer's Supplementary Documents*, pp. 5:1–42, O'Reilly & Associates, Inc., Sebastopol, CA, 1994.

Ritchie, 1988.
D. M. Ritchie, "Early Kernel Design," private communication, March 1988.

Rozier et al., 1988.
M. Rozier, V. Abrossimov, F. Armand, I. Boule, M. Gien, M. Guillemont, F. Herrmann, C. Kaiser, S. Langlois, P. Leonard, & W. Neuhauser, "Chorus Distributed Operating Systems," *USENIX Computing Systems*, vol. 1, no. 4, pp. 305–370, Fall 1988.

Tevanian, 1987.
A. Tevanian, "Architecture-Independent Virtual Memory Management for Parallel and Distributed Environments: The Mach Approach," *Department of Computer Science, Carnegie-Mellon University*, available from http://reports-archive.adm.cs.cmu.edu/cs.html, December 1987.

CHAPTER 3

Kernel Services

3.1 Kernel Organization

The FreeBSD kernel can be viewed as a service provider to user processes. Processes usually access these services through system calls. Some services, such as process scheduling and memory management, are implemented as processes that execute in kernel mode or as routines that execute periodically within the kernel. In this chapter, we describe how kernel services are provided to user processes, and we explain some of the ancillary processing done by the kernel. Then we describe the basic kernel services provided by FreeBSD and provide details of their implementation.

System Processes

All FreeBSD user-level processes originate from a single process that is crafted by the kernel at startup. Table 3.1 lists the most important of the processes that are created immediately and exist always. They are ***kernel processes***, and they function wholly within the kernel. Kernel processes execute code that is compiled into the kernel's load image and operate with the kernel's privileged execution mode. Often these processes have many threads. For example, the *intr* process starts a kernel thread for each device to handle interrupts for that device.

After creating the kernel processes, the kernel creates the first process to execute a program in user mode; it serves as the parent process for all subsequent processes. The first user-mode process is the **init** process—historically, process 1. This process does administrative tasks, such as spawning getty processes for each terminal on a machine, collecting exit status from orphaned processes, and handling the orderly shutdown of a system from multiuser to single-user operation. The **init** process is a user-mode process, running outside the kernel (see Section 15.4).

Table 3.1 Permanent kernel processes.

Name	Description
audit	writes system call tracing records to their output file
bufdaemon	maintains a supply of clean buffers by writing out dirty buffers when the supply of clean buffers gets too low
crypto	handles encrypting/decrypting of data streams
geom	g_event handles configuration tasks g_up handles data coming from devices and being delivered to processes g_down handles data coming from processes and being delivered to devices
idle	runs when there is nothing else to do
intr	one thread for each hardware interrupt
pagedaemon	writes parts of the address space of a process to secondary storage to support the paging facilities of the virtual-memory system
syncer	ensures that dirty file data is written after 30 seconds
vmdaemon	schedules the transfer of whole processes from main memory to secondary storage when system resources are low
vnlru	maintains a supply of free vnodes by cleaning up the least recently used ones
yarrow	collects entropy data to supply seeding for kernel random numbers and the **/dev/random** device

System Entry

Entrances into the kernel can be categorized according to the event or action that initiates them:

- Hardware interrupt
- Hardware trap
- Software-initiated trap

Hardware interrupts arise from external events, such as an I/O device needing attention or a clock reporting the passage of time. (For example, the kernel depends on the presence of a real-time clock or interval timer to maintain the current time of day, to drive process scheduling, and to initiate the execution of system timeout functions.) Hardware interrupts occur ***asynchronously*** and may not relate to the context of the currently executing process.

Hardware traps may be either synchronous or asynchronous but are related to the current executing process. Examples of hardware traps are those generated as a result of an illegal arithmetic operation, such as dividing by zero.

Software-initiated traps are used by the system to force the scheduling of an event, such as process rescheduling or network processing, as soon as possible. Software-initiated traps are implemented by setting a flag that is checked whenever a process is preparing to exit from the kernel. If the flag is set, the software-interrupt code runs instead of exiting from the kernel.

System calls are a special case of a software-initiated trap—the machine instruction used to initiate a system call typically causes a hardware trap that is handled specially by the kernel.

Run-Time Organization

The kernel can be logically divided into a ***top half*** and a ***bottom half***, as shown in Figure 3.1. The top half of the kernel provides services to processes in response to system calls or traps. This software can be thought of as a library of routines shared by all processes. The top half of the kernel executes in a privileged execution mode, in which it has access both to kernel data structures and to the context of user-level processes. The context of each process is contained in two areas of memory reserved for process-specific information. The first of these areas is the ***process structure***, which has historically contained the information that is necessary even if the process has been swapped out. In FreeBSD, this information includes the identifiers associated with the process, the process's rights and privileges, its descriptors, its memory map, pending external events and associated actions, maximum and current resource utilization, and many other things. The second is the ***thread structure***, which has historically contained the information that is not necessary when the process is swapped out. In FreeBSD, the

Figure 3.1 Run-time structure of the kernel.

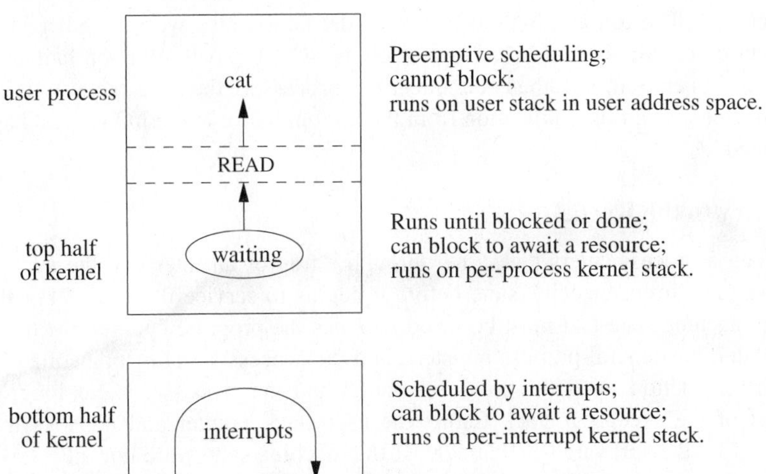
user process
cat
READ
waiting
top half
of kernel
bottom half
of kernel
interrupts
Preemptive scheduling;
cannot block;
runs on user stack in user address space.
Runs until blocked or done;
can block to await a resource;
runs on per-process kernel stack.
Scheduled by interrupts;
can block to await a resource;
runs on per-interrupt kernel stack.

thread-structure information of each process includes the hardware thread state block (TSB), its kernel stack, and minor additional information for debugging and creating a core dump. Deciding what was to be stored in the *process* structure and the *thread* structure was far more important in previous systems than it was in FreeBSD. As memory became a less limited resource, most of the *thread* structure was merged into the *process* structure for convenience (see Section 4.2).

The bottom half of the kernel comprises routines that are invoked to handle hardware interrupts. Activities in the bottom half of the kernel are ***synchronous*** with respect to the interrupt source but are ***asynchronous***, with respect to the top half, and the software cannot depend on having a specific (or any) process running when an interrupt occurs. Thus, the state information for the process that initiated the activity is not available. The top and bottom halves of the kernel communicate through data structures, generally organized around work queues.

The FreeBSD kernel is rarely preempted to run another user process while executing in the top half of the kernel—for example, while executing a system call—although it will explicitly give up the processor if it must wait for an event or for a shared resource. Its execution may be interrupted, however, by the need to run a real-time process or by interrupts for the bottom half of the kernel. When an interrupt is received, the kernel process that handles that device is scheduled to run. Normally these device-interrupt processes have a higher priority than user processes or processes running in the top half of the kernel. Thus, when an interrupt causes a device-interrupt process to be made runnable, it will usually preempt the currently running process. When a process running in the top half of the kernel wants to add an entry to the work list for a device, it needs to ensure that it will not be preempted by that device part way through linking the new element onto the work list. In FreeBSD, the work list is protected by a mutex. Any process (top or bottom half) seeking to modify the work list must first obtain the mutex. Once held, any other process seeking to obtain the mutex will wait until the process holding it has finished modifying the list and released the mutex.

Processes cooperate in the sharing of system resources, such as the disks and memory. The top and bottom halves of the kernel also work together in implementing certain system operations, such as I/O. Typically, the top half will start an I/O operation, and then relinquish the processor; then the requesting process will sleep, awaiting notification from the bottom half that the I/O request has completed.

Entry to the Kernel

When a process enters the kernel through a trap or an interrupt, the kernel must save the current machine state before it begins to service the event. For the PC, the machine state that must be saved includes the program counter, the user stack pointer, the general-purpose registers, and the processor status longword. The PC trap instruction saves the program counter and the processor status longword as part of the exception stack frame; the user stack pointer and registers must be saved by the software trap handler. If the machine state were not fully saved, the kernel could change values in the currently executing program in improper ways.

Since interrupts may occur between any two user-level instructions (and on some architectures between parts of a single instruction), and because they may be completely unrelated to the currently executing process, an incompletely saved state could cause correct programs to fail in mysterious and not easily reproducible ways.

The exact sequence of events required to save the process state is completely machine dependent, although the PC provides a good example of the general procedure. A trap or system call will trigger the following events:

- The hardware switches into kernel (supervisor) mode, so that memory-access checks are made with kernel privileges, references to the stack use the per-process kernel stack, and privileged instructions can be executed.
- The hardware pushes onto the per-process kernel stack the program counter, processor status longword, and information describing the type of trap. (On architectures other than the PC, this information can include the system-call number and general-purpose registers as well.)
- An assembly-language routine saves all state information not saved by the hardware. On the PC, this information includes the general-purpose registers and the user stack pointer, also saved onto the per-process kernel stack.

After this preliminary state saving, the kernel calls a C routine that can freely use the general-purpose registers as any other C routine would, without concern about changing the unsuspecting process's state.

There are three major kinds of handlers, corresponding to particular kernel entries:

1. *Syscall*() for a system call
2. *Trap*() for hardware traps and for software-initiated traps other than system calls
3. The appropriate device-driver interrupt handler for a hardware interrupt

Each type of handler takes its own specific set of parameters. For a system call, they are the system-call number and an exception frame. For a trap, they are the type of trap, the relevant floating-point and virtual-address information related to the trap, and an exception frame. (The exception-frame arguments for the trap and system call are not the same. The PC hardware saves different information based on different types of traps.) For a hardware interrupt, the only parameter is a unit (or board) number.

Return from the Kernel

When the handling of the system entry is completed, the user-process state is restored, and control returns to the user process. Returning to the user process reverses the process of entering the kernel:

- An assembly-language routine restores the general-purpose registers and user-stack pointer previously pushed onto the stack.
- The hardware restores the program counter and program status longword, and switches to user mode, so that future references to the stack pointer use the user's stack pointer, privileged instructions cannot be executed, and memory-access checks are done with user-level privileges.

Execution then resumes at the next instruction in the user's process.

3.2 System Calls

The most frequent trap into the kernel (after clock processing) is a request to do a system call. System performance requires that the kernel minimize the overhead in fielding and dispatching a system call. The system-call handler must do the following work:

- Verify that the parameters to the system call are located at a valid user address, and copy them from the user's address space into the kernel
- Call a kernel routine that implements the system call

Result Handling

Eventually, the system call returns to the calling process, either successfully or unsuccessfully. On the PC architecture, success or failure is returned as the carry bit in the user process's program status longword: If it is zero, the return was successful; otherwise, it was unsuccessful. On many machines, return values of C functions are passed back through a general-purpose register (for the PC, data register EAX). The routines in the kernel that implement system calls return the values that are normally associated with the global variable *errno*. After a system call, the kernel system-call handler leaves this value in the register. If the system call failed, a C library routine moves that value into *errno*, and sets the return register to −1. The calling process is expected to notice the value of the return register, and then to examine *errno*. The mechanism involving the carry bit and the global variable *errno* exists for historical reasons derived from the PDP-11.

There are two kinds of unsuccessful returns from a system call: those where kernel routines discover an error and those where a system call is interrupted. The most common case is a system call that is interrupted when it has relinquished the processor to wait for an event that may not occur for a long time (such as terminal input), and a signal arrives in the interim. When signal handlers are initialized by a process, they specify whether system calls that they interrupt should be restarted or whether the system call should return with an interrupted system call (EINTR) error.

When a system call is interrupted, the signal is delivered to the process. If the process has requested that the signal abort the system call, the handler then returns an error, as described previously. If the system call is to be restarted, however, the handler resets the process's program counter to the machine instruction that caused the system-call trap into the kernel. (This calculation is necessary because the program-counter value that was saved when the system-call trap was done is for the instruction after the trap-causing instruction.) The handler replaces the saved program-counter value with this address. When the process returns from the signal handler, it resumes at the program-counter value that the handler provided and reexecutes the same system call.

Restarting a system call by resetting the program counter has certain implications. First, the kernel must not modify any of the input parameters in the process address space (it can modify the kernel copy of the parameters that it makes). Second, it must ensure that the system call has not performed any actions that cannot be repeated. For example, in the current system, if any characters have been read from the terminal, the read must return with a short count. Otherwise, if the call were to be restarted, the already-read bytes would be lost.

Returning from a System Call

While the system call is running or sleeping with signals blocked, a signal may be posted to the process, or another process may attain a higher scheduling priority. After the system call completes, the system-call exit code checks to see whether either event has occurred.

The system-call exit code first checks for a posted signal. Such signals include signals that interrupted the system call, as well as signals that arrived while a system call was in progress but were held pending until the system call completed. Signals that are ignored, by default or by explicit programmatic request, are never posted to the process. Signals with a default action have that action taken before the process runs again (i.e., the process may be stopped or terminated as appropriate). If a signal is to be caught (and is not currently blocked), the system-call exit code arranges to have the appropriate signal handler called rather than have the process return directly from the system call. After the signal handler returns, the process will resume execution at system-call return (or system-call execution, if the system call is being restarted).

After checking for posted signals, the system-call exit code checks to see whether any process has a priority higher than that of the currently running one. If such a process exists, the system-call exit code calls the context-switch routine to cause the higher-priority process to run. At a later time, the current process will again have the highest priority and will resume execution by returning from the system call to the user process.

If a process has requested that the system do profiling, the system-call exit code also calculates the amount of time that has been spent in the system call—that is, the system time accounted to the process between the latter's entry into and exit from the kernel. This time is charged to the routine in the user's process that made the system call.

3.3 Traps and Interrupts

Traps, like system calls, occur synchronously for a process. Traps normally occur because of unintentional errors, such as division by zero or indirection through an invalid pointer. The process becomes aware of the problem either by catching a signal or by being terminated. Traps can also occur because of a page fault, in which case the system makes the page available and restarts the process without the process being aware that the fault occurred.

The trap handler is invoked like the system-call handler. First, the process state is saved. Next, the trap handler determines the trap type and then arranges to post a signal or to cause a pagein as appropriate. Finally, it checks for pending signals and higher-priority processes, and exits like the system-call handler except that it has no return value.

I/O Device Interrupts

Interrupts from I/O and other devices are handled by interrupt routines that are loaded as part of the kernel's address space. These routines handle the console terminal interface, one or more clocks, and several software-initiated interrupts used by the system for low-priority clock processing and for networking facilities.

Unlike traps and system calls, device interrupts occur asynchronously. The process that requested the service is unlikely to be the currently running process and may no longer exist! The process that started the operation will be notified that the operation has finished when that process runs again. As occurs with traps and system calls, the entire machine state must be saved, since any changes could cause errors in the currently running process.

Device-interrupt handlers run only on demand. Unlike the pre-multiprocessing versions of FreeBSD, modern FreeBSD kernels create a thread context for each device driver. Thus, just as one process cannot access the context of the previously running process, interrupt handlers cannot access any of the context of the previously running interrupt handler. The stack normally used by the kernel is part of a process context. Since each device has its own context, it also has its own stack on which to run.

Interrupts in pre-multiprocessing FreeBSD systems had no context, so they had to run to completion without sleeping. In modern FreeBSD kernels, interrupts can block to wait for resources. However, while blocked they cannot be invoked with another event, so to reduce the chance for lost interrupts, most handlers still run to completion without sleeping.

An interrupt handler is never invoked from the top half of the kernel. Thus, it must get all the information it needs from the data structures that it shares with the top half of the kernel—generally, its global work queue. Similarly, all information provided to the top half of the kernel by the interrupt handler must be communicated the same way.

Software Interrupts

Many events in the kernel are driven by hardware interrupts. For high-speed devices such as network controllers, these interrupts are scheduled at a high priority. A network controller must quickly acknowledge receipt of a packet and reenable the controller to accept more packets to avoid losing closely spaced packets. However, the further processing of passing the packet to the receiving process, although time-consuming, does not need to be done quickly. Thus, the further processing can be scheduled at a lower priority, so critical operations will not be blocked from executing longer than necessary.

The mechanism for performing lower-priority processing is called a ***software interrupt***. Typically, a high-priority interrupt creates a queue of work to be done at a lower-priority level. As with hardware devices in FreeBSD, each software interrupt has a process context associated with it. The software-interrupt processes are generally given a lower scheduling priority than the device-driver processes but a higher priority than those given to user processes. Whenever a hardware interrupt arrives, the process associated with the device driver will attain the highest priority and be scheduled to run. When there are no device-driver processes that are runnable, the highest priority software-interrupt process will be scheduled to run. If there are no software-interrupt processes that are runnable, then the highest priority user process will run. If either a software-interrupt process or a user process is running when an interrupt arrives and makes its device-driver process runnable, the scheduler will preempt the software-interrupt or user process to run the device-driver process.

The delivery of network packets to destination processes is handled by a packet-processing function that runs at a lower priority than the network-controller device driver. As packets come in, they are put onto a work queue and the controller is immediately reenabled. Between packet arrivals, the packet-processing process works to deliver the packets. Thus, the controller can accept new packets without having to wait for the previous packet to be delivered. In addition to network processing, software interrupts are used to handle time-related events and process rescheduling.

3.4 Clock Interrupts

The system is driven by a clock that interrupts at regular intervals. Each interrupt is referred to as a ***tick***. On the PC, the clock ticks 1000 times per second. At each tick, the system updates the current time of day as well as user-process and system timers.

Handling 1000 interrupts per second can be time consuming. To reduce the interrupt load, the kernel computes the number of ticks in the future at which an action may need to be taken. It then schedules the next clock interrupt to occur at that time. Thus, clock interrupts typically occur much less frequently than the 1000 ticks-per-second rate implies. This reduced interrupt rate is particularly helpful for systems with limited power budgets such as laptop computers and embedded systems as it allows them to spend much more time in low-power-consumption sleep mode.

Interrupts for clock ticks are posted at a high hardware-interrupt priority. After switching to the clock-device process, the *hardclock*() routine is called. It is important that the *hardclock*() routine finish its job quickly:

- If *hardclock*() runs for more than one tick, it will miss the next clock interrupt. Since *hardclock*() maintains the time of day for the system, a missed interrupt will cause the system to lose time.
- Because of *hardclock*()'s high interrupt priority, nearly all other activity in the system is blocked while *hardclock*() is running. This blocking can cause network controllers to miss packets.

So the time spent in *hardclock*() is minimized, less critical time-related processing is handled by a lower-priority software-interrupt handler called *softclock*(). In addition, if multiple clocks are available, some time-related processing can be handled by other routines supported by alternate clocks. On the PC there are two additional clocks that run at a different frequency than the system clock: the *statclock*(), which runs at 127 ticks per second to collect system statistics, and the *profclock*(), which runs at 8128 ticks per second to collect profiling information.

The work done by *hardclock*() is as follows:

- If the currently running process has a virtual or profiling interval timer (see Section 3.6), it decrements the timer and delivers a signal if the timer has expired.
- It increments the current time of day by the number of ticks since the previous call to *hardclock*().
- If the system does not have a separate clock for process profiling, the *hardclock*() routine does the operations normally done by *profclock*(), as described in the next section.
- If the system does not have a separate clock for statistics gathering, the *hardclock*() routine does the operations normally done by *statclock*(), as described in the next section.
- If *softclock*() needs to be run, it makes the softclock process runnable.

Statistics and Process Scheduling

On historic FreeBSD systems, the *hardclock*() routine collected resource-utilization statistics about what was happening when the clock interrupted. These statistics were used to do accounting, to monitor what the system was doing, and to determine future scheduling priorities. In addition, *hardclock*() forced context switches so that all processes would get a share of the CPU.

This approach has weaknesses because the clock supporting *hardclock*() interrupts on a regular basis. Processes can become synchronized with the system clock, resulting in inaccurate measurements of resource utilization (especially CPU) and inaccurate profiling [McCanne & Torek, 1993]. It is also possible to write programs that deliberately synchronize with the system clock to outwit the scheduler.

On architectures with multiple high-precision, programmable clocks—such as the PC—a statistics clock is run at a different frequency than the time-of-day clock. The FreeBSD *statclock*() runs at 127 ticks per second and is responsible for accumulating resource usage to processes. At each tick, it charges the currently running process with a tick; if the process has accumulated four ticks, it recalculates its priority. If the new priority is less than the current priority, it arranges for the process to be rescheduled. Thus, processes that become synchronized with the system clock still have CPU time accounted to them.

The *statclock*() also collects statistics on what the system was doing at the time of the tick (sitting idle, executing in user mode, or executing in system mode). Finally, it collects basic information on system I/O, such as which disk drives are currently active.

To allow the collection of more accurate profiling information, FreeBSD supports a profiling clock. When one or more processes are requesting profiling information, the profiling clock is set to run at a tick rate that is relatively prime to the main system clock (8128 ticks per second on the PC). At each tick, it checks to see if one of the processes that it has been asked to profile is running. If so, it obtains the current location of the program counter and increments a counter associated with that location in the profiling buffer associated with the process.

Timeouts

The remaining time-related processing involves processing timeout requests and periodically reprioritizing processes that are ready to run. These functions are handled by the *softclock*() routine.

When *hardclock*() completes, if there were any *softclock*() functions to be done, *hardclock*() schedules the softclock process to run.

The primary task of the *softclock*() routine is to arrange for the execution of periodic events, such as the following:

- Process real-time timer (see Section 3.6)
- Retransmission of dropped network packets
- Watchdog timers on peripherals that require monitoring
- System process-rescheduling events

An important event is the scheduling that periodically raises or lowers the CPU priority for each process in the system based on that process's recent CPU usage (see Section 4.4). The rescheduling calculation is done once per second. The scheduler is started at boot time, and each time that it runs, it requests that it be invoked again 1 second in the future.

On a heavily loaded system with many processes, the scheduler may take a long time to complete its job. Posting its next invocation 1 second after each completion may cause scheduling to occur less frequently than once per second. However, as the scheduler is not responsible for any time-critical functions, such as maintaining the time of day, scheduling less frequently than once a second is normally not a problem.

The data structure that describes waiting events is called the ***callout queue***. Figure 3.2 shows an example of the callout queue. When a process schedules an event, it specifies a function to be called, a pointer to be passed as an argument to the function, and the number of clock ticks until the event should occur.

The kernel maintains an array of queue headers, each representing a particular time. There is a pointer that references the queue header for the current time, marked "now" in Figure 3.2. The queue header that follows the currently referenced one represents events that are one tick in the future. The queue header after that is two ticks in the future. The list wraps around, so if the last queue header in the list represents time t, then the first queue header in the list represents time $t + 1$. The queue header immediately preceding the currently referenced one represents the time furthest in the future. In Figure 3.2 there are 200 queue headers, so the queue header immediately preceding the one marked "now" represents events that are 199 ticks in the future.

Each time the *hardclock*() routine runs, it increments the callout queue-head pointer. If the queue is not empty, it schedules the *softclock*() process to run. The

Figure 3.2 Timer events in the callout queue.

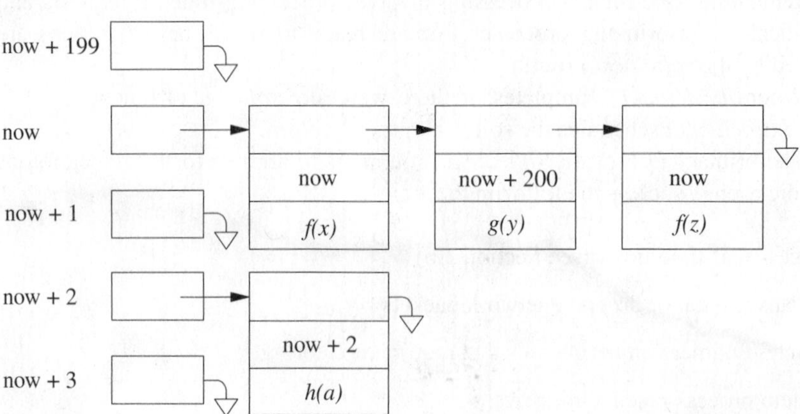

softclock() process scans the events in the current queue. It compares the current time to the time stored in the event structure. If the times match, the event is removed from the list and its requested function is called, being passed the argument specified when it was registered.

When an event *n* ticks in the future is to be posted, its queue header is calculated by taking the index of the queue labelled "now" in Figure 3.2, adding *n* to it, and then taking the resulting value modulo the number of queue headers. If an event is to occur further in the future than the number of queue headers, then it will end up on a list with other events that are to happen sooner. Thus, the actual time of the event is stored in its entry so that when the queue is scanned by *softclock*(), it can determine which events are current and which are to occur in the future. In Figure 3.2, the second entry in the "now" queue will be skipped on the current scan of the queue, but it will be handled 200 ticks in the future when *softclock*() next processes this queue.

An argument is provided to the callout-queue function when it is called so that one function can be used by multiple processes. For example, there is a single real-time timer function that sends a signal to a process when a timer expires. Every process that has a real-time timer running posts a timeout request for this function; the argument that is passed to the function is a pointer to the process structure for the process. This argument enables the timeout function to deliver the signal to the correct process.

Timeout processing is more efficient when the timeouts are specified in ticks. Time updates require only an integer decrement, and checks for timer expiration require only an integer comparison. If the timers contained time values, decrementing and comparisons would be more complex. The approach used in FreeBSD is based on the work of Varghese & Lauck [1987]. Another possible approach is to maintain a heap with the next-occurring event at the top [Barkley & Lee, 1988].

3.5 Memory-Management Services

The memory organization and layout associated with a FreeBSD process is shown in Figure 3.3. Each process begins execution with three memory segments: text, data, and stack. The data segment is divided into initialized data and uninitialized data (also known as bss). The text is read-only and is normally shared by all processes executing the file, whereas the data and stack areas can be written by, and are private to, each process. The text and initialized data for the process are read from the executable file.

An executable file is distinguished by being a plain file (rather than a directory, special file, or symbolic link) and by having one or more of its execute bits set. Each executable file has an exec header containing a ***magic number*** that specifies the type of the executable file. FreeBSD supports multiple executable formats including the following:

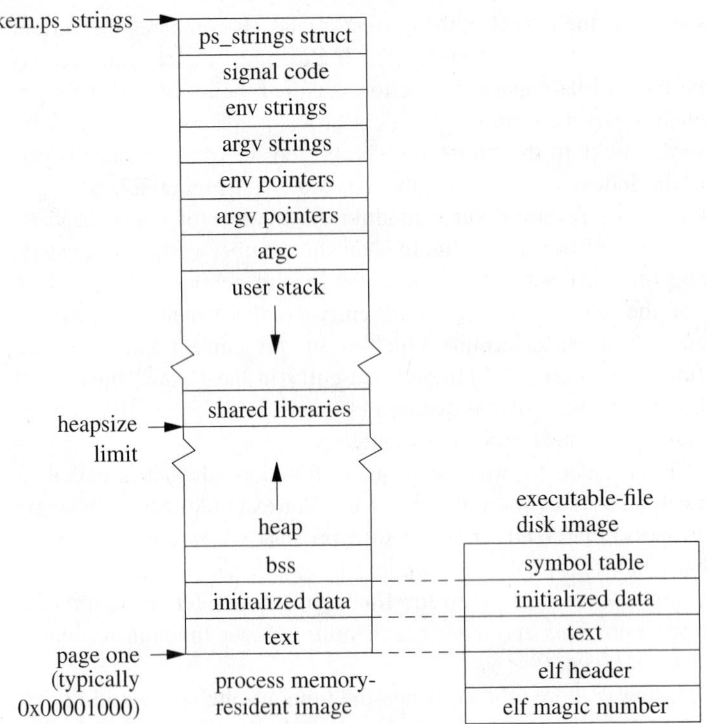

Figure 3.3 Layout of a FreeBSD process in memory and on disk.

1. Files that must be read by an ***interpreter***
2. Files that are directly executable including AOUT, ELF, and gzipped ELF

An executable file is initially parsed by the image activation (*imgact*) framework. The header of a file to be executed is passed through a list of registered image activators to find a matching format. When a matching format is found, the corresponding image activator prepares the file for execution.

Files falling into the first classification have as their magic number (located in the first 2 bytes of the file) the two-character sequence **#!** followed by the pathname of the interpreter to be used. This pathname is currently limited by a compile-time constant to 128 characters. For example, **#!/bin/sh** refers to the Bourne shell. The image activator that will be selected is the one that handles the invocation of interpreters. It will load and run the named interpreter, passing the name of the file that is to be interpreted as an argument. To prevent loops, FreeBSD allows only one level of interpretation, and a file's interpreter may not itself be interpreted.

For performance reasons, most files fall into the second classification and are directly executable. Information in the header of a directly executable file includes the architecture and operating system for which an executable was built and whether it is statically linked or uses shared libraries. The selected image activator can use information such as knowledge of the operating system for which an executable was compiled to configure the kernel to use the proper system call interpretation when running the program. For example, an executable built to run on Linux can be seamlessly run on FreeBSD by using the system-call dispatch vector that provides emulation of the Linux system calls.

The header also specifies the sizes of text, initialized data, uninitialized data, and additional information for debugging. The debugging information is not used by the kernel or by the executing program. Following the header is an image of the text, followed by an image of the initialized data. Uninitialized data are not contained in the executable file because they can be created on demand using zero-filled memory.

To begin execution, the kernel arranges to have the text portion of the file mapped into the low part of the process address space starting at the beginning of the second page of the virtual address space. The first page of the virtual address space is marked as invalid so that attempts to read or write through a null pointer will fault. The initialized data portion of the file is mapped into the address space following the text. An area equal to the uninitialized data region is created with zero-filled memory after the initialized data region. The stack is also created from zero-filled memory. Although the stack should not need to be zero filled, early UNIX systems made it so. In an attempt to save some startup time in 4.2BSD, the developers modified the kernel to not zero-fill the stack, leaving the random previous contents of the page instead. But concerns about surreptitious misuse of data from previously running programs and unrepeatable errors in previously working programs lead to restoration of the zero filling of the stack by the time that 4.3BSD was released.

Copying into memory the entire text and initialized data portion of a large program causes a long startup latency. FreeBSD avoids this startup time by ***demand paging*** the program into memory rather than preloading the program. In demand paging, the program is loaded in small pieces (pages) as it is needed rather than all at once before it begins execution. The system does demand paging by dividing up the address space into equal-size areas called pages. For each page, the kernel records the offset into the executable file of the corresponding data. The first access to an address on each page causes a page-fault trap in the kernel. The page-fault handler reads the correct page of the executable file into the process memory. Thus, the kernel loads only those parts of the executable file that are needed. Chapter 6 explains paging details.

It might seem more efficient to load the whole process at once rather than in many little pieces. However, most processes use less than half of their address space during their entire execution lifetime. The reason for the low utilization is that typical user commands have many options, only a few of which are used on any invocation. The code and data structures that support the unused options are not needed. Thus, the cost of loading the subset of pages that are used is lower than the cost of initially loading the whole process. In addition to the time saved by avoiding the loading of the entire process, demand paging also reduces the amount of physical memory that is needed to run the process.

The uninitialized data area can be extended with zero-filled pages using the system call *sbrk*, although most user processes use the library routine *malloc*(), a more programmer-friendly interface to *sbrk*. This allocated memory, which grows from the top of the original data segment, is called the ***heap***. On the PC, the stack grows down from the top of memory, whereas the heap grows up from the bottom of memory.

Above the user stack are areas of memory that are created by the system when the process is started. Directly above the user stack is the number of arguments (*argc*), the argument vector (*argv*), and the process environment vector (*envp*) set up when the program was executed. Following them are the argument and environment strings themselves. Next is the signal code, used when the system delivers signals to the process. At the top is the *ps_strings* structure, used by **ps** to locate the *argv* of the process.

Historically, most executables were statically linked. In a statically linked binary, all the library routines and system-call entry stubs are loaded into the binary image at the time that it is compiled. Today, most binaries are dynamically linked. A dynamically linked binary contains only the compiled application code and a list of the routines (library and system-call entry stubs) that it needs. When the executable is run, a set of shared libraries containing the routines that it needs to use are mapped into its address space as part of its startup. The first time that it calls a routine, that routine is located in the shared library and a dynamic linkage is created to it.

When the dynamic loader does the *mmap* system call to allocate space for the shared libraries, the kernel must find a place within the process address space to place them. The convention in FreeBSD is to place them just below the administrative lower limit for the stack. Since the stack will not be permitted to grow below the administrative stack size limit, there is no danger of the shared libraries being overwritten. A side effect of this implementation is that the stack limit cannot be safely changed after a binary begins running. Ideally, a bigger stack limit can be set by the process (such as the shell) before it starts the application. However, applications that know at startup that they will need a bigger stack can increase their stack limit and then call the *exec* system call on themselves to restart with their shared libraries relocated at the bottom of their new stack limit.

An alternative would be to place the shared libraries just above the heap limit. However, this would mean that the heap limit could not be increased once the binary began running. As applications much more frequently want to increase their heap size than their stack size, the stack limit was selected as the appropriate location to place the shared libraries.

A process requires the use of some global system resources. The kernel maintains a linked list of processes that has an entry for each process in the system. Among other data, the process entries record information on scheduling and on virtual-memory allocation. Because the entire process address space, including the kernel stack for the process, may be swapped out of main memory, the process entry must record enough information to be able to locate the process and to bring that process back into memory. In addition, information needed while the process is swapped out (e.g., scheduling information) must be maintained in the process entry rather than in the thread structure to avoid the kernel swapping in the process only to decide that it is not at a high enough priority to be run.

Other global resources associated with a process include space to record information about descriptors and page tables that record information about physical-memory utilization.

3.6 Timing Services

The kernel provides several different timing services to processes. These services include timers that run in real time and timers that run only while a process is executing.

Real Time

The system's time offset since January 1, 1970, Universal Coordinated Time (UTC), also known as the Epoch, is returned by the system call *gettimeofday*. Most modern processors (including the PC processors) maintain a battery-backup time-of-day register. This clock continues to run even if the processor is turned off. When the system boots, it consults the processor's time-of-day register to find out the current time. The system's time is then maintained by the clock interrupts. At each interrupt, the system increments its global time variable by an amount equal to the number of microseconds per tick. For the PC, running at 1000 ticks per second, each tick represents 1000 microseconds.

External Representation

Time is always exported from the system as microseconds, rather than as clock ticks, to provide a resolution-independent format. Internally, the kernel is free to select whatever tick rate best trades off clock-interrupt-handling overhead with timer resolution. As the tick rate per second increases, the resolution of the system timers improves, but the time spent dealing with hardclock interrupts increases. As processors become faster, the tick rate can be increased to provide finer resolution without adversely affecting user applications. Systems with real-time constraints often run the clock at 5000 or 10,000 ticks per second. As explained in Section 3.4, the kernel can usually eliminate most of the interrupts associated with a high tick rate.

All filesystem (and other) timestamps are maintained in UTC offsets from the Epoch. Conversion to local time, including adjustment for daylight saving time, is handled externally to the system in the C library.

Adjustment of the Time

Often, it is desirable to maintain the same time on all the machines on a network. It is also possible to keep more accurate time than that available from the basic processor clock. For example, hardware is readily available that listens to the set of radio stations that broadcast UTC synchronization signals in the United States. When processes on different machines agree on a common time, they will wish to change the clock on their host processor to agree with the networkwide time value. One possibility is to change the system time to the network time using the *settimeofday* system call. Unfortunately, the *settimeofday* system call will result in time running backward on machines whose clocks were fast. Time running backward can confuse user programs (such as **make**) that expect time to invariably increase. To avoid this problem, the system provides the *adjtime* system call [Mills, 1992]. The *adjtime* system call takes a time delta (either positive or negative) and changes the rate at which time advances by 10 percent, faster or slower, until the time has been corrected. The operating system does the speedup by incrementing the global time by 1100 microseconds for each tick and does the slowdown by incrementing the global time by 900 microseconds for each tick. Regardless, time increases monotonically, and user processes depending on the ordering of file-modification times are not affected. However, time changes that take tens of seconds to adjust will affect programs that are measuring time intervals by using repeated calls to *gettimeofday*.

Interval Time

The system provides each process with three interval timers. The real timer decrements in real time. An example of use for this timer is a library routine maintaining a wakeup-service queue. A SIGALRM signal is delivered to the process when this timer expires. The real-time timer is run from the timeout queue maintained by the *softclock*() routine (see Section 3.4).

The profiling timer decrements both in process virtual time (when running in user mode) and when the system is running on behalf of the process. It is designed to be used by processes to profile their execution statistically. A SIGPROF signal is delivered to the process when this timer expires. Each time that *profclock*() runs, it checks to see whether the currently running process has requested a profiling timer; if it has, *profclock*() decrements the timer and sends the process a signal when zero is reached.

The virtual timer decrements in process virtual time. It runs only when the process is executing in user mode. A SIGVTALRM signal is delivered to the process when this timer expires. The virtual timer is also implemented in *profclock*() as the profiling timer is, except that it decrements the timer for the current process only if it is executing in user mode and not if it is running in the kernel.

3.7 Resource Services

All systems have limits imposed by their hardware architecture and configuration to ensure reasonable operation and to keep users from accidentally (or maliciously) creating resource shortages. At a minimum, the hardware limits must be imposed on processes that run on the system. It is usually desirable to limit processes further, below these hardware-imposed limits. The system measures resource utilization and allows limits to be imposed on consumption either at or below the hardware-imposed limits.

Process Priorities

The default scheduling policy in the FreeBSD system is managed by the share scheduler that gives CPU scheduling priority to processes that have not used CPU time recently. This priority scheme tends to favor processes that execute for only short periods of time—for example, interactive processes. The priority selected for each process is maintained internally by the kernel. The calculation of the priority is affected by the per-process ***nice*** variable. Positive *nice* values mean that the process is willing to receive less than its share of the processor. Negative values of *nice* mean that the process wants more than its share of the processor. Most processes run with the default *nice* value of zero, asking neither higher nor lower access to the processor. It is possible to determine or change the *nice* currently assigned to a process, to a process group, or to the processes of a specified user. Many factors other than *nice* affect scheduling, including the amount of CPU time that the process has used recently, the amount of memory that the process has used recently, and the current load on the system.

In addition to the share scheduler described here, the FreeBSD system also has a real-time scheduler available. The real-time scheduler allows processes to precisely control their order of execution and the amount of time given to each process. The details of the share and real-time scheduling algorithms are described in Section 4.4.

Resource Utilization

As a process executes, it uses system resources such as the CPU and memory. The kernel tracks the resources used by each process and compiles statistics describing this usage. The statistics managed by the kernel are available to a process while the latter is executing. When a process terminates, the statistics are made available to its parent via the *wait* family of system calls.

The resources used by a process are returned by the system call *getrusage*. The resources used by the current process, or by all the terminated children of the current process, may be requested. The following information is included:

- The amount of user and system time used by the process

- The memory utilization of the process
- The paging and disk I/O activity of the process
- The number of voluntary and involuntary context switches taken by the process
- The amount of interprocess communication done by the process

The resource-usage information is collected at locations throughout the kernel. The CPU time is collected by the *statclock*() function, which is called either by the system clock in *hardclock*(), or, if an alternate clock is available, by the alternate-clock interrupt process. The kernel scheduler calculates memory utilization by sampling the amount of memory that an active process is using at the same time that it is recomputing process priorities. The *vm_fault*() routine recalculates the paging activity each time that it starts a disk transfer to fulfill a paging request (see Section 6.11). The I/O activity statistics are collected each time that the process has to start a transfer to fulfill a file or device I/O request, as well as when the general system statistics are calculated. The IPC communication activity is updated each time that information is sent or received.

Resource Limits

The kernel also supports limiting certain per-process resources. These resources include the following:

- The maximum amount of CPU time that can be accumulated
- The maximum bytes that a process can request be locked into memory
- The maximum size of a process's data segment
- The maximum size of a process's stack segment
- The maximum amount of private physical memory that a process may have at any given moment
- The maximum amount of private or shared physical memory that a process may have at any given moment
- The maximum amount of physical memory that a process may have dedicated to socket buffers
- The maximum size of a file that can be created by a process
- The maximum size of a core file that can be created by a process
- The maximum number of simultaneous open files for a process
- The maximum number of simultaneous processes allowed to a user

For each resource controlled by the kernel, two limits are maintained: a ***soft limit*** and a ***hard limit***. All users can alter the soft limit within the range of 0 to the corresponding hard limit. All users can (irreversibly) lower the hard limit, but only the superuser can raise the hard limit. If a process exceeds certain soft limits, a signal is delivered to the process to notify it that a resource limit has been exceeded. Normally, this signal causes the process to terminate, but the process may either catch or ignore the signal. If the process ignores the signal and fails to release resources that it already holds, further attempts to obtain more resources will result in errors.

Resource limits are generally enforced at or near the locations that the resource statistics are collected. The CPU time limit is enforced in the process context-switching function. The stack and data-segment limits are enforced by a return of allocation failure once those limits have been reached. The file-size limit is enforced by the filesystem.

Filesystem Quotas

In addition to limits on the size of individual files, the kernel optionally enforces limits on the total amount of space that a user or group can use on a filesystem. Our discussion of the implementation of these limits is deferred to Section 9.4.

3.8 Kernel Tracing Facilities

Operating-system kernels are large and complex pieces of software, encompassing thousands of lines of mainly C code, organized into dozens of subsystems and including hundreds of device drivers. Understanding what is happening within the operating system while it is running is important not only to developers of the code but also to the much larger group of people who use the system every day to get their work done. FreeBSD includes several facilities that allows users and administrators of the system to understand what is happening inside the system as it executes.

System-Call Tracing

The **ktrace** facility allows a user to get a detailed trace of the order of, arguments to, and results from all the system calls done by an application. This information includes such important details as pathnames being looked up, type and timing of signals being posted, and even the contents of all input and output operations.

The facility is available for any application without the need for prior compilation or inclusion of special hooks. Thus, it can be particularly helpful when trying to debug an application for which the source code is unavailable.

Tracing can be flexibly applied. It can be started at the time an application begins running or to an already running application. It can be applied to individual processes, to all the processes in a process group, or through inheritance to all current or future children processes.

The traces are generated in a compact binary format to keep them as dense as possible. The use of a binary format also minimizes the time spent collecting and writing the information while the application runs and avoids the need to do string processing in the kernel. The binary dump is converted to a human-readable format using the **kdump** program that converts the system call numbers to names, *ioctl* values to their macro names, system error numbers to their standard error strings, and displays the running time between and during system calls.

A similar facility is provided by the **truss** command popularized in System V and Solaris. Rather than having specialized hooks inside the kernel to collect tracing information, it collects its information by stopping and restarting the processes being monitored using the *ptrace* system call. As a result, it has higher overhead and provides less information than **ktrace**.

DTrace

The information collected by **ktrace** is limited to the set of information available from its fixed set of hooks in the kernel. Further, this set of hooks has to be limited to those pieces of information deemed to be most generally useful. If **ktrace** collected every possibly useful bit of information, it would generate an overwhelming amount of data for even trivial applications. Its other major limitation is that it collects information only about system calls. When trying to track down bugs or performance problems, one needs to analyze the entire software stack that includes the application itself, the libraries that it uses, and the system calls that it makes. The DTrace facility was developed to address all these issues [Cantrill et al., 2004]. Originally written for Sun's Solaris operating system, DTrace support was added to FreeBSD 8, and is present by default in kernels starting with FreeBSD 10.

DTrace greatly expands the set of information from system calls by adding thousands of hooks, referred to as tracepoints, that can identify many details of what is happening. To avoid the resulting avalanche of data, each tracepoint can be configured to conditionally collect and output its information. DTrace defines the D language that allows application developers and systems administrators to write a small D-language program to describe the information that they want to collect. They can specify the tracepoint that they are interested in inspecting and refine the information that they output. For example, a D program might monitor a routine that changes a reference counter to collect the highest value that it ever reached, or collect the total number of times that a resource was referenced rather than just blindly outputting some information every time the routine is called. Only those tracepoints that are useful to the analysis are activated, while all others are left dormant. With its ability to trigger only a small number of tracepoints at anyone one time, DTrace can collect detailed information on a narrow set of interesting events with low overhead and carefully bounded output.

The tracing information is expanded into the rest of the software stack by adding DTrace tracepoints to the system libraries and to the application itself. A standard set of tracepoints is available with no programming effort required by the library or application developers. The standard tracepoints are the set of all functions in a library, application, or the kernel itself, and include the ability to capture parameter information at every subroutine call and return. In addition to these function boundary tracepoints, many system libraries have had additional application-specific hooks added by their developers.

The tracing functionality in DTrace is implemented using ***probes*** and providers. A probe is a specific tracepoint within the running kernel, such as a function boundary, while a provider is a kernel module that supports a set of probes. The DTrace system was designed to be extended so that new kernel modules or services could have tracepoints that were not envisioned by the original authors. The providers found in FreeBSD are listed in Table 3.2. The mac_framework, sched, and vfs providers are unique to FreeBSD. A complete discussion of DTrace providers and how they are used by developers and administrators can be found in Gregg & Mauro [2011]. In this section, we describe only how DTrace interacts with the FreeBSD kernel and do not discuss how to use DTrace in general.

Before the advent of DTrace, any system to which logging or tracing was added demonstrated a significant ***probe effect***. Consider what happens when a function contains a conditional statement that determines whether to report a statistic. Whether or not the statistic is reported, the effect of having the conditional statement in the function, compared to no conditional statement being present at all, is measurable. The overhead seen by having the conditional statement is called the probe effect.

DTrace implements its probes by patching the executable when a probe is activated. For example, to monitor a call to a routine, the first instruction of the called routine is replaced with a call to the probe. The probe then collects its information, executes the instruction its call replaced, and returns to the instruction following the one that it patched. When the probe is deactivated, the original patched-instruction location with the call to the probe is replaced with the

Table 3.2 FreeBSD DTrace providers.

Name	Description
fbt	function-boundary tracing
io	block I/O probes
lockstat	probes for locking operations
profile	performance profiling probes
mac_framework	mandatory access control
nfscl	probes for the network-filesystem client
sched	process and thread scheduler
sctp	SCTP network protocol
sdt	statically defined tracing
syscall	system-call probes
vfs	filesystem operations

instruction that was originally at that location. This technique avoids any probe effect for inactive probes. Debuggers, such as **lldb**, use the same technique to add breakpoints to the program they are debugging. Patching an instruction stream that is currently executing is both tricky to do safely, and an explicit violation of the security and privacy of data structures on the system; thus, super-user privileges are required to enable kernel probes. DTrace is safe to use in production systems as it ensures that its patches to the program or kernel cannot cause either to behave incorrectly. An example of a precaution taken by DTrace to ensure safe operation is that it will not instrument a jump table, an operation that could easily lead to a system failure.

As part of the kernel build process, a separate program, **ctfconvert**, is executed against all the kernel's object files to generate updated object files that can be understood by DTrace. The **ctfconvert** program takes information from the debugging section of an object file and creates a new section .SUNW_ctf that contains type information for each function's arguments that can be used by DTrace. Every type that appears in the .SUNW_ctf section of the object file is converted into data that can be used by the function boundary trace provider to associate data types with function arguments, allowing userspace D scripts to interrogate function arguments in much the same way as the debugger allows a programmer to inspect program data with associated type information. All functions found in the debugging section are exposed to the user as individual tracepoints. The FreeBSD kernel contains over 45,000 function boundary tracepoints, or fbt probes, each of which can be triggered on entry to or exit from a routine in the kernel. Because the generation of the function boundary tracing probes happens automatically at system build time, new probes come into existence whenever new code is added to the FreeBSD kernel, relieving developers of the need to add tracepoints to the system by hand, and to keep the tracepoints up to date with other code changes. Function boundary tracepoints can change with each release of the operating system, which means that function boundary tracepoints may change or disappear, so cannot be depended upon in scripts when upgrading across major releases, for example, from FreeBSD 9 to FreeBSD 10. Compiler optimization or the redefinition of a function as static can also cause a function boundary tracepoint to disappear. Statically defined tracepoints (SDT) do not change unless they are specifically updated by a programmer and are therefore considered stable across major releases.

Tracepoints are reached through DTrace providers, each of which is a kernel module that exposes a uniform interface to the rest of the kernel. All DTrace providers expose a uniform API via a set of function pointers embedded in a DTrace-provider operations structure, *dtrace_pops*. Each provider registers itself with the DTrace system by calling the *dtrace_register*() routine that allows DTrace to track all the available providers and expose them to the user through the D programming language. The *dtrace_register*() routine passes the *dtrace_pops* structure for the provider as one of its arguments. Provider operations include enabling, disabling, suspending, and resuming probes, as well as retrieving argument names and values, from within the probe. DTrace understands not only functions but also basic types, such as integers, strings, and programmer-defined structures.

When the fbt module is loaded, tracepoints are created for the kernel using the kernel's linker functions. The *fbt_provide_module_function*() routine is responsible for disassembling the entry and exit points of each function in the kernel as well as all the loaded modules, building up a list of *fbt_probe_t* structures that contain the address of the functions that can be probed. The *fbt_probe_t* structure contains three key components used by DTrace when turning tracing on or off. The *fbtp_patchpoint* is the address of the instruction that needs to be replaced when tracing is enabled or disabled. When the *fbt_provide_module_function*() runs, it determines the address of the instruction that must later be replaced with a function call to the DTrace system during active tracing. The address of that instruction is stored in *fbtp_patchpoint*. At the same time, the instruction that must be replaced during tracing is put into the *fbtp_savedval* element of the structure and the instruction that will be used to cause the entry point to change is placed into *fbtp_patchval*. Whenever the DTrace command enables a tracepoint, the *fbtp_patchpoint* is set to the instruction stored in *fbtp_patchval*. When tracing is turned off, the instruction stored in *fbtp_savedval* is again placed back into *fbtp_patchpoint*. Storing the instructions during module load time makes the *fbt_enable*() and *fbt_disable*() routines shorter and safer than they would be if the functions to be traced had to be disassembled whenever the user enabled a tracepoint.

While the automatic generation of tracepoints for functions is a powerful feature of DTrace, the ability to add specific tracepoints not associated with a function boundary is an important part of the system. Any subsystem or collection of subsystems can be encapsulated as a provider to be monitored by developers and administrators. The collection of locking statistics for individual threads is an example of a DTrace provider that was written by hand into the kernel's source code. The DTrace lockstat provider piggybacks on the preexisting lockstat statistics collection by adding a probe to each of the lockstat macros.

The FreeBSD kernel provides several synchronization primitives, referred to collectively as locks, that are described fully in Section 4.3. To track the locking and unlocking actions of the kernel at a low level, it is necessary to know more than just the lock that is being requested. We often want to know if it was necessary to wait for the lock, and if so, which other thread blocked us from getting it. The information we want from a locking operation is not evident from the parameters to the lock call, but is embedded within the code implementing the lock. Locking statistics are collected by manually placing macros at key points in the locking-implementation code to record data about the lock when it is acquired or released. These locking statistics reside in the lockstat provider. The macros for collecting the lockstat statistics are written generically enough that they can be used in all the locking primitives in the system. When a lock is acquired, the macro is given a pointer to the lock object, a Boolean flag telling whether the lock was contested, the time that the thread started waiting for the the lock, and the kernel file name and the line number within the function from which the lock primitive was called. The macros call an appropriate function to collect statistics on how often the lock is acquired, average time that it is held, how often it is contested, and when it is contested, as well as the average time that the blocked thread had to wait. These statistics identify the contested locks in the kernel. One important way of improving system performance is to use finer-grain locking for the most highly contested locks in the system. For example, a single global lock controlling access to a hash table might be replaced with one lock per hash chain.

The lockstat DTrace provider is only available if the lockstat lock profiling has been compiled into the kernel. Each probe is defined by a *lockstat_probe* structure that contains the function and name of the probe, which is exported to the user as well as a probe number and probe identifier that the lockstat provider uses when the probes fire.

The macro shown in Figure 3.4 is placed into various locking functions to record data whenever a lock is acquired. The lockstat information is collected by the *lock_profile_obtain_lock_success*() function. The remainder of the macro implements the lockstat provider probe. The probe is active if its entry in the *lockstat_probemap* is non-NULL, which occurs only when a probe is activated via the lockstat provider's *lockstat_enable*() routine. Configuring the kernel to collect lockstat statistics introduces a fixed amount of overhead. The lockstat DTrace provider introduces a variable amount of overhead depending on which probes are active at any time.

Kernel Tracing

Any large software system usually includes a logging system to aid in debugging problems that arise after the software has been released and FreeBSD is no different. The kernel tracing facility (KTR) is a set of logging facilities that can be compiled into the kernel with a configuration option. This tracing facility primarily helps debug the kernel as compared to the other tracing described in this section that primarily helps debug user-level processes.

Figure 3.4 Lockstat probe macro.

```
#define LOCKSTAT_PROFILE_OBTAIN_LOCK_SUCCESS(probe, lockptr,
        wascontested, startwaittime, file, line)
do {
    uint32_t id;
    lock_profile_obtain_lock_success(lockptr, wascontested,
        startwaittime, file, line);
    if ((id = lockstat_probemap[(probe)]))
        lockstat_probe_func(id, (uintptr_t)(lockptr), 0, 0);
} while (0)
```

```
struct ktr_entry {
        u_int64_t ktr_timestamp;
        int ktr_cpu;
        int ktr_line;
        const   char *ktr_file;
        const   char *ktr_desc;
        struct  thread *ktr_thread;
        u_long  ktr_parms[KTR_PARMS];
    };
```

Figure 3.5 Kernel trace-entry structure.

Before the addition of KTR, developers would sprinkle calls to *printf*() throughout their code, and conditionally compile them in or out of the kernel using

```
#ifdef DEBUG
printf()
#endif DEBUG
```

statements. The KTR system introduced a single logging system for the kernel that could be shared by the entire source base and centrally controlled from kernel configuration files.

Kernel trace events are described by a *ktr_entry* structure, shown in Figure 3.5. Each entry contains a timestamp, the CPU on which the event occurred, the file and line of source code from which the event was logged, a programmer specified description, a pointer to the thread that executed the event, and up to six parameters.

Calls into the kernel tracing system are implemented as a set of macros, shown in Figure 3.6. Unlike the *printf*() routine, the kernel tracing facility does

Figure 3.6 Kernel tracing macros.

```
CTR0(event_mask, format)
CTR1(event_mask, format, p1)
CTR2(event_mask, format, p1, p2)
CTR3(event_mask, format, p1, p2, p3)
CTR4(event_mask, format, p1, p2, p3, p4)
CTR5(event_mask, format, p1, p2, p3, p4, p5)
CTR6(event_mask, format, p1, p2, p3, p4, p5, p6)
```

not allow for a variable number of arguments. Variable argument parsing is computationally expensive, and is not appropriate for a kernel logging facility because the extra CPU time expended might prevent developers from catching timing-related problems.

When support for the KTR system is compiled into the kernel, there is a statically sized array, used as a circular buffer, that contains all the trace events. It is important to size the event buffer correctly as it is possible to overwrite entries before they are read out of the kernel if many events are logged in a short amount of time.

If enabling KTR recorded all the more than the 1700 defined events, the system would grind to a near halt. Thus, the rate of event generation is controlled by tagging each event with a programmer-defined event mask. The event mask collects a related set of events so that recording them can be turned on or off as a group. When a kernel with KTR is first booted, the system's event mask is cleared so that no events are recorded. The event mask is set either from user level, using the *debug.ktr.mask sysctl*, or in the boot configuration file **/boot/loader.conf**, if events are to be recorded from the time the system boots.

Kernel tracing events can be recorded to disk using the asynchronous logging facility which runs as a kernel resident thread. It reads events from the kernel trace buffer and writes them to a file specified by the user using a *sysctl*. Writing events to a file, whether on local disk or a remote filesystem, introduces extra I/O load onto the system, which may make it inappropriate for finding timing-related problems in the system.

Exercises

3.1 Describe three types of system activity.

3.2 When can a routine executing in the top half of the kernel be preempted? When can it be interrupted?

3.3 Why are routines executing in the bottom half of the kernel precluded from using information located in the current user process?

3.4 Why does the system defer as much work as possible from high-priority interrupts to lower-priority software-interrupt processes?

3.5 What determines the shortest (nonzero) time period that a user process can request when setting a timer?

3.6 How does the kernel determine the system call for which it has been invoked?

3.7 How are initialized data represented in an executable file? How are uninitialized data represented in an executable file? Why are the representations different?

3.8 Describe how the "#!" mechanism can be used to make programs that require emulation appear as though they were normal executables.

3.9 What facilities does the DTrace facility provide that is not available in the **ktrace** facility?

*3.10 Describe the security implications of not zero filling the stack region at program startup.

*3.11 Why is the conversion from UTC to local time done by user processes rather than in the kernel?

*3.12 What is the advantage of having the kernel rather than an application restart an interrupted system call?

*3.13 Describe a scenario in which the timer-wheel algorithm used for the callout queue does not work well. Suggest an alternative data structure that runs more quickly than does the timer-wheel algorithm for your scenario.

*3.14 The SIGPROF profiling timer was originally intended to replace the *profil* system call to collect a statistical sampling of a program's program counter. Give two reasons why the *profil* facility had to be retained.

**3.15 What weakness in the process-accounting mechanism makes the latter unsuitable for use in a commercial environment?

References

Barkley & Lee, 1988.
R. E. Barkley & T. P. Lee, "A Heap-Based Callout Implementation to Meet Real-Time Needs," *USENIX Association Conference Proceedings*, pp. 213–222, June 1988.

Cantrill et al., 2004.
B. M. Cantrill, M. W. Shapiro, & A. H. Leventhal, "Dynamic Instrumentation of Production Systems," *USENIX Annual Technical Conference, General Track*, June 2004.

Gregg & Mauro, 2011.
B. Gregg & J. Mauro, *DTrace: Dynamic Tracing in Oracle Solaris, Mac OS X and FreeBSD,* Pearson Education, Upper Saddle River, NJ, 2011.

McCanne & Torek, 1993.
S. McCanne & C. Torek, "A Randomized Sampling Clock for CPU Utilization Estimation and Code Profiling," *USENIX Association Conference Proceedings*, pp. 387–394, January 1993.

Mills, 1992.
D. L. Mills, "The NTP Time Synchronization Protocol," RFC 1305, available from http://www.faqs.org/rfcs/rfc1305.html, March 1992.

Varghese & Lauck, 1987.
G. Varghese & T. Lauck, "Hashed and Hierarchical Timing Wheels: Data Structures for the Efficient Implementation of a Timer Facility," *Proceedings of the Eleventh Symposium on Operating Systems Principles*, pp. 25–38, November 1987.

PART II

Processes

CHAPTER 4

Process Management

4.1 Introduction to Process Management

A ***process*** is a program in execution. A process has an address space containing a mapping of its program's object code and global variables. It also has a set of kernel resources that it can name and on which it can operate using system calls. These resources include its credentials, signal state, and its descriptor array that gives it access to files, pipes, sockets, and devices. Each process has at least one and possibly many threads that execute its code. Every thread represents a virtual processor with a full context worth of register state and its own stack mapped into the address space. Every thread running in the process has a corresponding kernel thread, with its own kernel stack that represents the user thread when it is executing in the kernel as a result of a system call, page fault, or signal delivery.

A process must have system resources, such as memory and the underlying CPU. The kernel supports the illusion of concurrent execution of multiple processes by scheduling system resources among the set of processes that are ready to execute. On a multiprocessor, multiple threads of the same or different processes may execute concurrently. This chapter describes the composition of a process, the method that the system uses to switch between the process's threads, and the scheduling policy that it uses to promote sharing of the CPU. It also introduces process creation and termination, and details the signal and process-debugging facilities.

Two months after the developers began the first implementation of the UNIX operating system, there were two processes: one for each of the terminals of the PDP-7. At age 10 months, and still on the PDP-7, UNIX had many processes, the *fork* operation, and something like the *wait* system call. A process executed a new program by reading in a new program on top of itself. The first PDP-11 system (First Edition UNIX) saw the introduction of *exec*. All these systems allowed only one process in memory at a time. When a PDP-11 with memory management (a

KS-11) was obtained, the system was changed to permit several processes to remain in memory simultaneously, to reduce swapping. But this change did not apply to multiprogramming because disk I/O was synchronous. This state of affairs persisted into 1972 and the first PDP-11/45 system. True multiprogramming was finally introduced when the system was rewritten in C. Disk I/O for one process could then proceed while another process ran. The basic structure of process management in UNIX has not changed since that time [Ritchie, 1988].

The threads of a process operate in either ***user mode*** or ***kernel mode***. In user mode, a thread executes application code with the machine in a nonprivileged protection mode. When a thread requests services from the operating system with a system call, it switches into the machine's privileged protection mode via a protected mechanism and then operates in kernel mode.

The resources used by a thread are split into two parts. The resources needed for execution in user mode are defined by the CPU architecture and typically include the CPU's general-purpose registers, the program counter, the processor-status register, and the stack-related registers, as well as the contents of the memory segments that constitute FreeBSD's notion of a program (the text, data, shared library, and stack segments).

Kernel-mode resources include those required by the underlying hardware such as registers, program counter, and the stack pointer. These resources also include the state required for the FreeBSD kernel to provide system services for a thread. This ***kernel state*** includes parameters to the current system call, the current process's user identity, scheduling information, and so on. As described in Section 3.1, the kernel state for each process is divided into several separate data structures, with two primary structures: the ***process structure*** and the ***thread structure***.

The process structure contains information that must always remain resident in main memory, along with references to other structures that remain resident, whereas the thread structure tracks information that needs to be resident only when the process is executing such as its kernel run-time stack. Process and thread structures are allocated dynamically as part of process creation and are freed when the process is destroyed as it exits.

Multiprogramming

FreeBSD supports transparent multiprogramming: the illusion of concurrent execution of multiple processes or programs. It does so by ***context switching***—that is, by switching between the execution context of the threads within the same or different processes. A mechanism is also provided for ***scheduling*** the execution of threads—that is, for deciding which one to execute next. Facilities are provided for ensuring consistent access to data structures that are shared among processes.

Context switching is a hardware-dependent operation whose implementation is influenced by the underlying hardware facilities. Some architectures provide machine instructions that save and restore the hardware-execution context of a thread or an entire process including its virtual-address space. On others, the software must collect the hardware state from various registers and save it, then load those registers with the new hardware state. All architectures must save and restore the software state used by the kernel.

Context switching is done frequently, so increasing the speed of a context switch noticeably decreases time spent in the kernel and provides more time for execution of user applications. Since most of the work of a context switch is expended in saving and restoring the operating context of a thread or process, reducing the amount of the information required for that context is an effective way to produce faster context switches.

Scheduling

Fair scheduling of threads and processes is an involved task that is dependent on the types of executable programs and on the goals of the scheduling policy. Programs are characterized according to the amount of computation and the amount of I/O that they do. Scheduling policies typically attempt to balance resource utilization against the time that it takes for a program to complete. In FreeBSD's default scheduler, which we shall refer to as the timeshare scheduler, a process's priority is periodically recalculated based on various parameters, such as the amount of CPU time it has used, the amount of memory resources it holds or requires for execution, etc. Some tasks require more precise control over process execution called real-time scheduling. Real-time scheduling must ensure that threads finish computing their results by a specified deadline or in a particular order. The FreeBSD kernel implements real-time scheduling using a separate queue from the queue used for regular timeshared processes. A process with a real-time priority is not subject to priority degradation and will only be preempted by another thread of equal or higher real-time priority. The FreeBSD kernel also implements a queue of threads running at idle priority. A thread with an idle priority will run only when no other thread in either the real-time or timeshare-scheduled queues is runnable and then only if its idle priority is equal to or greater than all other runnable idle-priority threads.

The FreeBSD timeshare scheduler uses a priority-based scheduling policy that is biased to favor ***interactive programs***, such as text editors, over long-running batch-type jobs. Interactive programs tend to exhibit short bursts of computation followed by periods of inactivity or I/O. The scheduling policy initially assigns a high execution priority to each thread and allows that thread to execute for a fixed ***time slice***. Threads that execute for the duration of their slice have their priority lowered, whereas threads that give up the CPU (usually because they do I/O) are allowed to remain at their priority. Threads that are inactive have their priority raised. Jobs that use large amounts of CPU time sink rapidly to a low priority, whereas interactive jobs that are mostly inactive remain at a high priority so that, when they are ready to run, they will preempt the long-running lower-priority jobs. An interactive job, such as a text editor searching for a string, may become compute-bound briefly and thus get a lower priority, but it will return to a high priority when it is inactive again while the user thinks about the result.

Some tasks, such as the compilation of a large application, may be done in many small steps in which each component is compiled in a separate process. No individual step runs long enough to have its priority degraded, so the compilation as a whole impacts the interactive programs. To detect and avoid this problem, the scheduling priority of a child process is propagated back to its parent. When a new child process is started, it begins running with its parent's current priority. As the program that coordinates the compilation (typically **make**) starts many compilation steps, its priority is dropped because of the CPU-intensive behavior of its children. Later compilation steps started by **make** begin running and stay at a lower priority, which allows higher-priority interactive programs to run in preference to them as desired.

The system also needs a scheduling policy to deal with problems that arise from not having enough main memory to hold the execution contexts of all processes that want to execute. The major goal of this scheduling policy is to minimize ***thrashing***—a phenomenon that occurs when memory is in such short supply that more time is spent in the system handling page faults and scheduling processes than in user mode executing application code.

The system must both detect and eliminate thrashing. It detects thrashing by observing the amount of free memory. When the system has little free memory and a high rate of new memory requests, it considers itself to be thrashing. The system reduces thrashing by marking the least recently run process as not being allowed to run, allowing the pageout daemon to push all the pages associated with the process to backing store. On most architectures, the kernel also can push to backing store the kernel stacks of all the threads of the marked process. The effect of these actions is to cause the process and all its threads to be swapped out (see Section 6.12). The memory freed by blocking the process can then be distributed to the remaining processes, which usually can then proceed. If the thrashing continues, additional processes are selected to be blocked from running until enough memory becomes available for the remaining processes to run effectively. Eventually, enough processes complete and free their memory that blocked processes can resume execution. However, even if there is not enough memory, the blocked processes are allowed to resume execution after about 20 seconds. Usually, the thrashing condition will return, requiring that some other process be selected for being blocked (or that an administrative action be taken to reduce the load).

4.2 Process State

Every process in the system is assigned a unique identifier termed the ***process identifier*** (*PID*). PIDs are the common mechanism used by applications and by the kernel to reference processes. PIDs are used by applications when the latter send a signal to a process and when receiving the exit status from a deceased process. Two PIDs are of special importance to each process: the PID of the process itself and the PID of the process's parent process.

The layout of process state is shown in Figure 4.1. The goal is to support multiple threads that share an address space and other resources. A ***thread*** is the unit of execution of a process; it requires an address space and other resources, but it can share many of those resources with other threads. Threads sharing an

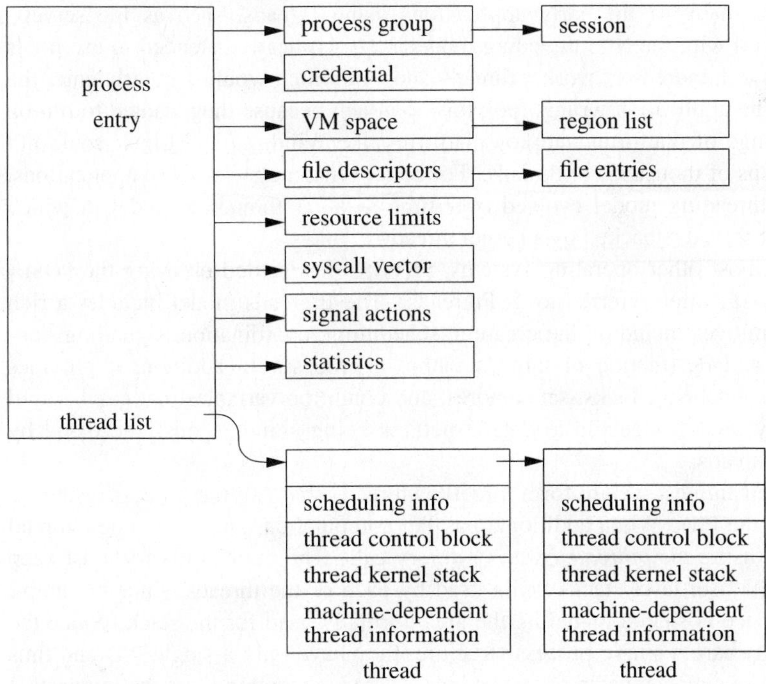

Figure 4.1 Process state.

address space and other resources are scheduled independently and in FreeBSD can all execute system calls simultaneously. The process state in FreeBSD is designed to support threads that can select the set of resources to be shared, known as variable-weight processes [Aral et al., 1989].

Each of the components of process state is placed into separate substructures for each type of state information. The process structure references all the substructures directly or indirectly. The thread structure contains just the information needed to run in the kernel: information about scheduling, a stack to use when running in the kernel, a ***thread state block*** (***TSB***), and other machine-dependent state. The TSB is defined by the machine architecture; it includes the general-purpose registers, stack pointers, program counter, processor-status word, and memory-management registers.

The first threading models that were deployed in systems such as FreeBSD 5 and Solaris used an N:M threading model in which many user level threads (N) were supported by a smaller number of threads (M) that could run in the kernel [Simpleton, 2008]. The N:M threading model was light-weight but incurred extra overhead when a user-level thread needed to enter the kernel. The model assumed that application developers would write server applications in which potentially thousands of clients would each use a thread, most of which would be idle waiting for an I/O request.

While many of the early applications using threads, such as file servers, worked well with the N:M threading model, later applications tended to use pools of dozens to hundreds of worker threads, most of which would regularly enter the kernel. The application writers took this approach because they wanted to run on a wide range of platforms and key platforms like Windows and Linux could not support tens of thousands of threads. For better efficiency with these applications, the N:M threading model evolved over time to a 1:1 threading model in which every user thread is backed by a kernel thread.

Like most other operating systems, FreeBSD has settled on using the POSIX threading API often referred to as Pthreads. The Pthreads model includes a rich set of primitives including the creation, scheduling, coordination, signalling, rendezvous, and destruction of threads within a process. In addition, it provides shared and exclusive locks, semaphores, and condition variables that can be used to reliably interlock access to data structures being simultaneously accessed by multiple threads.

In their lightest-weight form, FreeBSD threads share all the process resources including the PID. When additional parallel computation is needed, a new thread is created using the *pthread_create*() library call. The pthread library must keep track of the user-level stacks being used by each of the threads, since the entire address space is shared including the area normally used for the stack. Since the threads all share a single process structure, they have only a single PID and thus show up as a single entry in the **ps** listing. There is an option to **ps** that requests it to list a separate entry for each thread within a process.

Many applications do not wish to share all of a process's resources. The *rfork* system call creates a new process entry that shares a selected set of resources from its parent. Typically, the signal actions, statistics, and the stack and data parts of the address space are not shared. Unlike the lightweight thread created by *pthread_create*(), the *rfork* system call associates a PID with each thread that shows up in a **ps** listing and that can be manipulated in the same way as any other process in the system. Processes created by *fork*, *vfork*, or *rfork* initially have just a single thread structure associated with them. A variant of the *rfork* system call is used to emulate the Linux *clone*() functionality.

The Process Structure

In addition to the references to the substructures, the process entry shown in Figure 4.1 contains the following categories of information:

- Process identification: the PID and the parent PID
- Signal state: signals pending delivery and summary of signal actions
- Tracing: process tracing information
- Timers: real-time timer and CPU-utilization counters

The process substructures shown in Figure 4.1 have the following categories of information:

- Process-group identification: the process group and the session to which the process belongs
- User ***credential***s: the real, effective, and saved user and group identifiers; credentials are described more fully in Chapter 5
- Memory management: the structure that describes the allocation of virtual address space used by the process; the virtual-address space and its related structures are described more fully in Chapter 6
- File descriptors: an array of pointers to file entries indexed by the process's open file descriptors; also, the open file flags and current directory
- System call vector: the mapping of system call numbers to actions; in addition to current and deprecated native FreeBSD executable formats, the kernel can run binaries compiled for several other UNIX variants such as Linux and System V Release 4 by providing alternative system call vectors when such environments are requested
- Resource accounting: the *rlimit* structures that describe the utilization of the many resources provided by the system (see Section 3.7)
- Statistics: statistics collected while the process is running that are reported when it exits and are written to the accounting file; also includes process timers and profiling information if the latter is being collected
- Signal actions: the action to take when a signal is posted to a process
- Thread structure: the contents of the thread structure (described at the end of this section)

The state element of the process structure holds the current value of the process state. The possible state values are shown in Table 4.1. When a process is first

Table 4.1 Process states.

State	Description
NEW	undergoing process creation
NORMAL	thread(s) will be RUNNABLE, SLEEPING, or STOPPED
ZOMBIE	undergoing process termination

created with a *fork* system call, it is initially marked as NEW. The state is changed to NORMAL when enough resources are allocated to the process for the latter to begin execution. From that point onward, a process's state will be NORMAL until the process terminates. Its thread(s) will fluctuate among RUNNABLE—that is, preparing to be or actually executing; SLEEPING—that is, waiting for an event; and STOPPED—that is, stopped by a signal or the parent process. A deceased process is marked as ZOMBIE until it has freed its resources and communicated its termination status to its parent process.

The system organizes process structures into two lists. Process entries are on the *zombproc* list if the process is in the ZOMBIE state; otherwise, they are on the *allproc* list. The two queues share the same linkage pointers in the process structure, since the lists are mutually exclusive. Segregating the dead processes from the live ones reduces the time spent both by the *wait* system call, which must scan the zombies for potential candidates to return, and by the scheduler and other functions that must scan all the potentially runnable processes.

Most threads, except the currently executing thread (or threads if the system is running on a multiprocessor), are also in one of three queues: a ***run queue***, a ***sleep queue***, or a ***turnstile queue***. Threads that are in a runnable state are placed on a run queue, whereas threads that are blocked while awaiting an event are located on either a turnstile queue or a sleep queue. Stopped threads awaiting an event are located on a turnstile queue, a sleep queue, or they are on no queue. The run queues are organized according to thread-scheduling priority and are described in Section 4.4. The sleep and turnstile queues are organized in a data structure that is hashed by an event identifier. This organization optimizes finding the sleeping threads that need to be awakened when a wakeup occurs for an event. The sleep and turnstile queues are described in Section 4.3.

The *p_pptr* pointer and related lists (*p_children* and *p_sibling*) are used in locating related processes, as shown in Figure 4.2. When a process spawns a child process, the child process is added to its parent's *p_children* list. The child process also keeps a backward link to its parent in its *p_pptr* pointer. If a process has more than one child process active at a time, the children are linked together through their *p_sibling* list entries. In Figure 4.2, process B is a direct descendant of process A, whereas processes C, D, and E are descendants of process B and are

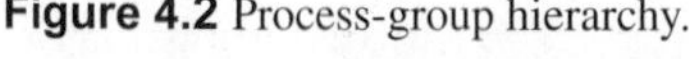

Figure 4.2 Process-group hierarchy.

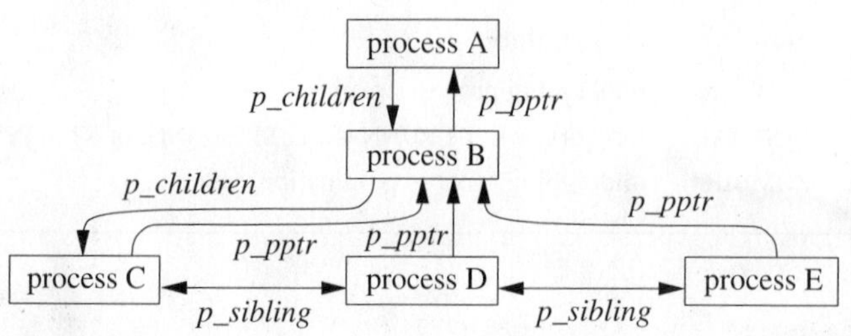

Table 4.2 Thread-scheduling classes.

Range	Class	Thread type
0 – 47	ITHD	bottom-half kernel (interrupt)
48 – 79	REALTIME	real-time user
80 – 119	KERN	top-half kernel
120 – 223	TIMESHARE	time-sharing user
224 – 255	IDLE	idle user

siblings of one another. Process B typically would be a shell that started a pipeline (see Sections 2.4 and 4.8) including processes C, D, and E. Process A probably would be the system-initialization process **init** (see Sections 3.1 and 15.4).

CPU time is made available to threads according to their ***scheduling class*** and ***scheduling priority***. As shown in Table 4.2, the FreeBSD kernel has two kernel and three user scheduling classes. The kernel will always run the thread in the highest-priority class. Any kernel-interrupt threads will run in preference to anything else followed by any runnable real-time threads. Any top-half-kernel threads are run in preference to runnable threads in the share and idle classes. Runnable timeshare threads are run in preference to runnable threads in the idle class. The priorities of threads in the real-time and idle classes are set by the applications using the *rtprio* system call and are never adjusted by the kernel. The bottom-half interrupt priorities are set when the devices are configured and never change. The top-half priorities are set based on predefined priorities for each kernel subsystem and never change.

The priorities of threads running in the timeshare class are adjusted by the kernel based on resource usage and recent CPU utilization. A thread has two scheduling priorities: one for scheduling user-mode execution and one for scheduling kernel-mode execution. The *td_user_pri* field associated with the thread structure contains the user-mode scheduling priority, whereas the *td_priority* field holds the current scheduling priority. The current priority may be different from the user-mode priority when the thread is executing in the top half of the kernel. Priorities range between 0 and 255, with a lower value interpreted as a higher priority (see Table 4.2). User-mode priorities range from 120 to 255; priorities less than 120 are used only by real-time threads or when a thread is asleep—that is, awaiting an event in the kernel—and immediately after such a thread is awakened. Threads asleep in the kernel are given a higher priority because they typically hold shared kernel resources when they awaken. The system wants to run them as quickly as possible once they get a resource so that they can use the resource and return it before another thread requests it and gets blocked waiting for it.

When a thread goes to sleep in the kernel, it must specify whether it should be awakened and marked runnable if a signal is posted to it. In FreeBSD, a kernel thread will be awakened by a signal only if it sets the PCATCH flag when it sleeps.

The *msleep*() interface also handles sleeps limited to a maximum time duration and the processing of restartable system calls. The *msleep*() interface includes a reference to a string describing the event that the thread awaits; this string is externally visible—for example, in **ps**. The decision of whether to use an interruptible sleep depends on how long the thread may be blocked. Because it is complex to handle signals in the midst of doing some other operation, many sleep requests are not interruptible; that is, a thread will not be scheduled to run until the event for which it is waiting occurs. For example, a thread waiting for disk I/O will sleep with signals blocked.

For quickly occurring events, delaying to handle a signal until after they complete is imperceptible. However, requests that may cause a thread to sleep for a long period, such as waiting for terminal or network input, must be prepared to have its sleep interrupted so that the posting of signals is not delayed indefinitely. Threads that sleep interruptibly may abort their system call because of a signal arriving before the event for which they are waiting has occurred. To avoid holding a kernel resource permanently, these threads must check why they have been awakened. If they were awakened because of a signal, they must release any resources that they hold. They must then return the error passed back to them by *sleep*(), which will be EINTR if the system call is to be aborted after the signal or ERESTART if it is to be restarted. Occasionally, an event that is supposed to occur quickly, such as a disk I/O, will get held up because of a hardware failure. Because the thread is sleeping in the kernel with signals blocked, it will be impervious to any attempts to send it a signal, even a signal that should cause it to exit unconditionally. The only solution to this problem is to change *sleep*()s on hardware events that may hang to be interruptible.

In the remainder of this book, we shall always use *sleep*() when referring to the routine that puts a thread to sleep, even when one of the *mtx_sleep*(), *sx_sleep*(), *rw_sleep*(), or *t_sleep*() interfaces is the one that is being used.

The Thread Structure

The thread structure shown in Figure 4.1 contains the following categories of information:

- Scheduling: the thread priority, user-mode scheduling priority, recent CPU utilization, and amount of time spent sleeping; the run state of a thread (runnable, sleeping); additional status flags; if the thread is sleeping, the ***wait channel***, the identity of the event for which the thread is waiting (see Section 4.3), and a pointer to a string describing the event
- TSB: the user- and kernel-mode execution states
- Kernel stack: the per-thread execution stack for the kernel
- Machine state: the machine-dependent thread information

Historically, the kernel stack was mapped to a fixed location in the virtual address space. The reason for using a fixed mapping is that when a parent forks, its run-time stack is copied for its child. If the kernel stack is mapped to a fixed address, the child's kernel stack is mapped to the same addresses as its parent kernel stack. Thus, all its internal references, such as frame pointers and stack-variable references, work as expected.

On modern architectures with virtual address caches, mapping the kernel stack to a fixed address is slow and inconvenient. FreeBSD removes this constraint by eliminating all but the top call frame from the child's stack after copying it from its parent so that it returns directly to user mode, thus avoiding stack copying and relocation problems.

Every thread that might potentially run must have its stack resident in memory because one task of its stack is to handle page faults. If it were not resident, it would page fault when the thread tried to run, and there would be no kernel stack available to service the page fault. Since a system may have many thousands of threads, the kernel stacks must be kept small to avoid wasting too much physical memory. In FreeBSD on the Intel architecture, the kernel stack is limited to two pages of memory. Implementors must be careful when writing code that executes in the kernel to avoid using large local variables and deeply nested subroutine calls to avoid overflowing the run-time stack. As a safety precaution, some architectures leave an invalid page between the area for the run-time stack and the data structures that follow it. Thus, overflowing the kernel stack will cause a kernel-access fault instead of disastrously overwriting other data structures. It would be possible to simply kill the process that caused the fault and continue running. However, the cleanup would be difficult because the thread may be holding locks or be in the middle of modifying some data structure that would be left in an inconsistent or invalid state. So the FreeBSD kernel panics on a kernel-access fault because such a fault shows a fundamental design error in the kernel. By panicking and creating a crash dump, the error can usually be pinpointed and corrected.

4.3 Context Switching

The kernel switches among threads in an effort to share the CPU effectively; this activity is called ***context switching***. When a thread executes for the duration of its time slice or when it blocks because it requires a resource that is currently unavailable, the kernel finds another thread to run and context switches to it. The system can also interrupt the currently executing thread to run a thread triggered by an asynchronous event, such as a device interrupt. Although both scenarios involve switching the execution context of the CPU, switching between threads occurs ***synchronously*** with respect to the currently executing thread, whereas servicing interrupts occurs ***asynchronously*** with respect to the current thread. In addition, interprocess context switches are classified as voluntary or involuntary. A voluntary context switch occurs when a thread blocks because it requires a resource that is unavailable. An involuntary context switch takes place when a thread executes for the duration of its time slice or when the system identifies a higher-priority thread to run.

Each type of context switching is done through a different interface. Voluntary context switching is initiated with a call to the *sleep*() routine, whereas an involuntary context switch is forced by direct invocation of the low-level context-switching mechanism embodied in the *mi_switch*() and *setrunnable*() routines. Asynchronous event handling is triggered by the underlying hardware and is effectively transparent to the system.

Thread State

Context switching between threads requires that both the kernel- and user-mode context be changed. To simplify this change, the system ensures that all of a thread's user-mode state is located in the thread structure while most kernel state is kept elsewhere. The following conventions apply to this localization:

- Kernel-mode hardware-execution state: Context switching can take place in only kernel mode. The kernel's hardware-execution state is defined by the contents of the TSB that is located in the thread structure.
- User-mode hardware-execution state: When execution is in kernel mode, the user-mode state of a thread (such as copies of the program counter, stack pointer, and general registers) always resides on the kernel's execution stack that is located in the thread structure. The kernel ensures this location of user-mode state by requiring that the system-call and trap handlers save the contents of the user-mode execution context each time that the kernel is entered (see Section 3.1).
- The process structure: The process structure always remains resident in memory.
- Memory resources: Memory resources of a process are effectively described by the contents of the memory-management registers located in the TSB and by the values present in the process and thread structures. As long as the process remains in memory, these values will remain valid and context switches can be done without the associated page tables being saved and restored. However, these values need to be recalculated when the process returns to main memory after being swapped to secondary storage.

Low-Level Context Switching

The localization of a process's context in that process's thread structure permits the kernel to perform context switching simply by changing the notion of the current thread structure and (if necessary) process structure, and restoring the context described by the TSB within the thread structure (including the mapping of the virtual address space). Whenever a context switch is required, a call to the *mi_switch*() routine causes the highest-priority thread to run. The *mi_switch*() routine first selects the appropriate thread from the scheduling queues, and then resumes the selected thread by loading its context from its TSB.

Voluntary Context Switching

A voluntary context switch occurs whenever a thread must await the availability of a resource or the arrival of an event. Voluntary context switches happen frequently in normal system operation. In FreeBSD, voluntary context switches are initiated through a request to obtain a lock that is already held by another thread or by a call to the *sleep*() routine. When a thread no longer needs the CPU, it is suspended, awaiting the resource described by a ***wait channel***, and is given a scheduling priority that should be assigned to the thread when that thread is awakened. This priority does not affect the user-level scheduling priority.

When blocking on a lock, the wait channel is usually the address of the lock. When blocking for a resource or an event, the wait channel is typically the address of some data structure that identifies the resource or event for which the thread is waiting. For example, the address of a disk buffer is used while the thread is waiting for the buffer to be filled. When the buffer is filled, threads sleeping on that wait channel will be awakened. In addition to the resource addresses that are used as wait channels, there are some addresses that are used for special purposes:

- When a parent process does a *wait* system call to collect the termination status of its children, it must wait for one of those children to exit. Since it cannot know which of its children will exit first, and since it can sleep on only a single wait channel, there is a quandary about how to wait for the next of multiple events. The solution is to have the parent sleep on its own process structure. When a child exits, it awakens its parent's process-structure address rather than its own. Thus, the parent doing the *wait* will awaken independently of which child process is the first to exit. Once running, it must scan its list of children to determine which one exited.
- When a thread does a *sigsuspend* system call, it does not want to run until it receives a signal. Thus, it needs to do an interruptible sleep on a wait channel that will never be awakened. By convention, the address of the signal-actions structure is given as the wait channel.

A thread may block for a short, medium, or long period of time depending on the reason that it needs to wait. A short wait occurs when a thread needs to wait for access to a lock that protects a data structure. A medium wait occurs while a thread waits for an event that is expected to occur quickly such as waiting for data to be read from a disk. A long wait occurs when a thread is waiting for an event that will happen at an indeterminate time in the future such as input from a user.

Short-term waits arise only from a lock request. Short-term locks include mutexes, read-writer locks, and read-mostly locks. Details on these locks are given later in this section. A requirement of short-term locks is that they may not be held while blocking for an event as is done for medium- and long-term locks. The only reason that a thread holding a short-term lock is not running is that it has been preempted by a higher-priority thread. It is always possible to get a short-term lock released by running the thread that holds it and any threads that block the thread that holds it.

A short-term lock is managed by a ***turnstile*** data structure. The *turnstile* tracks the current owner of the lock and the list of threads waiting for access to the lock. Figure 4.3 shows how *turnstile*s are used to track blocked threads. Across the top of the figure is a set of hash headers that allow a quick lookup to find a lock with waiting threads. If a *turnstile* is found, it provides a pointer to the thread

Figure 4.3 Turnstile structures for blocked threads.

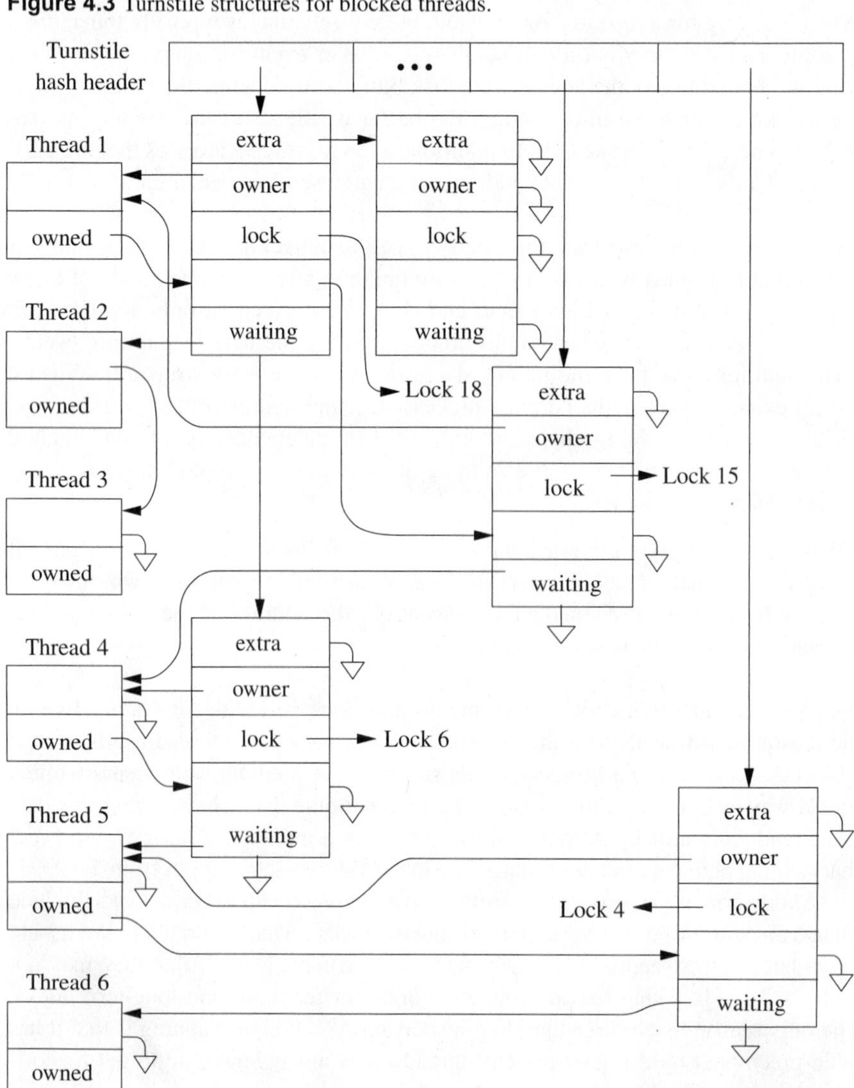

that currently owns the lock and lists of the threads that are waiting for exclusive and shared access. The most important use of the *turnstile* is to quickly find the threads that need to be awakened when a lock is released. In Figure 4.3, Lock 18 is owned by thread 1 and has threads 2 and 3 waiting for exclusive access to it. The *turnstile* in this example also shows that thread 1 holds contested Lock 15.

A *turnstile* is needed each time a thread blocks on a contested lock. Because blocking is common, it would be prohibitively slow to allocate and free a *turnstile* every time one is needed. So each thread allocates a *turnstile* when it is created. As a thread may only be blocked on one lock at any point in time, it will never need more than one *turnstile*. *Turnstile*s are allocated by threads rather than being incorporated into each lock structure because there are far more locks in the kernel than there are threads. Allocating one *turnstile* per thread rather than one per lock results in lower memory utilization in the kernel.

When a thread is about to block on a short-term lock, it provides its *turnstile* to be used to track the lock. If it is the first thread to block on the lock, its *turnstile* is used. If it is not the first thread to block, then an earlier thread's *turnstile* will be in use to do the tracking. The additional *turnstile*s that are provided are kept on a free list whose head is the *turnstile* being used to track the lock. When a thread is awakened and is being made runnable, it is given a *turnstile* from the free list (which may not be the same one that it originally provided). When the last thread is awakened, the free list will be empty and the *turnstile* no longer needed, so it can be taken by the awakening thread.

In Figure 4.3, the *turnstile* tracking Lock 18 was provided by thread 2 as it was the first to block. The spare *turnstile* that it references was provided by thread 3. If thread 2 is the first to be awakened, it will get the spare *turnstile* provided by thread 3 and when thread 3 is awakened later, it will be the last to be awakened so will get the no-longer-needed *turnstile* originally provided by thread 2.

A ***priority inversion*** occurs when a thread trying to acquire a short-term lock finds that the thread holding the lock has a lower priority than its own priority. The owner and list of blocked threads tracked by the *turnstile* allows ***priority propagation*** of the higher priority from the thread that is about to be blocked to the thread that holds the lock. With the higher priority, the thread holding the lock will run, and if, in turn, it is blocked by a thread with lower priority, it will propagate its new higher priority to that thread. When finished with its access to the protected data structure, the thread with the temporarily raised priority will release the lock. As part of releasing the lock, the propagated priority will be dropped, which usually results in the thread from which the priority was propagated getting to run and now being able to acquire the lock.

Processes blocking on medium-term and long-term locks use *sleepqueue* data structures rather than *turnstile*s to track the blocked threads. The *sleepqueue* data structure is similar to the *turnstile* except that it does not need to track the owner of the lock. The owner need not be tracked because *sleepqueue*s do not need to provide priority propagation. Threads blocked on medium- and long-term locks cannot proceed until the event for which they are waiting has occurred. Raising their priority will not allow them to run any sooner.

Sleepqueues have many similarities to *turnstiles* including a hash table to allow quick lookup of contested locks and lists of the threads blocked because they are awaiting shared and exclusive locks. When created, each thread allocates a *sleepqueue* structure. It provides its *sleepqueue* structure when it is about to be put to sleep and is returned a *sleepqueue* structure when it is awakened.

Unlike short-term locks, the medium- and long-term locks can request a time limit so that if the event for which they are waiting has not occurred within the specified period of time, they will be awakened with an error return that indicates that the time limit expired rather than the event occurring. Finally, long-term locks can request that they be interruptible, meaning that they will be awakened if a signal is sent to them before the event for which they are waiting has occurred.

Suspending a thread takes the following steps in its operation:

1. Prevents events that might cause thread-state transitions. Historically a global scheduling lock was used, but it was a bottleneck. Now each thread uses a lock tied to its current state to protect its per-thread state. For example, when a thread is on a run queue, the lock for that run queue is used; when the thread is blocked on a *turnstile*, the *turnstile*'s lock is used; when a thread is blocked on a sleep queue, the lock for the wait channels hash chain is used.

2. Records the wait channel in the thread structure and hashes the wait-channel value to check for an existing *turnstile* or *sleepqueue* for the wait-channel. If one exists, links the thread to it and saves the *turnstile* or *sleepqueue* structure provided by the thread. Otherwise places the *turnstile* or *sleepqueue* onto the hash chain and links the thread into it.

3. For threads being placed on a *turnstile*, if the current thread's priority is higher than the priority of the thread currently holding the lock, propagates the current thread's priority to the thread currently holding the lock. For threads being placed on a *sleepqueue*, sets the thread's priority to the priority that the thread will have when the thread is awakened and sets its SLEEPING flag.

4. For threads being placed on a *turnstile*, sort the thread into the list of waiting threads such that the highest priority thread appears first in the list. For threads being placed on a *sleepqueue*, place the thread at the end of the list of threads waiting for that wait-channel.

5. Calls *mi_switch*() to request that a new thread be scheduled; the associated mutex is released as part of switching to the other thread.

A sleeping thread is not selected to execute until it is removed from a *turnstile* or *sleepqueue* and is marked runnable. This operation is done either implicitly as part of a lock being released, or explicitly by a call to the *wakeup*() routine to signal that an event has occurred or that a resource is available. When *wakeup*() is invoked, it is given a wait channel that it uses to find the corresponding *sleepqueue* (using a hashed lookup). It awakens all threads sleeping on that wait channel. All threads waiting for the resource are awakened to ensure that none are inadvertently left sleeping. If only one thread were awakened, it might not request the resource on which it was sleeping. If it does not use and release the resource, any other threads waiting for that resource will be left sleeping forever. A thread that needs an empty disk buffer in which to write data is an example of a thread that may not request the resource on which it was sleeping. Such a thread can use any available buffer. If none is available, it will try to create one by requesting that a dirty buffer be written to disk and then waiting for the I/O to complete. When the I/O finishes, the thread will awaken and will check for an empty buffer. If several are available, it may not use the one that it cleaned, leaving any other threads to sleep forever as they wait for the cleaned buffer.

In instances where a thread will always use a resource when it becomes available, *wakeup_one*() can be used instead of *wakeup*(). The *wakeup_one*() routine wakes up only the first thread that it finds waiting for a resource as it will have been asleep the longest. The assumption is that when the awakened thread is done with the resource, it will issue another *wakeup_one*() to notify the next waiting thread that the resource is available. The succession of *wakeup_one*() calls will continue until all threads waiting for the resource have been awakened and had a chance to use it. Because the threads are ordered from longest to shortest waiting, that is the order in which they will be awakened and gain access to the resource.

When releasing a turnstile lock, all waiting threads are released. Because the threads are ordered from highest to lowest priority, that is the order in which they will be awakened. Usually they will then be scheduled in the order in which they were released. When threads end up being run concurrently, the adaptive spinning (described later in this section) usually ensures that they will not block. And because they are released from highest to lowest priority, the highest priority thread will usually be the first to acquire the lock. There will be no need for, and hence no overhead from, priority propagation. Rather, the lock will be handed down from the highest priority threads through the intermediate priorities to the lowest priority.

To avoid having excessive numbers of threads awakened, kernel programmers try to use locks and wait channels with fine-enough granularity that unrelated uses will not collide on the same resource. For example, they put locks on each buffer in the buffer cache rather than putting a single lock on the buffer cache as a whole.

Resuming a thread takes the following steps in its operation:

1. Removes the thread from its *turnstile* or *sleepqueue*. If it is the last thread to be awakened, the *turnstile* or *sleepqueue* is returned to it. If it is not the last thread to be awakened, a *turnstile* or *sleepqueue* from the free list is returned to it.

2. Recomputes the user-mode scheduling priority if the thread has been sleeping longer than one second.

3. If the thread had been blocked on a *turnstile*, it is placed on the run queue. If the thread had been blocked on a *sleepqueue*, it is placed on the run queue if it is in a SLEEPING state and if its process is not swapped out of main memory.

If the process has been swapped out, the *swapin* process will be awakened to load it back into memory (see Section 6.12); if the thread is in a STOPPED state, it is not put on a run queue until it is explicitly restarted by a user-level process, either by a *ptrace* system call (see Section 4.9) or by a continue signal (see Section 4.7).

If any threads are placed on the run queue and one of them has a scheduling priority higher than that of the currently executing thread, it will also request that the CPU be rescheduled as soon as possible.

Synchronization

The FreeBSD kernel supports both ***symmetric multiprocessing*** (SMP) and ***nonuniform memory access*** (NUMA) architectures. An SMP architecture is one in which all the CPUs are connected to a common main memory while a NUMA architecture is one in which the CPUs are connected to a non-uniform memory. With a NUMA architecture, some memory is local to a CPU and is quickly accessible while other memory is slower to access because it is local to another CPU or shared between CPUs. Throughout this book, references to multiprocessors and multiprocessing refer to both SMP and NUMA architectures.

A multiprocessing kernel requires extensive and fine-grained synchronization. The simplist form of synchronization is a critical section. While a thread is running in a critical section, it can neither be migrated to another CPU nor preempted by another thread. A critical section protects per-CPU data structures such as a run queue or CPU-specific memory-allocation data structures. A critical section controls only a single CPU, so it cannot protect systemwide data structures; one of the locking mechanisms described below must be used. While critical sections are useful for only a limited set of data structures, they are beneficial in those cases

Table 4.3 Locking hierarchy.

Level	Type	Sleep	Description
Highest	witness	yes	partially ordered sleep locks
	lock manager	yes	drainable shared/exclusive access
	condition variables	yes	event-based thread blocking
	shared-exclusive lock	yes	shared and exclusive access
	read-mostly lock	no	optimized for read access
	reader-writer lock	no	shared and exclusive access
	sleep mutex	no	spin for a while, then sleep
	spin mutex	no	spin lock
Lowest	hardware	no	memory-interlocked compare-and-swap

because they have significantly lower overhead than locks. A critical section begins by calling *critical_enter*() and continues until calling the function *critical_exit*().

Table 4.3 shows the hierarchy of locking that is necessary to support multiprocessing. The column labelled Sleep in Table 4.3 shows whether a lock of that type may be held when a thread blocks for a medium- or long-term sleep.

Although it is possible to build locks using single-memory operations [Dekker, 2013], to be practical, the hardware must provide a memory interlocked compare-and-swap instruction. The compare-and-swap instruction must allow two operations to be done on a main-memory location—the reading and comparing to a specified compare-value of the existing value followed by the writing of a new value if the read value matches the compare-value—without any other processor being able to read or write that memory location between the two memory operations. All the locking primitives in the FreeBSD system are built using the compare-and-swap instruction.

Mutex Synchronization

Mutexes are the primary method of short-term thread synchronization. The major design considerations for mutexes are as follows:

- Acquiring and releasing uncontested mutexes should be as fast as possible.
- Mutexes must have the information and storage space to support priority propagation. In FreeBSD, mutexes use *turnstile*s to manage priority propagation.
- A thread must be able to acquire a mutex recursively if the mutex is initialized to support recursion.

Mutexes are built from the hardware compare-and-swap instruction. A memory location is reserved for the lock. When the lock is free, the value of MTX_UNOWNED is stored in the memory location; when the lock is held, a pointer to the thread owning the lock is stored in the memory location. The compare-and-swap instruction tries to acquire the lock. The value in the lock is compared with MTX_UNOWNED; if it matches, it is replaced with the pointer to the thread. The instruction returns the old value; if the old value was MTX_OWNED, then the lock was successfully acquired and the thread may proceed. Otherwise, some other thread held the lock so the thread must loop doing the compare-and-swap until the thread holding the lock (and running on a different processor) stores MTX_OWNED into the lock to show that it is done with it.

There are currently two flavors of mutexes: those that block and those that do not. By default, threads will block when they request a mutex that is already held. Most kernel code uses the default lock type that allows the thread to be suspended from the CPU if it cannot get the lock.

Mutexes that do not sleep are called ***spin mutexes***. A spin mutex will not relinquish the CPU when it cannot immediately get the requested lock, but it will loop, waiting for the mutex to be released by another CPU. Spinning can result in deadlock if a thread interrupted the thread that held a mutex and then tried to acquire the mutex. To protect an interrupt thread from blocking against itself during the period that it is held, a spin mutex runs inside a critical section with interrupts disabled on that CPU. Thus, an interrupt thread can run only on another CPU during the period that the spin mutex is held.

Spin mutexes are specialized locks that are intended to be held for short periods of time. A thread may hold multiple spin mutexes, but it is required to release the mutexes in the opposite order from which they were acquired. A thread may not go to sleep while holding a spin mutex.

On most architectures, both acquiring and releasing an uncontested spin mutex are more expensive than the same operation on a nonspin mutex. Spin mutexes are more expensive than blocking locks because spin mutexes have to disable or defer interrupts while they are held to prevent races with interrupt handling code. As a result, holding spin mutexes can increase interrupt latency. To minimize interrupt latency and reduce locking overhead, FreeBSD uses spin mutexes only in code that does low-level scheduling and context switching.

The time to acquire a lock can vary. Consider the time to wait for a lock needed to search for an item on a list. The thread holding the search lock may have to acquire another lock before it can remove an item it has found from the list. If the needed lock is already held, it will block to wait for it. A different thread that tries to acquire the search lock uses adaptive spinning. Adaptive spinning is implemented by having the thread that wants the lock extract the thread pointer of the owning thread from the lock structure. It then checks to see if the thread is currently executing. If so, it spins until either the lock is released or the thread stops executing. The effect is to spin so long as the current lock holder is executing on another CPU. The reasons for taking this approach are many:

- Locks are usually held for brief periods of time, so if the owner is running, then it will probably release the lock before the current thread completes the process of blocking on the lock.
- If a lock holder is not running, then the current thread has to wait at least one context switch time before it can acquire the lock.
- If the owner is on a run queue, then the current thread should block immediately so it can lend its priority to the lock owner.
- It is cheaper to release an uncontested lock with a single atomic operation than a contested lock. A contested lock has to find the *turnstile*, lock the turnstile chain and *turnstile*, and then awaken all the waiters. So adaptive spinning reduces overhead on both the lock owner and the thread trying to acquire the lock.

The lower cost for releasing an uncontested lock explains the algorithm used to awaken waiters on a mutex. Historically, the mutex code would only awaken a single waiter when a contested lock was released, which left the lock in a contested state if there were more than one waiter. However, leaving a contested lock ensured that the new lock holder would have to perform a more expensive unlock operation. Indeed, all but the last waiter would have an expensive unlock operation. In the current FreeBSD system, all the waiters are awakened when the lock is released. Usually they end up being scheduled sequentially, which results in them all getting to do cheaper unlock operations. If they do all end up running concurrently, they will then use adaptive spinning and will finish the chain of lock requests sooner since the context switches to awaken the threads are performed in parallel rather than sequentially. This change in behavior was motivated by documentation of these effects noted in Solaris Internals [McDougall & Mauro, 2006].

It is wasteful of CPU cycles to use spin mutexes for resources that will be held for long periods of time (more than a few microseconds). For example, a spin mutex would be inappropriate for a disk buffer that would need to be locked throughout the time that a disk I/O was being done. Here, a sleep lock should be used. When a thread trying to acquire a medium- or long-term lock finds that the lock is held, it is put to sleep so that other threads can run until the lock becomes available.

Spin mutexes are never appropriate on a uniprocessor since the only way that a resource held by another thread will ever be released will be when that thread gets to run. Spin mutexes are always converted to sleep locks when running on a uniprocessor. As with the multi-processor, interrupts are disabled while the spin mutexes are held. Since there is no other processor on which the interrupts can run, interrupt latency becomes much more apparent on a uniprocessor.

Mutex Interface

The *mtx_init*() function must be used to initialize a mutex before it can be used. The *mtx_init*() function specifies a type that the witness code uses to classify a mutex when doing checks of lock ordering. It is not permissible to pass the same *mutex* to *mtx_init*() multiple times without intervening calls to *mtx_destroy*().

The *mtx_lock*() function acquires a mutual exclusion lock for the currently running kernel thread. If another kernel thread is holding the mutex, the caller will sleep until the mutex is available. The *mtx_lock_spin*() function is similar to the *mtx_lock*() function except that it will spin until the mutex becomes available. A critical section is entered when the spin mutex is obtained and is exited when the spin mutex is released. Interrupts are blocked on the CPU on which the thread holding the spin mutex is running. No other threads, including interrupt threads, can run on the CPU during the period that the spin mutex is held.

It is possible for the same thread to acquire a mutex recursively with no ill effects if the MTX_RECURSE bit was passed to *mtx_init*() during the initialization of the mutex. The witness module verifies that a thread does not recurse on a non-recursive lock. A recursive lock is useful if a resource may be locked at two or more levels in the kernel. By allowing a recursive lock, a lower layer need not check if the resource has already been locked by a higher layer; it can simply lock and release the resource as needed.

The *mtx_trylock*() function tries to acquire a mutual exclusion lock for the currently running kernel thread. If the mutex cannot be immediately acquired, *mtx_trylock*() will return 0; otherwise the mutex will be acquired and a nonzero value will be returned. The *mtx_trylock*() function cannot be used with spin mutexes.

The *mtx_unlock*() function releases a mutual exclusion lock; if a higher-priority thread is waiting for the mutex, the releasing thread will be put to sleep to allow the higher-priority thread to acquire the mutex and run. A mutex that allows recursive locking maintains a reference count showing the number of times that it has been locked. Each successful lock request must have a corresponding unlock request. The mutex is not released until the final unlock has been done, causing the reference count to drop to zero.

The *mtx_unlock_spin*() function releases a spin-type mutual exclusion lock; the critical section entered before acquiring the mutex is exited.

The *mtx_destroy*() function destroys a mutex so the data associated with it may be freed or otherwise overwritten. Any mutex that is destroyed must previously have been initialized with *mtx_init*(). It is permissible to have a single reference to a mutex when it is destroyed. It is not permissible to hold the mutex recursively or have another thread blocked on the mutex when it is destroyed. If these rules are violated, the kernel will panic.

Normally, a mutex is allocated within the structure that it will protect. For long-lived structures or structures that are allocated from a zone (structures in a zone are created once and used many times before they are destroyed), the time overhead of initializing and destroying it is insignificant. For a short-lived structure that is not allocated out of a zone, the cost of initializing and destroying an embedded mutex may exceed the time during which the structure is used. In addition, mutexes are large and may double or triple the size of a small short-lived structure (a mutex is often the size of a cache line, which is typically 128 bytes). To avoid this overhead, the kernel provides a pool of mutexes that may be borrowed for use with a short-lived structure. The short-lived structure does not need to reserve space for a mutex, just space for a pointer to a pool mutex. When the structure is allocated, it requests a pool mutex to which it sets its pointer. When it is done, the pool mutex is returned to the kernel and the structure freed. An example of a use of a pool mutex comes from the *poll* system call implementation that needs a structure to track a poll request from the time the system call is entered until the requested data arrives on the descriptor.

Lock Synchronization

Interprocess synchronization to a resource typically is implemented by associating it with a *lock* structure. The kernel has several lock managers that manipulate a lock. The operations provided by all the lock managers are:

- Request shared: Get one of many possible shared locks. If a thread holding an exclusive lock requests a shared lock, some lock managers will downgrade the exclusive lock to a shared lock while others simply return an error.
- Request exclusive: When all shared locks have cleared, grant an exclusive lock. To ensure that the exclusive lock will be granted quickly, some lock managers

stop granting shared locks when an exclusive lock is requested. Others grant new shared locks only for recursive lock requests. Only one exclusive lock may exist at a time, except that a thread holding an exclusive lock may get additional exclusive locks if the *canrecurse* flag was set when the lock was initialized. Some lock managers allow the *canrecurse* flag to be specified in the lock request.

- Request release: Release one instance of a lock.

In addition to these basic requests, some of the lock managers provide the following additional functions:

- Request upgrade: The thread must hold a shared lock that it wants to have upgraded to an exclusive lock. Other threads may get exclusive access to the resource between the time that the upgrade is requested and the time that it is granted. Some lock managers allow only a limited version of upgrade where it is granted if immediately available, but do not provide a mechanism to wait for an upgrade.
- Request exclusive upgrade: The thread must hold a shared lock that it wants to have upgraded to an exclusive lock. If the request succeeds, no other threads will have received exclusive access to the resource between the time that the upgrade is requested and the time that it is granted. However, if another thread has already requested an upgrade, the request will fail.
- Request downgrade: The thread must hold an exclusive lock that it wants to have downgraded to a shared lock. If the thread holds multiple (recursive) exclusive locks, some lock managers will downgrade them all to shared locks; other lock managers will fail the request.
- Request drain: Wait for all activity on the lock to end, and then mark it decommissioned. This feature is used before freeing a lock that is part of a piece of memory that is about to be released.

Locks must be initialized before their first use by calling their initialization function. Parameters to the initialization function may include the following:

- A top-half kernel priority at which the thread should run if it was blocked before it acquired the lock
- Flags such as *canrecurse* that allow the thread currently holding an exclusive lock to get another exclusive lock rather than panicking with a "locking against myself" failure
- A string that describes the resource that the lock protects, referred to as the ***wait channel*** message
- An optional maximum time to wait for the lock to become available

Not all types of locks support all these options. When a lock is no longer needed, it must be released.

As shown in Table 4.3, the lowest-level type of lock is the reader-writer lock. The reader-writer lock operates much like a mutex except that a reader-writer lock supports both shared and exclusive access. Like a mutex, it is managed by a *turnstile* so it cannot be held during a medium- or long-term sleep and provides priority propagation for exclusive (but not shared) locks. Reader-writer locks may be recursed.

Next up in Table 4.3 is the read-mostly lock. The read-mostly lock has the same capabilities and restrictions as reader-writer locks while they also add priority propagation for shared locks by tracking shared owners using a caller-supplied tracker data structure. Read-mostly locks are used to protect data that are read far more often than they are written. They work by trying the read without acquiring a lock assuming that the read will succeed and only fall back to using locks when the assumption fails. Reads usually happen more quickly but at a higher cost if the underlying resource is modified. The routing table is a good example of a read-mostly data structure. Routes are rarely updated, but are read frequently.

The remaining types of locks all permit medium- and long-term sleeping. None of these locks support priority propagation. The shared-exclusive locks are the fastest of these locks with the fewest features. In addition to the basic shared and exclusive access, they provide recursion for both shared and exclusive locks, the ability to be interrupted by a signal, and limited upgrade and downgrade capabilities.

The lock-manager locks are the most full featured but also the slowest of the locking schemes. In addition to the features of the shared-exclusive locks, they provide full upgrade and downgrade capabilities, the ability to be awakened after a specified interval, the ability to drain all users in preparation for being deallocated, and the ability to pass ownership of locks between threads and to the kernel.

Condition variables are used with mutexes to wait for conditions to occur. Threads wait on condition variables by calling *cv_wait*(), *cv_wait_sig*() (wait unless interrupted by a signal), *cv_timedwait*() (wait for a maximum time), or *cv_timedwait_sig*() (wait unless interrupted by a signal or for a maximum time). Threads unblock waiters by calling *cv_signal*() to unblock one waiter, or *cv_broadcast*() to unblock all waiters. The *cv_waitq_remove*() function removes a waiting thread from a condition-variable wait queue if it is on one.

A thread must hold a mutex before calling *cv_wait*(), *cv_wait_sig*(), *cv_timedwait*(), or *cv_timedwait_sig*(). When a thread waits on a condition, the mutex is atomically released before the thread is blocked, and then atomically reacquired before the function call returns. All waiters must use the same mutex with a condition variable. A thread must hold the mutex while calling *cv_signal*() or *cv_broadcast*().

Deadlock Prevention

The highest-level locking primitive prevents threads from deadlocking when locking multiple resources. Suppose that two threads, A and B, require exclusive access to two resources, R_1 and R_2, to do some operation as shown in Figure 4.4. If thread A acquires R_1 and thread B acquires R_2, then a deadlock occurs when

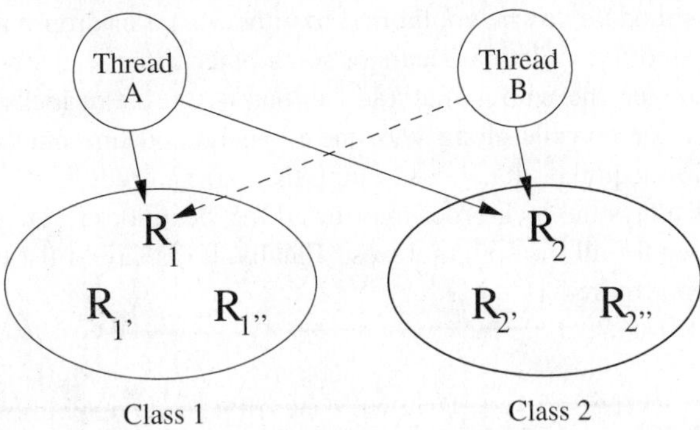

Figure 4.4 Partial ordering of resources.

thread A tries to acquire R_2 and thread B tries to acquire R_1. To avoid deadlock, FreeBSD maintains a partial ordering on all the locks. The two partial-ordering rules are as follows:

1. A thread may acquire only one lock in each class.
2. A thread may acquire only a lock in a higher-numbered class than the highest-numbered class for which it already holds a lock.

Figure 4.4 shows two classes. Class 1 with resources R_1, $R_{1'}$, and $R_{1''}$. Class 2 with resources R_2, $R_{2'}$, and $R_{2''}$. In Figure 4.4, Thread A holds R_1 and can request R_2 as R_1 and R_2 are in different classes and R_2 is in a higher-numbered class than R_1. However, Thread B must release R_2 before requesting R_1, since R_2 is in a higher class than R_1. Thus, Thread A will be able to acquire R_2 when it is released by Thread B. After Thread A completes and releases R_1 and R_2, Thread B will be able to acquire both of those locks and run to completion without deadlock.

Historically, the class members and ordering were poorly documented and unenforced. Violations were discovered when threads would deadlock and a careful analysis was done to figure out what ordering had been violated. With an increasing number of developers and a growing kernel, the ad hoc method of maintaining the partial ordering of locks became untenable. A witness module was added to the kernel to derive and enforce the partial ordering of the locks. The witness module keeps track of the locks acquired and released by each thread. It also keeps track of the order in which locks are acquired relative to each other. Each time a lock is acquired, the witness module uses these two lists to verify that a lock is not being acquired in the wrong order. If a lock order violation is detected, then a message is output to the console detailing the locks involved and the locations in the code in which they were acquired. The witness module also verifies that no locks that prohibit sleeping are held when requesting a sleep lock or voluntarily going to sleep.

The witness module can be configured to either panic or drop into the kernel debugger when an order violation occurs or some other witness check fails. When running the debugger, the witness module can output the list of locks held by the current thread to the console along with the filename and line number at which each lock was last acquired. It can also dump the current order list to the console. The code first displays the lock order tree for all the sleep locks. Then it displays the lock order tree for all the spin mutexes. Finally, it displays a list of locks that have not yet been acquired.

4.4 Thread Scheduling

The FreeBSD scheduler has a well-defined set of kernel-application programming interfaces (kernel APIs) that allow it to support different schedulers. Since FreeBSD 5.0, the kernel has had two schedulers available:

- The ULE scheduler first introduced in FreeBSD 5.0 and found in the file **/sys/kern/sched_ule.c** [Roberson, 2003]. The name is not an acronym. If the underscore in its filename is removed, the rationale for its name becomes apparent. This scheduler is used by default and is described later in this section.
- The traditional 4.4BSD scheduler found in the file **/sys/kern/sched_4bsd.c**. This scheduler is still maintained but no longer used by default.

Because a busy system makes millions of scheduling decisions per second, the speed with which scheduling decisions are made is critical to the performance of the system as a whole. Other UNIX systems have added a dynamic scheduler switch that must be traversed for every scheduling decision. To avoid this overhead, FreeBSD requires that the scheduler be selected at the time the kernel is built. Thus, all calls into the scheduling code are resolved at compile time rather than going through the overhead of an indirect function call for every scheduling decision.

The Low-Level Scheduler

Scheduling is divided into two parts: a simple low-level scheduler that runs frequently and a more complex high-level scheduler that runs at most a few times per second. The low-level scheduler runs every time a thread blocks and a new thread must be selected to run. For efficiency when running thousands of times per second, it must make its decision quickly with a minimal amount of information. To simplify its task, the kernel maintains a set of ***run queue***s for each CPU in the system that are organized from high to low priority. When a task blocks on a CPU, the low-level scheduler's sole responsibility is to select the thread from the highest-priority non-empty run queue for that CPU. The high-level scheduler is responsible for setting the thread priorities and deciding on which CPU's run queue they should be placed. Each CPU has its own set of run queues to avoid contention for access when two CPUs both need to select a new thread to run at the same time. Contention between run queues occurs only when the high-level scheduler decides to move a thread from the run queue of one CPU to the run queue of another CPU. The kernel tries to avoid moving threads between CPUs as the loss of its CPU-local caches slows it down.

All threads that are runnable are assigned a scheduling priority and a CPU by the high-level scheduler that determines in which run queue they are placed. In selecting a new thread to run, the low-level scheduler scans the run queues of the CPU needing a new thread from highest to lowest priority and chooses the first thread on the first nonempty queue. If multiple threads reside on a queue, the system runs them ***round robin***; that is, it runs them in the order that they are found on the queue, with equal amounts of time allowed. If a thread blocks, it is not put back onto any run queue. Instead, it is placed on a *turnstile* or a *sleepqueue*. If a thread uses up the ***time quantum*** (or ***time slice***) allowed it, it is placed at the end of the queue from which it came, and the thread at the front of the queue is selected to run.

The shorter the time quantum, the better the interactive response. However, longer time quanta provide higher system throughput because the system will incur less overhead from doing context switches and processor caches will be flushed less often. The time quantum used by FreeBSD is adjusted by the high-level scheduler as described later in this subsection.

Thread Run Queues and Context Switching

The kernel has a single set of run queues to manage all the thread scheduling classes shown in Table 4.2. The scheduling-priority calculations described in the previous section are used to order the set of timesharing threads into the priority ranges between 120 and 223. The real-time threads and the idle threads priorities are set by the applications themselves but are constrained by the kernel to be within the ranges 48 to 79 and 224 to 255, respectively. The number of queues used to hold the collection of all runnable threads in the system affects the cost of managing the queues. If only a single (ordered) queue is maintained, then selecting the next runnable thread becomes simple but other operations become expensive. Using 256 different queues can significantly increase the cost of identifying the next thread to run. The system uses 64 run queues, selecting a run queue for a thread by dividing the thread's priority by 4. To save time, the threads on each queue are not further sorted by their priorities.

The run queues contain all the runnable threads in main memory except the currently running thread. Figure 4.5 shows how each queue is organized as a doubly linked list of thread structures. The head of each run queue is kept in an array. Associated with this array is a bit vector, *rq_status*, that is used in identifying the nonempty run queues. Two routines, *runq_add*() and *runq_remove*(), are used to place a thread at the tail of a run queue, and to take a thread off the head of a run queue. The heart of the scheduling algorithm is the *runq_choose*() routine. The *runq_choose*() routine is responsible for selecting a new thread to run; it operates as follows:

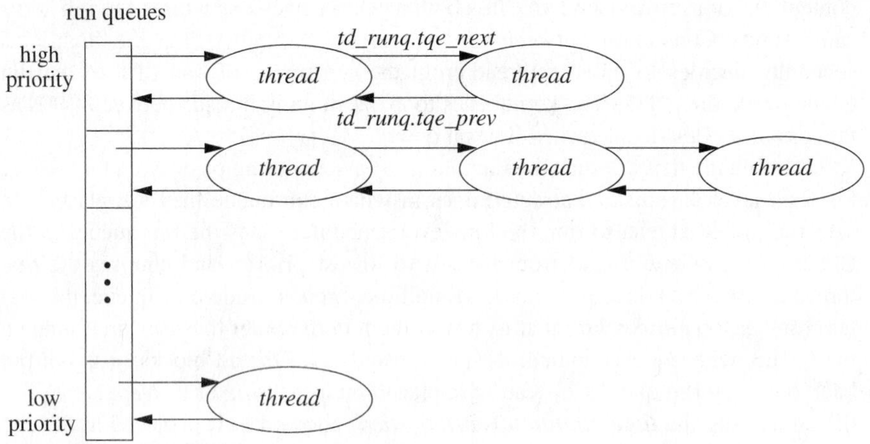

Figure 4.5 Queueing structure for runnable threads.

1. Ensures that our caller acquired the lock associated with the run queue.
2. Locates a nonempty run queue by finding the location of the first nonzero bit in the *rq_status* bit vector. If *rq_status* is zero, there are no threads to run, so selects an ***idle loop*** thread.
3. Given a nonempty run queue, removes the first thread on the queue.
4. If this run queue is now empty as a result of removing the thread, clears the appropriate bit in *rq_status*.
5. Returns the selected thread.

The context-switch code is broken into two parts. The machine-independent code resides in *mi_switch*(); the machine-dependent part resides in *cpu_switch*(). On most architectures, *cpu_switch*() is coded in assembly language for efficiency.

Given the *mi_switch*() routine and the thread-priority calculations, the only missing piece in the scheduling facility is how the system forces an involuntary context switch. Remember that voluntary context switches occur when a thread calls the *sleep*() routine. *Sleep*() can be invoked only by a runnable thread, so *sleep*() needs only to place the thread on a sleep queue and to invoke *mi_switch*() to schedule the next thread to run. Often, an interrupt thread will not want to *sleep*() itself but will be delivering data that will cause the kernel to want to run a different thread than the one that was running before the interrupt. Thus, the kernel needs a mechanism to request that an involuntary context switch be done at the conclusion of the interrupt.

This mechanism is handled by setting the currently running thread's TDF_NEEDRESCHED flag and then posting an ***asynchronous system trap*** (*AST*). An AST is a trap that is delivered to a thread the next time that thread is preparing to return from an interrupt, a trap, or a system call. Some architectures support ASTs directly in hardware; other systems emulate ASTs by checking an AST flag at the end of every system call, trap, and interrupt. When the hardware AST trap occurs or the AST flag is set, the *mi_switch*() routine is called instead of the current thread resuming execution. Rescheduling requests are made by the *sched_lend_user_prio*(), *sched_clock*(), *sched_setpreempt*(), and *sched_affinity*() routines.

With the advent of multiprocessor support, FreeBSD can preempt threads executing in kernel mode. However, such preemption is generally not done for threads running in the timesharing class, so the worst-case real-time response to events when running with the timeshare scheduler is defined by the longest path through the top half of the kernel. Since the system guarantees no upper bounds on the duration of a system call, when running with just the timeshare scheduler FreeBSD is decidedly not a hard real-time system.

Real-time and interrupt threads do preempt lower-priority threads. The longest path that preemption is disabled for real-time and interrupt threads is defined by the longest time a spinlock is held or a critical section is entered. Thus, when using real-time threads, microsecond real-time deadlines can be met. The kernel can be configured to preempt timeshare threads executing in the kernel with other higher-priority timeshare threads. This option is not used by default as the increase in context switches adds overhead and does not help make timeshare threads response time more predictable.

Timeshare Thread Scheduling

The goal of a multiprocessing system is to apply the power of multiple CPUs to a problem, or set of problems, to achieve a result in less time than it would run on a single-processor system. If a system has the same number of runnable threads as it does CPUs, then achieving this goal is easy. Each runnable thread gets a CPU to itself and runs to completion. Typically, there are many runnable threads competing for a few processors. One job of the scheduler is to ensure that the CPUs are always busy and are not wasting their cycles. When a thread completes its work, or is blocked waiting for resources, it is removed from the processor on which it was running. While a thread is running on a processor, it brings its working set—the instructions it is executing and the data on which it is operating—into the CPU's memory cache. Migrating a thread has a cost. When a thread is moved from one CPU to another, its CPU-cache working set is lost and must be removed from the CPU on which it was running and then loaded into the new CPU to which it has been migrated. The performance of a multiprocessing system with a naive scheduler that does not take this cost into account can fall beneath that of a single-processor system. The term ***processor affinity*** describes a scheduler that only migrates threads when necessary to give an idle processor something to do.

A multiprocessing system may be built with multiple processor chips. Each processor chip may have multiple CPU cores, each of which can execute a thread. The CPU cores on a single processor chip share many of the processor's resources, such as memory caches and access to main memory, so they are more tightly synchronized than the CPUs on other processor chips.

Handling processor chips with multiple CPUs is a derivative form of load balancing among CPUs on different chips. It is handled by maintaining a hierarchy of CPUs. The CPUs on the same chip are the cheapest between which to migrate threads. Next down in the hierarchy are processor chips on the same motherboard. Below them are chips connected by the same backplane. The scheduler supports an arbitrary depth hierarchy as dictated by the hardware. When the scheduler is deciding to which processor to migrate a thread, it will try to pick a new processor higher in the hierarchy because that is the lowest-cost migration path.

From a thread's perspective, it does not know that there are other threads running on the same processor because the processor is handling them independently. The one piece of code in the system that needs to be aware of the multiple CPUs is the scheduling algorithm. In particular, the scheduler treats each CPU on a chip as one on which it is cheaper to migrate threads than it would be to migrate the thread to a CPU on another chip. The mechanism for getting tighter affinity between CPUs on the same processor chip versus CPUs on other processor chips is described later in this section.

The traditional FreeBSD scheduler maintains a global list of runnable threads that it traverses once per second to recalculate their priorities. The use of a single list for all runnable threads means that the performance of the scheduler is dependent on the number of tasks in the system, and as the number of tasks grow, more CPU time must be spent in the scheduler maintaining the list.

The ULE scheduler was developed during FreeBSD 5.0 with major work continuing into FreeBSD 9.0, spanning 10 years of development. The scheduler was developed to address shortcomings of the traditional BSD scheduler on multiprocessor systems. A new scheduler was undertaken for several reasons:

- To address the need for processor affinity in multiprocessor systems
- To supply equitable distribution of load between CPUs on multiprocessor systems
- To provide better support for processors with multiple CPU cores on a single chip
- To improve the performance of the scheduling algorithm so that it is no longer dependent on the number of threads in the system
- To provide interactivity and timesharing performance similar to the traditional BSD scheduler.

The traditional BSD scheduler had good interactivity on large timeshare systems and single-user desktop and laptop systems. However, it had a single global run queue and consequently a single global scheduler lock. Having a single global run queue was slowed both by contention for the global lock and by difficulties implementing CPU affinity.

The priority computation relied on a single global timer that iterated over every runnable thread in the system and evaluated its priority while holding several highly contended locks. This approach became slower as the number of runnable threads increased. While the priority calculations were being done, processes could not *fork* or *exit* and CPUs could not context switch.

The ULE scheduler can logically be thought of as two largely orthogonal sets of algorithms; those that manage the affinity and distribution of threads among CPUs and those that are responsible for the order and duration of a thread's runtime. These two sets of algorithms work in concert to provide a balance of low latency, high throughput, and good resource utilization. The remainder of the scheduler is event driven and uses these algorithms to implement various decisions according to changes in system state.

The goal of equalling the exceptional interactive behavior and throughput of the traditional BSD scheduler in a multiprocessor-friendly and constant-time implementation was the most challenging and time consuming part of ULE's development. The interactivity, CPU utilization estimation, priority, and time slice algorithms together implement the timeshare scheduling policy.

The behavior of threads is evaluated by ULE on an event-driven basis to differentiate interactive and batch threads. Interactive threads are those that are thought to be waiting for and responding to user input. They require low latency to achieve a good user experience. Batch threads are those that tend to consume as much CPU as they are given and may be background jobs. A good example of the former is a text editor, and for the latter, a compiler. The scheduler must use imperfect heuristics to provide a gradient of behaviors based on a best guess of the category to which a given thread fits. This categorization may change frequently during the lifetime of a thread and must be responsive on timescales relevant to people using the system.

The algorithm that evaluates interactivity is called the interactivity score. The interactivity score is the ratio of voluntary sleep time to run time normalized to a number between 0 and 100. This score does not include time waiting on the run queue while the thread is not yet the highest priority thread in the queue. By requiring explicit voluntary sleeps, we can differentiate threads that are not running because of inferior priority versus those that are periodically waiting for user input. This requirement also makes it more challenging for a thread to be marked interactive as system load increases, which is desirable because it prevents the system from becoming swamped with interactive threads while keeping things like shells and simple text editors available to administrators. When plotted, the interactivity scores derived from a matrix of possible sleep and run times becomes a three-dimensional sigmoid function. Using this approach means that interactive tasks tend to stay interactive and batch tasks tend to stay batched.

A particular challenge is complex X Window applications such as Web browsers and office productivity packages. These applications may consume significant resources for brief periods of time, however the user expects them to remain interactive. To resolve this issue, a several-second history of the sleep and run behavior is kept and gradually decayed. Thus, the scheduler keeps a moving average that can tolerate bursts of behavior but will quickly penalize timeshare threads that abuse their elevated status. A longer history allows longer bursts but learns more slowly.

The interactivity score is compared to the interactivity threshold, which is the cutoff point for considering a thread interactive. The interactivity threshold is modified by the process ***nice*** value. Positive nice values make it more challenging for a thread to be considered interactive, while negative values make it easier. Thus, the nice value gives the user some control over the primary mechanism of reducing thread-scheduling latency.

A thread is considered to be interactive if the ratio of its voluntary sleep time versus its run time is below a certain threshold. The interactivity threshold is defined in the ULE code and is not configurable. ULE uses two equations to compute the interactivity score of a thread. For threads whose sleep time exceeds their run time, Eq 4.1 is used:

$$interactivity\ score = \frac{scaling\ factor}{sleep\ /\ run} \qquad \text{(Eq. 4.1)}$$

When a thread's run time exceeds its sleep time, Eq. 4.2 is used instead:

$$interactivity\ score = \frac{scaling\ factor}{run\ /\ sleep} + scaling\ factor \qquad \text{(Eq. 4.2)}$$

The scaling factor is the maximum interactivity score divided by two. Threads that score below the interactivity threshold are considered to be interactive; all others are noninteractive. The *sched_interact_update*() routine is called at several points in a threads existence—for example, when the thread is awakened by a *wakeup*() call—to update the thread's run time and sleep time. The sleep- and run-time values are only allowed to grow to a certain limit. When the sum of the run time and sleep time pass the limit, they are reduced to bring them back into range. An interactive thread whose sleep history was not remembered at all would not remain interactive, resulting in a poor user experience. Remembering an interactive thread's sleep time for too long would allow the thread to get more than its fair share of the CPU. The amount of history that is kept and the interactivity threshold are the two values that most strongly influence a user's interactive experience on the system.

Priorities are assigned according to the thread's interactivity status. Interactive threads have a priority that is derived from the interactivity score and are placed in a priority band above batch threads. They are scheduled like real-time round-robin threads. Batch threads have their priorities determined by the estimated CPU utilization modified according to their process nice value. In both cases, the available priority range is equally divided among possible interactive scores or percent-cpu calculations, both of which are values between 0 and 100. Since there are fewer than 100 priorities available for each class, some values share priorities. Both computations roughly assign priorities according to a history of CPU utilization but with different longevities and scaling factors.

The CPU utilization estimator accumulates run time as a thread runs and decays it as a thread sleeps. The utilization estimator provides the percent-cpu values displayed in **top** and **ps**. ULE delays the decay until a thread wakes to avoid periodically scanning every thread in the system. Since this delay leaves values unchanged for the duration of sleeps, the values must also be decayed before any user process inspects them. This approach preserves the constant-time and event-driven nature of the scheduler.

The CPU utilization is recorded in the thread as the number of ticks, typically 1 millisecond, during which a thread has been running, along with window of time defined as a first and last tick. The scheduler attempts to keep roughly 10 seconds of history. To accomplish decay, it waits until there are 11 seconds of history and then subtracts one-tenth of the tick value while moving the first tick forward 1 second. This inexpensive, estimated moving-average algorithm has the property of allowing arbitrary update intervals. If the utilization information is inspected after more than the update interval has passed, the tick value is zeroed. Otherwise, the number of seconds that have passed divided by the update interval is subtracted.

The scheduler implements round-robin through the assignment of time slices. A time slice is a fixed interval of allowed run time before the scheduler will select another thread of equal priority to run. The time slice prevents starvation among equal priority threads. The time slice times the number of runnable threads in a given priority defines the maximum latency a thread of that priority will experience before it can run. To bound this latency, ULE dynamically adjusts the size of slices it dispenses based on system load. The time slice has a minimum value to prevent thrashing and balance throughput with latency. An interrupt handler calls the scheduler to evaluate the time slice during every statclock tick. Using the statclock to evaluate the time slice is a stochastic approach to slice accounting that is efficient but only grossly accurate.

The scheduler must also work to prevent starvation of low-priority batch jobs by higher-priority batch jobs. The traditional BSD scheduler avoided starvation by periodically iterating over all threads waiting on the run queue to elevate the low-priority threads and decrease the priority of higher-priority threads that had been monopolizing the CPU. This algorithm violates the desire to run in constant time independent of the number of system threads. As a result, the run queue for batch-policy timeshare threads is kept in a similar fashion to the system callwheel, also known as a calendar queue. A calendar queue is one in which the queue's head and tail rotate according to a clock or period. An element can be inserted into a calendar queue many positions away from the head and gradually migrate toward the head. Because this run queue is special purpose, it is kept separately from the real-time and idle queues while interactive threads are kept along with the real-time threads until they are no longer considered interactive.

The ULE scheduler creates a set of three arrays of queues for each CPU in the system. Having per-CPU queues makes it possible to implement processor affinity in a multiprocessor system.

One array of queues is the ***idle queue***, where all idle threads are stored. The array is arranged from highest to lowest priority. The second array of queues is designated the realtime queue. Like the idle queue, it is arranged from highest to lowest priority.

The third array of queues is designated the timeshare queue. Rather than being arranged in priority order, the timeshare queues are managed as a calendar queue. A pointer references the current entry. The pointer is advanced once per system tick, although it may not advance on a tick until the currently selected queue is empty. Since each thread is given a maximum time slice and no threads may be added to the current position, the queue will drain in a bounded amount of time. This requirement to empty the queue before advancing to the next queue means that the wait time a thread experiences is not only a function of its priority but also the system load.

Insertion into the timeshare queue is defined by the relative difference between a thread's priority and the best possible timeshare priority. High-priority threads will be placed soon after the current position. Low-priority threads will be placed far from the current position. This algorithm ensures that even the lowest-priority timeshare thread will eventually make it to the selected queue and execute in spite of higher-priority timeshare threads being available in other queues. The difference in priorities of two threads will determine their ratio of run-time. The higher-priority thread may be inserted ahead of the lower-priority thread multiple times before the queue position catches up. This run-time ratio is what grants timeshare CPU hogs with different nice values, different proportional shares of the CPU.

These algorithms taken together determine the priorities and run times of timesharing threads. They implement a dynamic tradeoff between latency and throughput based on system load, thread behavior, and a range of effects based on user-scheduling decisions made with nice. Many of the parameters governing the limits of these algorithms can be explored in real time with the *sysctl kern.sched* tree. The rest are compile-time constants that are documented at the top of the scheduler source file (**/sys/kern/sched_ule.c**).

Threads are picked to run, in priority order, from the realtime queue until it is empty, at which point threads from the currently selected timeshare queue will be run. Threads in the idle queues are run only when the other two arrays of queues are empty. Real-time and interrupt threads are always inserted into the realtime queues so that they will have the least possible scheduling latency. Interactive threads are also inserted into the realtime queue to keep the interactive response of the system acceptable.

Noninteractive threads are put into the timeshare queues and are scheduled to run when the queues are switched. Switching the queues guarantees that a thread gets to run at least once every pass around the array of the timeshare queues regardless of priority, thus ensuring fair sharing of the processor.

Multiprocessor Scheduling

A principal goal behind the development of ULE was improving performance on multiprocessor systems. Good multiprocessing performance involves balancing affinity with utilization and the preservation of the illusion of global scheduling in a system with local scheduling queues. These decisions are implemented using a CPU topology supplied by machine-dependent code that describes the relationships between CPUs in the system. The state is evaluated whenever a thread becomes runnable, a CPU idles, or a periodic task runs to rebalance the load.

These events form the entirety of the multiprocessor-aware scheduling decisions.

The topology system was devised to identify which CPUs were symmetric multi-threading peers and then made generic to support other relationships. Some examples are CPUs within a package, CPUs sharing a layer of cache, CPUs that are local to a particular memory, or CPUs that share execution units such as in symmetric multi-threading. This topology is implemented as a tree of arbitrary depth where each level describes some shared resource with a cost value and a bitmask of CPUs sharing that resource. The root of the tree holds CPUs in a system with branches to each socket, then shared cache, shared functional unit, etc. Since the system is generic, it should be extensible to describe any future processor arrangement. There is no restriction on the depth of the tree or requirement that all levels are implemented.

Parsing this topology is a single recursive function called *cpu_search*(). It is a path-aware, goal-based, tree-traversal function that may be started from arbitrary subtrees. It may be asked to find the least- or most-loaded CPU that meets a given criteria, such as a priority or load threshold. When considering load, it will consider the load of the entire path, thus giving the potential for balancing sockets, caches, chips, etc. This function is used as the basis for all multiprocessing-related scheduling decisions. Typically, recursive functions are avoided in kernel programming because there is potential for stack exhaustion. However, the depth is fixed by the depth of the processor topology that typically does not exceed three.

When a thread becomes runnable as a result of a wakeup, unlock, thread creation, or other event, the *sched_pickcpu*() function is called to decide where it will run. ULE determines the best CPU based on the following criteria:

- Threads with hard affinity to a single CPU or short-term binding pick the only allowed CPU.
- Interrupt threads that are being scheduled by their hardware interrupt handlers are scheduled on the current CPU if their priority is high enough to run immediately.
- Thread affinity is evaluated by walking backwards up the tree starting from the last CPU on which it was scheduled until a package or CPU is found with valid affinity that can run the thread immediately.
- The whole system is searched for the least-loaded CPU that is running a lower-priority thread than the one to be scheduled.
- The whole system is searched for the least-loaded CPU.
- The results of these searches are compared to the current CPU to see if that would give a preferable decision to improve locality among the sleeping and waking threads as they may share some state.

This approach orders from most preferential to least preferential. The affinity is valid if the sleep time of the thread was shorter than the product of a time constant and a largest-cache-shared level in the topology. This computation coarsely models the time required to push state out of the cache. Each thread has a bitmap of allowed CPUs that is manipulated by **cpuset** and is passed to *cpu_search*() for every decision. The locality between sleeper and waker can improve producer/consumer type threading situations when they have shared cache state but it can also cause underutilization when each thread would run faster given its own CPU. These examples exemplify the types of decisions that must be made with imperfect information.

The next major multiprocessing algorithm runs when a CPU idles. The CPU sets a bit in a bitmask shared by all processors that says that it is idle. The idle CPU calls *tdq_idled*() to search other CPUs for work that can be migrated, or stolen in ULE terms, to keep the CPU busy. To avoid thrashing and excessive migration, the kernel sets a load threshold that must be exceeded on another CPU before some load will be taken. If any CPU exceeds this threshold, the idle CPU will search its run queues for work to migrate. The highest-priority work that can be scheduled on the idle CPU is then taken. This migration may be detrimental to affinity but improves many latency-sensitive workloads.

Work may also be pushed to an idle CPU. Whenever an active CPU is about to add work to its own run queue, it first checks to see if it has excess work and if another CPU in the system is idle. If an idle CPU is found, then the thread is migrated to the idle CPU using an ***interprocessor interrupt*** (***IPI***). Making a migration decision by inspecting a shared bitmask is much faster than scanning the run queues of all the other processors. Seeking out idle processors when adding a new task works well because it spreads the load when it is presented to the system.

The last major multiprocessing algorithm is the long-term load balancer. This form of migration, called ***push migration***, is done by the system on a periodic basis and more aggressively offloads work to other processors in the system. Since the two scheduling events that distribute load only run when a thread is added and when a CPU idles, it is possible to have a long-term imbalance where more threads are running on one CPU than another. Push migration ensures fairness among the runnable threads. For example, with three runnable threads on a two-processor system, it would be unfair for one thread to get a processor to itself while the other two had to share the second processor. To fulfill the goal of emulating a fair global run queue, ULE must periodically shuffle threads to keep the system balanced. By pushing a thread from the processor with two threads to the processor with one thread, no single thread would get to run alone indefinitely. An ideal implementation would give each thread an average of 66 percent of the CPU available from a single CPU.

The long-term load balancer balances the worst path pair in the hierarchy to avoid socket-, cache-, and chip-level imbalances. It runs from an interrupt handler in a randomized interval of roughly 1 second. The interval is randomized to prevent harmonic relationships between periodic threads and the periodic load balancer. In much the same way a stochastic sampling profiler works, the balancer picks the most- and least-loaded path from the current tree position and then recursively balances those paths by migrating threads.

The scheduler must decide whether it is necessary to send an IPI when adding a thread to a remote CPU, just as it must decide whether adding a thread to the current CPU should preempt the current thread. The decision is made based on the current priority of the thread running on the target CPU and the priority of the thread being scheduled. Preempting whenever the pushed thread has a higher priority than the currently running thread results in excessive interrupts and preemptions. Thus, a thread must exceed the timesharing priority before an IPI is generated. This requirement trades some latency in batch jobs for improved performance.

A notable omission to the load balancing events is thread preemption. Preempted threads are simply added back to the run queue of the current CPU. An additional load-balancing decision can be made here. However, the runtime of the preempting thread is not known and the preempted thread may maintain affinity. The scheduler optimistically chooses to wait and assume affinity is more valuable than latency.

Each CPU in the system has its own set of run queues, statistics, and a lock to protect these fields in a *thread-queue* structure. During migration or a remote wakeup, a lock may be acquired by a CPU other than the one owning the queue. In practice, contention on these locks is rare unless the workload exhibits grossly overactive context switching and thread migration, typically suggesting a higher-level problem. Whenever a pair of these locks is required, such as for load balancing, a special function locks the pair with a defined lock order. The lock order is the lock with the lowest pointer value first. These per-CPU locks and queues resulted in nearly linear scaling with well-behaved workloads in cases where performance previously did not improve with the addition of new CPUs and occasionally have decreased as new CPUs introduced more contention. The design has scaled well from single CPUs to 512-thread network processors.

Adaptive Idle

Many workloads feature frequent interrupts that do little work but need low latency. These workloads are common in low-throughput, high-packet-rate networking. For these workloads, the cost of waking the CPU from a low-power state, possibly with an IPI from another CPU, is excessive. To improve performance, ULE includes a feature that optimistically spins, waiting for load when the CPU has been context switching at a rate exceeding a set frequency. When this frequency lowers or we exceed the adaptive spin count, the CPU is put into a deeper sleep.

Traditional Timeshare Thread Scheduling

The traditional FreeBSD timeshare-scheduling algorithm is based on ***multilevel feedback queues***. The system adjusts the priority of a thread dynamically to reflect resource requirements (e.g., being blocked awaiting an event) and the amount of resources consumed by the thread (e.g., CPU time). Threads are moved between run queues based on changes in their scheduling priority (hence the word "feedback" in the name ***multilevel feedback queue***). When a thread other than the currently running thread attains a higher priority (by having that priority either assigned or given when it is awakened), the system switches to that thread immediately if the current thread is in user mode. Otherwise, the system switches to the higher-priority thread as soon as the current thread exits the kernel. The system tailors this ***short-term-scheduling algorithm*** to favor interactive jobs by raising the scheduling priority of threads that are blocked waiting for I/O for 1 or more seconds and by lowering the priority of threads that accumulate significant amounts of CPU time.

The time quantum is always 0.1 second. This value was empirically found to be the longest quantum that could be used without loss of the desired response for interactive jobs such as editors. Perhaps surprisingly, the time quantum remained unchanged over the 30-year lifetime of this scheduler. Although the time quantum was originally selected on centralized timesharing systems with many users, it has remained correct for decentralized laptops. While laptop users expect a response time faster than that anticipated by the original timesharing users, the shorter run queues on the single-user laptop made a shorter quantum unnecessary.

4.5 Process Creation

In FreeBSD, new processes are created with the *fork* family of system calls. The *fork* system call creates a complete copy of the parent process. The *rfork* system call creates a new process entry that shares a selected set of resources from its parent rather than making copies of everything. The *vfork* system call differs from *fork* in how the virtual-memory resources are treated; *vfork* also ensures that the parent will not run until the child does either an *exec* or *exit* system call. The *vfork* system call is described in Section 6.6.

The process created by a *fork* is termed a ***child process*** of the original ***parent process***. From a user's point of view, the child process is an exact duplicate of the parent process except for two values: the child PID and the parent PID. A call to *fork* returns the child PID to the parent and zero to the child process. Thus, a program can identify whether it is the parent or child process after a *fork* by checking this return value.

A *fork* involves three main steps:

1. Allocating and initializing a new process structure for the child process

2. Duplicating the context of the parent (including the thread structure and virtual-memory resources) for the child process

3. Scheduling the child process to run

The second step is intimately related to the operation of the memory-management facilities described in Chapter 6. Consequently, only those actions related to process management will be described here.

The kernel begins by allocating memory for the new process and thread entries (see Figure 4.1). These thread and process entries are initialized in three steps: One part is copied from the parent's corresponding structure, another part is zeroed, and the rest is explicitly initialized. The zeroed fields include recent CPU utilization, wait channel, swap and sleep time, timers, tracing, and pending-signal information. The copied portions include all the privileges and limitations inherited from the parent, including the following:

- The process group and session
- The signal state (ignored, caught, and blocked signal masks)
- The *p_nice* scheduling parameter
- A reference to the parent's credential
- A reference to the parent's set of open files
- A reference to the parent's limits

The child's explicitly set information includes:

- The process's signal-actions structure
- Zeroing the process's statistics structure
- Entry onto the list of all processes
- Entry onto the child list of the parent and the back pointer to the parent
- Entry onto the parent's process-group list
- Entry onto the hash structure that allows the process to be looked up by its PID
- A new PID for the process

The new PID must be unique among all processes. Early versions of BSD verified the uniqueness of a PID by performing a linear search of the process table. This search became infeasible on large systems with many processes. FreeBSD maintains a range of unallocated PIDs between *lastpid* and *pidchecked.* It allocates a new PID by incrementing and then using the value of *lastpid.* When the newly selected PID reaches *pidchecked,* the system calculates a new range of unused PIDs by making a single scan of all existing processes (not just the active ones are scanned—zombie and swapped processes also are checked).

The final step is to copy the parent's address space. To duplicate a process's image, the kernel invokes the memory-management facilities through a call to *vm_forkproc*(). The *vm_forkproc*() routine is passed a pointer to the initialized process structure for the child process and is expected to allocate all the resources that the child will need to execute. The call to *vm_forkproc*() returns through a different execution path directly into user mode in the child process and via the normal execution path in the parent process.

Once the child process is fully built, its thread is made known to the scheduler by being placed on the run queue. The alternate return path will set the return value of *fork* system call in the child to 0. The normal execution return path in the parent sets the return value of the *fork* system call to be the new PID.

4.6 Process Termination

Processes terminate either voluntarily through an *exit* system call or involuntarily as the result of a signal. In either case, process termination causes a status code to be returned to the parent of the terminating process (if the parent still exists). This termination status is returned through the *wait4* system call. The *wait4* call permits an application to request the status of both stopped and terminated processes. The *wait4* request can wait for any direct child of the parent, or it can wait selectively for a single child process or for only its children in a particular process group. *Wait4* can also request statistics describing the resource utilization of a terminated child process. Finally, the *wait4* interface allows a process to request status codes without blocking.

Within the kernel, a process terminates by calling the *exit*() routine. The *exit*() routine first kills off any other threads associated with the process. The termination of other threads is done as follows:

- Any thread entering the kernel from userspace will *thread_exit*() when it traps into the kernel.
- Any thread already in the kernel and attempting to sleep will return immediately with EINTR or EAGAIN, which will force them back out to userspace, freeing resources as they go. When the thread attempts to return to userspace, it will instead hit *exit*().

The *exit*() routine then cleans up the process's kernel-mode execution state by doing the following:

- Canceling any pending timers
- Releasing virtual-memory resources
- Closing open descriptors
- Handling stopped or traced child processes

With the kernel-mode state reset, the process is then removed from the list of active processes—the *allproc* list—and is placed on the list of ***zombie processes*** pointed to by *zombproc*. The process state is changed to show that no thread is currently running. The *exit*() routine then does the following:

- Records the termination status in the *p_xstat* field of the process structure
- Bundles up a copy of the process's accumulated resource usage (for accounting purposes) and hangs this structure from the *p_ru* field of the process structure
- Notifies the deceased process's parent

Finally, after the parent has been notified, the *cpu_exit*() routine frees any machine-dependent process resources and arranges for a final context switch from the process.

The *wait4* call works by searching a process's descendant processes for ones that have entered the ZOMBIE state (e.g., that have terminated). If a process in ZOMBIE state is found that matches the wait criterion, the system will copy the termination status from the deceased process. The process entry then is taken off the zombie list and is freed. Note that resources used by children of a process are accumulated only as a result of a *wait4* system call. When users are trying to analyze the behavior of a long-running program, they will find it useful to be able to obtain this resource usage information before the termination of a process. Although the information is available inside the kernel and within the context of that program, there is no interface to request it outside that context until process termination.

4.7 Signals

Signals were originally designed to model exceptional events, such as an attempt by a user to kill a runaway program. They were not intended to be used as a general ***interprocess-communication*** mechanism, and thus no attempt was made to make them reliable. In earlier systems, whenever a signal was caught, its action was reset to the default action. The introduction of job control brought much more frequent use of signals and made more visible a problem that faster processors also exacerbated: If two signals were sent rapidly, the second could cause the process to die, even though a signal handler had been set up to catch the first signal. At this time, reliability became desirable, so the developers designed a new framework that contained the old capabilities as a subset while accommodating new mechanisms.

The signal facilities found in FreeBSD are designed around a ***virtual-machine*** model, in which system calls are considered to be the parallel of a machine's hardware instruction set. Signals are the software equivalent of traps or interrupts, and signal-handling routines do the equivalent function of interrupt or trap service routines. Just as machines provide a mechanism for blocking hardware interrupts so that consistent access to data structures can be ensured, the signal facilities allow software signals to be masked. Finally, because complex run-time stack environments may be required, signals, like interrupts, may be handled on an alternate application-provided run-time stack. These machine models are summarized in Table 4.4

Table 4.4 Comparison of hardware-machine operations and the corresponding software virtual-machine operations.

Hardware Machine	Software Virtual Machine
instruction set	set of system calls
restartable instructions	restartable system calls
interrupts/traps	signals
interrupt/trap handlers	signal handlers
blocking interrupts	masking signals
interrupt stack	signal stack

FreeBSD defines a set of ***signals*** for software and hardware conditions that may arise during the normal execution of a program; these signals are listed in Table 4.5. Signals may be delivered to a process through application-specified ***signal handler***s or may result in default actions, such as process termination, carried out by the system. FreeBSD signals are designed to be software equivalents of hardware interrupts or traps.

Each signal has an associated action that defines how it should be handled when it is delivered to a process. If a process contains more than one thread, each thread may specify whether it wishes to take action for each signal. Typically, one thread elects to handle all the process-related signals such as interrupt, stop, and continue. All the other threads in the process request that the process-related signals be masked out. Thread-specific signals such as segmentation fault, floating point exception, and illegal instruction are handled by the thread that caused them. Thus, all threads typically elect to receive these signals. The precise disposition of signals to threads is given in the later subsection on posting a signal. First, we describe the possible actions that can be requested.

The disposition of signals is specified on a per-process basis. If a process has not specified an action for a signal, it is given a default action (see Table 4.5) that may be any one of the following:

- Ignoring the signal
- Terminating all the threads in the process
- Terminating all the threads in the process after generating a ***core file*** that contains the process's execution state at the time the signal was delivered
- Stopping all the threads in the process
- Resuming the execution of all the threads in the process

An application program can use the *sigaction* system call to specify an action for a signal, including these choices:

Table 4.5 Signals defined in FreeBSD.

Name	Default action	Description
SIGHUP	terminate process	terminal line hangup
SIGINT	terminate process	interrupt program
SIGQUIT	create core image	quit program
SIGILL	create core image	illegal instruction
SIGTRAP	create core image	trace trap
SIGABRT	create core image	abort
SIGEMT	create core image	emulate instruction executed
SIGFPE	create core image	floating-point exception
SIGKILL	terminate process	kill program
SIGBUS	create core image	bus error
SIGSEGV	create core image	segmentation violation
SIGSYS	create core image	bad argument to system call
SIGPIPE	terminate process	write on a pipe with no one to read it
SIGALRM	terminate process	real-time timer expired
SIGTERM	terminate process	software termination signal
SIGURG	discard signal	urgent condition on I/O channel
SIGSTOP	stop process	stop signal not from terminal
SIGTSTP	stop process	stop signal from terminal
SIGCONT	discard signal	a stopped process is being continued
SIGCHLD	discard signal	notification to parent on child stop or exit
SIGTTIN	stop process	read on terminal by background process
SIGTTOU	stop process	write to terminal by background process
SIGIO	discard signal	I/O possible on a descriptor
SIGXCPU	terminate process	CPU time limit exceeded
SIGXFSZ	terminate process	file-size limit exceeded
SIGVTALRM	terminate process	virtual timer expired
SIGPROF	terminate process	profiling timer expired
SIGWINCH	discard signal	window size changed
SIGINFO	discard signal	information request
SIGUSR1	terminate process	user-defined signal 1
SIGUSR2	terminate process	user-defined signal 2
SIGTHR	terminate process	used by thread library
SIGLIBRT	terminate process	used by real-time library

- Taking the default action
- Ignoring the signal
- Catching the signal with a ***handler***

A ***signal handler*** is a user-mode routine that the system will invoke when the signal is received by the process. The handler is said to catch the signal. The two signals SIGSTOP and SIGKILL cannot be masked, ignored, or caught; this restriction ensures that a software mechanism exists for stopping and killing runaway processes. It is not possible for a process to decide which signals would cause the creation of a core file by default, but it is possible for a process to prevent the creation of such a file by ignoring, blocking, or catching the signal.

Signals are posted to a process by the system when it detects a hardware event, such as an illegal instruction, or a software event, such as a stop request from the terminal. A signal may also be posted by another process through the *kill* system call. A sending process may post signals to only those receiving processes that have the same effective user identifier (unless the sender is the superuser). A single exception to this rule is the ***continue signal***, SIGCONT, which always can be sent to any descendant of the sending process. The reason for this exception is to allow users to restart a ***setuid*** program that they have stopped from their keyboard.

Like hardware interrupts, each thread in a process can mask the delivery of signals. The execution state of each thread contains a set of signals currently masked from delivery. If a signal posted to a thread is being masked, the signal is recorded in the thread's set of pending signals, but no action is taken until the signal is unmasked. The *sigprocmask* system call modifies the set of masked signals for a thread. It can add to the set of masked signals, delete from the set of masked signals, or replace the set of masked signals. Although the delivery of the SIGCONT signal to the signal handler of a process may be masked, the action of resuming that stopped process is not masked.

Two other signal-related system calls are *sigsuspend* and *sigaltstack*. The *sigsuspend* call permits a thread to relinquish the processor until that thread receives a signal. This facility is similar to the system's *sleep*() routine. The *sigaltstack* call allows a process to specify a run-time stack to use in signal delivery. By default, the system will deliver signals to a process on the latter's normal run-time stack. In some applications, however, this default is unacceptable. For example, if an application has many threads that have carved up the normal run-time stack into many small pieces, it is far more memory efficient to create one large signal stack on which all the threads handle their signals than it is to reserve space for signals on each thread's stack.

The final signal-related facility is the *sigreturn* system call. *Sigreturn* is the equivalent of a user-level load-processor-context operation. The kernel is passed a pointer to a (machine-dependent) context block that describes the user-level execution state of a thread. The *sigreturn* system call restores state and resumes execution after a normal return from a user's signal handler.

Posting of a Signal

The implementation of signals is broken up into two parts: posting a signal to a process and recognizing the signal and delivering it to the target thread. Signals may be posted by any process or by code that executes at interrupt level. Signal delivery normally takes place within the context of the receiving thread. When a signal forces a process to be stopped, the action can be carried out on all the threads associated with that process when the signal is posted.

A signal is posted to a single process with the *psignal*() routine or to a group of processes with the *gsignal*() routine. The *gsignal*() routine invokes *psignal*() for each process in the specified process group. The actions associated with posting a signal are straightforward, but the details are messy. In theory, posting a signal to a process simply causes the appropriate signal to be added to the set of pending signals for the appropriate thread within the process, and the selected thread is then set to run (or is awakened if it was sleeping at an interruptible priority level).

The disposition of signals is set on a per-process basis. The kernel first checks to see if the signal should be ignored, in which case it is discarded. If the process has specified the default action, then the default action is taken. If the process has specified a signal handler that should be run, then the kernel must select the appropriate thread within the process that should handle the signal. When a signal is raised because of the action of the currently running thread (for example, a segment fault), the kernel will only try to deliver it to that thread. If the thread is masking the signal, then the signal will be held pending until it is unmasked. When a process-related signal is sent (for example, an interrupt), then the kernel searches all the threads associated with the process, searching for one that does not have the signal masked. The signal is delivered to the first thread that is found with the signal unmasked. If all threads associated with the process are masking the signal, then the signal is left in the list of signals pending for the process for later delivery.

Each time that a thread returns from a call to *sleep*() (with the PCATCH flag set) or prepares to exit the system after processing a system call or trap, it uses the *cursig*() routine to check whether a signal is pending delivery. The *cursig*() routine determines the next signal that should be delivered to a thread by inspecting the process's signal list, *p_siglist*, to see if it has any signals that should be propagated to the thread's signal list, *td_siglist*. It then inspects the *td_siglist* field to check for any signals that should be delivered to the thread. If a signal is pending and must be delivered in the thread's context, it is removed from the pending set, and the thread invokes the *postsig*() routine to take the appropriate action.

The work of *psignal*() is a patchwork of special cases required by the process-debugging and job-control facilities and by intrinsic properties associated with signals. The steps involved in posting a signal are as follows:

1. Determine the action that the receiving process will take when the signal is delivered. This information is kept in the *p_sigignore* and *p_sigcatch* fields of the process's process structure. If a process is not ignoring or catching a signal, the default action is presumed to apply. If a process is being traced by its parent—that is, by a debugger—the parent process is always permitted to intercede before the signal is delivered. If the process is ignoring the signal, *psignal*()'s work is done and the routine can return.

2. Given an action, *psignal*() selects the appropriate thread and adds the signal to the thread's set of pending signals, *td_siglist*, and then does any implicit actions specific to that signal. For example, if the signal is the continue signal, SIGCONT, any pending signals that would normally cause the process to stop, such as SIGTTOU, are removed.

3. Next, *psignal*() checks whether the signal is being masked. If the thread is currently masking delivery of the signal, *psignal*()'s work is complete and it may return.

4. If the signal is not being masked, *psignal*() must either perform the action directly or arrange for the thread to execute so that the thread will take the action associated with the signal. Before setting the thread to a runnable state, *psignal*() must take different courses of action depending on the state of the thread as follows:

SLEEPING The thread is blocked awaiting an event. If the thread is sleeping noninterruptibly, then nothing further can be done. Otherwise, the kernel can apply the action—either directly or indirectly—by waking up the thread. There are two actions that can be applied directly. For signals that cause a process to stop, all the threads in the process are placed in the STOPPED state, and the parent process is notified of the state change by a SIGCHLD signal being posted to it. For signals that are ignored by default, the signal is removed from the signal list and the work is complete. Otherwise, the action associated with the signal must be done in the context of the receiving thread, and the thread is placed onto the run queue with a call to *setrunnable*().

STOPPED The process is stopped by a signal or because it is being debugged. If the process is being debugged, then there is nothing to do until the controlling process permits it to run again. If the process is stopped by a signal and the posted signal would cause the process to stop again, then there is nothing to do, and the posted signal is discarded. Otherwise, the signal is either a continue signal or a signal that would normally cause the process to terminate (unless the signal is caught). If the signal is SIGCONT, then all the threads in the process that were previously running are set running again. Any threads in the process that were blocked waiting on an event are returned to the SLEEPING state. If the signal is SIGKILL, then all the threads in the process are set running again no matter what, so that they can terminate the next time that they are scheduled to run. Otherwise, the signal causes the threads in the process to be made runnable, but the threads are not placed on the run queue because they must wait for a continue signal.

RUNNABLE, NEW, ZOMBIE

If a thread scheduled to receive a signal is not the currently executing thread, its TDF_NEEDRESCHED flag is set, so that the signal will be noticed by the receiving thread as soon as possible.

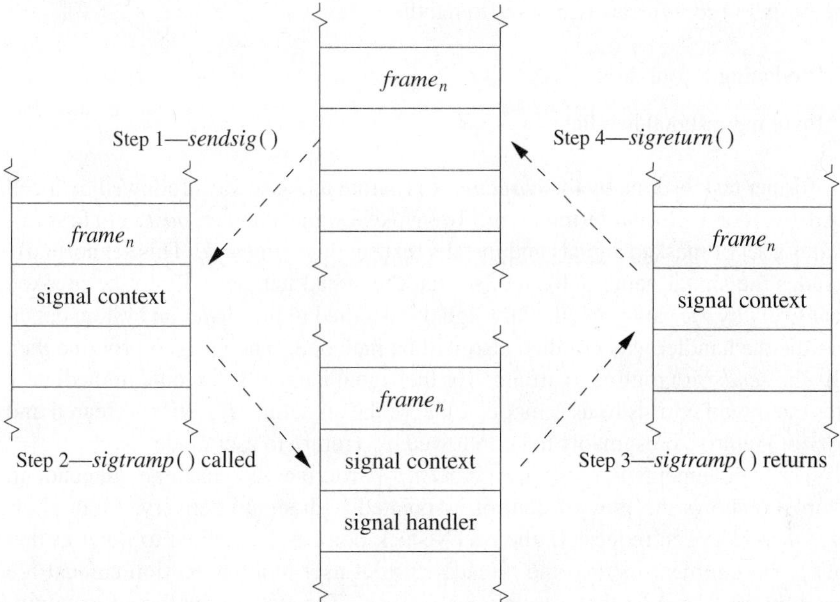

Figure 4.6 Delivery of a signal to a process. Step 1: The kernel places a signal context on the user's stack. Step 2: The kernel places a signal-handler frame on the user's stack and arranges to start running the user process in the *sigtramp*() code. When the *sigtramp*() routine starts running, it calls the user's signal handler. Step 3: The user's signal handler returns to the *sigtramp*() routine, which pops the signal-handler context from the user's stack. Step 4: The *sigtramp*() routine finishes by calling the *sigreturn* system call, which restores the previous user context from the signal context, pops the signal context from the stack, and resumes the user's process at the point at which it was running before the signal occurred.

Delivering a Signal

Most actions associated with delivering a signal to a thread are carried out within the context of that thread. A thread checks its *td_siglist* field for pending signals at least once each time that it enters the system by calling *cursig*().

If *cursig*() determines that there are any unmasked signals in the thread's signal list, it calls *issignal*() to find the first unmasked signal in the list. If delivering the signal causes a signal handler to be invoked or a core dump to be made, the caller is notified that a signal is pending, and the delivery is done by a call to *postsig*(). That is,

```
if (sig = cursig(curthread))
        postsig(sig);
```

Otherwise, the action associated with the signal is done within *issignal*() (these actions mimic the actions carried out by *psignal*()).

The *postsig*() routine has two cases to handle:

1. Producing a core dump
2. Invoking a signal handler

The former task is done by the *coredump*() routine and is always followed by a call to *exit*() to force process termination. To invoke a signal handler, *postsig*() first calculates a set of masked signals and installs that set in *td_sigmask*. This set normally includes the signal being delivered, so that the signal handler will not be invoked recursively by the same signal. Any signals specified in the *sigaction* system call at the time the handler was installed also will be included. The *postsig*() routine then calls the *sendsig*() routine to arrange for the signal handler to execute immediately after the thread returns to user mode. Finally, the signal in *td_siglist* is cleared and *postsig*() returns, presumably to be followed by a return to user mode.

The implementation of the *sendsig*() routine is machine dependent. Figure 4.6 shows the flow of control associated with signal delivery. If an alternate stack has been requested, the user's stack pointer is switched to point at that stack. An argument list and the thread's current user-mode execution context are stored by the kernel on the (possibly new) stack. The state of the thread is manipulated so that, on return to user mode, a call will be made immediately to a body of code termed the ***signal-trampoline code***. This code invokes the signal handler (between steps 2 and 3 in Figure 4.6) with the appropriate argument list, and, if the handler returns, makes a *sigreturn* system call to reset the thread's signal state to the state that existed before the signal. The signal-trampoline code, *sigcode*() contains several assembly-language instructions that are copied onto the thread's stack when the signal is about to be delivered. It is the responsibility of the trampoline code to call the registered signal handler, handle any possible errors, and then return the thread to normal execution. The trampoline code is implemented in assembly language because it must directly manipulate CPU registers, including those relating to the stack and return value.

4.8 Process Groups and Sessions

Each process in the system is associated with a ***process group***. The group of processes in a process group is sometimes referred to as a ***job*** and is manipulated as a single entity by processes such as the shell. Some signals (e.g., SIGINT) are delivered to all members of a process group, causing the group as a whole to suspend or resume execution, or to be interrupted or terminated.

Sessions were designed by the IEEE POSIX.1003.1 Working Group with the intent of fixing a long-standing security problem in UNIX—namely, that processes could modify the state of terminals that were trusted by another user's processes. A ***session*** is a collection of process groups, and all members of a process group are members of the same session. In FreeBSD, when a user first logs onto the system, he is entered into a new session. Each session has a ***controlling process***, which is normally the user's login shell. All subsequent processes created by the user are part of process groups within this session, unless he explicitly creates a new session. Each session also has an associated login name, which is usually the user's login name. This name can be changed by only the superuser.

Each session is associated with a terminal, known as its ***controlling terminal***. Each controlling terminal has a process group associated with it. Normally, only processes that are in the terminal's current process group read from or write to the terminal, allowing arbitration of a terminal between several different jobs. When the controlling process exits, access to the terminal is taken away from any remaining processes within the session.

Newly created processes are assigned process IDs distinct from all already-existing processes and process groups, and are placed in the same process group and session as their parent. Any process may set its process group equal to its process ID (thus creating a new process group) or to the value of any process group within its session. In addition, any process may create a new session, as long as it is not already a process-group leader.

Process Groups

A process group is a collection of related processes, such as a shell pipeline, all of which have been assigned the same ***process-group identifier***. The process-group identifier is the same as the PID of the process group's initial member; thus, process-group identifiers share the namespace of process identifiers. When a new process group is created, the kernel allocates a process-group structure to be associated with it. This process-group structure is entered into a process-group hash table so that it can be found quickly.

A process is always a member of a single process group. When it is created, each process is placed into the process group of its parent process. Programs such as shells create new process groups, usually placing related child processes into a group. A process can change its own process group or that of one of its child process by creating a new process group or by moving a process into an existing process group using the *setpgid* system call. For example, when a shell wants to set up a new pipeline, it wants to put the processes in the pipeline into a process group different from its own so that the pipeline can be controlled independently of the shell. The shell starts by creating the first process in the pipeline, which initially has the same process-group identifier as the shell. Before executing the target program, the first process does a *setpgid* to set its process-group identifier to the same value as its PID. This system call creates a new process group, with the child process as the ***process-group leader*** of the process group. As the shell starts each additional process for the pipeline, each child process uses *setpgid* to join the existing process group.

In our example of a shell creating a new pipeline, there is a ***race condition***. As the additional processes in the pipeline are spawned by the shell, each is placed in the process group created by the first process in the pipeline. These conventions are enforced by the *setpgid* system call. It restricts the set of process-group identifiers to which a process may be set to either a value equal to its own PID or to a value of another process-group identifier in its session. Unfortunately, if a pipeline process other than the process-group leader is created before the process-group leader has completed its *setpgid* call, the *setpgid* call to join the process group will fail. As the *setpgid* call permits parents to set the process group of their children (within some limits imposed by security concerns), the shell can avoid this race by making the *setpgid* call to change the child's process group both in the newly created child and in the parent shell. This algorithm guarantees that, no matter which process runs first, the process group will exist with the correct process-group leader. The shell can also avoid the race by using the *vfork* variant of the *fork* system call that forces the parent process to wait until the child process either has done an *exec* system call or has exited. In addition, if the initial members of the process group exit before all the pipeline members have joined the group—for example, if the process-group leader exits before the second process joins the group, the *setpgid* call could fail. The shell can avoid this race by ensuring that all child processes are placed into the process group without calling the *wait* system call, usually by blocking the SIGCHLD signal so that the shell will not be notified of a child exit until after all the children have been placed into the process group. As long as a process-group member exists, even as a zombie process, additional processes can join the process group.

There are additional restrictions on the *setpgid* system call. A process may join process groups only within its current session (discussed in the next section), and it cannot have done an *exec* system call. The latter restriction is intended to avoid unexpected behavior if a process is moved into a different process group after it has begun execution. Therefore, when a shell calls *setpgid* in both parent and child processes after a *fork*, the call made by the parent will fail if the child has already made an *exec* call. However, the child will already have joined the process group successfully, and the failure is innocuous.

Sessions

Just as a set of related processes are collected into a process group, a set of process groups are collected into a ***session***. A session is a set of one or more process groups and may be associated with a terminal device. The main uses for sessions are to collect a user's login shell and the jobs that it spawns and to create an isolated environment for a daemon process and its children. Any process that is not already a process-group leader may create a session using the *setsid* system call, becoming the ***session leader*** and the only member of the session. Creating a session also creates a new process group, where the process-group ID is the PID of the process creating the session, and the process is the process-group leader. By definition, all members of a process group are members of the same session.

A session may have an associated ***controlling terminal*** that is used by default for communicating with the user. Only the session leader may allocate a controlling terminal for the session, becoming a ***controlling process*** when it does so. A device can be the controlling terminal for only one session at a time. The terminal I/O system (described in Section 8.6) synchronizes access to a terminal by permitting only a single process group to be the foreground process group for a controlling terminal at any time. Some terminal operations are restricted to members of the session. A session can have at most one controlling terminal. When a session is created, the session leader is dissociated from its controlling terminal if it had one.

A login session is created by a program that prepares a terminal for a user to log into the system. That process normally executes a shell for the user, and thus the shell is created as the controlling process. An example of a typical login session is shown in Figure 4.7.

The data structures used to support sessions and process groups in FreeBSD are shown in Figure 4.8. This figure parallels the process layout shown in Figure 4.7. The *pg_members* field of a process-group structure heads the list of member processes; these processes are linked together through the *p_pglist* list entry in the process structure. In addition, each process has a reference to its process-group structure in the *p_pgrp* field of the process structure. Each process-group structure has a pointer to its enclosing session. The session structure tracks per-login information, including the process that created and controls the session, the controlling terminal for the session, and the login name associated with the session. Two processes wanting to determine whether they are in the same session can traverse their *p_pgrp* pointers to find their process-group structures and then compare the *pg_session* pointers to see whether the latter are the same.

Job Control

Job control is a facility first provided by the C shell [Joy, 1994] and today is provided by most shells. It permits a user to control the operation of groups of processes termed ***jobs***. The most important facilities provided by job control are the abilities to suspend and restart jobs and to do the multiplexing of access to the

Figure 4.7 A session and its processes. In this example, process 3 is the initial member of the session—the session leader—and is referred to as the controlling process if it has a controlling terminal. It is contained in its own process group, 3. Process 3 has spawned two jobs: One is a pipeline composed of processes 4 and 5, grouped together in process group 4, and the other one is process 8, which is in its own process group, 8. No process-group leader can create a new session; thus, process 3, 4, or 8 could not start its own session, but process 5 would be allowed to do so.

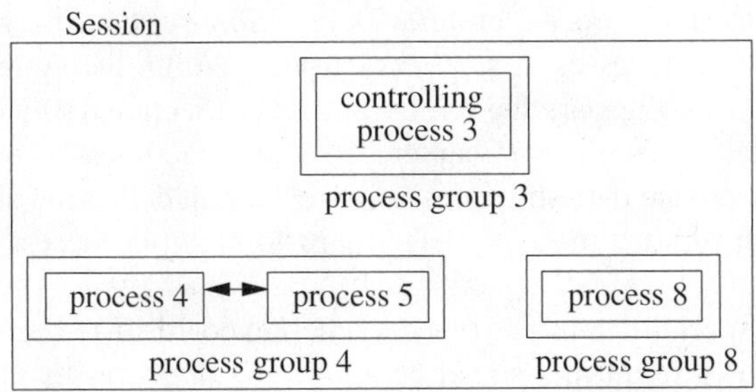

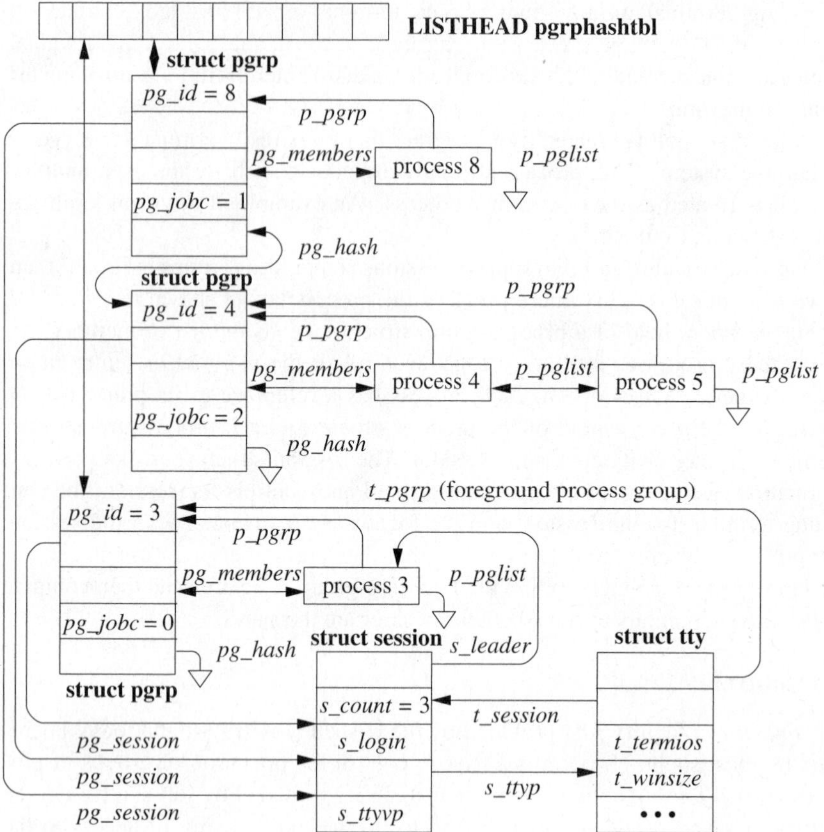

Figure 4.8 Process-group organization.

user's terminal. Only one job at a time is given control of the terminal and is able to read from and write to the terminal. This facility provides some of the advantages of window systems, although job control is sufficiently different that it is often used in combination with window systems. Job control is implemented on top of the process group, session, and signal facilities.

Each job is a process group. Outside the kernel, a shell manipulates a job by sending signals to the job's process group with the *killpg* system call, which delivers a signal to all the processes in a process group. Within the system, the two main users of process groups are the terminal handler (Section 8.6) and the interprocess-communication facilities (Chapter 12). Both facilities record process-group identifiers in private data structures and use them in delivering signals. The terminal handler, in addition, uses process groups to multiplex access to the controlling terminal.

For example, special characters typed at the keyboard of the terminal (e.g., control-C or control-\) result in a signal being sent to all processes in one job in the session; that job is in the ***foreground***, whereas all other jobs in the session are in the ***background***. A shell may change the foreground job by using the *tcsetpgrp*() function, implemented by the TIOCSPGRP *ioctl* on the controlling terminal. Background jobs will be sent the SIGTTIN signal if they attempt to read from the terminal, normally stopping the job. The SIGTTOU signal is sent to background jobs that attempt an *ioctl* system call that would alter the state of the terminal. The SIGTTOU signal is also sent if the TOSTOP option is set for the terminal, and an attempt is made to write to the terminal.

The foreground process group for a session is stored in the *t_pgrp* field of the session's controlling terminal *tty* structure (see Section 8.6). All other process groups within the session are in the background. In Figure 4.8, the session leader has set the foreground process group for its controlling terminal to be its own process group. Thus, its two jobs are in the background, and the terminal input and output will be controlled by the session-leader shell. Job control is limited to processes contained within the same session and to the terminal associated with the session. Only the members of the session are permitted to reassign the controlling terminal among the process groups within the session.

If a controlling process exits, the system revokes further access to the controlling terminal and sends a SIGHUP signal to the foreground process group. If a process such as a job-control shell exits, each process group that it created will become an ***orphaned process group***: a process group in which no member has a parent that is a member of the same session but of a different process group. Such a parent would normally be a job-control shell capable of resuming stopped child processes. The *pg_jobc* field in Figure 4.8 counts the number of processes within the process group that have the controlling process as a parent. When that count goes to zero, the process group is orphaned. If no action were taken by the system, any orphaned process groups that were stopped at the time that they became orphaned would be unlikely ever to resume. Historically, the system dealt harshly with such stopped processes: They were killed. In POSIX and FreeBSD, an orphaned process group is sent a hangup and a continue signal if any of its members are stopped when it becomes orphaned by the exit of a parent process. If processes choose to catch or ignore the hangup signal, they can continue running after becoming orphaned. The system keeps a count of processes in each process group that have a parent process in another process group of the same session. When a process exits, this count is adjusted for the process groups of all child processes. If the count reaches zero, the process group has become orphaned. Note that a process can be a member of an orphaned process group even if its original parent process is still alive. For example, if a shell starts a job as a single process A, that process then forks to create process B, and the parent shell exits; then process B is a member of an orphaned process group but is not an orphaned process.

To avoid stopping members of orphaned process groups if they try to read or write to their controlling terminal, the kernel does not send them SIGTTIN and SIGTTOU signals, and prevents them from stopping in response to those signals. Instead, their attempts to read or write to the terminal produce an error.

4.9 Process Debugging

FreeBSD provides a simple facility for controlling and debugging the execution of a process. This facility, accessed through the *ptrace* system call, permits a parent process to control a child process's execution by manipulating user- and kernel-mode execution states. In particular, with *ptrace*, a parent process can do the following operations on a child process:

- Attaches to an existing process to begin debugging it
- Reads and writes address space and registers
- Intercepts signals posted to the process
- Single steps and continues the execution of the process
- Terminates the execution of the process

The *ptrace* call is used almost exclusively by program debuggers, such as **lldb**.

When a process is being traced, any signals posted to that process cause it to enter the STOPPED state. The parent process is notified with a SIGCHLD signal and may interrogate the status of the child with the *wait4* system call. On most machines, ***trace traps***, generated when a process is single stepped, and ***breakpoint faults***, caused by a process executing a breakpoint instruction, are translated by FreeBSD into SIGTRAP signals. Because signals posted to a traced process cause it to stop and result in the parent being notified, a program's execution can be controlled easily.

To start a program that is to be debugged, the debugger first creates a child process with a *fork* system call. After the fork, the child process uses a *ptrace* call that causes the process to be flagged as "traced" by setting the P_TRACED bit in the *p_flag* field of the process structure. The child process then sets the trace trap bit in the process's processor status word and calls *execve* to load the image of the program that is to be debugged. Setting this bit ensures that the first instruction executed by the child process after the new image is loaded will result in a hardware trace trap, which is translated by the system into a SIGTRAP signal. Because the parent process is notified about all signals to the child, it can intercept the signal and gain control over the program before it executes a single instruction.

Alternatively, the debugger may take over an existing process by attaching to it. A successful attach request causes the process to enter the STOPPED state and to have its P_TRACED bit set in the *p_flag* field of its process structure. The debugger can then begin operating on the process in the same way as it would with a process that it had explicitly started.

An alternative to the *ptrace* system call is the **/proc** filesystem. The functionality provided by the **/proc** filesystem is the same as that provided by *ptrace*; it differs only in its interface. The **/proc** filesystem implements a view of the system process table inside the filesystem and is so named because it is normally mounted on **/proc**. It provides a two-level view of process space. At the highest level, processes themselves are named, according to their process IDs. There is also a special node called **curproc** that always refers to the process making the lookup request.

Each node is a directory that contains the following entries:

ctl A write-only file that supports a variety of control operations. Control commands are written as strings to the **ctl** file. The control commands are:

- **attach** Stops the target process and arranges for the sending process to become the debug control process.
- **detach** Continues execution of the target process and remove it from control by the debug process (that need not be the sending process).
- **run** Continues running the target process until a signal is delivered, a breakpoint is hit, or the target process exits.
- **step** Single steps the target process, with no signal delivery.
- **wait** Waits for the target process to come to a steady state ready for debugging. The target process must be in this state before any of the other commands are allowed.

The string can also be the name of a signal, lowercase and without the SIG prefix, in which case that signal is delivered to the process.

dbregs Sets the debug registers as defined by the machine architecture.

etype The type of the executable referenced by the **file** entry.

file A reference to the vnode from which the process text was read. This entry can be used to gain access to the symbol table for the process or to start another copy of the process.

fpregs The floating point registers as defined by the machine architecture. It is only implemented on machines that have distinct general-purpose and floating-point register sets.

map A map of the process's virtual memory.

mem The complete virtual memory image of the process. Only those addresses that exist in the process can be accessed. Reads and writes to this file modify the process. Writes to the text segment remain private to the process. Because the address space of another process can be accessed with *read* and *write* system calls, a debugger can access a process being debugged with much greater efficiency than it can with the *ptrace* system call. The pages of interest in the process being debugged are mapped into the kernel address space. The data requested by the debugger can then be copied directly from the kernel to the debugger's address space.

regs Allows read and write access to the register set of the process.

rlimit A read-only file containing the process's current and maximum limits.

status The process status. This file is read-only and returns a single line containing multiple space-separated fields that include the command name, the process id, the parent process id, the process group id, the session id, the controlling terminal (if any), a list of the process flags, the process start time, user and system times, the wait channel message, and the process credentials.

Each node is owned by the process's user and belongs to that user's primary group, except for the **mem** node, which belongs to the *kmem* group.

In a normal debugging environment, where the target does a *fork* followed by an *exec* by the debugger, the debugger should *fork* and the child should stop itself (with a self-inflicted SIGSTOP, for example). The parent should issue a *wait* and then an *attach* command via the appropriate **ctl** file. The child process will receive a SIGTRAP immediately after the call to *exec*.

Users wishing to view process information often find it easier to use the **procstat** command than to figure out how to extract the information from the **/proc** filesystem.

Exercises

4.1 For each state listed in Table 4.1, list the system queues on which a process in that state might be found.

4.2 Why is the performance of the context-switching mechanism critical to the performance of a highly multiprogrammed system?

4.3 What effect would increasing the time quantum have on the system's interactive response and total throughput?

4.4 What effect would reducing the number of run queues from 64 to 32 have on the scheduling overhead and on system performance?

4.5 Give three reasons for the system to select a new process to run.

4.6 Describe the three types of scheduling policies provided by FreeBSD.

4.7 What type of jobs does the timeshare scheduling policy favor? Propose an algorithm for identifying these favored jobs.

4.8 When and how does thread scheduling interact with memory-management facilities?

4.9 After a process has exited, it may enter the state of being a ZOMBIE before disappearing from the system entirely. What is the purpose of the ZOMBIE state? What event causes a process to exit from ZOMBIE?

4.10 Suppose that the data structures shown in Table 4.3 do not exist. Instead, assume that each process entry has only its own PID and the PID of its parent. Compare the costs in space and time to support each of the following operations:

a. Creation of a new process

b. Lookup of the process's parent

c. Lookup of all of a process's siblings

d. Lookup of all of a process's descendants

e. Destruction of a process

4.11 What are the differences between a mutex and a lock-manager lock?

4.12 Give an example of where a mutex lock should be used. Give an example of where a lock-manager lock should be used.

4.13 A process blocked without setting the PCATCH flag may never be awakened by a signal. Describe two problems a noninterruptible sleep may cause if a disk becomes unavailable while the system is running.

4.14 Describe the limitations a jail puts on the filesystem namespace, network access, and processes running in the jail.

*4.15 In FreeBSD, the signal SIGTSTP is delivered to a process when a user types a "suspend character." Why would a process want to catch this signal before it is stopped?

*4.16 Before the FreeBSD signal mechanism was added, signal handlers to catch the SIGTSTP signal were written as

```
catchstop()
{
    prepare to stop;
    signal(SIGTSTP, SIG_DFL);
    kill(getpid(), SIGTSTP);
    signal(SIGTSTP, catchstop);
}
```

This code causes an infinite loop in FreeBSD. Why does it do so? How should the code be rewritten?

*4.17 The process-priority calculations and accounting statistics are all based on sampled data. Describe hardware support that would permit more accurate statistics and priority calculations.

*4.18 Why are signals a poor interprocess-communication facility?

**4.19 A kernel-stack-invalid trap occurs when an invalid value for the kernel-mode stack pointer is detected by the hardware. How might the system gracefully terminate a process that receives such a trap while executing on its kernel-run-time stack?

**4.20 Describe alternatives to the `test-and-set` instruction that would allow you to build a synchronization mechanism for a multiprocessor FreeBSD system.

**4.21 A lightweight process is a thread of execution that operates within the context of a normal FreeBSD process. Multiple lightweight processes may exist in a single FreeBSD process and share memory, but each is able to do blocking operations, such as system calls. Describe how lightweight processes might be implemented entirely in user mode.

References

Aral et al., 1989.
Z. Aral, J. Bloom, T. Doeppner, I. Gertner, A. Langerman, & G. Schaffer, "Variable Weight Processes with Flexible Shared Resources," *USENIX Association Conference Proceedings*, pp. 405–412, January 1989.

Dekker, 2013.
Dekker, "Dekker Algorithm," *Wikipedia*, available from http://en.wikipedia.org/wiki/Dekkers_algorithm, November 2013.

Joy, 1994.
W. N. Joy, "An Introduction to the C Shell," in *4.4BSD User's Supplementary Documents*, pp. 4:1–46, O'Reilly & Associates, Inc., Sebastopol, CA, 1994.

McDougall & Mauro, 2006.
R. McDougall & J. Mauro, *Solaris Internals: Solaris 10 and OpenSolaris Kernel Architecture (2nd Edition),* Prentice Hall, Upper Saddle River, NJ, 2006.

Ritchie, 1988.
D. M. Ritchie, "Multi-Processor UNIX," private communication, April 25, 1988.

Roberson, 2003.
J. Roberson, "ULE: A Modern Scheduler For FreeBSD," *Proceedings of the USENIX BSDCon 2003*, pp. 17–28, September 2003.

Simpleton, 2008.
Caffeinated Simpleton, *A Threading Model Overview,* available from http://justin.harmonize.fm / Development / 2008 / 09 / 09 / threading-model-overview.html, September 2008.

CHAPTER 5

Security

Security is an integral part of contemporary operating-system design, from supporting multiple users and limiting their interactions via access-control, to mitigating software vulnerabilities via sandboxing, and implementing cryptographic protection of network and disk data. The FreeBSD security model addresses a broad range of use cases spanning classic UNIX servers and workstations, storage appliances, network routers and switches, Internet Service Provider hosting environments, and even hand-held devices. The security model has tracked these evolving needs through 30 years of contributions from active security research and development communities.

The kernel is the heart of FreeBSD's Trusted Computing Base (TCB), the minimum subset of system components that must be secure for the system as a whole to be secure. The kernel protects itself from userspace interference using processor rings and virtual memory; these CPU features also support the UNIX process model, which isolates application instances from one another. Processes not only offer robustness in the face of application bugs, but also provide the underlying assumption of isolation required to implement access control. The kernel also maintains a tamper-proof credential for each process that holds security information such as the user and groups on whose behalf the process acts. These credentials are used as inputs to interprocess and discretionary access controls such as filesystem permissions, which in turn allow administrators, application authors, and users to specify policies for data sharing in the system. More recent additions to the FreeBSD security feature set include lightweight jail virtualization, mandatory access control, the Capsicum capability model (used for sandboxing), and security event auditing (or logging).

The kernel's low-level security features are the foundation on which more complex userspace security models can be based. For example, while the kernel itself has no notion of user authentication, process credentials, root privilege, and filesystem permissions collectively protect the password file and allow controlled switching of users at login. As network security has become more important and threat models have expanded to include physical theft of computer systems, kernel cryptographic features such as secure pseudorandom number generation, encryption, and integrity checking have been introduced. These security features support contemporary cryptographic protocols such as IPSec, **ssh**, and full-disk encryption.

In this chapter, we consider the underlying model and its practical implementation; these design principles and low-level services directly affect the subsystems described throughout the remaining chapters.

5.1 Operating-System Security

Operating-system security is a broad topic spanning the kernel, filesystem layout, and userspace applications. Historic notions of operating-system security centered on authentication, access control, and security-event auditing—features explored and largely standardized between the 1960s and 1990s. These features limit and account for user access to data, and were initially found only in high-end computing systems with hardware support for memory protection: mainframes, minicomputers, servers, and later high-end workstations [Saltzer & Schroeder, 1975]. By the end of the 1990s, higher-end technologies had become available to personal workstations and notebook computers, and during the early 2000s, tablets and smart phones. Fundamental new technologies emerged in the consumer space including digital subscriber lines, local-area networks (LANs) wide-area networks (WANs), and wireless networking, making personal computing devices the epicenter, rather than the periphery, of computer security.

As a result, requirements for operating-system security have expanded to include features previously found only in research or high-assurance trusted systems. They also incorporate new technologies necessary to address the world of distributed systems that was unanticipated by earlier development. Some of these features center on the concept of a ***trusted computing base*** (***TCB***)—that self-protecting core in the operating system that provides confidence in its security [Anderson, 1972]. Others place individual computer systems securely in a global network context through services built on cryptography and cryptographic protocols, also products of the 1980s and 1990s.

BSD, and later FreeBSD, have been central to this evolution, as they provide a bridge for advanced operating systems from the traditional world of mainframe computers, first to commodity server hardware and personal computers (PCs), and later to a variety of embedded and mobile devices. FreeBSD has developed and adopted new security features to support the security requirements of personal workstations, network servers, and derived systems including the security models found in Juniper's Junos operating system (used throughout Juniper's router, switch, and firewall products) and Apple's Mac OS X and iOS operating systems (used on Apple Mac computers, and also the iPhone, iPod Touch, and iPad mobile devices) [Watson, 2013].

FreeBSD provides the following security features:

- a self-protecting Trusted Computing Base (TCB) spanning kernel and userspace;
- kernel isolation and process separation based on virtual memory;
- authentication and multiplexing of multiple simultaneous users;
- discretionary and mandatory access-control models;
- sandboxing facilities to contain potentially malicious code;
- a range of mitigation techniques such as stack protection;
- security-event auditing for accountability and intrusion detection;
- Yarrow-based **/dev/random** supporting hardware and software entropy sources;
- support for Trusted Platform Modules (TPMs);
- a cryptographic framework supporting hardware and software implementations;
- support for full-disk encryption and cryptographic integrity protection;
- distributed authentication models (e.g., Kerberos, x.509 certificates);
- cryptographically protected network protocols (e.g., **ssh**, TLS, IPSec); and
- binary updates to remedy vulnerabilities discovered after release.

This chapter focuses on the kernel's security model and facilities—foundations for userspace security, including the ubiquitous multiuser UNIX model.

5.2 Security Model

The core of the FreeBSD security model is a trusted, self-protecting kernel hosting a user ***process model***. Discretionary and mandatory access control constrain communication between processes and access to network and storage facilities. The privilege model allows controlled violation of access-control policies for the purposes of system operation and management. Collectively, these features support the definition of FreeBSD's TCB: a self-protecting core of the operating system that allows safe execution of untrustworthy code for mutually distrusting users. Other features, such as mandatory access control, a capability-system model, security event auditing, lightweight virtualization, and cryptographic features both reinforce and build on these low-level elements.

Process Model

The kernel relies on two hardware features to implement process isolation: virtual addressing, which constructs independent virtual-memory address spaces for each process, and rings, which restrict access to privileged CPU protection features while in user mode that otherwise might allow breaking out of process confinement. System calls (e.g., *syscall* on MIPS and *sysenter* on recent X86), virtual-memory traps, and interrupts allow transitions to and from the privileged kernel; system calls occur via hardware-supported call gates that allow safe transition of control from an untrusted user process to kernel execution on the same CPU. The kernel is permitted access to user process memory, but user processes are allowed neither access to kernel memory, nor to the memory of other processes. Exceptions are granted for the purposes of privileged system management, debugging, and certain types of interprocess communication (e.g., shared memory objects).

For most of the history of UNIX systems, only two hardware rings have been employed: user and supervisor modes. More recently, full system virtualization has popularized the use of additional rings, in which a hypervisor hosts a general-purpose operating-system kernel in much the same way that an operating-system kernel hosts user processes. FreeBSD is able to run on several such virtualization systems, and even host virtual machines itself, but they are not considered further in this chapter, which focuses on security within a single operating system instance.

Discretionary and Mandatory Access Control

Kernel services such as the filesystem, interprocess communication, and networking bridge process isolation. They are constrained by access-control policies, which include ***discretionary access control*** (***DAC***) and ***mandatory access control*** (***MAC***). As the name suggests, DAC protects objects at the discretion of the object owner—for example, ***file permissions*** or ***access control lists*** (***ACLs***). In contrast, MAC allows system administrators to impose mandatory rules across all processes. MAC policies often take the form of information-flow-based models (e.g., for confidentiality) or rule-based models (e.g., to constrain the scope of an application program to certain operations regardless of the user that runs it).

Separation of policy and enforcement is a key design goal, preventing code duplication (and associated bugs), making it easier to extend the security model as requirements change, and facilitating security review. Access-control implementation is therefore split across two places in the kernel: centralized implementations of policies, and more widely distributed enforcement points in various subsystems. For example, the function *vaccess_acl_posix1e*() in **subr_acl_posix1e.c** implements POSIX.1e ACL evaluation centrally, but is invoked by several individual filesystems to check accesses. Mandatory access control and system privilege checks are similarly structured.

Access control policies depend on the ***process credential*** to hold security metadata associated with a process, such as user IDs and MAC labels, that can be compared with metadata on filesystem objects, IPC objects, and other processes during access-control decision making. Credentials are maintained and protected within the kernel address space so that modifications can only be made in keeping with the security policy.

Trusted Computing Base (TCB)

One critical function of access control is protecting the integrity of the TCB itself from unauthorized modification that might render other security protections moot. The FreeBSD TCB consists of the boot loader, kernel, and userspace libraries and programs required to support boot to multi-user mode, user login, and system administration functions (e.g., setuid-root binaries). In practice, the TCB includes a significant fraction of the integrated FreeBSD userspace, from **/sbin/init**, **/etc/rc.d**, and the libraries and tools necessary to run them, such as **/lib/libc.so**, and **/bin/sh**, to user login and management components such as **/usr/sbin/sshd** and **/usr/bin/passwd**. In a typical FreeBSD installation, protection of the TCB occurs primarily through careful configuration of system users and file ownership: most system files are owned by the root user, and cannot be unmodified by any other users. Mandatory access-control policies, such as the Biba integrity model discussed in this chapter, supplements this discretionary form of access control.

Other Kernel-Security Features

Other key concepts described in this chapter include the kernel's privilege model, that allows selective exemption from access-control rules for the purposes of system bootstrap, management, and debugging. FreeBSD also implements a hybrid-capability-system model, ***Capsicum***, which provides APIs for ***application compartmentalization*** (running code within a ***sandbox***). Complex, security-aware applications such as Web browsers use Capsicum to limit access to ***ambient authority***, or the full rights of a user, for risky portions of their functionality (e.g., Web-page rendering). FreeBSD jails build on access-control and privilege features to provide operating-system virtualization. ***Security-event auditing*** logs security-critical events for administrator review and automated intrusion detection systems. Low-level cryptographic features in the kernel, such as the kernel's cryptography framework and Yarrow random number generator, support higher-level services such as GELI disk encryption and the IPSec network protocol.

5.3 Process Credentials

Process credentials represent the notion of a subject for a variety of security and resource-management purposes: they hold UNIX security metadata such as User IDs (UIDs) and Group IDs (GIDs), MAC labels, event auditing state, and references to current jail state and resource limits. These fields collectively encapsulate the rights that a process has within the system, which will vary based on the user owning the process, the groups of which the user is a member, the jail the process is in, the binary that the process is executing, and other properties, such as resource limits and MAC policies that may provide (or limit) finer-grained rights on a per-process basis. When the kernel makes an access-control decision during a system call or in a trap handler, the authorizing credential is checked against object properties such as file owners, permissions, and labels. It is also checked against global policies to determine whether the operation should be allowed to proceed.

User credentials, stored in the kernel *ucred* structure, are stored in kernel memory to protect them from undesired modification by user processes; they can be modified only according to system access-control rules. Each *proc* structure points to its process credential via the *p_ucred* field. Individual threads within a process also have credential references via their *td_ucred* field. Per-thread credentials act as a thread-local cache of the process credential that can be accessed read-only without acquiring the process lock, avoiding contention. Avoiding lock contention is particularly important during system calls that perform many access-control checks. For example, pathname lookup uses the credential to determine the portion of the file permissions bitmask that applies, and what privileges override it, for each looked-up intermediate directory.

Thread credentials are synchronized with the process credential by calling *cred_update_thread*() whenever system calls or traps enter the kernel, or when a thread modifies the process credential. This model allows system calls and traps to use a consistent credential for their duration, avoiding race conditions when credentials change (e.g., because of *setuid* in another thread) that might otherwise lead to inconsistent behavior. However, an important result of this design choice is that downgrading of privilege by one thread will not immediately affect in-flight operations in other threads, such as long-running I/O operations, that will continue using the credential present when the system call began.

The Credential Structure

Credentials are represented by the *ucred* structure, illustrated in Figure 5.1. The credential incorporates traditional UNIX IDs, including the effective, real, and saved UIDs and GIDs, and a variable-length list of additional GIDs, described by *cr_ngroups* (number of additional groups present), *cr_groups* (pointer to the group array), and *cr_agroups* (number of groups that will fit in the currently allocated array). Historically, the additional group list was a fixed-size array in the credential, but was moved to external, variable-size storage as larger group lists became common. The credential also includes a flags field, *cr_flags*, that currently stores a single flag, CRED_FLAG_CAPMODE, indicating that the process is in a Capsicum-capability-mode sandbox, discussed later in this chapter.

Credentials reference two additional classes of external data structures. Per-user resource usage policy and accounting utilize reference-counted data structures pointed to by *cr_uidinfo*, *cr_ruidinfo*, and *cr_loginclass*. Several optional security features conditionally allocate storage, including MAC (*cr_label*), security event auditing (*cr_audit*), and jail (*cr_prison*). Reference-counted shared objects not only save space by avoiding storing the same information for many credentials, but also provide for live reconfiguration of global subject state, such as changes to a jail's configuration.

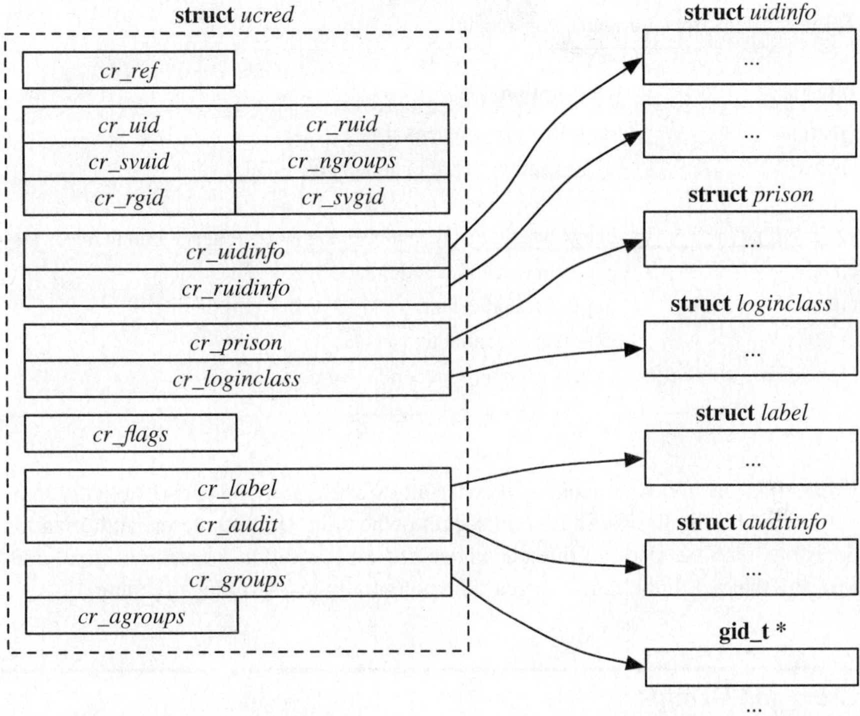

Figure 5.1 The credential structure.

Credential Memory Model

To conserve space, the credential structure is reference counted, copy-on-write, using the *cr_ref* field; any credential with a reference count greater than 1 is immutable. Modifications to credentials require that the original first be duplicated, then any updates done on the new instance, with the old credential reference replaced with the new one when ready. As credentials are rarely modified, this model conserves kernel memory and reduces cache footprint. Kernel functions managing credentials are shown in Table 5.1.

Access-Control Checks

Access-control checks accept a thread (almost always the current thread) or an explicit credential as an argument. The latter form handles cases where processes authorize operations in asynchronous contexts. For example, credentials are cached with each open file descriptor and propagated with I/O to the buffer cache. This propagation allows them to be used asynchronously with NFS write-behind.

Table 5.1 Functions for managing credentials.

Interface	Description
crget()	allocate a new credential
crhold()	increment reference count on credential
crfree()	release a reference on credential
crshared()	check whether a credential is shared (and hence immutable)
crcopy()	copy contents of a credential
crdup()	duplicate a credential
cru2x()	export a credential to userspace
cred_update_thread()	update a thread's credential from its process

Credentials cached with sockets likewise allow asynchronous packet delivery to be authorized by the firewall based on socket ownership. In both cases, authorization decisions may be made in threads whose credentials differ from the original context, but that act on behalf of the earlier (potentially less-privileged) context.

5.4 Users and Groups

Users and groups are inputs to several types of basic UNIX access control: interprocess access control that determines whether one process may signal, debug, or otherwise observe, another; discretionary access control, that includes file permissions and ACLs; and resource accounting and limits, that allow tracking and control of resource utilization. Users and groups are named by two independent 32-bit number spaces called ***user identifiers*** (***UID***s) and ***group identifiers*** (***GID***s). Users and groups are typically assigned to represent real-world users and the projects or organizations of which they are members. Pseudo-users are sometimes assigned to represent system roles, such as the ***superuser*** (***root user***), or the execution of services, such as the mail system, allowing them to be assigned ownership of files, resource limits, etc. Likewise, groups delegate access to system objects, such as the right to dial out on modems or the right to read audit trail files.

UIDs and GIDs are assigned by an external administrative authority, and are pushed into the kernel via system calls, such as at user login or when file ownership is set. Using an outside administrative authority allows user and group information to originate from databases in the filesystem, or from distributed directory services such as NIS or LDAP. In effect, the kernel user and group credential is a cache of authoritative data elsewhere—a property that must be understood by administrators because of its implications on deletion of users, removal from groups, etc. For example, removing a user from a group list in **/etc/group** does not affect existing user processes, which will continue to hold that GID in their credential. Likewise, deletion of a user from **/etc/master.passwd** does not terminate processes he or she may own, nor revoke his or her access to filesystem objects.

The credential of the first process, **init**, has its UID and GID fields set to zero. Zero is a reserved UID normally termed the superuser (usually given the user name *root*), that is trusted by the system and is permitted to do any supported kernel operation. Each additional process created with *fork* will inherit the credential of its parent, including its UIDs and GIDs.

User and group identifiers may then be manipulated using system calls such as *setuid* and *setgid*, subject to access-control rules, or may be set as a result of executing a ***set-user-identifier*** or ***set-group-identifier*** program. Credential manipulation rules are carefully structured so that privilege, once given up, can be reacquired only by executing authorized programs. When a user logs in, the login program (see Section 15.4) sets the UID and GIDs before running the user's login shell; thus, all later processes will inherit the appropriate identifiers.

UIDs and GIDs are stored with both subjects (process credentials) and objects (e.g., files and shared memory objects) to identify ownership for the purposes of resource accounting, resource limits, checking system privileges, and access control. As with processes, a set of controlled system calls, such as *chown* and *chgrp*, manipulates file-object ownership. Use of file ownership is described in Section 15.7.

Setuid and Setgid Binaries

Often, it is desirable to grant a user additional privileges. For example, a user who wants to send mail must be able to append the message to another user's mailbox file. Making the target mailbox writable by all users would permit a user other than its owner to modify messages in it (whether maliciously or unintentionally). To solve this problem, the kernel allows the creation of programs that are granted additional privileges while they are running—also a privileged operation. Programs that run with a different UID are called ***set-user-identifier*** (***setuid***) programs; programs that run with an additional group privilege are called ***set-group-identifier*** (***setgid***) programs [Ritchie, 1979]. When a setuid or setgid program is executed, the rights of the process are augmented to include those of the additional UID or GID associated with the program. The UID of the program is termed the ***effective UID*** of the process, whereas the original UID of the process is termed the ***real UID***. Similarly, executing a setgid program augments a process's permissions with those of the program's GID, and the effective GID and real GID are defined accordingly.

Systems can use setuid and setgid programs to provide controlled access to files or services. For example, the program that adds mail to a user's mailbox runs with the privileges of the superuser, which allow it to write to any file in the system. Thus, users do not need permission to write to other users' mailboxes, but can still do so by running this program. Naturally, such programs must be written carefully to have only a limited set of functionality!

The kernel stores a process's UID and GIDs in the process credential. Historically, GIDs were implemented as one distinguished GID (the effective GID) and a supplementary array of GIDs, which were logically treated as one set of GIDs. In FreeBSD, the distinguished GID is the first entry in the array of GIDs.

FreeBSD implements the setgid facility by setting the zeroth element of the supplementary groups array of the process that executed the setgid program to the group of the file. Because of the additional group, the setgid program may be able to access more files than can a user process that runs a program without the special privilege. To avoid losing the privileges associated with the group in the zeroth array element when running a setgid program, the login program duplicates the zeroth array element into the first array element when initializing the user's supplementary group array. Thus, when a setgid program is run and modifies the zeroth element, the user does not lose any privileges as the group that had been contained in the zeroth array element is still available in the first array element.

The setuid facility is implemented by the effective UID of the process being changed from that of the user to that of the program being executed. As with setgid, the protection mechanism will now permit access without any change or special knowledge that the program is running setuid. Since a process can have only a single UID at a time, it is possible to lose some privileges while running setuid. The previous real UID is still maintained as the real UID when the new effective UID is installed. The real UID, however, is not used for any validation checking.

A setuid process may wish to revoke its special privilege temporarily while it is running. For example, it may need its special privilege to access a restricted file at only the start and end of its execution. During the rest of its execution, it should have only the real user's privileges. In earlier versions of BSD, revocation of privilege was done by switching of the real and effective UIDs. Since only the effective UID is used for access control, this approach provided the desired semantics and a place to hide the special privilege. The drawback of this approach was that it was easy to lose track of the real and effective UIDs.

In FreeBSD, an additional identifier called the ***saved UID*** records the identity of setuid programs. When a program is *exec*'ed, its effective UID is copied to its saved UID. The first line of Table 5.2 shows an unprivileged program for which

Table 5.2 Actions affecting the real, effective, and saved UIDs.

Action	Real	Effective	Saved
1. exec-normal	R	R	R
2. exec-setuid	R	S	S
3. *seteuid*(R)	R	R	S
4. *seteuid*(S)	R	S	S
5. *seteuid*(R)	R	R	S
6. exec-normal	R	R	R

Key: R—real-user identifier; S—special-privilege user identifier.

the real, effective, and saved UIDs are all those of the real user. The second line of Table 5.2 shows a setuid program being run that causes the effective UID to be set to its associated special-privilege UID. The special-privilege UID has also been copied to the saved UID.

The *seteuid* system call sets only the effective UID; it does not affect the real or saved UIDs. The *seteuid* system call is permitted to set the effective UID to the value of either the real or the saved UID. Lines 3 and 4 of Table 5.2 show how a setuid program can give up and then reclaim its special privilege while continuously retaining its correct real UID. Lines 5 and 6 show how a setuid program can run a subprocess without granting the latter the special privilege. First, it sets its effective UID to the real UID. Then, when it *exec*'s the subprocess, the effective UID is copied to the saved UID, and all access to the special-privilege UID is lost. A similar saved GID mechanism permits processes to switch between the real GID and the initial effective GID.

5.5 Privilege Model

In FreeBSD, user processes are permitted access to kernel-managed objects (such as files and IPC primitives) subject to access-control policy; as described in the previous section, privileges are collectively granted to the root user. Privilege refers to a set of rights that, implicitly or explicitly, connote the ability to bypass the system access-control policy. We consider these two cases separately.

Implicit Privilege

Implicit privilege arises out of configuration of the system and its access-control policies, and describes rights held by a user or process that would allow it to violate integrity of the TCB or another security policy. Implicit privilege is best explained through an example: integrity of the system boot depends on the integrity of the kernel loaded from disk. In traditional UNIX systems, including FreeBSD in its default configuration, the kernel is owned by the root user, and protected by restrictive file permissions. If the kernel file were owned by a malicious user, or the permissions were not configured correctly, then system integrity could be violated. As a result, the root user is implicitly trusted to maintain the correct configuration and support integrity of the system. Implicit trust is not a property of the structure of the kernel access-control model, but an application of it.

Physical access to a system also holds implicit privilege in many computer systems, as access to the system might, for example, allow tampering with storage devices without passing through OS protections.

Explicit Privilege

In general, rights granted solely by access-control policies are enough to operate the system in its steady state. However, certain cases require that user processes be given additional explicit privilege that exempts them from access control to do critical system functions including:

- Kernel management operations that have global consequences across the system, such as rebooting, or configuring IPv4 addresses on a network interface.
- Kernel management operations that effectively grant kernel privilege, such as the loading of kernel modules. Misuse of these functions would violate integrity of the TCB.
- System management operations that imply system privileges, such as maintenance of system binaries (including the kernel).
- Configuring access-control policies and, particularly, setting up process credentials during the login process.
- Higher-level management operations that depend on bypassing per-object protections, such as backing up the system, or changing the owner or permissions on a file in the role of system administrator.
- Certain classes of debugging operations that offer insight into global behaviors normally limited to avoid information leaks, such as using DTrace or hardware-performance-monitoring counters on the kernel itself.

FreeBSD's privilege model is an outlet for these cases by allowing processes to execute with elevated privilege—i.e., outside the confines of the access-control policy. FreeBSD contains an explicit enumeration of kernel privileges in **sys/priv.h**, and call sites around the kernel invoke the functions *priv_check*() and *priv_check_cred*(), passing both an authorizing credential and the privilege requested to test centrally for privileges (an instance of the separation of policy and enforcement). Table 5.3 illustrates several examples of named privileges that support system management, credential management, and overriding discretionary access control. However, FreeBSD does not currently have a mechanism for fine-grained delegation of privileges to arbitrary processes—it instead relies on a simple check of the effective or, in certain cases involving resource limits, the real UID for the root user, sometimes known as the superuser policy. As the system starts its first process with a UID of 0, the implicit authority of the root user allows the system bootstrap to take place naturally, with privileges dropped when the login process switches to another UID.

The privilege model is augmented by FreeBSD jails, which restrict access to certain privileges for root users within jails, as discussed later in this chapter. Further, pluggable mandatory access-control policies can restrict or grant access to privileges. For example, the Biba integrity policy limits access to most, but not all, system privileges when the root user is executing a process without the policy's own notion of privilege. The limited system privilege allows Biba to restrict loading kernel modules when executing at low integrity, while still allowing overriding of discretionary access-control rules, subject to the integrity policy. The

Table 5.3 Example kernel privileges.

Privilege	Description
PRIV_ACCT	manage process accounting
PRIV_SETDUMPER	configure dump device
PRIV_KENV_SET	set kernel environmental variables
PRIV_KENV_UNSET	unset kernel environmental variables
PRIV_KLD_LOAD	load a kernel module
PRIV_KLD_UNLOAD	unload a kernel module
PRIV_CRED_SETUID	set the real UID
PRIV_CRED_SETEUID	set the effective UID to other than the real or saved UID
PRIV_CRED_SETGID	set the real GID
PRIV_CRED_SETEGID	set the effective GID to other than the real or saved GID
PRIV_CRED_SETGROUPS	set process additional groups
PRIV_VFS_READ	override vnode DAC read perm
PRIV_VFS_WRITE	override vnode DAC write perm
PRIV_VFS_ADMIN	override vnode DAC admin perm
PRIV_VFS_EXEC	override vnode DAC exec perm
PRIV_VFS_LOOKUP	override vnode DAC lookup perm
PRIV_NETINET_RESERVEDPORT	bind low port number
PRIV_NETINET_REUSEPORT	allow [rapid] port/address reuse
PRIV_NETINET_IPFW	administer IPFW firewall
PRIV_NETINET_DIVERT	create DIVERT sockets
PRIV_NETINET_PF	administer PF firewall

current privilege interfaces have been designed to support future introduction of a general-purpose and fine-grained privilege model.

5.6 Interprocess Access Control

Interprocess operations are system calls that allow one process (the subject) to monitor, manage, or debug another process (the target). As these operations bypass process isolation, they are subject to access control. Interprocess access controls are particularly tricky to enforce: ease of monitoring is in direct competition with information flow-centric controls (e.g., the historic choice to allow users to list each others' processes in UNIX), and it proves difficult to reason about the implied set of rights gained access to when debugging a second process. Interprocess access control is centralized in **kern_prot.c**, and falls into several categories.

Visibility

Process visibility controls access to *sysctl* nodes, such as those used by **ps** to list processes, and system calls, such as *sched_getparam*. The subject is always a process credential (*cr_cansee*), or process (*p_cansee*), and the target is the individual process being monitored.

The behavior of *cr_cansee* is controlled by two global tunables: *see_other_uids*, which limits process visibility between users; and *see_other_gids*, which limits visibility between processes with nonoverlapping group sets. For reasons of both ease-of-use and historic compatibility, displaying processes owned by other users and groups is enabled by default. Privilege can override both of these features.

Two other aspects are considered when authorizing process visibility: jail and MAC. Jail requires that, if the subject process is in a jail, then the target process must also be in the same jail. For information-flow MAC policies such as Biba or Multilevel Security, checks determine whether information may flow from the target to the subject.

Signals

Controls on signal delivery are much more complex than those on visibility: checks vary depending on whether the subject process, or just its credential, is available; signals may be authorized based on a common login session, not just the credentials involved; control depends on which specific signal is being sent; and application races in signal-handling have led to past security vulnerabilities, complicating access-control logic.

Two functions, *cr_cansignal*() and *p_cansignal*(), check signal delivery based on a subject credential or thread, target process, and signal number. The *p_cansignal*() function allows SIGCONT if the processes share a tty, and allows SIGTHR and other threading-related signals within groups of processes acting as a thread group. It then invokes *cr_cansignal*().

The *cr_cansignal*() function enforces a variety of checks, all of which must pass: if the subject is in a jail, then the object must be in the same jail; MAC must authorize signal delivery (e.g., via information flow checks); and UID and GID visibility rules are checked. If a process has changed credential since the last *execve*, that is, P_SUGID is set in the process's flags, then only certain signals can be delivered—for example, SIGKILL but not SIGTHR to prevent manipulation of internal process state. Finally, credentials are checked: if neither of the subject's real or effective UIDs match the target's real or saved UIDs, then privilege is required.

Scheduling Control

Scheduling checks occur when one process attempts to manipulate the scheduling properties of another process—for example, assigning a process to a CPU set, or changing its scheduling priority. *p_cansched*() accepts a subject thread and target process, and does a similar set of checks to signal delivery: jail protections are enforced, MAC is queried, UID and GID visibility constraints are enforced, and the subject real and effective UIDs are compared to the target's real UID. Privilege overrides UID-based checks.

Waiting on Process Termination

The *wait4* system call allows a parent process to wait for a child process termination; interfering with this mechanism, regardless of visibility and information flow goals, can have serious consequences for the correctness of shells or the **init** process, which must reap zombie processes to reclaim resources. Only jail and MAC checks are enforced here: a parent process is allowed to collect child termination information regardless of UID and GID differences.

Debugging

Control of debugging and tracing interfaces requires great care to avoid inappropriately granting a subject access to a target process's rights, confidential mappings, or data (e.g., passwords or private keys) in the target process address space. Thus, the rules authorizing debugging are complicated and are employed by various subsystems including conventional process debugging (*ptrace*), kernel tracing (*ktrace*), and also certain process-monitoring features, such as the *sysctl* nodes providing access to target process-address-space layout and file-descriptor information.

First, the global *unprivileged_proc_debug* tunable is checked to determine whether debugging features are available to unprivileged users (they are by default). Then, jail and MAC policies are allowed to authorize the operation, followed by UID and GID visibility rules.

The next category of checks is concerned with whether the subject process has a superset of the rights present in the target process—that is, whether full control of a target process grants the subject additional rights. First, the target process-group set is checked to ensure it is a subset of the subject's; then, the effective, real, and saved UIDs are similarly compared. Finally, credential change in the target (which might indicate that rights or data had been inherited from a UID no longer in the credential) is checked. Privilege can override any of these checks.

Two further rules are enforced: first, that debugging the **init** process is only permitted when the *securelevel* is less than or equal to zero; and second, that processes mid-*exec* cannot be debugged, as their credentials (or other properties) may be in a state of flux that could lead to an inconsistent access-control result.

5.7 Discretionary Access Control

Discretionary access control (***DAC***) allows each user to control the access rights granted over his or her objects to other users of the system. DAC is often contrasted with MAC: in DAC, object owners share (or not) access to objects at their own discretion, whereas in MAC, the system administrator determines when users are able to share data. The primary focus of DAC is filesystem objects: files, directories, fifos, and special devices. However, DAC controls access to System V and POSIX shared memory segments, semaphores, and queues.

FreeBSD has historically implemented the UNIX permissions model, in which each file or directory is associated with a short bitmask of rights, or file permissions. This model is simple, easy-to-understand, and consumes minimal resources: per-file 32-bit UID and GID inode fields are supplemented by a 32-bit file mode specifying rights granted to the file's group, and any other users on the system. More recently, ***access control lists*** (***ACLs***) have offered greater flexibility, at some cost to performance and administrative complexity, allowing object owners to specify rights for additional users and groups. FreeBSD supports two flavors of ACLs: POSIX.1e (more compatible with historic file permissions) and NFSv4 (more compatible with Windows and its CIFS protocol) [P1003.1e, 1998; Shepler et al., 2003].

The Virtual-Filesystem Interface and DAC

In early UNIX versions, the UNIX filesystem was solely responsible for implementing discretionary access control: it stored file ownership information, maintained the file permissions bitmask, and made checks when operations requiring authorization occurred. As the number of filesystem types increased, code implementing common access-control checks was centralized. Today, many virtual-filesystem interface (VFS)–linked kernel components, including system calls such as *open* and *execve*, IPC implementations such as local domain sockets and POSIX message queues, and the NFS server, request DAC checks before initiating I/O operations. Filesystems also invoke checks directly; for example, when performing pathname lookup or modifying file attributes.

Historically, a single vnode operation, *VOP_ACCESS*(), accepted a bitmask of coarse-grained VFS permissions that reflected underlying UNIX mode bits: VEXEC, VWRITE (optionally with VAPPEND), VREAD, and VADMIN. When NFSv4 ACLs were introduced, new VFS permissions were required reflecting finer-grained NFSv4 ACL permissions. For example, previously VWRITE encapsulated both the rights to modify a file's data and to unlink an entry within a directory, reflecting similar behavior in the UNIX file permissions bitmask. In NFSv4 ACLs, ACL_WRITE_DATA and ACL_DELETE_CHILD are separate permissions; as a result, VWRITE has now been subdivided into VWRITE and VDELETE_CHILD. A complete list of current permissions appears in Table 5.4.

VOP_ACCESS() continues to accept the older, more limited set of VFS permissions; a new vnode operation, *VOP_ACCESSX*(), accepts finer-grained permissions. All filesystems implement one of these two operations, relying on the VFS layer to provide a wrapper function where required: *vop_stdaccessx*(), for example, maps fine-grained VFS permissions into historic ones supported by older filesystems using *vfs_unixify_accmode*(). Filesystems implementing NFSv4 ACLs must implement the newer *VOP_ACCESSX*().

In addition to a VFS permissions bitmask, the vnode operations also accept the file or directory to be operated on, a process credential, and thread pointer.

Table 5.4 VFS-layer access-control permissions passed to vaccess().

Permission	Description
VEXEC	execute file/lookup in directory
VWRITE	file or directory write
VREAD	read file/list directory
VADMIN	file-owner operations such as *chmod*
VAPPEND	append file/insert in directory (always set with VWRITE)
VDELETE_CHILD	delete directory child
VREAD_ATTRIBUTES	stat file or directory
VWRITE_ATTRIBUTES	write file or directory timestamp
VDELETE	delete file or directory
VREAD_ACL	read file or directory ACL/mode
VWRITE_ACL	write file or directory ACL/mode
VWRITE_OWNER	change file or directory owner

Internal use of the same abstraction allows filesystems to implement multiple access-control models more easily: for example, UFS's *ufs_accessx*() selects between POSIX.1e and NFSv4 ACLs on a per-mountpoint basis (for a discussion of UFS, see Chapter 9). Internal to these vnode operations, the filesystem will load any necessary metadata (e.g., ACLs), and make filesystem-specific checks (e.g., file flags). Most filesystems rely on a subset of three model-specific but filesystem-independent authorization functions: *vaccess*() for UNIX permissions, *vaccess_acl_posix1e*() for POSIX.1e ACLs, or *vaccess_acl_nfs4*() for NFSv4 ACLs. Filesystems pass on the process credential from the vnode operation, but also extract and directly pass file metadata such as file type, owner, group, and mode, along with any ACLs required by the model. Access-control implementations compare credential data and VFS permissions bitmask with file ownership, UNIX mode bits, and ACL entries, returning success (0) or an *errno* value on failure.

Object Owners and Groups

All objects supporting DAC have an owner and group represented by a UID and GID pair stored as object metadata. For filesystem objects, the UID and GID are stored in the inode's *i_uid* and *i_gid* fields. For IPC objects, the UID and GID are stored as fields of the in-memory data structure describing the object.

Users have full access to objects they own, and can set the group field, permissions, and optional ACLs to control access by other users and groups. The semantics of the object GID depend on the ACL model used. For UNIX permissions, an object's group controls whether processes owned by other users will be affected by the group or "other" entries in the object's file permissions.

When a process creates a new object, the object inherits the process's effective UID as its owner. New files and directories inherit their groups from their parent directory at creation time. New IPC objects inherit their group from the creating process's effective GID. File UIDs and GIDs can be modified after creation using the *chown*, *fchown*, and *lchown* system calls. Changing a file's UID requires privilege (e.g., root access). A file's GID can be set by its owner to any group of which that user is a member.

UNIX Permissions

In the UNIX permissions model, each object has associated ***file permissions*** that describe the rights granted to the object's owner, group, and "other". In UFS, file permissions are stored as the lower 12 bits of the 16-bit file mode stored in the *i_mode* field; the remainder holds the inode's file type. A file's ownership and permissions can be queried using the *stat*, *lstat*, and *fstat* system calls; permissions may be set using the *chmod*, *lchmod*, and *fchmod* system calls.

When processes create filesystem objects, they specify initial permissions as an argument to the system call. Requested permissions will be masked by a process's *umask*, which specifies the maximum creation-time permissions that may be set on any object created by the process. Interpretation of the *umask* depends on whether ACLs are enabled on the filesystem. However, the commonly used *umask* of 022 allows new objects to be readable by any user on the system, but prevents them from being world-writable unless explicitly set that way using a separate system call.

File permissions are interpreted in the context of the accessing credential's effective UID, effective GID, and additional groups. These identifiers are compared with the *i_uid* and *i_gid* to select which portion of the file's permissions bitmask will be used in authorization. Each file has three sets of permission bits for read, write, or execute permission for each of owner, group, and "other". If the target object is a directory, then the read bit authorizes listing of entries in the directory, and the execute bit authorizes lookup of further files and subdirectories under it.

The *vaccess*() function combines credential, requested VFS permissions (mapped as shown in Table 5.5), and file owner, group, and permissions bitmask as follows:

1. If the UID of the file is the same as the effective UID of the thread, only the owner permissions apply; the group and other permissions are not checked.

2. If the UIDs do not match, but the GID of the file matches an effective or additional GID of the thread, only the group permissions apply; the owner and other permissions are not checked.

3. Only if the UID and GIDs of the thread fail to match those of the file are the permissions for all others checked. If these permissions do not allow the requested operation, it will fail.

Table 5.5 Mapping of VFS permissions to UNIX permissions.

VFS permission	UNIX file permission
VEXEC	S_IXUSR, S_IXGRP, S_IXOTH
VWRITE	S_IWUSR, S_IWGRP, S_IWOTH
VREAD	S_IRUSR, S_IRGRP, S_IROTH
VADMIN	file owner
VAPPEND	S_IWUSR, S_IWGRP, S_IWOTH
VDELETE_CHILD	*always denied*
VREAD_ATTRIBUTES	*always allowed*
VWRITE_ATTRIBUTES	*mapped to VADMIN*
VDELETE	*always denied*
VREAD_ACL	*always allowed*
VWRITE_ACL	*mapped to VADMIN*
VWRITE_OWNER	*mapped to VADMIN*

If the permissions present are insufficient to authorize the requested access, privilege will be checked and may override DAC protections.

Three additional mode bits relate to the UNIX security model. The setuid and setgid bits control credential UID and GID transition on execution of a binary as discussed earlier in the chapter. There is one further quirk: the ***sticky bit***. If present in a directory's permissions, the bit prevents users from unlinking children files or subdirectories that they do not own. This feature is used almost exclusively for the shared **/tmp** directory.

Access Control Lists (ACLs)

UNIX permissions allow users to protect or share data with little storage or performance overhead; however, the expressiveness of the model is limited. Group permissions are the only means by which a file owner can differentiate rights granted to specific users from rights granted to any other users of the system—but each file is limited to a single group. Any time a file or directory must have permissions assigned to a previously unused combination of users, a new group must be created—which under UNIX requires system-administrator intervention. In multiuser environments where UNIX groups represent projects or teams, the permissions model is unable to easily describe common setups such as having a directory be readable and writable by one group, read-only for a second group, but inaccessible to other users of the system.

File permissions may be seen as a degraded form of access control list (ACL): a per-object list of users, groups, and their individual assigned permissions. A full ACL implementation provides greater expressive power at the cost of increased complexity, storage overhead, and performance overhead. FreeBSD supports two ACL models: POSIX.1e, which emphasizes compatibility with UNIX permissions; and NFSv4, a newer model improving interoperability between the network filesystem (NFS) and Windows, now also used by Mac OS X. UFS supports simple UNIX permissions (the default), POSIX.1e ACLs, and NFSv4 ACLs. ZFS supports only NFSv4 ACLs (for a discussion of ZFS, see Chapter 10). Different ACL models may have markedly different semantics: not only may different rights be expressed, and different compatibility behavior be present for traditional UNIX permissions, but semantics such as the effect of entry ordering can differ. For example, POSIX.1e ACLs, as described by the user, are ordering independent (and will be sorted internally); in contrast, NFSv4 ACLs are interpreted differently based on the order in which entries are specified.

Each ACL is described by an *acl* data structure containing an array of *acl_entry* structures, illustrated in Figure 5.2. Each entry consists of a tag, ID, file permissions, entry type, and flags. The *tag* and *ID* identify the principal described by the entry—typically a UID or GID. The *entry_type* and *flags* fields are used only for NFSv4 ACLs: the former indicates whether a particular ACL entry grants or denies rights; the latter indicates how the ACL entry will be inherited. The *perm* field contains a bitmask of granted or denied rights specific to the ACL model.

System-call APIs are portable across models: the same system calls check, delete, get, and set ACLs on filesystem objects, as illustrated in Table 5.6. Each system call accepts an object name or file descriptor, a pointer to an *acl* structure in user memory, and an ACL type. ACLs set on files must be of the appropriate type, and valid for the target (e.g., default ACLs may be set only on directories); userspace programs can test an ACL for both internal consistency and applicability to a specific filesystem object via the *aclcheck*() system calls. Table 5.7 lists currently supported types; others may be added in the future as further ACL models are introduced. ACL models may allow more than one ACL to be set on a file at a time: for example, POSIX.1e supports both access and default ACLs on directories, controlling (respectively) access control and ACL inheritance.

Figure 5.2 ACLs consist of a **struct** *acl* embedding instances of **struct** *acl_entry*.

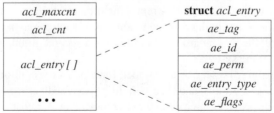

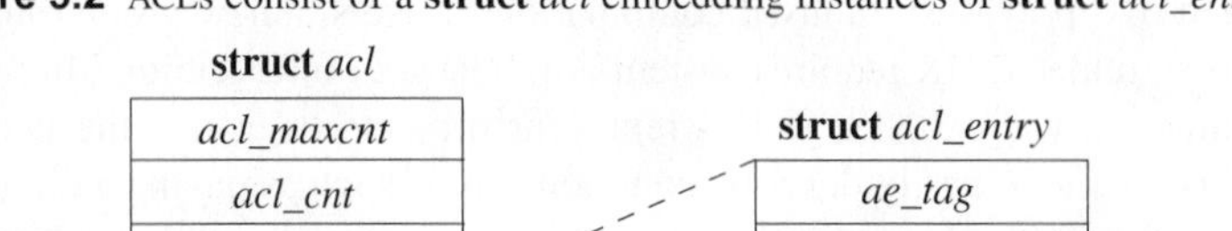

Table 5.6 ACL system calls are portable across different ACL models.

Interface	Description
__acl_aclcheck_fd()	check ACL is valid by file descriptor
__acl_aclcheck_file()	check ACL is valid by path (follow links)
__acl_aclcheck_link()	check ACL is valid by path (do not follow links)
__acl_delete_fd()	delete ACL by file descriptor
__acl_delete_file()	delete ACL by path (follow links)
__acl_delete_link()	delete ACL by path (do not follow links)
__acl_get_fd()	get ACL by file descriptor
__acl_get_file()	get ACL by path (follow links)
__acl_get_link()	get ACL by path (do not follow links)
__acl_set_fd()	set ACL by file descriptor
__acl_set_file()	set ACL by path (follow links)
__acl_set_link()	set ACL by path (do not follow links)

ACL-aware filesystems implement three ACL-related vnode operations: *VOP_GETACL*(), *VOP_SETACL*(), and *VOP_ACLCHECK*(). The ACL implementation is split across filesystem-independent VFS code and individual filesystems implementations. Code portable across ACL models and filesystems may be found in **vfs_acl.c**, and includes ACL system-call code and utility functions for managing ACL memory. Model-specific ACL code may be found in **subr_acl_posix1e.c** and **subr_acl_nfs4.c**. These files include functions for ACL evaluation replacing *vaccess*(). They check the validity of ACLs, and implement new-file/directory creation (e.g., ACL inheritance and mode initialization).

ACL-aware filesystems include three adaptations to implement ACLs: they provide filesystem-specific storage of ACLs by implementing *VOP_GETACL*() and *VOP_SETACL*(); they invoke VFS-layer ACL utility functions during file creation to ensure that the file mode and ACLs on a new object are properly initialized; and they invoke VFS-layer *vaccess*() variations, passing loaded ACLs as needed to

Table 5.7 ACL models may support multiple types of ACL.

Type	Description
ACL_TYPE_ACCESS	POSIX.1e access ACL
ACL_TYPE_DEFAULT	POSIX.1e default ACL
ACL_TYPE_NFS4	NFSv4 ACL

implement access-control checks for various ACL models.

UFS is able to store the file owner, group, and permissions in each file's inode because of their small size (4 bytes each). ACLs, however, are substantially larger (several hundred bytes); instead, they are stored in extended attributes outside of the inode. As a result, additional disk accesses are required to read and update ACLs. UFS uses system extended attributes, which prevents direct modification of ACL contents, even by the file owner. To centralize as much access-control logic as possible, UFS performs internal checks using the *VOP_ACCESSX*() vnode operation. *ufs_vaccessx*() loads ACLs and then invokes *vaccess*(), *vaccess_acl_posix1e*(), or *vaccess_acl_nfs4*() depending on the ACL model enabled on the filesystem.

POSIX.1e Access Control Lists

POSIX.1e ACLs extend UNIX permissions to provide greater expressive power, at the cost of greater complexity, storage requirements, and performance overheads. As in the file permissions model, files and directories have an owner UID, an associated GID, and file permissions bitmask that holds permissions for the owner, group, and "other", that make up the canonical entries in a file's ACL. POSIX.1e allows these permissions to be supplemented with further file permissions reflecting read, write, and execute rights for both additional users and additional groups.

All files and directories have access ACLs that direct access control during pathname lookup and file *open*. The access ACL directly solves many of the problems experienced with UNIX permissions in multi-user environments: the file owner can add additional entries that assign specific rights to multiple users and groups without encountering the single-group limit or requiring administrator intervention to create groups when working with small sets of users.

In POSIX.1e, ACLs have six possible tag values illustrated in Table 5.8. The object owner, group, and "other" entries are the canonical entries inherited from the UNIX model. The mask entry plays a key role in compatibility with the permissions model. Applications continue to request simple file permissions via

Table 5.8 POSIX.1e ACL entry tags.

Tag value	Description
ACL_USER_OBJ	object owner
ACL_USER	additional user
ACL_GROUP_OBJ	object group
ACL_GROUP	additional group
ACL_MASK	ACL mask
ACL_OTHER	object other

Table 5.9 Mapping of VFS permissions to POSIX.1e ACL permissions.

VFS permission	POSIX.1e ACL permission
VEXEC	ACL_EXECUTE
VWRITE	ACL_WRITE
VREAD	ACL_READ
VADMIN	file owner
VAPPEND	*mapped to VWRITE*
VDELETE_CHILD	*always denied*
VREAD_ATTRIBUTES	*always allowed*
VWRITE_ATTRIBUTES	*mapped to VADMIN*
VDELETE	*always denied*
VREAD_ACL	*always allowed*
VWRITE_ACL	*mapped to VADMIN*
VWRITE_OWNER	*mapped to VADMIN*

open, *mkdir*; set rights and masks via *chmod* and *umask*; and retrieve file modes via *stat*. Likewise, users may reasonably expect reasonable behavior when seeing permissions listed by **ls** or set via the **chmod** command. When only canonical entries are present on a file or directory, then the group bits in set or retrieved via permissions will affect the object-group ACL entry. However, if any additional user or group entries exist in an ACL, then a new mask entry will be present, whose value will be set or retrieved instead. During ACL evaluation, the mask entry limits the maximum rights granted by any noncanonical ACL entry. As a result, setting a conservative umask or file permissions will cause rights set via additional user and group fields to be limited to those the user specified for the file group. Likewise, the file-mode output of **ls** will provide a conservative (overly permissive) estimate of rights granted by any ACL present on the file, preferring to err on the side of suggesting less, rather than greater, protection than is actually present.

POSIX.1e ACL evaluation is implemented by *vaccess_acl_posix1e*() in **subr_acl_posix1e.c**. VFS permissions are mapped to POSIX.1e ACL permissions as shown in Table 5.9. It replaces *vaccess*()'s checks with the following algorithm that returns a result for the first ACL entry to match the thread's credential:

1. The file or directory's access ACL (type ACL_TYPE_ACCESS) is searched for object-owner, mask, and "other" entries, to be consulted at various points in evaluation.

2. If the credential's effective UID matches the object-owner ACL entry, then the access request is checked against the entry's permissions. If sufficient, success

is returned. If insufficient, appropriate privilege is checked to supplement the entry's permissions; if sufficient, success is returned. Otherwise, access is denied and no further entries are consulted.

3. If the credential's effective UID matches an additional user ACL entry, then the access request is checked against the entry's permissions—limited to those also granted by the ACL mask entry. If sufficient, success is returned. If insufficient, appropriate privilege is checked to supplement the entry's permissions; if sufficient, success is returned. Otherwise, access is denied and no further entries are consulted.

4. If either one of the credential's effective or additional GIDs matches the object-group entry or any of the additional group ACL entries, then the access request is checked against the entry's permissions—limited to those also granted by the ACL mask entry. If any entry is sufficient, success is returned.

5. If no group entries were sufficient without privilege, then any matching group entries will be retried with appropriate privilege checked to supplement the entry's permissions; if sufficient, success is returned. Otherwise, if there were any matching groups, access is denied and no further entries are consulted.

6. Finally, the ACL "other" entry will be consulted; if sufficient, success is returned. If insufficient, appropriate privilege is checked to supplement the entry's permissions; if sufficient, success is returned. Otherwise, access is denied.

A mask entry will always be present if any noncanonical ACL entries are present, and it applies to all entries but the object's owner and "other" entries. When multiple group entries match a credential, then best match, rather than first match, selects an entry. Privilege is checked for a matching entry only if the entry's permissions are insufficient—this limitation of privilege checking avoids unnecessary exercise of privilege, which in the future may be recorded in event-audit records.

In addition, directories may have default ACLs (type ACL_TYPE_DEFAULT) used when new objects are created in the directory; these entries are combined with the system-call mode field and process umask by *acl_posix1e_newfilemode*(). FreeBSD implements the behavior specified by POSIX.1e by allowing the umask to restrict all rights granted in the resulting ACL; this behavior differs from Linux in which the directory's mask entry is allowed to override the *umask*. Both models have merit: strict adherence to POSIX.1e causes users and applications aware of the permissions model to always get conservative behavior when setting the umask and file modes; allowing the mask to override the umask makes it possible to create project directories in which the directory owner need not worry about how process umasks are set for other users and can, instead, ensure that (for example) files are always group writable.

The UFS implementation of POSIX.1e ACLs uses the inode UID, GID, mode fields to hold canonical ACL entries. If an extended ACL is present, then additional entries are placed in an extended attribute. If an ACL mask entry is present, then the group permissions in the inode mode will be used for the mask entry, and permissions for the object-group entry will be stored in the extended attribute instead. This approach is consistent with file permissions passed via the system-call interface that also uses group bits for the file mask, and avoids extended-attribute operations when implementing *stat* and *chmod*.

NFSv4 Access Control Lists

Whereas POSIX.1e ACLs are designed for UNIX compatibility, the primary design consideration for NFSv4 ACLs is compatibility with Windows clients accessing a UNIX server via the Network File System or CIFS protocols. As such, NFSv4 ACLs are modeled on those found in Windows' filesystem NTFS. Largely because of inclusion of ZFS, FreeBSD has adopted Solaris semantics for NFSv4 ACLs. There are necessarily design tradeoffs: where in POSIX.1e ACLs, compatibility for users and applications that were aware only of the UNIX permissions model was a key goal, in NFSv4 ACLs, users may experience unexpected behavior as ACL entries override more UNIX-like expectations. For example, an ACL entry on a file granting deletion rights may override a lack of write permission on its parent directory, to provide greater compatibility with the Windows model.

In the NFSv4 ACL model, filesystem objects each have a single ACL of type ACL_TYPE_NFS4. In contrast to UNIX permissions and POSIX.1e ACLs, NFSv4 ACL evaluation takes into account all entries that match the credential's effective UID, effective GID, and additional groups, not just the first entry that matches the credential.

The set of tags supported by NFSv4 ACL entries is similar to those in POSIX.1e ACLs (see Table 5.10). An additional tag ACL_EVERYONE allows object owners to specify rights applicable to all users and groups. There is no notion of an ACL_MASK entry in NFSv4, although changes to file mode do affect ACL interpretation, and the mode is updated to reflect ACL changes.

NFSv4 defines four types of ACL entries: allow entries, deny entries, audit entries, and alarm entries. Only allow and deny entries are implemented in FreeBSD; setting ACL entries of other types will return an error. NFSv4 ACLs are

Table 5.10 NFSv4 ACL entry tags.

Tag value	Description
ACL_USER_OBJ	object owner
ACL_USER	additional user
ACL_GROUP_OBJ	object group
ACL_GROUP	additional group
ACL_EVERYONE	matches all users/groups

defined as deny by default: operations not explicitly authorized by ACL entries will be rejected. Further, explicit deny entries can block access that might otherwise be granted by other allow entries. An exception to deny by default in the FreeBSD implementation is that file owners are always allowed to get and set the file's mode and ACL, regardless of ACL contents. Table 5.11 contains a complete list of mappings from VFS permissions to NFSv4 ACL permissions.

NFSv4 ACL evaluation is implemented in *vaccess_acl_nfs4*(). The function begins by determining the set of NFSv4 ACL permissions that must be granted:

1. *access_mask* is initialized to the set of NFSv4 permissions corresponding to the requested VFS permissions, calculated by *_access_mask_from_accmode*().
2. If the filer owner is equal to the credential's effective UID, then ACL_READ_ACL, ACL_WRITE_ACL, ACL_READ_ATTRIBUTES, and ACL_WRITE_ATTRIBUTES are removed from *access_mask*.
3. If the target object is not a directory and ACL_APPEND_DATA is requested, then it is replaced with ACL_WRITE_DATA.

Next, *vaccess_acl_nfs4*() must determine whether or not the ACL and other properties, such as file mode and ownership, would grant the request:

4. *_acl_denies*() is invoked to iterate over and evaluate ACL entries: its conclusion will be stored in a local variable *denied*. Each time a matching allow

Table 5.11 Mapping of VFS permissions to NFSv4 ACL permissions.

VFS permission	NFSv4 ACL permission
VEXEC	ACL_EXECUTE
VWRITE	ACL_WRITE_DATA
VREAD	ACL_READ_DATA
VADMIN	file owner
VAPPEND	ACL_APPEND_DATA (directories); ACL_WRITE_DATA (files)
VDELETE_CHILD	ACL_DELETE_CHILD
VREAD_ATTRIBUTES	file owner; ACL_READ_ATTRIBUTES
VWRITE_ATTRIBUTES	file owner; ACL_WRITE_ATTRIBUTES
VDELETE	ACL_DELETE
VREAD_ACL	file owner; ACL_READ_ACL
VWRITE_ACL	file owner; ACL_WRITE_ACL
VWRITE_OWNER	ACL_WRITE_OWNER

entry is encountered, any rights it grants are removed from *access_mask*. If at any point a matching entry is encountered that denies remaining permissions in *access_mask*, then *denied* will be set to EPERM, with *_acl_denies*() returning immediately. If, while iterating over entries, *access_mask* reaches 0, *denied* will be set to 0, with *_acl_denies*() returning immediately. If the end of the ACL is reached without *access_mask* reaching 0, then *denies* will be set to EPERM, reflecting a default-deny model.

After *_acl_denies*() returns, several other factors are considered that may deny access:

5. If the original operation request included VADMIN, and the effective UID is not equal to the file owner, then *denied* will be set to EPERM.
6. If VEXEC has been requested, the object is not a directory, and the operation has not already been denied, then the equivalent file permissions for the ACL is calculated by *acl_nfs4_sync_mode_from_acl*(). Following the same rule enforced in *execve*, if the file mode does not include S_IXUSR, S_IXGRP, or S_IXOTH, then *denied* will be set to EACCES.

If after these tests *denied* is 0 (success), then *vaccess_acl_nfs4*() will return success. Otherwise, it continues:

7. If VEXPLICIT_DENY was set, and *_acl_denies*() did not fail because of a deny entry, then success can be returned. This test is used only during file unlink, where finding a VDELETE_CHILD deny entry can block unlink of a child in a directory, but failing to find an allow entry is not sufficient to cause it to fail: general write permission on the parent directory is also able to authorize unlink in the UNIX model.
8. Appropriate privilege will then be checked for any remaining ungranted rights, which may cause *vaccess_acl_nfs4*() to return success.
9. Finally, an error value is selected: if the operation would have required ownership of the file or directory, or involves unlinking, then EPERM will be returned; otherwise, EACCES will reflect a DAC failure.

Unlike POSIX.1e ACLs, ACL inheritance is combined in the single NFSv4 ACL, rather than stored in a separate default ACL. Per-ACL-entry flags indicate whether the entry is to be inherited by new files or subdirectories, and whether or not the entry is used for access control or just inheritance. *acl_nfs4_compute_inherited_acl*() computes the ACL of a newly created filesystem object given the parent's ACL and system-call requested permissions (combined with umask). *acl_nfs4_inherit_entries*() allows an entry to be inherited if it is not an object-owner, object-group, or everyone entry; if the entry is tagged as inheritable by directories or files; if the object is not a directory, then only file-inheritable entries are used; and if the entry type must be either allow or deny.

As with POSIX.1e ACLs, some effort has gone into UFS to allow what NFSv4 terms trivial ACLs to be stored only using inode fields; only if more complex ACLs are defined will they overflow into extended attributes. *acl_nfs4_is_trivial*() performs this calculation before writing out an ACL by first converting the ACL to a file mode, then converting it back to an ACL and determining whether it is semantically identical to the original ACL. Two NFSv4 ACLs are semantically identical if they have the same number of entries, and each entry has identical tag, ID, permissions, entry type, and flags.

5.8 Capsicum Capability Model

Through the mid-2000s, operating-system security research focused on multi-user systems: discretionary and mandatory access-control models, fine-grained privilege, auditing, and virtualization. As UNIX systems were scaled down for use in personal and mobile devices, such as laptop computers, phones, tablets, and embedded and appliance devices, the aims of local OS security changed significantly. Rather than control the interactions of multiple users, developers instead sought to limit the rights of applications, or even components of applications, to protect a single user, the system owner, from application vulnerabilities exploited by malicious content originating from the Internet. Conventional OS security notions such as users and groups sometimes found use in these environments (Android), and as well as in mandatory access-control schemes (iOS, SELinux), but have proven mediocre tools for the particular problem of ***application compartmentalization***, sometimes referred to as ***privilege separation***.

Application compartmentalization decomposes programs into multiple isolated components each running with different rights such that compromise of one component yields only its individual rights, rather than the the total rights of the composed application, mitigating the effects of a security vulnerability. In early work pioneered by Provos et al. [2002], and similar work by Kilpatrick [2003], the goal was to reduce the exposure of all-powerful root privilege to attacks in which arbitrary code execution was available to attackers (e.g., buffer overflows). In later application-level work by Reis & Gribble [2009], and OS work by Watson et al. [2010], compartmentalization is also applied to complex, security-aware applications without access to system privilege, such as Web browsers. The argument for this approach is straightforward: in computer systems with a single user, that user's access to his or her own data overshadows the importance of historic root access as all critical data on the system is available to the user without local privilege escalation.

Capsicum is a capability-based scheme first shipped in FreeBSD 9 to provide improved OS support for application compartmentalization. Capsicum adopts ideas from historic ***capability systems*** in which ***ambient authority*** is deemphasized: rather than allowing all processes to name all system objects, and then performing explicit access control based on permissions or labels, sandboxes gain access to objects through program-driven delegation. This approach matches the requirements of security-aware applications that must support their own distributed system or user-facing security models such as the World Wide Web's same-origin policy or powerboxes that grant file access to sandboxes via a privileged file-open dialog box.

Capsicum Application Structure

While simple Capsicum-enabled applications may consist of a single sandboxed process, in practice most complex applications consist of a set of tightly interconnected processes collectively known as a logical application. Often, one process will have ambient authority, acting as a gateway and source of global rights that will be selectively delegated to one or more sandboxed processes encapsulating specific protection domains. For example, the Capsicumized **gunzip**, illustrated in Figure 5.3, consists of two processes. The first process executes the main loop, walking a series of pathname arguments on the command line with the ambient authority required to open files by pathname. It selectively delegates open file descriptors to a second sandboxed process that reads data from a read-only input capability, performs potentially risky decompression operations on the data, and writes the decompressed data to a write-only output capability. In the event of a vulnerability in the decompression logic allowing arbitrary code execution, the attacker gains access to only the delegated capabilities rather than ambient authority that would allow access to all the user's files.

Trade-offs necessarily exist in multiprocess sandboxing designs: the security benefits of finer-grained compartmentalization must be weighed against context switch and interprocess communication performance overhead; and debugging multiprocess programs is substantially more difficult. For example, **gunzip** could be refined to use a new sandbox for each file being decompressed, further limiting the data and capabilities leaked as a result of an exploit in one of several files passed on the same command line. However, this restriction comes at the cost of additional per-file process creation and destruction. Capsicum has proven effective for use in a variety of high-risk applications, but research into the best approaches for applying compartmentalization to software along with methods for decreasing overhead, remains active.

Figure 5.3 Compartmentalized **gunzip** using Capsicum.

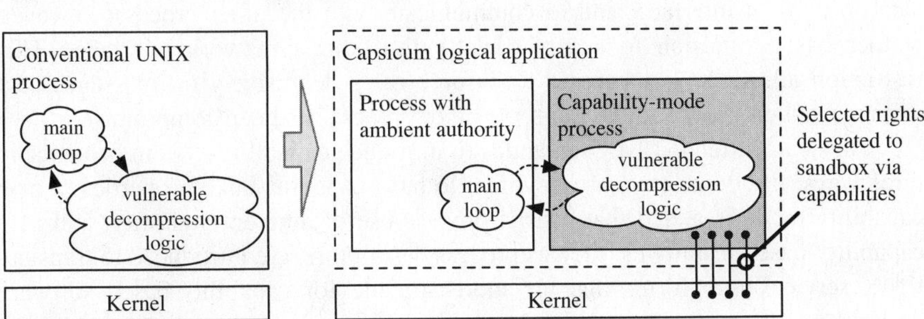

Capability Systems

Capsicum is a hybrid capability system that blends ideas from historic capability-system research with a contemporary UNIX design. In capability systems, tasks do operations on all resources via ***capabilities***—unforgeable tokens of authority. In capability-based operating systems, capabilities are communications endpoints that refer to objects; invocations on the capability are implemented via message passing to a process that implements the underlying object. Capabilities consist of not just a reference to an object, but also a mask of rights limiting the set of methods that can be invoked via the capability. Applications are constructed from sets of processes linked by capabilities; each process embodies a protection domain consisting of access to a subset of overall capabilities in the system. By minimizing capabilities held by each process, the scope of damage in the presence of a fault—or an exploited vulnerability—is also minimized.

Capabilities are unforgeable in that their integrity is protected by the TCB that prevents tasks from bypassing the protection model by constructing capabilities to arbitrary objects. For OS-based schemes, capabilities are maintained in kernel; userspace code uses per-process indices to identify on which capability a system call should operate. Processes can obtain capabilities by creating a new object, inheriting a capability from the parent process, being explicitly delegated the capability by another process (e.g., via message passing), or by deriving it from another capability that they already hold. Refinement allows processes to create new capabilities to objects for which they already hold a capability; rights on the new capability must be a subset of rights on the original capability.

Capability systems support the construction of both hierarchical and nonhierarchical security relationships between pairs of communicating processes. Hierarchical relationships are those in which one process holds a struct subset of rights of the other (asymmetric distrust). Nonhierarchical relationships are those in which the two processes have nonidentical sets of rights, and yet neither is a strict subset of the other (symmetric distrust). Both types of relationships are valuable in application compartmentalization.

Conventional sandboxing is hierarchical in that the sandbox has a strict subset of rights relative to the ambient process that created it—for example, as seen in our earlier **gunzip** example. An example of a useful nonhierarchical relationship is that found in an assured pipeline between two processes implementing a protocol proxy between two network interfaces. Each is granted the right to communicate on its own interface, and to communicate with the other process; however, neither has permission to access directly the other's network interface. This restriction allows both processes to enforce rules defensively on messages sent and received on its interface even if the other process has been compromised.

Capsicum extends UNIX semantics to introduce capability-system behavior in three ways: file descriptors are modified to have capability-like properties; a new capability mode is added that restrict process use of ambient authority; and new capability-based primitives, such as process descriptors, are introduced to translate UNIX services into forms that are more suitable for capability-based software designs.

Capabilities

In UNIX, file descriptors have many of the properties of capabilities: the kernel protects their integrity making them unforgeable, they encapsulate not just a reference to an object, but also reference-specific access rights, and may be inherited across *fork* or passed between processes using UNIX domain sockets. Despite these similarities, there are significant differences that require modification to the file-descriptor model to build a capability system. Perhaps the most important is that only a few of the many file-descriptor system calls are controlled by the existing per-descriptor *f_flag* access-right mask. For example, a read-only descriptor returned by *open* will not permit write I/O operations to be done; however, the *fchmod* system call is allowed regardless of *open*-time flags. There is also no way to refine rights on a file descriptor after it has been created but before delegating it on to other processes.

In Capsicum, these problems are solved by introducing a new type of file descriptor, the ***capability***, that allows rights to be restricted and refined in a fine-grained manner suitable for delegation to sandboxes. Capability rights, a selection of which is illustrated in Table 5.12, correspond to common operations on file descriptors. Once held, capabilities for objects may be passed as arguments to any system calls to which the original file descriptors could be passed, subject to appropriate rights being present. There is no one-to-one mapping of system calls to rights: system calls may require more than one right and a single right may authorize more than one system call. For example, the *write*, *writev*, *pwrite*, and *pwritev* system calls all require CAP_WRITE to authorize a write on the file

Table 5.12 Selection of capability rights.

Capability right	Authorizes file-descriptor operation
CAP_READ	read or receive
CAP_WRITE	write or send
CAP_SEEK	modify offset or read/write at a nonoffset location
CAP_FCHDIR	set working directory
CAP_FCHFLAGS	set file flags
CAP_FCHMOD	change file mode
CAP_FCHOWN	change file owner
CAP_LOOKUP	use as starting directory for at() operations
CAP_KQUEUE_EVENT	test for events on a kqueue
CAP_KQUEUE_CHANGE	modify events monitored on a kqueue
CAP_ACCEPT	accept sockets
CAP_LISTEN	set up a listen socket

descriptor. However, *pwrite* and *pwritev* also require CAP_SEEK as they write to locations other than the file descriptor's current offset. *lseek*, in contrast, requires only CAP_SEEK.

Capabilities are created using the *cap_rights_limit* system call, similar to *dup2*, which accepts an existing file descriptor (possibly already a capability) and a requested access-rights mask, returning a new capability with the new mask. The operation fails if the requested mask includes any rights not already held on the argument capability, enforcing a monotonic decrease in rights.

Capabilities are implemented via a struct *filecaps* embedded in each file-descriptor array entry, struct *filedescent*. The capability rights for a descriptor include a mask of basic CAP_ rights that authorize system calls on the descriptor, as shown in Figure 5.4. It also includes whitelists of specific *ioctl* and *fcntl* commands that are permitted. *ioctl* operations are device-specific, and so the regular mask on system calls alone provides insufficient granularity to usefully delegate device nodes to sandboxes. For example, the whitelist allows the high-availability storage daemon (**hastd**) to delegate kernel GEOM_GATE devices while permitting only suitable *ioctl* commands.

Figure 5.4 Each file-descriptor array entry has a capability mask that controls access.

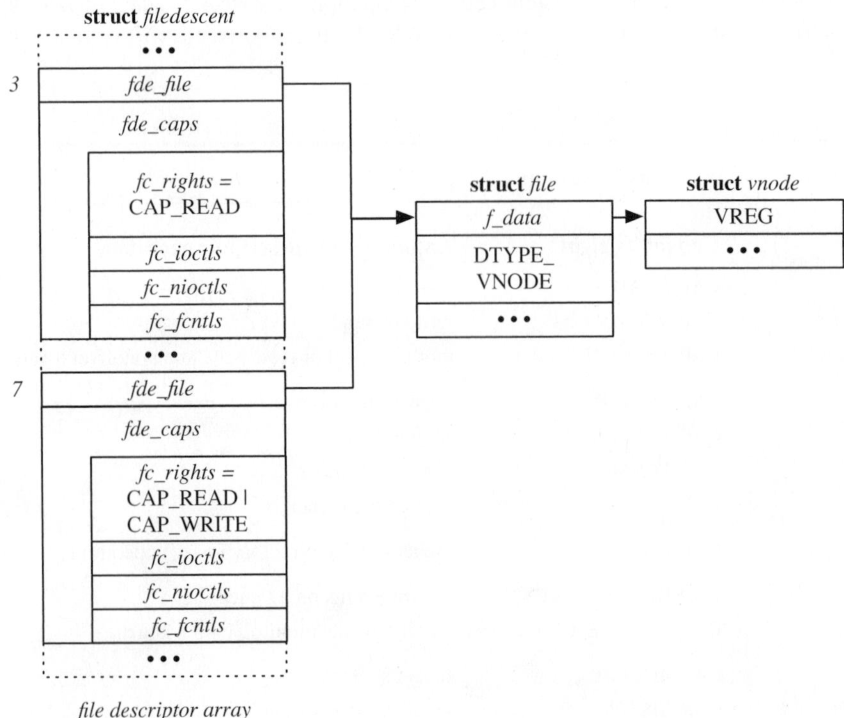

Capabilities are evaluated when a file descriptor is looked up in a system call, typically in *fget*(), which accepts a mask of required capability rights for the operation as an argument. *fget*() invokes *cap_rights*() to extract the set of rights for a file descriptor, and then passes it to *cap_check*() to confirm that the rights are sufficient to authorize the current system call on this specific object.

Capability Mode

In strict capability systems, global capabilities are assigned to the first process, from which all other capabilities will be directly or indirectly derived and then distributed through descendent processes as the system runs. In UNIX, access to global namespaces, such as the filesystem namespace accessible via *open*, gives processes the ability to acquire undelegated capabilities. Capsicum therefore differentiates between regular UNIX processes, which retain ambient authority, and those in capability mode, for which global namespace access is denied. Capability-mode processes must be delegated any rights they are to use, supporting fine-grained sandboxing based on a capability model. This hybrid approach allows portions of applications to run with the full rights of the user, but other components may have access to only explicitly delegated files, directories, devices, or network connections.

A process enters capability mode by invoking the *cap_enter* system call that sets the CRED_FLAG_CAPMODE flag on the *cr_flags* field of the process credential. A child process created with *fork* inherits the parent process credential, and so also inherits the capability-mode flag. Processes may query whether they are in capability mode using *cap_getmode*, but there is no system call to clear the flag and exit capability mode. Within capability mode, all system calls must implement capability discipline: their actions must be scoped to the current process or an object named using file-descriptor arguments.

System calls that naturally implement capability discipline when used with regular files and directory descriptor arguments are left unfettered: for example, the *read* and *write* system calls are not limited in capability mode. Similarly, certain system calls act only on the local process, such as *getuid* and *signal*, and are also not limited in capability mode. These calls are listed in **capabilities.conf**, which causes the SYF_CAPENABLED flag to be set in their system call descriptions when the kernel is compiled. When a capability-mode process invokes a system call without the SYF_CAPENABLED flag set, ECAPMODE will be returned by the system-call handler.

Certain system calls implement multiple functions, only some of which follow capability discipline. Their use may be permitted in capability mode, but certain aspects of their function are restricted. For example, *shm_open* is permitted in capability mode, but only to create anonymous, rather than named, shared memory objects. Likewise, while the *open* system call is entirely blocked because of its dependence on the global filesystem namespace, *openat* is permitted as long as it is used only to open files “under” the passed directory descriptor, rather than relative to the filesystem root or current working directory. Implementing filesystem subtree delegation proves tricky because of concurrency, and because the only effective technique appears to be to prevent use of ".." in capability-mode path lookup.

System calls implement restrictions using *IN_CAPABILITY_MODE*(), which checks whether the current thread should be limited. Sometimes checks are per-system call, such as in *shm_open*, but frequently, checks are done centrally, such as in *namei*(), which implements checks that lookups are under, rather than outside of, delegated directory descriptors for *openat*, *fchmodat*, etc.

5.9 Jails

Jail, first introduced in FreeBSD 4.0, is a lightweight operating-system based virtualization framework that allows safe delegation of subsets of a FreeBSD system to guest root users [Kamp & Watson, 2000]. Administrators of guest instances, known as jails, can hold root access, manage their own users and groups, install third-party software packages, and perform a variety of other administrative activities safely without putting the host system at risk. When configured to use ZFS, guest administrators can also manage data sets, set quotas, and prepare snapshots, all localized to their individual jail. Combined with more recent IPC and network-stack virtualization features, administrators can be granted the ability to manage networking properties such as routing, VLANs, and firewalls. As of FreeBSD 9.0, enhanced resource control allows resource limits to be set and strictly enforced for jails, including on CPU time, resident memory use, open files, swap use, number of processes, and number of threads.

Jails see widespread use in confining integrated system-scale applications, such as database/Web server combinations, where independently run services may require root privilege but must also safely cohabit a single server system. They are an especially popular tool for Internet Service Providers (ISPs) as customers can be granted administrative rights (including root privilege) for systems they manage, while also allowing high-density hosting—hundreds and even thousands of virtual instances on a single server. Security and hosting density are frequently cited benefits of virtualization, but there are others—not least, larger numbers of smaller and more specialized installations can be easier to manage, especially where applications have complex and sensitive package dependencies making combined upgrades tricky.

Jail's origins lie in the *chroot*, or change root, system call, which transforms a process's filesystem namespace by modifying the process-local root vnode (*fd_rdir*) to differ from the boot-time global root vnode. *chroot* saw early use in facilitating reproducible software builds, but in the 1990s it became a popular technique for confining system daemons such as anonymous FTP servers. The technique proved neither particularly convenient, nor particularly secure. In practice, changing a process's root directory proves tricky, as applications often require access to system configuration files, libraries, and IPC channels reached via the filesystem namespace. These requirements sometimes lead to replication of system content into a per-application root; for example, when BIND's **named** daemon runs *chroot*'ed for security, it requires its own **devfs** mount.

More importantly, *chroot* is by design a namespace transformation rather than a security tool: countless nonfilesystem system calls exist that permit access to global resources that may either allow "escape" from *chroot*'s constraints, or the ability to negatively impact system operation in ways that a sandboxing model would ideally not allow. For example, several supported architectures have machine-dependent system calls unrestricted by *chroot* that provide direct access to the hardware I/O space for root-owned processes. Finally, relevant to both usability and security, *chroot* required root privilege, as the ability to change the filesystem namespace affects the security of setuid binaries that rely on the sanctity of system directories such as **/usr/lib** and **/etc** for correct—and secure—operation; being able to change where these paths point can lead to security vulnerabilities.

Capsicum has now replaced *chroot* as the preferred means of confinement within a single application by virtue of an unprivileged sandboxing primitive and application-centered security model. Jails address the other important use case for *chroot*: the virtualization-like effect of giving a set of applications their own filesystem namespace. Jail reuses ideas from *chroot* for lightweight filesystem virtualization; it also addresses potential "escape" techniques and restricts or denies use of system services that might allow processes in a jail to have more global effects. This latter notion is necessarily configurable as the desirable limits on availability and scope of system services vary with the specific requirements of a deployment environment and its applications.

Jails are collections of processes with a common set of namespace transformations (including filesystem root), virtualized networking and IPC subsystems, and mutual visibility for interprocess operations. Within the kernel, each jail is represented by a reference-counted *prison* structure as illustrated in Figure 5.5. Each process is in exactly one jail by virtue of the *cr_prison* pointer in its process credential. At boot, the first user process, **init**, is placed in the statically allocated *prison0*. As with other credential properties, jail references are inherited across *exec* and *fork*, and so a new process will be in the same jail as its parent unless it is explicitly changed. Jails can be nested, which is represented by a tree of *prison* structures linked by their *pr_children*, *pr_sibling*, and *pr_parent* fields. Jails extend *chroot* with a number of restrictions that:

- Prevent further use of *chroot* from allowing "escape" by differentiating between each process's current root directory (*fd_rdir*) and jail root directory (*fd_jdir*). Both will be tested for (and blocked) when evaluating ".." lookups. With the introduction of nested jails, *pr_parent* pointers must be walked to check the root of each ancestor jail.
- Limit the set of privileges available to root-owned processes in jail; for example, the restrictions do not permit loading of kernel modules or direct kernel-memory access.

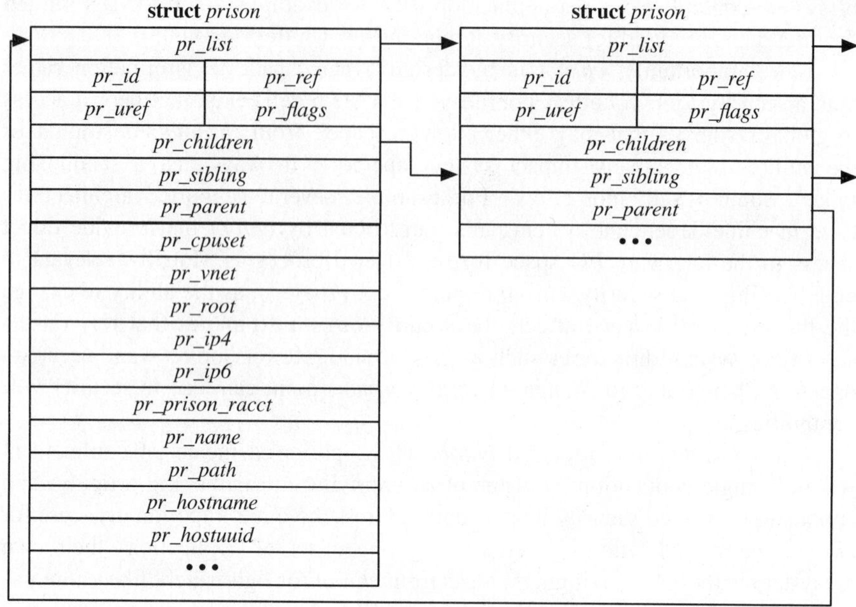

Figure 5.5 Prison structures are the in-kernel representations of jails.

- Block interprocess operations on processes not in the same jail; for example, they do not allow a jailed process to signal processes outside the jail, or in another jail, using *kill*, or attach a debugger to them using *ptrace*.
- Do not allow processes in a jail to *bind* sockets to IPv4 and IPv6 addresses that have not been delegated to the jail. Likewise, they force loopback network requests to *connect* only to sockets bound in the jail.
- Prevent jailed processes from opening terminal devices already in use by another jail, in order to prevent capture or forgery of user input via a pseudo-terminal.
- Limit use of the *mount* system call to jail-safe filesystems, marked as VFCF_JAIL in their VFS declaration: **nullfs**, **tmpfs**, **procfs devfs**, and ZFS.

Jail implements these protections using several strategies across various kernel subsystems. Entirely blocked services (such as jail-unsafe filesystems) are protected by calls to *jailed*() on the process's credential. The centralized *priv_check*() function calls out to *prison_priv_check*() to validate privileges requested by a jail against a whitelist; examples are shown in Table 5.13. Certain constraints are implemented by rewriting system-call arguments; for example, the use of IP addresses is scoped by rewriting *sockaddr_in* arguments to *bind* and *connect* to replace INADDR_ANY with the jail's own IP address. Finally, system calls such as *ptrace* have their arguments checked for appropriate scope:

Table 5.13 Example privileges permitted and denied to jailed processes.

Privilege	Available in Jail?
PRIV_ACCT	no
PRIV_SETDUMPER	no
PRIV_KENV_SET	no
PRIV_KENV_UNSET	no
PRIV_KLD_LOAD	no
PRIV_KLD_UNLOAD	no
PRIV_CRED_SETUID	yes
PRIV_CRED_SETEUID	yes
PRIV_CRED_SETGID	yes
PRIV_CRED_SETEGID	yes
PRIV_CRED_SETGROUPS	yes
PRIV_VFS_READ	yes
PRIV_VFS_WRITE	yes
PRIV_VFS_ADMIN	yes
PRIV_VFS_EXEC	yes
PRIV_VFS_LOOKUP	yes
PRIV_NETINET_RESERVEDPORT	yes
PRIV_NETINET_REUSEPORT	yes
PRIV_NETINET_IPFW	VNET-only
PRIV_NETINET_DIVERT	VNET-only
PRIV_NETINET_PF	VNET-only

p_candebug() checks that if an invoking process is in a jail, that the target process is in the same jail. Pseudo-terminal access is likewise scoped by tagging opened terminal devices with the jail of the process that first opened them; later attempts to *open* a device will fail if the process is not in the same jail.

The simplest way for a process to create a new jail is via the *jail* system call, which takes a *jail* structure specifying a new root directory, hostname, jail name, and lists of IPv4 and IPv6 addresses. The **jail** program is careful to close any open directory descriptors and resources from outside of the jail that might allow escape before executing the requested binary. Each jail is assigned a unique jail ID (JID), which can then be specified as an argument to other system calls that will act on the jail after creation. Processes can attach to an existing jail using the *jail_attach* system call, which allows new commands to be injected into the jail from outside; extreme care is also required to prevent the undesirable leakage of resources into the jail. Jails can be destroyed using the *jail_remove* system call, which will terminate any processes in the jail.

In FreeBSD 8.0, new system calls were introduced to ease management of increasingly flexible and configurable jails. The *jail_get* and *jail_set* system calls allow getting and setting sets of name-value variables on an existing jail by JID. Possible option names are shown in Table 5.14. In FreeBSD 8, jail was also integrated with the experimental VIMAGE facility, which allows IPC and network-stack virtualization, described in greater detail in Chapter 12 and Chapter 13. With this feature enabled, jailed root users can manage per-jail firewalls and routing tables, as well as use packet-sniffing tools such as **tcpdump**. Instead of delegating IP addresses, virtual (or real) network interfaces are assigned to jails.

Unlike hypervisor-based virtualization systems such as bhyve, jails share a single kernel across all instances; this allows significantly greater efficiency than virtual-machine approaches, supports more integrated scheduling and memory management, and facilitates sharing between virtual machines through regular OS-based IPC primitives such as pipes and sockets. Through **nullfs** mounts and ZFS copy-on-write features, jail storage footprints can be minimized—while also easing management of many virtual systems. On the other hand, jail-based virtualization is more visible to guest administrators who cannot upgrade the kernel version, use tools that require access to kernel memory, or directly access hardware. Jails also share a larger common TCB than hypervisor-based solutions such as Xen, where common attack surfaces between mutually distrusting guests are limited to a narrower hypercall interface and common paravirtualized backend drivers (described in Chapter 8). Since their development, the approach promoted by FreeBSD jails has also been adopted in other systems, including Solaris Zones and Linux Containers.

5.10 Mandatory Access-Control Framework

Mandatory access control (***MAC***) describes a class of security models in which system or security-administrator-defined policies constrain the behavior and interactions of all system users. Whereas in DAC, object owners protect (or share) objects at their own discretion, MAC enforces systemwide security invariants regardless of user preference. The security research literature has defined a diverse set of mandatory security policies, the most influential of which are described in the next section. There is also significant user-community interest in product-specific security customization for appliance and embedded systems, such as firewalls and smart phones. However, it is neither desirable to integrate all possible security models directly into FreeBSD, nor to encourage extensive and difficult-to-maintain local modifications of the OS kernel within every FreeBSD-derived product.

The MAC framework offers a logical solution to this problem: a kernel access-control-extension infrastructure able to represent many different policies, offering improved maintainability and significant flexibility supported by the OS vendor [Watson et al., 2003; Watson, 2012]. Similar to the device-driver framework and VFS, the MAC framework allows policies compiled into the kernel, or encapsulated in kernel modules, to modify the kernel security policy using

Table 5.14 Jail options used with jail_get() and jail_set().

Jail option	Description
jid	jail ID
children.max	maximum number of nested jails (0 prevents nested jail creation)
devfs_ruleset	specify a devfs ruleset to use within the jail
enforce_statfs	do not expose filesystems from other jails via stafs()
host	virtualized hostname flag
host.hostname	name returned by gethostname()
host.domainname	name returned by getdomainname()
host.hostuuid	jail UUID
host.hostid	value returned for kern.hostid sysctl()
ipv4	IPv4-enabled flag
ipv4.addr	IPv4 address list
ipv4.saddrsel	IPv4 automatic source-address selection flag
ipv6	IPv6-enabled flag
ipv6.addr	IPv6 address list
ipv6.saddrsel	IPv6 automatic source-address selection flag
name	jail name
path	root directory
persist	jail persists even without processes flag
securelevel	per-jail securelevel
vnet	virtualized network-stack flag
allow.set_hostname	permit setting kern.hostname sysctl()
allow.sysvipc	permit access to System V IPC
allow.raw_sockets	permit use of raw sockets
allow.chflags	allow setting system file flags
allow.mount	allow mounting jail-safe filesystems
allow.quotas	allow quota operations
allow.socket_af	allow unrestricted use of socket-address families
allow.mount.devfs	allow mounting devfs
allow.mount.nullfs	allow mounting nullfs
allow.mount.zfs	allow mounting ZFS
allow.mount.procfs	allow mounting procfs
allow.mount.tmpfs	allow mounting tmpfs

well-defined kernel-programming interfaces (KPIs). Policy modules can augment kernel access-control decisions, and make use of common policy infrastructure, such as object labelling, to avoid code replication or the need for direct kernel modification. Unlike filesystem stacking, previously proposed for access-control extension, the framework supports enforcement of ubiquitous policies spanning a broad range of kernel object types, from files to network interfaces. The framework also supports tight integration of access-control policies with the kernel concurrency model, unlike system-call interposition, another widely discussed technique for kernel access-control extension [Watson, 2007].

Mandatory Policies

Early mandatory security models focused on information flow, and require ubiquitous enforcement across all kernel services. Bell and LaPadula's ***multilevel security*** (***MLS***), protects confidentiality by controlling information flow through the operating system [Bell & LaPadula, 1973]. The Biba integrity policy is the logical dual of MLS, protecting integrity [Biba, 1977]. Fraser's low-watermark mandatory access control (LOMAC) is an integrity policy that tracks the dynamic flow of taint through a system [Fraser, 2000]. These models are concerned with maintaining invariants by permitting or denying operations that lead to the upgrade or downgrade of information. To have this effect, they place ***security labels*** holding policy-specific metadata on both subjects (credentials) and objects (files, sockets, etc.) to support access-control decisions.

In MLS, subject labels capture the user's security clearance and object labels capture an objects classification; in Biba and LOMAC, labels represent subject and object integrity. Information-flow control is imposed by controlling use of read and write functions; for example, in MLS, a user with a SECRET clearance is not permitted to "write down" secret data to a file marked UNCLASSIFIED; likewise, a user with a SECRET clearance is not permitted to "read up" top-secret data from a file marked TOP SECRET. Integrity models instead prevent the upward flow of lower-integrity data, blocking the upward write of data from low-integrity subjects to higher-integrity files. Biba prevents "read down" by blocking read operations on lower-integrity files, whereas LOMAC allows "read down" operations to succeed, but downgrades the subject label of the reader, preventing later writes to higher-integrity objects, maintaining the same information flow invariant.

Boebert's Type Enforcement (TE) and Badger's Domain and Type Enforcement (DTE) have also proven influential, with TE seeing widespread deployment in SELinux and McAfee's FreeBSD-based Sidewinder firewall [Boebert & Kain, 1985; Badger et al., 1995; Loscocco & Smalley, 2001]. Both models are flexible and fine-grained, with subjects and objects labelled with symbolic domains and types. An administrator-controlled rule set defines how these labels are interpreted, authorizing permitted interactions and domain transitions. Processes in the user_d domain might be allowed to read, but not write, objects of type system_t, regardless of filesystem ownership and permissions. Transitions between domains occur by executing specially labelled programs in a similar way to setuid binaries, subject to policy. Processes can also transition between domains dynamically, again subject to policy.

Finally, a broad class of hardening policies are also relevant, which take less principled approaches, but offer direct control over OS-level services and features in a more system-centered way, rather than relying on abstract information-flow or label-centered approaches. For example, the **ugidfw** filesystem firewall policy allows a global set of system-administrator-defined rules to control the interactions of users, groups, and files/directories like a network firewall. This policy is similar, notionally, to TE, but applies only to the filesystem, and relies on existing UID and GID elements of the process credential rather than on supplemental security labels.

Guiding Design Principles

The dual goals of explicit access-control extensibility and engagement with downstream system vendors lead to several philosophical and programmatic design principles:

1. Do not commit to a particular access-control policy as there is no consensus on a single true policy or even policy language. Policy is therefore captured by C code that can compute results dynamically, perhaps based on a configurable policy or labels, or that can implement purely static decisions.

2. Avoid policy-specific intrusions into kernel subsystems: encapsulate these details behind policy-agnostic kernel interfaces. This approach leads naturally to an object-centered design: access-control checks are relative to a subject (process credential), object, and method.

3. To avoid code redundancy, provide policy-agnostic infrastructure such as access-control instrumentation points, label storage, label APIs, and tracing. Where possible, user APIs are also policy-agnostic to permit shared command-line tools.

4. Policy authors determine their own security and performance trade-offs. The MAC framework supports heavy-weight policy designs (such as the ubiquitous labelling of network packets required by Biba and MLS), but only policies using those functions need pay for them.

5. Support multiple simultaneous and independent policies. Most commercial trusted systems include at least two different mandatory policies: MLS for confidentiality, and Biba for TCB protection. This approach allows third parties to extend the security model while base OS policies are in place. Where possible, provide predictable, deterministic, and ideally sensible compositions of simultaneously loaded policies.

6. Impose structures that simplify assurance arguments. In the parlance of Anderson, the MAC framework acts as a ***reference monitor***: tamper-proof, always invoked, and small enough to be subjected to analysis and tests [Anderson, 1972]. The goals of tamper resistance and nonbypassability are done through enforcement of access-control policies by the kernel. The goal of analyzability is done through separation of policy and mechanism. Access-control policies can be validated separately from the services they protect and the framework that allows their enforcement.

7. Design for an increasingly concurrent operating system kernel. As even hand-held systems have grown native parallelism, and demands on kernel scalability have grown, new security policies need not only to behave correctly, but also scale with the kernel features they protect.

Architecture of the MAC Framework

The MAC framework architecture, illustrated in Figure 5.6, consists of a thin service layer linking security-aware user applications, kernel services, and access-control-policy modules. Policies employ the framework's infrastructure to instrument policy-relevant kernel security decisions, store and retrieve security labels on objects, and dynamically compose with other loaded modules. In addition, the MAC framework implements a set of DTrace probes that support debugging and profiling using the D script language, see Section 3.8. The framework also exposes policy-independent but security-aware system calls so that policy-agnostic monitoring and management tools, such as **getfmac** and **setfmac**, can query and manipulate labels on objects. Several different interfaces are defined:

- The kernel services entry-point KPI is invoked by kernel services, such as the Virtual File System (VFS) and interprocess communication (IPC), to notify the MAC framework of object events such as allocation and destruction, and to do access-control checks. Roughly 240 entry points are defined, most representing

Figure 5.6 The MAC framework is a pluggable framework for kernel policy augmentation.

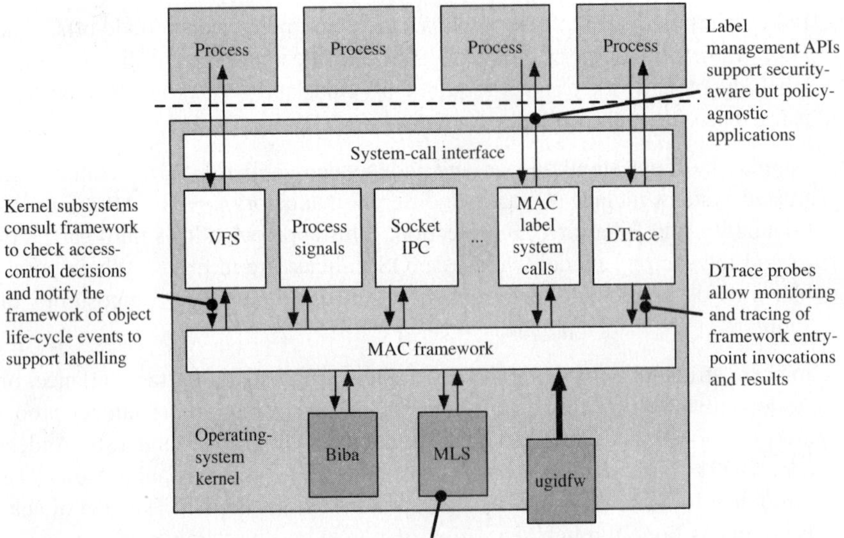

specific methods on particular object classes; generally, access-control entry points take the perspective that a subject (typically represented by a process credential) is invoking a method on an object. Kernel subsystems are responsible for providing opaque storage for labels on their objects in the form of a *void* * pointer to be maintained by the framework.

- The policy entry-point KPI sits between the MAC framework and registered policies. Many policy entry points correspond directly to kernel entry points, albeit with explicit *label* references added to the argument set. These label references are supplemented by policy life-cycle events and a library of infrastructure functions available to policies, such as memory allocation and label storage. Policy modules need to implement and invoke those KPIs that they require, and the specifics of how object labels are stored is opaque to policies to insulate them from changes in kernel implementation details.
- The label-management API allows userspace programs to query and set security labels on various object types including files, sockets, and processes without knowing the details of loaded policies.
- A set of DTrace probes allow framework operations to be monitored using D scripts: probes are available on entry and return from every MAC framework access-control entry point, providing access to arguments and return values so that decisions can be monitored or manipulated.

Framework Startup

To meet the nonbypassability requirements of a reference monitor, the MAC framework must be initialized and ready to handle access-control checks by the time the first user process, **init**, begins execution. Ubiquitously labelled policies, such as Biba and MLS, require that the framework be available significantly earlier to maintain security labels on all kernel objects from inception. As a result, the framework is initialized early in boot—shortly after the kernel memory allocator, console, and locking primitives become available, but before device probing and process creation have begun. Initialization occurs in several phases:

1. Framework data structures, locks, and memory allocation are initialized.
2. Policies compiled into the kernel or loaded before boot are registered.
3. The global *mac_late* is set, indicating that from this point onward, kernel objects controlled by the framework may be allocated.
4. The MAC framework steady state is entered and kernel boot continues.

Policies loaded after *mac_late* are not assured complete access to all events on all controlled objects, and are unable to rely on label memory being present for objects allocated prior to policy registration. These constraints are compatible with many UNIX-centric policies, and even some labelling policies, but not policies such as MLS and Biba that require ubiquitous labelling and control to enforce information-flow constraints. In practice, no special behavior currently appears to be necessary at kernel shutdown.

Policy Registration

Policies must register with the MAC framework to instrument access-control decisions, receive object life-cycle events, label object classes, and access framework services. The kernel linker identifies MAC policies in the kernel and modules using the linker set facility. Each policy declares a set of properties including whether or not the policy may be attached after boot (i.e., after *mac_late* is set), and whether the policy may be unloaded. These properties are stored in a statically allocated per-policy data structure, *mac_policy_conf*, illustrated in Figure 5.7, along with a reference to the complete set of policy entry points, stored in a *mac_policy_ops* structure.

When an entry point is invoked by a kernel service, the set of loaded policies is stabilized for the lifetime of that invocation; attempts to change the set of loaded policies must wait to let in-flight invocations drain before continuing. This design ensures consistent implementation of access-control checks, and the prevention of implementation races such as use of code in a policy after its containing module has been unloaded.

Figure 5.8 illustrates the policy life cycle: MAC policy *mpo_init*() and *mpo_destroy*() entry points are invoked, respectively, during policy registration and deregistration. Exclusive framework locks are held over both entry points to ensure that all steady-state entry-point invocations on the policy are bracketed by the two events, allowing safe policy initialization and cleanup.

Figure 5.7 MAC policies are described by *mac_policy_conf* and *mac_policy_ops* structures.

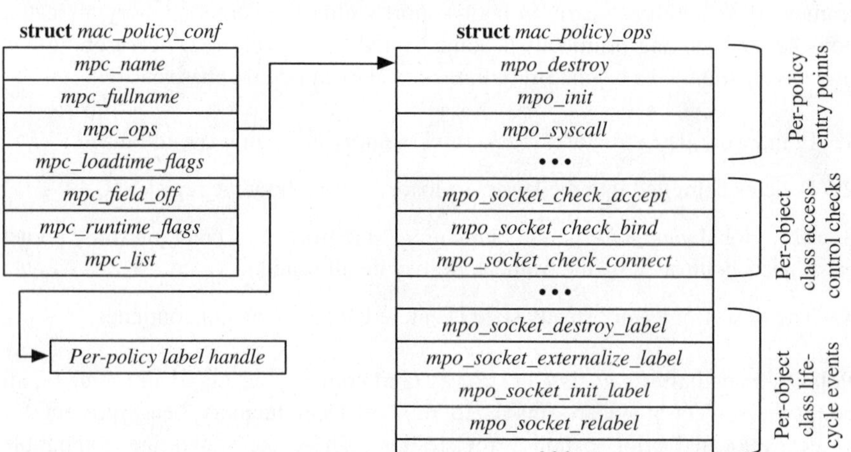

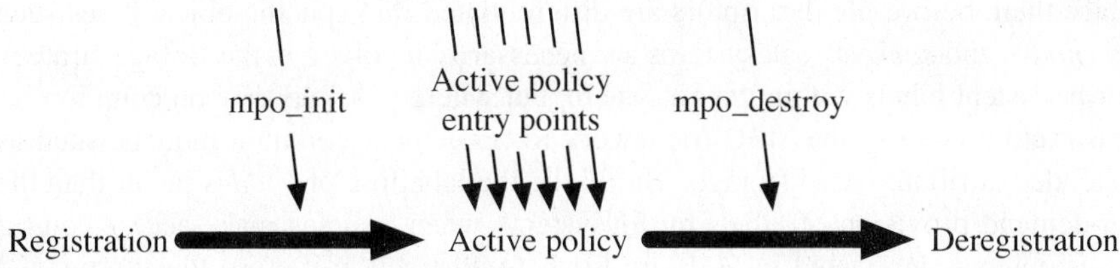

Figure 5.8 MAC policies have an explicit life cycle.

Framework Entry-Point Design Considerations

The kernel service entry point KPI is the means by which kernel subsystems, such as filesystems and the network stack, engage the reference monitor in security-relevant events and decisions. Wherever possible, the MAC framework takes the perspective that kernel subsystems implement objects whose instances may be labelled, and that policies may be adequately enforced through controls on method invocation. This approach is a natural fit for the kernel architecture, which often takes on an object-oriented structure, despite an absence of supporting language features in C.

In most cases, selection of the objects to protect is a straightforward result of analyzing the APIs offered to userspace via system calls: methods on sockets, pipes, and files seem natural to protect using the framework. In other cases, design choices are less clear: should all *sysctl* management-information base (MIB) nodes be independent objects each with their own labels, or should they be treated collectively as a single object with read and write methods? The MAC framework takes the latter approach on the basis that *sysctl* nodes frequently provide access to many individual back-end objects, as is the case with nodes that export process information for use by **ps**. Here, it is the underlying process labels that are used for authorization.

Once objects have been identified, selecting and placing entry points also requires careful thought: the more granular the KPI, the more expressive policies can be—however, this granularity is at the cost of policy complexity. A consistent approach to placing entry-point invocations is also important: the fewer the calling sites, the easier they are to validate—however, too few invocations lead to inadequate protection. MAC entry-point design is necessarily somewhat subjective, but generally requires placing the checks deep enough to allow both adequate insight into object types, and a single enforcement point for a particular level of abstraction.

As an example: in early versions of the MAC framework, access-control checks for files were done in the filesystems themselves—in later versions, these access-control checks were moved to the common VFS code invoking all filesystems to provide more consistent protection and simpler implementation. Placing VFS access control too high in the call stack for I/O system calls, however, would place them before file descriptors are differentiated into specific object types such as *vnode*s and *socket*s. Filesystems are necessarily involved in the storage strategy for persistent labels within the filesystem, but where possible, rely on common infrastructure code in the MAC framework to implement common models, such as extended attribute-based storage. Similarly, the labelling of *vnode*s rather than the on-demand provision of labels by filesystems when policies make access-control decisions was motivated by a desire to share abstractions across filesystems and provide a uniform caching model.

Policy Entry-Point Considerations

Most policy entry points are entered because of invocation of a corresponding kernel-service entry point:

- Object life-cycle events, such as socket creation and destruction
- Access-control requests checking a subject's use of a method on an object
- General and sometimes subject-free decision requests

Policy entry-point KPIs have been designed with great care to provide enough information so that policies can meet functional goals while also discouraging unsafe constructions that might, for example, lead to concurrency vulnerabilities, or excess dependence on kernel-internal binary interfaces that are subject to change between minor releases. Thus, it is desirable to limit policy-module exposure to kernel-internal data structures where not specifically required for policy semantics. It is simultaneously desirable to offer the flexibility to use those internal structures where required to avoid policy developers simply bypassing formal KPIs, which would be counter to the maintainability goals of the MAC framework.

Structuring the MAC framework to prevent bugs in policy modules, and the framework itself, is a central concern. Where possible, the framework employs language types to detect programmer errors; its structure also enables static analysis (such as completeness checking on controlling access to classes) through its use of symbols. Programmability and binary compatibility goals sometimes come into conflict. Earlier versions of the framework, prior to the advent of C99 sparse-static-structure initialization, declared policy entry points via an array of integer entry-point names and function pointers cast to *void* *. On face value, this approach offered stronger binary compatibility by allowing new entry points to be defined without disrupting current data-structure layouts. However, it also discards type information for arguments to entry-point functions. When we experimentally switched to explicit, typed entry-point functions, we discovered a number of previously unnoticed bugs in policy modules that had been incorrectly interpreting their arguments.

```
static int
vn_write(struct file *fp, struct uio *uio,
    struct ucred *active_cred, int flags, struct thread *td)
{
  ...
        vn_lock(vp, lock_flags | LK_RETRY);
  ...
#ifdef MAC
        error = mac_vnode_check_write(active_cred,
            fp->f_cred, vp);
        if (error == 0)
#endif
                error = VOP_WRITE(vp, uio, ioflag,
                    fp->f_cred);
  ...
        VOP_UNLOCK(vp, 0);
  ...
        return (error);
}
```

Figure 5.9 Example MAC framework invocation from VFS.

Kernel Service Entry-Point Invocation

To understand how the MAC framework is integrated into the kernel, and its relationship with policies, we will consider an example in the form of access-control checks that occur when a file is read. An excerpt from *vn_write*(), the kernel function implementing the *write* system call on files, is shown in Figure 5.9. When the MAC framework is compiled into the kernel, *vn_write*() calls *mac_vnode_check_write*() to authorize the request. The framework will return 0 to allow the *write* to continue, or in the event that one or more policies denies the request, a nonzero *errno* value is returned. In most cases, the framework is able to select the error number returned to userspace; this approach allows policies to indicate, for example, whether an error is a result of violation of a policy's rules (EACCES) or holds inadequate privilege (EPERM).

vn_write() passes several arguments into the entry point: the credential authorizing the write (*active_cred*), the credential cached in the file descriptor at the time of file open (*file_cred*), and the vnode on which the *write* is being done (*vp*). The stability of arguments to entry points is ensured by the kernel synchronization model's interaction with the calling code. Credential contents are copy-on-write, and references held by the calling thread and file descriptor prevent them from being garbage collected. The *vnode* is protected by a reference count, and *vnode* data, including the MAC label on the *vnode*, is stabilized by the *vnode* lock; *vn_write*() holds the lock over both check and use to ensure adequate atomicity. This construction avoids several critical races that might occur when using other security extension approaches, such as system-call interposition.

The arguments excluded from entry-point invocation are as interesting as those included. For example, *vn_write*()'s data pointer is not passed into the entry point as the data it references resides in the user address space where it cannot be accessed race-free with respect to the file-write operation that will follow. Similar design choices throughout the kernel service KPI discourage the expression of policies that cannot be safely represented within the kernel synchronization model.

Policy Composition

Kernel entry points correspond to one (or more) policy-level entry points, and will invoke any policy implementations of those entry points on each call. Policy entry-point invocation is nontrivial: access to the policy list must be synchronized to prevent races with policy load and unload, the subset of policies interested in the event must have their entry point implementations called, and the results of those calls must be sensibly composed. With one exception, the granting of system privileges, MAC framework polices are only able to restrict, not grant, rights, which leads to a simple composition in which the set of rights granted is the intersection of those granted by the base system and any registered policies. This meta-policy is simple, deterministic, predictable by developers, and above all, useful.

Policy entry points may be placed in three broad categories based on return type: event notifications that do not return a value, access-control checks that return an *errno* value, and decision functions that return a Boolean. The composition policy requires that for an access-control check to succeed, all policies expressing interest in the entry point must return success; as policies may return different error numbers in response to the same access-control check, a composition function, *mac_error_select*(), orders and selects from among available error values, as illustrated in Figure 5.10. Invocation of policy entry points and composition of the results are done using a set of composition macros that combine synchronization, selective policy invocation, and composition:

- *MAC_POLICY_PERFORM*() broadcasts event notifications to all interested policies. Events may relate to policy changes, label management, policy management, or kernel object life-cycle events.
- *MAC_POLICY_CHECK*() composes access-control results returned by multiple policies. Each policy contributes an *errno* value; these values are composed using *mac_error_select*(), a function that encodes an ordering of failure classes. Success is returned only if all interested policies accept the request.
- *MAC_POLICY_BOOLEAN*() composes boolean values returned by entry points augmenting general kernel decisions. A boolean "and" is used during IP

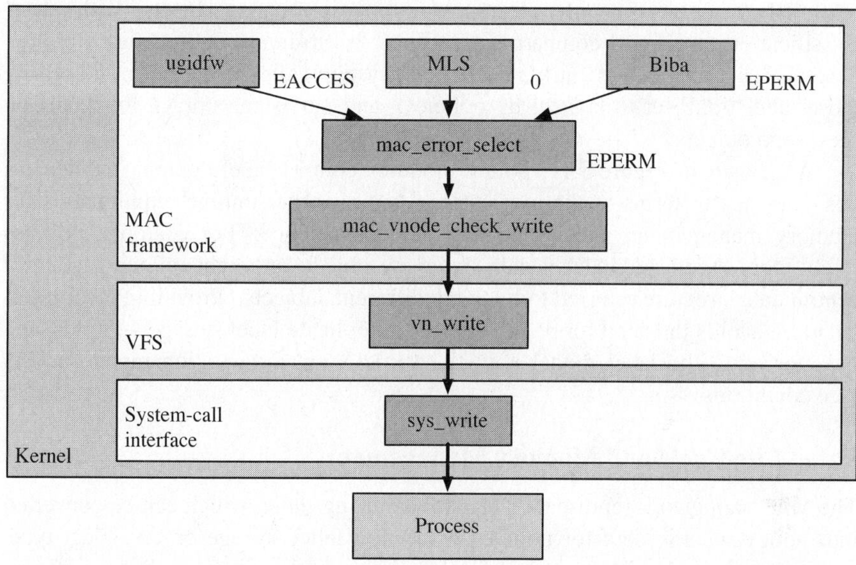

Figure 5.10 MAC policy results are combined using an explicit composition meta-policy.

fragment reassembly; for example, all interested policies must accept a fragment for it to be matched with a reassembly queue.

- *MAC_POLICY_GRANT*(), added in FreeBSD 7, is used in allowing policies to grant privileges. In contrast to *MAC_POLICY_CHECK*(), its composition function returns success if any interested policy returns 0.

Some MAC framework operations invoke more than one entry point. For example, a label-set system call will need to allocate and initialize temporary label storage for the object type, copy in and internalize the userspace version of the label, perform an access control check, set the label, and free the temporary storage, each of which requires a separate policy entry-point invocation. This sequence supports one of the more interesting aspects of policy composition: a two-phase commit on relabelling operations. This approach allows one policy to provide access-control logic limiting the setting of labels associated with another policy on an object; for example, the Biba policy can prevent MLS labels from being set on a high-integrity object by a low-integrity subject.

Object Labelling

Several access-control policies of interest require additional policy-specific metadata associated with subjects (process credentials), and often some or all objects (files, pipes, network interfaces, etc.). This metadata is referred to as a label, and provides subject- or object-specific information required to make access-control decisions. For example, Biba labels subjects and objects with integrity levels, and

MLS labels subjects with clearance information and objects with data-classification levels and compartments. The MAC framework provides a policy-agnostic label abstraction for kernel objects, system calls for querying and setting those labels (subject to control by policies), and persistent storage for labels on filesystem objects.

As shown in Figure 5.11, policy modules control label content and semantics—not just in terms of the bytes stored, but also the runtime requirements for memory management, synchronization, and persistence. For example, policies might store independent label data for every object, or might reference-count a central data structure referred to by many different subjects. Providing label infrastructure avoids the need for policy authors to replicate label storage facilities, and by integrating the label model with the kernel's synchronization model, avoids race conditions.

Label Life Cycle and Memory Management

The MAC framework represents label storage using *label*, which can be converted into policy-specific data for policies requesting label storage on an object type. In-memory kernel data structures for labelled kernel objects, including process credentials, virtual filesystem nodes, and IPC objects, are extended to hold references to labels, which are managed by the MAC framework. Table 5.15 enumerates the kernel data structures that have label storage; for some types, such as

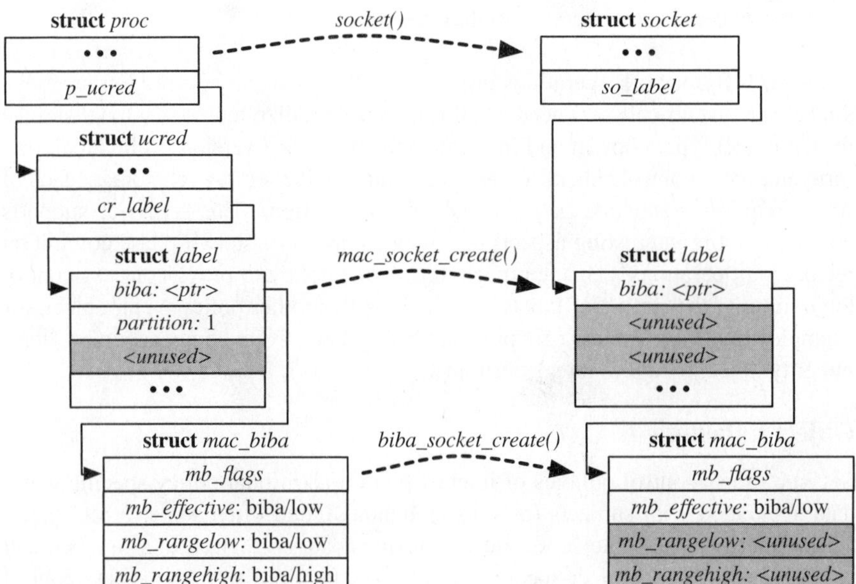

Figure 5.11 Policies impose semantics on the MAC framework's opaque label facility.

Table 5.15 Kernel object types supporting MAC labels.

Structure	Description
struct bpf_d	BPF packet sniffing device
struct devfs_dirent	devfs entry
struct ifnet	network interface
struct inpcb	IPv4/6 connection block
struct ip6q	IPv6 fragment queue
struct ipq	IPv4 fragment queue
struct ksem	POSIX semaphore
struct mbuf	in-flight packet
struct mount	filesystem mount
struct msg	System V message
struct msq	System V message queue
struct pipepair	IPC pipe
struct proc	process
struct semid_kernel	System V semaphore
struct shmfd	POSIX shared memory
struct shmid_kernel	System V shared memory
struct socket	BSD IPC socket
struct syncache	TCP syncache entry
struct ucred	process credential, represents subject
struct vnode	VFS node: files, directories, etc.

vnode, a label pointer is added to the data structure itself, referencing label storage allocated and managed by the framework; where kernel data structures already support a metadata scheme, such as *mbuf* tags, that facility holds the label data.

The *label* structure is opaque to both kernel subsystems and MAC policies; the former invoke kernel-service entry points to manage the field, and the latter employ two accessor functions, *mac_label_get*() and *mac_label_set*() to retrieve and set policy-specific opaque values of type *uintptr_t*, which is large enough to hold a pointer or an integer. Internally, the MAC framework implements *label* as an array of *uintptr_t* indexed by a per-policy slot number allocated on policy load if requested by the policy. However, that mechanism may be changed in the future.

As of FreeBSD 8, labels are allocated only when a policy specifically registers an initialization entry-point function for that object's label. As a result, policies loaded after boot may find that label structures are not present for objects instantiated before the policy was loaded, and must be able to handle that case. Alternatively, policies can be marked as unloadable after boot.

In the FreeBSD kernel, data-structure allocation occurs in a number of forms; most frequently, the slab allocator is used (described in Section 6.3), which caches partially initialized instances of objects to avoid complete reinitialization on each reuse. In other cases, the kernel's *malloc*() allocator is used, in which case full object reinitialization occurs on each allocation. In rare cases, a subsystem manages its own memory cache in more complex ways, such as the *vnode* cache, that leaves structures fully initialized and available for continued use until the memory is reclaimed because of pressure from the pageout daemon. The memory model for each labelled object is reflected in MAC framework and policy entry points, requiring variation in the handling of labels across object types.

Differing dispositions with respect to waiting for memory allocation under pressure are also propagated to MAC framework label allocation in the form of arguments, indicating whether sleeping is permitted, that are also exposed to policy entry points; failing to allocate a label will also lead to object allocation failure. Contexts that prevent sleeping include interrupt threads and kernel threads holding nonsleepable locks; in both of these scenarios, allowing unconditional (and therefore potentially sleeping) memory allocations could lead to deadlock; thus, allocations must be allowed to fail, with effects on the complexity of calling code, which must be able to handle that failure.

Kernel object allocation is significantly more complex than simply allocating memory: once memory is available, its fields must be initialized, including locks, and it must be hooked up to namespaces, etc. Similarly, label allocation is notionally separate from object creation and object association, the two mechanisms by which MAC policies may initialize their own label state in a given security context.

Object creation occurs when an API to create a new object is invoked: for example, a call to *open* may create a new file, *socket* a new socket, and *pipe* a new pipe. In these scenarios, the security properties of the new object (including any policy-specific MAC label data) will be initialized from sources such as the creating process's credential or the security properties of a parent object (such as a parent directory).

Object association occurs when the kernel associates an instance of a kernel data structure with an existing underlying object in persistent storage, for which the kernel data structure is simply a cache. For example, a specific file will have a *vnode* allocated for it only after it is pulled into the in-memory working set of the filesystem, and may be detached from the *vnode* if it falls out of the working set and the *vnode* must be reused for another file. In that scenario, label association occurs at the point where the *vnode* is associated with the on-disk file, at which point MAC policies are given the opportunity to set up policy-specific label states, perhaps derived from the mount point from which the file is being loaded, or from extended attributes from the on-disk file. Both the source of file label data and its interpretation are policy specific, but the MAC framework provides the necessary entry points to interpret and propagate label data as required. For kernel services such as the filesystem, creation and association operations implemented by policy modules are permitted to fail, in turn propagating failure back to the kernel service. This design prevents creation of a file if, for example, storage for its security label cannot be allocated in the filesystem.

Object destruction, which may represent the destruction of an actual object (such as a process exiting), or simply the recycling of in-memory storage for some persisting object (such as a file falling out of the vnode cache), also triggers the destruction of the object's label. The MAC framework is given the opportunity to release storage for the label, permitting policies to free any allocated storage or references associated with that label.

Label Synchronization

Where supported by the semantics of kernel locking, the MAC framework allows policy modules to borrow existing kernel locks on labelled objects. This design offers not only the benefit of improved performance by reducing the number of locks and locking operations, but also allows label access to be synchronized with object access, avoiding time-of-check-to-time-of-use races. Locking protocols are documented for each policy entry point, and enforced by locking assertions in debugging versions of the kernel, allowing policy developers to rely on synchronization properties.

In some cases, these semantics are insufficient for policy requirements: for example, if a policy shares mutable label data between multiple objects (such as a reference-counted sandbox descriptor), then additional synchronization may be required to protect policy data. Similar concerns may arise where read-write locking is used on an object, and a policy needs to mutate the label (taint tracking in LOMAC, for example) while only a read lock is held by the framework; here, the policy must provide supplemental locking to ensure mutual exclusion on label data.

Another interesting case is the process credential, which itself is a reference-counted, read-only object—an important performance optimization that reduces the memory overhead of credential data, and also allows for lock-free and thread-local use of credentials in almost all access-control scenarios. When the kernel needs to modify credentials, it will do a copy-on-write, allocating a new credential, copying old data, and modifying required fields; however, this design means that much of the time, credential data is shared among not just threads, but also processes. Performing credential copy-on-write cannot be done in arbitrary contexts because of memory allocation constraints and lock order, so the LOMAC policy uses an additional process label, protected by its own locks, to tag processes for taint propagation asynchronously on the next system-call return. However, existing object locking usually is able to protect label data for objects. The **mac_test** module validates that framework expectations for locking and label life cycles in entry points are maintained. Detailed coverage of specific object behavior can be found in Watson [2012].

Policy-Agnostic Label Management from Userspace

The MAC framework supports label manipulation by two classes of applications: those aware of MAC but unaware of specific policies, and those intended to manage the labels of specific MAC policies.

Policy-agnostic but MAC-aware applications, including traditional UNIX monitoring tools such as **/bin/ps**, **/bin/ls**, and **/sbin/ifconfig**, have been extended to display subject and object label information. New commands, such as **/bin/getfmac** and **/bin/setfmac**, have been added to set the MAC labels on system objects such as files. The system login process has also been extended to set labels on process credentials based on user classes defined in **/etc/login.conf**. These programs all treat labels in an abstract, policy-agnostic manner. The userland framework relies on a configuration file, **/etc/mac.conf**, to determine administrator-defined defaults for labels to query and list on files, interfaces, and processes.

Policy-specific applications are aware of the semantics of specific security policies, and if applicable, the security labels they place on objects. Depending on the nature of the the application, developers may choose to use the policy-agnostic interfaces provided by the MAC framework, or new policy-specific interfaces exported specifically by the policy. For example, applications that are aware of the semantics of MLS labels may perform labelling operations involving only MLS label elements via policy-agnostic labelling interfaces. On the other hand, the **ugidfw** policy module exports a rule list via the kernel *sysctl* management interface.

To implement these functions, the kernel provides new system calls and socket options to support querying and setting labels in a policy-agnostic format, including *mac_get_file*, *mac_get_fd*, *mac_set_file*, and *mac_set_fd*, that get and set labels on files and file descriptors. Applications handle MAC labels via the opaque *mac_t* type, which is implemented as a string buffer internally.

Labels manipulated by applications are multipart, consisting of a series of name and value pairs, allowing label components from different policies to be manipulated simultaneously (and with mutual atomicity) up and down the software stack. Applications can convert labels to and from an explicit text format for printing and user input; however, label parsing is generally left up to the kernel, a design trade-off that appears acceptable, but motivated an expansion of safe string-handling routines in the kernel. The string "biba/low,mls/10," for example, describes a label that consists of two elements: a low-integrity Biba label, and an MLS label of sensitivity 10. Applications may address all of the elements available on an object or any subset. In earlier MAC framework designs, we intended to allow the userspace framework for labels to be run-time extended using plug-in modules, as is the case for the kernel, but this design was abandoned in favor of a simpler approach.

5.11 Security Event Auditing

Security event auditing, often referred to simply as audit, is the secure, reliable, fine-grained, and configurable logging of security-relevant system events. Events of potential interest include security-related user authentication and authorization activities, as well as administrative events that affect system security, such as network interface reconfiguration or rebooting. Historically, OS vendors have provided audit facilities to support forensic analysis following compromise; however,

FreeBSD's audit system has been designed more broadly to also allow live intrusion detection and general-purpose system monitoring. For the purposes of this section, we are concerned primarily with the kernel portions of the audit implementation and their effect on general kernel design.

The FreeBSD event-auditing system was developed jointly by Apple and the FreeBSD Project during Common Criteria certification of Mac OS X, targeting the Common Access Protection Profile (CAPP). FreeBSD userspace audit libraries and tools are loosely compatible with Sun's Basic Security Module (BSM) APIs, and are separately distributed as OpenBSM. Its BSM-compatible APIs and file format have been significantly extended to support operating-system portability and operating-system features not present in Solaris—e.g., Capsicum in FreeBSD and catalogue operations in Mac OS X; it has also made byte-order independent. The FreeBSD and Mac OS X kernel audit implementations are also derived from the OpenBSM code base [Watson & Salamon, 2006].

Audit Events and Records

Auditable events are those that the audit system is able to log, which include kernel-centered activity (e.g., filesystem and network accesses) and user-level events (e.g., authentication). CAPP requires that the set of auditable events in an operating system include any exercise of the system's access-control policies, authentication, security management, and audit management. The kernel audit framework is primarily focused on capturing events originating in system calls, which reflect the actions of subjects (processes) on controlled kernel objects. User processes, such as **login** and **su**, may also submit audit records describing user-level events using the *audit* system call. The act of submitting an audit record via *audit* is also an auditable event that may need to be logged.

Each audited security event is described by an audit record that contains information on the subject responsible for the event (e.g., the process, user, and where they were logged in from), any objects affected by the event (e.g., files), and event-specific data (e.g., the new mode set on a file by *chmod*). Records are stored sequentially to files, referred to as audit trails. Auditing is subject to an audit pre-selection policy that specifies the subset of auditable events that will actually be logged—without this feature, even casual system usage would generate vast quantities of log data, filling disks rapidly, and severely impact performance. Audit trails can also be reduced, or filtered post-capture, to remove generated records that may be of less interest over time. For example, administrators might have a policy of keeping detailed file-access logs for 1 month, but login information for 12 months. Here, the **auditreduce** command thins the longs incrementally.

CAPP also describes attributable events, which may be traced back to an authenticated user—for example, a file access by a logged-in user, and nonattributable events that occur as part of system operation—for example, the starting of a security-relevant daemon during system boot. The idea of attribution required adding a new audit UID (AUID) in the process credential, illustrated in

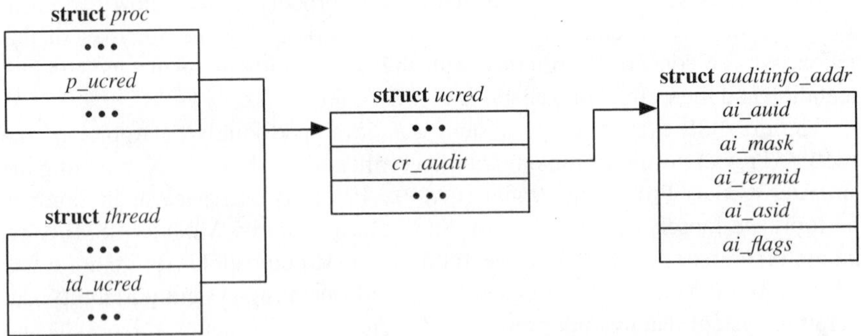

Figure 5.12 Audit-related additions to the process credential.

Figure 5.12. The AUID tracks the authenticated user who initiated an event, regardless of any UID changes that may have occurred as a result of executing setuid binaries. The process credential has also been extended to include the audit terminal and audit session that will be tagged onto each audit record generated for the process, and the audit mask, which together with global-audit configuration, will control which events will be audited for the process.

BSM Audit Records and Audit Trails

BSM audit trails are binary files made up of a sequence of machine-readable tokens, as illustrated in Figure 5.13. Tokens have a type, captured by its token

Figure 5.13 Records consist of tokens holding state, arguments, and return values.

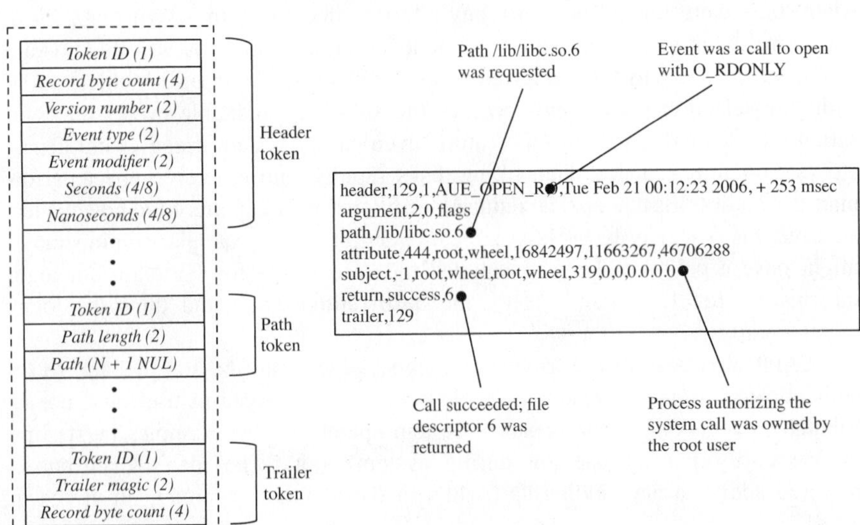

ID, and a value, whose parsing is type-specific; omission of a length field from most token types makes unrecognized tokens unparseable—arguably a weakness to the design, but one that saves considerable space. Records begin with one of several possible header tokens that will include the total length of the record, a timestamp, and an event type indicating what the record describes—for example, whether it is a *open* system call or event submitted by **login**. The header is followed by a series of data tokens holding credential information, arguments and return values for the event, and at the end, a trailer token terminating the record. In addition to record-oriented tokens, audit trail files also begin and end with stand-alone file tokens that contain start and stop timestamps.

While the FreeBSD kernel generates BSM directly, internal data structures used for the majority of in-kernel processing are not BSM-specific, so they could be easily replaced to add support for a new file format. However, records submitted by userspace via the *audit* system call also contain BSM.

Kernel-Audit Implementation

Key components of the kernel-audit implementation are illustrated in Figure 5.14 and include the following:

- System calls to set the global-audit configuration, including global pre-select parameters for unattributed events and trail rotation; this global-audit configuration is mostly used by **auditd**

Figure 5.14 The audit daemon and login process configure audit state for user processes.

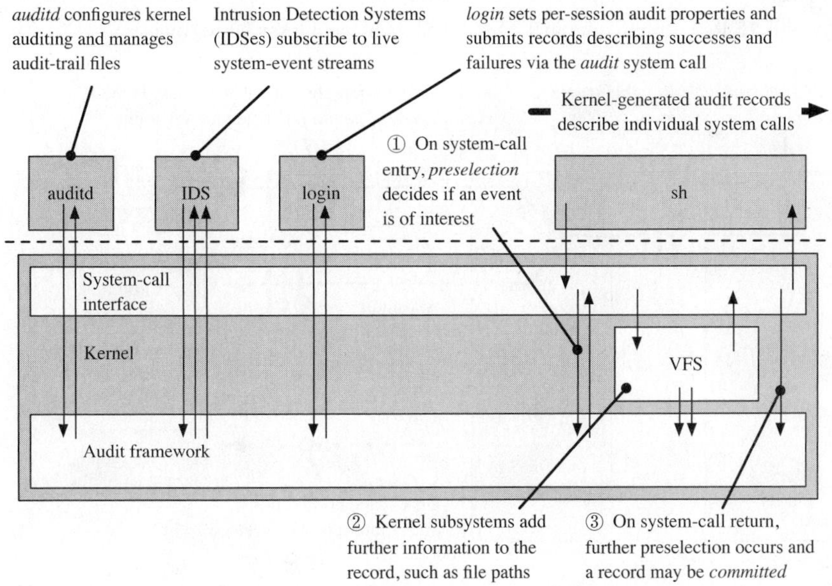

- Extensions to the process credential to hold the AUID and audit masks, managed with new system calls used by programs such as **login** and **sshd**
- System-call entry code that performs initial pre-selection and optionally allocates an audit record for the thread
- System-call instrumentation that captures arguments to the event, such as file paths or UIDs
- System-call return code that performs further pre-selection, once the system call return value is known, and commits the record to the global-audit queue
- The audit worker thread, responsible for managing delivery of records to the active audit trail and audit pipes; it also processes audit-trail rotation requests synchronously
- Audit pipe code responsible for further pipe-specific filtering that instruments both system call entry and return *ioctl*s to configure filtering

Mandatory monitoring and high reliability are both key requirements for the audit system: if an event is configured to be audited, then either the event occurs and is audited, or it must not be allowed to occur. Nonbypassability is implemented by performing auditing in the TCB; that is, the kernel and trustworthy user processes; access to the audit trail is strictly controlled to ensure integrity and confidentiality. Reliability, however, has a host of further implications, including the need to track remaining disk storage carefully to ensure that records for in-progress events can be stored. These requirements are quite different from those implemented by the system log daemon, **syslogd**, that is intended for public log

Figure 5.15 Records pass through a series of reliable and lossy kernel queues.

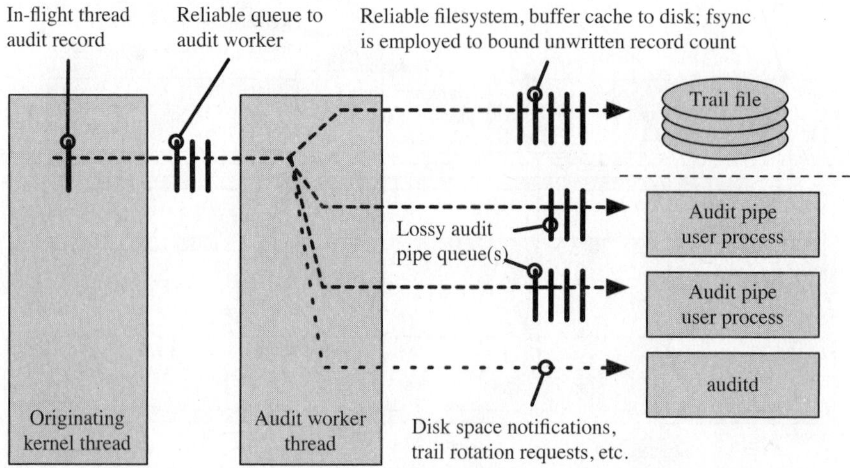

data, submittable by any user, and which will drop records rather than affect system availability when they are submitted too quickly or fill the disk.

Figure 5.15 illustrates the arrangement of queues in the system, each with different size and reliability properties. Individual threads may carry up to two audit records describing in-progress activities: an active kernel audit record, and an optional user-audit record submitted via *audit*. On system-call return, audit records are submitted to the global queue that is both reliable and bounded in length to prevent outstripping of available disk space. Once the audit worker thread has removed a record from the global queue, it will convert the record to BSM and optionally deliver it to the global-audit trail, based on global and per-process configuration, and to any open audit pipes, subject to either global configuration or per-pipe configuration, depending on how the pipe has been configured.

Figure 5.16 illustrates the data structures involved: the *thread* structure points at the current *kaudit_record*, if any, for the in-flight system call. This structure describes both a kernel-originated record, whose fields are stored in *audit_record*, with a bitmask showing which fields have been set so that they can be converted to tokens, and *k_udata*, that points at the BSM record as submitted from userspace. The global *audit_queue* is simply a linked list of outstanding records, along with metadata on queue limits and length.

Figure 5.16 Per-thread in-flight audit record and global-audit record queue.

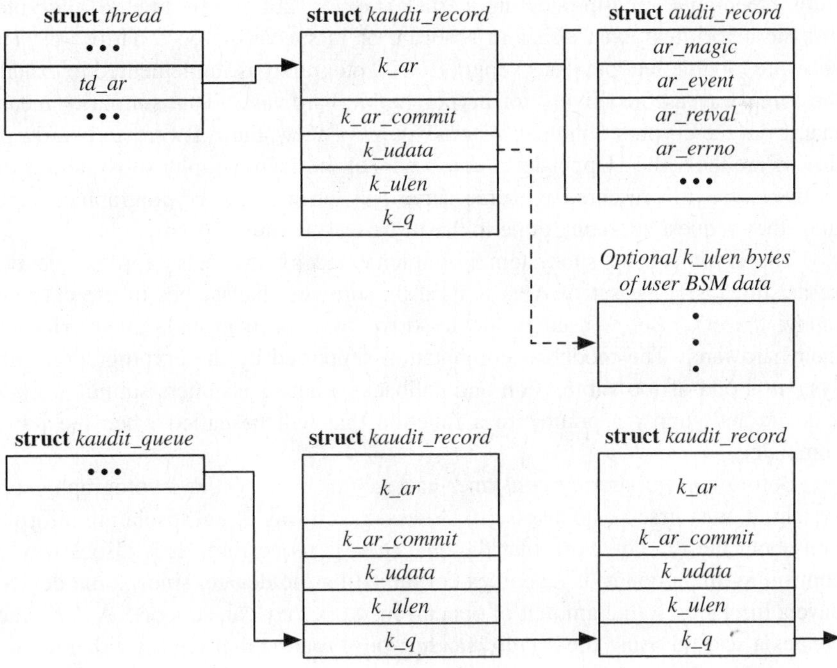

5.12 Cryptographic Services

The FreeBSD kernel integrates several low-level cryptographic services, including a framework supporting software and hardware implementations of common encryption and cryptographic hash functions, and a Yarrow-based cryptographic pseudo-random number generator. Higher-level services, such as full-disk encryption (GBDE and GEOM), the GSSAPI implementation used for NFS, and IPSec, depend integrally on these low-level cryptographic services to provide local and distributed security. Random numbers support many other kernel services, some with significant security implications; the kernel is well-placed to collect entropy inputs to pseudo-random number generation. Cryptographic and random-number generation services are also made available to userspace via **/dev/crypto**, **/dev/random**, and the *kern.arandom sysctl*.

Cryptographic Framework

Underlying cryptographic services such as GELI and IPSec is a set of APIs and libraries that support cryptography. The cryptographic subsystem in FreeBSD supports both symmetric and asymmetric cryptography. Symmetric cryptography, used by IPSec, uses the same key to encrypt data as it does to decrypt it. Asymmetric cryptography, which implements public-key encryption, uses one key to encrypt data and another key to decrypt it. This section describes how symmetric cryptography is implemented as it relates to a specific client, IPSec.

The cryptographic subsystem was ported from OpenBSD and optimized for a fully preemptive multiprocessing kernel [Leffler, 2003]. In FreeBSD, cryptographic algorithms exist either in software or in special-purpose hardware. The software module that provides support for cryptography is implemented in exactly the same way as the drivers for cryptographic hardware. This similarity means that, from the cryptography subsystem's point of view, the software and hardware drivers are the same. Upper-level consumers of the cryptography subsystem, such as IPSec, are all presented with the same API whether the cryptographic operations they request are being done in hardware or software.

The cryptography subsystem is implemented by two sets of APIs and two kernel threads. One set of APIs is used by software that wishes to use cryptography; the other set is used by device-driver writers to provide an interface to their hardware. The model of computation supported by the cryptographic subsystem is one of job submission and callbacks where consumers submit work to a queue and supply a pointer to a function that will be called when the job is completed.

Before a cryptography consumer can submit work to the cryptography subsystem, it must first create a session. A session is a way of encapsulating information about the type of work that the consumer is requesting. It is also a way of controlling the amount of resources consumed on the device, since some devices have a limitation to the amount of concurrent work they can support. A consumer creates a session using the *crypto_newsession*() routine that returns either a valid session identifier or an error.

crp_sid
crp_ilen
crp_olen
crp_etype
crp_flags
crp_buf
crp_opaque
crp_desc
crp_callback

struct *cryptop*

Figure 5.17 Cryptographic descriptor.

Once the consumer has a proper session identifier, it then requests a cryptographic descriptor, shown in Figure 5.17. The consumer fills in the fields of the cryptographic descriptor, including supplying an appropriate callback in the *crp_callback* element. When the descriptor is ready, it is handed to the cryptographic subsystem via the *crypto_dispatch*() routine that puts it on a queue to be processed. When the work is complete, the callback is invoked. All callbacks have this form:

```
int (*crp_callback)(
    struct cryptop *arg);
```

If an error has occurred, the error code is contained in the *crp_etype* field of the cryptographic descriptor that is passed to the callback.

A set of device drivers provides the low-level interface to specialized cryptographic hardware. Each driver provides three function pointers to the cryptographic subsystem when it registers itself. Driver registration is done via a call to the *crypto_register*() routine.

```
crypto_register(
    u_int32_t driverid,
    int alg,
    u_int16_t maxoplen,
    u_int32_t flags,
    int (*newsession)(void*, u_int32_t*, struct cryptoini*),
    int (*freesession)(void*, u_int64_t),
    int (*process)(void*, struct cryptop *, int),
    void *arg);
```

The *newsession*() or *freesession*() routines are called by the cryptographic subsystem whenever the *crypto_newsession*() or *crypto_freesession*() routines are called by a consumer. The *process*() routine is called by the *crypto_proc*() kernel thread to pass operations into the device.

The lower half of the cryptographic subsystem uses two software interrupt threads and two queues to control the underlying hardware. Whenever there are requests on the *crp_q* queue, the *crypto_proc*() thread dequeues them and sends them to the underlying device, using the *crypto_invoke*() routine. Once invoked, the underlying hardware has the responsibility to handle the request. The only requirement is that when the hardware has completed its work, the device driver associated with the hardware must invoke *crypto_done*() that either enqueues the callback on the *crp_ret_q* queue or, more rarely, directly calls the consumer's callback. The *crp_ret_q* queue is provided because the *crypto_done*() routine often will be called from an interrupt context, and running the consumer's callback with interrupts locked out will degrade the interactive performance of the system. When running in an interrupt context, the callback will be queued and then handled later by the *crypto_ret_proc* software interrupt thread. This use of queues and software interrupt threads effectively decouples the kernel from any possible performance issues introduced by a variety of cryptographic hardware.

Unfortunately, there are several problems with the system just described:

- Using multiple threads requires two context switches per cryptographic operation. The context switches are nontrivial and severely degrade throughput.
- Some callback routines do little work, and so moving all callbacks out of the device driver's interrupt-service routine adds another context switch that is expensive and unnecessary.
- The dispatch queue batches operations, but many consumers of the cryptographic subsystem, including IPSec, do not batch operations, so this shunting of work into the dispatch queue is unnecessary overhead.

To address these performance problems, several changes were made to the cryptographic subsystem. Cryptographic drivers are now supplied a hint if there is more work to follow when work is submitted to them. The drivers can decide whether to batch work based on this hint and, where requests are not batched, completely bypass the *crp_q* queue. Cryptographic requests whose callback routines are short mark their requests so that the underlying device executes them directly instead of queueing them on the *crypto_ret_q* queue. The optimization of bypassing the *crypto_req_q* queue is especially useful to consumers of the **/dev/crypto** device, whose callback routine awakens only the thread that wrote to it. All these optimizations are described more fully in Leffler [2003].

Random-Number Generator

Random (or unpredictable) numbers are relied on throughout the FreeBSD kernel and userspace. For example, some network protocols use randomly generated identifiers rather than globally managed identifiers to benefit from unique names for hosts and users (e.g., UUIDs) while avoiding the cost of global registries.

Strong random numbers—those unpredictable to even a motivated adversary—are of particular importance to security and robustness. They generate:

- PIDs, and stack canaries, used for exploit mitigation;
- IP IDs, TCP initial sequence numbers (ISN), and the key for TCP SYN cookies (described in Section 14.3);
- authentication and encryption keys and initialization vectors (IV)s used in network protocols: kernel includes IPSec, and SCTP; userspace includes TLS, **ssh**, Kerberos, and GSSAPI;
- authentication and encryption keys, IVs used for GELI and GBDE;
- initial UFS inode generation numbers for NFS file handles;
- salt for cryptographic hashes used in the system password database; and
- keys, IVs, and nonces for third-party applications such as pretty-good privacy (PGP) e-mail encryption.

Computers are by design highly deterministic, making unpredictable numbers hard to acquire in the volumes that may be required by software. Even when in-hardware random-number generators are present, there are open questions about their effectiveness as they can suffer biases and supply-chain attacks that are difficult to identify or mitigate. Software developers therefore rely on pseudo-random number generators (PRNGs) to generate sequences of numbers that, given a smaller secret key (or seed) as an initial input, will prove effectively unpredictable to attackers. Seeds are generated by collecting entropy from around the system to which attackers will not have access: explicit hardware entropy sources, the layout and probe time of hardware busses and peripherals present in the system, unique serial numbers, and unpredictable timings from the system—e.g., interpacket and interrupt arrival times.

While the kernel is well-placed to collect entropy, generating and protecting seeds are technically challenging: weak or improperly protected seeds may allow attackers to reduce the search space for keys (or even completely reconstruct past pseudo-random sequences). Given adequate processing and a strong cryptographic number generator, however, not all inputs to the seed need be unpredictable, so systems can safely include sources that might be accessible to some attackers. For example, interpacket arrival times contribute usefully to the seed even if some adversaries might be able to sniff the same wireless network.

Entropy is fed into the in-kernel random-number generator, which provides a stream of pseudo-random bytes for in-kernel use. Entropy is exported to userspace via **/dev/random** and the *kern.arandom sysctl*. Sometimes the generator provides the random data directly—for example, *read* system calls on **/dev/random**. In other cases, differing security and performance trade-offs allow use of a cheaper generator seeded from the strong generator; for example, the *arc4random*() interface used in the network stack, and the *kern.arandom sysctl* used for stack-canary initialization by the C runtime.

A key concern in random-number generator designs is perfect forward secrecy (PFS), which guarantees that information about random numbers produced at a later time cannot attack random numbers generated earlier in the sequence. For example, PFS prevents adversaries that may gain access to a system following a theft (or via export of random numbers) from gaining an advantage in breaking keys that protect on-disk storage or communications with another party the previous day. PFS is done through intermittently reseeding the generator with new entropy; the reseeding interval controls the window over which an attacker who has compromised the system can derive information about earlier random sequences. Some care must be taken, however: if entropy is mixed into the generator too frequently, then an attacker may be able to gain information about the entropy source by inspecting generator output over time.

To address these concerns, FreeBSD employs the Yarrow cryptographic pseudo-random number generator to generate sequences of random numbers for use throughout the system [Kelsey et al., 1999; Murray, 2002]. Yarrow itself has four major components: an entropy accumulator that gathers entropy samples in one of two pools using a cryptographic hash; a reseed mechanism that, at routine intervals, reseeds the generator key; a generation mechanism that generates a pseudo-random sequence from the key; and reseed control that determines at what interval reseeding from fresh entropy should occur. These structures are directly reflected in the software implementation.

An important design choice in Yarrow is using existing strong cryptographic primitives, such as triply-DES and SHA-1 in the design, which comes at significant performance cost, but avoids use of custom cryptographic primitives that have seen less cryptanalysis. The FreeBSD implementation supports multiple cryptographic hashes and encryption algorithms, an extension to the original design; by default, AES and SHA-256 are used—both defined after Yarrow was published.

FreeBSD is able to collect entropy samples, which include both a timestamp and context-dependent data (e.g., packet headers). Configurable entropy sources include:

- low-level hardware interrupt processing,
- scheduling of a hardware interrupt to a thread,
- scheduling of a software interrupt (SWIs) to a thread,
- packet headers injected via Ethernet interfaces,
- packet headers injected via point-to-point interfaces,
- attach times during boot-time hardware enumeration,
- keyboard and mouse input,
- hardware random-number sources, such as Intel's `rdrand` instruction, and
- entropy preserved in a file across reboot.

Entropy gathering occurs throughout the kernel. Individual sources will check whether they are enabled before invoking *random_harvest*(). A timestamp is collected, typically via the high-precision cycle counter available in most contemporary CPU designs. However, some older architectures may not support the cycle counter, in which case a slower real-time clock will be used. Sources also pass a pointer to optional data, its length, an estimated number of bits of entropy in the sample, and the entropy source type.

The function *random_harvestq_internal*() enqueues entropy samples to a global linked list, with further processing deferred to a dedicated kernel thread to avoid performing computationally intensive hashes in performance-sensitive contexts such as interrupt handling. If the queue is full, then the sample is discarded to bound memory use. *random_kthread*() wakes up 10 times a second to drain the pending queue of samples and inject them into Yarrow via *random_process_event*(). *random_kthread*() also samples high-volume dedicated hardware entropy sources such as `rdrand` at the same interval by invoking *live_entropy_sources_feed*(). This sampling interval, combined with limits on linked-list size, bounds the total amount of entropy that can be collected each second, and therefore limits the amount of CPU capacity that will be spent on computationally expensive hashing.

As entropy events arrive in Yarrow, they are alternately injected into either the slow pool or the fast pool, which each consist of an instance of the selected cryptographic hash function. The maximum entropy that a pool can store is limited by the width of the hash: 160 bits for SHA-1 and 256 bits for SHA-256 The complete sample, including data and timestamp, is passed to the hash, and the entropy estimate provided by the caller updates the per-source running estimate. The fast pool will reseed Yarrow when any one source has contributed at least 100 bits of accumulated entropy. The slow pool will reseed Yarrow when any two sources have both contributed at least 160 bits of accumulated entropy. Yarrow's authors call for the use of statistical tests to help measure entropy gathered from sources. However, devising valid statistical tests has proven to be tricky and they are the most criticized aspect of the algorithm. FreeBSD relies solely on a programmer estimate of entropy in each sample.

This approach spreads entropy from different sources over time to prevent a particularly fast, low-quality (or even compromised) source of entropy from diluting the pool—while still allowing strong fast-moving sources to reseed frequently. When a reseed occurs, the contents of the fast-pool hash are always included; slow-pool contents are only included when a slow reseed is triggered. The cryptographic hash is applied multiple times to ensure that if hash context and key size differ, then all bits of stored entropy are evenly distributed over all bits of keying material.

Yarrow's generator runs only when randomness is required, as opposed to entropy accumulation, which runs whenever entropy samples are available. Thus, generator cost is proportional to randomness consumed, whereas accumulator cost is proportional to entropy sampled, and there is greater tolerance for the performance overhead of a contemporary encryption algorithm versus a cheaper cryptographic hash. Yarrow's seed is not used directly as a key; instead, it is used by *generator_gate*() to generate a short-lived current key. This approach prevents the same encryption key from being used too many times, which might otherwise allow output cycles to arise in the PRNG. Key generation feeds output bits from the PRNG back in as keying material; as it does not introduce any new entropy, it does not constitute reseeding. By default, the key will be regenerated every 10 output blocks.

When a *read* system call occurs on **/dev/random**, Yarrow is queried to determined whether it has been seeded; if not, it will block. If it has been seeded, then it is invoked to do counter-mode encryption using the current key. While some systems differentiate **random** and **urandom** devices, offering blocking and non-blocking entropy sources, FreeBSD simply provides the output of Yarrow directly to both device nodes, so once unblocked by seeding, Yarrow will provide unlimited randomness on either device.

The **/dev/random** framework offers significant pluggability and flexibility, allowing both new entropy sources and new cryptographic PRNGs to be introduced. In the current implementation, FreeBSD passes all entropy sources through Yarrow, but can be configured to allow direct use of hardware randomness sources if desired. Direct use of hardware randomness may be suitable on low-end embedded devices where cryptographic schemes are particularly expensive, or where a high level of trust can be placed in hardware sources. The authors of Yarrow have since published a new scheme, Fortuna, that may in the long term replace Yarrow in FreeBSD; the framework should allow both implementations to live side by side, with compile-time or run-time selection. Another potential future direction would be to replicate PRNG instances across CPUs, rather than using a single instance that requires communication between processors.

5.13 GELI Full-Disk Encryption

GELI is a GEOM class that offers cryptographic privacy and integrity protection for storage devices that might be lost or stolen. Its primary concern is ensuring that, once a shutdown has occurred, confidential data cannot be recovered from the disk without access to suitable cryptographic keys or passphrases. A secondary concern is detecting corruption of on-disk data if the device is recovered.

Confidentiality and Integrity Protection

Confidentiality is ensured by applying symmetric encryption to each sector before it is written to the disk, and decryption when the sector is read back in. While a provider is active (e.g., while the filesystem is mounted), its encryption keys are held in memory; when the provider is detached, or on system shutdown, keying material is discarded. GELI can also be configured to discard keying material when a system is suspended, requiring that it be present when the notebook is resumed to load further data from disk. Encryption occurs at measurable computational cost, but requires only one additional sector of metadata storage (at the end of the device) to support any number of data sectors. The default (and recommended) encryption algorithm is the advanced-encryption standard (AES) AES-XTS, an AES-derived block cipher designed for use with storage devices.

Optional integrity protection is done by calculating keyed cryptographic hashes for disk sectors on write; sector hashes are validated on each read from disk. Sector-level verification failures are coerced into read failures that must be handled by the filesystem or application. Integrity checking comes with additional computational costs, but also requires that hash values be stored for each on-disk sector. The hash cannot be stored within a 512-byte sector while maintaining filesystem sector-size expectations; to mitigate this overhead, GELI coalesces multiple 512-byte sectors into 4-Kbyte sectors with one hash in each underlying disk sector, resulting in about an 11 percent storage overhead. The recommended cryptographic hash is HMAC SHA-256; integrity protection is disabled by default. GELI makes use of the kernel cryptographic framework, and is therefore able to use offloaded or CPU-accelerated cryptography, substantially improving performance.

Key Management

Each GELI partition is protected by two underlying cryptographic keys: a data-encryption key and an initialization-vector key that collectively make up the GELI per-provider master key. Separate per-block keys for data encryption, initialization vectors (IVs), and integrity checking are generated from the master key using cryptographic hashes rather than using the master key directly. This approach avoids reusing the same keys for multiple purposes (e.g., confidentiality and authentication), a practice heavily discouraged in contemporary cryptography.

Master keys are stored encrypted on the disk and must be decrypted before the provider can be attached. Typical use decrypts the master key using one or both of a passphrase entered on the console ("something you know") and a keyfile stored on a removable USB device ("something you have"). Up to two copies of the master keying material, encrypted using different passphrases or keyfiles, may be stored in on-disk metadata. This approach allows, for example, the daily user of a corporate notebook to specify one passphrase and key, but the employer to retain its own recovery passphrase or key in a vault to be used if the user passphrase is forgotten or USB stick is lost. GELI can also operate with randomly generated keys for swap partitions, entirely preventing data persistence across reboot.

Protecting the master key on-disk is critical to the security of GELI. Instances of the master are protected on disk with a derived key generated by passing a concatenation of the on-disk keyfile, on-disk salt, and user passphrase (optionally strengthened using PKCS#5v2) through unkeyed HMAC SHA-512. The master-key encryption key is generated by running HMAC SHA-512 over the string "\x01" keyed with the derived key. The same encryption algorithm and key length are used for the master key as are configured for block storage. The decrypted master key is validated by passing the derived key into HMAC SHA-512 over the string

"\x00" and comparing it with the decrypted verification hash. The comparison will fail if the passphrase or keyfile do not match on-disk storage.

Once decrypted, the master keys are stored in memory for the lifetime of the provider. The implementation is careful to zero memory that holds keys once they are no longer required. Zeroing memory is especially important for the passphrase and keyfile, which are not used after the GELI instance has attached.

Starting GELI

GELI providers are attached automatically at system boot, or explicitly at runtime using the **/sbin/geli** command. During boot, suitably configured instances will be discovered using GELI's taste method, *g_eli_taste*(), which will be called as GEOM itself discovers new devices and partitions. After boot, the *ioctl* system call is used by **/sbin/geli** to trigger GELI's config method, *g_eli_config*(), which will configure a new GELI provider for a device or partition.

Only GELI instances marked as G_ELI_FLAG_BOOT will be automatically started; required key files must have been preloaded by the boot loader, and GELI may need to suspend the boot before root-filesystem mount to interactively requested a user passphrase. For post-boot attachment, keying material and passphrase are passed explicitly in the configuration request. After the root filesystem has been mounted, auto-starting new GELI instances is disabled, and only a user-driven configuration is supported.

GELI's metadata is found in the last sector of the underlying device or partition. GELI supports several multiple on-disk layout versions, allowing backward compatibility despite an evolving feature set; version 7 of the disk trailer appears in Figure 5.18. The metadata includes the encrypted master keys protecting all data stored in the GELI instance. Other information, such as the encryption algorithm, key length, and salt, is unencrypted. Metadata is decoded by *g_eli_taste*() into a *g_eli_metadata* structure that initializes the *g_eli_softc* data structure, shown in Figure 5.19, which holds information about the attached provider.

Figure 5.18 GELI v7 on-disk metadata, including encrypted master keys.

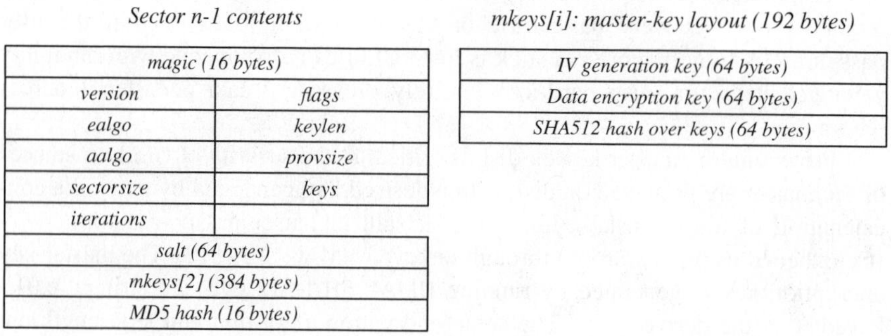

Sector n-1 contents

magic (16 bytes)	
version	*flags*
ealgo	*keylen*
aalgo	*provsize*
sectorsize	*keys*
iterations	
salt (64 bytes)	
mkeys[2] (384 bytes)	
MD5 hash (16 bytes)	

mkeys[i]: master-key layout (192 bytes)

IV generation key (64 bytes)
Data encryption key (64 bytes)
SHA512 hash over keys (64 bytes)

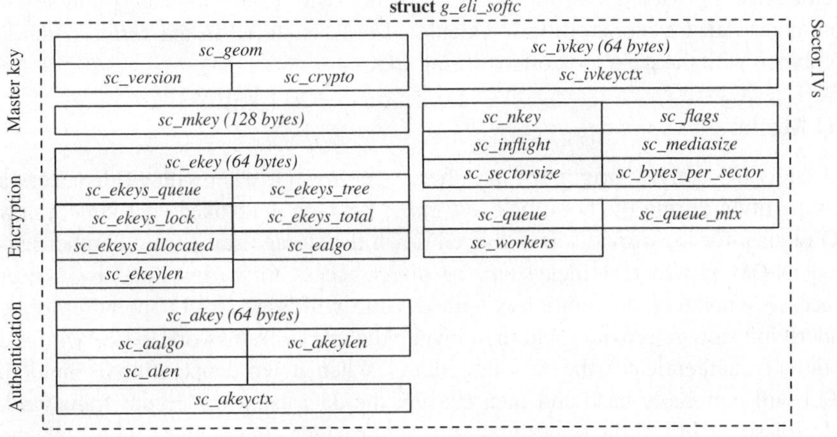

Figure 5.19 The g_eli_softc structure describes active GELI sessions.

Cryptographic Block Protection

GELI uses per-sector IVs to prevent identical data written to different sectors from having the same ciphertext, which might allow attackers to gain insight into on-disk layout and content. With most encryption algorithms, the per-sector IV is calculated by passing HMAC SHA-256, keyed with the master key's IV generation key, over the little-endian representation of the sector's byte offset. GELI caches a partially calculated version of the hash in its *softc* structure for performance reasons. AES-XTS, the default encryption algorithm, takes sector number as a direct argument, and so does not require explicit IV calculations by GELI.

Recent versions of GELI vary per-sector encryption keys across the disk to limit direct reuse of the underlying master-key data-encryption key. A key number is associated with each 512 Mbyte chunk of the disk; keys are calculated by passing a concatenation of the string "ekey" with the little-endian representation of the key number to HMAC SHA-512 keyed with the master-key data-encryption key. Because this calculation is expensive, GELI maintains a red-black tree of cached calculated key value. Entries in the cache are reference-counted so that the cryptographic framework can prevent cache entries from being freed while they are in use.

When suitably configured, GELI will generate and check keyed cryptographic hashes on sector data. This approach imposes an additional metadata overhead for each block; to minimize this overhead, GELI providers with authentication enabled will typically be configured to use larger (4-Kbyte) block sizes, reducing overhead. As with per-block encryption keys and IVs, per-block authentication keys are generated by passing a concatenation of the provider's data-encryption key and sector offset in bytes through SHA-256. As the hash of the data-encryption key is common to all blocks, a partially calculated hash is stored in the *softc*, which is combined with the per-block offset during I/O.

I/O Model

All GELI I/O activity originates in either *g_eli_taste*(), when GEOM discovers a new partition during the boot, or *g_eli_start*(), which is invoked each time a new I/O request for the provider is delivered down the storage stack from another layered GEOM provider, a filesystem, or direct access to a **/dev** node by a user process. When a read operation is fielded, GELI will issue an I/O operation to the underlying storage provider and then invoke the crypto framework to decrypt (and optionally authenticate) the resulting data. When a write operation is fielded, GELI will optionally hash and then encrypt the data using the crypto framework before issuing I/O to the underlying storage provider. Interactions with both the underlying provider and crypto framework are asynchronous: GELI provides callback functions that will be invoked when the operation completes. Both success and failure are returned to GEOM by invoking *g_io_request*() that will, in turn, trigger notification to the GEOM consumer that initiated the I/O operation.

GELI creates a pool of per-CPU worker threads to process cryptographic operations to avoid congesting the GEOM thread that would otherwise synchronously execute I/O start and completion events including encryption, decryption, and hashing. The *g_eli_worker*() routine implements the thread worker body, which sleeps on the *g_eli_softc* structure pointer and extracts new work from *sc_queue* using *g_eli_takefirst*() when signalled. A GELI instance is marked as suspended by *g_eli_suspend_one*(), which it does by setting G_ELI_FLAG_SUSPEND in *sc_flags*. Once suspended, all I/O requests will be stalled. Suspension clears *softc* keying material, which must be restored before I/O can be resumed. I/O is resumed by *g_eli_ctl_resume*() clearing the G_ELI_FLAG_SUSPEND flag.

Limitations

As with all security features, GELI must be used with an awareness of its threat model and guarantees. For example, integrity protection can detect sector data that was written without access to a master key for the provider. It is unable, however, to detect "replay attacks" in which an older version of a sector replaces a newer version, as both will pass integrity checks. Multiple losses of the same storage device therefore leave the disk vulnerable to rewinding—a difficult problem to address, and one that GELI documents as outside of its threat model. GELI also excludes a number of other attacker models including:

- Online snooping of encrypted I/O traffic on its way to the disk rather than offline analysis, for example, **tcpdump** of iSCSI traffic carrying GELI-protected data.
- Social engineering to gain access to the key or passphrase. Any encryption scheme that depends on a remembered passphrase can be broken if the person can be tricked into giving up the passphrase.

It does, however, provide significant benefit in limiting the access of an attacker who has acquired a stolen notebook.

Exercises

5.1 Describe the difference between discretionary and mandatory access controls.

5.2 How do definitions of "implicit privilege" and "explicit privilege" affect TCB protection in FreeBSD? What are the potential risks and benefits to implementing a flexible, fine-grained privilege model?

5.3 Is it possible for a file to have UNIX permissions set such that its owner cannot read it, even though a group can? Is this situation possible if the owner is a member of the group that can read the file? Explain your answers.

*5.4 How do distributed authentication and authorization systems, such as Kerberos or NFS, interact with local authentication and access control?

*5.5 When should distributed-filesystem access-control enforcement occur on the client, and when on the server?

*5.6 Access control has changed significantly between historic DAC and MAC models, and more contemporary approaches such as Capsicum. What similar considerations might apply to the more traditional audit framework present in FreeBSD?

5.7 FreeBSD uses a model in which the first process starts with complete privilege, which is discarded as events such as user authentication take place. This model has proven a problem in the past when system login services, such as **sshd, have had security vulnerabilities that yielded root privilege. How might the model be restructured so that user authentication takes place without any privilege, and privilege is escalated rather than dropped?

**5.8 What sort of hardware support would make it more efficient for the kernel to implement the FreeBSD security policies?

**5.9 This chapter has primarily considered the protection of objects maintained by a single instance of the operating system, such as local files and IPC objects. As virtualization becomes more prevalent, how might hypervisor and operating system access-control models interact?

References

Anderson, 1972.
J. P. Anderson, "Computer Security Technology Planning Study," Technical Report, Electronic Systems Division, Air Force Systems Command, Hanscom Field, Bedford, MA, October 1972.

Badger et al., 1995.
L. Badger, D. F. Sterne, D. L. Sherman, K. M. Walker, & S. A. Haghighat, "Practical Domain and Type Enforcement for UNIX," *Proceedings of the 1995 IEEE Symposium on Security and Privacy*, IEEE, May 1995.

Bell & LaPadula, 1973.
D. E. Bell & L. J. LaPadula, "Secure computer systems: Mathematical foundations and model," Technical Report M74-244, The MITRE Corporation, Bedford, MA, May 1973.

Biba, 1977.
K. Biba, "Integrity considerations for secure computer systems," Technical Report TR-3153, The MITRE Corporation, Bedford, MA, April 1977.

Boebert & Kain, 1985.
W. E. Boebert & R. Y. Kain, "A practical alternative to hierarchical integrity policies.," *Proceedings of the 8th National Computer Security Conference*, October 1985.

Fraser, 2000.
T. Fraser, "LOMAC: Low Water-Mark Integrity Protection for COTS Environments," *Proceedings of the 2000 IEEE Symposium on Security and Privacy*, IEEE, May 2000.

Kamp & Watson, 2000.
P. Kamp & R. Watson, "Jails: Confining the Omnipotent Root," *Proceedings of the Second International System Administration and Networking Conference (SANE)*, available from http://docs.freebsd.org/44doc/papers/jail/, May 2000.

Kelsey et al., 1999.
J. Kelsey, B. Schneier, & N. Ferguson, "Yarrow-160: Notes on the Design and Analysis of the Yarrow Cryptographic Pseudorandom Number Generator," *Proceedings of the Sixth Annual Workshop on Selected Areas in Cryptography*, available from https://www.schneier.com/paper-yarrow.html, August 1999.

Kilpatrick, 2003.
D. Kilpatrick, "Privman: A Library for Partitioning Applications," *Proceedings of the USENIX Annual Technical Conference*, pp. 273–284, June 2003.

Leffler, 2003.
S. J. Leffler, "Cryptographic Device Support for FreeBSD," *Proceedings of BSDCon 2003*, September 2003.

Loscocco & Smalley, 2001.
P. A. Loscocco & S. D. Smalley, "Integrating Flexible Support for Security Policies into the Linux Operating System," *Proceedings of the USENIX Annual Technical Conference*, USENIX Association, June 2001.

Murray, 2002.
M. R. V. Murray, "An Implementation of the Yarrow PRNG for FreeBSD," *Proceedings of BSDCon 2002*, available from https://www.usenix.org/legacy/event/bsdcon02/murray.html, February 2002.

P1003.1e, 1998.
P1003.1e, "Unpublished Draft Standard for Information Technology—Portable Operating System Interface (POSIX)—Part 1: System Application Program Interface—Amendment: Protection, Audit and Control Interfaces [C Language] IEEE Standard 1003.1e Draft 17," Editor Casey Schaufler, Institute of Electrical and Electronic Engineers, Piscataway, NJ, 1998.

Provos et al., 2002.
N. Provos, M. Friedl, & P. Honeyman, "Preventing Privilege Escalation," *Proc. of the 12th USENIX Security Symposium*, pp. 207–225, August 2002.

Reis & Gribble, 2009.
C. Reis & S. D. Gribble, "Isolating Web Programs in Modern Browser Architectures," *EuroSys '09: Proceedings of the 4th ACM European Conference on Computer Systems*, pp. 219–232, April 2009.

Ritchie, 1979.
D. M. Ritchie, "Protection of Data File Contents," *United States Patent*, no. 4,135,240, United States Patent Office, Washington, DC, January 16, 1979. Assignee: Bell Telephone Laboratories, Inc., Murray Hill, NJ, Appl. No.: 377,591, Filed: July 9, 1973.

Saltzer & Schroeder, 1975.
J. H. Saltzer & M. D. Schroeder, "The Protection of Information in Computer Systems," *Proceedings of the IEEE*, vol. 63, no. 9, pp. 1278–1308, September 1975.

Shepler et al., 2003.
S. Shepler, B. Callaghan, D. Robinson, R. Thurlow, C. Beame, M. Eisler, & D. Noveck, "Network File System (NFS) version 4 Protocol," RFC 3530, available from http://www.faqs.org/rfcs/rfc3530.html, April 2003.

Watson, 2007.
R. N. M. Watson, "Exploiting concurrency vulnerabilities in system call wrappers," *WOOT07: Proceedings of the first USENIX Workshop on Offensive Technologies*, USENIX Association, Boston, MA, August 2007.

Watson, 2012.
R. N. M. Watson, "New approaches to operating system security extensibility," Technical Report UCAM-CL-TR-818, University of Cambridge, Computer Laboratory, William Gates Building, 15 JJ Thomson Avenue, Cambridge CB3 0FD, April 2012.

Watson, 2013.
R. N. M. Watson, "A Decade of OS access-control extensibility," *Communications of the ACM*, vol. 56, no. 2, pp. 52–63, February 2013.

Watson et al., 2003.
R. N. M. Watson, B. Feldman, A. Migus, & C. Vance, "Design and Implementation of the TrustedBSD MAC Framework," *Proceedings of the Third DARPA Information Survivability Conference and Exhibition (DISCEX)*, IEEE, April 2003.

Watson et al., 2010.
R. N. M. Watson, B. Laurie, J. Anderson, & K. Kennaway, "Capsicum:

Practical Capabilities for UNIX," *Proceedings of the 19th USENIX Security Symposium*, August 2010.

Watson & Salamon, 2006.
R. N. M. Watson & W. Salamon, "The FreeBSD Audit System," *Proceedings of UKUUG LISA 2006*, March 2006.

CHAPTER 6

Memory Management

6.1 Terminology

A central component of any operating system is the ***memory-management system***. As the name implies, memory-management facilities are responsible for the management of memory resources available on a machine. These resources are typically layered in a hierarchical fashion, with memory-access times inversely related to their proximity to the CPU (see Figure 6.1). The primary memory system is ***main memory***; the next level of storage is ***secondary storage*** or ***backing storage***. Main-memory systems usually are constructed from random-access memories, whereas secondary stores are placed on disk drives. In certain workstation environments, the common two-level hierarchy is a three-level hierarchy, with the

Figure 6.1 Hierarchical layering of memory.

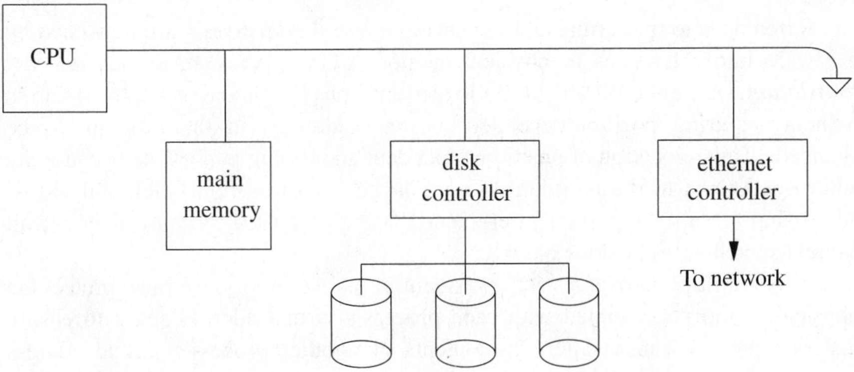

addition of file-server machines or network-attached storage connected to a workstation via a local-area network [Gingell et al., 1987].

Each level in this hierarchy may have its own hierarchy. For example, there are usually several layers of caches between the CPU and the main memory. The secondary storage often has dynamic- or flash-memory caches to speed access to the moving-head disk drives.

In a multiprogrammed environment, it is critical for the operating system to share available memory resources effectively among the processes. The operation of any memory-management policy is directly related to the memory required for a process to execute. That is, if a process must reside entirely in main memory for it to execute, then a memory-management system must be oriented toward allocating large units of memory. On the other hand, if a process can execute when it is only partially resident in main memory, then memory-management policies are likely to be substantially different. Memory-management facilities usually try to optimize the number of runnable processes that are resident in main memory. This goal must be considered with the goals of the scheduler (Section 4.4) so that conflicts that can adversely affect overall system performance are avoided.

Although the availability of secondary storage permits more processes to exist than can be resident in main memory, it also requires additional algorithms that can be complicated. Space management typically requires algorithms and policies different from those used for main memory, and a policy must be devised for deciding when to move processes between main memory and secondary storage.

Processes and Memory

Each process operates in a ***virtual address space*** that is defined by the architecture of the underlying hardware on which it executes. A virtual address space is a range of memory locations that a process references independently of the physical memory present in the system. In other words, the virtual address space of a process is independent of the physical address space of the CPU. For a machine to support virtual memory, we also require that the whole of a process's virtual address space does not need to be resident in main memory for that process to execute.

References to the virtual address space—***virtual addresses***—are translated by hardware into references to physical memory. This operation, termed ***address translation***, permits programs to be loaded into physical memory at any location without requiring position-dependent virtual addresses in the program to be changed. This relocation of position-dependent addressing is possible because the addresses known to the program do not change. Address translation and virtual addressing are also important in efficient sharing of a CPU, because they permit context switching to be done quickly.

When multiple processes are coresident in main memory, we must protect the physical memory associated with each process's virtual address space to ensure that one process cannot alter the contents of another process's virtual address space unless they explicitly choose to share parts of their address space. This protection is implemented in hardware and is usually tightly coupled with the implementation of address translation. Consequently, the two operations usually are defined and implemented together as hardware termed the ***memory-management unit*** (***MMU***).

Virtual memory can be implemented in many ways, some of which are software based, such as ***overlays***. Most effective virtual-memory schemes are, however, hardware based. In these schemes, the virtual address space is divided into fixed-size units, termed ***pages***, as shown in Figure 6.2. Virtual-memory references are resolved by the address-translation unit to a page in main memory and an offset within that page. Hardware protection is applied by the memory-management unit on a page-by-page basis.

Paging

Address translation provides the implementation of virtual memory by decoupling the virtual address space of a process from what is contained in the physical address space of the CPU. Each page of virtual memory is marked as ***resident*** or ***nonresident*** in main memory. If a process references a location in virtual memory that is not resident, a hardware trap termed a ***page fault*** is generated. The servicing of page faults, or ***paging***, permits processes to execute even if they are only partially resident in main memory.

Coffman & Denning [1973] characterize paging systems by three important policies:

1. When the system loads pages into memory—the ***fetch policy***
2. Where the system places pages in memory—the ***placement policy***
3. How the system selects pages to be removed from main memory when pages are unavailable for a placement request—the ***replacement policy***

Figure 6.2 Paged virtual-memory scheme.

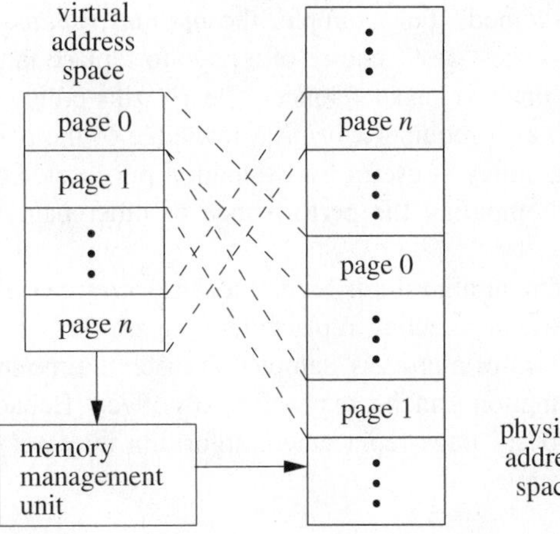

The performance of modern computers is heavily dependent on one or more high-speed hardware caches to reduce the need to access the much slower main memory. The placement policy should ensure that contiguous pages in virtual memory make the best use of the processor-memory cache and the address-translation cache [Kessler & Hill., 1992]. FreeBSD uses superpages to ensure good placement. Under a ***pure demand-paging*** system, a demand-fetch policy is used, in which only the missing page is fetched, and replacements occur only when main memory is full. In practice, paging systems do not implement a pure demand-paging algorithm. Instead, the fetch policy often is altered to do ***prepaging***—fetching pages of memory other than the one that caused the page fault—and the replacement policy is invoked before main memory is full.

Replacement Algorithms

The replacement policy is an important aspect of any paging system. There are many algorithms from which we can select in designing a replacement strategy for a paging system. Much research has been carried out in evaluating the performance of different page-replacement algorithms [Jiang et al., 2005; Bansal & Modha, 2004; Belady, 1966; Marshall, 1979; King, 1971].

A process's paging behavior for a given input is described in terms of the pages referenced over the time of the process's execution. This sequence of pages, termed a ***reference string***, represents the behavior of the process at discrete times during the process's lifetime. Corresponding to the sampled references that constitute a process's reference string are real-time values that reflect whether the associated references resulted in a page fault. A useful measure of a process's behavior is the ***fault rate***, which is the number of page faults encountered during processing of a reference string, normalized by the length of the reference string.

Page-replacement algorithms typically are evaluated in terms of their effectiveness on reference strings that have been collected from execution of real programs. Formal analysis can also be used, although it is difficult to do unless many restrictions are applied to the execution environment. The most common metric used in measuring the effectiveness of a page-replacement algorithm is the fault rate.

Page-replacement algorithms are defined by the criteria that they use for selecting pages to be reclaimed. For example, the ***optimal replacement policy*** [Denning, 1970] states that the "best" choice of a page to replace is the one with the longest expected time until its next reference. Clearly, this policy is not applicable to dynamic systems, as it requires *a priori* knowledge of the paging characteristics of a process. The policy is useful for evaluation purposes, however, as it provides a yardstick for comparing the performance of other page-replacement algorithms.

Practical page-replacement algorithms require a certain amount of state information that the system uses in selecting replacement pages. This state typically includes the reference pattern of a process, sampled at discrete time intervals. On some systems, this information can be expensive to collect [Babaoğlu & Joy, 1981]. As a result, the "best" page-replacement algorithm may not be the most efficient.

Working-Set Model

The working-set model helps identify the set of pages that a process is actively using. The working-set model assumes that processes exhibit a slowly changing ***locality of reference***. For a period of time, a process operates in a set of subroutines or loops, causing all its memory references to refer to a fixed subset of its address space, termed the ***working set***. The process periodically changes its working set, abandoning certain areas of memory and beginning to access new ones. After a period of transition, the process defines a new set of pages as its working set. In general, if the system can provide the process with enough pages to hold that process's working set, the process will experience a low page-fault rate. If the system cannot provide the process with enough pages for the working set, the process will run slowly and will have a high page-fault rate.

Precise calculation of the working set of a process is impossible without *a priori* knowledge of that process's memory-reference pattern. However, the working set can be approximated by various means. One method of approximation is to track the number of pages held by a process and that process's page-fault rate. If the page-fault rate increases above a high watermark, the working set is assumed to have increased, and the number of pages held by the process is allowed to grow. Conversely, if the page-fault rate drops below a low watermark, the working set is assumed to have decreased, and the number of pages held by the process is reduced.

Swapping

Swapping is the term used to describe a memory-management policy in which entire processes are moved to and from secondary storage when main memory is in short supply. Swap-based memory-management systems usually are less complicated than are demand-paged systems, since there is less bookkeeping to do. However, pure swapping systems typically are less effective than are paging systems, since the degree of multiprogramming is lowered by the requirement that processes be fully resident to execute. Swapping is sometimes combined with paging in a two-tiered scheme, whereby paging satisfies memory demands until a severe memory shortfall requires drastic action, in which case swapping is used.

In this chapter, a portion of secondary storage that is used for paging or swapping is termed a ***swap area*** or ***swap space***. The hardware devices on which these areas reside are termed ***swap devices***.

Advantages of Virtual Memory

There are several advantages to the use of virtual memory on computers capable of supporting this facility properly. Virtual memory allows large programs to be run on machines with main-memory configurations that are smaller than the program size. On machines with a moderate amount of memory, it allows more programs to be resident in main memory to compete for CPU time, as the programs do not need to be completely resident. When programs use sections of their program or data space for some time, leaving other sections unused, the unused sections do not need to be present. Also, the use of virtual memory allows programs to start up faster, since they generally require only a small section to be loaded before they begin processing arguments and determining what actions to take. Other parts of a program may not be needed at all during individual runs. As a program runs, additional sections of its program and data spaces are paged in as needed (***demand paging***). Finally, there are many algorithms that are more easily programmed by sparse use of a large address space than by careful packing of data structures into a small area. Such techniques are too expensive for use without virtual memory, but they may run much faster when that facility is available, without using an inordinate amount of physical memory.

On the other hand, the use of virtual memory can degrade performance. It is more efficient to load a program all at one time than to load it entirely in small sections on demand. There is a cost for each operation, including saving and restoring state and determining which page must be loaded, so some systems use demand paging for only those programs that are larger than some minimum size.

Hardware Requirements for Virtual Memory

Nearly all versions of UNIX have required some form of memory-management hardware to support transparent multiprogramming. To protect processes from modification by other processes, the memory-management hardware must prevent programs from changing their own address mapping. The FreeBSD kernel runs in a privileged mode (***kernel mode*** or ***system mode***) in which memory mapping can be controlled, whereas processes run in an unprivileged mode (***user mode***). There are several additional architectural requirements for support of virtual memory. The CPU must distinguish between resident and nonresident portions of the address space, must suspend programs when they refer to nonresident addresses, and must resume programs' operation once the operating system has placed the required section in memory. Because the CPU may discover missing data at various times during the execution of an instruction, it must provide a mechanism to save the machine state so that the instruction can be continued or restarted later. This ability to restart an instruction is called a precise exception. The CPU may implement restarting by saving enough state when an instruction begins that the state can be restored when a fault is discovered. Alternatively, instructions could delay any modifications or side effects until after any faults would be discovered so that the instruction execution does not need to back up before restarting. On some computers, instruction backup requires the assistance of the operating system.

Most machines designed to support demand-paged virtual memory include hardware support for the collection of information on program references to memory. When the system selects a page for replacement, it must save the contents of that page if they have been modified since the page was brought into memory. The hardware usually maintains a per-page flag showing whether the page has been modified. Many machines also include a flag recording any access to a page for use by the replacement algorithm.

6.2 Overview of the FreeBSD Virtual-Memory System

The FreeBSD virtual-memory system is based on the Mach 2.0 virtual-memory system [Tevanian, 1987; Rashid et al., 1987], with updates from Mach 2.5 and Mach 3.0. The Mach virtual-memory system was adopted because it features efficient support for sharing and a clean separation of machine-independent and machine-dependent features, as well as multiprocessor support. Although parts of the original Mach abstractions persist, little of the code still remains. None of the original Mach system-call interface remains. It has been replaced with the interface first proposed for 4.2BSD that has been widely adopted by the UNIX industry; the FreeBSD interface is described in Section 6.5.

The virtual address space of most architectures is divided into two parts: address space dedicated to the kernel at high addresses and address space dedicated to run user processes at low addresses. A typical address space layout is shown in Figure 6.3. Here, the kernel and its associated data structures reside at the top of the address space. The initial text and data areas of the user process start near the beginning of memory. By default, the first 4 or 8 Kbyte of memory are kept off-limits to the process. The reason for this restriction is to limit the ability to convert a kernel null-pointer dereference into a privilege escalation attack. This restriction also eases program debugging; indirecting through a null pointer will cause an invalid address fault instead of reading or writing the program text.

Memory allocations made by the running process using the *malloc*() library routine are done in the memory that starts immediately following the data area and grows to higher addresses. The argument vector and environment vectors are at the top of the user portion of the address space. The user's stack starts just below these vectors and grows to lower addresses.

Figure 6.3 Layout of virtual address space.

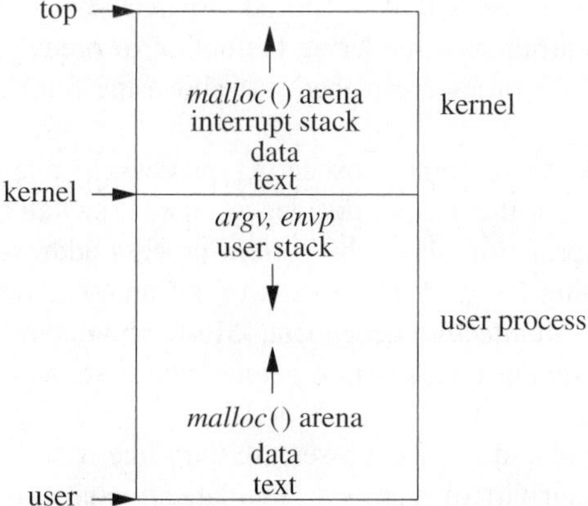

For a process running on an architecture with 64 bits of address space, its stack is mapped so far above its *malloc*() arena that the two spaces should never run into each other as the process would run out of memory resources long before the two address spaces would meet.

For processes running on 32-bit architectures, the top 1 Gbyte of the address space is reserved for use by the kernel. Systems with many small processes making heavy use of kernel facilities such as networking can be configured to use the top 2 Gbyte for the kernel. The remaining 3 Gbyte or 2 Gbyte of address space is available for use by processes. Unless administratively limited, the stack and *malloc*() arena of a process can each grow until they meet.

The kernel's address space on a 64-bit architecture is usually large enough to support a fixed and permanent mapping to all the physical memory on the machine. This direct mapping to the physical address space greatly simplifies many kernel operations since the kernel can always directly read any page of physical memory.

On a 32-bit architecture, the physical memory usually exceeds the address space dedicated to the kernel. Thus, the kernel must set aside part of its address space to temporarily map in physical pages that it needs to read. Each time that it wants to read a new physical page, it must find an existing page that it can unmap to make room for the new page. It must then manipulate its memory mapping, invalidating the old mapping and any caching associated with that mapping, and then enter the new mapping. The cost of cache invalidation on multiprocessor machines is high because the cache on every CPU must be invalidated.

User Address-Space Management

The virtual-memory system implements protected address spaces into which can be mapped data sources (***objects***) such as files, or private and anonymous pieces of swap space. Physical memory is used as a cache of recently used pages from these objects and is managed by a global page-replacement algorithm.

In FreeBSD and other modern UNIX systems that support the *mmap* system call, address-space usage is less structured. Shared library implementations may place text or data arbitrarily, rendering the notion of predefined regions obsolete. By default, shared libraries are placed just above the run-time configured maximum heap area.

At any time, the currently executing process is mapped into the virtual address space. When the system decides to context switch to another process, it must save the information about the current-process address mapping, then load the address mapping for the new process to be run. The details of this address-map switching are architecture dependent. Most architectures need to change only a few memory-mapping registers that point to the base, and to give the length of memory-resident page tables.

Both the kernel and user processes use the same basic data structures for the management of their virtual memory. The data structures used to manage virtual memory are as follows:

vmspace	Structure that encompasses both the machine-dependent and machine-independent structures describing a process's address space
vm_map	Highest-level data structure that describes the machine-independent virtual address space
vm_map_entry	Structure that describes the mapping from a virtually contiguous range of addresses that share protection and inheritance attributes to the backing-store *vm_object*
vm_object	Structure that describes a source of data such as physical memory or other resources containing instructions or data
shadow vm_object	Special *vm_object* that represents modified copy of original data, described in Section 6.5.
vm_page	The lowest-level data structure that represents the physical memory being used by the virtual-memory system

In the remainder of this section, we describe briefly how all these data structures fit together. The remainder of this chapter describes the details of the structures and how the structures are used.

Figure 6.4 shows a typical process address space and associated data structures. The *vmspace* structure encapsulates the virtual-memory state of a particular process, including the machine-dependent and machine-independent data structures, as well as statistics. The machine-dependent *vm_pmap* structure is opaque to all but the lowest level of the system and contains all information necessary to manage the memory-management hardware. This *pmap layer* is the subject of Section 6.13 and is ignored for the remainder of the current discussion. The

Figure 6.4 Data structures that describe a process address space.

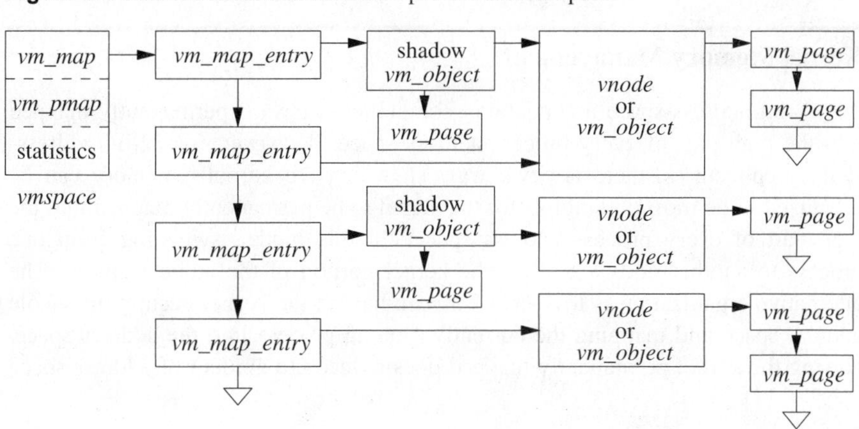

machine-independent data structures include the address space that is described by a *vm_map* structure. The *vm_map* points to an ordered linked list of *vm_map_entry* structures, a binary-search tree for speeding up lookups during memory allocation and page-fault handling, and a pointer to the associated machine-dependent *vm_pmap* structure contained in the *vmspace*. A *vm_map_entry* structure describes a virtually contiguous range of addresses that have the same protection and inheritance attributes. Every *vm_map_entry* points to a chain of *vm_object* structures that describes sources of data (objects) that are mapped at the indicated address range. At the tail of the *vm_object* chain is the original mapped data object, usually representing a persistent data source, such as a file. Interposed between that *vm_object* and the map entry are zero or more transient *shadow vm_objects* that represent modified copies of the original data. These shadow *vm_objects* are discussed in detail in Section 6.5.

Each *vm_object* structure contains an ordered list of *vm_page* structures representing the physical-memory cache of the *vm_object*. A *vm_page* structure is most commonly and quickly found using the radix tree maintained for each *vm_object*. The page is keyed within this radix tree by its logical offset from the start of the *vm_object*. The cached pages are also kept in an ordered list to provide fast iteration over all the pages within a range of virtual addresses. The *vm_page* structure also records the type of, and a pointer to, the *pager* structure (not shown) that contains information on how to page in or page out data from its backing store.

At boot time, the kernel allocates an array of *vm_page* structures with an entry for every page of physical memory managed by the virtual-memory system where page N is entry N in the array. The structure also contains the status of the page (e.g., modified or referenced) and links for various paging queues.

All structures have the necessary interlocks for multithreading in a multiprocessor environment. The locking is fine grained, with at least one lock per instance of a data structure. Many of the structures have different locks protecting their individual fields.

6.3 Kernel Memory Management

For 64-bit address-space architectures, the kernel is always permanently mapped into the high part of every process address space. However, for 32-bit address-space architectures, there are two ways in which the kernel's memory can be organized. The most common is for the kernel to be permanently mapped into the high part of every process address space. In this model, switching from one process to another does not affect the kernel portion of the address space. The alternative organization is to switch between having the kernel occupy the whole address space and mapping the currently running process into the address space. Having the kernel permanently mapped does reduce the amount of address space

Table 6.1 Kernel memory allocator hierarchy.

Level	Purpose
buckets	per-CPU allocation of objects
zones	allocation of objects from a keg to buckets
kegs	collection of slabs holding a particular type of object
slabs	allocation of a set of objects from a vmem arena
vmem	multiple-of-page allocations within the *vm_map*
vm_map	kernel address space partitioning

available to a large process (and the kernel), but it also reduces the cost of data copying. Many system calls require data to be transferred between the currently running user process and the kernel. With the kernel permanently mapped, the data can be copied via the efficient block-copy instructions. If the kernel is alternately mapped with the process, data copying requires either the use of temporary mappings or the use of special instructions that copy to and from the previously mapped address space. Both of these approaches are up to a factor of 2 slower than the standard block-copy instructions. Since up to one-third of the kernel time is spent in copying between the kernel and user processes, slowing this operation by a factor of 2 significantly slows system throughput.

When the kernel is permanently mapped into the address space, it is able to freely read and write the address space of the user process but the converse is not true. The kernel's range of virtual address space is marked inaccessible to all user processes. Writing is restricted so user processes cannot tamper with the kernel's data structures. Reading is restricted so user processes cannot watch sensitive kernel data structures, such as the terminal input queues, that include such things as users typing their passwords.

Usually, the hardware dictates which organization can be used. All the architectures supported by FreeBSD map the kernel into the top of the address space.

When the system boots, the first task that the kernel must do is to set up data structures to describe and manage its address space. Table 6.1 lists the kernel's hierarchy of allocators to manage its address space. The relationship of the elements of the hierarchy are shown in Figure 6.5. The remainder of this section describes this hierarchy starting from the low-level *vm_map* up to the per-CPU-level buckets.

Kernel Maps and Submaps

Like any process, the kernel has a *vm_map* with a corresponding set of *vm_map_entry* structures that describe the use of a range of addresses (see

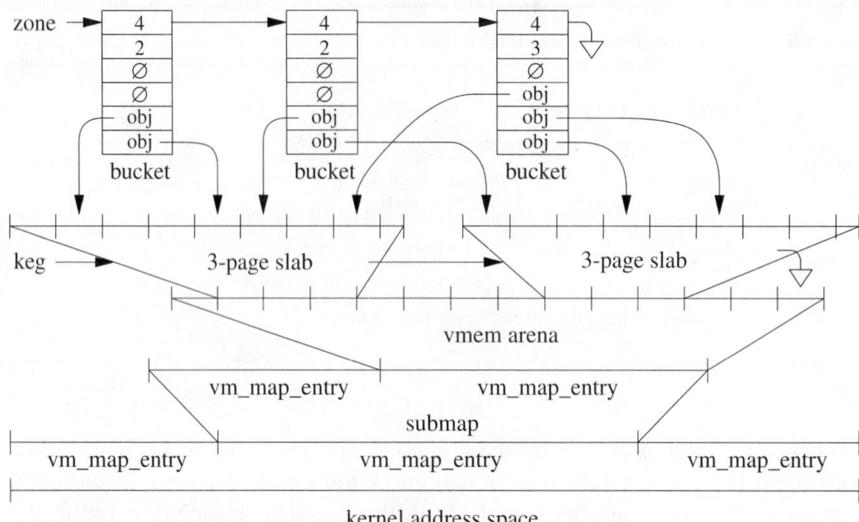

Figure 6.5 Kernel memory allocator hierarchy.

Figure 6.6). Submaps are a special kernel-only construct used to isolate and constrain address-space allocation for kernel subsystems. One use is in subsystems that require contiguous pieces of the kernel address space. To avoid intermixing of unrelated allocations within an address range, that range is covered by a submap, and only the appropriate subsystem can allocate from that map. Maps associate data objects with similar sizes and lifetimes to minimize internal and external fragmentation respectively. Parts of the kernel may also require addresses with particular alignments or even specific addresses. Both can be ensured by use of submaps. Finally, submaps can be used to limit statically the amount of address space and hence the physical memory consumed by a subsystem.

An example layout of the kernel map is shown in Figure 6.6. The kernel's address space is described by the *vm_map* structure shown in the upperleft corner of the figure. Pieces of the address space are described by the *vm_map_entry* structures that are linked in ascending address order from K0 to K8 on the *vm_map* structure. Here, the kernel text, initialized data, uninitialized data, and initially allocated data structures reside in the range K0 to K1 and are represented by the first *vm_map_entry*. The next *vm_map_entry* is associated with the address range from K2 to K6. This piece of the kernel address space is being managed via a submap headed by the referenced *vm_map* structure. This submap currently has two parts of its address space used: the address range K2 to K3, and the address range K4 to K5. These two address ranges represent the kernel *exec* arguments arena and the *pipe* buffer arena, respectively. The final part of the kernel address space is being managed in the kernel's main map, the address range K7 to K8 representing the kernel I/O staging area.

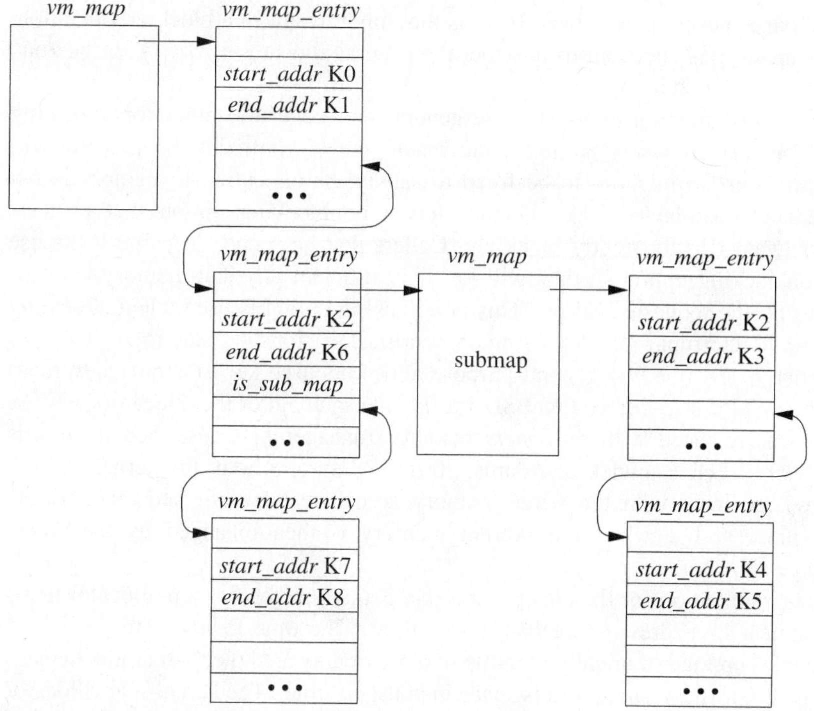

Figure 6.6 Kernel address-space maps.

Kernel Address-Space Allocation

The virtual-memory system implements a set of primitive functions for allocating and freeing the page-aligned, page-size virtual-memory ranges that the kernel uses. These ranges may be allocated either from the main kernel-address map or from a submap. The allocation routines take a map and size as parameters but do not take an address. Thus, specific addresses within a map cannot be selected. There are different allocation routines for obtaining pageable and nonpageable memory ranges.

Pageable kernel virtual memory is allocated with *kmap_alloc_wait*(). A pageable range has physical memory allocated on demand, and this memory can be written out to backing store by the pageout daemon (described in Section 6.12) as part of the latter's normal replacement policy. The *kmap_alloc_wait*() function will block until address space is available. The *kmap_free_wakeup*() function deallocates kernel pageable memory and wakes up any processes waiting for address space in the specified map. Currently, pageable kernel memory is used for temporary storage of *exec* arguments and for pipe buffering.

A nonpageable, or ***wired***, range has physical memory assigned at the time of the call, and this memory is not subject to replacement by the pageout daemon.

Wired pages never cause a page fault as that might result in a blocking operation. Wired memory is allocated from either the general allocator *malloc*(), or the zone allocator described in the last two subsections of this section.

The base functions used by the general and zone allocators for allocating wired memory are *kmem_malloc*() and *kmem_free*(). Normally, the allocator will block to wait for memory to be freed to satisfy the allocation if memory is not immediately available. The allocator has a nonblocking option that protects callers against inadvertently blocking. Callers that hold non-sleepable locks use the nonblocking option so they will fail if insufficient physical memory is available to fill the requested range. This nonblocking option is used when allocating memory at interrupt time and during other critical sections of code.

Historically, the two general-purpose allocators used kernel submaps to manage their address space. In FreeBSD 10, the management of the allocators address space was replaced with the *vmem* resource manager first described in Solaris [Bonwick, 1994; Bonwick & Adams, 2001]. At system boot, the kernel address ranges associated with the wired-memory arena are fully allocated in a single large piece and that piece of kernel memory is then managed by the *vmem* resource allocator.

The motivation for the change to *vmem* is that the kernel-map allocator tends to fragment its address space badly over time. The time to find a free piece of space goes up logarithmically with the number of allocated pieces that it is managing. By contrast, *vmem* allocates space in constant-time. The kernel-map allocator uses a first-fit strategy while *vmem* uses an approximation to a best-fit strategy. Best fit results in lower fragmentation and less wasted memory.

The data structures that *vmem* uses to manage its address-space arena are shown in Figure 6.7. The granularity that it manages are single pages of memory. Shown across the bottom of Figure 6.7 is the set of pages that it is managing. The arena is broken up into the free memory (hashed) and allocated memory (white). Each piece of free or allocated memory is described by a boundary tag. All the boundary tags are linked together in a segment list sorted from lowest to highest address.

The boundary tags that reference allocated memory are kept in a hash table using their starting address as their hash key. When a piece of memory is freed, its boundary tag is looked up and removed from the hash table. If either (or both) of its neighbors on the sorted list of boundary tags is free, they can be coalesced. The resulting free piece is then placed on the appropriate freelist. When coalescing has occurred, any unneeded boundary tags are freed. Taking the memory off the hash list when it is freed helps to detect multiple attempts to free the same memory. A second attempt to free it will not find it on the hash list and can issue an appropriate error.

The boundary tags that reference free memory are on power-of-two freelists where freelist[n] is a list of free segments that are in the range 2^n to $2^{n+1}-1$. To allocate a segment, we search the appropriate freelist for a segment large enough to satisfy the allocation. This approach, called segregated fit, approximates best fit because any segment on the chosen freelist is a good fit [Wilson et al., 1995].

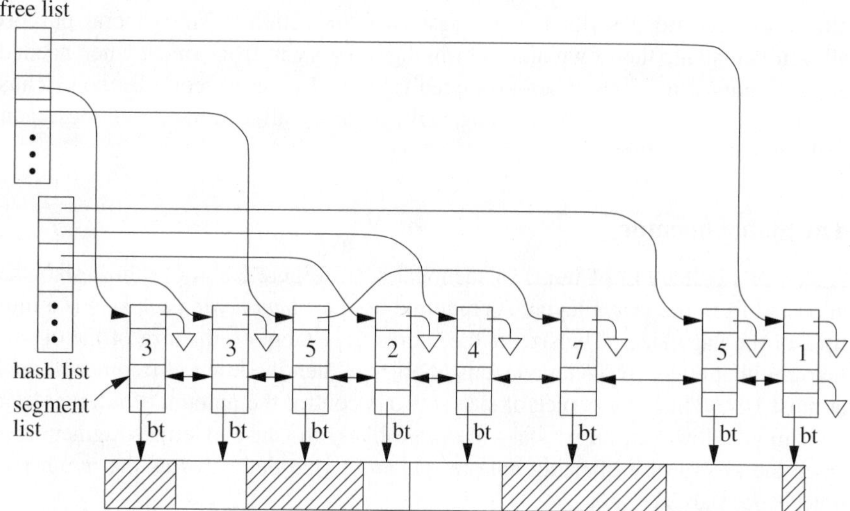

Figure 6.7 Vmem data structures. Key: bt—boundary tag.

Approximations to best fit are appealing because they exhibit low fragmentation in practice for a wide variety of workloads [Johnstone & Wilson, 1998].

The algorithm for selecting a free segment depends on the allocation policy specified in the allocation request. Given a requested size in the range 2^n to $2^{n+1}-1$, the following policies are available:

- VM_BESTFIT: Search for the smallest segment on freelist[n] that can satisfy the allocation. If none are found, search for the smallest segment on freelist[n + 1] that can satisfy the allocation.
- VM_INSTANTFIT: If the size is exactly 2^n, take the first segment on freelist[n]. Otherwise, take the first segment on freelist[n+1]. Any segment on this freelist is necessarily large enough to satisfy the allocation, yielding constant-time performance with a reasonably good fit. Instant fit is the default in FreeBSD because it guarantees constant-time performance, provides low fragmentation in practice, and is easy to implement.
- VM_NEXTFIT: Ignore the freelists altogether and search the arena for the next free segment after the one previously allocated. This option is not supported in FreeBSD 10. The *vmem* in Solaris supports it for allocating resources like process identifiers.

There are many other techniques for choosing a suitable free segment in logarithmic time such as keeping all free segments in a size-sorted tree. For a through survey, see Wilson et al. [1995].

Each *vmem* arena is protected by a single lock as allocations from the *vmem* arena are infrequent. Most of the allocations are done by the general-purpose allocators that are described in the last two subsections. The general purpose allocators manage their own arenas bringing memory in from *vmem* when needed, and returning it to *vmem* when prompted to do so by the pageout daemon. Thus, the fine-grained locking for handling multi-threaded allocations are in these general purpose allocators.

The Slab Allocator

A slab is a collection of items of identical size. Figure 6.8 shows how slabs are allocated from the *vmem* layer. As required by the *vmem* layer, each slab is a multiple of the page size. The size of the slab is dependent on the size of the objects that it will contain. If a slab contains N objects, then the internal fragmentation is at most 1/N. Thus, the choice of slab size can control the amount of internal fragmentation. However, larger slabs are more likely to cause external fragmentation since the probability of being able to reclaim a slab decreases as the number of objects per slab increases.

In the Solaris implementation of *vmem*, the size selected for the slab when allocating large objects must be big enough to hold at least eight of the objects so that waste is at most 12.5 percent. Objects smaller than an eighth of a page are allocated on a single-page slab.

FreeBSD 11 does not implement the Solaris policy. It limits the slab size to a single page unless the object itself needs more than one page. Here, the allocation will be the number of pages required to hold one object. Historically, the reason for the single-page limitation was to reduce fragmentation in the kernel submap used by the slab allocator. Since the running time for the kernel-map allocator was logarithmic in the number of map entries, the time to allocate memory for the slab was affected by fragmentation. Going to primarily single-page requests mitigated this bad behavior.

With the addition of the *vmem* allocator, these concerns have been reduced because it allocates in constant-time regardless of fragmentation. However, the FreeBSD developers chose to gain more operational experience with the *vmem*

Figure 6.8 Slab data structures.

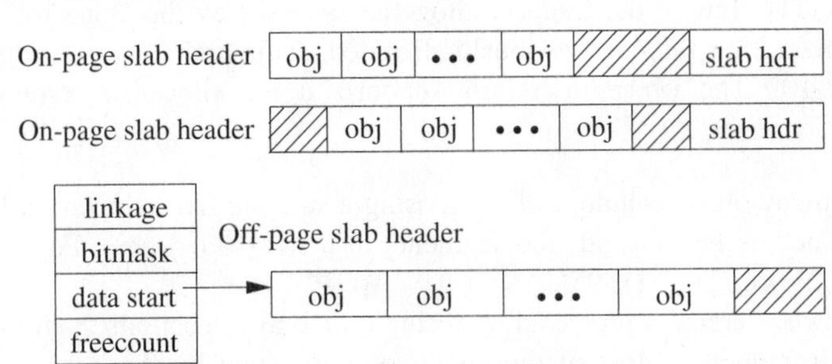

allocator before putting it out in a production release with a more challenging workload.

Figure 6.8 shows three slabs. The top two slabs place the header that describes the slab internally to the memory that holds the objects. The bottom slab places the header that describes the slab in a separate allocation external to the memory that holds the objects. The decision on whether to place the header internally or externally is based primarily on the size of the objects. An external header is used if doing so makes it possible to fit an extra object in the memory. For example, if an object is a power-of-2 size, then an internal header would allow one fewer objects per slab than would be possible if an external header were used.

Most slabs have some unused space. FreeBSD 11 always puts the unused space at the end. In Solaris, the unused space is sprinkled between the front and back in cache-alignment sized steps to improve cache line utilization (hardware caching is described in Section 6.11). For example, if the cache line is 64 bytes and the slab has 160 unused bytes, the slabs will start the object allocations at 0-, 64-, and 128-byte offsets. Solaris reports significant performance improvement using this scheme [Bonwick & Adams, 2001].

When an object is freed, the zone manager must determine the slab to which it belongs to be able to return it. In Solaris, the slab is found using a hash table that maps the address of the object to its corresponding slab header in the same way that the *vmem* system uses a hash table to find the appropriate boundary tag. Instead of using a hash table, FreeBSD stores a pointer in the *vm_page* structure that refers back to the slab header. The *vm_page* structure is found by using *pmap_kextract*() to get the physical page address from the slab's virtual address. The physical address indexes the array of *vm_page* structures. Since every slab uses at least one page, there is always a *vm_page* structure available to store the back pointer. Because wired memory is not on any page queue, the existing page-queue linkage field can be used for this purpose. Thus, no extra space must be added to the *vm_page* structure to support this functionality.

Because the kernel must allocate a *vm_page* structure for every physical page of memory on the machine, it is desirable to keep the *vm_page* structure as small as possible. To keep their size small, *vm_page* structures do not contain a mutex to control access to their fields like most other kernel data structures. Rather, there is a pool of mutexes from which a *vm_page* selects a lock using a hash of its address. The result is some lock contention when multiple pages hash to the same lock, but is far better than a single global lock.

The off-page slab header in Figure 6.8 shows its important fields. Slabs are allocated and managed by kegs, described later in this section. Kegs use the linkage fields to track the slabs that they are managing. The use of objects is tracked using the bitmask and the freecount. The bitmask has one bit per object, set when it is free and cleared if it is in use. The freecount tracks the number of available objects in the slab. When it reaches zero, all the objects have been allocated. Finally the data-start field points to the starting location of the first object in the slab. If the objects are offset from the beginning of the slab, the data-start pointer will reflect the offset.

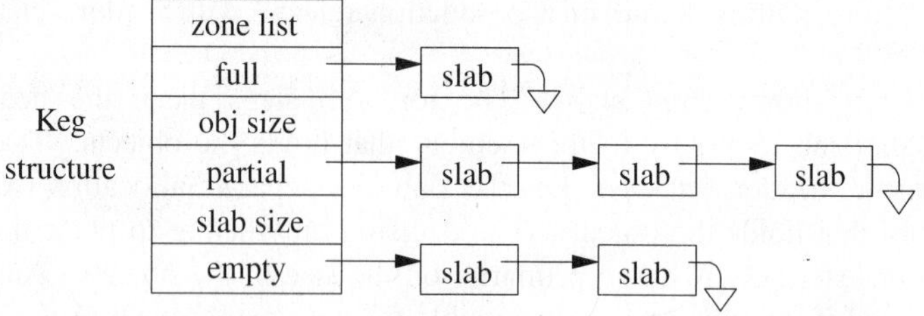

Figure 6.9 Keg data structure.

The Keg Allocator

A keg is a collection of slabs of items of identical size. Slabs are allocated to the keg as necessary. Figure 6.9 shows how the keg data structure manages its collection of slabs. The keg tracks the number of pages in each of its slabs, the number of objects held in each of its slabs, and a list of its client zones. Typically, a keg has a single client zone, but it may have more than one. The keg maintains its slabs in three lists:

- Those whose objects are currently all allocated
- Those whose objects are currently partially allocated
- Those whose objects are currently all free

When an allocation request is made to a keg, it first tries to allocate from a slab on its partially allocated list. If the partially allocated list has no slabs, it tries to allocate from a slab on its fully populated slab list. If the fully populated slab list has no slabs, it calls the *vmem* layer to allocate a new slab of its selected number of pages. The slab is broken up into the number of objects that it can hold as described above. The newly allocated slab has the requested object removed and is placed on the partially allocated list.

When an item is freed, it is returned to the slab from which it came. If it is the first object to be freed, the slab will move from the empty list to the partial list. If it is the last object to be freed, the slab will move from the partial list to the fully populated list.

Items in a keg with a single client zone are type stable. The memory in the keg will not be used for any other purpose. A structure in the keg need only be initialized the first time that it is handed out for use. Later uses may assume that the initialized values will retain their contents as of the previous free.

Objects are handed out and returned as needed. Only when the pageout daemon does a memory callback is an unused slab of objects uninitialized and the slab freed. A callback is provided on each object in the slab to allow any persistent state to be cleaned up before the slab memory is freed.

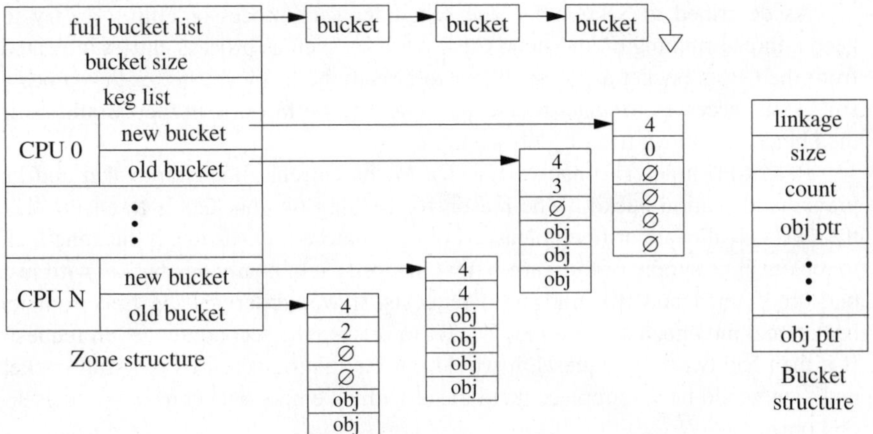

Figure 6.10 Zone and bucket data structures.

The Zone Allocator

A zone manages a set of objects in one or more kegs. The zone allocator keeps track of the active and free items, and provides functions for allocating items from the zone and for releasing them back to make them available for later use. Figure 6.10 shows how the zone allocator manages the objects in its zone. A zone typically gets its objects from a single keg, though it may source its objects from multiple kegs. The role of the zone is to fill buckets with objects that it then makes available to service allocation requests.

The details of a bucket are shown on the right of Figure 6.10. A bucket holds an array of pointers to available objects. The size field gives the size of the array and count is the number of available objects in the array. The count is equal to size when the array is full and zero when it is empty.

Unlike the global lock used by *vmem* and the slab allocator, each zone and its keg have their own locks, so different zones can be accessed simultaneously without blocking. As described in the next two subsections on kernel *malloc*() and the kernel zone allocator, most zones are used for specific objects such as vnodes, process entries, etc. A set of zones are used by *malloc*() to supply power-of-two sized objects ranging in size from 16 bytes to the number of bytes in a page. Since each power-of-2 has its own zone, allocations for one power-of-2 size does not block allocations for other power-of-2 sizes.

High demand on a single zone can still lead to lock contention. To aid performance on multiprocessor systems, a zone provides separate buckets of objects to each CPU on the system. Each CPU is able to allocate or free objects from its two buckets without the need for any lock. The only requirement is that it needs to put a critical section around the insertion and removal of an object from one of its buckets. As described in Section 4.3, a critical section prevents the currently running thread from being preempted or moved to a different CPU.

As described in Section 4.4, the scheduler uses processor affinity to try to keep a thread running on the same CPU. Objects such as process entries allocated from the CPU's bucket are more likely to already be in the cache for that processor. Thus, accesses to that structure are likely to be faster than they would be if the object was drawn from a global pool.

Each CPU holds two buckets of size M, its current allocation bucket and its previous allocation bucket. The reason for holding two buckets is to ensure that the CPU can allocate or free at least M objects before it needs to get the zone lock to replenish its supply or to return a full bucket. If it had only one bucket with just one object in it and two allocation requests, it would service the first from its bucket and then need to get a new bucket to service the second allocation request. If it then had two free requests, it would put the first object in its now-full bucket and then would need to replace that bucket with an empty bucket to return the second object.

By having two buckets, it can simply switch the two buckets to continue servicing requests. If both buckets become full, it can turn in a full one and replace it with an empty one. Or, if both become empty, it can turn in an empty one and replace it with a full one. Once it has turned in one bucket, it will be able to service at least M allocation or free requests before having to replace one of its buckets.

The zone keeps a list of full buckets. When a CPU requests a full bucket, the zone returns one from its list. If the list becomes empty, the zone allocates an empty bucket (from a bucket zone) and requests that its keg fill it with objects. When a CPU has emptied a bucket, it returns it to its bucket zone.

The level of contention for the keg lock can be controlled by the size of the bucket. If the number of objects held by a bucket doubles, the number of requests to the keg drops by at least half. FreeBSD tunes the size of the bucket based on the measured contention. Low rates of contention get smaller buckets; high rates of contention get larger buckets.

The contention is measured by doing a *trylock*() for the keg lock when it is needed. If the *trylock*() fails because some other CPU has the lock, the thread does a blocking lock. Once it gets the lock, it increments the desired bucket size for its keg. Unlike the Solaris implementation, it is not necessary to notify every CPU that the bucket size has changed. The size of each bucket is stored in its header, so the bucket size can change over time. As new buckets are created, they will have the larger size. Eventually, the older and smaller buckets will be retired and all the buckets will have the new size. The more actively a bucket is used, the more quickly it will be replaced, so the remaining small buckets are not involved in creating lock contention.

Zones only release memory when requested to do so by the paging daemon. Thus, if there is a spike in demand for a zone, it will have a long list of full buckets. When the paging daemon requests that memory be handed back, the zone walks its list of full buckets and, for each bucket, returns all its objects to its keg and frees the bucket. In turn, the keg returns the objects to its slabs. Once the return of objects from the zone to the keg is completed, the keg returns all the slabs on its full list to *vmem*. The *vmem* layer then unwires and frees its areas of unused pages so that they are available for other uses. When allocating the freed areas in the future, the *vmem* layer must first request that the kernel mapping layer populate them with wired pages.

During periods of heavy paging activity, the paging daemon can request that the size of buckets be reduced. If memory becomes critically low, the paging daemon can request that the per-CPU caches be flushed. Per-CPU cache flushing requires binding a flushing thread to each CPU in succession so that it can access the private per-CPU bucket pointers.

The zone allocator provides the *uma_zone_set_max*() function to set the upper limit of items in the zone. The limit on the total number of items in the zone includes the allocated and free items, including the items in the per-CPU caches. On multiprocessor systems, it may not be possible to allocate a new item for a particular CPU because the limit has been hit and all the free items are in the caches of the other CPUs. It is not possible to reclaim buckets from the CPU caches because the caches are not protected by locks. Only a thread running on the CPU itself can enter a critical section to manipulate the cache.

Kernel *Malloc*

The kernel provides a generalized nonpageable memory-allocation and freeing mechanism that can handle requests of arbitrary size, as well as allocate memory at interrupt time. *Malloc*() is the preferred way to allocate kernel memory other than large, fixed-size structures that are better handled by the zone allocator. This mechanism has an interface similar to that of the well-known memory allocator provided for applications programmers through the C library routines *malloc*() and *free*(). Like the C library interface, the allocation routine takes a parameter specifying the size of memory that is needed. The range of sizes for memory requests are not constrained. The free routine takes a pointer to the storage being freed, but it does not require the size of the piece of memory being freed.

Often, the kernel needs a memory allocation for the duration of a single system call. In a user process, such short-term memory would be allocated on the run-time stack. Because the kernel has a limited run-time stack, it is not feasible to allocate even moderate blocks of memory on it. Consequently, such memory must be allocated dynamically. For example, when the system must translate a pathname, it must allocate a 1-Kbyte buffer to hold the name. Other blocks of memory must be more persistent than a single system call and have to be allocated from dynamic memory. Examples include protocol control blocks that remain throughout the duration of a network connection.

The design specification for a kernel memory allocator is similar, but not identical, to the design criteria for a user-level memory allocator. One criterion for a memory allocator is that it make good use of the physical memory. Use of memory is measured by the amount of memory needed to hold a set of allocations at any point in time. Percentage utilization is expressed as

$$utilization = \frac{requested}{required}$$

Here, *requested* is the sum of the memory that has been requested and not yet freed; *required* is the amount of memory that has been allocated for the pool from which the requests are filled. An allocator requires more memory than requested because of fragmentation and a need to have a ready supply of free memory for future requests. A perfect memory allocator would have a utilization of 100 percent. In practice, a 50 percent utilization is considered good [Korn & Vo, 1985].

Good memory utilization in the kernel is more important than in user processes. Because user processes run in virtual memory, unused parts of their address space can be paged out. Thus, pages in the process address space that are part of the required pool and are not being requested do not need to tie up physical memory. Since the kernel malloc arena is not paged, all pages in the required pool are held by the kernel and cannot be used for other purposes. To keep the kernel-utilization percentage as high as possible, the kernel should release unused memory in the required pool rather than hold it, as is typically done with user processes.

The most important criterion for a kernel memory allocator is that it be fast. A slow memory allocator will degrade the system performance because memory allocation is done frequently. Speed of allocation is more critical when executing in the kernel than it is in user code because the kernel must allocate many data structures that user processes can allocate cheaply on their run-time stack. In addition, the kernel represents the platform on which all user processes run, and if it is slow, it will degrade the performance of every process that is running.

Another problem with a slow memory allocator is that programmers of frequently used kernel interfaces will think that they cannot afford to use the memory allocator as their primary one. Instead, they will build their own memory allocator on top of the original by maintaining their own pool of memory blocks. Multiple allocators reduce the efficiency with which memory is used. The kernel ends up with many different free lists of memory instead of a single free list from which all allocations can be drawn. For example, consider the case of two subsystems that need memory. If they have their own free lists, the amount of memory tied up in the two lists will be the sum of the greatest amount of memory that each of the two subsystems has ever used. If they share a free list, the amount of memory tied up in the free list may be as low as the greatest amount of memory that either subsystem used. As the number of subsystems grows, the savings from having a single free list grow.

The kernel memory allocator uses a hybrid strategy. Small allocations are done using a power-of-2 list strategy. Using the zone allocator, the kernel creates a set of zones with one for each power-of-two between 16 and the page size. The allocation simply requests a block of memory from the appropriate zone. Usually, the zone will have an available piece of memory in one of the buckets of the CPU on which it is running that it can return. Only if the CPUs buckets are both empty will the zone allocator have to do a full allocation. As described in the zone allocator subsection, when forced to do an additional allocation, it fills a whole bucket with the appropriately sized pieces. This strategy speeds future allocations because several pieces of memory become available as a result of the call into the allocator.

Freeing a small block is also fast. The memory is simply returned to the zone from which it came.

Because of the inefficiency of power-of-2 allocation strategies for allocations larger than a page, the allocation method for blocks larger than a page is based on allocating pieces of memory in multiples of pages. The algorithm switches to the slower but more memory-efficient strategy for allocation sizes larger than a page using the *vmem* allocator. This value is chosen because the power-of-2 algorithm yields sizes of 2, 4, 8, 16, . . ., *n* pages, whereas the large block algorithm that allocates in multiples of pages yields sizes of 2, 3, 4, 5, . . ., *n* pages. Thus, for allocations of greater than one page, the large block algorithm will use less than or equal to the number of pages used by the power-of-2 algorithm, so the threshold between the large and small allocators is set at one page.

Large allocations are first rounded up to be a multiple of the page size. The allocator then uses the algorithm described in the previous subsection to find space in the *vmem* arena.

Because the size is not specified when a block of memory is freed, the allocator must keep track of the sizes of the pieces that it has handed out. Many allocators increase the allocation request by a few bytes to create space to store the size of the block in a header just before the allocation. However, this strategy doubles the memory requirement for allocations that request a power-of-two-size block. Therefore, the kernel memory allocators store the size externally. For allocations up to the size of a page that are allocated from a zone, the zone allocator associates the size information with the memory page. Locating the allocation size outside the allocated block improved utilization far more than expected. The reason is that many allocations in the kernel are for blocks of memory whose size is exactly a power of 2. The size of these requests would be nearly doubled if the more typical strategy were used. Now they can be accommodated with no wasted memory.

The allocator can be called from anywhere in the kernel. Clients show their willingness (and ability) to wait with a flag to the allocation routine. For clients that are willing to wait, the allocator guarantees that their request will succeed. Thus, these clients do not need to check the return value from the allocator. If memory is unavailable and the client cannot wait, the allocator returns a null pointer. These clients must be prepared to cope with this (typically infrequent) condition. Clients that cannot wait because they hold a short-term lock often release it, wait for memory to become available, then reacquire their lock. The other strategy is to give up and hope to succeed later.

Kernel Zone Allocator

Some commonly allocated items in the kernel such as process, thread, vnode, and control-block structures are not well handled by the general purpose *malloc*() interface. These structures share several characteristics:

- They tend to be large and hence wasteful of space. For example, the process structure is about 550 bytes, which when rounded up to a power-of-2 size requires 1024 bytes of memory.

- They tend to be common. Because they are individually wasteful of space, collectively they waste too much space compared to a denser representation.
- They are often linked together in long lists. If the allocation of each structure begins on a page boundary, then the list pointers will all be at the same offset from the beginning of the page. When traversing these structures, the linkage pointers will all be competing for a small set of hardware cache lines causing many steps along the list to produce a cache miss, making the list traversal slow.
- These structures often contain many lists and locks that must be initialized before use. If there is a dedicated pool of memory for each structure, then these substructures need to be initialized only when the pool is first created rather than after every allocation.

For these reasons, FreeBSD allocates a separate zone for each of these kernel structures. Thus, there is a zone that contains only process structures, another that contains only vnodes, etc.

A new zone is created with the *uma_zcreate*() function. It must specify the size of the items to be allocated and register two sets of functions. The first set is called whenever an item is allocated or freed from the zone. These routines typically track the number of allocated items. The second set is called whenever memory is allocated or freed from the zone's keg. When a new slab of memory is allocated to the zone's keg, all the locks and list heads for each object in the new slab are initialized. When making allocations from the zone, the kernel knows that the locks and list heads are already initialized and ready for use. Similarly, they need not be destroyed when the structure is freed. Only when memory is reclaimed from the zone's keg is it necessary to destroy the locks.

Items are allocated with *uma_zalloc*(), which takes a zone identifier returned by *uma_zcreate*(). Items are freed with *uma_zfree*(), which takes a zone identifier and a pointer to the item to be freed. No size is needed when allocating or freeing, since the item size was set when the zone was created.

The creation of separate zones runs counter to the desire to keep all memory in a single pool to maximize utilization efficiency. However, the benefits from segregating memory for the set of structures for which the zone allocator is appropriate outweighs the efficiency gains from keeping them in the general pool. The zone allocator minimizes the waste of the separate pools by freeing memory from a zone based on a reduction in demand for objects from the zone and when notified of a memory shortage by the pageout daemon.

6.4 Per-Process Resources

As we have already seen, a process requires a process entry and a kernel stack. The next major resource that must be allocated is its virtual memory. The initial virtual-memory requirements are defined by the header in the process's executable. These requirements include the space needed for the program text, the initialized data, the uninitialized data, and the run-time stack. During the initial startup of the program, the kernel will build the data structures necessary to describe these four areas. Most programs need to allocate additional memory. The kernel typically provides this additional memory by expanding the uninitialized data area.

Most FreeBSD programs use shared libraries. The header for the executable will describe the libraries that it needs (usually the C library, and possibly others). The kernel is not responsible for locating and mapping these libraries during the initial execution of the program. Finding, mapping, and creating the dynamic linkages to these libraries is handled by an interpreter specified in the header. For ELF binaries, the interpreter is **/libexec/ld-elf.so**. This startup code runs before control is passed to the main entry point of the program.

FreeBSD Process Virtual-Address Space

The initial layout of the address space for a process is shown in Figure 6.11. As discussed in Section 6.2, the address space for a process is described by that process's *vmspace* structure. The contents of the address space are defined by a list of *vm_map_entry* structures, each structure describing a ***region*** of virtual address space that resides between a *start* and an *end* address. A region describes a range of memory that is being treated in the same way. For example, the text of a program is a region that is read-only and executable, and is demand paged from the file on disk that contains it. Thus, the *vm_map_entry* also contains the protection mode to be applied to the region that it describes. Each *vm_map_entry* structure also has a pointer to the *vm_object* that provides the initial data for the region. Finally, each *vm_map_entry* structure has an offset that describes where within the *vm_object* the mapping begins.

The example shown in Figure 6.11 represents a process just after it has started execution. The first two map entries both point to the same *vm_object*; here, that *vm_object* is the executable. The executable consists of two parts: the text of the program that resides at the beginning of the file and the initialized data area that follows at the end of the text. Thus, the first *vm_map_entry* describes a read-only region that maps the text of the program. The second *vm_map_entry* describes the copy-on-write region that maps the initialized data of the program that follows the program text in the file (copy-on-write is described in Section 6.6). The offset field in the entry reflects this different starting location. The third and fourth *vm_map_entry* structures describe the uninitialized data and stack areas, respectively. Both of these areas are represented by ***anonymous vm_objects***. An anonymous *vm_object* provides a zero-filled page on first use and arranges to store modified pages in the swap area if memory becomes tight. Anonymous *vm_object*s are described in more detail later in this section.

Page-Fault Dispatch

When a process attempts to access a piece of its address space that is not currently resident, a page fault occurs. The page-fault handler in the kernel is presented with the virtual address that caused the fault and the type of access that was

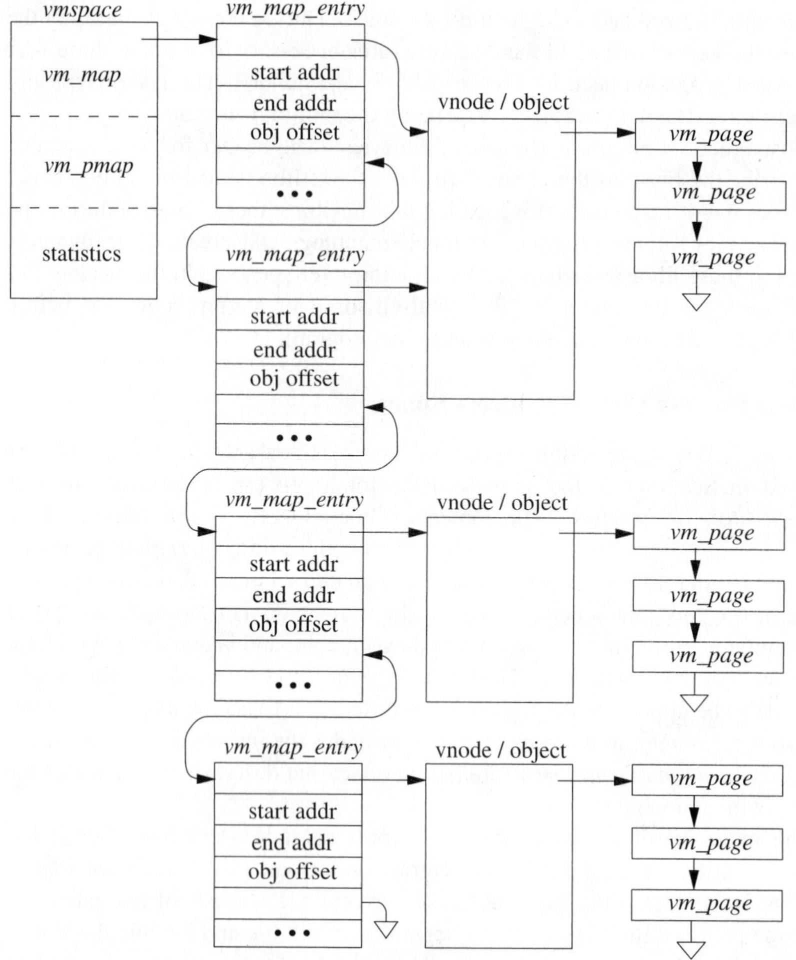

Figure 6.11 Layout of an address space.

attempted (execute, read, or write). The fault is handled with the following four steps:

1. Find the *vmspace* structure for the faulting process; from that structure, find the binary-search tree for its *vm_map_entries*.
2. Look up the faulting address. If the lookup fails, the faulting address is not within any valid part of the address space for the process, so send the process a segment fault signal. Lookups are done using Tarjan and Sleator's top-down splay algorithm. This algorithm reorders the tree so that the most recently found entry is moved to the top of the tree. Recently found entries remain near the top of the tree. The benefit of this algorithm is that it takes advantage

of the frequent locality of page faults. The drawback is that lookups often need to exclusively acquire the tree's lock to do the permutation causing lock contention between page-faulting threads sharing the same address space.

3. Having found a *vm_map_entry* that contains the faulting address, convert that address to an offset within the underlying *vm_object*. Calculate the offset within the *vm_object* as

```
object_offset = fault_address
        - vm_map_entry->start_address
        + vm_map_entry->object_offset
```

   Subtract off the start address to give the offset into the region mapped by the *vm_map_entry*. Add in the object_offset to give the absolute offset of the page within the *vm_object*.

4. Present the absolute object_offset to the underlying *vm_object*, which allocates a *vm_page* structure and uses its pager to fill the page. The *vm_object* then returns a pointer to the *vm_page* structure, which is mapped into the faulting location in the process address space.

Once the appropriate page has been mapped into the faulting location, the page-fault handler returns and reexecutes the faulting instruction.

Mapping to *Vm_objects*

A *vm_object* holds information about either a file or an area of anonymous memory. Whether a file is mapped by a single process in the system or by many processes in the system, it will always be represented by a single *vm_object*. Thus, the *vm_object* is responsible for maintaining all the state about those pages of a file that are resident. All references to that file will be described by *vm_map_entry* structures that reference the same *vm_object*. A *vm_object* never stores the same page of a file in more than one physical-memory page, so all mappings will get a consistent view of the file.

A *vm_object* stores the following information:

- A collection of the pages for that *vm_object* that are currently resident in main memory; a page may be mapped into multiple address spaces, but it is always claimed by exactly one *vm_object*
- A count of the number of *vm_map_entry* structures or other *vm_object*s that reference the *vm_object*
- The size of the file or anonymous area described by the *vm_object*
- The number of memory-resident pages held by the *vm_object*
- For shadow objects, a pointer to the next *vm_object* in the chain (shadow objects are described in Section 6.5)

- The type of ***pager*** for the *vm_object*; the pager is responsible for providing the data to fill a page and for providing a place to store the page when it has been modified (pagers are covered in Section 6.10)

There are three types of *vm_object*s in the system:

- *Named vm_object*s represent files; they may also represent hardware devices that are able to provide mapped memory such as frame buffers.
- *Anonymous vm_object*s represent areas of memory that are zero filled on first use; they are abandoned when they are no longer needed.
- *Shadow vm_object*s hold private copies of pages that have been modified; they are abandoned when they are no longer referenced.

Shadow and all anonymous *vm_object*s (other than POSIX *shmem*) are often referred to as "internal" *vm_object*s in the source code. The type of a *vm_object* is defined by the type of pager that it uses to fulfill page-fault requests.

A named *vm_object* uses the device pager if it maps a hardware device, the vnode pager if it is backed by a file in the filesystem, or the swap pager if it backs a POSIX *shmem* object. The device pager services a page fault by returning the appropriate physical address for the device being mapped. Since the device memory is separate from the main memory on the machine, it will never be selected by the pageout daemon. Thus, the device pager never has to handle a pageout request.

The vnode pager provides an interface to *vm_object*s that represent files in the filesystem. The vnode pager keeps a reference to a vnode that represents the file being mapped in the *vm_object*. The vnode pager services a pagein request by doing a read on the vnode; it services a pageout request by doing a write to the vnode. Thus, the file itself stores the modified pages. In cases where it is not appropriate to modify the file directly, such as an executable that does not want to modify its initialized data pages, the kernel must interpose a shadow *vm_object* between the *vm_map_entry* and the *vm_object* representing the file; see Section 6.5.

Anonymous or POSIX *shmem vm_object*s use the swap pager. An anonymous or POSIX *shmem vm_object* services pagein requests by getting a page of memory from the free list and zeroing that page. When a pageout request is made for a page for the first time, the swap pager is responsible for finding an unused page in the swap area, writing the contents of the page to that space, and recording where that page is stored. If a pagein request comes for a page that had been previously paged out, the swap pager is responsible for finding where it stored that page and reading back the contents into a free page in memory. A later pageout request for that page will cause the page to be written out to the previously allocated location.

Shadow *vm_object*s also use the swap pager. They work just like anonymous or POSIX *shmem vm_object*s, except that the swap pager does not need to provide their initial pages. The initial pages are created by the *vm_fault*() routine by copying existing pages in response to copy-on-write faults.

Further details on the pagers are given in Section 6.10.

Vm_objects

Each virtual-memory *vm_object* has a pager type, pager handle, and pager private data associated with it. The *vm_objects* that map files have a vnode-pager type associated with them. The handle for the vnode-pager type is a pointer to the vnode on which to do the I/O, and the private data is the size of the vnode at the time that the mapping was done. Every vnode that maps a file has a *vm_object* associated with it. When a fault occurs for a file that is mapped into memory, the *vm_object* associated with the file can be checked to see whether the faulted page is resident. If the page is resident, it can be used. If the page is not resident, a new page is allocated, and the vnode pager is requested to fill the new page.

Caching in the virtual-memory system is done by a *vm_object* that is associated with a file or region that it represents. Each *vm_object* contains pages that are the cached contents of its associated file or region. All *vm_objects* are reclaimed as soon as their reference count drops to zero. Pages associated with reclaimed *vm_objects* are moved to the free list. Each *vm_object* that represents anonymous memory is reclaimed as part of cleaning up a process as it exits. However, *vm_objects* that refer to files are persistent. When the reference count on a vnode drops to zero, it is stored on a ***least recently used*** (***LRU***) list known as the vnode cache; vnodes are described in Section 7.3. The vnode does not release its *vm_object* until the vnode is reclaimed and reused for another file. Unless there is pressure on the memory, the *vm_object* associated with the vnode will retain its pages. If the vnode is reactivated and a page fault occurs before the associated page is freed, that page can be used rather than being reread from disk.

This cache is similar to the text cache found in earlier versions of BSD in that it provides performance improvements for short-running but frequently executed programs. Frequently executed programs include those used to list the contents of directories, show system status, or perform the intermediate steps involved in compiling a program. For example, consider a typical application that is made up of multiple source files. Each of several compiler steps must be run on each file in turn. The first time that the compiler is run, the executable files associated with its various components are read in from the disk. For each file compiled thereafter, the previously created executable files are found, as well as any previously read header files, alleviating the need to reload them from disk each time.

Vm_objects to Pages

When the system is first booted, the kernel looks through the physical memory on the machine to find out how many pages are available. After the physical memory that will be dedicated to the kernel has been deducted, all the remaining pages of physical memory are described by *vm_page* structures. These *vm_page* structures are all initially placed on the memory free list. As the system starts running and processes begin to execute, they generate page faults. Each page fault is matched to the *vm_object* that covers the faulting piece of address space. The first time that a piece of a *vm_object* is faulted, it must allocate a page from the free list and must initialize that page either by zero-filling it or by reading its contents from the filesystem. That page then becomes associated with the *vm_object*. Thus, each *vm_object* has its current set of *vm_page* structures linked to it.

If memory becomes scarce, the paging daemon will search for pages that have not been used actively. Before these pages can be used by a new *vm_object*, they must be removed from all the processes that currently have them mapped, and any modified contents must be saved by the *vm_object* that owns them. Once cleaned, the pages can be removed from the *vm_object* that owns them and can be placed on the free list for reuse. The details of the paging system are described in Section 6.12.

6.5 Shared Memory

In Sections 6.2 and 6.4, we explained how the address space of a process is organized. This section shows the additional data structures needed to support shared address space between processes. Traditionally, the address space of each process was completely isolated from the address space of all other processes running on the system. The only exception was read-only sharing of program text. All interprocess communication was done through well-defined channels that passed through the kernel: pipes, sockets, files, and special devices. The benefit of this isolated approach is that, no matter how badly a process destroys its own address space, it cannot affect the address space of any other process running on the system. Each process can precisely control when data are sent or received; it can also precisely identify the locations within its address space that are read or written. The drawback of this approach is that all interprocess communication requires at least two system calls: one from the sending process and one from the receiving process. For high volumes of interprocess communication, especially when small packets of data are being exchanged, the overhead of the system calls dominates the communications cost.

Shared memory provides a way to reduce interprocess-communication costs dramatically. Two or more processes that wish to communicate map the same piece of read–write memory into their address space. Once all the processes have mapped the memory into their address space, any changes to that piece of memory are visible to all the other processes, without any intervention by the kernel. Thus, interprocess communication can be achieved without any system-call overhead other than the cost of the initial mapping. The drawback to this approach is that, if a process that has the memory mapped corrupts the data structures in that memory, all the other processes mapping that memory also see the corrupted data structures. In addition, there is the complexity faced by the application developer who must develop data structures to control access to the shared memory and must cope with the race conditions inherent in manipulating and controlling such data structures that are being accessed concurrently.

Some UNIX variants have a kernel-based semaphore mechanism to provide the needed serialization of access to the shared memory. However, both getting and setting such semaphores require system calls. The overhead of using such semaphores is comparable to that of using the traditional interprocess-communication methods. Unfortunately, these semaphores have all the complexity of shared memory, yet confer little of its speed advantage. The primary reason to introduce the complexity of shared memory is for the commensurate speed gain. If this gain is to be obtained, most of the data-structure locking needs to be done in the shared memory segment itself. The kernel-based semaphores should be used for only those rare cases where there is contention for a lock and one process must wait. Consequently, modern interfaces, such as POSIX Pthreads, are designed such that the semaphores can be located in the shared memory region. The common case of setting or clearing an uncontested semaphore can be done by the user process, without calling the kernel. There are two cases where a process must perform a system call. If a process tries to set an already-locked semaphore, it must call the kernel to block until the semaphore is available. This system call has little effect on performance because the lock is contested, so it is impossible to proceed, and the kernel must be invoked to do a context switch anyway. If a process clears a semaphore that is wanted by another process, it must call the kernel to awaken that process. Since most locks are uncontested, the applications can run at full speed without kernel intervention.

Mmap Model

When two processes wish to create an area of shared memory, they must have some way to name the piece of memory that they wish to share, and they must be able to describe its size and initial contents. The system interface describing an area of shared memory accomplishes all these goals by using files as the basis for describing a shared memory segment. A process creates a shared memory segment by using

```
void *addr = mmap(
    void *addr,         /* base address */
    size_t len,         /* length of region */
    int prot,           /* protection of region */
    int flags,          /* mapping flags */
    int fd,             /* file to map */
    off_t offset);      /* offset to begin mapping */
```

to map the file referenced by descriptor *fd*, starting at file offset *offset* into its address space, starting at *addr* and continuing for *len* bytes with access permission *prot*. The *flags* parameter allows a process to specify whether it wants to make a *shared* or *private* mapping. Changes made to a shared mapping are written back to the file and are visible to other processes. Changes made to a private mapping are not written back to the file and are not visible to other processes. Two processes that wish to share a piece of memory request a shared mapping of the same file into their address space. Thus, the existing and well-understood filesystem namespace identifies shared objects. The contents of the file are used as the initial value of the memory segment. All changes made to the mapping are reflected back into the contents of the file, so long-term state can be maintained in the shared memory region, even across invocations of the sharing processes.

Some applications want to use shared memory purely as a short-term interprocess-communication mechanism. They need an area of memory that is initially zeroed and whose contents are abandoned when they are done using it. Such processes want neither to pay the relatively high startup cost associated with paging in the contents of a file to initialize a shared memory segment nor to pay the shutdown costs of writing modified pages back to the file when they are done with the memory. Although FreeBSD does provide the limited and quirky naming scheme of the System V *shmem* interface as a rendezvous mechanism for such short-term shared memory (see Section 7.2), the designers ultimately decided that all naming of memory objects for *mmap* should use the filesystem namespace. To provide an efficient mechanism for short-term shared memory, mappings that do not require stability across system reboots use the MAP_NOSYNC flag to avoid the overhead of periodic syncing of dirty pages. When this flag is specified, dirty pages are only written to the filesystem when memory is in high demand.

When a mapping is no longer needed, it can be removed using

```
munmap(void *addr, size_t len);
```

The *munmap* system call removes any mappings that exist in the address space, starting at *addr* and continuing for *len* bytes. There are no constraints between previous mappings and a later *munmap*. The specified range may be a subset of a previous *mmap*, or it may encompass an area that contains many *mmap*'ed files. When a process exits, the system does an implied *munmap* over its entire address space.

During its initial mapping, a process can set the protections on a page to allow reading, writing, and/or execution. The process can change these protections later by using

```
mprotect(const void *address, int length, int protection);
```

This feature can be used by debuggers when they are trying to track down a memory-corruption bug. By disabling writing on the page containing the data structure that is being corrupted, the debugger can trap all writes to the page and verify that they are correct before allowing them to occur.

Traditionally, programming for real-time systems has been done with specially written operating systems. In the interests of reducing the costs of real-time applications and of using the skills of the large body of UNIX programmers, companies developing real-time applications now use UNIX-based systems for writing these applications. Two fundamental requirements of a real-time system are guaranteed maximum latencies and predictable execution times. Predictable execution time is difficult to provide in a virtual-memory-based system, since a page fault may occur at any point in the execution of a program, resulting in a potentially large delay while the faulting page is retrieved from the disk or network. To avoid paging delays, the system allows a process to force its pages to be resident, and not paged out, by using

```
mlock(const void *address, size_t length);
```

As long as the process limits its accesses to the locked area of its address space, it can be sure that it will not be delayed by page faults. To prevent a single process from acquiring all the physical memory on the machine to the detriment of all other processes, the system imposes a resource limit to control the amount of memory that may be locked. Typically, this limit is set to no more than one-third of the physical memory, and it may be set to zero by a system administrator who does not want random processes to be able to monopolize system resources.

When a process has finished with its time-critical use of an *mlock*'ed region, it can release the lock on the pages using

```
munlock(const void *address, size_t length);
```

After the *munlock* call, the pages in the specified address range are still accessible, but they may be paged out if memory is needed and they are not accessed.

An application may need to ensure that certain records are committed to disk without forcing the writing of all the dirty pages of a file done by the *fsync* system call. For example, a database program may want to commit a single piece of metadata without writing back all the dirty blocks in its database file. A process does this selective synchronization using

```
msync(void *address, int length, int flags);
```

Only those modified pages within the specified address range are written back to the filesystem. The *msync* system call has no effect on anonymous regions.

Shared Mapping

When multiple processes map the same file into their address space, the system must ensure that all the processes view the same set of memory pages. As shown in Sections 6.2 and 6.4, each file that is being used actively by a client of the virtual-memory system is represented by a *vm_object*. Each mapping that a process has to a piece of a file is described by a *vm_map_entry* structure. An example of two processes mapping the same file into their address space is shown in Figure 6.12. When a page fault occurs in one of these processes, the process's *vm_map_entry* references the *vm_object* to find the appropriate page. Since all mappings reference the same *vm_object*, the processes will all get references to the same set of

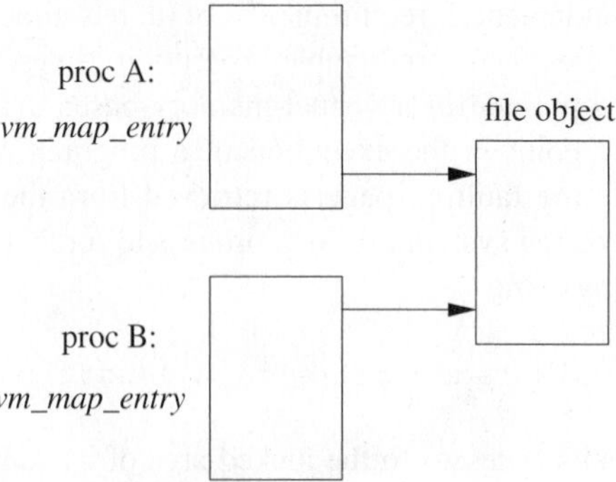

Figure 6.12 Multiple mappings to a file.

physical memory, thus ensuring that changes made by one process will be visible in the address spaces of the other processes as well.

Two processes sharing a mapping do not have to place it at the same virtual address in their address spaces. Moreover, a process may have two or more *vm_map* entries to the same file (or region of that file) in its address space. For example, when running an executable, a process has a *vm_map* entry referencing the text portion of the executable and a *vm_map* entry referencing the initialized-data portion of the executable.

Private Mapping

A process may request a ***private mapping*** of a file. A private mapping has two main effects:

1. Changes made to the memory mapping the file are not reflected back into the mapped file.
2. Changes made to the memory mapping the file are not visible to other processes mapping the file.

An example of the use of a private mapping would be during program debugging. The debugger will request a private mapping of the program text so that, when it sets a breakpoint, the modification is not written back into the executable stored on the disk and is not visible to the other (presumably nondebugging) processes executing the program.

The kernel uses shadow *vm_object*s to prevent changes made by a process from being reflected back to the underlying *vm_object*. The use of a shadow *vm_object* is shown in Figure 6.13. When the initial private mapping is requested, the file *vm_object* is mapped into the requesting-process address space, with copy-on-write semantics.

If the process attempts to write a page of the *vm_object*, a page fault occurs and traps into the kernel. If this fault is the first for the private mapping to the

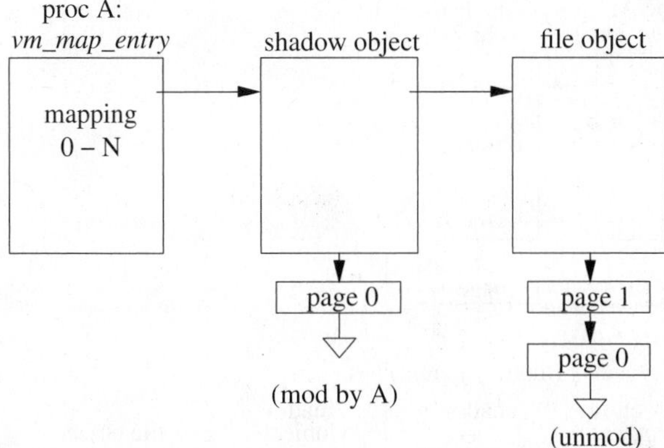

Figure 6.13 Use of a shadow *vm_object* for a private mapping.

vm_object, then a new shadow *vm_object* must be created. First, a new shadow *vm_object* is allocated with a pager type of swap (pagers are described in Section 6.10). The new shadow *vm_object* is set to point to the original *vm_object* that it will shadow. The faulting *vm_map_entry* is then changed to reference the shadow *vm_object*. The kernel makes a copy of the page to be modified and hangs it from the shadow *vm_object*. In this example, process A has modified page 0 of the file *vm_object*. The kernel has copied page 0 to the shadow *vm_object* that is being used to provide the private mapping for process A.

If free memory is limited, it would be better simply to move the modified page from the file *vm_object* to the shadow *vm_object*. The move would reduce the immediate demand on the free memory, because a new page would not have to be allocated. The drawback to this optimization is that, if there is a later access to the file *vm_object* by some other process, the kernel will have to allocate a new page. The kernel will also have to pay the cost of doing an I/O operation to reload the page contents. In FreeBSD, the virtual-memory system never moves a page from a file *vm_object* rather than copying it.

When a page fault for the private mapping occurs, the kernel traverses the list of *vm_object*s headed by the *vm_map_entry*, looking for the faulted page. The first *vm_object* in the chain that has the desired page is the one that is used. If the search gets to the final *vm_object* on the chain without finding the desired page, then the page is requested from that final *vm_object*. Thus, pages on a shadow *vm_object* will be used in preference to the same pages in the file *vm_object* itself. The details of page-fault handling are given in Section 6.11.

When a process removes a mapping from its address space (either explicitly from an *munmap* request or implicitly when the address space is freed on process exit), pages held by its shadow *vm_object* are not written back to the file *vm_object*. The shadow-*vm_object* pages are simply placed back on the memory free list for immediate reuse.

When a process forks, it does not want changes to its private mappings made after it forked to be visible in its child; similarly, the child does not want its

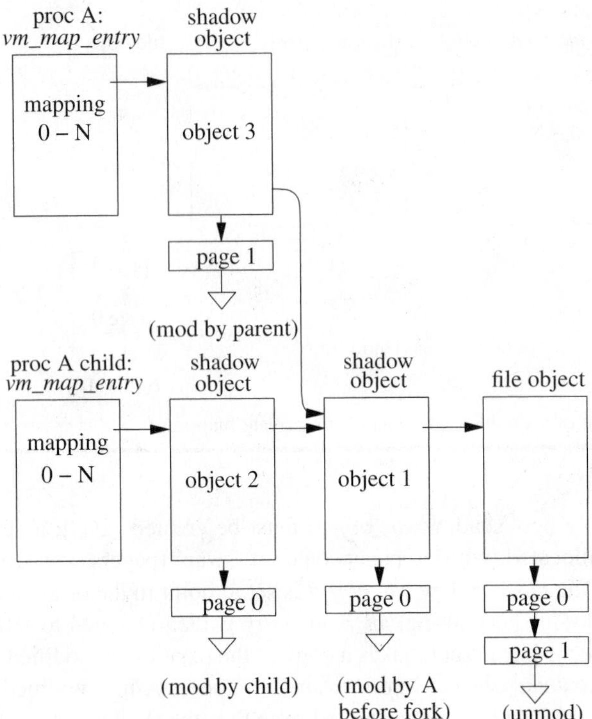

Figure 6.14 Shadow-object chains.

changes to be visible in its parent. The result is that each process needs to create a shadow *vm_object* if it continues to make changes in a private mapping. When process A in Figure 6.13 forks, a set of shadow-*vm_object* chains is created, as shown in Figure 6.14. In this example, process A modified page 0 before it forked and then later modified page 1. Its modified version of page 1 hangs off its new shadow *vm_object*, so those modifications will not be visible to its child. Similarly, its child has modified page 0. If the child were to modify page 0 in the original shadow *vm_object*, that change would be visible in its parent. Thus, the child process must make a new copy of page 0 in its own shadow *vm_object*.

If the system runs short of memory, the kernel may need to reclaim inactive memory held in a shadow *vm_object*. The kernel assigns to the swap pager the task of backing the shadow *vm_object*. The swap pager sets up data structures (described in Section 6.10) that can describe the entire contents of the shadow *vm_object*. It then allocates enough swap space to hold the requested shadow pages and writes them to that area. These pages can then be freed for other uses. If a later page fault requests a swapped-out page, then a new page of memory is allocated and its contents are reloaded with an I/O from the swap area.

Collapsing of Shadow Chains

When a process with a private mapping removes that mapping either explicitly with an *munmap* system call or implicitly by exiting, its parent or child process may be left with a chain of shadow *vm_object*s. Usually, these chains of shadow *vm_object*s can be collapsed into a single shadow *vm_object*, often freeing up memory as part of the collapse. Consider what happens when process A exits in Figure 6.14. First, shadow *vm_object* 3 can be freed along with its associated page of memory. This deallocation leaves shadow *vm_object*s 1 and 2 in a chain with no intervening references. Thus, these two *vm_object*s can be collapsed into a single shadow *vm_object*. Since they both contain a copy of page 0, and since only the page 0 in shadow *vm_object* 2 can be accessed by the remaining child process, the page 0 in shadow *vm_object* 1 can be freed along with shadow *vm_object* 1 itself.

If the child of process A were to exit instead, then shadow *vm_object* 2 and the associated page of memory could be freed. Shadow *vm_object*s 1 and 3 would then be in a chain that would be eligible for collapse. Here, there are no common pages, so *vm_object* 3 would retain its own page 1 and acquire page 0 from shadow *vm_object* 1. *Vm_object* 1 would then be freed. In addition to merging the pages from the two *vm_object*s, the collapse operation requires a similar merger of any swap space that has been allocated by the two *vm_object*s. If page 2 had been copied to *vm_object* 3 and page 4 had been copied to *vm_object* 1, but these pages were later reclaimed, the pager for *vm_object* 3 would hold a swap block for page 2, and the pager for *vm_object* 1 would hold a swap block for page 4. Before freeing *vm_object* 1, its swap block for page 4 would have to be moved over to *vm_object* 3.

A performance problem can arise if either a process or its children repeatedly fork. Without some intervention, they can create long chains of shadow *vm_object*s. If the processes are long-lived, the system does not get an opportunity to collapse these shadow-*vm_object* chains. Traversing these long chains of shadow *vm_object*s to resolve page faults is time consuming, and many inaccessible pages can build up forcing the system to needlessly page them out to reclaim them.

One alternative would be to calculate the number of live references to a page after each copy-on-write fault. When only one live reference remained, the page could be moved to the shadow *vm_object* that still referenced it. When all the pages had been moved out of a shadow *vm_object*, it could be removed from the chain. For example, in Figure 6.14, when the child of process A wrote to page 0, a copy of page 0 was made in shadow *vm_object* 2. At that point, the only live reference to page 0 in *vm_object* 1 was from process A. Thus, the page 0 in *vm_object* 1 could be moved to *vm_object* 3. That would leave *vm_object* 1 with no pages, so it could be reclaimed leaving *vm_object*s 2 and 3 pointing at the file *vm_object* directly. Unfortunately, this strategy would add considerable overhead to the page-fault handling routine which would noticeably slow the overall performance of the system, so FreeBSD does not make this optimization.

FreeBSD uses a lower-cost heuristic to reduce the copying of shadow pages. When a page of a top-level shadow object is faulted, the kernel checks whether a lower-level shadow object contains a copy of the page. If that lower-level shadow object has the page and is referenced only by the top-level shadow object, (i.e., in principle the chain could be collapsed) the page is moved rather than copied from the lower-level shadow object to the top-level shadow object and mapped with write access.

Private Snapshots

When a process makes read accesses to a private mapping of a *vm_object*, it continues to see changes made to that *vm_object* by other processes that are writing to the *vm_object* through the filesystem or that have a shared mapping to the *vm_object*. When a process makes a write access to a private mapping of an *vm_object*, a snapshot of the corresponding page of the *vm_object* is made and is stored in the shadow *vm_object*, and the modification is made to that snapshot. Thus, further changes to that page made by other processes that are writing to the page through the filesystem or that have a shared mapping to the *vm_object* are no longer visible. However, changes to unmodified pages of the *vm_object* continue to be visible. This mix of changing and unchanging parts of the file can be confusing.

To provide a more consistent view of a file, a process may want to take a snapshot of the file at the time that it is initially privately mapped. Historically, both Mach and 4.4BSD provided a copy *vm_object* whose effect was to take a snapshot of a *vm_object* at the time that the private mapping was set up. The copy *vm_object* tracked changes to a *vm_object* by other processes and kept original copies of any pages that changed. Only Mac OS/X implemented copy *vm_object*s, and there are no major applications that depend on them. The copy-*vm_object* code in the virtual-memory system was large and complex, and it noticeably slowed virtual-memory performance. Consequently, copy *vm_object*s were deemed unnecessary and were removed from FreeBSD as part of the early cleanup and performance work done on the virtual-memory system. Applications that want to get a snapshot of a file can do so by reading it into their address space or by making a copy of it in the filesystem and then referring to the copy.

6.6 Creation of a New Process

Processes are created with a *fork* system call. The *fork* is usually followed shortly thereafter by an *exec* system call that overlays the virtual address space of the child process with the contents of an executable image that resides in the filesystem. The process then executes until it terminates voluntarily by exiting or involuntarily by receiving a signal. In Sections 6.6 to 6.9, we trace the management of the memory resources used at each step in this cycle.

A *fork* system call duplicates the address space of an existing process, creating an identical child process. The *fork* set of system calls is the only way that new processes are created in FreeBSD. *Fork* duplicates all the resources of the original process (except for its *kqueue* descriptors) and copies that process's address space.

The virtual-memory resources of the process that must be allocated include the child's process structure and its associated substructures, and its kernel stack. In addition, the kernel can be requested through the *procctl* system call to reserve storage (either memory, filesystem space, or swap space) used to back the process. The general outline of the implementation of a *fork* is as follows:

- If requested to do so, reserve virtual address space for the child process
- Allocate a process entry and thread structure for the child process, and fill it in
- Copy to the child the parent's process group, credentials, file descriptors, limits, and signal actions
- Allocate a new kernel stack, copying the bottom frame that returns from the system call in the current one to initialize it
- Allocate a *vmspace* structure
- Duplicate the address space by creating copies of the parent *vm_map_entry* structures marked copy-on-write
- Arrange for the child process to return 0, to distinguish its return value from the new PID that is returned to the parent process

The allocation and initialization of the process structure, and the arrangement of the return value, were covered in Chapter 4. The remainder of this section discusses the other steps involved in duplicating a process.

Reserving Kernel Resources

The first resource to be reserved when an address space is duplicated is the required virtual address space. To avoid running out of memory resources, the kernel must ensure that it does not promise to provide more virtual memory than it is able to deliver. The total virtual memory that can be provided by the system is limited to the amount of physical memory available for paging plus the amount of swap space that is provided. A few pages are held in reserve to stage I/O between the swap area and main memory.

The reason for this restriction is to ensure that processes get synchronous notification of memory limitations. Specifically, a process should get an error back from a system call (such as *sbrk*, *fork*, or *mmap*) if there are insufficient resources to allocate the needed virtual memory. If the kernel promises more virtual memory than it can support, it can deadlock trying to service a page fault. Trouble arises when it has no free pages to service the fault and no available swap space to save an active page. Here, the kernel has no choice but to send a kill signal to the process unfortunate enough to be page faulting. Such asynchronous notification of insufficient memory resources is unacceptable.

Excluded from this limit are those parts of the address space that are mapped read-only, such as the program text. Any pages that are being used for a read-only part of the address space can be reclaimed for another use without being saved because their contents can be refilled from the original source. Also excluded from this limit are parts of the address space that map shared files. The kernel can reclaim any pages that are being used for a shared mapping after writing their contents back to the filesystem from which they are mapped. Here, the filesystem is being used as an extension of the swap area. Finally, any piece of memory that is used by more than one process (such as an area of anonymous memory being shared by several processes) needs to be counted only once toward the virtual-memory limit.

The limit on the amount of virtual address space that can be allocated causes problems for applications that want to allocate a large piece of address space but want to use the piece only sparsely. For example, a process may wish to make a private mapping of a large database from which it will access only a small part. Because the kernel has no way to guarantee that the access will be sparse, when requested to reserve space, it takes the pessimistic view that the entire file will be modified and denies the request if it has insufficient resources.

Tracking the outstanding virtual memory accurately and determining when to limit further allocation is a complex task. Because most processes use only about half of their virtual address space, limiting outstanding virtual memory to the sum of process address spaces is needlessly conservative. However, allowing greater allocation runs the risk of running out of virtual-memory resources. Although FreeBSD calculates the outstanding-memory load, it only enforces a total memory limit if the *vm.overcommit sysctl* has been enabled. Because the *vm.overcommit* follows the conservative approach of limiting outstanding virtual memory to the sum of process address spaces, *vm.overcommit* is turned off by default. Thus, it does not enforce any total memory limit so it can be made to promise more than it can deliver. When memory resources run out, it picks a process to kill favoring processes with large memory use. An important future enhancement will be to develop a heuristic for better determining when virtual-memory resources are in danger of running out and need to be limited. As a stopgap measure, FreeBSD 10 added the *procctl* system call that can be accessed using the **protect** utility to allow the system administrator to identify processes that are critical to system operation and should not be considered as candidates to be killed.

Duplication of the User Address Space

The next step in *fork* is to allocate and initialize a new process structure. This operation must be done before the address space of the current process is duplicated because it records state in the process structure. From the time that the process structure is allocated until all the needed resources are allocated, the parent process is locked against swapping to avoid deadlock. The child is in an inconsistent state and cannot yet run or be swapped, so the parent is needed to complete the copy of its address space. To ensure that the child process is ignored by the scheduler, the kernel sets the process's state to NEW during the entire *fork* procedure.

Historically, the *fork* system call operated by copying the entire address space of the parent process. When large processes fork, copying the entire user address space is expensive and wasteful if the *fork* is followed immediately by an *exec*, which discards all the existing pages before allocating the new pages for the program that it has been requested to run. All the pages that are on secondary storage must be read back into memory to be copied. If there is not enough free memory for both complete copies of the process, this memory shortage will cause the system to begin paging to create enough memory to do the copy (see Section 6.12). The copy operation may result in parts of the parent and child processes being paged out, as well as the paging out of parts of unrelated processes.

The technique used by FreeBSD to create processes without this overhead is called ***copy-on-write***. Rather than copy each page of a parent process, both the child and parent processes resulting from a fork are given references to the same physical pages. The page tables are changed to prevent either process from modifying a shared page. Instead, when a process attempts to modify a page, the kernel is entered with a protection fault. On discovering that the fault was caused by an attempt to modify a shared page, the kernel simply copies the page and changes the protection field for the page to allow modification once again. Only pages modified by one of the processes need to be copied. Because processes that fork typically overlay the child process with a new image with *exec* shortly thereafter, this technique significantly improves the performance of *fork*.

Using copy-on-write for *fork* is done by traversing the list of *vm_map_entry* structures in the parent and creating a corresponding entry in the child. Each entry must be analyzed and the appropriate action taken:

- If the entry maps a shared region, the child can take a reference to it.
- If the entry maps a privately mapped region (such as the data area or stack), the child must create a copy-on-write mapping of the region. The parent must be converted to a copy-on-write mapping of the region. If either process later tries to write the region, it will create a shadow object to hold the modified pages.

With the virtual-memory resources allocated, the system sets up the kernel- and user-mode state of the new process. It then clears the NEW flag and places the process's thread on the run queue; the new process can then begin execution.

Creation of a New Process Without Copying

When a process (such as a shell) wishes to start another program, it will generally *fork*, do a few simple operations such as redirecting I/O descriptors and changing signal actions, and then start the new program with an *exec*. In the meantime, the parent shell suspends itself with *wait* until the new program completes. For such operations, it is not necessary for both parent and child to run simultaneously, and therefore only one copy of the address space is required. This frequently occurring set of system calls led to the implementation of the *vfork* system call. Although it is extremely efficient, *vfork* has peculiar semantics and is generally considered to be an architectural blemish.

The implementation of *vfork* will always be more efficient than the copy-on-write implementation because the kernel avoids copying the address space for the child. Instead, the kernel simply passes the parent's address space to the child and suspends the parent. The child process does not need to allocate any virtual-memory structures, receiving the *vmspace* structure and all its pieces from its parent. The child process returns from the *vfork* system call with the parent still suspended. The child does the usual activities in preparation for starting a new program, then calls *exec*. Now the address space is passed back to the parent process, rather than being abandoned, as in a normal *exec*. Alternatively, if the child process encounters an error and is unable to execute the new program, it will *exit*. Again, the address space is passed back to the parent instead of being abandoned.

With *vfork*, the entries describing the address space do not need to be copied, and the page-table entries do not need to be set to read-only and then cleared of read-only. *Vfork* is likely to remain more efficient than copy-on-write or other schemes that must duplicate the process's virtual address space. The architectural quirk of the *vfork* call is that the child process may modify the contents and even the size of the parent's address space while the child has control. Although modification of the parent's address space is bad programming practice, some programs have been known to take advantage of this quirk.

6.7 Execution of a File

The *exec* system call was described in Sections 2.4 and 3.1; it replaces the address space of a process with the contents of a new program obtained from an executable file. During an *exec*, the target executable image is validated and then the arguments and environment are copied from the current process image into a temporary area of pageable-kernel virtual memory.

To do an *exec*, the system must allocate resources to hold the new contents of the virtual address space, set up the mapping for this address space to reference the new image, and release the resources being used for the existing virtual memory.

The first step is to check whether the kernel has been requested to reserve memory resources for the new executable image. If it has, a space reservation must be made for the space needed by the new executable. *Exec* does this reservation without first releasing the currently assigned space, because the system must be able to continue running the old executable until it is sure that it will be able to run the new one. If the system released the current space and the memory reservation failed, the *exec* would be unable to return to the original process. Once the reservation is made, the address space and virtual-memory resources of the current process are then freed as though the process were exiting; this mechanism is described in Section 6.9.

Now the process has only a kernel stack. The kernel now allocates a new *vmspace* structure and creates the list of four or five *vm_map_entry* structures:

1. A copy-on-write, fill-from-file entry maps the text segment. A copy-on-write mapping is used, rather than a read-only one, to allow active text segments to have debugging breakpoints set without affecting other users of the binary.
2. A private (copy-on-write), fill-from-file entry maps the initialized data segment.
3. An anonymous zero-fill-on-demand entry maps the uninitialized data segment.
4. An anonymous zero-fill-on-demand entry maps the stack segment.
5. For dynamically loaded binaries (most of them), a copy-on-write, fill-from-file entry maps the runtime loader. Execution will begin in the loader that will map the needed shared libraries, link the program with the libraries, and finish by invoking the program.

No further operations are needed to create a new address space during an *exec* system call; the remainder of the work involves copying the arguments and environment out to the top of the new stack. Initial values are set for the registers: The program counter is set to the entry point, and the stack pointer is set to point to the argument vector. The new process image is then ready to run.

6.8 Process Manipulation of Its Address Space

Once a process begins execution, it has several ways to manipulate its address space. The system has always allowed processes to expand their uninitialized data area (usually done with the *malloc*() library routine). The stack is grown on an as-needed basis. The FreeBSD system also allows a process to map files and devices into arbitrary parts of its address space and to change the protection of various parts of its address space, as described in Section 6.5. This section describes how these address-space manipulations are done.

Change of Process Size

A process can change its size during execution by explicitly requesting more data space with the *sbrk* system call. Also, the stack segment will be expanded automatically if an invalid address fault is encountered because of an attempt to grow the stack below the end of the stack region. In either case, the size of the process address space must be changed. The size of the request is always rounded up to a multiple of page size. New pages are marked fill-with-zeros, since there are no contents initially associated with new sections of the address space.

The first step of enlarging a process's size is to check whether the new size would violate the size limit for the process segment involved. If the new size is in range, the following steps are taken to enlarge the data area:

1. Verify that the address space of the requested size immediately following the current end of the data area is not already mapped.

2. If requested, verify that the virtual-memory resources are available.

3. If the existing *vm_map_entry* is the only reference to the swap *vm_object*, increment the *vm_map_entry*'s ending address by the requested size and increase the size of the swap *vm_object* by the same amount. If the swap *vm_object* has two or more references (as it would after a process forked), a new *vm_map_entry* must be created with a starting address immediately following the end of the previous fixed-size entry. Its ending address is calculated to give it the size of the request. It will be backed by a new swap *vm_object*. Until this process forks again, the new entry and its swap *vm_object* will be able to continue growing.

If the change is to reduce the size of the data segment, the operation is easy: Any memory allocated to the pages that will no longer be part of the address space is freed. The ending address of the *vm_map_entry* is reduced by the size. If the requested size reduction is bigger than or equal to the range defined by the *vm_map_entry*, the entire entry is freed, and the remaining reduction is applied to the *vm_map_entry* that precedes it. This algorithm is applied until the entire reduction has been made. Future references to these addresses will result in invalid address faults, as access is disallowed when the address range has been deallocated.

File Mapping

The *mmap* system call requests that a file be mapped into an address space. The system call may request either that the mapping be done at a particular address or that the kernel pick an unused area. If the request is for a particular address range, the kernel first checks to see whether that part of the address space is already in use. If it is in use, the kernel first does an *munmap* of the existing mapping, then proceeds with the new mapping.

The kernel implements the *mmap* system call by traversing the list of *vm_map_entry* structures for the process. The various types of overlap to consider are shown in Figure 6.15. The five types are as follows:

1. The new mapping exactly overlaps an existing mapping. The old mapping is deallocated as described in Section 6.9. The new mapping is created in its place as described in the paragraph following this list.

2. The new mapping is a subset of the existing mapping. The existing mapping is split into three pieces (two pieces if the new mapping begins at the beginning or ends at the end of the existing mapping). The existing *vm_map_entry* structure is augmented with one or two additional *vm_map_entry* structures: one mapping the remaining part of the existing mapping before the new mapping, and one mapping the remaining part of the existing mapping following the new mapping. Its overlapped piece is replaced by the new mapping, as described in the paragraph following this list.

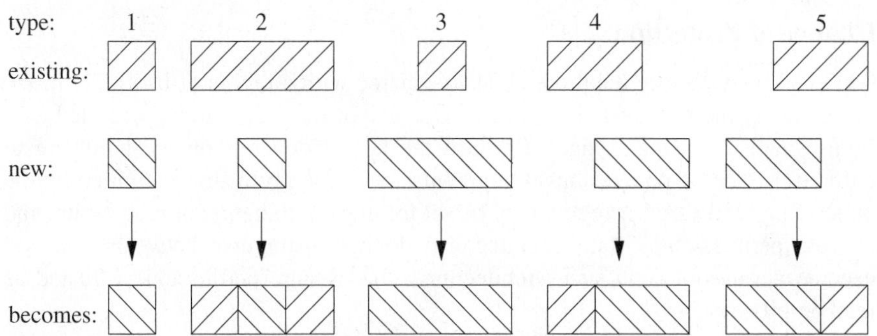

Figure 6.15 Five types of overlap that the kernel must consider when adding a new address mapping.

3. The new mapping is a superset of an existing mapping. The old mapping is deallocated as described in Section 6.9, and a new mapping is created as described in the paragraph following this list.

4. The new mapping starts partway into and extends past the end of an existing mapping. The existing mapping has its length reduced by the size of the unmapped area. Its overlapped piece is replaced by the new mapping, as described in the paragraph following this list.

5. The new mapping extends into the beginning of an existing mapping. The existing mapping has its starting address incremented and its length reduced by the size of the covered area. Its overlapped piece is replaced by the new mapping, as described in the paragraph following this list.

In addition to these five basic types of overlap, a new mapping request may span several existing mappings. Specifically, a new request may be composed of zero or one of type 4, zero to many of type 3, and zero or one of type 5. When a mapping is shortened, any shadow pages associated with it are released because they are no longer needed.

Once the old mapping to the address range has been removed, the kernel allocates a *vm_map_entry* to describe the new mapping to the address range. If the *vm_object* being mapped is already being mapped by another process, the new *vm_map_entry* gets a reference to the existing *vm_object*. This reference is obtained in the same way, as described in Section 6.6, when a new process is being created and needs to map each of the regions in its parent. If this request is a mapping of a file, then the kernel sets the new *vm_map_entry* to reference its *vm_object*. If this is a mapping to an anonymous region, then the kernel sets the new *vm_map_entry* to reference its *vm_object* but sets the MAP_ENTRY_NEEDS_COPY flag so that a new shadow *vm_object* will be created if a page in the *vm_object* is modified.

Change of Protection

A process may change the protections associated with a region of its virtual memory by using the *mprotect* system call. The size of the region to be protected may be as small as a single page. Because the kernel depends on the hardware to enforce the access permissions, the granularity of the protection is limited by the underlying hardware. A region may be set for any combination of read, write, and execute permissions. Many architectures do not distinguish between read and execute permissions; on such architectures, the execute permission is treated as read permission.

The kernel implements the *mprotect* system call by finding the existing *vm_map_entry* structure or structures that cover the region specified by the call. If the existing permissions are the same as the request, then no further action is required. Otherwise, the new permissions are compared to the maximum protection value associated with the *vm_map_entry*. The maximum value is set at *mmap* time and reflects the maximum value allowed by the underlying file. If the new permissions are valid, one or more new *vm_map_entry* structures may have to be set up to describe the new protections. The set of overlap conditions that must be handled is similar to that described in the previous subsection. Any *vm_map_entries* wholly contained within the *mprotect*'ed range can simply change their permissions. For *vm_map_entries* that have to be split, the *vm_map_entry* on the unchanged address range retains it old permissions and the *vm_map_entry* on the *mprotect*'ed address range changes to the new permissions. Instead of replacing the *vm_object* underlying the new *vm_map_entry* structures, these *vm_map_entry* structures still reference the same *vm_object*; the difference is that they grant different access permissions to it.

6.9 Termination of a Process

The final change in process state that relates to the operation of the virtual-memory system is *exit*; this system call terminates a process, as described in Chapter 4. The part of *exit* that is discussed here is the release of the virtual-memory resources of the process. There are two sets of virtual-memory resources that need to be freed:

1. The user portions of the address space, both memory and swap space
2. The kernel stack

The first set of resources is freed in *exit*. The kernel stack is freed in *wait*. The release of the kernel stack is delayed because it must be used until the process relinquishes the processor for the final time.

The first step—freeing the user address space—is identical to the one that occurs during *exec* to free the old address space. The free operation proceeds entry by entry through the list of *vm_map_entry* structures associated with the address space. The first step in freeing an entry is to call the machine-dependent routines to unmap and free up any page table or data structures that are associated with the *vm_map_entry*. The next step is to traverse its list of shadow *vm_objects*. If the entry is the last reference to a shadow *vm_object*, then any physical pages or swap space that is associated with the *vm_object* can be freed. If the shadow *vm_object* is still referenced by other *vm_map_entry* structures, its resources cannot be freed. Finally, if the underlying *vm_object* referenced by the *vm_map_entry* is losing its last reference, then that *vm_object* is a candidate for deallocation. If it is a *vm_object* that will never have any chance of a future reuse (such as an anonymous *vm_object* associated with a stack or uninitialized data area), then its resources are freed as though it were a shadow *vm_object*. However, if the *vm_object* is associated with a vnode (e.g., it maps a file such as an executable), the *vm_object* will persist until the vnode is reused for another purpose. Until the vnode is reused, the *vm_object* and its associated pages will be available for reuse by newly executing processes or by processes mapping in a file.

With all its resources free, the exiting process finishes detaching itself from its process group and notifies its parent that it is done. The process has now become a zombie process—one with no resources. Its parent will collect its exit status with a *wait* call. Because the process structure and kernel stack are allocated using the zone allocator, they will normally be retained for future use by another process rather than being broken down and their memory pages reclaimed. Thus, there is nothing for the virtual-memory system to do when *wait* is called: All virtual-memory resources of a process are removed when *exit* is done. On *wait*, the system just returns the process status to the caller, releases the process structure and kernel stack back to the zone allocator, and frees the space in which the resource-usage information was kept.

6.10 The Pager Interface

The pager interface provides the mechanism by which data are moved between backing store and physical memory. The FreeBSD pager interface is an evolution of the interface present in Mach 2.0 as evolved by 4.4BSD. The interface is page based, with all data requests made in multiples of the page size. The *vm_page* structures are passed around as descriptors providing the backing-store offset and physical-memory address of the desired data. This interface should not be confused with the Mach 3.0 external paging interface [Young, 1989], where pagers are typically user applications outside the kernel and are invoked via asynchronous remote procedure calls using the Mach interprocess-communication mechanism. The FreeBSD interface is internal in the sense that the pagers are compiled into the kernel and pager routines are invoked via simple function calls.

Each virtual-memory *vm_object* has a pager type, pager handle, and pager private data associated with it. Conceptually, the pager describes a logically contiguous piece of backing store, such as a chunk of swap space or a disk file. The pager type identifies the pager responsible for supplying the contents of pages within the *vm_object*. Each pager registers a set of functions that define its operations. These function sets are stored in an array indexed by pager type. When the kernel needs to perform a pager operation, it uses the pager type to index into the array of pager functions and then selects the routine that it needs such as getting or putting pages. For example,

```
(*pagertab[object->type]->pgo_putpages)
    (object, vmpage, count, flags, rtvals);
```

writes *count* pages starting with page *vmpage* from *object*.

A pager type is specified when a *vm_object* is created to represent a file, device, or piece of anonymous memory. The pager manages the *vm_object* throughout its lifetime. When a page fault occurs for a virtual address mapping a particular *vm_object*, the fault-handling code allocates a *vm_page* structure and converts the faulting address to an offset within the *vm_object*. This offset is recorded in the *vm_page* structure, and the page is added to the collection of pages cached by the *vm_object*. The page frame and *vm_object* are then passed to the underlying pager routine. The pager routine is responsible for filling the page referenced by the *vm_page* structure with the appropriate contents for that offset of the *vm_object* that it represents.

The pager is also responsible for saving the contents of a dirty page if the system decides to write out the page to backing store. When the pageout daemon decides that a particular page is no longer needed, it requests the *vm_object* that owns the page to free the page. The *vm_object* first passes the page with the associated logical offset to the underlying pager to be saved for future use. The pager is responsible for finding an appropriate place to save the page and doing any I/O necessary for the save. When it is done, the pager marks the page as clean and notifies the *vm_object* that the page has been written so that the pageout daemon can move the *vm_page* structure to the cache or free list for future use.

There are seven routines associated with each pager type; see Table 6.2. The *pgo_init*() routine is called at boot time to do any one-time type-specific initializations, such as allocating a pool of private pager structures. The *pgo_alloc*() routine associates a pager with a *vm_object* as part of the creation of the *vm_object*. The *pgo_dealloc*() routine disassociates a pager from a *vm_object* as part of the destruction of the *vm_object*.

The *pgo_getpages*() function is called to return one or more pages of data from a pager. The main use of this routine is by the page-fault handler. The *pgo_putpages*() function writes back one or more pages of data. This routine is called by the pageout daemon to write back one or more pages asynchronously, and by *msync* to write back one or more pages synchronously or asynchronously. Both the get and put routines are called with an array of pointers to *vm_page* structures and a count indicating the affected pages.

The *pgo_haspage*() routine queries a pager to see whether it has data at a particular backing-store offset. This routine is used in the ***clustering*** code of the page-fault handler to determine whether pages on either side of a faulted page can be read in as part of a single I/O operation. It is also used when collapsing chains

Table 6.2 Operations defined by a pager.

Operation	Description
pgo_init()	initialize pager
pgo_alloc()	allocate pager
pgo_dealloc()	deallocate pager
pgo_getpages()	read page(s) from backing store
pgo_putpages()	write page(s) to backing store
pgo_haspage()	check whether backing store has a page
pgo_pageunswapped()	remove a page from backing store (swap pager only)

of *vm_object*s to determine if the allocated pages of a shadow *vm_object* completely obscure the allocated pages of the *vm_object* that it shadows.

The four most commonly used pagers supported by the system are described in the next four subsections.

Vnode Pager

The vnode pager handles *vm_object*s that provide the physical memory for caching data from files in a filesystem. Whenever a file is opened either explicitly by *open* or implicitly by *exec*, the system must find an existing vnode that represents it or, if there is no existing vnode for the file, allocate a new vnode for it. Part of allocating a new vnode is to allocate a *vm_object* to hold the pages of the file and to associate the vnode pager with the *vm_object*. The *vm_object* handle is set to point to the vnode and the private data stores the size of the file. Any time the vnode changes size, the *vm_object* is informed by a call to *vnode_pager_setsize*().

When a pagein request is received by the vnode pager *pgo_getpages*() routine, it is passed an array of pointers to physical pages, the size of the array, and the index into the array of the page that is required to service the page fault. Only the required page must be read, but the *pgo_getpages*() routine is encouraged to provide as many of the others as it can easily read at the same time. For example, if the required page is in the middle of the block of a file, the filesystem will usually read the entire file block since the file block can be read with a single I/O operation. The larger read will fill in the required page along with the pages surrounding it.

The kernel has two types of I/O operations: mapped and unmapped. Mapped I/O requires that the physical pages be mapped into the kernel's address space. The I/O is done using a physical-I/O buffer that maps the pages to be read into the kernel address space long enough for the pager to call the device-driver strategy routine to load the pages with the file contents. Once the pages are filled, the kernel mapping can be dropped, the physical-I/O buffer can be released, and the pages can be returned.

Unmapped I/O does not require the physical pages to be mapped into the kernel's address space. Many devices have the ability to do I/O on unmapped pages through the use of a hardware I/O map. For these devices, it is not necessary for the kernel to map them into its address space. Rather the *vm_page* structures can be passed directly to the device. The device can copy the physical page numbers into its I/O map and proceed with the I/O operation. The details of using the hardware I/O map are described in Section 8.8.

When the vnode pager is asked to save a page to be freed, it simply arranges to write the page back to the part of the file from which the page came. The request is made with the *pgo_putpages*() routine, which is passed an array of pointers to physical pages, the size of the array, and the index into the array of the page that must be written. Only the required page must be written, but the *pgo_putpages*() routine is encouraged to write as many of the others as it can easily handle at the same time. The filesystem will write out all the pages that are in the same filesystem block as the required page. As with the *pgo_getpages*() routine, the pages are mapped into the kernel long enough to do the write operation only if the device to which they are being written does not have the ability to do I/O on unmapped pages.

If a file is being privately mapped, then modified pages cannot be written back to the filesystem. Such private mapping must use a shadow *vm_object* with a swap pager for all pages that are modified. Thus, a privately mapped *vm_object* will never be asked to save any dirty pages to the underlying file.

Historically, the BSD kernel had separate caches for the filesystems and the virtual memory. FreeBSD has eliminated the filesystem buffer cache by replacing it with the virtual-memory cache. Each vnode has a *vm_object* associated with it, and the blocks of the file are stored in the pages associated with the *vm_object*. The file data is accessed using the same pages whether they are mapped into an address space or accessed via read and write. An added benefit of this design is that the filesystem cache is no longer limited by the address space in the kernel that can be dedicated to it. Absent other demands on the system memory, it can all be dedicated to caching filesystem data.

The ZFS filesystem integrated from OpenSolaris is the one exception to the integrated buffer cache. ZFS has its own set of memory that it manages by itself. Files that are *mmap*'ed from ZFS must be copied to the virtual-memory managed memory. In addition to requiring two copies of the file in memory, extra copying occurs every time an *mmap*'ed ZFS file is being accessed through the read and write interfaces. As detailed in Section 10.5, ZFS would require extensive restructuring to integrate its buffer cache into the virtual-memory infrastructure.

Device Pager

The device pager handles *vm_object*s representing memory-mapped hardware devices. Memory-mapped devices provide an interface that looks like a piece of memory. An example of a memory-mapped device is a frame buffer, which presents a range of memory addresses with one word per pixel on the screen. The kernel provides access to memory-mapped devices by mapping the device memory into a process's address space. The process can then access that memory without further operating-system intervention. Writing to a word of the frame-buffer memory causes the corresponding pixel to take on the appropriate color and brightness. The device pager can also be used to create user-level mappings of kernel buffers. For example, a network driver can make its buffers available to a user-level application to allow the application to access their contents directly.

The device pager is fundamentally different from the other three pagers described in this section in that it does not fill provided physical-memory pages with data. Instead, it creates and manages its own *vm_page* structures, each of which describes a page of the device space. The head of the list of these pages is kept in the pager private-data area of the *vm_object*. This approach makes device memory look like wired physical memory. Thus, no special code should be needed in the remainder of the virtual-memory system to handle device memory.

When a device object is mapped, the device-pager allocation routine will validate the desired range by calling the device *d_mmap*() routine. If the device allows the requested access for all pages in the range, an empty page list is created in the private-data area of the *vm_object* that manages the device mapping. The device-pager allocation routine does not create *vm_page* structures immediately—they are created individually by the *pgo_getpages*() routine as they are referenced. The reason for this late allocation is that some devices export a large memory range in which either not all pages are valid or the pages may not be accessed for common operations. Complete allocation of *vm_page* structures for these sparsely accessed devices would be wasteful.

The first access to a device page will cause a page fault and will invoke the device-pager *pgo_getpages*() routine. The device pager creates a *vm_page* structure, initializes the latter with the appropriate *vm_object* offset and a physical address returned by the device *d_mmap*() routine, and flags the page as fictitious. This *vm_page* structure is added to the collection of all such allocated pages for the *vm_object*. Since the fault code has no special knowledge of the device pager, it has preallocated a physical-memory page to fill and has associated that *vm_page* structure with the *vm_object*. The device-pager routine removes that *vm_page* structure from the *vm_object*, returns the structure to the free list, and inserts its own *vm_page* structure in the same place.

The device-pager *pgo_putpages*() routine expects never to be called and will panic if it is. This behavior is based on the assumption that device-pager pages are never entered into any of the paging queues and hence will never be seen by the pageout daemon. However, the device-pager must be prepared to be called if an application does an *msync* on a part of its address space that is mapped to a range of device memory. Although there is nothing that needs to be done, this operation brings up an exception to the higher-level virtual-memory system's ignorance of device memory: The *vm_object* page-cleaning routine will skip pages that are flagged as fictitious.

Finally, when a device is unmapped, the device-pager deallocation routine is invoked. This routine deallocates all the *vm_page* structures that it allocated.

Physical-Memory Pager

The physical-memory pager handles *vm_object*s that contain nonpagable memory. It is used to make a copy of the current time-of-day structure accessible to user processes to permit them to get the time of day without the need to do a system call. It is also used for a page of data that the kernel shares with all processes that contains the signal trampoline code. The trampoline code used to be placed at the top of the stack for each process. To make stack overflow exploits more difficult, the stack region is marked as nonexecutable. So the trampoline code was moved to a kernel text page that is made read-only and executable to every process. The System V shared-memory interface uses the physical-memory pager when it has been configured to use nonpagable memory instead of the default swappable memory.

The first access to a physical-memory-pager page will cause a page fault and will invoke the *pgo_getpages*() routine. Like the swap pager, the physical-memory pager zero-fills pages when they are first faulted. Unlike the swap pager, the page is marked as unmanaged so that it will not be considered for replacement by the pageout daemon. Unmanaged pages never require finding all the instances of their mappings, so the associated data structure used to find all mappings (described in Section 6.13) need not be allocated. Marking its pages unmanaged makes the memory for the physical-memory pager look like wired physical memory. Thus, no special code is needed in the remainder of the virtual-memory system to handle physical-memory-pager memory.

The *pgo_putpages*() routine of the physical-memory-pager does not expect to be called, and it panics if it is. This behavior is based on the assumption that physical-memory-pager pages are never entered into any of the paging queues and hence will never be seen by the pageout daemon. However, it is possible to *msync* a range of memory backed by the physical-memory pager. This operation brings up an exception to the higher-level virtual-memory system's ignorance of physical-memory-pager memory: The *vm_object* page-cleaning routine will skip pages that are flagged as unmanaged.

Finally, when a *vm_object* using a physical-memory pager is freed, each of its pages has its unmanaged flag cleared and is released back to the list of free pages.

Swap Pager

The term swap pager refers to two functionally different pagers. In the most common use, swap pager refers to the pager that is used by *vm_object*s that manage anonymous memory. This pager has sometimes been referred to as the default pager because it is the pager that is used if no other pager has been requested. It provides what is commonly known as ***swap space***: nonpersistent backing store that is zero filled on first reference. When an anonymous *vm_object* is first created, it is assigned the default pager. The default pager allocates no resources and provides no storage backing. The default pager handles page faults (*pgo_getpage*()) by zero filling and page queries (*pgo_haspage*()) as not held. The expectation is that free memory will be plentiful enough that it will not be necessary to swap out any pages. The *vm_object* will simply create zero-filled pages during the process lifetime that can all be returned to the free list when the process exits. When a *vm_object* is freed with the default pager, no pager cleanup is required since no pager resources were allocated.

However, on the first request by the pageout daemon to remove an allocated page from an anonymous *vm_object*, the default pager replaces itself with the swap pager. The role of the swap pager is swap-space management: figuring out where to store dirty pages and how to find dirty pages when they are needed again. Shadow *vm_object*s require that these operations be efficient. A typical shadow *vm_object* is sparsely populated: It may cover a large range of pages, but only those pages that have been modified will be in the shadow *vm_object*'s backing store. In addition, long chains of shadow *vm_object*s may require numerous pager queries to locate the correct copy of a *vm_object* page to satisfy a page fault. Hence, determining whether a pager contains a particular page needs to be fast, preferably requiring no I/O operations. A final requirement of the swap pager is that it can do asynchronous writeback of dirty pages. This requirement was necessitated by the original pageout daemon, which was a single-threaded process. If a single-threaded pageout daemon blocked waiting for a page-clean operation to complete before starting the next operation, it often could not keep enough memory free in times of heavy memory demand. Even with asynchronous I/O, by the time of FreeBSD 10 it was necessary to create multiple pageout-daemon threads to keep up with the memory demand on busy systems.

In theory, any pager that meets these criteria can be used as the swap pager. In Mach 2.0, the vnode pager was used as the swap pager. Special paging files could be created in any filesystem and registered with the kernel. The swap pager would then suballocate pieces of the files to back particular anonymous *vm_object*s. One obvious advantage of using the vnode pager is that swap space can be expanded by the addition of more swap files or the extension of existing ones dynamically (i.e., without rebooting or reconfiguring of the kernel). The main disadvantage is that the filesystem does not provide as much bandwidth as direct access to the disk.

The desire to provide the highest possible disk bandwidth led to the creation of a special raw-partition pager to use as the swap pager for FreeBSD. Previous versions of BSD also used dedicated disk partitions, commonly known as swap partitions, so this partition pager became the swap pager. The remainder of this section describes how the swap pager is implemented and how it provides the necessary capabilities for backing anonymous *vm_object*s.

In 4.4BSD, the swap pager preallocated a fixed-size structure to describe the backing space for the *vm_object*. For a large *vm_object*, the structure would be large even if only a few pages of the *vm_object* were written to backing store. Worse, the size of the *vm_object* was frozen at the time of allocation. Thus, if the anonymous area continued to grow (such as the stack or heap of a process), a new *vm_object* had to be created to describe the expanded area. On a system that was short of memory, the result was that a large process could acquire many anonymous *vm_object*s. Changing the swap pager to handle growing *vm_object*s dramatically reduced this *vm_object* proliferation. Another problem with the 4.4BSD swap pager was that it used a block list to track the swap space usage. The block list grew in size as the swap area became fragmented. The system tends to swap when it is low on memory. To avoid potential deadlocks, kernel memory should not be allocated at such times. The 4.4BSD swap pager's simplistic management of the swap space led to fragmentation, slow allocation under load, and deadlocks brought on by its need to allocate kernel memory during periods of shortage. For all these reasons, the swap pager was completely rewritten in FreeBSD 4.0.

Swap space tends to be sparsely allocated. On average, a process only accesses about half of its allocated address space during its lifetime. Thus, only about half the pages in a *vm_object* ever come into existence. Unless the machine is under heavy memory pressure and the process is long-lived, most of the pages in the *vm_object* that do come into existence will never be written to backing store. So the new swap pager replaced the old fixed-size block map for each *vm_object* with a method that allocates a structure for each set of swap blocks that gets allocated. Each structure tracks the swap blocks used by an aligned and contiguous region of 32 pages belonging to the *vm_object*. A large *vm_object* with two pages swapped out will use at most two of these structures, and only one if the two swapped pages are close to each other (as they often are). The amount of memory required to track swap space for a *vm_object* is proportional to the number of pages that have been written to swap rather than to the size of the *vm_object*. The size of the *vm_object* is no longer frozen when its first page is swapped out, since any pages that are part of its larger size can be accommodated.

The structures that track swap space usage are kept in a global hash table managed by the swap pager. While it might seem logical to store the structures separately on lists associated with the *vm_object* of which they are a part, the single global hash table has two important advantages:

1. It ensures a short time to determine whether a page of a *vm_object* has been written to swap. If the structures were linked onto a list headed by the *vm_object*, then *vm_object*s with many swapped pages would require the traversal of a long list. The long list could be shortened by creating a hash table for every *vm_object*, but that would require much more memory than simply allocating a single large hash table that could be used by all *vm_object*s.

2. It allows operations that need to scan all the allocated swap blocks to have a centralized place to find them rather than needing to scan all the anonymous *vm_object*s in the system. An example is the *swapoff* system call that removes a swap partition from use. It needs to page in all the blocks from the device that is to be taken out of service.

The free space in the swap area is managed with a bitmap with one bit for each page-size block of swap space. The bitmap for the entire swap area is allocated when the swap space is first added to the system. This initial allocation reduces the need to allocate kernel memory during critical low-memory swapping operations.

Doing a linear scan of the swap-block bitmaps to find free space would be unacceptably slow. Thus, the bitmap is organized in a radix-tree structure with free-space hinting in the radix-node structures. The use of radix-tree structures makes swap-space allocation and release a constant-time operation. To reduce fragmentation, the radix tree can allocate large contiguous chunks at once, skipping over smaller fragmented chunks.

A future improvement would be to keep track of the different-size free areas as swap allocations are done similarly to the way that the filesystem tracks the different sizes of free space. This free-space information would increase the probability of doing contiguous allocation and improve locality of reference.

Swap blocks are allocated at the time that swap out is done. They are freed when the page is brought back in and becomes dirty or the *vm_object* is freed.

The swap pager is responsible for managing the I/O associated with the *pgo_putpages*() request. Once it identifies the set of pages within the *pgo_putpages*() request that it will be able to write, it must allocate a buffer and have those pages mapped into it. Because the swap pager does not synchronously wait while the I/O is done, it does not regain control after the I/O operation completes. Therefore, it marks the buffer with a callback flag and sets the routine for the callback to be *swp_pager_async_iodone*().

When the write completes, *swp_pager_async_iodone*() is called. Each written page is marked as clean, has its busy bit cleared, and calls the *vm_page_io_finish*() routine to notify the pageout daemon that the write has completed and to awaken any processes waiting for it. The swap pager then unmaps the pages from the buffer and releases it. A count of pageouts-in-progress is kept for the pager associated with each *vm_object*; this count is decremented when the pageout completes and, if the count goes to zero, a *wakeup*() is issued. This operation is done so that a *vm_object* that is deallocating a swap pager can wait for the completion of all pageout operations before freeing the pager's references to the associated swap space.

Because the swap pager uses the physical I/O buffers shared with other kernel subsystems and a fixed number of these buffers are allocated when the system is booted, the swap pager must take care to ensure that it does not use more than its fair share. Once this limit is reached, the *pgo_putpages*() operations block until one of the swap pager's outstanding writes completes. This unexpected blocking of the pageout daemon is an unfortunate side effect of pushing the buffer management down into the pagers. Any single pager hitting its buffer limit stops the pageout daemon. While the pageout daemon might want to perform additional I/O operations using other I/O resources such as the network, it is prevented from doing so. Worse, the failure of any single pager can deadlock the system by preventing the pageout daemon from running.

6.11 Paging

When the memory-management hardware detects an invalid virtual address, it generates a trap to the system. This page-fault trap can occur for several reasons. Most BSD programs are created in a format that permits the executable image to be paged into main memory directly from the filesystem. When a program in a demand-paged format is first run, the kernel marks as invalid the pages for the text and initialized-data regions of the executing process. The text and initialized data regions share a *vm_object* that provides fill-on-demand from the filesystem. As part of mapping in the *vm_object*, the kernel traverses the collection of pages associated with the *vm_object* and marks them as resident in the newly created process. For regions that are writable (such as the initialized data of the executable), the pages are marked as copy-on-write. For a heavily used executable with most of its pages already resident, this prepaging reduces many of its initial page faults. As missing pages of the text or initialized-data region are first referenced, or write attempts are made on pages in the initialized-data region, page faults occur.

Page faults can also occur when a process first references a page in the uninitialized-data region of a program. Here, the anonymous *vm_object* managing the region automatically allocates memory to the process and initializes the newly assigned page to zero. Other types of page faults arise when previously resident pages have been reclaimed by the system in response to a memory shortage.

The handling of page faults is done with the *vm_fault*() routine; this routine services all page faults. Each time *vm_fault*() is invoked, it is provided the virtual address that caused the fault. The first action of *vm_fault*() is to traverse the *vm_map_entry* list of the faulting process to find the entry associated with the fault. The routine then computes the logical page within the underlying *vm_object* and traverses the list of *vm_objects* to find or create the needed page. Once the page has been found, *vm_fault*() must call the machine-dependent layer to validate the faulted page and return to restart the process.

The details of calculating the address within the *vm_object* are described in Section 6.4. Having computed the offset within the *vm_object* and determined the *vm_object*'s protection and *vm_object* list from the *vm_map_entry*, the kernel is ready to find or create the associated page. The page-fault-handling algorithm is shown in Figure 6.16. In the following overview, the lettered points are references to the tags down the left side of the code.

A. The loop traverses the list of shadow, anonymous, and file *vm_objects* until it either finds a *vm_object* that holds the sought-after page or reaches the final *vm_object* in the list. If no page is found, the final *vm_object* will be requested to produce it.

B. A *vm_object* with the desired page has been found. If the page is busy, another process may be in the middle of faulting it in, so this process is blocked until the page is no longer busy. Since many things could have happened to the affected *vm_object* while the process was blocked, it must

```
/*
 * Handle a page fault occurring at the given address,
 * requiring the given permissions, in the map specified.
 * If successful, insert the page into the associated
 * physical map.
 */
int vm_fault(
    vm_map_t map,
    vm_offset_t addr,
    vm_prot_t type)
{
RetryFault:
    lookup address in map returning object/offset/prot;
    first_object = object;
    first_page = NULL;
[A] for (;;) {
        page = lookup page at object/offset;
[B]     if (page found) {
            if (page busy)
                block and goto RetryFault;
            remove from paging queues;
            mark page as busy;
            break;
        }
[C]     if (object has nondefault pager or
            object == first_object) {
            page = allocate a page for object/offset;
            if (no pages available)
                block and goto RetryFault;
        }
[D]     if (object has nondefault pager) {
            scan for pages to cluster;
            call pager to fill page(s);
            if (IO error)
                return an error;
            if (pager has page)
                break;
            if (object != first_object)
                free page;
        }
        /* no pager, or pager does not have page */
[E]     if (object == first_object)
            first_page = page;
        next_object = next object;
```

Figure 6.16 Page-fault handling (part 1 of 2).

```
[F]     if (no next object) {
            if (object != first_object) {
                object = first_object;
                page = first_page;
            }
            first_page = NULL;
            zero fill page;
            break;
        }
        object = next_object;
    }
[G] /* appropriate page has been found or allocated */
    orig_page = page;
[H] if (object != first_object) {
        if (fault type == WRITE) {
            copy page to first_page;
            deactivate page;
            page = first_page;
            first_page = NULL;
            object = first_object;
        } else {
            prot &= ~WRITE;
            mark page copy-on-write;
        }
    }
[I] if (prot & WRITE)
        mark page not copy-on-write;
    enter mapping for page;
    enter read-only mapping for clustered pages;
[J] activate and unbusy page;
    if (first_page != NULL)
        unbusy and free first_page;
}
```

Figure 6.16 Page-fault handling (part 2 of 2).

restart the entire fault-handling algorithm. If the page was not busy, the algorithm exits the loop with the page.

C. Anonymous *vm_objects* (such as those used to represent shadow *vm_objects*) do not upgrade from the default pager to the swap pager until the first time that they need to write a page to backing store. Thus, if a *vm_object* has a pager other than the default pager, then there is a chance that the page previously existed but was paged out. If the *vm_object* has a nondefault pager, then the kernel needs to allocate a page to give to the pager to be filled (see D). The special case for the *vm_object* being the first *vm_object* is to avoid a race condition with two processes trying to get the same page. The first process through will create the sought-after page in the first *vm_object* but keep it marked as busy. When the second process tries to fault the same page, it will find the page created by the first process and block on it (see B). When the first process completes the pagein processing, it will unlock the first page, causing the second process to awaken, retry the fault, and find the page created by the first process.

D. Before calling the pager, check to see if any of the eight pages on either side of the faulting page are eligible to be brought in at the same time. To be eligible, a page must be part of the *vm_object* and neither already in memory nor part of another I/O operation. The pager is given the range of possible pages and told which one is the required page. It must return the required page if it holds a copy of it. The other pages are produced only if they are held by the *vm_object* and can be easily read at the same time. If the required page is present in the file or swap area, the pager will bring it back into the newly allocated page. If the pagein succeeds, then the sought-after page has been found. If the page never existed, then the pagein request will fail. Unless this *vm_object* is the first, the page is freed and the search continues. If this *vm_object* is the first, the page is not freed, so it will act as a block to further searches by other processes (as described in C).

E. If the kernel created a page in the first *vm_object* but did not use that page, it will have to remember that page so it can use the page in a shadow object or free the page when the pagein is done (see J).

F. If the search has reached the end of the *vm_object* list and has not found the page, then the fault is on an anonymous *vm_object* chain, and the first *vm_object* in the list will handle the page fault using the page allocated in C. The *first_page* entry is set to NULL to show that it does not need to be freed, the page is zero filled, and the loop is exited.

G. The search exits the loop with `page` as the page that has been found or allocated and initialized, and `object` as the owner of that page. The page has been filled with the correct data at this point.

H. If the *vm_object* providing the page is not the first *vm_object*, then this mapping must be private, with the first *vm_object* being a shadow *vm_object* of the *vm_object* providing the page. If pagein is handling a write fault, then the contents of the page that it has found have to be copied to the page that it allocated for the first *vm_object*. Having made the copy, it can release the *vm_object* and page from which the copy came, since the first *vm_object* and first page will be used to finish the page-fault service. If pagein is handling a read fault, it can use the page that it found, but it has to mark the page copy-on-write to avoid the page being modified in the future.

I. If pagein is handling a write fault, then it has made any copies that were necessary, so it can safely make the page writable. As any pages around the required page that were brought into memory as part of the clustering were not copied, they are mapped read-only so that if a write is done on one of them, the full page-fault analysis will be done and a copy made at that time if it is necessary to do so.

J. As the page and possibly the *first_page* are released, any processes waiting for that page of the *vm_object* will get a chance to run to get their own references.

Note that the page, *vm_map*, and *vm_object* locking has been elided in Figure 6.16 to simplify the explanation.

Hardware-Cache Design

Because the speed of CPUs has increased far more rapidly than the speed of main memory, most machines today require the use of a memory cache to allow the CPU to operate near its full potential.

Code that describes the operation of a hardware cache is given in Figure 6.17. An actual cache is entirely implemented in hardware, so the loop shown in Figure 6.17 would really be done by parallel comparisons rather than iteratively. Historically, most machines had a direct-mapped cache. With a direct-mapped cache, an access to byte B followed by an access to byte B + (CACHELINES × LINESIZE) would cause the cached data for byte B to be lost. Most modern caches are N-way set associative where N is typically 8 for high-speed caches such as the L1 cache, and 64 for lower-speed but larger caches such as the L3 cache. An N-way set-associative cache allows access of N different memory regions that overlap the same cache memory without destroying the previously cached data. But on the Nth + 1 access at that offset, an earlier cached value is lost.

There are several cache-design choices that require cooperation with the virtual-memory system. The design option with the biggest effect is whether the cache uses virtual or physical addressing. A physically addressed cache takes the address from the CPU, runs it through the ***memory-management unit*** (***MMU***) to get the address of the physical page, then uses this physical address to find out whether the requested memory location is available in the cache. Although a translation lookaside buffer (described in the next subsection) significantly reduces the average latency of the translation, there is still a delay in going through the MMU. A virtually addressed cache uses the virtual address as that address comes from the CPU to find out whether the requested memory location is available in the cache. The virtual-address cache is faster than the physical-address cache because it avoids the time to run the address through the MMU. However, the virtual-address cache must be flushed completely after each context switch, because virtual addresses from one process are indistinguishable from the virtual addresses of another process. By contrast, a physical-address cache does not need to be flushed after a context switch. In a system with many short-running processes, a virtual-

```
struct cache {
    vm_offset_t key;           /* address of data */
    char        data[LINESIZE]; /* cache data */
} cache[CACHELINES][SETSIZE];

/*
 * If present, get data for addr from cache. Otherwise fetch
 * entire line of data containing addr from main memory,
 * place in cache, and return it.
 */
hardware_cache_fetch(vm_offset_t addr)
{
    vm_offset_t set, key, line;

    key = addr - (addr % LINESIZE);
    line = (addr / LINESIZE) % CACHELINES;
    for (set = 0; set < SETSIZE; set++)
        if (cache[line][set].key == key)
            break;
    if (set < SETSIZE)
        return (cache[line][set].data);
    set = select_replacement_set(line);
    cache[line][set].key = key;
    return (cache[line][set].data = fetch_from_RAM(key));
}
```

Figure 6.17 Hardware-cache algorithm. Key: LINESIZE—Number of bytes in each cache line, typically 64 or 128 bytes; CACHELINES—Number of lines in the cache, 8192 is a typical size; SETSIZE—1 for a direct mapped cache, 2 for 2-way set associative, 4 for 4-way set associative, etc.

---

address cache gets flushed so frequently that it is seldom useful.

A further refinement to the virtual-address cache is to add a process tag to the key field for each cache line. At each context switch, the kernel loads a hardware context register with the tag assigned to the process. Each time an entry is recorded in the cache, both the virtual address and the process tag that faulted it are recorded in the key field of the cache line. The cache looks up the virtual address as before, but when it finds an entry, it compares the tag associated with that entry to the hardware context register. If they match, the cached value is returned. If they do not match, the correct value and current process tag replace the old cached value. When this technique is used, the cache does not need to be flushed completely at each context switch, since multiple processes can have entries in the cache. The drawback is that the kernel must manage the process tags. Usually, there are fewer tags (8 to 16) than there are processes. The kernel must assign the tags to the active set of processes. When an old process drops out of the active set to allow a new one to enter, the kernel must flush the cache entries associated with the tag that it is about to reuse. Another major drawback to virtual caches with process tags are aliases. An alias is the same page of data that is mapped to different virtual addresses in different processes. An example of an alias is a shared library that is mapped to different locations in the address space of different processes. First, the cache is polluted with duplicate read-only data that reduce its efficiency. Second, two processes using shared memory for IPC have to prevent aliases to avoid stale data by flushing their tag's cache entries on every context switch.

A final consideration is a write-through versus a write-back cache. A write-through cache writes the data back to main memory at the same time as it is writing to the cache, forcing the CPU to wait for the memory access to conclude. A write-back cache writes the data to only the cache, delaying the memory write until an explicit request or until the cache entry is reused. The write-back cache allows the CPU to resume execution more quickly and permits multiple writes to the same cache block to be consolidated into a single memory write. However, the writes must be forced any time it is necessary for the data to be visible to a DMA request for a device or to other CPUs on a multiprocessor.

Hardware Memory Management

The MMU implements address translation and access control when virtual memory is mapped onto physical memory. One common MMU design uses memory-resident ***forward-mapped page tables***. These page tables are large contiguous arrays indexed by the virtual address. There is one element, or ***page-table entry*** (***PTE***), in the array for each virtual page in the address space. This element contains the physical page to which the virtual page is mapped, as well as access permissions, status bits telling whether the page has been referenced or modified, and a bit showing whether the entry contains valid information. For a 4-Gbyte address space with 4-Kbyte virtual pages and a 32-bit page-table entry, 1 million entries, or 4 Mbyte, would be needed to describe an entire address space. Since most processes use little of their address space, most of the entries would be invalid, and allocating 4 Mbyte of physical memory per process would be wasteful. Thus, most page-table structures are hierarchical, using two or more levels of mapping. A 64-bit architecture using its entire address space would need five or six levels of page tables. Implementations in 2014 limit the address space to a 48-bit address space that can be handled with four levels of page tables. With a hierarchical structure, different portions of the virtual address space index the various levels of the page tables. The intermediate levels of the table contain the addresses of the next lower level of the page table. The kernel can mark as unused large contiguous regions of an address space by inserting invalid entries at the higher levels of the page table, eliminating the need for invalid page descriptors for each individual unused virtual page.

The translation of a virtual address to a physical address during an access by a 32-bit CPU using a two-level page table and 4 Kbyte pages is shown in Figure 6.18 and proceeds as follows:

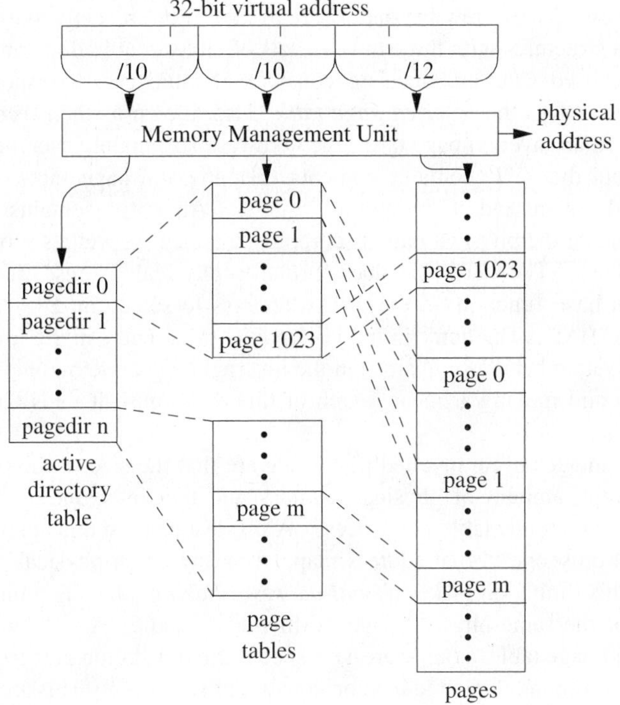

Figure 6.18 Two-level page table.

1. The 10 most significant bits of the virtual address are used to index into the active-directory table.
2. If the selected directory-table entry is valid and the access permissions grant the access being made, the next 10 bits of the virtual address are used to index into the page-table page referenced by the directory-table entry.
3. If the selected page-table entry is valid and the access permissions match, the final 12 bits of the virtual address are combined with the physical page referenced by the page-table entry to form the physical address of the access.

This hierarchical page-table structure requires the hardware to make frequent memory references to translate a virtual address. To speed the translation process, most page-table-based MMUs also have a small, fast, hardware cache of recent address translations, a structure known commonly as a ***translation lookaside buffer*** (***TLB***) that works much like the hardware cache described in the previous subsection. When a memory reference is translated, the TLB is first consulted and, only if a valid entry is not found there, the page-table structure for the current process is traversed. Because most programs exhibit spatial locality in their memory-access patterns, the typical 1024-entry TLB is large enough to hold their working set.

As address spaces grew beyond 32 to 48 and, more recently, 64 bits, simple indexed data structures with three to six levels of tables required to handle address translation caused CPU architects to consider alternatives. A response to this page-table growth is the ***inverted page table***, also known as the ***reverse-mapped page table***. In an inverted page table, the hardware still maintains a memory-resident table, but that table contains one entry per physical page and is indexed by physical address instead of by virtual address. An entry contains the virtual address to which the physical page is currently mapped, as well as protection and status attributes. The hardware does virtual-to-physical address translation by computing a hash function on the virtual address to select an entry in the hash anchor table (HAT). The entry in the HAT points to an entry in the inverted page table. The system handles collisions in the inverted page table by linking together table entries and making a linear search of this chain until it finds the matching virtual address.

The advantages of an inverted page table are that the size of the table is proportional to the amount of physical memory and that only one global table is needed, rather than one table per process. A disadvantage to this approach is that there can be only one virtual address mapped to any given physical page at any one time. This limitation makes ***virtual-address aliasing***—having multiple virtual addresses for the same physical page—difficult to handle. As it is with the forward-mapped page table, a hardware TLB speeds the translation process.

A final common MMU organization consists of just a TLB. This architecture is the simplest hardware design. It gives the software maximum flexibility by allowing the latter to manage translation information in whatever structure it desires. However, unlike the other hardware-based TLBs, a software-based TLB miss raises an exception to the kernel that runs a handler to fill the missing TLB entry.

Superpages

Typical hardware today has a TLB with 1024 entries. A TLB does a set-associative lookup, meaning that when presented with a virtual address, it must simultaneously compare that address with every entry that it holds. The larger the number of entries, the longer it takes for the TLB to produce an answer. If the TLB takes longer than reading the memory, then it ceases to be useful. The reason for the slow growth of the size of TLBs is that they generally aim to produce an answer in less than one clock cycle of the CPU, which limits the number of entries that they can compare.

The size of hardware TLBs has grown much more slowly than the size of the main memory. Thus, the working-set size of a typical process has grown more quickly than the ability of the TLB to reference it. On a machine with 4-Kbyte pages and a 1024-entry TLB, the maximum-size working set that fits in the TLB is 4 Mbyte. As soon as the working-set size of the program exceeds 4 Mbyte, the TLB begins to miss translations, thus requiring one or more extra memory references to read the page-table entries to resolve the location of a virtual page. While most of these memory references will be in one of the processor's memory caches, accessing those caches is typically a factor of 10 slower than resolving the address in the TLB. The small working-set size becomes even more acute on 64-bit architectures that are also limited to 1024-entry TLBs.

As the hardware vendors have been unable to increase the size of the TLB, their solution to the small working-set problem is to create ***superpages***. Most hardware allows for multiple page sizes. The page sizes available are dependent on the architecture. Common sizes in addition to the standard 4-Kbyte pages are 8-Kbyte, 64-Kbyte, 512-Kbyte, 2-Mbyte, and 4-Mbyte pages.

The PC architecture has a 4-Kbyte regular-size page. Unlike many other architectures, it provides only a single alternate superpage size: 4-Mbyte superpages on chips that support a maximum of 4 Gbyte of physical memory and 2-Mbyte superpages on chips that support more than 4 Gbyte of physical memory. The smaller superpage size on the machines with more physical memory is because the additional address bits required to address the larger memory require page table entries to be 64-bits rather than 32-bits. Thus, each 4-Kbyte page table references only half as much address space. An address space may have a mix of regular and superpages but virtual addresses must be aligned to page-size boundaries. Standard-size pages must begin on 4-Kbyte boundaries and 2-Mbyte superpages must begin on 2-Mbyte boundaries. Note that recent 64-bit Intel and AMD processors also support 1 Gbyte superpages.

A process using entirely 2-Mbyte superpages to back its address space can fit a working set of 2 Gbyte into the same 1024-entry TLB. While a 2-Gbyte working set is large for an application running on a 32-bit architecture, it is quite common for applications running on a 64-bit architecture.

The implementation of superpages on the PC architecture is shown in Figure 6.19. The pointer in the first level of the page table is set to point to a superpage rather than to a second level of page tables. A flag bit in the top-level page table entry is set to indicate that the pointer references a superpage rather than the usual second-level page table. As can be seen in Figure 6.19, superpages may be mixed with regular pages within an address space. Although the hardware treats the superpage as a single entity, the software still maintains all 1024 *vm_page* structures for its component 4-Kbyte pages. Maintaining the *vm_page* structures is necessary so that if a superpage is demoted, the kernel can track the individual 4-Kbyte pages from which it is built.

Providing hardware support for superpages is simple and, when used appropriately, is quite effective at relieving pressure on the TLB. The difficult part is devising the software solution for using them. Some operating systems simply provide an interface to allow applications to request superpages for part or all of their address space. This approach rarely works as many application writers are unaware of the ability to ask for superpages or the need to do so. Many of the application writers that do ask for superpages do so in an inappropriate context and just end up wasting system resources and slowing everything down.

The best solution (and the one used by FreeBSD) is to have the operating system monitor its running processes and assign superpages to those parts of the processes for which they will provide clear benefit [Navarro et al., 2002]. Here, the application writers do not have to concern themselves with superpages knowing that they will be used where appropriate.

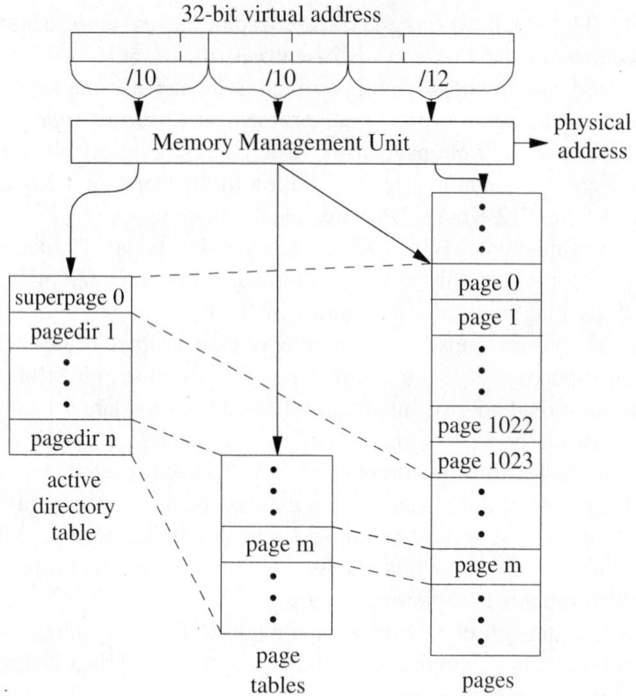

Figure 6.19 Superpage hardware operation.

The kernel must be conservative in choosing to use a superpage within a process. The savings from using a superpage are reduced misses in the TLB. As described below, the potential cost of using a superpage is extra memory-to-memory copies or additional disk I/O. It does not take many memory-to-memory copies or additional disk I/O to completely wipe out any savings of TLB misses and indeed can quickly add up to more cost than benefit, which makes the application and potentially the entire system run more slowly than if superpages were not used. Thus, FreeBSD delays the promotion to superpages until it is clear that they will be a performance win. While some promotion opportunities are missed, those that are made nearly always provide a net improvement in performance.

Consideration of using a superpage begins with a superpage reservation. Superpages for a process are considered on a region-by-region basis (a region is defined by an area of the process memory described by a *vm_map_entry* structure; see Section 6.4). On the first page fault for each region of memory, the virtual-memory system must decide whether the region should be eligible to use superpages. A region containing a mapped file must be of at least superpage size to be eligible for a superpage reservation. Since such a region rarely grows, if it is not already at least the size of a superpage, it is unlikely that it ever will be superpage size. By contrast, anonymous memory such as a stack or a heap is always eligible for a superpage reservation since it often grows. Additionally, kernel memory allocation is always given a reservation.

When a region is denied a superpage reservation, the first and all subsequent page faults are provided with a normal 4-Kbyte page. If a region is granted a superpage reservation, then a superpage is assigned to the part of the region that includes the faulted page. However, only the single 4-Kbyte page within the superpage corresponding to the fault is initialized and placed into the process page table. Each superpage has a population map to track its used pages. As the process faults in additional parts of the superpage, the corresponding 4-Kbyte pages get initialized and added into its page table and the appropriate entry in its population map is updated.

When a *vm_object* first gets mapped, the virtual-memory system records its offset into a superpage. Thus, if a *vm_object*'s mapping begins at a 7-Mbyte offset and the system has 2-Mbyte superpages, the *vm_object* is marked as beginning at a 1-Mbyte offset. If another process asks to map the same *vm_object*, the virtual memory system will place the *vm_object* in that new process at the same offset as it did in the first *vm_object*. The purpose for tracking and using the alignment is to avoid the need to copy data around in memory to get necessary alignment. If the application demands a particular alignment that does not match the current superpage alignment, then that process will have to map that *vm_object* using regular 4-Kbyte page-table entries.

A superpage reservation is eligible for promotion when it faults every page in its reservation. On the PC architecture, promotion means that the 4-Kbyte page-table page holding the references to all the individual 4-Kbyte pages is replaced with a pointer to the superpage itself (see Figure 6.19).

The superpage is marked read-only unless it has modified every page in its reservation. The reason that it is made read-only is that the superpage active-directory entry has only a single bit to indicate that the page has been modified. If the superpage were made writable and only a single byte in the superpage is modified, the virtual-memory system would have no way of knowing where in the superpage the modification had occurred. When it came time to write the page to backing store, it would have to write the entire 2-Mbyte page. Thus, when a read-only superpage is modified, it is demoted back to small pages so that the modifications can be tracked on a 4-Kbyte by 4-Kbyte basis. Only when all the small pages are modified is it promoted to a writable superpage.

This conservative approach ensures that the kernel does not get forced into doing extra I/O, thus wiping out the TLB-miss savings. In practice, this approach works well. Applications either have a large area that they change constantly such as a matrix multiplication, or an area that they mostly read such as a database.

Providing superpage reservations requires a steady supply of superpages to be available. To this end, the virtual-memory system must take the stream of cached and freed 4-Kbyte pages and defragment them back into superpages. The cached and free pages are kept on buddy lists that aggregate the small pages back into bigger groups. For architectures that support more than one superpage size, the buddy lists track all the useful page sizes as the smaller groups are aggregated into bigger groups and eventually make their way up to maximum-size superpages. When servicing page faults for non-reserved areas of address space, the 4-Kbyte memory page is taken from a list of pages that have few if any buddies, thus preserving the larger pieces. The result may be that a cache page with known content is used rather than a free page with no useful contents. But the benefit of having more superpages available usually outweighs the loss of a page that is typically not used again.

The pageout daemon (described in Section 6.12) remains unchanged. It continues to move pages between its lists based on its best estimate of when and how they will be used most effectively. The superpages used for reservations are built from only pages on the cached and free lists. The parts of reserved superpages that have not been faulted are counted as free or cached. Thus, the rate at which pages are consumed from the cache and free lists does not change, which means that the pageout daemon is not forced to run faster than it did before superpages were added.

We have considered changing the pageout daemon to allow it to grab more actively referenced pages to fill out holes in the buddy lists. The question then arises as to how many actively referenced 4-Kbyte pages the pageout daemon can take to complete a superpage before the filesystem-cache performance is too heavily impacted. It does not take many filesystem rereads of lost cache data to wipe out the TLB-miss savings from a a single superpage. And the cost is even higher if the filesystem-cache page was dirty and had to be written to reclaim the page only to have it reread again. For all of these reasons, we have so far avoided these changes to the pageout daemon.

The performance improvements of superpages is shown in Table 6.3. These numbers are taken from much more extensive results in Navarro et al. [2002]. Of the more than 20 workloads studied in the paper, the only one that showed a slowdown (-1.7 percent) was for one of the programs in Spec Float 2000.

The first results column in the table shows the improvements on an architecture with four superpage sizes while the second column shows the PC architecture with only a single 4-Mbyte superpage size. Having multiple superpage sizes

Table 6.3 Performance of superpages.

Benchmark	Page sizes available 8K/64K/512K/4M	4M only
Spec Int 2000	11%	5%
Spec Float 2000	11%	6%
Web	2%	0%
Image rotation	23%	16%
Link FreeBSD kernel	33%	19%
Fast Fourier Transform	55%	55%
Matrix transposition	655%	586%

typically doubles the benefit derived from superpages. The primary reason for the higher performance is the greater number of superpages available and, hence, greater opportunity to use them.

6.12 Page Replacement

The service of page faults and other demands for memory may be satisfied from the free list for some time, but eventually memory must be reclaimed for reuse. Some pages are reclaimed when processes exit. On systems with a large amount of memory and low memory demand, exiting processes may provide enough free memory to fill demand. This case arises when there is enough memory for the kernel and for all pages that have ever been used by any current process. Obviously, many computers do not have enough main memory to retain all pages in memory. Thus, it eventually becomes necessary to move some pages to secondary storage—back to the filesystem or to the swap space. Bringing in a page is demand driven. For paging it out, however, there is no immediate indication when a page is no longer needed by a process. The kernel must implement some strategy for deciding which pages to move out of memory so that it can replace these pages with the ones that are currently needed in memory. Ideally, the strategy will choose pages for replacement that will not be needed soon. An approximation to this strategy is to find pages that have not been used actively or recently.

The 4.4BSD system implemented demand paging with a page-replacement algorithm that approximated global least recently used [Easton & Franaszek, 1979]. In FreeBSD, the one-bit use field for each page has been augmented with an activity counter to approximate global least actively used. Both these algorithms are examples of a ***global page-replacement algorithm***: one in which the choice of a page for replacement is made according to systemwide criteria. A ***local page-replacement algorithm*** would choose a process for which to replace a page and then chose a page based on per-process criteria. Although the algorithm in FreeBSD is similar in nature to that in 4.4BSD, its implementation is considerably different.

The kernel scans physical memory on a regular basis, considering pages for replacement. The use of a systemwide list of pages forces all processes to compete for memory on an equal basis. Note that it is also consistent with the way that FreeBSD treats other resources provided by the system. A common alternative to allowing all processes to compete equally for memory is to partition memory into multiple independent areas, each localized to a collection of processes that compete with one another for memory. This scheme is used, for example, by the VMS operating system [Kenah & Bate, 1984]. With this scheme, system administrators can guarantee that a process, or collection of processes, will always have a minimal percentage of memory. Unfortunately, this scheme can be difficult to administer. Allocating too small a number of pages to a partition can result in underutilization of memory and excessive I/O activity to secondary-storage devices, whereas setting the number too high can result in excessive swapping [Lazowska & Kelsey, 1978].

The kernel divides the main memory into five lists:

1. *Wired*: Wired pages are locked in memory and cannot be paged out. Typically, these pages are being used by the kernel or the physical-memory pager, or they have been locked down with *mlock*. In addition, all the pages being used to hold the thread stacks of loaded (i.e., not swapped-out) processes are also wired.

2. *Active*: Active pages are being used by one or more regions of virtual memory. Although the kernel can page them out, doing so is likely to cause an active process to fault them back again.

3. *Inactive*: Inactive pages may be dirty and have contents that are still known, but they are not usually part of any active region. If the contents of the page are dirty, the contents must be written to backing store before the page can be reused. Once the page has been cleaned, it is moved to the cache list. If the system becomes short of memory, the pageout daemon may try to move active pages to the inactive list in the hopes of finding pages that are not really in use. The selection criteria that are used by the pageout daemon to select pages to move from the active list to the inactive list are described later in this section. When the free-memory and cache lists drop too low, the pageout daemon traverses the inactive list to create more cache and free pages.

4. *Cache*: Cache pages have contents that are still known, but they are not part of any mapping. If they are faulted into an active region, they will be moved from the cache list to the active list. If they are used for a read or a write, they will be moved from the cache list first to the buffer cache and eventually released to the inactive list. An *mlock* system call can reclaim a page from the cache list and wire it. Pages on the cache list are similar to inactive pages except that they are not dirty, either because they are unmodified since they were paged in or because they have been written to their backing store. They can be claimed for a new use when a page is needed.

5. *Free*: Free pages have no useful contents and will be used to fulfill new page-fault requests.

The pages of main memory that can be used by user processes are those on the active, inactive, cache, and free lists. Requests for new pages are usually taken first from the free list if it has pages available, otherwise they will be taken from the cache list. Cache pages will be used in preference to free-list pages that are part of a large cluster of pages or a superpage.

Ideally, the kernel would maintain a working set for each process in the system. It would then know how much memory to provide to each process to minimize the latter's page-fault behavior. The FreeBSD virtual-memory system does not use the working-set model because it lacks accurate information about the reference pattern of a process. It does track the number of pages held by a process via the ***resident-set size***, but it does not know which of the resident pages constitute the working set. In 4.3BSD, the count of resident pages was used in making decisions on whether there was enough memory for a process to be swapped in when that process wanted to run. This feature was not carried over to the FreeBSD virtual-memory system. Although it works well during periods of high memory demand, memory is so abundant on current machines that swapping never happens, so it was not worth the effort to incorporate it into FreeBSD systems.

Paging Parameters

The memory-allocation needs of processes compete constantly, through the page-fault handler, with the overall system goal of maintaining a minimum threshold of pages in the inactive, cache, and free lists. As the system operates, it monitors main-memory utilization and attempts to run the pageout daemon frequently enough to keep the amount of inactive, cache, and free memory at or above the minimum threshold shown in Table 6.4. When the page-allocation routine, *vm_page_alloc*(), determines that more memory is needed, it awakens the pageout daemon.

The number of pages to be reclaimed by the pageout daemon is a function of the memory needs of the system. As more memory is needed by the system, more pages are scanned. This scanning causes the number of pages freed to increase. The pageout daemon determines the memory needed by comparing the number of available-memory pages against several parameters that are calculated during system startup. The desired values for the paging parameters are communicated to the pageout daemon through global variables that may be viewed or changed with *sysctl*. Likewise, the pageout daemon records its progress in global counters that may be viewed or reset with *sysctl*. Progress is measured by the number of pages scanned over each interval that it runs.

The goal of the pageout daemon is to maintain the inactive, cache, and free queues between the minimum and target thresholds shown in Table 6.4. The pageout daemon achieves this goal by moving pages from more active queues to less active queues to reach the indicated ranges. It never moves pages to the free list. Rather, pages from the anonymous areas of exiting processes are placed on the free list. It moves pages from the inactive list to the cache list to keep the sum of free and cached pages near its target. It moves pages from the active list to the inactive list to maintain the inactive list near its target.

Table 6.4 Available-memory thresholds.

Pool	Minimum	Target
Free + Cache	3.7%	9%
Inactive	0%	4.5%

The Pageout Daemon

Page replacement is done by the ***pageout daemon***. The paging policy of the pageout daemon is embodied in the *vm_pageout*() and *vm_pageout_scan*() routines. When the pageout daemon reclaims pages that have been modified, it is responsible for writing them to the swap area. Thus, the pageout daemon must be able to use normal kernel-synchronization mechanisms, such as *sleep*(). It therefore runs as a separate process, with its own process structure and kernel stack. Like **init**, the pageout daemon is created by an internal *fork* operation during system startup (see Section 15.4); unlike **init**, however, it remains in kernel mode after the fork. The pageout daemon simply enters *vm_pageout*() and never returns. Unlike some other users of the disk I/O routines, the pageout process needs to perform its disk operations asynchronously so that it can continue scanning in parallel with disk writes.

When running on systems with many CPUs, the demand for pages can vastly exceed the number of pages that a single pageout daemon can provide. Starting in FreeBSD 10, the paging daemon was multithreaded so that it would be able to keep up with heavy paging demand.

Historically, the pages were handled by a least recently used algorithm. The drawback to this algorithm is that a sudden burst of memory activity can flush many useful pages from the cache. To mitigate this behavior, FreeBSD uses a least actively used algorithm to preserve pages that have a history of usage so that they will be favored over the once-used pages brought in during a period of high memory demand.

When a page is first brought into memory, it is given an initial usage count of 5. Further usage information is gathered by the pageout daemon during its periodic scans of memory. As each page of memory is scanned, its reference bit is checked. If the bit is set, it is cleared and the usage counter for the page is incremented (up to a limit of 64) by the number of references to the page. If the reference bit is clear, the usage counter is decremented. When the usage counter reaches 0, the page is moved from the active list to the inactive list. Pages that are repeatedly used build up large usage counts that will cause them to remain on the active list much longer than pages that are used just once.

The goal of the pageout daemon is to keep the number of pages on the inactive, cache, and free lists within their desired ranges. Whenever an operation that uses pages causes the amount of free memory to fall below the minimum thresholds, the pageout daemon is awakened. The pageout-handling algorithm is shown in Figure 6.20. In the following overview, the lettered points are references to the tags down the left side of the code.

A. The pageout daemon calculates the number of pages that need to be moved from the inactive list to the cache list. To avoid saturating the I/O system, the pageout daemon limits the number of I/O operations that it will start concurrently.

B. Scans the inactive list until the desired number of pages are moved. Skips over busy pages, since they are likely being paged out and can be moved later when they are clean.

```
/*
 * Vm_pageout_scan does the dirty work for the pageout daemon.
 */
void vm_pageout_scan(void)
{
[A] page_shortage = free_target -
        (free_count + cache_count);
    max_writes_in_progress = 32;
[B] for (page = FIRST(inactive list); page; page = next) {
        next = NEXT(page);
        if (page_shortage < 0)
            break;
        if (page busy)
            continue;
[C]     if (page is referenced) {
            update page active count;
            move page to end of active list;
            continue;
        }
        if (page is invalid) {
            move page to front of free list;
            page_shortage--;
            continue;
        }
        if (page is clean) {
            move page to end of cache list;
            page_shortage--;
            continue;
        }
[D]     if (first time page seen dirty) {
            mark page as seen dirty;
            move to end of inactive list;
            continue;
        } else if (max_writes_in_progress > 0) {
            check for cluster of dirty pages around page;
            start asynchronous write of page cluster;
            move to end of inactive list;
            page_shortage--;
            max_writes_in_progress--;
        }
    }
[E] page_shortage = free_target + inactive_target
        - (free_count + cache_count + inactive_count);
```

Figure 6.20 Pageout handling (part 1 of 2).

```
[F] for (page = FIRST(active list); page; page = next) {
        next = NEXT(page);
        if (page_shortage <= 0)
            break;
        if (page is referenced) {
            update page active count;
            move page to end of active list;
            continue;
        }
[G]     decrement page active count;
        if (page active count > 0) {
            move page to end of active list;
            continue;
        }
        page_shortage--;
        move page to end of inactive list;
    }
[H] if (targets not met)
        request swap-out daemon to run;
[I] if (nearly all memory and swap in use)
        kill biggest unprotected process;
}
```

Figure 6.20 Pageout handling (part 2 of 2).

C. If we find a page that has been referenced, then it has been moved to the inactive list prematurely, so update its usage count and move it back to the active list. Pages with invalid contents (usually caused by an I/O error) are removed from their *vm_object* and moved to the free list. Pages that are clean can be moved to the cache list.

D. Dirty pages need to be paged out, but flushing a page is extremely expensive compared to freeing a clean page. Thus, dirty pages are given extra time on the inactive queue by cycling them through the queue twice before being flushed. They cycle through the list once more while being cleaned. This extra time on the inactive queue will reduce unnecessary I/O caused by prematurely paging out an active page. The clustering checks for up to 16 dirty pages on either side of the selected page. The pager is only required to write the selected page. However, it may write as many of the clustered dirty pages as it finds convenient. The scanning of the inactive list stops initiating new writes if the number of pageouts in progress hits its limit. In 4.4BSD, the I/O completions were handled by the pageout daemon. FreeBSD requires that pagers track their own I/O operations including the appropriate updating of the written pages. The written-page update at I/O completion does not move the page from the inactive list to the cache list. Rather, the page remains on the inactive list until it is eventually moved to the cache list during a future pass of the pageout daemon.

E. The pageout daemon calculates the number of pages that need to be moved from the active list to the inactive list. As some will eventually need to be moved to the cache list, enough pages must be moved to the inactive list to leave it at its target level after the cache list has been filled.

F. Scan the active list until the desired number of pages are moved. If we find a page that has been referenced since our last scan, update its usage count and move it to the end of the active list.

G. The page is not active, so decrements its usage count. If its usage is still above zero, moves it to the end of the active list. Otherwise, moves it to the inactive list.

H. If the page-count targets have not been met, the swap-out daemon is started (see next subsection) to try to clear additional memory.

I. If the kernel has been configured to not impose any limits on the amount of virtual memory that it will grant, then it can find that it has nearly filled its memory and swap space. It avoids going into deadlock by killing off the largest unprotected process.

Note that the page and *vm_object* locking has been elided in Figure 6.20 to simplify the explanation.

Even when no additional pages are needed, the pageout daemon is awakened often enough to ensure that it will scan all the pages on the active list once every *vm_pageout_update_period* seconds. The default is to scan every active page once every 10 minutes. A 1-minute interval would be better, but checking all of active memory on large memory machines once per minute would put too much of a non-work load on the system. And even a 10-minute scan eliminates the worst-case behaviors when no scanning is done for long periods of time.

Swapping

Although swapping is generally avoided, there are several times when it is used in FreeBSD to address a serious memory shortage. Swapping is done in FreeBSD when any of the following situations occur:

- The system becomes so short of memory that the paging process cannot free memory fast enough to satisfy the demand. For example, a memory shortfall may happen when multiple large processes are run on a machine lacking enough memory for the minimum working sets of the processes.
- Processes are completely inactive for more than 10 seconds. Otherwise, such processes would retain a few pages of memory associated with their thread stacks. Swapping out idle threads is disabled by default as the extra delay in restarting them is not worth the small amount of memory that is reclaimed.

Swap operations completely remove a process from main memory, including the process page tables, the pages of the data and the stack segments that are not already in swap space, and the thread stacks.

Process swapping is invoked only when paging is unable to keep up with memory needs or when short-term memory needs warrant swapping a process. In general, the swap-scheduling mechanism does not do well under heavy load; system performance is much better when memory scheduling can be done by the page-replacement algorithm than when the swap algorithm is used.

Swap out is driven by the swap-out daemon, *vmdaemon*. The swap-out policy of the *vmdaemon* is embodied in the *vm_daemon*() routine. If the swapping of idle processes is enabled and the pageout daemon can find any processes that have been sleeping for more than 10 seconds (*swap_idle_threshold2*, the cutoff for considering the time sleeping to be "a long time"), it will swap them all out. Such processes have the least likelihood of making good use of the memory that they occupy; thus, they are swapped out even if they are small. If none of these processes are available, the pageout daemon will swap out all processes that has been sleeping for as briefly as 2 seconds (*swap_idle_threshold1*). These criteria attempt to avoid swapping entirely until the pageout daemon is clearly unable to keep enough memory free.

In 4.4BSD, if memory was still desperately low, the swap-out daemon would select to swap out the runnable process that had been resident the longest. Once swapping of runnable processes had begun, the processes eligible for swapping would take turns in memory so that no process was frozen out entirely. The FreeBSD swap-out daemon will not select a runnable processes to swap out. So, if the set of runnable processes do not fit in memory, the machine will effectively deadlock. Current machines have enough memory that this condition usually does not arise. If it does, FreeBSD avoids deadlock by killing the largest process. If the condition begins to arise in normal operation, the 4.4BSD algorithm will need to be restored.

The mechanics of performing a swap out are simple. The swapped-in process flag P_INMEM is cleared to show that the process is not resident in memory. The PS_SWAPPINGOUT flag is set while the swap out is being done so that neither a second swap out nor a swap in is attempted at the same time. If a runnable process is to be swapped (which currently never happens), it needs to be removed from the runnable process queue. The kernel stacks for the threads of the process are then marked as pageable, which allows the stack pages, along with any other remaining pages for the process, to be paged out via the standard pageout mechanism. The swapped-out process cannot be run until after it is swapped back into memory.

The Swap-In Process

Swap-in operations are done by the swapping process, ***swapper*** (process 0). This process is the first one created by the system when the latter is started. The swap-in policy of the swapper is embodied in the *scheduler*() routine. This routine swaps processes back in when memory is available and they are ready to run. At any time, the swapper is in one of three states:

1. *Idle*: No swapped-out processes are ready to be run. Idle is the normal state.
2. *Swapping in*: At least one runnable process is swapped out, and *scheduler*() attempts to find memory for it.
3. *Swapping out*: The system is short of memory, or there is not enough memory to swap in a process. Under these circumstances, *scheduler*() awakens the pageout daemon to free pages and to swap out other processes until the memory shortage abates.

If more than one swapped-out process is runnable, the first task of the swapper is to decide which process to swap in. This decision may affect the decision about whether to swap out another process. Each swapped-out process is assigned a priority based on:

- The length of time it has been swapped out
- Its *nice* value
- The amount of time it was asleep since it last ran

In general, the process that has been swapped out longest or was swapped out because it had slept for a long time before being swapped will be brought in first. Once a process is selected, the swapper checks to see whether there is enough memory free to swap in the process. Historically, the system required as much memory to be available as was occupied by the process before that process was swapped. Under FreeBSD, this requirement was reduced to a requirement that the number of pages on the free and cache lists be at least equal to the minimum free-memory threshold. If there is enough memory available, the process is brought back into memory. The kernel stacks for the threads of the process are swapped in immediately, but the process loads the rest of its working set by demand paging from the backing store. Thus, not all the memory that is needed by the process is used immediately. Earlier BSD systems tracked the anticipated demand and would only swap in runnable processes as free memory became available to fulfill their expected needs. FreeBSD allows all swapped-out runnable processes to be swapped in as soon as there is enough memory to load their thread stacks.

The procedure for swap in of a process is the reverse of that for swap out:

1. Memory is allocated for the kernel stack of each of the threads of the process and they are read back from swap space.
2. The process is marked as resident, and its runnable threads are returned to the run queue (i.e., those threads that are not stopped or sleeping).

After the swap in completes, the process is ready to run like any other, except that it has no resident pages. It will bring in the pages that it needs by faulting them.

6.13 Portability

Everything discussed in this chapter up to this section has been part of the machine-independent data structures and algorithms. These parts of the virtual-memory system require little change when FreeBSD is ported to a new architecture. This section will describe the machine-dependent parts of the virtual-memory system: the parts of the virtual-memory system that must be written as part of a port of FreeBSD to a new architecture. The role of the machine-dependent parts of the virtual-memory system are to manage the page tables used by the hardware ***memory-management unit*** (see Section 6.11) to control access to process and kernel memory.

Often, a port to another architecture with a similar memory-management organization can be used as a starting point for a new port. The 32-bit PC architecture uses the typical two-level page-table organization shown in Figure 6.21. An address space is broken into 4-Kbyte virtual pages, with each page identified by a 32-bit entry in the ***page table***. Each page-table entry contains the physical page number assigned to the virtual page, the access permissions allowed, modify and reference information, and a bit showing that the entry contains valid information. The 4 Mbyte of page-table entries are likewise divided into 4-Kbyte ***page-table pages***, each of which is described by a single 32-bit entry in the ***directory table***. Directory-table entries are nearly identical to page-table entries: They contain access bits, modify and reference bits, a valid bit, and the physical page number of the page-table page described. One 4-Kbyte

Figure 6.21 Two-level page-table organization. Key: V—page-valid bit; M—page-modified bit; R—page-referenced bit; ACC—page-access permissions.

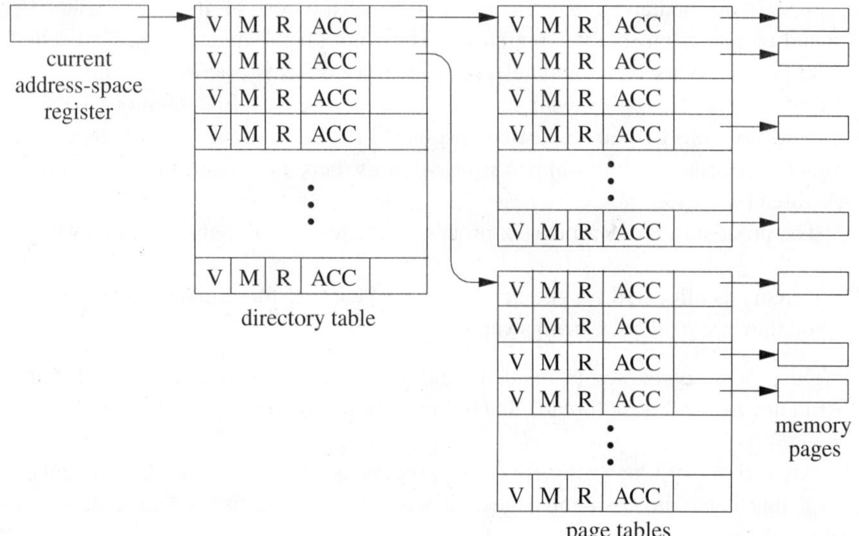

page—1024 directory-table entries—covers the maximum-size 4-Gbyte address space. The CR3 hardware register contains the physical address of the directory table for the currently active process. The 64-bit PC architecture is similar except that it needs more levels of page tables.

The Role of the *pmap* Module

The machine-dependent code describes how the ***physical mapping*** is done between the user-processes and kernel virtual addresses and the physical addresses of the main memory. This mapping function includes management of access rights in addition to address translation. The physical-mapping module, usually referred to as the ***pmap module***, manages machine-dependent translation and access tables that are used either directly or indirectly by the memory-management hardware. For example, on the PC, the *pmap* maintains the memory-resident directory and page tables for each process, as well as for the kernel. The machine-dependent state required to describe the translation and access rights of a single page is often referred to as a *mapping* or ***mapping structure***.

The FreeBSD *pmap* interface shares many design characteristics with the *pmap* interface in Mach 3.0. FreeBSD has added many functions to optimize range operations such as prefaulting whole files and destroying an entire address space. The *pmap* module is intended to be logically independent of the higher levels of the virtual-memory system. The interface deals strictly in machine-independent page-aligned virtual and physical addresses and in machine-independent protections. The machine-independent page size may be a multiple of the architecture-supported page size. Thus, *pmap* operations must be able to affect more than one physical page per logical page. The machine-independent protection is a simple encoding of read, write, and execute permission bits. The *pmap* must map all possible combinations into valid architecture-specific values.

A process's *pmap* is considered to be a cache of mapping information kept in a machine-dependent format. As such, it does not need to contain complete state for all valid mappings. Mapping state is the responsibility of the machine-independent layer. With one exception, the *pmap* module may throw away mapping state at its discretion to reclaim resources. The exception is wired mappings, which should never cause a fault that reaches the machine-independent *vm_fault*() routine. Thus, state for wired mappings must be retained in its *vm_pmap* structure until it is removed explicitly.

In general, *pmap* routines may act either on a set of mappings defined by a virtual address range or on all mappings for a particular physical address. Being able to act on individual or all virtual mappings for a physical page requires that the mapping information maintained by the *pmap* module be easily found by both virtual and physical addresses. For architectures such as the PC that support memory-resident page tables, the virtual-to-physical, or forward lookup, may be a simple emulation of the hardware page-table traversal. Physical-to-virtual, or reverse, lookup uses a list of *pv_entry* structures, described in the next subsection, to find all the page-table entries referencing a page. The list may contain multiple entries only if ***virtual-address aliasing*** is allowed.

There are two strategies that can be used for management of *pmap* memory resources, such as user-directory or page-table memory. The traditional and easiest approach is for the *pmap* module to manage its own memory. Under this strategy, the *pmap* module can grab a fixed amount of wired physical memory at system boot time, map that memory into the kernel's address space, and allocate pieces of the memory as needed for its own data structures. The primary benefit is that this approach isolates the *pmap* module's memory needs from those of the rest of the system and limits the *pmap* module's dependencies on other parts of the system. This design is consistent with a layered model of the virtual-memory system in which the *pmap* is the lowest, and hence self-sufficient, layer.

The disadvantage is that this approach requires the duplication of many of the memory-management functions. The *pmap* module has its own memory allocator and deallocator for its private heap—a heap that is statically sized and cannot be adjusted for varying systemwide memory demands. For an architecture with memory-resident page tables, it must keep track of noncontiguous chunks of processes' page tables, because a process may populate its address space sparsely. Handling this requirement entails duplicating much of the standard list-management code, such as that used by the *vm_map* code.

An alternative approach, used by the PC, is to use the higher-level virtual-memory code recursively to manage some *pmap* resources. Here, the 4-Kbyte directory table for each user process is mapped into the address space of the kernel as part of setting up the process and remains resident until the process exits. While a process is running, its page-table entries are mapped into a virtually contiguous 4-Mbyte array of page-table entries in the kernel's address space. This organization leads to an obscure memory-saving optimization, exploited in the PC *pmap* module, where the kernel's page-table page describing the 4-Mbyte user page-table range can double as the user's directory table. The kernel also maintains alternate maps to hold individual page-table pages of other nonrunning processes if it needs to access their address space.

Using the same page-allocation routines as all the other parts of the system ensures that physical memory is allocated only when needed and from the systemwide free-memory pool. Page tables and other *pmap* resources also can be allocated from pageable kernel memory. This approach easily and efficiently supports large sparse address spaces, including the kernel's own address space.

The *vm_pmap* data structures are contained in the machine-dependent include directory in the file **pmap.h**. Most of the code for these routines is in the machine-dependent source directory in the file **pmap.c**. The main tasks of the *pmap* module are these:

- System initialization and startup (*pmap_bootstrap*( ), *pmap_init*( ), *pmap_growkernel*( ))
- Allocation and deallocation of mappings of physical to virtual pages (*pmap_enter*( ), *pmap_remove*( ), *pmap_qenter*( ), *pmap_qremove*( ))

- Change of access and wiring attributes for mappings (*pmap_change_wiring*(), *pmap_remove_all*(), *pmap_remove_write*(), *pmap_protect*())
- Maintenance of physical page-usage information (*pmap_clear_modify*(), *pmap_is_modified*(), *pmap_ts_referenced*())
- Initialization of physical pages (*pmap_copy_page*(), *pmap_zero_page*())
- Management of internal data structures (*pmap_pinit*(), *pmap_release*())

Each of these tasks is described in the following subsections.

Initialization and Startup

The first step in starting up the system is for the loader to bring the kernel image from a disk or the network into the physical memory of the machine. The kernel load image looks much like that of any other process; it contains a text segment, an initialized data segment, and an uninitialized data segment. The loader places the kernel contiguously near the beginning of physical memory. Unlike a user process that is demand paged into memory, the text and data for the kernel are read into memory in their entirety. Following these two segments, the loader zeros an area of memory equal to the size of the kernel's uninitialized memory segment. After loading the kernel, the loader passes control to the starting address given in the kernel executable image. When the kernel begins executing, it is either executing with the MMU turned off using the direct physical addresses or with a minimal predefined set of page tables.

The first task undertaken by the kernel is to set up the kernel *vm_pmap*, and any other data structures that are necessary to describe the kernel's virtual address space. On the PC, the initial setup includes allocating and initializing the directory and page tables that map the statically loaded kernel image and memory-mapped I/O address space, allocating a fixed amount of memory for kernel page-table pages, allocating and initializing the kernel stack for the initial process, reserving special areas of the kernel's address space, and initializing assorted critical *vm_pmap*-internal data structures. When done, it is possible to enable the MMU or switch to the fully configured page tables. In either case, the kernel begins running in the context of process zero.

Once the kernel is running in its virtual address space, it proceeds to initialize the rest of the system. It determines the size of the physical memory, then calls *pmap_bootstrap*() and *vm_page_startup*() to set up the initial *vm_pmap* data structures, to allocate the *vm_page* structures, and to create a small, fixed-size pool of memory, which the kernel memory allocators can use so that they can begin responding to memory allocation requests. Next, it makes a call to set up the machine-independent portion of the virtual-memory system. It concludes with a call to *pmap_init*(), which allocates all resources necessary to manage multiple user address spaces and synchronizes the higher-level kernel virtual-memory data structures with the kernel *vm_pmap*.

The *pmap_init*() function allocates a minimal amount of wired memory to use for kernel page-table pages. The page-table space is expanded dynamically by the *pmap_growkernel*() routine as it is needed while the kernel is running. Once allocated, it is never freed. The limit on the size of the kernel's address space is selected at boot time. On 64-bit architectures, the kernel is typically given an address space large enough to directly map all of physical memory. On 32-bit architectures, the kernel is typically given a maximum of 1 Gbyte of address space.

In 4.4BSD, the memory managed by the buffer cache was separate from the memory managed by the virtual-memory system. Since all the virtual-memory pages were used to map process regions, it was sensible to create an inverted page table. This table was an array of *pv_entry* structures. Each *pv_entry* described a single address translation and included the virtual address, a pointer to the associated *vm_pmap* structure for that virtual address, a link for chaining together multiple entries mapping this physical address, and additional information specific to entries mapping page-table pages. Building a dedicated table was sensible, since all valid pages were referenced by a *vm_pmap*, yet few had multiple mappings.

With the merger of the buffer cache into the virtual-memory system in FreeBSD, many pages of memory are used to cache file data that is not mapped into any process address space. Thus, preallocating a table of *pv_entry* structures is wasteful, since many of them would go unused. So, FreeBSD allocates *pv_entry* structures on demand as pages are mapped into a process address space.

Figure 6.22 shows the *pv_entry* references for a set of pages that have a single mapping. The purpose of the *pv_entry* structures is to identify the address space that has the page mapped. The machine-dependent part of each *vm_page* structure contains the head of a list of *pv_entry* structures and a count of the number of entries on the list. In Figure 6.22, the *vm_object* has cached its pages 5, 18, and 79. The list heads in the machine-dependent structures of these *vm_page* structures would each point to a single *pv_entry* structure labelled in the figure with the number of the *vm_page* structure that references them. Not shown in Figure 6.22 is that each *vm_pmap* structure also maintains a list of all the *pv_entry* structures that reference it.

Figure 6.22 Physical pages with a single mapping.

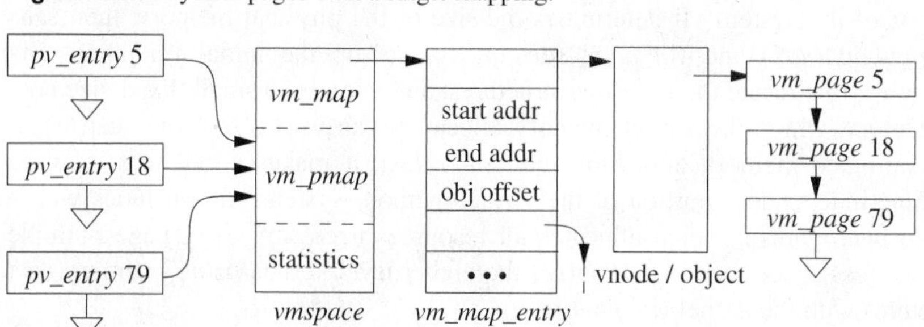

Each *pv_entry* can reference only one physical map. When a *vm_object* becomes shared between two or more processes, each physical page of memory may become mapped into two or more sets of page tables. To track these multiple references, the *pmap* module must create chains of *pv_entry* structures, as shown in Figure 6.23. Copy-on-write is an example of the need to find all the mappings of a page as it requires that the page tables be set to read-only in all the processes sharing the *vm_object*. The *pmap* module can implement this request by walking the collection of pages cached by the *vm_object* to be made copy-on-write. For each page, it traverses that page's list of *pv_entry* structures. It then makes the appropriate change to the page-table entry associated with each *pv_entry* structure.

A system with many shared *vm_object*s can require many *pv_entry* structures, which can use an unreasonable amount of the kernel memory. The alternative would be to keep a list associated with each *vm_object* of all the *vm_map_entry* structures that reference it. When it becomes necessary to modify the mapping of all the references to the page, the kernel could traverse this list, checking the address space associated with each *vm_map_entry* to see if it held a reference to the page. For each page found, it could make the appropriate update.

The *pv_entry* structures consume more memory but reduce the time to do a common operation. For example, consider a system running 1000 processes that all share a common library. Without the *pv_entry* list, the cost to change a page to copy-on-write would require checking all 1000 processes. With the *pv_entry* list, only those processes using the page would need to be inspected.

Figure 6.23 Physical pages with multiple mappings.

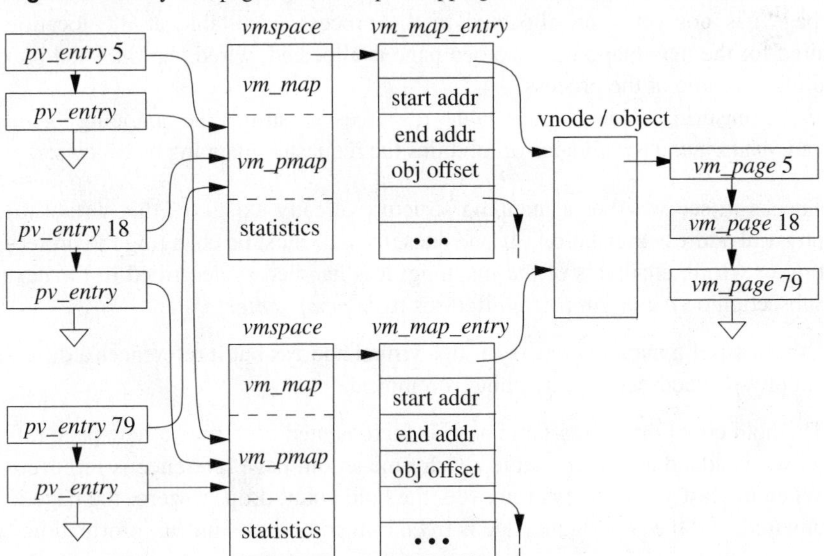

Mapping Allocation and Deallocation

The primary responsibility of the *pmap* module is validating (allocating) and invalidating (deallocating) mappings of physical pages to virtual addresses. The physical pages represent cached portions of a *vm_object* that is providing data from a file or an anonymous memory region. A physical page is bound to a virtual address because that *vm_object* is being mapped into a process's address space either explicitly by *mmap* or implicitly by *fork* or *exec*. Physical-to-virtual address mappings are not created at the time that the *vm_object* is mapped; instead, their creation is delayed until the first reference to a particular page is made. At that point, an access fault will occur, and *pmap_enter*() will be called. The *pmap_enter*() function is responsible for any required side effects associated with creation of a new mapping. Such side effects are largely the result of entering a second translation for an already mapped physical page—for example, as the result of a copy-on-write operation. Typically, this operation requires flushing uniprocessor or multiprocessor TLB or cache entries to maintain consistency.

In addition to its use to create new mappings, *pmap_enter*() may also be called to modify the wiring or protection attributes of an existing mapping or to rebind an existing mapping for a virtual address to a new physical address. The kernel can handle changing attributes by calling the appropriate interface routine, described in the next subsection. Changing the target physical address of a mapping is simply a matter of first removing the old mapping and then handling it like any other new mapping request.

The *pmap_enter*() function is the only routine that cannot lose state or delay its action. When called, it must create a mapping as requested, and it must validate that mapping before returning to the caller. On the PC, *pmap_enter*() must first check whether a page-table entry exists for the requested address. If a physical page has not yet been allocated to the process page-table at the location required for the new mapping, a zeroed page is allocated, wired, and inserted into the directory table of the process.

After ensuring that all page-table resources exist for the mapping being entered, *pmap_enter*() validates or modifies the requested mapping as follows:

1. Checks to see whether a mapping structure already exists for this virtual-to-physical address translation. If one does, the call must be changing the protection or wiring attributes of the mapping; it is handled as described in the next subsection on *pmap_protect*(). Returns from *pmap_enter*().

2. Otherwise, if a mapping exists for this virtual address but it references a different physical address, that mapping is removed.

3. The hold count on a page-table page is incremented each time a new page reference is added and decremented each time an old page reference is removed. When the last valid page is removed, the hold count drops to zero, the page is unwired, and the page-table page is freed as it contains no useful information.

4. A page-table entry is created and validated, the hold count is set to 1, and the cache and TLB entries are flushed as necessary.

5. If the physical address is outside the range managed by the *pmap* module (e.g., a frame-buffer page), no *pv_entry* structure is needed. Otherwise, for the case of a new mapping for a physical page that is mapped into an address space, a *pv_entry* structure is created.

6. For machines with a virtually indexed cache, a check is made to see whether this physical page already has other mappings. If it does, all mappings may need to be marked cache inhibited, to avoid cache inconsistencies.

When a *vm_object* is unmapped from an address space, either explicitly by *munmap* or implicitly on process exit, the *pmap* module is invoked to invalidate and remove the mappings for all physical pages caching data for the *vm_object*. Unlike *pmap_enter*(), *pmap_remove*() can be called with a virtual-address range encompassing more than one mapping. Hence, the kernel does the unmapping by looping over all virtual pages in the range, ignoring those for which there is no mapping and removing those for which there is one.

The *pmap_remove*() function on the PC is simple. It loops over the specified address range, invalidating individual page mappings. Since *pmap_remove*() can be called with large sparsely allocated regions, such as an entire process virtual-address range, it needs to skip invalid entries within the range efficiently. It skips invalid entries by first checking the directory-table entry for a particular address and, if an entry is invalid, skipping to the next 4-Mbyte boundary. When all page mappings have been invalidated, any necessary global cache flushing is done.

To invalidate a single mapping, the kernel locates and marks as invalid the appropriate page-table entry. The reference and modify bits for the page are saved in the page's *vm_page* structure for future retrieval. If this mapping was a user mapping, the hold count for the page-table page is decremented. When the count reaches zero, the page-table page can be reclaimed because it contains no more valid mappings. When a user page-table page is removed from the kernel's address space (i.e., as a result of removing the final valid user mapping from that page), the process's directory table must be updated. The kernel does this update by invalidating the appropriate directory-table entry. If the physical address from the mapping is outside the managed range, nothing more is done. Otherwise, the *pv_entry* structure is found and is deallocated.

The *pmap_qenter*() and *pmap_qremove*() are faster versions of the *pmap_enter*() and *pmap_remove*() functions that can be used by the kernel to create and remove temporary mappings quickly. They can only be used on non-pageable mappings in the address space of the kernel. For example, the buffer-cache management routines use these routines to map file pages into kernel memory so that they can be read or written by the filesystem.

Change of Access and Wiring Attributes for Mappings

An important role of the *pmap* module is to manipulate the hardware access protections for pages. These manipulations may be applied to all mappings covered by a virtual-address range within a *vm_pmap* via *pmap_protect*(), or they may be applied to all mappings of a particular physical page across *vm_pmaps* via *pmap_remove_write*() and *pmap_remove_all*(). There are two features common to both calls. First, either form may be called with a protection value of VM_PROT_NONE to remove a range of virtual addresses or to remove all mappings for a particular physical page, which it does by calling *pmap_remove*(). Second, these routines should never add write permission to the affected mappings. Thus, calls including VM_PROT_WRITE should make no changes. This restriction is necessary for the copy-on-write mechanism to function properly. The request to make the page writable is made only in the *vm_map_entry* structure. When a later write attempt on the page is made by the process, a page fault will occur. The page-fault handler will inspect the *vm_map_entry* and determine that the write should be permitted. If it is a copy-on-write page, the fault handler will make any necessary copies before calling *pmap_enter*() to enable writing on the page. Thus, write permission on a page is added only via calls to the *pmap_enter*() function.

The *pmap_protect*() function is used primarily by the *mprotect* system call to change the protection for a region of process address space (though its functionality is also duplicated in *pmap_enter*() as described in step 1 of the previous subsection). The strategy is similar to that of *pmap_remove*(): Loop over all virtual pages in the range and apply the change to all valid mappings that are found. Invalid mappings are left alone.

For the PC, *pmap_protect*() first checks for the special cases. If the requested permission is VM_PROT_NONE, it calls *pmap_remove*() to handle the revocation of all access permission. If VM_PROT_WRITE is included, it just returns immediately. For a normal protection value, *pmap_protect*() loops over the given address range, skipping invalid mappings. For valid mappings, the page-table entry is looked up, and, if the new protection value differs from the current value, the entry is modified and any TLB and cache flushing is done. As occurs with *pmap_remove*(), any global cache actions are delayed until the entire range has been modified.

The *pmap_remove_write*() function is used internally by the virtual-memory system to set read-only permission when a copy-on-write operation is set up (e.g., during *fork*). The *pmap_remove_all*() function removes all access permissions before doing page replacement to force all references to a page to block pending the completion of its operation.

The addition of write enable must be done on a page-by-page basis by the page-fault handling routine as described for *pmap_protect*(). Otherwise, *pmap_remove_write*() and *pmap_remove_all*() traverse the list of *pv_entry* structures for the requested page, invalidating the individual mappings as described in the previous subsection. As occurs with *pmap_protect*(), the entry is checked to ensure that it is changing before expensive TLB and cache flushes are done. Note that TLB and cache flushing differ from those for *pmap_remove*(), since they must invalidate entries from multiple process contexts, rather than invalidating multiple entries from a single process context.

The *pmap_change_wiring*() function is called to wire or unwire a single machine-independent virtual page within a *vm_pmap*. As described in the previous subsection, wiring informs the *pmap* module that a mapping should not cause a hardware fault that reaches the machine-independent *vm_fault*() code. Wiring is typically a software attribute that has no effect on the hardware MMU state: it simply tells the *pmap* not to throw away state about the mapping. As such, if a *pmap* module never discards state, then it is not strictly necessary for the module even to track the wired status of pages. The only side effect of not tracking wiring information in the *vm_pmap* is that the *mlock* system call cannot be completely implemented without a wired page-count statistic.

The PC *pmap* implementation maintains wiring information. An unused bit in the page-table-entry structure records a page's wired status. The *pmap_change_wiring*() function sets or clears this bit when it is invoked with a valid virtual address. Since the wired bit is ignored by the hardware, there is no need to modify the TLB or cache when the bit is changed.

Maintenance of Physical Page-Usage Information

The machine-independent page-management code needs to be able to get basic information about the usage and modification of pages from the underlying hardware. The *pmap* module facilitates the collection of this information without requiring the machine-independent code to understand the details of the mapping tables by providing a set of interfaces to query and clear the reference and modify bits. The pageout daemon can call *vm_page_test_dirty*() to determine whether a page is dirty. If the page is dirty, the pageout daemon can write it to backing store and then call *pmap_clear_modify*() to clear the modify bit. The *pmap_clear_modify*() routine clears the modified bit in the attribute array and then loops over all *pv_entry* structures associated with the physical page, clearing the hardware-maintained page-table-entry bits. This final step may involve TLB or cache flushes along the way or afterward. Similarly, when the pageout daemon wants to update the active count for a page, it uses *pmap_ts_referenced*() to count and clear the number of uses of the page since it was last scanned.

One important feature of the query routines is that they should return valid information even if there are currently no mappings for the page in question. Thus, referenced and modified information cannot just be gathered from the hardware-maintained bits of the various page-table or TLB entries; rather, there must be a place where the information is retained when a mapping is removed.

For the PC, the modified information for a page is stored in the *dirty* field of its *vm_page* structure. Initially cleared, the information is updated by calling the *vm_page_test_dirty*() routine whenever a mapping for a page is considered for removal. The *vm_page_test_dirty*() routine first checks the *dirty* field and, if it is set, returns immediately. Since this attribute array contains only past information, it still needs to check status bits in the page-table entries for currently valid mappings of the page. This information is checked by calling the machine-dependent *pmap_is_modified*() routine that traverses the *pv_entry* structures associated with the physical page, examining the modified bit for the *pv_entry*'s associated page-table entry. It can return TRUE as soon as it encounters a set bit or FALSE if the bit is not set in any page-table entry. If it returns TRUE, *vm_page_test_dirty*() sets the *dirty* field before returning.

The referenced information for a page is stored in the *act_count* field and as a flag of its *vm_page* structure. Initially cleared, the information is updated periodically by the pageout daemon. As it scans memory, the pageout daemon calls the *pmap_ts_referenced*() routine to collect a count of references to the page. The *pmap_ts_referenced*() routine returns zero if it is not passed a managed physical page. Otherwise, it traverses the *pv_entry* structures associated with the physical page, examining and clearing the referenced bit for the *pv_entry*'s associated page-table entry. It returns the number of referenced bits that it found.

Initialization of Physical Pages

Two interfaces are provided to allow the higher-level virtual-memory routines to initialize physical memory. The *pmap_zero_page*() function takes a physical address and fills the page with zeros. The *pmap_copy_page*() function takes two physical addresses and copies the contents of the first page to the second page. Since both take physical addresses, the *pmap* module will most likely have to first map those pages into the kernel's address space before it can access them.

Each CPU in the PC implementation has a pair of kernel virtual addresses reserved for zeroing and copying pages. The *pmap_zero_page*() function maps the specified physical address into the reserved virtual address, calls *bzero*() to clear the page, and then removes the temporary mapping with the single translation-invalidation primitive used by *pmap_remove*(). Similarly, *pmap_copy_page*() creates mappings for both physical addresses, uses *bcopy*() to make the copy, and then removes both mappings.

Management of Internal Data Structures

The remaining *pmap* interface routines are used for management and synchronization of internal data structures. The *pmap_pinit*() function creates an instance of the machine-dependent *vm_pmap* structure. It is used by the *vmspace_fork*() and *vmspace_exec*() routines when creating new address spaces during a *fork* or *exec*. The *pmap_release*() function deallocates the *vm_pmap*'s resources. It is used by the *vmspace_free*() routine when cleaning up a vmspace when a process exits.

Exercises

6.1 What does it mean for a machine to support virtual memory? What four hardware facilities are typically required for a machine to support virtual memory?

6.2 What is the relationship between paging and swapping on a demand-paged virtual-memory system? Explain whether it is desirable to provide both mechanisms in the same system. Can you suggest an alternative to providing both mechanisms?

6.3 What three policies characterize paging systems?

6.4 What is ***copy-on-write***? In most UNIX applications, the *fork* system call is followed almost immediately by an *exec* system call. Why does this behavior make it particularly attractive to use copy-on-write in implementing *fork*?

6.5 Explain why the *vfork* system call will always be more efficient than a clever implementation of the *fork* system call.

6.6 When a process exits, all its pages may not be placed immediately on the memory free list. Explain this behavior.

6.7 Why does the kernel have both the traditional *malloc*() and *free*() interface and the zone allocator? Explain when each type of interface is useful.

6.8 What is the purpose of superpages? Why is it needed?

6.9 What purpose does the pageout-daemon process serve in the virtual-memory system?

6.10 What is clustering? Where is it used in the virtual-memory system?

6.11 Why is the historic use of the ***sticky bit*** to lock a process image in memory no longer useful in FreeBSD?

6.12 Give two reasons for swapping to be initiated.

*6.13 The 4.3BSD virtual-memory system had a text cache that retained the identity of text pages from one execution of a program to the next. How does the caching of vnode *vm_objects* in FreeBSD improve on the performance of the 4.3BSD text cache?

**6.14 FreeBSD reduces the length of shadow chains by checking at each copy-on-write fault whether the *vm_object* taking the fault completely shadows the *vm_object* below it in the chain. If it does, a collapse can be done. One alternative would be to calculate the number of live references to a page after each copy-on-write fault and, if only one reference remains, to move that page to the *vm_object* that references it. When the last page is removed, the chain can be collapsed. Implement this algorithm and compare its cost to the current algorithm.

**6.15 The *pv_entry* structures could be replaced by keeping a list associated with each *vm_object* of all the *vm_map_entry* structures that reference it. If each *vm_map_entry* structure had only a single list pointer in it, only the final *vm_object* would be able to reference it. Shadow *vm_objects* would have to find their final *vm_object* to find their referencing *vm_map_entry* structure. Implement an algorithm to find all the references to the pages of a shadow *vm_object* using this scheme. Compare its cost with that of the current algorithm using *pv_entry* structures.

**6.16 Port the code from 4.3BSD that would forcibly swap out runnable processes when the paging rate gets too high. Run three or more processes that each have a working set of 40 percent of the available memory. Compare the performance of this benchmark using the 4.3BSD algorithm and the current algorithm.

References

Babaoğlu & Joy, 1981.
Ö. Babaoğlu & W. N. Joy, "Converting a Swap-Based System to Do Paging in an Architecture Lacking Page-Referenced Bits," *Proceedings of the Eighth Symposium on Operating Systems Principles*, pp. 78–86, December 1981.

Bansal & Modha, 2004.
S. Bansal & D. Modha, "CAR: Clock with Adaptive Replacement," *Proceedings of the Third USENIX Conference on File and Storage Technologies*, pp. 187–200, April 2004.

Belady, 1966.
L. A. Belady, "A Study of Replacement Algorithms for Virtual Storage Systems," *IBM Systems Journal*, vol. 5, no. 2, pp. 78–101, April 1966.

Bonwick, 1994.
J. Bonwick, "The Slab Allocator: An Object-Caching Kernel Memory Allocator," *Proceedings of the 1994 USENIX Annual Technical Conference*, pp. 87–98, June 1994.

Bonwick & Adams, 2001.
J. Bonwick & J. Adams, "Magazines and Vmem: Extending the Slab Allocator to Many CPUs and Arbitrary Resources," *Proceedings of the 2001 USENIX Annual Technical Conference*, pp. 15–34, June 2001.

Coffman & Denning, 1973.
E. G. Coffman, Jr. & P. J. Denning, *Operating Systems Theory,* p. 243, Prentice-Hall, Englewood Cliffs, NJ, 1973.

Denning, 1970.
P. J. Denning, "Virtual Memory," *Computer Surveys*, vol. 2, no. 3, pp. 153–190, September 1970.

Easton & Franaszek, 1979.
M. C. Easton & P. A. Franaszek, "Use Bit Scanning in Replacement Decisions," *IEEE Transactions on Computing*, vol. 28, no. 2, pp. 133–141, February 1979.

Gingell et al., 1987.
R. Gingell, J. Moran, & W. Shannon, "Virtual Memory Architecture in SunOS," *USENIX Association Conference Proceedings*, pp. 81–94, June 1987.

Jiang et al., 2005.

S. Jiang, F. Chen, & X. Zhang, "CLOCK-Pro: An Effective Improvement of the CLOCK Replacement," *USENIX Annual Technical Conference, General Track*, pp. 323–336, June 2005.

Johnstone & Wilson, 1998.

M. Johnstone & P. Wilson, "The Memory Fragmentation Problem: Solved?," *ISMM'98 Proceedings of the ACM International Symposium on Memory Management*, pp. 26–36, available from ftp://ftp.dcs.gla.ac.uk/pub/drastic/gc/wilson.ps, October 1998.

Kenah & Bate, 1984.

L. J. Kenah & S. F. Bate, *VAX/VMS Internals and Data Structures,* Digital Press, Bedford, MA, 1984.

Kessler & Hill., 1992.

R. E. Kessler & M. D. Hill., "Page Placement Algorithms for Large Real-Indexed Caches.," *ACM Transactions on Computer Systems*, vol. 10, no. 4, pp. 338–359, available from ftp://ftp.cs.wisc.edu/markhill/Papers/tocs92_coloring.pdf, July 1992.

King, 1971.

W. F. King, "Analysis of Demand Paging Algorithms," *IFIP*, pp. 485–490, North Holland, Amsterdam, 1971.

Korn & Vo, 1985.

D. Korn & K. Vo, "In Search of a Better Malloc," *USENIX Association Conference Proceedings*, pp. 489–506, June 1985.

Lazowska & Kelsey, 1978.

E. D. Lazowska & J. M. Kelsey, "Notes on Tuning VAX/VMS," Technical Report 78-12-01, Department of Computer Science, University of Washington, Seattle, WA, December 1978.

Marshall, 1979.

W. T. Marshall, "A Unified Approach to the Evaluation of a Class of 'Working Set Like' Replacement Algorithms," PhD Thesis, Department of Computer Engineering, Case Western Reserve University, Cleveland, OH, May 1979.

Navarro et al., 2002.

J. Navarro, S. Iyer, P. Druschel, & A. Cox, "Practical, transparent operating system support for superpages," *USENIX 5th Symposium on Operating Systems Design and Implementation*, pp. 89–104, available from http://www.usenix.org / publications / library / proceedings / osdi02 / tech / navarro.html, December 2002.

Rashid et al., 1987.

R. Rashid, A. Tevanian, M. Young, D. Golub, R. Baron, D. Black, W. Bolosky, & J. Chew, "Machine-Independent Virtual Memory Management for Paged Uniprocessor and Multiprocessor Architectures," *Operating Systems Review*, vol. 21, no. 4, pp. 31–39, October 1987.

Tevanian, 1987.

A. Tevanian, "Architecture-Independent Virtual Memory Management for

Parallel and Distributed Environments: The Mach Approach," *Department of Computer Science, Carnegie-Mellon University*, available from http://reports-archive.adm.cs.cmu.edu/cs.html, December 1987.

Wilson et al., 1995.

P. Wilson, M. Johnstone, M. Neely, & D. Boles, "Dynamic Storage Allocation: A Survey and Critical Review," *Proceedings of the International Workshop on Memory Management*, available from http://citeseer.nj.nec.com/wilson95dynamic.html, September 1995.

Young, 1989.

M. W. Young, *Exporting a User Interface to Memory Management from a Communication-Oriented Operating System,* CMU-CS-89-202, Department of Computer Science, Carnegie-Mellon University, November 1989.

PART III

I/O System

CHAPTER 7

I/O System Overview

Figure 7.1 shows an overview of the entire kernel. This chapter focuses on the upper part of that figure. It describes the management and operation of file descriptors, the virtual filesystem interface (VFS), the facilities provided by the kernel to the filesystems operating under the VFS, and the provision that the kernel makes for stacking multiple filesystems.

Figure 7.1 Kernel I/O structure.

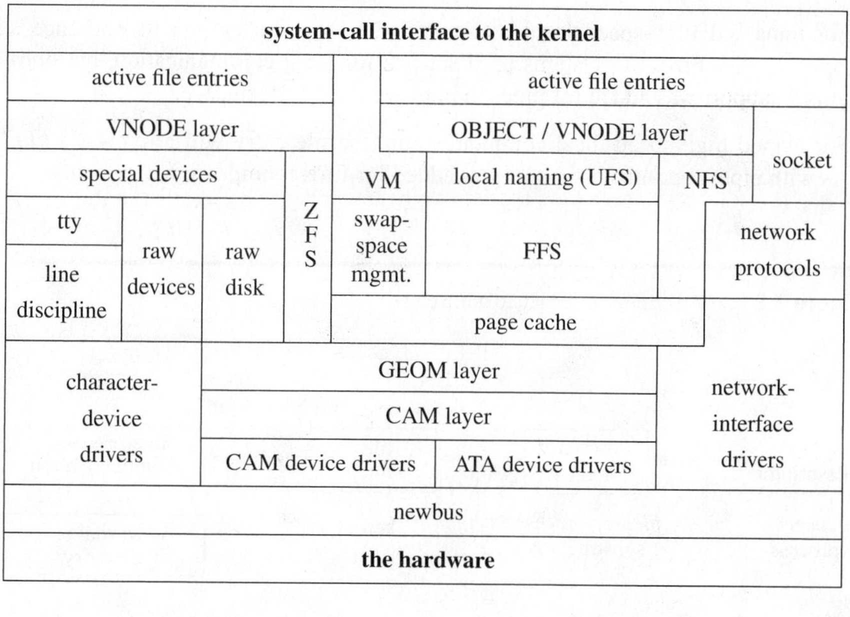

system-call interface to the kernel
active file entries
active file entries
VNODE layer
OBJECT / VNODE layer
socket
special devices
VM
local naming (UFS)
NFS
tty
Z F S
swap-space mgmt.
network protocols
line discipline
raw devices
raw disk
FFS
page cache
character-device drivers
GEOM layer
CAM layer
network-interface drivers
CAM device drivers
ATA device drivers
newbus
the hardware

Chapter 8 will describe the lower part of Figure 7.1. It covers the various types of device drivers in the system, their aggregation and delivery by their client subsystems, and the infrastructure needed to support and operate them.

7.1 Descriptor Management and Services

For user processes, all I/O is done through descriptors. The user interface to descriptors was described in Section 2.7. This section describes how the kernel manages descriptors and how it provides descriptor services, such as locking and polling.

System calls that refer to open files take a file descriptor as an argument to specify the file. The file descriptor is used by the kernel to index into the ***descriptor table*** for the current process (kept in the *filedesc* structure, a substructure of the process structure for the process) to locate a ***file entry***, or ***file structure***. The relationships of these data structures are shown in Figure 7.2.

The file entry provides a file type and a pointer to an underlying object for the descriptor. The object types supported in FreeBSD are shown in Table 7.1:

- For data files, the file entry points to a ***vnode*** structure that references a substructure containing the filesystem-specific information described in Chapters 9 through 11. The vnode layer is described in Section 7.3. Special files do not have data blocks allocated on the disk; they are handled by the *special-device* filesystem that calls appropriate drivers to handle I/O for them.
- For access to interprocess communication including networking, the FreeBSD file entry may reference a ***socket***.
- For unnamed high-speed local communication, the file entry will reference a ***pipe***. Earlier FreeBSD systems used sockets for local communication, but optimized support was added for pipes to improve their performance.
- For named high-speed local communication, the file entry will reference a ***fifo***. As with pipes, optimized support was added for fifos to improve performance.

Figure 7.2 File-descriptor reference to a file entry.

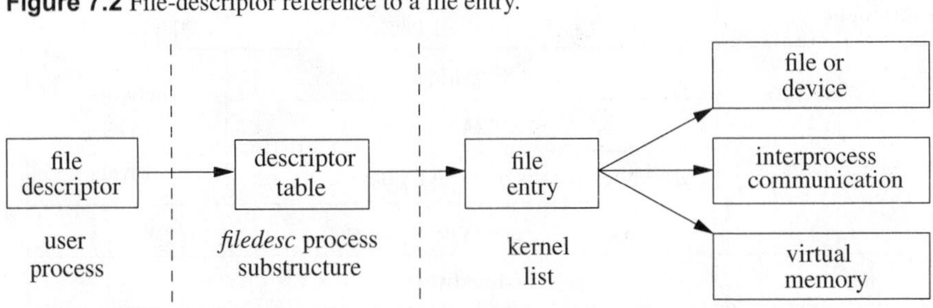

Table 7.1 File descriptor types.

Descriptor	Object referenced
VNODE	file or device
SOCKET	communications endpoint
PIPE	pipe
FIFO	named pipe
MQUEUE	POSIX message queue
KQUEUE	event queue
CRYPTO	cryptographic hardware
SHM	POSIX shared memory
SEM	POSIX semaphore
PTS	pseudo-teletype master device
DEV	device not referenced by a vnode
PROCDESC	process

- For POSIX.1-2004-compliant named high-speed local communication, the file entry will reference a message queue. As with pipes, optimized support was added for message queues to improve performance.
- For notification of kernel events, the file entry will reference a ***kqueue***. The ***kqueue*** interface is described at the end of this section.
- For systems that have cryptographic support in hardware, the file entry will provide direct access to that hardware.
- For POSIX.1-2004-compliant shared memory (using the *shm_open* system call), the file entry will reference a shared-memory object. Before FreeBSD 7.0, POSIX shared memory was implemented with files.
- For POSIX.1-2004-compliant semaphores (using the *sem_open* system call), the file entry will reference a semaphore.
- For a pseudo-terminals device pair, file entries reference a pseudo-terminal's master and slave devices. Pseudo-terminals are described in Section 8.6.
- For compatibility with Linux, a file entry may reference a device directly rather than through the vnode interface.
- For capability mode in which processes are unable to use PIDs, because PIDs are a global namespace, a file entry references a process. The descriptor for this file entry allows systems running in capability mode to create and manage child processes without recourse to PIDs. The uses for processes referenced by descriptors are described in Section 5.7.

The virtual-memory system supports the mapping of files into a process's address space. Here, the file descriptor must reference a vnode or a POSIX shared-memory region that will be partially or completely mapped into the user's address space.

Open File Entries

The set of file entries is the focus of activity for file descriptors. They contain the information necessary to access the underlying objects and to maintain common information.

The file entry is an object-oriented data structure. Each entry contains a type and an array of function pointers that translate the generic operations on file descriptors into the specific actions associated with their type. The operations that must be implemented for each type are as follows:

- Read from the descriptor
- Write to the descriptor
- Truncate the descriptor
- Change the mode or owner of the descriptor
- Poll the descriptor
- Do *ioctl* operations on the descriptor
- Collect *stat* information for the descriptor
- Check to see if there are any *kqueue* events pending for the descriptor
- Close and possibly deallocate the object associated with the descriptor

Note that there is no *open*() routine defined in the object table. FreeBSD treats descriptors in an object-oriented fashion only after they are created. This approach was taken because the various descriptor types have different characteristics. Generalizing the interface to handle all types of descriptors at open time would have complicated an otherwise simple interface. Vnode descriptors are created by the *open* system call; socket descriptors are created by the *socket* system call; fifo descriptors are created by the *pipe* system call; message queues are created using the *mq_open* system call.

Each file entry has a pointer to a data structure that contains information specific to the instance of the underlying object. The data structure is opaque to the routines that manipulate the file entry. A reference to the data structure is passed on each call to a function that implements a file operation. All state associated with an instance of an object must be stored in that instance's data structure; the underlying objects are not permitted to manipulate the file entry themselves.

The *read* and *write* system calls do not take an offset in the file as an argument. Instead, each read or write updates the current ***file offset*** in the file according to the number of bytes transferred. The offset determines the position in the file for the next read or write. The offset can be set directly by the *lseek* system call. Since more than one process may open the same file, and each such process needs its own offset for the file, the offset cannot be stored in the per-object data structure. Thus, each *open* system call allocates a new file entry, and the open file entry contains the offset.

Some semantics associated with all file descriptors are enforced at the descriptor level, before the underlying system call is invoked. These semantics are maintained in a set of flags associated with the descriptor. For example, the flags record whether the descriptor is open for reading, writing, or both reading and writing. If a descriptor is marked as open for reading only, an attempt to write it will be caught by the descriptor code. Thus, the functions defined for performing reading and writing do not need to check the validity of the request; we can implement them knowing that they will never receive an invalid request.

The application-visible flags are described in the next subsection. In addition to the application-visible flags, the flags field also has information on whether the descriptor holds a shared or exclusive lock on the underlying file. The locking primitives could be extended to work on sockets, as well as on files. However, the descriptors for a socket rarely refer to the same file entry. The only way for two processes to share the same socket descriptor is for a parent to share the descriptor with its child by forking or for one process to pass the descriptor to another in a message.

Each file entry has a reference count. A single process may have multiple references to the entry because of calls to the *dup* or *fcntl* system calls. Also, file structures are inherited by the child process after a *fork*, so several different processes may reference the same file entry. Thus, a read or write by either process on the twin descriptors will advance the file offset. This semantic allows two processes to read the same file or to interleave output to the same file. Another process that has independently opened the file will refer to that file through a different file structure with a different file offset. This functionality was the original reason for the existence of the file structure; the file structure provides a place for the file offset between the descriptor and the underlying object.

Each time that a new reference is created, the reference count is incremented. When a descriptor is closed (in any one of three ways: (1) explicitly with a *close*: (2) implicitly after an *exec* because the descriptor has been marked as close-on-exec: or (3) on process exit), the reference count is decremented. When the reference count drops to zero, the file entry is freed.

The close-on-exec flag is kept in the descriptor table rather than in the file entry. This flag is not shared among all the references to the file entry because it is an attribute of the file descriptor itself. The close-on-exec flag is the only piece of information that is kept in the descriptor table rather than being shared in the file entry.

Management of Descriptors

The *fcntl* system call manipulates the file structure. It can be used to make the following changes to a descriptor:

- Duplicate a descriptor as though by a *dup* system call.

- Get or set the close-on-exec flag. When a process *fork*s, all the parent's descriptors are duplicated in the child. The child process then *exec*s a new process. Any of the child's descriptors that were marked close-on-exec are closed. The remaining descriptors are available to the newly executed process.
- Set the *no-delay* (*O_NONBLOCK*) flag to put the descriptor into nonblocking mode. In nonblocking mode, if any data are available for a read operation, or if any space is available for a write operation, an immediate partial read or write is done. If no data are available for a read operation, or if a write operation would block, the system call returns an error (EAGAIN) showing that the operation would block, instead of putting the process to sleep. This facility is not implemented for local filesystems in FreeBSD, because local-filesystem I/O is always expected to complete within a few milliseconds.
- Set the *synchronous* (*O_FSYNC*) flag to force all writes to the file to be written synchronously to the disk.
- Set the *direct* (*O_DIRECT*) flag to request that the kernel attempt to write the data directly from the user application to the disk rather than copying it via kernel buffers.
- Set the *append* (*O_APPEND*) flag to force all writes to append data to the end of the file, instead of at the descriptor's current location in the file. This feature is useful when, for example, multiple processes are writing to the same log file.
- Set the *asynchronous* (*O_ASYNC*) flag to request that the kernel watch for a change in the status of the descriptor, and arrange to send a signal (SIGIO) when a read or write becomes possible.
- Send a signal to a process when an exception condition arises, such as when urgent data arrive on an interprocess-communication channel.
- Set or get the process identifier or process-group identifier to which the two I/O-related signals in the previous steps should be sent.
- Test or change the status of a lock on a range of bytes within an underlying file. Locking operations are described later in this section.

The implementation of the *dup* system call is easy. If the process has reached its limit on open files, the kernel returns an error. Otherwise, the kernel scans the current process's descriptor table, starting at descriptor zero, until it finds an unused entry. The kernel allocates the entry to point to the same file entry as does the descriptor being duplicated. The kernel then increments the reference count on the file entry and returns the index of the allocated descriptor-table entry. The *fcntl* system call provides a similar function, except that it specifies a descriptor from which to start the scan.

Sometimes, a process wants to allocate a specific descriptor-table entry. Such a request is made with the *dup2* system call. The process specifies the descriptor-table index into which the duplicated reference should be placed. The kernel implementation is the same as for *dup*, except that the scan to find a free entry is changed to close the requested entry if that entry is open and then to allocate the entry as before. No action is taken if the new and old descriptors are the same.

The system implements getting or setting the close-on-exec flag via the *fcntl* system call by making the appropriate change to the flags field of the associated descriptor-table entry. Other attributes that *fcntl* manipulates operate on the flags in the file entry. However, the implementation of the various flags cannot be handled by the generic code that manages the file entry. Instead, the file flags must be passed through the object interface to the type-specific routines to do the appropriate operation on the underlying object. For example, manipulation of the non-blocking flag for a socket must be done by the socket layer, since only that layer knows whether an operation can block.

The implementation of the *ioctl* system call is broken into two major levels. The upper level handles the system call itself. The *ioctl* call includes a descriptor, a command, and pointer to a data area. The command argument encodes what the size is of the data area for the parameters and whether the parameters are input, output, or both input and output. The upper level is responsible for decoding the command argument, allocating a buffer, and copying in any input data. If a return value is to be generated and there is no input, the buffer is zeroed. Finally, the *ioctl* is dispatched through the file-entry *ioctl* function, along with the I/O buffer, to the lower-level routine that implements the requested operation.

The lower level does the requested operation. Along with the command argument, it receives a pointer to the I/O buffer. The upper level has already checked for valid memory references, but the lower level may do more precise argument validation because it knows more about the expected nature of the arguments. However, it does not need to copy the arguments in or out of the user process. If the command is successful and produces output, the lower level places the results in the buffer provided by the top level. When the lower level returns, the upper level copies the results to the process.

Asynchronous I/O

Historically, UNIX systems did not have the ability to do asynchronous I/O beyond the ability to do background writes to the filesystem. An asynchronous I/O interface was defined by the POSIX.1b-1993 realtime group. Shortly after its ratification, an implementation was added to FreeBSD.

An asynchronous read is started with *aio_read*; an asynchronous write is started with *aio_write*. The kernel builds an asynchronous I/O request structure that contains all the information needed to do the requested operation. If the request cannot be immediately satisfied from kernel buffers, the request structure is queued for processing by an asynchronous kernel-based I/O daemon and the system call returns. The next available asynchronous I/O daemon handles the request using the usual kernel synchronous I/O path.

When the daemon finishes the I/O, the asynchronous I/O structure is marked as finished along with a return value or error code. The application uses the *aio_error* system call to poll to find if the I/O is complete. This call is implemented by checking the status of the asynchronous I/O request structure created by the kernel. If an application gets to the point where it cannot proceed until an I/O completes, it can use the *aio_suspend* system call to wait until an I/O is done. Here, the application is put to sleep on its asynchronous I/O request structure and is awakened by the asynchronous I/O daemon when the I/O completes. Alternatively, the application can request that a specified signal be sent when the I/O is done.

The *aio_return* system call gets the return value from the asynchronous request once *aio_error*, *aio_suspend*, or the arrival of a completion signal has indicated that the I/O is done. FreeBSD has also added the nonstandard *aio_waitcomplete* system call that combines the functions of *aio_suspend* and *aio_return* into a single operation. For either *aio_return* or *aio_waitcomplete*, the return information is copied out to the application from the asynchronous I/O request structure and the asynchronous I/O request structure is then freed.

File-Descriptor Locking

Early UNIX systems had no provision for locking files. Processes that needed to synchronize access to a file had to use a separate "lock file." A process would try to create a lock file. If the creation succeeded, then the process could proceed with its update; if the creation failed, the process would wait and then try again. This mechanism had three drawbacks:

1. Processes consumed CPU time by looping over attempts to create locks.
2. Locks left lying around because of system crashes had to be removed (normally in a system-startup command script).
3. Processes running as the special system-administrator user, the ***superuser***, are always permitted to create files, and so were forced to use a different mechanism.

Although it is possible to work around all these problems, the solutions are not straightforward, so a mechanism for locking files was added in 4.2BSD.

The most general locking schemes allow multiple processes to update a file concurrently. Several of these techniques are discussed in Peterson [1983]. A simpler technique is to serialize access to a file with locks. For standard system applications, a mechanism that locks at the granularity of a file is sufficient. So, 4.2BSD and 4.3BSD provided only a fast, whole-file locking mechanism. The semantics of these locks include allowing locks to be inherited by child processes and releasing locks only on the last close of a file.

Certain applications require the ability to lock pieces of a file. Locking facilities that support a byte-level granularity are well understood. Unfortunately, they are not powerful enough to be used by database systems that require nested hierarchical locks, but are complex enough to require a large and cumbersome implementation compared to the simpler whole-file locks. Because byte-range locks are mandated by the POSIX standard, the developers added them to BSD reluctantly.

The semantics of byte-range locks come from the initial implementation of locks in System V, which included releasing all locks held by a process on a file every time a *close* system call was done on a descriptor referencing that file. The 4.2BSD whole-file locks are removed only on the last close. A problem with the POSIX semantics is that an application can lock a file, then call a library routine that opens, reads, and closes the locked file. Calling the library routine will have the unexpected effect of releasing the locks held by the application. Another problem is that a file must be open for writing to be allowed to get an exclusive lock. A process that does not have permission to open a file for writing cannot get an exclusive lock on that file. To avoid these problems, yet remain POSIX compliant, FreeBSD provides separate interfaces for byte-range locks and whole-file locks. The byte-range locks follow the POSIX semantics; the whole-file locks follow the traditional 4.2BSD semantics. The two types of locks can be used concurrently; they will serialize against each other properly.

Both whole-file locks and byte-range locks use the same implementation; the whole-file locks are implemented as a range lock over an entire file. The kernel handles the other differing semantics between the two implementations by having the byte-range locks be applied to processes, whereas the whole-file locks are applied to descriptors. Because descriptors are shared with child processes, the whole-file locks are inherited. Because the child process gets its own process structure, the byte-range locks are not inherited. The last-close versus every-close semantics are a small bit of special-case code in the close routine that checks whether the underlying object is a process or a descriptor. It releases locks on every call if the lock is associated with a process and only when the reference count drops to zero if the lock is associated with a descriptor.

Locking schemes can be classified according to the extent that they are enforced. A scheme in which locks are enforced for every process without choice is said to use ***mandatory locks***, whereas a scheme in which locks are enforced for only those processes that request them is said to use ***advisory locks***. Clearly, advisory locks are effective only when all programs accessing a file use the locking scheme. With mandatory locks, there must be some override policy implemented in the kernel. With advisory locks, the policy is left to the user programs. In the FreeBSD system, programs with superuser privilege are allowed to override any protection scheme. Because many of the programs that need to use locks must also run as the superuser, 4.2BSD implemented advisory locks rather than creating an additional protection scheme that was inconsistent with the UNIX philosophy or that could not be used by privileged programs. The use of advisory locks carried over to the POSIX specification of byte-range locks and is retained in FreeBSD.

The FreeBSD file-locking facilities allow cooperating programs to apply advisory *shared* or *exclusive* locks on ranges of bytes within a file. Only one process may have an exclusive lock on a byte range, whereas multiple shared locks may be present. A shared and an exclusive lock cannot be present on a byte range at the same time. If any lock is requested when another process holds an exclusive lock, or an exclusive lock is requested when another process holds any lock, the lock request will block until the lock can be obtained. Because shared and exclusive locks are only advisory, even if a process has obtained a lock on a file, another process may access the file if it ignores the locking mechanism.

So that there are no races between creating and locking a file, a lock can be requested as part of opening a file. Once a process has opened a file, it can manipulate locks without needing to close and reopen the file. This feature is useful, for example, when a process wishes to apply a shared lock, to read information, to determine whether an update is required, and then to apply an exclusive lock and update the file.

A request for a lock will cause a process to block if the lock cannot be obtained immediately. In certain instances, this blocking is unsatisfactory. For example, a process that wants only to check whether a lock is present would require a separate mechanism to find out this information. Consequently, a process can specify that its locking request should return with an error if a lock cannot be obtained immediately. Being able to request a lock conditionally is useful to *daemon* processes that wish to service a spooling area. If the first instance of the daemon locks the directory where spooling takes place, later daemon processes can easily check to see whether an active daemon exists. Since locks exist only while the locking processes exist, locks can never be left active after the processes exit or if the system crashes.

The implementation of locks is done on a per-filesystem basis. The implementation for the local filesystems is described in Section 9.5. A network-based filesystem has to coordinate locks with a central lock manager that is usually located on the server exporting the filesystem. Client lock requests must be sent to the lock manager. The lock manager arbitrates among lock requests from processes running on its server and from the various clients to which it is exporting the filesystem. The most complex operation for the lock manager is recovering lock state when a client or server is rebooted or becomes partitioned from the rest of the network. The FreeBSD network-based lock manager is described in Chapter 11.

Multiplexing I/O on Descriptors

A process sometimes wants to handle I/O on more than one descriptor. For example, consider a remote login program that wants to read data from the keyboard and to send them through a socket to a remote machine. This program also wants to read data from the socket connected to the remote end and to write them to the screen. If a process makes a read request when there are no data available, it is normally blocked in the kernel until the data become available. In our example, blocking is unacceptable. If the process reads from the keyboard and blocks, it will be unable to read data from the remote end that are destined for the screen. The user does not know what to type until more data arrive from the remote end, so the session deadlocks. Conversely, if the process reads from the remote end when there are no data for the screen, it will block and will be unable to read from the terminal. Again, deadlock would occur if the remote end were waiting for input before sending any data. There is an analogous set of problems to blocking on the writes to the screen or to the remote end. If a user has stopped output to his screen by typing the stop character, the write will block until the user types the start character. In the meantime, the process cannot read from the keyboard to find out that the user wants to flush the output.

FreeBSD provides four mechanisms that permit multiplexing I/O on descriptors: ***polling I/O***, ***kernel-event polling***, ***nonblocking I/O***, and ***signal-driven I/O***. Polling is done with the *select* or *poll* system call, described in the next subsection. Kernel-event polling is done with the *kevent* system call, described in the following subsection. Operations on nonblocking descriptors finish immediately, partially complete an input or output operation and return a partial count, or return an error that shows that the operation could not be completed at all. Descriptors that have signalling enabled cause the associated process or process group to be notified when the I/O state of the descriptor changes.

There are four possible alternatives that avoid the blocking problem:

1. Set all the descriptors into nonblocking mode. The process can then try operations on each descriptor in turn to find out which descriptors are ready to perform I/O. The problem with this busy-waiting approach is that the process must run continuously to discover whether there is any I/O to be done, wasting CPU cycles.

2. Enable all descriptors of interest to signal when I/O can be done. The process can then wait for a signal to discover when it is possible to perform I/O. The drawback to this approach is that signals are expensive to catch. Hence, signal-driven I/O is impractical for applications that do moderate to large amounts of I/O.

3. Have the system provide a method for asking which descriptors are capable of performing I/O. If none of the requested descriptors are ready, the system can put the process to sleep until a descriptor becomes ready. This approach avoids the problem of deadlock because the process will be awakened whenever it is possible to perform I/O and will be told which descriptor is ready. The drawback is that the process must do two system calls per operation: one to poll for the descriptor that is ready to perform I/O and another to perform the operation itself.

4. Have the process register with the system all the events including I/O on descriptors that it is interested in tracking. Have the system provide a system call for asking which events have occurred. If none of the registered events have occurred, the system can put the process to sleep until a registered event occurs. When the system call returns, the process is given a list of the events that have occurred [Accetta et al., 1986; Lemon, 2001].

The first approach is available in FreeBSD as nonblocking I/O. It typically is used for output descriptors because the operation typically will not block. Rather than doing a *select*, *poll*, or *kevent*, which nearly always succeeds, followed immediately by a *write*, it is more efficient to try the *write* and revert to using *select*, *poll*, or *kevent* only during periods when the *write* returns a blocking error.

The second approach is available in FreeBSD as signal-driven I/O. It typically is used for rare events, such as the arrival of out-of-band data on a socket. For such rare events, the cost of handling an occasional signal is lower than that of checking constantly with *select*, *poll*, or *kevent* to find out whether there are any pending data.

The third approach is available in FreeBSD via the *select* or *poll* system call. Although less efficient than the fourth approach, it is a more widely available interface.

The fourth approach is available in FreeBSD via the *kevent* system call. In addition to tracking the status of multiple descriptors, it handles other notifications such as file modification monitoring, signals, asynchronous I/O events (AIO), child process state change monitoring and timers that support nanosecond resolution. Like *select* and *poll*, *kqueue* can timeout when no I/O is possible. An interface similar in functionality to *kevent* is available in Linux as *epoll* and in Windows and Solaris as *completion ports*.

The *select* and *poll* interfaces provide the same information. They differ only in their programming interface. The *select* interface was first developed in 4.2BSD with the introduction of socket-based interprocess communication. The *poll* interface was introduced in System V several years later with its competing STREAMS-based interprocess communication. Although STREAMS has fallen into disuse, the *poll* interface has proven popular enough to be retained. The FreeBSD kernel supports both interfaces.

The *select* system call is of the form

```
int error = select(
    int numfds,
    fd_set *readfds,
    fd_set *writefds,
    fd_set *exceptfds,
    struct timeval *timeout);
```

It takes three masks of descriptors to be monitored, corresponding to interest in reading, writing, and exceptional conditions. In addition, it takes a timeout value for returning from *select* if none of the requested descriptors becomes ready before a specified amount of time has elapsed. The *select* call returns the same three masks of descriptors after modifying them to show the descriptors that are able to perform reading, to perform writing, or that have an exceptional condition. If none of the descriptors has become ready in the timeout interval, *select* returns showing that no descriptors are ready for I/O. If a timeout value is given and a descriptor becomes ready before the specified timeout period, the time that *select* spends waiting for I/O to become ready is subtracted from the time given.

The *poll* interface copies in an array of *pollfd* structures, one array entry for each descriptor of interest. The *pollfd* structure contains three elements:

- The file descriptor to poll

- A set of flags describing the information being sought
- A set of flags set by the kernel showing the information that was found

The flags specify availability of normal or out-of-band data for reading and the availability of buffer space for normal or out-of-band data writing. The return flags can also specify that an error has occurred on the descriptor, that the descriptor has been disconnected, or that the descriptor is not open. These error conditions are raised by the *select* call by indicating that the descriptor with the error is ready to perform I/O. When the application attempts to perform the I/O, the error is returned by the *read* or *write* system call. Like the *select* call, the *poll* call takes a timeout value to specify the maximum time to wait. If none of the requested descriptors becomes ready before the specified amount of time has elapsed, the *poll* call returns. If a timeout value is given and a descriptor becomes ready before the specified timeout period, the time that *poll* spends waiting for I/O to become ready is subtracted from the time given.

Implementation of *Select*

The implementation of *select* is divided into a generic top layer and many device- or socket-specific bottom pieces. At the top level, *select* or *poll* decodes the user's request and then calls the appropriate lower-level poll functions. The *select* and *poll* system calls have different top layers to determine the sets of descriptors to be polled but use all the same device- and socket-specific bottom pieces. Only the *select* top layer will be described here. The *poll* top layer is implemented in a completely analogous way.

The data structures used to support the *select* and *poll* system calls are shown in Figure 7.3. A *selfd* structure tracks each request. Across the top of Figure 7.3 is the list of threads waiting for I/O to become available on a set of descriptors. Each of these threads has a *seltd* structure that heads the list of *selfd* structures tracking the descriptors of interest to the thread. This list is protected by the mutex in the *seltd* structure. Down the lefthand side of Figure 7.3 is the set of sockets and devices that have threads waiting for I/O to become possible. Each of these sockets and devices has a *selinfo* structure that heads the list of *selfd* structures tracking the threads interested in the socket or device. This list is protected by a pool mutex allocated the first time an entry is referenced from the *selinfo* structure.

The *select* top level takes the following steps:

1. Copies and validates the descriptor masks for read, write, and exceptional conditions. Performing validation requires checking that each requested descriptor is currently open by the process.
2. For each descriptor with a bit set in at least one select mask, calls the poll routine for the socket or device. If the descriptor is not able to perform any of the requested I/O operations, the poll routine records that the thread wants to

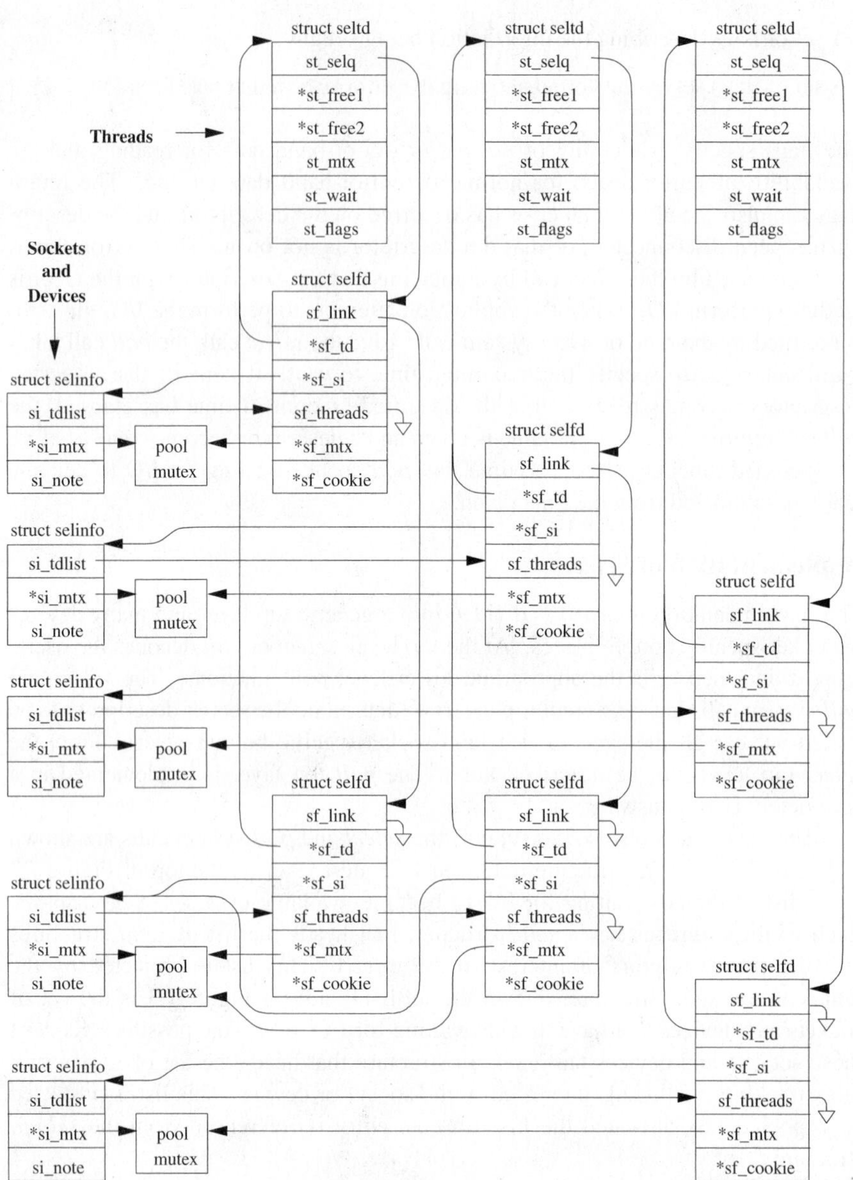

Figure 7.3 Select data structures.

perform I/O by allocating a *selfd* structure and linking it into the requesting thread's *seltd* structure and the associated socket or device *selinfo* structure as shown in Figure 7.3. When I/O becomes possible for the descriptor—usually as a result of an interrupt—a notification will be issued for all the threads selecting on it by traversing the list of *selfd* structures headed by the *selinfo* structure for the socket or device and awakening each of the associated threads.

3. Because the selection process may take a long time, the kernel does not want to block out I/O during the time it takes to poll all the requested descriptors. Instead, the kernel arranges to detect the occurrence of I/O that may affect the status of the descriptors being polled. When such I/O occurs, the associated socket or device traverses the list of *setfd* structures, headed by its *selinfo* structure, setting the PENDING flag in the flags field of the associated thread's *seltd* structure and marks the associated *setfd* structure as ready to do I/O. If the top-level select code finds that the PENDING flag for the thread has been set while it has been performing the polling, and it has not found any descriptors that are ready to perform an operation, then the top level knows that the polling results are incomplete. It traverses the list of *selfd* structures headed by its *seltd* structure to find and return the available descriptors.

4. If no descriptors are ready and the *select* specified a timeout, the kernel posts a timeout for the requested amount of time. The thread blocks on the *st_wait* condition variable in its *seltd* structure. Normally, a descriptor will become ready and the thread will be notified by *selwakeup*(). When the thread is awakened, it traverses the list of *selfd* structures headed by its *seltd* structure and returns the available descriptors. If none of the descriptors become ready before the timer expires, the thread returns with a timed-out error and an empty list of available descriptors. If a timeout value is given and a descriptor becomes ready before the specified timeout period, the time that *select* spent waiting for I/O to become ready is subtracted from the time given.

Kqueues and *Kevents*

The *select* and *poll* interfaces are limited because they are unable to handle other potentially interesting activities in which an application might want to engage such as signals, filesystem changes, and asynchronous I/O completions. Further, the *select* and *poll* system calls do not scale well with increasing numbers of descriptors. Their inefficiency comes from being stateless. The kernel does not keep any record of the application's interest between system calls and must recalculate it and build up the associated data structures every time that *select* or *poll* is called. In addition, the application must scan the entire list of events that it passed to the kernel to determine which events occurred.

The *kevent* interface is provided to mitigate both of these problems. *Kevent* is a generic notification interface that allows an application to select from a wide range of event sources, and be notified of activity on these sources in a scalable and efficient manner. The interface may be extended to cover future event sources without changing the application interface.

An application registers the events in which it is interested. When one or more of these events occur, the kernel returns a list containing just the occurring events to the application. Thus, the kernel need only build the set of event notification structures once and the application is notified of just those events that have occurred. The cost of the interface is a function of the number of events that occur rather than the number of events being checked. The savings are most evident for applications checking for many events that happen only infrequently.

The types of events that can be monitored using the *kevent* system are shown in Table 7.2. In addition to the events that can be checked by the *select* and *poll* interfaces, *kevent* can also track changes to files including being renamed, deleted, or having their attributes updated. It also subsumes the *aio_error* and *aio_suspend* system calls to monitor and wait for an asynchronous I/O. The process still needs to use *aio_return* system call to get the I/O completion status and to free the kernel data structures associated with the I/O once the *kevent* system call has notified it that the I/O has completed. It can track the posting of signals to a process and when the process *forks*, *execs*, or *exits*. It can create and monitor timers and provides event monitoring defined and triggered by user-level applications.

A process uses the *kqueue* system call to get a descriptor to use as a handle on which to register the events that it wishes to track. This descriptor is then used to get notification of the registered events as they occur. Additional events may be added and previously requested events deleted as the process runs.

Figure 7.4 shows the data structures set up when a *kqueue* is created. Each event in which an application registers interest is recorded using a *knote*. Each event has an identifier such as a descriptor number for a file or socket descriptor-based event, a process identifier for a process-based event, a signal number for a signal-based event, or an application-defined identifier for a timer- or user-based event. Event registration also includes a filter describing the action of interest such as reading or writing as well as further refinements such as a minimum read/write size, whether this is a one-time request or should be reported until canceled. The registration maps the filter to a filter function that will be called each time an event occurs for that identifier to decide whether it merits being reported.

The *kqueue* structure links the *knote*s it is tracking into one of two lists: an array indexed by descriptor for descriptor-identified events or a table hashed by the identifier for all other types of events. The *knote* structure is also linked into a *knote*-list for the event-generating entity that it is monitoring.

Table 7.2 Events that may be monitored with *kevents*

Event name	Operation tracked
EVFILT_READ	Descriptor has data to read
EVFILT_WRITE	Descriptor has buffer space to write
EVFILT_AIO	Asynchronous I/O associated with descriptor has completed
EVFILT_VNODE	Information associated with a file has changed
EVFILT_PROC	Status of a process has changed
EVFILT_SIGNAL	A signal has been posted for a process
EVFILT_TIMER	An event-based timer has expired
EVFILT_USER	Application defined and triggered events

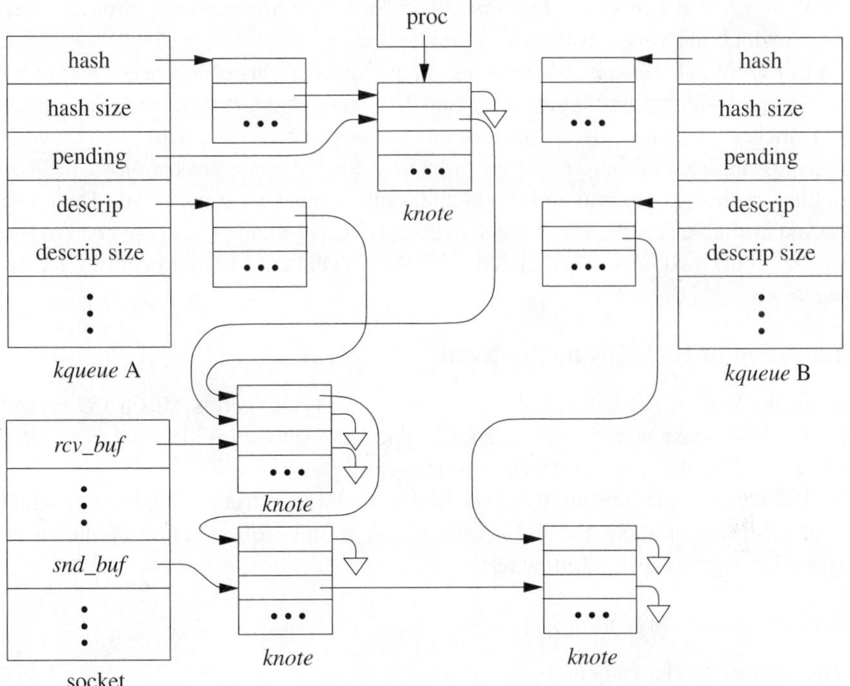

Figure 7.4 The data structures supporting an event queue.

When an event occurs, the event-generating entity traverses its *knote* list invoking the filter function for each *knote* on the list to let it know that an event has occurred. The filter function decides if the event merits reporting. For example, a filter concerned with reading will not care that buffer space has become available and return zero to indicate that it is not interested. But if enough data has arrived to exceed the specified read threshold, it will return nonzero to indicate that it should be added to its *kqueue* pending list.

Time will pass before the application next calls or awakens from a sleep in the *kevent* system call to collect any pending events. During this time, the event may no longer be relevant. For example, the buffering space for which a process has been waiting may have been used up by the time it goes to collect the event. So, as the *kevent* system call walks the list of pending events, it calls the associated filter function to verify that the event is still relevant. If it is still relevant, it is copied out to the application along with any filter-function-specific information such as number of bytes available to be read. If it is not relevant, it is dropped from the pending list. By validating the data immediately before returning it, the *kevent* system call will never return stale results. To further ensure valid results, any time that a resource is reclaimed (such as a descriptor when it is last closed or a process when it exits), any *knote*s associated with it are removed from all three lists on which they may reside and are reclaimed.

In Figure 7.4, *kqueue A* is tracking three events: status of a process identified by its process-identifier (referenced from the *kqueue* hash table), data availability of a socket identified by its descriptor number (referenced from the *kqueue* descriptor table), and buffer space availability for the same socket. *Kqueue B* is tracking buffer space availability on the same socket as *Kqueue A*. Data has become available for reading at the socket and a status change has happened to the process so the two *knote*s associated with these events are on the pending list for *kqueue A*.

Movement of Data Inside the Kernel

Within the kernel, I/O data are described by an array of vectors. Each ***I/O vector*** or ***iovec*** has a base address and a length. The I/O vectors are identical to the I/O vectors used by the *readv* and *writev* system calls.

The kernel maintains another structure, called a ***uio*** structure, that holds additional information about the I/O operation. A sample *uio* structure is shown in Figure 7.5; it contains the following:

- A pointer to the *iovec* array
- The number of elements in the *iovec* array
- The file offset at which the operation should start
- The sum of the lengths of the I/O vectors

Figure 7.5 An *uio* structure.

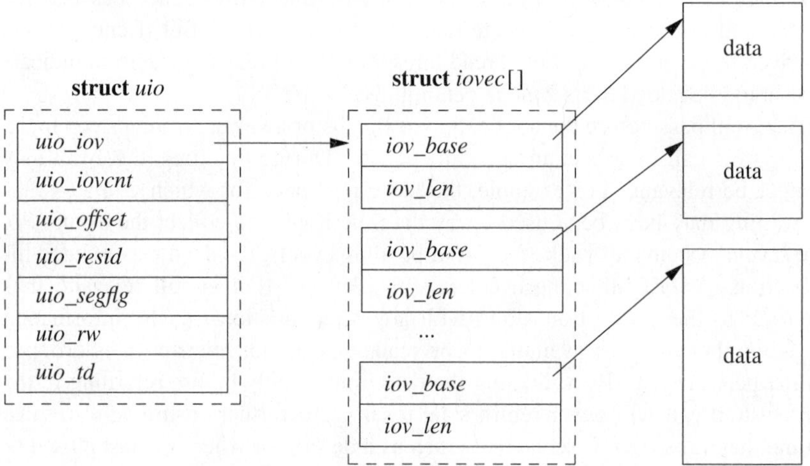

- A flag showing whether the source and destination are both within the kernel or whether the source and destination are split between the user and the kernel
- A flag showing whether the data are being copied from the *uio* structure to the kernel (UIO_WRITE) or from the kernel to the *uio* structure (UIO_READ)
- A pointer to the thread whose data area is described by the *uio* structure (the pointer is NULL if the *uio* structure describes an area within the kernel)

All I/O within the kernel is described with *iovec* and *uio* structures. System calls such as *read* and *write* that are not passed an *iovec* create a *uio* to describe their arguments; this *uio* structure is passed to the lower levels of the kernel to specify the parameters of an I/O operation. Eventually, the *uio* structure reaches the part of the kernel responsible for moving the data to or from the process address space: the filesystem, the network, or a device driver. In general, these parts of the kernel do not interpret *uio* structures directly. Instead, they arrange a kernel buffer to hold the data and then use *uiomove*() to copy the data to or from the buffer or buffers described by the *uio* structure. The *uiomove*() routine is called with a pointer to a kernel data area, a data count, and a *uio* structure. As it moves data, it updates the counters and pointers of the *iovec* and *uio* structures by a corresponding amount. If the kernel buffer is not as large as the areas described by the *uio* structure, the *uio* structure will point to the part of the process address space just beyond the location completed most recently. Thus, while servicing a request, the kernel may call *uiomove*() multiple times, each time giving a pointer to a new kernel buffer for the next block of data.

Character device drivers that do not copy data from the process generally do not interpret the *uio* structure. Instead, there is one low-level kernel routine that arranges a direct transfer to or from the address space of the process. Here, a separate I/O operation is done for each *iovec* element, calling back to the driver with one piece at a time.

7.2 Local Interprocess Communication

The socket interfaces are not the only APIs that provide interprocess communication. Applications that wish to divide up work on a single host use semaphores, messages queues, and shared memory to communicate between their processes. Each type of local IPC has different performance characteristics and provides a different form of communication. The local IPC mechanisms originally supported in FreeBSD are derived from System V, as described in Bach [1986]. For this reason, they are often referred to as System V semaphores, mutexes, and shared memory. While most applications use the socket-based IPC mechanisms, a small but pertinent subset of applications make use of the System V IPC mechanisms, especially semaphores and shared memory. For example, X11 uses System V shared-memory segments between the X server and applications to avoid sending large images (and especially, continuously updated images) over sockets. PosgreSQL uses System V semaphores for synchronisation. The **ipcs** command lists open System V IPC objects and can be used to discover the extent of their use on a FreeBSD system.

The biggest drawback of the System V IPC is that it introduced a new, flat, number-oriented object namespace but with filesystem-like permissions. As a result of it being flat, applications cannot use directories to reserve portions of the namespace safely, and weird hash functions are used to convert useful string names into possibly colliding numbers. Unlike other IPC objects, no file descriptor is associated with these objects. Some implementations (notably Linux) store these objects in special filesystems below **/dev**. This implementation is better than the System V approach as it makes jail-like virtualisation possible.

As POSIX added specifications for IPC mechanisms, they were implemented in FreeBSD: shared memory in FreeBSD 4.3, semaphores in FreeBSD 5.0, and message queues in FreeBSD 7.0. The POSIX IPC manages to both improve on System V by building it using file descriptors while simultaneously repeating its mistake of having a flat namespace. POSIX shared-memory objects and semaphores are seeing increasing use as replacements for System V IPC objects as they work well with both multi-threaded synchronisation and multi-process synchronisation. As described in Section 5.8, Capsicum uses a version of the POSIX shared-memory interface to create a file descriptor associated with an anonymously backed *vm_object* that can then be shared using file descriptor passing. Prior to this addition, the only mechanism for sharing memory was to rendezvous using the filesystem namespace and *mmap* or to agree on a name to use in the System V shared-memory namespace.

Every type of IPC must make it possible for independently executing processes to rendezvous and find the resources they are sharing. This piece of information must be known to all of them and must be unique enough that no other process could come across the same information by accident. Historically, UNIX used the filesystem namespace for rendezvous. It has the benefit of being hierarchical with permissions to provide fine-grained access control. Applications that wanted to share memory would pick a common file that each would map into its address space.

The System V IPC introduced a new ***key***-based namespace. A key is a long integer that is treated by the cooperating processes as an opaque piece of data, meaning that they do not attempt to decipher or attribute any meaning to it. The library routine, *ftok*(), is used to generate a key from a pathname. As long as each process uses the same pathname, they are guaranteed to get the same key.

All of the local System V IPC subsystems were designed and implemented to be used in a similar way. A summary of all the user-level System V APIs is given in Table 7.3, and an excellent introduction to using them can be found in Stevens [1999]. Once a process has a key, it uses it to create or retrieve the relevant object, using a subsystem specific *get* call, which is similar to a file *open* or *creat*. To create an object, the IPC_CREAT flag is passed as an argument to the *get* call. All *get* calls return an integer to be used in all subsequent local IPC system calls. Just like

Table 7.3 System V local IPC, user-level APIs.

Subsystem	Create	Control	Communicate
System V semaphores	semget	semctl	semop
POSIX semaphores (5.0)	sem_open	sem_init, sem_destroy	sem_post, sem_wait
System V message queues	msgget	mesgctl	msgrcv, msgsnd
POSIX message queues (7.0)	mq_open	mq_unlink, mq_setattr	mq_receive, mq_send
System V shared memory	shmget	shmctl, shmdt	n/a
POSIX shared memory (4.3)	shm_open	shm_unlink	n/a

a file descriptor, this integer is used to identify the object that the process is manipulating.

Each System V IPC subsystem has its own way of operating on the underlying object, and these functions are described in the following sections. All control operations, such as retrieving statistics or removing a previously created object, are handled by a subsystem-specific *ctl* routine.

Semaphores

A semaphore is the smallest atom of IPC available to a set of cooperating processes. Each semaphore contains a short integer that can be increased or decreased. A process that attempts to reduce the value of the semaphore below 0 will either be blocked or, if called in a nonblocking mode, will return immediately with an errno value of EAGAIN. The concept of semaphores and how they are used in multiprocess programs was originally proposed in Dijkstra & Genuys [1968].

Unlike the semaphores described in most computer science textbooks, semaphores in FreeBSD are grouped into arrays so that the code in the kernel can protect the process using them from causing a deadlock. Deadlocks were discussed in terms of locking within the kernel in Section 4.3 but are discussed here are well.

With System V semaphores, the deadlock occurs between two user-level processes rather than between kernel threads. A deadlock occurs between two processes, A and B, when they both attempt to take two semaphores, S_1 and S_2. If process A acquires S_1 and process B acquires S_2, then a deadlock occurs when process A tries to acquire S_2 and process B tries to acquire S_1 because there is no way for either process to give up the semaphore that the other one needs to make progress. It is always important when using semaphores that all cooperating processes acquire and release them in the same order to avoid this situation.

The implementation of semaphores in System V protected against deadlock by forcing the users of the API to group their semaphores into arrays and to perform semaphore operations as a sequence of events on the array. If the sequence submitted in the call could cause a deadlock, then an error was returned. The section on semaphores in Bach [1986] points out that this complexity should never have been placed in the kernel, but in order to adhere to the previously defined API, the same complexity exists in FreeBSD as well. At some point in the future, the kernel should provide a simpler form of semaphores to replace the current implementation.

Creating and attaching to a semaphore is done with the System V *semget* or the POSIX *sem_open* system call. Although semaphores were designed to look like file descriptors, they are not stored in the file descriptor table. All the semaphores in the system are contained in a single table in the kernel, whose size and shape are described by several tunable parameters. This table is protected by a global semaphore lock so that multiple processes are protected from partially creating entries in it. This lock is only taken when creating or attaching to a semaphore and is not a bottleneck in the actual use of existing semaphores.

Once a process has created a semaphore, or attached to a preexisting one, it calls the System V *semop* system call or the POSIX *sem_post* and *sem_wait* system calls to perform operations on it. The operations on the semaphore are passed to the system call as an array. Each element of the array includes the semaphore number to operate on (the index into the array returned by the previous System V *semget* or the POSIX *sem_open* call), the operation to perform, and a set of flags. The operation is a misnomer because it is not a command but simply a number. If the number is positive, then the corresponding semaphore's value is increased by that amount. If the operation is 0 and the semaphore's value is not 0, then either the process is put to sleep until the value is 0 or, if the IPC_NOWAIT flag was passed, EAGAIN is returned to the caller. When the operation is negative, there are several possible outcomes. If the value of the semaphore was greater than the absolute value of the operation, then the value of the operation is subtracted from the semaphore and the call returns. If subtracting the absolute value of the operation from the semaphore would force its value to be less than zero, then the process is put to sleep, unless the IPC_NOWAIT flag was passed. Here, EAGAIN is returned to the caller.

All of this logic is implemented in the System V *semop* system call or the POSIX *sem_post* and *sem_wait* system calls. The call first does some rudimentary checks to make sure that it has a chance of succeeding, including making sure there is enough memory to execute all the operations in one pass and that the calling process has the proper permissions to access the semaphore. Each semaphore ID returned to a process by the kernel has its own mutex to protect against multiple processes modifying the same semaphore at the same time. The routine locks this mutex and then attempts to perform all the operations passed to it in the array. It walks the array and attempts to perform each operation in order. There is the potential for this call to sleep before it completes all its work. If this situation occurs, then the code rolls back all its work before it goes to sleep. When it reawakens, the routine starts at the beginning of the array and attempts to perform the operations again. Either the routine will complete all its work, return with an appropriate error, or go back to sleep. Rolling back all the work is necessary to guarantee the idempotence of the routine. Either all the work is done or none of it is.

Message Queues

A message queue facilitates the sending and receiving of typed, arbitrary-length messages. The sending process adds messages at one end of the queue, and the receiving process removes messages from the other. The queue's size and other characteristics are controlled by a set of tunable kernel parameters. Message queues are inherently half duplex, meaning that one process is always the sender and the other is the receiver, but there are ways to use them as a form of full duplex communication, as we will see later.

The messages passed between the endpoints contain a type and a data area, as shown in Figure 7.6. This data structure should not be confused with the *mbufs* that are used by the networking code (see Section 12.3). MSGMNB is a tunable kernel parameter that defines the size of a message queue, and therefore the largest possible message that can be sent between two processes, and is set to 2048 by default.

Message queues can be used to implement either a pure first-in first-out queue, where all messages are delivered in the order in which they were sent, or a priority queue, where messages with a certain type can be retrieved ahead of others. This ability is provided by the *type* field of the message structure.

When a process sends a message, it invokes the System V *msgsnd* system call or the POSIX *mq_send* system call, which checks all the arguments in the call for correctness and then attempts to get enough resources to place the message into the queue. If there aren't enough resources, and the caller did not pass the IPC_NOWAIT flag, then the caller is put to sleep until such time as resources are available. The resources come from a pool of memory that is allocated by the kernel at boot time. The pool is arranged in fixed segments whose length is defined by MSGSSZ. The memory pool is managed as a large array so the segments can be located efficiently. Once the kernel has enough resources, it copies the message into the segments in the array and updates the rest of the data structures related to this queue.

The kernel data structures that control the message queues in the system are protected by a single lock which is taken and held by both the System V *msgsnd* and *msgrcv* system calls or the POSIX *mq_receive* and *mq_send* system calls for the duration of their execution. The use of a single lock for both routines protects the queue from being read and written simultaneously, possibly causing data corruption. It is also a performance bottleneck because it means that all other message queues are blocked when any one of them is being used.

Figure 7.6 Message data structure.

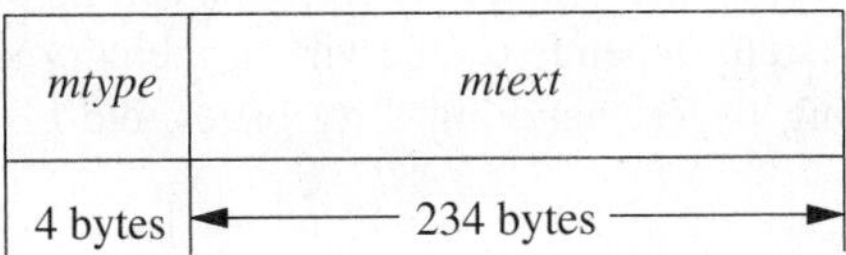

To retrieve a message from the queue, a process calls the System V *msgrcv* system call or the POSIX *mq_receive* system call. If the processes are using the queue as a simple fifo, then the receiver passes a 0 in the *msgtype* argument to this call to retrieve the first available message in the queue. To retrieve the first message in the queue of a particular type, a positive integer is passed. Processes implement a priority queue by using the type as the priority of the message. To implement a full duplex channel, each process picks a different type—say, 1 and 2. Messages of type 1 are from process A, and messages of type 2 are from process B. Process A sends messages with type 1 and receives messages with type 2, while process B does exactly the opposite.

After acquiring the message queue mutex, the receive routine finds the correct queue from which to retrieve data, and if there is an appropriate message, it returns data from the segments to the caller. If no data are available and the caller specified the IPC_NOWAIT flag, then the call returns immediately; otherwise, the calling process is put to sleep until there are data to be returned. When a message is retrieved from a message queue, its data are deallocated after they have been delivered to the receiving process.

Shared Memory

Shared memory is used when two or more processes need to communicate large amounts of data between them. Each process stores data in the shared memory just as it would within its own, per-process, memory. Care must be taken to serialize access to the shared memory so that processes do not write over each other. Hence, shared memory is often used with semaphores to synchronize read and write access.

Processes that are using shared memory are really sharing virtual memory (see Chapter 6). When a process creates a segment of shared memory by calling the System V *shmget* system call or the POSIX *shm_open* system call, the kernel allocates a set of virtual memory pages and places a pointer to them in the shared memory handle that is then returned to the calling process. To actually use the shared memory within a process, the System V interface must call the *shmat* system call, which attaches the virtual memory pages into the calling process. The attach routine uses the shared memory handle passed to it as an argument to find the relevant pages and returns an appropriate virtual address to the caller. Once this call completes, the process can then access the memory pointed to by the returned address as it would any other kind of memory. The POSIX interface creates and attaches the memory in its *shm_open* system call.

When the process is through using the shared memory, it detaches from it using the System V *shmdt* system call or the POSIX *shm_unlink* system call. This routine does not free the associated memory, because other processes may be using it, but it removes the virtual memory mapping from the calling process.

The shared memory subsystem depends on the virtual memory system to do most of the real work (mapping pages, handling dirty pages, etc.), so its implementation is relatively simple.

7.3 The Virtual-Filesystem Interface

In early UNIX systems, the file entries directly referenced the local filesystem ***inode***. An inode is a data structure that describes the contents of a file; it is more fully described in Section 9.2. This approach worked fine when there was a single filesystem implementation. However, with the advent of multiple filesystem types, the architecture had to be generalized. The new architecture had to support importing of filesystems from other machines, including those that were running different operating systems.

One alternative would have been to connect the multiple filesystems into the system as different file types. However, this approach would have required massive restructuring of the internal workings of the system, because current directories, references to executables, and several other interfaces used inodes instead of file entries as their point of reference. Thus, it was easier and more logical to add a new object-oriented layer to the system below the file entry and above the inode. This new layer was first implemented by Sun Microsystems, which called it the virtual-node, or *vnode*, layer. Interfaces in the system that had referred previously to inodes were changed to reference generic vnodes. A vnode used by a local filesystem would refer to an inode. A vnode used by a remote filesystem would refer to a protocol control block that described the location and naming information necessary to access the remote file.

Contents of a Vnode

The vnode is an extensible object-oriented interface. It contains information that is generically useful independent of the underlying filesystem object that it represents. The information stored in a vnode includes the following:

- Flags are used for identifying generic attributes. An example of a generic attribute is a flag to show that a vnode represents an object that is the root of a filesystem.
- The various reference counts include the number of file entries that are open for reading and/or writing that reference the vnode, the number of file entries that are open for writing that reference the vnode, and the number of pages and buffers that are associated with the vnode.
- A pointer to the mount structure describes the filesystem that contains the object represented by the vnode.
- Various information to perform file read-ahead.
- A reference to the *vm_object* associated with the vnode.
- A reference to state about special devices, sockets, and fifos.
- A mutex to protect the flags and counters within the vnode.

- A lock-manager lock to protect parts of the vnode that may change while it has an I/O operation in progress.
- Fields used by the name cache to track the names associated with the vnode.
- A pointer to the set of vnode operations defined for the object. These operations are described in the next subsection.
- A pointer to private information needed for the underlying object. For the local filesystem, this pointer will reference an inode; for NFS, it will reference an nfsnode.
- The type of the underlying object (e.g., regular file, directory, character device, etc.) is given. The type information is not strictly necessary, since a vnode client could always call a vnode operation to get the type of the underlying object. However, because the type often is needed, the type of underlying objects does not change, and it takes time to call through the vnode interface, the object type is cached in the vnode.
- There are clean and dirty buffers associated with the vnode. Each valid buffer in the system is identified by its associated vnode and the starting offset of its data within the object that the vnode represents. All the buffers that have been modified but have not yet been written back are stored on their vnode dirty-buffer list. All buffers that have not been modified or have been written back since they were last modified are stored on their vnode clean list. Having all the dirty buffers for a vnode grouped onto a single list makes the cost of doing an *fsync* system call to flush all the dirty blocks associated with a file proportional to the amount of dirty data. In some UNIX systems, the cost is proportional to the smaller of the size of the file or the size of the buffer pool. The list of clean buffers is used to free buffers when a file is deleted. Since the file will never be read again, the kernel can immediately cancel any pending I/O on its dirty buffers, then reclaim all its clean and dirty buffers and place them at the head of the buffer free list, ready for immediate reuse.
- A count is kept of the number of buffer write operations in progress. To speed the flushing of dirty data, the kernel does this operation by doing asynchronous writes on all the dirty buffers at once. For local filesystems, this simultaneous push causes all the buffers to be put into the disk queue so that they can be sorted into an optimal order to minimize seeking. For remote filesystems, this simultaneous push causes all the data to be presented to the network at once so that it can maximize their throughput. System calls that cannot return until the data are on stable store (such as *fsync*) can sleep on the count of pending output operations, waiting for the count to reach zero.

The position of vnodes within the system was shown in Figure 7.1. The vnode itself is connected into several other structures within the kernel, as shown in Figure 7.7. Each mounted filesystem within the kernel is represented by a generic mount structure that includes a pointer to a filesystem-specific control

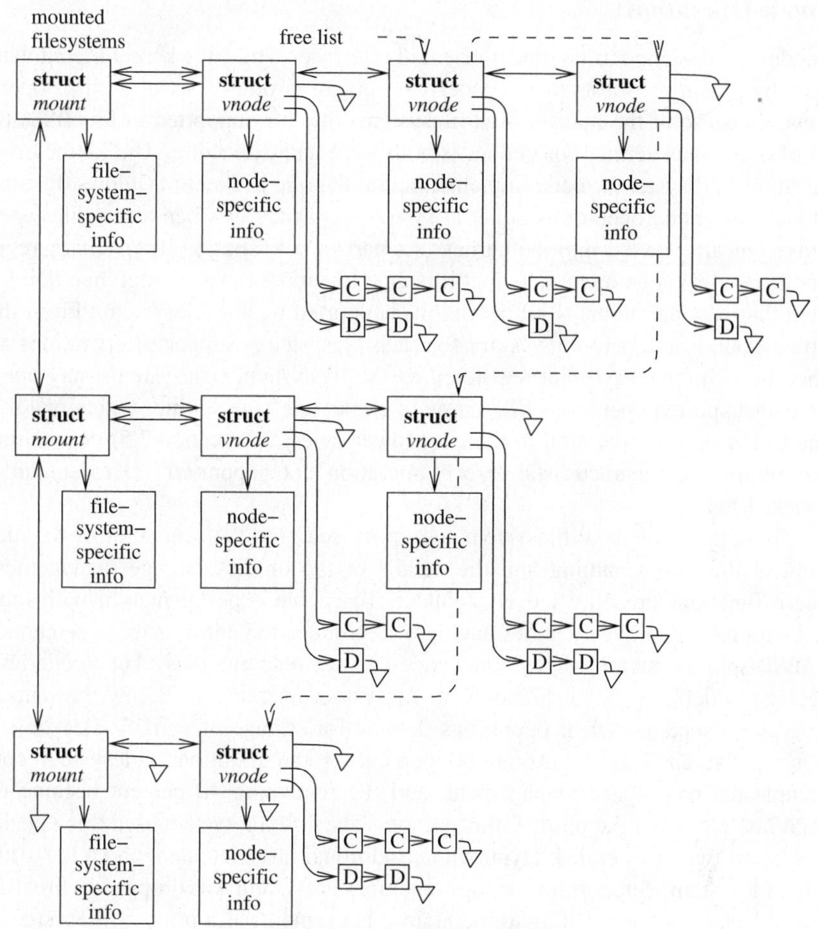

Figure 7.7 Vnode linkages. Key: D—dirty buffer; C—clean buffer.

block. All the vnodes associated with a specific mount point are linked together on a list headed by this generic mount structure. When the filesystem is being unmounted, the kernel needs to traverse this list to release all the vnodes associated with the mount point.

The subset of vnodes that are actively being used are also linked together on a list headed by the generic mount structure. Thus, when it is doing a *sync* system call for a filesystem, the kernel traverses this list of active vnodes to visit just the subset of the filesystem's vnodes that may need to have data written to disk.

Also shown in the figure are the lists of clean and dirty buffers associated with each vnode. Finally, there is a free list that links together all the vnodes in the system that are inactive (not currently referenced). The free list is used when a filesystem needs to allocate a new vnode so that the latter can open a new file; see Section 7.4.

Vnode Operations

Vnodes are designed as an object-oriented interface. Thus, the kernel manipulates them by passing requests to the underlying object through a set of defined operations. Because of the many varied filesystems that are supported in FreeBSD, the set of operations defined for vnodes is both large and extensible. Unlike the original Sun Microsystems vnode implementation, the one in FreeBSD allows dynamic addition of vnode operations either at system boot time or when a new filesystem is dynamically loaded into the kernel. As part of activating a filesystem, it registers the set of vnode operations that it is able to support. The kernel then builds a table that lists the union of all operations supported by any filesystem. From that table, it builds an operations vector for each filesystem. Supported operations are filled in with the entry point registered by the filesystem. Filesystems may opt to have unsupported operations filled in with either a default routine (typically a routine to bypass the operation to the next lower layer; see Section 7.5) or a routine that returns the characteristic error "operation not supported" [Heidemann & Popek, 1994].

In 4.3BSD, the local filesystem code provided both the semantics of the hierarchical filesystem naming and the details of the on-disk storage management. These functions are only loosely related. To enable experimentation with other disk-storage techniques without having to reproduce the entire naming semantics, 4.4BSD split the naming and storage code into separate modules. The vnode-level operations define a set of hierarchical filesystem operations. Below the naming layer are a separate set of operations defined for storage of variable-size objects using a flat namespace. About 60 percent of the traditional filesystem code became the namespace management, and the remaining 40 percent became the code implementing the on-disk file storage. The 4.4BSD system used this division to support two distinct disk layouts: the traditional fast filesystem and a log-structured filesystem. Support for the log-structured filesystem was dropped in FreeBSD due to lack of anyone willing to maintain it but remains as a primary filesystem in NetBSD. The naming and disk-storage scheme are described in Chapter 8.

Pathname Translation

The translation of a pathname requires a series of interactions between the vnode interface and the underlying filesystems. The pathname-translation process proceeds as follows:

1. The pathname to be translated is copied in from the user process or, for a remote filesystem request, is extracted from the network buffer.

2. The starting point of the pathname is determined as either the root directory or the current directory (see Section 2.9). The vnode for the appropriate directory becomes the *lookup directory* used in the next step.

3. The vnode layer calls the filesystem-specific *lookup*() operation and passes to that operation the remaining components of the pathname and the current

lookup directory. Typically, the underlying filesystem will search the *lookup directory* for the next component of the pathname and will return the resulting vnode (or an error if the name does not exist).

4. If an error is returned, the top level returns the error. If the pathname has been exhausted, the pathname lookup is done, and the returned vnode is the result of the lookup. If the pathname has not been exhausted, and the returned vnode is not a directory, then the vnode layer returns the "not a directory" error. If there are no errors, the top layer checks to see whether the returned directory is a mount point for another filesystem. If it is, then the *lookup directory* becomes the mounted filesystem; otherwise, the *lookup directory* becomes the vnode returned by the lower layer. The lookup then iterates with step 3.

Although it may seem inefficient to call through the vnode interface for each pathname component, doing so usually is necessary. The reason is that the underlying filesystem does not know which directories are being used as mount points. Since a mount point will redirect the lookup to a new filesystem, it is important that the current filesystem not proceed past a mounted directory. Although it might be possible for a local filesystem to be knowledgeable about which directories are mount points, it is nearly impossible for a server to know which of the directories within its exported filesystems are being used as mount points by its clients. Consequently, the conservative approach of traversing only a single pathname component per *lookup*() call is used. There are a few instances where a filesystem will know that there are no further mount points in the remaining path, and will traverse the rest of the pathname. An example is crossing into a *portal*, described in Section 7.5.

Exported Filesystem Services

The vnode interface has a set of services that the kernel exports from all the filesystems supported under the interface. The first of these is the ability to support the update of generic mount options. These options include the following:

noexec Do not execute any files on the filesystem. This option is often used when a server exports binaries for a different architecture that cannot be executed on the server itself. The kernel will even refuse to execute shell scripts; if a shell script is to be run, its interpreter must be invoked explicitly.

nosuid Do not honor the set-user-id or set-group-id flags for any executables on the filesystem. This option is useful when a filesystem of unknown origin is mounted.

nodev Do not allow any special devices on the filesystem to be opened. FreeBSD now uses a special-device filesystem to manage all its special devices and no longer implements special device nodes in the regular filesystem (see Section 8.1). However, some legacy systems still use special device nodes, so this option can be used to explicitly ignore their interpretation.

noatime When reading a file, do not update its access time. This option is useful on filesystems where there are many files being frequently read and performance is more critical than updating the file access time (which is rarely ever important).

sync Request that all I/O to the filesystem be done synchronously.

It is not necessary to unmount and remount the filesystem to change these flags; they may be changed while a filesystem is mounted. In addition, a filesystem that is mounted read-only can be upgraded to allow writing. Conversely, a filesystem that allows writing may be downgraded to read-only provided that no files are open for modification. The system administrator can forcibly downgrade the filesystem to read-only by requesting that any files open for writing have their access revoked.

Another service exported from the vnode interface is the ability to get information about a mounted filesystem. The *statfs* system call returns a buffer that gives the numbers of used and free disk blocks and inodes, along with the filesystem mount point, and the device, location, or program from which the filesystem is mounted. The *getfsstat* system call returns information about all the mounted filesystems. This interface avoids the need to track the set of mounted filesystems outside the kernel, as is done in some other UNIX variants.

7.4 Filesystem-Independent Services

The vnode interface not only supplies an object-oriented interface to the underlying filesystems but also provides a set of management routines that can be used by the client filesystems. These facilities are described in this section.

When the final file-entry reference to a file is closed, the usage count on the vnode drops to zero and the vnode interface calls the *inactive*() vnode operation. The *inactive*() call notifies the underlying filesystem that the file is no longer being used. The filesystem will often use this call to write dirty data back to the file but will not typically reclaim the memory holding file data. The filesystem is permitted to cache the file so that the latter can be reactivated quickly (i.e., without disk or network I/O) if the file is reopened.

In addition to the *inactive*() vnode operation being called when the reference count drops to zero, the vnode is placed on a systemwide free list. Unlike many vendor's vnode implementations, which have a fixed number of vnodes allocated to each filesystem type, the FreeBSD kernel keeps a single systemwide collection of vnodes. When an application opens a file that does not currently have an in-memory vnode, the client filesystem calls the *getnewvnode*() routine to allocate a new vnode. The kernel maintains two lists of free vnodes: those that have data pages cached in memory and those that do not have any data pages cached in memory. The preference is to reuse vnodes with no cached pages, since the reuse of a vnode with cached pages will cause all the cached pages associated with that vnode to lose their identity. If the vnodes were not classified separately, then an application that walked the filesystem tree doing *stat* calls on each file that it encountered would eventually flush all the vnodes referencing data pages, thus losing the identity of all the cached pages in the kernel. So when allocating a new vnode, the *getnewvnode*() routine first checks the front of the free list of vnodes with no cached pages and only if that list is empty does it select from the front of the list of vnodes with cached pages.

Having selected a vnode, the *getnewvnode*() routine then calls the vnode's *reclaim*() operation to notify the filesystem currently using that vnode that it is about to be reused. The *reclaim*() operation writes back any dirty data associated with the underlying object, removes the underlying object from any lists that it is on (such as hash lists used to find it), and frees up any auxiliary storage that was being used by the object. The vnode is then returned for use by the new client filesystem.

The benefit of having a single global vnode table is that the kernel memory dedicated to vnodes is used more efficiently than when several filesystem-specific collections of vnodes are used. Consider a system that is willing to dedicate memory for 1000 vnodes. If the system supports 10 filesystem types, then each filesystem type will get 100 vnodes. If most of the activity moves to a single filesystem (e.g., during the compilation of a kernel located in a local filesystem), all the active files will have to be kept in the 100 vnodes dedicated to that filesystem while the other 900 vnodes sit idle. In a FreeBSD system, all 1000 vnodes could be used for the active filesystem, allowing a much larger set of files to be cached in memory. If the center of activity moved to another filesystem (e.g., compiling a program on an NFS mounted filesystem), the vnodes would migrate from the previously active local filesystem over to the NFS filesystem. Here, too, there would be a much larger set of cached files than if only 100 vnodes were available using a partitioned set of vnodes.

The *reclaim*() operation is a disassociation of the underlying filesystem object from the vnode itself. This ability, combined with the ability to associate new objects with the vnode, provides functionality with usefulness that goes far beyond simply allowing vnodes to be moved from one filesystem to another. By replacing an existing object with an object from the *dead* filesystem—a filesystem in which all operations except *close* fail—the kernel revokes the object. Internally, this revocation of an object is provided by the *vgone*() routine.

This revocation service is used for session management, where all references to the controlling terminal are revoked when the session leader exits. Revocation works as follows: All open terminal descriptors within the session reference the vnode for the special device representing the session terminal. When *vgone*() is called on this vnode, the underlying special device is detached from the vnode and is replaced with the dead filesystem. Any further operations on the vnode will result in errors, because the open descriptors no longer reference the terminal. Eventually, all the processes will exit and will close their descriptors, causing the reference count to drop to zero. The *inactive*() routine for the dead filesystem returns the vnode to the front of the free list for immediate reuse because it will never be possible to get a reference to the vnode again.

The revocation service supports forcible unmounting of filesystems. If the kernel finds an active vnode when unmounting a filesystem, it simply calls the *vgone*() routine to disassociate the active vnode from the filesystem object. Processes with open files or current directories within the filesystem find that they have simply vanished, as though they had been removed. It is also possible to downgrade a mounted filesystem from read–write to read-only. Instead of access being revoked on every active file within the filesystem, only those files with a nonzero number of references for writing have their access revoked.

Finally, the ability to revoke objects is exported to processes through the *revoke* system call. This system call can be used to ensure controlled access to a device such as a pseudo-terminal port. First, the ownership of the device is changed to the desired user and the mode is set to owner-access only. Then the device name is revoked to eliminate any interlopers that already had it open. Thereafter, only the new owner is able to open the device.

The Name Cache

Name-cache management is another service that is provided by the vnode management routines. The interface provides a facility to add a name and its corresponding vnode, to lookup a name to get the corresponding vnode, and to delete a specific name from the cache. In addition to providing a facility for deleting specific names, the interface also provides an efficient way to invalidate all names that reference a specific vnode. Each vnode has a list that links together all their entries in the name cache. When the references to the vnode are to be deleted, each entry on the list is purged. Each directory vnode also has a second list of all the cache entries for names that are contained within it. When a directory vnode is to be purged, it must delete all the name-cache entries on this second list. A vnode's name-cache entries must be purged each time it is reused by *getnewvnode*() or when specifically requested by a client (e.g., when a directory is being renamed).

The cache-management routines also allow for negative caching. If a name is looked up in a directory and is not found, that name can be entered in the cache, along with a null pointer for its corresponding vnode. If the name is later looked up, it will be found in the name table, and thus the kernel can avoid scanning the entire directory to determine that the name is not there. If a name is added to a directory, then the name cache must lookup that name and purge it if it finds a negative entry. Negative caching provides a significant performance improvement because of path searching in command shells. When executing a command, many shells will look at each path in turn, searching for the executable. Commonly run executables will be searched for repeatedly in directories in which they do not exist. Negative caching speeds these searches.

The name cache does not solve the performance problems for directories with many entries that are actively having names added and deleted. Each time a name is to be added, the entire directory must be scanned to ensure that the name does not already exist. Similarly, when a name is deleted, the directory must be scanned to find the name to be deleted. For a directory with many entries, these linear scans are slow even if all the directory blocks are in the ***buffer cache***.

To avoid these costs, directories above a certain size are read into a hashed database in the kernel memory. Every name in the directory is stored in the database along with its location in the directory. Any free space in the directory is also noted in the database. When a file is to be deleted, its name is found in the database, the needed write operation is queued for the directory block to be updated, and the newly freed space is noted in the database for future use. When a new entry is to be created, the database is consulted to find out if it already exists. If it does not exist, a piece of free space of the needed size is allocated in the directory and the needed write operation is queued for the directory block to be updated. Thus, the database eliminates all linear scans of the directory.

A fixed-size arena is set aside to hold the directory databases. When a new directory is activated, its needed space is reclaimed from the least recently used directory's database. If the rate of turnover of directory databases is too high, the kernel will consider raising the size of the arena. Conversely, if other demands on the kernel memory arise and the turnover rate is low, the kernel will decrease the size of the arena.

Buffer Management

Historically, UNIX systems divided the main memory into two primary pools. The first was the virtual-memory pool that was used to cache process pages. The second was the buffer pool and was used to cache filesystem data. The main memory was divided between the two pools when the system booted and there was no memory migration between the pools once they were created.

With the addition of the *mmap* system call, the kernel supported the mapping of files into the address space of a process. If a file is mapped in with the MAP_SHARED attribute, changes made to the mapped file are to be written back to the disk and should show up in *read* calls done by other processes. Providing these semantics is difficult if there are copies of a file in both the buffer cache and the virtual-memory cache. Thus, FreeBSD merged the buffer cache and the virtual-memory cache into a single-page cache.

As described in Chapter 6, virtual memory is divided into a pool of pages holding the contents of files and a pool of anonymous pages holding the parts of a process that are not backed by a file such as its stack and heap. Pages backed by a file are identified by their vnode and logical block number. Rather than rewrite all the filesystems to lookup pages in the virtual-memory pool, a buffer-cache emulation layer was written. The emulation layer has the same interface as the old buffer-cache routines but works by looking up the requested file pages in the virtual-memory cache. When a filesystem requests a block of a file, the emulation layer calls the virtual-memory system to see if it is in memory. If it is not in memory, the virtual-memory system arranges to have it read. Normally, the pages in the virtual-memory cache are not mapped into the kernel address space. However, a filesystem often needs to inspect the blocks that it requests—for example, if it is a directory or filesystem metadata. Thus, the buffer-cache emulation layer must not only find the requested block but also allocate some kernel address space and map the requested block into it. The filesystem then uses the buffer to read, write, or manipulate the data and, when done, releases the buffer. On release, the buffer may be held briefly but soon is dissolved by releasing the kernel mapping, dropping the reference count on the virtual-memory pages and releasing the header.

The virtual-memory system does not have any way to describe blocks that are identified as a block associated with a disk. A small remnant of the buffer cache remains to hold these disk blocks that are used to hold filesystem metadata such as superblocks, bitmaps, and inodes.

The internal kernel interface to the buffer-cache emulation layer is simple. The filesystem allocates and fills buffers by calling the *bread*() routine. *Bread*() takes a vnode, a logical block number, and a size, and returns a pointer to a locked buffer. The details on how a buffer is created are given in the next subsection. Any other thread that tries to obtain the buffer will be put to sleep until the buffer is released.

A buffer can be released in one of four ways. If the buffer has not been modified, it can simply be released through use of *brelse*(), which checks for any threads that are waiting for it. If any threads are waiting, they are awakened. Otherwise, the buffer is dissolved by returning its contents back to the virtual-memory system, releasing its kernel address-space mapping and releasing the buffer.

If the buffer has been modified, it is called ***dirty***. Dirty buffers must eventually be written back to their filesystem. Three routines are available based on the urgency with which the data must be written. In the typical case, *bdwrite*() is used. Since the buffer may be modified again soon, it should be marked as dirty but should not be written immediately. After the buffer is marked as dirty, it is returned to the dirty-buffer list and any threads waiting for it are awakened. The heuristic is that, if the buffer will be modified again soon, the I/O would be wasted. Because the buffer is typically held for 20 to 30 seconds before it is written, a thread doing many small writes will not repeatedly access the disk or network.

If a buffer has been filled completely, then it is unlikely to be written again soon, so it should be released with *bawrite*(). The *bawrite*() routine schedules an I/O on the buffer but allows the caller to continue running while the output completes.

The final case is *bwrite*(), which ensures that the write is complete before proceeding. Because *bwrite*() can introduce a long latency to the writer, it is used only when a process explicitly requests the behavior (such as the *fsync* system call), when the operation is critical to ensure the consistency of the filesystem after a system crash, or when a stateless remote filesystem protocol such as NFS is being served. A buffer that is written using *bawrite*() or *bwrite*() is placed on the appropriate output queue. When the output completes, the *brelse*() routine is called to awaken any threads that are waiting for it or, if there is no immediate need for it, to dissolve the buffer.

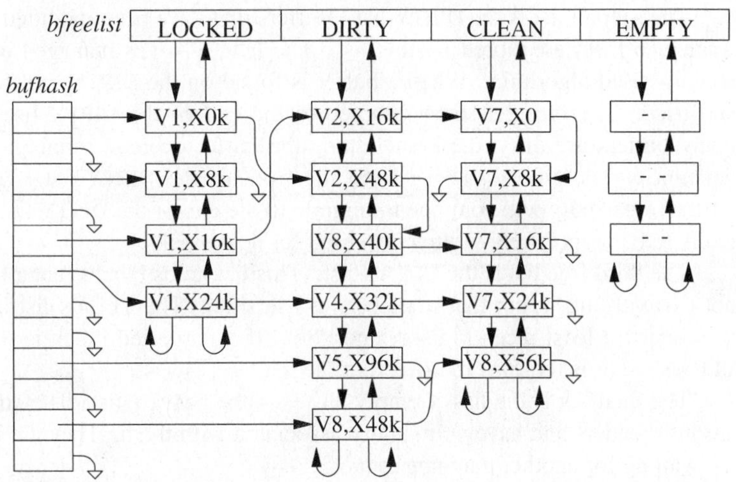

Figure 7.8 Snapshot of the buffer pool. Key: V—vnode; X—file offset.

Some buffers, though clean, may be needed again soon. To avoid the overhead of repeatedly creating and dissolving buffers, the buffer-cache emulation layer provides the *bqrelse*() routine to let the filesystem notify it that it expects to use the buffer again soon. The *bqrelse*() routine places the buffer on a clean list rather than dissolving it.

Figure 7.8 shows a snapshot of the buffer pool. A buffer with valid contents is contained on exactly one *bufhash* hash chain. The kernel uses the hash chains to determine quickly whether a block is in the buffer pool and, if it is, to locate it. A buffer is removed only when its contents become invalid or it is reused for different data. Thus, even if the buffer is in use by one thread, it can still be found by another thread, although it will be locked so that it will not be used until its contents are consistent.

In addition to appearing on the hash list, each unlocked buffer appears on exactly one free list. The first free list is the LOCKED list. Buffers on this list cannot be flushed from the cache. This list was originally intended to hold superblock data; in FreeBSD, it holds only buffers being written in background. In a background write, the contents of a dirty buffer are copied to another anonymous buffer. The anonymous buffer is then written to disk. The original buffer can continue to be used while the anonymous buffer is being written. Background writes are used primarily for fast and continuously changing blocks such as those that hold filesystem allocation bitmaps. If the block holding the bitmap was written normally, it would be locked and unavailable while it waited on the disk queue to be written. Thus, applications trying to write files in the area described by the bitmap would be blocked from running while they waited for the write of the bitmap to finish so that they could update the bitmap. By using background writes for bitmaps, applications are rarely forced to wait to update a bitmap.

The second list is the DIRTY list. Buffers that have been modified, but not yet written to disk, are stored on this list. The DIRTY list is managed using a least recently used algorithm. When a buffer is found on the DIRTY list, it is removed and used. The buffer is then returned to the end of the DIRTY list. When too many buffers are dirty, the kernel starts the buffer daemon running. The buffer daemon writes buffers starting from the front of the DIRTY list. Thus, buffers written repeatedly will continue to migrate to the end of the DIRTY list and are not likely to be prematurely written or reused for new blocks.

The third free list is the CLEAN list. This list holds blocks that a filesystem is not currently using but that it expects to use soon. The CLEAN list is also managed using a least recently used algorithm. If a requested block is found on the CLEAN list, it is returned to the end of the list.

The final list is the list of empty buffers—the EMPTY list. The empty buffers are just headers and have no memory associated with them. They are held on this list waiting for another mapping request.

When a new buffer is needed, the kernel first checks to see how much memory is dedicated to the existing buffers. If the memory in use is below its permissible threshold, a new buffer is created from the EMPTY list. Otherwise, the oldest buffer is removed from the front of the CLEAN list. If the CLEAN list is empty, the buffer daemon is awakened to clean up and release a buffer from the DIRTY list.

Implementation of Buffer Management

Having looked at the functions and algorithms used to manage the buffer pool, we now turn our attention to the implementation requirements for ensuring the consistency of the data in the buffer pool. Figure 7.9 shows the support routines that implement the interface for getting buffers. The primary interface to getting a buffer is through *bread*(), which is called with a request for a data block of a specified size for a specified vnode. There is also a related interface, *breadn*(), that both gets a requested block and starts read-ahead for additional blocks. *Bread*() first calls *getblk*() to find out whether the data block is available in an existing buffer. If the block is available in a buffer, *getblk*() calls *bremfree*() to take the buffer off whichever free list it is on and to lock it; *bread*() can then return the buffer to the caller.

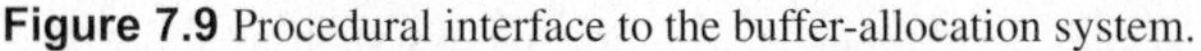

Figure 7.9 Procedural interface to the buffer-allocation system.

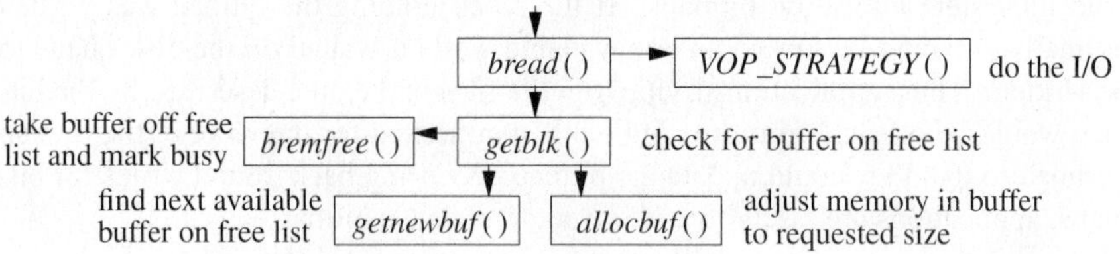

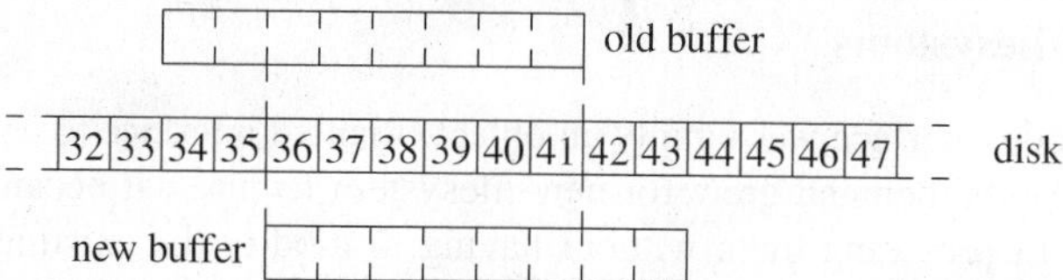

Figure 7.10 Potentially overlapping allocation of buffers.

If the block is not already in an existing buffer, *getblk*() calls *getnewbuf*() to allocate a new buffer, using the algorithm described in the previous subsection. The new buffer is then passed to *allocbuf*(), which is responsible for determining how to constitute the contents of the buffer.

The common case is that the buffer is to contain a logical block of a file. Here, *allocbuf*() must request the needed block from the virtual-memory system. If the virtual-memory system does not already have the needed block, it arranges to get it brought into its page cache. The *allocbuf*() routine then allocates an appropriately sized piece of kernel address space and requests the virtual-memory system to map the needed file block into that address space. The buffer is then marked filled and returned through *getblk*() and *bread*().

The other case is that the buffer is to contain a block of filesystem metadata such as a bitmap or an inode block that is associated with a disk device rather than a file. Because the virtual memory does not (currently) have any way to track such blocks, they can be held in memory only within buffers. Here, *allocbuf*() must call the kernel *malloc*() routine to allocate memory to hold the block. The *allocbuf*() routine then returns the buffer to *getblk*() and *bread*() marked busy and unfilled. Noticing that the buffer is unfilled, *bread*() passes the buffer to the *strategy*() routine for the underlying filesystem to have the data read in. When the read completes, the buffer is returned.

To maintain the consistency of the filesystem, the kernel must ensure that a disk block is mapped into, at most, one buffer. If the same disk block were present in two buffers, and both buffers were marked dirty, the system would be unable to determine which buffer had the most current information. Figure 7.10 shows a sample allocation. In the middle of the figure are the blocks on the disk. Above the disk an old buffer is shown containing a 4096-byte fragment for a file that presumably has been removed or shortened. The new buffer is going to be used to hold a 4096-byte fragment for a file that is presumably being created and that will reuse part of the space previously held by the old file. The kernel maintains the consistency by purging old buffers when files are shortened or removed. Whenever a file is removed, the kernel traverses the file's list of dirty buffers. For each buffer, the kernel cancels its write request and dissolves the buffer so that the buffer cannot be found in the buffer pool again. For a file being partially truncated, only the buffers following the truncation point are invalidated. The system can then allocate the new buffer, knowing that the buffer maps the corresponding disk blocks uniquely.

7.5 Stackable Filesystems

The early vnode interface was simply an object-oriented interface to an underlying filesystem. As the demand grew for new filesystem features, it became desirable to find ways of providing them without having to modify the existing and stable filesystem code. One approach was to provide a mechanism for stacking several filesystems on top of one another other [Rosenthal, 1990]. The stacking ideas were refined and implemented in the 4.4BSD system [Heidemann & Popek, 1994]. The implementation of the stacking has been refined in FreeBSD, but the semantics remain largely unchanged from those found in 4.4BSD. The bottom of a vnode stack tends to be a disk-based filesystem, whereas the layers used above it typically transform their arguments and pass on those arguments to a lower layer.

In all UNIX systems, the *mount* command takes a special device as a source and maps that device onto a directory mount point in an existing filesystem. When a filesystem is mounted on a directory, the previous contents of the directory are hidden; only the contents of the root of the newly mounted filesystem are visible. To most users, the effect of the series of mount commands done at system startup is the creation of a single seamless filesystem tree.

Stacking also uses the *mount* command to create new layers. The *mount* command pushes a new layer onto a vnode stack; an *unmount* command removes a layer. Like the mounting of a filesystem, a vnode stack is visible to all processes running on the system. The *mount* command identifies the underlying layer in the stack, creates the new layer, and attaches that layer into the filesystem namespace. The new layer can be attached to the same place as the old layer (covering the old layer) or to a different place in the tree (allowing both layers to be visible). An example is shown in the next subsection.

If layers are attached to different places in the namespace, then the same file will be visible in multiple places. Access to the file under the name of the new layer's namespace will go to the new layer, whereas that under the old layer's namespace will go to only the old layer.

When a file access (e.g., an *open*, *read*, *stat*, or *close*) occurs to a vnode in the stack, that vnode has several options:

- Perform the requested operations and return a result.
- Pass the operation without change to the next-lower vnode on the stack. When the operation returns from the lower vnode, it may modify the results or simply return them.
- Modify the operands provided with the request and then pass it to the next-lower vnode. When the operation returns from the lower vnode, it may modify the results, or simply return them.

If an operation is passed to the bottom of the stack without any layer taking action on it, then the interface will return the error "operation not supported."

Vnode interfaces released before 4.4BSD implemented vnode operations as indirect function calls. The requirements that intermediate stack layers bypass operations to lower layers and that new operations can be added into the system at boot or module load time mean that this approach is no longer adequate. Filesystems must be able to bypass operations that may not have been defined at the time that the filesystem was implemented. In addition to passing through the function, the filesystem layer must also pass through the function parameters, which are of unknown type and number.

To resolve these two problems in a clean and portable way, the kernel places the vnode operation name and its arguments into an argument structure. An example access-check call and its implementation for the UFS filesystem are shown in Figure 7.11. Note that the *vop_access_args* structure is normally declared in a header file, but here it is declared at the function site to simplify the example. The

Figure 7.11 Call to and function header for *access* vnode operation.

```
{
    ...
    /*
     * Check for read permission on file ``vp''.
     */
    if (error = VOP_ACCESS(vp, VREAD, cred, td))
        return (error);
    ...
}

/*
 * Check access permission for a file.
 */
int ufs_access(
    struct vop_access_args {
        struct vnodeop_desc *a_desc; /* operation descrip. */
        struct vnode *a_vp;          /* file to be checked */
        int a_mode;                  /* access mode sought */
        struct ucred *a_cred;        /* user seeking access */
        struct thread *a_td;         /* associated thread */
    } *ap);
{

    if (permission granted)
        return (1);
    return (0);
}
```

argument structure is passed as a single parameter to the vnode operation. Thus, all calls on a vnode operation will always have exactly one parameter, which is the pointer to the argument structure. If the vnode operation is one that is supported by the filesystem, then it will know what the arguments are and how to interpret them. If it is an unknown vnode operation, then the generic bypass routine can call the same operation in the next-lower layer, passing to the operation the same argument structure that it received. In addition, the first argument of every operation is a pointer to the vnode operation description. This description provides the information about the operation to a bypass routine, including the operation's name and the location of the operation's parameters.

Simple Filesystem Layers

The simplest filesystem layer is *nullfs*. It makes no transformations on its arguments, simply passing through all requests that it receives and returning all results that it gets back. Although it provides no useful functionality if it is simply stacked on top of an existing vnode, *nullfs* can provide a loopback filesystem by mounting the filesystem rooted at its source vnode at some other location in the filesystem tree. The code for *nullfs* is also an excellent starting point for designers who want to build their own filesystem layers. Examples that could be built include a compression layer or an encryption layer.

A sample vnode stack is shown in Figure 7.12. The figure shows a local filesystem on the bottom of the stack that is being exported from **/local** via an NFS layer. Clients within the administrative domain of the server can import the **/local** filesystem directly because they are all presumed to use a common mapping of UIDs to user names.

The *umapfs* filesystem works much like the *nullfs* filesystem in that it provides a view of the file tree rooted at the **/local** filesystem on the **/export** mount point. In addition to providing a copy of the **/local** filesystem at the **/export** mount point, it transforms the credentials of each system call made to files within

Figure 7.12 Stackable vnodes.

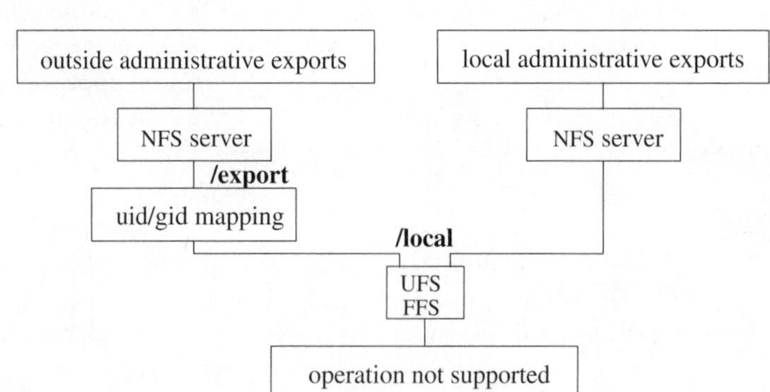

the **/export** filesystem. The kernel does the transformation using a mapping that was provided as part of the *mount* system call that created the *umapfs* layer.

The **/export** filesystem can be exported to clients from an outside administrative domain that uses different UIDs and GIDs. When an NFS request comes in for the **/export** filesystem, the *umapfs* layer modifies the credential from the foreign client by mapping the UIDs used on the foreign client to the corresponding UIDs used on the local system. The requested operation with the modified credential is passed down to the lower layer corresponding to the **/local** filesystem, where it is processed identically to a local request. When the result is returned to the mapping layer, any returned credentials are mapped inversely so that they are converted from the local UIDs to the outside UIDs, and this result is sent back as the NFS response.

There are three benefits to this approach:

1. There is no cost of mapping imposed on the local clients.
2. There are no changes required to the local filesystem code or the NFS code to support mapping.
3. Each outside domain can have its own mapping. Domains with simple mappings consume small amounts of memory and run quickly; domains with large and complex mappings can be supported without detracting from the performance of simpler environments.

Vnode stacking is an effective approach for adding extensions, such as the *umapfs* service.

The Union Filesystem

The *union* filesystem is another example of a middle filesystem layer. Like the *nullfs*, it does not store data but just provides a namespace transformation. It is loosely modeled on the work on the 3-D filesystem [Korn & Krell, 1989], on the Translucent filesystem [Hendricks, 1990], and on the Automounter [Pendry & Williams, 1994]. The *union* filesystem takes an existing filesystem and transparently overlays the latter on another filesystem. Unlike most other filesystems, a union mount does not cover up the directory on which the filesystem is mounted. Instead, it shows the logical merger of both directories and allows both directory trees to be accessible simultaneously [Pendry & McKusick, 1995].

A small example of a union-mount stack is shown in Figure 7.13. Here, the bottom layer of the stack is the **src** filesystem that includes the source for the **shell** program. Being a simple program, it contains only one source and one header file. The upper layer that has been union mounted on top of **src** initially contains just the **src** directory. When the user changes directory into **shell**, a directory of the same name is created in the top layer. Directories in the top layer corresponding to directories in the lower layer are created only as they are encountered while the top layer is traversed. If the user were to run a recursive

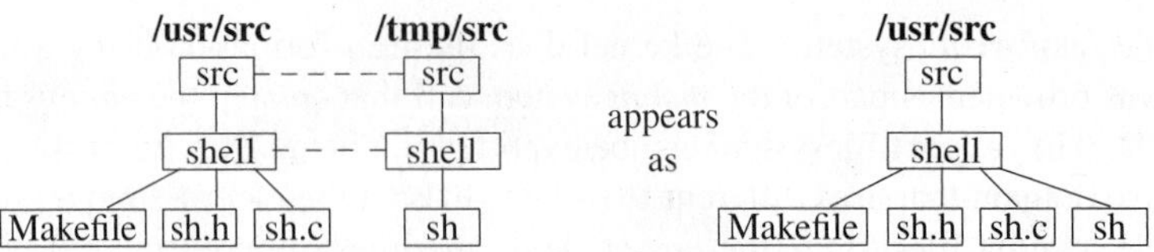

Figure 7.13 A union-mounted filesystem. The **/usr/src** filesystem is on the bottom, and the **/tmp/src** filesystem is on the top.

traversal of the tree rooted at the top of the union-mount location, the result would be a complete tree of directories matching the underlying filesystem. In our example, the user now types **make** in the **shell** directory. The **sh** executable is created in the upper layer of the union stack. To the user, a directory listing shows the sources and executable all apparently together, as shown on the right in Figure 7.13.

All filesystem layers, except the top one, are treated as though they were read-only. If a file residing in a lower layer is opened for reading, a descriptor is returned for that file. If a file residing in a lower layer is opened for writing, the kernel first copies the entire file to the top layer and then returns a descriptor referencing the copy of the file. The result is that there are two copies of the file: the original unmodified file in the lower layer and the modified copy of the file in the upper layer. When the user performs a directory listing, any duplicate names in the lower layer are suppressed. When a file is opened, a descriptor for the file in the uppermost layer in which the name appears is returned. Thus, once a file has been copied to the top layer, instances of the file in lower layers become inaccessible.

The tricky part of the *union* filesystem is handling the removal of files that reside in a lower layer. Since the lower layers cannot be modified, the only way to remove a file is to hide it by creating a whiteout directory entry in the top layer. A whiteout is an entry in a directory that has no corresponding file; it is distinguished by having an inode number of 1. If the kernel finds a whiteout entry while searching for a name, the lookup is stopped and the "no such file or directory" error is returned. Thus, the file with the same name in a lower layer appears to have been removed. If a file is removed from the top layer, it is necessary to create a whiteout entry for it only if there is a file with the same name in the lower level that would reappear.

When a process creates a file with the same name as a whiteout entry, the whiteout entry is replaced with a regular name that references the new file. Because the new file is being created in the top layer, it will mask out any files with the same name in a lower layer. When a user performs a directory listing, whiteout entries and the files that they mask usually are not shown. However, there is an option that causes them to appear.

One feature that has long been missing in UNIX systems is the ability to recover files after they have been deleted. For the union filesystem, the kernel can implement file recovery trivially by simply removing the whiteout entry to expose the underlying file. For filesystems that provide file recovery, users can recover files by using a special option to the remove command. Processes can recover files by using the *undelete* system call.

When a directory whose name appears in a lower layer is removed, a whiteout entry is created just as it would be for a file. However, if the user later attempts to create a directory with the same name as the previously deleted directory, the union filesystem must treat the new directory specially to avoid having the previous contents from the lower-layer directory reappear. When a directory that replaces a whiteout entry is created, the union filesystem sets a flag in the directory metadata to show that this directory should be treated specially. When a directory scan is done, the kernel returns information about only the top-level directory; it suppresses the list of files from the directories of the same name in the lower layers.

The *union* filesystem can be used for many purposes:

- It allows several different architectures to build from a common source base. The source pool is NFS mounted onto each of several machines. On each host machine, a local filesystem is union mounted on top of the imported source tree. As the build proceeds, the objects and binaries appear in the local filesystem that is layered above the source tree. This approach not only avoids contaminating the source pool with binaries, but also speeds the compilation because most of the filesystem traffic is on the local filesystem.
- It allows compilation of sources on read-only media such as CD-ROMs. A local filesystem is union mounted above the CD-ROM sources. It is then possible to change into directories on the CD-ROM and to give the appearance of being able to edit and compile in that directory.
- It allows creation of a private source directory. The user creates a source directory in her own work area and then union mounts the system sources underneath that directory. This feature is possible because the restrictions on the *mount* command have been relaxed. If the *sysctl* **vfs.usermount** option has been enabled, any user can do a mount if she owns the directory on which the mount is being done and she has appropriate access permissions on the device or directory being mounted (read permission is required for a read-only mount, read–write permission is required for a read–write mount). Only the user who did the mount or the superuser can unmount a filesystem.

Other Filesystems

There are several other filesystems included as part of FreeBSD. The *portal* filesystem mounts a process onto a directory in the file tree. When a pathname that traverses the location of the portal is used, the remainder of the path is passed to the process mounted at that point. The process interprets the path in whatever way it sees fit, then returns a descriptor to the calling process. This descriptor may be for a socket connected to the portal process. If it is, further operations on the descriptor will be passed to the portal process for the latter to interpret. Alternatively, the descriptor may be for a file elsewhere in the filesystem.

Consider a portal process mounted on **/dialout** used to manage a bank of dialout modems. When a process wanted to connect to an outside number, it would open **/dialout/15105551212/28800** to specify that it wanted to dial 1-510-555-1212 at 28800 baud. The portal process would get the final two pathname components. Using the final component, it would determine that it should find an unused 28800-baud modem. It would use the other component as the number to which to place the call. It would then write an accounting record for future billing, and would return the descriptor for the modem to the process.

An interesting use of the portal filesystem is to provide an Internet service directory. For example, with an Internet portal process mounted on **/net**, an open of **/net/tcp/McKusick.COM/smtp** returns a TCP socket descriptor to the calling process that is connected to the SMTP server on **McKusick.COM**. Because access is provided through the normal filesystem, the calling process does not need to be aware of the special functions necessary to create a TCP socket and to establish a TCP connection [Stevens & Pendry, 1995].

There are several filesystems that are designed to provide a convenient interface to kernel information. The *procfs* filesystem is normally mounted at **/proc** and provides a view of the running processes in the system. Its primary use is for debugging, but it also provides a convenient interface for collecting information about the processes in the system. A directory listing of **/proc** produces a numeric list of all the processes in the system. The **/proc** interface is more fully described in Section 4.9.

The *fdesc* filesystem is normally mounted on **/dev/fd** and provides a list of all the active file descriptors for the currently running process. An example where this is useful is specifying to an application that it should read input from its standard input. Here, you can use the pathname **/dev/fd/0** instead of having to come up with a special convention, such as using the name "–" to tell the application to read from its standard input.

The *linprocfs* emulates a subset of the Linux process filesystem and is normally mounted on **/compat/linux/proc**. It provides similar information to that provided by the **/proc** filesystem, but in a format expected by Linux binaries.

Finally, there is the *cd9660* filesystem. It allows ISO-9660-compliant filesystems, with or without Rock Ridge extensions, to be mounted. The ISO-9660 filesystem format is most commonly used on CD-ROMs.

Exercises

7.1 Where are the read and write attributes of an open file descriptor stored?

7.2 Why is the close-on-exec bit located in the per-process descriptor table instead of in the system file table?

7.3 Why are the file-table entries reference counted?

7.4 What three shortcomings of lock files are addressed by the FreeBSD descriptor-locking facilities?

7.5 What two problems are raised by mandatory locks?

7.6 Why is the implementation of *select* split between the descriptor-management code and the lower-level routines?

7.7 Describe how the *process selecting flag* is used in the implementation of *select*.

7.8 The *syncer* daemon starts as part of system boot. Once every second, it does an *fsync* on any vnodes that it finds that have been dirty for 30 seconds. What problem could arise if this daemon were not run?

7.9 When is a vnode placed on the free list?

7.10 Why must the lookup routine call through the vnode interface once for each component in a pathname?

7.11 Give three reasons for revoking access to a vnode.

7.12 Why are the buffer headers allocated separately from the memory that holds the contents of the buffer?

7.13 Asynchronous I/O is provided through the *aio_read* and *aio_write* systems calls rather than through the traditional *read* and *write* system calls. What problems arise with providing asynchronous I/O in the existing read–write interface?

*7.14 Why are there both a CLEAN list and a DIRTY list instead of all buffers being managed on one list?

*7.15 If a process reads a large file, the blocks of the file will fill the virtual memory cache completely, flushing out all other contents. All other processes in the system then will have to go to disk for all their filesystem accesses. Write an algorithm to control the purging of the buffer cache.

*7.16 Vnode operation parameters are passed between layers in structures. What alternatives are there to this approach? Explain why your approach is more or less efficient, compared to the current approach, when there are less than five layers in the stack. Also compare the efficiency of your solution when there are more than five layers in the stack.

References

Accetta et al., 1986.

M. Accetta, R. Baron, W. Bolosky, D. Golub, R. Rashid, A. Tevanian, & M. Young, "Mach: A New Kernel Foundation for UNIX Development," *USENIX Association Conference Proceedings*, pp. 93–113, June 1986.

Bach, 1986.

M. J. Bach, *The Design of the UNIX Operating System,* Prentice-Hall, Englewood Cliffs, NJ, 1986.

Dijkstra & Genuys, 1968.
E. Dijkstra & F. Genuys, editor, "Cooperating Sequential Processes," in *Programming Languages*, pp. 43–112, Academic Press, New York, NY, 1968.

Heidemann & Popek, 1994.
J. S. Heidemann & G. J. Popek, "File-System Development with Stackable Layers," *ACM Transactions on Computer Systems*, vol. 12, no. 1, pp. 58–89, February 1994.

Hendricks, 1990.
D. Hendricks, "A Filesystem for Software Development," *USENIX Association Conference Proceedings*, pp. 333–340, June 1990.

Korn & Krell, 1989.
D. Korn & E. Krell, "The 3-D File System," *USENIX Association Conference Proceedings*, pp. 147–156, June 1989.

Lemon, 2001.
J. Lemon, "Kqueue: A Generic and Scalable Event Notification Facility," *Proceedings of the Freenix Track at the 2001 USENIX Annual Technical Conference*, pp. 141–154, June 2001.

Pendry & McKusick, 1995.
J. Pendry & M. K. McKusick, "Union Mounts in 4.4BSD-Lite," *USENIX Association Conference Proceedings*, pp. 25–33, January 1995.

Pendry & Williams, 1994.
J. Pendry & N. Williams, "AMD: The 4.4BSD Automounter Reference Manual," in *4.4BSD System Manager's Manual*, pp. 13:1–57, O'Reilly & Associates, Inc., Sebastopol, CA, 1994.

Peterson, 1983.
G. Peterson, "Concurrent Reading While Writing," *ACM Transactions on Programming Languages and Systems*, vol. 5, no. 1, pp. 46–55, January 1983.

Rosenthal, 1990.
D. Rosenthal, "Evolving the Vnode Interface," *USENIX Association Conference Proceedings*, pp. 107–118, June 1990.

Stevens, 1999.
R. Stevens, *UNIX Network Programming Volume 2, Second Edition,* Prentice-Hall, Englewood Cliffs, NJ, 1999.

Stevens & Pendry, 1995.
R. Stevens & J. Pendry, "Portals in 4.4BSD," *USENIX Association Conference Proceedings*, pp. 1–10, January 1995.

CHAPTER 8

Devices

8.1 Device Overview

This chapter describes the part of the system that interfaces with the hardware as is shown in the bottom part of Figure 7.1. Historically, the device interface was static and simple. Devices were discovered as the system was booted and did not change thereafter. Filesystems were built in a partition of a single disk. When a disk driver received a request from a filesystem to write a block, it would add the base offset of the partition and perform a bounds check based on information from its disk label. It would then do the requested I/O and return the result or error to the filesystem. A typical disk driver could be written in a few hundred lines of code.

As the system has evolved, the complexity of the I/O system has increased with the addition of new functionality. The new functionality can be broken into three categories:

1. Disk management
2. I/O routing and control
3. Networking

Each of these areas is handled by a new subsystem in FreeBSD.

Disk management consists of organizing the myriad ways that disks can be used to build a filesystem. A disk may be broken up into several slices, each of which can be used to support a different operating system. Each of these slices may be further subdivided into partitions that can be used to support filesystems as they did historically. However, it is also possible to combine several slices and/or partitions to create a virtual partition on which to build a filesystem that spans several disks. The virtual partition may concatenate several partitions to stripe the filesystem across several disks, thus providing a high-bandwidth filesystem, or the underlying partitions may be put together in a Redundant Array of Inexpensive Disks (RAID) to provide a higher level of reliability and accessibility than a single disk. Or, the partitions may be organized into two equal-size groups and mirrored to provide an even higher level of reliability and accessibility than RAID. The aggregation of physical disk partitions into a virtual partition in these ways is referred to as volume management.

Rather than building all this functionality into all the filesystems or disk drivers, it has been abstracted out into the GEOM (geometry) layer. The GEOM layer takes as input the set of disks available on the system. It is responsible for doing volume management. At a low level, volume management creates, maintains, and interprets the slice tables and the disk labels defining the partitions within each slice. At a higher level, GEOM combines the physical disk partitions through striping, RAID, or mirroring to create the virtual partitions that are exported to the filesystem layer above. The virtual partition appears to the filesystem as a single large disk. As the filesystem does I/O within the virtual partition, the GEOM layer determines which disk(s) are involved and breaks up and dispatches the I/O request to the appropriate physical drives. The operation of the GEOM layer is described in Section 8.7.

The PC I/O Architecture

Historically, architectures had only one or two I/O busses and types of disk controllers. As described in the next subsection, a modern PC today can have several types of disks connected to the machine through five or more different types of interfaces. The complexity of these disk controllers rivals that of the entire early UNIX operating system. Early controllers could only handle one disk I/O at a time. Today's controllers can typically juggle up to 64 simultaneous requests through a scheme called tagged queueing. A request works its way through the controller being posted as it is received, scheduled to be done, completed, and reported back to the requester. I/O may also be cached in the controller to allow future requests to be handled more quickly. Another task handled by the controller is to provide a replacement with an alternate good sector for a disk sector with a permanent error.

The PC I/O architecture is shown in Figure 8.1. Far greater detail is available at Arch [2014]. On the left of the figure is one or more CPUs that have a high-speed interconnect to the system's main memory and the graphics memory that drives the system display. Note that the L1 and L2 caches are not shown in this picture because they are considered as part of the CPU. Historically, the memory and graphics were connected to the CPU via the northbridge bus. Modern Intel and AMD CPUs have subsumed the roles of the memory controller and the graphics controller. Here, they have converged with the system-on-chip design of small embedded architectures.

Beneath the CPUs is the Peripheral Controller Hub (PCH) that connects all the I/O busses to the system. These busses include the following:

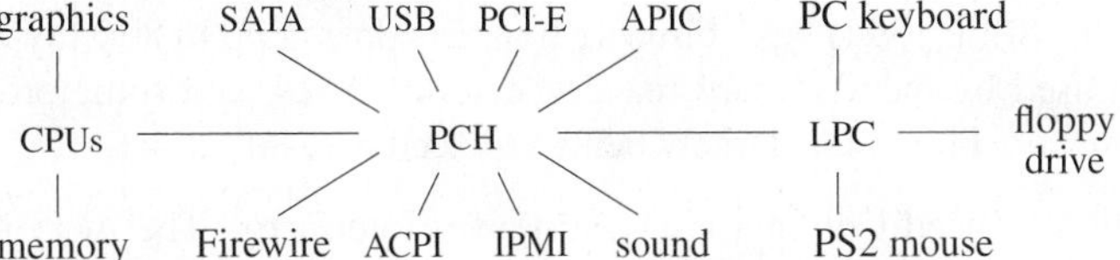

Figure 8.1 The PC I/O architecture. Key: PCH—Peripheral Controller Hub; SATA—Serial Advanced Technology Attachment; USB—Universal Serial Bus; PCI-E—Peripheral Component Interconnect Express; APIC—Advanced Programmable Interrupt Controller; ACPI—Advanced Configuration and Power Interface; IPMI—Intelligent Platform Management Interface; LPC—Low Pin Count interface.

- The SATA (Serial Advanced Technology Attachment) bus. SATA has replaced the parallel ATA bus that was common in earlier PC designs. SATA supports the ability to hot-plug drives and transfer data at up to 600 Mbyte per second. Devices connected via SATA have a one-to-one relationship between the device and a port: there is no daisy chaining of devices as was present in earlier busses such as SCSI. Commercially available systems have at least two and usually more SATA ports available. Switching from a parallel to a serial bus allowed the size of the connectors and cables to be shrunk to the point where having one cable per device does not present any cable routing or space problems even in laptop systems.
- The USB (Universal Serial Bus). The USB provides a high-speed input typically used for external hard disks, removable flash disks, video cameras, scanners, and printers, as well as human input devices such as keyboards, mice, and joysticks. USB 2.0 provides speeds up to 48 Mbyte per second, while USB 3.0 provides speeds up to 500 Mbyte per second.
- The PCI (Peripheral Component Interconnect) and PCI-E (Peripheral Component Interconnect Express) busses. These busses provide a well-designed architecture for high-speed throughput and automated autoconfiguration for modern I/O cards. The older PCI bus uses a parallel interface and a simple bus topology, while the newer PCI-E bus uses a star topology and a serial interface that allows multiple channels to bond together to increase the bandwidth to the peripheral. These busses also have the advantage of being available on many other computer architectures besides the PC.
- The APIC (Advanced Programmable Interrupt Controller). The APIC maps the device interrupts to IRQ (Interrupt ReQuest) values for the CPU. Most modern machines use an IOAPIC (I/O Advanced Programmable Interrupt Controller) that provides much finer-grain control over the device interrupts. All processors since the Pentium Pro (1997) have had an LAPIC (Local Advanced Programmable Interrupt Controller) that works with the IOAPIC to support distribution of interrupts among the CPUs.

- The Firewire (IEEE 1394) bus. Firewire transfers data at up to 80 Mbyte per second. It is used by memory-card readers, external disks, and some professional digital cameras. Firewire is largely being replaced by USB.

- The ACPI (Advanced Configuration and Power Interface). The ACPI is present on all mobile systems, desktops, and servers. It provides topology and discovery information to the kernel for system resources like PCI/PCI-E busses and APICs. It controls various components, including power and sleep buttons, back-light intensity of screens, and cooling fans and status lights. It also controls power-saving modes for the CPU, chassis, and system peripherals [ACPI, 2013].

- IPMI (Intelligent Platform Management Interface). The IPMI subsystem is provided on many server-class machines to allow for remote monitoring and control of the system over a network connection. The network connection may be shared with a network port on the system or a completely separate network port may be present allowing for complete out-of-band control of the machine. IPMI provides access to various environmental registers including component temperatures, fan speeds, and power levels. It may also offer a serial-over-LAN capability where a virtual serial console is available over the network.

- Support for the AC97 (Audio CODEC) sound standard. This standard allows a single DSP (Digital Signal Processor) to be used to support both a modem and sound.

- The Low Pin Count (LPC) interface. A specialized combination of general-purpose I/O pins, it can be used to emulate legacy interfaces. These interfaces include access to floppy disks, serial ports, and the PS2 keyboard and mouse ports. Most machines connect the keyboard and mouse through the USB port, but some systems still provide PS2 ports for legacy devices. The emulation happens transparently in the Basic Input Output System (BIOS) code via the System Management Interrupt. The result is that the kernel sees what appears to be classic controller. For example, the kernel might detect a legacy serial port but it is really soft emulation in the BIOS controlling pins assigned to the serial port on the LPC. The LPC exists as a transition technology as the last remnants of first-generation PC devices are retired.

The Structure of the FreeBSD Mass Storage I/O Subsystem

There were several disk subsystems in early versions of FreeBSD. The first support for ATA and SCSI disks came from Mach 2.5 and were present in FreeBSD 1.0. Both of these were highly device specific. Efforts to replace both resulted in CAM (Common Access Method), introduced in FreeBSD 3.0, and the new ATA driver, introduced in FreeBSD 4.0. As the ATA effort was proceeding, the CAM maintainers attempted to have it become a CAM attachment. However, the strange reservation and locking rules of the ATA register-file model was a poor match for the CAM implementation, so the ATA implementation, with the exception of the CD-ROM driver, remained separate until FreeBSD 9.0 when the CAM implementation replaced it.

CAM is an ANSI (American National Standards Institute) standard (X3.232-1996). A revised and enhanced version of CAM was proposed by the X3T10 group but was never approved [ANSI, 2002]. Although originally used for SCSI, CAM is a way of interfacing host-bus adapter (HBA) drivers (software-interface-module drivers in CAM terminology), midlayer *transport* glue, and peripheral drivers. This layering provides a powerful abstraction that separates the physical bus protocol from the logical device protocol, making it suitable for many modern I/O systems. While CAM seems unlikely to ever be approved as a standard, it still provides a useful framework for implementing a storage subsystem.

The FreeBSD CAM implementation supports SPI (SCSI Parallel Interface), Fibre Channel [ANSI, 2003], UMASS (USB Mass Storage), IEEE 1394 (Firewire), SAS (Serial Attached SCSI), SATA, and iSCSI (Internet SCSI). It has peripheral drivers for disks (da), cdrom (cd), tapes (sa), tape changers (ch), processor devices (pt), and enclosure services (ses). Additionally, there is the target emulator that allows a computer to emulate any of the supported devices and a pass-through interface that allows user applications to send I/O requests to any CAM-controlled peripheral. The operation of the CAM layer is described in Section 8.8.

The structure of the FreeBSD Disk I/O subsystem is shown in Figure 8.2. As the figure shows, disk drives may be attached to the system through many busses.

Fibre Channel was once the fastest and most expensive disk connection technology, employing fiberoptic or high-speed copper serial links. Such disk systems are usually used on large servers or when the data must travel farther than just within the case of the computer or to an adjacent rack. Its use is declining in favor of cheaper iSCSI and SAS.

The more common fast choice is a controller that plugs into the PCI-E bus, such as a SAS controller, which can typically support 8 to 16 devices directly attached, and hundred of devices attached via a switched network of bus expanders. SAS disks generally are faster and more reliable under heavy load than the more consumer-desktop-oriented SATA disks. SAS allows for transfer speeds

Figure 8.2 The structure of the FreeBSD disk I/O subsystem.

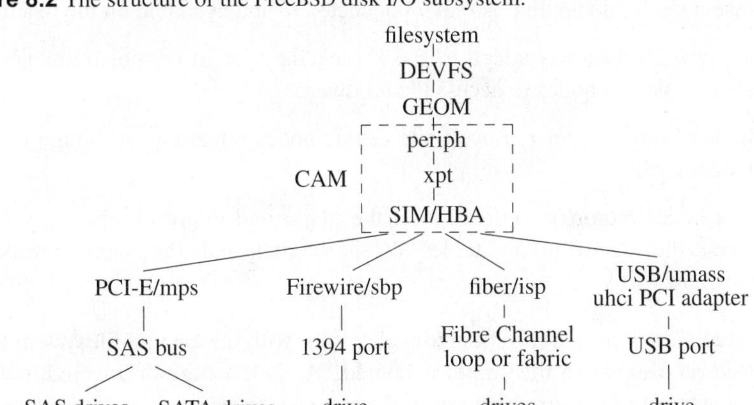

up to 1.2 Gbyte per second, twice the speed of the cheapest and most ubiquitous SATA disks.

Serial interface SATA disks may also be connected through the other busses available on the PC architecture. These include Firewire and USB. Usually, the disks are connected through an interface that acts as a bridge from the interface to a PCI bus. The USB and Firewire busses may also support other types of devices that will be directly connected to their device drivers rather than be managed by the CAM layer. The iSCSI interface is a way to connect disk drives and disk enclosures directly to a TCP/IP network. It provides many of the benefits of Fibre Channel but at a fraction of the cost.

Network device drivers provide another important piece of functionality within the kernel and are covered in Section 8.5.

Autoconfiguration is the procedure carried out by the system to recognize and enable the hardware devices present in a system. Historically, autoconfiguration was done just once when the system was booted. In current machines, particularly portable machines such as laptop computers, devices routinely come and go while the machine is operating. Thus, the kernel must be prepared to configure, initialize, and make available hardware when it arrives and to drop operations with hardware that has departed. FreeBSD uses a device-driver infrastructure called ***newbus*** to manage the devices on the system. Newbus builds a tree rooted at an abstract *root0* node and descends in a treelike structure down the various I/O paths and terminates at the various devices connected to the machine. On a uniprocessor system, the root0 node is synonymous with the CPU. On a multiprocessor system the root0 node is logically connected to each of the CPUs. Device autoconfiguration is described in Section 8.9, which gives the details of configuring devices when they appear and cleaning up after them when they disappear.

Device Naming and Access

Historically, FreeBSD used static device nodes located in **/dev** to provide access to the hardware devices on the system. This approach had several problems:

- The device nodes are persistent entities in the filesystem and do not necessarily represent the hardware that is really connected to and available on the machine.
- When new hardware is added to the kernel, the system administrator needs to create new device nodes to access the hardware.
- If the hardware is later removed, the device nodes remain even though they are no longer usable.
- Device nodes require coordination of the major and minor numbering schemes between the device-driver tables in the kernel and the shell scripts that create them.

FreeBSD 5 replaced the static **/dev** directory with the DEVFS filesystem that is mounted on **/dev** when the kernel is booted. As devices are discovered, either at boot or while the system is running, their names appear in the **/dev** filesystem.

When a device disappears or becomes unavailable, its entries in **/dev** disappear. DEVFS has several benefits over the old static **/dev** directory:

- Only devices that are currently available appear in **/dev**.
- Adding a device to the system causes its device nodes to appear in **/dev**, obviating the need for a system administrator to create new device nodes.
- It is no longer necessary to coordinate device major and minor numbers between the kernel and device-creation scripts or filesystem device nodes.

One benefit of the old static **/dev** was that device nodes could be given nonstandard names, access permissions, owners, or groups. To provide the same flexibility, DEVFS has a rule-set mechanism that allows these changes to be automated in the new **/dev** implementation. These rule sets can be put in place when the system is booted and can be created or modified at any time that the system is running. Each rule provides a pattern to identify the device nodes to be affected. For each matched device node, it specifies one or more actions that should be taken. Actions include creating a symbolic link to provide a nonstandard name as well as setting nonstandard permissions, owner, or group. The rule sets are checked and applied whenever a new device node is created or destroyed. They may also be checked and applied when explicitly requested to do so by the system administrator, either manually or through a system-initiated script.

Zero or more *dev_t* entries (major and minor numbers) in **/dev** may be created by the device drivers each time that a *device_t* is created as part of the autoconfiguration process. Most device drivers create a single **/dev** entry, but network device drivers do not create any entries, whereas disk devices may create dozens. Additional entries may appear in **/dev** as the result of cloning devices. For example, a cloning device such as a pseudo-terminal creates a new device each time that it is opened.

8.2 I/O Mapping from User to Device

Computers store and retrieve data through supporting peripheral I/O devices. These devices typically include mass-storage devices, such as disk drives, archival-storage devices, and network interfaces. Storage devices such as disks are accessed through I/O controllers that manage the operation of their attached devices according to I/O requests from the CPU.

Many hardware device peculiarities are hidden from the user by high-level kernel facilities, such as the filesystem and socket interfaces. Other such peculiarities are hidden from the bulk of the kernel itself by the I/O system. The I/O system consists of buffer-caching systems, general device-driver code, and drivers for specific hardware devices that must finally address peculiarities of the specific devices. An overview of the entire kernel is shown in Figure 7.1. The bottom third of the figure comprises the various I/O systems.

There are three main kinds of I/O in FreeBSD: the ***character-device*** interface, the ***filesystem***, and the ***socket*** interface with its related network devices. The character interface appears in the filesystem namespace and provides unstructured access to the underlying hardware. The network devices do not appear in the filesystem; they are accessible through the socket interface. Character devices are described in Section 8.3. The disk devices used by the filesystems are described in Section 8.4. The fast filesystem is described in Chapter 9; the Zettabyte filesystem (ZFS) is described in Chapter 10. The network devices used by the socket interface are described in Section 8.5. Sockets are described in Chapter 12.

A character-device interface comes in two styles that depend on the characteristics of the underlying hardware device. For some character-oriented hardware devices, such as terminal multiplexers, the interface is truly character oriented, although higher-level software, such as the terminal driver, may provide a line-oriented interface to applications. However, for block-oriented devices such as disks, a character-device interface is an *unstructured* or *raw* interface. For this interface, I/O operations do not go through the filesystem or the page cache; instead, they are made directly between the device and buffers in the application's virtual address space. Consequently, the size of the operations must be a multiple of the underlying ***block size*** required by the device and, on some machines, the application's I/O buffer must be aligned on a suitable boundary.

Internal to the system, I/O devices are accessed through a set of entry points provided by each device's ***device driver***. A character-device interface uses a *cdevsw* structure. A *cdevsw* structure is created for each device as the device is configured either at the time that the system is booted or later when the device is attached to the system.

All devices in the system are managed by the DEVFS filesystem. As devices are configured, entries are created for the device in the **/dev** filesystem. Each entry in the **/dev** filesystem has a direct reference to its corresponding *cdevsw* entry. When a program accesses a device directly by calling the *open*() system call with a path that terminates within the DEVFS filesystem, such as **/dev/cu**, the DEVFS filesystem searches for a matching entry in its internal list of devices and, if it finds a match, calls the the *open*() routine that is present in the device's *cdevsw*. When opened, most devices allocate new state to handle their new consumer. Devices that can only be opened by one user will return an error when a second user attempts to call *open*().

Device Drivers

A device driver is divided into three main sections:

1. Autoconfiguration and initialization routines
2. Routines for servicing I/O requests (the top half)
3. Interrupt service routines (the bottom half)

The autoconfiguration portion of a driver is responsible for ***probing*** for a hardware device to see whether the latter is present and to initialize the device and any associated software state that is required by the device driver. This portion of the driver is typically called only once, either when the system is initialized or, for transient devices, when they are connected to the system. Autoconfiguration is described in Section 8.9.

The section of a driver that services I/O requests is invoked because of system calls or by the virtual-memory system. This portion of the device driver executes synchronously in the top half of the kernel and is permitted to block by calling the *sleep*() routine. We commonly refer to this body of code as the ***top half*** of a device driver.

Interrupt service routines are invoked when the system fields an interrupt from a device. Consequently, these routines cannot depend on any per-process state. In FreeBSD, an interrupt has its own thread context, so it can block if it needs to do so. However, the cost of extra thread switches is sufficiently high that for good performance device drivers should attempt to avoid blocking. We commonly refer to a device driver's interrupt service routines as the ***bottom half*** of a device driver.

In addition to these three sections of a device driver, an optional ***crash-dump*** routine may be provided. This routine, if present, is invoked when the system recognizes an unrecoverable error and wishes to record the contents of physical memory for use in postmortem analysis. Most device drivers for disk controllers provide a crash-dump routine. The use of the crash-dump routine is described in Section 15.5.

I/O Queueing

Device drivers typically manage one or more queues of I/O requests in their normal operation. When an input or output request is received by the top half of the driver, it is recorded in a data structure that is placed on a per-device queue for processing. When an input or output operation completes, the device driver receives an interrupt from the controller. The interrupt service routine removes the appropriate request from the device's queue, notifies the requester that the command has completed, and then starts the next request from the queue. The I/O queues are the primary means of communication between the top and bottom halves of a device driver.

Because I/O queues are shared among asynchronous routines, access to the queues must be synchronized. Routines in both the top and bottom half of the device driver must acquire the mutex associated with the queue before manipulating it to avoid corruption from simultaneous modifications (mutexes are described in Section 4.3). For example, a bottom-half interrupt might try to remove an entry that had not yet been fully linked in by the top half. Synchronization among multiple processes starting I/O requests is also serialized through the mutex associated with the queue.

Interrupt Handling

Interrupts are generated by devices to signal that an operation has completed or that a change in status has occurred. On receiving a device interrupt, the system schedules the appropriate device-driver interrupt-service routine with one or more parameters that uniquely identify the device that requires service. These parameters are needed because device drivers typically support multiple devices of the same type. If the interrupting device's identity were not supplied with each interrupt, the driver would be forced to poll all the potential devices to identify the device that interrupted.

The system arranges for the unit-number parameter to be passed to the interrupt-service routine for each device by installing the address of an auxiliary glue routine in the interrupt-vector table. This glue routine, rather than the actual interrupt service routine, is invoked to service the interrupt; it takes the following actions:

1. Collects the relevant hardware parameters and places them in the space reserved for them by the device
2. Updates statistics on device interrupts
3. Schedules the interrupt service thread for the device
4. Clears the interrupt-pending flag in the hardware
5. Returns from the interrupt

Because a glue routine is interposed between the interrupt-vector table and the interrupt-service routine, special-purpose instructions, which cannot be generated from C, and which are needed by the hardware to support interrupts, can be kept out of the device driver. This interposition of a glue routine permits device drivers to be written without assembly language.

8.3 Character Devices

Almost all peripherals on the system, except network interfaces, have a character-device interface. A character device usually maps the hardware interface into a byte stream, similar to that of the filesystem. Character devices of this type include terminals (e.g., **/dev/ttyu0**), line printers (e.g, **/dev/lp0**), an interface to physical main memory (**/dev/mem**), and a bottomless sink for data and an endless source of end-of-file markers (**/dev/null**). Some of these character devices, such as terminal devices, may display special behavior on line boundaries but, in general, are still treated as byte streams.

Devices such as high-speed graphics interfaces may have their own buffers or may always do I/O directly into the address space of the user; they, too, are classed as character devices. Some of these drivers may recognize special types of records and thus be further from the plain byte-stream model.

The character interface for disks is also called the ***raw-device interface***; it provides an unstructured interface to the device. Its primary task is to arrange for direct I/O to and from the device. The disk driver handles the asynchronous nature of I/O by maintaining and ordering an active queue of pending transfers. Each entry in the queue specifies whether it is for reading or writing, the main-memory address for the transfer, the device address for the transfer (usually a disk sector number), and the transfer size (in bytes).

All other restrictions of the underlying hardware are passed through the character interface to its clients, making character-device interfaces the furthest from the byte-stream model. Thus, the user process must abide by the sectoring restrictions imposed by the underlying hardware. For magnetic disks, the file offset and transfer size must be a multiple of the sector size. The character interface does not copy the user data into a kernel buffer before putting them on an I/O queue. Instead, it arranges to have the I/O done directly to or from the address space of the process. The size and alignment of the transfer is limited by the physical device. However, the transfer size is not restricted by the maximum size of the internal buffers of the system because these buffers are not used.

The character interface is typically used by only those system-utility programs that have an intimate knowledge of the data structures on the disk. The character interface also allows user-level prototyping; for example, the 4.2BSD filesystem implementation was written and largely tested as a user process that used a raw disk interface before the code was moved into the kernel.

Character devices are described by entries in the *cdevsw* structure. The entry points in this structure (see Table 8.1) are used to support raw access to block-oriented devices such as disks, as well as normal access to character-oriented devices through the terminal driver. Raw devices support a subset of the entry points that correspond to those entry points found in block-oriented devices. The base set of entry points for all device drivers is described in this section; the additional set of entry points for block-oriented devices is given in Section 8.4.

Table 8.1 Entry points for character and raw device drivers.

Entry point	Function
open()	open the device
close()	close the device
read()	do an input operation
write()	do an output operation
ioctl()	do an I/O control operation
poll()	poll device for I/O readiness
stop()	stop output on the device
mmap()	map device offset to memory location
reset()	reinitialize device after a bus reset

Raw Devices and Physical I/O

Most raw devices differ from filesystems only in the way that they do I/O. Whereas filesystems read and write data to and from kernel buffers, raw devices transfer data to and from user buffers. Bypassing kernel buffers eliminates the memory-to-memory copy that must be done by filesystems but also denies applications the benefits of data caching. In addition, for devices that support both raw and filesystem access, applications must take care to preserve consistency between data in the kernel buffers and data written directly to the device. The raw device should be used only when the filesystem is unmounted or mounted read-only. Raw-device access is used by many filesystem utilities such as the filesystem check program, **fsck**, and by programs that read and write backup media such as **dump**.

Because raw devices bypass kernel buffers, they are responsible for managing their own buffer structures. Most devices borrow swap buffers to describe their I/O. The read and write routines use the *physio*() routine to start a raw I/O operation (see Figure 8.3). The *strategy* parameter identifies a block-device strategy

Figure 8.3 Algorithm for physical I/O.

```
void physio(
    device dev,
    struct uio *uio,
    int ioflag);
{
    allocate a swap buffer;
    while (uio is not exhausted) {
        mark the buffer busy for physical I/O;
        set up the buffer for a maximum-size transfer;
        use device maximum I/O size to bound
            the transfer size;
        check user read/write access at uio location;
        lock the part of the user address space
            involved in the transfer into RAM;
        map the user pages into the buffer;
        call dev->strategy() to start the transfer;
        wait for the transfer to complete;
        unmap the user pages from the buffer;
        unlock the part of the address space previously
            locked;
        deduct the transfer size from the total number
            of data to transfer;
    }
    free swap buffer;
}
```

routine that starts I/O operations on the device. The buffer is used by *physio*() in constructing the request(s) made to the strategy routine. The device, read–write flag, and *uio* parameters completely specify the I/O operation that should be done. The maximum transfer size for the device is checked by *physio*() to adjust the size of each I/O transfer before the latter is passed to the strategy routine. This check allows the transfer to be done in sections according to the maximum transfer size supported by the device.

Raw-device I/O operations request the hardware device to transfer data directly to or from the data buffer in the user program's address space described by the *uio* parameter. Thus, unlike I/O operations that perform direct memory access (DMA) from buffers in the kernel address space, raw I/O operations must check that the user's buffer is accessible by the device and must lock it into memory for the duration of the transfer.

Character-Oriented Devices

Character-oriented I/O devices are typified by terminal ports, although they also include printers and other character- or line-oriented devices. These devices are usually accessed through the terminal driver, described in Section 8.6. The close tie to the terminal driver has heavily influenced the structure of character device drivers. For example, several entry points in the *cdevsw* structure exist for communication between the generic terminal handler and the terminal-multiplexer hardware drivers.

Entry Points for Character Device Drivers

A device driver for a character device is defined by its entries in a *cdevsw* structure:

open Opens the device in preparation for I/O operations. A device's open entry point will be called for each *open* system call on a special-device file or, internally, when a device is prepared for mounting a filesystem with the *mount* system call. The *open*() routine will commonly verify the integrity of the associated medium. For example, it will verify that the device was identified during the autoconfiguration phase and, for disk drives, that a medium is present and ready to accept commands.

close Closes a device. The *close*() routine is called after the final client interested in using the device terminates. These semantics are defined by the higher-level I/O facilities. Disk devices have nothing to do when a device is closed and thus use a null *close*() routine. Devices that support access to only a single client must mark the device as available once again.

read Reads data from a device. For raw devices, this entry point normally just calls the *physio*() routine with device-specific parameters. For terminal-oriented devices, a read request is passed immediately to the terminal driver. For other devices, a read request requires that the specified data be copied into the kernel's address space, typically with the *uiomove*() routine (see the end of Section 7.1), and then be passed to the device.

write Writes data to a device. This entry point is a direct parallel of the read entry point: raw devices use *physio*(), terminal-oriented devices call the terminal driver to do this operation, and other devices handle the request internally.

ioctl Performs an operation other than a read or write. This entry point originally provided a mechanism to get and set device parameters for terminal devices; its use has expanded to other types of devices as well. Historically, *ioctl* operations have varied widely from device to device.

poll Checks the device to see whether data are available for reading or space is available for writing data. The poll entry point is used by the *select* and *poll* system calls in checking file descriptors associated with device special files. For raw devices, a poll operation is meaningless since data are not buffered. Here, the entry point is set to *seltrue*(), a routine that returns true for any poll request.

mmap Maps a device offset into a memory address. This entry point is called by the virtual-memory system to convert a logical mapping to a physical address. For example, it converts an offset in **/dev/mem** to a kernel address.

kqfilter Adds the device to the kernel event list for the calling thread. Kernel events are described in Section 7.1.

8.4 Disk Devices

Disk devices fill a central role in the UNIX kernel and thus have additional features and capabilities beyond those of the typical character device driver. Historically, UNIX provided two interfaces to disks. The first was a character-device interface that provided direct access to the disk in its raw form. This interface is still available in FreeBSD and is described in Section 8.3. The second was a block-device interface that converted from the user abstraction of a disk as an array of bytes to the structure imposed by the underlying physical medium. Block devices were accessible directly through appropriate device special files. Block devices were eliminated in FreeBSD 5 because they were not needed by any common applications and added considerable complexity to the kernel.

Entry Points for Disk Device Drivers

Device drivers for disk devices contain all the usual character device entry points described in Section 8.3. In addition to those entry points there are two entry points that are used only for disk devices:

strategy Starts a read or write operation, and return immediately. I/O requests to or from filesystems located on a device are translated by the system into calls to the block I/O routines *bread*() and *bwrite*(). These block I/O routines in turn call the device's strategy routine to read or write data not in the memory cache. Each call to the strategy routine specifies a pointer to a *buf* structure containing the parameters for an I/O request. If the request is synchronous, the caller must sleep (on the address of the *buf* structure) until I/O completes.

dump If performing a dump has been configured during system startup, writes all physical memory to the configured device. Typically, the dump entry point saves the contents of physical memory on secondary storage into an area used for swapping. To speed the dump and to save space, the system can be configured to perform a mini-dump that writes only the physical memory in use by the kernel. The system automatically performs a dump when it detects an unrecoverable error and is about to ***crash***. The dump is used in postmortem analysis to help find the problem that caused the system to crash. The dump routine is invoked with context switching and interrupts disabled; thus, the device driver must poll for device status rather than wait for interrupts. At least one disk device is expected to support this entry point.

Sorting of Disk I/O Requests

The kernel provides a generic *disksort*() routine that can be used by all the disk device drivers to sort I/O requests into a drive's request queue using an ***elevator sorting algorithm***. This algorithm sorts requests in a cyclic, ascending, block order, so that requests can be serviced with minimal one-way scans over the drive. This ordering was originally designed to support the normal read-ahead requested by the filesystem and also to counteract the filesystem's random placement of data on a drive. With the improved placement algorithms in the current filesystem, the effect of the *disksort*() routine is less noticeable; *disksort*() produces the largest effect when there are multiple simultaneous users of a drive.

The *disksort*() algorithm is shown in Figure 8.4. A drive's request queue is made up of two lists of requests ordered by block number. The first is the active list; the second is the next-pass list. The request at the front of the active list shows the current position of the drive. If the next-pass list is not empty, it is made up of requests that lie before the current position. Each new request is sorted into either the active or the next-pass list, according to the request's location. When the heads reach the end of the active list, the next-pass list becomes the active list, an empty next-pass list is created, and the drive begins servicing the new active list.

Disk sorting can also be important on machines that have a fast processor and do not sort requests within the device driver. Here, if a write of several Mbyte is honored in order of queueing, it can block other processes from accessing the disk

```
void disksort(
    drive queue *dq,
    buffer *bp);
{
    if (active list is empty) {
        place the buffer at the front of the active list;
        return;
    }
    if (request lies before the first active request) {
        locate the beginning of the next-pass list;
        sort bp into the next-pass list;
    } else
        sort bp into the active list;
}
```

Figure 8.4 Algorithm for *disksort*().

while it completes. Sorting requests provides some scheduling, which more fairly distributes accesses to the disk controller.

Most modern disk controllers accept several concurrent I/O requests. The controller then sorts these requests to minimize the time needed to service them. If the controller could always manage all outstanding I/O requests, then there would be no need to have the kernel do any sorting. However, most controllers can handle only about 15 outstanding requests. Since a busy system can easily generate bursts of activity that exceed the number that the disk controller can manage simultaneously, disk sorting by the kernel is still necessary.

Disk Labels

A disk may be broken up into several partitions, each of which may be used for a separate filesystem or swap area. A disk label contains information about the partition layout and usage including type of filesystem, swap partition, or unused. For the fast filesystem, the partition usage contains enough additional information to enable the filesystem check program (**fsck**) to locate the alternate superblocks for the filesystem. The disk label also contains any other driver-specific information.

Having labels on each disk means that partition information can be different for each disk and that it carries over when the disk is moved from one system to another. It also means that, when previously unknown types of disks are connected to the system, the system administrator can use them without changing the disk driver, recompiling, and rebooting the system.

The label is located near the beginning of each drive—usually, in block zero. It must be located near the beginning of the disk to enable it to be used in the first-level bootstrap. Most architectures have hardware (or first-level) bootstrap code stored in read-only memory (ROM). When the machine is powered up or the reset button is pressed, the CPU executes the hardware bootstrap code from the ROM. The hardware bootstrap code typically reads the first few sectors on the disk into the main memory, then branches to the address of the first location that it read. The program stored in these first few sectors is the second-level bootstrap. Having the disk label stored in the part of the disk read as part of the hardware bootstrap allows the second-level bootstrap to have the disk-label information. This information gives it the ability to find the root filesystem and hence the files, such as the kernel, needed to bring up FreeBSD. The size and location of the second-level bootstrap are dependent on the requirements of the hardware bootstrap code. Since there is no standard for disk-label formats and the hardware bootstrap code usually understands only the vendor label, it is usually necessary to support both the vendor and the FreeBSD disk labels. Here, the vendor label must be placed where the hardware bootstrap ROM code expects it; the FreeBSD label must be placed out of the way of the vendor label but within the area that is read in by the hardware bootstrap code so that it will be available to the second-level bootstrap.

For example, on the PC architecture, the BIOS expects sector 0 of the disk to contain boot code, a slice table commonly referred to as the Master Boot Record (MBR), and a ***magic number***. MBR slices can be used to break the disk up into several pieces. The BIOS brings in sector 0 and verifies the magic number. The sector 0 boot code then searches the MBR table to determine which slice is marked active. This boot code then brings in the operating-system-specific bootstrap from the active slice and, if marked bootable, runs it. This operating-system specific bootstrap includes the disk label described above and the code to interpret it.

The MBR is limited to 32-bit block numbers providing access to only the first 2 Tbyte of the disk, thus leaving the remainder hidden from the MBR and tricky to use. The MBR is also limited to a maximum of four partitions on the disk. The replacement for the MBR for the PC architecture is the globally unique identifier partition table (GPT) label that has 64-bit block numbers providing access to 8 zettabyte. It also permits up to 128 partitions on the disk.

Booting a disk with a GPT label requires an Extended Firmware Interface (EFI) BIOS. To allow use of GPT labels on legacy systems without the EFI BIOS, FreeBSD supports a hybrid mode that contains a compatibility MBR at sector 0 of the disk, and a GPT label at sector 1. This configuration allows a legacy BIOS to boot the disk via the MBR label. The MBR label references a boot-loader program that understands the GPT label and can continue the boot process using the GPT information. Even if the disk is larger than 2 Tbyte, the boot chain is contained at the front of the disk and is safe from the limits of the MBR. Another advantage of the GPT label is that its expanded support for partitions makes the BSD disk label redundant. Thus, FreeBSD systems partitioned with GPT will typically not have a BSD disk label.

8.5 Network Devices

All the networking protocols and facilities of FreeBSD ultimately rest atop some form of networking device driver. A networking device driver is responsible for taking network data as packets and transmitting or receiving them on some underlying physical media. The most common type of network driver in the FreeBSD kernel works with Ethernet hardware [Xerox, 1980]. Unlike most other devices in the kernel, network devices are completely asynchronous. They receive data whenever it happens to arrive and send data without waiting for any type of acknowledgment. It is the responsibility of the socket API described in Chapter 12, and the network protocols described in Chapters 13 and 14 to present a more easily understood model. The socket API presents applications with a sequenced byte stream and looks more like reading or writing a local file.

Entry Points for Network Drivers

All network devices are described by a data structure called an *ifnet* that encapsulates the running state of the device and exposes most of the functions that the kernel uses to interact with the underlying hardware. The functions defined for a network device driver are shown in Table 8.2. Two functions that are not included in the *ifnet* structure that are essential to the proper functioning of a network device are the driver's *attach* and *detach* routines. Whether a network device is discovered at system boot time or dynamically during run time, the first function that must be called is the driver's *attach* routine. The *attach* routine is responsible for talking directly to the hardware to set up hardware registers and allocate resources for use by the driver. The *attach* routine also fills in the methods of the *ifnet* structure with the correct functions for working with the device and thereby hooks the device into the rest of the networking subsystems so that network protocols and

Table 8.2 Functions defined for network drivers.

Function	Description
if_init	initialize the underlying device
if_ioctl	configure and control the device
if_output	send a packet
if_start	start the device's transmit hardware
if_transmit	start output
if_qflush	flush underlying queues
if_input	called asynchronously on packet reception
if_reassign	reassign to a virtual network instance
if_resolvemulti	resolve a multicast address

facilities can use the hardware. The driver's *detach* routine is called when a device is turned off or otherwise removed from the system and is responsible for freeing the resources and destroying the associations created by the *attach* routine.

Configuration and Control

All network device drivers expose a single routine to the kernel that configures and controls the underlying device. A generic I/O control routine or *ioctl* is stored in the driver's *ifnet* structure when the device driver is first loaded into the kernel. The driver's *ioctl* routine is responsible for enabling, disabling, and resetting the device. It also turns special device-specific features on and off at runtime. Each message that can be sent to the device driver is encoded as a macro and is checked via a switch statement in the driver's *ioctl* routine. Table 8.3 lists the most commonly implemented control messages. Each message is encoded as a socket *ioctl* and most have both a set and a get form. The set form, shown here, has an S in the message name, as in SIOCSIFFLAGS. The get form replaces the S with a G so that SIOCGIFFLAGS retrieves the current set of flags from the device. User programs and networking subsystems call the driver's *ioctl* routine using a generic function provided for this purpose. Only the kernel calls the driver-specific *ioctl* routine directly. The messages that handle multicast addresses, which are maintained in a device-specific data structure, use ADD and DEL instead of get and set.

The details of many of the features controlled by the driver's *ioctl* routine are device specific, but their meaning to the kernel is generic enough for us to describe them in general. Each networking device in the system can be in one of two states, either UP or DOWN. The state of the device does not reflect whether it is turned on or initialized, but whether it will receive or transmit packets. A device may be fully initialized and yet not be up. The up and down state of a device is an administrative control that can be set any time during the life of the kernel, so long as the device's hardware has been properly initialized. The SIOCIFFLAGS message is responsible for setting the device's administrative state as well as a few

Table 8.3 Network driver control messages.

Message	Description
SIOCSIFADDR	set network address on interface
SIOCSIFFLAGS	set interface flags
SIOCADDMULTI	add a multicast address to the device's list
SIOCDELMULTI	delete a multicast address from the device's list
SIOCSIFMTU	set the interface's maximum transfer unit
SIOCSIFMEDIA	set media-specific features for the device
SIOCSIFCAP	set capabilities on the device

other features. These features include promiscuous mode, where a device can receive all the packets that pass by it on the network, rather than just the packets that it knows are bound for it. Each device knows which packets are meant for it because the device's network layer address is set via the SIOCSIFADDR message. Many network devices can support different native sizes of packets called the ***maximum transmission unit*** (*MTU*). For Ethernet, the standard is still 1500 bytes but often can be increased to 9000, 16,384, or 64 Kbyte. The device's native packet size is controlled via the SIOCSIFMTU message. The last two messages in the table control different device-specific features. Earlier network devices could only communicate at a single speed and over a single low-level medium such as coaxial cable. Modern devices can often operate at various speeds from 10 Mbit per second up through one or 10 Gbit. Most devices will automatically set themselves up to communicate at their top speed, but it is possible to change the speed of the device by using the SIOCSIFMEDIA *ioctl*. Features unrelated to the medium on which the network is built, such as support for Virtual LANs (VLANs) and various types of hardware offloading, where the device takes over part of the work normally done by the kernel's networking software, are called ***capabilities*** and are controlled through the SIOCSIFCAP *ioctl*.

Packet Reception

Network data can appear at any time on a network device; there is no need for an application to have made any sort of request. The data arriving on the device might be a request for a service that the system is providing, such as a Web or domain name server. When data arrive at a network device, they are held in memory buffers within the network device until the kernel transfers them into its own buffers. The device's memory buffers are often maintained as a ring as shown in

Figure 8.5 Packet ring. Owner key: D—owned by the device; K—owned by the kernel.

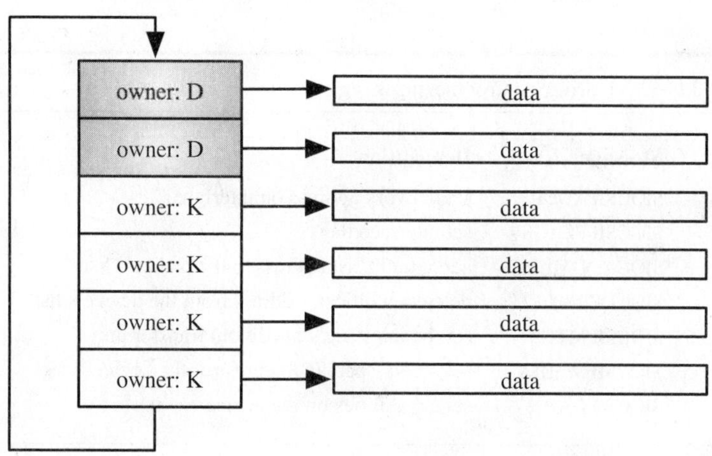

Figure 8.5. The underlying hardware places data in the ring via DMA and the kernel empties the ring in response to some form of interrupt. Using a ring as the shared data structure between the kernel and the device provides a buffer between the lower-level hardware and the kernel executing on the CPU. The ring makes it easier to do work in batches, decreasing the overhead incurred by the kernel when it retrieves data from the device. Whenever data is received by the network device, it interrupts the kernel, asking it to retrieve the data that has been received. Storing the data in a ring allows the device to continue to receive data while the kernel is simultaneously retrieving data from the ring. If there is more than one packet present in the receive ring when the kernel services the device interrupt, it can retrieve the data in batches, reducing the number of expensive interrupts that need to be processed.

A receive ring is made up of receive descriptors, each of which contains a pointer to some memory where the received data resides as well as an ownership bit that describes its validity. In Figure 8.5, "D" marks buffers owned by the device and "K" marks buffers owned by the kernel. Specifically, a "K" ownership bit tells the kernel it can read the data out of the memory associated with the receive descriptor. When the device receives data, it places it into the memory of the next descriptor that it owns. When the data has all been moved, the device changes the setting of the ownership bit to "K" to show that the data is now owned by the kernel. The device can continue to place data in the ring without the aid of the kernel until the ring is full, that is, all descriptors are owned by the kernel. When data is delivered into the receive ring, the device will trigger some form of interrupt, signalling the kernel to retrieve the data. The kernel will then read as many packets as are available in the ring up to some pre-set maximum. It will pass them into the networking subsystems through whatever function pointer the driver's *attach* routine placed into the *if_input* entry in the driver's *ifnet* structure. Often, the *if_input* routine is associated with the type of hardware that the device is supporting such as Ethernet or Wireless. The kernel returns the descriptors to the device by setting the ownership bit back to "D" once it has copied the data into its own buffers.

The ring structure is used to buffer the packets between the device and the kernel. A kernel running on a processor that is faster than the underlying network hardware will be able to keep the ring nearly empty as it should be able to keep up with the underlying hardware. On a system with high-speed networking hardware, such as a 10-Gbit Ethernet (Nm 10GbE), the adapter ring makes it possible for the underlying device to absorb periodic bursts of packets and then have the kernel read each burst of packets in a single batch.

Packet Transmission

Every *ifnet* structure contains a queue of data to be transmitted called the interface queue. Whenever some part of the kernel wants to transmit data on a network device, it enqueues the data on the device's interface queue and then calls the *if_start*() routine stored in the device's *ifnet* structure. The pointer to the *if_start*() routine was placed in the driver's *ifnet* structure by the *attach*() routine when the device was first initialized.

Packet transmission is similar to packet reception in that the kernel and the device again share a ring data structure called the transmit ring. The transmit ring acts as a buffer between the kernel and the device into which the kernel writes data and from which the device reads it and transmits it on the underlying hardware. A transmit ring is made up of transmit descriptors that are nearly identical to receive descriptors. They contain a pointer to memory and an ownership bit. The only differences between receive and transmit descriptors pertain to statistics and special device features such as packet timestamping and checksum offloading. During transmission, the roles of the kernel and the device are reversed, with the kernel writing data into the transmit ring, changing the state of the ownership bit, and then telling the device that there is data in the ring to be sent. The driver's *if_start*() routine removes the data from the interface queue and places it into the transmit ring.

8.6 Terminal Handling

Before the advent of bitmapped displays and Web browsers, most users of UNIX systems interacted with the computer through some type of terminal. Terminals were either line-oriented teletypes, which meant that the user could only make changes to a single line of text before submitting it to the system, or they were screen based, with the most commonly available terminals providing a screen 80 characters wide by 24 lines high. The plethora of different terminals that could be hooked to a UNIX system meant that the parts of the kernel that handled interactions with terminals eventually grew to be complex. Users of modern UNIX systems interact with terminals less than their predecessors but programmers and systems administrators continue to use some form of terminal-based command-line interface to have effective and direct control over the system. Terminals also provide the most efficient and low-overhead method of controlling a system. Bitmapped displays and Web servers require far more resources from the system than does a simple terminal. In common FreeBSD-embedded and purpose-built systems such as routers, switches, and storage systems, the ability to interact with the system via a terminal is a requirement, whereas a Web interface communicating to a Web server is considered a luxury.

The terminal handling facilities in FreeBSD incorporate three separate subsystems: the tty driver, serial-device drivers, and the pseudo-terminal driver. The most common type of user session in FreeBSD uses a ***pseudo-terminal***, provided by the *pts* driver. The pseudo-terminal driver provides support for a device pair, termed the master and slave devices. The slave device provides a process with an interface identical to the one described for terminals in this section. Anything written on the master device is provided to the slave device as input, and anything written on the slave device is presented to the master device as input. The driver for the master device emulates all hardware-support details described in the rest of this section.

Pseudo-terminals are used by **xterm**, as well as the remote-login program **ssh**. In a typical use, **xterm** opens the master side of a pseudo-terminal and directs the keystrokes from the window manager to its input while taking its output and drawing the characters in its window. It forks a process that opens the slave side of the pseudo-terminal and then runs the user's preferred shell with the slave set up as the standard input, output, and error. As each keystroke is typed by the user, it is written into the master side of the pseudo-terminal, where it is processed by the ***line discipline*** and eventually emerges as input to the user's shell. Output from the shell is written into the slave side of the pseudo-terminal, where it is processed by the line discipline and eventually emerges from the master side and is displayed in the **xterm** window. Each pseudo-terminal opened by the system appears in the **/dev/pts** directory of the DEVFS filesystem.

The pseudo-terminal driver commonly processes data one character at a time using the character-device interface described in the user-interface subsection later in this section. As each character is typed at the keyboard or arrives from a user over the network, it is presented as input to the master side of the pseudo-terminal. The input of characters is independent of process requests to read user input from the slave side of the pseudo-terminal. Characters are processed when they are received and are stored until a process requests them, thus allowing ***type-ahead***. When a pseudo-terminal supports user interaction with the system, terminal input represents the keystrokes of the user, and terminal output is displayed on the user's screen. When we use the term *terminal*, we are describing a concept that applies to both pseudo-terminals and hardwired terminal devices.

Terminal-Processing Modes

FreeBSD supports several modes of terminal processing. Much of the time, keyboard input is in ***canonical mode*** (also commonly referred to as ***cooked mode*** or ***line mode***), in which input characters are echoed by the operating system as they are typed by the user but are buffered internally until a newline character is received. Only after the receipt of a newline character is the entire line made available to the shell or other process reading from the keyboard. If the process attempts to read from the keyboard before a complete line is ready, the process will sleep until a newline character is received, regardless of a partial line already having been received. The common case where a carriage return behaves like a newline character and causes the line to be made available to the waiting process is implemented by the operating system and is configurable by the user or process. In canonical mode, the user may correct typing errors, deleting the most recently typed character with the ***erase character***, deleting the most recent word with the ***word-erase character***, or deleting the entire current line with the ***kill character***. Other special characters generate signals sent to processes associated with the keyboard; these signals may abort processing or may suspend it. Additional characters start and stop output, flush output, or prevent special interpretation of the succeeding character. The user can type several lines of input, up to an implementation-defined limit, without waiting for input to be read and removed from the input queue. The user can specify the special processing characters or can selectively disable them.

Editors and programs that communicate with other computers generally run in ***noncanonical mode*** (also commonly referred to as ***raw mode*** or ***character-at-a-time mode***). In this mode, the system makes each typed character available to be read as input as soon as that character is received. All special-character input processing is disabled, no erase or other line-editing processing is done, and all characters are passed to the program reading from the keyboard.

In addition to processing input characters, the terminal interface must do certain processing on output. Most of the time, this processing is simple: newline characters are converted to a carriage return plus a line feed. In addition to performing character processing, the terminal output routines must manage flow control, both with the user (using stop and start characters) and with the process. Because users absorb output slowly in comparison with computer peripherals, a program writing to a terminal may produce output much faster than that output can be handled by the user. When a process has filled the terminal output queue, it will be put to sleep and will be restarted when enough output has drained.

Most of the character processing done for terminal interfaces is independent of whether it is associated with a pseudo-terminal or a real hardware device. Therefore, most of this processing is done by common routines in the *tty driver*, or terminal handler. A hardware interface is supported by a specific device driver, which is responsible for receiving and transmitting characters and for handling some of the synchronization with the process doing output. The hardware driver is called by the tty driver to do output; in turn, it calls the tty driver with input characters as they are received. The pseudo-terminal interface acts as a software emulation of an asynchronous serial interface, making it indistinguishable from real hardware to the rest of the kernel.

Earlier versions of FreeBSD implemented a flexible abstraction for the handling of terminal lines, called a line discipline. The line discipline was implemented as a set of routines that were called through a structure of function pointers, allowing the line discipline to be specialized for different types of devices. After hardware-based terminals became obsolete, there was no longer a need to have a flexible line-discipline system, since the only terminals that remain are virtual (i.e., xterm) and they all share a common control language. The integration of the new terminal layer in FreeBSD 8 removed all but the original terminal line discipline that handles interactive character processing. To maintain internal-interface compatibility, the line discipline routines remain and are called from within the tty driver and the various serial device drivers that are a part of FreeBSD.

The terminal line-discipline routines translate between the lower-layer hardware devices and the abstract implementation of the terminal. The main functions provided by the line discipline are listed in Table 8.4. Like all device drivers, a terminal driver is divided into the top half, which runs synchronously when called to process a system call, and the bottom half, which runs asynchronously when characters are presented to it from a pseudo-terminal or hardware device. The line discipline provides routines that perform common terminal processing for both the top and bottom halves of a terminal driver.

Table 8.4 Entry points for the TTY line discipline.

Routine	Usage
ttydisc_open	initial entry to discipline
ttydisc_close	exit from discipline
ttydisc_read	read from line
ttydisc_write	write to line
ttydisc_ioctl	control operations
ttydisc_rint	received character
ttydisc_getc	get character to output
ttydisc_modem	modem carrier transition

All the devices that can be placed beneath the tty device support the normal set of character device-driver entry points specified by the character-device switch. When a new serial device is attached to the system, it calls the *tty_alloc*() routine to hook a new *ttydevsw* structure into the system. Several of the system calls (*read*, *write*, and *ioctl*) immediately transfer control to the line discipline when called. The standard terminal-polling routine *ttypoll*() usually is used as the device driver *poll* entry in the character-device switch. The *open* and *close* routines are similar; the line-discipline open entry is called when a line first enters a discipline. Similarly, the discipline *close*() routine is called to exit from a discipline. All these routines are called from above in response to a corresponding system call.

The remaining line-discipline entries are called by the bottom half of the device driver to report input or status changes detected at interrupt time. The *ttydisc_rint* (receiver interrupt) entry is called with each character received on a line. The corresponding entry for outputting characters is the *ttydisc_getc* routine, which is called by the output routine to fetch characters from the line discipline to output. Transitions in modem-control lines may be detected by the hardware driver. Here, the *ttydisc_modem* routine is called passing the new state.

User Interface

The terminal line discipline is derived from a discipline that was present in System V, as modified by the POSIX standard, and then was modified further to provide reasonable compatibility with previous 4.2BSD line disciplines. The base structure used to describe terminal state in System V was the termio structure. The base structure used by POSIX and by FreeBSD is the ***termios structure***.

The standard programmatic interface for control of the terminal line discipline is the *ioctl* system call. This call sets and gets values for special processing characters and modes, sets and gets hardware serial line parameters, and performs other control operations. Most *ioctl* operations require one argument in addition to a file descriptor and the command; the argument is the address of an integer or structure from which the system gets parameters or into which information is placed. Because the POSIX Working Group thought that the *ioctl* system call was difficult and undesirable to specify—because of its use of arguments that varied in size, in type, and in whether they were being read or written—the group members chose to introduce new interfaces for each of the *ioctl* calls that they believed were necessary for application portability. Each of these calls is named with a *tc* prefix. In the FreeBSD system, each of these calls is translated (possibly after preprocessing) into an *ioctl* call.

The following set of *ioctl* commands apply specifically to the standard terminal line discipline. This list is not exhaustive, although it presents all the commands that are used commonly.

TIOCGETA TIOCSETA	Gets (sets) the termios parameters for this line, including line speed, behavioral parameters, and special characters such as erase and kill characters.
TIOCSETAW	Sets the termios parameters for this line after waiting for the output buffer to drain (but without discarding any characters from the input buffer).
TIOCSETAF	Sets the termios parameters for this line after waiting for the output buffer to drain and discarding any characters from the input buffer.
TIOCFLUSH	Discards all characters from the input and output buffers.
TIOCDRAIN	Waits for the output buffer to drain.
TIOCEXCL TIOCNXCL	Gets (releases) exclusive use of the line.
TIOCCBRK TIOCSBRK	Clears (sets) the terminal hardware BREAK condition for the line.
TIOCGPGRP TIOCSPGRP	Gets (sets) the process group associated with this terminal (see the next subsection).
TIOCOUTQ	Returns the number of characters in the terminal's output buffer.
TIOCSTI	Enters characters into the terminal's input buffer as though they were typed by the user.
TIOCNOTTY	Disassociates the current controlling terminal from the process (see the next subsection).
TIOCSCTTY	Makes the terminal the controlling terminal for the process (see the next subsection).
TIOCSTART TIOCSTOP	Starts (stops) output on the terminal.

TIOCGWINSZ TIOCSWINSZ	Gets (sets) the terminal or window size for the terminal line; the window size includes width and height in characters and (optionally, on graphical displays) in pixels.

Process Groups, Sessions, and Terminal Control

The process-control (job-control) facilities, described in Section 4.8, depend on the terminal I/O system to control access to the terminal. Each job (a process group that is manipulated as a single entity) is known by a process-group ID.

Each terminal structure contains a pointer to an associated session. When a process creates a new session, that session has no associated terminal. To acquire an associated terminal, the session leader must make an *ioctl* system call using a file descriptor associated with the terminal and specifying the TIOCSCTTY flag. When the *ioctl* succeeds, the session leader is known as the ***controlling process***. In addition, each terminal structure contains the process group ID of the foreground process group. When a session leader acquires an associated terminal, the terminal process group is set to the process group of the session leader. The terminal process group may be changed by making an *ioctl* system call using a file descriptor associated with the terminal and specifying the TIOCSPGRP flag. Any process group in the session is permitted to become the foreground process group for the terminal.

Signals that are generated by characters typed at the terminal are sent to all the processes in the terminal's foreground process group. By default, some of those signals cause the process group to stop. The shell creates jobs as process groups, setting the process group ID to be the PID of the first process in the process group. Each time it places a new job in the foreground, the shell sets the terminal process group to the new process group. Thus, the terminal process group is the identifier for the process group that is currently in control of the terminal—that is, for the process group running in the *foreground*. Other process groups may run in the *background*. If a background process attempts to read from the terminal, its process group is sent another signal, which stops the process group. Optionally, background processes that attempt terminal output may be stopped as well. These rules for control of input and output operations apply to only those operations on the controlling terminal.

When a user disconnects from a terminal—for example, when a network connection is lost—the session leader of the session associated with the terminal is sent a SIGHUP signal. If the session leader exits, the controlling terminal is revoked, and that invalidates any open file descriptors in the system for the terminal. This revocation ensures that processes holding file descriptors for a terminal cannot access the terminal after the terminal is acquired by another user. The revocation operates at the vnode layer. It is possible for a process to have a read or write sleeping for some reason—for example, it was in a background process group. Since such a process would have already resolved the file descriptor through the vnode layer, a single read or write by the sleeping process could complete after the *revoke* system call. To avoid this security problem, the system checks a terminal generation number when a process wakes up from sleeping on a terminal and, if the number has changed, restarts the read or write system call.

Terminal Operations

We now examine the operation of the pseudo-terminal device driver. Each time that the master side of a previously unused pseudo-terminal device is opened, by using the *sys_posix_openpt*() routine, the pseudo-terminal driver's alloc routine is called. The alloc routine initializes the *tty* structure, associating the set of function pointers that are part of the pts driver's *ttydevsw* structure with the underlying terminal device. Once the pseudo-terminal has been allocated, all other operations proceed through the device filesystem, where the terminal device driver's routines are called. The *ttydev_open*() routine is called to open the device that backs the pseudo-terminal, and it is the open routine that sets up the line discipline by calling the *ttydisc_open*() routine. The tty driver is sufficiently abstract that it can handle devices that are implemented in hardware as well as the pseudo-terminal, which is implemented purely in software.

Terminal Output (Upper Half)

After a terminal has been opened, a write on the resulting file descriptor produces output to be transmitted. Writes to the pseudo-terminal result in calls to the *ptsdev_write*() routine with a file pointer, a *uio* structure describing the data to be written, and a flag specifying whether the I/O is nonblocking. The tty structure is contained in the file structure passed into the write routine. The line discipline routines are called directly from the *ptsdev_write*() routine to send the data.

The main routine that handles the output of characters is the *ttydev_write*() routine. It is responsible for copying data into the kernel from the user process and for placing the translated data onto the pseudo-terminal's output queue. The *ttydev_write*() routine first checks whether the current process is allowed to write to the terminal at this time. The user may set a *tty* option to allow only the foreground process to do output. If this option is set, and if the terminal line is the controlling terminal for the process, then the process should do output immediately only if it is in the foreground process group (i.e., if the process groups of the process and of the terminal are the same). If the process is not in the foreground process group, and a SIGTTOU signal would cause the process to be suspended, a SIGTTOU signal is sent to the process group of the process. Here, the write will be attempted again when the user moves the process group to the foreground. If the process is in the foreground process group, or a SIGTTOU signal would not suspend the process, the write proceeds as usual.

When *ttydev_write*() has confirmed that the write is permitted, it enters a loop that copies the data to be written into the kernel, checks for any output translation that is required, and places the data on the output queue for the terminal. It prevents the queue from becoming overfull by blocking if the queue fills before all characters have been processed. The limit on the queue size, the ***high watermark***, is dependent on the output line speed; for pseudo-terminals, the line speed is set to the maximum baud rate so that they will get the maximum high watermark of several thousand characters. The ***low watermark*** is set to about half of the high watermark. When forced to wait for output to drain before proceeding, *ttydisc_write*() sets a flag in the *tty* structure state, TF_HIWAT_OUT, to request that it be awakened when the queue drops below the low watermark.

Once errors, permissions, and flow control have been checked, *ttydisc_getc*() copies the user's data into a local buffer in chunks of 256 characters at most, using *uiomove*(). (A value of 256 is used because the buffer is stored on the stack and so it cannot be large.) When the terminal driver is configured in noncanonical mode, no per-character translations are done, and the entire buffer is processed at once. In canonical mode, the terminal driver locates groups of characters requiring no translation by scanning through the output string, looking up each character in turn in a table that marks characters that might need translation (e.g., newline), or characters that need expansion (e.g., tabs). Each group of characters that requires no special processing is placed into the output queue using *memcpy*(). Trailing special characters are output with *ttydisc_reprint*().

The *ttydisc_write*() routine handles the translation of special characters by first searching the output for characters that might need post processing. Regular characters are then output and the special characters are handled through a post-processing routine. The following translations may be done, depending on the terminal mode:

- Tabs may be expanded to spaces.
- Newlines may be replaced with a carriage return plus a line feed.

As soon as data are placed on the output queue of a terminal, its device driver is awakened to let it know that it can start output. Unless output is already in progress or has been suspended by receipt of a *stop* character, a wakeup will be sent to the thread associated with the device. For a pseudo-terminal, the wakeup is sent to a thread sleeping on the master side and, if not already running, awakens it so that it can consume the data. For a hardware terminal, the wakeup is sent to the thread associated with the device that begins sending the characters out of the serial line. Once all the data have been processed and have been placed into the output queue, *ttydisc_write*() returns an indication that the *write* completed successfully.

Terminal Output (Lower Half)

Characters are removed from the output queue either by the thread running on the master side of the pseudo-terminal or by the hardware device driver. Whenever the number of characters on the output queue drops below the low watermark, the output routine checks to see if the TS_SO_OLOWAT flag is set to show that a thread is waiting for space in the output queue and should be awakened. In addition, *selwakeup*() is called, and if a thread is recorded in *t_wsel* as selecting for output, that thread is notified. The output continues until the output queue is empty.

Terminal Input

Unlike output, terminal input is not started by a system call but instead arrives asynchronously when the terminal line receives characters from a remote login session or locally from the keyboard. Thus, the input processing in the terminal system occurs mostly at interrupt time.

When a character arrives over the network from a remote login session, the locally running remote-login daemon writes it into the master side of the pseudo-terminal. The master side of the pseudo-terminal will pass the character as input to the terminal line discipline for the receiving terminal through the latter's *ttydisc_rint* entry. For locally attached hardware such as a keyboard, the input character will be passed by the device driver directly to the receiving tty device driver input entry. In either case, the input character is passed as an integer. The bottom 8 bits of the integer are the actual character. Characters received from locally connected hardware may have hardware-detected parity errors, break characters, or framing errors. Such errors are shown by setting flags in the upper bits of the integer.

The interpretation of terminal input is done in the *ttydisc_rint* routine. When a *break* condition is detected (a longer-than-normal character with only 0 bits), it is ignored, or an interrupt character or a null is passed to the process, depending on the terminal mode. Input characters are echoed if desired. In noncanonical mode, characters are placed into the raw input queue without interpretation. Otherwise, most of the work done by the *ttydisc_rint*() routine is to check for characters with special meanings and to take the requested actions. Other characters are placed into the raw queue. In canonical mode, if the received character is a carriage return or another character that causes the current line to be made available to the program reading the terminal, the contents of the raw queue are added to the canonicalized queue and any processes waiting for input or selecting for input on the device are awakened. In noncanonical mode, any process selecting for input on the device or sleeping on the raw queue awaiting input for a *read* are awakened. If the terminal has been set for signal-driven I/O using *fcntl* and the FASYNC flag, a SIGIO signal is sent to the process group controlling the terminal.

Eventually, a *read* call is made on the file descriptor for the terminal device. Like all calls to read from a character-special device, this one results in a call to the device driver's read routine with a device pointer, a *uio* structure describing the data to be read, and a flag specifying whether the I/O is nonblocking. Terminal device drivers use the device pointer to locate the *tty* structure for the device and then call the line discipline *ttydisc_read* entry to process the system call.

The *ttydisc_read* routine first checks to see whether the process is part of the session and the process group currently associated with the terminal. If the process is a member of the session currently associated with the terminal, if any, and is a member of the current process group, the read proceeds. Otherwise, if a SIGTTIN would suspend the process, a SIGTTIN is sent to that process group. Here, the read will be attempted again when the user moves the process group to the foreground. Otherwise, an error is returned. Finally, *ttydisc_read*() checks for data in the appropriate queue (the canonical queue in canonical mode, the raw queue in noncanonical mode). If no data are present, *ttydisc_read*() returns the error EAGAIN if the terminal is using nonblocking I/O; otherwise, it sleeps on the address of the raw queue. When *ttydisc_read*() is awakened, it restarts processing from the beginning because the terminal state or process group might have changed while it was asleep.

When characters are present in the queue for which *ttydisc_read*() is waiting, they are removed from the queue one at a time with *ttydisc_getc*() and are copied out to the user's buffer. In canonical mode, certain characters receive special processing as they are removed from the queue: The delayed-suspension character causes the current process group to be stopped with signal SIGTSTP, and the end-of-file character terminates the read without being passed back to the user program. If there was no previous character, the end-of-file character results in the read returning zero characters, and that is interpreted by user programs as indicating end-of-file. However, most special processing of input characters is done when the character is entered into the queue. For example, translating carriage returns to newlines based on the ICRNL flag must be done when the character is first received because the newline character wakes up waiting processes in canonical mode. In noncanonical mode, the characters are not examined as they are processed.

Characters are processed and returned to the user until the character count in the *uio* structure reaches zero, the queue is exhausted, or, if in canonical mode, a line terminator is reached. When the *read* call returns, the returned character count will be the amount by which the requested count was decremented as characters were processed.

After the read completes, if terminal output was blocked by a stop character being sent because the queue was filling up, and the queue is now less than 20 percent full, a start character (normally XON, control-Q) is sent.

Closing of Terminal Devices

When the final reference to a terminal device is closed, or the *revoke* system call is made on the device, the device *close*() routine is called. The kernel checks to make sure that there are no open references to the terminal before calling the line discipline's *close*() routine and then cleaning up all the state associated with the terminal. The line-discipline close entry, *ttydisc_close*(), flushes any pending output. Finally, the device close routine frees the queues that were associated with the device, clears any knotes associated with the terminal, and wakes up any processes that were waiting on the terminal.

8.7 The GEOM Layer

The GEOM layer provides a modular transformation framework for disk-I/O requests. This framework supports an infrastructure in which classes can do nearly arbitrary transformations on disk-I/O requests on their path from the upper kernel to the device drivers and back. GEOM can support both automatic data-directed configuration and manual, or script-directed, configuration.

Transformations in GEOM include the following:

- Simple base and bounds calculations needed for disk partitioning
- Aggregation of disks to provide a RAID, mirrored, or stripped logical volume
- A cryptographically protected logical volume
- Collection of I/O statistics
- I/O optimization such as disk sorting
- Journaled I/O transactions

Unlike many of its predecessors, GEOM is both extensible and topologically agnostic.

Terminology and Topology Rules

GEOM is object oriented and consequently borrows much context and semantics from the object-oriented terminology. A transformation is the concept of a particular way to modify I/O requests. Examples include partitioning a disk, mirroring two or more disks, and operating several disks together in a RAID.

A class implements one particular transformation. Examples of classes are a master boot record (MBR) disk partition, a BSD disk label, a RAID array, a transaction journal, or encryption.

An instance of a class is called a geom. In a typical FreeBSD system, there will be one geom of class MBR for each disk. The MBR subdivides a disk into as many as four pieces. There will also be one geom of class BSD for each slice with a BSD disk label.

A provider is the front gate at which a geom offers service. A typical provider is a logical disk, for example, **/dev/da0s1**. All providers have three main properties: name, media size, and sector size.

A consumer is the back end through which a geom connects to another geom provider and through which I/O requests are sent. For example, an MBR label will typically be a consumer of a disk and a provider of disk slices.

The topological relationship between these entities are as follows:

- A class has zero or more geom instances.
- A geom is derived from exactly one class.
- A geom has zero or more consumers.
- A geom has zero or more providers.
- A consumer can be attached to only one provider.
- A provider can have multiple consumers attached.
- The GEOM structure may not have loops; it must be an acyclic directed graph. From an object-oriented perspective GEOM implements a system of single inheritance because a consumer can only be attached to one provider.

All geoms have a rank number assigned that detects and prevents loops in the acyclic directed graph. This rank number is assigned as follows:

- A geom with no attached consumers has a rank of one.
- A geom with attached consumers has a rank one higher than the highest rank of the geoms of the providers to which its consumers are attached.

Figure 8.6 shows a sample GEOM configuration. At the bottom is a geom that communicates with the CAM layer and produces the da0 disk. It has two consumers. On the right is the DEVFS filesystem that exports the complete disk image as **/dev/da0**. On the left is stacked an MBR geom that interprets the MBR label found in the first sector of the disk to produce the two slices da0s1 and da0s2. Both of these slices have DEVFS consumers that export them as **/dev/da0s1** and **/dev/da0s2**. The first of these two slices has a second consumer, a BSD label geom, that interprets the BSD label found near the beginning of the slice. The BSD label subdivides the slice into as many as eight (possibly overlapping) partitions, da0s1a through da0s1h. All the defined partitions have DEVFS consumers that export them as **/dev/da0s1a** through **/dev/da0s1h**. When one of these partitions is mounted, the filesystem that has mounted it also becomes a consumer of that partition.

Changing Topology

The basic operations are *attach*, which attaches a consumer to a provider, and *detach*, which breaks the bond. Several more complex operations are available to simplify automatic configuration.

Tasting is a process that happens whenever a new class or new provider is created. It provides the class a chance to automatically configure an instance on providers that it recognizes as its own. A typical example is the MBR disk-partition class that will look for the MBR label in the first sector and, if found and valid, will instantiate a geom to multiplex according to the contents of the MBR.

Figure 8.6 A sample GEOM configuration.

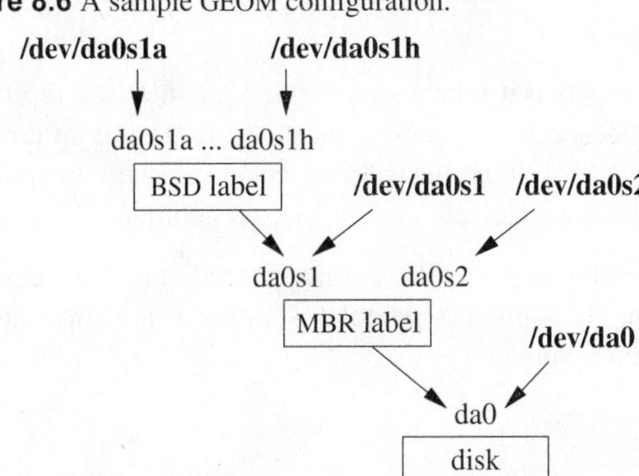

Exactly what a class does to recognize if it should accept the offered provider is not defined by GEOM, but the sensible set of options are:

- Examine specific data structures on the disk.
- Examine properties like sector size or media size for the provider.
- Examine the rank number of the provider's geom.
- Examine the method name of the provider's geom.

A new class will be offered to all existing providers and a new provider will be offered to all classes.

Configure is the process where the administrator issues instructions for a particular class to instantiate itself. For example, a BSD label module can be specified with a level of override forcing a BSD disk-label geom to attach to a provider that was not found palatable during the taste operation. A configure operation is typically needed when first labelling a disk.

Orphaning is the process by which a provider is removed while it potentially is still being used. When a geom orphans a provider, all future I/O requests will bounce on the provider with an error code set by the geom. All consumers attached to the provider will receive notification about the orphaning and are expected to act appropriately. A geom that came into existence as a result of a normal taste operation should self-destruct unless it has a way to keep functioning without the orphaned provider. Single-point-of-operation geoms, like those interpreting a disk label, should self-destruct. Geoms with redundant points of operation, such as those supporting a RAID or a mirror, will be able to continue as long as they do not lose quorum.

An orphaned provider may not result in an immediate change in the topology. Any attached consumers are still attached. Any opened paths are still open. Any outstanding I/O requests are still outstanding. A typical scenario is:

- A device driver detects a disk has departed and orphans the provider for it.
- The geoms on top of the disk receive the orphaning event and orphan all their providers. Providers that are not in use will typically self-destruct immediately. This process continues in a recursive fashion until all relevant pieces of the tree have responded to the event.
- Eventually the traversal stops when it reaches the device geom at the top of the tree. The geom will refuse to accept any new requests by returning an error. It will sleep until all outstanding I/O requests have been returned (usually as errors). It will then explicitly close, detach, and destroy its geom.
- When all the geoms above the provider have disappeared, the provider will detach and destroy its geom. This process percolates all the way down through the tree until the cleanup is complete.

While this approach seems byzantine, it does provide the maximum flexibility and robustness in handling disappearing devices. Ensuring that the tree does not unravel until all the outstanding I/O requests have returned guarantees that no applications will be left hanging because a piece of hardware has disappeared.

Spoiling is a special case of orphaning used to protect against stale metadata. It is probably easiest to understand spoiling by going through an example. Consider the configuration shown in Figure 8.6 that has disk da0 above which is an MBR geom that provides da0s1 and da0s2. On top of da0s1, a BSD geom provides da0s1a through da0s1h. Both the MBR and BSD geoms have autoconfigured based on data structures on the disk media. Now consider the case where da0 is opened for writing and the MBR is modified or overwritten. The MBR geom now would be operating on stale metadata unless some notification system can inform it otherwise. To avoid stale metadata, the opening of da0 for writing causes all attached consumers to be notified, resulting in the eventual self-destruction of the MBR and BSD geoms. When da0 is closed, it will be offered for tasting again, and if the data structures for MBR and BSD are still there, new geoms will instantiate themselves.

To avoid the havoc of changing a disk label for an active filesystem, changing the size of open geoms can be done only with their cooperation. If any of the paths through the MBR or BSD geoms were open (for example, as a mounted filesystem), they would have propagated an exclusive-open flag downward, rendering it impossible to open da0 for writing. Conversely, the exclusive-open flag requested when opening da0 to rewrite the MBR would render it impossible to open a path through the MBR geom until da0 is closed. Spoiling only happens when the write count goes from zero to nonzero, and the tasting only happens when the write count goes from nonzero to zero.

Figure 8.7 Using a mirror module to copy an active filesystem.

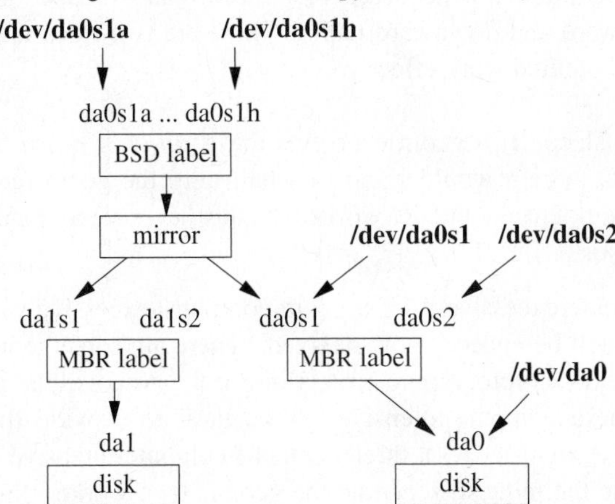

Insert is an operation that allows a new geom to be instantiated between an existing consumer and provider. Delete is an operation that allows a geom to be removed from between an existing consumer and provider. These capabilities can be used to move an active filesystem. For example, as shown in Figure 8.7, we could insert a mirror module into the GEOM stack pictured in Figure 8.6. The mirror operates on da0s1 and da1s1 between the BSD label consumer and its MBR label provider da0s1. The mirror is initially configured with da0s1 as its only copy and consequently is transparent to the I/O requests on the path. Next, we ask it to mirror da0s1 to da1s1. When the mirror copy is complete, we drop the mirror copy on da0s1. Finally, we delete the mirror geom from the path instructing the BSD label consumer to consume from da1s1. The result is that we moved a mounted filesystem from one disk to another while it was being used.

Operation

The GEOM system needs to be able to operate in a multiprocessor kernel. The usual method for ensuring proper operation is to use mutex locks on all the data structures. Because of the large size and complexity of the code and data structures implementing the GEOM classes, prior to FreeBSD 10 GEOM used a single-threading approach rather than traditional mutex locking to ensure data structure consistency. This mode of operation continues to be available using two threads to operate its stack: a *g_down* thread to process requests moving from the consumers at the top to the providers at the bottom, and a *g_up* thread to process requests moving from the providers at the bottom to the consumers at the top. Requests entering the GEOM layer at the top are queued awaiting the *g_down* thread. The *g_down* thread pops each request from the queue, moves it down through the stack, and out through the provider. Similarly, results coming back from the providers are queued awaiting the *g_up* thread. The *g_up* thread pops each request from the queue, moves it up through the stack, and sends it back out to the consumer. Because there is only ever a single thread running up and down in the stack, the only locking that is needed is on the few data structures that coordinate between the upward and downward paths. There are two rules required to make this single-thread method work effectively:

1. A geom can never sleep. If a geom ever puts the *g_up* or *g_down* thread to sleep, the entire I/O system would grind to a halt until the geom reawakens. The GEOM framework checks that its worker threads never sleep, panicking if they attempt to do so.

2. No geom can compute excessively. If a geom computes excessively, pending requests or results will be unacceptably delayed. There are some geoms, such as the one that provides cryptographic protection for filesystems, that are compute intensive. These compute-intensive geoms have to provide their own threads. When the *g_up* or *g_down* thread enters a compute-intensive geom, it will simply enqueue the request, schedule the geom's own worker thread, and

proceeded on to process the next request in its queue. When scheduled, the compute-intensive geom's thread will do the needed work and then enqueue the result for the *g_up* or *g_down* thread to finish pushing the request through the stack.

While a queued model of processing is flexible, it does give up performance to provide that flexibility. Each enqueue and dequeue operation requires processor resources, and the queues themselves need to be protected by locks so that two threads cannot update the queue data structure at the same time. To mitigate the bottleneck of a single thread in the I/O path, and to reduce the context switch overhead of switching to and from the *g_up* and *g_down* threads, FreeBSD 10 added a direct dispatch mode to GEOM. Each GEOM class has two flags that it can set, G_DIRECT_UP and G_DIRECT_DOWN, to indicate that I/O can pass through the class via direct dispatch in the indicated direction. To accept direct-dispatch, a module must add locking to protect its data structures so that the module can run concurrent threads. When direct dispatch is used, the thread making the request calls directly into the module rather than queueing its request to be run by the *g_down* or *g_up* thread. All I/O requests into the GEOM layer are checked to see if they can be delivered directly to the underlying class. Direct calls are made to any module that is marked as accepting direct dispatch in the direction of the I/O. Direct calls are also made for any I/O that is of zero effective length, meaning that it has no data but there is some command to the underlying class. An I/O request that does not meet these requirements is queued for the class to process later, using the *g_down* and *g_up* threads.

The set of commands that may be passed through the GEOM stack are read, write, and delete. The read and write commands have the expected semantics. Delete specifies that a certain range of data is no longer used and that it can be erased or freed. Technologies like flash-adaptation layers can arrange to erase the relevant blocks so that they are ready to be reassigned, and cryptographic devices may fill random bits into the range to reduce the amount of data available for attack. A delete request has no assurance that the data really will be erased or made unavailable unless guaranteed by specific geoms in the graph. If a secure-delete semantic is required, a geom that converts a delete request into a sequence of write requests should be pushed.

Topological Flexibility

GEOM is both extensible and topologically agnostic. The extensibility of GEOM makes it easy to write a new class of transformation. In the last few years several new classes have been written, including:

- *gcache* that provides a kernel-memory cache of ***backing storage*** such as a disk.
- *geli* that encrypts data sent to a backing store and decrypts data retrieved from a backing store. For example, providing an encrypted filesystem is simply a matter of stacking a geli class on top of a disk class.

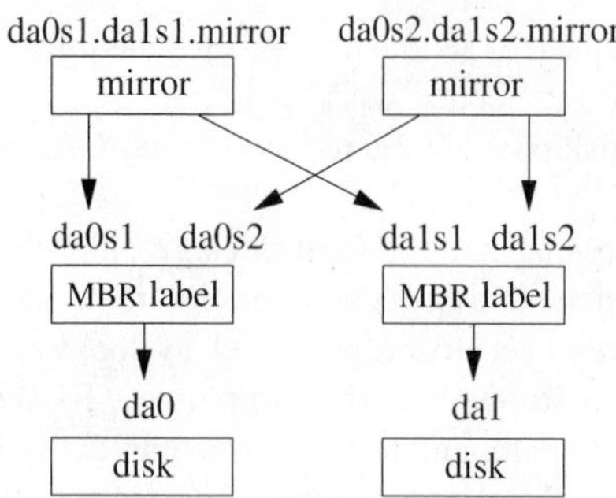

Figure 8.8 Fixed class hierarchy.

- *gjournal* that does block-level journaling of data sent to a backing store. All writes get logged and are later replayed if the system crashes before they are made to the backing store. Thus, it can provide journaling for any filesystem without needing to know anything about the filesystem's structure.
- *gsched* that provides alternate scheduling policies for a backing store.
- *gvirstor* that sets up a virtual storage device of an arbitrarily large size. The *gvirstor* class allows users to overcommit on storage (free filesystem space). The concept is also known as "thin provisioning" in virtualization environments. The *gvirstor* class is implemented on the level of physical storage devices.

In a departure from many previous volume managers, GEOM is topologically agnostic. Most volume-management implementations have strict notions of how classes can fit together, but often only a single fixed hierarchy is provided. Figure 8.8 shows a typical hierarchy. It requires that the disks first be divided into partitions, and then the partitions can be grouped into mirrors, which are exported as volumes.

With fixed hierarchies, it is impossible to express intent efficiently. In the fixed hierarchy of Figure 8.8, it is impossible to mirror two physical disks and

Figure 8.9 Flexible class hierarchy.

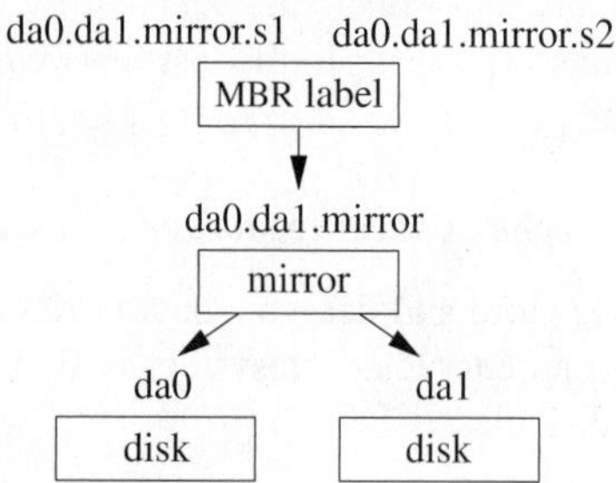

then partition the mirror into slices as is done in Figure 8.9. Instead, one is forced to make slices on the physical volumes and then create mirrors for each of the corresponding slices, resulting in a more complex configuration. Being topologically agnostic means that different orderings of classes are treated no differently than existing orderings. GEOM does not care in which order things are done. The only restriction is that cycles in the graph are not allowed.

8.8 The CAM Layer

To reduce the complexity of the individual disk drivers, much of the complexity of handling a modern controller has been abstracted into a set of routines that provide a Common Access Method (CAM) layer that sits between the GEOM and the device-driver layers. The CAM layer handles the device-independent tasks of resource allocation and command routing. These tasks include the tracking of requests and notifications between the controller and its clients. They also include the routing of requests across the many I/O busses to get the request to the correct controller.

The CAM layer leaves to the device driver the device-specific operations such as the setup and teardown of the DMA maps needed to do the I/O. CAM also allows device drivers to manage I/O timeouts and initial bus error-recovery measures. Some device drivers can become complex. For example, the Fibre Channel device driver has much code to handle operations, such as asynchronous topology changes as drives are removed and attached. A driver responds to a CAM request by converting the virtual address to store the data to the appropriate physical address. It then marshals the device-independent parameters like I/O request, physical address to store the data, and transfer length into a firmware-specific format, and then executes the command. When the I/O completes, the driver returns the results to the CAM layer.

In addition to disks, the CAM layer manages any other storage device that might be connected to the system such as tape and removable flash memory drives. For other character devices such as keyboard and mice, CAM will not be involved.

The CAM subsystem provides a uniform and modular system for the implementation of drivers to control various devices and to use different host adapters through host-adapter drivers. The CAM system is made up of three layers:

1. The CAM peripheral layer that provides open, close, strategy, attach, and detach operations for the supported devices. CAM-supported devices include: direct access (da) SCSI disk drives, ATA and SATA (sa) disk drives, cdrom (cd) CD-ROM drives, sequential access (sa) tape drives, and changer (ch) jukeboxes. Each peripheral driver builds an I/O command specific to the protocol for its devices, and then passes that command to the transport layer for execution. The driver also interprets the results of the I/O commands and takes corrective actions for errors. CAM starts by building a protocol-specific I/O command using a CAM control block (CCB) tailored either to SCSI or ATA devices.

The CCB contains a command descriptor block containing the command to be sent to the device. For example, the SCSI command "READ_10, block_offset, count" gets back a status of success or various error codes. If there is an error, the drive may also include sense data to give more information about the cause of the error.

2. The CAM Transport (XPT) layer schedules and dispatches I/O commands, acting as a switch between the myriad of peripheral device instances and the host bus adapters to which they belong. It also assists the device drivers with error recovery by allowing I/O to be frozen and and unfrozen at a device or subsystem level. For example, a disk device might be able to handle 64 commands, and the controller it is attached to might be able to handle 256 commands, but when more than 4 disks are attached to the controller, scheduling and arbitration needs to be done in the transport layer.

3. The CAM *software interface module* or *host bus adapter* interface layer provides bus routing to devices. Its job is to allocate a path to the requested device, send a CCB action request to the device, and then collect notification of the I/O completion from the device. It is also responsible for identifying errors that have happened at the protocol and bus layers, and notifying the transport and peripheral layers that it is done with error recovery actions.

The operation of the CAM layer is most easily understood by tracing an I/O request through it.

The Path of a SCSI I/O Request Through the CAM Subsystem

The path of a SCSI request through the CAM I/O subsystem is shown in Figure 8.10. In the FreeBSD framework, the filesystem sees a single contiguous disk. I/O requests are based on block numbers within this idealized disk. In

Figure 8.10 The path of a SCSI I/O request through the CAM subsystem.

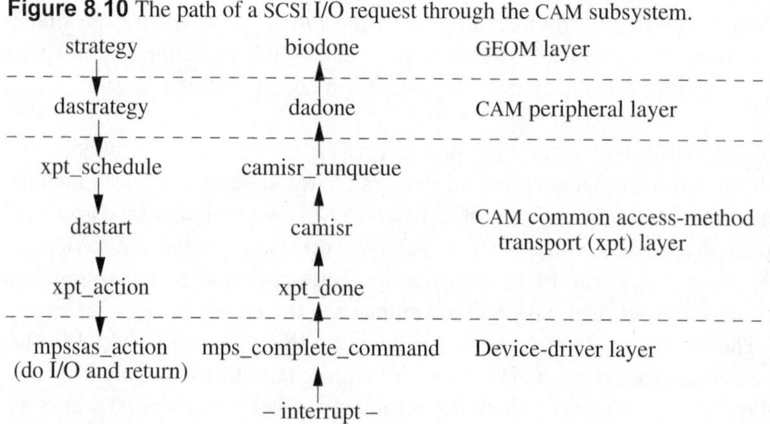

Figure 8.10, the filesystem determines a set of blocks on which it wants to perform I/O, and it passes this request down to the GEOM layer by calling the *strategy*() routine.

The GEOM layer takes the request and determines the disk to which the request should be sent. In this example, the request is on a *da* SCSI disk. When a request spans several disks, the GEOM layer breaks up the original request into a set of separate I/O requests for each of the disks on which the original request resides. Each of the new requests is passed down to the CAM layer by calling the appropriate *strategy*() routine for the associated disk (the *dastrategy*() routine in Figure 8.10).

The CAM *dastrategy*() routine gets the request and calls *bioq_disksort*(), which puts the request on the disk queue of the specified SCSI disk. The *dastrategy*() routine finishes by calling the *xpt_schedule*() function.

The *xpt_schedule*() function allocates and constructs a CCB to describe the operation that needs to be done. If the disk supports tagged queueing, an unused tag is allocated, if it is available. If tagged queueing is not supported or a tag is not available, the request is left on the queue of requests pending for the disk. If the disk is ready to accept a new command, the *xpt_schedule*() routine calls the drive start routine set up for it (*dastart*() in this example).

The *dastart*() routine takes the first request off the disk's queue and begins to service it using the CCB that was constructed by *dastrategy*(). Because the command is destined for a SCSI disk, *dastart*() needs to build a SCSI READ_10 command based on the information in the CCB. The resulting SCSI command that includes a READ_10 header, a pointer to the virtual address that references the data to be transferred, and a transfer length is placed in the CCB and given the type XPT_SCSI_IO. The *dastart*() routine then calls the *xpt_action*() routine to determine the bus and controller (adapter) to which the command should be sent.

The *xpt_action*() routine returns a pointer to a *cam_path* structure that describes the controller to be used and has a pointer to the controller's action routine. In this example, we are using the Adaptec SCSI controller whose action routine is *mpssas_action*(). The *xpt_action*() routine queues the CCB with its *cam_path* and schedules it to be processed.

The request is processed by calling the controller-specific action routine, *mpssas_action*(). The *mpssas_action*() routine gets the CCB and converts its generic SCSI command into a hardware-specific *SCSI control block* (SCB) to handle the command. The SCB is filled out from information in the CCB. It is also filled out with any hardware-specific information and a DMA request descriptor is set up. The SCB is then passed to the driver firmware to be executed. Having completed its task, the CAM layer returns to the caller of *dastrategy*().

The controller fulfills the request and uses DMAs to transfer the data to or from the location given in the SCB. When done, a completion interrupt arrives from the controller. The interrupt causes the *mps_complete_command*() routine to be run. The *mps_complete_command*() routine updates the CCB associated with the completed SCB from information in the SCB (command completion status or sense information if there was an error). It then frees the previously allocated

DMA resources and the completed SCB, and passes the completed CCB back to the CAM layer by calling *xpt_done*().

The *xpt_done*() routine inserts the associated CCB into the completion notification queue and posts a software interrupt request for *camisr*(), the CAM interrupt service routine. When *camisr*() runs, *camisr_runqueue*() removes the CCB from the completion notification queue and calls the specified completion function, which maps to *dadone*() in this example.

The *dadone*() routine will call the *biodone*() routine, which notifies the GEOM layer that one of its I/O requests has finished. The GEOM layer aggregates all the separate disk I/O requests together. When the last I/O operation finishes, it updates the original I/O request passed to it by the filesystem to reflect the result (either successful completion or details on any errors that occurred). The filesystem is then notified of the final result by calling the *biowait*() routine.

ATA Disks

Like SCSI disks, support for SATA and ATA drives has been abstracted into a module that is part of the CAM layer referred to as the ATA module. The ATA module handles the device-independent tasks of the tracking requests and notifications between the controller and its clients.

The handling of ATA I/O requests by the CAM layer is similar to that described for SCSI disks. Device-specific operations are left to the device driver. The device driver responds to a request for an ATA disk by marshaling the device-independent parameters in the CCB. It converts the type of the I/O request, the virtual address to store the data, and the transfer length into a firmware-specific format, and then executes the command. When the I/O completes, the driver places the results back in the CCB similar to the way it is done by the SCSI driver.

The ATA driver start routine handles TRIM commands that improve the efficiency of solid-state disks (SSDs). While SSDs use the same hardware interconnect as spinning magnetic disks, the way they operate internally is different. One difference is that an SSD must erase a block before it can be rewritten. It also must carefully manage the erasing and rewriting of its flash memory blocks so that the blocks are used evenly. The TRIM command is a part of the ATA specification that allow a filesystem to inform an SSD that a block or set of blocks are no longer in use and may be erased. The ATA driver maintains a separate queue of requests to trim data from a device, and these requests are executed at the beginning of its *adastart*() routine so that space is freed before the process of writing new data begins. TRIM is also available to SAS solid state disks via the *da* driver.

8.9 Device Configuration

Autoconfiguration is the procedure carried out by the system to recognize and enable the hardware devices present in a system. Autoconfiguration works by systematically probing the possible I/O busses on the machine. For each I/O bus that is found, each type of device attached to it is interpreted and, depending on this type, the necessary actions are taken to initialize and configure the device.

The first FreeBSD implementation of autoconfiguration was derived from the original 4.2BSD code with the addition of many special-case hacks. The 4.4BSD release introduced a new, more machine-independent configuration system that was considered for FreeBSD but was ultimately rejected in favor of the ***newbus*** scheme, which first appeared in FreeBSD 3.0 to support the Alpha architecture. It was brought over to the PC platform for FreeBSD 4.0. Newbus included machine-independent routines and data structures for use by machine-dependent layers, and provided a framework for dynamic allocation of data structures for each device.

A key design goal of the newbus system was to expose a stable application binary interface (ABI) to driver writers. A stable ABI is especially important for externally or vendor-maintained loadable kernel modules because their source code is often not available to recompile if the interface is changed.

To help achieve ABI stability, the device and devclass structures are hidden from the rest of the kernel with a simple function-call-based API to access their contents. If the structures were passed to the device driver directly, any change to the structure would require that all the drivers to which it is passed be recompiled. Changes to these data structures do not require a recompilation of all the drivers. Only the access functions to the data structures need to be recompiled.

Some hardware devices, such as the interface to the console terminal, are required for system operation. Other devices, however, may not be needed and their inclusion in the system may needlessly waste system resources. Devices that might be present in different numbers, at different addresses, or in different combinations are difficult to configure in advance. However, the system must support them if they are present and must fail gracefully if they are not present. To address these problems, FreeBSD supports two configuration procedures. The first is a static configuration procedure that is performed when a bootable system image is created. The second is a dynamic loading capability that allows kernel drivers and modules to be added to a running system as needed. Thus, the statically configured kernel can be small with just enough capability to get the system up and running. Once running, additional functionality can be added as needed.

Allowing code to be loaded dynamically into the kernel raises many security problems. Code running outside the kernel is limited in the damage that it can do because it does not run in privileged mode and cannot directly access the hardware. The kernel runs with full privilege and access to the hardware. If the kernel loads a module containing malicious code, it can inflict wide-ranging damage within the system. Kernels can be loaded across the network from a central server. If the kernel allows dynamic loading of modules, they could also come across the network, so there are numerous added points for malfeasance.

An important consideration in deciding whether to enable dynamic loading of kernel modules is to develop a scheme to verify the source of and lack of corruption in any code before that code is permitted to be loaded and used. A group of vendors have formed the Trusted Computing Group (TCG) to specify a hardware module called a Trusted Platform Module (TPM) that keeps a running SHA-1 hash of the software installed on the system to detect the loading of bad programs or modules. It is implemented as a microcontroller-based device similar to a smart card that is attached to the motherboard [TCG, 2003]. Other groups are doing work to limit the potential harm of kernel modules by running them with page protections that limit their access to the rest of the kernel [Chiueh et al., 2004]. The drawback to disabling dynamic loading is that any hardware that is not included in the kernel configuration file will be unavailable for use.

The initial kernel configuration is done by the **/usr/sbin/config** program. A configuration file is created by the system administrator that contains a list of drivers and kernel options. Historically, the configuration file defined both the set of hardware devices that might be present on a machine and the location where each device might be found. Since FreeBSD 10, hardware devices have been discovered dynamically as the various bus drivers probe and attach. The location of legacy devices for non-plug-and-play (non-self-identifying) busses are given in a **/boot/device.hints** file that is loaded with the kernel. The other use for hints is to hardwire a unit number to a location. Currently only CAM can hardwire unit numbers, although hard wiring could be implemented for any bus. The configuration procedure generates many files that define the initial kernel configuration. These files control the kernel compilation.

The autoconfiguration phase is done first during system initialization to identify the set of devices that are present on a machine. In general, autoconfiguration recurses through a tree of device interconnections, such as busses and controllers to which other devices attach. For example, a system might be configured with two SCSI host adapters (controllers) and four disk drives that are connected in any

Figure 8.11 Alternative drive configurations.

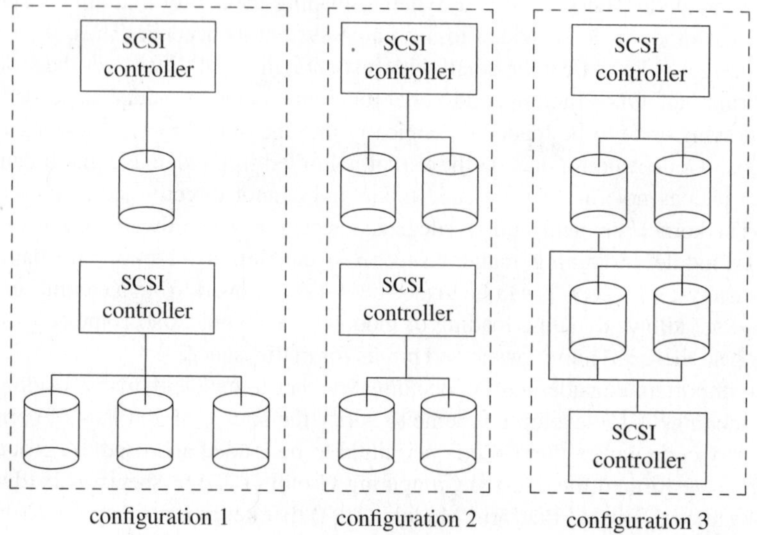

of the configurations shown in Figure 8.11. Autoconfiguration works in one of two ways at each level in the tree:

1. *Identifying* each possible location at which a device might be present and checking to see what type of device (if any) is there

2. *Probing* for devices at each of the possible locations where the device might be attached

The first approach of identifying predefined locations for devices is needed for older busses like ISA that were not designed to support autoconfiguration and are still present in some embedded systems boards such as those built around the ARM, MIPS, and PPC architectures. The second mechanism of probing for devices can be used only when a fixed set of locations is possible and when devices at those locations are self-identifying, such as devices connected to a SATA, SCSI, or PCI bus. Devices that can be probed dynamically implement a *probe* routine that is called during the first phase of the autoconfiguration process.

Devices that are recognized during the probing phase of the autoconfiguration process are attached and made available for use. The *attach* function for a device initializes and allocates resources for the device. The *attach* function for a bus or controller must probe for devices that might be attached at that location. If the *attach* function fails, the hardware was found but is nonfunctional, which results in a console message being printed. Devices that are present but not recognized may be configured once the system is running and has loaded other kernel modules. The *attach* function for busses is allowed to reserve resources for devices that are detected on the bus but for which no device driver is currently loaded in the system.

This scheme permits device drivers to allocate system resources for only those devices that are present in a running system. It allows the physical device topology to be changed without requiring the system load image to be regenerated. It also prevents crashes resulting from attempts to access a nonexistent device. In the remainder of this section, we consider the autoconfiguration facilities from the perspective of the device-driver writer. We examine the device-driver support required to identify hardware devices that are present on a machine and the steps needed to attach a device once its presence has been noted.

Device Identification

To participate in autoconfiguration, a device driver must register the set of functions shown in Table 8.5. Devices are an abstract concept in FreeBSD. In addition to the traditional disks, tapes, network interfaces, keyboards, terminal lines, and so on, FreeBSD will have devices that operate all the pieces that make up the I/O infrastructure such as the SCSI bus controller, the bridge controller to the PCI bus, and the bridge controller to the ISA bus. The top-level device is the root of the I/O system and is referred to as the root. On a uniprocessor system, the root logically resides at the I/O pins of the CPU. On a multiprocessor

Table 8.5 Functions defined for autoconfiguration.

Function	Description
device_probe	probe device presence
device_identify	find a device that cannot be probed
device_attach	attach a device
device_detach	detach a device
device_shutdown	system about to shut down
device_suspend	suspend device
device_resume	resume device

system, the root is logically connected to the I/O pins of each of the CPUs. The root0 device is handcrafted at boot time for each architecture supported by FreeBSD.

Autoconfiguration begins with a request to the root0 bus to configure all its children. When a bus is asked to configure its children, it calls the *device_identify*() routine of each of its possible device drivers. The result is a set of children that have been added to the bus either by the bus itself or by the *device_identify*() routines of one of its drivers. Next, the *device_probe*() routine of each of the children is called. The *device_probe*() routine that bids the highest for the device will then have its *device_attach*() routine called. The result is a set of devices corresponding to each of the busses that are directly accessible to root0. Each of these new devices is then given the opportunity to probe for or identify devices below them. The identification process continues until the topology of the I/O system has been determined.

Modern busses can directly identify the things that are connected to them. Older busses such as ISA use the *device_identify*() routine to bring in devices that are found only because of hints.

As an example of the device hierarchy, the device controlling the PCI bus may probe for a disk controller, which in turn will probe for possible targets that might be attached, such as disk drives. The autoconfiguration mechanism provides much flexibility, allowing a controller to determine the appropriate way in which to probe for additional devices attached to the controller.

As autoconfiguration proceeds, a device-driver *device_probe*() routine is called for each device that is found. The system passes to the *device_probe*() routine a description of the device's location and possibly other details such as I/O register location, memory location, and interrupt vectors. The *device_probe*() routine usually just checks to see if it recognizes the hardware.

It is possible that there is more than one driver that can operate a device. Each matching driver returns a priority that shows how well it matches the hardware. Success codes, shown in Table 8.6, are values less than or equal to zero, with the highest (least negative) value representing the best match. Failure codes are represented by positive values using the usual kernel error codes.

Table 8.6 Return codes for device_probe routine.

Probe Return Code	Value	Description
BUS_PROBE_SPECIFIC	0	only this driver can use this device
BUS_PROBE_VENDOR	-10	vendor-supplied driver
BUS_PROBE_DEFAULT	-20	base OS default driver
BUS_PROBE_LOW_PRIORITY	-40	older, less desirable drivers
BUS_PROBE_GENERIC	-100	generic driver for this type of device
BUS_PROBE_HOOVER	-500	generic driver for all devices on this bus
BUS_PROBE_NOWILDCARD	-200000	no wildcard device matches

If a driver returns a success code that is less than zero, it must not assume that it will be the same driver whose *device_attach*() routine will be called. In particular, it must not assume that any values stored in the device local-storage area will be available for its *device_attach*() routine. Any resources allocated during the probe must be released and reallocated if its *device_attach*() routine is called. By returning a success code of zero, a driver can assume that it will be the one attached. However, well-written drivers will not have their *device_attach*() routine use the device local-storage area because they may, one day, have their return value downgraded to a value less than zero. Typically, the resources used by a device are identified by the bus (parent device), and it is the bus that prints them out when the devices are probing.

Once the *device_probe*() routine has had the opportunity to identify the device and select the most appropriate driver to operate it, the selected driver's *device_attach*() routine is called. Attaching a device is separated from probing so that drivers can bid for devices. Probe and attach are also separate so that drivers can separate out the identification part of the configuration from the attaching part. Most device drivers use the *device_attach*() routine to initialize the hardware device and any software state. The *device_attach*() routine is also responsible for either creating the dev_t entries (for disks and character devices) or for network devices, registering the device with the networking system.

Devices that represent pieces of hardware such as a SATA controller will respond to verify that the device is present and to set or at least identify the device's interrupt vector. For disk devices, the *device_attach*() routine may make the drive available to higher levels of the kernel such as GEOM. GEOM will let its classes taste the disk drive to identify its geometry and possibly initialize the partition table that defines the placement of filesystems on the drive.

Autoconfiguration Data Structures

The autoconfiguration system in FreeBSD includes machine-independent data structures and support routines. The data structures allow machine- and bus-dependent information to be stored in a general way and allow the autoconfiguration process to be driven by the configuration data, rather than by compiled-in rules. The **/usr/sbin/config** program constructs many of the tables from information in the kernel-configuration file and from a machine-description file. The **/usr/sbin/config** program is thus data-driven as well and contains no machine-dependent code.

Figure 8.12 shows the data structures used by autoconfiguration. The basic building block is the *device* structure. Each piece of the I/O hierarchy will have its own device structure. The name and description fields identify the piece of hardware represented by the device structure. In Figure 8.12, the name of the device is *pci1*. Device names are globally unique. There can be only one pci1 device in the system. Knowing its name is enough to find it, unlike filesystems where there can be many files with the same name in different paths. This namespace is related by convention to the namespace that **/dev** entries have, but such a relationship is not required.

Each device is a member of a device class represented by a *devclass* structure that has two important roles. The first role of the devclass structure is to keep track of a list of drivers for devices in that class. Devices referenced from a devclass do not have to use the same driver. Each device structure references its best matching driver from the list available for the devclass. The list of candidate drivers is traversed, allowing every driver to probe each device that is identified as a member of the class. The best matching driver will be attached to the device. For example, the pci devclass contains a list of drivers suitable for probing against devices that may be plugged into a PCI bus. In Figure 8.12, there are drivers to

Figure 8.12 Autoconfiguration data structures for pci1.

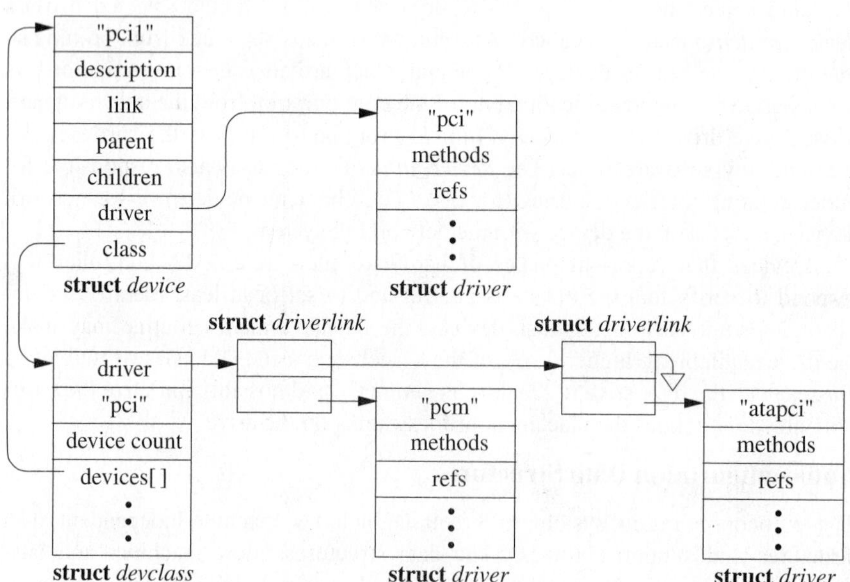

match *pcm* (sound cards) and *atapci* (PCI-based ATA-disk controllers).

The second role of the devclass structure is to manage the mapping from a user-friendly device name such as pci1 to its device structure. The name field in the devclass structure contains the root of a family of names—in this example, pci. The number following the root of the name—1 in this example—indexes into the array of pointers to device structures contained in the devclass. The name in the referenced device structure is the full name, pci1.

When a device structure first comes into existence, it will follow these steps:

1. The parent device typically determines the existence of a new child device by doing a bus scan. The new device is created as a child of the parent. In Figure 8.12, the autoconfiguration code would begin a scan of pci1 and discover an ATA disk controller.

2. The parent device starts a probe-and-attach sequence for the new child device. The probe iterates through drivers in the parent device's devclass until a driver is found that claims the device (i.e., the probe succeeds). The device structure sets its driver field to point at the selected driver structure and increments the reference count in the selected driver. In Figure 8.12, the atapci driver matches the ATA disk controller, atadisk.

3. Once a usable driver is found, the new device is registered with the devclass of the same name as the driver. The registration is done by allocating the next

Figure 8.13 Autoconfiguration data structures for atapci0.

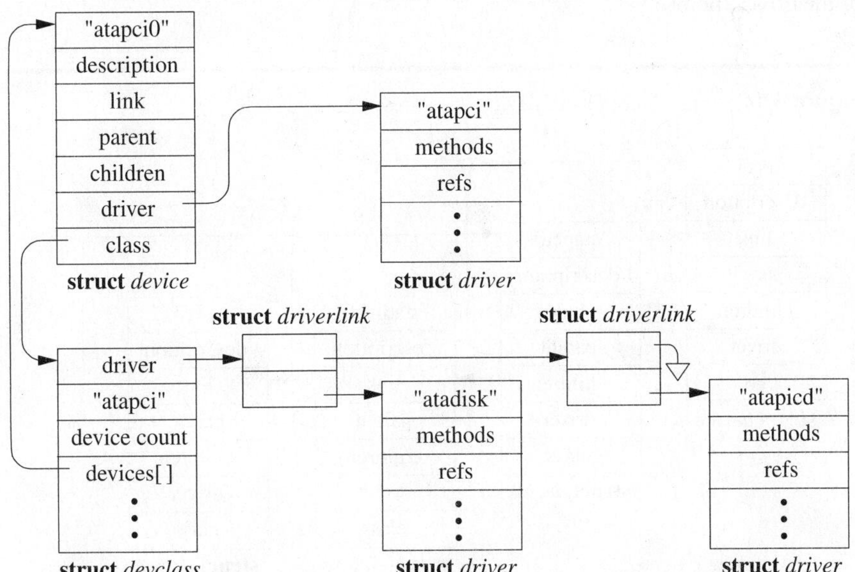

available unit number and setting a pointer from the corresponding entry in the devclass's array of device-structure pointers back to the device. In Figure 8.12, the atapci driver was matched, so the device would be bound to the atapci devclass. The resulting device configuration is shown in Figure 8.13. The key observation is that two different devclasses are involved in this three-step process.

The hierarchy of device structures is shown in Figure 8.14. Each device structure has a parent pointer and a list of children. In Figure 8.14, the pci device that manages the PCI bus is shown at the top and has as its only child the atapci device that operates ATA disks on the PCI bus. The atapci device has the pci device as its parent and has two children, one for each of the ATA disks that are attached. The devices representing the two drives have the atapci device as their parent. Because they are leaf nodes, they have no children.

To get a better idea of the I/O hierarchy, an annotated copy of the output of the **/usr/sbin/devinfo** program from the first author's test machine is shown in Figure 8.15. The output has been trimmed down from its original 250 lines to show just the branch from the root of the tree to the system's two ATA disks. The tree starts at root0, representing the I/O pins on the CPU. That leads to the high-speed bus that connects to the memory and the root0 (for example, northbridge) interconnect to the I/O bus. One of these busses is the pcib0 (for example, southbridge) connection to the PCI bus. The PCI bus is managed by the pci0 device, which as you can see from the figure, has many drivers available for the myriad of devices that may be connected to it. In this example, the one device that we show is the atapci0 device representing the PCI-based ATA disk controller. The final two devices shown in Figure 8.15 are atadisk0 and atadisk1 that manage the operation of the drives themselves.

Figure 8.14 Sample hierarchy of device structures.

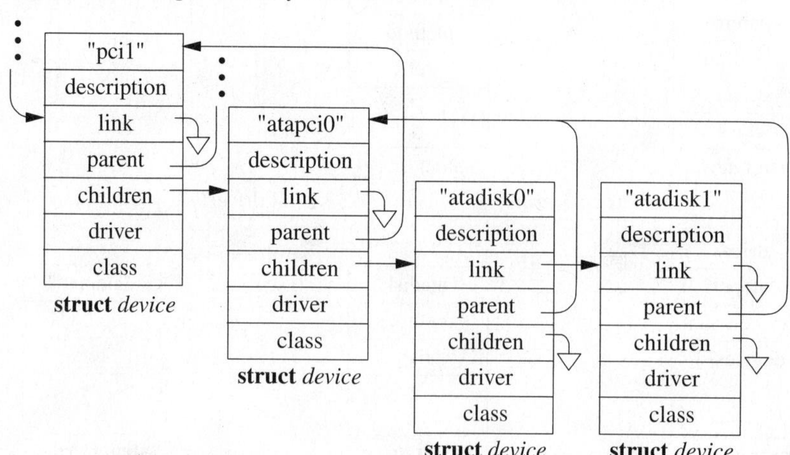

```
root0
    description: System root bus
    devclass: root, drivers: nexus
    children: nexus0

  nexus0
      devclass: nexus, drivers: acpi, legacy, npx
      children: npx0, legacy0

    legacy0
        description: legacy system
        devclass: legacy, drivers: eisa, isa, pcib
        children: eisa0, pcib0

      pcib0 /* southbridge */
          description: Intel 82443BX (440 BX) host to PCI bridge
          devclass: pcib, drivers: pci
          children: pci0
      pcib1
          description: PCI-PCI bridge
          devclass: pcib, drivers: pci
          children: pci1

        pci0
            description: PCI bus
            devclass: pci, drivers: agp, ahc, amr, asr, atapci,
                bfe, bge, ciss, csa, domino, dpt, eisab, emujoy,
                fxp, fixup_pci, hostb, ignore_pci, iir, ips,
                isab, mly, mode0, pcib, pcm, re, sio, uhci, xl
            children: agp0, pcib1, isab0, atapci0, ahc0, xl0

          atapci0
              description: Intel 82371AB PIIX4 IDE controller
              devclass: atapci, drivers: atadisk, atapicd
              children: atadisk0, atadisk1
              class: mass storage, subclass: ATA
              I/O ports: 0xffa0-0xffaf

            atadisk0
                devclass: atadisk, drivers: none
                interrupt request lines: 0xe
                I/O ports: 0x1f0-0x1f7, 0x3f6

            atadisk1
                devclass: atadisk, drivers: none
                interrupt request lines: 0xf
                I/O ports: 0x170-0x177, 0x376
```

Figure 8.15 Sample configuration output.

Resource Management

As part of configuring and operating devices, the autoconfiguration code needs to manage hardware resources such as interrupt-request lines, I/O ports, and device memory. To aid device-driver writers in this task, FreeBSD provides a framework for managing these resources. To participate in bus-resource management, a bus device driver must register the set of functions shown in Table 8.7. Low-level devices such as those that operate individual disk drives do not have the global knowledge of resource utilization needed to allocate scarce systemwide resources such as interrupt-request lines. They may register a generic bypass routine for resources that they do not have the needed information to allocate. When called, the bypass routine simply calls the corresponding routine registered by their parent. The result is that the request will work its way up the device tree until it reaches a high-enough level that it can be resolved.

Often a high-level node in the tree will not have enough information to know how much of a resource to allocate. Thus, it will reserve a range of resources, leaving it to the lower-level nodes to allocate and activate the specific resources that they need from the reservation made by the higher-level node.

Table 8.7 Functions defined for device resource allocation.

Function	Description
bus_alloc_resource	allocate a bus resource
bus_set_resource	set up a range for a resource
bus_activate_resource	activate allocated resource
bus_deactivate_resource	deactivate allocated resource
bus_release_resource	release ownership of a resource
bus_delete_resource	free a released resource
bus_get_resource	get the range for a resource
bus_get_resource_list	get a resource list
bus_probe_nomatch	call following a failed probe
bus_driver_added	new driver added to devclass
bus_add_child	attach an identified device
bus_child_detached	notice to parent of detached child
bus_setup_intr	initialize an interrupt
bus_config_intr	set interrupt trigger mode and polarity
bus_teardown_intr	disable an interrupt
bus_read_ivar	read an instance variable
bus_write_ivar	write an instance variable
bus_child_present	check for device still present
bus_print_child	print device description

The actual management of the allocated resources is handled by the kernel resource manager that was described in Section 6.3. The usual allocate and free routines have been expanded to allow different levels in the tree to manage different parts of these two functions. Thus, allocation breaks into three steps:

1. Setting the range for the resource
2. Initial allocation of the resource
3. Activating the resource

Similarly, resource freeing is done in three steps:

1. Deactivating the resource
2. Releasing ownership of the resource to the parent bus
3. Freeing it

It is common for a high-level part of the tree to allocate a resource and then have a low-level driver activate and use the resource that it allocated. Some busses reserve space for their children that do not have drivers associated with them. Having the allocation and freeing broken up into three steps gives maximum flexibility in partitioning the allocation and freeing processes.

The *bus_driver_added*(), *bus_add_child*(), and *bus_child_detached*() functions allow the device to be aware of changes in the I/O hardware so that it can respond appropriately. The *bus_driver_added*() function is called by the system when a new driver is loaded. The driver is added to some devclass, and then all current devices in that devclass have *bus_driver_added*() called to allow them to possibly match any unclaimed devices using the new driver. The *bus_add_child*() function is used during the identify phase of configuring some busses. It allows a bus device to create and initialize a new child device (for example, setting values for instance variables). The *bus_child_detached*() function is called by a driver when it decides that its hardware is no longer present (for example, a cardbus card is removed). It calls *bus_child_detached*() on its parent to allow it to do a detach of the child.

The *bus_probe_nomatch*() routine gives the device a last-ditch possibility to take some action after autoconfiguration has failed. It may try to find a generic driver that can run the device in a degraded mode, or it may simply turn the device off. If it is unable to find a driver that can run the device, it notifies the **devd** daemon, a user-level process started when the system is booted. The **devd** daemon uses a table to locate and load the proper driver. The loading of kernel modules is described in Section 15.4.

The *bus_read_ivar*() and *bus_write_ivar*() routines manage a bus-specific set of instance variables of a child device. The intention is that each different type of bus defines a set of appropriate instance variables such as ports and interrupt-request lines for the ISA bus.

8.10 Device Virtualization

Most virtualization systems support full virtualization in which guest operating systems use conventional bare-metal interfaces directly, including CPU, virtual memory, and timers, as well as drivers for off-the-shelf network-interface cards (NICs) and storage devices. Full virtualization allows guests to operate entirely unaware of the virtualized environment: a substantial simplification.

Full virtualization incurs performance overhead because of the costs of intercepting and emulating processor and I/O operations not permitted outside the CPU's supervisor ring. Bare-metal device drivers necessarily make assumptions about memory use that, while suitable for DMA-enabled devices on the PCI bus, make it difficult for virtualization systems to use OS-like virtual-memory optimizations such as moving memory pages between virtual machines to avoid data copying (page flipping). Finally, lack of virtualization awareness limits the opportunity for multiple virtual machines operating on the same physical hardware to exploit that locality for performance gain—for example, by forcing communication to take place using TCP/IP over emulated network interfaces rather than using shared memory.

In contrast, paravirtualization makes guest operating systems explicitly aware of virtualization, improving performance and integration at the cost of requiring software adaptation. For example, the bhyve hypervisor integrated with the FreeBSD kernel supports paravirtualized network and storage devices via the Virtio interface. Virtio is used with full-machine emulators such as Qemu. FreeBSD supports not only paravirtualized devices on the stand-alone Xen hypervisor, but also paravirtualized CPU features such as interprocessor interrupts and inter-virtual-machine communication.

With paravirtualization, host and guest environments (or for Xen, pairs of guest domains) implement a split device-driver model in which device-driver back ends implement device simulations for host-OS o physical devices that serve paravirtualization-aware device-driver front ends in the guest operating system. The back and front ends communicate via well-defined protocols reminiscent of communications between conventional device drivers and real physical devices, but with design choices more suited to virtualized environments.

Interaction with the Hypervisor

Explicit awareness of virtualization offers both performance and functionality benefits. Just as user processes make system calls to invoke operating-system kernel services, kernels themselves invoke hypercalls to request services from the hypervisor or virtualization framework. Using hypervisor features directly provides immediate benefits to the guest OS: support for hardware without native virtualization features (e.g., earlier X86 CPUs); performance improvements through batching of operations such as page-table updates; general system-performance improvements through scheduling features such as a yield hypercall; and avoidance of expensive emulation of peripheral devices such as NICs and storage devices where more appropriate performance optimizations can be made for virtualized environments.

Some hypervisors, such as FreeBSD's bhyve, are embedded within existing operating-system kernels. Here, paravirtualization support is primarily focused on improving device-driver performance. Stand-alone hypervisors, such as Xen, offer richer inter-virtual-machine communications interfaces reminiscent of operating-system IPC primitives. This approach explicitly allows virtual machines both to provide services to, and to consume services offered by, other virtual machines; paravirtualized device drivers are just one such service.

Hypercalls provide basic synchronous communication between a virtual machine and a hypervisor. However, the bulk of paravirtualized device-driver communication occurs via shared memory rings either between guest and host (e.g., in bhyve), or between multiple guests (e.g., under Xen). As with shared-memory interprocess communication on conventional OS kernels, avoiding copies via the hypervisor leads to big performance gains for bulk data transfer. Shared memory is configured using hypercalls, which are also used for event notification on the ring. In principle, entering the hypervisor can be entirely avoided in the steady state if a pair of communicating virtual machines, or host and guest, are running concurrently on different CPUs; they can likewise avoid (or suppress) signalling and rely on independently occurring context switches. In practice, communication protocols between device-driver front and back ends in Xen utilize dynamic page mappings that require hypercalls, and Virtio communication between front and back ends is often synchronous within a kernel-scheduled thread, even if requested operations can be processed asynchronously.

Paravirtualization models vary in the semantics that they offer. For example, Virtio has been designed assuming direct access to guest memory from the host, more reminiscent of kernel access to user processes. As a result, communication rings can reference buffers that do not have strong page alignment. In contrast, Xen's paravirtualized interfaces are designed to support back-end drivers operating in another domain. Thus, shared memory pages referenced by communication rings must be explicitly configured by pairs of guests using hypercalls.

Virtio

Virtio provides a simple, hypervisor-neutral, and performant interface for paravirtualized device drivers [Russell, 2008]. First introduced in Linux for use with both guest- and kernel-based virtual machines (KVMs), Virtio is now used across a range of virtualization systems, including FreeBSD's bhyve hypervisor. Virtio defines several interfaces and mechanisms: a virtual-ring primitive used for bulk communication and a PCI-based model for device enumeration and feature negotiation. It also defines conventions for paravirtualized terminal access, memory ballooning, entropy provision, network interfaces, block storage, and the SCSI HBA driver.

Virtio is designed for virtualization systems in which back-end device implementations are able to read and write guest operating-system memory directly. Direct memory access is possible when a hypervisor implements virtualized devices itself, or when the host shares an address space (typically a UNIX process) with the virtual-machine guest. For example, bhyve combines an in-kernel hypervisor with a userspace process implementing configuration, memory management, and device emulation. The bhyve user process donates memory pages to the guest while retaining direct memory access to them. This assumption of address-space sharing facilitates copy avoidance: shared communication rings between the front and back ends can refer to memory allocated and managed "as normal" in the guest kernel. As a result, bhyve's user process can do scatter-gather I/O directly from guest buffer-cache and socket-buffer memory when emulating a device. Less tight address-space integration, as with Xen, incurs overhead as it requires either more data copying or dynamic mapping of pages containing buffers.

The host exposes access to devices via a virtual PCI bus in the guest. The lowest-level front-end driver in the guest, **vtpci**, implements a bus to which other paravirtualized front-end drivers attach. Virtio devices are discovered via PCI enumeration, with each device offered to potential drivers to probe and attach. Table 8.8 lists the vtpci bus implemented interfaces described in **virtio_bus_if.m**. Front-end device drivers can use these interfaces to probe for matching back-end instances, negotiate supported feature sets with the back-end, configure communication queues to the back end, and subscribe to event notification to be delivered via emulated interrupts. Table 8.9 lists the optional interfaces described in **virtio_if.m**. Device drivers can optionally implement these interfaces to receive callbacks on successful device-driver attach and to be notified of back-end configuration changes (e.g., changes in virtual block-device size originating in the back end).

Virtio's core communications primitive is the virtual queue, or virtqueue, that allows front- and back-end implementations to exchange chained buffers via a shared-memory communications ring. Each ring is described by a *vring* structure that points to an array of descriptor entries and two indexed control rings used to transfer ownership of buffers between endpoints. The key data structures for virtqueues are illustrated in Figure 8.16.

Table 8.8 Virtio bus services exported to Virtio device drivers.

Bus method	Description
negotiate_features	negotiate intersection of driver, virtual queue, and host features
with_features	test whether feature is negotiated
alloc_virtqueues	allocate and configure a new virtual queue for driver
setup_intr	configure interrupt for driver
stop	deliver reset to back-end implementation
reinit	deliver reset to back-end implementation with acknowledgment
reinit_complete	notify back-end implementation of completed reset
notify_vq	notify back-end implementation of event on virtual queue
read_device_config	allow driver to read per-device configuration registers
write_device_config	allow driver to write per-device configuration registers

Table 8.9 Interfaces exposed by Virtio device drivers to the Virtio bus.

Bus method	Description
attach_completed	invoked when device-driver attach is successful
config_change	notify device driver of configuration change from hypervisor

Descriptor entries describe scatter-gather buffers in guest memory, that will typically carry requests and either data the front end would like to write/transmit, or space in which the back end should store read/received data. The descriptor array consists of a set of *vring_desc* entries, each of which contains a guest-physical address, length, flags indicating read/write status, and the *next* field that points to the optional next entry in a scatter-gather list; chains are terminated by a descriptor without the VRING_DESC_F_NEXT flag set. A typical chain's first entry points to a command header, with later entries pointing to buffered data or buffer space.

Figure 8.16 Virtio virtqueue data structures. The ring[] elements in the *vring_avail* are descriptor-chain indices, whereas ring[] elements in *vring_used* are arrays of *vring_used_elem* structures.

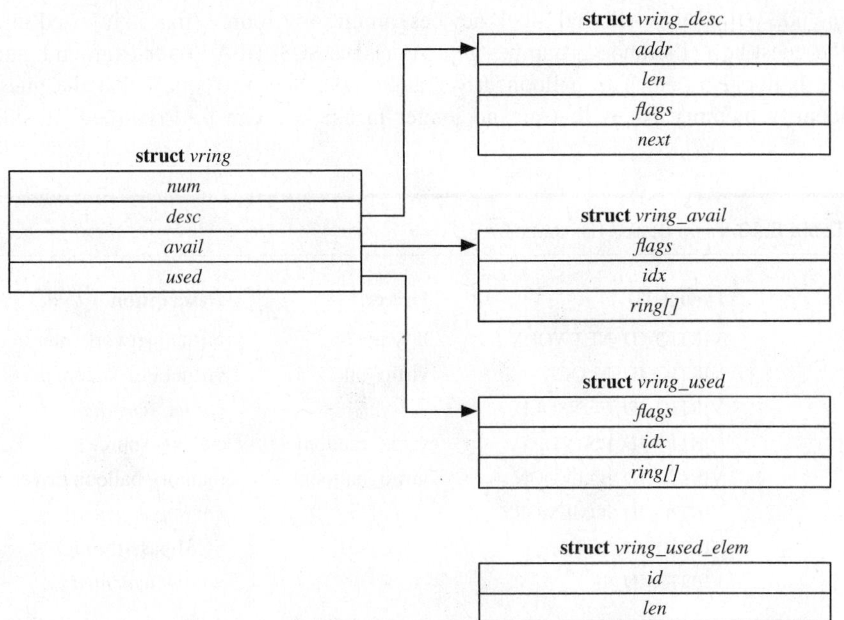

The available ring, described by *vring_avail*, allows the front end to pass chained buffers to the back end (e.g., to request that a filled buffer be written to disk, or request that a buffer be filled with a read from disk). The used ring, described by *vring_used*, allows the back end to return ownership of chains to the front end once it has been used (e.g., to acknowledge that the disk write is complete, or filled with data from a disk read). The *vring_used_elem* structure contains a length reporting the size of data copied from the back end, whereas the lengths in the descriptor array describe the space that is available. Notice that if supported by the device type, back-end drivers are able to return used buffer chains in a different order from that in which they were made available. Reordering is appropriate for the block-storage back end, for example, where reordering I/O operations using elevator sorting can improve performance without harming semantics.

The *idx* fields in both rings are incremented each time a new chained buffer has been successfully made available or used. The guest and host may be executing on different CPUs. Careful use of memory barriers following updates to the descriptor-ring and used-element entries is required to ensure that changes to these entries are visible to all CPUs before the changes to the *idx* fields become visible [Harris & Fraser, 2007]. Once an update has taken place, the host or guest can optionally notify the other party, either via a virtual PCI write in the paravirtualized driver, or via an interrupt to the guest kernel, that will propagate the interrupt to the device driver. Batching of requests is a key performance optimization. During steady-state processing, front and back-end implementations can avoid overhead by switching from per-packet notifications to polled operation.

Table 8.10 lists the Virtio device drivers implemented by FreeBSD, which include virtual network and block devices, an entropy source (that is injected into the guest kernel's random-number generator), the SCSI HBA driver front end, and the balloon driver. The balloon driver allows the host to request that the guest identify memory pages that are no longer in use and can be "returned" to the

Table 8.10 Virtio device IDs and drivers.

Device ID	Driver	Description
VIRTIO_ID_NETWORK	if_vtnet	virtual network interface
VIRTIO_ID_BLOCK	virtio_blk	virtual block storage
VIRTIO_ID_CONSOLE	-	*not implemented*
VIRTIO_ID_ENTROPY	virtio_random	entropy source
VIRTIO_ID_BALLOON	virtio_balloon	memory balloon driver
VIRTIO_ID_IOMEMORY	-	*not implemented*
VIRTIO_ID_SCSI	virtio_scsi	SCSI pass-through
VIRTIO_ID_9P	-	*not implemented*

hypervisor to assist with memory pressure elsewhere in the system. In the event that these pages are required by the guest again in the future, touching the pages will restore them—albeit in a re-zeroed state. The balloon driver helps the host avoid swapping guest pages, which can lead to poor performance as competing host and guest virtual memory systems identify unused pages and swap them causing thrashing.

Individual paravirtualized device drivers closely resemble traditional device drivers, implementing kernel interfaces such as *disks* (see Section 8.4) and *ifnet* (see Section 8.5). Device communications occur via virtqueues rather than programmed I/O or DMA descriptor rings. The Virtio block-storage front end utilizes a single ring to push storage requests to the back end; in contrast, the network front end uses pairs of rings, one for receive and the other for transmit, for each virtual NIC queue. Virtio's feature negotiation support has proven especially important for network device drivers. Feature negotiation allows Virtio to determine the availability of features such as checksum offload, TCP-segmentation offload (TSO), large-receive offload (LRO), and multiqueue.

On the other side of virtual queues, back-end implementations are responsible for mapping virtual devices into underlying OS services. Virtual block devices are often mapped into filesystem images embedded on ordinary files; sometimes, however, they are passed through to underlying OS-exposed block devices such as partitions on SCSI disks. Read and write requests are submitted to the host kernel via normal I/O system calls—often using the *preadv* and *pwritev* variants that can accept scatter-gather arguments drawn from the host memory mappings of chained buffers, avoiding additional copying in the back end.

Network devices require more complexity. They are most frequently handled by associating a virtual interface in the host (e.g., an **if_tun** or **if_tap** interface) with back-end driver instances. Providing access to link-layer bridging, IP-layer routing, and optionally, network-address translation via the host network stack allows the host's network interfaces to be shared. Virtual network interfaces often allow communication between guests running on the same host. Where low-level network access is not available to the back-end implementation (e.g., for security reasons), it may be desirable to proxy network-layer traffic from the guest via sockets in the host network stack, requiring substantially more implementation complexity.

Xen

The Xen hypervisor takes a fundamentally different perspective on virtualization than do OS-centered approaches such as bhyve. The hypervisor is a stand-alone piece of software akin to a microkernel rather than a module integrated with a conventional kernel, with implications for the guest-OS device drivers [Barham et al., 2003; Chisnall, 2007]. Whereas Virtio focused on providing efficient paravirtualized device support optimized for shared memory access between host and guest, Xen implements an overt service model between a set of virtual machines, known as domains, running over a common hypervisor.

The first domain running over Xen, domain 0, bootstraps the system, creates and manages user domains, and provides services to those domains. The hypervisor has direct support for only a few CPU-oriented hardware devices (such as local APICs). Device drivers for storage controllers, network interface cards, and other more complex devices run in domain 0, which is granted direct hardware access. Domain 0 can then forward requests received from front-end device drivers to their physical counterparts. It can also support greater resource sharing in back-end drivers by mapping virtual disks into images stored in a filesystem on a physical device or by bridging a virtual network interface into a virtual switch connected to both other user domains and physical devices.

Although placing back-end drivers in domain 0 is common, the model is flexible: any guest can provide back-end services to another. This flexibility allows what is known as domain 0 disaggregation, the decomposition of a single privileged domain 0 into several driver domains to reduce both privileges and attack surfaces available to less trustworthy guests—not dissimilar to the reasons given for compartmentalization using Capsicum in Chapter 5. This decomposition is facilitated by the increasing prevalence of I/O Memory Management Units (IOMMUs), described later in this section, that allow safe delegation, or pass-through, of physical devices (such as PCI-connected storage controllers or network interfaces) to guests. Although FreeBSD 10 is not able to operate as the boot-time domain 0, it can implement device-driver back ends, including exporting ZFS-backed storage, allowing it to act as a driver domain and as a simple consumer guest. Future releases are slated to include support for operating as domain 0, made easier by the advent of hardware-assisted virtualization combined with increasingly mature paravirtualization support.

Among the services offered to user domains by domain 0 is XenStore, a rendezvous service for inter-guest communication, and a set of back-end drivers for network interfaces and block storage. Guests use XenStore to enumerate back- and front-end device configurations during boot, and to offer and look up grant table references, which instantiate shared memory between domains, and event channels, which deliver inter-domain signalling. Together, these facilities discover virtual devices and configure and implement communication rings between front- and back-end drivers, similar to Virtio's virtqueues.

Different combinations of processors and operating systems require different levels of guest-OS adaptation for Xen. At one extreme, earlier Intel and AMD processors do not have fully virtualizable instruction sets, requiring guest operating systems to use Xen in fully paravirtualized (PV) mode. In effect, the FreeBSD PV kernel is its own X86-like platform target with a customized virtual memory subsystem and other substantial kernel changes. The guest kernel runs in ring 1 rather than 0 (which is occupied by Xen itself), and hypercalls are substituted for unvirtualizable privileged instructions. A PV kernel must use explicit hypercalls to do operations such as:

- Access a low-level console;

- Implement lazy floating-point unit (FPU) context switching;
- Implement unvirtualizable descriptor-update instructions;
- Request page-table changes and trigger TLB flushes;
- Receive interrupt-like event notifications from timers and I/O devices; and
- Send Inter-Processor Interrupts (IPIs) required for multi-processor operation.

At the other extreme, pure Hardware Virtual Machine (HVM) mode relies on more recently introduced Intel Virtualization Technology (VT) and AMD Virtualization (AMD-V) CPU features such as nested page tables that allow kernels to execute a range of privileged operations despite running under a hypervisor. Combined with emulations of conventional hardware devices borrowed from Qemu, HVM mode allows entirely unmodified guest operating systems to run over Xen.

In practice, however, the preferred configuration for FreeBSD over Xen combines aspects of both approaches: the kernel uses hardware-supported extended page tables to avoid a modified virtual-memory subsystem, while also using paravirtualized device drivers and other hypervisor features to improve performance. Table 8.11 shows a subset of Xen hypercalls, some used only in PV mode, others used in both PV and HVM modes. Hypercalls continue to be used for the following types of operations even in HVM mode:

Table 8.11 Xen hypercalls used in PV and HVM modes.

Hypercall	Mode	Description
console_io	PV	I/O to and from Xen virtual console
fpu_taskswitch	PV	modify privileged cr0 register for FPU context switching
iret	PV	implement unvirtualizable interrupt return instruction
mmuext_op	PV	notify hypervisor of page-table updates; TLB flushes
set_gdt	PV	implement unvirtualizable global-descriptor table update
update_descriptor	PV	implement unvirtualizable update of descriptor registers
update_va_mapping	PV	map or unmap a page in virtual memory
event_channel_op	PV/HVM	allocate, bind, use, and close event channels
grant_table_op	PV/HVM	manipulate shared-memory grant tables
memory_op	PV/HVM	adjust physical page reservation; map page into guest
sched_op	PV/HVM	invoke hypervisor scheduler operations such as yield
vcpu_op	PV/HVM	control per-virtual CPU properties such as periodic timers
xen_version	PV/HVM	query Xen version
multicall	PV/HVM	batch a series of hypervisor requests via one hypercall

- Scheduler and timer operations, such as the *set_singleshot_timer* virtual CPU (VCPU) hypercall, which schedules an upcall after a suitable interval;
- Mapping page grants delegating memory from other domains; and
- Loading binaries into new virtual machines.

For the remainder of this section, we will be concerned primarily with how FreeBSD uses paravirtualized features when operating over Xen HVM. Xen discovery and initialization begins early in the X86 boot in *xen_hvm_init*():

1. The `cpuid` instruction detects whether Xen is present. If so, the kernel will be configured to use paravirtualized features.
2. The hypercall region, a memory page holding code that invokes hypercalls, is allocated from kernel memory and initialized with the help of the hypervisor using emulated write-model-specific-register (`wrmsr`) instructions. Xen will select the hypercall implementation most suitable for the current CPU architecture; Intel VT will use `vmcall`, and AMD-V will use `vmmcall`.
3. The *xen_version* hypercall queries available Xen features; used for PV mode, and by paravirtualized drivers that may run on PV or HVM systems, to determine whether the distinction between guest physical page numbers and machine page numbers is visible to the guest. On HVM, nested page tables mask this distinction.
4. The *cpu_ops* operation vector is updated so that Xen versions of CPU initialization, CPU resume, and IPI support are used rather than the default X86 versions.
5. The *memory_op* hypercall is invoked to set up the Xen shared_info page, a read-write page shared with the hypervisor itself. The page holds event-channel masks, per-CPU information, and time-keeping information such as skew and rate adjustment information to convert a timestamp-counter (TSC) value to wall-clock time.
6. The *hvm_op* hypercall is invoked to set up an explicit event-channel callback, used to notify the guest of events on communication rings in a way similar to normal interrupt delivery.
7. An emulated I/O instruction triggers Xen to disable emulations of conventional devices used with full-machine virtualization. Only paravirtualized drivers will attach, improving performance and preventing confusion caused by duplicate attachments of the same block or network devices.
8. Finally, each virtual CPU invokes the *vcpu_op* hypercall to register its per-CPU *vcpu_info* structure, which contains the CPU's event-channel, architectural, and time state.

These initialization steps may be re-run following virtual-machine suspend/resume or migration, as the guest may find changes in CPU and Xen features and configuration. For example, communication rings to device-driver back ends must be reestablished, as they will now be hosted by different domains, requiring shared memory and event channels to be rediscovered.

Whereas Virtio provided an emulated PCI bus that regular bus drivers could enumerate, Xen provides guest configuration data explicitly via XenStore, a filesystem-like hierarchical key-value database holding system configuration information published by domain 0. XenStore contains named subtrees for each live domain including configuration information such as its UUID, target physical memory usage used by the **balloon**, an enumeration of front-end and back-end devices to configure (along with grant-table and event-channel state required to communicate with corresponding drivers in other domains), and per-device configuration information (e.g., whether an instance of the **netfront** driver supports TCP Segmentation Offload (TSO)). XenStore is implemented by the **xenstore** front-end device driver, whose back end is accessed via shared-memory rings and event channels that, of necessity, cannot be bootstrapped using XenStore. Instead, XenStore resources are configured using the shared_info page initialized by the hypervisor during early boot.

XenStore information on device topology and configuration, sometimes referred to as XenBus, populates two synthetic-Newbus busses in the guest: **xenbus_back** and **xenbus_front**, that respectively attach back-end and front-end device drivers within the guest. XenBus provides several abstractions to paravirtualized drivers, such as convenient wrappers that can be used by front-end drivers to delegate access to shared-memory rings to back-end drivers in other domains. These busses are rooted in the **xenpci** driver in FreeBSD 10. The driver is named **xenpci** because it is visible in PCI-bus enumeration in the guest, and is able to own and handle PCI-like interrupts and own memory resources. Use of Xen's event-channel mechanism is preferred over the use of emulated interrupts, so in FreeBSD 11 this driver is replaced by a new root for Xen-provided paravirtualized devices, **xenpv**. This change eliminates the last remnants of PCI-emulation reliance in HVM configurations.

A full list of paravirtualized device drivers can be found in Table 8.12. Where device drivers are configured using XenBus, their back ends declare an explicit "type" allowing driver front ends to discover it. Three low-level paravirtualized drivers are configured without help from XenBus and are attached unconditionally to **nexus** or **xenpci**:

1. The **console** device driver supports low-level I/O via a virtual console (used only for PV guests).
2. The **control** driver services management messages from domain 0, such as requests to shutdown or reboot.
3. The **timer** driver implements FreeBSD's internal event timer mechanism using Xen's timer and event-channel primitives instead of using an emulated local APIC.

Table 8.12 Xen paravirtualized device drivers.

Driver	XenBus Type	Description
balloon	-	transfers physical memory to/from the guest
console	-	Xen low-level console device
control	-	handles management requests from domain 0
timer	-	paravirtualized in-kernel timer implementation
xenbus_back	-	XenBus: bus for back-end devices
xenbus_front	-	XenBus: bus for front-end devices
xenpci	-	synthetic PCI device used for HVM interrupt handling
xenstore	-	XenStore front end
blkback	vbd	virtual block device: back end
blkfront	vbd	virtual block device: front end
netback	vif	virtual network interface: back end
netfront	vif	virtual network interface: front end

As with Virtio, communication between device-driver front and back ends is done using a common ring-buffer implementation. In Xen, however, these ring buffers represent communication between guests rather than the hierarchical host-guest relationship found with in-OS hypervisors such as bhyve. Ring buffers are layered over two hypervisor primitives: shared memory configured using grant tables that authorize access to selected memory pages in one domain by another, and event channels that provide an interrupt-like wakeup mechanism. Rings pass requests and responses that may themselves contain further grants referencing pages to be mapped into the remote domain. Alternatively, data will be copied into the rings, or copied by the hypervisor, to avoid the overhead of page-table manipulation and TLB flushes.

Xen grant tables are the mechanism by which memory pages may be shared with, transferred to, or received from a second domain. Each domain has its own grant table stored as an array of grant-table entries in memory shared with the hypervisor, as shown in Figure 8.17. Each entry describes one "grant":

Figure 8.17 Xen grant-table entries control and track memory sharing between domains.

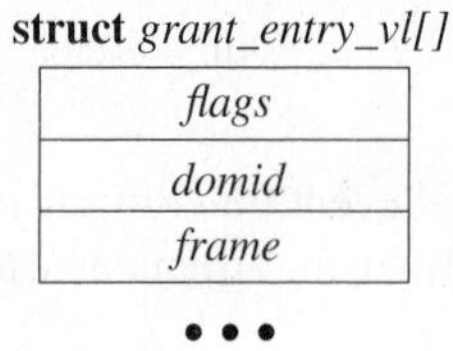

struct *grant_entry_vl[]*

flags
domid
frame

• • •

authorization to share or transfer a page owned by the domain, or a request to receive a page from another domain. The table is allocated by the guest kernel, initialized, and then shared with the hypervisor via the *memory_op* hypercall during boot.

Each grant-table entry describes a single grant operation. Entries sharing or transferring a page to another domain specify the physical page number in the source domain, and the remote domain identifier to which the page will be sent. Entries authorizing receipt of a page will identify the remote domain, a local page which will be replaced with the transferred page and a grant-table reference. Grant-table references are simply integer indexes into a source domain's grant table, and may be sent to other domains as data via requests and responses in communication rings. Grant-table entries also contain a *flags* field that the domain uses to select the operation to perform and whether the grant or mapping should be read-only. Grant-table entry flags also allow the hypervisor to export status bits indicating whether the page is currently mapped in a remote domain (here its grant status cannot be changed, as Xen does not support revocation while the page is in use), and to confirm that a page has been accepted for transfer by the remote domain. Table 8.13 shows the possible flag values.

Domains must use an explicit hypercall, *grant_table_op*, to notify the hypervisor of one or more grant-table entries authorizing receipt of grants from a remote domain. In contrast, sharing a page with or transferring a page to a remote domain does not use an explicit call as the hypervisor can look up the grant-table entry in the sender's memory using the grant reference when a mapping request occurs in the recipient. Xen does not support revocation of shared pages while they are mapped by the remote domain; instead, the sender must wait for the GTF_reading and GTF_writing flags to be cleared by the hypervisor, at which time GTF_permit_access can be cleared. Atomic operations and memory barriers safely expose writes to the grant table between guest and hypervisor.

Device-driver front ends allocate and share memory with back ends, rather than vice versa. This approach minimizes modification to front-end memory allocation which is helpful for less virtualization-aware guest operating systems, and

Table 8.13 Xen grant-table entry operations, domain flags, and hypervisor flags.

Type	Name	Description
Operation	GTF_permit_access	grant a domain access to a local page
Operation	GTF_accept_transfer	accept transfer of page to local domain
Domain flag	GTF_readonly	export or import page read-only
Hypervisor flag	GTF_reading	page mapped for reading by remote domain
Hypervisor flag	GTF_writing	page mapped for writing by remote domain
Hypervisor flag	GTF_transfer_committed	transfer of page completed

also helps avoid data copies. Front-end drivers will rely on XenBus's *xenbus_grant_ring* () function to share locally allocated rings with back-end drivers that will communicate references to the back end via XenStore. Grant references embedded in requests and responses sent via these rings share and transfer pages containing buffers (e.g., network packets and disk blocks). These grants and references will be managed directly using interfaces defined in **gnttab.c**, such as *gnttab_grant_foreign_access_ref*(), which grants a remote domain shared access to a page, *gnttab_end_foreign_access_ref*(), which cancels a grant of a shared page with a remote domain, and *gnttab_grant_foreign_transfer_ref*(), which accepts transfer of a page from a remote domain.

Grant tables, with the help of XenStore, allow shared memory to be configured between device-driver front and back ends. Event management is required to construct higher-level communication primitives, such as blocking rings for requests and responses. In Xen, event management is done via event channels that allow interrupt-like callbacks to be triggered within a domain by the hypervisor (for physical- and virtual-device interrupts) and other domains (for split device drivers and other interdomain communication). This mechanism implements Inter-Processor Interrupts (IPIs) between VCPUs within a single domain, used by FreeBSD for interprocessor synchronization.

Domains enumerate event channels using event ports, integers associated with bits in a per-guest global bitmask stored in the domain's *shared_info* structure. The size of the bitmask limits the number of unique event sources from which a domain can receive notifications; for 32-bit domains, the mask is 1024-bit; for 64-bit guests, 4096 bits. These limits can be avoided through use of the new FIFO event channel facility in more recent Xen versions, but this is not yet supported by FreeBSD. When an event channel fires, the bit corresponding to its event port in the bitmask will be set to 1; if the bit transitions from 0 to 1, then an upcall will be delivered, subject to a per-VCPU flag in the *vcpu_info* structure allowing interrupts to be disabled for that virtual CPU.

The upcall is delivered in the style of a traditional software interrupt; FreeBSD handles this code in **xen_intr.c** that routes interrupts via *intr_execute_handlers*(). After the event-channel bit has been set, further upcall invocation is suppressed until the bit has been cleared by the guest. Event ports are allocated and bound to particular event sources using *event_channel_op* hypercall operations:

- *bind_pirq* returns an event port allowing domain 0 to receive interrupts from underlying physical devices.
- *bind_virq* returns an event port for per-domain virtual devices, such as timers.
- *bind_ipi* returns an event port allowing a domain to deliver an IPI to another VCPU in the same domain.
- *alloc_unbound* and *bind_interdomain* allow a pair of cooperating domains to allocate and bind a pair of event ports, establishing a two-way interdomain event channel for a variety of purposes including ring buffer events.

Domains can deliver events on interdomain event channels using the *send* operation, and close no-longer-required event ports using the *close* operation. Domains can also bind an event port to a particular VCPU using the *bind_vcpu* operation. These functions are configurable enough to expose them up the **xen_intr** stack as though event channels were a Programmable Interrupt Controller (PIC), thus allowing the device-driver stack to remain oblivious to the implementation details. As with grant-table references, event-port numbers can be shared between domains as integers embedded in messages, and distributed using XenStore to configure virtual interrupts linking both halves of split device drivers.

Using grant-table entries and event channels, domains are able to implement ring buffers suitable for carrying requests and responses between device driver front ends and back ends. As with Virtio rings, Xen communication rings consist of a ring buffer allowing one party to send requests to, and receive responses from, another party. Unlike Virtio rings, request and response messages are embedded in the ring directly, with the option of referring to shared pages or event channels via grant-table references and event-port numbers. An event channel associated with each ring allows a recipient to receive an upcall when the ring transitions from empty to non-empty, and a sender to receive an upcall when the ring transitions from full to non-full. Macros defined in **ring.h** differentiate domain-private versions of request and response head and tail indices from versions in shared memory, allowing multiple requests or responses to be inserted before an event is delivered to amortize event-delivery costs.

As with Virtio's virtual block device, Xen's **blkback** and **blkfront** use a single ring to carry requests and responses between the device-driver front and back ends. The front end temporarily delegates read-only pages to the back end to provide data to write to the virtual device, and writable pages into which data can be read from the virtual device. The block-device back end in FreeBSD is able to direct I/O to any underlying block device in the driver domain, including raw-disk devices and ZFS volumes.

Also similar to Virtio's virtual network-interface device, Xen's **netback** and **netfront** use a pair of rings to implement transmit and receive rings for virtual network interfaces. The back end exposes the other end of the virtual interface as a **if_xnb** device in the driver domain, which can then be bridged to conventional Ethernet using the FreeBSD **if_bridge** driver. Techniques originally developed for physical-network-interface performance optimization such as checksum offloading, TCP Segmentation Offload, and Large Receive Offload apply equally well to virtual network interfaces, and are typically utilized to mitigate domain-switching costs.

Device Pass-Through

Another increasingly common approach is delegation of physical device access to virtual machines, rather than virtualizing devices. This approach requires hardware support, implemented using IOMMUs that virtualize the address space seen by DMA engines on peripherals in the same manner that the CPU's memory-management unit (MMU) virtualizes memory access for the processor. This approach safely delegates access to I/O ports and DMA descriptor rings to guest virtual machines. For example, for suitably virtualization-aware network interface cards, this approach delegates specific descriptor rings to the guest allowing direct Ethernet access with few performance overheads.

Device delegation offers different configuration and performance tradeoffs: for example, it is unsuitable if the host operating system instance wishes to impose fine-grained policies on network access, use virtual disks rather than physical ones, or if communication is to be between virtual machines rather than to remote systems. When a device must be shared by multiple virtual machines, the IOMMU alone is insufficient: the device itself must be aware of multiple virtual machines and be able to impose OS-originated policy on their interactions. For example, a virtualization-aware NIC would allow the host or domain 0 operating system instance an opportunity to control NIC-side rules for distributing packets to specific receive rings, and limiting packets that can be sent on specific transmit rings; individual guest virtual machines will then be able to interact directly with the NIC using those rings without trapping to the hypervisor or host operating system.

Exercises

8.1 Describe the differences between the PCI and USB busses.

8.2 Why was the **/dev** filesystem added to FreeBSD 5?

8.3 Give an example of a network interface that is useful without an underlying hardware device.

8.4 Give two reasons why the addresses of a network interface are not in the network-interface data structure.

8.5 Describe two tasks performed by a network-interface output routine.

8.6 Why is the identity of the network interface on which each message is received passed upward with the message?

8.7 Name the two devices that make up a pseudo-terminal. Explain the role of each of these pieces.

8.8 What are the two modes of terminal input? Which mode is most commonly in use when users converse with an interactive screen editor?

8.9 Explain why there are two character queues for dealing with terminal input. Describe the use of each.

8.10 What signal is sent to what process associated with a terminal if a network connection breaks in the middle of a session?

8.11 Name the three layers between the filesystem and the disk. Briefly describe the purpose of each layer.

8.12 Give an example of a GEOM provider and a GEOM consumer.

8.13 What happens if two GEOM consumers try to operate at the same time?

8.14 Draw a sequence of pictures showing what happens to the GEOM configuration in Figure 8.6 when the disk becomes unavailable.

8.15 Name the three layers within CAM. Briefly describe the service that each of these layers provides.

8.16 Can the CAM layer handle the setup and tear down of the DMA maps for one of its device drivers? Why or why not?

8.17 What is the purpose of the **/usr/sbin/config** program?

8.18 Give two reasons why it is unsafe to allow a kernel to load code dynamically.

8.19 Why are device probing and attaching done as two separate steps?

8.20 Describe the purpose of the device structure.

8.21 Run the **/usr/sbin/devinfo** program on a FreeBSD machine and identify the hardware associated with each of the leaf nodes.

8.22 Name the three steps used for resource allocation and freeing. Why are these functions broken into three separate steps?

**8.23 All devices are currently attached once in a depth-first search. But some devices may offer services needed by devices higher up the tree. Describe devices that fall into this class and give a plan to build a multipass-attach approach into newbus to handle them.

References

ACPI, 2013.

ACPI, *Advanced Configuration and Power Interface Specification,* available from http://www.acpi.info/, November 2013.

ANSI, 2002.

ANSI, "Common Access Method draft standard," X3T10, available from http://www.t10.org, January 2002.

ANSI, 2003.

ANSI, "Fibre Channel draft standard," T11, available from http://www.t11.org, January 2003.

Arch, 2014.

Arch, *PC Architecture,* available from http://www.intel.com/design/chipsets/865PE/pix/865PE_schematic.gif, and http://www.just2good.co.uk/chipset.php, March 2014.

Barham et al., 2003.

P. Barham, B. Dragovic, K. Fraser, S. Hand, T. Harris, A. Ho, R. Neugebauer, I. Pratt, & A. Warfield, "Xen and the Art of Virtualization,"

Proceedings of the Nineteenth ACM Symposium on Operating Systems Principles, pp. 164–177, October 2003.

Chisnall, 2007.
D. Chisnall, *The Definitive Guide to the Xen Hypervisor,* Prentice Hall Press, Upper Saddle River, NJ, 2007.

Chiueh et al., 2004.
T. Chiueh, P. Pardhan, & G. Venkitachalam, *Intra-Address Space Protection Using Segmentation Hardware,* available from http://www.ecsl.cs.sunysb.edu/palladium.html, March 2004.

Harris & Fraser, 2007.
T. Harris & K. Fraser, "Concurrent Programming Without Locks," *ACM Transactions on Computer Systems*, vol. 25, no. 2, Association for Computing Machinery, May 2007.

Russell, 2008.
R. Russell, "Virtio: Towards a De-facto Standard for Virtual I/O Devices," *ACM SIGOPS Operating Systems Review*, vol. 42, no. 5, pp. 95–103, September 2008.

TCG, 2003.
TCG, *Trusted Computing Group TPM Specification Version 1.2,* available from http://www.trustedcomputinggroup.org/, October 2003.

Xerox, 1980.
Xerox, "The Ethernet, a Local Area Network: Data Link Layer and Physical Layer Specification," X3T51/80-50, Xerox Corporation, Stamford, CT, October 1980.

CHAPTER 9

The Fast Filesystem

9.1 Hierarchical Filesystem Management

The operations defined for local filesystems are divided into two parts. Common to all local filesystems are hierarchical naming, locking, quotas, attribute management, and protection. These features, which are independent of how data are stored, are provided by the UFS code described in the first seven sections of this chapter. The other part of the local filesystem, the filestore, is concerned with the organization and management of the data on the storage media. Storage is managed by the datastore filesystem operations that are provided by the FFS code described in the final two sections of this chapter. We use the acronym UFS when referring to the fast filesystem in this book.

The vnode operations defined for performing hierarchical filesystem operations are shown in Table 9.1. The most complex of these operations is that for performing a lookup. The filesystem-independent part of the lookup is described

Table 9.1 Hierarchical filesystem operations.

Operation done	Operator names
pathname searching	*lookup*
name creation	*create, mknod, link, symlink, mkdir*
name change/deletion	*rename, remove, rmdir*
attribute manipulation	*access, getattr, setattr*
object interpretation	*open, readdir, readlink, mmap, close*
process control	*advlock, ioctl, poll*
object management	*lock, unlock, inactive, reclaim*

in Section 7.4. The algorithm used to lookup a pathname component in a directory is described in Section 9.3.

There are five operators for creating names. The operator used depends on the type of object being created. The *create* operator creates regular files and also is used by the networking code to create AF_LOCAL domain sockets. The *link* operator creates additional names for existing objects. The *symlink* operator creates a symbolic link (see Section 9.3 for a discussion of symbolic links). The *mknod* operator creates character special devices (for compatibility with other UNIX systems that still use them); it is also used to create fifos. The *mkdir* operator creates directories.

There are three operators for changing or deleting existing names. The *rename* operator deletes a name for an object in one location and creates a new name for the object in another location. The implementation of this operator is complex when the kernel is dealing with the movement of a directory from one part of the filesystem tree to another. The *remove* operator removes a name. If the removed name is the final reference to the object, the space associated with the underlying object is reclaimed. The *remove* operator operates on all object types except directories; they are removed using the *rmdir* operator.

Three operators are supplied for object attributes. The kernel retrieves attributes from an object using the *getattr* operator and stores them using the *setattr* operator. Access checks for a given user are provided by the *access* operator.

Five operators are provided for interpreting objects. The *open* and *close* operators have only peripheral use for regular files, but when they are used on special devices, they notify the appropriate device driver of device activation or shutdown. The *readdir* operator converts the filesystem-specific format of a directory to the standard list of directory entries expected by an application. Note that the interpretation of the contents of a directory is provided by the hierarchical filesystem-management layer; the filestore code considers a directory as just another object holding data. The *readlink* operator returns the contents of a symbolic link. As with directories, the filestore code considers a symbolic link as just another object holding data. The *mmap* operator prepares an object to be mapped into the address space of a process.

Three operators are provided to allow process control over objects. The *poll* operator allows a process to find out whether an object is ready to be read or written. The *ioctl* operator passes control requests to a special device. The *advlock* operator allows a process to acquire or release an advisory lock on an object. None of these operators modifies the object in the filestore. They are simply using the object for naming or directing the desired operation.

There are four operations for management of the objects. The *inactive* and *reclaim* operators were described in Section 7.3. The *lock* and *unlock* operators allow the callers of the vnode interface to provide hints to the code that implements operations on the underlying objects. Stateless filesystems such as NFS ignore these hints. Stateful filesystems, however, can use hints to avoid doing extra work. For example, an *open* system call requesting that a new file be created requires two steps. First, a *lookup* call is done to see if the file already exists. Before the lookup is started, a *lock* request is made on the directory being searched. While scanning through the directory checking for the name, the lookup code also identifies a location within the directory that contains enough space to hold the new name. If the lookup returns successfully (meaning that the name does not already exist), the *open* code verifies that the user has permission to create the file. If the caller is not eligible to create the new file, then they are expected to call *unlock* to release the lock that they acquired during the lookup. Otherwise, the *create* operation is called. If the filesystem is stateful and has been able to lock the directory, then it can simply create the name in the previously identified space because it knows that no other processes will have had access to the directory. Once the name is created, an *unlock* request is made on the directory. If the filesystem is stateless, then it cannot lock the directory, so the *create* operator must rescan the directory to find space and to verify that the name has not been created since the lookup.

9.2 Structure of an Inode

To allow files to be allocated concurrently and to provide random access within files, FreeBSD uses the concept of an index node, or ***inode***. The inode contains information about the contents of the file, as shown in Figure 9.1. This information includes the following:

- The type and access mode for the file
- The file's owner and group-access identifiers
- The time that the file was created, when it was most recently read and written, and when its inode was most recently updated by the system
- The size of the file in bytes
- The number of physical ***block***s used by the file (including blocks used to hold indirect pointers and extended attributes)
- The number of directory entries that reference the file
- The kernel and user-setable flags that describe characteristics of the file
- The generation number of the file (a randomly selected number assigned to the inode each time that the latter is allocated to a new file; the generation number is used by NFS to detect references to deleted files)
- The block size of the data blocks referenced by the inode (typically the same as, but sometimes larger than, the filesystem block size)
- The size of the extended attribute information

Notably missing in the inode is the filename. Filenames are maintained in directories rather than in inodes because a file may have many names, or links, and the name of a file can be large (up to 255 bytes in length). Directories are described in Section 9.3.

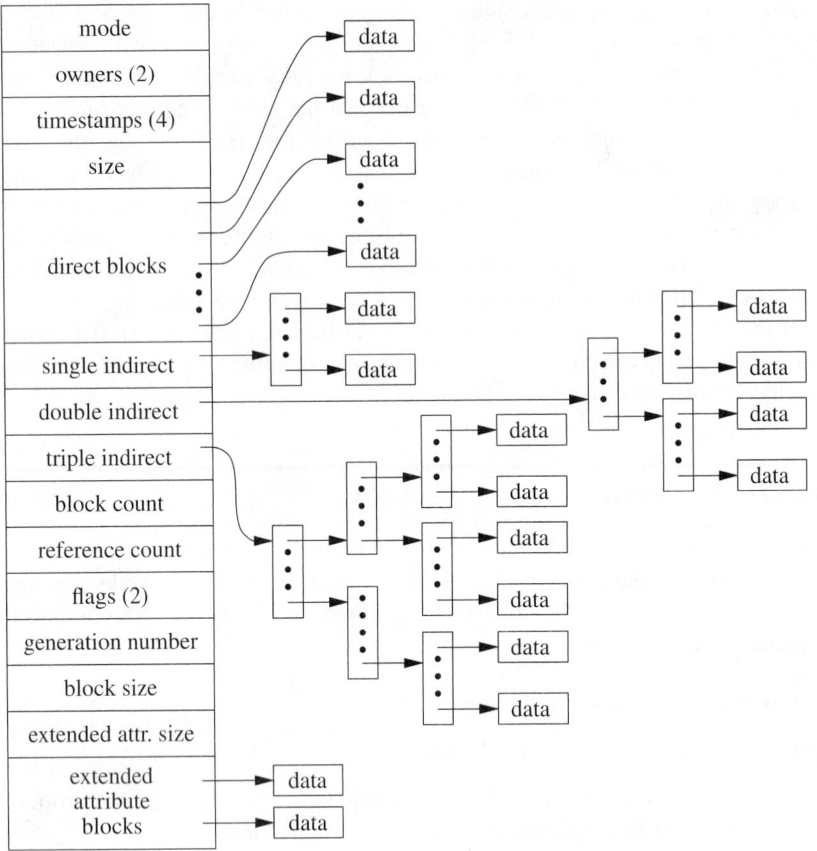

Figure 9.1 The structure of an inode.

To create a new name for a file, the system increments the count of the number of names referring to that inode. Then the new name is entered in a directory, along with the number of the inode. Conversely, when a name is deleted, the entry is deleted from a directory, and the name count for the inode is then decremented. When the name count reaches zero, the system deallocates the inode by putting all the inode's blocks back on a list of free blocks.

The inode also contains an array of pointers to the blocks in the file. The system can convert from a logical block number to a physical sector number by indexing into the array using the logical block number. A null array entry shows that no block has been allocated and will cause a block of zeros to be returned on a read. On a write of such an entry, a new block is allocated, the array entry is updated with the new block number, and the data are written to the disk.

Inodes are fixed in size, and most files are small, so the array of pointers must be small for efficient use of space. The first 12 array entries are allocated in the inode itself. For typical filesystems, this implementation allows the first 384

Kbyte of data to be located directly via a simple indexed lookup.

For somewhat larger files, Figure 9.1 shows that the inode contains a single indirect pointer that points to a ***single indirect block*** of pointers to data blocks. To find the 100th logical block of a file, the system first fetches the block identified by the indirect pointer and then indexes into the 88th block (100 minus 12 direct pointers) and fetches that data block.

For files that are bigger than a few Mbyte, the single indirect block is eventually exhausted; these files must resort to using a ***double indirect block***, which is a pointer to a block of pointers to pointers to data blocks. For files of multiple Tbyte, the system uses a ***triple indirect block***, which contains three levels of pointers before reaching the data block.

Although indirect blocks appear to increase the number of disk accesses required to get a block of data, the overhead of the transfer is typically much lower. In Section 7.4, we discuss the management of the cache that holds recently used disk blocks. The first time that a block of indirect pointers is needed, it is brought into the cache. Further accesses to the indirect pointers find the block already resident in memory; thus, they require only a single disk access to get the data.

Changes to the Inode Format

Traditionally, the FreeBSD fast filesystem (which we shall refer to in this book as UFS1) [McKusick et al., 1984] and its derivatives have used 32-bit pointers to reference the blocks used by a file on the disk. The UFS1 filesystem was designed in the early 1980s when the largest disks were 330 Mbyte. There was debate at the time whether it was worth squandering 32 bits per block pointer rather than using the 24-bit block pointers of the filesystem that it replaced. Luckily, the futurist view prevailed, and the design used 32-bit block pointers. Over the 20 years since it has been deployed, storage systems have grown to hold over a Pbyte of data. Depending on the block size configuration, the 32-bit block pointers of UFS1 run out of space in the 1 to 4 Tbyte range. While some stopgap measures can be used to extend the maximum-size storage systems supported by UFS1, by 2002 it became clear the only long-term solution was to use 64-bit block pointers. Thus, we decided to build a new filesystem, UFS2, that would use 64-bit block pointers.

We considered the alternatives between trying to make incremental changes to the existing UFS1 filesystem versus importing another existing filesystem such as XFS [Sweeney et al., 1996], or ReiserFS [Reiser, 2001]. We also considered writing a new filesystem from scratch so that we could take advantage of recent filesystem research and experience. We chose to extend the UFS1 filesystem because this approach allowed us to reuse most of the existing UFS1 code base. The benefits of this decision were that UFS2 was developed and deployed quickly, it became stable and reliable rapidly, and the same code base could be used to support both UFS1 and UFS2 filesystem formats. Over 90 percent of the code base is shared, so bug fixes and feature or performance enhancements usually apply to both filesystem formats.

The on-disk inodes used by UFS1 are 128 bytes in size and have only two unused 32-bit fields. It would not be possible to convert to 64-bit block pointers without reducing the number of direct block pointers from 12 to 5. Doing so would dramatically increase the amount of wasted space, since only direct block pointers can reference fragments, so the only alternative is to increase the size of the on-disk inode to 256 bytes.

Once one is committed to changing to a new on-disk format for the inodes, it is possible to include other inode-related changes that were not possible within the constraints of the old inodes. While it was tempting to throw in everything that has ever been suggested over the last 20 years, we felt that it was best to limit the addition of new capabilities to those that were likely to have a clear benefit. Every new addition adds complexity that has a cost both in maintainability and performance. Obscure or little-used features may add conditional checks in frequently executed code paths such as read and write, slowing down the overall performance of the filesystem even if they are not used.

Extended Attributes

A major addition in UFS2 is support for extended attributes. Extended attributes are a piece of auxiliary data storage associated with an inode that can be used to store auxiliary data that is separate from the contents of the file. The idea is similar to the concept of data forks used in the Apple filesystem [Apple, 2003]. By integrating the extended attributes into the inode, it is possible to provide the same integrity guarantees as are made for the contents of the file. Specifically, the successful completion of an *fsync* system call ensures that the file data, the extended attributes, and all names and paths leading to the names of the file are in stable store.

The current implementation has space in the inode to store up to two blocks of extended attributes. The new UFS2 inode format had room for up to five additional 64-bit pointers. Thus, the number of extended attribute blocks could have been between one to five blocks. We chose to allocate two blocks to the extended attributes and to leave the other three as spares for future use. By having two, all the code had to be prepared to deal with an array of pointers, so if the number is expanded into the remaining spares in the future, the existing implementation will work without changes to the source code. By saving three spares, we provided a reasonable amount of space for future needs. And if the decision to allow only two blocks proves to be too little space, one or more of the spares can be used to expand the size of the extended attributes in the future. If vastly more extended attribute space is needed, a spare could be used as an indirect pointer to extended attribute data blocks.

Figure 9.2 shows the format used for the extended attributes. The first field of the header of each attribute is its length. Applications that do not understand the namespace or name can simply skip over the unknown attribute by adding the length to their current position to get to the next attribute. Thus, many different applications can share the usage of the extended attribute space, even if they do not understand each other's data types.

The first of two initial uses for extended attributes is to support an ***access control list***, generally referred to as an ACL. An ACL replaces the group permissions for a file with a more specific list of the users that are permitted to access the files. The ACL also includes a list of the permissions that each user is granted. These permissions include the traditional read, write, and execute permissions along with other properties such as the right to rename or delete the file [Rhodes, 2014].

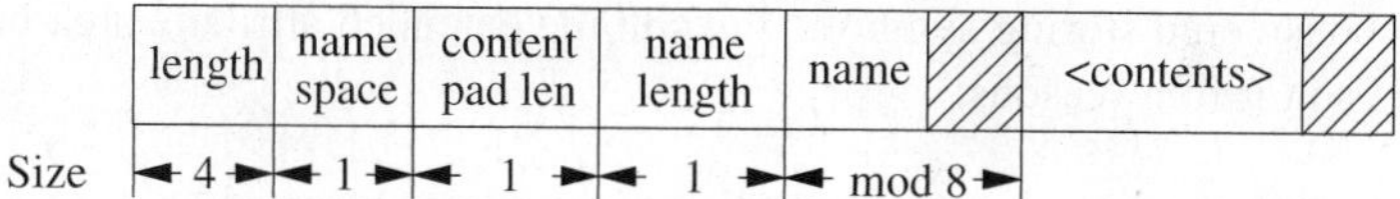

Figure 9.2 Format of extended attributes. The header of each attribute has a 4-byte length, 1-byte namespace class, 1-byte content pad length, 1-byte name length, and name. The name is padded so that the contents start on an 8-byte boundary. The contents are padded to the size shown by the "content pad length" field. The size of the contents can be calculated by subtracting from the length the size of the header (including the name) and the content pad length.

Earlier implementations of ACLs were done with a single auxiliary file per filesystem that was indexed by the inode number and had a small fixed-size area to store the ACL permissions. The small size was intended to keep the size of the auxiliary file reasonable, since it had to have space for every possible inode in the filesystem. There were two problems with this implementation. The fixed size of the space per inode to store the ACL information meant that it was not possible to give access to long lists of users. The second problem was that it was difficult to commit changes atomically to the ACL list for a file, since an update required that both the file inode and the ACL file be written to have the update take effect [Watson, 2000].

Both problems with the auxiliary file implementation of ACLs are fixed by storing the ACL information directly in the extended-attribute data area of the inode. Because of the large size of the extended attribute data area (a minimum of 8 Kbyte and typically 64 Kbyte), long lists of ACL information can be easily stored. Space used to store extended attribute information is proportional to the number of inodes with extended attributes and the size of the ACL lists that they use. Atomic update of the information is much easier, since writing the inode will update the inode attributes and the set of data that the inode references including the extended attributes in one disk operation. While it would be possible to update the old auxiliary file on every *fsync* system call done on the filesystem, the cost of doing so would be prohibitive. Here, the kernel knows if the extended attribute data block for an inode is dirty and can write just that data block during an *fsync* call on the inode.

The second use for extended attributes is for data labeling. Data labels provide permissions for a ***mandatory access control*** (***MAC***) framework enforced by the kernel. As described in Section 5.10, the kernel's MAC framework permits dynamically introduced system-security modules to modify system security functionality. This framework can be used to support a variety of new security services, including traditional labelled mandatory access control models. The framework provides a series of entry points that are called by code supporting various kernel services, especially with respect to access control points and object creation. The framework then calls out to security modules to offer them the opportunity to modify security behavior at those MAC entry points. Thus, the filesystem does not codify how the labels are used or enforced. It simply stores the labels associated with the inode and produces them when a security module needs to query them to do a permission check [Watson, 2001; Watson et al., 2003].

We considered storing symbolic links in the extended attribute area but chose not to do so for four reasons:

1. Most symbolic links fit within the 120 bytes normally used to store the direct and indirect pointers, and thus do not need a disk block to be allocated to hold them.
2. If the symbolic link is large enough to require storage in a disk block, the time to access an extended storage block is the same as the time to access a regular data block.
3. Since symbolic links rarely have any extended attributes, there would be no savings in storage, since a filesystem fragment would be needed whether it was stored in a regular data block or in an extended storage block.
4. If the symbolic link were stored in an extended storage block, it would take more time to traverse down the attribute list to find it.

New Filesystem Capabilities

Several other improvements were made when the enlarged inode format was created. We decided to get an early jump on the year 2038 problem when the 32-bit time fields overflow (specifically, Tue Jan 19 03:14:08 2038 GMT, which could be a really ugly way to usher in the first author's 84th birthday). We expanded the time fields (which hold seconds-since-1970) for access, modification, and inode-modification times from 32 bits to 64 bits. At plus or minus 136 billion years, this expansion should carry us from well before the universe was created until long after our sun has burned itself out. We left the nanoseconds fields for these times at 32 bits because we did not feel that added resolution was going to be useful in the foreseeable future. We considered expanding the time to only 48 bits. We chose to go to 64 bits, since 64 bits is a native size that can be easily manipulated with existing and likely future architectures. Using 48 bits would have required an extra unpacking or packing step each time the field was read or written. Also, going to 64 bits ensures enough bits for all likely measured time so it will not have to be enlarged.

We also added a new time field (also 64 bits) to hold the birth time (also commonly called the creation time) of the file. The birth time is set when the inode is first allocated and is not changed thereafter. It has been added to the structure returned by the *stat* system call so that applications can determine its value and so that archiving programs such as **dump**, **tar**, and **pax** can save this value along with the other file times. The birth time was added to a previously spare field in the *stat* system-call structure so that the size of the structure did not change. Thus, old versions of programs that use the *stat* call continue to work.

To date, only the **dump** program has been changed to save the birth-time value. This new version of **dump**, which can dump both UFS1 and UFS2 filesystems, creates a new dump format that is not readable by older versions of **restore**. The updated version of **restore** can identify and restore from both old and new dump formats. The birth times are only available and setable from the new dump format.

The *utimes* system call sets the access and modification times of a file to a specified set of values. It is used primarily by archive retrieval programs to set a newly extracted file's times back to those associated with the file's times in the archive. With the addition of birth time, we added a new system call that allows the setting of access, modification, and birth times. However, we realized that many existing applications will not be changed to use the new *utimes* system call. The result will be that the files that they retrieved from archives will have a newer birth time than access or modification times.

To provide a sensible birth time for applications that are unaware of the birth-time attribute, we changed the semantics of the *utimes* system call so that if the birth time was newer than the value of the modification time that it was setting, it would set the birth time to the same time as the modification time. An application that is aware of the birth-time attribute can set both the birth time and the modification time by doing two calls to *utimes*. First, it calls *utimes* with a modification time equal to the saved birth time, and then it calls *utimes* a second time with a modification time equal to the (presumably newer) saved modification time. For filesystems that do not store birth times, the second call will overwrite the first call resulting in the same values for access and modification times as they would have previously received. For filesystems that support birth time, it will be properly set. Most happily for the application writers, they will not have to compile the name of *utimes* conditionally for BSD and non-BSD systems. They just write their applications to call the standard interface twice knowing that all supported times will be set correctly on all systems and filesystems. Applications that value speed of execution over portability can use the new version of the *utimes* system call that allows all time values to be set with one call.

File Flags

FreeBSD has two system calls, *chflags* and *fchflags*, that set the 32-bit user-flags word in the inode. The flags are included in the *stat* structure so that they can be inspected.

The owner of the file or the superuser can set the low 16 bits. Currently, there are flags defined to mark a file as append-only, immutable, and not needing to be dumped. An immutable file may not be changed, moved, or deleted. An append-only file is immutable, except data may be appended to it. The user append-only and immutable flags may be changed by the owner of the file or the superuser.

Only the superuser can set the high 16 bits. Currently, there are flags defined to mark a file as append-only and immutable. Once set, the append-only and immutable flags in the top 16 bits cannot be cleared when the system is secure.

The kernel runs with four different levels of security. Any superuser process can raise the security level, but only the **init** process can lower that level (the **init** program is described in Section 15.4). Security levels are defined as follows:

–1. Permanently insecure mode: Always run system in level 0 mode (must be compiled into the kernel).

0. Insecure mode: Immutable and append-only flags may be turned off. All devices can be read or written, subject to their permissions.

1. Secure mode: The superuser-settable immutable and append-only flags cannot be cleared; disks for mounted filesystems and kernel memory (**/dev/mem** and **/dev/kmem**) are read-only.

2. Highly secure mode: This mode is the same as secure mode, except that disks are always read-only whether mounted or not. This level precludes even a superuser process from tampering with filesystems by unmounting them, but it also inhibits formatting of new filesystems.

Normally, the system runs with level 0 security while in single-user mode, and with level 1 security while in multiuser mode. If level 2 security is desired while the system is running in multiuser mode, it should be set in the **/etc/rc** startup script (the **/etc/rc** script is described in Section 15.4).

Files marked immutable by the superuser cannot be changed except by someone with physical access to either the machine or the system console. Files marked immutable include those that are frequently the subject of attack by intruders (e.g., **login** and **su**). The append-only flag is typically used for critical system logs. If an intruder breaks in, he will be unable to cover his tracks. Although simple in concept, these two features improve the security of a system dramatically. However, there are some serious limitations to this security model:

- Immutable files can only be updated when system is single-user.
- Append-only files can only be rotated when system is single-user.
- Direct hardware access is restricted.

The biggest limitation is that all startup activities must be protected. The reason for this limitation is that a kernel always has some bug that can be exploited to cause it to crash and reboot. During the reboot process, it is running in insecure mode; thus, if an exploit script can be injected anywhere during the time that the system is starting up, the system can be compromised. The set of startup activities includes:

- Startup scripts and their containing directories
- All binaries executed during startup
- All libraries used during startup
- Many configuration files used during startup

Finding and locking down all these files and directories is very difficult and if even one is missed, it is possible to break into the system.

One change in the UFS2 inode format was to split the flags field into two separate 32-bit fields: one for flags that can be set by applications (as in UFS1) and a new field for flags maintained strictly by the kernel. An example of a kernel flag is the SNAPSHOT flag used to label a file as being a snapshot. Another kernel-only flag is OPAQUE, which is used by the union filesystem to mark a directory that should not make the layers below it visible. By moving these kernel flags from the high 16 bits of the user-flags field into a separate kernel-flags field, they will not be accidentally set or cleared by a naive or malicious application.

Dynamic Inodes

A common complaint about the UFS1 filesystem is that it preallocates all its inodes at the time that the filesystem is created. For filesystems with millions of files, the initialization of the filesystem can take several hours. Additionally, the filesystem creation program, **newfs**, had to assume that every filesystem would be filled with many small files and allocate a lot more inodes than were likely to ever be used. If a UFS1 filesystem uses up all its inodes, the only way to get more is to dump, rebuild, and restore the filesystem. The UFS2 filesystem resolves these problems by dynamically allocating its inodes. The usual implementation of dynamically allocated inodes requires a separate filesystem data structure (typically referred to as the inode file) that tracks the current set of inodes. The management and maintenance of this extra data structure adds overhead and complexity and often degrades performance.

To avoid these costs, UFS2 preallocates a range of inode numbers and a set of blocks for each cylinder group (cylinder groups are described in Section 9.10). Initially, each cylinder group has two blocks of inodes allocated (a typical block holds 128 inodes). When the blocks fill up, the next block of inodes in the set is allocated and initialized. The set of blocks that may be allocated to inodes is held as part of the free-space reserve until all other space in the filesystem is allocated. Only then can it be used for file data.

In theory, a filesystem could fill, using up all the blocks set aside for inodes. Later, after large files have been removed and many small files created to replace them, the filesystem might find itself unable to allocate the needed inodes because all the space set aside for inodes was still in use. Here, it would be necessary to reallocate existing files to move them to new locations outside the inode area. Such code has not been written as we do not expect that this condition will arise in practice, since the free-space reserve used on most filesystems (8 percent) exceeds the amount of space needed for inodes (typically less than 6 percent). On these systems, only a process running with root privileges would ever be able to allocate the inode blocks. Should the code prove necessary in real use, it can be written at that time. Until it is written, filesystems hitting this condition will return an "out of inodes" error on attempts to create new files.

A side benefit of dynamically allocating inodes is that the time it takes to create a new filesystem in UFS2 is about 1 percent of the time that it takes in UFS1. A filesystem that would take one hour to build in a UFS1 format can be built in under a minute in the UFS2 format. While filesystem creations are not a common operation, having them build quickly does matter to the system administrators that have to do such tasks with some regularity.

The cost of dynamically allocating inodes is one extra disk write for every 128 new inodes that are created. Although this cost is low compared to the other costs of creating 128 new files, some systems administrators might want to preallocate more than the minimal number of inodes. If such a demand arises, it would be trivial to add a flag to the **newfs** program to preallocate additional inodes at the time that the filesystem is created.

Inode Management

Most of the activity in the local filesystem revolves around inodes. As described in Section 7.4, the kernel keeps a list of active and recently accessed vnodes. The decisions regarding how many and which files should be cached are made by the vnode layer based on information about activity across all filesystems. Each local filesystem will have a subset of the system vnodes to manage. Each uses an inode supplemented with some additional information to identify and locate the set of files for which it is responsible. Figure 9.3 shows the location of the inodes within the system.

Reviewing the material in Section 7.1, each process has a ***process open-file table*** that has slots for up to a system-imposed limit of file descriptors; this table is maintained as part of the process state. When a user process opens a file (or socket), an unused slot is located in the process's open-file table; the small integer file descriptor that is returned on a successful *open* is an index value into this table.

The per-process file-table entry points to a system *open-file entry*, which contains information about the underlying file or socket represented by the descriptor. For files, the file table points to the vnode representing the open file. For the local filesystem, the vnode references an inode. It is the inode that identifies the file itself.

The first step in opening a file is to find the file's associated inode. The lookup request is given to the filesystem associated with the directory currently being searched. When the local filesystem finds the name in the directory, it gets the inode number of the associated file. First, the filesystem searches its collection of inodes to see whether the requested inode is already in memory. To avoid performing a linear scan of all its entries, the system keeps a set of hash chains with each entry keyed by inode number and filesystem identifier; see Figure 9.4. If the inode is not in the table, such as the first time a file is opened, the filesystem must request a new vnode. When a new vnode is allocated to the local filesystem, a new structure to hold the inode is allocated.

The next step is to locate the disk block containing the inode and to read that block into a buffer in system memory. When the disk I/O completes, the inode is copied from the disk buffer into the newly allocated inode entry. In addition to the

Figure 9.3 Layout of kernel tables.

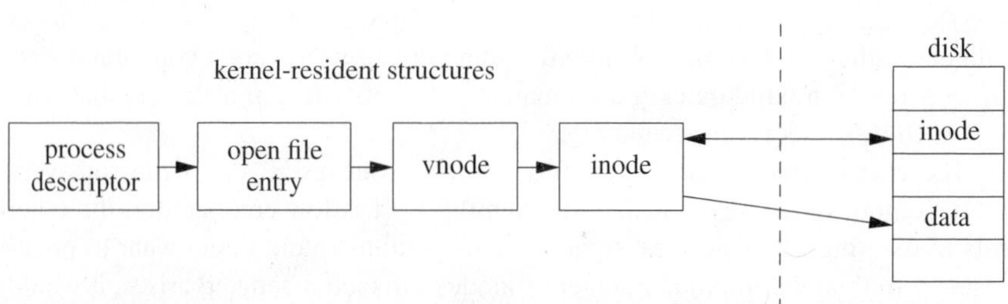

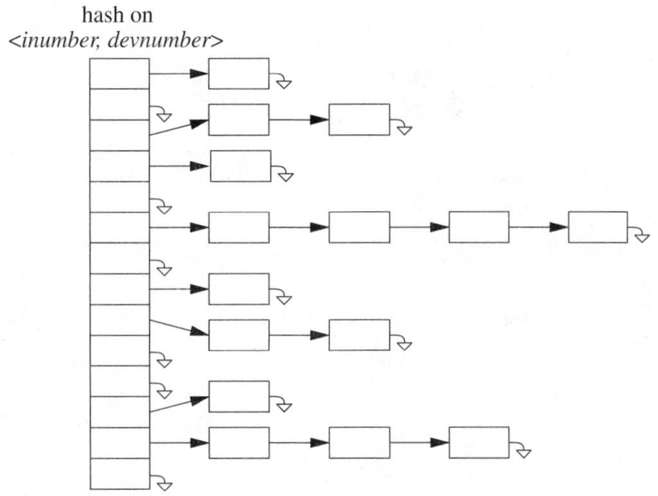

Figure 9.4 Structure of the inode table.

information contained in the disk portion of the inode, the inode table itself maintains supplemental information while the inode is in memory. This information includes the hash chains described previously, as well as flags showing the inode's status, reference counts on its use, and information to manage locks. The information also contains pointers to other kernel data structures of frequent interest, such as the superblock for the filesystem containing the inode.

When the last reference to a file is closed, the local filesystem is notified that the file has become inactive. When it is inactivated, the inode times will be updated, and the inode may be written to disk. However, it remains on the hash list so that it can be found if it is reopened. After being inactive for a period determined by the vnode layer, based on demand for vnodes in all the filesystems, the vnode will be reclaimed. When a vnode for a local file is reclaimed, the inode is removed from the previous filesystem's hash chain and, if the inode is dirty, its contents are written back to disk. The space for the inode is then deallocated, so that the vnode will be ready for use by a new filesystem client.

9.3 Naming

Filesystems contain files, most of which contain ordinary data. Certain files are distinguished as directories and contain pointers to files that may themselves be directories. This hierarchy of directories and files is organized into a tree structure; Figure 9.5 shows a small filesystem tree. Each of the circles in the figure represents an inode with its corresponding inode number inside. Each of the arrows represents a name in a directory. For example, inode 4 is the **/usr** directory with entry **.**, that points to itself, and entry **..**, that points to its parent, inode 2, the root of the filesystem. It also contains the name **bin**, which references directory inode 7, and the name **foo**, which references file inode 6.

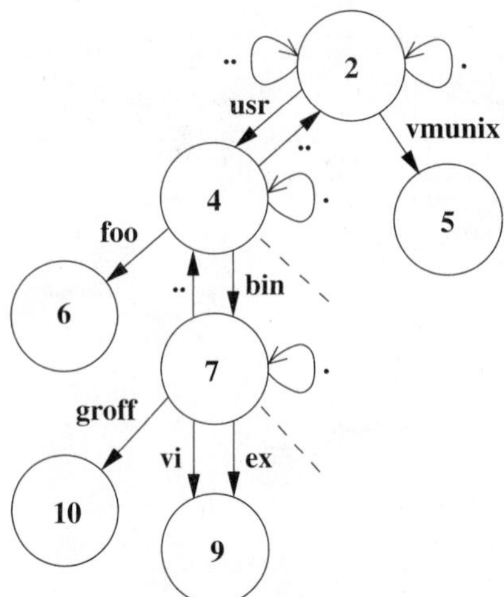

Figure 9.5 A small filesystem tree.

Directories

Directories are allocated in units called chunks; Figure 9.6 shows a typical directory chunk. The size of a chunk is chosen such that each allocation can be transferred to disk in a single operation. The ability to change a directory in a single operation makes directory updates atomic. Chunks are broken up into variable-length directory entries to allow filenames to be of nearly arbitrary length. No directory entry can span multiple chunks. The first four fields of a directory entry are of fixed length and contain the following:

1. The inode number, an index into a table of on-disk inode structures; the selected entry describes the file (inodes were described in Section 9.2)
2. The size of the entry in bytes
3. The type of the entry
4. The length of the filename contained in the entry in bytes

The remainder of an entry is of variable length and contains a null-terminated filename padded to a 4-byte boundary. The maximum length of a filename in a directory is 255 characters.

The filesystem records free space in a directory by having entries accumulate the free space in their size fields. Thus, some directory entries are larger than required to hold the entry name plus fixed-length fields. Space allocated to a directory should always be accounted for completely by the total of the sizes of the directory's entries. When an entry is deleted from a directory, the system coalesces the entry's space into the previous entry in the same directory chunk by increasing the size of the previous entry by the size of the deleted entry. If the first entry of a directory chunk is free, then the pointer to the entry's inode is set to zero to show that the entry is unallocated.

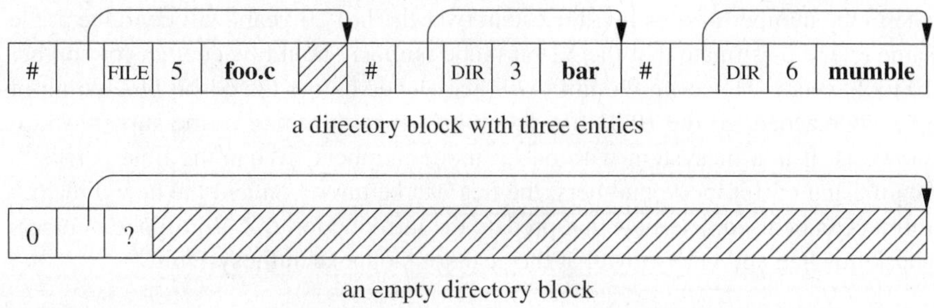

Figure 9.6 Format of directory chunks.

When creating a new directory entry, the kernel must scan the entire directory to ensure that the name does not already exist. While doing this scan, it also checks each directory block to see if it has enough space in which to put the new entry. The space need not be contiguous. The kernel will compact the valid entries within a directory block to coalesce several small unused spaces into a single space that is big enough to hold the new entry. The first block that has enough space is used. The kernel will neither compact space across directory blocks nor create an entry that spans two directory blocks as it always wants to be able to do directory updates by writing a single directory block. If no space is found when scanning the directory, a new block is allocated at the end of the directory.

Applications obtain chunks of directories from the kernel by using the *getdirentries* system call. For the local filesystem, the on-disk format of directories is identical to that expected by the application, so the chunks are returned uninterpreted. When directories are read over the network or from non-BSD filesystems, such as Apple's HFS, the *getdirentries* system call has to convert the on-disk representation of the directory to that described.

Normally, programs want to read directories one entry at a time. This interface is provided by the directory-access routines. The *opendir*() function returns a structure pointer that is used by *readdir*() to get chunks of directories using *getdirentries*; *readdir*() returns the next entry from the chunk on each call. The *closedir*() function deallocates space allocated by *opendir*() and closes the directory. In addition, there is the *rewinddir*() function to reset the read position to the beginning, the *telldir*() function that returns a structure describing the current directory position, and the *seekdir*() function that returns to a position previously obtained with *telldir*().

The UFS1 filesystem uses 32-bit inode numbers. While it is tempting to increase these inode numbers to 64 bits in UFS2, doing so would require that the directory format be changed. There is much code that works directly on directory entries. Changing directory formats would entail creating many more filesystem-specific functions that would increase the complexity and maintainability issues with the code. Furthermore, the current APIs for referencing directory entries use 32-bit inode numbers. As a result, even if the underlying filesystem supported 64-bit inode numbers, they could not currently be made visible to user applications. In the short term, applications are not running into the 4-billion-files-per-filesystem limit that 32-bit inode numbers impose. If we assume that the growth rate in the number of files per filesystem over the last 20 years will continue at the same rate, we estimate that the 32-bit inode number should be enough for another 10 to 20 years. However, the limit will be reached before the 64-bit block limit of UFS2 is reached, so the UFS2 filesystem has reserved a flag in the superblock to show that it is a filesystem with 64-bit inode numbers. When the time comes to begin using 64-bit inode numbers, the flag can be turned on and the new directory format can be used. Kernels that predate the introduction of 64-bit inode numbers check this flag and will know that they cannot mount such filesystems.

Finding of Names in Directories

A common request to the filesystem is to look up a specific name in a directory. The kernel usually does the lookup by starting at the beginning of the directory and going through it, comparing each entry in turn. First, the length of the sought-after name is compared with the length of the name being checked. If the lengths are identical, a string comparison of the name being sought and the directory entry is made. If they match, the search is complete; if they fail, either in the length or in the string comparison, the search continues with the next entry. Whenever a name is found, its name and containing directory are entered into the systemwide name cache described in Section 7.4. Whenever a search is unsuccessful, an entry is made in the cache showing that the name does not exist in the particular directory. Before starting a directory scan, the kernel looks for the name in the cache. If either a positive or negative entry is found, the directory scan can be avoided.

Another common operation is to look up all the entries in a directory. For example, many programs do a *stat* system call on each name in a directory in the order that the names appear in the directory. To improve performance for these programs, the kernel maintains the directory offset of the last successful lookup for each directory. Each time that a lookup is done in that directory, the search is started from the offset at which the previous name was found (instead of from the beginning of the directory). For programs that step sequentially through a directory with n files, search time decreases from $Order(n^2)$ to $Order(n)$.

One quick benchmark that demonstrates the maximum effectiveness of the cache is running the *ls −l* command on a directory containing 600 files. On a system that retains the most recent directory offset, the amount of system time for this test is reduced by 85 percent. Unfortunately, the maximum effectiveness is much greater than the average effectiveness. Although the cache is 90 percent effective when hit, it is applicable to only about 25 percent of the names being looked up. Despite the amount of time spent in the lookup routine itself decreasing substantially, the improvement is diminished because more time is spent in the routines that that routine calls. Each cache miss causes a directory to be accessed twice—once to search from the middle to the end and once to search from the beginning to the middle.

These caches provide good directory lookup performance but are ineffective for large directories that have a high rate of entry creation and deletion. Each time a new directory entry is created, the kernel must scan the entire directory to ensure that the entry does not already exist. When an existing entry is deleted, the kernel must scan the directory to find the entry to be removed. For directories with many entries, these linear scans are time consuming.

The approach to solving this problem is to introduce dynamic directory hashing that retrofits a directory indexing system to UFS [Dowse & Malone, 2002]. To avoid repeated linear searches of large directories, the dynamic directory hashing builds a hash table of directory entries on the fly when the directory is first accessed. This table avoids directory scans on later lookups, creates, and deletes. Unlike filesystems originally designed with large directories in mind, these indices are not saved on disk and so the system is backward compatible. The drawback is that the indices need to be built the first time that a large directory is encountered after each system reboot. The effect of the dynamic directory hashing is that large directories in UFS cause minimal performance problems.

When we built UFS2, we contemplated solving the large directory update problem by changing to a more complex directory structure such as one that uses B-trees. This technique is used in many modern filesystems such as XFS [Sweeney et al., 1996], JFS [Best, 2000], ReiserFS [Reiser, 2001], and in later versions of Ext2 [Phillips, 2001]. We decided not to make the change at the time that UFS2 was first implemented for two reasons. First, we had limited time and resources, and we wanted to get something working and stable that could be used in the time frame of FreeBSD 5. By keeping the same directory format, we were able to reuse all the directory code from UFS1, did not have to change numerous filesystem utilities to understand and maintain a new directory format, and were able to produce a stable and reliable filesystem in the time frame available to us. Second, we felt that we could retain the existing directory structure because of the dynamic directory hashing that was added to FreeBSD.

Borrowing the technique used by the Ext2 filesystem, a flag was also added to show that an on-disk indexing structure is supported for directories [Phillips, 2001]. This flag is unconditionally turned off by the existing implementation of UFS. In the future, if an implementation of an on-disk directory-indexing structure is added, the implementations that support it will not turn the flag off. Index-supporting kernels will maintain the indices and leave the flag on. If an old non-index-supporting kernel is run, it will turn off the flag so that when the filesystem is once again run under a new kernel, the new kernel will discover that the indexing flag has been turned off and will know that the indices may be out of date and have to be rebuilt before being used. The only constraint on an implementation of the indices is that they have to be an auxiliary data structure that references the old linear directory format.

Pathname Translation

We are now ready to describe how the filesystem looks up a pathname. The small filesystem introduced in Figure 9.5 is expanded to show its internal structure in Figure 9.7. Each of the files in Figure 9.5 is shown expanded into its constituent inode and data blocks. As an example of how these data structures work, consider how the system finds the file **/usr/bin/vi**. It must first search the root directory of the filesystem to find the directory **usr**. It first finds the inode that describes the root directory. By convention, inode 2 is always reserved for the root directory of a filesystem; therefore, the system finds and brings inode 2 into memory. This inode shows where the data blocks are for the root directory. These data blocks must also be brought into memory so that they can be searched for the entry for

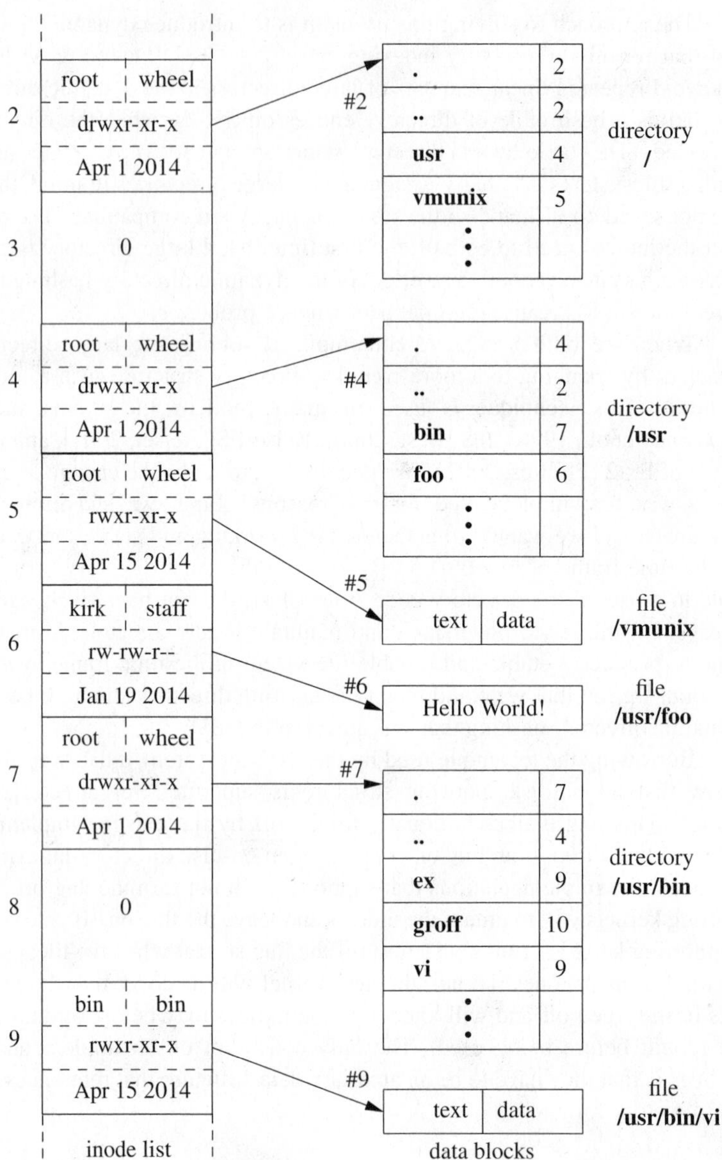

Figure 9.7 Internal structure of a small filesystem.

usr. Having found the entry for **usr**, the system knows that the contents of **usr** are described by inode 4. Returning once again to the disk, the system fetches inode 4 to find where the data blocks for **usr** are located. Searching these blocks, it finds the entry for **bin**. The **bin** entry points to inode 7. Next, the system brings in inode 7 and its associated data blocks from the disk to search for the entry for **vi**. Having found that **vi** is described by inode 9, the system can fetch this inode and the blocks that contain the **vi** binary. The first time after booting that this lookup is done, many I/O operations will be done. Thereafter, the various filesystem caches will ensure that these I/O operations will not need to be repeated.

Links

As shown in Figure 9.8, each file has a single inode, but multiple directory entries in the same filesystem may reference that inode (i.e., the inode may have multiple names). Each directory entry creates a ***hard link*** of a filename to the inode that describes the file's contents. The link concept is fundamental; inodes do not reside in directories but exist separately and are referenced by links. When all the links to an inode are removed, the inode is deallocated. If one link to a file is removed and the filename is recreated with new contents, the other links will continue to point to the old inode. Figure 9.8 shows two different directory entries, **foo** and **bar**, that reference the same file; thus, the inode for the file shows a reference count of 2.

The system also supports a ***symbolic link***, or ***soft link***. A symbolic link is implemented as a file that contains a pathname. When the system encounters a symbolic link while looking up a component of a pathname, the contents of the symbolic link are prepended to the rest of the pathname; the lookup continues with the resulting pathname. If a symbolic link contains an absolute pathname, that absolute pathname is used. Otherwise, the contents of the symbolic link are evaluated relative to the location of the link in the file hierarchy (not relative to the current working directory of the calling process).

A symbolic link is illustrated in Figure 9.9. Here, there is a hard link, **foo**, that points to the file. The other reference, **bar**, points to a different inode whose contents are a pathname of the referenced file. When a process opens **bar**, the system interprets the contents of the symbolic link as a pathname to find the file

Figure 9.8 Hard links to a file.

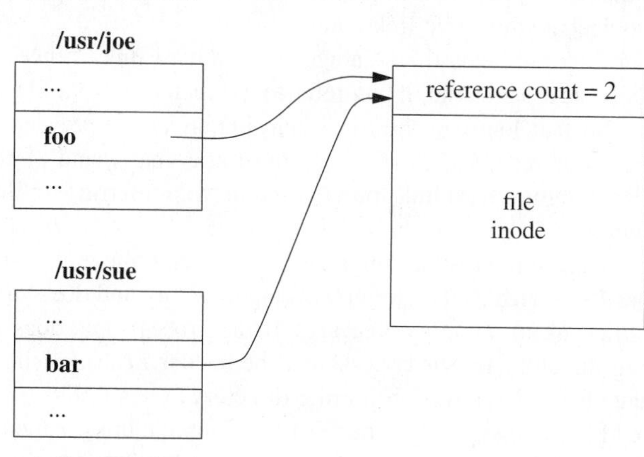

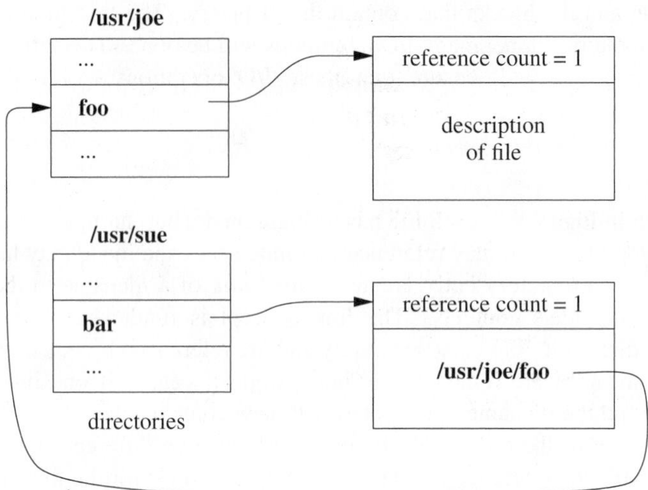

Figure 9.9 Symbolic link to a file.

the link references. Symbolic links are treated like data files by the system, rather than as part of the filesystem structure; thus, they can point at directories or files on other filesystems. If a filename is removed and replaced, any symbolic links that point to it will access the new file. Finally, if the filename is not replaced, the symbolic link will point at nothing, and any attempt to access it will return an error.

When *open* is applied to a symbolic link, it returns a file descriptor for the file pointed to, not for the link itself. Otherwise, it would be necessary to use indirection to access the file pointed to—and that file, rather than the link, is what is usually wanted. For the same reason, most other system calls that take pathname arguments also follow symbolic links. Sometimes, it is useful to be able to detect a symbolic link when traversing a filesystem or when making an archive tape. In this situation, the *lstat* system call is available to get the status of a symbolic link, instead of the object at which that link points.

A symbolic link has several advantages over a hard link. Since a symbolic link is maintained as a pathname, it can refer to a directory or to a file on a different filesystem. So that loops in the filesystem hierarchy are prevented, unprivileged users are not permitted to create hard links (other than **.** and **..**) that refer to a directory. The design of hard links prevents them from referring to files on a different filesystem.

There are several interesting implications of symbolic links. Consider a process that has **/usr/keith** as its current working directory and does *cd* **src**, where **src** is a symbolic link to directory **/usr/src**. If the process then does a *cd* **..**, the current working directory for the process will be in **/usr** instead of in **/usr/keith**, as it would have been if **src** were a normal directory instead of a symbolic link. The kernel could be changed to keep track of the symbolic links that a process has traversed and to interpret **..** differently if the directory has been reached through a symbolic link. There are two problems with this implementation. First, the kernel would have to maintain a potentially unbounded amount of information. Second, no program could depend on being able to use **..**, since it could not be sure how the name would be interpreted.

Many shells keep track of symbolic-link traversals. When users change directory through **..** from a directory that was entered through a symbolic link, the shell returns them to the directory from which they came. Although the shell might have to maintain an unbounded amount of information, the worst that will happen is that the shell will run out of memory. Having the shell fail will affect only the user silly enough to traverse endlessly through symbolic links. Tracking of symbolic links affects only change-directory commands in the shell; programs can continue to depend on **..** to reference its true parent. Thus, tracking symbolic links outside the kernel in a shell is reasonable.

Since symbolic links may cause loops in the filesystem, the kernel prevents looping by allowing at most eight symbolic link traversals in a single pathname translation. If the limit is reached, the kernel produces an error (ELOOP).

9.4 Quotas

Resource sharing always has been a design goal for the BSD system. By default, any single user can allocate all the available space in the filesystem. In certain environments, uncontrolled use of disk space is unacceptable. Consequently, FreeBSD includes a quota mechanism to restrict the amount of filesystem resources that a user or members of a group can obtain. The quota mechanism sets limits on both the number of files and the number of disk blocks that a user or members of a group may allocate. Quotas can be set separately for each user and group on each filesystem.

Quotas support both ***hard*** and ***soft limits***. When a process exceeds its soft limit, a warning is printed on the user's terminal; the offending process is not prevented from allocating space unless it exceeds its hard limit. The idea is that users should stay below their soft limit between login sessions but may use more resources while they are active. If a user fails to correct the problem for longer than a grace period, the soft limit starts to be enforced as the hard limit. The grace period is set by the system administrator and is 7 days by default. These quotas are derived from a larger resource-limit package that was developed at the University of Melbourne in Australia by Robert Elz [Elz, 1984].

Quotas connect into the system primarily as an adjunct to the allocation routines. When a new block is requested from the allocation routines, the request is first validated by the quota system with the following steps:

1. If there is a user quota associated with the file, the quota system consults the quota associated with the owner of the file. If the owner has reached or exceeded their limit, the request is denied.

2. If there is a group quota associated with the file, the quota system consults the quota associated with the group of the file. If the group has reached or exceeded its limit, the request is denied.

3. If the quota tests pass, the request is permitted and is added to the usage statistics for the file.

When either a user or group quota would be exceeded, the allocator returns a failure as though the filesystem were full. The kernel propagates this error up to the process doing the *write* system call.

Quotas are assigned to a filesystem after it has been mounted. A system call associates a file containing the quotas with the mounted filesystem. By convention, the file with user quotas is named **quota.user**, and the file with group quotas is named **quota.group**. These files typically reside either in the root of the mounted filesystem or in the **/var/quotas** directory. For each quota to be imposed, the system opens the appropriate quota file and holds a reference to it in the mount-table entry associated with the mounted filesystem. Figure 9.10 shows the mount-table reference. Here, the root filesystem has a quota on users but has none on groups. The **/usr** filesystem has quotas imposed on both users and groups. As quotas for different users or groups are needed, they are taken from the appropriate quota file.

Quota files are maintained as an array of quota records indexed by user or group identifiers; Figure 9.11 shows a typical record in a user quota file. To find the quota for user identifier *i*, the system seeks to the offset $i \times$ **sizeof**(quota structure) in the quota file and reads the quota structure at that offset. Each quota structure contains the limits imposed on the user for the associated filesystem. These limits include the hard and soft limits on the number of blocks and inodes that the user may have, the number of blocks and inodes that the user currently has allocated, and the time that the soft limit should start being enforced as the hard limit. The group quota file works in the same way, except that it is indexed by group identifier.

Active quotas are held in system memory in a data structure known as a *dquot* entry; Figure 9.12 shows two typical entries. In addition to the quota limits and usage extracted from the quota file, the *dquot* entry maintains information about

Figure 9.10 References to quota files.

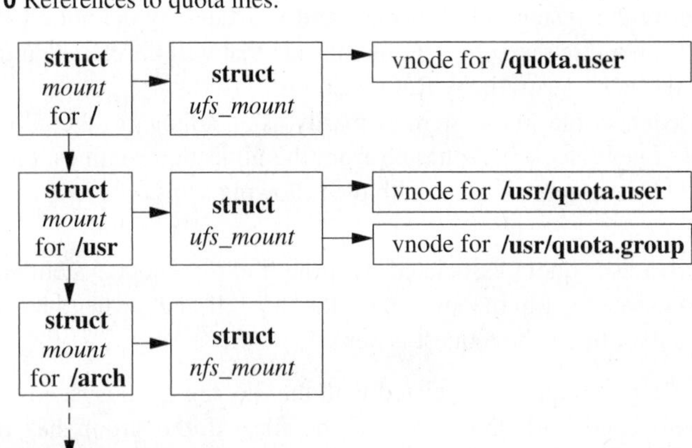

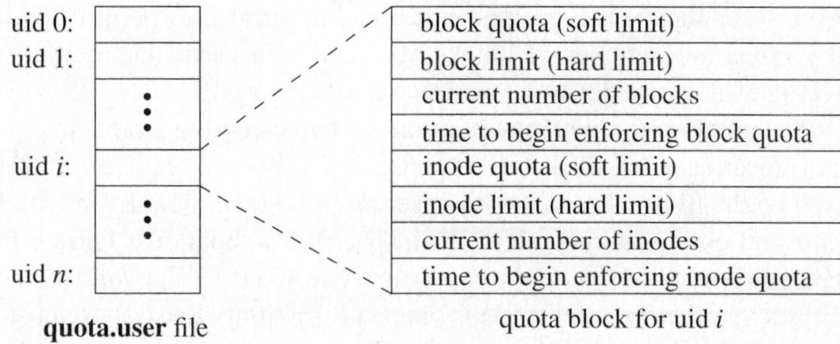

Figure 9.11 Contents of a quota record.

the quota while the quota is in use. This information includes fields to allow fast access and identification. Quotas are checked by the *chkdq*() routine. Since quotas may have to be updated on every write to a file, *chkdq*() must be able to find and manipulate them quickly. Thus, the task of finding the *dquot* structure associated with a file is done when the file is first opened for writing. When an access check is done to check for writing, the system checks to see whether there is either a user or a group quota associated with the file. If one or more quotas exist, the inode is set up to hold a reference to the appropriate *dquot* structures for as long as the inode is resident. The *chkdq*() routine can determine that a file has a quota simply by checking whether the *dquot* pointer is nonnull; if it is, all the necessary information can be accessed directly. If a user or a group has multiple files open

Figure 9.12 Dquot entries.

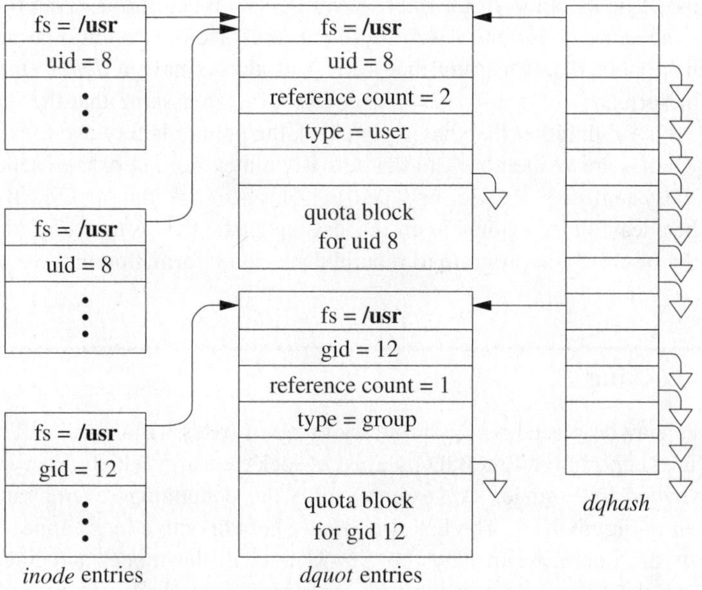

on the same filesystem, all inodes describing those files point to the same *dquot* entry. Thus, the number of blocks allocated to a particular user or a group can always be known easily and consistently.

The number of *dquot* entries in the system can grow large. To avoid performing a linear scan of all the *dquot* entries, the system keeps a set of hash chains keyed on the filesystem and on the user or group identifier. Even with hundreds of *dquot* entries, the kernel needs to inspect only about five entries to determine whether a requested *dquot* entry is memory resident. If the *dquot* entry is not resident, such as the first time a file is opened for writing, the system must reallocate a *dquot* entry and read in the quota from disk. The *dquot* entry is reallocated from the least recently used *dquot* entry. So that it can find the oldest *dquot* entry quickly, the system keeps unused *dquot* entries linked together in an LRU chain. When the reference count on a *dquot* structure drops to zero, the system puts that *dquot* onto the end of the LRU chain. The *dquot* structure is not removed from its hash chain, so if the structure is needed again soon, it can still be located. Only when a *dquot* structure is recycled with a new quota record is it removed and relinked into the hash chain. The *dquot* entry on the front of the LRU chain yields the least recently used *dquot* entry. Frequently used *dquot* entries are reclaimed from the middle of the LRU chain and are relinked at the end after use.

The hashing structure allows *dquot* structures to be found quickly. However, it does not solve the problem of how to discover that a user has no quota on a particular filesystem. If a user has no quota, a lookup for the quota will fail. The cost of going to disk and reading the quota file to discover that the user has no quota imposed would be prohibitive. To avoid doing this work each time that a new file is accessed for writing, the system maintains nonquota *dquot* entries. When an inode owned by a user or group that does not already have a *dquot* entry is first accessed, a dummy *dquot* entry is created that has infinite values filled in for the quota limits. When the *chkdq*() routine encounters such an entry, it will update the usage fields but will not impose any limits. When the user later writes other files, the same *dquot* entry will be found, thus avoiding additional access to the on-disk quota file. Ensuring that a file will always have a *dquot* entry improves the performance of writing data, since *chkdq*() can assume that the *dquot* pointer is always valid, rather than having to check the pointer before every use.

Quotas are written back to the disk when they fall out of the cache, whenever the filesystem does a sync, or when the filesystem is unmounted. If the system crashes, leaving the quotas in an inconsistent state, the system administrator must run the **quotacheck** program to rebuild the usage information in the quota files.

9.5 File Locking

Locks may be placed on any arbitrary range of bytes within a file. These semantics are supported in FreeBSD by a list of locks, each of which describes a lock of a specified byte range. An example of a file containing several range locks is shown in Figure 9.13. The list of currently held or active locks appears across the top of the figure, headed by the *i_lockf* field in the inode, and linked together through the *lf_next* field of the lock structures. Each lock structure identifies the

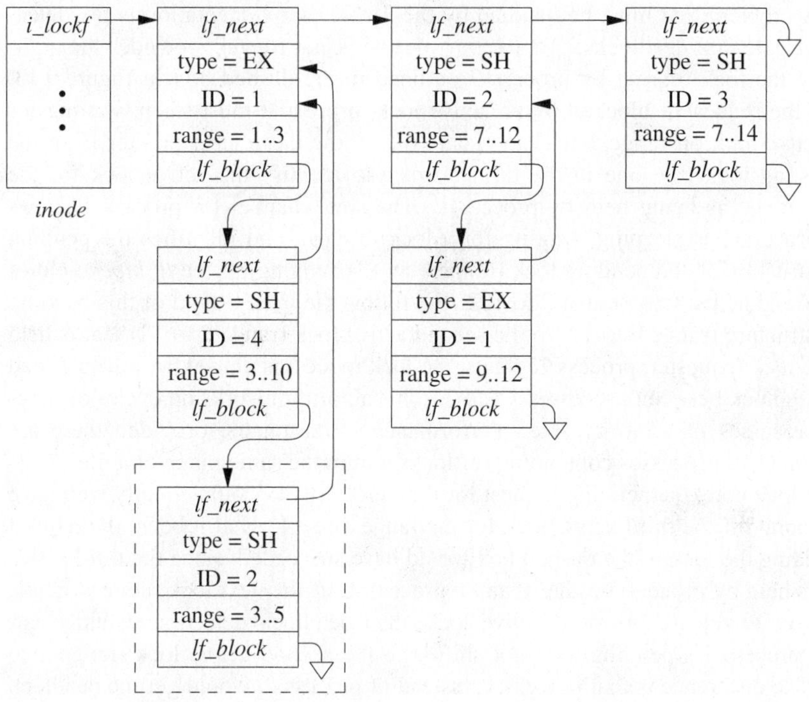

Figure 9.13 A set of range locks on a file.

type of the lock (exclusive or shared), the byte range over which the lock applies, and the identity of the lock holder. A lock may be identified either by a pointer to a process entry or by a pointer to a file entry. A process pointer is used for POSIX-style range locks; a file-entry pointer is used for BSD-style whole file locks. The examples in this section show the identity as a pointer to a process entry. In this example, there are three active locks: an exclusive lock held by process 1 on bytes 1 to 3, a shared lock held by process 2 on bytes 7 to 12, and a shared lock held by process 3 on bytes 7 to 14.

In addition to the active locks, there are other processes that are sleeping, waiting to get a lock applied. Pending locks are headed by the *lf_block* field of the active lock that prevents them from being applied. If there are multiple pending locks, they are linked through their *lf_block* fields. New lock requests are placed at the end of the list; thus, processes tend to be granted locks in the order that they requested the locks. Each pending lock uses its *lf_next* field to identify the active lock that currently blocks it. In the example in Figure 9.13, the first active lock has two other locks pending. There is also a pending request for the range 9 to 12 that is currently linked onto the second active entry. It could equally well have been linked onto the third active entry, since the third entry also blocks it. When an active lock is released, all pending entries for that lock are awakened, so they can retry their request. If the second active lock were released, the result would be that its currently pending request would move over to the blocked list for the last active entry.

A problem that must be handled by the locking implementation is the detection of potential deadlocks. To see how deadlock is detected, consider the addition of the lock request by process 2 outlined in the dashed box in Figure 9.13. Since the request is blocked by an active lock, process 2 must sleep, waiting for the active lock on range 1 to 3 to clear. We follow the *lf_next* pointer from the requesting lock (the one in the dashed box), to identify the active lock for the 1-to-3 range as being held by process 1. The wait channel for process 1 shows that process 1 is sleeping, waiting for a lock to clear, and identifies the pending lock structure as the pending lock (range 9 to 12) hanging off the *lf_block* field of the second active lock (range 7 to 12). We follow the *lf_next* field of this pending lock structure (range 9 to 12) to the second active lock (range 7 to 12) that is held by the lock requester, process 2. Thus, the lock request is denied, as it would lead to a deadlock between processes 1 and 2. This algorithm works on cycles of locks and processes of arbitrary size. Performance is reasonable provided there are fewer than 50 processes contending for locks within the same range of a file.

As we note, the pending request for the range 9 to 12 could equally well have been hung off the third active lock for the range 7 to 14. Had it been, the request for adding the lock in the dashed box would have succeeded, since the third active lock is held by process 3 rather than by process 2. If the next lock request on this file were to release the third active lock, then deadlock detection would occur when process 1's pending lock got shifted to the second active lock (range 7 to 12). The difference is that process 1, instead of process 2, would get the deadlock error.

When a new lock request is made, it must first be checked to see whether it is blocked by existing locks held by other processes. If it is not blocked by other processes, it must then be checked to see whether it overlaps any existing locks already held by the process making the request. There are five possible overlap cases that must be considered; these possibilities are shown in Figure 9.14. The assumption in the figure is that the new request is of a type different from that of the existing lock (i.e., an exclusive request against a shared lock, or vice versa). If the existing lock and the request are of the same type, the analysis is a bit simpler. The five cases are as follows:

Figure 9.14 Five types of overlap considered by the kernel when a range lock is added.

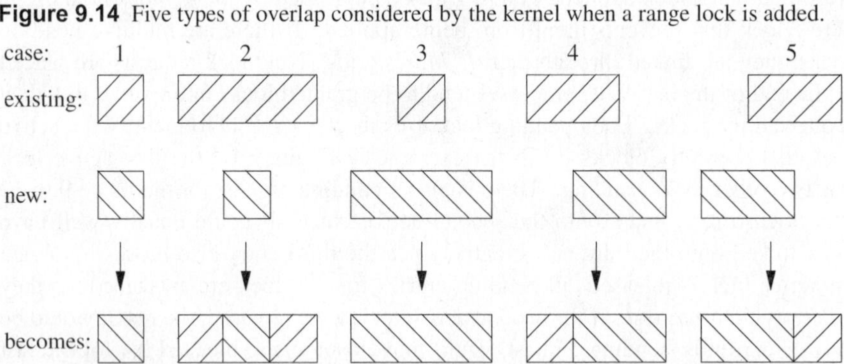

1. The new request exactly overlaps the existing lock. The new request replaces the existing lock. If the new request downgrades from exclusive to shared, all requests pending on the old lock are awakened.

2. The new request is a subset of the existing lock. The existing lock is broken into three pieces (two if the new lock begins at the beginning or ends at the end of the existing lock). If the type of the new request differs from that of the existing lock, all requests pending on the old lock are awakened, so they can be reassigned to the correct new piece, blocked on a lock held by some other process, or granted.

3. The new request is a superset of an existing lock. The new request replaces the existing lock. If the new request downgrades from exclusive to shared, all requests pending on the old lock are awakened.

4. The new request extends past the end of an existing lock. The existing lock is shortened, and its overlapped piece is replaced by the new request. All requests pending on the existing lock are awakened, so they can be reassigned to the correct new piece, blocked on a lock held by some other process, or granted.

5. The new request extends into the beginning of an existing lock. The existing lock is shortened, and its overlapped piece is replaced by the new request. All requests pending on the existing lock are awakened, so they can be reassigned to the correct new piece, blocked on a lock held by some other process, or granted.

In addition to the five basic types of overlap outlined, a request may span several existing locks. Specifically, a new request may be composed of zero or one of type 4, zero or more of type 3, and zero or one of type 5.

Figure 9.15 Locks before addition of exclusive-lock request by process 1 on range 3..13.

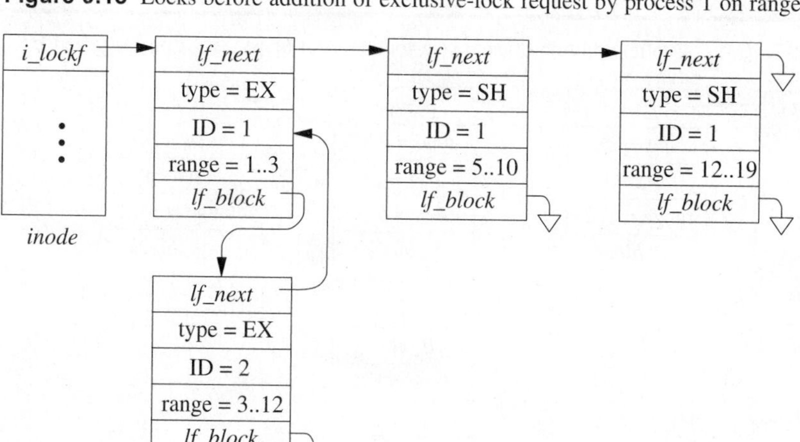

To understand how the overlap is handled, we can consider the example shown in Figure 9.15. This figure shows a file that has all its active range locks held by process 1, plus a pending lock for process 2.

Now consider a request by process 1 for an exclusive lock on the range 3 to 13. This request does not conflict with any active locks (because all the active locks are already held by process 1). The request does overlap all three active locks, so the three active locks represent a type 4, type 3, and type 5 overlap, respectively. The result of processing the lock request is shown in Figure 9.16. The first and third active locks are trimmed back to the edge of the new request, and the second lock is replaced entirely. The request that had been held pending on the first lock is awakened. It is no longer blocked by the first lock but is blocked by the newly installed lock, so it now hangs off the blocked list for the second lock. The first and second locks could have been merged because they are of the same type and are held by the same process. However, the current implementation makes no effort to do such merges because range locks are normally released over the same range that they were created. If the merge were done, it would probably have to be split again when the release was requested.

Lock-removal requests are simpler than addition requests; they need only to consider existing locks held by the requesting process. Figure 9.17 shows the five possible ways that a removal request can overlap the locks of the requesting process. They include:

1. The unlock request exactly overlaps an existing lock. The existing lock is deleted, and any lock requests that were pending on that lock are awakened.

2. The unlock request is a subset of an existing lock. The existing lock is broken into two pieces (one if the unlock request begins at the beginning or ends at the end of the existing lock). Any locks that were pending on that lock are awakened so that they can be reassigned to the correct new piece, blocked on a lock held by some other process, or granted.

Figure 9.16 Locks after addition of exclusive-lock request by process 1 on range 3..13.

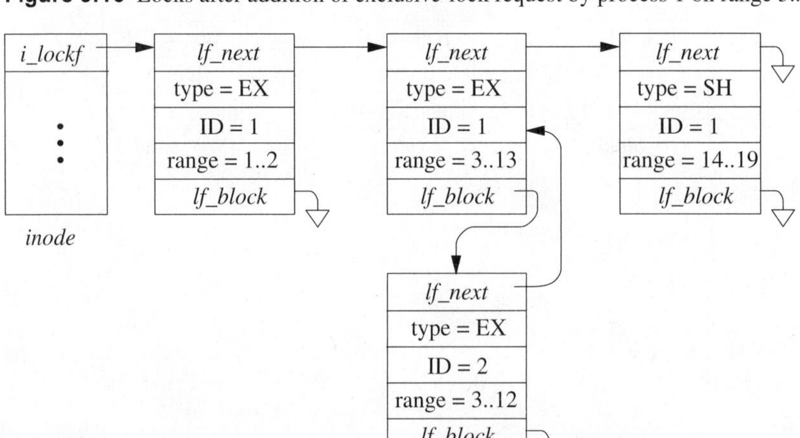

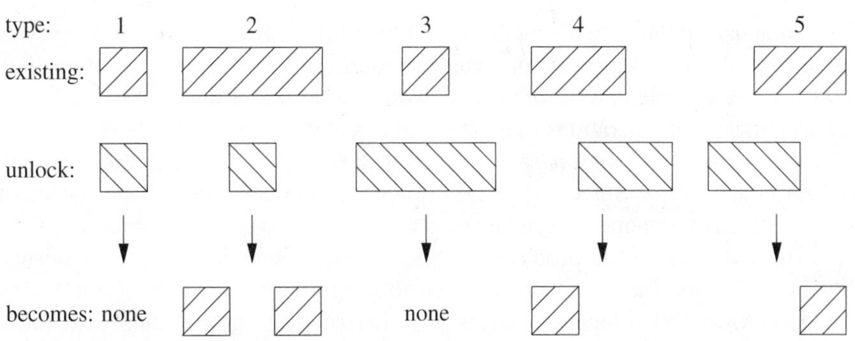

Figure 9.17 Five types of overlap considered by the kernel when a range lock is deleted.

3. The unlock request is a superset of an existing lock. The existing lock is deleted, and any locks that were pending on that lock are awakened.
4. The unlock request extends past the end of an existing lock. The end of the existing lock is shortened. Any locks that were pending on that lock are awakened so that they can be reassigned to the shorter lock, blocked on a lock held by some other process, or granted.
5. The unlock request extends into the beginning of an existing lock. The beginning of the existing lock is shortened. Any locks that were pending on that lock are awakened so that they can be reassigned to the shorter lock, blocked on a lock held by some other process, or granted.

In addition to the five basic types of overlap outlined, an unlock request may span several existing locks. Specifically, a new request may be composed of zero or one of type 4, zero or more of type 3, and zero or one of type 5.

9.6 Soft Updates

In filesystems, ***metadata*** (e.g., directories, inodes, and free block maps) gives structure to raw storage capacity. Metadata provides pointers and descriptions for linking multiple disk sectors into files and identifying those files. To be useful for persistent storage, a filesystem must maintain the integrity of its metadata in the face of unpredictable system crashes, such as power interruptions and operating system failures. Because such crashes usually result in the loss of all information in volatile main memory, the information in nonvolatile storage (i.e., disk) must always be consistent enough to reconstruct deterministically a coherent filesystem state. Specifically, the on-disk image of the filesystem must have no dangling pointers to uninitialized space, no ambiguous resource ownership caused by multiple pointers, and no unreferenced live resources. Maintaining these invariants generally requires sequencing (or atomic grouping) of updates to small on-disk metadata objects.

Traditionally, the UFS filesystem used synchronous writes to properly sequence stable storage changes. For example, creating a file involves first allocating and initializing a new inode and then filling in a new directory entry to point to it. With the synchronous write approach, the filesystem forces an application that creates a file to wait for the disk write that initializes the on-disk inode. As a result, filesystem operations like file creation and deletion proceed at disk speeds rather than processor/memory speeds [McVoy & Kleiman, 1991; Ousterhout, 1990; Seltzer et al., 1993]. Since disk access times are long compared to the speeds of other computer components, synchronous writes reduce system performance.

The metadata update problem can also be addressed with other mechanisms. For example, one can eliminate the need to keep the on-disk state consistent by using NVRAM technologies, such as an uninterruptible power supply or Flash RAM [Moran et al., 1990; Wu & Zwaenepoel, 1994]. Filesystem operations can proceed as soon as the block to be written is copied into the stable store, and updates can propagate to disk in any order and whenever it is convenient. If the system fails, unfinished disk operations can be completed from the stable store when the system is rebooted.

Another approach is to group each set of dependent updates as an atomic operation with some form of write-ahead logging [Chutani et al., 1992; Hagmann, 1987] or shadow-paging [Chamberlin & Astrahan, 1981; Rosenblum & Ousterhout, 1992; Stonebraker, 1987]. These approaches augment the on-disk state with a log of filesystem updates on a separate disk or in stable store. Filesystem operations can then proceed as soon as the operation to be done is written into the log. If the system fails, unfinished filesystem operations can be completed from the log when the system is rebooted. Many modern filesystems successfully use write-ahead logging to improve performance compared to the synchronous write approach.

In Ganger & Patt [1994], an alternative approach called ***soft updates*** was proposed and evaluated in the context of a research prototype. Following a successful evaluation, a production version of soft updates was written for FreeBSD. With soft updates, the filesystem uses delayed writes (i.e., write-back caching) for metadata changes, tracks dependencies between updates, and enforces these dependencies at write-back time. Because most metadata blocks contain many pointers, cyclic dependencies occur frequently when dependencies are recorded only at the block level. Therefore, soft updates track dependencies on a per-pointer basis, which allows blocks to be written in any order. Any still-dependent updates in a metadata block are rolled back before the block is written and rolled forward afterwards. Thus, dependency cycles are eliminated as an issue. With soft updates, applications always see the most current copies of metadata blocks, and the disk always sees copies that are consistent with its other contents.

Update Dependencies in the Filesystem

Several important filesystem operations consist of a series of related modifications to separate metadata structures. To ensure recoverability in the presence of unpredictable failures, the modifications often must be propagated to stable storage in a specific order. For example, when creating a new file, the filesystem allocates an inode, initializes it, and constructs a directory entry that points to it. If the system goes down after the new directory entry has been written to disk but before the initialized inode is written, consistency may be compromised since the contents of the on-disk inode are unknown. To ensure metadata consistency, the initialized inode must reach stable storage before the new directory entry. We refer to this requirement as an ***update dependency*** because safely writing the directory entry depends on first writing the inode. The ordering constraints map onto three simple rules:

1. Never point to a structure before it has been initialized (e.g., an inode must be initialized before a directory entry references it).
2. Never reuse a resource before nullifying all previous pointers to it (e.g., an inode's pointer to a data block must be nullified before that disk block may be reallocated for a new inode).
3. Never reset the old pointer to a live resource before the new pointer has been set (e.g., when renaming a file, do not remove the old name for an inode until after the new name has been written).

There are eight filesystem activities that require update ordering to ensure postcrash recoverability: file creation, file removal, directory creation, directory removal, file/directory rename, block allocation, indirect block manipulation, and free map management.

The two main resources managed by the filesystem are inodes and data blocks. Two bitmaps are used to maintain allocation information about these resources. For each inode in the filesystem, the inode bitmap has a bit that is set if the inode is in use and cleared if it is free. For each block in the filesystem, the data block bitmap has a bit that is set if the block is free and cleared if it is in use. Each filesystem is broken down into fixed-size pieces called cylinder groups (described more fully in Section 9.10). Each cylinder group has a cylinder-group block that contains the bitmaps for the inodes and data blocks residing within that cylinder group. For a large filesystem, this organization allows just those subpieces of the filesystem bitmap that are actively being used to be brought into the kernel memory. Each of these active cylinder-group blocks is stored in a separate I/O buffer and can be written to disk independently of the other cylinder-group blocks.

When a file is created, three metadata structures located in separate blocks are modified. The first is a new inode, which is initialized with its type field set to the new file type, its link count set to one to show that it is live (i.e., referenced by some directory entry), its permission fields set as specified, and all other fields set to default values. The second is the inode bitmap, which is modified to show that the inode has been allocated. The third is a new directory entry, which is filled in with the new name and a pointer to the new inode. To ensure that the bitmaps always reflect all allocated resources, the bitmap must be written to disk before the inode or directory entry. Because the inode is in an unknown state until after it has been initialized on the disk, rule #1 specifies that there is an update dependency requiring that the relevant inode be written before the relevant directory entry. Although not strictly necessary, most BSD fast filesystem implementations also immediately write the directory block before the system call creating the file returns. This second synchronous write ensures that the filename is on stable storage if the application later does an *fsync* system call. If the second synchronous write were not done, then the *fsync* call would have to be able to find all the unwritten directory blocks containing a name for the file and write them to disk. A similar update dependency between an inode and a new directory entry exists when the new directory entry adds a second name for the inode (a.k.a. a hard link), since the addition of the second name requires the filesystem to increment the link count in the inode and write the inode to disk before the entry may appear in the directory.

When a file is deleted, a directory block, an inode block, and one or more cylinder group bitmaps are modified. In the directory block, the relevant directory entry is "removed" by reclaiming its space or by nullifying the inode pointer. In the inode block, the relevant inode's type field, link count, and block pointers are zeroed out. The deleted file's blocks and inode are then added to the appropriate free block/inode maps. Rule #2 specifies that there are update dependencies between the directory entry and the inode and between the inode and any modified free map bits. To keep the link count conservatively high (and reduce complexity in practice), the update dependency between a directory entry and inode also exists when removing one of multiple names (hard links) for a file.

Creation and removal of directories is largely as just described for regular files. However, the **..** entry is a link from the child directory to the parent, which adds additional update dependencies. Specifically, during creation, the parent's link count must be incremented on disk before the new directory's **..** pointer is written. Likewise, during removal, the parent's link count must be decremented after the removed directory's **..** pointer is nullified. (Note that this nullification is implicit in deleting the child directory's pointer to the corresponding directory block.)

When a new block is allocated, its bitmap location is updated to reflect that it is in use and the block's contents are initialized with newly written data or zeros. In addition, a pointer to the new block is added to an inode or indirect block. To ensure that the on-disk bitmap always reflects allocated resources, the bitmap must be written to disk before the pointer. Also, because the contents of the newly allocated disk location are unknown, rule #1 specifies an update dependency between the new block and the pointer to it. Because enforcing this update dependency with synchronous writes can reduce data creation throughput by a factor of two [Ganger & Patt, 1994], many implementations ignore it for regular data blocks. This implementation decision reduces integrity and security, since newly allocated blocks generally contain previously deleted file data. Soft updates allow all block allocations to be protected in this way with near-zero performance reduction.

Manipulation of indirect blocks does not introduce fundamentally different update dependencies, but they do merit separate discussion. Allocation, both of indirect blocks and of blocks pointed to by indirect blocks, is as just discussed. File deletion, and specifically deallocation, is more interesting for indirect blocks. Because the inode reference is the only way to identify indirect blocks and blocks connected to them (directly or indirectly), nullifying the inode's pointer to an indirect block is enough to eliminate all recoverable pointers to said blocks. Once the pointer is nullified on disk, all its blocks can be freed. The exception to this rule is when a file is partially truncated. Here, the pointer from the inode to the indirect block remains. Some of the indirect block pointers will be zeroed and and their corresponding blocks freed while the rest of the pointers are left intact.

When a file is being renamed, two directory entries are affected. A new entry (with the new name) is created and set to point to the relevant inode, and the old entry is removed. Rule #3 states that the new entry should be written to disk before the old entry is removed to avoid having the file unreferenced on reboot. If link counts are being kept conservatively, rename involves at least four disk updates in sequence: one to increment the inode's link count, one to add the new directory entry, one to remove the old directory entry, and one to decrement the link count. If the new name already existed, then the addition of the new directory entry also acts as the first step of file removal as discussed above. Interestingly, *rename* is the one POSIX file operation that should have an atomic update to multiple user-visible metadata structures to provide ideal semantics. POSIX does not require said semantics and most implementations, including FreeBSD, cannot provide it.

On an active filesystem, the bitmaps change constantly. Thus, the copy of the bitmaps in the kernel memory often differs from the copy that is stored on the disk. If the system halts without writing out the incore state of the bitmaps, some of the recently allocated inodes and data blocks may not be reflected in the out-of-date copies of the bitmaps on the disk. As a result, the filesystem check program, **fsck**, must be run over all the inodes in the filesystem to ascertain which inodes and blocks are in use and bring the bitmaps up to date [McKusick & Kowalski, 1994]. An added benefit of soft updates is that they track the writing of the bitmaps to disk and use this information to ensure that no newly allocated inodes or pointers to newly allocated data blocks will be written to disk until after the bitmap that references them has been written to disk. This guarantee ensures that there will never be an allocated inode or data block that is not marked in the on-disk bitmap. This guarantee, together with the other guarantees made by the soft update code, means that it is no longer necessary to run **fsck** after a system crash.

The next 12 subsections describe the soft-updates data structures and their use in enforcing the update dependencies just described. The structures and algorithms described eliminate all synchronous write operations from the filesystem except for the partial truncation of a file and the *fsync* system call, which explicitly requires that all the state of a file be committed to disk before the system call returns.

The key attribute of soft updates is dependency tracking at the level of individual changes within cached blocks. Thus, for a block containing 128 inodes, the system can maintain up to 128 dependency structures with one for each inode in the buffer. Similarly, for a buffer containing a directory block containing 50 names, the system can maintain up to 50 dependency structures with one for each name in the directory. With this level of detailed dependency information, circular dependencies between blocks are not problematic. For example, when the system wishes to write a buffer containing inodes, those inodes that can be safely written can go to the disk. Any inodes that cannot yet be safely written are temporarily rolled back to their safe values while the disk write proceeds. After the disk write completes, such inodes are rolled forward to their current values. Because the buffer is locked throughout the time that the contents are rolled back, the disk write is being done, and the contents are rolled forward, any processes wishing to use the buffer will be blocked from accessing it until it has been returned to its correct state.

Dependency Structures

The soft-updates implementation uses a variety of data structures to track pending update dependencies among filesystem structures. Table 9.2 lists the dependency structures used in the BSD soft-updates implementation, their main functions, and the types of blocks with which they can be associated. These dependency structures are allocated and associated with blocks as various file operations are completed. They are connected to the incore blocks with which they are associated by a pointer in the corresponding buffer header. Two common aspects of all listed dependency structures are the *worklist* structure and the states used to track the progress of a dependency.

The *worklist* structure is really just a common header included as the first item in each dependency structure. It contains a set of linkage pointers and a type field to show the type of structure in which it is embedded. The *worklist* structure allows several different types of dependency structures to be linked together into a single list. The soft-updates code can traverse one of these heterogeneous lists, using the type field to determine which kind of dependency structure it has encountered, and take the appropriate action with each.

The typical use for the *worklist* structure is to link together a set of dependencies associated with a buffer. Each buffer in the system has a pointer to a *worklist* added to it. Any dependencies associated with that buffer are linked onto its *worklist*. After the buffer has been locked and just before the buffer is to be written, the I/O system passes the buffer to the soft-updates code to let it know that a disk write is about to be started. The soft-updates code then traverses the list of dependencies associated with the buffer and does any needed rollback operations. After the disk write completes but before the buffer is unlocked, the I/O system calls the soft-updates code to let it know that a write has completed. The soft-updates code then traverses the list of dependencies associated with the buffer, does any needed roll-forward operations, and deallocates any dependencies that are fulfilled by the data in the buffer having been written to disk.

Another important list maintained by the soft-updates code is the *tasklist* that contains background tasks for the work daemon. Dependency structures are generally added to the *tasklist* during the disk-write completion routine, describing tasks that have become safe given the disk update but which may need to block for locks or I/O and therefore cannot be completed during the interrupt handler. Once per second, the *syncer* daemon (in its dual role as the soft-updates work daemon) wakes up and calls into the soft-updates code to process any items on the *tasklist*. The work done for a dependency structure on this list is type-dependent. For example, for a *freeblks* structure, the listed blocks are marked free in the block bitmaps. For a *dirrem* structure, the associated inode's link count is decremented, possibly triggering file deletion.

Most dependency structures have a set of flags that describe the state of completion of the corresponding dependency. Dirty cache blocks can be written to the

Table 9.2 Soft updates and dependency tracking.

Name	Function	Associated Structures
bmsafemap	tracks bitmap dependencies (points to lists of dependency structures for recently allocated blocks and inodes)	cylinder-group block
inodedep	tracks inode dependencies (information and list head pointers for all inode-related dependencies, including changes to the link count, the block pointers, and the file size)	inode block
allocdirect	tracks inode-referenced blocks (linked into lists pointed to by an inodedep and a bmsafemap to track inode's dependence on the block and bitmap being written to disk)	data block or indirect block or directory block
indirdep	tracks indirect block dependencies (points to list of dependency structures for recently allocated blocks with pointers in the indirect block)	indirect block
allocindir	tracks indirect-block-referenced block (linked into lists pointed to by an indirdep and a bmsafemap to track the indirect block's dependence on that block and bitmap being written to disk)	data block or indirect block or directory block
pagedep	tracks directory-block dependencies (points to lists of diradd and dirrem structures)	directory block
diradd	tracks dependency between a new directory entry and the referenced inode	inodedep and directory block
mkdir	tracks new directory creation (used in addition to standard diradd structure when doing a mkdir)	inodedep and directory block
dirrem	tracks dependency between a deleted directory entry and the unlinked inode	first pagedep then tasklist
freefrag	tracks a single block or fragment to be freed as soon as the corresponding block (containing the inode with the now-replaced pointer to it) is written to disk	first inodedep then tasklist
freeblks	tracks all the block pointers to be freed as soon as the corresponding block (containing the inode with the now-zeroed pointers to them) is written to disk	first inodedep then tasklist
freefile	tracks the inode that should be freed as soon as the corresponding block (containing the inode block with the now-reset inode) is written to disk	first inodedep then tasklist

disk at any time. When the I/O system hands the buffer to the soft-updates code (before and after a disk write), the states of the associated dependency structures determine what actions are taken. Although the specific meanings vary from structure to structure, the three main flags and their general meanings are:

ATTACHED The ATTACHED flag shows that the buffer with which the dependency structure is associated is not currently being written. When a disk write is started for a buffer with a dependency that must be rolled back, the ATTACHED flag is cleared in the dependency structure to show that it has been rolled back in the buffer. When the disk write completes, updates described by dependency structures that have the ATTACHED flag cleared are rolled forward, and the ATTACHED flag is set. Thus, a dependency structure can never be deleted while its ATTACHED flag is cleared, since the information needed to do the roll-forward operation would then be lost.

DEPCOMPLETE The DEPCOMPLETE flag shows that all associated dependencies have been completed. When a disk write is started, the update described by a dependency structure is rolled back if the DEPCOMPLETE flag is clear. For example, in a dependency structure that is associated with newly allocated inodes or data blocks, the DEPCOMPLETE flag is set when the corresponding bitmap has been written to disk.

COMPLETE The COMPLETE flag shows that the update being tracked has been committed to the disk. For some dependencies, updates will be rolled back during disk writes when the COMPLETE flag is clear. For example, for a newly allocated data block, the COMPLETE flag is set when the contents of the block have been written to disk.

In general, the flags are set as disk writes complete, and a dependency structure can be deallocated only when its ATTACHED, DEPCOMPLETE, and COMPLETE flags are all set. Consider the example of a newly allocated data block that will be tracked by an *allocdirect* structure. The ATTACHED flag will initially be set when the allocation occurs. The DEPCOMPLETE flag will be set after the bitmap allocating that new block is written. The COMPLETE flag will be set after the contents of the new block are written. If the inode claiming the newly allocated block is written before both the DEPCOMPLETE and COMPLETE flags are set, the ATTACHED flag will be cleared while the block pointer in the inode is rolled back to zero, the inode is written, and the block pointer in the inode is rolled forward to the new block number. Where different, the specific meanings of these flags in the various dependency structures are described in the subsections that follow.

Bitmap Dependency Tracking

Bitmap updates are tracked by the *bmsafemap* structure shown in Figure 9.18. Each buffer containing a cylinder-group block will have its own *bmsafemap* structure. As with every dependency structure, the first entry in the *bmsafemap*

bmsafemap
worklist
cylgrp_bp
allocindir head
inodedep head
new blk head
allocdirect head

Figure 9.18 Bitmap update dependencies.

structure is a *worklist* structure. Each time an inode, direct block, or indirect block is allocated from the cylinder group, a dependency structure is created for that resource and linked onto the appropriate *bmsafemap* list. Each newly allocated inode will be represented by an *inodedep* structure linked to the *bmsafemap inodedep head* list. Each newly allocated block directly referenced by an inode will be represented by an *allocdirect* structure linked to the *bmsafemap allocdirect head* list. Each newly allocated block referenced by an indirect block will be represented by an *allocindir* structure linked to the *bmsafemap allocindir head* list. Because of the code's organization, there is a small window between the time a block is first allocated and the time at which its use is known. During this period of time, it is described by a *newblk* structure linked to the *bmsafemap new blk head* list. After the kernel chooses to write the cylinder-group block, the soft-updates code will be notified when the write has completed. At that time, the code traverses the inode, direct block, indirect block, and new block lists, setting the DEPCOMPLETE flag in each dependency structure and removing said dependency structure from its dependency list. Having cleared all its dependency lists, the *bmsafemap* structure can be deallocated. There are multiple lists as it is slightly faster and more type-safe to have lists of specific types.

Inode Dependency Tracking

Inode updates are tracked by the *inodedep* structure shown in Figure 9.19. The *worklist* and *state* fields are as described for dependency structures in general. The *filesystem ptr* and *inode number* fields identify the inode in question. When an inode is newly allocated, its *inodedep* is attached to the *inodedep head* list of a *bmsafemap* structure. Here, *deps list* chains additional new *inodedep* structures and *dep bp* points to the cylinder-group block that contains the corresponding bitmap. Other *inodedep* fields are explained in later subsections.

Before detailing the rest of the dependencies associated with an inode, we need to discuss the steps involved in updating an inode on disk as pictured in Figure 9.20.

1. The kernel calls the vnode operation, VOP_UPDATE, which requests that the disk-resident part of an inode (referred to as a dinode) be copied from its in-memory vnode structure to the appropriate disk buffer. This disk buffer holds the contents of an entire disk block, which is usually big enough to include

inodedep
worklist
state
deps list
dep bp
hash list
filesystem ptr
inode number
nlink delta
saved inode ptr
saved size
pending ops head
buffer wait head
inode wait head
buffer update head
incore update head

Figure 9.19 Inode update dependencies.

128 dinodes. Some dependencies are fulfilled only when the inode has been written to disk. These dependencies need dependency structures to track the progress of the writing of the inode. Therefore, during step 1, a soft update routine, *softdep_update_inodeblock*(), is called to move *allocdirect* structures from the *incore update* list to the *buffer update* list and to move *freefile*, *freeblks*, *freefrag*, *diradd*, and *mkdir* structures (described below) from the *inode wait* list to the *buffer wait* list.

Figure 9.20 Inode update steps.

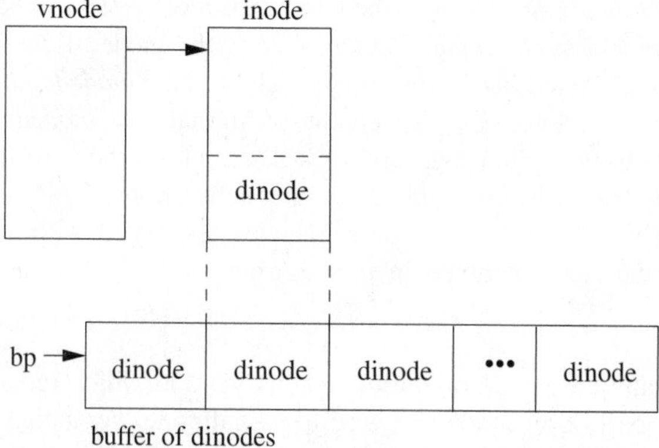

2. The kernel calls the vnode operation, VOP_STRATEGY, that prepares to write the buffer containing the dinode, pointed to by *bp* in Figure 9.20. A soft-updates routine, *softdep_disk_io_initiation*(), identifies *inodedep* dependencies and calls *initiate_write_inodeblock*() to do rollbacks as necessary.

3. Output completes on the buffer referred to by *bp* and the I/O system calls a routine, *biodone*(), to notify any waiting processes that the write has finished. The *biodone*() routine then calls a soft-updates routine, *softdep_disk_write_complete*(), that identifies *inodedep* dependencies and calls *handle_written_inodeblock*() to revert rollbacks and clear any dependencies on the *buffer wait* and *buffer update* lists.

Direct-Block Dependency Tracking

Figure 9.21 illustrates the dependency structures involved in allocation of direct blocks. Recall that the key dependencies are that, before the on-disk inode points to a newly allocated block, both the corresponding bitmap block and the new

Figure 9.21 Direct block allocation dependencies.

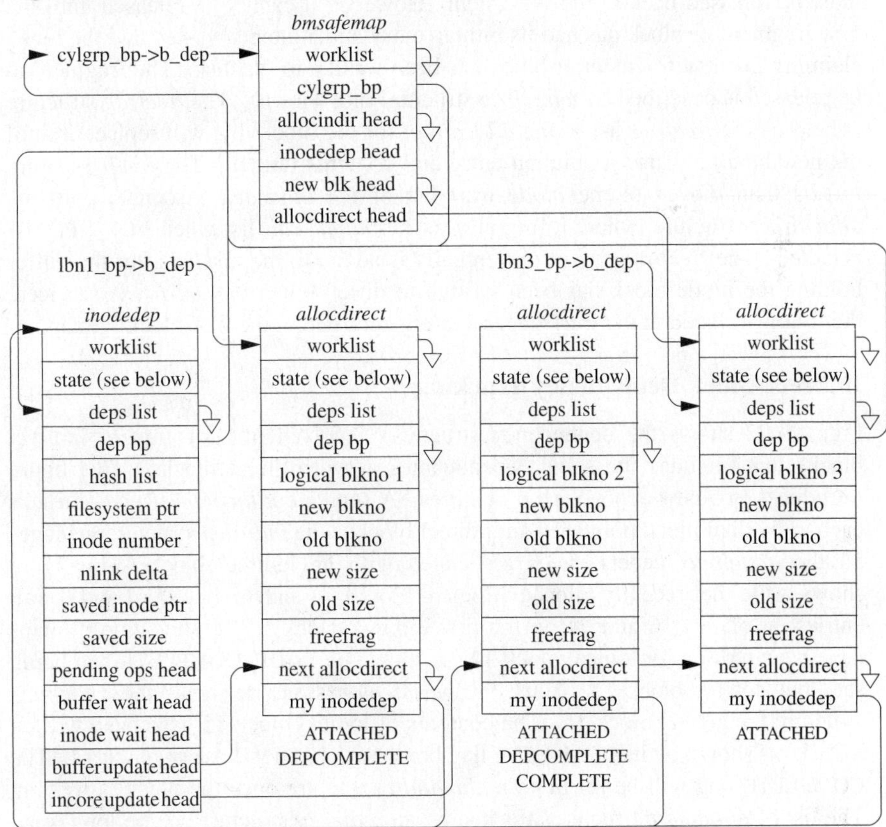

block itself must be written to the disk. The order in which the two dependencies complete is not important. The figure introduces the *allocdirect* structure that tracks blocks directly referenced by the inode. The three recently allocated logical blocks (1, 2, and 3) shown are each in a different state. For logical block 1, the bitmap block dependency is complete (as shown by the DEPCOMPLETE flag being set), but the block itself has not yet been written (as shown by the COMPLETE flag being cleared). For logical block 2, both dependencies are complete. For logical block 3, neither dependency is complete, so the corresponding *allocdirect* structure is attached to a *bmsafemap allocdirect head* list (recall that this list is traversed to set DEPCOMPLETE flags after bitmap blocks are written). The COMPLETE flag for logical blocks 1 and 3 will be set when their initialized data blocks are written to disk. The figure also shows that logical block 1 existed at a time that VOP_UPDATE was called, which is why its *allocdirect* structure resides on the *inodedep buffer update* list. Logical blocks 2 and 3 were created after the most recent call to VOP_UPDATE and thus their structures reside on the *inodedep incore update* list.

For files that grow in small steps, a direct block pointer may first point to a fragment that is later promoted to a larger fragment and eventually to a full-size block. When a fragment is replaced by a larger fragment or a full-size block, it must be released back to the filesystem. However, it cannot be released until the new fragment or block has had its bitmap entry and contents written and the inode claiming the new fragment or block has been written to the disk. The fragment to be released is described by a *freefrag* structure (not shown). The *freefrag* structure is held on the *freefrag* list of the *allocdirect* for the block that will replace it until the new block has had its bitmap entry and contents written. The *freefrag* structure is then moved to the *inode wait* list of the *inodedep* associated with its *allocdirect* structure, where it migrates to the *buffer wait* list when VOP_UPDATE is called. The *freefrag* structure eventually is added to the *tasklist* after the buffer holding the inode block has been written to disk. When the *tasklist* is serviced, the fragment listed in the *freefrag* structure is returned to the free-block bitmap.

Indirect-Block Dependency Tracking

Figure 9.22 shows the dependency structures involved in allocation of indirect blocks that includes the same dependencies as with direct blocks. This figure introduces two new dependency structures. A separate *allocindir* structure tracks each individual block pointer in an indirect block. The *indirdep* structure manages all the *allocindir* dependencies associated with an indirect block. The figure shows a file that recently allocated logical blocks 14 and 15 (the third and fourth entries, at offsets 16 and 24, in the first indirect block). The allocation bitmaps have been written for logical block 14 (as shown by its DEPCOMPLETE flag being set), but not for block 15. Thus, the *bmsafemap* structure tracks the *allocindir* structure for logical block 15. The contents of logical block 15 have been written to disk (as shown by its COMPLETE flag being set), but not those of block 14. The COMPLETE flag will be set in 14's *allocindir* structure once the block is written. The list of *allocindir* structures tracked by an *indirdep* structure can be long (e.g., up to 4096 entries for 32-Kbyte indirect blocks). To avoid traversing lengthy dependency structure lists in the I/O routines, an *indirdep* structure maintains a

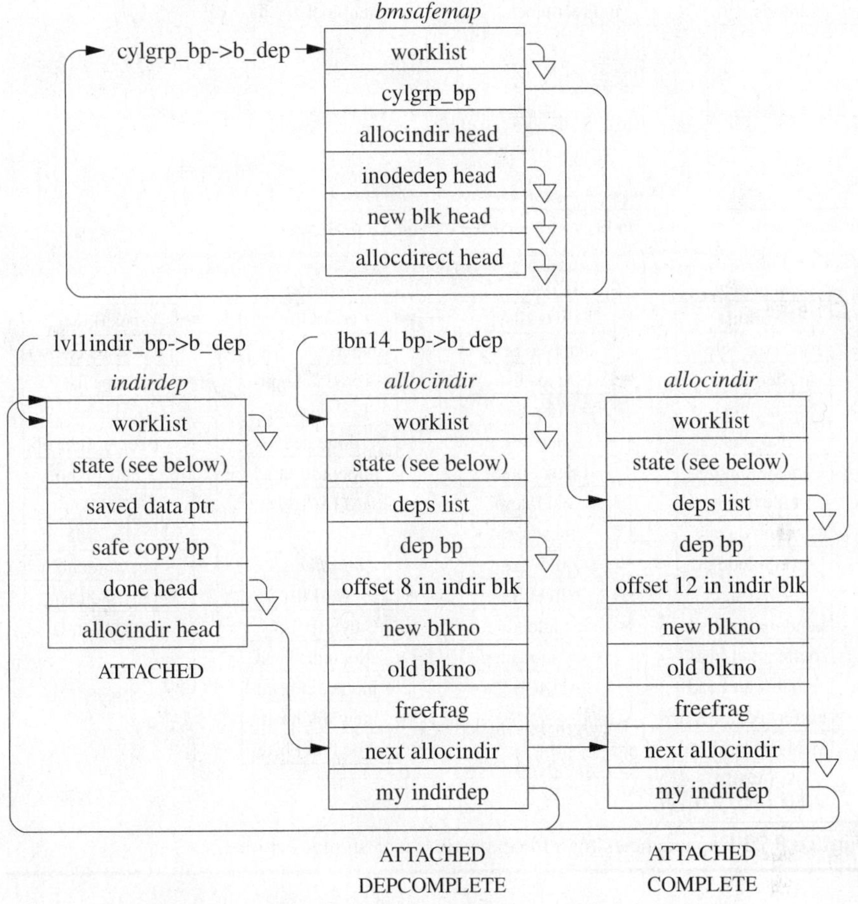

Figure 9.22 Indirect block allocation dependencies.

second version of the indirect block: the *saved data ptr* always points to the buffer's up-to-date copy and the *safe copy ptr* points to a version that includes only the subset of pointers that can be safely written to disk (and NULL for the others). The up-to-date copy is used for all filesystem operations and the copy with the subset of pointers that can be safely written to disk is used for disk writes. When the *allocindir head* list becomes empty, the *saved data ptr* and *safe copy ptr* point to identical blocks and the *indirdep* structure (and the safe copy) can be deallocated.

Dependency Tracking for New Indirect Blocks

Figure 9.23 shows the structures associated with a file that recently expanded into its single-level indirect block. Specifically, this expansion involves *inodedep* and *indirdep* structures to manage dependency structures for the inode and indirect block, an *allocdirect* structure to track the dependencies associated with the indirect block's allocation, and an *allocindir* structure to track the dependencies

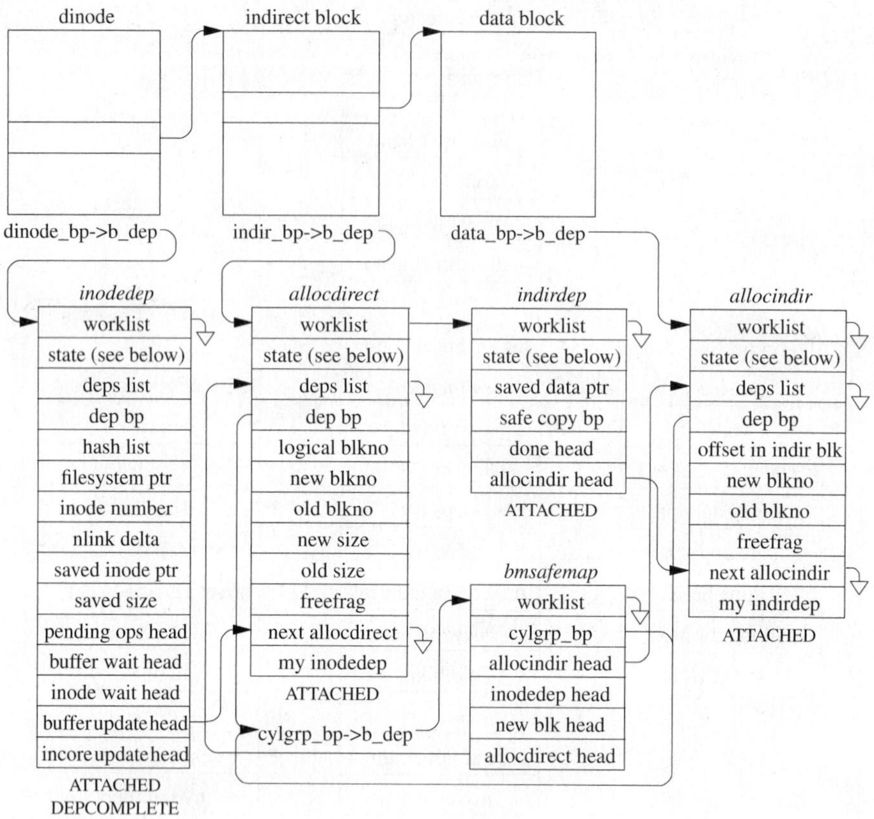

Figure 9.23 Dependencies for a file expanding into an indirect block.

associated with a newly allocated block pointed to by the indirect block. These structures are used as described in the previous three subsections. Neither the indirect block nor the data block that it references have had their bitmaps set, so they do not have their DEPCOMPLETE flag set and are tracked by a *bmsafemap* structure. The bitmap entry for the inode has been written, so the *inodedep* structure has its DEPCOMPLETE flag set. The use of the *buffer update head* list by the *inodedep* structure shows that the incore inode has been copied into its buffer by a call to VOP_UPDATE. Neither of the dependent pointers (from the inode to the indirect block and from the indirect block to the data block) can be safely included in disk writes yet, since the corresponding COMPLETE and DEPCOMPLETE flags are not set. Only after the bitmaps and the contents have been written will all the flags be set and the dependencies complete.

New Directory-Entry Dependency Tracking

Figure 9.24 shows the dependency structures for a directory that has two new entries, **foo** and **bar**. This figure introduces two new dependency structures. A separate *diradd* structure tracks each individual directory entry in a directory block. The *pagedep* structure manages all the *diradd* dependencies associated

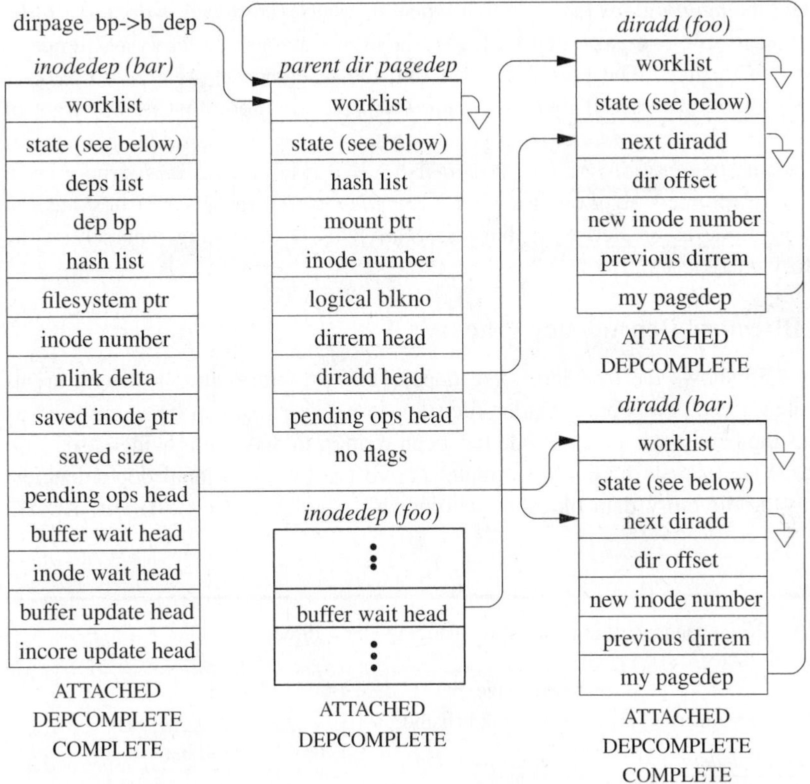

Figure 9.24 Dependencies associated with adding new directory entries.

with a directory block. For each new file, there is an *inodedep* structure and a *diradd* structure. Both files' inodes have had their bitmaps written to disk, as shown by the DEPCOMPLETE flags being set in their *inodedep* structures. The inode for **foo** has been updated with VOP_UPDATE but has not yet been written to disk, as shown by the COMPLETE flag on its *inodedep* structure not being set and by its *diradd* structure still being linked onto its *buffer wait* list. Until the inode is written to disk with its increased link count, the directory entry may not appear on disk. If the directory page is written, the soft-updates code will roll back the creation of the new directory entry for **foo** by setting its inode number to zero. After the disk write completes, the rollback is reversed by restoring the correct inode number for **foo**.

The inode for **bar** has been written to disk, as shown by the COMPLETE flag being set in its *inodedep* and *diradd* structures. When the inode write completed, the *diradd* structure for **bar** was moved from the *inodedep buffer wait* list to the *inodedep pending ops* list. The *diradd* also moved from the *pagedep diradd* list to the *pagedep pending ops* list. Since the inode has been written, it is safe to allow the directory entry to be written to disk. The *diradd* entries remain on the *inodedep* and *pagedep pending ops* list until the new directory entry is written to disk. When the entry is written, the *diradd* structure is freed. One reason to maintain the *pending ops* list is so that when an *fsync* system call is done on a file, the kernel is able to ensure that both the file's contents and directory reference(s) are written to disk. The kernel ensures that the reference(s) are written by performing a lookup to see if there is an *inodedep* for the inode that is the target of the *fsync*. If it finds an *inodedep*, it checks to see if it has any *diradd* dependencies on either its *pending ops* or *buffer wait* lists. If it finds any *diradd* structures, it follows the pointers to their associated *pagedep* structures and flushes out the directory inode associated with that *pagedep*. This backtracking recurses on the directory *inodedep*.

New Directory Dependency Tracking

Figure 9.25 shows the two additional dependency structures involved with creating a new directory. For a regular file, the directory entry can be committed as soon as the newly referenced inode has been written to disk with its increased link count. When a new directory is created, there are two additional dependencies: writing the directory data block containing the . and .. entries (MKDIR_BODY)

Figure 9.25 Dependencies associated with adding a new directory.

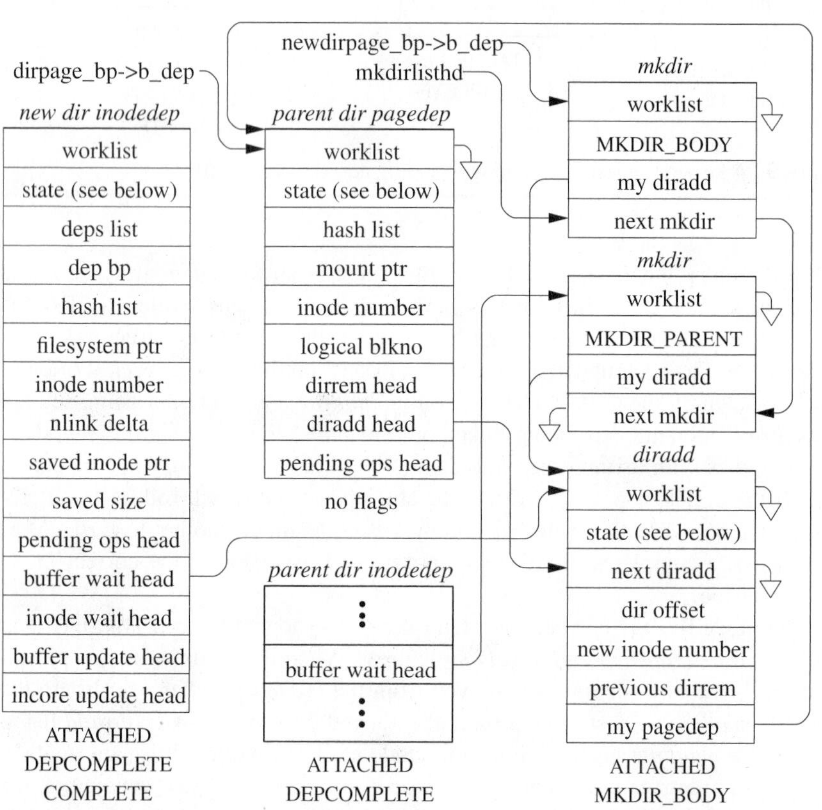

and writing the parent inode with the increased link count for .. (MKDIR_PARENT). These additional dependencies are tracked by two *mkdir* structures linked to the associated *diradd* structure. The soft-updates design dictates that any given dependency will correspond to a single buffer at any given point in time. Thus, two structures are used to track the action of the two different buffers. When each completes, it clears its associated flag in the *diradd* structure. The MKDIR_PARENT is linked to the *inodedep* structure for the parent directory. When that directory inode is written, the link count will be updated on disk. The MKDIR_BODY is linked to the buffer that contains the initial contents of the new directory. When that buffer is written, the entries for **.** and **..** will be on disk. The last *mkdir* to complete sets the DEPCOMPLETE flag in the *diradd* structure so that the *diradd* structure knows that these extra dependencies have been completed. Once these extra dependencies have been completed, the handling of the directory *diradd* proceeds exactly as it would for a regular file.

All *mkdir* structures in the system are linked together on a list. This list is needed so that a *diradd* can find its associated *mkdir* structures and deallocate them if it is prematurely freed (e.g., if a *mkdir* system call is immediately followed by a *rmdir* system call of the same directory). Here, the deallocation of a *diradd* structure must traverse the list to find the associated *mkdir* structures that reference it. The deletion would be faster if the *diradd* structure were simply augmented to have two pointers that referenced the associated *mkdir* structures. However, these extra pointers would double the size of the *diradd* structure to speed an infrequent operation.

Directory-Entry Removal-Dependency Tracking

Figure 9.26 shows the dependency structures involved with the removal of a directory entry. This figure introduces one new dependency structure, the *dirrem* structure, and a new use for the *pagedep* structure. A separate *dirrem* structure tracks each individual directory entry to be removed in a directory block. In addition to

Figure 9.26 Dependencies associated with removing a directory entry.

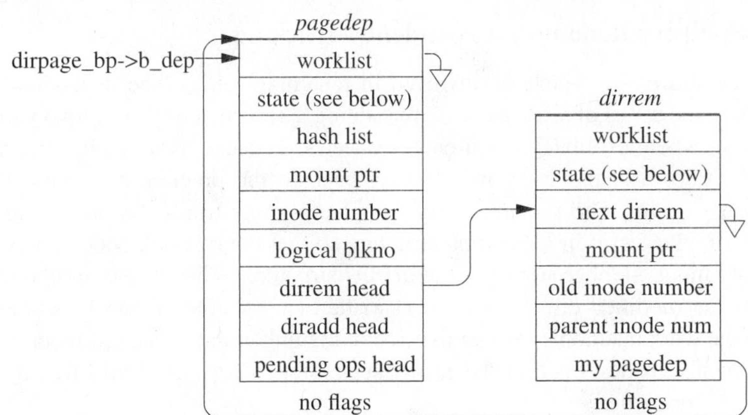

previously described uses, *pagedep* structures associated with a directory block manage all *dirrem* structures associated with the block. After the directory block is written to disk, the *dirrem* request is added to the work daemon's *tasklist* list. For file deletions, the work daemon will decrement the inode's link count by one. For directory deletions, the work daemon will decrement the inode's link count by two, truncate its size to zero, and decrement the parent directory's link count by one. If the inode's link count drops to zero, the resource reclamation activities described in the "file and directory inode reclamation" section are started.

File Truncation

When a file is truncated to zero length without soft updates enabled, the block pointers in its inode are saved in a temporary list, the pointers in the inode are zeroed, and the inode is synchronously written to disk. When the inode write completes, the list of its formerly claimed blocks is added to the free-block bitmap. With soft updates, the block pointers in the inode being truncated are copied into a *freeblks* structure, the pointers in the inode are zeroed, and the inode is marked dirty. The *freeblks* structure is added to the *inode wait* list, and it migrates to the *buffer wait* list when VOP_UPDATE is called. The *freeblks* structure is eventually added to the *tasklist* after the buffer holding the inode block has been written to disk. When the *tasklist* is serviced, the blocks listed in the *freeblks* structure are returned to the free-block bitmap.

File and Directory Inode Reclamation

When the link count on a file or directory drops to zero, its inode is zeroed to show that it is no longer in use. When running without soft updates, the zeroed inode is synchronously written to disk, and the inode is marked as free in the bitmap. With soft updates, information about the inode to be freed is saved in a *freefile* structure. The *freefile* structure is added to the *inode wait* list, and it migrates to the *buffer wait* list when VOP_UPDATE is called. The *freefile* structure eventually is added to the *tasklist* after the buffer holding the inode block has been written to disk. When the *tasklist* is serviced, the inode listed in the *freefile* structure is returned to the free inode map.

Directory-Entry Renaming Dependency Tracking

Figure 9.27 shows the structures involved in renaming a file. The dependencies follow the same series of steps as those for adding a new file entry, with two variations. First, when a rollback of an entry is needed because its inode has not yet been written to disk, the entry must be set back to the previous inode number rather than to zero. The previous inode number is stored in a *dirrem* structure. The DIRCHG flag is set in the *diradd* structure so that the rollback code knows to use the old inode number stored in the *dirrem* structure. The second variation is that, after the modified directory entry is written to disk, the *dirrem* structure is added to the work daemon's *tasklist* list so that the link count of the old inode will be decremented as described in the earlier section on "Directory-Entry Removal-Dependency Tracking."

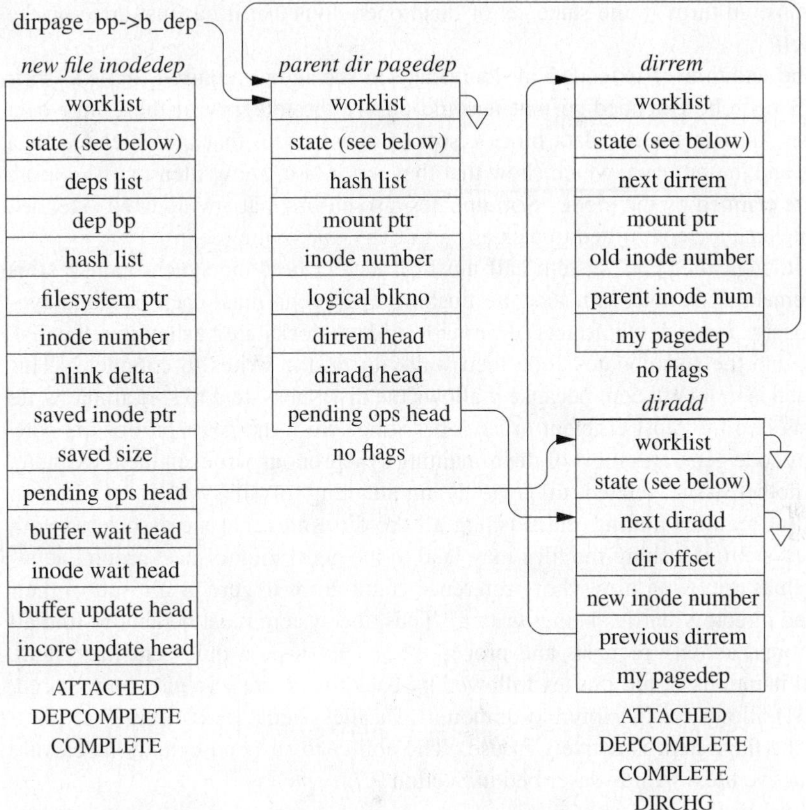

Figure 9.27 Dependencies associated with renaming a directory entry.

Fsync Requirements for Soft Updates

The *fsync* system call requests that the specified file be written to stable storage and that the system call not return until all its associated writes have completed. The task of completing an *fsync* requires more than simply writing all the file's dirty data blocks to disk. It also requires that any unwritten directory entries that reference the file also be written, as well as any unwritten directories between the file and the root of the filesystem. Simply getting the data blocks to disk can be a major task. First, the system must check to see if the bitmap for the inode has been written, finding the bitmap and writing it if necessary. It must then check for, find, and write the bitmaps for any new blocks in the file. Next, any unwritten data blocks must go to disk. Following the data blocks, any first-level indirect blocks that have newly allocated blocks in them are written, followed by any double indirect blocks, then triple indirect blocks. Finally, the inode can be written that will ensure that the contents of the file are on stable store. Ensuring that all names for the file are also on stable store requires data structures that can determine whether there are any uncommitted names and, if so, in which directories they occur. For each directory containing an uncommitted name, the soft-updates code must go through the same set of flush operations that it has just done on the file itself.

The addition of extended attribute data to the inode required that the soft-updates code be extended so that it could ensure the integrity of these new data blocks. As with the file data blocks, soft updates ensure that the extended data blocks and the bitmaps, which show that they are in use, are written to disk before they are claimed by the inode. Soft updates also ensure that any updated extended attribute data are committed to disk as part of an *fsync* of the file.

Although the *fsync* system call must ultimately be done synchronously, this requirement does not mean that the flushing operations must each be done synchronously. Instead, whole sets of bitmaps or data blocks are pushed into the disk queue, and the soft-updates code then waits for all the writes to complete. This approach is more efficient because it allows the disk subsystem to sort all the write requests into the most efficient order for writing. Still, the *fsync* part of the soft-updates code generates most of the remaining synchronous writes in the filesystem.

Another issue related to *fsync* is unmounting of filesystems. Doing an **unmount** requires finding and flushing all the dirty files that are associated with the filesystem. Flushing the files may lead to the generation of background activity, such as removing files whose reference count drops to zero as a result of their nullified directory entries being written. Thus, the system must be able to find all background activity requests and process them. Even on a quiescent filesystem, several iterations of file flushes followed by background activity may be required. FreeBSD allows for the forcible unmount of a filesystem, which may take place while the filesystem is actively in use. The ability to suspend operations cleanly on an active filesystem is described in Section 9.7.

File-Removal Requirements for Soft Updates

For correct operation, a directory's **..** entry should not be removed until after the directory is persistently unlinked. Correcting this dependency ordering in the soft-updates code introduced a delay of up to 2 minutes between the time a directory is unlinked and the time that it is really deallocated (when the **..** entry is removed). Until the directory's **..** entry is really removed, the link count on its parent will not be decremented. Thus, when a user removes one or more directories, the link count of their former parent still reflects that they are present for several minutes. This delayed link count decrement not only causes some questions from users, but also causes some applications to break. For example, the *rmdir* system call will not remove a directory that has a link count over two. This restriction means that a directory that recently had directories removed from it cannot be removed until its former directories have been fully deleted.

To fix these link-count problems, the soft-updates implementation augments the inode *nlink* field with a new field called *effnlink*. The *nlink* field is still stored as part of the on-disk metadata and reflects the true link count of the inode. The *effnlink* field is maintained only in kernel memory and reflects the final value that the *nlink* field will reach once all its outstanding operations are completed. All interactions with user applications report the value of the *effnlink* field, which results in the illusion that everything has happened immediately.

When a file is removed on a filesystem running with soft updates, the removal appears to happen quickly, but the process of removing the file and returning its blocks to the free list may take up to several minutes. Before UFS2, the space held by the file did not show up in the filesystem statistics until the removal of the file had been completed. Thus, applications that clean up disk space such as the news expiration program would often vastly overshoot their goal. They work by removing files and then checking to see if enough free space has showed up. Because of the time lag in having the free space recorded, they would remove far too many files. To resolve problems of this sort, the soft-updates code now maintains a counter that keeps track of the amount of space that is held by the files that the soft-updates code is in the process of removing. This counter of pending space is added to the actual amount of free space as reported by the kernel (and thus by utilities like **df**). The result of this change is that free space appears immediately after the *unlink* system call returns or the **rm** utility finishes.

The second and related change to soft updates has to do with avoiding false out-of-space errors. When running with soft updates on a nearly full filesystem with high turnover rate (for example, when installing a whole new set of binaries on a root partition), the filesystem can return a filesystem full error even though it reports that it has plenty of free space. The filesystem full message happens because soft updates have not managed to free the space from the old binaries in time for it to be available for the new binaries.

The initial attempt to correct this problem was to have the process that wished to allocate space simply wait for the free space to show up. The problem with this approach is that it often had to wait for up to a minute. In addition to making the application seem intolerably slow, it usually held a locked vnode that could cause other applications to get blocked waiting for it to become available (often referred to as a lock race to the root of the filesystem). Although the condition would clear in a minute or two, users often assumed that their system had hung and would reboot.

To remedy this problem, the solution devised for UFS2 is to co-opt the process that would otherwise be blocked and put it to work helping soft updates process the files to be freed. The more processes trying to allocate space, the more help that is available to soft updates and the faster free blocks begin to appear. Usually, enough space shows up in under 1 second that the processes can return to their original task and complete. The effect of this change is that soft updates can now be used on small, nearly full filesystems with high turnover.

Although the common case for deallocation is for all data in a file to be deleted, the *truncate* system call allows applications to delete only part of a file. This semantic creates slightly more complicated update dependencies, including the need to have deallocation dependencies for indirect blocks and the need to consider partially deleted data blocks. Because it is so uncommon, the soft-updates implementation does not optimize this case; the conventional synchronous write approach is used instead.

One concern with soft updates is the amount of memory consumed by the dependency structures. In daily operation, we have found that the additional dynamic memory load placed on the kernel memory allocation area is about equal to the amount of memory used by vnodes plus inodes. For each 1000 vnodes in the system, the additional peak memory load from soft updates is about 300 Kbyte. The one exception to this guideline occurs when large directory trees are removed. Here, the filesystem code can get arbitrarily far ahead of the on-disk state, causing the amount of memory dedicated to dependency structures to grow without bound. The soft-update code was modified to monitor the memory load for this case and not allow it to grow past a tunable upper bound. When the bound is reached, new dependency structures can only be created at the rate at which old ones are retired. The effect of this limit is to slow down the rate of removal to the rate at which the disk updates can be done. While this restriction slows the rate at which soft updates can normally remove files, it is still considerably faster than the traditional synchronous-write filesystem. In steady-state, the soft-update remove algorithm requires about one disk write for each 10 files removed, whereas the traditional filesystem requires at least two writes for every file removed.

Soft-Updates Requirements for fsck

As with the dual tracking of the true and effective link count, the changes needed to **fsck** became evident through operational experience. In a non-soft-updates filesystem implementation, file removal happens within a few milliseconds. Thus, there is a short period of time between the directory entry being removed and the inode being deallocated. If the system crashes during a bulk tree removal operation, there are usually no inodes lacking references from directory entries, though in rare instances there may be one or two. By contrast, in a system running with soft updates, many seconds may elapse between the time when the directory entry is deleted and the inode is deallocated. If the system crashes during a bulk tree removal operation, there are usually tens to hundreds of inodes lacking references from directory entries. Historically, **fsck** placed any unreferenced inodes into the **lost+found** directory. This action is reasonable if the filesystem has been damaged because of disk failure that results in the loss of one or more directories. However, it results in the incorrect action of stuffing the **lost+found** directory full of partially deleted files when running with soft updates. Thus, the **fsck** program was modified to check that a filesystem is running with soft updates and clear out, rather than save, unreferenced inodes (unless **fsck** has determined that unexpected damage has occurred to the filesystem, in which case the files are saved in **lost+found**).

A peripheral benefit of soft updates is that **fsck** can trust the allocation information in the bitmaps. Thus, it only needs to check the subset of inodes in the filesystem that the bitmaps show are in use. Although some of the inodes marked "in use" may be free, none of those marked "free" will ever be in use.

9.7 Filesystem Snapshots

A filesystem ***snapshot*** is a frozen image of a filesystem at a given instant in time. Snapshots support several important features: the ability to provide backups of the filesystem at several times during the day, the ability to do reliable dumps of live filesystems, and (most important for soft updates) the ability to run a filesystem check program on an active system to reclaim lost blocks and inodes.

Creating a Filesystem Snapshot

Implementing snapshots has proven to be straightforward. Taking a snapshot entails the following steps:

1. A *snapshot file* is created to track later changes to the filesystem; a snapshot file is shown in Figure 9.28. This snapshot file is initialized to the size of the filesystem's partition, and its file block pointers are marked as zero, which means "not copied." A few strategic blocks are allocated, such as those holding copies of the superblock and cylinder-group maps.
2. A preliminary pass is made over each of the cylinder groups to copy it to its preallocated backing block. Additionally, the block bitmap in each cylinder group is scanned to determine which blocks are free. For each free block that is found, the corresponding location in the snapshot file is marked with a distinguished block number (1) to show that the block is "not used." There is no need to copy those unused blocks if they are later allocated and written.
3. The filesystem is marked as "wanting to suspend." In this state, processes that wish to invoke system calls that will modify the filesystem are blocked from running, while processes that are already in progress on such system calls are permitted to finish them. These actions are enforced by inserting a gate at the top of every system call that can write to a filesystem. The set of gated system calls includes *write*, *open* (when creating or truncating), *fhopen* (when creating or truncating), *mknod*, *mkfifo*, *link*, *symlink*, *unlink*, *chflags*, *fchflags*, *chmod*, *lchmod*, *fchmod*, *chown*, *lchown*, *fchown*, *utimes*, *lutimes*, *futimes*, *truncate*,

Figure 9.28 Structure of a snapshot file.

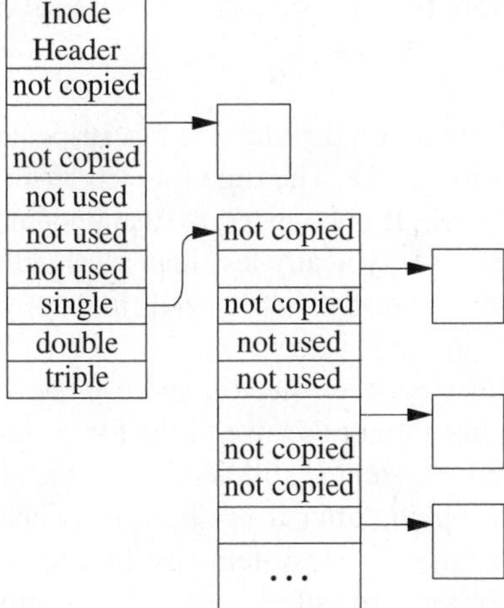

ftruncate, *rename*, *mkdir*, *rmdir*, *fsync*, *sync*, *unmount*, *undelete*, *quotactl*, *revoke*, and *extattrctl*. In addition, gates must be added to *pageout*, *ktrace*, local-domain socket creation, and core dump creation. The gate tracks activity within a system call for each mounted filesystem. A gate has two purposes. The first is to suspend processes that want to enter the gated system call during periods when the filesystem that the process wants to modify is suspended. The second is to keep track of the number of processes that are running inside the gated system call for each mounted filesystem. When a process enters a gated system call, a counter in the mount structure for the filesystem that it wants to modify is incremented. When the process exits a gated system call, the counter is decremented.

4. The filesystem's status is changed from "wanting to suspend" to "fully suspended." This status change is done by allowing all system calls currently writing to the filesystem being suspended to finish. The transition to "fully suspended" is complete when the count of processes within gated system calls drops to zero.

5. The filesystem is synchronized to disk as if it were about to be unmounted.

6. Any cylinder groups that were modified after they were copied in step 2 are recopied to their preallocated backing block. Additionally, the block bitmap in each recopied cylinder group is rescanned to determine which blocks were changed. Newly allocated blocks are marked as "not copied," and newly freed blocks are marked as "not used." The details on how these modified cylinder groups are identified is described at the end of this subsection. The amount of space initially claimed by a snapshot is small, usually less than a tenth of one percent.

7. With the snapshot file in place, activity on the filesystem resumes. Any processes that were blocked at a gate are awakened and allowed to proceed with their system call.

8. Blocks claimed by any snapshots that existed at the time that the current snapshot was taken are expunged from the new snapshot for reasons described in the next subsection.

During steps 3 through 6, all write activity on the filesystem is suspended. Steps 3 and 4 complete in at most a few milliseconds. The time for step 5 is a function of the number of dirty pages in the kernel. It is bounded by the amount of memory that is dedicated to storing file pages. It is typically less than a second and is independent of the size of the filesystem. Typically, step 6 needs to recopy only a few cylinder groups, so it also completes in less than a second.

The splitting of the bitmap copies between steps 2 and 6 is the way that we avoid having the suspend time be a function of the size of the filesystem. By making the primary copy pass while the filesystem is still active, and then having only a few cylinder groups in need of recopying after it has been suspended, we keep the suspend time down to a small and usually filesystem-size-independent time.

The details of the two-pass algorithm are as follows. Before starting the copy and scan of all the cylinder groups, the snapshot code allocates a "progress" bitmap whose size is equal to the number of cylinder groups in the filesystem. The purpose of the "progress" bitmap is to keep track of which cylinder groups have been scanned. Initially, all the bits in the "progress" map are cleared. The first pass is completed in step 2 before the filesystem is suspended. In this first pass, all the cylinder groups are scanned. When the cylinder group is read, its corresponding bit is set in the "progress" bitmap. The cylinder group is then copied, and its block map is consulted to update the snapshot file as described in step 2. Since the filesystem is still active, filesystem blocks may be allocated and freed while the cylinder groups are being scanned. Each time a cylinder group is updated because of a block being allocated or freed, its corresponding bit in the "progress" bitmap is cleared. Once this first pass over the cylinder groups is completed, the filesystem is "suspended."

Step 6 now becomes the second pass of the algorithm. The second pass need only identify and update the snapshot for any cylinder groups that were modified after it handled them in the first pass. The changed cylinder groups are identified by scanning the "progress" bitmap and rescanning any cylinder groups whose bits are zero. Although every bitmap would have to be reprocessed in the worst case, in practice only a few bitmaps need to be recopied and checked.

Maintaining a Filesystem Snapshot

Each time an existing block in the filesystem is modified, the filesystem checks whether that block was in use at the time that the snapshot was taken (i.e., it is not marked "not used"). If so, and if it has not already been copied (i.e., it is still marked "not copied"), a new block is allocated from among the "not used" blocks and placed in the snapshot file to replace the "not copied" entry. The previous contents of the block are copied to the newly allocated snapshot file block, and the write to the original is then allowed to proceed. Whenever a file is removed, the snapshot code inspects each of the blocks being freed and claims any that were in use at the time of the snapshot. Those blocks marked "not used" are returned to the free list.

When a snapshot file is read, reads of blocks marked "not copied" return the contents of the corresponding block in the filesystem. Reads of blocks that have been copied return the contents in the copied block (e.g., the contents that were stored at that location in the filesystem at the time that the snapshot was taken). Writes to snapshot files are not permitted. When a snapshot file is no longer needed, it can be removed in the same way as any other file; its blocks are simply returned to the free list, and its inode is zeroed and returned to the free inode list.

Snapshots may live across reboots. When a snapshot file is created, the inode number of the snapshot file is recorded in the superblock. When a filesystem is mounted, the snapshot list is traversed and all the listed snapshots are activated. The only limit on the number of snapshots that may exist in a filesystem is the size of the array in the superblock that holds the list of snapshots. Currently, this array can hold up to 20 snapshots.

Multiple snapshot files can exist concurrently. As just described, earlier snapshot files would appear in later snapshots. If an earlier snapshot is removed, a later snapshot would claim its blocks rather than allowing them to be returned to the free list. This semantic means that it would be impossible to free any space on the filesystem except by removing the newest snapshot. To avoid this problem, the snapshot code goes through and expunges all earlier snapshots by changing its view of them to being zero-length files. With this technique, the freeing of an earlier snapshot releases the space held by that snapshot.

When a block is overwritten, all snapshots are given an opportunity to copy the block. A copy of the block is made for each snapshot in which the block resides. Overwrites typically occur only for inode and directory blocks. File data usually are not overwritten. Instead, a file will be truncated and then reallocated as it is rewritten. Thus, the slow and I/O intensive block copying is infrequent.

Deleted blocks are handled differently. The list of snapshots is consulted. When a snapshot is found in which the block is active ("not copied"), the deleted block is claimed by that snapshot. The traversal of the snapshot list is then terminated. Other snapshots for which the block is active are left with an entry of "not copied" for that block. The result is that when they access that location, they will still reference the deleted block. Since snapshots may not be modified, the block will not change. Since the block is claimed by a snapshot, it will not be allocated to another use. If the snapshot claiming the deleted block is deleted, the remaining snapshots will be given the opportunity to claim the block. Only when none of the remaining snapshots wants to claim the block (i.e., it is marked "not used" in all of them) will it be returned to the freelist.

Large Filesystem Snapshots

Creating and using a snapshot requires random access to the snapshot file. The creation of a snapshot requires the inspection and copying of all the cylinder-group maps. Once in operation, every write operation to the filesystem must check whether the block being written needs to be copied. The information on whether a blocks needs to be copied is contained in the snapshot file metadata (its indirect blocks). Ideally, this metadata would be resident in the kernel memory throughout the lifetime of the snapshot. In FreeBSD, the entire physical memory on the machine can be used to cache file data pages if the memory is not needed for other purposes. Unfortunately, data pages associated with disks can only be cached in pages mapped into the kernel's physical memory. On a 32-bit architecture, only about 10 Mbyte of kernel memory is dedicated to such purposes. Even on 64-bit architectures, only about 100 Mbyte of kernel memory is dedicated to such purposes. If we allow up to half of this space to be used for any single snapshot, the largest snapshot whose metadata that we can hold in memory is 11 Gbyte or 110 Gbyte. Without help, such a tiny cache would be hopeless in trying to support a multiterabyte snapshot.

In an effort to support multiterabyte snapshots with the tiny metadata cache available, it is necessary to observe the access patterns on typical filesystems. The snapshot is only consulted for files that are being written. The filesystem is organized around cylinder groups that map small contiguous areas of the disk (see Section 9.9). Within a directory, the filesystem tries to allocate all the inodes and files in the same cylinder group. When moving between directories, different cylinder groups are usually inspected. Thus, the widely random behavior occurs from movement between cylinder groups. Once file-writing activity settles down into a cylinder group, only a small amount of snapshot metadata needs to be consulted. That metadata will easily fit in even the tiny kernel metadata cache, so the need is to find a way to avoid thrashing the cache when moving between cylinder groups.

The technique used to avoid thrashing when moving between cylinder groups is to build a look-aside table of all the blocks that were copied while the snapshot was made. This table lists the blocks associated with all the snapshot metadata blocks, the cylinder-group maps, the superblock, and blocks that contain active inodes. When a copy-on-write fault occurs for a block, the first step is to consult this table. If the block is found in the table, then no further searching needs to be done in any of the snapshots. If the block is not found, then the metadata of each active snapshot on the filesystem must be consulted to see if a copy is needed. This table lookup saves time because it not only avoids faulting in metadata for widely scattered blocks, but it also avoids the need to consult potentially many snapshots.

Another problem with snapshots on large filesystems is that they aggravate existing deadlock problems. When there are multiple snapshots associated with a filesystem, they are kept in a list ordered from oldest to youngest. When a copy-on-write fault occurs, the list is traversed, letting each snapshot decide if it needs to copy the block that is about to be written. Originally, each snapshot inode had its own lock. A deadlock could occur between two processes, each trying to do a write. Consider the example in Figure 9.29. It shows a filesystem with two snapshots: snap1 and snap2. Process A holds snapshot 1 locked, and process B holds snapshot 2 locked. Both snap1 and snap2 have decided that they need to allocate a new block in which to hold a copy of the block being written by the process that holds them locked. The writing of the new block in snapshot 1 will cause the kernel running in the context of process A to scan the list of snapshots that will get blocked at snapshot 2 because it is held locked by process B. Meanwhile, the writing of the new block in snapshot 2 will cause the kernel running in the context of process B to scan the list of snapshots that will get blocked at snapshot 1 because it is held locked by process A.

The resolution to the deadlock problem is to allocate a single lock that is used for all the snapshots on a filesystem. When a new snapshot is created, the kernel checks whether there are any other snapshots on the filesystem. If there are, the per-file lock associated with the new snapshot inode is released and replaced with the lock used for the other snapshots. With only a single lock, the access to the

Figure 9.29 Snapshot deadlock scenario.

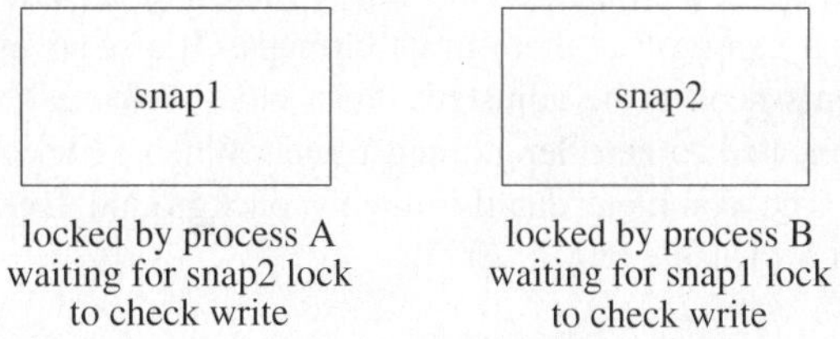

snapshots as a whole is serialized. Thus, in Figure 9.29, process B will hold the lock for all the snapshots and will be able to make the necessary checks and updates while process A will be held waiting. Once process B completes its scan, process A will be able to get access to all the snapshots and will be able to run successfully to completion. Because of the added serialization of the snapshot lookups, the look-aside table described earlier is important to ensure reasonable performance of snapshots. In gathering statistics on our running systems, we found that the look-aside table resolves nearly half of the snapshot copy-on-write lookups. Thus, we found that the look-aside table keeps the contention for the snapshot lock to a reasonable level.

Background fsck

Traditionally, after an unclean system shutdown, the filesystem check program, **fsck**, has had to be run over all the inodes in a filesystem to ascertain which inodes and blocks are in use and to correct the bitmaps. This check is a painfully slow process that can delay the restart of a big server for an hour or more. The current implementation of soft updates guarantees the consistency of all filesystem resources, including the inode and block bitmaps. With soft updates, the only inconsistency that can arise in the filesystem (barring software bugs and media failures) is that some unreferenced blocks may not appear in the bitmaps and some inodes may have to have overly high link counts reduced. Thus, it is completely safe to begin using the filesystem after a crash without first running **fsck**. However, some filesystem space may be lost after each crash. Thus, there is value in having a version of **fsck** that can run in the background on an active filesystem to find and recover any lost blocks and adjust inodes with overly high link counts. A special case of the overly high link count is one that should be zero. Such an inode will be freed as part of reducing its link count to zero. This garbage collection task is less difficult than it might at first appear, since this version of **fsck** only needs to identify resources that are not in use and cannot be allocated or accessed by the running system.

With the addition of snapshots, the task becomes simple, requiring only minor modifications to the standard **fsck**. When run in background cleanup mode, **fsck** starts by taking a snapshot of the filesystem to be checked. **Fsck** then runs over the snapshot filesystem image doing its usual calculations just as in its normal operation. The only other change comes at the end of its run, when it wants to write out the updated versions of the bitmaps. Here, the modified **fsck** takes the set of blocks that it finds were in use at the time of the snapshot and removes this set from the set marked as in use at the time of the snapshot—the difference is the set of lost blocks. It also constructs the list of inodes whose counts need to be adjusted. **Fsck** then calls a new system call to notify the filesystem of the identified lost blocks so that it can replace them in its bitmaps. It also gives the set of inodes whose link counts need to be adjusted; those inodes whose link count is reduced to zero are truncated to zero length and freed. When **fsck** completes, it releases its snapshot. The complete details of how background **fsck** is implemented can be found in McKusick [2002; 2003].

User-Visible Snapshots

Snapshots may be taken at any time. When taken every few hours during the day, they allow users to retrieve a file that they wrote several hours earlier and later deleted or overwrote by mistake. Snapshots are much more convenient to use than dump tapes and can be created much more frequently.

The snapshot described above creates a frozen image of a filesystem partition. To make that snapshot accessible to users through a traditional filesystem interface, the system administrator uses the vnode driver, *vnd*. The *vnd* driver takes a file as input and produces a character-device interface to access it. The *vnd* character device can then be used as the input device for a standard **mount** command, allowing the snapshot to appear as a replica of the frozen filesystem at whatever location in the namespace that the system administrator chooses to mount it.

Live Dumps

Once filesystem snapshots are available, it becomes possible to dump live filesystems safely. When **dump** notices that it is being asked to dump a mounted filesystem, it can simply take a snapshot of the filesystem and dump the snapshot instead of dumping the live filesystem. When **dump** completes, it releases the snapshot.

9.8 Journaled Soft Updates

This section describes the work to add "journaling lite" to soft updates and its incorporation into the FreeBSD fast filesystem. Because soft updates prevent most inconsistencies, the journal need only track those inconsistencies that soft updates fail to address. Specifically, the journal contains the information needed to recover the block and inode resources that have been freed but whose freed status failed to make it to disk before a system failure. After a crash, a variant of the venerable **fsck** program runs through the journal to identify and free the lost resources. Only if an inconsistency between the log and filesystem is detected is it necessary to run the whole-filesystem **fsck**. The journal is tiny, 16 Mbyte is usually enough, independent of filesystem size. Although journal processing needs to be done before restarting, the processing time is typically just a few seconds and, in the worst case, a minute. It is not necessary to build a new filesystem to use soft-updates journaling. The addition or deletion of soft-updates journaling to existing FreeBSD fast filesystems is done using the **tunefs** program.

Background and Introduction

The soft-updates dependency-tracking system was adopted by FreeBSD in 1998 as an alternative to the popular journaled-filesystem technique and is described in Section 9.6. While the runtime performance and consistency guarantees of soft updates are comparable to journaled filesystems [Seltzer et al., 2000], it relies on an expensive and time-consuming background filesystem recovery operation after a crash as is described in Section 9.7. This section outlines a method for eliminating an expensive background or foreground whole-filesystem check operation by using a small journal that logs the only two inconsistencies possible in soft updates. The first is allocated but unreferenced blocks; the second is incorrectly high link counts. Incorrectly high link counts include unreferenced inodes that were being deleted and files that were unlinked but open [Ganger et al., 2000]. This journal allows a journal-analysis program to complete recovery in just a few seconds independent of filesystem size.

Compatibility with Other Implementations

Journaling is enabled via **tunefs** and only requires a few spare superblock fields and 16 Mbyte of free blocks for the journal. These minimal requirements make it easily enabled on existing FreeBSD filesystems. The journal's filesystem blocks are placed in an inode named **.sujournal** in the root of the filesystem and filesystem flags are set such that older nonjournaling kernels will trigger a full filesystem check when mounting a previously journaled volume. When mounting a journaled filesystem, older kernels clear a flag that shows that journaling is being done so that when the filesystem is next encountered by a kernel that does journaling, it will know that that the journal is invalid and will ensure that the filesystem is consistent and clear the journal before resuming use of the filesystem.

Journal Format

The journal is kept as a circular log of segments containing records that describe metadata operations. If the journal fills, the filesystem must complete enough operations to expire journal entries before allowing new operations. In practice, the journal almost never fills.

Each journal segment contains a unique sequence number and a timestamp that identifies the filesystem mount instance so old segments can be discarded during journal processing. Journal entries are aggregated into segments to minimize the number of writes to the journal. Each segment contains the last valid sequence number at the time it was written to allow **fsck** to recover the head and tail by scanning the entire journal. Segments are variably sized as some multiple of the disk block size and are written atomically to avoid read/modify/write cycles in running filesystems.

The journal analysis has been incorporated into the **fsck** program. This incorporation into the existing **fsck** program has several benefits. The existing startup scripts already call **fsck** to see if it needs to be run in the foreground or background. For filesystems running with journaled soft updates, **fsck** can request to run in the foreground and do the needed journaled operations before the filesystem is brought online. If the journal fails for some reason, it can instead report that a full **fsck** needs to be run as the traditional fallback. Thus, this new functionality can be introduced without any change to the way that system administrators start up their systems. Finally, the invoking of **fsck** means that after the journal has been processed, it is possible for debugging purposes to fall through and run a complete check of the filesystem to ensure that the journal is working properly.

The journal entry size is 32 bytes, providing a dense representation allowing for 128 entries per 4-Kbyte sector. The journal is created in a single area of the filesystem in as contiguous an allocation as is available. We considered spreading it out across cylinder groups to optimize locality for writes but it ended up being so small that this approach was not practical and would make scanning the entire journal during cleanup too slow.

The journal blocks are claimed by a named immutable inode. This approach allows user-level access to the journal for debugging and statistics-gathering purposes as well as providing backwards compatibility with older kernels that do not support journaling. We have found that a journal size of 16 Mbyte is enough in even the most tortuous and worst-case benchmarks. A 16-Mbyte journal can cover over 500,000 namespace operations or 16 Gbyte of outstanding allocations (assuming a standard 32-Kbyte block size).

Modifications That Require Journaling

This subsection describes the operations that must be journaled so that the information needed to clean up the filesystem is available to **fsck**.

Increased Link Count

A link count may be increased through a hard link or file creation. The link count is temporarily increased during a rename. Here, the operation is the same. The inode number, parent inode number, directory offset, and initial link count are all recorded in the journal. Soft updates guarantee that the inode link count will be increased and stable on disk before any directory write. The journal write must occur before the inode write that updates the link count and before the bitmap write that allocates the inode if it is newly allocated.

Decreased Link Count

The inode link count is decreased through unlink or rename. The inode number, parent inode, directory offset, and initial link count are all recorded in the journal. The deleted directory entry is guaranteed to be written before the link is adjusted down. As with increasing the link count, the journal write must happen before all other writes.

Unlink While Referenced

Unlinked yet referenced files pose a problem for journaled filesystems. In UNIX, an inode's storage is not reclaimed until after the final name is removed and the last reference is closed. Simply leaving the journal entry valid while waiting for applications to close their dangling references is untenable as it will easily exhaust journal space. A solution that scales to the total number of inodes in the filesystem is required. At least two approaches are possible: a replication of the inode allocation bitmap, or a linked list of inodes to be freed. We have chosen to use the linked-list approach.

In the linked-list case, which is employed by several filesystems (xfs, ext4, etc.), the superblock contains the inode number that serves as the head of a singly linked list of inodes to be freed, with each inode storing a pointer to the next inode on the list. The advantage of this approach is that at recovery time, **fsck** need only examine a single pointer in the superblock that will already be in memory. The disadvantage is that the kernel must keep an in-memory doubly linked list so that it can rapidly remove an inode once it is unreferenced. This approach ingrains a filesystem-wide lock in the design and incurs nonlocal writes when maintaining the list. In practice, we have found that unreferenced inodes occur rarely enough that this approach is not a bottleneck.

Removal from the list may be done lazily but must be completed before any re-use of the inode. Additions to the list must be stable before reclaiming journal space for the final unlink but otherwise may be delayed long enough to avoid needing the write at all if the file is quickly closed. Addition and removal involve only a single write to update the preceding pointer to the following inode.

Change of Directory Offset

Any time a directory compaction moves an entry, a journal entry must be created that describes the old and new locations of the entry. The kernel does not know at the time of the move whether a remove will follow it, so currently all offset changes are journaled. Without this information, **fsck** would be unable to disambiguate multiple revisions of the same directory block.

Block Allocation and Free

When performing either block allocation or free, whether it is a fragment, indirect block, directory block, direct block, or extended attributes, the record is the same. The inode number of the file and the offset of the block within the file are recorded using negative offsets for indirect blocks and extents. Additionally, the disk block address and number of fragments are included in the journal record. The journal entry must be written to disk before any allocation or free.

When freeing an indirect block, only the root of the indirect block tree is logged. Thus, for truncation we need a maximum of 15 journal entries, 12 for direct blocks and 3 for indirect blocks. These 15 journal entries allow us to free a large amount of space with a minimum of journaling overhead. During recovery, **fsck** will follow indirect blocks and free any descendants including other indirect blocks. For this algorithm to work, the contents of the indirect block must remain valid until the journal record is free so that user data is not confused with indirect block pointers.

Additional Requirements of Journaling

Some operations that had not previously required tracking under soft updates need to be tracked when journaling is introduced. This subsection describes these new requirements.

Cylinder-Group Rollbacks

Soft updates previously did not require any rollbacks of cylinder groups as they were always the first or last write in a group of changes. When a block or inode has been allocated but its journal record has not yet been written to disk, it is not safe to write the updated bitmaps and associated allocation information. The routines that write blocks with *bmsafemap* dependencies now rollback any allocations with unwritten journal operations.

Inode Rollbacks

The inode link count must be rolled back to the link count as it existed before any unwritten journal entries. Allowing it to grow beyond this count would not cause filesystem corruption but it would prohibit the journal recovery from adjusting the link count properly. Soft updates already prevent the link count from decreasing before the directory entry is removed as a premature decrement could cause filesystem corruption.

When an unlinked file has been closed, its inode cannot be returned to the inode freelist until its zeroed-out block pointers have been written to disk so that its blocks can be freed and it has been removed from the on-disk list of unlinked files. The unlinked-file inode is not completely removed from the list of unlinked files until the next pointer of the inode that precedes it on the list has been updated on disk to point to the inode that follows it on the list. If the unlinked-file inode is the first inode on the list of unlinked files, then it is not completely removed from the list of unlinked files until the head-of-unlinked-files pointer in the superblock has been updated on disk to point to the inode that follows it on the list.

Reclaiming Journal Space

To reclaim journal space from previously written records, the kernel must know that the operation the journal record describes is stable on disk. This requirement means that when a new file is created, the journal record cannot be freed until writes are completed for a cylinder group bitmap, an inode, a directory block, a directory inode, and possibly some number of indirect blocks. When a new block is allocated, the journal record cannot be freed until writes are completed for the new block pointer in the inode or indirect block, the cylinder group bitmap, and the block itself. Block pointers within indirect blocks are not stable until all parent indirect blocks are fully reachable on disk via the inode indirect block pointers. To simplify fulfillment of these requirements, the dependencies that describe these operations carry pointers to the oldest segment structure in the journal containing journal entries that describe outstanding operations.

Some operations may be described by multiple entries. For example, when making a new directory, its addition creates three new names. Each of these names is associated with a reference count on the inode to which the name refers. When one of these dependencies is satisfied, it may pass its journal entry reference to another dependency if another operation on which the journal entry depends is not yet complete. If the operation is complete, the final reference on the journal record is released. When all references to journal records in a journal segment are released, its space is reclaimed and the oldest valid segment sequence number is adjusted. We can only release the oldest free journal segment, since the journal is treated as a circular queue.

Handling a Full Journal

If the journal ever becomes full, we must prevent any new journal entries from being created until more space becomes available from the retirement of the oldest valid entries. An effective way to stop the creation of new journal records is to suspend the filesystem using the mechanism in place for taking snapshots. Once suspended, existing operations on the filesystem are permitted to complete, but new operations that wish to modify the filesystem are put to sleep until the suspension is lifted.

We do a check for journal space before each operation that will change a link count or allocate a block. If we find that the journal is approaching a full condition, we suspend the filesystem and expedite the progress on the soft-updates work-list processing to speed the rate at which journal entries are retired. As the operation that did the check has already started, it is permitted to finish, but future operations are blocked. Thus, operations must be suspended while there is still enough journal space to complete operations already in progress. When enough journal entries have been freed, the filesystem suspension is lifted and normal operations resume.

In practice, we had to create a minimal-size journal (4 Mbyte) and run scripts designed to create huge numbers of link-count changes, block allocations, and block frees to trigger the journal-full condition. Even under these tests, the filesystem suspensions were infrequent and brief, lasting under a second.

The Recovery Process

This subsection describes the use of the journal by **fsck** to clean up the filesystem after a crash.

Scanning the Journal

To perform recovery, the **fsck** program must first scan the journal from start to end to discover the oldest valid sequence number. We contemplated keeping journal head and tail pointers, however, that would require extra writes to the superblock area. Because the journal is small, the extra time spent scanning it to identify the head and tail of the valid journal seemed a reasonable tradeoff to reduce the run-time cost of maintaining the journal head and tail pointers. As a result, the **fsck** program must discover the first segment containing a still-valid sequence number and work from there. Journal records are then resolved in order. Journal records are marked with a timestamp that must match the filesystem mount time as well as a CRC to protect the validity of the contents.

Adjusting Link Counts

For each journal record recording a link increase, **fsck** needs to examine the directory at the offset provided and see whether the directory entry for the recorded inode number exists on disk. If it does not exist, but the inode link count was increased, then the recorded link count needs to be decremented.

For each journal record recording a link decrease, **fsck** needs to examine the directory at the offset provided and see whether the directory entry for the recorded inode number exists on disk. If it has been deleted on disk, but the inode link count has not been decremented, then the recorded link count needs to be decremented.

Compaction of directory offsets for entries that are being tracked complicates the link adjustment scheme presented above. Since directory blocks are not written synchronously, **fsck** must look up each directory entry in all its possible locations.

When an inode is added and removed from a directory multiple times, **fsck** is not able to assess the link count correctly given the algorithm presented above. The chosen solution is to preprocess the journal and link all entries related to the same inode together. In this way, all operations not known to be committed to the disk can be examined concurrently to determine how many links should exist relative to the known stable count that existed before the first journal entry. Duplicate records that occur when an inode is added and deleted multiple times at the same offset are discarded, resulting in a coherent count.

Updating the Allocated Inode Map

Once the link counts have been adjusted, **fsck** must free any inodes whose link count has fallen to zero. In addition, **fsck** must free any inodes that were unlinked but still in use at the time that the system crashed. The head of the list of unreferenced inode is in the superblock as described earlier in this section. The **fsck** program must traverse this list of unlinked inodes and free them.

The first step in freeing an inode is to add all its blocks to the list of blocks that need to be freed. Next, the inode needs to be zeroed to show that it is not in use. Finally, the inode bitmap in its cylinder group must be updated to reflect that the inode is available and all the appropriate filesystem statistics updated to reflect the inode's availability.

Updating the Allocated Block Map

Once the journal has been scanned, it provides a list of blocks that were intended to be freed. The journal entry lists the inode from which the block was to be freed. For recovery, **fsck** processes each free record by checking to see if the block is still claimed by its associated inode. If it finds that the block is no longer claimed, it is freed.

For each block that is freed, either by the deallocation of an inode or through the identification process described above, the block bitmap in its cylinder group must be updated to reflect that it is available and all the appropriate filesystem statistics updated to reflect its availability. When a fragment is freed, the fragment availability statistics must also be updated.

Performance

Journaling adds extra running time and memory allocations to the traditional soft-updates requirements as well as additional I/O operations to write the journal. The overhead of the extra running time and memory allocations was immeasurable in the benchmarks that we ran. The extra I/O was mostly evident in the increased delay for individual operations to complete. Operation completion time is usually only evident to an application when it does an *fsync* system call that causes it to wait for the file to reach the disk. Otherwise, the extra I/O to the journal only becomes evident in benchmarks that are limited by the filesystem's I/O bandwidth before journaling is enabled. In summary, a system running with journaled soft updates will never run faster than one running soft updates without journaling. So, systems with small filesystems such as an embedded system will usually want to run soft updates without journaling and take the time to run **fsck** after system crashes.

The primary purpose of the journaling project was to eliminate long filesystem check times. A 40 Tbyte volume may take an entire day and a considerable amount of memory to check. We have run several scenarios to understand and validate the recovery time.

A typical operation for developers is to run a parallel buildworld. Crash recovery from this case demonstrates time to recover from moderate write workload. A 250 Gbyte disk was filled to 80 percent with copies of the FreeBSD source tree. One copy was selected at random and an 8-way buildworld proceeded for 10 minutes before the box was reset. Recovery from the journal took 0.9 seconds. An additional run with traditional **fsck** was used to verify the safe recovery of the filesystem. The **fsck** took about 27 minutes, or 1800 times as long.

A testing volunteer with a 92-percent full 11 Tbyte volume spanning 14 drives on a 3ware RAID controller generated hundreds of megabytes of dirty data by writing random length files in parallel before resetting the machine. The resulting recovery operation took less than one minute to complete. A normal **fsck** run takes about 10 hours on this filesystem.

Future Work

This subsection describes some areas we have not yet explored that may give further performance improvements to our implementation.

Rollback of Directory Deletions

Doing a rollback of a directory addition is easy. The new directory entry has its inode number set to zero to show that it is not really allocated. However, rollback of directory deletions is much more difficult as the space may have been claimed by a new allocation. There are times when being able to roll back a directory deletion would be convenient. For example, when a file is renamed, a directory rollback could be used to prevent the removal of an old name before a new name reaches the disk. Here, we have considered using a distinguished inode number that the filesystem would recognize internally as being in use, but which would not be returned to the user application. However, at present we cannot rollback deletes, which requires any delete journaling to be written to disk before the writing of affected directory blocks.

Truncate and Weaker Guarantees

As a potential optimization, the *truncate* system call instead may choose to record the intended file size and operate more lazily, relying on the log to recover any partially completed operations correctly. This approach also allows us to perform partial truncations asynchronously. Further, the journal allows for the weakening of other soft dependency guarantees although we have not yet fully explored these reduced guarantees and do not know if they provide any real benefit.

Tracking File-Removal Dependencies

This subsection gives a short example describing the dependencies that track the removal of a file when using journaled soft updates. These five ordering constraints must be maintained:

1. The journal must record the location in the directory that has the name to be deleted and the inode number associated with the name.
2. The filename in the on-disk copy of the directory must be deleted.
3. The journal must record the blocks to be deleted. The inode describing the file must be deallocated by zeroing out its on-disk dinode. The writing of the journal entry must precede the writing of the zeroed-out on-disk inode.
4. The blocks formerly referenced by the inode for the file must be released to the free-space bitmap, and the inode must be released to the free-inode bitmap.
5. The journal must record the successful completion of the removal.

These five constraints are maintained by soft updates as follows:

1. The buffer containing the journal entry with the name and inode number to be deleted adds a dependency structure to start the file deletion.
2. Some time in the next 30 seconds after step 1, the kernel will decide to write the journal buffer. When notified that the journal entry has been written, the block of the directory containing the name to be deleted is read into a kernel buffer. The entry is deleted by changing the entry that precedes it to point to the entry that follows it (see Section 9.3). Before releasing the buffer, a set of dependencies must be constructed, as shown in Figure 9.26. If this deletion is the first dependency for the directory block, it needs to have a *pagedep* structure allocated that is linked onto the dependency list for the buffer. Next, a *dirrem* structure is allocated that records the inode number of the entry being deleted. The *dirrem* structure is linked onto the *dirrem* list of the *pagedep* structure for the directory block. The buffer is then marked dirty and it is unlocked and released.
3. Some time in the next 30 seconds after step 2, the kernel will decide to write the dirty directory buffer. When the write completes, the *pagedep* associated with the buffer is passed to soft updates for processing. One processing step is to handle each of the *dirrem* entries. Each *dirrem* entry causes the inode formerly referenced by the directory to have its reference count decremented by one. If the reference count drops to zero (meaning that the last name for the file was removed), then the inode must be deallocated and freed. Before zeroing out the contents of the on-disk dinode, its list of allocated blocks must be saved in a *freeblks* structure and information needed to free the inode must be saved in a *freefile* structure. A journal entry containing the *freeblks* and *freefile*

information must be added to the journal buffer. The block of the filesystem containing the dinode to be freed is read into a kernel buffer, as shown in Figure 9.20. The part of the buffer containing the dinode is zeroed out. If the deallocation is the first dependency for the dinode, it must have an *inodedep* structure allocated that is linked onto the dependency list for the buffer. The *freeblks* and *freefile* structures are linked onto the *buffer wait* list of the *inodedep* structure. A reference to the journal entry is also added to the *inodedep*. The buffer is then marked dirty and it is unlocked and released. The *dirrem* structure is freed as is the *pagedep* structure if it is no longer tracking any dependencies.

4. Some time in the next 30 seconds after step 3, the kernel will decide to write the buffer containing the zeroed-out dinode. If the buffer containing the journal dependency has not yet been written, the zeroed-out dinode is replaced with its original contents and the write is allowed to proceed. When the write completes, the zeroed-out dinode is put back into the buffer and the buffer marked as still dirty (needing to be written). When a write on the buffer finds that the journal entry has been written, the write of the zeroed-out dinode is allowed to proceed. When the write completes, the *inodedep* associated with the buffer is passed to soft updates for processing. One processing step is to handle each of the *buffer wait* entries. The handling of the *freeblks* entry causes all its listed blocks to be marked free in the appropriate cylinder-group bitmaps. The handling of the *freefile* entry causes the deleted inode to be marked free in the appropriate cylinder-group bitmap. The *freeblks* and *freefile* structures are freed as is the *inodedep* structure if it is no longer tracking any dependencies. A journal dependency is added to the buffer containing the bitmaps.

5. Some time in the next 30 seconds, the kernel will decide to write the buffer containing the bitmaps. When the write completes, the journal dependency is processed that writes an entry to the journal to show that the block and inode release has been completed.

The file has now been completely removed and ceases to be tracked by soft updates.

9.9 The Local Filestore

The next two sections of this chapter describe the organization and management of data on storage media. Historically, FreeBSD provided three different filestore managers: the traditional Berkeley Fast Filesystem (FFS), the Log-Structured Filesystem, and the Memory-Based Filesystem. These storage managers shared the same code for all the filesystem naming semantics and differed only in the management of their data on storage media. The Log-Structured Filesystem filestore manager has been replaced by ZFS described in Chapter 10. The Memory-Based Filesystem filestore manager has been replaced by an implementation optimized for operating in virtual memory.

Overview of the Filestore

The FFS filestore was designed at a time when file caches were small and thus files needed to be read from the disk often. It is willing to do extra disk seeks while writing to place files likely to be accessed together in the same general location on the disk. This approach minimizes disk seeks needed to read these files. By contrast, ZFS was designed at a time when file caches were large and thus most file reads would not need to access the disk. Hence, ZFS optimizes its write speed by grouping blocks in the order in which they are written. ZFS is willing to accept more disk seeks to read files on the rare occasions when they are not in the cache.

The operations defined for doing the datastore filesystem operations are shown in Table 9.3. These operators are fewer and semantically simpler than are those used for managing the namespace.

There are two operators for allocating and freeing objects. The *valloc* operator creates a new object. The identity of the object is a number returned by the operator. The mapping of this number to a name is the responsibility of the namespace code. An object is freed by the *vfree* operator. The object to be freed is identified by only its number.

The attributes of an object are changed by the *update* operator. This layer performs no interpretation of these attributes; they are simply fixed-size auxiliary data stored outside the main data area of the object. They are typically file attributes, such as the owner, group, permissions, and so on. Note that the extended attribute space is updated using the *read* and *write* interface as that interface is already prepared to read and write arbitrary length data to and from user-level processes.

There are five operators for manipulating existing objects. The *vget* operator retrieves an existing object from the filestore. The object is identified by its number and must have been created previously by *valloc*. The *read* operator copies data from an object to a location described by a *uio* structure. The *blkatoff* operator is similar to the *read* operator, except that the *blkatoff* operator simply returns a pointer to a kernel memory buffer with the requested data instead of copying the data. This operator is designed to increase the efficiency of operations where the namespace code interprets the contents of an object (i.e., directories) instead of just returning the contents to a user process. The *write* operator copies data to an object from a location described by a *uio* structure. The *fsync* operator requests that all data associated with the object be moved to stable storage (usually by writing them all to disk). There is no need for an analog of *blkatoff* for writing, as the

Table 9.3 Datastore filesystem operations.

Operation Done	Operator Names
object creation and deletion	*valloc, vfree*
attribute update	*update*
object read and write	*vget, blkatoff, read, write, fsync*
change in space allocation	*truncate*

kernel can simply modify a buffer that it received from *blkatoff*, mark that buffer as dirty, and then perform an *fsync* operation to have the buffer written back.

The final datastore operation is *truncate*. This operation changes the amount of space associated with an object. Historically, it could be used only to decrease the size of an object. In FreeBSD, it can be used both to increase and decrease the size of an object. When the size of a file is increased, a hole in the file is created. Usually, no additional disk space is allocated; the only change is to update the inode to reflect the larger file size. When read, holes are treated by the system as zero-valued bytes.

Each disk drive has one or more subdivisions, or *partitions*. Each such partition can contain only one filestore, and a filestore never spans multiple partitions. While a filesystem may use multiple disk partitions to perform striping or RAID, the aggregation and management of the parts that make up the filesystem are managed by a lower-level driver in the kernel. The filesystem code always has the view of operating on a single contiguous partition.

The filestore is responsible for the management of the space within its disk partition. Within that space, its responsibility is the creation, storage, retrieval, and removal of files. It operates in a flat namespace. When asked to create a new file, it allocates an inode for that file and returns the assigned number. The naming, access control, locking, and attribute manipulation for the file are all handled by the hierarchical filesystem-management layer above the filestore.

The filestore also handles the allocation of new blocks to files as the latter grow. Simple filesystem implementations, such as those used by early microcomputer systems, allocate files contiguously, one after the next, until the files reach the end of the disk. As files are removed, holes occur. To reuse the freed space, the system must compact the disk to move all the free space to the end. Files can be created only one at a time; for the size of a file other than the final one on the disk to be increased, the file must be copied to the end and then expanded.

As we saw in Section 9.2, each file in a filestore is described by an inode; the locations of its data blocks are given by the block pointers in its inode. Although the filestore may cluster the blocks of a file to improve I/O performance, the inode can reference blocks scattered anywhere throughout the partition. Thus, multiple files can be written simultaneously and all the disk space can be used without the need for compaction.

The filestore implementation converts from the user abstraction of a file as an array of bytes to the structure imposed by the underlying physical medium. Consider a typical medium of a magnetic disk with fixed-size sectoring. Although the user may wish to write a single byte to a file, the disk supports reading and writing only in multiples of sectors. Here, the system must read in the sector containing the byte to be modified, replace the affected byte, and write the sector back to the disk. This operation—converting random access to an array of bytes to reads and writes of disk sectors—is called *block I/O*.

First, the system breaks the user's request into a set of operations to be done on ***logical block***s of the file. Logical blocks describe block-size pieces of a file. The system calculates the logical blocks by dividing the array of bytes into filestore-size pieces. Thus, if a filestore's block size is 32,768 bytes, then logical block 0 would contain bytes 0 to 32,767, logical block 1 would contain bytes 32,768 to 65,535, and so on.

The data in each logical block are stored in a ***physical block*** on the disk. A physical block is the location on the disk to which the system maps a logical block. A physical disk block is constructed from one or more contiguous sectors. For a disk with 4096-byte sectors, a 32,768-byte filestore block would be built up from 8 contiguous sectors. Although the contents of a logical block are contiguous on disk, the logical blocks of the file do not need to be laid out contiguously. The data structure used by the system to convert from logical blocks to physical blocks is described in Section 9.2.

User I/O to a File

Although the user may wish to write a single byte to a file, the disk hardware can read and write only in multiples of sectors. Hence, the system must arrange to read in the sector containing the byte to be modified, to replace the affected byte, and to write back the sector to the disk.

Processes may read data in sizes smaller than a disk block. The first time that a small read is required from a particular disk block, the block will be transferred from the disk into a kernel buffer. Later reads of parts of the same block then require only copying from the kernel buffer to the memory of the user process. Multiple small writes are treated similarly. A buffer is allocated from the cache when the first write to a disk block is made, and later writes to part of the same block are then likely to require only copying into the kernel buffer and no disk I/O.

In addition to providing the abstraction of arbitrary alignment of reads and writes, the block buffer cache reduces the number of disk I/O transfers required by filesystem accesses. Because system-parameter files, commands, and directories are read repeatedly, their data blocks are usually in the buffer cache when they are needed. Thus, the kernel does not need to read them from the disk every time that they are requested.

Figure 9.30 shows the flow of information and work required to access a file on the disk. The abstraction shown to the user is an array of bytes. These bytes are collectively described by a file descriptor that refers to some location in the array. The user can request a write operation on the file by presenting the system with a pointer to a buffer and with a request for some number of bytes to be written. As Figure 9.30 shows, the requested data do not need to be aligned with the beginning or end of a logical block. Further, the size of the request is not constrained to a single logical block. In the example shown, the user has requested data to be written to parts of logical blocks 1 and 2. Since the disk can transfer data only in multiples of sectors, the filestore must first arrange to read in the data for any part of the block that is to be left unchanged. The system must arrange an intermediate staging area for the transfer. This staging is done through one or more system buffers, described in Section 7.4.

In our example, the user wishes to modify data in logical blocks 1 and 2. The operation iterates over five steps:

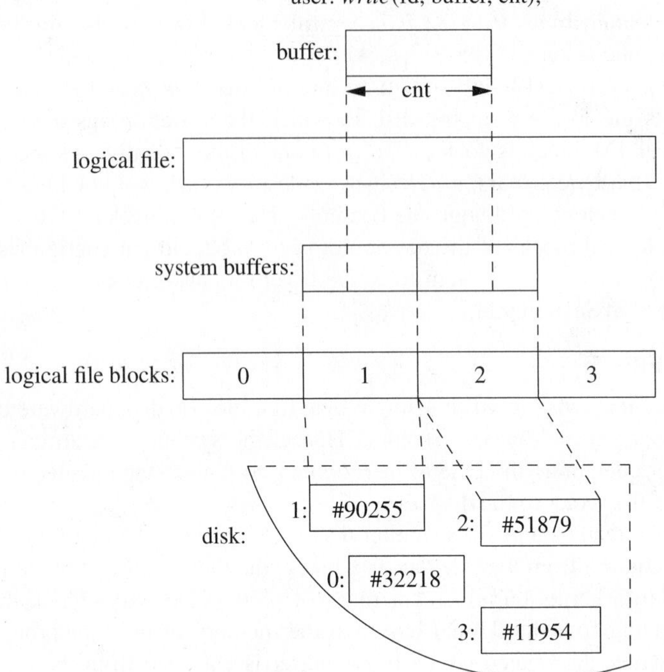

Figure 9.30 The block I/O system.

1. Allocate a buffer.
2. Determine the location of the corresponding physical block on the disk.
3. Request the disk controller to read the contents of the physical block into the system buffer and wait for the transfer to complete.
4. Do a memory-to-memory copy from the beginning of the user's I/O buffer to the appropriate portion of the system buffer.
5. Write the block to the disk and continue without waiting for the transfer to complete.

If the user's request is incomplete, the process is repeated with the next logical block of the file. In our example, the system fetches logical block 2 of the file and is able to complete the user's request. Had an entire block been written, the system could have skipped step 3 and have simply written the data to the disk without first reading in the old contents. This incremental filling of the write request is transparent to the user's process because that process is blocked from running during the entire procedure. The filling is transparent to other processes; because the inode is locked during the process, any attempted access by any other process will be blocked until the write has completed.

If the system crashes while data for a particular block are in the cache but have not yet been written to disk, the filesystem on the disk will be incorrect and those data will be lost. The consistency of critical filesystem data is maintained using the techniques described in Section 9.6, but it is still possible to lose recently written application data. So that lost data are minimized, writes for dirty buffer blocks are forced, at most, 30 seconds after they are written. There is also a system call, *fsync*, that a process can use to force all dirty blocks of a single file to be written to disk immediately; this synchronization is useful for ensuring database consistency or before removing an editor backup file.

9.10 The Berkeley Fast Filesystem

A traditional UNIX filesystem is described by its ***superblock***, which contains the basic parameters of the filesystem. These parameters include the number of data blocks in the filesystem, a count of the maximum number of files, and a pointer to the ***free list***, which is a list of all the free blocks in the filesystem.

A 150-Mbyte traditional UNIX filesystem consists of 4 Mbyte of inodes followed by 146 Mbyte of data. That organization segregates the inode information from the data; thus, accessing a file normally incurs a long seek from the file's inode to its data. Files in a single directory typically are not allocated consecutive slots in the 4 Mbyte of inodes, causing many nonconsecutive disk blocks to be read when many inodes in a single directory are accessed.

The allocation of data blocks to files also is suboptimal. The traditional filesystem implementation uses a 512-byte physical block size. However, the next sequential data block often is not on the same cylinder, so seeks between 512-byte data transfers are required frequently. This combination of small block size and scattered placement severely limits filesystem throughput.

The first work on the UNIX filesystem at Berkeley attempted to improve both the reliability and the throughput of the filesystem. The developers improved reliability by staging modifications to critical filesystem information so that the modifications could be either completed or repaired cleanly by a program after a crash [McKusick & Kowalski, 1994]. Doubling the block size of the filesystem improved the performance of the 4.0BSD filesystem by a factor of more than two when compared with the 3BSD filesystem. This doubling caused each disk transfer to access twice as many data blocks and eliminated the need for indirect blocks for many files. In the remainder of this section, we shall refer to the filesystem with these changes as the 3BSD filesystem.

The performance improvement in the 3BSD filesystem gave a strong indication that increasing the block size was a good method for improving throughput. Although the throughput had doubled, the 3BSD filesystem was still using only about 4 percent of the maximum disk throughput. The main problem was that the order of blocks on the free list quickly became scrambled as files were created and removed. Eventually, the free-list order became entirely random, causing files to have their blocks allocated randomly over the disk. This randomness forced a seek before every block access. Although the 3BSD filesystem provided transfer rates of up to 175 Kbyte per second when it was first created, the scrambling of the free list caused this rate to deteriorate to an average of 30 Kbyte per second after a few weeks of moderate use. There was no way of restoring the performance of a 3BSD filesystem except to recreate the system.

Organization of the Berkeley Fast Filesystem

The first version of the current BSD filesystem appeared in 4.2BSD [McKusick et al., 1984]. This version is still in use today as UFS1. In the FreeBSD filesystem organization (as in the 3BSD filesystem organization), each disk drive contains one or more filesystems. A FreeBSD filesystem is described by its superblock, located at the beginning of the filesystem's disk partition. Because the superblock contains critical data, it is replicated to protect against catastrophic loss. This replication is done when the filesystem is created. Since most of the superblock data do not change, the copies do not need to be referenced unless a disk failure causes the default superblock to be corrupted. The data in the superblock that does change include a few flags and some summary information that can easily be recreated if an alternative superblock has to be used.

To allow support for filesystem fragments as small as a single 512-byte disk sector, the minimum size of a filesystem block is 4096 bytes. The block size can be any power of 2 greater than or equal to 4096. The block size is recorded in the filesystem's superblock, so it is possible for filesystems with different block sizes to be accessed simultaneously on the same system. The block size must be selected at the time that the filesystem is created; it cannot be changed subsequently without the filesystem being rebuilt.

The BSD filesystem organization divides a disk partition into one or more areas, each of which is called a ***cylinder group***. Historically, a cylinder group comprised one or more consecutive cylinders on a disk. Although FreeBSD still uses the same data structure to describe cylinder groups, the practical definition of them has changed. When the filesystem was first designed, it could get an accurate view of the disk geometry including the cylinder and track boundaries and could accurately compute the rotational location of every sector. Modern disks hide this information, providing fictitious numbers of blocks per track, tracks per cylinder, and cylinders per disk. Indeed, in modern RAID arrays, the "disk" that is presented to the filesystem may really be composed from a collection of disks in the RAID array. While some research has been done to figure out the true geometry of a disk [Griffin et al., 2002; Lumb et al., 2002; Schindler et al., 2002], the complexity of using such information effectively is high. Modern disks have greater numbers of sectors per track on the outer part of the disk than the inner part, which makes calculating the rotational position of any given sector complex. So when the design for UFS2 was drawn up, we decided to get rid of all the rotational layout code found in UFS1 and simply assume that laying out files with numerically close block numbers (sequential being viewed as optimal) would give the best performance. Thus, the cylinder-group structure is retained in UFS2, but it is used only as a convenient way to manage logically close groups of blocks. The rotational layout code had been disabled in UFS1 since the late 1980s, so as part of the code base cleanup it was removed entirely.

Each cylinder group must fit into a single filesystem block. When creating a new filesystem, the **newfs** utility calculates the maximum number of blocks that can be packed into a cylinder-group map based on the filesystem block size. It then allocates the minimum number of cylinder groups needed to describe the filesystem. A filesystem with 32-Kbyte blocks typically has 1.4 cylinder groups per Gbyte.

Each cylinder group contains bookkeeping information that includes a redundant copy of the superblock, space for inodes, a bitmap describing available blocks in the cylinder group, and summary information describing the usage of data blocks within the cylinder group. The bitmap of available blocks in the cylinder group replaces the traditional filesystem's free list. For each cylinder group in UFS1, a static number of inodes is allocated at filesystem-creation time. The default policy is to allocate one inode per four filesystem fragments, with the expectation that this amount will be far more than will ever be needed. For each cylinder group in UFS2, the default is to reserve bitmap space to describe one inode per two filesystem fragments. In either type of filesystem, the default may be changed only at the time that the filesystem is created.

The rationale for using cylinder groups is to create clusters of inodes that are spread over the disk close to the blocks that they reference, instead of them all being located at the beginning of the disk. The filesystem attempts to allocate file blocks close to the inodes that describe them to avoid long seeks between getting the inode and getting its associated data. Also, when the inodes are spread out, there is less chance of losing all of them in a single disk failure.

Although we decided to come up with a new on-disk inode format for UFS2, we chose not to change the format of the superblock, the cylinder group maps, or the directories. Additional information needed for the UFS2 superblock and cylinder groups is stored in spare fields of the UFS1 superblock and cylinder groups. Maintaining the same format for these data structures allows a single code base to be used for both UFS1 and UFS2. Because the only difference between the two filesystems is in the format of their inodes, code can dereference pointers to superblocks, cylinder groups, and directory entries without need to check what type of filesystem is being accessed. To minimize conditional checking of code that references inodes, the on-disk inode is converted to a common incore format when the inode is first read in from the disk and converted back to its on-disk format when it is written back. The effect of this decision is that there are only nine out of several hundred routines that are specific to UFS1 versus UFS2. The benefit of having a single code base for both filesystems is that it dramatically reduces the maintenance cost. Outside the nine filesystem format-specific functions, fixing a bug in the code fixes it for both filesystem types. A common code base also meant that as the multiprocessing support was added, it only needed to be done once for the UFS family of filesystems.

Boot Blocks

The UFS1 filesystem reserved an 8-Kbyte space at the beginning of the filesystem in which to put a boot block. While this space seemed huge compared to the 1-Kbyte boot block that it replaced, over time it has become increasingly difficult to cram the needed boot code into this space. Consequently, we decided to revisit the boot-block size in UFS2.

The boot code has a list of locations to check for boot blocks. A boot block can be defined to start at any 8-Kbyte boundary. We set up an initial list with four possible boot-block sizes: none, 8 Kbyte, 64 Kbyte, and 256 Kbyte. Each of these locations was selected for a particular purpose. Filesystems other than the root filesystem do not need to be bootable, so they can use a boot-block size of zero. Also, filesystems on tiny media that need every block that they can get, such as flash-based disks, can use a zero-size boot block. For architectures with simple boot blocks, the traditional UFS1 8-Kbyte boot block can be used. More typically, the 64-Kbyte boot block is used (for example, on the PC architecture with its need to support booting from a myriad of busses and disk drivers).

We added the 256-Kbyte boot block in case some future architecture or application needs to set aside a particularly large boot area. This space reservation is not strictly necessary, since new sizes can be added to the list at any time, but it can take a long time before the updated list is propagated to all the boot programs and loaders out on the existing systems. By adding the option for a huge boot area now, we can ensure it will be readily available should it be needed on short notice in the future.

An unexpected side effect of using a 64-Kbyte boot block for UFS2 is that if the partition had previously had a UFS1 filesystem on it, the superblock for the former UFS1 filesystem may not be overwritten. If an old version of **fsck** that does not first look for a UFS2 filesystem is run and finds the UFS1 superblock, it can incorrectly try to rebuild the UFS1 filesystem, destroying the UFS2 filesystem in the process. So when building UFS2 filesystems, the **newfs** utility looks for old UFS1 superblocks and zeros them out.

Optimization of Storage Utilization

Data are laid out such that large blocks can be transferred in a single disk operation, greatly increasing filesystem throughput. A file in the new filesystem might be composed of 32,768-byte data blocks, as compared to the 1024-byte blocks of the 3BSD filesystem; disk accesses would thus transfer up to 32 times as much information per disk transaction. In large files, several blocks can be allocated consecutively, so even larger data transfers are possible before a seek is required.

The main problem with larger blocks is that most BSD filesystems contain primarily small files. A uniformly large block size will waste space. For large blocks to be used without significant waste, small files must be stored more efficiently. To increase space efficiency, the filesystem allows the division of a single filesystem block into one or more ***fragments***. The fragment size is specified at the time that the filesystem is created; each filesystem block optionally can be broken into two, four, or eight fragments, each of which is addressable. The lower bound on the fragment size is constrained by the disk-sector size, which is typically 4096 byte. The block map associated with each cylinder group records the space available in a cylinder group in fragments; to determine whether a block is available, the system examines aligned fragments. Figure 9.31 shows a piece of a block map from a filesystem with 16,384-byte blocks and 4096-byte fragments, hereinafter referred to as a 16,384/4096 filesystem.

bits in map	----	--11	11--	1111
fragment numbers	0-3	4-7	8-11	12-15
block numbers	0	1	2	3

Figure 9.31 Example of the layout of blocks and fragments in a 16,384/4096 filesystem. Each bit in the map records the status of a fragment; a "-" means that the fragment is in use, whereas a "1" means that the fragment is available for allocation. In this example, fragments 0 through 5, 10, and 11 are in use, whereas fragments 6 through 9 and 12 through 15 are free. Fragments of adjacent blocks cannot be used as a full block, even if they are large enough. In this example, fragments 6 through 9 cannot be allocated as a full block; only fragments 12 through 15 can be coalesced into a full block.

On a 16,384/4096 filesystem, a file is represented by zero or more 16,384-byte blocks of data, possibly including a single fragmented block. If the system must fragment a block to obtain space for a few data, it makes the remaining fragments of the block available for allocation to other files. As an example, consider a 44,000-byte file stored on a 16,384/4096 filesystem. This file would use two full-size blocks and one three-fragment portion of another block. If no block with three aligned fragments were available at the time that the file was created, a full-size block would be split, yielding the necessary fragments and a single unused fragment. This remaining fragment could be allocated to another file as needed.

Reading and Writing to a File

Having opened a file, a process can do reads or writes on it. The procedural path through the kernel is shown in Figure 9.32. If a read is requested, it is channeled through the *ffs_read*() routine. The *ffs_read*() routine is responsible for converting the read into one or more reads of logical file blocks. A logical block request is then handed off to *ufs_bmap*(). The *ufs_bmap*() routine is responsible for converting a logical block number to a physical block number by interpreting the direct and indirect block pointers in an inode. The *ffs_read*() routine requests the block I/O system to return a buffer filled with the contents of the disk block. If two or more logically sequential blocks are read from a file, the process is assumed to be reading the file sequentially. Here, *ufs_bmap*() returns two values: first, the disk address of the requested block and then the number of contiguous blocks that follow that block on disk. The requested block and the number of contiguous blocks that follow it are passed to the *cluster*() routine. If the file is being accessed sequentially, the *cluster*() routine will do a single large I/O on the entire range of sequential blocks. If the file is not being accessed sequentially (as determined by a seek to a different part of the file preceding the read), only the requested block or a subset of the cluster will be read. If the file has had a long series of sequential reads, or if the number of contiguous blocks is small, the system will issue one or more requests for read-ahead blocks in anticipation that the process will soon want those blocks. The details of block clustering are described at the end of this section.

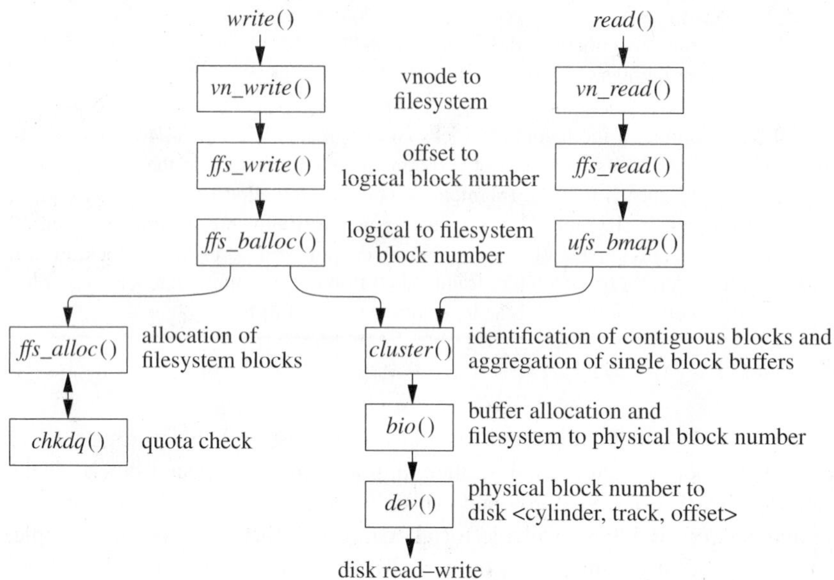

Figure 9.32 Procedural interface to reading and writing.

Each time that a process does a *write* system call, the system checks to see whether the size of the file has increased. A process may overwrite data in the middle of an existing file—in which case space would usually have been allocated already (unless the file contains a hole in that location). If the file must be extended, the request is rounded up to the next fragment size, and only that much space is allocated (see "Allocation Mechanisms" later in this section for the details of space allocation). The *write* system call is channeled through the *ffs_write*() routine. The *ffs_write*() routine is responsible for converting the write into one or more writes of logical file blocks. A logical block request is then handed off to *ffs_balloc*(). The *ffs_balloc*() routine is responsible for interpreting the direct and indirect block pointers in an inode to find the location for the associated physical block pointer. If a disk block does not already exist, the *ffs_alloc*() routine is called to request a new block of the appropriate size. After calling *chkdq*() to ensure that the user has not exceeded his quota, the block is allocated, and the address of the new block is stored in the inode or indirect block. The address of the new or already-existing block is returned, and *ffs_write*() allocates a buffer to hold the contents of the block. The user's data are copied into the returned buffer, and the buffer is marked as dirty. If the buffer has been filled completely, it is passed to the *cluster*() routine. When a maximum-size cluster has been accumulated, a noncontiguous block is allocated, or a seek is done to another part of the file, and the accumulated blocks are grouped together into a single I/O operation that is queued to be written to the disk. If the buffer has not been filled completely, it is not considered immediately for writing. Instead, the buffer is held in the expectation that the process will soon want to add more data to it. It is not released until it is needed for some other block—that is, until it has reached the head of the free list or until a user process does an *fsync* system call. When a file acquires its first dirty block, it is placed on a 30-second timer queue. If it still has dirty blocks when the timer expires, all its dirty buffers are written. If it subsequently is written again, it will be returned to the 30-second timer queue.

Repeated small write requests may expand the file one fragment at a time. The problem with expanding a file one fragment at a time is that data may be copied many times as a fragmented block expands to a full block. Fragment reallocation can be minimized if the user process writes a full block at a time, except for a partial block at the end of the file. Since filesystems with different block sizes may reside on the same system, the filesystem interface provides application programs with the optimal size for a read or write. This facility is used by the standard I/O library that many application programs use and by certain system utilities, such as archivers and loaders, that do their own I/O management. To avoid excessive copying for slowly growing files, the filesystem allows only direct blocks of files to refer to fragments.

If the layout policies (described at the end of this section) are to be effective, a filesystem cannot be kept completely full. A parameter, termed the ***free-space reserve***, gives the minimum percentage of filesystem blocks that should be kept free. If the number of free blocks drops below this level, only the superuser is allowed to allocate blocks. This parameter can be changed any time that the filesystem is unmounted. When the number of free blocks approaches zero, the filesystem throughput tends to be cut in half because the filesystem is unable to localize blocks in a file. If a filesystem's throughput drops because of overfilling, it can be restored by removal of files until the amount of free space once again reaches the minimum acceptable level. Users can restore locality to get faster access rates for files created during periods of little free space by copying the file to a new one and removing the original one when enough space is available.

Layout Policies

Each filesystem is parameterized so that it can be adapted to the characteristics of the application environment in which it is being used. These parameters are summarized in Table 9.4. In most situations, the default parameters work well, but in an environment with only a few large files or an environment with just a few huge directories, the performance can be enhanced by adjusting the layout parameters accordingly.

Table 9.4 Important parameters maintained by the filesystem.

Name	Default	Meaning
minfree	8%	minimum percentage of free space
avgfilesize	16K	expected average file size
filesperdir	64	expected number of files per directory
maxbpg	2048	maximum blocks per file in a cylinder group
maxcontig	8	maximum contiguous blocks that can be transfered in one I/O request

The filesystem layout policies are divided into two distinct parts. At the top level are global policies that use summary information to make decisions regarding the placement of new inodes and data blocks. These routines are responsible for deciding the placement of new directories and files. They also build contiguous block layouts and decide when to force a long seek to a new cylinder group because there is insufficient space left in the current cylinder group to do reasonable layouts.

Below the global-policy routines are the local-allocation routines. These routines use a locally optimal scheme to lay out data blocks. The local-allocation routines are responsible for managing the allocation bitmaps and ensuring that resources are not double allocated. Thus, the policy layer does not have to worry about requesting an already allocated block. If the implementation layer finds that a requested block is already allocated, it simply scans through the map to find the closest available free block. The result of this separation is that once the implementation layer is working properly, filesystem designers are free to try out whatever hair-brained policy ideas that they want without fear of corrupting the filesystem. The implementation layer for FFS was written and debugged in 1982 and has not been changed since. Further refinements to the filesystem have been done at the policy layer. Separating policy from implementation is an important design principle when designing software systems, especially when they are mission-critical systems. The policy layer allows new ideas to be implemented and tested quickly. Once validated, those ideas can be deployed without danger of compromising the integrity of the system.

Two methods for improving filesystem performance are to increase the locality of reference to minimize seek latency [Trivedi, 1980] and to improve the layout of data to make larger transfers possible [Nevalainen & Vesterinen, 1977]. The global layout policies try to improve performance by clustering related information. They cannot attempt to localize all data references but must instead try to spread unrelated data among different cylinder groups. If too much localization is attempted, the local cylinder group may run out of space, forcing further related data to be scattered to nonlocal cylinder groups. Taken to an extreme, total localization can result in a single huge cluster of data resembling the 3BSD filesystem. The global policies try to balance the two conflicting goals of localizing data that are concurrently accessed while spreading out unrelated data.

One allocatable resource is inodes. Inodes of files in the same directory frequently are accessed together. For example, the list-directory command, **ls**, may access the inode for each file in a directory. The inode layout policy tries to place all the inodes of files in a directory in the same cylinder group. To ensure that files are distributed throughout the filesystem, the system uses a different policy to allocate directory inodes. When a directory is being created in the root of the filesystem, it is placed in a cylinder group with a greater-than-average number of free blocks and inodes, and with the smallest number of directories. The intent of this policy is to allow inode clustering to succeed most of the time. When a directory is created lower in the tree, it is placed in a cylinder group with a greater-than-average number of free blocks and inodes near its parent directory. The intent of this policy is to reduce the distance tree-walking applications must seek as they move from directory to directory in a depth-first search while still allowing inode clustering to succeed most of the time.

The filesystem allocates inodes within a cylinder group using a first-free strategy. Although this method allocates the inodes randomly within a cylinder group, it keeps the allocation down to the smallest number of inode blocks possible. Even when all the possible inodes in a cylinder group are allocated, they can be accessed with 10 to 20 disk transfers. This allocation strategy puts a small and constant upper bound on the number of disk transfers required to access the inodes for all the files in a directory. In contrast, the 3BSD filesystem typically requires one disk transfer to fetch the inode for each file in a directory.

The other major resource is the data blocks. Data blocks for a file typically are accessed together. The policy routines try to place data blocks for a file in the same cylinder group, preferably laid out contiguously. The problem with allocating all the data blocks in the same cylinder group is that large files quickly use up the available space, forcing a spillover to other areas. Further, using all the space also causes future allocations for any file in the cylinder group to spill to other areas. Ideally, none of the cylinder groups should ever become completely full. The heuristic chosen is to redirect block allocation to a different cylinder group after every few Mbyte of allocation. The spillover points are intended to force block allocation to be redirected when any file has used about 25 percent of the data blocks in a cylinder group. In day-to-day use, the heuristics appear to work well in minimizing the number of completely filled cylinder groups. Although this heuristic appears to benefit small files at the expense of larger files, it really aids both file sizes. The small files are helped because there are nearly always blocks available in the cylinder group for them to use. The large files benefit because they are able to use the contiguous space available in the cylinder group and then to move on, leaving behind the blocks scattered around the cylinder group. Although these scattered blocks are fine for small files that need only a block or two, they slow down big files that are best stored on a single, large group of blocks that can be read in a few disk revolutions.

The newly chosen cylinder group for block allocation is the next cylinder group that has a greater-than-average number of free blocks left. Although big files tend to be spread out over the disk, several Mbyte of data typically are accessible before a seek to a new cylinder group is necessary. Thus, the time to do one long seek is small compared to the time spent in the new cylinder group doing the I/O.

In an effort to speed random access to files and to speed the checking of metadata by **fsck**, the filesystem holds the first 4 percent of the data blocks in each cylinder group for the use of metadata. The policy routines preferentially place metadata in the metadata area and everything else in the blocks that follow the metadata area. The size of the metadata area does not need to be precisely calculated as it is used just as a hint of where to place the metadata by the policy routines. If the metadata area fills up, then the metadata can be placed in the regular-blocks area, and if the regular-blocks area fills up, then the regular blocks can be placed in the metadata area. This decision happens on a cylinder group by cylinder group basis, so some cylinder groups can overflow their metadata area while others do not overflow it. The policy is to place all metadata in the same cylinder group as their inode. Spreading the metadata across cylinder groups generally results in reduced filesystem performance.

The one exception to the metadata placement policy is for the first indirect block of the file. The policy is to place the first (single) indirect block inline with the file data (e.g., it tries to lay out the first 12 direct blocks contiguously, followed immediately by the indirect block, followed immediately by the data blocks referenced from the indirect block). Putting the first indirect block inline with the data rather than in the metadata area is to avoid two extra seeks when reading it. These two extra seeks would noticeably slow down access to a file that uses only the first few blocks referenced from its indirect block.

Only the second and third level indirects, along with the indirects that they reference, are allocated in the metadata area. The nearly contiguous allocation of this metadata close to the inode that references them noticeably improves the random access time to the file as well as speeding up the running time of **fsck**. Also, the disk track cache is often filled with much of a file's metadata when the second-level indirect block is read, thus often speeding up even the sequential reading time for the file.

In addition to putting indirect blocks in the metadata area, it is also helpful to put the blocks holding the contents of directories there, too. Putting the contents of directories in the metadata area gives a speedup to directory tree traversal since the data is a short seek away from where the directory inode was read and may already be in the disk's track cache from other directory reads done in its cylinder group.

Allocation Mechanisms

The global-policy routines call local-allocation routines with requests for specific blocks. The local-allocation routines will always allocate the requested block if it is free; otherwise, they will allocate a free block of the requested size that is closest to the requested block. If the global layout policies had complete information, they could always request unused blocks and the allocation routines would be reduced to simple bookkeeping. However, maintaining complete information is costly; thus, the global layout policy uses heuristics based on the partial information that is available.

If a requested block is not available, the local allocator uses a three-level allocation strategy:

1. Use the next available block closest to the requested block in the same cylinder group.

2. If the cylinder group is full, quadratically hash the cylinder-group number to choose another cylinder group in which to look for a free block. Quadratic hash is used because of its speed in finding unused slots in nearly full hash tables [Knuth, 1975]. Filesystems that are parameterized to maintain at least 8 percent free space rarely need to use this strategy. Filesystems used without free space typically have so few free blocks available that almost any allocation is random; the most important characteristic of the strategy used under such conditions is that it be fast.

3. Apply an exhaustive search to all cylinder groups. This search is necessary because the quadratic rehash may not check all cylinder groups.

The task of managing block and fragment allocation is done by *ffs_balloc*(). If the file is being written and a block pointer is zero or points to a fragment that is too small to hold the additional data, *ffs_balloc*() calls the allocation routines to obtain a new block. If the file needs to be extended, one of two conditions exists:

1. The file contains no fragmented blocks (and the final block in the file contains insufficient space to hold the new data). If space exists in a block already allocated, the space is filled with new data. If the remainder of the new data consists of more than a full block, a full block is allocated and the first full block of new data are written there. This process is repeated until less than a full block of new data remains. If the remaining new data to be written will fit in less than a full block, a block with the necessary number of fragments is located; otherwise, a full block is located. The remaining new data are written into the located space. However, to avoid excessive copying for slowly growing files, the filesystem allows only direct blocks of files to refer to fragments.
2. The file contains one or more fragments (and the fragments contain insufficient space to hold the new data). If the size of the new data plus the size of the data already in the fragments exceeds the size of a full block, a new block is allocated. The contents of the fragments are copied to the beginning of the block and the remainder of the block is filled with new data. The process then continues as in step 1. Otherwise, a set of fragments big enough to hold the data is located; if enough of the rest of the current block is free, the filesystem can avoid a copy by using that block. The contents of the existing fragments, appended with the new data, are written into the allocated space.

The *ffs_balloc*() routine is also responsible for allocating blocks to hold indirect pointers. It must also deal with the special case in which a process seeks past the end of a file and begins writing. Because of the constraint that only the final block of a file may be a fragment, *ffs_balloc*() must first ensure that any previous fragment has been upgraded to a full-size block.

On completing a successful allocation, the allocation routines return the block or fragment number to be used; *ffs_balloc*() then updates the appropriate block pointer in the inode. Having allocated a block, the system is ready to allocate a buffer to hold the block's contents so that the block can be written to disk.

The procedural description of the allocation process is shown in Figure 9.33. *Ffs_balloc*() is the routine responsible for determining when a new block must be allocated. It first calls the layout-policy routine *ffs_blkpref*() to select the most desirable block based on the preference from the global-policy routines that were described earlier in this section. If a fragment has already been allocated and needs to be extended, *ffs_balloc*() calls *ffs_realloccg*(). If nothing has been allocated yet, *ffs_balloc*() calls *ffs_alloc*().

Ffs_realloccg() first tries to extend the current fragment in place. Consider the sample block of an allocation map with two fragments allocated from it,

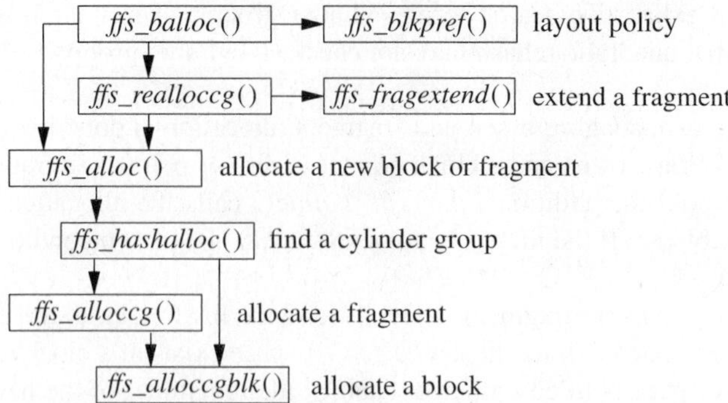

Figure 9.33 Procedural interface to block allocation.

shown in Figure 9.34. The first fragment can be extended from a size 2 fragment to a size 3 or a size 4 fragment, since the two adjacent fragments are unused. The second fragment cannot be extended, as it occupies the end of the block, and fragments are not allowed to span blocks. If *ffs_realloccg*() is able to expand the current fragment in place, the map is updated appropriately and it returns. If the fragment cannot be extended, *ffs_realloccg*() calls the *ffs_alloc*() routine to get a new fragment. The old fragment is copied to the beginning of the new fragment, and the old fragment is freed.

The bookkeeping tasks of allocation are handled by *ffs_alloc*(). It first verifies that a block is available in the desired cylinder group by checking the filesystem summary information. If the summary information shows that the cylinder group is full, *ffs_alloc*() quadratically rehashes through the summary information looking for a cylinder group with free space. Having found a cylinder group with space, *ffs_alloc*() calls either the fragment-allocation routine or the block-allocation routine to acquire a fragment or block.

The block-allocation routine is given a preferred block. If that block is available, it is returned. If the block is unavailable, the allocation routine tries to find another block in the same cylinder group that is close to the requested block. It looks for an available block by scanning forward through the free-block map, starting from the requested location until it finds an available block.

The fragment-allocation routine is given a preferred fragment. If that fragment is available, it is returned. If the requested fragment is not available, and the filesystem is configured to optimize for space utilization, the filesystem uses a best-fit strategy for fragment allocation. The fragment-allocation routine checks the cylinder-group summary information, starting with the entry for the desired

Figure 9.34 Sample block with two allocated fragments.

entry in table	1	-	-	1	1	-	-	-
allocated fragments	size 2			size 3				

bits in map	decimal value
-111--11	115

Figure 9.35 Map entry for a 32,768/4096 filesystem.

size, and scanning larger sizes until an available fragment is found. If there are no fragments of the appropriate size or larger, then a full-size block is allocated and is broken up.

If a fragment of an appropriate size is listed in the fragment summary, then the allocation routine expects to find it in the allocation map. To speed up the process of scanning the potentially large allocation map, the filesystem uses a table-driven algorithm. Each byte in the map is treated as an index into a ***fragment-descriptor table***. Each entry in the fragment-descriptor table describes the fragments that are free for that corresponding map entry. Thus, by doing a logical AND with the bit corresponding to the desired fragment size, the allocator can determine quickly whether the desired fragment is contained within a given allocation-map entry. As an example, consider the entry from an allocation map for the 32,768/4096 filesystem shown in Figure 9.35. The map entry shown has already been fragmented, with a single fragment allocated at the beginning and a size 2 fragment allocated in the middle. Remaining unused is another size 2 fragment and a size 3 fragment. Thus, if we look up entry 115 in the fragment table, we find the entry shown in Figure 9.36. If we were looking for a size 3 fragment, we would inspect the third bit and find that we had been successful; if we were looking for a size 4 fragment, we would inspect the fourth bit and find that we needed to continue. The C code that implements this algorithm is as follows:

```
for (i = 0; i < MAPSIZE; i++)
    if (fragtbl[allocmap[i]] & (1 << (size - 1)))
        break;
```

Using a best-fit policy has the benefit of minimizing disk fragmentation; however, it has the undesirable property of maximizing the number of fragment-to-fragment copies that must be made when a process writes a file in many small pieces. To avoid this behavior, the system can configure filesystems to optimize for time rather than for space. The first time that a process does a small write on a filesystem configured for time optimization, it is allocated a best-fit fragment. On the second small write, however, a full-size block is allocated, with the unused portion being freed. Later small writes are able to extend the fragment in place, rather than requiring additional copy operations. Under certain circumstances,

Figure 9.36 Fragment-table entry for entry 115.

entry in table	0	0	0	0	0	1	1	0
available fragment size	8	7	6	5	4	3	2	1

this policy can cause the disk to become heavily fragmented. The system tracks this condition and automatically reverts to optimizing for space if the percentage of fragmentation reaches one-half of the minimum free-space limit.

Block Clustering

Most machines running FreeBSD do not have separate I/O processors. The main CPU must take an interrupt after each disk I/O operation; if there is more disk I/O to be done, it must select the next buffer to be transferred and must start the operation on that buffer. Before the advent of track-caching controllers, the filesystem obtained its highest throughput by leaving a gap after each block to allow time for the next I/O operation to be scheduled. If the blocks were laid out without a gap, the throughput would suffer because the disk would have to rotate nearly an entire revolution to pick up the start of the next block.

Track-caching controllers have a large buffer in the controller that continues to accumulate the data coming in from the disk even after the requested data have been received. If the next request is for the immediately following block, the controller will already have most of the block in its buffer, so it will not have to wait a revolution to pick up the block. Thus, for the purposes of reading, it is possible to nearly double the throughput of the filesystem by laying out the files contiguously rather than leaving gaps after each block.

Unfortunately, the track cache is less useful for writing. Because the kernel does not provide the next data block until the previous one completes, there is still a delay during which the controller does not have the data to write, and it ends up waiting a revolution to get back to the beginning of the next block. One solution to this problem is to have the controller give its completion interrupt after it has copied the data into its cache, but before it has finished writing them. This early interrupt gives the CPU time to request the next I/O before the previous one completes, thus providing a continuous stream of data to write to the disk.

This approach has one seriously negative side effect. When the I/O completion interrupt is delivered, the kernel expects the data to be on stable store. Filesystem integrity and user applications using the *fsync* system call depend on these semantics. These semantics will be violated if the power fails after the I/O completion interrupt but before the data are written to disk. Some vendors eliminate this problem by using nonvolatile memory for the controller cache and providing microcode restart after power fail to determine which operations need to be completed. Because this option is expensive, few controllers provide this functionality.

Newer disks resolve this problem with a technique called ***tag queueing***. With tag queueing, each request passed to the disk driver is assigned a unique numeric tag. Most disk controllers supporting tag queueing will accept at least 16 pending I/O requests. After each request is finished, the tag of the completed request is returned as part of the completion interrupt. If several contiguous blocks are presented to the disk controller, it can begin work on the next one while the tag for the previous one is being returned. Thus, tag queueing allows applications to be accurately notified when their data has reached stable store without incurring the penalty of lost disk revolutions when writing contiguous blocks.

One approach to dealing with disks that report completion before the data are on stable store is the Coerced Cache Eviction Project in which the disk cache is forcibly flushed at each ordering point to maintain consistency in its journaling filesystem [Rajimwale et al., 2011]. Another approach is the No-Order File System in which the filesystem is redesigned to provide crash consistency without ordering writes by employing a technique called backpointer-based consistency [Chidambaram et al., 2012].

To maximize throughput on systems without tag queueing or nonvolatile controller memory, the FreeBSD system implements I/O clustering. Clustering helps improve performance on all systems by reducing the number of I/O requests through the aggregation of many small requests into a smaller number of big ones. Clustering was first done by Santa Cruz Operations [Peacock, 1988] and Sun Microsystems [McVoy & Kleiman, 1991]; the idea was later adapted to 4.4BSD and thus to FreeBSD [Seltzer et al., 1993]. As a file is being written, the allocation routines try to allocate up to *maxcontig* (typically 256 Kbyte) of data in contiguous disk blocks. Instead of the buffers holding these blocks being written as they are filled, their output is delayed. The cluster is completed when the limit of *maxcontig* of data is reached, the file is closed, or the cluster cannot grow because the next sequential block on the disk is already in use by another file. If the cluster size is limited by a previous allocation to another file, the filesystem is notified and is given the opportunity to find a larger set of contiguous blocks into which the cluster may be placed. If the reallocation is successful, the cluster continues to grow. When the cluster is complete, the buffers making up the cluster of blocks are aggregated and passed to the disk controller as a single I/O request. The data can then be streamed out to the disk in a single uninterrupted transfer.

A similar scheme is used for reading. If the *ffs_read*() discovers that a file is being read sequentially, it inspects the number of contiguous blocks returned by *ufs_bmap*() to look for clusters of contiguously allocated blocks. It then allocates a set of buffers big enough to hold the contiguous set of blocks and passes them to the disk controller as a single I/O request. The I/O can then be done in one operation. Although read clustering is not needed when track-caching controllers are available, it reduces the interrupt load from systems that have them, and it speeds low-cost systems that do not have them.

For clustering to be effective, the filesystem must be able to allocate large clusters of contiguous blocks to files. If the filesystem always tried to begin allocation for a file at the beginning of a large set of contiguous blocks, it would soon use up its contiguous space. Instead, it uses an algorithm similar to that used for the management of fragments. Initially, file blocks are allocated via the standard algorithm described in the previous two subsections. Reallocation is invoked when the standard algorithm does not result in a contiguous allocation. The reallocation code searches a cluster map that summarizes the available clusters of blocks in the cylinder group. It allocates the first free cluster that is large enough to hold the file and then moves the file to this contiguous space. This process continues until the current allocation has grown to a size equal to the maximum permissible I/O operation (*maxcontig*). At that point, the I/O is done and the process of allocating space begins again.

Unlike fragment reallocation, block reallocation to different clusters of blocks does not require extra I/O or memory-to-memory copying. The data to be written are held in delayed write buffers. Within that buffer is the disk location to which

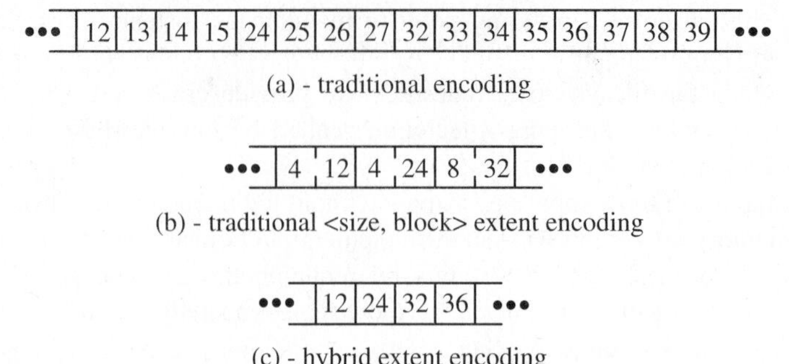

Figure 9.37 Alternative file metadata representations.

the data are to be written. When the block cluster is relocated, it takes little time to walk the list of buffers in the cluster and to change the disk addresses to which they are to be written. When the I/O occurs, the final destination has been selected and will not change.

To speed the operation of finding clusters of blocks, the filesystem maintains a cluster map with 1 bit per block (in addition to the map with 1 bit per fragment). It also has summary information showing how many sets of blocks there are for each possible cluster size. The summary information allows it to avoid looking for cluster sizes that do not exist. The cluster map is used because it is faster to scan than is the much larger fragment bitmap. The size of the map is important because the map must be scanned bit by bit. Unlike fragments, clusters of blocks are not constrained to be aligned within the map. Thus, the table-lookup optimization done for fragments cannot be used for lookup of clusters.

The filesystem relies on the allocation of contiguous blocks to achieve high levels of performance. The fragmentation of free space may increase with time or with filesystem utilization. This fragmentation can degrade performance as the filesystem ages. The effects of utilization and aging were measured on over 50 filesystems at Harvard University. The measured filesystems ranged in age, since initial creation, from one to three years. The fragmentation of free space on most of the measured filesystems caused performance to degrade no more than 10 percent from that of a newly created empty filesystem. The most severe degradation measured was 30 percent on a highly active filesystem that had many small files and was used to spool USENET news [Seltzer et al., 1995].

Extent-Based Allocation

With the addition of dynamic block reallocation in the early 1990s [Seltzer & Smith, 1996], the UFS1 filesystem has had the ability to allocate most files contiguously on the disk. The metadata describing a large file consist of indirect blocks with long runs of sequential block numbers, as shown in Figure 9.37(a). For quick access while a file is active, the kernel tries to keep all a file's metadata in memory. With UFS2, the space required to hold the metadata for a file is doubled as every block pointer grows from 32 bits to 64 bits. To provide a more compact representation, many filesystems use an extent-based representation. A typical extent-based representation uses pairs of block numbers and lengths. Figure 9.37(b) represents the same set of block numbers as Figure 9.37(a) in an extent-based format. If the file can be laid out nearly contiguously, this representation provides a compact description. However, randomly or slowly written files can end up with many noncontiguous block allocations, which will produce a representation that requires more space than the one used by UFS1. This representation also has the drawback that it can require much computation to perform random-access to the file, since the block number needs to be computed by adding up the sizes starting from the beginning of the file until the desired seek offset is reached.

To gain most of the efficiencies of extents without the random access inefficiencies, UFS2 has added a field to the inode that will allow that inode to use a larger block size. Small, slowly growing, or sparse files set this value to the regular filesystem block size and represent their data in the traditional way shown in Figure 9.37(a). However, when the filesystem detects a large, dense file, it can set this inode-block-size field to a value 2 to 16 times the filesystem block size. Figure 9.37(c) represents the same set of block numbers as Figure 9.37(a), with the inode-block-size field set to 4 times the filesystem block size. Each block pointer references a piece of disk storage that is four times larger, which reduces the metadata storage requirement by 75 percent. Since every block pointer other than possibly the last one references an equal-size block, computation of random access offsets is just as fast as in the traditional metadata representation. Unlike the traditional extent-based representation that can double the metadata space requirement for certain datasets, this representation will always result in less space dedicated to metadata.

The drawback to this approach is that once a file has committed to using a larger block size, it can only use blocks of that size. If the filesystem runs out of big blocks, then the file can no longer grow, and either the application will get an "out-of-space" error or the filesystem has to recreate the metadata with the standard filesystem block size. The current plan is to write the code to recreate the metadata. While recreating the metadata usually will cause a long pause, we expect that condition to be rare and not a noticeable problem in real use.

Exercises

9.1 What are the seven classes of operations handled by the hierarchical filesystem?

9.2 What is the purpose of the inode data structure?

9.3 How does the system select an inode for replacement when a new inode must be brought in from disk?

9.4 Why are directory entries not allowed to span chunks?

9.5 Describe the steps involved in looking up a pathname component.

9.6 Why are hard links not permitted to span filesystems?

9.7 Describe how the interpretation of a symbolic link containing an absolute pathname is different from that of a symbolic link containing a relative pathname.

9.8 Explain why unprivileged users are not permitted to make hard links to directories but are permitted to make symbolic links to directories.

9.9 How can hard links be used to gain access to files that could not be accessed if a symbolic link were used instead?

9.10 How does the system recognize loops caused by symbolic links? Suggest an alternative scheme for doing loop detection.

9.11 How do quotas differ from the file-size resource limits described in Section 5.12?

9.12 How does the kernel determine whether a file has an associated quota?

9.13 Draw a picture showing the effect of processing an exclusive-lock request by process 1 on bytes 7 to 10 to the lock list shown in Figure 9.15. Which of the overlap cases of Figure 9.14 apply to this example?

9.14 In the absence of soft updates, which three FFS operations must be done synchronously to ensure that the filesystem can always be recovered deterministically after a crash (barring unrecoverable hardware errors)?

9.15 What are the guarantees made by the *fsync* system call?

9.16 Name the five ordering constraints that must be maintained when a file is removed. Describe how soft updates maintains this ordering.

9.17 Give three uses for a filesystem snapshot.

9.18 Describe the eight steps needed to take a filesystem snapshot.

9.19 What are the three states that a block may have in a snapshot? Describe the actions taken by a snapshot for each of these states when a write occurs. Describe the actions taken by a snapshot for each of these states when a block is released.

9.20 What are the four classes of operations handled by the datastore filesystem?

9.21 Under what circumstances can a write request avoid reading a block from the disk?

9.22 What is the difference between a logical block and a physical block? Why is this distinction important?

9.23 Give two reasons why increasing the basic block size in the old filesystem from 512 bytes to 1024 bytes more than doubled the system's throughput.

9.24 How many blocks and fragments are allocated to a 31,200-byte file on a FFS with 4096-byte blocks and 1024-byte fragments? How many blocks and fragments are allocated to this file on a FFS with 4096-byte blocks and

512-byte fragments? Also, answer these two questions assuming that an inode has only 6 direct block pointers instead of 12.

9.25 Explain why the FFS maintains a 5 to 10 percent reserve of free space. What problems would arise if the free-space reserve were set to zero?

9.26 What is a quadratic hash? Describe for what it is used in the FFS, and why it is used for that purpose.

9.27 Why are the allocation policies for inodes different from those for data blocks?

9.28 Under what circumstances does block clustering provide benefits that cannot be obtained with a disk-track cache?

*9.29 Give an example where the file-locking implementation is unable to detect a potential deadlock.

*9.30 What problems would arise if files had to be allocated in a single contiguous piece of the disk? Consider the problems created by multiple processes, random access, and files with holes.

**9.31 Design a system that allows the security level of the system to be lowered while the system is still running in multiuser mode.

**9.32 Inodes could be allocated dynamically as part of a directory entry. Instead, the inode allocation region is reserved when the filesystem is created. Why is the latter approach used?

References

Apple, 2003.

Apple, *Mac OS X Essentials, Chapter 9 Filesystem, Section 12 Resource Forks,* available from http://developer.apple.com/techpubs/macosx/Essentials/SystemOverview/FileSystem/chapter_9_section_12.html, 2003.

Best, 2000.

S. Best, *JFS overview,* available from http://www-128.ibm.com/developerworks/library/l-jfs.html, January 2000.

Chamberlin & Astrahan, 1981.

D. Chamberlin & M. Astrahan, "A History and Evaluation of System R," *Communications of the ACM*, vol. 24, no. 10, pp. 632–646, October 1981.

Chidambaram et al., 2012.

V. Chidambaram, T. Sharma, A. Arpaci-Dusseau, & R. Arpaci-Dusseau, "Consistency Without Ordering," *Proceedings of the Tenth USENIX Conference on File and Storage Technologies*, available from http://pages.cs.wisc.edu/~vijayc/nofs.htm, February 2012.

Chutani et al., 1992.

S. Chutani, O. Anderson, M. Kazar, W. Mason, & R. Sidebotham, "The Episode File System," *USENIX Association Conference Proceedings*, pp. 43–59, January 1992.

Dowse & Malone, 2002.
I. Dowse & D. Malone, "Recent Filesystem Optimizations on FreeBSD," *Proceedings of the Freenix Track at the 2002 USENIX Annual Technical Conference*, pp. 245–258, June 2002.

Elz, 1984.
K. R. Elz, "Resource Controls, Privileges, and Other MUSH," *USENIX Association Conference Proceedings*, pp. 183–191, June 1984.

Ganger et al., 2000.
G. Ganger, M. K. McKusick, C. Soules, & Y. Patt, "Soft Updates: A Solution to the Metadata Update Problem in File Systems," *ACM Transactions on Computer Systems*, vol. 18, no. 2, pp. 127–153, May 2000.

Ganger & Patt, 1994.
G. Ganger & Y. Patt, "Metadata Update Performance in File Systems," *USENIX Symposium on Operating Systems Design and Implementation*, pp. 49–60, November 1994.

Griffin et al., 2002.
J. L. Griffin, J. Schindler, S. W. Schlosser, J. S. Bucy, & G. R. Ganger, "Timing-Accurate Storage Emulation," *Proceedings of the USENIX Conference on File and Storage Technologies*, pp. 75–88, January 2002.

Hagmann, 1987.
R. Hagmann, "Reimplementing the Cedar File System Using Logging and Group Commit," *ACM Symposium on Operating Systems Principles*, pp. 155–162, November 1987.

Knuth, 1975.
D. Knuth, *The Art of Computer Programming, Volume 3—Sorting and Searching,* pp. 506–549, Addison-Wesley, Reading, MA, 1975.

Lumb et al., 2002.
C. R. Lumb, J. Schindler, & G. R. Ganger, "Freeblock Scheduling Outside of Disk Firmware," *Proceedings of the USENIX Conference on File and Storage Technologies*, pp. 275–288, January 2002.

McKusick, 2002.
M. K. McKusick, "Running fsck in the Background," *Proceedings of the BSDCon 2002 Conference*, pp. 55–64, February 2002.

McKusick, 2003.
M. K. McKusick, "Enhancements to the Fast Filesystem to Support Multi-terabyte Storage Systems," *Proceedings of the BSDCon 2003 Conference*, pp. 79–90, September 2003.

McKusick et al., 1984.
M. K. McKusick, W. N. Joy, S. J. Leffler, & R. S. Fabry, "A Fast File System for UNIX," *ACM Transactions on Computer Systems*, vol. 2, no. 3, pp. 181–197, Association for Computing Machinery, August 1984.

McKusick & Kowalski, 1994.
M. K. McKusick & T. J. Kowalski, "fsck: The UNIX File System Check Program," in *4.4BSD System Manager's Manual*, pp. 3:1–21, O'Reilly & Associates, Inc., Sebastopol, CA, 1994.

McVoy & Kleiman, 1991.
L. McVoy & S. Kleiman, "Extent-Like Performance from a UNIX File

System," *USENIX Association Conference Proceedings*, pp. 33–44, January 1991.

Moran et al., 1990.
J. Moran, R. Sandberg, D. Coleman, J. Kepecs, & B. Lyon, "Breaking Through the NFS Performance Barrier," *Proceedings of the Spring 1990 European UNIX Users Group Conference*, pp. 199–206, April 1990.

Nevalainen & Vesterinen, 1977.
O. Nevalainen & M. Vesterinen, "Determining Blocking Factors for Sequential Files by Heuristic Methods," *The Computer Journal*, vol. 20, no. 3, pp. 245–247, August 1977.

Ousterhout, 1990.
J. Ousterhout, "Why Aren't Operating Systems Getting Faster as Fast as Hardware?," *Summer USENIX Conference*, pp. 247–256, June 1990.

Peacock, 1988.
J. Peacock, "The Counterpoint Fast File System," *USENIX Association Conference Proceedings*, pp. 243–249, January 1988.

Phillips, 2001.
D. Phillips, "A Directory Index for Ext2," *Proceedings of the USENIX Fifth Annual Linux Showcase and Conference*, November 2001.

Rajimwale et al., 2011.
A. Rajimwale, V. Chidambaram, D. Ramamurthi, A. Arpaci-Dusseau, & R. Arpaci-Dusseau, "Coerced Cache Eviction and Discreet-Mode Journaling: Dealing with Misbehaving Disks," *Proceedings of 41st Annual International Conference on Dependable Systems and Networks*, available from http://pages.cs.wisc.edu/~vijayc/cce.htm, June 2011.

Reiser, 2001.
H. Reiser, *The Reiser File System,* available from http://www.namesys.com/res_whol.shtml, January 2001.

Rhodes, 2014.
T. Rhodes, *FreeBSD Handbook, Chapter 3, Section 3.3 File System Access Control Lists,* available from http://www.FreeBSD.org/doc/en_US.ISO8859-1/books/handbook/fs-acl.html, March 2014.

Rosenblum & Ousterhout, 1992.
M. Rosenblum & J. Ousterhout, "The Design and Implementation of a Log-Structured File System," *ACM Transactions on Computer Systems*, vol. 10, no. 1, pp. 26–52, Association for Computing Machinery, February 1992.

Schindler et al., 2002.
J. Schindler, J. L. Griffin, C. R. Lumb, & G. R. Ganger, "Track-Aligned Extents: Matching Access Patterns to Disk Drive Characteristics," *Proceedings of the USENIX Conference on File and Storage Technologies*, pp. 259–274, January 2002.

Seltzer et al., 1993.
M. Seltzer, K. Bostic, M. K. McKusick, & C. Staelin, "An Implementation of a Log-Structured File System for UNIX," *USENIX Association Conference Proceedings*, pp. 307–326, January 1993.

Seltzer et al., 2000.
M. Seltzer, G. Ganger, M. K. McKusick, K. Smith, C. Soules, & C. Stein,

"Journaling versus Soft Updates: Asynchronous Meta-data Protection in File Systems," *Proceedings of the San Diego USENIX Conference*, pp. 71–84, June 2000.

Seltzer & Smith, 1996.
M. Seltzer & K. Smith, "A Comparison of FFS Disk Allocation Algorithms," *Winter USENIX Conference*, pp. 15–25, January 1996.

Seltzer et al., 1995.
M. Seltzer, K. Smith, H. Balakrishnan, J. Chang, S. McMains, & V. Padmanabhan, "File System Logging Versus Clustering: A Performance Comparison," *USENIX Association Conference Proceedings*, pp. 249–264, January 1995.

Stonebraker, 1987.
M. Stonebraker, "The Design of the POSTGRES Storage System," *Very Large DataBase Conference*, pp. 289–300, September 1987.

Sweeney et al., 1996.
A. Sweeney, D. Doucette, W. Hu, C. Anderson, M. Nishimoto, & G. Peck, "Scalability in the XFS File System," *USENIX Association Conference Proceedings*, pp. 1–14, January 1996.

Trivedi, 1980.
K. Trivedi, "Optimal Selection of CPU Speed, Device Capabilities, and File Assignments," *Journal of the ACM*, vol. 27, no. 3, pp. 457–473, July 1980.

Watson, 2000.
R. Watson, "Introducing Supporting Infrastructure for Trusted Operating System Support in FreeBSD," *Proceedings of the BSDCon 2000 Conference*, September 2000.

Watson, 2001.
R. Watson, "TrustedBSD: Adding Trusted Operating-System Features to FreeBSD," *Proceedings of the Freenix Track at the 2001 USENIX Annual Technical Conference*, pp. 15–28, June 2001.

Watson et al., 2003.
R. Watson, W. Morrison, C. Vance, & B. Feldman, "The TrustedBSD MAC Framework: Extensible Kernel Access Control for FreeBSD 5.0," *Proceedings of the Freenix Track at the 2003 USENIX Annual Technical Conference*, pp. 285–296, June 2003.

Wu & Zwaenepoel, 1994.
M. Wu & W. Zwaenepoel, "eNVy: A Non-Volatile, Main Memory Storage System," *International Conference on Architectural Support for Programming Languages and Operating Systems (ASPLOS)*, pp. 86–97, October 1994.

CHAPTER 10

The Zettabyte Filesystem

10.1 Introduction

The Zettabyte filesystem is generally referred to as simply ZFS [Bonwick et al., 2003]. It is in a class of filesystems that never overwrite existing data. A benefit of never overwriting is that snapshots (read-only) and clones (writable) are easy and cheap. Many of them can be created with no performance hit.

ZFS has the property that the on-disk filesystem state is never inconsistent. Filesystem changes are accumulated in memory. Periodically, all the changes are gathered up and written to disk. When all the changes are on stable storage, ZFS makes a checkpoint of the new filesystem state. The checkpoint is made by doing a single write to update the ***uberblock*** to reference the new filesystem state (the uberblock is analogous to the superblock of a UFS filesystem). Thus, a ZFS filesystem moves from one consistent state to the next without ever passing through an inconsistent state.

ZFS takes advantage of the abundant processor power available with current multi-core CPUs. Because they are much faster than storage, ZFS can afford to checksum everything. The checksums are used to detect:

- Bit rot on disks
- Phantom writes
- Misdirected reads and writes
- DMA parity errors
- Bugs in disk drivers and disk firmware
- Accidental overwrite of disk data

- Verification of reconstructed data (e.g., if you have a 3-way mirror, and one disk dies, nonchecksumming systems would just choose a "good" disk at random from which to read the data). ZFS reads the data and then verifies the checksum, so if a "good" disk has a few bad blocks, it can read from the other good disk instead. Data verification can also be used with RAIDZ when it has multiple levels of redundancy.

ZFS allows the use of inexpensive mechanical disks. Because of the redundancy available with RAIDZ and the error detection provided by checksums, ZFS can quickly and easily recover from disk failure.

Unlike the rest of FreeBSD, which is broken into many layers, ZFS is written as one big monolithic piece. The modules that make up ZFS along with the piece of FreeBSD that they most closely resemble is shown in Table 10.1. Figure 10.1 compares the layers of UFS and ZFS. The traditional FreeBSD layering is:

- Filesystem namespace management: UFS layer
- Cache management: virtual memory page-cache layer
- Filesystem storage organization: FFS layer
- Volume management: GEOM layer

ZFS subsumes all these layers:

- Filesystem namespace management: the ZFS POSIX Layer (ZPL) and ZFS Attribute Processor (ZAP) have a role similar to the UFS layer.
- Filesystem storage management: the Data Management Unit (DMU) and ZFS Intent Log (ZIL) have a role like the FFS layer. The Dataset and Snapshot Layer

Table 10.1 ZFS modules.

Acronym	Name	Layer	FreeBSD Analog
ZPL	ZFS POSIX Layer	object set	UFS
ZAP	ZFS Attribute Processor	object set	UFS
DMU	Data Management Unit	object set	FFS
ZIL	ZFS Intent Log	object set	FFS
DSL	Dataset and Snapshot Layer	metaobject set	FFS
SPA	Storage Pool Allocator	storage	GEOM
ZVOL	ZFS Volume	storage	GEOM
ZIO	ZFS I/O	storage	GEOM
RAIDZ	RAID with variable-size stripes	storage	GEOM
VDEV	Virtual Device	storage	GEOM
ARC	Adaptive Replacement Cache	cache	VM page cache
L2ARC	Level 2 Adaptive Replacement Cache	cache	VM swap space

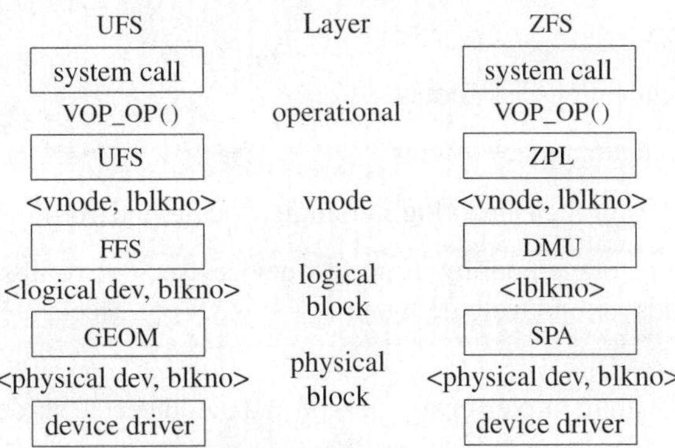

Figure 10.1 Comparison of UFS and ZFS layering.

(DSL) manages snapshots as does the FFS layer. However, these two modules of ZFS provide much additional functionality that has no analog in the other FreeBSD filesystems. As described in the next section, these modules operate in the Meta-Object Set (MOS) layer that is separate from the filesystem layers rather than being a part of the filesystem.

- Volume management: The Storage Pool Allocator (SPA) module manages block placement. The ZFS I/O (ZIO) module orchestrates I/O. The Virtual Device (VDEV) module aggregates disks into RAIDZ groups. ZFS also provides ZFS volumes (ZVOLs) that appear as traditional fixed-size disk partitions, much like the role of the GEOM layer.
- Cache management: The Adaptive Replacement Cache (ARC) has a role similar to that of the virtual memory page cache. The Level 2 Adaptive Replacement Cache (L2ARC) has a role similar to that of the virtual memory swap area and acts as a slower-access backing store for the memory-based ARC cache.

The result of this monolithic design is that ZFS has many features that include:

- Massive scale supporting petabyte-size storage pools with data structures that allow scalability to zettabytes.
- POSIX filesystems with features similar to UFS that include support for NFSv4 and Server Message Block (SMB) remote filesystem functionality such as selectable case insensitivity, unicode normalization, ACLs, and special flags needed for anti-virus support.
- ZVOLs that can be shared over iSCSI.
- Support for millions of snapshots and clones.
- Selective data compression and deduplication.
- Data integrity from checksums and data redundancy.

- A variable block size.
- Architecture-independent on-disk format.
- Pooled storage shared among filesystems.
- Disk-level redundancy through mirroring and single, double, and triple parity RAID.
- Support for a hybrid storage pool by using fast devices such as solid-state disks (SSDs) to cache reads and nonvolatile memory (NVRAM) to accelerate synchronous writes.
- Intelligent prefetch with multiple streams per file and autodetected stride patterns.
- Space management that includes several types of quotas and reservations.
- A simple administrative model that has the filesystem as the administrative control point with delegated administration and integration between mountpoints and NFS shares.
- Fast remote replication and backups.
- Availability on many platforms including FreeBSD, Linux, Mac OS/X, and Illumos.

Figure 10.2 ZFS module layering. See Table 10.1 for acronyms.

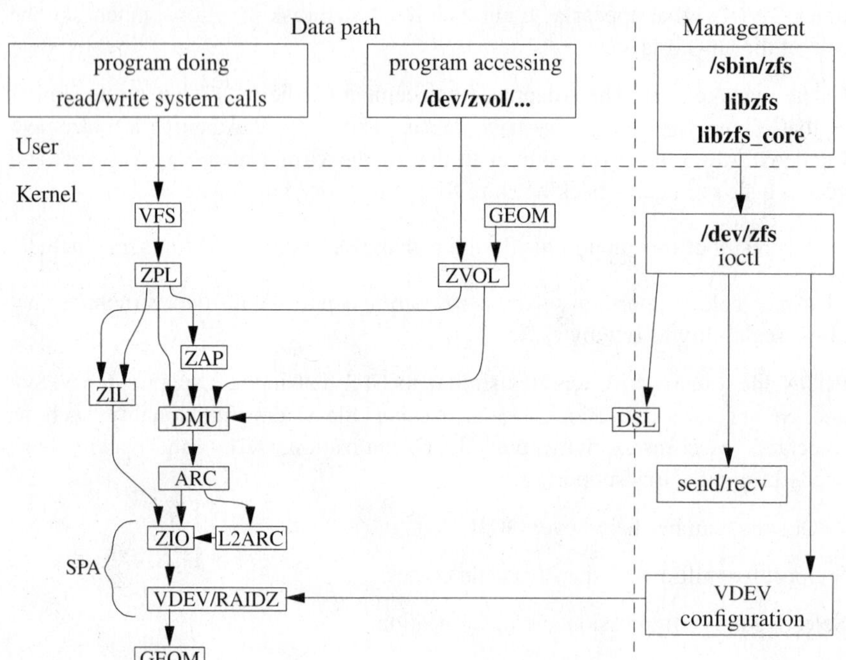

• Stability derived from its use in production by the world's biggest companies since 2006.

10.2 ZFS Organization

Figure 10.2 shows the relationship of the ZFS modules. The remainder of this chapter explains the interactions of these modules.

Traditional filesystems like UFS each manage their own set of disk blocks that are stored at a range of offsets on a single device. Each filesystem is given a fixed-size set of blocks when it is first created and the size of that set does not change. When a filesystem runs out of blocks, it cannot borrow blocks from another filesystem. If a filesystem has an excess of blocks, it cannot make them available to another filesystem.

ZFS removes the space-management role from the traditional filesystem model. It creates a pool of space that is then handed out as needed to the set of filesystems using the pool. The DSL and SPA modules implementing the Meta-Object Set (MOS) layer shown in Table 10.1 and Figure 10.3 manage the pool of space and make it available to the filesystem modules of the object-set layer. Thus, space in the pool can move between filesystems as needed. The arrows in Figure 10.3 represent a single block pointer, while the triangles represent indirect blocks mapping a potentially large set of blocks.

At the top is the uberblock that points to a data structure that describes an array of meta-objects. These meta-objects include filesystems, snapshots, clones, ZVOLs, and the space map describing the allocated and free blocks in the pool. Creating a new snapshot or filesystem requires allocating a new metadata object, a

Figure 10.3 ZFS organization.

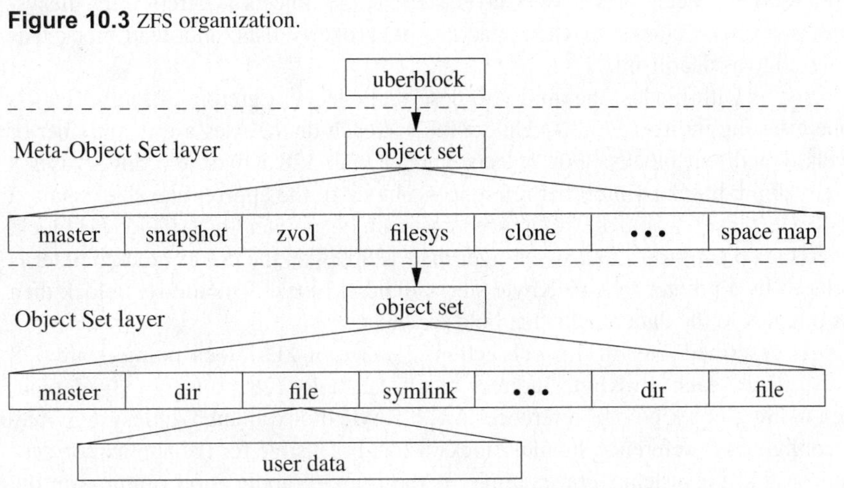

task that is about as difficult as creating a new file in a filesystem. When a filesystem needs to allocate space, its request is handled by the SPA module that finds an available block of the requested size in the space map. When the filesystem (and all its clones and snapshots) no longer need the block, it is returned to the pool. In general, the blocks of the pool are shared among all the filesystems that the pool contains. For administrative reasons, it is possible both to limit the maximum amount of space that a filesystem can use and to ensure that some minimum amount of space is reserved for a filesystem to use.

Each object set in the MOS, such as a filesystem, references a data structure that describes its array of objects. These objects include the usual things found in a filesystem such as directories, files, symbolic links, etc. Each of these filesystem objects then references an array of blocks that contain the object's data.

The allocation, expansion, and eventual freeing of the contents of all these objects is managed by the DMU module. The tree-structured POSIX-semantic directory structure is managed by the ZPL module. The ZAP module stores a key-to-value hashtable in an on-disk object. Its original use was for directory entries (each directory is implemented as a ZAP object). Its use later was expanded to store object attributes and many other types of metadata in other parts of ZFS. Finally, the ZIL module ensures that changes are not lost between filesystem checkpoints.

ZFS Dnode

ZFS stores the metadata for a file in a ***dnode*** that is analogous to the inode of UFS. Like that inode used in UFS, a dnode describes an object that may change in size from tiny to huge. The dnode is managed by the DMU. One use for dnodes is to describe filesystem objects such as files, directories, etc. When used for this purpose, the dnode is embedded with a ***znode*** that is managed by the ZPL and contains the metadata required to support POSIX semantics. Unlike the inode, dnodes also describe objects in the MOS layer such as the objects that represent filesystems, snapshots, clones, ZVOLs, space maps, property lists, and dead-block lists (referred to as deadlists).

Just as with inodes, the ability to describe objects of greatly different sizes is done by using indirect blocks. Unlike inodes, each dnode uses a fixed number of levels of indirect blocks. For objects smaller than 128 Kbyte, the dnode uses a single, direct-block pointer that references a block of the appropriate size. Thus, a 12-Kbyte object would be referenced by a single pointer to a 12-Kbyte block. When the object grows to a size bigger than 128 Kbyte, the direct-block pointer is replaced by a pointer to a 16-Kbyte single indirect block. The indirect block then has pointers to the data blocks that hold the object.

As described later in this subsection, the size of ZFS block pointers are 128 bytes. Thus, each 16-Kbyte indirect block can hold 128 pointers. By default, each indirect-block pointer references a 128-Kbyte block, though a filesystem may be configured to reference smaller blocks if that is sensible for the application running on that filesystem. For example, if the primary application running on the filesystem is a database that reads and writes widely separated 4-Kbyte records, the filesystem can be configured to allocate 4-Kbyte blocks to reduce the need to copy an entire 128-Kbyte block when only 4 Kbyte of it has been modified.

When the object grows beyond the size that can be described by a single-level indirect block, its dnode is promoted to use two levels of indirect blocks. The dnode's block pointer references a 16-Kbyte second-level block. The single-level block that it previously referenced is moved to be referenced from the first pointer in the new second-level indirect block. As the object continues to grow, additional first-level indirect blocks are allocated and referenced from the second-level indirect block.

If the object outgrows the size that can be described by a two-level set of indirect blocks, the dnode grows to support a three-level hierarchy, similarly to the way it was expanded to support a two-level hierarchy.

One important use of dnodes is to reference ZAP objects. A ZAP object stores a key-to-value hashtable. They were first used for directories that map from names to object numbers. An object number is an index into an *objset* dnode array that maps the object number to the location of the object on the disk. Directories require fast entry lookup, new entry insertion, old entry deletion, and full-directory scanning. All these properties are provided by ZAP objects. Because the ZAP module is flexibly written and these directory-like properties are needed in many other contexts, ZAP objects are used to store attribute and property lists along with many other types of metadata in the DSL and the SPA.

ZFS Block Pointers

Figure 10.4 shows a ZFS block-pointer structure. Unlike the traditional UFS 8-byte block pointer that references a block number within a disk partition, the ZFS block pointer is a 128-byte structure that can contain pointers to as many as three copies of a block, each on a different disk along with the block's size and its checksum. By keeping the checksum separate from the data, errors such as misdirected reads and writes can be detected. If the checksum were stored in the data block itself, a misdirected read or write would appear to be correct since both the data and the checksum would have been misdirected.

By default, ZFS checksums every block that it is managing. With multiple-core processors being common, the CPU cost of performing the checksum is insignificant in comparison to the cost of performing an I/O operation.

For systems with multiple disks, the first line of defense against data corruption or loss is RAID. If a disk block or even an entire disk is lost, the RAID disk structure can recover the data. For systems with only a single disk such as a laptop, and as a secondary backup for systems with multiple disks running with RAID, ZFS by default provides double redundancy for all metadata. Thus, all ZFS block pointers that reference metadata will have two of the three block-pointer fields in use. Filesystems can be configured to have all data replicated. Here, all block-pointers that reference user data will have two of the three block-pointer fields in use. When running in this mode, ZFS uses triple redundancy for all metadata. Thus, metadata block pointers will have all three block-pointer fields in use.

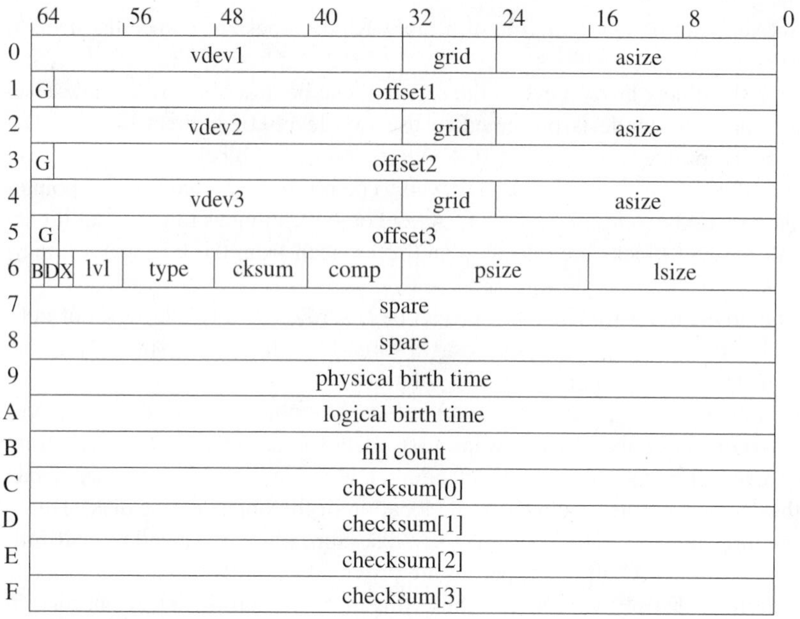

<table>
<tr><th></th><th>64</th><th>56</th><th>48</th><th>40</th><th>32</th><th>24</th><th>16</th><th>8 0</th></tr>
<tr><td>0</td><td colspan="4">vdev1</td><td>grid</td><td colspan="3">asize</td></tr>
<tr><td>1</td><td>G</td><td colspan="7">offset1</td></tr>
<tr><td>2</td><td colspan="4">vdev2</td><td>grid</td><td colspan="3">asize</td></tr>
<tr><td>3</td><td>G</td><td colspan="7">offset2</td></tr>
<tr><td>4</td><td colspan="4">vdev3</td><td>grid</td><td colspan="3">asize</td></tr>
<tr><td>5</td><td>G</td><td colspan="7">offset3</td></tr>
<tr><td>6</td><td>B D X lvl</td><td>type</td><td>cksum</td><td>comp</td><td colspan="2">psize</td><td colspan="2">lsize</td></tr>
<tr><td>7</td><td colspan="8">spare</td></tr>
<tr><td>8</td><td colspan="8">spare</td></tr>
<tr><td>9</td><td colspan="8">physical birth time</td></tr>
<tr><td>A</td><td colspan="8">logical birth time</td></tr>
<tr><td>B</td><td colspan="8">fill count</td></tr>
<tr><td>C</td><td colspan="8">checksum[0]</td></tr>
<tr><td>D</td><td colspan="8">checksum[1]</td></tr>
<tr><td>E</td><td colspan="8">checksum[2]</td></tr>
<tr><td>F</td><td colspan="8">checksum[3]</td></tr>
</table>

Figure 10.4 Description of a block pointer. Key: vdev—virtual device identifier; grid—RAIDZ layout information (reserved for future use); asize—allocated size (including RAIDZ parity and gang-block headers); G—gang-block flag; offset—offset into virtual device; B—byteorder (endianness) flag; D—deduplication flag; X—unused flag; lvl—number of levels of indirection for data described by this block pointer; type—DMU object type; cksum—checksum function identifier; comp—compression function identifier; psize—physical size (after compression); lsize—logical size; physical birth time—transaction group in which the block was physically allocated, zero if same as logical birth time; logical birth time—transaction group in which the block was logically allocated; fill count—number of nonzero blocks under this block pointer; checksum[ ]—256-bit checksum of the data described by this block pointer.

Each block has an associated birth time. Birth time is measured as the number of checkpoints that have been taken since the ZFS pool was created. When the pool is first created, the transaction group (TXG) is set to zero. Each time that a checkpoint is done, the transaction group is incremented. The problem with using seconds since the epoch for the birth time is that seconds since the epoch can fail to be monotonically increasing if the battery maintaining the hardware clock fails or if a time daemon sets incorrect time information. Self-consistency is ensured by using transaction groups rather than seconds since the epoch. It also ensures that if two checkpoints are taken less than 1 second apart, the birth times of blocks from the two checkpoints can be distinguished. As described in the next section, the birth time is needed to determine when a block has no references so that it can be freed.

The dedup flag identifies a block that is in the deduplication table. The flag is used when trying to free a block. If the deduplication flag is set, ZFS must find the corresponding entry in the deduplication table and decrement its reference count as the block can only be freed when the reference count reaches zero. The deduplication table is huge so it typically does not fit in memory. Pieces of it are brought in when needed. Thus, checking for a block in the deduplication table is expensive, especially if the required block of the deduplication table is not in memory. If the deduplication flag is not set, ZFS can avoid the cost of looking it up in the deduplication table.

Most blocks have only a logical birth time that is equal to the TXG in which they were created. Only deduplication blocks need a physical birth time. The first time a block is written, it gets just a logical birth time. When the same contents are written again, the deduplication module creates a new block pointer to the original copy. The new block pointer has a logical birth time of the current TXG but a physical birth time of the TXG of the original block's logical birth time. The reason that the physical birth time is needed is so that when the filesystem is traversed after a disk failure to reconstruct the RAIDZ, the kernel knows the actual times that blocks were created and hence knows which ones need to be reconstructed.

Normally, when the SPA needs to allocate a block of a given size, it is able to do so. However, when the pool of unused blocks becomes small, there may not be a single block of space large enough to fulfill the request. Here, the SPA must allocate two or more smaller pieces to make up the bigger block. These smaller pieces are described by an array of pointers in a structure called a gang-block header. The gang-block flag is set when the reference in the block pointer is to one of these gang-block headers so that header can be interpreted by the I/O system to gather together the pieces that make up the block.

Each block pointer has three sizes associated with it:

1. lsize – the logical size of the block
2. psize – the physical size of the block, which may be smaller than the logical size if it has been compressed.
3. asize – the allocated size on the disk including RAIDZ parity and gang-block headers.

For blocks that reference indirect blocks, the level of the referenced block is also maintained. Since any given dnode uses a fixed number of indirection levels as described earlier in this subsection, maintaining the level count in the block pointer is used purely as a consistency check and is not needed for normal operation. Similarly, the type field is known, so it is used only as a consistency check.

ZFS *objset* Structure

The *objset* structure describes a set of objects. An *objset* structure is used to describe the set of objects in a filesystem, a snapshot, a clone, or a ZVOL. When used in this role, their closest analogy to UFS is that of the superblock, which is the data structure that describes all the objects in a filesystem. Another important use of the *objset* structure is to describe the collection of objects that make up the MOS.

The objects in the MOS include the descriptors for all the filesystems, clones, snapshots, and ZVOLs in the pool along with their relationships to each other. The MOS also includes a master node that includes properties that apply to the pool and space-map objects that identify the used and available blocks in the pool.

10.3 ZFS Structure

Having described the most important ZFS data structures, it is now possible to describe the layout of a ZFS pool in more detail. Figure 10.5 shows a typical ZFS pool that is anchored at its top by an uberblock.

Two 256-Kbyte blocks of space are reserved for volume labels at the beginning and end of every device in the ZFS pool. Half of each of these four volume labels are used to store redundant copies of information specific to the device. The other half of each of these four labels holds an array of 128 uberblocks. The final step to complete a checkpoint is to write out the uberblock. When the pool is created, the initial uberblock is written to the zeroth entry in each of the uberblock arrays on all the devices. The uberblock for the first checkpoint (TXG number one) is written to the first entry in all the uberblock arrays of up to three of the devices that are selected at random. After all 128 entries in an uberblock array

Figure 10.5 ZFS Structure.

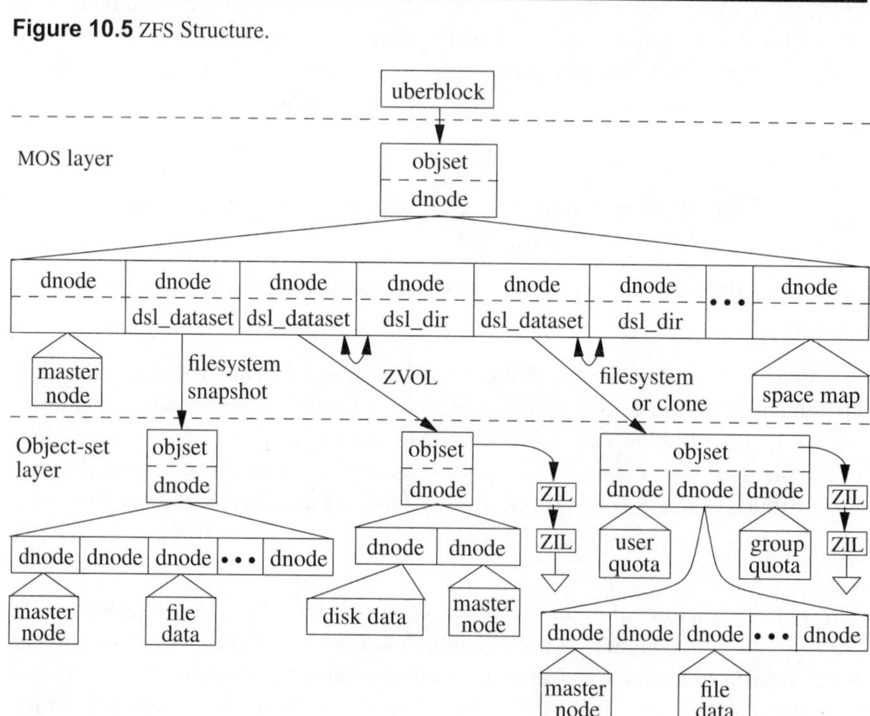

have been used, the checkpoint location of the uberblock update reverts to the zeroth entry in that uberblock array.

The MOS Layer

A single block pointer contained in the uberblock references an *objset* structure that describes the set of objects making up the MOS layer. The MOS contains the data structures managed by the DSL that tracks datasets, which include chains of snapshots, trees of clones, the active filesystems, and ZFS volumes (ZVOLs) that appear like traditional fixed-size disk partitions. The DSL is also responsible for tracking filesystem properties and the deadlists. The MOS also contains data structures managed by the Storage Pool Allocator (SPA) that tracks allocated versus freed blocks. The SPA module is also responsible for handling compression and deduplication as well as I/O queueing and scheduling. Thus, the MOS manages filesystems while the volume manager found in traditional filesystem layering manages blocks.

Each of the objects in the MOS is described by a dnode. One important object in the MOS is the first dnode, often referred to as the master node. The master node contains pool-wide information including pool-wide property lists and configurations, recent error logs, and operational statistics. Another important object in the MOS layer is the dnode that contains the space map. The space map identifies the allocation of blocks within the pool.

Most of the dnodes in the MOS are used to describe a filesystem, clone, snapshot, or ZVOL. Each of these dnodes has a *dsl_dataset* structure embedded within it. This structure serves two main purposes:

1. It keeps a set of pointers to track the relationship of snapshots and clones to their associated filesystem.
2. It contains the object number of the deadlist that tracks when blocks are no longer referenced and can be freed.

The management of relationships and the operation of deadlists is described in the next section.

The *dsl_dataset* structure within all these dnodes, except those for snapshots, points to a second dnode object in the MOS that contains an embedded *dsl_dir* structure. The *dsl_dir* structure contains:

- The object number of the MOS object for its parent's *dsl_dir*.
- The object number of the ZAP object listing its children's *dsl_dir*s.
- The object number of the ZAP object listing its properties. Its properties include typical filesystem properties such as whether to honor the set-user-identifier flag on executables, whether to maintain access time on files and directories, etc. The ZAP object also records the use of compression and, if enabled, the compression algorithm being used.

- The object number of the ZAP object that lists all its clones.
- Block accounting for all filesystems and clones mounted below it.
- Its quota and reservation byte counts.
- For clones, the object number of the MOS object for the snapshot from which they were created.

The relationships between a filesystem and its clones and snapshots is shown in Figure 10.6. ZFS can take snapshots and make clones of both filesystems and ZVOLs, so everything described below in the context of filesystems applies equally to ZVOLs. Clones cannot be taken of a filesystem or another clone; they can only be taken from a snapshot. It is possible to create multiple clones from the same snapshot. When a clone is promoted to being a filesystem, the previous filesystem is demoted to being a clone. Clone promotion does not change the datasets' names, mountpoints, or contents. Renaming operations must be done separately.

The Object-Set Layer

Each of the *dsl_dataset* structures in the MOS layer has a block pointer that points to an *objset* structure in the object-set layer. The bottom half of Figure 10.5 shows three distinct organizations of the *objset*. From left to right in the object-set layer, they are:

1. A snapshot of a filesystem or a clone (see number 3). The organization of the snapshot is the same as that of a filesystem or clone except that since it cannot be changed, it does not need to track user or group quotas. A snapshot does keep a copy of the user and group quotas as they existed at the time that the snapshot was made so that they are available for use after a rollback is done or a clone is made. They are stored in the *objset* as is done for a filesystem, but are not shown in Figure 10.5.
2. ZVOLs have a single dnode in their *objset* that references an array of two dnodes. The first dnode references an array of block pointers that is the size of the device partition with one pointer per 4-Kbyte block. The other dnode describes the master node. It is a ZAP object that records ZVOL-specific information.

Figure 10.6 Filesystem, clone, and snapshot relationships.

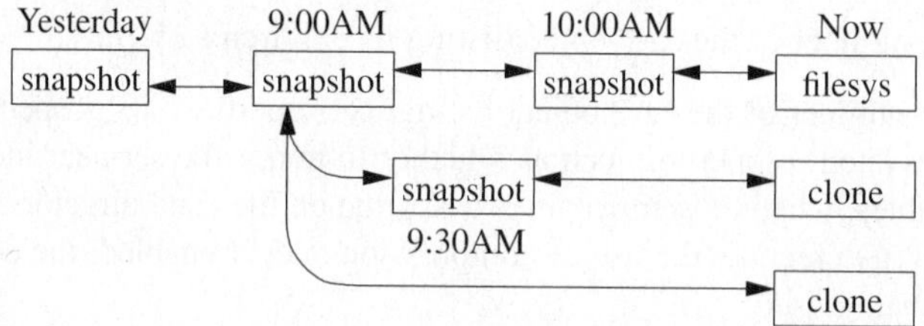

3. Filesystems have three dnodes in their *objset*. Two are ZAP objects that record the user and group space usage for a filesystem. The third references the filesystem's array of the files and directories. The first dnode of the array is its master node, described later in this section. Clones of filesystems have the same *objset* organization as a filesystem, while clones of ZVOLs have the same *objset* organization as a ZVOL.

The filesystem master node is a ZAP object that contains the following information:

- It records the object number of the root inode.
- It records the objects numbers for the user and group quota files.
- It records the ZAP object number that tracks the set of files that have been unlinked but cannot be reclaimed because they are still referenced by an open file descriptor. The ZAP object simply records a list of the unlinked object numbers. Objects are added when they become unlinked and removed when their final reference is closed. Use of the ZAP object ensures that these operations can be done in constant time. After a reboot, the list is traversed to remove the unlinked and now unreferenced files.

The layout of a snapshot mirrors that of the object set that it snapshots. The snapshot of a filesystem in Figure 10.6 shows how its structure mirrors that of a filesystem. A snapshot of a ZVOL has a structure that mirrors that of a ZVOL. Similarly, the layout of a clone of a filesystem or ZVOL snapshot is the same as that of the object that it is cloning.

Each of the *objset*s that describe a filesystem, clone, or ZVOL has a *zil_header* structure embedded within it that points to a linked list of blocks containing the ZIL intent log. The ZIL records all the changes since the last checkpoint for recovery after a crash.

10.4 ZFS Operation

Unlike overwriting filesystems like UFS that continuously update their on-disk state, ZFS collects all filesystem updates in memory. Periodically, it writes all the changes to an unused disk area to create a checkpoint. None of the changes to the on-disk state are visible until the final write of the checkpoint is made, which is to update the root of the ZFS pool, the uberblock. Thus, a ZFS filesystem is always consistent; that is, it transitions from one consistent state to a new consistent state.

Each checkpoint is taken across the entire pool and affects every filesystem, snapshot, clone, and ZVOL in the pool at the same time. ZFS calls these checkpoints transaction groups, abbreviated to TXGs. Snapshots taken across several filesystems that all fall within the same checkpoint will all be consistent at the same instant in time. Thus, two different snapshots within the same pool with the same TXG will be precisely synchronized with each other in time. Conversely, it is difficult to get consistent snapshots across two different pools because it would require the precise coordination when they take a checkpoint.

Many operations in ZFS, such as the way that writes to files appear atomic to different processes doing *write* system calls to the same file, are handled similarly to those of traditional overwriting filesystems like UFS. This section will not describe functionality that is similar to the UFS functionality described in Chapter 9. This section details the operations performed by the ZFS filesystem that differ significantly from the way they are performed in UFS.

Writing New Data to Disk

All updates to the filesystems, clones, and ZVOLs within a pool are accumulated in memory until a specified time has passed (default is 5 seconds), 64 Mbyte of dirty data have been accumulated, or an administrative action is taken that requires a checkpoint such as a snapshot request. To flush the new data to disk, ZFS must take a checkpoint of the pool.

Taking a checkpoint requires that all modifications to the filesystem, made since the previous checkpoint, be saved to disk. The first step is to get a consistent state for the filesystem, which requires that all system calls modifying filesystem data must be complete. ZFS uses a technique similar to the one described in Section 9.7 as step 3 of taking a snapshot in UFS. Specifically, processes that are already in progress on such system calls are permitted to finish those system calls. The checkpoint proceeds once all the in-progress system calls have finished.

It may take several seconds to write out all the disk blocks making up the checkpoint. Allowing no modifications during that entire period would cause an unacceptable delay to applications running on the system. To avoid this delay, all the dirty blocks that will be written to make the checkpoint are tagged with their transaction group (TXG). New modifications to the filesystems, clones, and ZVOLs are tagged with a new transaction group. If a modification finds that the block it needs to modify is marked as being part of a checkpoint in progress, ZFS makes a copy of that block in memory and the modification is made to the copy. The copied blocks become part of the next checkpoint. As I/O completes on the blocks that are part of the current checkpoint, ZFS must decide how to handle the in-memory buffers. If they were not copied, they can be marked as available for current use. If they were copied, then their contents are now out of date so the memory holding the out-of-date copy is freed.

Figure 10.7 shows the nine steps that must be taken to flush the changes for a file to which data has been added since the last checkpoint:

1. All the blocks of new data must be written. If the write has been done over existing data, the modified data block must be written to a new location as ZFS never overwrites any existing data.

2. Typically, the update requires an update of a block pointer in one of the file's indirect blocks. Since the indirect block has been modified, it will need to be written to a new location, which means the indirect block that references it

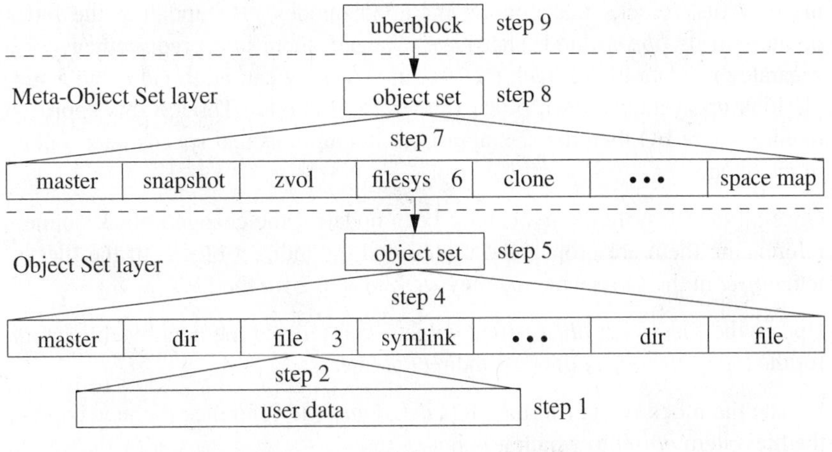

Figure 10.7 Nine steps to create a checkpoint.

will need to be modified. These modifications continue up the indirect tree until they reach the dnode for the file.

3. Update the dnode for the file to reference the new block location for the top of its indirect pointers. Since ZFS cannot overwrite the existing dnode when it has changed, it must write a copy of the block containing the dnode with the updated size and new block pointer.

In UFS, reading in an inode requires allocating a piece of memory that is the size of an inode including the space needed to store the on-disk dinode, reading in the disk block that contains the inode, copying the dinode from the disk block to the newly allocated memory, and then releasing the disk buffer. Writing an inode back to disk requires reading in the disk block that contains the inode, copying the modified inode into the appropriate part of the buffer, and then writing the updated buffer back to the disk.

In ZFS, reading in a dnode begins by allocating a piece of memory that is the size of the in-memory dnode. The in-memory dnode does not contain the on-disk dnode; it includes only a pointer to the on-disk part. ZFS reads in and locks in memory the disk block that contains the on-disk dnode. It then sets the pointer in the dnode to point to its on-disk part in the disk buffer. Writing the dnode back to the disk requires only that the disk buffer containing the modified dnode be written to its new location.

The benefit of the ZFS approach is less memory-to-memory copies and fewer I/O operations at the expense of using more memory. For a system with 100,000 cached nodes, UFS will use 50 Mbyte of memory while ZFS typically uses 200 Mbyte and can use up to 1.6 Gbyte of memory.

The original log-structured filesystem (LFS) collected all the modified inodes together in sets of 64 that could then be packed into a 16-Kbyte block. The drawback to this approach is that it required another metadata file that mapped from inode number to disk location. ZFS simply writes all the in-memory disk blocks that contain modified dnodes. By updating the block pointers in its *objset* dnode that have changed, there is no requirement for a separate metadata file to track their location as they can be found using a simple look up at their known offset in the *objset* dnode. Though this approach requires more I/O than the LFS approach, it simplifies and speeds later lookup of the dnodes.

4. Once all the filesystem *dnode*s have been updated, the changed block pointers referencing them are propagated up through the indirect blocks of the filesystem *objset* in the same way that they were in step 2 for the file.

5. Update the filesystem *objset* dnode object to reference the new block location for the top of the *objset* dnode's indirect pointers.

6. Update the block pointer in the MOS *dsl_dataset* to reference the new copy of the filesystem *objset* to which it points.

7. Once all the *dsl_dataset* pointers have been updated to point to their new *objset* objects, the changed block pointers referencing them are propagated up through the indirect blocks of the MOS *objset* in the same way that they were in steps 2 and 4 for the file and filesystem *objset*s.

8. Update the MOS *objset* dnode object to reference the new block location for the top of its indirect pointers.

9. Once all these updates have been written to their disk locations, the last step in checkpoint creation is to update the block pointer in the uberblock to point at the new MOS *objset* and update its TXG transaction group to reflect the new checkpoint. The updated uberblock is then written to its new locations as is described in Section 10.3.

Logging

ZFS keeps all ZPL-level changes logged in memory. The log is handled by the ZFS Intent Log (ZIL). Examples of log entries are:

- Write these 700 bytes of data to this offset of this file,
- Change the permissions of this file to this mode, or
- Create a new symbolic link in this directory with this name that points to this path.

Unlike logs associated with traditional overwriting filesystems that are needed to bring the filesystem back into a consistent state, ZFS is always consistent so its only requirement for its log is to retain any changes between checkpoints that need to be persistent. An example of the need for persistence is the *fsync* system call that needs to ensure the associated file is stable before returning. Because of the time and I/O operations required to do a ZFS checkpoint, *fsync* is implemented by forcing a log write, not by doing a checkpoint.

Traditional filesystems often log only filesystem metadata changes as metadata tends to be much smaller than the data updates and returning to a consistent state requires only that the metadata be recovered. When performing an *fsync* on a file, a traditional filesystem can commit modified data by overwriting the same disk blocks that held the previous value of the data. The traditional filesystem can also overwrite a file's inode to reflect any newly allocated blocks. ZFS has to log both data and metadata because it does not have the option of just flushing the data and inode to disk to synchronize them. ZFS reduces the overhead of writing file data to both the log and the disk by allocating a disk block, writing the data to it, and then placing a pointer to that data in the log. When the next checkpoint is made, ZFS can reference the already-written block. By default, ZFS only allocates and writes blocks of size 32 Kbyte and larger, but the *logbias* property allows the setting of a lower threshold.

The high volume of data being written to the ZFS log can often be a throughput-performance bottleneck. The logging bottleneck can be alleviated by using a solid-state disk (SSD) to store the log. The log often does not need all the space available on the SSD. ZFS can use the remaining space on the SSD to extend its in-memory ARC cache by pushing less actively read items to the SSD. ZFS refers to this SSD cache as its L2ARC.

Recovery of a ZFS pool starts from the last checkpoint. When the pool is first opened, the kernel must read in an uberblock array from every device and scan through them to find the uberblock with the highest TXG value as that will represent the most current checkpointed state of the ZFS pool. If an uberblock array on a device is unreadable or corrupted, the kernel reads an alternative copy of the uberblock array from that device.

Once the uberblock has been found, ZFS has to find and claim all the log blocks. The blocks are claimed by updating the MOS space map to show that all the log blocks are allocated. This reclaim must happen when the pool is first opened and before any other modifications are made to it to ensure that the log blocks are not overwritten by later writes. The log blocks are identified by looking up the *objset* for all the filesystems, ZVOLs, and clones listed in the MOS. Each of these *objset*s contains an intent-log header that points to its linked list of log blocks. The pool then starts processing a new transaction group (TXG).

The processing of filesystems, ZVOLs, and clones is completely analogous. In the rest of this section filesystems are described, but the description applies equally to ZVOLs and clones. Recovery for each filesystem then proceeds as follows:

1. The filesystem is mounted.
2. ZFS plays forward through its intent log whose list head is contained in its *objset* structure. Each of the operations contained in the log is made to the filesystem.
3. The blocks from the fully replayed log are freed.
4. The filesystem begins accepting new requests.

In the normal course of events, the transaction_completes with a new uberblock being written. If the system crashes before the new uberblock has been written, then all the recovery work is lost and must be done again when the system is restarted. No data will be lost as any writes that were done before the crash will be to parts of the disk that were previously unallocated, so none of the existing filesystem data will have been corrupted. Any modifications accepted for the filesystems that had completed step 4 above will have been added to their intent log. Thus, these changes will be included in the filesystem when the system successfully completes its recovery process.

RAIDZ

Traditional layered design separates the filesystem implementation from the disk-storage implementation. Thus, the storage layer has no knowledge of the data being stored on it. RAID is typically used in modern storage systems. Since the size and organization of the data is unknown to the storage layer, each stripe in the RAID array is a fixed-size. For example, consider a traditional RAID running with four data disks plus a single parity disk. If the disks have a 4-Kbyte sector size, the stripe size is 16 Kbyte using one sector on each of the four data drives plus a 4-Kbyte sector on the parity drive. If an application writes a 24-Kbyte block, this RAID will write one full-size stripe and then have to read in a 16-Kbyte stripe, replace the first 8 Kbyte of the 16-Kbyte stripe, recalculate the parity, and write out the new 8 Kbyte of data and the updated 4-Kbyte parity sector. If a disk fails, the RAID reconstructs by reading every stripe, rebuilds the bad 4-Kbyte block, and writes the rebuilt block back to the replacement disk. The rebuild time can be reduced by using dirty-region logging to keep track of the stripes that are in use, but it comes at a cost of increased complexity and reduced performance.

Because ZFS integrates its RAIDZ disk-storage implementation with its filesystem implementation, it can support a variable-size stripe. Instead of writing fixed-size stripes, each block that it writes fills in the amount of space that it requires. Each block that is written is referenced by a block pointer that contains the size of the block so the disk-storage implementation can determine the size of the stripe to use. Figure 10.8 shows the layout of blocks on a RAIDZ-1 pool constructed from five disks with a single parity per stripe. Each block requires a parity sector for each four blocks of data sectors. A block that is not a multiple of four sectors requires a parity block for its residual set of sectors. To get double redundancy (RAIDZ-2), each block would require two parity sectors for each three blocks of data sectors. The smallest possible allocation on RAIDZ-N is N + 1 sectors constructed from N parity sectors plus one data sector.

In Figure 10.8, the first block has two parity and eight data sectors. The second and third blocks have one parity sector and three data sectors. The fourth block exhibits the worst overhead with one parity and one data sector. The fifth block has fourteen data and four parity sectors. The sixth block contains one parity sector, four data sectors, and an unused sector. To avoid the creation of

	disk 1	disk2	disk 3	disk 4	disk 5
stripe 1	P0	D0	D2	D4	D6
stripe 2	P1	D1	D3	D5	D7
stripe 3	P0	D0	D1	D2	P0
stripe 4	D0	D1	D2	P0	D0
stripe 5	P0	D0	D4	D8	D11
stripe 6	P1	D1	D5	D9	D12
stripe 7	P2	D2	D6	D10	D13
stripe 8	P3	D3	D7	P0	D0
stripe 9	D1	D2	D3	X	P0
stripe 10	D0	D1	X	P0	D0
stripe 11	D3	D6	D9	P1	D1
stripe 12	D4	D7	D10	P2	D2
stripe 13	D5	D8			

Figure 10.8 Layout of blocks in a RAIDZ disk pool. The blocks have been written sequentially and are shown alternating between light and dark backgrounds.

unallocatable segments, ZFS requires all allocations be a multiple of N + 1 sectors. In Figure 10.8, N is equal to one, so allocations must be a multiple of two. Since the sixth block uses five sectors, its allocation must be rounded up to six sectors thus charging the odd-size block for the wasted space. If the sixth block is freed and the space is later reallocated to a block with one parity and three data sectors, the two-sector residual space will still be usable for a block containing one parity and one data sector. Had the allocation for the sixth block not been rounded up, the residual space would have been a single sector that could not be used. The seventh data block containing a single parity and two data sectors also needs to allocate an unused sector. The eighth and final block contains three parity and nine data sectors. The parity sectors for a given block are all on the same disk. The disk holding the parity for a block is the one on which the block begins. Thus, parity blocks are distributed among the disks.

If a disk fails, the RAIDZ reconstructs it by traversing the pool's filesystems and rebuilding each block that it encounters using the block's size to determine its stripe size. An added benefit of this approach is that reconstruction time is often lowered since ZFS need only rebuild the part of the disk holding allocated data. Despite the slowdown from random reads to the data to be rebuilt, the need to rebuild just the allocated data is faster than rebuilding the whole disk when the allocated data use less than about half of the disk. However, in worst-case scenarios of pools configured to use 4-Kbyte blocks, such as those supporting databases or virtual-disk images with totally random block placement and most of the disk space allocated, ZFS reconstruction may take 10 times longer to complete.

Snapshots

Taking a snapshot in ZFS is quick and easy, and for reasons explained later in this section, there are no limits on the number of snapshots that can be taken. The steps involved in taking a snapshot are:

- Take a checkpoint.
- Allocate a new dnode in the MOS to contain the new *dsl_dataset* that will represent the snapshot.
- Copy the block pointer from the *dsl_dataset* of the filesystem being snapshotted to the *dsl_dataset* in the newly allocated snapshot dnode. Until at least the next checkpoint is taken, the block pointers of both the snapshot and the filesystem will reference the same *objset* block. The next checkpoint made after any change in the filesystem will create a new copy of the filesystem *objset*. The block pointer in the snapshot will continue to reference the old *objset*, while the block pointer in the filesystem will reference the new *objset*.
- Link the new dnode into the head of the filesystem's snapshot list (as it is the youngest snapshot).
- Add the new snapshot's name and object number into the snapshot name list for the filesystem.
- Move the filesystem's deadlist to the snapshot. Since the filesystem's deadlist contains blocks that it no longer references, they will not be referenced by the snapshot. The freeing of deadlists is described in a later subsection.

At this point, the new snapshot is complete and is ready to be accessed.

ZFS Block Allocation

Space allocation is handled by the SPA module. It manages all the space in the pool and makes it available to filesystems, clones, and ZVOLs as it is needed. The SPA uses the space map in the MOS to identify the allocation of blocks within the pool. Rather than having a single map to describe the entire pool, the blocks are broken up into fixed-size groups analogous to the way that UFS breaks a filesystem up into cylinder groups, each with a fixed-size block map. Unlike cylinder-group maps, ZFS maps are described using base-length pairs similar to those used to describe space in an extent-based filesystem. A disk will typically be described by about 200 of these fixed-size maps. The next subsection describes how blocks are freed back to the pool.

A ZFS allocation proceeds as follows:

1. Select a disk from which to do the allocation. The preference is to choose the disk with the most free space.
2. From among the fixed-size space maps describing the space on the disk, select the one that is least fragmented.

3. Allocate a chunk of space with the needed size that is closest to the previous allocation.

In addition to managing the space map, the SPA also handles related operations such as compression and deduplication, and it determines block layout into a RAIDZ stripe as well as the stripe's parity calculation. Finally, the SPA manages the scheduling, queueing, and completion handling of the block I/O operations.

Freeing Blocks

The first implementations of nonoverwriting filesystems were described as log-structured filesystems [Rosenblum & Ousterhout, 1992]. A production version of a log-structured filesystem, LFS, was released as part of 4.4BSD [McKusick et al., 1996; Seltzer et al., 1993]. New data were appended to the filesystem partition until they reached the end of the partition. A garbage collection process was run over the filesystem partition to find the blocks that were no longer being referenced. The filesystem operations then resumed until these blocks had been used at which point another garbage collection pass was done. While this technique for managing free space worked, and much research was done on ways to minimize its effect, it still produced awkward pauses that made production use difficult [Blackwell et al., 1995].

In the 1990's, two commercial implementations of nonoverwriting filesystems were started, ZFS by Sun Microsystems and the Write Anywhere File Layout (WAFL) filesystem by Network Appliance (NetApp) [Hutchinson et al., 1999]. Both of these implementations chose to track the used and available blocks continuously as is done in traditional filesystems but used different techniques.

WAFL keeps and updates a complete block list. In WAFL, each block has a 256-bit word associated with it. Bit 0 in the word is set to show that the block is in use in the active filesystem. Bit 1 is set to show that the block is in use in snapshot 1, bit 2 is set to show that the block is in use in snapshot 2, etc. When all bits in the word are 0, the block is free and available for use. When a new snapshot is made, WAFL allocates an available bit number for it and then makes a pass over the entire bitmap, copying all the set bits in bit 0 to the new snapshot's bit column. Freeing a snapshot makes a pass over the entire bitmap, clearing the bit in the snapshot's bit location. Thus, the cost to create or delete a WAFL snapshot is proportional to the size of the filesystem and the number of snapshots is limited to the width of the block-map word. ZFS does not have these limitations.

ZFS tracks its used and available blocks using space maps, birth time, and deadlists. The benefit of the ZFS approach is that it never has to traverse its space map when creating or freeing a snapshot, clone, or ZVOL. When a filesystem needs a new block, it requests one from the SPA that allocates it from the pool's space map. The current transaction group (TXG) is recorded in the block's pointer. The block then becomes part of an object in the filesystem. Over time, the filesystem or clone may be snapshotted, which will also reference the block.

When an object in a filesystem is overwritten, truncated, or deleted, its blocks will be released. For each block freed from an object, the kernel must determine whether to free it. The kernel checks the block pointer's birth time and, if it was born after the most recent (youngest) snapshot, it is not referenced by any snapshots so the block can be freed (i.e., the SPA can return the block to the pool's space map). Otherwise, the block must be remembered for later freeing by adding it to the filesystem's deadlist. Each *dsl_dataset* contains the object number of its deadlist. The deadlist of a given dataset (filesystem, ZVOL, clone, or snapshot) is the list of blocks referenced by the previous snapshot and possibly some older snapshots, but not referenced by the dataset.

When a snapshot is freed, the kernel needs to free any blocks referenced only by that snapshot [Ahrens, 2005]. Figure 10.9 shows the four lifetimes of blocks that need to be considered when freeing "this snap." The kernel must determine the blocks to be freed and those that need to remain on a deadlist. It iterates over the blocks in the "next snap" deadlist (blocks A and B in Figure 10.9). Each block is removed from the list and the block's birth time is compared to the birth time of "prev snap." If the block was born before "prev snap" (block A), then the kernel cannot free it, so it adds the block to the deadlist of "this snap." Otherwise, the block was born after "prev snap" (block B), so the kernel must free it. Having emptied the deadlist of "next snap," the kernel sets the deadlist of "next snap" to the deadlist of "this snap." Finally, the kernel removes "this snap" from the linked list of snapshots and from the directory of snapshot names.

While the implementation is simple, the algorithm is subtle. The blocks that the kernel must free are those that are referenced by only the snapshot the kernel is deleting (block B). The blocks to be deleted must meet four constraints:

1. They were born after "prev snap,"
2. They were born before "this snap,"
3. They died after "this snap," and
4. They died before the "next snap."

The blocks on the "next snap" deadlist are those that meet constraints 2, 3, and 4. They are live in "this snap," but dead in the "next snap." Thus, to find the blocks that meet all constraints, the kernel examines all the blocks on the deadlist

Figure 10.9 Four lifetimes of blocks considered by the kernel when a snapshot is deleted.

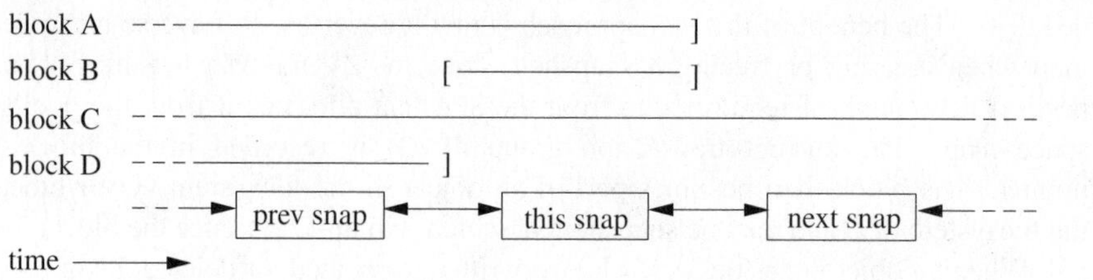

```
block A   ---————————————————————————————]
block B                        [—————————]
block C   ---——————————————————————————————————————————————---
block D   ---————————————————]
          --→ [prev snap] ←——→ [this snap] ←——→ [next snap] ←---
time ——→
```

of "next snap" and finds those that meet constraint 1 (i.e., if the block's birth time is after the "prev snap"). Note that the argument applies if "next snap" is the live filesystem.

To confirm that the kernel left the correct blocks on the deadlist of "next snap," observe that the deadlist of "this snap" contains the blocks that were live in "prev snap" and dead in "this snap" (block D). If "this snap" did not exist, then the blocks would be live in "prev snap" and dead in "next snap," and therefore should be on the deadlist of "next snap." Additionally, the blocks that were live for both "prev snap" and "this snap" but dead in "next snap" (block A) should be on the deadlist of "next snap."

Originally, the deadlist contained the object number of an object that contained an array of all the dead-block pointers associated with the filesystem, ZVOL, snapshot, or clone. Since every block on the list has to be considered for deletion, snapshot deletion time is proportional to the size of its deadlist. As the number of deleted or changed blocks grows, the size of the deadlists also grows. Because the only blocks that could be deleted are those in the transaction group that covers the snapshot or clone being deleted, the deadlist was reorganized.

To decouple the removal time of a snapshot from the size of the deadlist, the deadlist has now been split into separate lists organized by the ranges of transaction groups between each of the snapshots that existed at the time the snapshot was created. The new deadlist contains the object number of a ZAP object that maps the first transaction group of a specific range of birth times to an object that contains an array of all the dead block pointers for just that range of birth times. Typically, only one of these lists needs to be scanned when the snapshot is deleted, which improves snapshot deletion time as it only needs to consider the subset of blocks that it will need to free. If several snapshots have been deleted between the snapshot being deleted and the one that currently precedes it, then several lists will need to be traversed, but all the blocks on the traversed lists will need to be freed. Thus, with this new organization, the time required at snapshot removal time is a function of the number of blocks that the snapshot will free independent of the number of other blocks that remain.

The elegance of this design is that it places no limit on the number of snapshots that can be created and it never needs to traverse the entire block-allocation map, so snapshot creation and removal times are not affected by the size of the disk space being managed.

Deduplication

ZFS provides deduplication on a pool-wide basis [Bonwick, 2009]. Deduplication is implemented in the SPA module. Logically, when a new block is created, the pool is checked to see if a block with identical contents already exists. If an identical block does exist, the existing block is referenced rather than creating a duplicate copy of it. Deduplication is most useful when there are many duplicate blocks, such as when many instances of the same virtual-machine image are being stored among the filesystems in the pool.

To speed the check for an existing block with a given value, ZFS computes a hash of each unique block and stores it in the MOS in a ZAP table that maps from hash to block location. Rather than computing both a hash and a checksum for each block, the checksum is used as the hash. The hash must use a function such as SHA-256 that uniquely identifies data with very high probability. Thus, when using deduplication, the *fletcher4* checksumming function, which is faster to compute but more likely to have collisions, is replaced with SHA-256.

When a block is to be written, ZFS computes its hash and then checks the table to see if a block with that hash already exists. If it does, a pointer to the existing block is created and the reference count associated with the block is incremented. Otherwise, the hash, the new block's location, and a reference count of 1 are inserted into the table and the block is written to disk.

Not all users of the pool need to participate in deduplication. Only filesystems and ZVOLs that administratively elect to participate have their blocks deduplicated. The size of the hash-to-block mapping table is proportional to the number of blocks allocated to the participating filesystems and ZVOLs. When the table grows too large to be kept entirely in memory, write throughput to the participating filesystems and ZVOLs slows dramatically as new allocations have to wait for the needed part of the table to be read into memory to check whether they are a duplicate. Because of the cost of deduplication, most administrators only enable deduplication on filesystems and ZVOLs on which there are likely to be many duplicate blocks. The administrators further limit the number of filesystems participating in deduplication to a level that provides enough memory to keep the entire table resident.

Note that redundant copies of blocks that have been made for reliability are not deduplicated. As described in Section 10.2, ZFS supports up to three copies of a block referenced from its block pointer. When the first instance of the block is created, all the requested copies will be made. Later instances of the block will have block pointers that also reference all the copies of the data.

Remote Replication

As with all filesystems, ZFS must be able to provide a mechanism for performing backup both locally and remotely. Backup is handled by the DMU layer that understands how to traverse the data structures of any type of *objset* to create a data stream much like the UFS **dump** creates a data stream from a filesystem image using its knowledge of the filesystem's on-disk data structures. ZFS refers to creating this data stream as a *send* operation.

The stream of data can be directed locally or over a network to a remote backup site where it can be stored as a blob of data on a tape or disk, or it can be interpreted by the DMU layer to create another copy of the contents. ZFS refers to accepting a data stream as a *receive* operation. This functionality is similar to a UFS **dump** stream that can be stored as a blob of data on a tape or disk or immediately reconstructed into a filesystem using the **restore** program.

Much like the UFS **dump** program, ZFS is able to send either the complete contents of a snapshot (equivalent to a full dump) or just the differences between two snapshots (equivalent to an incremental dump).

10.5 ZFS Design Tradeoffs

This section compares the design tradeoffs between a traditional overwriting filesystem versus ZFS's nonoverwriting architecture. The biggest difference between the two architectures is the tradeoff between reading and writing. Writes in a traditional filesystem architecture are scattered across the disk as data for different files being written at the same time may be scattered far apart on the disk. Additionally, the metadata for those files will typically be stored separately from the file data. The payoff for the scattered writes is that when the file is later read, its data will all be clustered together even if they were written over a long period of time (as would be the case for a log file). The nonoverwriting filesystem does all its writes sequentially. All the modified file data along with any metadata changes are collected and written together. The result of the sequential writing is that a file can end up requiring many random accesses when it is later read. ZFS mitigates the reading cost by dedicating enough memory to the ARC to be able to keep all actively accessed files resident. ZFS also attempts to prefetch data when files are being read.

The areas in which ZFS's architecture works well are as follows:

- When disk pools are less than half full, RAIDZ can reconstruct a failed disk faster than fixed-size RAID since it only needs to copy the blocks that are in use.
- Traditional filesystems using RAID have to handle a condition known as the RAID write hole. Each update to a RAID stripe requires writing to several disks which cannot be done atomically. Thus, unprotected RAID stripes can become damaged during a crash or power outage. For example, if two of five disks are written and the power fails, the data and parity for that stripe are inconsistent. Therefore, if a disk fails, the RAID reconstruction process generates garbage the next time any data is read from that stripe. The write-hole problem can be avoided by using nonvolatile memory to hold data until all the disks in a stripe have been written. However, nonvolatile memory is expensive and when full, the system must pause and wait for enough I/O to complete to release some of it. Because ZFS never overwrites existing data, it can avoid the write-hole problem by waiting for all disk I/O to complete before creating a new checkpoint.
- Moving allocation and freeing of storage out of the filesystems, and managing it as part of the pool optimizes the utilization of the space since individual filesystems do not need to be over-provisioned for their highest expected usage scenarios.
- The tight integration of ZFS's architecture means that all the features work well together. For example, snapshots work the same when taken on filesystems, clones, and ZVOLs.
- Administration is easier because the pool is aware of the relationships between all the filesystems, clones, and snapshots. Thus, it keeps track of how everything should be mounted (subsuming the need to maintain **/etc/fstab**), allows properties to be inherited down the tree rather than needing to be set individually, and organizes NFS exports (subsuming the need to maintain **/etc/exports**).

The areas in which ZFS's architecture works less well than UFS are as follows:

- As implemented, ZFS's block cache must fit in the kernel's address space. Thus, it works well only on 64-bit systems.
- Like all nonoverwriting filesystems, ZFS operates best when at least a quarter of its disk pool is free. Write throughput becomes poor when the pool gets too full. By contrast, UFS can run well to 95 percent full and acceptably to 99 percent full.
- Traditional RAID implementations have a fixed overhead for the parity. For example, with five drives, one-fifth of the space will be dedicated to parity. With a RAIDZ pool filled with sector-size blocks, half of the space will be dedicated to parity, effectively reducing it to the density of a mirror. This scenario arises when using disks with 4-Kbyte sectors to build pools configured to use 4-Kbyte blocks such as those supporting databases or ZVOLs.
- ZFS caches its data in its ARC that is not part of the unified-memory cache managed by the virtual memory. The result is that when *mmap* is used on a ZFS file, read faults are first read into the ARC and then copied to a page in the unified-memory cache. When dirty unified-memory pages are flushed, they must be copied to an ARC buffer and then written by ZFS. To ensure coherency whenever *mmap* has been used on a ZFS file, reads and writes to that file need to check whether, for each page in the transfer, the requested page is present in the unified-memory cache and, if present, use that page to do the I/O. If the page is not present in the unified-memory cache, then the I/O can proceed normally from the ARC. This approach provides coherency between memory-mapped and I/O access at the expense of wasted memory due to having two copies of the file in memory and extra overhead caused by the need to copy the contents between the two copies.

  Similarly, when using *sendfile* on a file in ZFS, it must be copied from the ARC to the unified-memory cache thereby losing the benefits of the no-copy semantics of *sendfile*. The primary use of *sendfile* is by Web-server applications like Apache.

  Integrating ZFS's ARC into the unified-memory cache would require massive changes. The problem is easily seen in Figure 10.1. The unified-memory cache operates at the vnode interface level and the ARC operates at the physical block level. The pages in the ARC are identified by their block number on a device. The ARC representation is efficient because access to an unmodified file in a filesystem and access to the same file in a snapshot will reference the same entry in the ARC. By contrast, the unified-memory cache identifies pages by their vnode and logical block number. In the unified-memory cache, access to an unmodified file in a filesystem and access to the same file in a snapshot will reference different pages even though their contents are identical. The benefit of this approach is that modification of the file's copy of a block will not affect the snapshot's copy of that block.

ZFS was designed to manage and operate enormous filesystems easily, which it does well. Its design assumed that it would have many fast 64-bit CPUs with large amounts of memory to support these enormous filesystems. When these resources are available, it works extremely well. However, it is not designed for or well suited to run on resource-constrained systems using 32-bit CPUs with less than 8 Gbyte of memory and one small, nearly-full disk, which is typical of many embedded systems.

Exercises

10.1 What is the purpose of the dnode data structure?

10.2 List five problems that ZFS's checksums can detect.

10.3 What is the role of ZFS's Meta-Object Set?

10.4 What is the role of ZFS's Object Set?

10.5 Why does the ZFS block pointer contain three disk addresses?

10.6 Why is the ZFS checksum stored in its block pointer?

10.7 Given that ZFS's on-disk state is always consistent, why does it need a log?

10.8 Why does ZFS checksum using SHA-256 instead of *fletcher4* when doing deduplication?

*10.9 Much of the time required to rebuild a RAIDZ disk pool after replacing a disk arises from all the random reads it requires. Describe an algorithm that would reduce the time to perform these random reads.

**10.10 Describe a design for integrating the unified-memory cache into ZFS.

References

Ahrens, 2005.

M. Ahrens, "It Is Magic," Unpublished Blog entry, available from http://www.mckusick.com/bookrefs/is_it_magic.html, November 2005.

Blackwell et al., 1995.

T. Blackwell, J. Harris, & M. Seltzer, "Heuristic Cleaning Algorithms in Log-Structured File Systems," *USENIX Association Conference Proceedings*, pp. 277–288, January 1995.

Bonwick, 2009.

J. Bonwick, "ZFS Deduplication," Unpublished Blog entry, available from http://www.mckusick.com/bookrefs/zfs_dedup.html, November 2009.

Bonwick et al., 2003.

J. Bonwick, M. Ahrens, V. Henson, M. Maybee, & M. Shellenbaum, "The

Zettabyte File System," Unpublished Paper, available from http://www.mckusick.com/bookrefs/zfs_overview.pdf, November 2003.

Hutchinson et al., 1999.
N. Hutchinson, S. Manley, M. Federwisch, G. Harris, D. Hitz, S. Kleiman, & S. O'Malley, "Logical vs. Physical File System Backup," *USENIX 3rd Symposium on Operating Systems Design and Implementation*, pp. 239–250, available from https://www.usenix.org / legacy / publications / library / proceedings / osdi99 / full_papers / hutchinson / hutchinson_html / hutchinson.html, February 1999.

McKusick et al., 1996.
M. McKusick, K. Bostic, M. Karels, & J. Quarterman, *The Design and Implementation of the 4.4BSD Operating System,* Addison-Wesley, Reading, MA, 1996.

Rosenblum & Ousterhout, 1992.
M. Rosenblum & J. Ousterhout, "The Design and Implementation of a Log-Structured File System," *ACM Transactions on Computer Systems*, vol. 10, no. 1, pp. 26–52, Association for Computing Machinery, February 1992.

Seltzer et al., 1993.
M. Seltzer, K. Bostic, M. K. McKusick, & C. Staelin, "An Implementation of a Log-Structured File System for UNIX," *USENIX Association Conference Proceedings*, pp. 307–326, January 1993.

CHAPTER 11

The Network Filesystem

A commonly provided user-level service in any collection of UNIX systems is the network filesystem (NFS) that allows a set of computers connected to a network to share files. NFS provides client computers with a namespace and a set of file access semantics similar to the capabilities of a local filesystem. Providing local-filesystem semantics in a distributed system is a challenging problem. Sections 11.1 and 11.2 cover the development of NFSv2 and NFSv3. Section 11.3 describes NFSv4 which attempts to address the problems discovered in the first 25 years of deploying NFS. NFSv3 is the most widely used version in 2014, but NFSv4 is rapidly overtaking it in popularity. FreeBSD supports all three versions of NFS.

11.1 Overview

The most commercially successful and widely available remote-filesystem protocol on UNIX systems is NFS, originally designed and implemented by Sun Microsystems [Sandberg et al., 1985; Walsh et al., 1985]. There are two important components to the success of NFS. First, Sun placed the protocol specification for NFS in the public domain. Second, Sun sold that implementation to anyone who wanted it, for less than the cost the company would have incurred to implement it. Thus, most vendors chose to buy the Sun implementation. They were willing to buy from Sun because they knew that they could always legally write their own implementation. The 4.4BSD implementation was written from the protocol specification rather than being incorporated from Sun because of the developers' desire to be able to redistribute it freely in source form.

The first widely released implementation of NFS was version 2 by Sun in 1984. Although version 3 was expected to be released within a year or two of version 2, it suffered several iterations of hugely complicated proposals before an incremental improvement on version 2 was finally released in 1992. The final release of 4.4BSD included an implementation of NFS that supported both versions 2 and 3. FreeBSD's NFS implementation is a direct descendant of the code released in 4.4BSD.

Although versions 2 and 3 of NFS were designed entirely within Sun, the growing set of companies providing NFS-based products put increasing pressure on Sun to bring others into the design of NFS version 4. After much political maneuvering, Sun agreed to pass the responsibility for defining the specification of NFS version 4 to the Internet Engineering Task Force (IETF). Version 4 greatly expands the functionality of the earlier versions of NFS.

Sun's NFS is not the only remote filesystem protocol currently in use. Research at Carnegie-Mellon lead to the Andrew filesystem (AFS) [Howard, 1988]. AFS was commercialized by Transarc and eventually became part of the Distributed Computing Environment promulgated by the Open Software Foundation and was supported by many vendors. It was designed to handle widely distributed servers and clients, and also to work well with mobile computers that operate while detached from the network for long periods. AFS did not see wide commercial use.

In the Microsoft family of operating systems, remote filesystem access is provided by the Common Internet File System (CIFS), which runs on top of the Server Message Block (SMB) protocol [SNIA, 2002]. In FreeBSD, support for SMB and CIFS client and server is provided by *Samba*, which resides in **/usr/ports/net/samba**. Since this book deals with the kernel, and *Samba* runs mostly external to the kernel, we will not discuss it further.

NFS was designed as a client-server application. Its implementation is divided into a client part that imports filesystems from other machines and a server part that exports local filesystems to other machines. The general model is shown in Figure 11.1. In FreeBSD, the kernel can be configured to support just the client, just the server, or both client and server. Many goals went into the NFS design:

- The protocol is designed to be stateless. Because there is no state to maintain or recover, NFS can continue to operate even during periods of client or server failures. Thus, it was thought to be much more robust than a system that operates with state.
- NFS is designed to support UNIX filesystem semantics. However, its design also allows it to support the possibly less-rich semantics of other filesystem types, such as the MS-DOS filesystem.
- The protection and access controls follow the UNIX semantics of having the process present a UID and set of groups that are checked against the file's owner, group, and other access modes. The security check is done by filesystem-dependent code that can do more or fewer checks based on the capabilities of the filesystem that it is supporting. For example, the MS-DOS filesystem cannot implement the full UNIX security validation, and it makes access decisions solely based on the UID.
- The protocol design is transport independent. Although it was originally built using the UDP datagram protocol in version 2, it was easily moved to the TCP

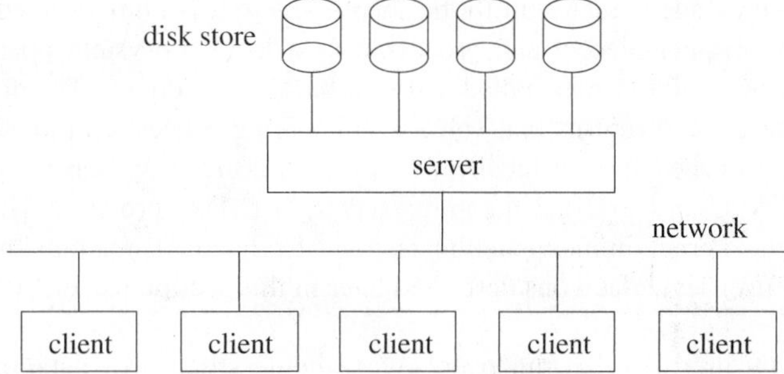

Figure 11.1 The division of NFS between client and server.

stream protocol in version 3. It has also been ported to run over numerous other non-IP-based protocols.

Some of the design decisions limit the set of applications for which NFS is appropriate:

- The design envisions clients and servers being connected on a local, fast network. The NFS protocol does not work well over slow links. When using an unreliable protocol, such as UDP as the transport, it does not work well between clients and servers with intervening gateways. It also works poorly in mobile computing environments that have extended periods of disconnected operation.
- The caching model assumes that most files will not be shared. Performance suffers when files are heavily shared.
- The stateless protocol requires some loss of traditional UNIX semantics. Filesystem locking (*flock*) has to be implemented by a separate stateful daemon. Deferral of the release of space in an unlinked file until the final process has closed the file is approximated with a heuristic that sometimes fails.

Despite these limitations, NFS proliferated because it makes a reasonable tradeoff between semantics and performance; its low cost of adoption has now made it ubiquitous.

11.2 Structure and Operation

NFS operates as a typical client–server application. The server receives ***remote procedure call*** (***RPC***) requests from its various clients. An RPC operates much like a local procedure call: the client makes a procedure call and then waits for the result while the procedure executes. For a remote procedure call, the parameters must be marshalled together into a message. ***Marshalling*** includes replacing pointers by the data to which they point and converting data into network byte order. The message is then sent to the server, where it is unmarshalled (separated out into its original pieces) and processed as a local filesystem operation. The result must be similarly marshalled and sent back to the client. The client unmarshalls the result and returns that value to the calling process as though the result were being returned from a local procedure call [Birrell & Nelson, 1984]. NFS uses Sun's RPC and external data-representation (XDR) protocols [Reid, 1987]. Although the kernel implementation is done by hand to get maximum performance, the user-level daemons described later in this section use the RPC and XDR libraries.

The NFS protocol can run over any available stream- or datagram-oriented protocol but the most common choice is TCP because it provides better service over a wide range of network types from local to wide area. Each NFS RPC message may need to be broken into multiple packets to be sent across the network. A motivating factor to move away from running NFS over a datagram protocol, such as UDP, is that any single RPC may be broken into up to six packets; if any of these packets are lost, the entire RPC is lost and needs to be resent. When running over a stream protocol, such as TCP, the RPC will still be broken into several packets; however, individual lost packets, rather than the entire message, will be retransmitted by TCP. The problems with running NFS over an unreliable datagram protocol are exacerbated on high-bandwidth local-area networks. NFS messages will always fit into a single UDP datagram but the underlying network usually requires the messages to be split, a process called IP fragmentation. Each IP packet contains an identifier that allows large packets, that were broken up, to be reassembled when they are received by the server. The IP identifier field is only 16 bits, which means that once a concurrent and highly fragmented workload is present, the birthday paradox kicks in where different streams have a high probability of selecting overlapping IP-identifier sequences. The server's network stack will now reassemble the UDP datagrams incorrectly, leading to datagrams with failed checksums that require retransmission. The ensuing poor performance is the main reason use of NFS over UDP is heavily discouraged even for local-area networks. In FreeBSD, NFS over UDP is retained primarily for use in network booting. For a more complete discussion of IP fragmentation see Section 13.1.

The set of RPC requests that a client can send to a server, under version 3 of the protocol, is shown in Table 11.1. After the server handles each request, it responds with the appropriate data or with an error code explaining why the request could not be completed. As noted in the table, many operations are ***idempotent***. An idempotent operation is one that can be repeated several times without the final result being changed or an error being caused. For example, writing the same data to the same offset in a file is idempotent because it will yield the same result whether it is done once or many times. However, trying to remove the same file more than once is nonidempotent because the file will no longer exist after the first try. Idempotency is an issue when the server is slow or when an RPC acknowledgment is lost and the client retransmits the RPC request. The retransmitted RPC will cause the server to attempt the same operation again. For a nonidempotent request, such as a request to remove a file, the retransmitted RPC,

Table 11.1 NFS, Version 3, RPC requests.

RPC request	Action	Idempotent
NULL	query the presence of the server	yes
GETATTR	get file attributes	yes
SETATTR	set file attributes	yes
LOOKUP	look up file name	yes
ACCESS	check access permission	yes
READLINK	read from symbolic link	yes
READ	read from file	yes
WRITE	write to file	yes
COMMIT	commit cached data on a server to stable storage	yes
CREATE	create file	no
REMOVE	remove file	no
RENAME	rename file	no
LINK	create link to file	no
SYMLINK	create symbolic link	no
MKNOD	create a special device	no
MKDIR	create directory	no
RMDIR	remove directory	no
READDIR	read from directory	yes
READDIRPLUS	extended read from directory	yes
FSSTAT	get dynamic filesystem attributes	yes
FSINFO	get static filesystem attributes	yes
PATHCONF	retrieve POSIX information	yes

if undetected by the server recent-request cache [Juszczak, 1989], will cause a "no such file" error to be returned, because the file will have been removed already by the first RPC. Users may be confused by the error because they believe that they are attempting to remove an existing file.

Each file on the server is identified by a unique ***file handle***. A file handle is the token by which clients refer to files on a server. The handles are passed in operations, such as read and write, that reference a file. A file handle is created by the server when a pathname-translation request (lookup) is sent from a client to the server. The server must find the requested file or directory and ensure that the requesting user has access permission. If permission is granted, the server returns a file handle for the requested file to the client. The file handle identifies the file in future access requests by the client. A file handle is meant to be opaque to the client. The client is not allowed to peek into or infer any information from the file handle but only to present it to the server as part of routine file operations. Servers are free to build file handles from whatever information they find convenient.

In the FreeBSD NFS implementation, each filesystem can decide what data goes into a file handle. In ZFS, the file handle is created from the underlying file ID. ZFS is covered in Chapter 10.

In UFS, covered in Chapter 9, the file handle is built from a filesystem identifier, an inode number, and a ***generation number***. The server creates a unique filesystem identifier for each of its locally mounted filesystems. A generation number is assigned to an inode each time that the latter is allocated to represent a new file. The generation number is selected by using the kernel's random-number generator. The kernel ensures that the same generation value is never used for two consecutive allocations of the same underlying inode or file ID.

The purpose of the file handle is to provide the server with enough information to find the file in future requests. The generation number verifies that the file handle still references the same file that it referenced when the file was first accessed. Using a generation number allows the server to detect when a file has been deleted, and a new file is later created using the same inode or file ID. Although the new file has the same filesystem identifier and inode number, it is a completely different file from the one that the previous file handle referenced. Since the generation number is included in the file handle, a previously used generation number for an inode will not match the new generation number in the same inode. When a file handle representing a previous version of the file is presented to the server by a client, the server refuses to accept it and instead returns the "stale file handle" error message.

The use of the generation number ensures that the file handle is time stable. Distributed systems define a ***time-stable identifier*** as one that refers uniquely to some entity both while that entity exists and for a long time after it is deleted. A time-stable identifier allows a system to remember an identity across transient failures and allows the system to detect and report errors for attempts to access deleted entities.

Versions 2 and 3 of the NFS protocol are ***stateless***. Being stateless means that the server does not need to maintain any information about which clients it is serving or about the files that they currently have open. Every RPC request that is received by the server is completely self-contained. The server does not need any additional information beyond that contained in the RPC to fulfill the request. For example, a read request will include the credential of the user doing the request, the file handle on which the read is to be done, the offset in the file to begin the read, and the number of bytes to be read. This information allows the server to open the file, verify that the user has permission to read it, seek to the appropriate point, read the desired contents, and close the file. In practice, the server caches recently accessed file data. However, if there is enough activity to push the file out of the cache, the file handle provides the server with enough information to reopen the file.

The benefit of a stateless protocol is that there is no need to do state recovery after a client or server has crashed and rebooted or after the network has been partitioned and reconnected. Because each RPC is self-contained, the server can simply begin servicing requests as soon as it begins running; it does not need to know which files its clients have open. Indeed, it does not even need to know which clients are currently using it as a server.

There are drawbacks to a stateless protocol. First, the semantics of the local filesystem imply state. When files are unlinked, they continue to be accessible until the last reference to them is closed. Because NFS knows neither which files are open on clients nor when those files are closed, it cannot properly know when to free file space. As a result, it always frees the space at the time of the unlink of the last link to the file. Clients that want to preserve the freeing-on-last-close semantics convert *unlink*s of open files to *rename*s to obscure names on the server. The names are in the form *.nfs.ttttttt.xxxx4.4*, where the *ttttttt* is the number of CPU ticks since the system booted and *xxxx* is replaced with the hexadecimal value of the process identifier. The ticks are successively incremented until an unused name is found. When the last close is done on the client, the client sends an unlink of the obscure filename to the server. This heuristic works for file access on only a single client; if one client has the file open and another client removes the file, the file will still disappear from the first client at the time of the remove. Other stateful semantics include the advisory locking described in Section 9.5. The locking semantics cannot be handled by the NFS protocol. Under versions 2 and 3 of the NFS protocol, they are handled by a separate lock manager; the FreeBSD version of NFS implements them using the user-level **rpc.lockd** daemon. Locking is handled differently under version 4 of the protocol (see Section 11.3).

The second drawback of a stateless protocol is related to performance. Under version 2 of the NFS protocol, all operations that modify the filesystem must be committed to stable storage before the RPC can be acknowledged. Most servers do not have battery-backed memory; the stable-store requirement means that all written data must be on the disk before they can reply to the RPC. For a growing file, an update may require up to three synchronous disk writes: one for the inode to update its size, one for the indirect block to add a new data pointer, and one for the new data. At a minimum, a single write to a filesystem log is required. Each synchronous write takes several milliseconds; this delay severely restricts the write throughput for any given client file.

Version 3 of the NFS protocol eliminated some of the synchronous writes by adding a new asynchronous write RPC request. When such a request is received by the server, it is permitted to acknowledge the RPC without writing the new data to stable storage. Typically, a client will do a series of asynchronous write requests followed by a commit RPC request when it reaches the end of the file or it runs out of buffer space to store the file. The commit RPC request causes the server to write any unwritten parts of the file to stable store before acknowledging the commit RPC. The server benefits by having to write the inode and indirect blocks for the file only once per batch of asynchronous writes, instead of on every write RPC request. The client benefits from having higher throughput for file writes. The client does have the added overhead of having to save copies of all asynchronously written buffers until a commit RPC is done because the server may crash before having written one or more of the asynchronous buffers to stable store. Each time the client does an asynchronous write RPC, the server returns a cookie, which acts as a verification token. When the client sends the commit RPC, the acknowledgment to that RPC also includes a cookie. The client uses the cookie to determine whether the server has rebooted between a call to write data and a later call to commit it. The cookie is guaranteed to be the same throughout a single boot session of the server and to be different each time the server reboots where uncommitted data may be lost. If the cookie changes, the client knows that it must retransmit all asynchronous write RPCs done since the last commit RPC that were verified with the old cookie value.

The NFS protocol does not specify the granularity of the buffering that should be used when files are written. Most implementations of NFS utilize 8-Kbyte buffers when working on file blocks in system memory. If an application writes 10 bytes in the middle of a block, the client reads the entire block from the server, modifies the requested 10 bytes, and then writes the entire block back to the server. The FreeBSD implementation also uses 8-Kbyte buffers, but it keeps additional information that describes which bytes in the buffer are modified. If an application writes 10 bytes in the middle of a block, the client reads the entire block from the server, modifies the requested 10 bytes, but then writes back only the 10 modified bytes to the server. The block read is necessary to ensure that, if the application later reads back other unmodified parts of the block, it will get valid data. Writing back only the modified data has two benefits:

1. Fewer bytes are sent over the network, reducing contention for a scarce resource.
2. Nonoverlapping modifications to a file are not lost. If two different clients simultaneously modify different parts of the same file block, both modifications will show up in the file since only the modified parts are sent to the server. When clients send back entire blocks to the server, changes made by the first client will be overwritten by data read before the first modification was made and then will be written back by the second client.

Another performance problem that comes from the stateless nature of the NFS protocol is that the server must check permissions for each I/O operation that a client requests. The server does not support, nor understand, the concept of an open file; it only handles I/O operations based on the paths that are sent by the clients. Checking the permissions on each request requires extra filesystem accesses on the server, resulting in higher overhead per operation.

The FreeBSD NFS Implementation

The NFS implementation that appears in FreeBSD was written by Rick Macklem at the University of Guelph, using the specifications of the Version 2 protocol published by Sun Microsystems [Macklem, 1994a; Sun Microsystems, 1989]. He later extended it to support the protocol extensions found in version 3 [Callaghan et al., 1995; Pawlowski et al., 1994], and has most recently added support for version 4 of the protocol [Haynes & Noveck, 2014]. Table 11.1 lists the functionality in the version 3 protocol. Version 3 of the protocol provides the following:

- Sixty-four-bit file offsets and sizes
- An access RPC that provides server permission checking on file open, rather than having the client guess whether the server will allow access
- An append option on the write RPC
- A defined way to make special device nodes and fifos
- Optimization of bulk directory access
- The ability to batch writes into several asynchronous RPCs followed by a commit RPC to ensure that the data are on stable storage
- Additional information about the capabilities of the underlying filesystem

In addition to the version 2 and version 3 support, Rick Macklem made several other extensions to the BSD NFS implementation; the extended version became known as the Not Quite NFS (NQNFS) protocol [Macklem, 1994b]. The NQNFS extensions added support for extended file attributes to support FreeBSD filesystem functionality more fully and a variant of short-term ***leases*** with delayed-write client caching that provided distributed cache consistency and improved performance [Gray & Cheriton, 1989]. Although the NQNFS extensions were never widely adopted in version 3 implementations, they were instrumental in proving the value of using leases in NFS. The leasing technology was adopted for use in the NFS version 4 protocol, not only for cache consistency and improved performance, but also as a mechanism to bound the recovery time for locks.

The NFS implementation distributed in FreeBSD supports clients and servers running any of versions 2, 3, or 4 of the NFS protocol. The code that implemented the experimental NQNFS protocol was removed during the development of FreeBSD 5.

The FreeBSD client and server implementations of NFS are kernel resident. NFS interfaces to the network with sockets via the kernel RPC layer. The kernel RPC layer contains calls to the in-kernel versions of the socket routines *sosend*() and *soreceive*() (see Chapter 12 for a discussion of the socket interface) and frees the NFS daemons from having to handle socket communication on their own.

The less time-critical operations, such as the mounting and unmounting of remote filesystems, as well as determination of which filesystems may be exported and to what set of clients they may be exported are managed by user-level system daemons. For the server side to function, the **portmap**, **mountd**, and **nfsd** daemons must be running. For full NFS functionality, the **rpc.lockd** and **rpc.statd** daemons must also be running.

The **portmap** acts as a clearing house for the services provided by the machine on which it is running. Whenever any RPC daemon is started, it tells the

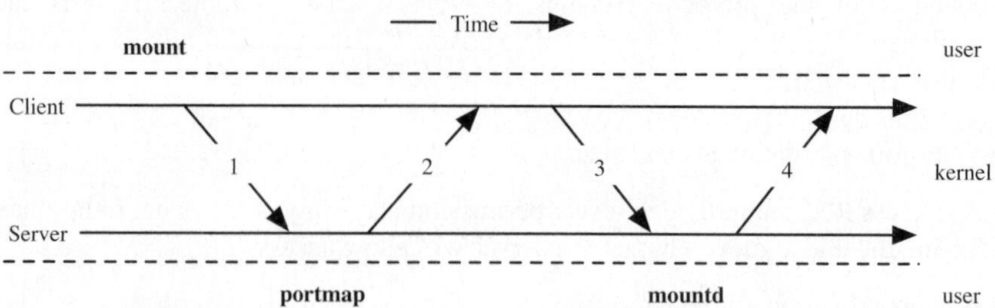

Figure 11.2 Daemon interaction when a remote filesystem is mounted. Step 1: The client's **mount** process sends a message to the well-known port of the server's **portmap** daemon, requesting the port address of the server's **mountd** daemon. Step 2: The server's **portmap** daemon returns the port address of its server's **mountd** daemon. Step 3: The client's **mount** process sends a request to the server's **mountd** daemon with the pathname of the filesystem that it wants to mount. Step 4: The server's **mountd** daemon requests a file handle for the desired mount point from its kernel. If the request is successful, the file handle is returned to the client's **mount** process. Otherwise, the error from the file-handle request is returned. If the request is successful, the client's **mount** process does a *mount* system call, passing in the file handle that it received from the server's **mountd** daemon.

portmap daemon to what port number it is listening and what RPC services it is prepared to serve. When a client wishes to make an RPC call to a given service, it will first contact the **portmap** daemon on the server machine to determine whether a service is available and, if it is available, the port number to which RPC messages should be sent.

The interactions between the client and server daemons when a remote filesystem is mounted are shown in Figure 11.2. The **mountd** daemon handles two important functions:

1. On startup and after a hangup signal, **mountd** reads the **/etc/exports** file and creates a list of hosts and networks to which each local filesystem may be exported. It passes this list into the kernel using the *mount* system call; the kernel links the list to the associated local filesystem mount structure so that the list is readily available for consultation when an NFS request is received.

2. Client mount requests are directed to the **mountd** daemon. After verifying that the client has permission to mount the requested filesystem, **mountd** returns a file handle for the requested mount point. This file handle is used by the client for later traversal into the filesystem.

The NFS server is implemented as a set of kernel libraries that are invoked by a pool of service threads that remain perpetually resident in the kernel. The user level **nfsd** daemon creates, and fills in, a structure that it passes to the *nfssvc* system call that tells the kernel how many NFS daemon threads to run. Typical servers run four to six **nfsd** kernel threads but more may be used to increase throughput if the underlying hardware has sufficient resources. Other than starting the kernel **nfsd** master thread, the user level NFS daemon does very little work. The **nfsd** kernel threads rely on the kernel RPC and service libraries.

Any kernel thread that wishes to provide an RPC creates a transport object and then registers it with the service layer. To create a datagram-based transport service the thread uses the *svc_dg_create*() routine while creating a connection-oriented service is accomplished with the *svc_vc_create*() routine. After the transport is created, it must be registered with the service, in order to start receiving RPCs, via the *svc_reg*() routine. All versions of NFS for both datagram and connection oriented protocols register the *nfssvc_program*() entry point, which demultiplexes incoming requests into the correct parts of the protocol libraries. Once the demultiplexing is complete, the **nfsd** kernel thread verifies the sender and then passes the request to the appropriate local filesystem for processing. When the result comes back from the filesystem, it is returned to the requesting client. Each individual request results in a kernel thread invoking *nfssvc_program*(), which returns once its work is complete. The maximum degree of concurrency on the server is determined by the number of **nfsd** kernel threads that are running.

For connection-oriented transport protocols, such as TCP, there is one connection for each client-to-server mount point. For datagram-oriented protocols, such as UDP, the server creates a fixed number of incoming RPC sockets when it starts its **nfsd** daemons; clients create one socket for each imported mount point. The socket for a mount point is created in the kernel in response to the **mount** command on the client calling the *nmount*() system call. The client side uses it to communicate with the **mountd** daemon on the server. Once the client-to-server connection is established, the daemon processes on a connection-oriented protocol may perform additional verification, such as authentication. If the connection breaks while the mount point is still active, the client will attempt a reconnect with a new socket.

For version 2 and version 3 of the NFS protocol, the **rpc.lockd** daemon manages locking requests for remote files. Client locking requests are exported from the kernel through a fifo, **/var/run/lock**. The **rpc.lockd** daemon reads the locking request from the fifo and sends the lock request across the network to the **rpc.lockd** daemon on the server that holds the file. The daemon running on the server opens the file to be locked and uses the *flock* system call to acquire the requested lock. Once the lock has been acquired, the server daemon sends a message back to the client daemon. The client daemon writes the lock status into the fifo, which is then read by the kernel and passed up to the user application. The release of the lock is handled similarly. If the **rpc.lockd** daemon is not run, then lock requests on NFS files will fail with an "operation not supported" error.

The **rpc.statd** daemon cooperates with **rpc.statd** daemons on other hosts to provide a status-monitoring service. The daemon accepts requests from programs running on the local host (typically **rpc.lockd**) to monitor the status of specified hosts. If a monitored host crashes and restarts, the daemon on the crashed host will notify the other daemons that it crashed when it is restarted. When notified of a crash, or when a daemon determines that a remote host has crashed because of its lack of response, it will notify the local program(s) that requested the monitoring service. If the **rpc.statd** daemon is not run, then locks held by clients on a host that crashed may be held indefinitely. By using the **rpc.statd** service, crashes will be discovered and the locks held by a crashed host will be released.

The client side can operate without any daemons running, but the system administrator can improve performance by running several **nfsiod** daemons. As with the server, for full functionality the client must run the **rpc.lockd** and **rpc.statd** daemons.

The purpose of the **nfsiod** daemons is to perform asynchronous read-ahead and write-behind. The daemons are typically started when the kernel begins running multiuser, and are started via the *nfsiod_setup*() routine. They are completely kernel resident, providing a process context for the NFS RPC client side. In their absence, each read or write of an NFS file that cannot be serviced from the local client cache must be done in the context of the requesting process. The process sleeps while the RPC is sent to the server, the RPC is handled by the server, and a reply is sent back. No read-ahead is done and write operations proceed at the disk-write speed of the server. When present, the **nfsiod** daemons provide a separate context in which to issue RPC requests to a server. When a file is written, the data are copied into the buffer cache on the client. The buffer is then passed to a waiting **nfsiod** that does the RPC to the server and awaits the reply. When the reply arrives, **nfsiod** updates the local buffer to mark that buffer as written. Meanwhile, the process that did the write can continue running. The NFS protocol flushes all the blocks of a file to the server when that file is closed. If all the dirty blocks have been written to the server when a process closes a file that it has been writing, it will not have to wait for them to be flushed.

When reading a file, the client first hands a read-ahead request to the **nfsiod** that does the RPC to the server. It then looks up the buffer that it has been requested to read. If the sought-after buffer is already in the cache because of a previous read-ahead request, then it can proceed without waiting. Otherwise, it must do an RPC to the server and wait for the reply. The interactions between the client and server daemons when I/O is done are shown in Figure 11.3.

Client–Server Interactions

A local filesystem is unaffected by network service disruptions. It is always available to the users on the machine unless there is a catastrophic event, such as a disk or power failure. Since the entire machine hangs or crashes, the kernel does not need to concern itself with how to handle the processes that were accessing the filesystem. By contrast, the client end of a network filesystem must have ways to handle processes that are accessing remote files when the client is still running but the server becomes unreachable or crashes. Each NFS mount point is provided with three alternatives for dealing with server unavailability:

1. The default is a hard mount that will continue to try to contact the server indefinitely to complete the filesystem access. This type of mount is appropriate when processes on the client that access files in the filesystem do not tolerate

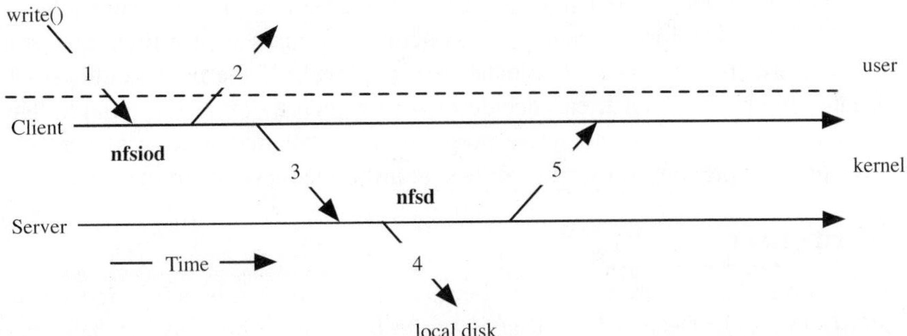

Figure 11.3 Daemon interaction when I/O is done. Step 1: The client's process does a *write* system call. Step 2: The data to be written are copied into a kernel buffer on the client, and the *write* system call returns. Step 3: An **nfsiod** daemon awakens inside the client's kernel, picks up the dirty buffer, and sends the buffer to the server. Step 4: The incoming write request is delivered to the next available **nfsd** daemon running inside the kernel on the server. The server's **nfsd** daemon writes the data to the appropriate local disk and waits for the disk I/O to complete. Step 5: After the I/O has completed, the server's **nfsd** daemon sends back an acknowledgment of the I/O to the waiting **nfsiod** daemon on the client. On receipt of the acknowledgment, the client's **nfsiod** daemon marks its local buffer as clean.

I/O system calls that return transient errors. A hard mount is used for processes for which access to the filesystem is critical for normal system operation. It is also useful if the client has a long-running program that simply wants to wait for the server to resume operation (e.g., after the server is taken down for maintenance).

2. The other extreme is a soft mount that retries an RPC a specified number of times, and then the corresponding system call returns with a transient error. For a connection-oriented protocol, the actual RPC request is not retransmitted; instead, NFS depends on the protocol retransmission to do the retries. If a response is not returned within the specified time, the corresponding system call returns with a transient error. The problem with this type of mount is that most applications do not expect a transient error return from I/O system calls (since they never occur on a local filesystem). Often, they will mistakenly interpret the transient error as a permanent error and will exit prematurely. An additional problem is deciding how long to set the timeout period. If it is set too low, error returns will start occurring whenever the NFS server is slow because of heavy load or when the network is heavily loaded. Alternately, a large retry limit can result in a process being hung for a long time because of a crashed server or network partitioning.

3. Most system administrators take a middle ground by using an interruptible mount that will wait forever like a hard mount but checks to see whether a termination signal is pending for any process that is waiting for a server

response. If a signal (such as an interrupt) is sent to a process waiting for an NFS server, the corresponding I/O system call returns with a transient error. Normally, the process is terminated by the signal. If the process chooses to catch the signal, then it can decide how to handle the transient failure. This mount option allows interactive programs to be aborted when a server fails, while allowing long-running processes to await the server's return.

Security Issues

NFS versions 2 and 3 are not secure because the protocol was not designed with security in mind. Despite several attempts to fix security problems in these versions, NFS security is still limited. In particular, the security work only addresses authentication; file data are sent over the network in clear text. Even if someone is unable to get your server to send him or her a sensitive file, he or she can just wait until a legitimate user accesses it, and then can pick it up as it goes by on the net. Much of the work that went into version 4 addressed both authentication and data security. As version 4 moves into general use, NFS filesystems will be able to be run more securely than previously.

NFS export control is at the granularity of local filesystems. Associated with each local filesystem mount point is a list of the hosts to which that filesystem may be exported. A local filesystem may be exported to a specific host, to all hosts that match a subnet mask, or to all other hosts (the world). For each host or group of hosts, the filesystem can be exported read-only or read–write. In addition, a server may specify a set of subdirectories within the filesystem that may be mounted. However, this list of mount points is enforced by only the **mountd** daemon. If a malicious client wishes to do so, it can access any part of a filesystem that is exported to it.

The final determination of exportability is made by the list maintained in the kernel. As a result, even if a rogue client manages to snoop the net and to steal a file handle for the mount point of a valid client, the kernel will refuse to accept the file handle unless the client presenting that handle is on the kernel's export list. When NFS is running with TCP, the check is done once when the connection is established. When NFS is running with UDP, the check must be done for every RPC request.

The NFS server also permits limited remapping of user credentials. Typically, the credential for the superuser is not trusted and is remapped to the low-privilege user "nobody." The credentials of all other users can be accepted as given or also mapped to a default user (typically "nobody"). Use of the client UID and GID list unchanged on the server implies that the UID and GID space are common between the client and server (i.e., UID N on the client must refer to the same user on the server). One of the main problems in the deployment of NFS in large, heterogeneous environments is the need for a unified UID and GID space. The system administrator can support more complex UID and GID mappings by using the **umapfs** filesystem described in Section 7.5.

NFSv3 can use Kerberos to authenticate users of the system. A fuller discussion of the use of Kerberos within NFS is presented in Section 11.3 .

Techniques for Improving Performance

Remote filesystems face a challenging performance problem: providing both a coherent network-wide view of the data and delivering that data quickly are often conflicting goals. The server can maintain coherency easily by keeping a single repository for the data and sending them out to each client when the clients need them; this approach tends to be slow because every data access requires the client to wait for an RPC round-trip time. The delay is further aggravated by the huge load that it puts on a server that must service every I/O request from its clients. To increase performance and to reduce server load, remote filesystem protocols attempt to cache frequently used data on the clients themselves. If the cache is designed properly, the client will be able to satisfy many of its own I/O requests directly from the cache. Performing these accesses is faster than communicating with the server, reducing latency on the client and load on the server and network. The hard part of client caching is keeping the caches coherent—that is, ensuring that each client quickly replaces any cached data that are modified by writes done on other clients. If one client writes a file that is later read by a second client, the second client wants to see the data written by the first client, rather than the stale data that were in the file previously. There are two main ways that the stale data may be read accidentally:

1. If the second client has stale data sitting in its cache, the client may use those data because it does not know that newer data are available.

2. The first client may have new data sitting in its cache but may not yet have written those data back to the server. Here, even if the second client asks the server for up-to-date data, the server may return the stale data because it does not know that one of its clients has a newer version of the file in that client's cache.

The second of these problems is related to the way that client writing is done. Synchronous writing requires that all writes be pushed through to the server during the *write* system call. This approach is the most consistent because the server always has the most recently written data. It also permits any write errors, such as "filesystem out of space," to be propagated back to the client process via the *write* system-call return. With an NFS filesystem using synchronous writing, error returns most closely parallel those from a local filesystem. Unfortunately, this approach restricts the client to only one write per RPC round-trip time.

An alternative to synchronous writing is delayed writing, where the *write* system call returns as soon as the data are cached on the client; the data are written to the server sometime later. This approach permits client writing to occur at the rate of local storage access up to the size of the local cache. Also, for cases where file truncation or deletion occurs shortly after writing, the write to the server may be avoided entirely because the data have already been deleted. Avoiding the data push saves the client time and reduces load on the server.

There are some drawbacks to delayed writing. To provide full consistency, the server must notify the client when another client wants to read or write the file so that the delayed writes can be written back to the server. There are also problems with the propagation of errors back to the client process that issued the *write* system call. For example, a semantic change is introduced by delayed-write caching when the file server is full. Here, delayed-write RPC requests can fail with an "out of space" error. If the data are sent back to the server when the file is closed, the error can be detected only if the application checks the return value from the *close* system call. For delayed writes, written data may not be sent back to the server until after the process that did the write has exited—long after it can be notified of any errors. The only solution is to modify programs writing an important file to do an *fsync* system call and to check for an error return from that call instead of depending on getting errors from *write* or *close*. Finally, there is a risk of the loss of recently written data if the client crashes before the data are written back to the server.

A compromise between synchronous writing and delayed writing is asynchronous writing. The write to the server is started during the *write* system call, but the *write* system call returns before the write completes. This approach reduces the risk of data loss because of a client crash but negates the possibility of reducing server write load by discarding writes when a file is truncated or deleted.

Since NFS has no way of knowing when write sharing might occur, it tries to bound the period of inconsistency by writing the data back when a file is closed. Files that are open for long periods are written back when their oldest dirty data becomes 30 seconds old. Thus, the NFS implementation does a mix of asynchronous and delayed writing, but it always pushes all writes to the server on close. Pushing the delayed writes on close negates much of the performance advantage of delayed writing because the delays that were avoided in the *write* system calls are observed in the *close* system call. With this approach, the server is always aware of all changes made by its clients with a maximum delay of 30 seconds and usually sooner, because most files are open only briefly for writing.

The server maintains read consistency by always having a client verify the contents of its cache before using that cache. When a client reads data, it first checks for the data in its cache. Each cache entry is stamped with an attribute that shows the most recent time that the server says that the data were modified. If the data are found in the cache, the client sends a timestamp RPC request to its server to find out when the data were last modified. If the modification time returned by the server matches that associated with the cache, the client uses the data in its cache; otherwise, it arranges to replace the data in its cache with the new data.

The problem with checking with the server on every cache access is that the client still experiences an RPC round-trip delay for each file access, and the server is still inundated with RPC requests, although they are considerably quicker to handle than are full I/O operations. To reduce this client latency and server load, most NFS implementations track how recently the server has been asked about each cache block. The client then uses a tunable parameter that is typically set at a few seconds to delay asking the server about a cache block. If an I/O request finds a cache block and the server has been asked about the validity of that block within the delay period, the client does not ask the server again, but just uses the block. Because certain blocks are used many times in succession, the server will be asked about them only once, rather than on every access. For example, the directory block for the **/usr/include** directory will be accessed once for each **#include** in a source file that is being compiled. The drawback to this approach is that changes made by other clients may not be noticed for up to the delay number of seconds.

A more consistent approach used by some network filesystems is to use a ***callback*** mechanism where the server keeps track of all the files that each of its clients has cached. When a cached file is modified, the server notifies the clients holding that file so that they can purge it from their cache. This algorithm dramatically reduces the number of queries from the client to the server, with the effect of decreasing client I/O latency and server load [Howard et al., 1988]. The drawback is that this approach introduces state into the server because the server must remember the clients that it is serving and the set of files that they have cached. If the server crashes, it must rebuild this state before it can begin running again. Rebuilding the server state is a significant problem when everything is running properly; it gets even more complicated and time-consuming when it is aggravated by network partitions that prevent the server from communicating with some of its clients [Mogul, 1993].

The FreeBSD NFS implementation uses asynchronous writes while a file is open but synchronously waits for all data to be written when the file is closed. This approach gains the speed benefit of writing asynchronously, yet ensures that any delayed errors will be reported no later than the point at which the file is closed. The implementation will query the server about the attributes of a file at most once every 3 seconds. This 3-second period reduces network traffic for files accessed frequently, yet ensures that any changes to a file are detected with no more than a 3-second delay. Although these heuristics provide tolerable semantics, they are noticeably imperfect.

11.3 NFS Evolution

Over its 25-year history, the NFS protocol has had to evolve to meet changing technology and user requirements. Many of the features that were considered experimental extensions to version 3 of NFS, as well as the work done in NQNFS, have been codified and included as fully fledged features in the latest versions of the protocol, NFS version 4.0 and 4.1. NFS version 3, in particular, depended on external daemons for certain operations, such as locking, that have now been subsumed into the base protocol in version 4, obviating the need for supplementary daemons. The scale of the work undertaken to update NFS for version 4 was monumental, with the initial update to version 4.0 spanning over 250 pages of description [Shepler et al., 2003]. Version 4.1, an update to version 4.0, is described in an even larger, 600-page-plus document, although much of the length of the update can be attributed to the more extensive description of each of the possible NFS operations [Shepler et al., 2010]. FreeBSD contains an implementation of both a client and server that supports the NFS protocol up through version 4.1. This section describes the design and implementation of both of the protocols as if they were one. The differences between the major version and the revision will be noted only when absolutely necessary. The NFSv4.0 RFC lists four goals for the latest version of the protocol:

- Improved access and good performance on the Internet. The protocol should not only do well in a high-bandwidth/low-latency network such as a LAN, but also over a low-bandwidth/high-latency network such as a WAN. The earlier versions of the protocol operate poorly over WANs.
- Strong security with negotiation built into the protocol. When NFS was first designed, computers that were powerful enough to run a UNIX-like operating system were generally used in medium to large installations and were not carried around by individuals who might connect them to an insecure network and then expect to get full access to their files on a server. The advent of mobile computing and pervasive, high-speed, wireless networking has made it so that all network protocols must address security concerns, and NFS is no different. Version 4 of the protocol had security mechanisms designed into it from the beginning.
- Good cross-platform interoperability. NFS was designed so that computers running UNIX-like operating systems, with similar directory structures and file operations, could share a centralized store of files. The adaptation of NFS to non-UNIX environments required rethinking the protocol so that more types of clients could interoperate with NFS servers.
- Designed for protocol extensions. A shortcoming of both version 2 and version 3 of the NFS protocol was that it was virtually impossible to extend once it had been deployed. An inability to evolve the protocol has meant that necessary changes took a long time to get into the field.

Revision 4.1 of the NFS protocol adds a few new goals:

- Correct significant structural weaknesses and oversights discovered in version 4.0 of the protocol
- Add clarity and specificity to areas left unaddressed or not addressed in enough detail in version 4.0 of the protocol
- Add specific features based on experience with the existing protocol and recent industry developments
- Provide protocol support for clustered-server deployments including providing scalable parallel access to files distributed across multiple servers

NFSv4 is a significantly different protocol from its predecessors. A fundamental change in NFSv4 is the move to a stateful protocol. Many of the new features in version 4, such as caching, delegation, and locking, require that the server maintain state. Another significant change comes at the lowest level of the protocol where the 20 standard RPCs present in version 3 of the protocol have been replaced with two regular procedures, NULL and COMPOUND, and two callback procedures, CB_NULL and CB_COMPOUND. The operations that were previously encoded as their own RPCs in NFS versions 2 and 3 (see Section 11.2) are now encoded as operations within the COMPOUND or CB_COMPOUND RPCs. The COMPOUND procedure encapsulates, in a single RPC call, several NFS operations that are to be carried out by the server. When a server receives a COMPOUND RPC, it attempts to perform the operations encapsulated therein, in the order in which they are encoded into the message. If an error occurs in processing any of the operations received in the COMPOUND RPC, processing immediately stops and an error is returned. Encapsulating multiple operations into a single message can help to improve the performance of NFS by reducing the number of round trips that each operation requires. In practice, it has not been possible to group operations within the COMPOUND RPCs because too often one operation is dependent on the successful completion of a previous operation. Although the current implementation of NFSv4 in FreeBSD groups between 3 and 5 operations, the number of messages needed to do an operation in NFSv4 is the same as NFSv3.

Comparing the set of operations available in NFSv4, shown in Table 11.2 with the RPCs that were given in Table 11.1 shows that there are more than twice as many available in NFSv4. The new operations exist to support new features available in NFSv4 including locking, which was handled by a separate protocol under previous versions of NFS, delegations, which allow for local open and lock operations to be carried out on the client; and more aggressive caching of file data and attributes.

A significant change between previous versions of NFS, and NFSv4 is the addition of explicit OPEN and CLOSE operations. Integrating support for features that require state, such as locking and caching, lead to the addition of OPEN and CLOSE, which bring the filesystem semantics present in NFSv4 closer to those of a stateful local filesystem such as UFS. In previous versions of NFS, all the client needed to manipulate a file on the server was the file's handle. NFSv4 requires clients to open a file and obtain a file handle specific to that file before it can perform operations such as reading and writing data.

The original version of NFS targeted UNIX and UNIX-like operating systems in which there was always a single unique filesystem root. Systems such as Windows have a root for each filesystem that appears as the drive letter, C:, D: etc. Version 4 of the protocol tries to address the ***multiple-root problem*** by having the server maintain a pseudo-filesystem hierarchy that brings back the concept of a single root to the filesystem tree. The motivation for providing a single namespace comes from the way that many users access their files. They progressively browse the directory and file hierarchy through a graphical chooser or via tab completion on the command line.

A way to reduce the load on the server and to improve the user's experience on the client is to allow the client to cache as much file and metadata as possible. Removing round trips between the client and server by keeping copies of data at the client is a well-known technique for improving performance in a distributed

Table 11.2 NFS Version 4 operations (part 1 of 2).

Operation	Action
ACCESS	check Access Rights
BACKCHANNELCTL	modify the back channel
BINDCONNNTOSESS	bind connection to session
CLOSE	close file
COMMIT	commit cached data
CREATE	create a non-regular file object
CREATESESSION	create Session
DELEGPURGE	purge delegations awaiting recovery
DELEGRETURN	return delegation
DESTROYCLIENTID	destroy client ID
DESTROYSESSION	destroy session
EXCHANGEID	exchange client ID
FREESTATEID	free state ID
GETATTR	get attributes
GETDEVINFO	get device information
GETDEVLIST	get device list
GETDIRDELEG	get directory delegation
GETFH	get current filehandle
LAYOUTCOMMIT	commit layout
LAYOUTGET	get layout
LAYOUTRETURN	return layout
LINK	create link to a file
LOCK	create lock
LOCKT	test for lock
LOCKU	unlock file
LOOKUP	lookup filename
LOOKUPP	lookup parent directory
NVERIFY	verify difference in attributes

system. Caching data at the client introduces the problem discussed in Section 11.2, maintaining the coherence of data over many systems which must be handled carefully to avoid cases where data are mangled or lost by conflicting changes submitted by different clients. If two clients have opened and modified the same file, and those modifications occur on copies of the data that are locally cached at the client, then the server has no way of knowing which modification is correct and which should be thrown away. To avoid cache-coherency problems, NFSv4 only allows a client to cache information if either it is the only one writing data to the file or if all clients are only reading from the file. When a server

Table 11.2 NFS Version 4 operations (part 2 of 2).

Operation	Action
OPEN	open a regular file
OPENATTR	open named attribute directory
OPEN_CONFIRM	confirm open
OPEN_DOWNGRADE	reduce open file access
PUTFH	set current filehandle
PUTPUBFH	set public filehandle
PUTROOTFH	set root filehandle
READ	read from file
READDIR	read directory
READLINK	read symbolic link
RECLAIMCOMPL	lock reclaiming complete
RELEASE_LOCKOWNER	release lockowner
REMOVE	remove filesystem object
RENAME	rename directory entry
RENEW	renew a lease
RESTOREFH	restore saved filehandle
SAVEFH	save current filehandle
SECINFO	obtain available security
SECINFONONAME	obtains security info on file handle
SEQUENCE	contains session ID
SETATTR	set attributes
SETCLIENTID	negotiate client ID
SETCLIENTID_CONFIRM	confirm client ID
SETSSV	set secret state verifier
TESTSTATEID	validate state ID
VERIFY	verify same attributes
WANTDELEG	ask for delegation not based on open
WRITE	write to file

allows a client to cache data, it is said to be delegating responsibility for that data to the client. To properly support delegation, the protocol must also have a way to regain control over the data it delegated, for example, if a second client requests to open a file for writing. To regain control over a delegated piece of data, the server uses a callback mechanism to contact the client to which it has delegated the data and tell the client that the data can no longer be cached. In the absence of delegations, NFSv4 reverts to caching data, similarly to the way it was cached in NFSv3, by having the client periodically check for file change with the server.

Table 11.3 Unified namespace.

Mount Point	Volume	Exported?
/	disk1	Y
/usr	disk2	N
/usr/ports	disk3	Y

Namespace

A problem users encounter when browsing a server's filesystem under version 2 or 3 of NFS is reaching a dead end in the directory hierarchy caused by having to cross a mount point. On a simple server, all the underlying filesystems might be exported to all clients, but exporting to all clients would be an unusual case. More commonly, a subset of the filesystems are exported, such as those in Table 11.3, where there are two exported filesystems, **/** and **/usr/ports** bracketing one that is not exported. In previous versions of NFS, users that had changed their directory to the root would not be able to see **/usr/ports** from the root directory because the /usr volume was not exported, leaving a hole in the directory hierarchy. NFSv4 servers maintain a complete hierarchy of their exported filesystems filling in any holes with pseudo-filesystems that appear to the client as read-only exports.

Representing a unified namespace to the client requires the server to handle four operations differently from all others. The LOOKUP, GETATTR, GETFH, and SECINFO operations are the only client requests that are allowed to cross mount-points on the server. The function *nfsrvd_compound*(), which handles all COMPOUND RPCs for the server, checks to see if the operation is one of the four listed above and returns an error to the client if any other operation attempts to cross a mount point. It is by allowing these four operations to cross mount points that the client and server can present a unified filesystem hierarchy to the user.

Attributes

Version 3 of the NFS protocol contained limited support for file attributes. Attributes are metadata that are associated with a file, such as its size, and the times at which it was created, modified, and accessed. The original 13 file attributes that were available in NFSv3 proved to be insufficient for more modern filesystems that store more metadata. Information such as whether the file has been recently archived or the maximum supported file size, only some of which may be supported by a filesystem, are handled as attributes within NFSv4.

Clients have the ability to request attributes on an operation-by-operation basis, which means that the client can be highly specific about what it wants to know about the server or any object stored on it. The attributes that the server supports are themselves communicated as an attribute between the server and the client. The OPEN operation only asks for 2 attributes, the most recent modification time of the file and a server-generated change value that is used by the client to determine if the file or any of its associated metadata have been changed. The attribute is generated by the server, stored by the client, and used periodically after a successful OPEN call to make sure that the file has not changed on the server. A file can change when it is opened by multiple writers or when a user local to the server modifies the file directly. The ACCESS operation, which determines if the user can access an object, asks for 16 different attributes, including the file's owner and group, the file's mode, and the largest read request that the server will support. Unlike previous versions of NFS, the owner and group for a filesystem object are not a numeric user id and group id. Rather, they are strings that encode the user and domain name of the system, for example, gnn@FreeBSD.org.

The RFC defines three groups of attributes for version 4 of NFS. Required attributes are those pieces of metadata that every server must provide and every client must be able to handle. Examples of required attributes are file size, file type, and whether the server supports links. Recommended attributes are those that the authors of the RFC felt would be best for servers to support but are not strictly necessary. An example of a recommended attribute is an access-control list. The next subsection discusses recommended attributes such as whether a file should be considered as hidden by the Windows operating system, the maximum size of files, links and names supported by the server, and many others. The NFSv4 RFC includes 43 recommended attributes.

A goal for the NFSv4 protocol is extensibility, which includes being able to extend the set of attributes that can be associated with a filesystem object. Named attributes make extensibility of the attribute system in the field possible. A named attribute can be thought of as a key/value pair, where both the key and value are uninterpreted strings that can be associated with any filesystem object. The implementation of named attributes is dependent on the server, but the most common implementation creates a directory of named attributes. This attribute directory is sometimes referred to as a ***fork file***. Each attribute appears as a file in this attribute directory. Each attribute file can be opened, read, and written to modify the named attribute. Named attributes are not supported by the FreeBSD 10 NFSv4 server.

Clients request attributes by using the GETATTR operation that is encoded into a COMPOUND RPC, with other operations such as ACCESS and OPEN. Unlike previous versions of NFS, attributes are not sent in a fixed-size structure. They are requested when the client sets specific bits in a bit array. The implementation of NFSv4 in FreeBSD uses a set of macros to simplify handling the bits in the attribute array. The server replies to each GETATTR query from the client using the same 64-bit-wide array to indicate to the client which of the requested attributes are present. A single routine, *nfsv4_fillattr*(), does all the work of encoding attributes on the server. Centralizing the handling of attributes makes the code easier to manage and update. Clients can also set attributes on filesystem objects on the server by using the SETATTR operation. An example of setting an attribute is changing the access control list on an object, as discussed in the next subsection.

Access Control Lists

Although it is possible to use UNIX-style users, groups, and mode bits to control access to a set of files, such a system is limited in several ways. The first limitation is that there are clients such as Windows that do not understand UNIX user and group IDs, or UNIX mode bits. The second, and more important, limitation is that users and groups do not scale well in a heterogeneous environment. If two different departments both allocate user and group numbers independently, there is a high likelihood of a collision should these users and groups ever attempt to share a single filesystem. Forcing one set of users to change their user and group IDs can be a daunting task if there are many files that need to have their user and group IDs changed. Finally, the traditional UNIX model is often too coarse grained for large organizations that have multiple layers of security. For these reasons NFSv4 has added support for ***Access Control Lists*** (***ACL***s) to the protocol.

An ACL can express a specific set of permissions on any object in the filesystem, including files, directories, and links. Several filesystems present in FreeBSD including UFS and ZFS have built-in support for ACLs. For information on how ACLs are represented in a filesystem, see Section 5.7. ACLs in NFSv4 are a way of communicating the ACLs present in the filesystem over the network. The structures for ACLs are shared between NFSv4 and the on-disk filesystems ZFS and UFS. ACLs are contained in attributes, which is why setting or retrieving an ACL is done with the SETATTR and GETATTR operations rather than with a dedicated set of operations just for ACLs. Several operations can handle ACLs including: OPEN, CREATE, SETATTR, and GETATTR.

Caching, Delegation, and Callbacks

One way to improve the performance of a distributed system is to cache as much data and do as many operations at the client as possible. There are three caching scenarios in a distributed filesystem:

1. A file is being read by one or more clients. The file can be cached at all the clients at the same time as long as there are no updates to the file's data, and only minor changes to its metadata, such as changes to its time of last access.
2. A file is being written by a single client. The client that is writing the file may cache writes locally so that updates to the file are batched before being sent to the server, thereby improving write performance.
3. A file is being both read and written simultaneously on several clients and, therefore, cannot be cached at any of the clients but must be updated and accessed only on the server.

To properly handle all three of these scenarios and the inevitable transitions between them, NFSv4 provides clients with the ability to work with files locally through a mechanism called ***delegation***. NFSv4 maintains control over delegated files via a series of callbacks from the server to the client. Caching and delegation are intimately related with normal file operations. This section illustrates these

2

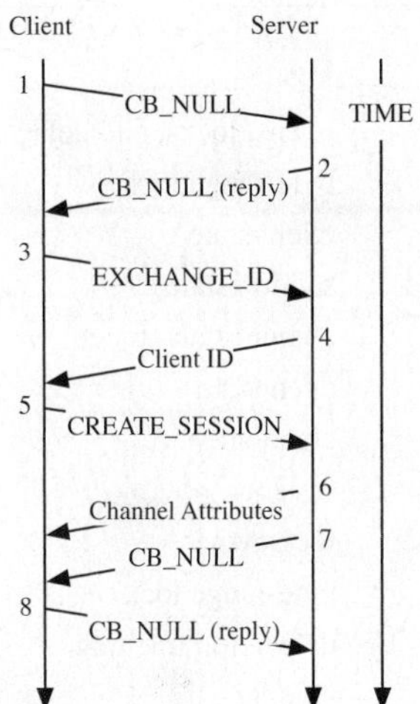

Figure 11.4 Mounting an NFSv4 Filesystem. Step 1: Client looks for the server with a CB_NULL RPC. Step 2: The Server replies to the CB_NULL. Step 3: Client requests a client ID from the server with an EXCHANGE_ID call. Step 4: The Server replies with a valid client ID constructed from their server's boot time and an incrementing boot count. Step 5: Client establishes a session with a CREATE_SESSION RPC. Step 6: The Server returns a set of communication parameters to the client establishing the session. Step 7: The Server checks to see whether the client is running the **nfscbd** daemon with its own CB_NULL call. Step 8: The client's **nfscbd** daemon replies to the CB_NULL RPC.

mechanisms by describing how the client and server establish communication and how they work together during the typical operation where clients are opening, closing, reading, and writing files.

Before a client can open a file, it must first mount the filesystem exported by the server, at which time several key structures are created. An NFSv4 client begins the mounting process by testing to see if the server exists using a CB_NULL message. If the client receives a correct reply, it then establishes a session with the server. Mounting an NFSv4 filesystem requires the creation of two persistent pieces of information shared by the client and the server. A ***client ID*** is created to identify the client and a ***session ID*** identifies all operations between the client and the server. The client ID is a unique 64-bit value that identifies each client from the server's perspective. The client establishes its identity with the server by using an EXCHANGE_ID operation. The EXCHANGE_ID operation is the first of a two-part operation that establishes the identity of the client on the server. The *exchange_id*() service executing in the server's kernel allocates an *nfsclient* structure that tracks all the client's interactions with the server. The *nfsclient* structure is retained until either the client unmounts all the filesystems that it has mounted from the server or the server or client crash. The process of mounting a filesystem is shown in Figure 11.4.

Table 11.4 Client and server data structures.

Structure	Use	Owner
nfsstate	opens, locks, and delegations	Server
nfslock	byte-range lock	server
nfsclient	client state	Server
nfsdsession	session state	Server
nfsclowner	owner of an object	Client
nfsclopen	open state	Client
nfsclclient	client state	Client
nfsclsession	session	client
nfscllockowner	lock owner	Client
nfscllock	byte-range lock	Client
nfscldeleg	delegation tracking	Client
nfscllayout	layout	Client
nfscldevinfo	device information	Client

Structures in the FreeBSD NFS implementation are named such that they can be easily identified as belonging either to the client or the server code. All structures that are part of the client software have the letters "cl" embedded between "nfs" and the structure's descriptive name. Thus, the structure that encapsulates the client's state in the client code is named *nfsclclient*, while the server structure that encapsulates the client's state is named *nfsclient*. Table 11.4 lists several of the client and server structures.

When the server is contacted by a client with an EXCHANGE_ID call, it searches its client hash list for a pre-existing instance of the client and if no pre-existing client is found, initializes a new *nfsclient* structure. Each client is assigned a unique client ID based on the boot time of the server and an incrementing counter. The combination of the boot time and the counter make client IDs unique across server reboots. This information is used by the client to detect when it must recover state from a crashed server. The boot time increases whenever the server is rebooted; a client that sends a request with an out-of-date client ID will receive an error from the server.

The second part of establishing initial communication between a client and server is the creation of a ***session***. The next operation after the EXCHANGE_ID must be a CREATE_SESSION as no other operations can take place until a session has been created. All operations in NFSv4, other than the establishment of the client ID, occur as part of a session.

The session concept was added during the update to NFSv4.1 and does not exist in version 4.0. One reason sessions were added was to provide ***exactly once semantics***. On the server side, each session has associated with it a set of available slots. Operations posted to a slot will always be serialized; they will never be run in parallel. If a client wants to serialize a set of calls, for example, a series of locking operations, it will use the same slot on the server for all the locking calls so that the RPC calls are serialized on that single slot. Operations that do not require serialization, such as reads, can be spread across the slots to increase parallelism and receive the fastest level of service from the server.

A session describes all the state necessary for the client and server to communicate, including several parameters that influence resource allocation and performance. The parameters negotiated as part of setting up a session include the maximum number of concurrent requests the session can carry at any one time, the maximum number of operations per request, and the maximum number of replies that the server can cache. Fine-grained performance tuning can be

Figure 11.5 Session and client structure (server side).

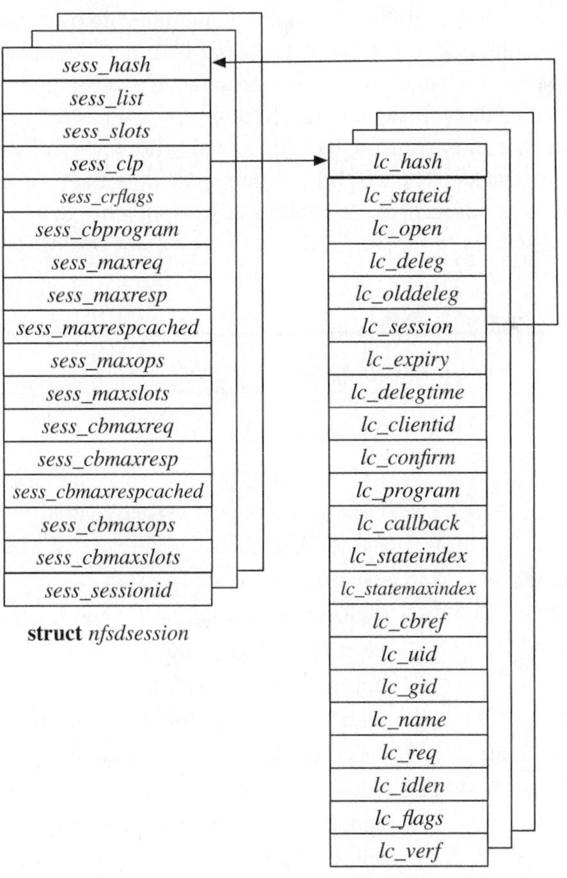

implemented using the session parameters, as they allow the server to express what it can handle in terms of parallelism and the amount of state it is willing to maintain on behalf of each client. To create a session, the client sends its client ID to the server along with its set of requested communications parameters. The server responds with a session ID and a possibly modified set of communications parameters. If the parameters are unacceptable to either the client or the server, then an error is returned and the session is not created. Once the client and server have created a session, the structures shown in Figure 11.5 are in place. The session structure on both the client and the server contain the negotiated communication parameters for use by the kernel when filesystem operations are executed. To complete the mounting process the server sends a CB_NULL RPC to the client and waits for a reply. If the server receives a reply to its CB_NULL call, it can then allow the client to cache data through the delegation process. If there is no reply to the CB_NULL RPC then the server will never grant a delegation to the client but will allow the client to receive file services. The callback mechanism is not used to test the network path between the client and server, as the client and server have already demonstrated their ability to properly communicate over the network. The server sends the call back to the client to ensure that the client is running the call back service, which is what allows the server to recall a delegation.

The need to handle callbacks in the NFSv4 protocol has led to the creation of a new daemon that must run on the client and whose job it is to receive and respond to the callbacks. The **nfscbd** program is an optional daemon that must be run if the client is to receive delegations. It is **nfscbd** that responds to the CB_NULL RPCs sent by the server, and to which all CB_COMPOUND RPCs will be

Table 11.5 NFS Version 4.1 callback operations from server to client.

Operation	Action
CB_GETATTR	get attributes
CB_SEQUENCE	backchannel sequencing and control
CB_RECALL	recall a delegation
CB_LAYOUTRECALL	recall a layout
CB_RECALL_ANY	notify client of aging delegations
CB_RECALL_SLOT	decrease number of available slots
CB_NOTIFY	directory change notification
CB_PUSH_DELEG	offer previously requested delegation
CB_WANTS_CANCELED	cancel pending delegation requests
CB_RECALLABLE_OBJ_AVAIL	inform client previously denied requests may now be granted
CB_NOTIFY_LOCK	notify client of lock availability
CB_NOTIFY_DEVICEID	tell client device id changed

sent. The full complement of callback operations is given in Table 11.5. The daemon itself is simple; like the NFS daemons described in Section 11.2, it is implemented by a set of kernel libraries that register a callback, *nfscb_program*(), with the kernel RPC service. The *nfscb_program*() interprets the CB_COMPOUND or CB_NULL RPC that it receives and takes the appropriate action. While it would be possible to add the callback functionality directly into the **nfsd** program, it is cleaner and simpler to place it in its own daemon.

Once the client and state IDs and client and session structures are set up, the client can ask for services from the server.

NFSv4 uses delegations combined with a system of callbacks to provide clients the ability to cache both data and metadata. Figure 11.6 shows a typical delegation and recall scenario. A delegation is a recallable right granted by the server to the client that allows the client to perform operations locally for a fixed

Figure 11.6 Delegating and recalling delegations. Step 1: Client A opens file **foo.txt** and wishes to cache it locally. Step 2: The server replies to the OPEN and includes an OPEN_DELEGATE_WRITE delegation type. Step 3: Client B asks the server for **foo.txt**, the same file that client A asked for in Step 1. Step 4: The server informs client A, via a CB_COMPOUND callback, that it must return the delegation for **foo.txt**. Step 5: Client A flushes any of its pending changes to **foo.txt** and returns the delegation by sending a DELEG_RETURN message to the server. Step 6: The server finishes the open and grants a file handle for **foo.txt** to client B with a delegation type of DELEGATE_NONE.

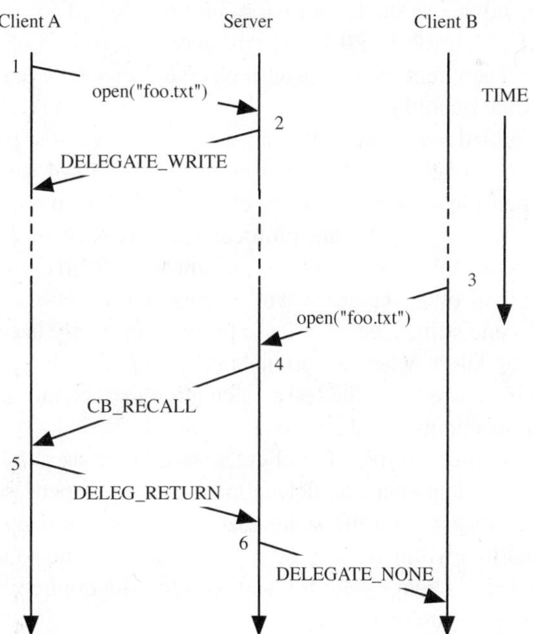

but extendable period of time without consulting the server. Delegations are always under the control of the server and may be revoked at any time. There are two important problems that NFSv4 has to handle with respect to delegations. The first is that the server must be able to revoke a delegation. Revoking a delegation requires the server to contact the client, which reverses the normal client-server relationship seen in previous versions of NFS. The second problem is that the client or server may crash or they may be unable to communicate for some period of time because of a network partition. If the server is unable to retrieve a delegation from a client, then it cannot allow other clients to proceed with operations on the same file. To prevent files from being caught in this deadlock situation, the server only allows the client to use a delegation for a fixed period of time, which is called a lease.

A lease is a piece of data that acts as a contract between the client and server, permitting an activity that is valid until some expiration time. As long as a client holds a valid lease, it knows that the server will not violate the terms of the contract, for example, by handing out a conflicting lock to another client. The server maintains a single lease for each client and the lease covers all the state including delegations and locks that are granted to the client. When the client first contacts the server and establishes a session, it will ask for the lease time via a GETATTR request and the server will return the lease time, which by default is 120 seconds. The client must renew the lease before the lease period ends. A lease is only considered stale by the server if it is older than five times the lease duration. If the client fails to renew the lease, it must return all the delegations and locks that were previously granted by the server. Several common operations, including opening or locking files, will cause the lease time to be extended. The server will respond with an error of NFS4ERR_EXPIRED to any operation from a client whose client ID has expired. The client must contact the server before the lease has expired if it wants to continue to hold the lock.

Leases are issued using time intervals rather than absolute times to avoid the requirement of time-of-day clock synchronization. If NFSv4 used absolute times for its leases, then the server and all its clients would need to have their clocks synchronized, via an external time protocol such as NTP or PTP, so that they would all share the same concept of the current time [Mills, 1992; IEEE, 2008]. By using an interval time, the server and clients can all have completely unsynchronized clocks and still execute the lease protocol correctly because each system has the ability to know when a certain amount of time has passed. A small amount of slop is allowed into the lease calculation to account for differing clock speeds between the clients and the server.

The server attempts to maintain client state as long as possible and will not forcibly remove a client that has delegations or active opens so long as it has enough resources to maintain the state. Each server has a maximum number of active clients that it is willing to service, 1000 by default, and so long as this number is not exceeded, a client's state ID, and therefore its implied lease, can remain active on the server for up to a week.

Each session has only one lease expiration time associated with it and all operations that must operate under a lease, including locking and delegations, are constrained by the same timeout. Although there is a specific operation to renew a lease it is rarely used because any operation initiated by the client that contains a valid client ID extends the lease time. Operations that extend the lease include OPEN, CLOSE, READ, WRITE, LOCK, and several others. When a lease has almost expired, and no other operation has taken place that might extend it, the client will attempt to extend the lease using the RENEW operation. If the request to renew the lease is granted, then operations can continue as before, with the new lease expiration being another 120 seconds into the future. When the server denies the request, the client loses all its locks and share reservations that it had in place up to the point when it received the denial from the server.

Clients that open a file exclusively for reading where no client is attempting to write, may cache data from the opened file and may also repeatedly open the same file without contacting the server. If a server has delegated control of a file to a client and then another client attempts to open the file for writing, the server must invalidate the original delegation and the first client must return the delegation to the server before the second client can be given access to the file.

Locking

Previous versions of NFS did not include support for file or record locking as part of the protocol. Limited support for locking was provided in NFSv3 by an out-of-band protocol and an external daemon, the Network Lock Manager. NFSv4 distinguishes between two cases when dealing with locks: a byte-range lock and a lock on an entire file, which is referred to in the protocol as a share reservation. Whole-file locking is handled through the OPEN RPC. When a client opens a file it specifies the type of access that it wishes to have: read, write, or both. It also specifies the level of control it wishes to maintain over the entire file in the form of a set of *share deny* bits, as shown in Table 11.6. During on open file operation, the client

Table 11.6 Open share types.

Share Type	Purpose
OPENSHARE_ACCESS_READ	read access
OPENSHARE_ACCESS_WRITE	write access
OPENSHARE_ACCESS_BOTH	read and write access
OPENSHARE_DENY_NONE	no file lock
OPENSHARE_DENY_READ	read file lock
OPENSHARE_DENY_WRITE	write file lock
OPENSHARE_DENY_BOTH	both read and write file locks

can indicate that it needs exclusive control over read, write, or both operations. A client that does not need to lock a file in any way specifies a share deny of none.

The server maintains a global structure that is a hashed list of all locks relating to files. Whenever a file is opened, a new *nfslockfile* structure is allocated and added to the *nfslockhash* table whether the client is asking the server to lock the file or a byte range within it. An *nfslockfile* structure exists for all open files so that there is one common place to which the server can refer to check on or allocate locking state in the future.

Byte-range locks are acquired and released via a separate set of RPC calls: LOCK, LOCKU, and LOCKT, which respectively lock, unlock, and test for byte-range locks. A single, large, routine, *nfsrv_lockctrl*() is at the center of all byte-range-locking operations and is called by the server's *nfsrvd_lock*(), *nfsrvd_locku*(), and *nfsrvd_lockt*() routines, which map to the RPC operations listed above. File locking is handled via the *nfsrv_open*() routine as described earlier in this section. Prior to locking a byte range, the *nfsrv_lockctrl*() routine must first check to make sure that there are no conflicting delegations or conflicting locks. A conflicting delegation would exist only if another client had been granted a write delegation in the past. The write delegation must be recalled by the callback mechanism before the lock can be granted. Read delegations do not conflict with locks because the lock does not deny a client the ability to read data. The server locks a range of bytes within a file by adding an *nfslock* structure to the

Figure 11.7 NFSv4 locking data structures.

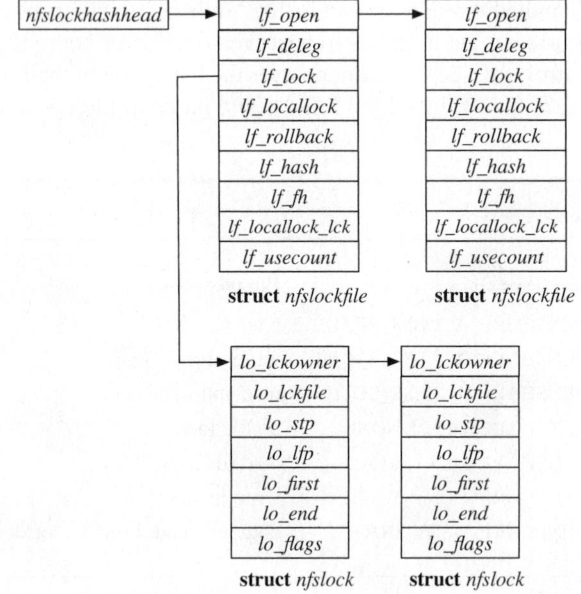

nfslockfile structure associated with the underlying file. When the client requests a byte-range lock, the server looks up the *nfslockfile* structure for the underlying file and searches the *lf_lock* list for any conflicting locks. If no conflicting lock is found, then a new *nfslock* structure is allocated and added to the list of locks for the file. The list of locks is kept in increasing order of byte range so that only a single pass over the list is necessary to find potential conflicts as well as the proper location to add or coalesce entries. All the actual changes to the file's locking state are handled by the *nfsrv_updatelock*() routine, which is responsible for adding and removing lock structures from the file's *lf_lock* list. Figure 11.7 shows an example containing two files, one of which has two byte-range locks. Acquiring a lock is considered a heavyweight operation in which much state may be passed between the client and the server. Reading and writing data, which should be the majority of the work of the protocol, should not be burdened with the state needed to maintain control of a lock.

Both share reservations and byte-range locks are acquired under the same lease that is used for delegations. The lease limits the time that the client can maintain a lock on a file or piece of a file without a renewal.

Security

Versions 2 and 3 of NFS had little support for security features. Since the original goal of the NFS protocol was to enable the sharing of files within a single workgroup, and certainly within a single organizational domain, it did not seem necessary to have heavyweight mechanisms for authenticating, encrypting, or validating data. Network filesystems are now deployed widely within companies and across more hostile environments, such as the Internet, so NFSv4 has integrated support for various levels of security directly into the protocol. There are three components that interact to provide security within NFSv4: an authentication system, a library that secures data within the RPC layer, and NFSv4 itself.

A system that wishes to provide a secure communication environment must have a way to authenticate participants such as users and hosts. Authentication is the process by which a participant, such as a user, proves to some other participant, such as a remote file server, that the participant is who it claims to be. NFSv4 relies on version 5 of the Kerberos Network Authentication Service to provide authentication between participants of the system [Neuman et al., 2005]. The Kerberos systems acts as a trusted third party that is used by both clients and servers to verify the truthfulness of various assertions that are made by participants in the system. A client wishing to communicate with a server using Kerberos must first contact a Kerberos authentication server to acquire the proper credentials, referred to in Kerberos as a ticket. A ticket has a limited lifetime to protect against a malicious entity gaining permanent access to the system. Using the ticket, the client can authenticate itself to the server and perform various cryptographic operations that allow the client and server to encrypt their data and communicate privately. Kerberos is a relatively complex network security protocol and will not be covered in further detail here. Interested readers are recommended to the RFC cited above for further information on the Kerberos protocol. For the purposes of our discussion within NFSv4 Kerberos should be thought of as the system that hands out, to both clients and servers, the keys to lock and unlock data transported over the network.

An authentication system is a necessary requirement to implement a secure network-based filesystem, but it does not really have any ability to secure or verify the data that is exchanged in the system. Securing data in NFSv4 is done using the RPCSEC_GSS protocol that depends on the Generic Security Service Application Program Interface (GSSAPI) [Eisler et al., 1997; Linn, 2000]. Three parameters describe the mechanism, service, and quality of protection that secures data between the client and the server. When taken together, these three parameters are referred to as the security-triple and each unique security triple is referred to as a flavor. There are three possible services that can be provided by the GSSAPI. The authentication service guarantees that a user or other entity wishing to gain access to a piece of data is the user or entity that they claim to be. NFSv4 uses Kerberos to authenticate users and systems, and so does not use the authentication service in GSS. The integrity service guarantees that the data has not been tampered with in transit but does not prevent an attacker from reading the data from the network while they are in transit between the client and server. The privacy service encrypts the data between the client and server so that an attacker cannot read the data while they are in transit. The actual encryption and decryption of data is done by the RPC libraries in the kernel and not by NFS directly, which has little or no direct knowledge of how data is secured.

The only situation in which NFSv4 deals directly with security, rather than relying on other protocols or libraries, is when a client needs to know the choice of security protocols that it can use with a server. An NFS client starts by assuming that there is only minimal security implemented on the server. At some point, perhaps as early as when a filesystem is mounted by the client, the server can respond with an NFS4ERR_WRONGSEC error, forcing the client to negotiate security parameters with the server. The client sends a SECINFO operation in response to the NFS4ERR_WRONGSEC message and receives back from the server a security flavor. If the security flavor is RPCSEC_GSS, then the reply to the SECINFO operation also contains a security triple, indicating the type of security and quality of security service that the server supports. Servers may return a list of security triples and the client picks the first one that it can support.

Data security in NFSv4 is available on a filesystem by filesystem basis, meaning that many different operations may fail with an NFS4ERR_WRONGSEC reply and necessitate the negotiation of security parameters.

Crash Recovery

A distributed system such as NFS must gracefully handle several common error conditions such that applications using the service can treat it as they would a local filesystem. Maintaining this illusion of consistency requires the protocol to have mechanisms that prevent recoverable or transient errors from permanently interrupting the service. While it should not be a common occurrence, the client or the server may crash, leading to an inconsistent state among the communicating systems. A more common problem is a network partition, where a client and server that were once able to communicate can no longer reach each other for some period of time. Network partitions may be brief, but if the state on the client and server get out of sync during the period when the client and server cannot communicate, then they must have a way to agree on a consistent state once the partition is repaired. From the point of view of both the client and server, it is impossible, without some help from the protocol, to determine whether a system has crashed or whether a temporary network partition has occurred. The NFSv4 protocol has mechanisms that handle regaining consistent state after a network partition or the failure of either the client or server system.

A client that has crashed and restarted would like to return to a correct running state as quickly as possible. Even though a client has crashed and restarted, the server continues to hold state for the client. Each client has an associated client ID. All state for the client is maintained at the server until the server restarts or the client dismounts all its mounted filesystems and destroys its session and client ID with explicit DESTROY_SESSION and DESTROY_CLIENTID RPC calls. Even if the client restarts within the lease period, it will still have to create a new client ID with the server via the EXCHANGE_ID mechanism described earlier in this section. Establishing a new client ID lets the server know that the client has restarted, at which point the server can invalidate and free all state associated with the previous incarnation of the client. After establishing a new client ID, the client can again use the NFS service.

Recovering from a server crash is a more complicated process than that required when a client restarts. When a server experiences a restart, it must take care to restore any locking state that existed prior to the system restarting. A client that attempts an operation with a server that has restarted will find that both its session and client IDs are invalid, and will have to establish new values for both before it can again use the service. A client that had locking state stored on the server must then go through a reclamation process to reacquire the locks that it previously held.

When a server restarts, it takes several steps to make sure that it is in a consistent state before it continues serving files to its clients. All NFSv4 servers record the time at which they were booted, in seconds since the epoch, and place that time into all client and state IDs. When a server is restarted, its boot time will have changed and any requests that contain a client or state ID from a previous incarnation of the server will receive an NFS4ERR_BAD_SESSION error, informing the client that it must reestablish itself with the server. During normal operation, the NFSv4 server makes a record of certain operations in a local file that recovers state after a server crash. The local state file includes a list of all the previous boot times of the server to guard against a collision in boot times. The server's boot time is used to construct client and state IDs and a collision could allow stale client or state IDs to go unnoticed, resulting in file corruption. Following the list of previous boot times is a set of variable-size entries containing client IDs and

Table 11.7 Open claims.

Claim	Purpose
NULL	normal open() by name
FH	normal open() via file handle
DELEGATE_CUR	open a file by name based on a delegation
DELEG_CUR_FH	open a file handle based on a delegation
PREVIOUS	reclaim open file by file handle
DELEG_PREV	recliam delegation by file name
DELEG_PREV_FH	reclaim delegation by file handle

flags. The flags indicate whether the client has active state associated with it or whether the state has been revoked.

When the server starts up, it sets a grace period of 15 seconds before it will grant new locks. During the grace period, clients are expected to reestablish any claims to state on the server, such as locks, via a reclamation process. The OPEN RPC contains a *claim* argument that shows whether the client is trying to reclaim state on the server. In normal operation, the claim argument is set to NULL, but when a client is forced to reestablish state with the server, its OPEN RPCs will contain a claim outlined in Table 11.7.

The client must also reclaim any locks that it had when the server restarted. A lock can be reclaimed by sending a LOCK RPC with the reclaim bit set. Once the client has completed the process of reclaiming all its state, it sends a RECLAIM_COMPLETE message to the server, at which point the server can discard the client's previous state records from its state file.

The local state file is created when the server is started via a call to the *nfsrv_setupstable*() routine. Any time the state file is written to by the server, it is also backed up via a call to *nfsrv_backupstable*() as an extra, paranoid measure to protect against the corruption of the state file during a system crash.

Exercises

11.1 Describe the functions done by an NFS client.

11.2 Describe the functions done by an NFS server.

11.3 Describe three benefits that NFSv3 derives from being stateless.

11.4 Name two new features added to version 4 of the NFS protocol.

11.5 Give two reasons why TCP is a better protocol to use than UDP for handling the NFS RPC protocol.

11.6 Describe the contents of a file handle in FreeBSD. How is a file handle used?

11.7 When is a new generation number assigned to a file? What purpose does the generation number serve?

11.8 Describe the three ways that an NFS client can handle filesystem-access attempts when its server crashes or otherwise becomes unreachable.

11.9 Give two reasons why leases are given a limited lifetime.

11.10 What is a callback? When is it used? Which daemon sends callbacks? Which daemon receives them?

11.11 What are the two types of locking that are supported in NFSv4?

11.12 Describe how an NFSv4 server recovers after a crash.

*11.13 Give a network time diagram that shows the process of a client acquiring a record lock within a file, writing data to the record, and releasing the lock.

**11.14 Assume that leases have an unlimited lifetime. Design a system for recovering the lease state after a client or server crash.

References

SNIA, 2002.
Storage Networking Industry Association SNIA, *Common Internet File System (CIFS) Technical Reference,* available from www.snia.org/tech_activities/CIFS/CIFS-TR-1p00_FINAL.pdf, March 2002.

Birrell & Nelson, 1984.
A. D. Birrell & B. J. Nelson, "Implementing Remote Procedure Calls," *ACM Transactions on Computer Systems*, vol. 2, no. 1, pp. 39–59, Association for Computing Machinery, February 1984.

Callaghan et al., 1995.
B. Callaghan, B. Pawlowski, & P. Staubach, "NFS: Network File System Version 3 Protocol Specification," RFC 1813, available from http://www.faqs.org/rfcs/rfc1813.html, June 1995.

Eisler et al., 1997.
M. Eisler, A. Chiu, & L. Ling, "RPCSEC_GSS Protocol Specification," RFC 2203, available from http://www.faqs.org/rfcs/rfc2203.html, September 1997.

Gray & Cheriton, 1989.
C. Gray & D. Cheriton, "Leases: An Efficient Fault-Tolerant Mechanism for Distributed File Cache Consistency," *Proceedings of the Twelfth Symposium on Operating Systems Principles*, pp. 202–210, December 1989.

Haynes & Noveck, 2014.
T. Haynes & D. Noveck, *NFS Version 4 Protocol (rfc3530bis Draft 33),*

available from https://datatracker.ietf.org/doc/draft-ietf-nfsv4-rfc3530bis/, April 2014.

Howard, 1988.
J. Howard, "An Overview of the Andrew File System," *USENIX Association Conference Proceedings*, pp. 23–26, January 1988.

Howard et al., 1988.
J. Howard, M. Kazar, S. Menees, D. Nichols, M. Satyanarayanan, R. Sidebotham, & M. West, "Scale and Performance in a Distributed File System," *ACM Transactions on Computer Systems*, vol. 6, no. 1, pp. 51–81, Association for Computing Machinery, February 1988.

IEEE, 2008.
IEEE, *1588-2008 - IEEE Standard for a Precision Clock Synchronization Protocol for Networked Measurement and Control Systems*, July 2008.

Juszczak, 1989.
C. Juszczak, "Improving the Performance and Correctness of an NFS Server," *USENIX Association Conference Proceedings*, pp. 53–63, January 1989.

Linn, 2000.
J. Linn, "Generic Security Service Application Program Interface Version 2, Update 1," RFC 2743, available from http://www.faqs.org/rfcs/rfc2743.html, January 2000.

Macklem, 1994a.
R. Macklem, "The 4.4BSD NFS Implementation," in *4.4BSD System Manager's Manual*, pp. 6:1–14, O'Reilly & Associates, Inc., Sebastopol, CA, 1994.

Macklem, 1994b.
R. Macklem, "Not Quite NFS, Soft Cache Consistency for NFS," *USENIX Association Conference Proceedings*, pp. 261–278, January 1994.

Mills, 1992.
D. L. Mills, "The NTP Time Synchronization Protocol," RFC 1305, available from http://www.faqs.org/rfcs/rfc1305.html, March 1992.

Mogul, 1993.
J. Mogul, "Recovery in Spritely NFS," Research Report 93/2, Digital Equipment Corporation Western Research Laboratory, Palo Alto, CA, June 1993.

Neuman et al., 2005.
C. Neuman, T. Yu, S. Hartman, & K. Raeburn, "The Kerberos Network Authentication Service (V5)," RFC 4120, available from http://www.faqs.org/rfcs/rfc4120.html, July 2005.

Pawlowski et al., 1994.
B. Pawlowski, C. Juszczak, P. Staubach, C. Smith, D. Lebel, & D. Hitz, "NFS Version 3: Design and Implementation," *USENIX Association Conference Proceedings*, pp. 137–151, June 1994.

Reid, 1987.
Irving Reid, "RPCC: A Stub Compiler for Sun RPC," *USENIX Association Conference Proceedings*, pp. 357–366, June 1987.

Sandberg et al., 1985.
R. Sandberg, D. Goldberg, S. Kleiman, D. Walsh, & B. Lyon, "Design and Implementation of the Sun Network Filesystem," *USENIX Association Conference Proceedings*, pp. 119–130, June 1985.

Shepler et al., 2003.
S. Shepler, B. Callaghan, D. Robinson, R. Thurlow, C. Beame, M. Eisler, & D. Noveck, "Network File System (NFS) version 4 Protocol," RFC 3530, available from http://www.faqs.org/rfcs/rfc3530.html, April 2003.

Shepler et al., 2010.
S. Shepler, M. Eisler, & D. Noveck, *Network File System (NFS) Version 4 Minor Version 1 Protocol,* available from http://www.ietf.org/rfc/rfc5661.txt, January 2010.

Sun Microsystems, 1989.
Sun Microsystems, "NFS: Network File System Protocol Specification," RFC 1094, available from http://www.faqs.org/rfcs/rfc1094.html, March 1989.

Walsh et al., 1985.
D. Walsh, B. Lyon, G. Sager, J. Chang, D. Goldberg, S. Kleiman, T. Lyon, R. Sandberg, & P. Weiss, "Overview of the Sun Network File System," *USENIX Association Conference Proceedings*, pp. 117–124, January 1985.

PART IV

Interprocess Communication

CHAPTER 12

Interprocess Communication

FreeBSD provides a rich set of interprocess-communication facilities intended to support the construction of ***distributed programs*** built on top of communications primitives. Support for these facilities is described in this chapter.

No one mechanism can provide for all types of interprocess communication. The subsystems that provide IPC in FreeBSD 10 can be broken down into two areas. The first provides for IPC on a single system and includes support for ***semaphores***, ***message queues***, and ***shared memory***. These subsystems were described in Section 7.2. The second is the socket interface, which provides a uniform communication API for network communication.

The socket API is deeply entwined with the network subsystem. The overall architecture of the network system is described in this chapter and is then referenced and refined in Chapters 13 and 14, which describe the implementation of network layer and transport layer protocols respectively. You will find it easiest to understand the material in the following two chapters if you read this chapter first.

12.1 Interprocess-Communication Model

There were several goals in the design of the interprocess-communication enhancements to UNIX. The most immediate need was to provide access to communication networks such as the Internet [Cerf, 1978]. Previous work in providing network access had focused on the implementation of the network protocols, exporting the transport facilities to applications via special-purpose—and often awkward—interfaces [Cohen, 1977; Gurwitz, 1981]. As a result, each new network implementation resulted in a different application interface, requiring most existing programs to be altered significantly or rewritten completely. For 4.2BSD, the interprocess-communication facilities were intended to provide a sufficiently general interface to allow network-based applications to be constructed independently of the underlying communication facilities.

The second goal was to allow multiprocess programs, such as distributed databases, to be implemented. The UNIX ***pipe*** requires all communicating processes to be derived from a common parent process. The use of pipes forced systems to be designed with a somewhat contorted structure. New communication facilities were needed to support communication between unrelated processes residing locally on a single host computer and residing remotely on multiple host machines.

Finally, it became important to provide new communication facilities to allow construction of local-area network services, such as file servers. The intent was to provide facilities that could be used easily in supporting resource sharing in a distributed environment and not to build a distributed UNIX system.

The interprocess-communication facilities were designed to support the following:

- Transparency: Communication between processes should not depend on whether the processes are on the same machine.
- Efficiency: The applicability of any interprocess-communication facility is limited by the performance of the facility. A naive implementation of interprocess communication often results in a modular but inefficient implementation because most interprocess communication facilities, especially those related to networks, are broken down into many layers. At each layer boundary, the software must do some work, either adding information to a message or removing it. FreeBSD only introduces layers where they are absolutely necessary for the proper functioning of the system and does not introduce arbitrary and unnecessary layers.
- Compatibility: Existing naive processes should be usable in a distributed environment without change. A naive process is characterized as a process that does its work by reading from the standard input file and writing to the standard output file. A sophisticated process uses knowledge about the richer set of interfaces provided by the kernel to do its work. A major reason UNIX has been successful is the operating system's support for modularity by naive processes that act as byte-stream filters. Although sophisticated applications such as web servers and screen editors exist, they are far outnumbered by the collection of naive application programs.

While designing the interprocess-communication facilities, the developers identified the following requirements to support these goals, and they developed a unifying concept for each:

- The system must support communication networks that use different sets of protocols, different naming conventions, different hardware, and so on. The notion of a ***communication domain*** was defined for these reasons. A communication domain embodies the standard semantics of communication and naming. Different networks have different standards for naming communication endpoints, which may also vary in their properties. In one network, a name may be a fixed address for a communication endpoint, whereas in another it may be used to locate a process that can move between locations. The semantics of communication can include the cost associated with the reliable transport of data, the support for multicast transmissions, the ability to pass access rights or capabilities, and so on.

- A unified abstraction for an endpoint of communication that can be manipulated with a file descriptor is needed. The ***socket*** is the abstract object from which messages are sent and received. Sockets are created within a communication domain, just as files are created within a filesystem. Unlike files, however, sockets exist only as long as they are referenced. Once the file descriptor that represents a socket is closed, and its reference count drops to zero, the socket is freed.

- The semantic aspects of communication must be made available to applications in a controlled and uniform way. Applications must be able to request different styles of communication, such as reliable byte stream or unreliable datagram, and these styles must be provided consistently across all communication domains. All sockets are typed according to their communication semantics. Types are defined by the semantic properties that a socket supports. These properties are:

  1. In-order delivery of data
  2. Unduplicated delivery of data
  3. Reliable delivery of data
  4. Connection-oriented communication
  5. Preservation of message boundaries
  6. Support for out-of-band messages

Pipes have the first four properties, but not the fifth or sixth. An out-of-band message is one that is delivered to the receiver outside the normal stream of incoming, in-band data and is usually associated with an urgent or exceptional condition. A connection is a mechanism that protocols use to avoid having to transmit the identity of the sending socket with each packet of data. Instead, the identity of each endpoint of communication is exchanged before transmission of any data and is maintained at each end so that it can be presented at any time. On the other hand, connectionless communications require a source and destination address associated with each transmission. A ***datagram socket*** provides unreliable, connectionless packet communication; a ***stream socket*** provides a reliable, connection-oriented byte stream that may support out-of-band data transmission; and a ***sequenced-packet socket*** provides a sequenced, reliable, unduplicated connection-based communication that preserves message boundaries. The socket API is extensible and other types of sockets can be and have been added to the system.

Processes must be able to locate endpoints of communication so that they can rendezvous without prior knowledge, so sockets can be named. A socket's name is meaningfully interpreted only within the context of the communication domain in which the socket is created. The names used by most applications are human-readable strings. However, the name for a socket that is used within a communication domain is usually a low-level address. Rather than placing name-to-address translation functions in the kernel, FreeBSD provides a userspace library for application programs to use in translating names to addresses.

Use of Sockets

Since the creation of the sockets API, several excellent books have been written about socket programming from the user's perspective [Stevens et al., 2003]. This section includes a brief description of a client and server program communicating over a reliable byte stream in the IPv4 communication domain. The client is described first and the server second. For more detailed information on writing network applications, please see the cited references.

A program that wants to use a socket creates it with the *socket* system call:

```
int sock = socket(AF_INET, SOCK_STREAM, 0);
```

The type of socket is selected according to the characteristic properties required by the application. In this example, reliable communication is required, so a stream socket (type = SOCK_STREAM) is selected. The *domain* parameter specifies the communication domain (or *address family*; see Section 12.4) in which the socket should be created, here the IPv4 Internet (domain = AF_INET). The final parameter, the *protocol*, can give a specific communication protocol for use in supporting the socket's operation. Protocols are specified by well-known (standard) constants specific to each communication domain. When zero is used, the system picks an appropriate protocol. The *socket* system call returns a file descriptor (a small integer; see Section 7.1) that is then used in all later socket operations.

After a socket has been created, the next step depends on the type of socket being used. Since this example is connection oriented, the sockets require a connection before being used. Creating a connection between two sockets usually requires that each socket have an address bound to it, which is simply a way of identifying each endpoint of the communication.

Applications may explicitly specify a socket's address or may permit the system to assign one. The address to be used with a socket must be given in a ***socket address structure***. The format of addresses can vary among domains; to permit a wide variety of different formats, the system treats addresses as variable-length byte arrays, which are prefixed with a length and a tag that identifies their format. Each domain has its own addressing format, which can always be mapped into the most generic one.

A connection is initiated with a *connect* system call:

```
int error, sock;
struct sockaddr_in rmtaddr;
int rmtaddrlen = sizeof(struct sockaddr_in);

error =
    connect(sock, (struct sockaddr *)&rmtaddr, rmtaddrlen);
```

When the connect call completes, the client has a fully functioning communication endpoint on which it can send and receive data.

A server follows a different path once it has created a socket. It must bind itself to an address and then accept incoming connections from clients. The call to bind an address to a socket is as follows:

```
int error, sock, addrlen = sizeof(struct sockaddr_in);
struct sockaddr_in addr;

error =
    bind(sock, (struct sockaddr*)&localaddr, localaddrlen);
```

where *sock* is the descriptor created by a previous call to *socket.*

For several reasons, binding a name to a socket was separated from creating a socket. First, sockets are potentially useful without names. If all sockets had to be named, users would be forced to devise meaningless names without reason. Second, in some communication domains, it may be necessary to supply additional information to the system before binding a name to a socket—for example, the "type of service" required when a socket is used. If a socket's name had to be specified at the time that the socket was created, supplying this information would not be possible without further complicating the interface.

In the *server process*, the socket must be marked to specify that incoming connections are to be accepted on it by using the *listen* system call:

```
int error, sock, backlog = 5;

error = listen(sock, backlog);
```

The *backlog* parameter used in the *listen* call specifies an upper bound on the number of pending connections that should be queued for acceptance. Having an upper bound on the listen queue is one way to prevent resource exhaustion in the kernel.

Connections are then received, one at a time, with the *accept* call:

```
int newsock, sock;
struct sockaddr_in clientaddr;
int clientaddrlen = sizeof(struct sockaddr_in);

newsock = accept(sock, (struct sockaddr *)&clientaddr,
            clientaddrlen);
```

Table 12.1 Sending and receiving data on a socket.

Routine	Connected	Flags	Address Info	Ancillary Data	Scatter Gather
read/write	Y	N	N	N	N
readv/writev	Y	N	N	N	Y
recv/send	Y	Y	N	N	N
recvfrom/sendto	Y	Y	Y	N	N
recvmsg/sendmsg	Y	Y	Y	Y	Y

The *accept* call returns a new connected socket, as well as the address of the client, by specifying the *clientaddr* and *clientaddrlen* parameters. The new socket is the one through which communication can take place. The original socket, *sock*, is used solely for managing the queue of connection requests in the server.

A variety of calls are available for sending and receiving data; these calls are summarized in Table 12.1. The richest of these interfaces are the *sendmsg* and *recvmsg* calls that can handle scatter-gather operations, specify an address on transmission and reception, supply optional flags, and handle specially interpreted ***ancillary data*** or control information. The message header structure that is used by *sendmsg* and *recvmsg* is shown in Figure 12.1. Ancillary data may include

Figure 12.1 Data structures for the *sendmsg* and *recvmsg* system calls.

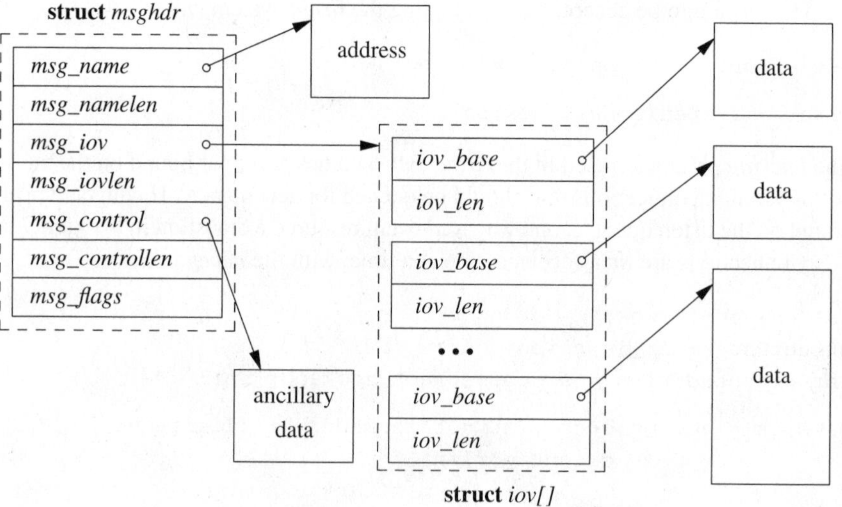

protocol-specific data, such as addressing or options, and also specially interpreted data, called access rights. Further details of the usage of the message header structure are given in Section 12.6.

In addition to these system calls, several other calls are provided to access miscellaneous services. The *getsockname* call returns the locally bound address of a socket, whereas the *getpeername* call returns the address of the socket at the remote end of a connection. The *shutdown* call terminates data transmission or reception at a socket, and two *ioctl*-style calls—*setsockopt* and *getsockopt*—can be used to set and retrieve various parameters that control the operation of a socket or of the underlying network protocols. Sockets are discarded with the normal *close* system call.

The interface to the interprocess-communication facilities was purposely designed to be orthogonal to the existing standard system interfaces—that is, to the *open*, *read*, and *write* system calls. This decision was made to avoid overloading the familiar interface with undue complexity. In addition, the developers thought that using an interface that was completely independent of the filesystem would improve the portability of software because, for example, pathnames would not be involved. Backward compatibility, for the sake of naive processes, was still deemed important. Thus, the familiar read–write interface was augmented to permit access to the new communication facilities wherever that made sense (e.g., when connected stream sockets were used).

12.2 Implementation Structure and Overview

The interprocess-communication facilities are layered on top of the networking facilities, as shown in Figure 12.2. Data flows from the application through the socket layer to the networking layer and vice versa. State required by the socket layer is fully encapsulated within it, whereas any protocol-related state is maintained in data structures that are specific to the supporting protocols. Responsibility for storage associated with transmitted data is passed from the socket layer to

Figure 12.2 Interprocess-communication implementation layering. The boxes on the left name the standard layers; the boxes on the right name specific examples of the layers that might be used by an individual socket.

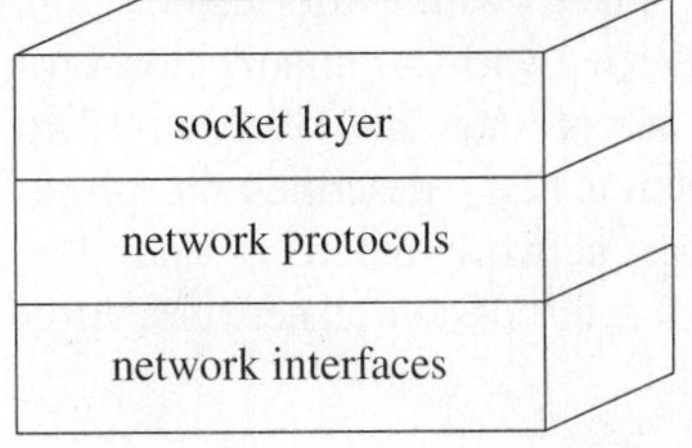

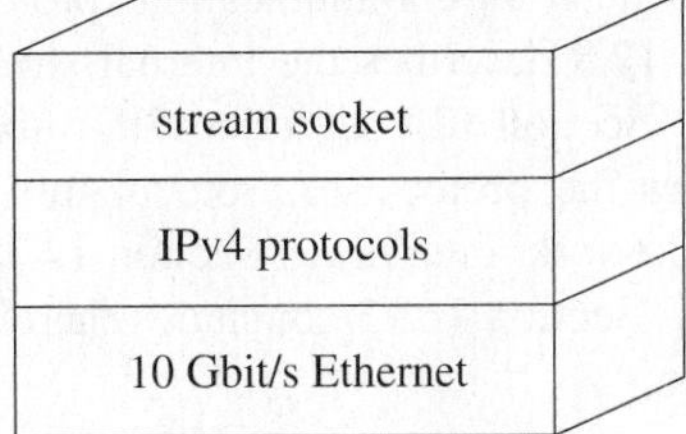

Table 12.2 Socket-layer support routines.

Routine	Function
socreate()	create a new socket
sobind()	bind a name to a socket
solisten()	mark a socket as listening for connection requests
soclose()	close a socket
soabort()	abort connection on a socket
soaccept()	accept a pending connection on a socket
soconnect()	initiate a connection to another socket
soconnect2()	create a connection between two sockets
sodisconnect()	initiate a disconnect on a connected socket
sosend()	send data
soreceive()	receive data
soshutdown()	shut down data transmission or reception
sosetopt()	set the value of a socket option
sogetopt()	get the value of a socket option

the network layer. Consistent adherence to this rule assists in simplifying details of storage management. Within the socket layer, the socket data structure is the focus of all activity. The system-call interface routines manage the actions related to a system call, collecting the system-call parameters (see Section 3.2) and converting user data into the format expected by the socket-layer routines. Most of the socket abstraction is implemented within the socket-layer routines. All socket-layer routines have names with a *so* prefix, and they directly manipulate socket data structures and manage the synchronization between asynchronous activities; these routines are listed in Table 12.2.

The remainder of this chapter focuses on the implementation of the socket layer. Section 12.3 discusses how memory is managed at the socket layer and below in the networking subsystem; Section 12.4 covers the socket and related data structures; Section 12.5 presents the algorithms for connection setup; Section 12.6 discusses data transfer; and Section 12.7 describes connection shutdown. Throughout these sections, references to the supporting facilities provided by the network-communication protocols are made with little elaboration. Section 12.8 describes the internal structure of the network-communication protocols. Section 12.9 describes the socket-to-protocol interface. Section 12.10 describes the protocol-to-protocol interface. Section 12.11 describes the protocol-to-network interface. Section 12.12 describes network buffering and flow control. Section 12.13 concludes the chapter with a discussion of network virtualization.

12.3 Memory Management

The requirements placed on a memory-management scheme by interprocess-communication and network protocols tend to be substantially different from those of other parts of the operating system. Although all require the efficient allocation and reclamation of memory, communication protocols in particular need memory in widely varying sizes. Memory is needed for variable-size structures such as communication protocol packets. Protocol implementations must frequently prepend headers or remove headers from packetized data. As packets are sent and received, buffered data may need to be divided into packets, and received packets may be combined into a single record. In addition, packets and other data objects must be queued when awaiting transmission or reception. A special-purpose memory-management facility exists for use by the interprocess-communication and networking systems to address these needs.

Mbufs

The memory-management facilities revolve around a data structure called an ***mbuf*** (see Figure 12.3). Mbufs, or memory buffers, vary in size depending on what they contain. All mbufs contain a fixed *m_hdr* structure that keeps track of various bits of bookkeeping about the mbuf. An mbuf that contains only data has space for 224 bytes (256 bytes total for the mbuf minus 32 bytes for the mbuf header). All structure sizes are calculated for 64-bit processors.

Figure 12.3 Memory-buffer (mbuf) data structure.

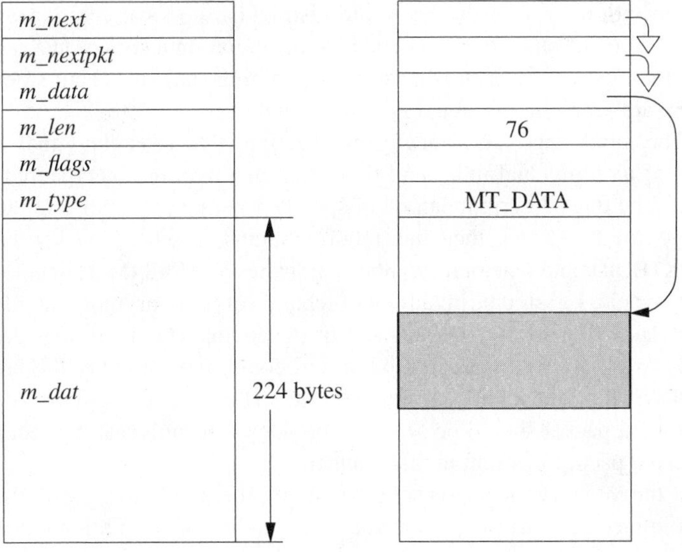

For large messages, the system can associate larger sections of data with an mbuf by referencing an external mbuf cluster from a private virtual memory area. The size of an mbuf cluster may vary by architecture, as specified by the macro MCLBYTES, and is 2 Kbyte on the X86.

Data are stored either in the internal data area or in an external cluster, but never in both. To access data in either location, a data pointer within the mbuf is used. In addition to the data-pointer field, a length field is also maintained. The length field shows the number of bytes of valid data to be found at the data-pointer location. The data and length fields allow routines to trim data efficiently at the start or end of an mbuf. In deletion of data at the start of an mbuf, the pointer is incremented and the length is decremented. To delete data from the end of an mbuf, the length is decremented, but the data pointer is left unchanged. When space is available within an mbuf, data can be added at either end. This flexibility to add and delete space without copying is particularly useful in communication-protocol implementation. Protocols routinely strip protocol information off the front or back of a message before the message's contents are handed to a higher-layer processing module, or they add protocol information as a message is passed to lower layers.

Multiple mbufs can be linked together to hold an arbitrary quantity of data. This linkage is done with the *m_next* field of the mbuf. By convention, a chain of mbufs linked through the *m_next* field is treated as a single object. For example, the communication protocols build packets from chains of mbufs. A second field, *m_nextpkt*, links objects built from chains of mbufs into lists of objects. Throughout our discussions, a collection of mbufs linked together with the *m_next* field will be called a chain; chains of mbufs linked together with the *m_nextpkt* field will be called a queue.

Each mbuf is typed according to its use. This type serves two purposes. The only operational use of the type is to distinguish optional components of a message in an mbuf chain that is queued for reception on a socket data queue. Otherwise, the type information is used in maintaining statistics about storage use and, if there are problems, as an aid in tracking mbufs.

The mbuf flags are logically divided into two sets: flags that describe the usage of an individual mbuf and those that describe an object stored in an mbuf chain. The flags describing an mbuf specify whether the mbuf references external storage (M_EXT), whether the mbuf contains a set of packet header fields (M_PKTHDR), and whether the mbuf completes a record (M_EOR). A packet normally would be stored in an mbuf chain (of one or more mbufs) with the M_PKTHDR flag set on the first mbuf of the chain. The mbuf flags describing the packet would be set in the first mbuf and could include either the broadcast flag (M_BCAST) or the multicast flag (M_MCAST). The latter flags specify that a transmitted packet should be sent as a broadcast or multicast, respectively, or that a received packet was sent in that manner.

If the M_PKTHDR flag is set on an mbuf, the mbuf has a second set of header fields immediately following the standard header. This addition causes the mbuf

Table 12.3 Important fields in (mbuf) data structure with M_PKTHDR.

Field	Description
rcvif	interface mbuf was received from
tags	list of tags for use by various networking subsystems
len	total packet length
flowid	packet ID: 4-tuple of source and destination network addresses and ports
csum_flags	checksum and offload features
fibnum	forwarding information base to use
rsstype	receive-side steering hash to steer packet to a queue
ether_vtag	ethernet VLAN tag
tso_segsz	TCP segmentation offload segment size
csum_data	packet checksum data

data area to shrink from 224 bytes to 168 bytes. The packet header shown in Table 12.3 is only used on the first mbuf of a chain. It includes several fields: a pointer to the interface on which the packet was received, the total length of the packet, a field relating to packet checksum calculation, and a pointer to a list of arbitrary tags.

An mbuf that uses external storage is marked with the M_EXT flag. Here, a different header area overlays the internal data area of an mbuf. The fields in this header, which is shown in Figure 12.4, describe the external storage, including the start of the buffer and its size. One field is designated to point to a routine to free the buffer, in theory allowing various types of buffers to be mapped by mbufs. In the current implementation, the free function is not used and the external storage is assumed to be a standard mbuf cluster. An mbuf may be both a packet header and have external storage. Here, the standard mbuf header is followed by the packet header and then the external storage header.

The ability to refer to mbuf clusters from an mbuf permits data to be referenced by different entities within the network code without a memory-to-memory copy operation. When multiple copies of a block of data are required, the same mbuf cluster is referenced from multiple mbufs. Since the mbuf headers are transient, the reference count for the clusters cannot be stored in the *m_ext* structure. Instead, the reference counts for clusters are managed as a separate array referenced from the mbufs that are sharing mbuf clusters. The array is large enough for every mbuf cluster that could be allocated by the system. The memory dedicated to mbufs and clusters is set based on the kernel parameter *maxusers*, which is itself based on the amount of physical memory in the system. Basing the amount of memory dedicated to the networking subsystem on the amount of physical memory gives a good default value but can be increased when a system is dedicated to networking tasks such as a Web server, firewall, or router.

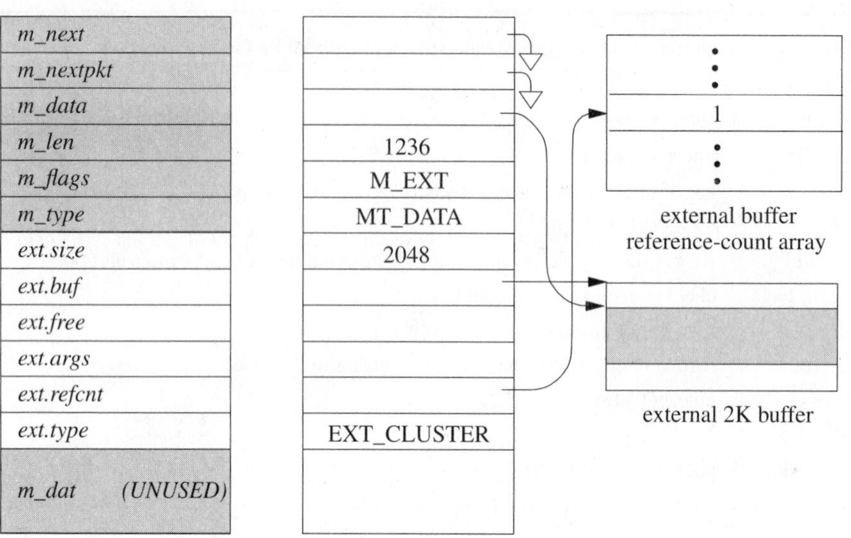

Figure 12.4 Memory-buffer (mbuf) data structure with external storage.

Mbufs have fixed-size, rather than variable-size, data areas for several reasons. First, the fixed size minimizes memory fragmentation. Second, communication protocols are frequently required to prepend or append headers to existing data areas, to split data areas, or to trim data from the beginning or end of a data area. The mbuf facilities are designed to handle such changes without reallocation or copying whenever possible.

Since the mbuf is the central object of all the networking subsystems, it has undergone changes with each large change in the code. It now contains a flags field and two optional sets of header fields. The data pointer replaces a field used as an offset in the initial version of the mbuf. The use of an offset was not portable when the data referenced could be in an mbuf cluster. The addition of a flags field allowed the use of a flag indicating external storage. Earlier versions tested the magnitude of the offset to see whether the data were in the internal mbuf data area. The addition of the broadcast flag allowed network-level protocols to know whether packets were received as link-level broadcasts, as was required for standards conformance. Several other flags have been added for use by specific protocols and to handle fragment processing.

The optional header fields have undergone the largest changes since 4.4BSD. The two headers were originally designed to avoid redundant calculations of the size of an object, to make it easier to identify the incoming network interface of a received packet, and to generalize the use of external storage by an mbuf. Since FreeBSD 5, the packet header has been expanded to include information on checksum calculation (a traditionally expensive operation that can now be done in hardware) as well as on the management of flows of packets, quality of service parameters, a receive-side scaling hash to steer packets to particular hardware queues, and an arbitrary set of ***tags***.

Tags are fixed-size structures that can point to arbitrary pieces of memory and are used to store information relevant to different modules within the networking subsystem. Each tag has a link to the next tag in the list, a 16-bit ID, a 16-bit length, and a 32-bit cookie and a module-defined type. The cookie identifies the module that owns the tag. The type is a piece of data that is private to the module that describes to the module the type of tag it is handling. Tags carry the information about a packet that should not be placed into the packet itself and they are often used as an extension mechanism for the networking subsystem. Instead of modifying the mbuf structures, and thereby losing binary compatibility between versions of FreeBSD, new networking modules can define their own tags as a way of communicating arbitrary out-of-band information between different components of the network stack. Examples of these tags are given in Section 13.7.

Storage-Management Algorithms

Providing the system with a network stack capable of multiprocessing required a complete rework of the memory-allocation algorithms underlying the mbuf code. Whereas previous versions of BSD allocated memory with the system allocator and then carved it up for mbufs and clusters, such a simple technique does not work when using multiple CPUs.

As is described in detail in Section 6.3, FreeBSD allocates virtual memory among a series of lists for use by the network memory allocation code. Each CPU has its own private container of mbufs and clusters. There is also a single, general pool of mbufs and clusters from which allocations are attempted when a per-CPU list is empty or to which memory is freed when a per-CPU list is full. A uniprocessor system acts as if it is a multiprocessor system with one CPU, which means that it has one per-CPU list as well as the general one.

Mbuf-allocation requests specify either that they must be fulfilled immediately or that they can wait for available resources. If a request is marked as "can wait" and the requested resources are unavailable, the process is put to sleep to await available resources. A nonblocking request will fail if no resources are available. Although a nonblocking allocation request is no longer necessary for code that executes at interrupt level, the networking code still operates assuming nonblocking is required. If mbuf allocation has reached its limit or memory is unavailable, the mbuf-allocation routines ask the network-protocol modules to give back any available resources that they can spare.

An mbuf-allocation request is made through a call to *m_get*(), *m_gethdr*(), or through an equivalent macro. An mbuf is retrieved from the currently running CPU's per-CPU list by the *mb_alloc*() function and is initialized. For *m_gethdr*(), the mbuf is initialized with the optional packet header. The MCLGET macro adds an mbuf cluster to an mbuf.

Release of mbuf resources is straightforward: *m_free*() frees a single mbuf and *m_freem*() frees a chain of mbufs. When an mbuf that references an mbuf cluster is freed, the reference count for the cluster is decremented. Mbuf clusters are placed onto the currently running CPU's per-CPU list when their reference counts reach zero.

Mbuf Utility Routines

Many useful utility routines exist for manipulating mbufs within the kernel networking subsystem. The *m_copym*() routine makes a copy of an mbuf chain starting at a logical offset, in bytes, from the start of the data. This routine may be used to copy all or only part of a chain of mbufs. If an mbuf is associated with an mbuf cluster, the copy will reference the same data by incrementing the reference count on the cluster. The *m_copydata*() function is similar, but it copies data from an mbuf chain into a caller-provided buffer. This buffer is not an mbuf, or chain, but an area of memory such as an I/O buffer elsewhere in the kernel.

The *m_adj*() routine adjusts the data in an mbuf chain by a specified number of bytes, removing data from either the front or back. No data are ever copied; *m_adj*() operates purely by manipulating the offset and length fields in the mbuf structures. The *mtod*() macro takes a pointer to an mbuf header and a data type, and returns a pointer to the data in the buffer, cast to the given type.

The *m_pullup*() routine rearranges an mbuf chain such that a specified number of bytes reside in a contiguous data area within the mbuf (not in external storage). This operation is used so that objects such as protocol headers are contiguous and can be treated as normal data structures. If there is room, *m_pullup*() will increase the size of the contiguous region up to the maximum size of a protocol header in an attempt to avoid being called in the future.

The *M_PREPEND*() macro adjusts an mbuf chain to prepend a specified number of bytes of data. If possible, space is made in place, but an additional mbuf may have to be allocated at the beginning of the chain. It is currently impossible to prepend data within an mbuf cluster because different mbufs might refer to data in different portions of the cluster.

12.4 IPC Data Structures

Sockets are the objects used by processes communicating over a network. A socket's type defines the basic set of communication semantics, whereas the communication domain defines auxiliary properties important to the use of the socket and may refine the set of available communication semantics. Table 12.4 shows the four types of sockets currently supported by the system. To create a new socket, applications must specify its type and the communication domain. The request may also indicate a specific network protocol to be used by the socket. If no protocol is specified, the system selects an appropriate protocol from the set of protocols supported by the communication domain. If the communication domain is unable to support the type of socket requested (i.e., no suitable protocol is available), the request will fail.

Sockets are described by a *socket* data structure that is dynamically created at the time of a *socket* system call. Communication domains are described by a ***domain*** data structure that is statically defined within the system based on the system's configuration (see Section 15.3). Communication protocols within a domain are described by a *protosw* structure that is also statically defined within the system for each protocol implementation configured. Having these structures

Table 12.4 Socket types supported by the system.

Name	Type	Properties
SOCK_STREAM	stream	reliable, sequenced data transfer; may support out-of-band data
SOCK_DGRAM	datagram	unreliable, unsequenced data transfer, with message boundaries preserved
SOCK_SEQPACKET	sequenced packet	reliable, sequenced data transfer, with message boundaries preserved
SOCK_RAW	raw	direct access to the underlying communication protocols

defined statically reduces communication startup time and reduces the complexity of the implementation because there is no need to support the dynamic addition and deletion of protocols or domains at run time.

When a request is made to create a socket, the system uses the value of the communication domain to search linearly the list of configured domains. If the domain is found, the domain's table of supported protocols is consulted for a protocol appropriate for the type of socket being created or for the specific protocol requested. A wildcard entry may exist for a raw socket. Should multiple protocol

Figure 12.5 Communication-domain data structure.

dom_family	AF_INET
dom_name	"internet"
dom_init	...
dom_destroy	...
dom_externalize	...
dom_dispose	...
dom_protosw	inetsw
dom_protoswNPROTOSW	*&inetsw[19]*
dom_next	0
dom_rtattach	in_inithead
dom_rtdttach	in_detachhead
dom_rtoffset	32
dom_maxrtkey	sizeof(struct sockaddr_in)
dom_ifattach	...
dom_ifdttach	...

entries satisfy the request, the first is selected. This section describes the domain structure. The *protosw* structure that lists a domain's supported protocols is discussed in Section 12.8.

The ***domain*** structure is shown in Figure 12.5. The *dom_name* field is the string that names the communication domain. The *dom_family* field identifies the ***address family*** used by the domain; some possible address-family values are shown in Table 12.5. Address families refer to the addressing structure of a domain. An address family generally has an associated ***protocol family***. Protocol families refer to the suite of communication protocols of a domain used to support the communication semantics of a socket. The *dom_protosw* field points to the table of functions that implement the protocols supported by the communication domain, and the *dom_protoswNPROTOSW* pointer marks the end of the table. The remaining entries contain pointers to domain-specific routines used in the management and transfer of access rights and fields relating to routing and network interface initialization for the domain.

The *socket* data structure is shown in Figure 12.6. Storage for the *socket* structure is allocated by the zone allocator (described in Section 6.3). Sockets contain information about their type, the supporting protocol in use, and their state. States are shown in Table 12.6. Data being transmitted or received are queued at the socket as a list of mbuf chains. Various fields are present for managing queues of sockets created during connection establishment. Each socket structure also holds a process-group identifier. The process-group identifier is used in delivering the SIGURG and SIGIO signals. SIGURG is sent when

Table 12.5 Address families.

Name	Description
AF_LOCAL	local communication
AF_UNIX	deprecated name for AF_LOCAL
AF_INET	Internet Version 4
AF_INET6	Internet Version 6
AF_IEE80211	IEEE 802.11 WiFi
AF_IPX	Novell Internetworking Packet Exchange
AF_ATM	Asynchronous Transfer Mode
AF_KEY	IPSec Key Management
AF_ISO	OSI network protocols
AF_CCITT	CCITT protocols, e.g., X.25
AF_SNA	IBM System Network Architecture (SNA)
AF_DLI	direct link interface
AF_APPLETALK	AppleTalk network
AF_ROUTE	communication with kernel routing layer
AF_LINK	raw link-layer access

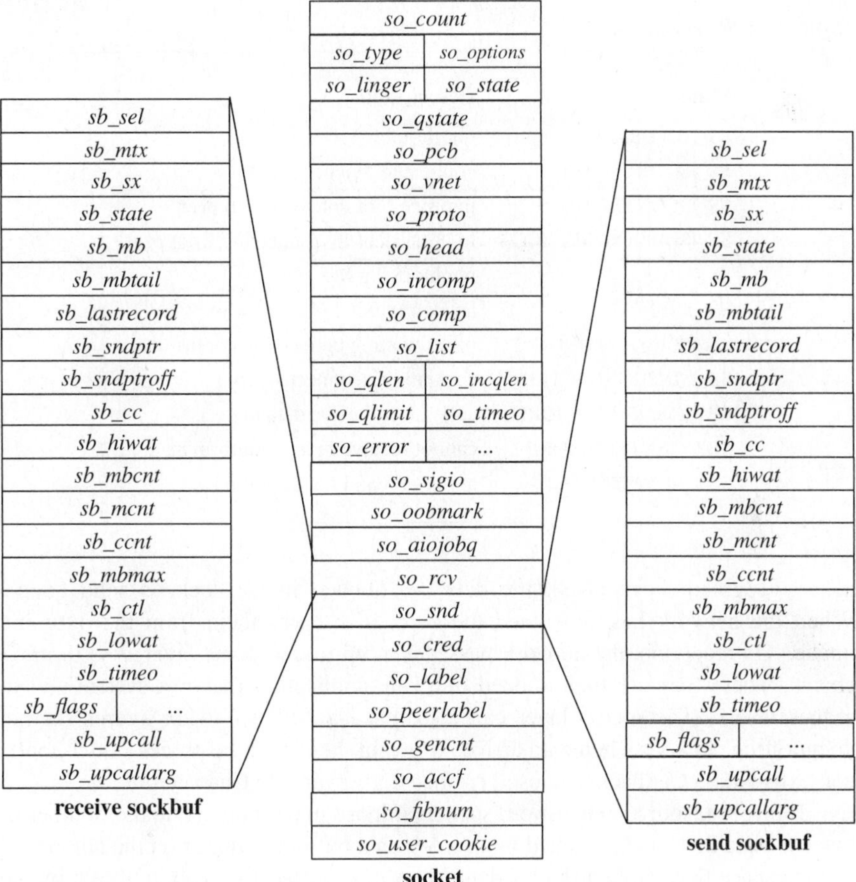

Figure 12.6 Socket data structure.

an urgent condition exists for a socket, and SIGIO is used by the asynchronous I/O facility (see Section 7.1). The socket contains an error field, which is needed for storing asynchronous errors to be reported to the owner of the socket.

Sockets are located using a process's file descriptor via a file entry. When a socket is created, the *f_data* field of the file structure is set to point at the socket structure, and the *f_ops* field is set to point to the set of routines defining socket-specific file operations. Here, the socket structure is a direct parallel of the ***vnode*** structure used by the filesystems.

The socket structure acts as a queueing point for data being transmitted and received. As data enter the system as a result of system calls, such as *write* or *send*, the socket layer passes the data to the networking subsystem as a chain of mbufs for transmission. If the supporting protocol module decides to postpone transmission of the data, or if a copy of the data are to be maintained until an

Table 12.6 Socket states.

State	Description
SS_NOFDREF	no file-table reference
SS_ISCONNECTED	connected to a peer
SS_ISCONNECTING	in process of connecting to peer
SS_ISDISCONNECTING	in process of disconnecting from peer
SS_NBIO	nonblocking I/O
SS_ASYNC	asynchronous I/O notification
SS_ISCONFIRMING	peer awaiting connection confirmation
SS_ISDISCONNECTED	socket is disconnected from peer
SBS_CANTSENDMORE	cannot send more data to peer
SBS_CANTRCVMORE	cannot receive more data from peer
SBS_RCVATMARK	at out-of-band mark on input

acknowledgment is received, the data are queued in the socket's send queue. When the network has consumed the data, it discards them from the outgoing queue. On reception, the network passes data up to the socket layer, also in mbuf chains, where they are then queued until the application makes a system call to request them. The socket layer can also make a *callback* to an internal kernel client of the network when data arrive, allowing the data to be processed without a context switch. Callbacks are used by the NFS server (see Chapter 11).

To avoid resource exhaustion, sockets impose upper bounds on the number of bytes of data that can be queued in a socket data buffer as well as on the amount of storage space that can be used for data. This ***high watermark*** is initially set by the protocol, although an application can change the value up to a system maximum. The network protocols can examine the high watermark and use the value in flow-control policies. A ***low watermark*** also is present in each socket data buffer. The low watermark allows applications to control data flow by specifying a minimum number of bytes required to satisfy a reception request, with a default of 1 byte and a maximum of the high watermark. For output, the low watermark sets the minimum amount of space available before transmission can be attempted; the default is the size of an mbuf cluster. These values also control the operation of the *select* system call when it is used to test for ability to read or write the socket.

When connection indications are received at the communication-protocol level, the connection may require further processing to complete. Depending on the protocol, that processing may be done before the connection is returned to the listening process, or the listening process may be allowed to confirm or reject the connection request. Sockets used to accept incoming connection requests maintain two associated queues of sockets. The list of sockets headed by the *so_incomp* field represents a queue of connections that must be completed at the protocol level before being returned. The *so_comp* field heads a list of sockets that are ready to be returned to the listening process. Like the data queues, the queues of connections also have an application-controllable limit. The limit applies to both queues. Because the limit may include sockets that cannot yet be accepted, the system enforces a limit 50 percent larger than the nominal limit.

Although a connection may be established by the network protocol, the application may choose not to accept the established connection or may close down the connection immediately after discovering the identity of the client. A network protocol may delay completion of a connection until after the application has obtained control with the *accept* system call. The application might then accept or reject the connection explicitly with a protocol-specific mechanism. Otherwise, if the application does a data transfer, the connection is confirmed; if the application closes the socket immediately, the connection is rejected.

Socket Addresses

Sockets may be labelled so that peers can connect to them. The socket layer treats an address as an opaque object. Applications supply and receive addresses as tagged, variable-length arrays of bytes. Addresses are placed in mbufs within the socket layer. A structure called a *sockaddr*, shown in Figure 12.7, is used as a template for referring to the identifying tag and length of each address. Most protocol layers support a single address type as identified by the tag, known as the address family.

It is common for addresses passed in by an application to reside in mbufs only long enough for the socket layer to pass them to the supporting protocol for transfer into a fixed-size address structure—for example, when a protocol records an address in a protocol control block. The *sockaddr* structure is the common means by which the socket layer and network-support facilities exchange addresses. The size of the generic data array was chosen to be large enough to hold many types of addresses directly, although generic code cannot depend on having sufficient space in a *sockaddr* structure for an arbitrary address. For example, the local communication domain (formerly known as the UNIX domain) stores filesystem pathnames in mbufs and allows socket names as large as 104 bytes, as shown in Figure 12.8. Both IPv4 and IPv6 use a fixed-size structure that combines a network address and a port number. The difference is in the size of the address (4 bytes for IPv4 and 16 bytes for IPv6) and in the fact that IPv6 address structures carry other information including the scope and flow information. Both Internet protocols reserve space for addresses in a protocol-specific control-block data structure and free up mbufs that contain addresses after copying the addresses.

Figure 12.7 Socket-address template structure.

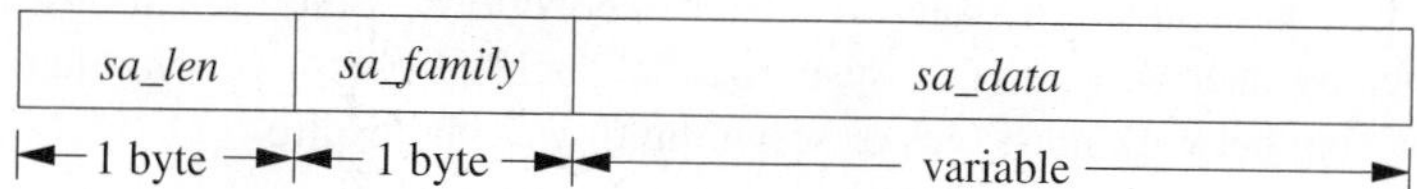

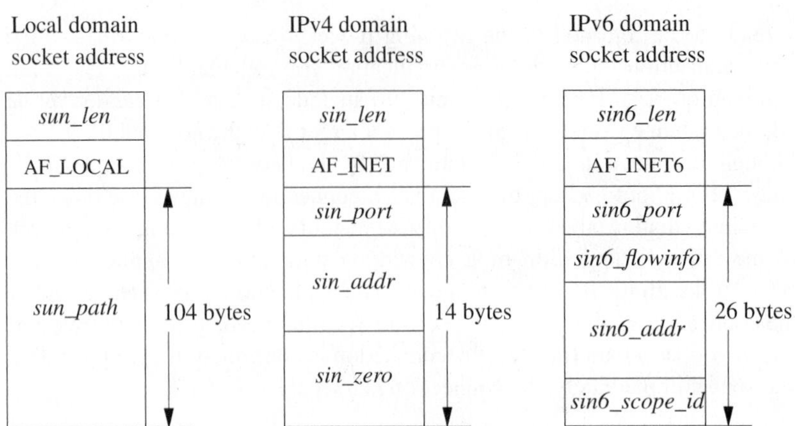

Figure 12.8 Local-domain, IPv4, and IPv6 address structures.

Locks

Section 4.3 discussed the need for locking structures in a multiprocessing kernel. The networking subsystem uses these locks internally to protect its data structures.

When multiprocessing features were first introduced, the entire networking subsystem was placed, with the rest of the kernel, under the giant lock. During the development of FreeBSD 5, several pieces of networking code were modified to run without the giant lock. As of FreeBSD 10, all parts of the networking system are locked using fine-grained locks and never resort to using the giant lock. Specific instances of networking-subsystem locks are discussed in the section in which they are most relevant.

12.5 Connection Setup

For two processes to pass information between them, an ***association*** must be established. The steps involved in creating an association (*socket*, *connect*, *listen*, *accept*, etc.) were described in Section 12.1. This section describes the operation of the socket layer in establishing associations. Since the state associated with a connectionless transfer of data is fully encapsulated in each message that is sent, our discussion will focus on connection-oriented associations established with the *connect*, *listen*, and *accept* system calls.

Connection establishment in the client–server model is asymmetric. A client actively initiates a connection to obtain service, whereas a server passively accepts connections to provide service. Figure 12.9 shows the state-transition diagram used by a socket to initiate or accept connections. State transitions are initiated either by user actions (i.e., system calls) or by protocol actions that result from receiving network messages or servicing timers that expire.

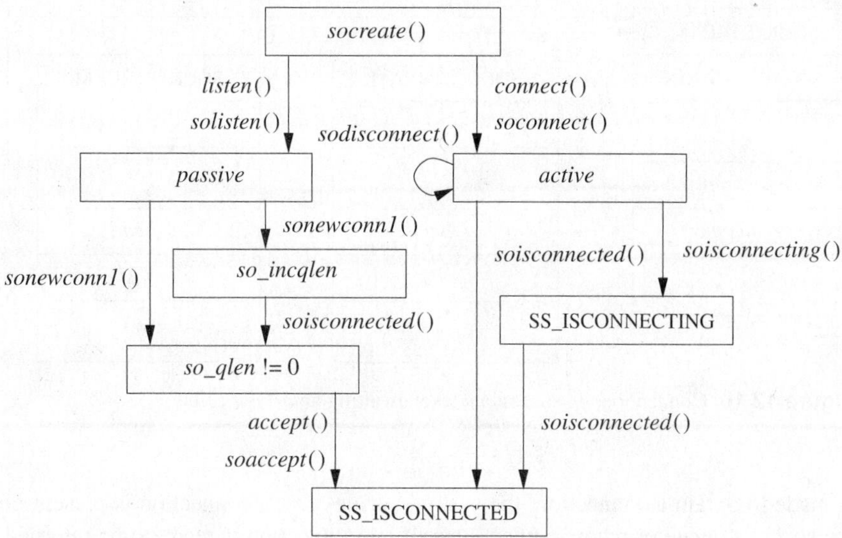

Figure 12.9 Socket state transitions during process rendezvous.

Sockets are normally used to send and receive data. When they are used in establishing a connection, they are treated somewhat differently. If a socket is to be used to accept a connection, the *listen* system call must be used. The *listen* call invokes *solisten*(), which notifies the supporting protocol that the socket will be receiving connections, establishes an empty list of pending connections at the socket (through the *so_comp* field), and then marks the socket as *accepting connections*, SO_ACCEPTCON. At the time a *listen* is done, a backlog parameter is specified by the application. This parameter sets a limit on the number of incoming connections that the system will queue awaiting acceptance by the application. The system enforces a maximum on this limit to prevent resource exhaustion. Once a socket is set up to receive connections, the remainder of the work in creating connections is managed by the protocol layers. For each connection established at the server side, a new socket is created with the *sonewconn*() routine. These new sockets may be placed on the socket's queue of partially established connections (see Figure 12.10) while the connections are being completed, or they may be placed directly into the queue of connections ready to be passed to the application via the *accept* call. The new sockets might be ready to be passed to the application either because no further protocol action is necessary to establish the connection or because the protocol allows the listening process to confirm or reject the connection request. In the latter case, the socket is marked as *confirming* (state bit SS_CONFIRMING) so that the pending connection request will be confirmed or rejected as needed. Once sockets on the queue of partly established connections are ready, they are moved to the queue of connections completed and pending acceptance by an application. When an *accept* system call

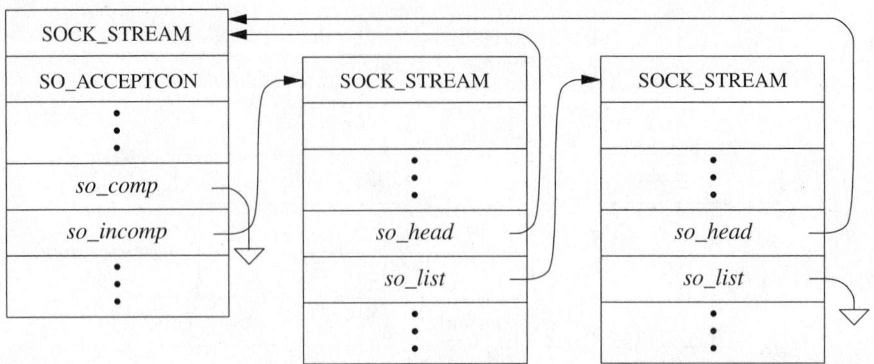

Figure 12.10 Connections queued at a socket awaiting an *accept* call.

is made to obtain a connection, the system verifies that a connection is present on the socket's queue of ready connections. If no connection is ready to be returned, the system puts the process to sleep until one arrives (unless nonblocking I/O is being used with the socket, in which case an EAGAIN error is returned). When a connection is available, the associated socket is removed from the queue, a new file descriptor is allocated to reference the socket, and the result is returned to the caller. If the *accept* call indicates that the peer's identity is to be returned, the peer's address is obtained from the protocol layer and is copied into the supplied buffer.

On the client side, an application requests a connection with the *connect* system call, supplying the address of the peer socket to which to connect. The system verifies that a connection attempt is not already in progress for that socket and then invokes *soconnect*() to initiate the connection. The *soconnect*() routine first checks the socket to see whether the latter is already connected. If the socket is already connected, and supports a connection-oriented protocol, the connection is first dropped and then an EINVAL error is returned to the caller. With the socket in an unconnected state, *soconnect*() makes a request to the protocol layer to initiate the new connection. Once the connection request has been passed to the protocol layer, if the connection request is incomplete, the system puts the process to sleep to await notification by the protocol layer that a completed connection exists. A nonblocking connect may return at this point, but a process awaiting a completed connection will awaken only when the connection request has been completed—either successfully or with an error condition. If the socket supports a datagram protocol, *soconnect*() sets a destination network address for the socket so that the program can use the *write* system call to send data, rather than the commonly used *send* or *sendmsg* calls.

A socket's state during connection establishment is managed jointly by the socket layer and the supporting protocol layer. The socket's state value is never altered directly by a protocol; to promote modularity, all modifications are performed by surrogate socket-layer routines, such as *soisconnected*(). These routines modify the socket state as indicated and notify any waiting processes. The supporting protocol layers never use synchronization or signalling facilities to directly modify the socket structure. Errors that are detected asynchronously are communicated to a socket in its *so_error* field. The socket layer always inspects the value of *so_error* on return from a call to *sleep*(); this field reports errors detected asynchronously by the protocol layers. For example, if a connection request fails because the protocol layer detects that the requested service is unavailable, the *so_error* field is set to ECONNREFUSED before the requesting process is awakened.

12.6 Data Transfer

Most of the work done by the socket layer lies in sending and receiving data. Note that the socket layer itself explicitly refrains from imposing any structure on data transmitted or received via sockets other than optional record boundaries. Within the overall interprocess-communication model, any data interpretation or structuring is logically isolated in the implementation of the communication domain. An example of this logical isolation is the ability to pass file descriptors between processes using local-domain sockets.

Sending and receiving data can be done with any one of several system calls. The system calls vary according to the amount of information to be transmitted and received, and according to the state of the socket doing the operation. For example, the *write* system call may be used with a socket that is in a connected state, since the destination of the data is known to the socket. The *sendto* or *sendmsg* system calls, however, allow the process to specify the destination for a message explicitly. Likewise, when data are received, the *read* system call allows a process to receive data on a connected socket without receiving the sender's address; the *recvfrom* and *recvmsg* system calls allow the process to retrieve the incoming message and the sender's address. The differences between these calls were summarized in Section 12.1. The *recvmsg* and *sendmsg* system calls allow scatter-gather I/O with multiple user-provided buffers. In addition, *recvmsg* reports additional information about a received message, such as whether it was expedited (out of band), whether it completes a record, or whether it was truncated because a buffer was too small. The decision to provide many different system calls rather than only a single general interface is debatable. It would have been possible to implement a single system-call interface and to provide simplified interfaces to applications via user-level library routines. However, the single system call would have to be the most general call, which has somewhat higher overhead. Internally, all transmission and reception requests are converted to a uniform format and are passed to the socket-layer *sendit*() and *recvit*() routines, respectively.

Transmitting Data

The *sendit*() routine is responsible for gathering all the system-call parameters from the application into the kernel's address space (except for the actual data) and for invoking the *sosend*() routine to do the transmission. The parameters may include the following components, illustrated in Figure 12.1:

- An address to which data will be sent, if the socket has not been connected
- Optional *ancillary data* (control data) associated with the message; ancillary data can include protocol-specific data associated with a message, protocol option information, or access rights
- Normal data, specified as an array of buffers (see Section 7.1)
- Optional flags, including out-of-band and end-of-record flags

The *sosend*() routine handles most of the socket-level data-transmission options, including requests for transmission of out-of-band data and for transmission without network routing. This routine is also responsible for checking socket state—for example, seeing whether a required connection has been made, whether transmission is still possible on the socket, and whether a pending error should be reported rather than transmission attempted. In addition, *sosend*() is responsible for putting processes to sleep when their data transmissions exceed the space available in the socket's send buffer. The actual transmission of data is done by the supporting communication protocol; *sosend*() copies data from the user's address space into mbufs in the kernel's address space and then makes calls to the protocol to transfer the data.

Most of the work done by *sosend*() lies in checking the socket state, handling flow control, checking for termination conditions, and breaking up an application's transmission request into one or more protocol transmission requests. The request must be broken up only when the size of the user's request plus the number of data queued in the socket's send data buffer exceeds the socket's high watermark. It is not permissible to break up a request if the protocol is atomic, because each request made by the socket layer to the protocol modules implicitly indicates a boundary in the data stream. Most datagram protocols are of this type. Honoring each socket's high watermark ensures that no process or group of processes can monopolize system resources.

For sockets that guarantee reliable data delivery, a protocol will normally maintain a copy of all transmitted data in the socket's send queue until receipt is acknowledged by the receiver. Protocols that provide no assurance of delivery normally accept data from *sosend*() and directly transmit the data to the destination without keeping a copy, but *sosend*() itself does not distinguish between reliable and unreliable delivery.

If a socket has insufficient space in its send buffer to hold all the data to be transmitted, *sosend*() uses the following strategy: If the protocol is atomic, *sosend*() verifies that the message is no larger than the send buffer size; if the message is larger, it returns an EMSGSIZE error. If the available space in the send queue is less than the send low watermark, the transmission is deferred. If the process is not using nonblocking I/O, the process is put to sleep until more space is available in the send buffer; otherwise, an EAGAIN error is returned. When space is available, a protocol transmit request is formulated according to the available space in the send buffer. The *sosend*() routine copies data from the user's address space into mbuf clusters whenever the data are larger than the minimum cluster size (specified by MINCLSIZE). If a transmission request for a nonatomic protocol is large, each protocol transmit request will normally contain a full mbuf cluster. Although additional data could be appended to the mbuf chain before delivery to the protocol, it is preferable to pass the data to lower levels immediately, which allows better pipelining because data reach the bottom of the protocol stack earlier and can begin physical transmission sooner. This procedure is repeated until no space remains; it resumes each time additional space becomes available. This strategy tends to preserve the application-specified message size and helps to avoid fragmentation at the network level. The latter benefit is important because system performance is significantly improved when data-transmission units are large—for example, the size of an mbuf cluster.

When the receiver or network is slower than the transmitter, the underlying connection-based transmission protocols usually apply some form of flow control to delay the sender's transmission. Here, the amount of data that the receiver will allow the sender to transmit can decrease to a size that the sender's natural transmission size drops below its optimal value. To retard this effect, *sosend*() delays transmission rather than breaking up the data to be transmitted in the hope that the receiver will reopen its flow-control window and allow the sender to perform optimally. The effect of this scheme is subtle and is also related to the networking subsystem's optimized handling of incoming data packets that are a multiple of the machine's page size.

Receiving Data

The *soreceive*() routine receives data queued at a socket. As the counterpart to *sosend*(), *soreceive*() appears at the same level in the internal software structure and does similar tasks. Three types of data may be queued for reception at a socket: in-band data, out-of-band data, and ancillary data, such as access rights. In-band data may also be tagged with the sender's address. Handling of out-of-band data varies by protocol. They may be placed at the beginning of the receive buffer or at the end of the buffer to appear in order with other data, or they may be managed in the protocol layer separately from the socket's receive buffer. In the first two cases, they are returned by normal receive operations. In the final case, they are retrieved through a special interface when requested by the user. These options allow varying styles of urgent data transmission.

The *soreceive*() routine checks the socket's state, including the receive data buffer, for incoming data, errors, or state transitions, and processes queued data according to their type and the actions specified by the caller. A system-call request may specify that only out-of-band data should be retrieved (MSG_OOB) or that data should be returned but not removed from the data buffer (by specifying the MSG_PEEK flag). Receive calls normally return as soon as the low watermark is reached. Because the default is one byte, the call returns when any data are present. The MSG_WAITALL flag specifies that the call should block until it can return all the requested data, if possible. Alternatively, the MSG_DONTWAIT flag causes the call to act as though the socket was in nonblocking mode, returning EAGAIN rather than blocking.

Data present in the receive data buffer are organized in one of several ways, depending on whether message boundaries are preserved. There are three common cases for stream, datagram, and sequenced-packet sockets. In the general case, the receive data buffer is organized as a list of messages (see Figure 12.11). Each message can include a sender's address (for datagram protocols), ancillary data, and normal data. Depending on the protocol, it is also possible for expedited or out-of-band data to be placed into the normal receive buffer. Each mbuf chain on a list represents a single message or, for the final chain, a possibly incomplete record. Protocols that supply the sender's address with each message place a single mbuf containing the address at the front of message. Immediately following any address is an optional mbuf containing any ancillary data. Regular data mbufs follow the ancillary data. Names and ancillary data are distinguished by the type field in an mbuf; addresses are marked as MT_SONAME, whereas

Figure 12.11 Data queueing for datagram socket.

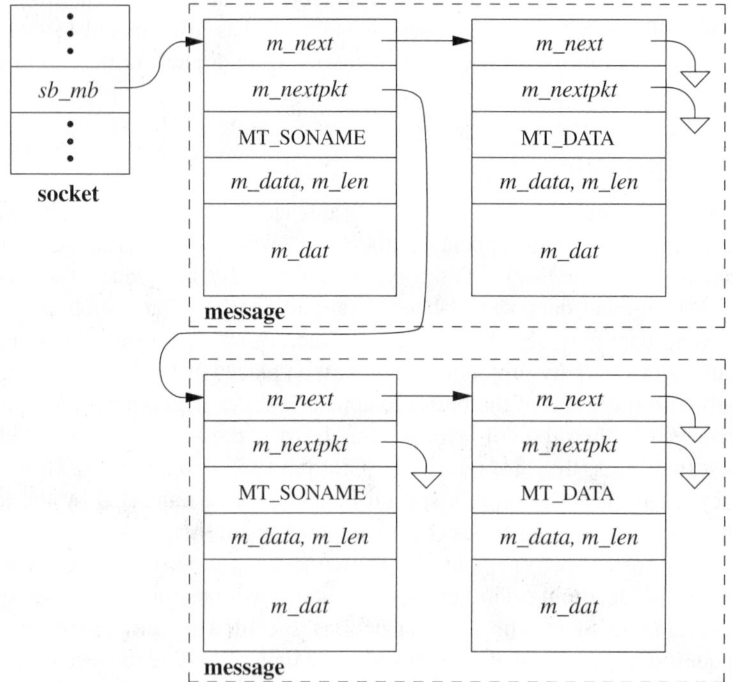

ancillary data are tagged as MT_CONTROL. Each message other than the final one is considered to be terminated. The final message is terminated implicitly when an atomic protocol is used, such as most datagram protocols. Sequenced-packet protocols could treat each message as an atomic record, or they could support records that could be arbitrarily long, as is done in SCTP, which is described in Section 14.7. In the latter case, the final record in the buffer might or might not be complete, and a flag on the final mbuf, M_EOR, marks the termination of a record. Record boundaries (if any) are generally ignored by a stream protocol. However, transition from out-of-band data to normal data in the buffer, or presence of ancillary data, causes logical boundaries. A single receive operation never returns data that cross a logical boundary. Note that the storage scheme used by sockets allows them to compact data of the same type into the minimal number of mbufs required to hold those data.

On entry to *soreceive*(), a check is made to see whether out-of-band data are being requested. Whenever out-of-band data are available from the protocol layer, they are returned to the caller immediately on request. Otherwise, data from the normal queue have been requested. The *soreceive*() function first checks whether the socket is in *confirming* state, with the peer awaiting confirmation of a connection request. If it is, no data can arrive until the connection is confirmed, and the protocol layer is notified that the connection should be completed. The *soreceive*() routine then checks the receive data buffer character count to see whether data are available. If they are, the call returns with at least the data currently available. If no data are present, *soreceive*() consults the socket's state to find out whether data might be forthcoming. Data may no longer be received because the socket is disconnected (and a connection is required to receive data) or because the reception of data has been terminated with a *shutdown* by the socket's peer. In addition, if an error from a previous operation was detected asynchronously, the error needs to be returned to the user; *soreceive*() checks the *so_error* field after checking for data. If no data or error exists, data might still arrive, and if the socket is not marked for nonblocking I/O, *soreceive*() puts the process to sleep to await the arrival of new data.

When data arrive for a socket, the supporting protocol notifies the socket layer by calling *sorwakeup*(). *Soreceive*() can then process the contents of the receive buffer, observing the data-structuring rules described previously. *Soreceive*() first removes any address that must be present, then optional ancillary data, and finally normal data. If the application has provided a buffer for the receipt of ancillary data, they are passed to the application in that buffer; otherwise, they are discarded. The removal of data is slightly complicated by the interaction between in-band and out-of-band data managed by the protocol. The location of the next out-of-band datum can be marked in the in-band data stream and used as a record boundary during in-band data processing. That is, when out-of-band data are received by a protocol that holds out-of-band data separately from the normal buffer, the corresponding point in the in-band data stream is marked. Then, when a request is made to receive in-band data, only data up to the mark will be returned. This mark allows applications to synchronize the in-band and out-of-band data streams so that, for example, received data can be flushed up to the point at which out-of-band data are received. Each socket has a field, *so_oobmark*, that contains the character offset from the front of the receive data buffer to the point in the data stream at which the last out-of-band message was received. When in-band data are removed from the receive buffer, the offset is updated so that data past the mark will not be mixed with data preceding the mark. The SS_RCVATMARK bit in a socket's state field is set when *so_oobmark* reaches zero to show that the out-of-band data mark is at the beginning of the socket receive buffer. An application can test the state of this bit with the SIOCATMARK *ioctl* call to find out whether all in-band data have been read up to the point of the mark.

Once data have been removed from a socket's receive buffer, *soreceive*() updates the state of the socket and notifies the protocol layer that data have been received by the user. The protocol layer can use this information to release internal resources, to trigger end-to-end acknowledgment of data reception, to update flow-control information, or to start a new data transfer. Finally, if any access rights were received as ancillary data, *soreceive*() passes them to a communication-domain-specific routine to convert them from their internal representation to the external representation.

The *soreceive*() function returns a set of flags that are supplied to the caller of the *recvmsg* system call via the *msg_flags* field of the *msghdr* structure (see Figure 12.1). The possible flags include MSG_EOR to specify that the received data complete a record for a nonatomic sequenced-packet protocol, MSG_OOB to specify that expedited (out-of-band) data were received from the normal socket receive buffer, MSG_TRUNC to specify that an atomic record was truncated because the supplied buffer was too small, and MSG_CTRUNC to specify that ancillary data were truncated because the control buffer was too small.

12.7 Socket Shutdown

Although closing a socket and reclaiming its resources appears at first glance to be a straightforward operation, it can be complicated. The complexity arises because of the implicit semantics of the *close* system call. In certain situations (e.g., when a process exits), a *close* call is never expected to fail. However, when a socket promising reliable delivery of data is closed with data still queued for transmission or awaiting acknowledgment of reception, the socket must attempt to transmit the data, perhaps indefinitely, for the *close* call to maintain the socket's advertised semantics. If the socket discards the queued data to allow the *close* to complete successfully, it violates its promise to deliver data reliably. Discarding data can cause naive processes, which depend on the implicit semantics of *close*, to work unreliably in a network environment. However, if sockets block until all data have been transmitted successfully, then, in some communication domains, a *close* may never complete!

In an effort to address this problem, the socket layer compromises yet maintains the semantics of the *close* system call. Figure 12.12 shows the possible state

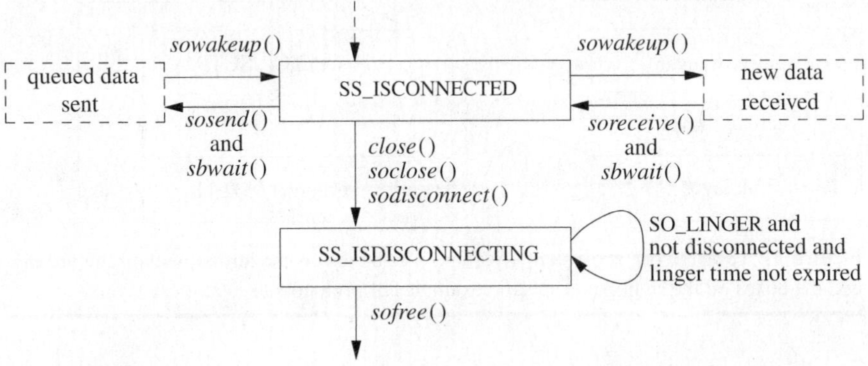

Figure 12.12 Socket-state transitions during shutdown.

transitions for a socket from a connected to a closed state. In normal operation, closing a socket causes any queued but unaccepted connections to be discarded. If the socket is in a connected state, a disconnect is initiated. The socket is marked to indicate that a file descriptor is no longer referencing it, and the close operation returns successfully. When the disconnect request completes, the network support notifies the socket layer, and the socket resources are reclaimed. The network layer may attempt to transmit any data queued in the socket's send buffer, although there is no guarantee that it will. However, commonly used connection-oriented protocols generally attempt to transmit any queued data asynchronously after the *close* call returns, preserving the normal semantics of *close* on a file.

Alternatively, a socket may be marked explicitly to force the application process to linger when closing until pending data have drained and the connection has shut down. This option is marked in the *socket* data structure using the *setsockopt* system call with the SO_LINGER option. When an application indicates that a socket is to linger, it also specifies a duration for the lingering period. The application can then block for as long as the specified duration while waiting for pending data to drain. If the lingering period expires before the disconnect is completed, the socket layer then notifies the network that it is closing, possibly discarding any data still pending. Some protocols handle the linger option differently. In particular, if the linger option is set with a duration of zero, the protocol may discard pending data rather than attempt to deliver them asynchronously.

12.8 Network-Communication Protocol Internal Structure

The network subsystem is logically divided into three layers as shown in Figure 12.13. These three layers manage the following tasks:

1. Interprocess data transport

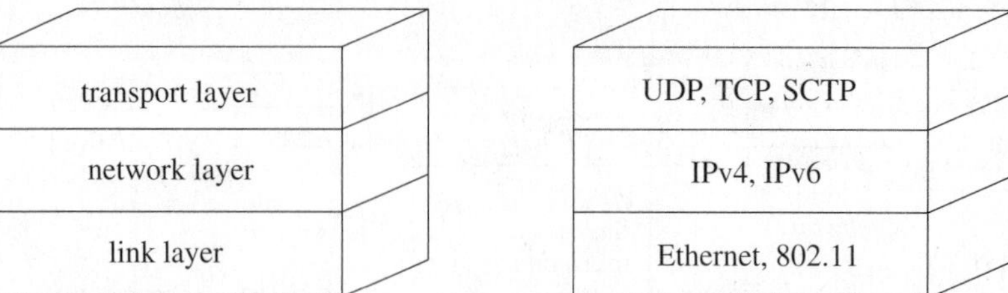

Figure 12.13 Network subsystem layering. The boxes on the left name the standard layers; the boxes on the right name specific examples of protocols used at those layers.

2. Internetwork addressing and message routing
3. Data-link layer

The first two layers are made up of modules that implement communication protocols. The software in the third layer handles protocols, such as Ethernet and WiFi, that are responsible for encapsulating and decapsulating packets over physical or wireless links.

The topmost layer in the network subsystem is termed the ***transport layer***. The transport layer must provide an addressing structure that permits communication between sockets and any protocol mechanisms necessary for socket semantics, such as reliable data delivery. The second layer, the ***network layer***, is responsible for the delivery of data destined for remote transport or for network-layer protocols. In providing internetwork delivery, the network layer must manage a private routing database or use the systemwide facility for routing messages to their destination host. Beneath the network layer is the ***datalink layer***, which handles the differences between various hardware standards for networking, such as Ethernet and WiFi. The ***link layer*** is responsible for transporting messages between hosts connected to a common transmission medium. The link layer is mainly concerned with driving the network devices involved and performing any necessary link-level protocol ***encapsulation*** and ***decapsulation***. The transport, network, and link layers of the network subsystem correspond to the transport, network, and link layers of the ISO Open Systems Interconnection Reference Model [ISO, 1984], respectively.

The internal structure of the networking software is not directly visible to users. Instead, all networking facilities are accessed through the socket layer. Each communication protocol that permits access to its facilities exports a set of user request routines to the socket layer. These routines are used by the socket layer in providing access to network services.

The layering described here is a logical layering, meaning that the software that implements network services may use more or fewer communication protocols according to the design of the network architecture being supported. For example, raw sockets often use a null implementation at one or more layers. At the opposite extreme, tunneling of one protocol through another uses one network protocol to encapsulate and deliver packets for another protocol and involves multiple instances of some layers.

Data Flow

Early versions of BSD were used as end systems in a network. They were either the source or destination of communication. Although many installations used a workstation as an office router, dedicated hardware did the more complex tasks of

Figure 12.14 Example of inbound flow of a data packet in the network subsystem. Key: Ethernet—Ethernet header; IPv4—Internet Version 4 Protocol header; TCP—Transmission Control Protocol header.

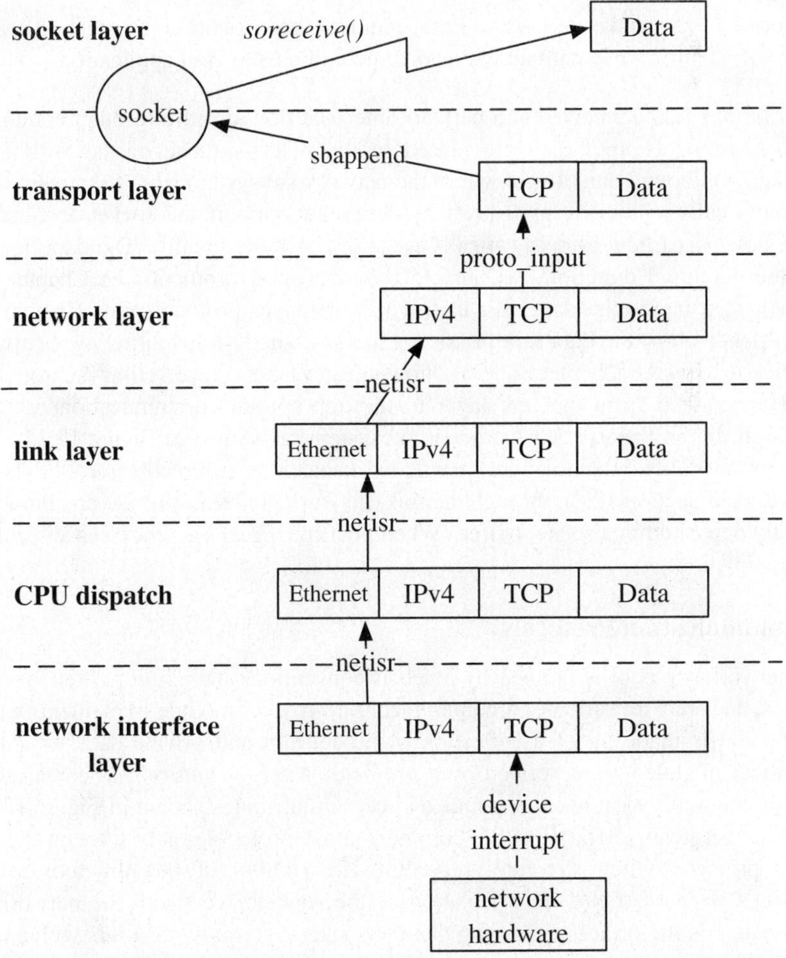

bridging and routing. At the time of the original design and implementation of the networking subsystem, the possibility of securing data by encrypting packets was still far too computationally slow. Since that initial design, many different uses have been made of the code. Bridges and routers can be built out of stock parts and the advent of specialized cryptographic accelerators has made packet encryption practical in almost any environment. These facts conspire to make discussion of data flow within the network subsystem more complex than it was in earlier systems.

There are four paths through a network node:

Inbound — Destined for this node and possibly a user-level application

Outbound — Originating on this node and destined, via a network, for another

Forward — Whether bridged or routed, the packets are not for this node but to be sent on to another network or host

Error — A packet has arrived that requires the network subsystem to send a response without the involvement of a user-level application.

Inbound data received at a network interface flow upward through communication protocols until they are placed in the receive queue of the destination socket. Outbound data flow down to the network subsystem from the socket layer through calls to the transport-layer modules that support the socket abstraction. The downward flow of data typically is started by system calls. The data flowing in the outbound direction are handled by a transport protocol (see Chapter 14), which then hands the data over to the network layer protocols (see Chapter 13) and thence on to the data link protocols, and are finally transmitted by a network device driver (see Chapter 8). Data flowing upward are received asynchronously and are passed from the link layer to the appropriate communication protocol through direct dispatch via the netisr subsystem, as shown in Figure 12.14. The system handles inbound network traffic by dispatching it directly from the device driver (see Section 12.8), through the link, network, and transport layers, until it is finally deposited in a socket buffer. When possible, FreeBSD processes all packets to completion.

Communication Protocols

A network protocol is defined by a set of conventions including packet formats, states, and state transitions. A communication-protocol module implements a protocol and is made up of a collection of procedures and private data structures. Protocol modules are described by a ***protocol-switch structure*** that contains the set of externally visible entry points and certain attributes shown in Figure 12.15. The socket layer interacts with a communication protocol solely through the latter's protocol-switch structure, recording the address of the structure in the socket's *so_proto* field. This isolation of the socket layer from the networking subsystem is important in ensuring that the socket layer provides users with a consistent interface to all the protocols supported by a system. When a socket is

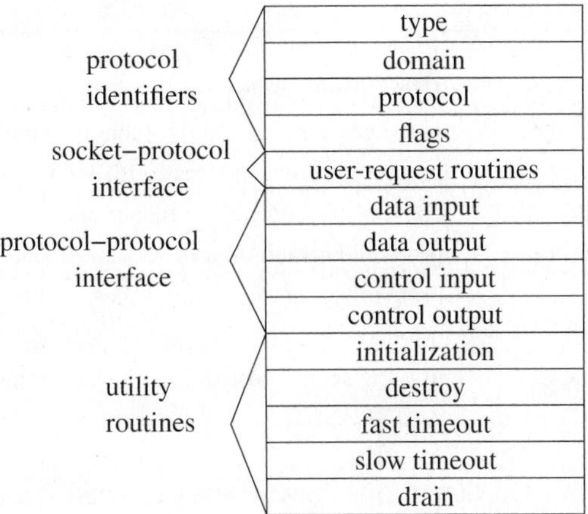

Figure 12.15 Protocol-switch structure.

created, the socket layer looks up the domain for the protocol family to find the array of protocol-switch structures for the family (see Section 12.4). A protocol is selected from the array based on the type of socket supported (the type field) and, optionally, a specific protocol number (the protocol field). The protocol switch has a back pointer to the domain (the domain field). Within a protocol family, every protocol capable of supporting a socket directly (for example, most transport protocols) must provide a protocol-switch structure describing the protocol. Lower-level protocols such as network-layer protocols may also have protocol-switch entries, although whether they do can depend on conventions within the protocol family.

Before a protocol is first used, the protocol's initialization routine is invoked. Thereafter, the protocol will be invoked for timer-based actions every 200 milliseconds if the fast timeout entry is present, and every 500 milliseconds if the slow timeout entry point is present. In general, protocols use the slower timer for most timer processing; the major use of the fast timeout is for delayed-acknowledgment processing in reliable transport protocols. The drain entry is provided so that the system can notify the protocol if the system is low on memory and would like any noncritical data to be discarded.

Protocols may pass data between their layers in chains of mbufs (see Section 12.3) using the data input and data output routines. The data input routine passes data up toward the user, whereas the data output routine passes data down toward the network. Similarly, control information passes up and down via the control-input and control-output routines. The table of ***user-request routines*** is the interface between a protocol and the socket level; they are described in detail in Section 12.9.

In general, a protocol is responsible for storage space occupied by any of the arguments passed downward via these procedures and must either pass the space

Table 12.7 Protocol flags.

Flag	Description
PR_ATOMIC	messages sent separately, each in a single packet
PR_ADDR	protocol presents address with each message
PR_CONNREQUIRED	connection required for data transfer
PR_WANTRCVD	protocol notified on user receipt of data
PR_RIGHTS	protocol supports passing access rights
PR_IMPLOPCL	implied open/close
PR_LASTHDR	used by secure protocols to check for last header

onward or dispose of it. On output, the lowest level reached must free space passed as arguments; on input, the highest level is responsible for freeing space passed up to it. Auxiliary storage needed by protocols is allocated from the mbuf pool. This space is used temporarily to formulate messages or to hold variable-size socket addresses. Mbufs allocated by a protocol for private use must be freed by that protocol when they are no longer in use.

The flags field in a protocol's protocol-switch structure describes the protocol's capabilities and certain aspects of its operation that are pertinent to the operation of the socket level; the flags are listed in Table 12.7. Protocols that are connection based specify the PR_CONNREQUIRED flag, so that socket routines will never attempt to send data before a connection has been established. If the PR_WANTRCVD flag is set, the socket routines will notify the protocol when the user has removed data from a socket's receive queue. This notification allows a protocol to implement acknowledgment on user receipt and also to update flow-control information based on the amount of space available in the receive queue. The PR_ADDR field indicates that any data placed in a socket's receive queue by the protocol will be preceded by the address of the sender. The PR_ATOMIC flag specifies that each *user* request to send data must be done in a single protocol-send request; it is the protocol's responsibility to maintain record boundaries on data to be sent. This flag also implies that messages must be received and delivered to processes atomically. The PR_RIGHTS flag indicates that the protocol supports the transfer of access rights; this flag is currently used by only those protocols in the local communication domain. Connection-oriented protocols that allow the user to set up, send data, and tear down a connection all in a single *sendto* call have the PR_IMPLOPCL flag set. The PR_LASTHDR flag is used by secure protocols, such as IPSec, where several headers must be processed to get the actual data.

12.9 Socket-to-Protocol Interface

The interface from the socket routines to the communication protocols is through the table of user-request routines and the control-output routine defined in the

Table 12.8 User-request routines.

Entry point	Description
pru_attach()	attach protocol to socket
pru_detach()	detach protocol from socket
pru_bind()	bind name to socket
pru_listen()	listen for connections
pru_connect()	establish connection to peer
pru_accept()	accept connection from peer
pru_disconnect()	disconnect from peer
pru_shutdown()	will not send any more data
pru_rcvd()	have taken data; more room now
pru_send()	protocol-specific send routine
pru_abort()	abort connection and detach
pru_control()	control protocol operation (*ioctl*)
pru_sense()	sense socket status (*fstat*)
pru_rcvoob()	retrieve out-of-band data
pru_sosend()	generic send routine
pru_soreceive()	receive system call
pru_sopoll()	check the socket for data
pru_sockaddr()	fetch socket's address
pru_peeraddr()	fetch peer's address
pru_connect2()	connect two sockets
pru_sosetlabel()	set a MAC label on a socket
pru_bindat()	local socket-specific bind for capability system
pru_connectat()	local socket-specific connect for capability system
pru_flush()	flush data on connection
pru_close()	close operation

protocol-switch structure for each protocol. When the socket layer requires services of a supporting protocol, it makes a call to a function in Table 12.8. The control-output routine implements the *getsockopt* and *setsockopt* system calls; the user-request routines are used for all other operations. Calls to the control-output routine specify SOPT_GET to get the current value of an option, or SOPT_SET to set the value of an option.

Protocol User-Request Routines

Calls to the user-request routines have a routine-specific signature, but the first argument is always a pointer to a *socket* structure that specifies the socket for which the operation is intended. An mbuf data chain is supplied for output operations and for certain other operations where a result is to be returned. A pointer to a *sockaddr* structure is supplied for address-oriented requests, such as *pru_bind*(), *pru_connect*(), and *pru_send*() (when an address is specified—e.g., the *sendto* call). Where it is used, the *control* parameter is a pointer to an optional mbuf chain containing protocol-specific control information passed via the *sendmsg* call. Each protocol is responsible for disposal of the data mbuf chains on output operations. A nonzero return value from a user-request routine indicates an error number that should be passed to higher-level software. A description of each of the possible requests follows:

- *pru_attach*(): attach protocol to socket. When a protocol is first bound to a socket (with the *socket* system call), the protocol module's *pru_attach*() routine is called. It is the responsibility of the protocol module to allocate any resources necessary. The *attach* routine will always precede any of the other operations and will occur only once per socket.

- *pru_detach*(): detach protocol from socket. This operation is the inverse of the attach routine and is used at the time that a socket is deleted. The protocol module may deallocate any resources that it allocated for the socket in a previous *pru_attach*() call.

- *pru_bind*(): bind address to socket. When a socket is initially created, it has no address bound to it. This routine binds an address to an existing socket. The protocol module must verify that the requested address is valid and is available for use.

- *pru_listen*(): listen for incoming connections. A ***listen request*** indicates that the user wishes to listen for incoming connection requests on the associated socket. The protocol module should make any state changes needed to meet this request (if possible). A call to the listen routine always precedes any request to accept a connection.

- *pru_connect*(): connect socket to peer. The ***connect request*** routine indicates that the user wants to establish an association. The *addr* parameter describes the peer to which a connection is desired. The effect of a connect request may vary depending on the protocol. Stream protocols use this request to initiate establishment of a network connection. Datagram protocols simply record the peer's address in a private data structure, where they use it as the destination address of all outgoing packets and as a source filter for incoming packets. There are no restrictions on how many times a connect routine may be used after an attach, although most stream protocols allow only one connect call.

- *pru_accept*(): accept pending connection. Following a successful listen request and the arrival of one or more connections, this routine is called to indicate that the user is about to accept a socket from the queue of sockets ready to be returned. The socket supplied as a parameter is the socket that is being accepted; the protocol module is expected to fill in the supplied buffer with the address of the peer connected to the socket.

- *pru_disconnect*(): disconnect connected socket. This routine eliminates an association created with the connect routine. It is used with datagram sockets before a new association is created; it is used with stream protocols only when the socket is closed.

- *pru_shutdown*(): shut down socket data transmission. This call indicates that no more data will be sent. The protocol may, at its discretion, deallocate any data structures related to the shutdown or the protocol may leave all that work for its *pru_detach*() routine. The module may also notify a connected peer of the shutdown at this time.

- *pru_rcvd*(): data were received by user. This routine is called only if the protocol entry in the protocol-switch table includes the PR_WANTRCVD flag. When the socket layer removes data from the receive queue and passes them to the user, this routine will be called in the protocol module. This routine may be used by the protocol to trigger acknowledgments, refresh windowing information, initiate data transfer, and so on. This routine is also called when an application attempts to receive data on a socket that is in the *confirming* state, indicating that the protocol must accept the connection request before data can be received (see Section 12.5).

- *pru_send*(): send user data. Each user request to send data is translated into one or more calls to the protocol module's *pru_send*() routine. A protocol may indicate that a single user send request must be translated into a single call to the *pru_send*() routine by specifying the PR_ATOMIC flag in its protocol description. The data to be sent are presented to the protocol as a chain of mbufs, and an optional address is supplied in the *addr* parameter. The protocol is responsible for preserving the data in the socket's send queue if it is not able to send them immediately or if it may need them at some later time (e.g., for retransmission). The protocol must eventually pass the data to a lower level or free the mbufs.

- *pru_abort*(): abnormally terminate service. This routine effects an abnormal termination of service. The protocol should delete any existing associations.

- *pru_control*(): perform control operation. The ***control request*** routine is called when a user does an *ioctl* system call on a socket and the *ioctl* is not intercepted by the socket routines. This routine allows protocol-specific operations to be provided outside the scope of the common socket interface. The *cmd* parameter contains the actual *ioctl* request code. The *data* parameter contains any data relevant to the command being issued and the *ifp* parameter contains a pointer to a network-interface structure if the *ioctl* operation pertains to a particular network interface.

- *pru_sense*(): sense socket status. The ***sense request*** routine is called when the user makes an *fstat* system call on a socket; it requests the status of the associated socket. This call returns a standard *stat* structure that typically contains only the optimal transfer size for the connection (based on buffer size, windowing information, and maximum packet size).

- *pru_rcvoob*(): receive out-of-band data. This routine requests that any ***out-of-band*** data now available are to be returned. An mbuf is passed to the protocol module, and the protocol should either place data in the mbuf or attach new mbufs to the one supplied if there is insufficient space in the single mbuf. An error may be returned if out-of-band data are not (yet) available or have already been consumed. The *flags* parameter contains any options, such as MSG_PEEK, that should be observed while this request is carried out.

- *pru_sosend*(): a generic routine, usable by system calls, as well as the kernel, to send data using a protocol.

- *pru_soreceive*(): routine that implements the kernel's part of the *recv* and *recvmsg* system calls.

- *pru_sopoll*(): check a socket to see if it has any available data. Used by both the *select* and *poll* system calls.

- *pru_sockaddr*(): retrieve local socket address. This routine returns the local address of the socket if one has been bound to the socket. The address is returned in the *nam* parameter, which is a pointer to a *sockaddr* structure.

- *pru_peeraddr*(): retrieve peer socket address. This routine returns the address of the peer to which the socket is connected. The socket must be in a connected state for this request to succeed. The address is returned in the *nam* parameter, which is a pointer to a *sockaddr* structure.

- *pru_connect2*(): connect two sockets without binding addresses. In this routine, the protocol module is supplied two sockets and is asked to establish a connection between the two without binding any addresses, if possible. The system uses this call in implementing the *socketpair* system call.

- *pru_sosetlabel*(): Set a MAC label on a socket.

- *pru_bindat*(): PF_LOCAL specific bind routine for use with Capsicum and capabilities.

- *pru_connectat*(): PF_LOCAL specific connect routine for use with Capsicum and capabilities.

- *pru_flush*(): used only by SCTP to flush input or output data.

- *pru_close*(): close down the connection associated with a socket.

Protocol Control-Output Routine

A call to the control-output routine is of the form

```
int (*pr->pr_ctloutput)(
      struct socket *so,
      struct sockopt *sopt);
```

where *so* is the socket to be modified and *sopt* is a socket option structure.

```
enum sopt_dir { SOPT_GET, SOPT_SET };

struct sockopt {
    enum    sopt_dir sopt_dir;
    int     sopt_level;
    int     sopt_name;
    void   *sopt_val;
    size_t  sopt_valsize;
    struct  thread *sopt_td;
};
```

The direction is either SOPT_SET to set an option or SOPT_GET to retrieve it. The *sopt_level* member indicates the layer of software that should interpret the option request. A *sopt_level* of SOL_SOCKET is specified to control an option at the socket layer. When the option is to be processed by a protocol module below the socket layer, *level* is set to the appropriate protocol number (the same number used in the *socket* system call). Each level has its own set of option names; this name is interpreted only by the targeted layer of software. The rest of the structure contains a pointer to the value being passed into or out of the module, the size of the pointed-to data, and a pointer to a thread structure. If the operation takes place wholly inside the kernel, then the pointer to the thread structure is null.

In supporting the *getsockopt* and *setsockopt* system calls, the socket layer always invokes the control-output routine of the protocol attached to the socket. To access lower-level protocols, each control-output routine must pass control-output requests that it does not intend to perform downward to the next protocol in the protocol hierarchy. Chapter 14 describes some of the options provided by the protocols in the Internet-communication domain.

12.10 Protocol-to-Protocol Interface

The interface between protocol modules uses the *pr_usrreqs*() routines as well as the *pr_ctloutput*() routine. The *pr_usrreqs*() and *pr_ctloutput*() routines are used by the socket layer to communicate with protocols.

Although imposing a standard calling convention for all a protocol's entry points might theoretically permit an arbitrary interconnection of protocol modules, it would be difficult in practice. Crossing a protocol-family boundary—for example, between IPv4 and IPX—would require a network address to be converted from the format of the caller's domain to the format of the receiver's domain. Consequently, connection of protocols in different communication domains is not generally supported, and calling conventions for the routines listed in the preceding paragraph are typically standardized on a per-domain basis. (However, the system does support encapsulation of packets from one protocol into packets of a protocol in another family to tunnel one protocol through another.)

In this section, we briefly examine the general framework and calling conventions of protocols. In Chapter 14, we examine specific protocols to see how they fit into this framework.

pr_output

Each protocol has a different calling convention for its output routine. This lack of standardization is a reason that protocol modules cannot be freely interchanged with each other in arbitrary stacks, such as is done in the STREAMS system [Ritchie, 1984]. Thus far, interface standardization has not been considered necessary because each protocol stack tends to stand on its own without ever borrowing from others. An arbitrary stacking of protocol modules would also complicate the interpretation of network addresses in each module, since each module would have to check to make sure that the address made some sense to them in their domain.

The simplest example of a protocol output routine often uses a calling convention designed to send a single message on a connection; for example,

```
int (*pr_output)(
    register struct inpcb *inp,
    struct mbuf *msg,
    struct sockaddr *addr
    struct mbuf *control,
    struct thread *td);
```

would send a message contained in *msg* on a socket described by protocol control block *inp*. Special address and control information are passed in *addr* and *control*, respectively.

pr_input

Upper-level protocol input routines are usually called by the network software-interrupt task once the network-level protocol has located the protocol identifier. They have stricter conventions than do output routines because they are called via the protocol switch. Depending on the protocol family, they may receive a pointer to a control block identifying the connection, or they may have to locate the control block from information in the received packet. A typical calling convention is

```
void (*pr_input)(
    struct mbuf *msg,
    int hlen);
```

In this example, the incoming packet is passed to a transport protocol in an mbuf *msg* with the network protocol header still in place for the transport protocol to use, as well as the length of the header, *hlen*, so that the header can be removed. The protocol does the endpoint-level demultiplexing based on information in the network and transport headers.

pr_ctlinput

This routine passes *control* information (i.e., information that might be passed to the user but does not consist of data) *upward* from one protocol module to another. The common calling convention for this routine is

```
void (*pr_ctlinput)(
    int cmd,
    struct sockaddr *addr,
    void* opaque);
```

Table 12.9 Control-input routine requests.

Request	Description
PRC_IFDOWN	network interface transition to down
PRC_ROUTEDEAD	select new route if possible
PRC_IFUP	network interface has come back up
PRC_QUENCH	some receiver said to slow down
PRC_QUENCH2	DEC congestion bit says slow down
PRC_MSGSIZE	message size forced packet to be dropped
PRC_HOSTDEAD	remote host is down
PRC_HOSTUNREACH	remote host is unreachable
PRC_UNREACH_NET	no route to network
PRC_UNREACH_HOST	no route to host
PRC_UNREACH_PROTOCOL	protocol not supported by destination
PRC_UNREACH_PORT	port number not in use at destination
PRC_UNREACH_SRCFAIL	source routing failed
PRC_REDIRECT_NET	routing redirect for a network
PRC_REDIRECT_HOST	routing redirect for a host
PRC_REDIRECT_TOSNET	routing redirect for type of service and network
PRC_REDIRECT_TOSHOST	routing redirect for type of service and host
PRC_TIMXCEED_INTRANS	packet lifetime expired in transit
PRC_TIMXCEED_REASS	lifetime expired on reassembly queue
PRC_PARAMPROB	header-parameter problem detected
PRC_UNREACH_ADMIN_PROHIB	packet administratively prohibited

The *cmd* parameter is a value shown in Table 12.9. The *addr* parameter is the remote address to which the condition applies. Many of the requests have been derived from the Internet Control Message Protocol (ICMP) [Postel, 1981] and from error messages defined in the 1822 host (Internet Message Processor) convention [BBN, 1978]. Some protocols may pass additional parameters internally, such as local addresses or more specific information.

12.11 Protocol-to-Network Interface

The lowest layer in the set of protocols that constitutes a protocol family must interact with one or more network interfaces to transmit and receive packets. It is assumed that any routing decisions have been made before a packet is sent to a network interface; a routing decision is necessary to locate any interface at all. Although there are four paths through any network stack, there are only two cases concerning protocols and network interfaces that we should consider: transmission of a packet and receipt of a packet. We shall consider each separately. The interactions between the kernel device-driver software and network interface hardware was described in Section 8.5.

Network Interfaces and Link-Layer Protocols

Each network interface configured in a system defines a link-layer path through which messages can be sent and received. A *link-layer path* is a path that allows a

Figure 12.16 Network-interface data structures. The fields marked in bold are broken out and described more fully in figures shown later in this section.

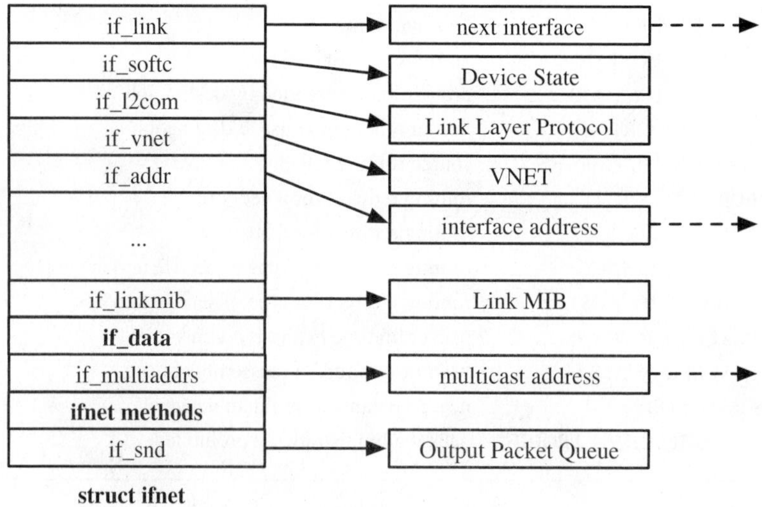

message to be sent via a single transmission to its destination, without network-level forwarding. Normally, a hardware device is associated with this interface, although there are software-based interfaces such as the *loopback* interface. In addition to manipulating the hardware device, a network-interface module is responsible for encapsulation and decapsulation of any link-layer protocol header required to deliver a message to its destination. For common interface types, the link-layer protocol is implemented in a separate sublayer that is shared by various hardware drivers. The selection of the interface to use in sending a packet is a routing decision carried out at the network-protocol layer. An interface may have addresses in one or more address families. Each address is set when the device is brought into a running state using an *ioctl* system call on a socket in the appropriate domain. This operation is implemented by the protocol family after the network interface verifies the operation. The network-interface abstraction provides protocols with a consistent interface to all hardware devices that may be present on a machine.

An interface and its addresses are defined by the structures shown in Figure 12.16. As interfaces are found at startup time, the *ifnet* structures are initialized and are placed on a linked list. The network-interface module generally maintains the *ifnet* interface data structure as part of a larger structure that also contains information used in operating the underlying hardware device. Similarly, the *ifaddr* interface-address structure is often part of a larger structure containing additional protocol information about the interface or its address. Because network socket addresses are variable in size, each protocol is responsible for allocating the space referenced by the address, mask, and broadcast or destination address pointers in the *ifaddr* structure.

Each network interface is identified in two ways: a character string identifying the driver plus a unit number for the driver (e.g. *cxgbe0*), and a binary systemwide index number. The index is used as a shorthand identifier—for example, when a route that refers to the interface is established. As each interface is initialized, the system creates an array of pointers to the *ifnet* structures for the interfaces. It can thus locate an interface quickly given an index number, whereas the lookup using a string name is less efficient. Some operations, such as interface address assignment, name the interface with a string for the user's convenience because performance is not critical. Other operations, such as route establishment, pass a newer style of identifier that can use either a string or an index. The new identifier uses a *sockaddr* structure in a new address family, AF_LINK, indicating a link-layer address. The family-specific version of the structure is a *sockaddr_dl* structure, shown in Figure 12.17, which may contain up to three identifiers. It includes an interface name as a string plus a length, with a length of zero denoting the absence of a name. It also includes an interface index as an integer, with a value of zero indicating that the index is not set. Finally, it may include a binary link-level address, such as an Ethernet address, and the length of the address. An address of this form is created for each network interface as the interface is configured by the system and is returned in the list of local addresses for the system along with network protocol addresses (see later in this subsection). Figure 12.17

struct *sockaddr_dl*	example struct *sockaddr_dl*
sdl_len	20
sdl_family	AF_LINK
sdl_index	1
sdl_type	IFT_ETHER
sdl_nlen	6
sdl_alen	6
sdl_slen	0
sdl_data	'c' 'x' 'g' 'b' 'e' '0' 00:07:43:c2:59:0b

Figure 12.17 Link-layer address structure. The box on the left names the elements of the *sockaddr_dl* structure. The box on the right shows sample values for these elements for an Ethernet interface. The *sdl_data* array may contain a name (if *sdl_nlen* is nonzero), a link-layer address (if *sdl_alen* is nonzero), and an address selector (if *sdl_slen* is nonzero). For an Ethernet, *sdl_data* contains a name followed by a unit number, *cxgbe0*, followed by a 6-byte Ethernet address.

shows a structure describing an Ethernet interface that is the first interface on the system; the structure contains the interface name, the index, and the link-layer (Ethernet) address.

The interface data structure includes an *if_data* structure, broken out in Table 12.10, which contains the externally visible description of the interface. It includes the link-layer type of the interface, the maximum network-protocol packet size that is supported, and the sizes of the link-layer header and address. It also contains numerous statistics, such as packets and bytes sent and received, input and output errors, and other data required by the **netstat** program and network-management protocols. The statistics are a subset of the statistics maintained by the network card. They are copied periodically from registers on the network interface into the *if_data* structure. Most network interfaces expose a much larger set of statistics via the **sysctl** subsystem.

The state of an interface and certain externally visible characteristics are stored in the *if_flags* field described in Table 12.11. The first set of flags characterizes an interface. If an interface is connected to a network that supports transmission of ***broadcast*** messages, the IFF_BROADCAST flag will be set, and the interface's address list will contain a broadcast address to be used in sending and receiving such messages. If an interface is associated with a point-to-point hardware link (e.g., a leased line circuit), the IFF_POINTOPOINT flag will be set, and the interface's address list will contain the address of the host on the other side of the connection. Note that the broadcast and point-to-point attributes are mutually exclusive. These addresses and the local address of an interface are used by network-layer protocols in filtering incoming packets. The IFF_MULTICAST flag is set by interfaces that support multicast packets in addition to IFF_BROADCAST. A multicast address is used to send a packet to a group of hosts rather than a single host on the network. A network has many multicast addresses available. A group

Table 12.10 Per *ifnet* meta-data and statistics. Fields marked in bold and italic record statistics at run time for use by other tools such as **netstat**.

Field	Description
ifi_type	link layer type, i.e. Ethernet, 802.11
ifi_physical	physical layer type, i.e. 100baseT, 10GBaseT
ifi_addrlen	media address length
ifi_hdrlen	media header length
ifi_link_state	current link state
ifi_vhid	CARP vhid
ifi_baudrate_pf	baudrate power factor
ifi_datalen	length of this data structure
ifi_mtu	maximum transmission unit for this interface
ifi_metric	routing metric
ifi_baudrate	speed of the network
ifi_ipackets	packets received on interface
ifi_ierrors	input errors on interface
ifi_opackets	packets sent on interface
ifi_oerrors	output errors on interface
ifi_collisions	collisions during transmit
ifi_ibytes	total number of bytes received
ifi_obytes	total number of bytes sent
ifi_imcasts	packets received via multicast
ifi_omcasts	packets sent via multicast
ifi_iqdrops	packets dropped on input by this interface
ifi_noproto	packets destined for unsupported protocol

that wishes to receive packets selects an available address and then every member of the group signs up to receive packets sent to that multicast address. Packets sent to the group's selected multicast address are received by all members of the group that have requested to receive it.

Additional interface flags describe the operational state of an interface. An interface sets the IFF_RUNNING flag after it has allocated system resources and has posted an initial read on the device that it manages. This state bit avoids multiple-allocation requests when an interface's address is changed. The IFF_UP flag is set when the interface is configured and is ready to transmit messages. The IFF_PROMISC flag is set by network-monitoring programs to enable promiscuous reception when they wish to receive packets for all destinations rather than only those destined for the local system. Packets addressed to other systems are passed to the monitoring packet filter but are not delivered to network protocols. The IFF_ALLMULTI flag is similar, but it only applies to multicast packets and is used

Table 12.11 Network interface flags.

Flag	Description
IFF_UP	interface is available for use
IFF_BROADCAST	broadcast is supported
IFF_DEBUG	enable debugging in the interface software
IFF_LOOPBACK	interface is for software loopback
IFF_POINTOPOINT	interface is for a point-to-point link
IFF_SMART	interface manages its own routes
IFF_DRV_RUNNING	interface resources have been allocated
IFF_NOARP	interface does not support ARP
IFF_PROMISC	interface receives packets for all destinations
IFF_ALLMULTI	interface receives all multicast packets
IFF_DRV_OACTIVE	interface is busy doing output
IFF_SIMPLEX	interface cannot receive its own transmissions
IFF_LINK0	link-layer specific
IFF_LINK1	link-layer specific
IFF_LINK2	link-layer specific
IFF_ALTPHYS	using alternate physical connection
IFF_MULTICAST	multicast is supported
IFF_CANTCONFIG	cannot configure interface via *ioctl*
IFF_PPROMISC	user-requested promiscuous mode
IFF_MONITOR	user-requested monitor mode
IFF_STATICARP	interface only uses static ARP
IFF_DYING	interface is being shutdown
IFF_RENAMING	interface is being renamed

by multicast-forwarding agents. The IFF_SIMPLEX flag is set by Ethernet drivers whose hardware cannot receive packets that they send. Here, the output function simulates reception of broadcast and (depending on the protocol) multicast packets that have been sent. Finally, the IFF_DEBUG flag can be set to enable any optional driver-level diagnostic tests or messages. Three flags are defined for use by individual link-layer drivers (IFF_LINK0, IFF_LINK1, and IFF_LINK2). They can be used to select link-layer options, such as Ethernet medium type.

Interface addresses and flags are set with *ioctl* requests. The requests specific to a network interface pass the name of the interface as a string in the input data structure, with the string containing the name for the interface type plus the unit number. Either the SIOCSIFADDR or the SIOCAIFADDR request is used initially to define each interface's addresses. The former sets a single address for the protocol on this interface. The latter adds an address, with an associated address mask and broadcast address. It allows an interface to support multiple addresses for the

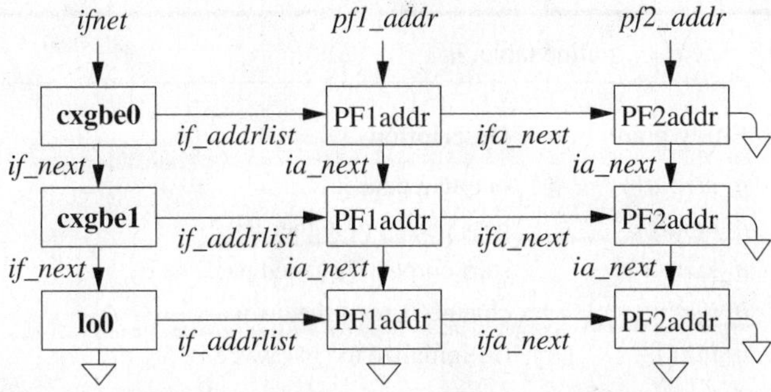

Figure 12.18 Network-interface and protocol data structures. The linked list of *ifnet* structures appears on the left side of the figure. The *ifaddr* structures storing the addresses for each interface are on a linked list headed in the *ifnet* structure and shown as a horizontal list. The *ifaddr* structures for most protocols are linked together as well, shown in the vertical lists headed by *pf1_addr* and *pf2_addr*.

same protocol. In either case, the protocol allocates an *ifaddr* structure and sufficient space for the addresses and any private data, and appends the structure onto the list of addresses for the network interface. In addition, most protocols keep a list of addresses for the protocol. The result appears like a two-dimensional linked list, as shown in Figure 12.18. An address can be deleted with the SIOCDIFADDR request.

The SIOCSIFFLAGS request can be used to change an interface's state and to do site-specific configuration. The destination address of a point-to-point link is set with the SIOCSIFDSTADDR request. Corresponding operations exist to read each value. Protocol families also can support operations to set and read the broadcast address. Finally, the SIOCGIFCONF request can be used to retrieve a list of interface names and protocol addresses for all interfaces and protocols configured in a running system. Similar information is returned by a newer mechanism based on the *sysctl* system call with a request in the routing protocol family (see Sections 12.4 and 13.5). These requests permit developers to construct network processes, such as a routing daemon, without detailed knowledge of the system's internal data structures.

The *ifnet* contains a table of function pointers that is filled in by the device driver when the device is initialized. The routines, shown in Table 12.12, define the kernel-programming interface (KPI) for working with network devices. The *if_input*() and *if_output*() routines are described in the following subsections.

The *if_ioctl*() routine is responsible for controlling the underlying device. The state of the device, the hardware features that are enabled, the flags that are set, and whether it is able to receive or send packets, are all controlled by a set of commands that are sent via the *if_ioctl*() routine.

One of the more complex operations carried out by the *if_ioctl*() routine is maintenance of the interface's multicast filters. Network-interface devices that operate over broadcast media, such as Ethernet and WiFi, all have the ability to receive packets destined for a multicast address that is meant to reach any

Table 12.12 The *ifnet* routine table.

Entry point	Description
if_output()	output a packet
if_input()	pass packet to higher layer
if_start()	start output of queued packets
if_ioctl()	change state of the device
if_init()	(re)initialize the hardware
if_resolvemulti()	modify multicast-address list
if_qflush()	flush any device-level queues
if_transmit()	directly transmit a packet without queueing
if_reassign()	move interface to a different VNET

interested listener on the local network. To receive packets with a multicast address as its destination, the network card implements a hardware filter. The filter accepts just the packets in the filtered multicast group so that the card does not need to see every packet on the network to know whether one of them has the selected multicast address set. Each network card manufacturer has its own scheme for filtering multicast packets and there has never been a unified way for the kernel to map this feature of the card into a single data structure. The kernel keeps a list of multicast addresses that user programs have asked it to listen for in a list pointed to by the *if_multiaddrs* field of the *ifnet* structure. Whenever a program joins or leaves a multicast group, a command is issued to the *if_ioctl*() routine of the driver telling the driver that the multicast-address list has now changed. It is the responsibility of the driver to reprogram the network-device hardware so that the device's filtering hardware matches what is expected by the kernel. The current implementation is somewhat lacking in terms of performance in the face of large multicast lists. Each update to the list often requires reprogramming the network-device hardware, because most network-device hardware does not provide fine-grained access to the underlying hardware tables. Whenever an entry is added to or removed from the *if_multiaddrs* list, the driver clears the hardware tables and then adds the updated list, entry by entry, until hardware has an updated view of the multicast address list. If hardware designers provided a proper API that allowed driver writers to add or remove single addresses directly from the hardware list, it would ease doing such operations.

The *if_resolvemulti*() routine exists to map a network-layer address to a hardware-layer multicast address. Each type of network device has a different way of mapping network-layer multicast addresses to link-layer multicast addresses and therefore must have a device-specific function to perform the mapping. The mapping is commonly handled by a link-layer protocol module such as Ethernet.

Packet Transmission

Once a network-layer protocol has chosen an interface, the protocol transmits a fully formatted network-level packet with the following call (where *ifp* is a pointer to the selected network-interface structure):

```
int (*if_output)(
    struct ifnet *ifp,
    struct mbuf *msg,
    struct sockaddr *dst,
    struct rtentry *rt);
```

Between network-layer protocols and the hardware devices is a layer of software responsible for resolving next-hop hardware addresses and adding link-layer information such as Ethernet hardware addresses to the packet. The output routine for the link-layer protocol modifies the packet header (*msg*) based on the destination address (*dst*) and route entry (*rtentry*) information. Once the fully formed packet reaches hardware, it may be transmitted immediately or held in the device for later transmission. In reality, transmission may not be immediate or successful. Typically, the device's transmit routine copies the packet into the device's transmit buffers or queues the packet. For unreliable media, such as Ethernet or wireless LANs, successful transmission means only that the packet has been placed on the wire or transmitted by radio without a collision. In contrast, a reliable point-to-point network such as *X.25* can guarantee proper delivery of a packet or give an error indication for each packet that was not successfully transmitted. The model employed in the networking system attaches no promise of delivery to the packets presented to a network interface and thus corresponds most closely to the Ethernet. Errors returned by the output routine are only those that can be detected immediately and are normally trivial in nature (network down, no buffer space, address format not handled, etc.). If errors are detected after the call has returned, the protocol is not notified.

When messages are transmitted in a broadcast network such as Ethernet, each network interface must formulate a link-layer address for each outgoing packet. The network layer for each protocol family selects a destination address for each message and then uses that address to select the appropriate network interface to use. This destination address is passed to the link layer's output routine as a *sockaddr* structure. The link layer is responsible for mapping the destination network-layer address into an address for the link-layer protocol associated with the transmission medium that the interface supports. This mapping may be a simple algorithm, it may require a table lookup, or it may require more involved techniques such as use of the address-resolution protocol described in Section 13.1.

Packet Reception

Network interfaces receive packets and dispatch packets to the appropriate network-layer protocol according to information encoded in the link-layer protocol header. Each protocol family must have one or more protocols that constitute the network layer described in Section 12.8. Prior to FreeBSD 5, network packets were processed by a kernel thread running a network-interrupt service routine (*netisr*). Though still referred to as the netisr subsystem, the FreeBSD kernel now processes received network packets using a ***run-to-completion*** model of data processing also referred to as direct dispatch. Each packet is carried up through as many layers of the networking code as possible. Packets that are not destined for a user process, such as those that are being forwarded to other nodes in the network, are processed until they are transmitted on to the next hop in the path to their ultimate destination. Earlier versions of FreeBSD had many points in the networking code, including between devices and protocols, where packets might be placed on a queue to be picked up and processed later. Using queues allows for a clean separation between various modules in the network stack, but it also introduces a performance penalty because of the cost of context switching between kernel threads and thrashing in the CPU's cache. The direct-dispatch model allows the system to carry out as much work as possible with a single thread whose data relevant to the current processing operation is still in the CPU's cache. Kernel threads that handle packet reception may be pinned to a particular CPU so that the maximum amount of cache coherency can be maintained throughout the packet reception process. Only when the kernel can no longer make progress processing a received packet does it place the packet on a queue for handling by another thread to execute later.

Protocols register protocol-handling functions with the netisr subsystem by calling *netisr_register*(). On receiving a packet, a device driver places the received data into an mbuf, records the interface on which the packet was received in the mbuf's packet header structure, and passes the packet to the lower part of the link-layer protocol via a call to *netisr_dispatch*(). The *netisr_dispatch*() routine makes the decision about whether to use direct dispatch and where an inbound packet should be processed. When using direct dispatch, the *netisr_dispatch*() can choose to pin the thread that is handling an inbound packet to a particular CPU. The system administrator can request that the old approach of queueing the packet and using a separate kernel thread to process all incoming packets be used. Queueing works best when many uniformly spaced packets arrive in periodic bursts. Here, the queue can hold the burst of packets that can then be processed during the slack period before the next burst. With direct dispatch, if packets arrive faster than they can be processed, all the CPUs will be busy handling earlier packets and the excess unclaimed packets will be lost by the network hardware when new packets arrive and overwrite older unclaimed ones.

The netisr module is used twice in the case of Ethernet packets. From the *ether_input*() routine, a packet is first sent through the netisr system so that the kernel can decide whether to process the packet on the current CPU, another CPU based on a tunable dispatching policy, or queued for later processing by a different kernel thread. Systems that expect to receive many packets typically process packets via direct dispatch, allowing the packet processing to run to completion.

Once a decision has been made on where to process the packet, it is passed into the netisr system again via the *ether_demux*() routine that handles passing the packet into the network-layer protocol. The *ether_demux*() routine uses the packet's ether type, a 16-bit value that indicates the network-layer protocol, to dispatch the packet via the netisr subsystem into the appropriate network-layer protocol. Each network-layer protocol accepts only an mbuf chain as an argument. By the time the packet reaches the network-layer protocol, the mbuf chain already has all the information necessary to complete processing of the packet for both network and transport-layer protocols.

12.12 Buffering and Flow Control

A major factor affecting the performance of a protocol is the buffering policy. Lack of a proper buffering policy can force packets to be dropped, cause false windowing information to be emitted by protocols, fragment memory, and degrade system performance. Because of these problems, most systems allocate a fixed pool of memory to the networking system and impose a policy optimized for normal network operation.

At boot time, a fixed amount of memory is allocated by the networking system for mbufs and mbuf clusters. More system memory may be requested for mbuf clusters as the need arises, up to a preconfigured limit. Although the kernel memory allocator can reclaim unused memory from zones, it has been configured never to reclaim memory from the zones used for mbufs and mbuf clusters. Because of the wide and frequent swings in network buffer needs, the network developers have found it more efficient to let the mbuf memory pool stay at its high-watermark usage level.

Protocol Buffering Policies

When a socket is created, the protocol reserves a protocol-selected amount of buffer space for send and receive queues. These amounts define the high watermarks used by the socket routines in deciding when to block and unblock a process.

Protocols that provide connection-level flow control, such as TCP and SCTP, select a space reservation based on the expected bandwidth and round-trip time for the connection. In operation, windows sent to peers are calculated based on the amount of free space in the socket's receive queue, and utilization of the send window received from a peer is dependent on the space available in the send queue.

Queue Limiting

Incoming packets from the network are always received unless memory allocation fails or the kernel fails to collect them from the network interface before the arrival of another packet. The default operation of the FreeBSD networking system is to use direct dispatch that carries every packet it receives through to its destination, whether that is a socket for an application on the host or transmitting it through another network interface. When the netisr subsystem has been set up to queue packets as they are received instead of running them to completion, each received packet is queued for later processing. Each queue has an upper bound on its length and any packets exceeding that bound are discarded. As explained in Section 12.11, direct dispatch is implicitly input limited when the system is too busy to collect packets from the network interface.

It is possible for a host to be overwhelmed by excessive network traffic if it is forwarding packets from a high-bandwidth network to a low-bandwidth network. As a defense mechanism, the output-queue limits can be adjusted to control network-traffic load on the system. Dropping packets is likely to increase the load on the network as applications and protocols retransmit the dropped packets. However, excessive buffering leads to large network delays and slows the feedback to TCP, which should tell TCP to slow down. The queue limit should be sufficiently high that transient overload can be handled by buffering, but not high enough to cause ***buffer bloat*** in routers [Gettys & Nichols, 2011].

The queuing in the netisr system is a single coarse knob that is tuned for the whole system. Network applications such as routers require a more complex set of queueing mechanisms. The ALTQ and Dummynet subsystems provide finer-grained control over selecting when packets are dropped. The Dummynet subsystem is discussed in Section 13.8.

12.13 Network Virtualization

With the increasing power of computer systems, it is now possible to have services running simultaneously that once would have required several separate machines. There are two basic ways in which the increased power of computing has been harnessed. One way is to virtualize the underlying hardware, introducing a layer of software on which several complete and isolated systems can execute at the same time. Hardware virtualization is not a new idea, but systems are now inexpensive and powerful enough that the use of virtualization software is common in the industry [Creasy, 1981]. Another way to harness the power of modern computing systems for multiple disparate purposes is to virtualize the services themselves. Virtualization is what an operating system does with the underlying hardware, making it appear to multiple programs that each of them has exclusive use of the machine. One type of software virtualization discussed in Section 5.9 are jails, which are containers for entire sets of programs running on top of FreeBSD.

The networking and interprocess-communication subsystems in FreeBSD have been virtualized so that many copies of the network subsystem can run in parallel. The framework that virtualizes the network subsystems is referred to as VIMAGE. Each virtual network stack is a world unto itself, with its own set of sockets and network interfaces. The implementation of the FreeBSD network

```
struct vnet {
    LIST_ENTRY(vnet)  vnet_le;      /* all vnets list */
    u_int             vnet_magic_n;
    u_int             vnet_ifcnt;
    u_int             vnet_sockcnt;
    void             *vnet_data_mem;
    uintptr_t         vnet_data_base;
};
```

Figure 12.19 The vnet structure.

stack relies on a collection of kernel global variables that maintain the data structures for all the network services. With the introduction of VIMAGE, each data structure had to be virtualized, meaning that if there are N instances of the network stack there are also N instances of each global variable. The global variables defined by the stack are collected in a special *linker set*, which is a collection of global variables that are encapsulated by the linker when a program, such as the kernel, is built. The kernel uses the linker set, *set_vnet*, to create new instances of the network stack's global state whenever a new vnet instance is created. To reduce the overhead of finding a global variable in a particular instance, a simple offset is used from the base of the memory containing the virtualized global variables. A memory offset is the fastest way to effect a lookup of the proper variable but it requires that the memory blocks containing the global variables be exactly the same size and laid out the same way in memory. If kernel developers had to do all this work themselves, it would be both tedious and error prone. A small set of macros are used to declare variables that are global to the network stack. The VNET_DEFINE macro is used throughout the kernel to set up global variables to be used by VIMAGE. When modules need to refer to externally defined variables, they use the VNET_DECLARE macro. Each virtualized global variable name is preceded by the characters *V_*, which is a convention used in the kernel to denote virtualized global variables. A complete set of each virtual stack's global state is kept in a vnet structure, shown in Figure 12.19. All vnets are kept on a singly-linked list and contain a count of the number of interfaces and sockets that are currently in use by the virtual network instance. The global variables are accessed via the *vnet_data_mem* pointer. Programmers do not access the global data members directly but instead use the macros discussed above to indicate the global variable that they are trying to access. When VIMAGE is not compiled into a kernel, all the macros that handle the indirection and variable lookup are null and empty, meaning there is no performance penalty for variable access when only a single network stack is in use.

Virtualized network stacks in FreeBSD 10 are inextricably tied to jails. A vnet is created via a call to *vnet_alloc*() that is called from the *jail_set* system call. Each jail may contain only one vnet. All the network stack's global state is initialized using the same kernel routines in the virtualized and nonvirtualized cases, with the VNET_ macros handling the proper indexing and offsets at run time.

Mapping IPC-related system calls to vnet instances is handled in the kernel using the credential structure associated with a thread. If a jail has been created with a vnet instance then every process in the jail has a valid pointer to a vnet instance in its *prison* structure. The system call then executes using the global variables ultimately pointed to from the *prison* structure. User applications and system-management programs, such as **netstat** do not expose vnet IDs to users of the system, but instead they, too, are a part of the jail and cannot see any data structures not already encapsulated in the jail. When a user outside the jail, such as a system administrator, wishes to look at the vnet instance inside a jail, he or she uses the *jexec* command, which executes the requested program from within the jail, thereby removing the need for anyone using the system to know the VNET ID of a vnet instance.

Exercises

12.1 What limitation in the use of pipes inspired the developers to design alternative interprocess-communication facilities?

12.2 Why are the FreeBSD interprocess-communication facilities designed to be independent of the filesystem for naming sockets?

12.3 Why is interprocess communication layered on top of networking in FreeBSD, rather than the other way around?

12.4 Would a screen editor be considered a naive or a sophisticated program, according to the definitions given in this chapter? Explain your answer.

12.5 What are out-of-band data? What types of sockets support the communication of out-of-band data? Describe one use for out-of-band data.

12.6 Give two requirements that interprocess communication places on a memory-management facility.

12.7 How many mbufs and mbuf clusters would be needed to hold a 3024-byte message? Draw a picture of the necessary mbuf chain and any associated mbuf clusters.

12.8 Why does an mbuf have two link pointers? For what is each pointer used?

12.9 Each socket's send and receive data buffers have high and low watermarks. For what are these watermarks used?

12.10 Consider a socket with a network connection that is queued at the socket awaiting an *accept* system call. Is this socket on the queue headed by the *so_comp* or by the *so_incomp* field in the socket structure? What is the use of the queue that does not contain the socket?

12.11 Describe two types of protocols that would immediately place incoming connection requests into the queue headed by the *so_comp* field in the socket structure.

12.12 How does the protocol layer communicate an asynchronous error to the socket layer?

12.13 Sockets explicitly refrain from interpreting the data that they send and receive. Do you believe that this approach is correct? Explain your answer.

12.14 Why does the *sosend*() routine ensure there is enough space in a socket's send buffer before making a call to the protocol layer to transmit data?

12.15 How is the type information in each mbuf used in the queueing of data at a datagram socket? How is this information used in the queueing of data at a stream socket?

12.16 Why does the *soreceive*() routine optionally notify the protocol layer when data are removed from a socket's receive buffer?

12.17 What might cause a connection to linger forever when closing?

12.18 Describe a deadlock between two processes, A and B, that are sharing two semaphores, S_1 and S_2.

12.19 How can a message queue implement a priority queue? How can it be used to allow full duplex communication?

12.20 Why doesn't the *shmdt* system call free the underlying shared memory?

*12.21 What effect might storage compaction have on the performance of network-communication protocols?

**12.22 Why is releasing mbuf-cluster storage back to the system complicated? Explain why it might be desirable.

**12.23 In the original design of the interprocess-communication facilities, a reference to a communication domain was obtained with a *domain* system call,

```
int d; d = domain("inet");
```

(where *d* is a descriptor, much like a file descriptor), and sockets then were created with

```
s = socket(type, d, protocol);
int s, type, protocol;
```

What advantages and disadvantages does this scheme have compared to the one that is used in FreeBSD? What effect does the introduction of a domain descriptor type have on the management and use of descriptors within the kernel?

**12.24 Design and implement a simple replacement for local IPC semaphores that operates on a single semaphore instead of an array. The new system should adhere to the original API to the extent that it should implement a *semget*, *semctl*, and *semop* routine.

References

BBN, 1978.
BBN, "Specification for the Interconnection of Host and IMP," Technical Report 1822, Bolt, Beranek, and Newman, Cambridge, MA, May 1978.

Cerf, 1978.
V. Cerf, "The Catenet Model for Internetworking," Technical Report IEN 48, SRI Network Information Center, Menlo Park, CA, July 1978.

Cohen, 1977.
D. Cohen, "Network Control Protocol (NCP) Software," University of Illinois Software Distribution, University of Illinois, Champaign-Urbana, IL, 1977.

Creasy, 1981.
R. J. Creasy, "The origin of the VM/370 time-sharing system," *IBM J. Res. Dev.*, pp. 483–490, September 1981.

Gettys & Nichols, 2011.
J. Gettys & K. Nichols, "Bufferbloat: Dark Buffers in the Internet," *ACM Queue*, available from http://queue.acm.org/detail.cfm?id=2071893, November 2011.

Gurwitz, 1981.
R. F. Gurwitz, "VAX-UNIX Networking Support Project—Implementation Description," Technical Report IEN 168, SRI Network Information Center, Menlo Park, CA, January 1981.

ISO, 1984.
ISO, "Open Systems Interconnection: Basic Reference Model," ISO 7498, International Organization for Standardization, available from the American National Standards Institute, 1430 Broadway, New York, NY 10018, 1984.

Postel, 1981.
J. Postel, "Internet Control Message Protocol," RFC 792, available from http://www.faqs.org/rfcs/rfc792.html, September 1981.

Ritchie, 1984.
D. Ritchie, "A Stream Input-Output System," *AT&T Bell Laboratories Technical Journal*, vol. 63, no. 8-2, pp. 1897–1910, October 1984.

Stevens et al., 2003.
R. Stevens, B. Fenner, & A. M. Rudoff, *UNIX Network Programming Volume 1: The Sockets Networking API, Third Edition,* Addison-Wesley, Reading, MA, 2003.

CHAPTER 13

Network-Layer Protocols

Chapter 12 presented the network-communications architecture of FreeBSD. This chapter examines the network protocols implemented within this framework. The FreeBSD system supports several major communication domains including IPv4, IPv6, Xerox Network Systems (NS), ISO/OSI, and the local domain (formerly known as the UNIX domain). The local domain does not include network protocols because it operates entirely within a single system. This chapter studies the portions of the TCP/IP protocols that implement the network-layer software. The protocols that make up the network layer of the TCP/IP software are responsible for moving packets between intermediate hosts in the Internet. Because the TCP/IP protocols implement a packet-switched network, there is a logical split between the components that handle, hop-by-hop, packets that reside in the network layer, and the components that present those packets as streams or datagrams to user programs, that reside in the transport layer. The transport layer protocols, including UDP, TCP, and SCTP, are discussed in Chapter 14.

Currently, there are two sets of defined protocols for the network layer of the Internet. IPv4 is the network-layer protocol that most programmers are familiar with and that has been developed and defined over a period of three decades. IPv6 is the next generation of the IP protocol and is now being deployed as an eventual replacement for IPv4. Both IPv4 and IPv6, and their attendant control and error protocols, are presented in this chapter, which describes the overall architecture of the IPv4 protocols and examines their operation according to the structure defined in Chapter 12. It then discusses changes the developers made in the system that were motivated by aspects of the IPv6 protocols and their implementation. Following the examination of the IPv4 and IPv6 network protocols is a discussion of the routing system that is integral to the network-layer protocols and the security protocols that are also implemented at the network layer. The chapter finishes with a discussion of the various packet-processing frameworks that exist within FreeBSD and which are also deeply enmeshed in the network layer.

13.1 Internet Protocol Version 4

The TCP/IP suite was developed under the sponsorship of DARPA for use on the ARPANET [DARPA, 1983; McQuillan & Walden, 1977]. The protocols are commonly known as TCP/IP, although TCP and IP are only two of the many protocols in the suite. These protocols do not assume a reliable subnetwork that ensures delivery of data. Instead, IPv4 was devised for a model in which hosts were connected to networks with varying characteristics and the networks were interconnected by routers. The ***Internet Protocols*** are responsible for host-to-host addressing and routing, packet forwarding, and packet fragmentation and reassembly. Unlike the transport protocols, they do not always operate for a socket on the local host, but may forward packets, receive packets for which there is no local socket, or generate error packets in response to these situations. The Internet protocols were designed for packet-switching networks using datagrams sent over links such as Ethernet that provide no indication of delivery.

The internetworking model leads to the use of at least two protocol layers. One layer operates end to end between two hosts involved in a conversation. It is based on a lower-level protocol that operates on a hop-by-hop basis, forwarding each message through intermediate routers to the destination host. In general, there exists at least one protocol layer above the other two: the application layer, which uses the transport protocols to implement a service or system. The three layers correspond roughly to levels 3 (network), 4 (transport), and 7 (application) in the ISO Open Systems Interconnection reference model [ISO, 1984].

The protocols that support this model have the layering illustrated in Figure 13.1. The Internet Protocol (IP) implements the network-layer protocol in the ISO model. In a packet-switched network, datagrams move hop by hop from the originating host to the destination via intermediate routers. IP provides the

Figure 13.1 TCP/IP protocol layering.

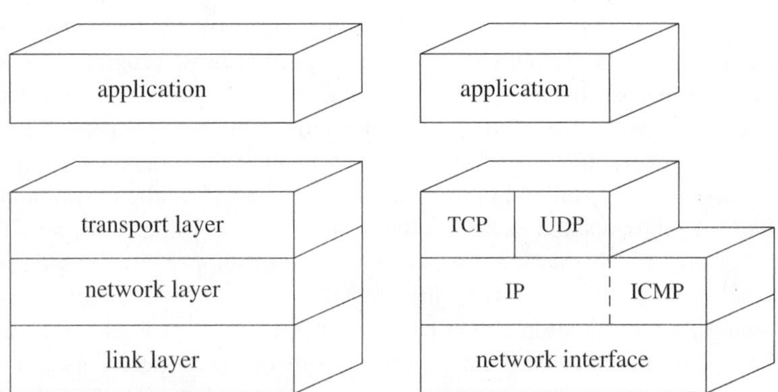

Key: TCP—Transmission Control Protocol; UDP—User Datagram Protocol; IP—Internet Protocol; ICMP—Internet Control Message Protocol.

network-level services of host addressing, routing, and, if necessary, packet fragmentation and reassembly if intervening networks cannot send an entire packet in one piece. The transport protocols use the services of IP. The User Datagram Protocol (UDP), Transmission Control Protocol (TCP) and Stream Control Transmission Protocol (SCTP) are transport-level protocols that provide additional facilities to applications that use IP. At the network layer, IP uses host addresses to identify endpoints in the network, while each protocol specifies a port identifier so that local and remote sockets can be identified. TCP provides connection-oriented, reliable, unduplicated, and flow-controlled transmission of data; it supports the stream socket type in the Internet domain. UDP provides a data checksum for checking integrity in addition to a port identifier, but otherwise adds little to the services provided by IP. UDP is the protocol used by datagram sockets in the Internet domain. The Internet Control Message Protocol (ICMP) is used for error reporting and for other simple network-management tasks; it is logically a part of IP but, like the transport protocols, is layered above IP. It usually is not accessed by users. Raw access to the IP and ICMP protocols is possible through ***raw sockets*** (see Section 13.6 for information on this facility).

All fields in the Internet protocols that are larger than a byte are expressed in ***network byte order***, with the most-significant byte first. When the IP protocols were first designed, hardware manufacturers disagreed on the order in which bytes ought to be stored in memory. Some manufacturers stored data in big-endian format, which is the same as network byte order, while others, including Intel, stored data in little-endian format. The FreeBSD network implementation uses a set of routines or macros to convert 16-bit and 32-bit integer fields between host and network byte order on hosts (such as X86 systems) that have a different native ordering. While X86 systems continue to use little-endian format, many embedded processors, particularly those used for building network routers and switches, use big-endian format. Converting between big- and little-endian byte formats introduces overhead that router and switch vendors do not want to incur, and so their systems are built with processors whose native memory format matches network byte order. On big-endian systems, the conversion macros are empty and are optimized out by the compiler.

The functions IP performs are illustrated by the contents of its packet header, shown in Figure 13.2. The header identifies source and destination hosts and the destination protocol, and it contains header and packet lengths. The identification and fragment fields are used when a packet or fragment must be broken into smaller sections for transmission on its next hop and to reassemble the fragments when they arrive at the destination. The fragmentation flags are *Don't Fragment* and *More Fragments*; the latter flag plus the offset are enough information to assemble the fragments of the original packet at the destination.

IP options are present in an IP packet if the header length field has a value larger than the 20-byte minimum. The *no-operation* option and the *end-of-option-list* option are each one byte in length. All other options are self-encoding, with a type and length preceding any additional data. Hosts and routers are able to skip over options that they do not implement. Examples of existing

0 3	4 7	8 15	16 31
version	IHL	type of service	total length
ID			fragment flags and offset
time to live		protocol	header checksum
source address			
destination address			
options			

Figure 13.2 IPv4 header. IHL is the Internet header length specified in units of 4 bytes. Options are delimited by IHL. All field lengths are given in bits.

options are the timestamp and record-route options, which are updated by each router that forwards a packet, and the source-route options, which supply a complete or partial route to the destination. These options are used rarely and most network operators silently drop packets with the source-route option because it makes it difficult to manage traffic on the network.

IPv4 Addresses

An IPv4 address is a 32-bit number that identifies the network on which a host resides and uniquely identifies a network interface on that host. It follows that a host with network interfaces attached to multiple networks has multiple addresses. Network addresses are assigned in blocks by Regional Internet Registries (RIRs) to Internet Service Providers (ISPs), which then allocate addresses to companies or individual users. If address assignment were not done in this centralized way, conflicting addresses could arise in the network and it would be impossible to route packets correctly.

Historically, IPv4 addresses were rigidly divided into three classes (A, B, and C) to address the needs of large, medium, and small networks [Postel, 1981a]. Three classes proved to be too restrictive and also too wasteful of address space. The current IPv4 addressing scheme is called Classless Inter-Domain Routing (CIDR) [Fuller et al., 1993]. In the CIDR scheme, each organization is given a contiguous group of addresses described by a single value and a ***netmask***. Using CIDR a site administrator can create multiple subnetworks each with its own netmask, without having to ask for a new address allocation from their ISP. The netmask determines to which subnetwork an address belongs. For example, a network might have a group of addresses defined by a 16-bit netmask, which means that the network is defined by the first 16 bits. The remaining 16 bits can potentially be used to identify hosts in the network, or be used to create a series of subnetworks, each of which have their own more narrowly scoped netmask. Figure 13.3 shows a network with a 16-bit netmask and two subnetworks, each with a 24-bit netmask. With this scheme the allocated network is broken up into 256 subnetworks and each subnetwork may have up to 253 hosts. The host part of each subnetwork

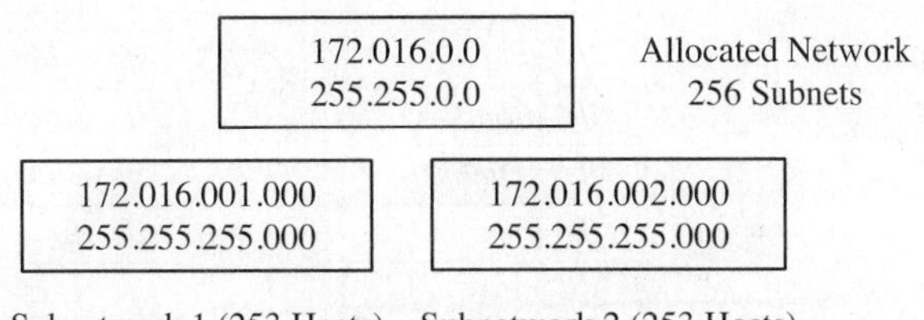

Figure 13.3 Allocating subnetworks.

address is 8 bits. Each subnetwork can only have 253 hosts because two addresses are held back for use in broadcasting packets and one is held back for the router. Networks need not be allocated on byte boundaries, but they must be a contiguous set of bits at the high end of the address. Because of this constraint, bit masks are described by a single number specifying the number of bits that represent the network part of the address. For example:

```
128.32.96.0/20
```

represents an address with a netmask of

```
0xfffff000.
```

Each Internet address assigned to a network interface is maintained in an *in_ifaddr* structure that contains a protocol-independent interface-address structure as well as additional information for use in the Internet domain (see Figure 13.4). When an interface's network mask is specified, it is recorded in the *ia_subnetmask* field of the address structure. The only time that a class-based address is used is when an interface's address is set without specifying a netmask. The system interprets local Internet addresses using the *ia_subnetmask* value. An address is considered to be local to the subnet if the field under the subnetwork mask matches the subnetwork field of an interface address.

Broadcast Addresses

On networks capable of supporting broadcast datagrams, 4.2BSD used the address with a host part of zero for broadcasts. After 4.2BSD was released, the Internet broadcast address was defined as the address with a host part of all 1s [Mogul, 1984]. This change and the introduction of subnets complicated the recognition of broadcast addresses. Hosts may use a host part of 0s or 1s to signify broadcast, and some may understand the presence of subnets, whereas others may not. For these reasons, 4.3BSD and later BSD systems set the broadcast address for each interface to be the host value of all 1s but allow the alternate address to be set for backward compatibility. If the network is subnetted, the subnet field of the broadcast address contains the normal subnet number. The logical broadcast address for the network is calculated when the address is set; this address would be the standard broadcast address if subnets were not in use. This address is needed by the IP input routine to filter input packets. On input, FreeBSD recognizes and accepts

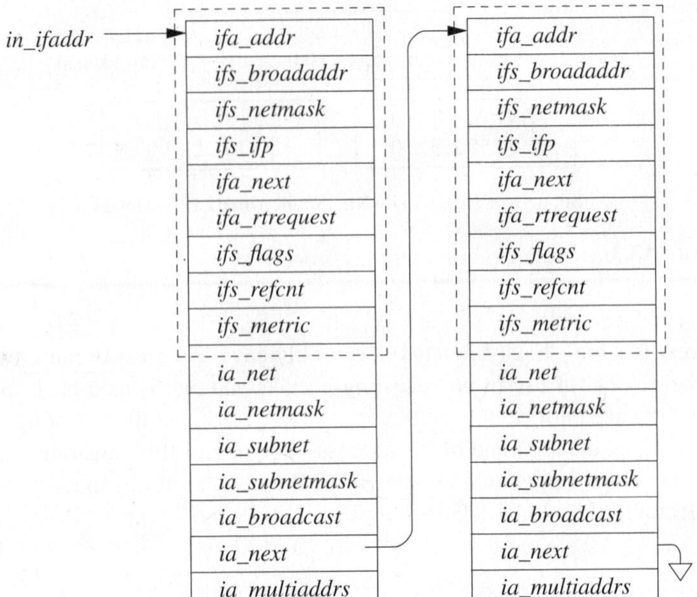

Figure 13.4 Internet interface-address structure (*in_ifaddr*).

subnet and network broadcast addresses with host parts of all 0s or all 1s, as well as the address with 32 bits of 1 ("broadcast on this physical link"). Routers always drop packets where the destination address is set to the broadcast address, which prevents broadcast packets from leaving the local subnet and causing a ***broadcast storm***.

Internet Multicast

Many link-layer network technologies, such as Ethernet, have the ability to send a single packet to a group of hosts. Being able to multicast data to a group of interested listeners is an efficient way to implement certain types of protocols, such as automatic configuration of local network parameters. IP provides a similar facility at the network-protocol level, using link-layer multicast where available [Deering, 1989]. IP multicasts are sent using destination addresses with high-order bits set to 1110. Unlike host addresses, multicast addresses do not contain network and host portions; instead, the entire address names a group, such as a group of hosts using a particular service. These groups are created dynamically and the members of the group change over time. IP multicast addresses map directly to physical multicast addresses on networks such as the Ethernet, using the low 24 bits of the IP address along with a constant 24-bit prefix to form a 48-bit link-layer address.

For a socket to use multicast, it must join a multicast group using the *setsockopt* system call. This call informs the link layer that it should receive multicasts for the corresponding link-layer address, and it also sends a multicast membership report using the Internet Group Management Protocol (IGMP) [Cain et al., 2002]. Routers and switches receive all multicast packets from directly attached networks and forward multicast datagrams as needed to group members on other networks. This function is similar to the role of routers that forward normal (unicast) packets, but the criteria for packet forwarding are different, and a packet can be forwarded to multiple neighboring networks. The purpose of IGMP is to allow switches and routers to track which hosts are interested in receiving data for a group or set of groups. Without a protocol such as IGMP, a network switch that received a multicast packet on one of its ports would not know to which other ports to forward that packet: and as a result, the packet would either be flooded to all ports or dropped. Flooding a packet to all ports is an inefficient use of network resources. Routers and switches are configured to drop packets that arrive for a group for which no connected host or network has asked for IGMP.

Link-Layer Address Resolution

Before a host can communicate with the broader Internet, it must first be able to talk to its neighbors. Hosts communicating with the IPv4 network protocol use the ***address-resolution protocol*** (ARP) to locate and communicate with their neighbors on the network. ARP is a link-level protocol that provides a dynamic address-translation mechanism for networks that support broadcast or multicast communication [Plummer, 1982]. ARP maps 32-bit IPv4 addresses to 48-bit media-access-control (MAC) addresses, such as those used by Ethernet and the wireless 802.11 link-layer protocols. Although ARP is not specific either to IPv4 protocol addresses or to Ethernet, the FreeBSD network subsystem supports only that combination, although it makes provision for additional combinations to be added. ARP is incorporated into the network-interface layer, although it logically sits between the network and link layers.

ARP maintains a set of translations from network addresses to link-layer addresses. When an address-translation request is made to the ARP service by a network-layer protocol, and the requested address is not in ARP's set of known translations, an ARP message is created that specifies the requested network address for the unknown link-layer address. This message is then broadcast by the interface with the expectation that a host attached to the network will know the translation—usually because the host is the intended target of the original message. If a response is received promptly, the ARP service uses the response to update its translation tables and to resolve the pending request, and the requesting network interface is then called to transmit the original message.

This algorithm is complicated by the need to avoid stale translation data, to minimize broadcasts when a target host is down, and to deal with failed translation requests. In addition, it is necessary to deal with packets for which transmission is attempted before the translation is completed. The ARP translation tables are implemented using a link-layer table (*lltable*) made up of link-layer entry structures (*llentry*). Both the *lltable* and *llentry* data structures are generic enough to handle different types of network to link-layer translation protocols such as the IPv6 neighbor-discovery protocol described in Section 13.3. Each *lltable* structure

Table 13.1 Link-layer entry.

Field	Description
lle_next	next entry in the table
lle_lock	lock on the entry
lle_tbl	back pointer to our link-layer table
lle_head	back pointer to our table's address lists
lle_refcnt	reference count for this entry
lle_timer	this entry's callout timer
lle_free	entry specific free routine
la_hold	list of packets awaiting address resolution
la_numheld	number of packets held awaiting resolution
la_expire	time at which this entry expires
la_flags	flags: valid, create new entry, delete entry
la_asked	how many times have we asked for this address?
la_preempt	ask for resolution before timeout occurs
ln_byhint	reachability hint for neigbor discovery
ln_state	state for neighbor discovery: incomplete, reachable, stale
ln_router	neighbor is via a router
ln_ntick	used by neighbor discovery timer
ll_addr	the resolved hardware address for the next hop

contains pointers to three functions, one to look up a translation, a second to free an entry, and a third to dump the table in some convenient format for display to a user. Every link-layer translation protocol creates its own table and populates the function pointer elements such that the kernel can call the relevant functions when necessary.

Every entry in the ARP table is contained in an *llentry* structure, shown in Table 13.1. Two of the challenges to implementing ARP are the need to time out entries so they do not get stale, and to hold packets from being transmitted until a proper reply to an ARP request is received. The *llentry* structure has elements to address both of these challenges specifically. Each entry has an *lle_timer* element that is used to set and reset a call-out timer for each entry in the table. When the timeout fires, the *arptimer*() routine is called and it cleans up and removes the stale entry. Entries have a limited lifetime to prevent a mapping from an IPv4 address to a link-layer address from remaining in the system, possibly after a host has had its IPv4 address change, either through the action of an administrator or because the host has been assigned a new IPv4 address via a protocol such as the dynamic host-configuration protocol (DHCP). A stale entry in the ARP table would prevent one host from reaching another host until the stale entry was cleared by an administrator. The default timeout for ARP entries is 20 minutes.

The timeout attempts to strike a balance between having a stale entry in the table and generating excessive ARP requests on the network. If hosts do not change their IPv4 addresses often, then having a longer timeout makes sense because ARP requests are overhead from the point of view of the network's user, as the ARP packets carry no user data.

Unlike many other network-layer protocols, ARP is not a transport protocol, yet it must hold packets for later transmission. When an IPv4 packet is ready to be transmitted by the system, the ARP table is checked by the *arpresolve*() routine to see if the kernel has a mapping for the destination's hardware address. If no such mapping exists, the *arpresolve*() routine must first prepare and transmit a request for the proper mapping. The *arpresolve*() routine cannot block the entire system while waiting for a reply, but it also cannot drop the IPv4 packet that it has been given for translation. IPv4 packets that arrive for transmission before an ARP entry has been resolved are placed on the *la_hold* queue until a proper ARP reply has been received or a timeout occurs. The *la_hold* queue is limited in size so that a malicious process cannot exhaust the kernel's store of mbufs by transmitting at a high rate to a destination that will not reply to an ARP request.

13.2 Internet Control Message Protocols (ICMP)

The ***Internet Control Message Protocols*** (***ICMP***) are the control- and error-message protocols for IPv4 [Postel, 1981b] and IPv6 [Conta et al., 2006]. Although they are layered above IP for input and output operations, they are really an integral part of IP. Most ICMP messages are received and implemented by the kernel. ICMP messages may also be sent and received via a raw IP socket (see Section 13.6).

ICMP messages fall into three general classes. One class includes various errors that may occur somewhere in the network and that may be reported back to the originator of the packet provoking the error. Such errors include routing failures (network or ***host unreachable***), expiration of the time-to-live field in a packet, or a report by the destination host that the target protocol or port number is not available. Error packets include the IP header plus at least 8 additional bytes of the packet that encountered the error. The second message class may be considered as router-to-host control messages. Instances of such messages include the *routing redirect* message that informs a host that a better route is available for a host or network, and router advertisements that provide a simple way for a host to discover its next-hop router. The final message class includes network management, testing, and measurement packets. These packets include a network-address request and reply, a network-mask request and reply, an echo request and reply, a timestamp request and reply, and a generic information request and reply.

All the actions and replies required by an incoming ICMP message are done by the relevant ICMP module. ICMPv4 and ICMPv6 packets follow a similar trajectory through the network code, the only difference being the use of the number 6 in the routines relating to IPv6. The discussion that follows describes the path of ICMPv4 packets through the network stack, but the reader is encouraged to seek out and review the ICMPv6 related functions to see how closely they resemble their IPv4 counterparts. ICMP packets are received from IP via the normal protocol-input entry point because ICMP has its own protocol number (1). The ICMP input routines handle three major cases. If the packet is an error, such as *port unreachable*, then the message is processed and delivered to any higher-level protocol that might need to know it, such as the one that initiated the communication. Messages that require a response—for example, an *echo*—are processed and then sent back to their source with the *icmp_reflect*() routine. Finally, if there are any sockets listening for ICMP messages, they are given a copy of the message by a call to *rip_input*() at the end of the *icmp_input*() routine.

When error indications are received, a generic address is constructed in a *sockaddr* structure. The address and error code are reported to each network protocol's control-input entry, *pr_ctlinput*(), by the *icmp_input*() routine. For example, an ICMP *port unreachable* message causes errors for only those connections with the specified remote port and protocol.

Routing changes suggested by redirect messages are processed by the *rtredirect*() routine, which verifies that the router from which the message was received was the next-hop ***gateway*** in use for the destination, and checks that the new gateway is on a directly attached network. If these tests succeed, the kernel routing tables are modified accordingly.

Once an incoming ICMP message has been processed by the kernel, it is passed to *rip_input*() for reception by any ICMP raw sockets. The raw sockets can also be used to send ICMP messages. The network test program **ping** works by sending ICMP echo requests on a raw socket and listening for corresponding replies.

ICMP is also used by other Internet network protocols to generate error messages. Many different errors may be detected by IP, especially on systems used as IP routers. The *icmp_error*() function constructs an error message of a specified type in response to an IP packet. Most error messages include a portion of the original packet that caused the error, as well as the type and code for the error. The source address for the error packet is selected according to the context. If the original packet was sent to a local system address, that address is used as the source. Otherwise, an address is used that is associated with the interface on which the packet was received, as when forwarding is done; the source address of the error message can then be set to the address of the router on the network closest to (or shared with) the originating host. Also, when IP forwards a packet via the same network interface on which that packet was received, it may send a redirect message to the originating host if that host is on the same network. The *icmp_error*() routine accepts an additional parameter for redirect messages: the address of the new router to be used by the host.

ICMPv6 has one responsibility that is not shared by ICMPv4, which is to handle various ***neighbor-discovery*** messages. Neighbor discovery is the protocol that allows IPv6 hosts to autoconfigure their network parameters. Unlike ARP, the neighbor-discovery protocols do not sit directly on top of the link-layer protocols, such as Ethernet and 802.11, but instead sit atop the ICMPv6 protocol. All the neighbor-discovery messages, including router and neighbor solicitation, neighbor advertisements, and router redirects, first pass through the ICMPv6 module before reaching the neighbor-discovery software.

13.3 Internet Protocol Version 6

After many successful years of deploying and using IPv4, several issues arose that caused the Internet community to start working on new versions of the Internet protocols. The motivation for the new versions was that the original Internet was running out of addresses [Gross & Almquist, 1992]. Several solutions had been proposed and implemented within the IPv4 protocols to handle this problem, including subnetting, and Classless Inter-Domain Routing (CIDR) [Fuller et al., 1993; Mogul & Postel, 1985] but neither of them proved sufficient. Several different proposals were made to replace the IPv4 protocols completely, and it took several years to make a final decision. Work on the new generation of the Internet protocols has been proceeding since the early 1990s, but it was not until 2003 that the protocol was rolled out by any large vendors. To date, the adoption of the new protocols has been limited because of the huge installed base of IPv4 hosts that must be converted.

FreeBSD includes an IPv6 networking domain that contains an implementation of the IPv6 protocols. The domain supports the entire suite of protocols from the network through the transport layers. The protocols are described in a large set of RFCs starting with Deering & Hinden [1998]. During the development of IPv6, several open-source implementations were written. Each implementation supported a different subset of the full features of IPv6 according to the needs of its authors. The one that eventually had the most complete set was developed by the KAME project [KAME, 2003] and is the implementation that was adopted by FreeBSD. A complete discussion of IPv6 is beyond the scope of this book. This section discusses the areas of IPv6 that make it different from IPv4 and the changes that had to be made to FreeBSD to accommodate those differences.

There are several major differences between IPv4 and IPv6 including:

- 128-bit addresses at the network layer
- Packet fragmentation discouraged
- Emphasis on automatic configuration
- Native support for security protocols

The biggest factor driving the move to a new protocol was the need for more addresses. The first change to be made between IPv4 and IPv6 was to enlarge the size of an address. An IPv4 address is 32 bits, which is theoretically large enough to address over 4 billion interfaces. There are two primary reasons why that theoretical maximum has never been reached. First is the need to control the size of the routing tables in the core Internet routers. Internet routing is most efficient when many addresses can be communicated by a single address, the address of the router to that network. If each address required its own route, there would be over 4 billion addresses in every routing table in the Internet, which would not be possible given the current state of network hardware and software. Thus, addresses are aggregated into blocks, and these blocks are assigned to ISPs, which then carve them up into smaller blocks for their customers. The customers then take these blocks and break them down further, through subnetting, and finally assign individual addresses to particular computers. At each level of this hierarchy, some addresses are kept aside for future use, which leads to the second source of IP address waste, overallocation. Because it is expensive and difficult to renumber a large installation of machines, customers request more addresses than they need in an attempt to prevent ever having to renumber their networks. This overallocation has lead to several calls for companies and ISPs to return unused addresses [Nesser, 1996]. For these reasons, the size of the IP address space was extended to 128 bits. The number of addresses available in IPv6 has been compared to numbering all the atoms in the universe or giving every person on the earth over a billion IP addresses.

As the Internet has been embraced by people who are not computer scientists and engineers, a major stumbling block has been the difficulty of setting up and maintaining an Internet-connected host. Companies have teams of professionals who do this work, but for a small company the task can be daunting. These difficulties led the designers of IPv6 to include several types of ***autoconfiguration*** into the protocol. Ideally, anyone using IPv6 can turn on a computer, connect a network cable to it, and be on the Internet in a matter of minutes. This goal has not been fully achieved, but it does explain many of the design decisions in the IPv6 protocols.

Even before the Internet was a commercial success, network researchers and operators understood that the original protocols did not provide any security to users of the network. The lack of security had two causes: the first was the initial emphasis of Internet development on sharing information; the second was that until the end of the 1990s the United States government prohibited the export of any security-related software. IPv6 includes a set of security protocols (IPSec) that are defined for IPv4 as well. IPSec is a standard part of IPv6 and is covered in Section 13.7.

IPv6 Addresses

IPv6 defines several types of addresses:

Unicast — Just like a unicast address in IPv4, the IPv6 unicast address is a 128-bit quantity that uniquely identifies an interface on a host.

Multicast — An address that identifies a set of interfaces participating in some form of group communication. A packet sent to a multicast address is delivered to all interfaces in the network that are bound to that address.

Anycast Anycast addresses are used to identify common services. The network will route a packet sent to an anycast address to the nearest interface bound to that address. Nearest is measured by the number of hops the packet would have to make between the source and destination.

Note that unlike IPv4, IPv6 does not have the concept of a broadcast address that is received by all interfaces on a particular link. The role of broadcast addresses in IPv4 is to provide a way for hosts to discover services even when they do not yet have their own IP address. Broadcast packets are wasteful in that they are delivered to every host on a link, even if that host does not provide the relevant service. Rather than using broadcast addresses as a way for a host to find a service, IPv6 uses a well-known multicast address for each service being offered. Hosts that are prepared to provide a service register to listen on the well-known multicast address assigned to that service.

The 128-bit addresses in IPv6 necessitated creating new structures to hold them and new interfaces to handle them. While it is reasonably easy to work with the traditional dotted-quad notation of IPv4 (i.e., 192.168.1.1), writing out an IPv6 address textually requires a bit more work, which is why the addressing architecture of IPv6 received its own RFC [Deering & Hinden, 2006]. When an IPv6 address is written, it is represented as a set of colon-separated hex bytes. The value between each set of colons represents a 16-bit value. For example, the string

```
fd69:0:0:8:0:0:200C:417A
```

represents a local unicast address in the IPv6 network, similar to the IPv4 addresses defined in RFC 1918. When written out as text, a portion of the address that contains zeros may be abbreviated with a double colon:

```
fd69::8:0:0:200C:417A
```

The first set of two zeros was eliminated in this address. When an address is abbreviated, only one set of zeros may be removed. For the run of zeros being eliminated, either all zeros must be removed or none. The following are examples of improper abbreviations of the preceding address:

```
fd69::0:8:0:0:200C:417A
fd69::8::200C:417A
```

The first example does not subsume the entire first set of zeros. The second example is ambiguous because you cannot tell how to divide the four zeros between the two areas marked with double colons.

Unicast and multicast addresses are differentiated by the bits set at the beginning of the address. All globally routable unicast addresses begin with the bits

Table 13.2 Well-known IPv6 addresses.

Address	Description
FF02::1	all nodes multicast address (link local)
FF02::2	all routers multicast address (link local)
FF05::2	all routers multicast address (site local)
FF02:0:0:0:0:1:FF00::/104	solicited node address
::1	the loopback address
::	the unspecified address

001, while multicast addresses start with 1111 1111. Examples of the most common addresses are shown in Table 13.2. The unspecified address is used by a host that has not yet been assigned an address when it is in the process of bringing up its network interface. The solicited-node address is used during neighbor discovery, which is covered later in this section.

A piece of baggage that was not carried over from IPv4 to IPv6 was the concept of network classes in addresses. IPv6 always uses the CIDR style of marking the boundary between the network prefix (hereafter referred to simply as the prefix) and the interface identifier, which is what identifies an interface on a particular host. The following examples all define the same fictitious network that has a 60-bit prefix:

```
fd69:0000:0000:1230:0000:0000:0000:0000/60
fd69::1230:0:0:0:0/60
fd69:0:0:1230::/60
```

IPv6 Packet Formats

When IPv6 was being designed, one goal was to reduce the amount of work necessary for a router to forward a packet. This reduction was addressed as follows:

- Simplification of the packet header. Comparing the IPv6 packet header in Figure 13.5 to the IPv4 header shown in Figure 13.2, we see that there are four fewer fields in the IPv6 header and that only one of them needs to be modified while the packet is in transit: the ***hop limit***. The hop limit is decremented every time the packet is forwarded by a router until the hop limit reaches 0, at which point the packet is dropped.
- The packet header is a fixed size. The IPv6 header never carries any options or padding within it. Options processing in IPv4 is an expensive operation that must be carried out whenever an IPv4 packet is sent, forwarded, or received.

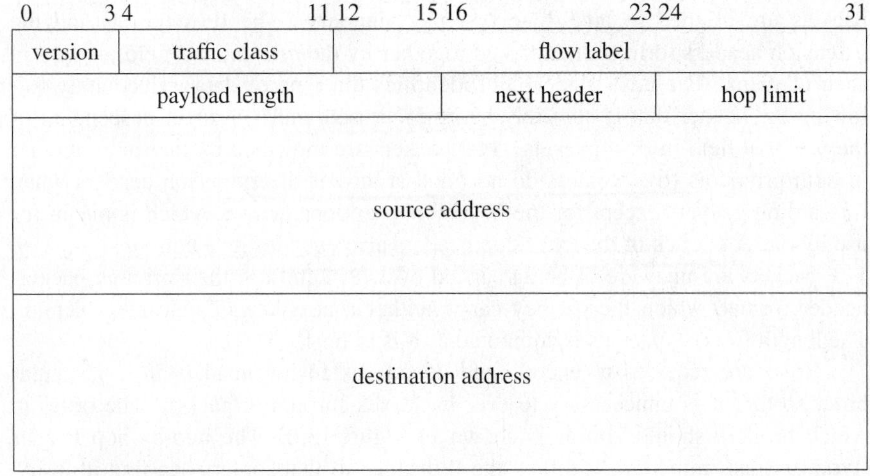

Figure 13.5 IPv6 packet header.

- IPv6 removed fragmentation at the network layer. Avoiding packet fragmentation simplifies packet forwarding as well as processing by hosts, since hosts are where the reassembly of fragmented packets takes place.

- The IPv6 header does not contain a checksum. Checksums are expensive to calculate and the IPv4 checksum only protected the IPv4 header. Since all modern transport protocols include a checksum over their data, a checksum at the IPv6 layer was deemed redundant.

All these simplifications make processing IPv6 packets less compute intensive than processing those of IPv4. Completely removing features that were inconvenient, such as options or fragmentation, would have decreased the acceptance of IPv6. Instead, the designers came up with a way to add these features, and several others, without polluting the base packet header. Extra features and upper-layer protocols in IPv6 are handled by ***extension headers***. An example packet is shown in Figure 13.6. All extension headers begin with a next-header field as well as an 8-bit length field that shows the length of the extension in units of 8 bytes. All

Figure 13.6 Extension headers. Key: AH—authentication header (type 51); ESP—encapsulating-security payload (type 50).

next: 0	next: 51 length: 1	next: 50 length: 4	next: 6 length: 6	
IP	hop by hop	AH	ESP	TCP

packets are aligned to an 8-byte (64-bit) boundary. The IPv6 header and the extension headers form a chain linked together by the *next-header* field, present in each of them. The next-header field identifies the type of data immediately following the header that is currently being processed and is a direct descendant of the *protocol* field in IPv4 packets. TCP packets are indicated by the same number in both protocols (6). Routers do not look at any of the extension headers when forwarding packets except for the hop-by-hop options header, which is meant for use by routers. Each of the extension headers also encodes its length in some way. TCP packets are unaware of being carried over IPv6 and use their original packet-header format, which means they carry neither a next-header field nor a length. The length for TCP packets is computed as it is in IPv4.

Hosts are required to encode and decode extension headers in a particular order so that it is unnecessary to ever backtrack through a packet. The order in which headers should appear is shown in Figure 13.6. The hop-by-hop header (type 0) must immediately follow the IP header so that routers can find it easily. The authentication header (AH) and encapsulating-security payload (ESP) headers are used by security protocols that are discussed in Section 13.7 and must come before the TCP header and data, since the information in the security headers must be retrieved before they can be used to authenticate and decrypt the TCP header and data.

Changes to the Socket API

It has always been the policy of the Internet Engineering Task Force (IETF) to specify protocols and not implementations. For IPv6, this rule was bent so that application developers would have an API to which they could code and speed the migration of applications to IPv6. The designers took the original sockets interface, as it was then implemented in BSD, and specified extensions [Gilligan et al., 1999] that are included in FreeBSD. There were several goals in extending the sockets API:

- The changes should not break existing applications. The kernel should provide backward compatibility for both source and binary.
- Minimize the number of changes needed to get IPv6 applications up and running.
- Ensure interoperability between IPv6 and IPv4 hosts.
- Addresses carried in data structures should be 64-bit aligned to obtain optimum performance on 64-bit architectures.

Adding a new address type was easy because all the routines that handle addresses, such as *bind*, *accept*, *connect*, *sendto*, and *recvfrom*, already work with addresses as opaque entities. A new data structure, *sockaddr_in6*, was defined to hold information about IPv6 endpoints as shown in Figure 13.7. The *sockaddr_in6* structure is similar to the *sockaddr_in* shown in Section 12.4. It contains the length of the structure, the family (which is always AF_INET6), a 16-bit port that identifies the transport-layer endpoint, a flow identifier, network-layer address, and

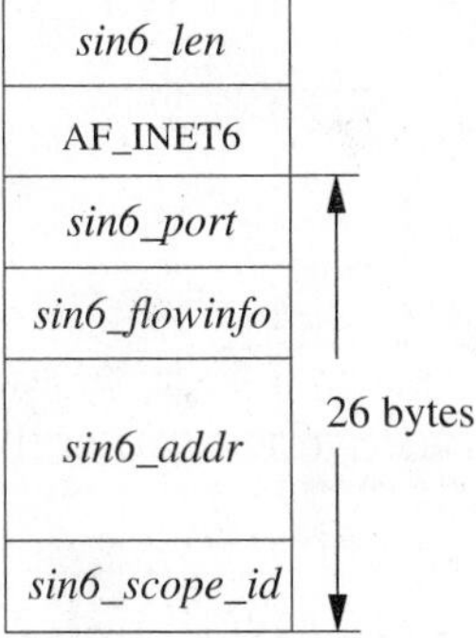

Figure 13.7 IPv6-domain socket-address structure.

a scope identifier. Many proposals have been put forth for the use of the flow information and scope identifier, but these fields are currently unused. The flow information is intended as a way of requesting special handling for packets within the network. For example, a real-time audio stream might have a particular flow label so that it would be given priority over less time-critical traffic. Although the idea is simple to explain, its implementation in a network where no one entity controls all the equipment is problematic. At present, there is no way to coordinate what a flow label means when it leaves one network and enters another. Until this conundrum is solved, the flow label will be used only in private network deployments and research labs.

IPv6 defines several scopes in which an address can be used. In IPv4, all addresses are global in scope, meaning that they are valid no matter where they are found on the Internet. The defined scopes in IPv6 are link local, site local, organization local, and global. An address in a lesser scope may not be passed out to a broader scope. For example, a link-local address will not be forwarded to another link by a router.

Working with 128-bit addresses by hand is clumsy and error prone. Applications are expected to deal almost exclusively with named entities for IPv6 by using the domain name system (DNS) [Thomson & Huitema, 1995]. The original API for looking up an address from a hostname, *gethostbyname*(), was specific to the IPv4 protocol, so a new API was added to lookup any type of address given a name. When a client wishes to find a server, it uses the *getaddrinfo*() routine:

```
int getaddrinfo(
        char *name,
        const char *servname,
        const struct addrinfo *hints,
        struct addrinfo **res);
```

The *getaddrinfo*() routine can work with any address family because the third argument is a structure that specifies the address family and the last argument is a similar structure that contains the address type being returned along with the

Table 13.3 Fields of the *addrinfo* structure.

Field	Description
ai_flags	specify type of address to return
ai_family	address family for socket (AF_INET, AF_INET6, ...)
ai_socktype	socket type (SOCK_DGRAM, SOCK_STREAM, SOCK_SEQPACKET, ...)
ai_protocol	protocol for socket (PROTO_UDP, PROTO_TCP, PROTO_SCTP, ...)
ai_addrlen	length of appropriate socket-address
ai_addr	socket-address for socket
ai_canonname	string name of the host and service being sought
ai_next	pointer to next in list

properly formatted address. Services are looked up using the structure shown in Table 13.3, which includes fields for the address family, socket type, and protocol being sought, as well as the string name of the host.

Autoconfiguration

A goal of IPv6 is to make adding a computer to the network a simpler process, one that requires less human intervention. The mechanisms and protocols that are used to reach this goal are called autoconfiguration. For a host to be automatically configured it has to be able to discover several pieces of information from the network without any prior knowledge. The host must be able to automatically figure out its own address, the address of its next-hop router, and the network prefix of the link to which it is attached. To communicate with other hosts on its link and with its next-hop router, a host needs the link-level addresses for those other systems. These questions are answered by the neighbor-discovery protocol that is a part of IPv6 and is defined in Narten et al. [2007]. Neighbor discovery either enhances or replaces disparate protocols that were a part of IPv4 and unifies them in a set of ICMPv6 messages [Conta et al., 2006]. Neighbor discovery uses ICMPv6 and is available on any system running IPv6. The first step of the neighbor-discovery protocol is router discovery used to find its next-hop router. The second step is the neighbor discovery, which is used to get the addresses of its neighbors.

A host finds its next-hop router in two different ways. IPv6 routers periodically send router-advertisement messages to the *all-nodes* multicast address. The format of a router-advertisement message is shown in Figure 13.8. The code field is currently always zero and the flags are unused. They are intended to allow for future extensions to the protocol. All hosts configured to pick up these multicast packets will see the router advertisement and process it. Although router advertisements are sent often enough to make sure that all hosts on a link know the location of their router and know when it has failed, this mechanism is insufficient

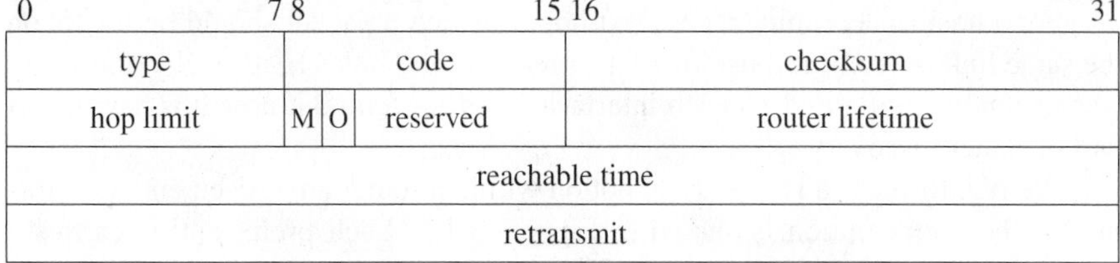

Figure 13.8 Router advertisement. Key: M—managed flag; O—other flag.

for bringing a new host up on the link. When a host first connects to the network, it sends a ***router-solicitation*** message to the *all-routers* multicast address. A router that receives a valid solicitation must immediately send a router advertisement in response. The advertisement will be sent to the multicast address of all nodes unless the router knows that it can successfully send a unicast response to the host that sent the solicitation. Router advertisements include a retransmit timer value that tells the receiving host how many milliseconds to wait between sending its neighbor solicitations. The retransmit timer controls the number of neighbor-solicitation messages any one host can send and keeps the overhead of such traffic from overwhelming the network. A router may send an option with the advertisement that includes the link-layer address of the router. If the link-layer address option is included, the receiving hosts will not need to perform neighbor discovery before sending packets to the router.

Each host maintains a linked list of its router entries. A single router entry is shown in Figure 13.9. Whenever a router advertisement is received, it is passed to the *defrtrlist_update*() routine that checks the message to see if it represents a new router and, if so, places a new entry at the head of the default router list. Each router advertisement message contains a lifetime field. This lifetime controls how long an entry may stay in the default router list. Whenever *defrtrlist_update*() receives a router advertisement for a router that is already present in the default router list, that router's expiration time is extended.

Figure 13.9 Router entry.

rtaddr
flags
rtlifetime
expire
ifp

struct *nd_defrouter*

For a host to determine if the next hop to which a packet should be sent is on the same link as itself, it must know the prefix for the link. Historically, the prefix was manually configured on each interface in the system, but now it is handled as part of router discovery.

Prefix information is sent as an option within a router advertisement. The format of the prefix option is shown in Figure 13.10. Each prefix option carries a 128-bit address. The number of valid bits in this address is given by the prefix-length field of the option. For example, the prefix given in the preceding example would be sent in a prefix option with

```
fd69:0000:0000:1230:0000:0000:0000:0000
```

encoded into the prefix field and 60 stored in the prefix-length field. Each prefix is only valid for the period shown by the valid lifetime. Later router advertisements that contain prefix options will have valid lifetimes that move into the future. The preferred lifetime controls the period of time that the prefix should be used by the host and may be shorter than the valid lifetime. A prefix that has passed the valid lifetime cannot be used. A prefix that has passed the preferred lifetime may be used but will trigger a new solicitation. The response to the solicitation will be either the same prefix or a new prefix with a new valid lifetime. When a host discovers that it has a prefix whose lifetime has expired, the prefix is removed from the interface with which it is associated, and the expired prefix no longer determines whether a destination address is on the local link. One way to support a backup router would be to send out its advertisement with an expired preferred lifetime, but a long valid lifetime. If the primary router with a valid preferred lifetime is available, it will be used, but if it goes down or times out, the backup router can be found and used.

Figure 13.10 Prefix option. Key: O—onlink flag; A—auto flag.

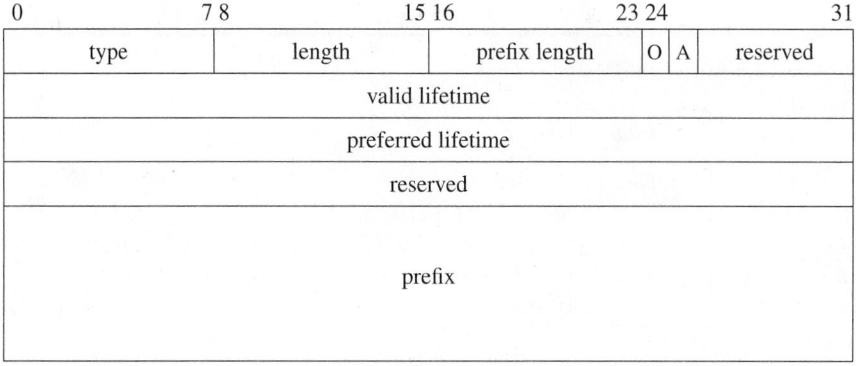

0 – 7	8 – 15	16 – 23	24 – 31		
type	length	prefix length	O	A	reserved
valid lifetime					
preferred lifetime					
reserved					
prefix					

All options encoded into neighbor- and router-discovery messages are appended immediately after the message being sent. For example, the prefix option follows the router-advertisement message to which it relates. All options start with a nonzero type and a length that specifies the number of bytes present in the option. Router- and neighbor-discovery packets are contained within ICMPv6 packets that are themselves contained in IPv6 packets. The IPv6 packet length contains the size of the IPv6 header, the ICMPv6 header, ICMPv6 options, and any message. When unpacking a router or neighbor advertisement, the IPv6 packet length is used to ensure that the packet is valid. If the kernel finds that the length given in the packet is too short to encompass any options, then the packet is discarded.

When a host has a packet for another host on its link, including its next-hop router, it must find the link-layer address of the host to which it wishes to send the packet. In IPv4, this process was handled by the address-resolution protocol (ARP); see Section 13.1. A problem with ARP is that it is Ethernet specific and has encoded in it assumptions about link-layer addresses that makes it difficult to adapt to other link types.

A host learns the link-layer addresses of its neighbors using a pair of messages: the neighbor solicitation and the neighbor advertisement. When the kernel wants to send an IPv6 packet to another host, the packet eventually passes through the *ip6_output*() routine, which does various checks on the packet to make sure that it is suitable for transmission. All properly formed packets are then passed down to the neighbor-discovery module via the *nd6_output*() routine. In earlier versions of FreeBSD, the *nd6_output*() routine handled mapping the IPv6 address to the link-layer address through a lookup in the routing table. After the link-layer address tables were removed from the routing table, a new routine, *nd6_output_lle*() was introduced to handle the mapping process. The *nd6_output_lle*() routine is now called by all the other IPv6 routines to pass packets down toward the interface layer. The *nd6_output*() routine is maintained for backwards compatibility but is now a simple wrapper around *nd6_output_lle*(). Once the packet has a correct link-layer destination address, it is passed to a network-interface driver via the driver's *if_output*() routine. The relationships between the various protocol modules are shown in Figure 13.11. The neighbor-discovery module does not have an *nd_input*() routine because it receives messages via the ICMPv6 module. This inversion of the protocol layering allows the neighbor-discovery protocol to be independent of the link layer. In IPv4, the ARP module is hooked into the network interface so that it can send and receive messages. The connection between ARP and the underlying link-layer interfaces means that the ARP code must understand every link type that the system supports.

Link-layer addresses are stored in their own link-layer table, and that is where *nd6_output_lle*() attempts to look up the link-layer address for the packets that are passed to it. When the host does not yet know the link-layer address for the destination, the outgoing packet must be held until neighbor discovery completes. The

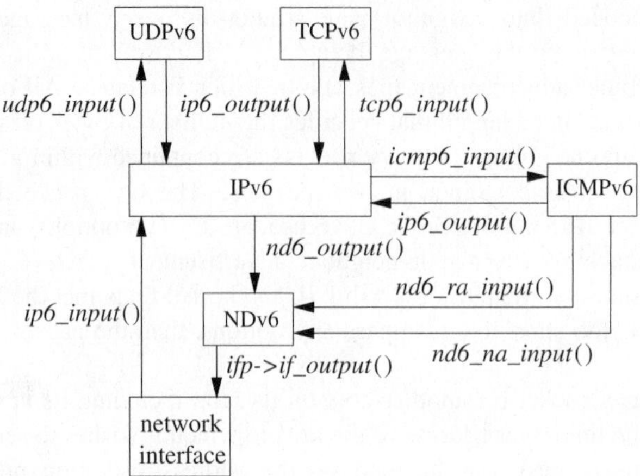

Figure 13.11 IPv6-module relationships. *nd6_ra_input*()—router-advertisement input routine; *nd6_na_input*()—neighbor-advertisement input routine.

outgoing packet is added to the end of the list of packets pointed to by the *ln_hold* field of the *llentry* structure. The *nd6_output_lle*() routine does not wait for the neighbor advertisement but returns. When a response is received as a neighbor advertisement, it is processed by the IPv6 and ICMPv6 modules and is finally passed into the neighbor-discovery module by a call to the *nd6_na_input*() routine, as shown in Figure 13.11. The *nd6_na_input*() routine records the link-layer address and checks to see if any packets were being held for transmission to that destination. If there are packets awaiting transmission, the *nd6_output_lle*() routine is invoked to send them. A link-layer address for the saved packet's destination is now in the system, so *nd6_output_lle*() will copy the link-layer address into the mbuf chain and invoke the network interface's *if_output*() routine to transmit the packet.

Once per second, the *nd6_timer*() routine walks the neighbor-discovery link-layer address list as well as the default-router and interface lists and removes the entries that have passed their expiration time. Removing stale entries prevents the system from trying to send data to a host that has failed or become unreachable.

13.4 Internet Protocols Code Structure

The interface between the transport- and network-layer protocols in FreeBSD is defined by a small set of routines, which either take packets from the transport layers and encapsulate them for transmission, or take network-layer packets that have arrived on one interface and forward them out via another interface. The routines that implement the IPv4 and IPv6 protocols are similar in structure and will be described in this section.

Output

The calling convention for IPv4's output routine is

```
int ip_output(
    struct mbuf *msg,
    struct mbuf *opt,
    struct route *ro,
    int flags,
    struct ip_moptions *imo,
    struct inpcb *inp);
```

The parameter *msg* is an mbuf chain containing the packet to be sent, including a skeletal IP header; *opt* is an optional mbuf containing IP options to be inserted into the header. If the route *ro* is given, it contains a reference to a routing entry (*rtentry* structure) that specifies a route to the destination from a previous call and in which any new route will be left for future use. Cached routes were moved from the network layer into the transport-layer protocols in FreeBSD 5.2 (see the TCP host-cache metrics described in Section 14.4). The cached route should appear as a TCP host-cache metric, but as of FreeBSD 10 it has not been added, so the *ro* entry is never specified. Unless a cached route is passed down through the *ro* parameter, a route lookup must be performed for each packet. The *flags* may allow the use of broadcast or may indicate that the routing tables should be bypassed. If present, *imo* includes options for multicast transmissions. The protocol control block, *inp*, is used by the IPSec subsystem (see Section 13.7) to hold data about security associations for the packet.

```
int ip6_output(
    struct mbuf *m0,
    struct ip6_pktopts *opt,
    struct route_in6 *ro,
    int flags,
    struct ip6_moptions *im6o,
    struct ifnet **ifpp,
    struct inpcb *inp)
```

The IPv6 output routine takes nearly the same arguments as the IPv4 output routine. The only additional parameter is a pointer *ifpp* where the IPv6 module can let the transport layer know something about the physical interface on which the packet was output. The returned interface pointer is currently used only in recording statistics about how many packets were transmitted on an interface.

The outline of the work performed by *ip_output*() is as follows:

- Insert any IP options.
- Fill in the remaining header fields (IP version, zero offset, header length, and a new packet identification) if the packet contains an IP pseudo-header.

- Determine the route (i.e., outgoing interface and next-hop address).
- Check whether the destination is a multicast address. If it is, determine the outgoing interface and hop count.
- Check whether the destination is a broadcast address; if it is, check whether broadcast is permitted.
- Do any IPSec manipulations that are necessary on the packet such as encryption.
- See if there are any filtering rules that would modify the packet or prevent the system from sending it.
- If the packet size is no larger than the maximum packet size for the outgoing interface, compute the checksum and call the interface output routine.
- If the packet size is larger than the maximum packet size for the outgoing interface, break the packet into fragments and send each in turn.

If no route reference is passed as a parameter, an internal routing-reference structure is used temporarily. A route structure that is passed from the caller is checked to see that it is a route to the same destination and that it is still valid. If either test fails, the old route is freed. After these checks, if there is no route, *in_rtalloc_ign*() is called to allocate a route. The route returned includes a pointer to the outgoing interface. The interface information includes the maximum packet size, flags including broadcast and multicast capability, and the output routine. If the route is marked with the RTF_GATEWAY flag, the network-layer address of the next-hop router is given by the route; otherwise, the packet's destination is the next-hop destination. If routing is to be bypassed because of a MSG_DONTROUTE option or a SO_DONTROUTE option, a directly attached network shared with the destination is sought. If there is no directly attached network, an error is returned. Once the outgoing interface and next-hop destination are found, enough information is available to send the packet.

As described in Section 12.11, the interface output routine normally validates the destination address and places the packet on its output queue, returning errors only if the interface is down, the output queue is full, or the destination address is not understood.

The *ip6_output*() routine follows the same pattern as the one presented for *ip_output*() but adds a few IPv6-specific steps. Unlike the IPv4 protocol, in which the header is a single entity, an IPv6 packet is made up of a chain of smaller headers, all of which must be processed before the packet can be transmitted. Many of the differences between the IPv6 and IPv4 output routines exist to handle extension-header processing. A packet that does not contain extension headers, such as hop-by-hop options, is simpler to construct than a similar IPv4 packet. One other difference between the IPv4 and IPv6 output routines is the need to handle the scoping rules for the packet. Section 13.2 describes how IPv6 packets all have a scope: link local, site local, organization local, and global. Deciding what scope a packet belongs to is handled in the *ip6_output*() routine and is based on the source address attached to the interface on which the packet will be transmitted. Because the scope is based on the interface that the packet will be transmitted on, it must be calculated after the packet's route is selected, as well as having been passed through any packet filters, including IPSec. One core concept in IPv6 was to prevent packets from being fragmented as they had been in IPv4. Fragmentation complicates the packet-processing code, not only in hosts but also in the intermediate routers, as well as in firewalls and other systems internal to a network. Unfortunately, practical concerns required the ability to fragment packets to be retrofitted into the IPv6 code. Retrofitting fragmentation into the output routine has caused it to be even more complex than the similar code in IPv4, as can be seen by reading the last section of *ip6_output*().

Input

In Section 12.11, we described the reception of a packet by a network interface. The netisr subsystem then runs the packet through the various upper-layer protocols via direct dispatch. The IPv4 and IPv6 input routines are invoked when network interfaces receive messages for one of these protocols. The input routine, *ip_input*() or *ip6_input*(), is called with an mbuf that contains the packet to be processed. A packet is processed in one of four ways: it is passed as input to a higher-level protocol, it encounters an error that is reported back to the source, it is dropped because of an error, or it is forwarded to the next hop on its path to its destination. In outline form, the steps in the processing of a packet on input are as follows:

1. Verify that the packet is at least as long as an IPv4 or IPv6 header and ensure that the header is contiguous.
2. For IPv4, checksum the header of the packet and discard the packet if there is an error.
3. Verify that the packet is at least as long as the header indicates and drop the packet if it is not. Trim any padding from the end of the packet.
4. Do any filtering or security functions required by *ipfw* or IPSec.
5. Process any options associated with the header.
6. Check whether the packet is for this host. If it is, continue processing the packet. If it is not, and if the system is acting as a router, try to forward the packet; otherwise, drop it.
7. If the packet has been fragmented, keep it until all its fragments are received and reassembled, or until it is too old to keep.
8. Pass the packet to the input routine of the next-higher-level protocol.

When the incoming packet is passed into the input routine, one field of the *mbuf* is a pointer to the interface on which the packet was received. This information is passed to the next protocol, to the forwarding function, or to the error-reporting function. If any error is detected and is reported to the packet's originator, the source address of the error message will be set according to the incoming packet's destination and the incoming interface.

The decision whether to accept a received packet for local processing by a higher-level protocol is not simple. If a host has multiple addresses, the packet is accepted if its destination matches any one of those addresses. If any of the attached networks support broadcast and the destination is a broadcast address, the packet is also accepted.

The IPv4 input routine uses a simple and efficient scheme for locating the input routine for the receiving protocol of an incoming packet. The protocol field in the packet is 8 bits long; thus, there are 256 possible protocols. Fewer than 256 protocols are defined or implemented, and the Internet protocol switch has far fewer than 256 entries. Therefore, *ip_input*() uses a 256-element mapping array to map from the protocol number to the protocol-switch entry of the receiving protocol. Each entry in the array is initially set to the index of a raw IP entry in the protocol switch. Then, for each protocol with a separate implementation in the system, the corresponding map entry is set to the index of the protocol in the IP protocol switch. When a packet is received, IP simply uses the protocol field to index into the mapping array and calls the input routine of the appropriate protocol. Locating the next-layer protocol for IPv6 is different from the IPv4 case because IPv6 packets are linked together by their *next-header* fields. Instead of simply passing the packet up to the next layer directly via a single call through the *inet6sw* array, the *ip6_input*() routine can call many input routines including *udp6_input*(), *tcp6_input*(), *sctp6_input*(), or any other, high-level protocol-input routine until one of them returns a value of IPPROTO_DONE. The loop that walks the chain of IPv6 headers can be seen at the end of the *ip6_input*() routine.

Forwarding

Implementations of IP traditionally have been designed for use by either hosts or routers, rather than by both. A system was either an endpoint for packets or a router. Routers forward packets between hosts on different networks but only use upper-level protocols for maintenance functions. Traditional host systems do not incorporate packet-forwarding functions; instead, if they receive packets not addressed to them, they simply drop the packets. 4.2BSD was the first common implementation that attempted to provide both host and router services in normal operation. This approach meant that 4.2BSD hosts connected to multiple networks could serve as routers and hosts, reducing the requirement for dedicated router hardware. Early routers were expensive and not especially powerful. Alternatively, the existence of router-function support in ordinary hosts made it more likely for misconfiguration errors to result in problems on the attached networks. The most serious problem had to do with forwarding of a broadcast packet because of a misunderstanding by either the sender or the receiver of the packet's destination. The packet-forwarding router functions are disabled by default in

FreeBSD. They may be enabled at run time, on a per-protocol basis, by setting either or both of the *net.inet.ip.forwarding* or *net.inet6.ip6.forwarding* sysctl variables. Hosts not configured as routers never attempt to forward packets or to return error messages in response to misdirected packets. As a result, far fewer misconfiguration accidents occur.

The procedure for forwarding IP packets received at a router but destined for another host is the following:

1. Check that forwarding is enabled. If it is not, drop the packet.
2. Check that the destination address is one that can be forwarded.
3. Save some important components of the received message in case an error message must be generated in response.
4. Determine the route to be used in forwarding the packet.
5. If the outgoing route uses the same interface as that on which the packet was received, and if the originating host is on that network, send a redirect message to the originating host.
6. Handle any IPSec updates that must be made to the packet header.
7. Call the appropriate output routine, either *ip_output*() for IPv4 or *nd6_output*() for IPv6, to send the packet to its destination or to the next-hop gateway.
8. If an error is detected, send an ICMP error message to the source host.

Multicast transmissions are handled separately from other packets. Systems may be configured as multicast routers independently from other routing functions. Multicast routers receive all incoming multicast packets and forward those packets to local receivers and group members on other networks according to group memberships and the remaining hop count of incoming packets.

13.5 Routing

The networking system was designed for a heterogeneous network environment, in which a collection of local-area networks are connected at one or more points through routers, as shown in Figure 13.12. Routers are nodes with multiple network interfaces, one on each local- or wide-area network. In such an environment, issues related to packet routing are important. For others, the network system provides simple mechanisms on which more involved policies can be implemented. These mechanisms ensure that, as these problems become better understood, their solutions can be incorporated into the system. Note that at the time of the original design of this part of the system, a network node that forwarded network-level packets was generally known as a ***gateway***. The current term is ***router***. We use both terms interchangeably, in part because the kernel data structures continue to use the name ***gateway***.

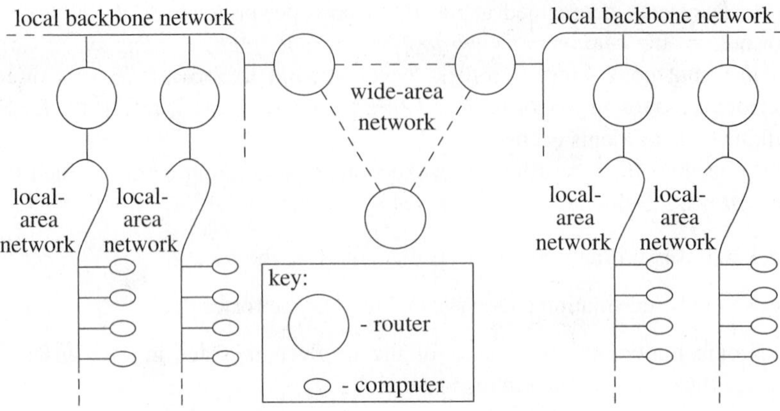

Figure 13.12 Example of the topology for which routing facilities were designed.

The routing facilities were designed for use by singly connected and multiply connected hosts, as well as by routers. There are several components involved in routing, illustrated in Figure 13.13. The design of the routing system places some components within the kernel and others at user level. Routing is an overbroad term. In a complex modern network, there are at least three major components to a routing system. The gathering and maintenance of route information (i.e., which interfaces are up, what the cost is to use each available link, etc.) as well as the implementation of routing policies (which interfaces can be used to forward traffic) are handled at user level by routing daemons. The actual forwarding of packets, which is the selection of the interface on which a packet will be sent, is split between two tables stored in the kernel. Earlier versions of FreeBSD maintained both routing and forwarding information in a single, per-protocol routing table. A more modern design, which splits routing information and forwarding information, was adopted as part of FreeBSD 8. Section 13.1 covers examples of the

Figure 13.13 Routing design.

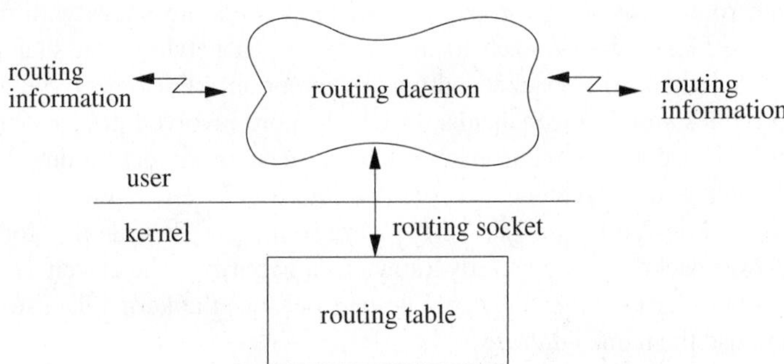

forwarding information base (FIB) that describes ARP and neighbor discovery. Removing the forwarding information from the routing table improved the performance of the system by removing lock contention on the routing table. In the earlier design, routing updates and forwarding lookups contended on the same set of locks to do their work, resulting in decreased performance for some networking workloads. A second important advantage to a split design is that the APIs for accessing each type of data are now cleaner and it is possible to easily replace the FIB with hardware, as is done in modern routing and switching gear.

The ***routing mechanism*** is a simple lookup that provides a next-hop route (a specific network interface) for each outbound packet, while the forwarding mechanism provides the next-hop address to be used when transmitting the packet. The current design places enough information in the kernel for packets to be sent on their way without external help; all other components are outside the kernel. User-level routing daemons communicate with the kernel via a routing socket to manipulate the kernel forwarding table and to listen for internal changes such as interfaces being brought up or down. Each of these components is described in this section.

Kernel Routing Tables

The kernel routing mechanism implements a routing table for looking up next-hop routes. It includes two distinct portions: a data structure describing each specific route (a routing entry) and a lookup algorithm to find the correct route for each possible destination. This subsection describes the entries in the routing table, and the next subsection explains the lookup algorithm. A destination is described by a *sockaddr* structure with an address family, a length, and a value. Routes are classified as either host (direct) or network (indirect) routes. The host–network distinction determines whether the route applies to a specific host or to a group of hosts with a portion of their addresses in common, based on a prefix of the address. For host routes, the destination address of a route must exactly match the desired destination; the address family, length, and bit pattern of the destination must match those in the route. For network routes, the destination address in the route is paired with a mask. The route matches any address that contains the same bits as the destination in the positions indicated by bits set in the mask. A host route is a special case of a network route, in which all the mask bits are set, and thus no bits are ignored in the comparison. Another special case is a ***wildcard route***—a network route with an empty mask. Such a route matches every destination and serves as a default route for unknown destinations. This fallback network route is usually pointed to a router that can then make more informed routing decisions.

The other major distinction between types of routes is either direct or indirect. A direct route is one that leads directly to the destination: The first hop of the path is the entire path, and the destination is on a network shared with the source. Most routes are indirect: the route specifies a router on a local network that is the first-hop destination for the packet. Much of the literature (especially for Internet protocols) refers to a local–remote decision, where an implementation checks first whether a destination is local to an attached network or is remote. In the first case, a packet is sent locally (via the link layer) to the destination; in the latter case, it is sent to a router that can forward it to the destination. In the FreeBSD implementation, the local–remote decision is made as part of the routing lookup. If the best route is direct, then the destination is local. Otherwise, the route is indirect, the destination is remote, and the route entry specifies the router for the destination. In either case, the route specifies only the first-hop gateway—a link-level interface to be used in sending packets—and the destination for the packets in this hop if different from the final destination. This information allows a packet to be sent via a local interface to a destination directly reachable via that interface—either the final destination or a router on the path to the destination. This distinction is needed when the link-layer encapsulation is done. If a packet is destined for a peer that is not directly connected to the source, the packet header will contain the address of the eventual destination, whereas the link-layer protocol header will address the intervening router.

The network system maintains a set of routing tables used by protocols to select a network interface to use when delivering a packet to its destination. These tables are composed of *rtentry* structures as shown in Table 13.4.

An *rtentry* structure, contains a reference to the destination address and mask, unless the route is to a host, in which case the mask is implicit. The destination address, address mask, and gateway address are different sizes and thus are placed in separately allocated memory. Routing entries also contain a reference to a network interface, a set of flags that characterize the route, and optionally, a gateway address. The flags indicate a route's type (host or network, direct or indirect) and the other attributes shown in Table 13.5. If the route is a member of a virtual networking instance, the route entry will reference the virtual network. The route entry also contains a set of metrics and a mutex for locking the entry. The RTF_HOST flag in a routing-table entry indicates that the route applies to a single

Table 13.4 Elements of a routing-table entry (*rtentry*) structure.

Element	Description
rt_nodes[2]	internal and leaf radix nodes (with references to destination and mask)
rt_gateway	address of the router/next hop
rt_flags	flags; see Table 13.5
rt_refcnt	reference count
rt_ifp	reference to interface, *ifnet*
rt_ifa	reference to interface address, *ifaddr*
rt_rmx	route metrics (e.g., MTU)
rt_fibnum	virtual network instance
rt_mtx	mutex for locking the entry (kernel only)

Table 13.5 Route-entry flags.

Flag	Description
RTF_UP	route is valid
RTF_GATEWAY	destination is a gateway
RTF_HOST	host entry (net otherwise)
RTF_REJECT	host or net unreachable
RTF_DYNAMIC	created dynamically (by redirect)
RTF_MODIFIED	modified dynamically (by redirect)
RTF_DONE	message confirmed
RTF_XRESOLVE	external daemon resolves name
RTF_LLINFO	generated by link layer
RTF_LLDATA	add or delete L2 information
RTF_STATIC	manually added by administrator
RTF_BLACKHOLE	just discard packets (during updates)
RTF_PROTO1	protocol-specific routing flag
RTF_PROTO2	protocol-specific routing flag
RTF_PROTO3	protocol-specific routing flag
RTF_PINNED	route is immutable
RTF_LOCAL	route represents a local address
RTF_BROADCAST	route represents a bcast address
RTF_MULTICAST	route represents an mcast address
RTF_STICKY	return to source over the same path

host, using an implicit mask containing all the bits of the address. The RTF_GATEWAY flag in a routing-table entry indicates that the route is to a router and that the link-layer header should be filled in from the *rt_gateway* field, instead of from the final destination address. The route entry contains a field that can be used by the link layer to cache a reference to the *direct* route for the router. The RTF_UP flag is set when a route is installed. When a route is removed, the RTF_UP flag is cleared, but the route entry is not freed until all users of the route have noticed the failure and have released their references. The route entry contains a reference count because it is allocated dynamically and cannot be freed until all references have been released. Other flags (RTF_REJECT and RTF_BLACKHOLE) mark the destination of the route as being unreachable, causing either an error or a silent failure when an attempt is made to send to the destination. Reject routes are useful when a router receives packets for a cluster of addresses from the outside, but may not have routes for all hosts or networks in the cluster at all times. Packets with unreachable destinations should not be sent outside the cluster via a default route because the default router would send back such packets for delivery within the cluster. ***Black-hole routes*** are used during routing transients when a new route may become available shortly.

Many connection-oriented protocols wish to retain information about the characteristics of a particular network path. Some of this information can be estimated dynamically for each connection, such as the round-trip time or path MTU. It is useful to cache such information so that the estimation does not need to begin anew for each connection [Mogul & Deering, 1990]. The routing entry contains a set of *route metrics* stored in a *rt_metrics_lite* structure that may be set externally or may be determined dynamically by the protocols. These metrics include the maximum packet size for the path, called the ***maximum transmission unit*** (MTU); the lifetime for the route; and the number of packets that have been sent using this route.

Routing Lookup

Given a set of routing entries describing various destinations, from specific hosts to a wildcard route, a routing lookup algorithm is required. The lookup algorithm in FreeBSD uses a variation of the *radix search trie* [Sedgewick, 1990]. (The initial design was to use a PATRICIA search, also described in Sedgewick [1990], which differs only in the details of storage management.) The radix search algorithm provides a way to find a bit string, such as a network address, in a set of known strings. Although the modified search was implemented for routing lookups, the radix code is implemented in a more general way so that it can be used for other purposes. For example, the filesystem code uses a radix tree to manage information about clients to which filesystems can be exported. Each kernel route entry begins with the data structures for the radix tree, including an internal radix node and a leaf node that refers to the destination address and mask.

The radix search algorithm uses a binary tree of nodes beginning with a root node for each address family. Figure 13.14 shows an example of a radix tree. A search begins at the root node and descends through internal nodes until a leaf node is found. Each internal node requires a test of a specific bit in the string, and the search descends in one of two directions depending on the value of that bit. The internal nodes contain an index of the bit to be tested, as well as a precomputed byte index and mask for use in the test. A leaf node is marked with a bit index of −1, which terminates the search. For example, a search for the address 127.0.0.1 (the loopback address) with the tree in Figure 13.14 would start at the head and would branch left when testing bit 0, branch right at the node for bit 1, and branch right on testing bit 31. This search leads to the leaf node containing a host route specific to that host; such a route does not contain a mask but uses an implicit mask with all bits set.

This lookup technique tests the minimum number of bits required to distinguish among a set of bit strings. Once a leaf node is found, either it specifies the specific bit string in question or that bit string is not present in the tree. This algorithm allows a minimal number of bits to be tested in a string to look up an unknown, such as a host route; however, it does not provide for partial matching as required by a routing lookup for a network route. Thus, the routing lookup uses a modified radix search, in which each network route includes a mask, and nodes

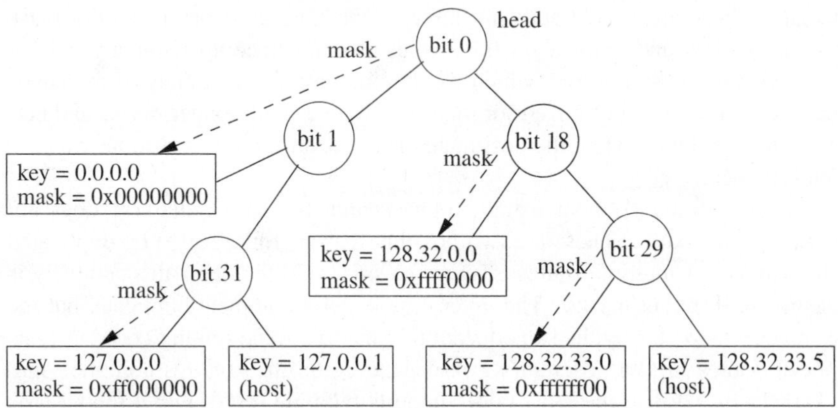

Figure 13.14 Example radix tree. This simplified example of a radix tree contains routes for the IPv4 protocol family, which uses 32-bit addresses. The circles represent internal nodes, beginning with the head of the tree at the top. The bit position to be tested is shown within the circle. Leaf nodes are shown as rectangles containing a key (a destination address, listed as four decimal bytes separated by dots) and the corresponding mask (in hexadecimal). Some interior nodes are associated with masks found lower in the tree, as indicated by dashed arrows.

are inserted into the tree such that longer masks are found earlier in the search [Sklower, 1991]. Interior nodes for subtrees with a common prefix are marked with a mask for that prefix. Masks generally select a prefix from an address, although the mask does not need to specify a contiguous portion of the address. As the routing lookup proceeds, the internal nodes that are passed are associated with masks that increase in specificity. If the route that is found at the leaf after the lookup is a network route, the destination is masked before comparison with the key, thus matching any destination on that network. If the leaf node does not match the destination, an interior node visited during the route lookup should refer to the best match. After a lookup does not find a match at the leaf node, the lookup procedure iterates backward through the tree, using a parent pointer in each node. At each interior node that contains a mask, a search is made for the part of the destination under that mask from that point. For example, a search for the address 128.32.33.7 in the tree in Figure 13.14 would test bits 0, 18, and 29 before arriving at the host route on the right (128.32.33.5). Because this address is not a match, the search moves up one level, where a mask is found. The mask is a 24-bit prefix, and it is associated with the route to 128.32.33.0, which is the best match. If the mask was not a prefix (in the code, a route with a mask specifying a prefix is called a normal route), a search would have been required for the value 128.32.33.7 starting from this point.

The first match found is the best match for the destination; that is, it has the longest mask for any matching route. Matches are thus found by a combination of a radix search, testing 1 bit per node on the way down the tree, plus a full comparison under a mask at the leaf node. If the leaf node (either host or network) does not match, the search backtracks up the tree, checking each parent with a mask until a match is found. This algorithm avoids a complete comparison at each step when searching down the tree, which would eliminate the efficiency of the radix-search algorithm. It is optimized for matches to routes with longer masks and performs least efficiently when the best match is the default route (the route with the shortest mask).

Another complication of using a radix search is that a radix tree does not allow duplicated keys. There are two possible reasons for a key to be duplicated in the tree: either multiple routes exist to the same destination or the same key is present with different masks. The latter case is not a complete duplicate, but the two routes would occupy the same location in the tree. The routing code supports duplicate routes in two different ways, depending on the features compiled into the kernel. By default, the radix code supports multiple routes that differ in only the mask. When the addition of a route causes a key to be duplicated, the affected routes are chained together from a single leaf node. The routes are chained in order of mask significance, the most specific mask first. If the masks are contiguous, longer masks are considered to be more specific (with a host route considered to have the longest possible mask). If a routing lookup visits a node with a duplicated key when doing a masked comparison (either at the leaf node or while moving back up the tree), the comparison is repeated for each duplicate node on the chain, with the first successful comparison producing the best match.

Duplicate routes to different gateways are referred to as equal-cost multi-path routes (ECMP) and are supported by the RADIX_MPATH feature. ECMP routes can be used to balance traffic load across multiple links as well as to provide the ability for a single link to fail without the total loss of connectivity to the next hop in the network. When ECMP routes are used for failover, one gateway may go over a valid but less-preferred route to the destination. A less-preferred route might transit a slower or more expensive link. The use of multi-path routes allows the system to failover gracefully when one link goes down. Enabling ECMP changes the routine used to look up a route as well as the way in which multiple routes are stored in a radix trie's leaf nodes.

Each radix trie has a single *radix_node_head* structure that contains both data about the trie, and a set of pointers to functions to use when performing operations on it. The *rnh_matchaddr*() field is filled in appropriately at the time that the table is initialized to point to the correct routine to return a matching route. When ECMP routing is in use, the *rtalloc_mpath_fib*() routine is ultimately used to look up a route rather than *rtalloc_fib*(). When ECMP routes are used to load balance traffic across a set of links, the matching algorithm uses a Modulo-N hash to choose the gateway to forward any single packet. The Modulo-N hash is calculated to guarantee that packets with the same source and destination information always cross the same link. If two packets from the same flow cross different links there is the chance that they will arrive at their destination out of order, causing a drop in network performance, (see Section 14.5) [Thaler & Hopps, 2000]. When ECMP routes are used to implement failover links, where one link is unused until the failure of a primary link, each equal-cost route is given a weight that is used as part of the gateway selection algorithm. The route with the greatest weight will be used instead of any other equal-cost route. When a link goes down, the routing entry will remain in the trie but it will not be used to route packets. The next hop gateway will be selected from the remaining equal cost routes at the same leaf node in the tree.

Routing Redirects

A ***routing redirect message*** is a control request from a protocol to the routing system to modify an existing routing-table entry or to create a new routing-table entry. Protocols usually generate such requests in response to redirect messages that they receive from routers. Routers generate redirect messages when they recognize that a better route exists for a packet that they have been asked to forward. For example, if two hosts, A and B, are on the same network, and host A sends a packet to host B via a router C, then C will send a redirect message to A specifying that A should send packets directly to B.

On hosts where exhaustive routing information is too expensive to maintain (e.g., SOHO routers, cable modems, and other embedded systems), the combination of wildcard routing entries and redirect messages can be used to provide a simple routing-management scheme without the use of a higher-level policy process, such as a user-level routing daemon. Statistics are kept by the routing-table routines on the use of routing-redirect messages and on the latter's effect on the routing tables. A redirect causes the gateway for a route to be changed if the redirect applies to all destinations to which the route applies. A user-level routing daemon will normally clean up stale host routes, but most hosts do not run routing daemons.

Routing-Table Interface

A protocol accesses the routing tables through three types of routines: one to allocate a route, one to free a route, and one to process a routing-redirect control message. The routine *rtalloc*() allocates a route. It is called with a pointer to a *route* structure that contains the desired destination and a pointer that will be set to reference a *rtentry* structure that is the best match for the destination. Figure 13.15 shows the resulting route allocation. The destination is recorded so that later output operations can check whether the new destination is the same as the previous one, allowing the same route to be used. With the addition of VIMAGE, it was necessary to provide routines such as *rtalloc_ign_fib*() that allowed the caller to pass in an index for the kernel to use to pick the appropriate routing table. All route allocation routines eventually wind up calling *rtalloc_ign_fib*(), where the work of looking up a route takes place. The route returned is assumed to be held by the caller until released with a call to the RTFREE macro. All accesses to the routing table must be properly locked in FreeBSD and the RTFREE macro handles the locking as well as decrementing the route's reference count, freeing the route entry when the reference count reaches zero. Since a route can only be present in a single routing table, there is no need to have a specific *rtfree_fib*() routine. The

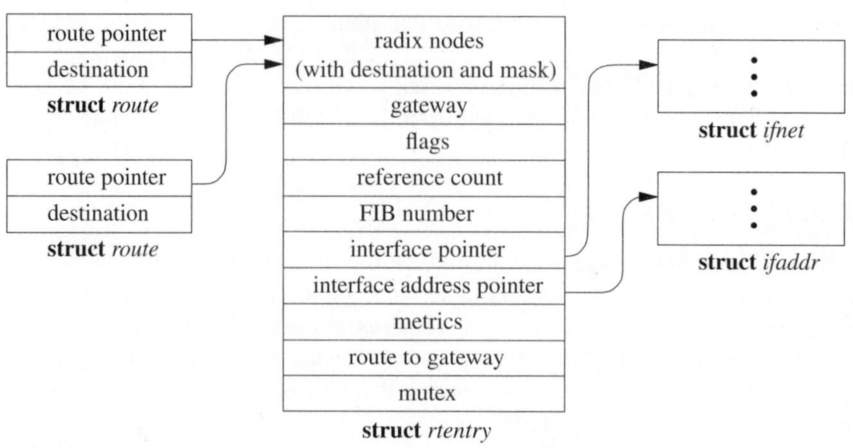

Figure 13.15 Data structures used in route allocation.

rtalloc_ign_fib() routine simply checks whether the route already contains a reference to a valid route. If no route is referenced or the route is no longer valid, *rtalloc_ign_fib*() calls the *rtalloc1_fib*() routine to look up a routing entry for the destination, passing a flag indicating whether the route will be used or is simply being checked.

The *rtredirect_fib*() routine is called to process a redirect control message. It is called with a destination address and mask, the new gateway to the referenced destination, and the source of the redirect. Redirects are accepted from only the current router for the destination. If a nonwildcard route exists to the destination, the gateway entry in the route is modified to point at the new gateway supplied; otherwise, a new host route is created. Routes to interfaces and routes to gateways that are not directly accessible from the host are ignored.

User-Level Routing Policies

The kernel routing facilities deliberately refrain from making policy decisions. Instead, ***routing policies*** are determined by user processes, which then add, delete, or change entries in the kernel routing tables. The decision to place policy decisions in a user process implies that routing-table updates may lag a bit behind the identification of new routes or the failure of existing routes. This period of instability is normally short if the routing process is implemented properly. Internet-specific advisory information, such as ICMP error messages, may also be read from raw sockets (described in Section 13.6).

Several routing-policy processes have been implemented. The system standard ***routing daemon***, **routed**, uses the Routing Information Protocol (RIP) [Hedrick, 1988]. Many sites that require the use of other routing protocols or more configuration options than are provided by **routed** use either a commercial package or the open-source Quagga Routing Suite [Ishiguro, 2003].

User-Level Routing Interface: Routing Socket

User-level processes that implement routing policy and protocols require an interface to the kernel routing table so that they can add, delete, and change kernel routes.

User level processes on FreeBSD use a socket to communicate with the kernel routing layer. A privileged process creates a raw socket in the routing protocol family, AF_ROUTE, and then passes messages to and from the kernel routing layer. A routing socket operates like a normal datagram socket, including queueing of messages received at the socket, except that communication takes place between a user process and the kernel. Messages include a header with a message type identifying the action, as listed in Table 13.6. Messages to the kernel are requests to add, modify, or delete a route, or are requests for information about the route to a specific destination. The kernel sends a message in reply with the original request, an indication that the message is a reply, and an error number for failures. Because routing sockets are raw sockets, each open routing socket receives a copy of the reply and must filter for the messages it wants. The message header includes a process ID and a sequence number so that each process can determine whether this message is a reply to its own request and can match replies with

Table 13.6 Routing-message types.

Message type	Description
RTM_ADD	add route
RTM_DELETE	delete route
RTM_CHANGE	change metrics or flags
RTM_GET	report route and metrics
RTM_LOSING	kernel suspects partitioning
RTM_REDIRECT	told to use different route
RTM_MISS	lookup failed on this address
RTM_LOCK	lock specified metrics
RTM_OLDADD	caused by SIOCADDRT
RTM_OLDDEL	caused by SIOCDELRT
RTM_RESOLVE	request to resolve link address
RTM_NEWADDR	address added to interface
RTM_DELADDR	address removed from interface
RTM_IFINFO	interface going up or down
RTM_IFANNOUNCE	network interface added or removed
RTM_NEWMADDR	multicast group membership being added to interface
RTM_DELMADDR	multicast group membership being deleted from interface
RTM_IEEE80211	802.11 wireless event

requests. The kernel also sends messages as indications of asynchronous events, such as redirects and changes in local interface state. These messages allow a daemon to monitor changes in the routing table made by other processes, events detected by the kernel, and changes to the local interface addresses and state. The routing socket is also used to deliver requests for external resolution of a link-layer route when the RTF_XRESOLVE flag is set on a route entry.

Requests to add or change a route include all the information needed for the route. The header has a field for the route flags listed in Table 13.5, and contains a *rt_metrics* structure of metrics that may be set or locked. Metrics that can be set on a route include the MTU and expiration time. The header also carries a bit vector that describes the set of addresses carried in the message; the addresses follow the header as an array of variable-size *sockaddr* structures. A destination address is required, as is a mask for network routes. A gateway address is generally required as well. The system normally determines the interface to be used by the route from the gateway address, using the interface shared with that gateway.

13.6 Raw Sockets

A ***raw socket*** allows privileged users direct access to a protocol other than those normally used for transport of user data—for example, network-level protocols. Raw sockets are intended for knowledgeable processes that wish to take advantage of some protocol feature not directly accessible through the normal interface or for the development of protocols built atop existing protocols. For example, the **ping** program is implemented using a raw ICMP socket (see Section 13.2). The raw IP socket interface attempts to provide an identical interface to the one a protocol would have if it were resident in the kernel.

The raw-socket support is built around a generic raw-socket interface, possibly augmented by protocol-specific processing routines. This section describes only the core of the raw-socket interface; details specific to particular protocols are not discussed. Some protocol families (including IPv4) use private versions of the routines and data structures described here.

Control Blocks

Every raw socket has a protocol control block of the form shown in Figure 13.16. Raw control blocks are kept on a singly linked list for performing lookups during packet dispatch. Associations may be recorded in fields referenced by the control block and may be used by the output routine in preparing packets for transmission. The *rcb_proto* field contains the protocol family and protocol number with which the raw socket is associated. The protocol, family, and addresses are used to filter packets on input, as described in the next subsection.

A raw socket is datagram oriented: each send or receive on the socket requires a destination address. Destination addresses are supplied by the user. If routing is necessary, it must be performed by an underlying protocol.

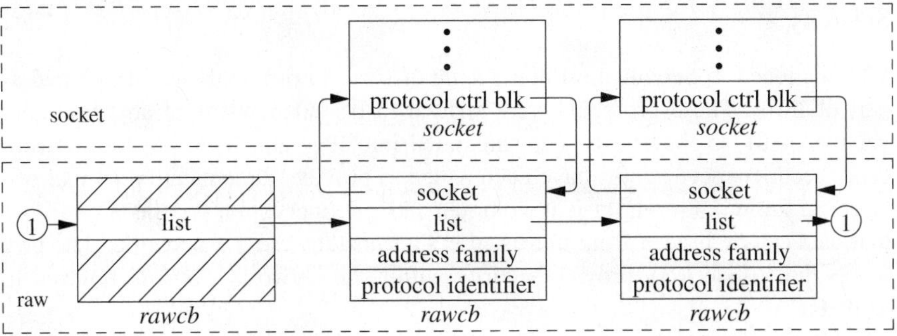

Figure 13.16 Raw-socket control block.

Input Processing

Input packets are assigned to raw sockets based on a simple pattern-matching scheme. Each protocol (and potentially some network interfaces) gives unassigned packets to the raw input routine with the call

```
void raw_input_ext(
        struct mbuf *msg,
        struct sockproto *proto,
        struct sockaddr *src)
```

Input packets are placed into the input queues of all raw sockets that match the header according to the following rules:

1. The protocol family of the socket and header agree.
2. If the protocol number in the socket is nonzero, then it agrees with that found in the packet header.

A basic assumption in the pattern-matching scheme is that protocol information in the control block and packet header (as constructed by the network interface and any raw input-protocol module) is in a canonical form that can be compared on a bit-for-bit basis. If multiple sockets match the incoming packet, the packet is copied as needed.

Output Processing

On output, each send request results in a call to the raw socket's *raw_usend* routine, which calls an output routine specific to the protocol or protocol family. Any necessary processing is done before the packet is delivered to the appropriate network interface.

13.7 Security

We mentioned in Section 13.3 that a suite of security protocols was developed as part of IPv6. These protocols were written to be independent of any particular version of IP, so they have been integrated into IPv4 and IPv6. At the network layer, security mechanisms have been added to provide authentication so that one host can know with whom it is communicating. Encryption has been added so that data can be hidden from untrusted entities as they cross a network. The protocols that collectively provide security within the network layer are referred to as IPSec.

Placing the security protocols at the network layer within the protocol stack was not an arbitrary decision. It is possible to place security at just about any layer within a communication system. For example, transport-layer security (TLS) supports communication security at the application layer and allows a client and a server to communicate securely over an arbitrary network. At the opposite end of the spectrum are the various protocols that support security over wireless networks working at the data-link layer. The decision to put security at the network layer was made for several reasons:

- The IP protocols act as a uniform platform in which to place the security protocols. Differences in underlying hardware, such as different types of network media, did not have to be taken into account when designing and implementing IPSec because if a piece of hardware could send and receive IP datagrams, then it could also support IPSec.
- Users need not do any work to use the security protocols. Because IPSec is implemented at the network, instead of the application layer, users who run network programs are automatically working securely as long as their administrators have properly configured the system.
- Key management can be handled in an automatic way by system daemons. The most difficult challenge in deploying network security protocols is giving out and canceling the keys used to secure the data. Since IPSec is handled in the kernel, and is not usually dealt with by users, it is possible to write daemons to handle the management of keys.

Security within the context of IPSec means several things:

- The ability to trust that a host is who it claims to be (authentication)
- Protection against the replay of old data
- Confidentiality of data (encryption)

Providing a security architecture for the Internet protocols is a complex problem. The relevant protocols are covered in several RFCs, and an overview is given in Kent & Atkinson [1998a].

IPSec Overview

The IPSec protocol suite provides a security framework for use by hosts and routers on the Internet. Security services, such as authentication and encryption, are available between two hosts, a host and a router, or two routers. When any two entities on the network (hosts or routers) are using IPSec for secure communication, they are said to have a ***security association*** (***SA***) between them. Each SA is unidirectional, which means that traffic is only secured between two points in the direction in which the SA has been set up. For a completely secure link two SAs are required, one in each direction.

SAs are uniquely identified by their destination address, the security protocol being used, and a ***security-parameter index*** (***SPI***), which is a 32-bit value that distinguishes among multiple SAs terminating at the same host or router. The SPI is the key used to look up relevant information in the security-association database that is maintained by each system running IPSec.

An SA can be used in two modes. In ***transport mode***, a portion of the IP header is protected as well as the IPSec header and the data. The IP header is only partially protected because it must be inspected by intermediate routers along the path between two hosts, and it is neither possible nor desirable, to require every possible router to run the IPSec protocols. One reason to run security protocols end to end is so intermediate routers do not have to be trusted with the data they are handling. Another reason is that security protocols are often computationally expensive and intermediate routers often do not have the computational power to decrypt and reencrypt every packet before it is forwarded.

Since only a part of the IP header is protected in transport mode, this type of SA only provides protection to upper-layer protocols, those that are completely encapsulated within the data section of the packet, such as UDP, TCP and SCTP. Figure 13.17 shows a transport-mode SA between hosts Alice and Bob, as well as the packet that would result. Alice sets up a normal IP packet with Bob as the destination. She then adds the IPSec header and data. Finally, she applies whatever

Figure 13.17 Security association in transport mode. Key: AH—authentication header; ESP—encapsulating-security payload; SPI—security-parameter index.

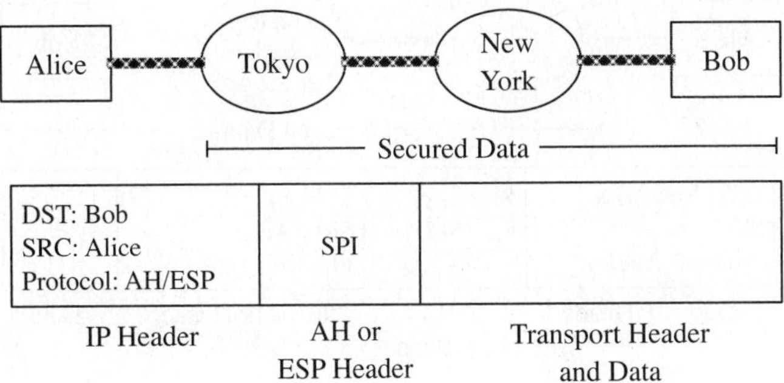

security protocol has been selected by the user and sends the packet, which travels through routers in Tokyo and New York and finally to Bob. Bob decrypts the packet by looking up the security protocol and keys in its security-association database.

The other mode is ***tunnel mode***, shown in Figure 13.18, where the entire packet is placed within an IP-over-IP tunnel [Simpson, 1995]. In tunneling, the entire packet, including all the headers and data, are placed as data within another packet and sent between two locations. Alice again wants to send a packet to Bob. When the packet reaches the Tokyo router, it is placed in a secure tunnel between Tokyo and New York. The entire original packet is placed inside a new packet and secured. The outer IP header identifies only the endpoints of the tunnel, the routers in Tokyo and New York, and does not give away any of the original packet's header information. When the packet reaches the end of the tunnel in New York, it is decrypted and then sent on to Bob, its original destination. In this example, neither Alice nor Bob knows that the data have been encrypted nor do they have to be running the IPSec protocols to participate in this secure communication.

Tunnel mode is only used for host-to-router or router-to-router communications and is most often seen in the implementation of ***virtual private networks*** that connect two private networks or that connect users to a corporate LAN over the public Internet.

Security Protocols

There are two security protocols specified for use with IPSec: the authentication header (AH) and the encapsulating-security payload (ESP), each of which provides different security services [Kent & Atkinson, 1998b; Kent & Atkinson, 1998c]. Both protocols are used with IPv4 and IPv6 without changes to their headers. This dual usage is possible because the packet headers are really IPv6 ***extension headers*** that properly encode information about the other protocols following them in the packet.

Figure 13.18 Security association in tunnel mode. Key: AH—authentication header; ESP—encapsulating-security payload; SPI—security-parameter index.

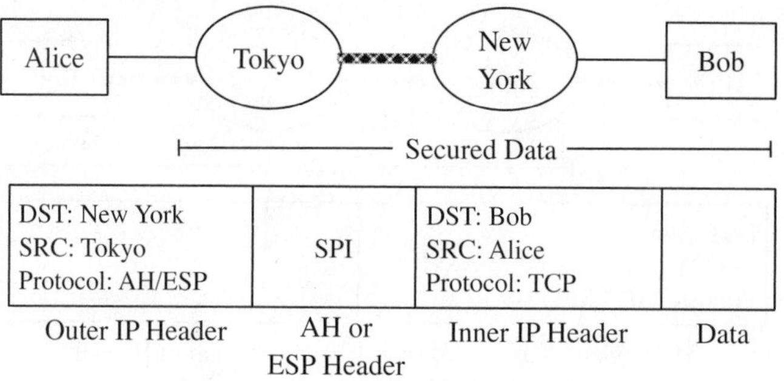

The AH protocol provides a packet-based authentication service as well as protection against an attacker attempting to replay old data. To understand how AH provides security, it is easiest to look at its packet header, shown in Figure 13.19. The *next-header* field identifies the type of packet that follows the current header. The *next-header* field uses the same value as the one that appears in the *protocol* field of an IPv4 packet: 6 for TCP, 17 for UDP, and 1 for ICMP. The *payload length* specifies the number of 32-bit words that are contained in the authentication header minus 2. The fudge factor of removing 2 from this number comes from the specification for IPv6 extension headers. The SPI is a 32-bit number that is used by each endpoint to look up relevant information about the security association.

Authentication is provided by computing an ***integrity-check value*** (***ICV***) over the packet. If an AH is used in transport mode, then only parts of the IP header are protected because some of the fields are modified by intermediate routers in transit and the changes are not predictable at the sender. In tunnel mode, the whole header is protected because it is encapsulated in another packet, and the ICV is computed over the original packet. The ICV is computed using the algorithm specified by the SPI with the result stored in the *authentication-data* field of the authentication header. The receiver uses the same algorithm, requested by the SPI to compute the ICV on the packet it received, and compares this value with the one found in the packet's *authentication-data* field. If the values are the same, then the packet is accepted; otherwise, it is discarded.

One possible attack on a communication channel is called a replay attack. An attacker attempts to insert malicious packets that duplicate packets sent in the past as if they were coming from the authentic source. To guard against a replay attack, the AH protocol uses a *sequence-number* field to uniquely identify each packet that is transmitted across an SA. This *sequence-number* field is distinct from the field of the same name in TCP. When an SA is established, both the sender and receiver set the *sequence number* field to zero. The sender increments the sequence number before transmitting a packet. The receiver implements a fixed-size sliding window, with its left edge being the lowest sequence number that it has seen and validated, and the right edge being the highest. When a new

Figure 13.19 Authentication header.

0 – 7	8 – 15	16 – 31
next header	payload length	reserved
security-parameters index (SPI)		
sequence-number field		
authentication data (variable)		

packet is received, its sequence number is checked against the window with three possible results:

1. The packet's sequence number is less than the sequence number on the left edge of the window and the packet is discarded.
2. The packet's sequence number is within the window. The receiver keeps a bitmap that tracks the packets that have been received within the window. The packet is checked to see if it is already marked in the bitmap. If it is in the bitmap, it is a duplicate and is discarded. If the packet is not a duplicate, it is inserted into the window and the bitmap is updated to show that its sequence number has been received.
3. The packet's sequence number is to the right of the current window. The ICV is verified and, if correct, the window is moved to the right to encompass the new sequence number value. The bitmap is updated to reflect that its sequence number has been received.

When the sequence number rolls over, after over 4 billion packets, the security association must be torn down and restarted. This restart is only a slight inconvenience because at gigabit Ethernet rates of 83,000 packets per second, it takes over 14 hours for the security sequence number to roll over, and a user-level daemon can automatically tear down and reestablish the link without human intervention.

All senders assume that a receiver is using the antireplay service and is always incrementing the sequence number, but it is not required for the receiver to implement the antireplay service, and it may be turned off at the discretion of the operator of the receiving system.

Figure 13.20 Encapsulating security-protocol header.

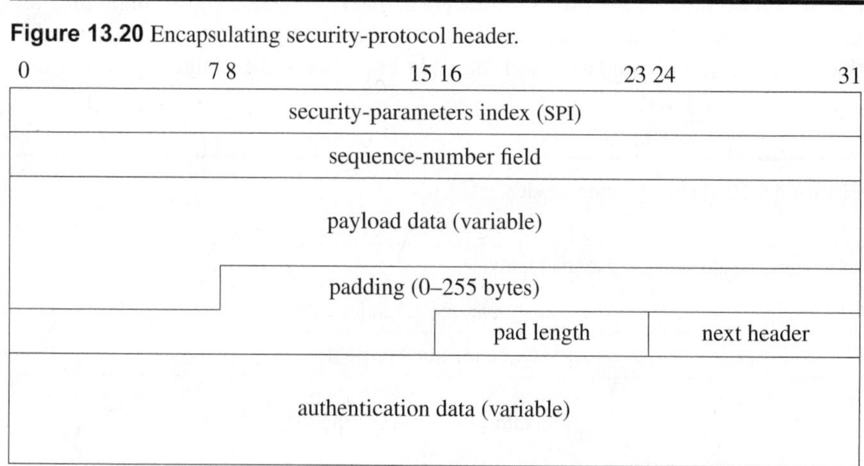

The ESP provides confidentiality using encryption. As with the AH, it is easiest to understand the ESP by examining its packet header, shown in Figure 13.20. The ESP header contains all the same fields as were found in the AH header, but it adds three more. The encrypted data sent using an ESP is stored in the *payload-data* field of the packet. The *padding* field that follows the payload data may be used for three purposes:

- The encryption algorithm might require that the data to be encrypted be some multiple number of bytes. The padding data is added to the data to be encrypted so that the chunk of data is of the correct size.
- Padding might be required to properly align some part of the packet. For example, the *pad-length* and *next-header* fields must be right-aligned in the packet, and the *authentication-data* field must be aligned on a 4-byte boundary.
- The padding may also be used to obscure the original size of the payload in an attempt to prevent an attacker from gaining information by watching the traffic flow.

Key Management

User-level applications cannot use IPSec in the same way that they use transport protocols like UDP and TCP. For example, an application cannot open a secure socket to another endpoint using IPSec. Instead, all SAs are kept in the kernel and managed using a new domain and protocol family called PF_KEY_V2 [McDonald et al., 1998].

The automated distribution of keys for use in IPSec is handled by the ***Internet Key Exchange* (*IKE*)** protocol [Harkins & Carrel, 1998]. User-level daemons that implement the IKE protocol, such as *Racoon*, interact with the kernel using PF_KEY_V2 sockets [Sakane, 2001]. As these daemons are not implemented in the kernel, they are beyond the scope of this book.

User-level applications interact with the security database by opening a socket of type PF_KEY. There is no corresponding AF_KEY address family. Key sockets are based on the routing-socket implementation and function much like a routing socket. Whereas the routing-socket API manipulates the kernel routing table, the key-socket API manages security associations and policies. Key sockets support a connectionless-datagram facility between user applications and the kernel. User-level applications send commands in packets to the kernel's security database. Applications can also receive messages from a key socket about changes to the security database such as the expiration of security associations.

The messages that can be sent using a key socket are shown in Table 13.7. Two groups of messages are defined for key sockets: a base set of messages that all start with a security-association database (SADB) and a set of extension messages that all start with SADB_X. The type of the message is the second part of the name. In FreeBSD, the extension messages manipulate a security-policy database (SPDB) that is separate from the SADB.

Table 13.7 PF_KEY messages.

Message type	Description
SADB_GETSPI	retrieve a unique security index from the kernel
SADB_UPDATE	update an existing security association
SADB_ADD	add a new security association with a known security index
SADB_DELETE	delete an existing security association
SADB_GET	retrieve information on a security association
SADB_ACQUIRE	sent to user-level daemons when kernel needs more information
SADB_REGISTER	tell the kernel this application can supply security information
SADB_EXPIRE	sent from the kernel to the application when an SA expires
SADB_FLUSH	tell the kernel to flush all SAs of a particular type
SADB_DUMP	tell the kernel to dump all SA information to the calling socket
SADB_X_PROMISC	this application wants to see all PF_KEY messages
SADB_X_PCHANGE	message sent to passive listeners
SADB_X_SPDUPDATE	update the security policy database (SPDB)
SADB_X_SPDADD	add an entry to the SPDB
SADB_X_SPDDELETE	delete an entry from the SPDB by policy index
SADB_X_SPDGET	get an entry from the SPDB
SADB_X_SPDACQUIRE	message sent by kernel to acquire an SA and policy
SADB_X_SPDDUMP	tell the kernel to dump its policy database to the calling socket
SADB_X_SPDFLUSH	flush the policy database
SADB_X_SPDSETIDX	add an entry in the SPDB by its policy index
SADB_X_SPDEXPIRE	tell the listening socket that an SPDB entry has expired
SADB_X_SPDDELETE2	delete an SPDB entry by policy identifier

Key: SA—security association; SADB—security-association database; SPDB—security-policy database.

Key-socket messages are made up of a base header, shown in Figure 13.21, and a set of extension headers. The base header contains information that is common to all messages. The version ensures that the application will work with the version of the key-socket module in the kernel. The command being sent is encoded in the *message-type* field. Errors are sent to the calling socket using the same set of headers that are used to send down commands. Applications cannot depend on all errors being returned by a *send* or *write* system call made on the socket, and they must check the error number of any returned message on the socket for proper error handling. The *errno* field is set to an appropriate error number before the message is sent to the listening socket. The type of security association that the application wants to manipulate is placed in the *SA-type* field

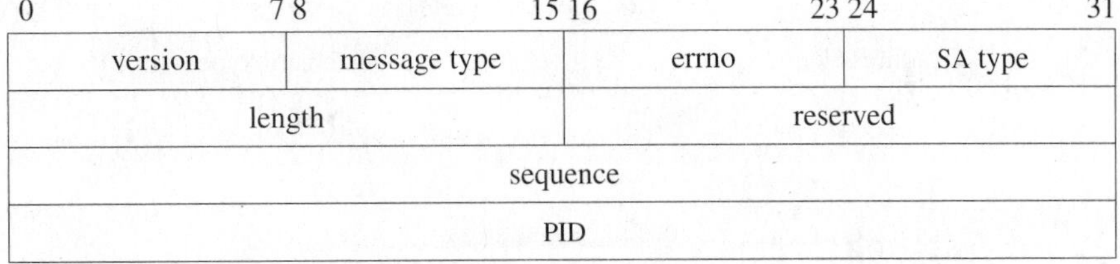

Figure 13.21 PF_KEY-base header.

of the packet. The length of the entire message, including the base header, all extension headers, and any padding that has been inserted, is stored in the *length* field. Each message is uniquely identified by its sequence and PID fields that match responses to requests. When the kernel sends a message to a listening process, the PID is set to 0.

The security-association database and security-policy database cannot be changed using the base header. To make changes, the application adds one or more ***extension headers*** to its message. Each extension header begins with a length and a type so that the entire message can be easily traversed by the kernel or an application. An association extension is shown in Figure 13.22. The association extension makes changes to a single security association, such as specifying the authentication or encryption algorithm to be used.

Whenever an association extension is used, an address extension must be present as well, since each security association is identified by the network addresses of the communicating endpoints. An address extension, shown in Figure 13.23. stores information on the IPv4 or IPv6 addresses using *sockaddr* structures.

One problem with the current PF_KEY implementation is that it is a datagram protocol and the message size is limited to 64 Kbyte. A 64-Kbyte limit is not important to users with small databases, but when a system using IPSec is deployed in a large enterprise, with hundreds and possibly thousands of simultaneous security associations, the SADB will grow large and this size limitation makes it more difficult to write user-level daemons to manage the kernel's security databases.

Figure 13.22 PF_KEY-association extension.

0 – 7	8 – 15	16 – 23	24 – 31
address length		extension type	
SPI			
replay	state	authorization	encrypt
flags			

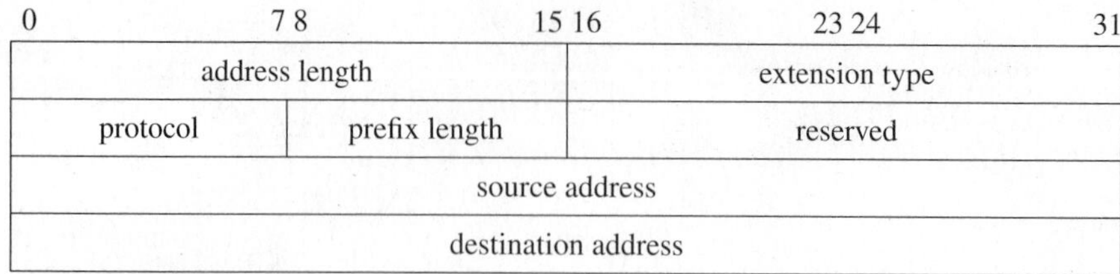

Figure 13.23 PF_KEY address extension.

A security-association structure is shown in Figure 13.24. Like many other data structures in FreeBSD, security-association structures are really objects implemented in C. Each security-association structure contains all the data related to a specific security association as well as the set of functions necessary to operate on packets associated with that association. The security-association database is stored as a doubly linked list of security-association structures. Each security association can be shared by more than one entity in the system, which is why it contains a reference count.

Figure 13.24 Security-association structure.

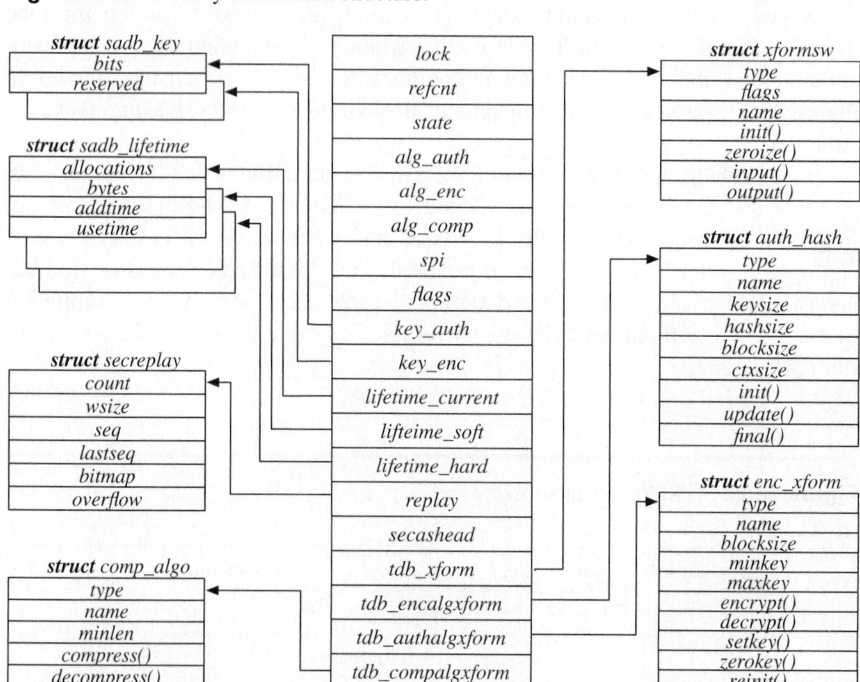

Security associations can be in four states: LARVAL, MATURE, DYING, and DEAD. When an SA is first being created, it is put into the LARVAL state, which indicates that it is not yet usable. Once an SA is usable, it moves to the MATURE state. An SA remains in the MATURE state until some event, such as the SA exceeding its lifetime, moves it to the DYING state. SAs in the DYING state can be revived if an application makes a request to use an SA with the same parameters before it is marked as DEAD.

The security-association structure contains all the information on a particular SA including the algorithms used, the SPI, and the key data. This information is used in processing packets for a particular association. The *lifetime* fields limit the usage of a particular SA. Although an SA is not required to have a lifetime, and so might not expire, recommended practice is to set a lifetime. Lifetimes can be given a time limit using the *addtime* and *usetime* fields of the *sadb_lifetime* structure, and can be given a data-processing limit using the *bytes* field. The three lifetime structures pointed to by the security association encode the current usage for the association and its hard and soft limits. When reached, the soft-lifetime value puts the SA into the DYING state to show that its useful life is about to end. When reached, the hard-lifetime value indicates that the SA is no longer usable. Once an SA passes the hard-lifetime limit, it is set to the DEAD state and can be reclaimed. The current-lifetime structure contains the present usage values for the SA—for example, how many bytes have been processed since the SA was created.

Each security-association structure has several tables of functions that point to routines that do the work on packets handled by that association. The *tdb_xform* table contains pointers to functions that implement the initialization, input, and output functions for a particular security protocol such as ESP or AH. The other three tables are specific to a protocol and contain pointers to the appropriate cryptographic functions for handling the protocol being used by the SA. The reason for having this plethora of tables is that the cryptographic subsystem ported from OpenBSD used these tables to encapsulate the functions that do the real work of cryptography. To simplify the maintenance of the code, this set of interfaces and tables was retained during the port. A useful side effect of having these tables is that it makes adding new protocols or cryptographic routines simple. The use of these tables is described later in this section.

User-level daemons interact with the IPSec framework via key sockets. Key sockets are implemented in the same way as other socket types. There is a domain structure, *keydomain*; a protocol-switch structure, *keysw*; a set of user-request routines, *key_usrreqs*; and an output routine, *key_output*(). Only those routines necessary for a connectionless-datagram type of protocol are implemented in the *key_usrreqs* structure. Any attempt to use a key socket in a connection-oriented way—for instance, calling *connect* on a key socket—will result in the kernel returning EINVAL to the caller.

When an application writes to a key socket, the message is eventually transferred down into the kernel and is handled by the *key_output*() routine. After some rudimentary error checking, the message is passed to *key_parse*(), which does more error checks, and then is finally shuttled off through a function-pointer switch called *key_types*. The functions pointed to by *key_types* are those that do the manipulation of the security-association and security-policy databases.

If the kernel needs to send a message to listening applications because of changes in the security databases, it uses the *key_sendup_mbuf*() routine to copy the message to one or more listening sockets. Each socket receives its own copy of the message.

IPSec Implementation

The IPSec protocols affect all areas of packet handling in the IPv4 and IPv6 protocol stacks. In some places, IPSec uses the existing networking framework, and in others, direct callouts are made to do some part of the security processing. We will look at three of the possible paths through the IPv4 stack: inbound, outbound, and forwarding.

One twist that IPSec adds to normal packet processing is the need to process some packets more than once. An example is the arrival of an encrypted packet bound for the current system. The packet will be processed once in its encrypted form and then a second time, by the same routines, after it has been decrypted. This multipass processing is unlike regular TCP or UDP processing where the IP header is stripped from the packet and the result is handed to the TCP or UDP modules for processing and eventual delivery to a socket. This ***continuation style*** of processing packets is one reason that the IPSec software makes extensive use of packet tags. Another reason to use packet tags is that parts of IPSec, namely the cryptographic algorithms, can be supported by special-purpose hardware accelerators. A hardware accelerator may do all or part of the security processing, such as checking a packet's authentication information or decrypting the packet payload and then passing the resulting packet into the protocol stack for final delivery to a waiting socket. The hardware needs some way to tell the protocol stack that it has completed the necessary work. It is neither possible, nor desirable, to store this information in the headers or data of the packet. Adding such information to a packet's header is an obvious security hole because a malicious sender could simply set the appropriate field and bypass the security processing. It would have been possible to extend the *mbuf* structure to handle this functionality, but packet

Table 13.8 IPSec packet tags.

Tag	Description
IPSEC_IN_DONE	inbound IPSec processing complete
IPSEC_OUT_DONE	outbound IPSec processing complete
IPSEC_IN_CRYPTO_DONE	inbound IPSec processing handled by hardware
IPSEC_OUT_CRYPTO_DONE	outbound IPSec processing handled by hardware

tags are a more flexible way of adding metadata to packets without modifying a key data structure in the network stack. The tags used by IPSec are described in Table 13.8.

As we saw in Section 13.4, when an IPv4 packet is received by the kernel, it is initially processed by *ip_input*(). The *ip_input*() routine does two checks on packets that are related to IPSec. The first is to see if the packet is really part of a tunnel. If a packet is being tunneled and it has been processed by the IPSec software already, it can bypass any filtering by filter hooks or the kernel's firewall code. The second check is done when a packet is to be forwarded. Routers can implement security policies on packets that are forwarded. Before a packet is passed to *ip_forward*(), it is checked by calling the *ipsec_getpolicy*() function to see if there is a policy that is associated with the packet itself. The *ipsec_getpolicybyaddr*() function is called to check if there is a policy associated with the address of the packet. If either function returns a pointer to a policy routine, the packet is passed to that policy routine to be checked. If the packet is rejected, it is silently dropped and no error is returned to the sender.

When *ip_input*() has determined that the packet is valid and is destined for the local machine, the protocol-stack framework takes over. The packet is passed to the appropriate input routine using the *pr_input* field of the *inetsw* structure. Although packets using different protocols have different entry points, they eventually wind up being passed to a single routine, *ipsec_common_input*(), for processing. The *ipsec_common_input*() routine attempts to find the appropriate security-association structure for the packet based on its destination address, the security protocol it is using, and the SPI. If an appropriate association is found, then control is passed to the input routine contained in the SA's *xform-switch* structure. The security-protocol's input routine extracts all the relevant data from the packet—for example, the key being used—and creates a cryptography-operation descriptor. This descriptor is then passed into the cryptographic routines. When the cryptographic routines have completed their work, they call a protocol-specific callback routine, which modifies the mbufs associated with the packet so that it may now be passed, unencrypted, back into the protocol stack via the *ip_input*() routine.

Applications do not know that they are using IPSec to communicate with other hosts in the Internet. For outbound packets, the use of IPSec is really controlled from within the *ip_output*() routine. When an outbound packet reaches the *ip_output*() routine, a check is made to see if there is a security policy that applies to the packet, either because of its destination address or because of the socket that sent it. If a security policy is found, then the packet is passed into the IPSec code via the *ipsec4_process_packet*() routine. If a security association has not been set up for this particular destination, one is created for it in the security-association database. The *ipsec4_process_packet*() uses the *output*() routine from the *xform switch* in the security association to pass off the packet to the security protocol's output routine. The security protocol's *output routine* uses the appropriate cryptographic routine to modify the packet for transmission. Once the packet has been modified appropriately, it is passed again into *ip_output*() but with the tag

IPSEC_OUT_DONE attached to it. This tag marks the packet as having completed IPSec processing, showing that it can now be transmitted like any other packet.

Underlying all the security protocols provided by IPSec is a set of APIs and libraries that support cryptography. The cryptographic subsystem in FreeBSD supports both symmetric and asymmetric cryptography. ***Symmetric cryptography***, used by IPSec, uses the same key to encrypt data as it does to decrypt them. ***Asymmetric cryptography***, which implements ***public-key encryption***, uses one key to encrypt data and another key to decrypt them. The cryptographic APIs are covered in detail in Section 5.12. Readers interested in how data are encrypted within the IPSec subsystem are encouraged to read the complete discussion found there.

13.8 Packet-Processing Frameworks

Most of the packets that are processed by a host pass through network-protocol modules such as TCP/IP. Some applications may need to get access to packets as they pass through the kernel without using the more common mechanisms provided by sockets. Over the last 20 years several different packet-processing frameworks have been developed in FreeBSD, from simple packet filtering to more complex frameworks in which new protocols can be developed. Packet-processing frameworks are used for debugging network problems, implementing firewalls, performing network address translation (NAT), and providing software for network-research testbeds.

Berkeley Packet Filter

The Berkeley Packet Filter (BPF) [McCanne & Jacobson, 1993], FreeBSD's packet sniffing system, is arguably the simplest packet-processing framework provided by the operating system. BPF provides a uniform user-level interface to all the operating system's network interfaces, allowing programs with root privilege to get access to raw packets as they pass by on the network. Most users do not interact directly with BPF but instead run programs such as **tcpdump** that use the packet-capture library, **libpcap**, to express easily understandable filtering rules that govern which packets are to be captured. The **tcpdump** program directs the BPF pseudo-device to read raw packets from a network device before any network protocols access them. Being implemented as a pseudo-device means that userspace programs can interact with BPF via the well-known *open*, *close*, *read*, *write*, and *ioctl* interfaces. The device nodes exposed by BPF are bi-directional, meaning that applications can not only receive packets but can also inject packets into the network from userspace.

BPF implements a simple high-speed packet-matching engine in software using a synthetic domain-specific assembly language. Comprising less than 30 instructions, the BPF virtual machine is general enough to do all the computational tasks of a CPU including fetching and storing data, mathematical operations, and branching. The simplicity and generality of the BPF instruction set make it possible to write complex filtering rules, have them compiled and optimized in userspace, and deliver the final instruction stream into the kernel. Separating the compilation and execution of BPF programs makes creating extensions easier and minimizes the amount of work that must be done on each packet during filtering, thereby reducing the overhead of deciding which packets to capture. One feature that the split between compilation and execution has made possible is just-in-time (JIT) compilation of filters to native machine code, which allows the kernel to avoid the overhead of virtual-machine instruction execution altogether.

For BPF to work when the system is transmitting packets, it must be hooked into each network driver's source code. A simple macro, BPF_MTAP, is provided for driver authors to use in their source code. The purpose of the macro is to take packets, from as near the hardware layer as possible, and feed them into BPF so that it can determine if the packets are of interest to a listener in userspace. On packet reception, the BPF_MTAP macro is called from the link-layer protocols, such as Ethernet. The BPF_MTAP macro is the only interface required by BPF to do its work. Providing a single macro that is easy to remember and use has made it possible to convince device-driver authors to include this code when writing software for new hardware.

Internally, the BPF_MTAP macro calls the *bpf_mtap*() function that contains the calls to the filtering and copying routines. The heart of the filtering code is in *bpf_filter*(), that executes the virtual assembly language to decide whether a packet matches a filter. When a packet matches a filter, it is copied into a buffer. Aside from data copying, the *catchpacket*() routine does all the tasks that are important to packet filtering: figuring out how much of the packet was captured, determining the length of the packet header, and timestamping the captured packet. How the packet is copied depends on the function that is passed as an argument to the *catchpacket*() routine. Copying packet data is an expensive operation. One optimization uses zero-copy buffers that combine virtual memory and a shared-memory protocol to share buffers directly between the kernel and userspace rather than requiring explicit copying. The *bpf_append_mbuf*() function contains a two-case switch statement that calls out to either *bpf_buffer_append_mbuf*() or *bpf_zerocopy_append_mbuf*(). The zero-copy code does a small bit of extra work to ensure that the buffers used to capture the packet data are reused as the packet moves toward userspace, reducing the number of times that the packet's data must be copied. The *bpf_buffer_append_mbuf*() code is simpler because it just loops over the packet data to copy it. However, the act of copying data between buffers is expensive and that is why the zero-copy code is available. Zero copy is more complex to implement but much faster at run time.

IP Firewalls

The job of a firewall is to inspect a packet and take an action based on the packet's contents. While BPF might copy the same packet to various listeners in userspace, it will neither modify nor drop the packet along the way. A firewall exists solely to modify or drop packets in transit. The kernel provides a generic set of hooks for use in implementing firewalls. All firewalls in FreeBSD are built using *pfil*, which stands for "packet filter." Firewalls register filtering functions with the *pfil* system, and these functions are executed whenever a packet passes through a *pfil* barrier point in the networking modules. The kernel has twenty one barrier points in the networking code where these functions may be added or removed at run time. Barrier points include the IPv6 and IPv4 input and output routines discussed in Section 13.4. Providing a generic packet filtering system in the kernel has enabled various developers to write firewall software without the need for them to modify the kernel on their own. When new network code is written, new barrier points are added in the appropriate places such that the firewall authors can extend their software further in a fully generic manner.

Firewalls register their hooks by calling the *pfil_add_hook*() routine, specifying the function to call and whether it should be called for packets that are inbound, outbound, or traveling in either direction. Once a hook is registered, it is called by *pfil_run_hooks*() whenever a packet reaches the barrier. The functions called from the *pfil_run_hooks*() routine can modify the mbuf that they are passed, for example, while performing network address translation. If a hook function returns a nonzero value, then packet processing ends and no other hooks are called. When a hook function decides to drop a packet, it is responsible for freeing the associated mbuf, which presents new module authors with the potential for memory leaks. All the firewalls in FreeBSD are built on top of this simple set of routines.

IPFW and Dummynet

The IP firewall (IPFW) system is both a firewall and generic packet-processing framework that can be used to manipulate IPv6 and IPv4 packets as they enter and exit the system. A single *pfil* hook, *ipfw_check_hook*(), is responsible for capturing packets from within the IPv6 and IPv4 input and output routines: *ip6_input*(), *ip6_output*(), *ip6_forward*(), *ip_input*(), *ip_output*(), and *ip_fastforward*(). In each of these functions, a single call to *pfil_run_hooks*() decides whether packet processing will continue.

IPFW contains a single central-dispatch function, *ipfw_chk*(), that decides the fate of all packets that are passed to it. Packets can be passed through unchanged, copied, diverted, subjected to network address translation, reassembled for further inspection, sent to *dummynet*, or dropped. The action taken on any packet is determined by the return value from the *ipfw_chk*() routine. The complete list of return values and their meanings is given in Table 13.9.

The *ipfw_chk*() routine does its work in two phases. In the first phase, *ipfw_chk*() dissects the packet gathering network addresses, the transport-protocol type, source, and destination ports, and any associated flags into a set of internal variables. The work done by *ipfw_chk*() is similar to that done in any of the IPv6 and IPv4 input routines. With the packet's state properly dissected, *ipfw_chk* moves on to phase two, where it decides what to do with the packet. A set of rules that are controlled at a high level by the administrator of the system dictates what should be done with the packet. The rules are stored in lists called chains. Each

Table 13.9 IPFW packet disposition based on *ipfw_chk*() return value.

Return Value	Description
IP_FW_PASS	accept the packet
IP_FW_DENY	drop the packet
IP_FW_DIVERT	divert the packet to a divert socket
IP_FW_TEE	copy the packet
IP_FW_DUMMYNET	send the packet to dummynet
IP_FW_NETGRAPH	send the packet to netgraph

rule contains a set of opcodes that control the action that should be taken at each position in the packet. A decision is made about the disposition of the packet when an opcode is reached that terminates packet processing. Table 13.10 shows the set of opcodes that result in an action being taken with the packet. The opcodes in IPFW mirror those in BPF.

Using a set of opcodes, rather than hard-coded individual functions, gives IPFW flexibility and reduces its code size. A single 1200-line loop is responsible

Table 13.10 IPFW action opcodes.

Opcode	Action
O_LOG	log the packet
O_PROB	probability, used for RED
O_CHECK_STATE	stateful filtering lookup
O_ACCEPT	accept the packet
O_DENY	drop the packet
O_REJECT	drop the packet and send an ICMP error
O_COUNT	update packet statistics
O_SKIPTO	jump to another rule in the chain
O_PIPE	send to a dummynet pipe
O_QUEUE	send to a dummynet queue
O_DIVERT	send to a divert socket
O_TEE	copy the packet
O_FORWARD_IP	forward to a different destination IPv4
O_FORWARD_IP6	forward to a different destination IPv6
O_NAT	send to Network Address Translation
O_REASS	reassemble packet

Table 13.11 IPFW IP opcodes.

Opcode	Action
O_IP_SRC	match IP source address
O_IP_SRC_ME	Is this host the source of the packet?
O_IP_DST	match IP destination address
O_IP_DST_ME	Is this host the destination of the packet?
O_IP_SRCPORT	match the source port
O_IP_DSTPORT	match the destination port
O_PROTO	match on transport protocol

for any action that can be taken with a packet. Having a centralized location for decisions about the disposition of a packet reduces the complexity of the code and also increases the likelihood that any errant bugs can be found quickly and repaired. Opcodes in IPFW can have data associated with them. For example, the IP opcodes all carry an address and a mask that can be used to check whether the packet's IP address matches the one in the rule that is currently being executed. A subset of the IP opcodes is given in Table 13.11.

Dummynet is a packet-processing framework that provides traffic shaping, packet delay emulation, and packet scheduling. The original purpose of dummynet was to provide a way to test network protocols such as TCP that have performance issues when their packet streams are subjected to variable networking delays or drops. It has grown into being a generic bandwidth-shaping tool used in various devices often at the edge of the network.

Dummynet passes all traffic through an object called a pipe. A pipe emulates a communication link driven by a scheduler that arbitrates access for several independent queues. The features of the pipe are programmable. Features include the pipe's bandwidth and delay. They also include the scheduling policy, the number and size of the queues, and the queues relative priorities. The system permits the dynamic creation of many pipes and queues, and the algorithms used in dummynet are designed to scale to tens of thousands of pipes and queues without introducing excessive overhead.

The dummynet system assigns every packet that it touches to a flow. A flow is a set of packets that match a pre-determined set of criteria, such as having the same destination address and port number. All packets that are part of a flow are processed similarly. Traffic shaping is carried out by dropping packets at the network layer as this approach forces protocols such as TCP to scale back their transmissions and results in a lower offered bandwidth. Dummynet can also delay packets by holding them in a pipe for a configurable amount of time. It is this delay property that was originally used for testing TCP in a laboratory environment.

Queues are served by a packet scheduler through one of the available scheduling policies listed in Table 13.12. The schedulers manage and shape packet flows as they traverse the system. Schedulers differ in the service guarantees they provide and their packet-processing cost. Better guarantees for minimum bandwidth or maximum delay require more effort, though state-of-the-art algorithms such as quick fair queueing (QFQ) perform well [Checconi et al., 2013]. Dummynet provides three weight-based schedulers. Each scheduler incurs a different amount of per-packet overhead when processing packets. The weighted round robin (WRR) scheduler has a constant run time but poor service guarantees, while a variant of weighted fair queueing (WFQ+) has optimal guarantees and a packet service time logarithmic in the number of flows. Finally, QFQ, has nearly optimal guarantees and constant processing time per packet. Other schedulers, including those based on priorities or other criteria, can be implemented as loadable kernel modules.

Packets are first classified by IPFW or another firewall before being passed into dummynet. As packets enter dummynet, an mbuf tag is attached to each mbuf via the *tag_mbuf*() routine. The mbuf tag contains a reference to the pipe to be used, as well as other metadata that associates the packet to a flow. The packet is then passed to the *dummynet_io*() routine that completes the classification and stores the packet into the correct queue, dropping the packet if the queue is full. When the link emulated by the pipe is ready to transmit a new packet, the scheduler selects the queue to serve and extracts a packet from it. Once this work is complete, a timer is set to run the scheduler again after a time equal to the packet length divided by the pipe's bandwidth. The resulting traffic exits the scheduler at exactly the programmed rate. Packets selected by the scheduler are put into a *delay line*, a FIFO queue from which packets are removed after a time equal to the delay associated with the pipe. The dummynet mbuf tag has an *output_time* field that tracks the time at which the packet needs to be transmitted. When packets are removed from the FIFO, they are reinserted into the network stack at the point from which they were intercepted. Depending on the configuration of the classifier, they may be reclassified and sent to another pipe.

Dummynet may have many queues and pipes that may need to be served. Thus, dummynet implements its own timer queue using a priority queue and processes it through a function, *dummynet_task*(), that is invoked on every timer tick.

Table 13.12 Dummynet schedulers.

Scheduler	Description
FIFO	first-in first-out queueing discipline
WRR	weighted round robin
WFQ+	weighted fair queueing
QFQ	quick fair queueing

Managing its own timer queue provides scalability at the price of some jitter in the output. The jitter seen in packets delayed by dummynet is directly related to the clock-tick setting in the kernel. The default tick rate of 1000 (see Section 3.4) will give good results down to 1 millisecond. To achieve finer granularity would require an increase in the kernel's tick rate.

Packet Filter (PF)

Although packet filter (PF) provides similar functionality to IPFW, it has a different structure and implementation. The PF system was originally developed under OpenBSD and then later ported to FreeBSD, where it has remained popular for building firewalls and network address translators. Like IPFW, PF uses *pfil* hooks to capture packets for examination. PF adds a hook in each of the inbound and outbound directions for both IPv4 and IPv6. The *pf_check_in*(), *pf_check_out*(), *pf_check6_in*(), and *pf_check6_out*() routines are the starting points for any packet filtering carried out by PF.

The purpose of a firewall is to decide whether to drop a packet. PF has two enumerated values, PF_PASS and PF_DROP, that control whether a packet will be allowed through a firewall. In addition to the enumerated values that determine whether a packet is passed or dropped, PF also uses a set of reason codes that explain the final disposition of the packet. The reason codes are listed in Table 13.13.

Table 13.13 PF reason codes.

Code	Reason
PFRES_MATCH	explicit match of a rule
PFRES_BADOFF	bad offset while trying to get headers
PFRES_FRAG	dropping following fragment
PFRES_SHORT	packet too short
PFRES_NORM	dropped during packet normalization
PFRES_MEMORY	ran out of memory
PFRES_TS	bad TCP Timestamp option
PFRES_CONGEST	IP input congestion
PFRES_IPOPTIONS	dropped because of IP options processing
PFRES_PROTCKSUM	protocol checksum invalid
PFRES_BADSTATE	state mismatch
PFRES_STATEINS	state insertion failure
PFRES_MAXSTATES	no more space in state table
PFRES_SRCLIMIT	source-node or connection limit
PFRES_SYNPROXY	TCP SYN proxy

When a packet enters the system, it is subjected to a series of tests starting in the *pf_test*() routine. Each of the test routines does some amount of work to dissect or reassemble the packet before passing it along to a higher-layer protocol test. The process of validating a packet proceeds in two phases. The first phase is called normalization and is where the contents are compared against rules set by the administrator. The IPv4, IPv6, and TCP protocols each have their own normalization routine: *pf_normalize_ip*(), *pf_normalize_ip6*(), and *pf_normalize_tcp*() respectively. All the rules in PF are stored in *pf_rule* structures that are linked together in a queue.

The second phase of packet processing happens after the packet has been normalized and subjected to any matching rules. The *pf_test*() routine dissects the IP header of the packet into a *pf_desc* descriptor structure. The *pf_desc* structure holds the state of the packet in a convenient form for the rest of the test routines. IP packets are demultiplexed in the *pf_test*() routine in much the same way that they are in *ip_input*(), except without the flexibility of the *inetsw* protocol switch. Instead of a lookup table, packets are passed directly into predetermined test functions based on their protocol type. Each transport-layer protocol, TCP, UDP, and ICMP is handled by a matching *pf_test*() routine: *pf_test_state_tcp*(), *pf_test_state_udp*(), and *pf_test_state_icmp*(). The test routines also handle all protocol specific state tracking.

Netgraph

The netgraph subsystem was designed to provide an easy way to develop new network protocols in the FreeBSD kernel and was first released as part of FreeBSD 3. Since its addition to the operating system, netgraph has been used to implement several protocols including the point-to-point protocol (PPP), the asynchronous-transfer mode protocol (ATM), and Bluetooth.

The core idea behind netgraph is that network protocols can be built around a data-flow model. In a data-flow model, packets flow between software modules, each of which does some small amount of work on the packet before passing it on to the next module. In netgraph the modules are referred to as nodes and the edges that connect the nodes are called hooks. The data flows across the set of hooks between the nodes of the graph. Nodes can be connected somewhat arbitrarily, although they may impose certain limitations on the number of connections they are willing to accept. Encapsulating the processing of packets into sufficiently fine-grained nodes can allow for greater software reuse than in a more monolithic design. A simple set of nodes can more easily be built up into a complex protocol in an experimental plug-and-play scenario similar to a set of childrens building blocks. A data-flow model also allows the possibility of adding or removing processing elements at run time—for example, when a protocol needs to attempt different types of encryption to establish a network connection with a peer. The different types of encryption can be encapsulated as nodes and then added and removed from the data path as needed at run time.

Nodes not only pass network packets across their hooks, but also respond to a set of control messages defined by each node. A node is configured using control messages. It can also expose counters and statistics to user-level programs via the control-message interface. Having a well-defined set of APIs both for packet processing and configuration allows the programmer to build a system that looks more like a traditional network router, with both a data plane and a control plane. In netgraph, the data plane is where network packets pass along the hooks between the nodes. The control plane is the set of messages that configures the nodes.

Netgraph, with its nodes and hooks, is an object-oriented design, where the nodes are objects and the hooks are methods. The object-oriented approach used by netgraph has advantages similar to other systems that create complex protocols out of smaller blocks, including STREAMS [Ritchie, 1984] and The Click Modular Router framework [Kohler et al., 2000]. There are more than 50 netgraph nodes available as part of FreeBSD, ranging from the simple *ng_echo* node that echos back every packet it receives, to those nodes that provide whole protocols such as PPP, ATM, and Bluetooth.

To build anything with netgraph, a set of nodes must be selected that are useful to implementing a protocol. The nodes are connected via their hooks into a graph. There are two main data structures used by netgraph, the *ng_node* and *ng_hook*. Every node in the graph maintains some basic information about itself, including a globally-unique name and details on how it is connected to other nodes. Each node also has a type, reference count, a set of flags, and a private data area in which the node can maintain statistics and internal state.

Nodes exist simultaneously on several lists in the system, including the global list of all nodes and the list of nodes for which there is work to do. The global list of all nodes tracks down a node when the user wants to send it a control message.

Each node exposes a set of functions via a function pointer table. Most nodes are written as loadable kernel modules (see Section 15.3). The functions exposed by the node relate to the different stages in a node's existence. When a node is activated, it is loaded as a module, initialized, and hooked to other nodes. While active, it receives and processes messages. When deactivated, it is disconnected from the rest of the nodes in the system and shutdown.

When the node is initialized, its *ng_constructor_t*() function is called to do any housekeeping chores required before the node can be used. When node A connects to a hook on node B, node B's *ng_newhook_t*() function is called. When a node is shut down, first the *ng_close_t*() and then the *ng_shutdown_t*() functions will be called. Control messages are received by the *ng_rcvmsg_t*() function while data arrives via the *ng_rcvdata_t*() entry point.

Each node has a set of associated hooks that dictate how the nodes are connected. The way in which nodes are connected defines how packets will be processed by the graph and represents the protocol being implemented. Hooks, like nodes, have textual names. Each hook is a first-class object in the system, and has its own type, flags, references, and private data. Hooks commonly record statistics about the data that cross them in their private-data area.

A simple example helps to understand how netgraph works. The example shown in Figure 13.25 uses two node types to build a simple network bridge. One

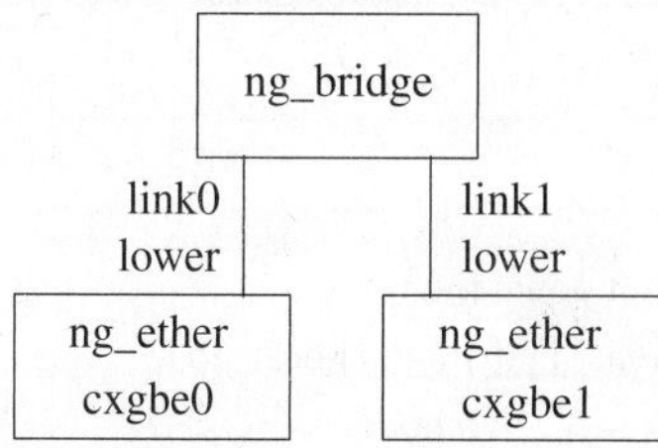

Figure 13.25 A simple network bridge.

is an Ethernet node, *ng_ether*, one of which is attached to each Ethernet interface in the system when the *ng_ether* module is loaded. The other is a bridge node, *ng_bridge*, that connects multiple Ethernet interfaces.

A bridge operates at a lower level than the Internet protocols, covered in Section 13.4, taking any Ethernet packet that arrives on one interface and forwarding it to one or more other interfaces. Network-layer protocols such as IPv4 and IPv6 are at a higher layer than Ethernet and do not come into play here. Packets are forwarded independent of their IPv4 or IPv6 addresses.

Our example bridge contains only two interfaces, cxgbe0 and cxgbe1. Every packet received on cxgbe0 is sent unchanged out of cxgbe1 and every packet received on cxgbe1 is sent out of cxgbe0. The bridge shown in Figure 13.25 is made up of three nodes. Each network interface is represented by its own *ng_ether* node, and the *ng_bridge* node ties them together. The *ng_ether* node has two hooks, *upper*() and *lower*() to which other nodes connect. The *lower*() hook is where all Ethernet packets received by the underlying interface appear for consumption by other nodes. Packets sent to the *upper*() hook are passed up into the network stack. When an *ng_ether* node is first initialized, its *upper*() and *lower*() hooks are connected so that packets flow from the underlying interface into the network stack.

To create a bridge, we must connect to the *ng_ether* node's *lower*() hook so that all the packets received on the underlying interface are sent to our bridge node and not into the network stack. The *ng_bridge* node has a set of numbered link hooks that can be connected to the *ng_ether* node's *lower*() hooks.

Like all netgraph nodes, the *ng_bridge* node exposes a set of functions. The *ng_bridge_newhook*() function is concerned with getting the name of the hook right. The code that does the work of passing packets is implemented in the node's *ng_bridge_rcvdata*() function.

When the *ng_bridge* node receives a packet, it must make several checks before deciding what to do with it. One of the more complex aspects of bridging a broadcast network like Ethernet is detecting when a loop has occurred. Loops can happen for several reasons, such as misconfiguration when adding new computers to the network or a piece of network equipment being damaged. If the network develops a loop, then packets can wind up being forwarded forever across a pair of interfaces, effectively destroying that segment of the network. To detect a loop,

Table 13.14 Netgraph base messages.

Message	Action
NGM_SHUTDOWN	shut down the node
NGM_MKPEER	create and attach a peer node
NGM_CONNECT	connect two nodes
NGM_NAME	give a node a name
NGM_RMHOOK	break a connection between two nodes
NGM_NODEINFO	get information about a node
NGM_LISTHOOKS	get the list of hooks for a node
NGM_LISTNAMES	get a list of all named nodes
NGM_LISTNODES	get a list of all nodes
NGM_LISTTYPES	list installed node types
NGM_TEXT_STATUS	get status as text string
NGM_BINARY2ASCII	convert **struct** *ng_mesg* to ASCII
NGM_ASCII2BINARY	convert ASCII representation to **struct** *ng_mesg*
NGM_TEXT_CONFIG	get or set node configuration

the system must record the link being used by each host based on the host's link-layer (Ethernet) source address. The system detects a loop when it observes a host using more than one link in a short period of time. When a loop is detected, the system outputs an error, drops the packet, and briefly turns the link off.

The first time the *ng_bridge* node sees a packet from a host, the loop detection code inserts an entry for the new host in the bridge's host table. The host table is implemented as a hash table indexed on the host's link-layer source address. The host's source address is stored as well as the link on which it is first seen by the *ng_bridge* node. On each subsequent reception of a packet from the same host, the packet will be found in the node's host table. After a host is looked up in the table, the code does the loop check. If the link on which this packet was received is not the same as the one stored in the host table, the system checks the age of this host's entry against the allowed minimum stable age for a host (one second). If a host has moved links in less than a second, the system considers the host to be in a loop condition. When a loop condition is detected, the offending link is disabled and all the hosts on the link are dropped from the link's tables. Links do not remain in a loop state forever. They are returned to a normal state by a timeout routine that is called once per second to do various house keeping duties for the *ng_bridge* node.

Netgraph nodes not only pass packets along their hooks, but they also respond to a set of control messages defined by the node. A small set of control messages are defined by the base class of netgraph. The basic messages are required to have minimal control over the nodes and include messages to instantiate, connect, control and shutdown the nodes. The set of base messages is shown in Table 13.14.

The *ng_bridge* nodes receive control messages on their *rcvmsg*() function. The receive-message function of a node looks much like an *ioctl*() routine in a network driver. The *ng_bridge_rcvmsg*() function takes an *item_p* structure and converts it into a message using the NGI_GET_MSG macro. The function knows nothing of the internals of the *item_p* structure, because it only knows how to interpret messages. The receive-message function decodes the message via a switch statement. Control messages in netgraph are encapsulated into a *ng_mesghdr* structure:

```
struct  ng_msghdr {
    u_char      version;                /* NGM_VERSION number */
    u_char      spare;                  /* pad to 4 bytes */
    u_int16_t   spare2;
    u_int32_t   arglen;                 /* length of data */
    u_int32_t   cmd;                    /* command identifier */
    u_int32_t   flags;                  /* message status */
    u_int32_t   token;                  /* match with reply */
    u_int32_t   typecookie;             /* node's type cookie */
    u_char      cmdstr[NG_CMDSTRSIZ];   /* cmd string + NULL */
} header;
```

All *ng_mesghdr* structures contain a generic header that describes the message being sent. Each node must decode the message to take the action that the message is requesting. While the header is standardized, the arbitrary node-specific data is contained in the *data* section following the header.

Every netgraph message header contains two pieces of information needed for a node to decode a message, the *typecookie* and the *cmd*. The *typecookie* is opaque data that identifies the type of node to which the message is being sent. Each node has its own *typecookie* and this *typecookie* is the first piece of data that is checked in processing an incoming control message. If the *typecookie* does not match that of the node trying to decode the message, then the message is invalid and an error is returned.

Once the *ng_bridge_recvmsg*() function has established that the message is for its consumption, it decodes the command by looking at the *cmd* element of the *ng_mesg* structure. The choice of messages is determined by the implementer of the node, but most nodes provide messages for getting and setting the node configuration, retrieving and clearing statistics, and resetting the node. Netgraph contains many convenience macros, such as NG_MKRESPONSE, to facilitate building nodes without programmers needing to concern themselves with the internals of the framework.

Netmap

The advent of networks and network interfaces that are capable of sustaining speeds of 1 and 10 gigabits per second has meant that the performance of some networking applications such as routers, switches, firewalls, and intrusion detection systems is limited by the amount of data that can be copied between the network interface and the user-level code that intends to operate on the packets. Several approaches avoid the overhead of copying data into userspace by running network applications in the kernel or bypassing the kernel completely and giving the application direct access to the underlying network interface. Each of these approaches has its drawbacks, including loss of generality, loss of virtual-memory protection, and higher maintenance costs. The *netmap* framework [Rizzo, 2012] provides a uniform userspace API for applications that require high-speed access to raw-packet data. Unlike a network protocol, the *netmap* framework does not process the packets in any way other than to make them available to userspace applications.

Applications using the *netmap* framework gain direct access to a network interface's packet rings. Packet rings were first described in Section 8.5 where the network-interface data structures are discussed. Each network device has one or more pairs of ring structures that point to memory buffers for receiving or transmitting packets. The rings normally pass packets into and out of the operating system's networking protocols. When an application starts using a network interface via *netmap*, the rings are mapped to a region of memory that is shared by both the application and the network interface. Packets that are received on the network interface continue to be placed by the device's DMA engine into the receive ring. Packets that the application wishes to transmit are placed into buffers referenced by the transmit ring. Proper synchronization between the kernel and userspace is maintained via the system-call interface with calls to request packet transmission and to be notified of packet reception. Data structure consistency is maintained because the kernel only manipulates the application's buffers while the application is blocked in a system call.

When an application wishes to use the netmap framework, it calls *open* on a special device, **/dev/netmap**. The file descriptor returned by the *open* call is used for all subsequent communication with the framework. Applications using *netmap* associate themselves with a particular interface by issuing an *ioctl* call with the NIOCREGIF command, passing in the textual name of the interface as the last argument to the system call. When an application registers for access to a network interface, the kernel disconnects the device's rings from the networking subsystems and makes them available to the application. Disconnecting the rings from the networking subsystems has the effect of stopping all traffic into and out of the normal networking protocols. The *netmap* framework has one pair of software-based packet rings that remain connected to the operating system's network stack and can be used by an application to pass packets into, and receive packets from, the operating system. An application using *netmap* can choose to process some packets but allow others to pass into the kernel's general networking framework. Packets pass into the kernel when the application receives packets from one of the hardware rings and places them into the software rings that are connected to the kernel. The application allows packets to flow out from the host network stack by taking packets from the software ring connected to the kernel and transmitting them on one of the hardware rings. Alternatively, an application can choose to process all the packets itself, thus preventing any packets from passing into the kernel's general networking framework. When a *netmap* application is using the device, any other program accessing the same network device through the *socket* API will no longer be able to receive or transmit packets on the interface, unless the application using the *netmap* framework allows packets to flow back into the kernel's general network framework.

An application using the *netmap* framework is responsible for updating and tracking the changes it has made to the receive and transmit rings. Figure 13.26 shows three steps taken when a netmap receive ring is updated by a userspace program:

1. The userspace program pointers shown after a netmap ring has been set up. The slots in the ring between the "head" pointer and the "tail" pointer, minus

Figure 13.26 Netmap receive-ring processing. Key: *—slot with undefined contents; h—slot held by the userspace program; R—packet ready for reception.

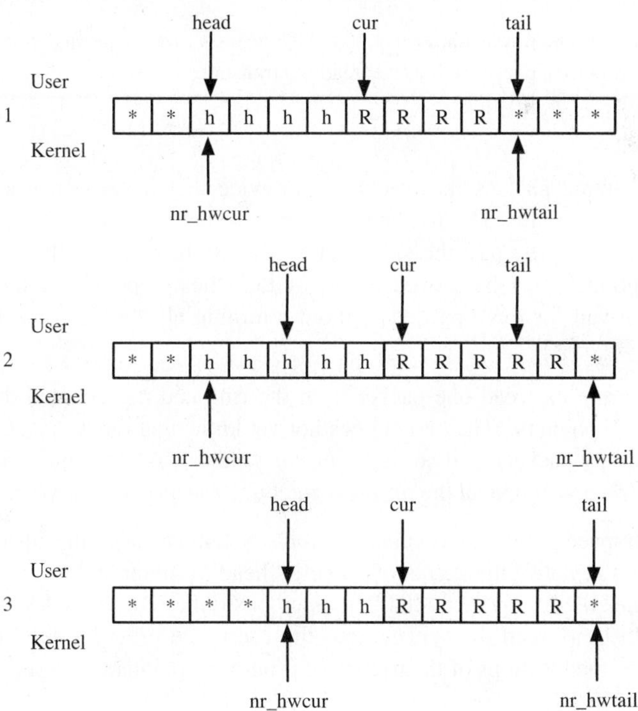

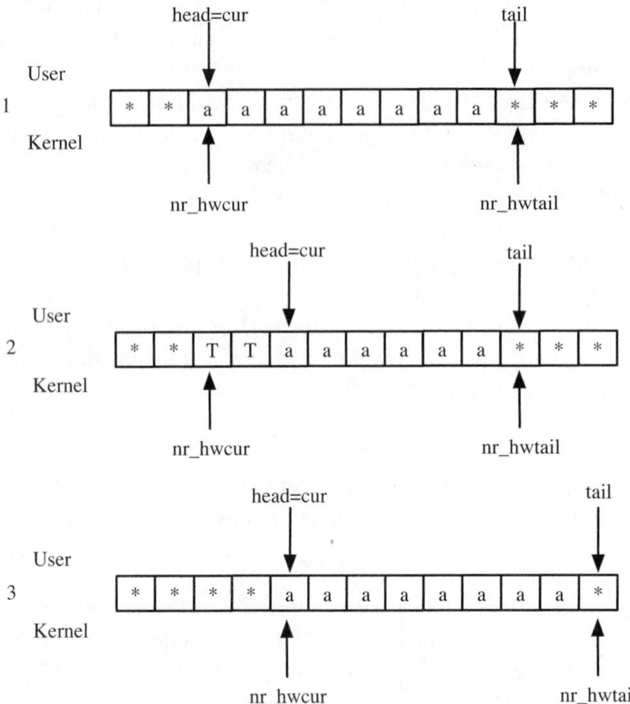

Figure 13.27 Netmap transmit-ring processing. Key: *—slot with undefined contents; a—available to place a packet; T—packet ready to transmit.

a slot, contain packets received by the device that have been passed to the userspace program. The userspace program processes packets and advances the "head" pointer past the slots that it is ready to return to the kernel. The "cur" pointer may be moved ahead of the "head" pointer if the program wants to wait for more packets without returning all the previous slots to the kernel.

2. The program has read one packet from the ring and has updated the "head" and "cur" pointers. The kernel does not yet know that the userspace program has read any packets, and so its *nr_hwcur* pointer has not been updated. The device driver will update the *nr_hwavail* counter as packets arrive in the ring.

3. The userspace program has called the *ioctl* system call with the NIOCRXSYNC command to notify the kernel of its new "head" pointer and to be notified by the kernel of the updated "tail" pointer position. The NIOCRXSYNC command does not read the packets into the userspace program but simply synchronizes the locations of the userspace program's pointers.

Writing packets to the ring is the opposite of reading them. Figure 13.27 shows three steps of a userspace program transmitting packets:

1. The slots between the "head" pointer and the "tail" pointer, minus one, that are available for transmission.
2. The program has filled two slots and advanced the "head" and "cur" pointers past the slots that are ready for transmission. The "cur" pointer may be moved further ahead if the program needs more slots before further transmissions.
3. The transmit ring following a NIOCTXSYNC command, which both notified the kernel of the data to send and updated the userspace program's pointers. The slots up to the "head" pointer, minus one, have been handed to the device for transmission, and the "tail" pointer has been advanced because more slots have become available.

Netmap file descriptors support the same actions available via the *ioctl* system call using the *select*, *poll*, and *kevent* system calls. These system calls rely on the polling framework or interrupts to wake up the threads blocked on the system calls. The interrupt service routine does not do any data processing. All accesses to the data occur in the context of the userspace program. The netmap framework is not limited to accessing network interfaces. The same functions can be used to access ports of the VALE virtual switch and dummynet pipes.

Exercises

13.1 Name two key data structures used in the networking subsystem that are important in ensuring that the socket-layer software is kept independent of the networking implementation.

13.2 Which routines in the protocol switch are called by the socket layer? Explain why each of these routines is called.

13.3 Assume that a reliably-delivered-message socket (SOCK_RDM) is a connectionless socket that guarantees reliable delivery of data and that preserves message boundaries. Which flags would a protocol that supported this type of socket have set in the *pr_flags* field of its protocol-switch entry?

13.4 Why is the name or address of a socket kept at the network layer rather than at the socket layer?

13.5 Why does FreeBSD not attempt to enforce a rigid protocol–protocol interface structure?

13.6 How does IPv4 identify the next-higher-level protocol that should process an incoming message? How might this dispatching differ in other networking architectures?

13.7 How many hosts can exist in an IPv4 subnet with a mask of 255.255.255.0?

13.8 What is a broadcast message? How are broadcast messages identified in IPv4? How are IPv6 broadcast messages identified?

13.9 Why does FreeBSD not forward broadcast messages?

13.10 Describe three ways in which IPv6 differs from IPv4.

13.11 In IPv6, what protocol replaces ARP for translating IP addresses to hardware addresses?

13.12 What does the networking code use the network mask, or prefix, of a link to determine?

13.13 What limitation of ARP does neighbor discovery overcome? How does it overcome this limitation?

13.14 Which routing policies are implemented in the kernel?

13.15 Describe three types of routes that can be found in the routing table that differ by the type of destination to which they apply.

13.16 What routing facility is designed mainly to support workstations?

13.17 What is a routing redirect? For what is it used?

13.18 Why are there separate protocols for authentication and encryption in IPSec?

13.19 Why is the cryptographic subsystem implemented using two queues and two kernel threads?

13.20 How is the protection offered to packets by IPSec different in tunnel mode and transport mode?

13.21 Name three different packet filtering systems included in FreeBSD. Which of the three filtering systems you choose is at the lowest layer of the networking subsystem?

13.22 What effect does the kernel's tick rate have on the packet-delay jitter in dummynet?

13.23 How are packets passed between nodes in the netgraph system?

13.24 Why are there no locks used between the kernel and userspace in the netmap system?

*13.25 Previous versions of FreeBSD stored ARP entries in the routing table. Give two reasons why moving the ARP entries to their own table was an improvement over the previous implementation.

*13.26 Why might a sender set the *Don't Fragment* flag in the header of an IP packet?

*13.27 What are three differences between how *pf* and *ipfw* filter packets?

*13.28 Explain why it is impossible to use the raw-socket interface to support parallel-protocol implementations—some in the kernel and some in user mode. What modifications to the system would be necessary to support this facility?

*13.29 Previous versions of the system used a hashed routing lookup for a destination as a host or as a network. Name two ways in which the radix search algorithm in FreeBSD is more capable.

*13.30 Compare the packet-processing overhead of BPF and netmap. Which is faster for receiving packets and why?

**13.31 What are the trade-offs between frequent and infrequent transmission of router advertisements in IPv6?

**13.32 Describe three paths that a packet can take through the networking code. How and where is each path chosen?

**13.33 Since IPSec may call routines in the network stack recursively, what requirement does this recursion place on the code?

**13.34 Support for multiple independent network stacks was added with the VIMAGE subsystem. Without using the linker-set support used in the current implementation, describe two other ways to provide similar support for independent stacks sharing a single kernel code image. What are the trade-offs made for each choice?

References

Cain et al., 2002.
B. Cain, S. Deering, I. Kouvelas, B. Fenner, & A. Thyagarajan, "Internet Group Management Protocol, Version 3," RFC 3376, available from http://www.faqs.org/rfcs/rfc3376.html, October 2002.

Checconi et al., 2013.
F. Checconi, L. Rizzo, & P. Valente, "QFQ: Efficient Packet Scheduling with Tight Guarantees," *IEEE/ACM Transactions on Networking*, vol. 21, no. 3, June 2013.

Conta et al., 2006.
A. Conta, S. Deering, & M. Gupta, "Internet Control Message Protocol (ICMPv6) for the Internet Protocol Version 6 (IPv6) Specification," RFC 4443, available from http://www.faqs.org/rfcs/rfc4443.html, March 2006.

DARPA, 1983.
DARPA, "A History of the ARPANET: The First Decade," Technical Report, Bolt, Beranek, and Newman, Cambridge, MA, April 1983.

Deering, 1989.
S. Deering, "Host Extensions for IP Multicasting," RFC 1112, available from http://www.faqs.org/rfcs/rfc1112.html, August 1989.

Deering & Hinden, 1998.
S. Deering & R. Hinden, "Internet Protocol, Version 6 (IPv6)," RFC 2460, available from http://www.faqs.org/rfcs/rfc2460.html, December 1998.

Deering & Hinden, 2006.
S. Deering & R. Hinden, "IP Version 6 Addressing Architecture," RFC 4291, available from http://www.faqs.org/rfcs/rfc4291.html, February 2006.

Fuller et al., 1993.
V. Fuller, T. Li, J. Yu, & K. Varadhan, "Classless Inter-Domain Routing (CIDR): An Address Assignment and Aggregation Strategy," RFC 1519, available from http://www.faqs.org/rfcs/rfc1519.html, September 1993.

Gilligan et al., 1999.
G. Gilligan, S. Thomson, J. Bound, & W. Stevens, "Basic Socket Interface Extensions for IPv6," RFC 2553, available from http://www.faqs.org/rfcs/rfc2553.html, March 1999.

Gross & Almquist, 1992.
P. Gross & P. Almquist, "IESG Deliberations on Routing and Addressing," RFC 1380, available from http://www.faqs.org/rfcs/rfc1380.html, November 1992.

Harkins & Carrel, 1998.
D. Harkins & D. Carrel, "The Internet Key Exchange (IKE)," RFC 2409, available from http://www.faqs.org/rfcs/rfc2409.html, November 1998.

Hedrick, 1988.
C. Hedrick, "Routing Information Protocol," RFC 1058, available from http://www.faqs.org/rfcs/rfc1058.html, June 1988.

Ishiguro, 2003.
K. Ishiguro, *Quagga,* available from www.quagga.net, August 2003.

ISO, 1984.
ISO, "Open Systems Interconnection: Basic Reference Model," ISO 7498, International Organization for Standardization, available from the American National Standards Institute, 1430 Broadway, New York, NY 10018, 1984.

KAME, 2003.
KAME, *Overview of KAME Project,* available from http://www.kame.net/project-overview.html#overview, December 2003.

Kent & Atkinson, 1998a.
S. Kent & R. Atkinson, "Security Architecture for the Internet Protocol," RFC 2401, available from http://www.faqs.org/rfcs/rfc2401.html, November 1998.

Kent & Atkinson, 1998b.
S. Kent & R. Atkinson, "IP Authentication Header," RFC 2402, available from http://www.faqs.org/rfcs/rfc2402.html, November 1998.

Kent & Atkinson, 1998c.
S. Kent & R. Atkinson, "IP Encapsulating Security Payload (ESP)," RFC 2406, available from http://www.faqs.org/rfcs/rfc2406.html, November 1998.

Kohler et al., 2000.
E. Kohler, R. Morris, B. Chen, J. Jannotti, & M. Kaashoek, "The click modular router," *ACM Transactions on Computer Systems*, vol. 18, no. 3, pp. 263–297, May 2000.

McCanne & Jacobson, 1993.
S. McCanne & V. Jacobson, "The BSD packet filter: A new architecture for user-level packet capture," *Proceedings of the USENIX Winter 1993 Conference*, pp. 259–269, January 1993.

McDonald et al., 1998.
D. McDonald, C. Metz, & B. Phan, "PF_KEY Key Management API, Version 2," RFC 2367, available from http://www.faqs.org/rfcs/rfc2367.html, July 1998.

McQuillan & Walden, 1977.
J. M. McQuillan & D. C. Walden, "The ARPA Network Design Decisions," *Computer Networks*, vol. 1, no. 5, pp. 243–289, August 1977.

Mogul, 1984.
J. Mogul, "Broadcasting Internet Datagrams," RFC 919, available from http://www.faqs.org/rfcs/rfc919.html, October 1984.

Mogul & Deering, 1990.
J. Mogul & S. Deering, "Path MTU Discovery," RFC 1191, available from http://www.faqs.org/rfcs/rfc1191.html, November 1990.

Mogul & Postel, 1985.
J. Mogul & J. Postel, "Internet Standard Subnetting Procedure," RFC 950, available from http://www.faqs.org/rfcs/rfc950.html, August 1985.

Narten et al., 2007.
T. Narten, E. Nordmark, W. Simpson, & H. Soliman, "Neighbor Discovery for IP Version 6 (IPv6)," RFC 4861, available from http://www.faqs.org/rfcs/rfc4861.html, September 2007.

Nesser, 1996.
P. Nesser, "An Appeal to the Internet Community to Return Unused IP Networks (Prefixes) to the IANA," RFC 1917, available from http://www.faqs.org/rfcs/rfc1917.html, February 1996.

Plummer, 1982.
D. Plummer, "An Ethernet Address Resolution Protocol," RFC 826, available from http://www.faqs.org/rfcs/rfc826.html, November 1982.

Postel, 1980.
J. Postel, "User Datagram Protocol," RFC 768, available from http://www.faqs.org/rfcs/rfc768.html, August 1980.

Postel, 1981a.
J. Postel, "Internet Protocol," RFC 791, available from http://www.faqs.org/rfcs/rfc791.html, September 1981.

Postel, 1981b.
J. Postel, "Internet Control Message Protocol," RFC 792, available from http://www.faqs.org/rfcs/rfc792.html, September 1981.

Ritchie, 1984.

D. Ritchie, "A Stream Input-Output System," *AT&T Bell Laboratories Technical Journal*, vol. 63, no. 8-2, pp. 1897–1910, October 1984.

Rizzo, 2012.

L. Rizzo, "netmap: A Novel Framework for Fast Packet I/O," *USENIX Annual Technical Conference*, pp. 101–112, June 2012.

Sakane, 2001.

S. Sakane, *Simple Configuration Sample of IPsec/Racoon,* available from http://www.kame.net/newsletter/20001119, September 2001.

Sedgewick, 1990.

R. Sedgewick, *Algorithms in C,* Addison-Wesley, Reading, MA, 1990.

Simpson, 1995.

W. Simpson, "IP in IP Tunneling," RFC 1853, available from http://www.faqs.org/rfcs/rfc1853.html, October 1995.

Sklower, 1991.

K. Sklower, "A Tree-Based Packet Routing Table for Berkeley UNIX," *USENIX Association Conference Proceedings*, pp. 93–99, January 1991.

Thaler & Hopps, 2000.

D. Thaler & C. Hopps, "Multipath Issues in Unicast and Multicast Next-Hop Selection," RFC 2991, available from http://www.faqs.org/rfcs/rfc2991.html, November 2000.

Thomson & Huitema, 1995.

S. Thomson & C. Huitema, "DNS Extensions to Support IP Version 6," RFC 1886, available from http://www.faqs.org/rfcs/rfc1886.html, December 1995.

CHAPTER 14

Transport-Layer Protocols

Chapter 13 covers network-layer protocols that are responsible for moving individual datagrams across the Internet. This chapter moves up a layer in the network stack to discuss protocols that handle end-to-end data movement. Unlike the network-layer protocols, IPv4 and IPv6, transport-layer protocols have no knowledge of intermediate systems such as routers. They only have knowledge of endpoints within the network, the senders and receivers of data.

The protocols at the network layer present data to applications as either individual messages or streams of bytes. The UDP protocol handles data in discrete messages. The TCP protocol handles data as streams of bytes. The SCTP protocol handles multiple streams of both data and discrete messages.

14.1 Internet Ports and Associations

At the network layer, packets are addressed to a host rather than to a process or communications port. As each packet arrives, its 8-bit protocol number identifies the transport-layer protocol that should receive it. Thus, packets identified as IPv4 are passed to *ip_input*(), while packets identified as IPv6 are passed to *ip6_input*().

Internet transport protocols use an additional identifier to designate the connection or communications port on the host. Most protocols (including SCTP, TCP, and UDP) use a 16-bit port number. Each transport protocol maintains its own mapping of port numbers to processes or descriptors. Thus, an ***association***, such as a connection, is fully specified by its transport protocol and 4-tuple <source address, destination address, source port, destination port>. When the local part of the address is set before the remote part, it is necessary to choose a unique port number to prevent collisions when the remote part is specified. For example, two applications on the same host might create a connection to the same service on a remote host, such as a Web server. The port number used to contact the remote system is the well-known web-port 80. For packets traveling from the server back to the applications to correctly reach the right socket, they must have an unambiguous port number at the originating host. When a connection is opened, FreeBSD picks an unused source port that is used for the duration of the connection, which ensures that the 4-tuple of all connections is unique.

Protocol Control Blocks

For each TCP- or UDP-based socket, a protocol control block (PCB) stored in an *inpcb* structure is created to hold network addresses, port numbers, routing information, and pointers to any auxiliary data structures. TCP creates a TCP control block stored in a *tcpcb* structure to hold the wealth of protocol state information necessary for its implementation. Internet control blocks for use with TCP are maintained in a hash table of doubly linked lists private to the TCP protocol module. Figure 14.1 shows the linkage between the socket data structure and these protocol-specific data structures.

Internet control blocks for use with UDP are kept in a similar table private to the UDP protocol module. Two separate tables are needed because each protocol

Figure 14.1 Internet-protocol data structures.

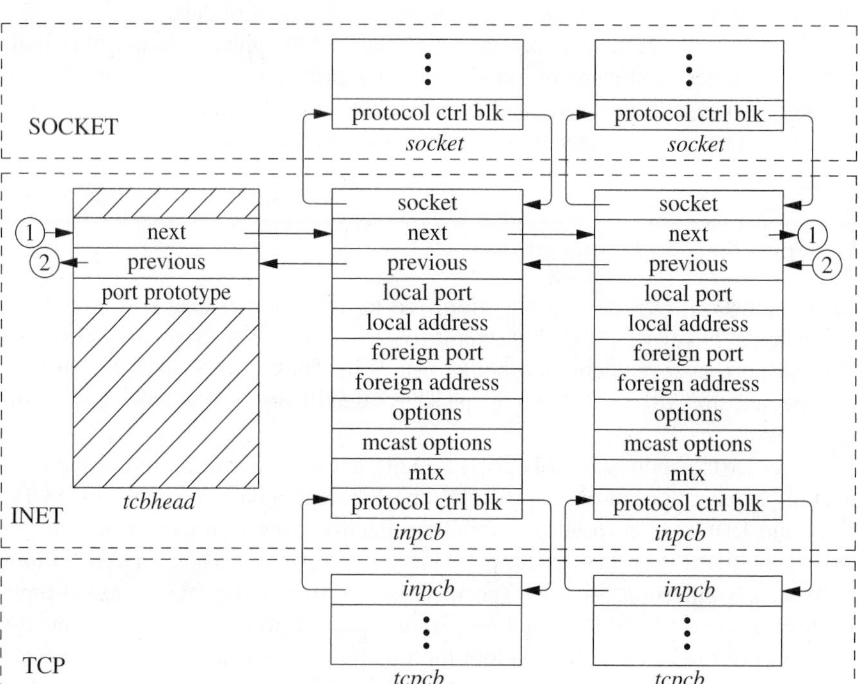

in the Internet domain has a distinct space of port identifiers. Common routines are used by the individual protocols to add new control blocks to a table, record the local and remote parts of an association, locate a control block by association, and delete control blocks. IP demultiplexes message traffic based on the protocol identifier specified in the protocol header, and each higher-level protocol is then responsible for checking its table of control blocks to direct a message to the appropriate socket.

14.2 User Datagram Protocol (UDP)

The ***user datagram protocol*** (***UDP***) [Postel, 1980] is a simple, unreliable datagram protocol that provides both peer-to-peer and multicast addressing with optional data checksums. In FreeBSD, checksums are enabled or disabled on a systemwide basis and cannot be enabled or disabled on individual sockets. UDP protocol headers are extremely simple, containing only the source and destination port numbers, the datagram length, and the data checksum. The host addresses for a datagram are provided by the IP header.

Initialization

When a new datagram socket is created, the socket layer locates the protocol-switch entry for UDP and calls the *udp_attach*() routine with the socket as a parameter. UDP uses *in_pcballoc*() to create a new protocol control block in its table of current sockets. It also sets the default limits for the socket send and receive buffers. Although datagrams are never placed in the send buffer, the limit is set as an upper limit on datagram size; the UDP protocol-switch entry contains the flag PR_ATOMIC, requiring that all data in a send operation be presented to the protocol at one time.

If the application program wishes to bind a port number—for example, the well-known port for some datagram service—it calls the *bind* system call. This request reaches UDP as a call to the *udp_bind*() routine. The binding may also specify a specific host address, which must be an address of an interface on this host. Otherwise, the address will be left unspecified, matching any local address on input, and with an address chosen as appropriate on each output operation. The binding is done by *in_pcbbind*(), which verifies that the chosen port number (or address and port) is not in use and then records the local part of the association in the socket's associated PCB.

To send datagrams, the system must know the remote part of an association. A program can specify this address and port with each send operation using *sendto* or *sendmsg*, or it can do the specification ahead of time with the *connect* system call. In either case, UDP uses the *in_pcbconnect*() function to record the destination address and port. If the local address was not bound, and if a route for the destination is found, the address of the outgoing interface is used as the local address. If no local port number was bound, one is chosen at the time of the send.

Output

A system call that sends data reaches UDP as a call to the *udp_send*() routine, which takes a chain of mbufs containing the data for the datagram. If the call provided a destination address, the address is passed as well; otherwise, the address from a prior *connect* call is used. The actual output operation is done by *udp_output*():

```
static int udp_output(
    struct inpcb *inp,
    struct mbuf *msg,
    struct mbuf *addr,
    struct mbuf *control,
    struct thread *td);
```

In this interface, *inp* is an IPv4 protocol control block, *msg* is a chain of mbufs that contain the data to be sent, and *addr* is an optional mbuf containing the destination address. The destination address could have been prespecified with a *connect* call; otherwise, it must be provided in the *send* call. The *control* argument is meant to contain ancillary data that can be passed to the protocol. The only allowable ancillary data for a UDP packet is a network-layer source address, which *udp_output*() passes to the lower layer as a *sockaddr_in* structure. The *td* argument is a pointer to a thread structure. Thread structures are discussed in Section 4.2 and are used within the network stack to identify the sender of a packet. UDP simply prepends its own header, fills in the UDP header fields and those of a prototype IP header, and calculates a checksum before passing the packet on to the IP module for output.

Input

All transport protocols that are layered directly on top of network-layer protocols such as IPv4 and IPv6 use the following calling convention when receiving packets from either protocol:

```
(void) (*pr_input)(
    struct mbuf *m,
    int off);
```

Each mbuf chain passed is a single complete packet to be processed by the protocol module. The packet includes the IP header at the front of the packet. The *off* parameter identifies offset at which the UDP packet begins, which is the length of the IP header. The UDP input routine *udp_input*() is typical of protocol input routines in that it first verifies that the length of the packet is at least as long as the IP plus UDP headers, and it uses *m_pullup*() to make the header contiguous. The *udp_input*() routine then checks that the packet is the correct length and calculates a checksum for the data in the packet. If any of these tests fail, the packet is discarded and the UDP error count is incremented. Finally, the protocol control block for the socket that is to receive the data is located by *in_pcblookup*() using the addresses and port numbers in the packet. There might be multiple control blocks with the same local port number but different local or remote addresses; if so, the control block with the best match is selected. An exact association matches best, but if none exists, a socket with the correct local port number but unspecified local address, remote port number, or remote address will match. A control block with unspecified local or remote addresses thus acts as a *wildcard* that receives packets for its port if no exact match is found. If a control block is located, the data and the address from which the packet was received are placed in the receive buffer of the indicated socket with *udp_append*(). If the destination address is a multicast address, copies of the packet are delivered to each socket with a matching address. If no receiver is found and if the packet was not addressed to a broadcast or multicast address, an ICMP port unreachable error message is sent to the originator of the datagram. The port unreachable error message normally has no effect, as the sender typically connects to this destination only temporarily, and the kernel destroys the association before new input is processed. However, if the sender still has a fully specified association, it may receive notification of the error.

Control Operations

UDP supports no control operations and passes calls to its *pr_ctloutput*() entry directly to IP. It has a simple *pr_ctlinput*() routine that receives notification of any asynchronous errors. Errors are passed to any datagram socket with the indicated destination; only sockets with a destination fixed by a *connect* call may be notified of errors asynchronously. Such errors are simply noted in the appropriate socket, and socket wakeups are issued if the process is selecting or sleeping while waiting for input.

When a UDP datagram socket is closed, the *udp_detach*() routine is called. The protocol control block and its contents are simply deleted with *in_pcbdetach*(); no other processing is required.

14.3 Transmission Control Protocol (TCP)

The most used protocol of the Internet protocol suite is the ***Transmission Control Protocol*** (***TCP***) [Cerf & Kahn, 1974; Postel, 1981]. TCP is a reliable connection-oriented stream-transport protocol on top of which many application protocols are layered. It includes several features not found in the other transport and network protocols described so far:

- Explicit and acknowledged connection initiation and termination
- Reliable, in-order, unduplicated delivery of data

- Flow control
- Out-of-band indication of urgent data
- Congestion avoidance and control

These features result in the TCP implementation being significantly more complicated than those for UDP and IP. These complications, along with the prevalence of the use of TCP, make the details of TCP's implementation more critical and more complex than the implementations of the simpler protocols.

A TCP connection is a bidirectional, sequenced stream of data transferred between two peers. The data may be transported in packets of varying sizes and at varying intervals—for example, when they support a login session over the network. The stream initiation and termination are explicit events at the start and end of the stream, and they occupy positions in the ***sequence space*** of the stream so that they can be acknowledged in the same way as data are. Sequence numbers are 32-bit numbers from a circular space; that is, comparisons are made modulo 2^{32}, so zero is the next sequence number after $2^{32} - 1$. The sequence numbers for each direction start with an arbitrary value, called the ***initial sequence number***, sent in the initial packet for a connection. Following Bellovin [1996], the TCP implementation selects the initial sequence number by computing a function over the 4-tuple local port, foreign port, local address, and foreign address that uniquely identifies the connection, and then adding a small offset based on the current time. The Bellovin algorithm prevents the spoofing of TCP connections by an attacker guessing the next initial sequence number for a connection, and the algorithm must be carried out while also guaranteeing that an old duplicate packet will not match the sequence space of a current connection.

Each packet of a TCP connection carries the sequence number of its first byte and (except during connection establishment) an acknowledgment of all contiguous data received thus far. A TCP packet is known as a ***segment*** because it begins at a specific location in the sequence space and has a specific length. Acknowledgments are specified as the sequence number of the next byte not yet received. Acknowledgments are cumulative and thus may acknowledge data received in more than one (or part of one) segment. A packet may or may not contain data, but it always contains the sequence number of the next datum to be sent.

Flow control in TCP is done with a ***sliding-window scheme***. Each packet with an acknowledgment contains a window advertisement, which is the number of bytes of data that the receiver is prepared to accept, beginning with the sequence number in the acknowledgment. The window is a 16-bit field, limiting the window to 64 Kbyte by default; however, the use of a larger window may be negotiated. Urgent data are handled similarly; if the flag indicating urgent data is set, the urgent-data pointer is used as a positive offset from the sequence number of the packet to indicate the extent of urgent data. Thus, TCP can send notification of urgent data without sending all intervening data, even if the flow-control window would not allow the intervening data to be sent.

The complete header for a TCP packet is shown in Figure 14.2. The flags include SYN and FIN, denoting the initiation (synchronization) and completion of a connection. Each of these flags occupies a sequence space of one. A complete connection thus consists of a SYN, zero or more bytes of data, and a FIN sent from each peer and acknowledged by the other peer. Additional flags indicate whether the *acknowledgment* field (ACK) and *urgent* fields (URG) are valid, a flag to request that data be pushed (flushed) to the user (PSH), and include a connection-abort signal (RST). Options are encoded in the same way as are IP options, either as a single byte or as a type, length, and value. Only the no-operation and end-of-options options are single bytes. The initial specification of TCP defined only one other option, which allows hosts to exchange the maximum segment (packet) size that they are willing to accept and is used only during initial connection establishment. Several other options have been defined and, to avoid confusion, the protocol standard allows these options to be used in data packets only if both endpoints include them during establishment of the connection.

TCP Connection States

The connection-establishment and connection-completion mechanisms of TCP are designed for robustness. They serve to frame the data that are transferred during a connection so that not only the data but also their extent are communicated reliably. In addition, the procedure is designed to discover old connections that have not terminated correctly because of a crash of one peer or loss of network connectivity. If such a ***half-open connection*** is discovered, it is aborted. Hosts choose new initial sequence numbers for each connection to lessen the chances that an old packet may be confused with a current connection.

The normal connection-establishment procedure is known as a ***three-way handshake***. Each peer sends a SYN to the other, and each in turn acknowledges

Figure 14.2 TCP packet header.

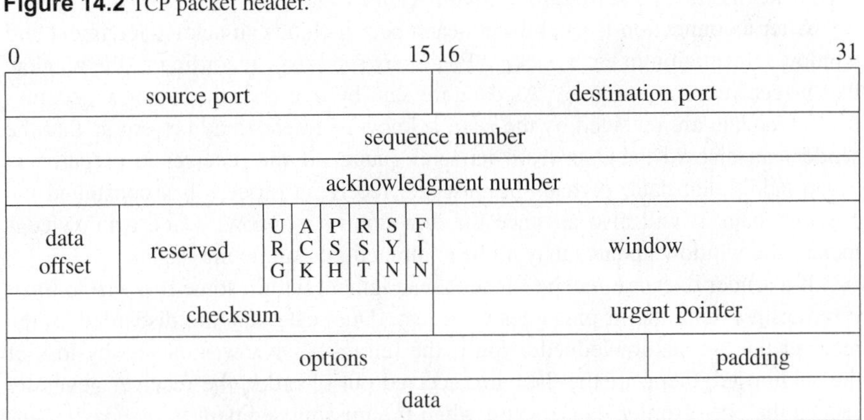

the other's SYN with an ACK. In practice, a connection is normally initiated by a client attempting to connect to a server listening on a well-known port. The client chooses a port number and initial sequence number, and uses these selections in the initial packet with a SYN. The server creates a SYN cache entry for the pending connection and sends a packet with its initial sequence number, a SYN, and an ACK of the client's SYN. The client responds with an ACK of the server's SYN, completing connection establishment. As the ACK of the first SYN is piggybacked on the second SYN, this procedure requires three packets, leading to the term three-way handshake. The protocol still operates correctly if both peers attempt to start a connection simultaneously, although the connection setup would then require four packets.

FreeBSD includes up to four options along with the SYN when initiating a connection. One contains the maximum segment size that the system is willing to accept [Jacobson et al., 1992]. The second of these options specifies a window-scaling value expressed as a binary shift value, allowing the window to exceed 65535 bytes. If both peers include this option during the three-way handshake, both scaling values take effect; otherwise, the window value remains in bytes. The third option is a timestamp. If this option is sent in both directions during connection establishment, it will also be sent in each packet during data transfer. The data field of the timestamp option includes a timestamp associated with the current sequence number and also echoes a timestamp associated with the current acknowledgment. Like the sequence space, the timestamp uses a 32-bit field and modular arithmetic. The unit of the timestamp field is not defined by the standard, although it must fall between 1 millisecond and 1 second. The value sent by each system must increase monotonically during a connection. FreeBSD always uses a value measured in milliseconds. These timestamps implement round-trip timing. They also serve as an extension of the sequence space to prevent old duplicate packets from being accepted; this extension is valuable when a large window or a fast path, such as an Ethernet, is used. The fourth option indicates support for selective acknowledgments, which allow a receiver to tell a sender if more than one packet has been lost in transit [Mathis et al., 1996].

After a connection is established, each peer includes an acknowledgment and window information in each packet. Each may send data according to the window that it receives from its peer. As data are sent by one end, the window becomes filled. As data are received by the peer, acknowledgments may be sent so that the sender can discard the data from its send queue. If the receiver is prepared to accept additional data, perhaps because the receiving process has consumed the previous data, it will also advance the flow-control window. Data, acknowledgments, and window updates may all be combined in a single message.

If a sender does not receive an acknowledgment within some reasonable time, it retransmits data that it presumes were lost. Duplicate data are discarded by the receiver but are acknowledged again if the retransmission was caused by loss of the acknowledgment. If the data are received out of order, the receiver generally retains the out-of-order data for use when the missing segment is received. Out-of-order data cannot be acknowledged because acknowledgments are cumulative.

Each peer may terminate data transmission at any time by sending a packet with the FIN bit. A FIN represents the end of the data (like an end-of-file indication). The FIN is acknowledged, advancing the sequence number by 1. The connection may continue to carry data in the other direction until a FIN is sent in that direction. The acknowledgment of the FIN terminates the connection. To guarantee synchronization at the conclusion of the connection, the peer sending the last ACK of a FIN must retain state long enough that any retransmitted FIN packets will have reached it or have been discarded; otherwise, if the ACK were lost and a retransmitted FIN were received, the receiver would be unable to repeat the acknowledgment. The interval is arbitrarily set to twice the expected ***maximum segment lifetime***, and is known as 2MSL. The default value for the maximum segment lifetime is 30 seconds, meaning that FreeBSD expects packets to exit the network after 1 minute.

The TCP input-processing module and timer modules must maintain the state of a connection throughout that connection's lifetime, meaning that in addition to processing data received on the connection, the input module must process SYN and FIN flags, as well as other state transitions. The list of states for one end of a TCP connection is given in Table 14.1. Figure 14.3 shows the finite-state machine

Table 14.1 TCP connection states. 2MSL—twice maximum segment lifetime.

State	Description
States involved while a connection becomes established	
CLOSED	closed
LISTEN	listening for connection
SYN SENT	active, have sent SYN
SYN RECEIVED	have sent and received SYN
State during an established connection	
ESTABLISHED	established
States involved when the remote end initiates a connection shutdown	
CLOSE WAIT	have received FIN, waiting for close
LAST ACK	have received FIN and close; awaiting FIN ACK
CLOSED	closed
States involved when the local end initiates a connection shutdown	
FIN WAIT 1	have closed, sent FIN
CLOSING	closed, exchanged FIN; awaiting FIN ACK
FIN WAIT 2	have closed, FIN is acknowledged; awaiting FIN
TIME WAIT	in 2MSL, quiet wait after close
CLOSED	closed

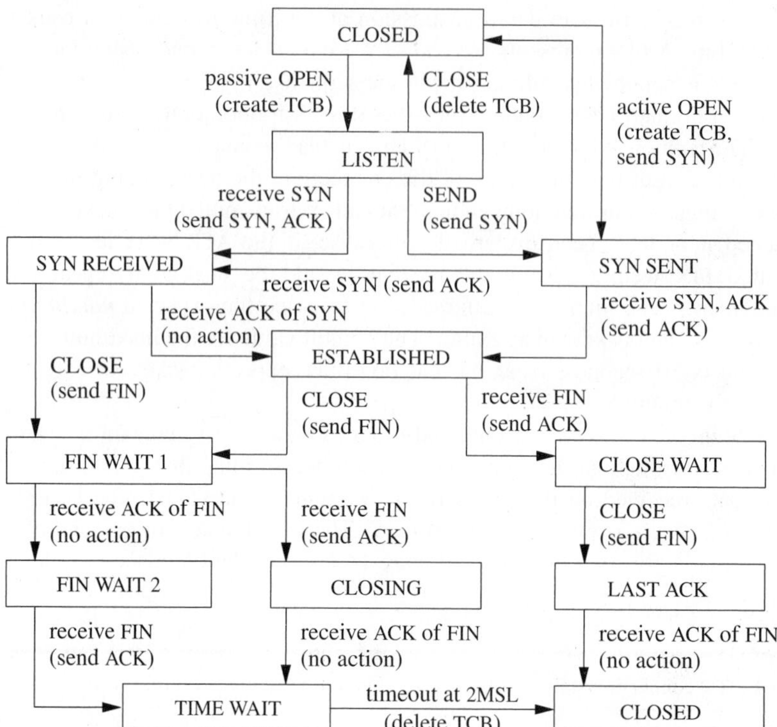

Figure 14.3 TCP state diagram. Key: TCB—TCP control block; 2MSL—twice maximum segment lifetime.

made up by these states, the events that cause transitions, and the actions during the transitions.

If a connection is lost because of a crash or timeout on one host, but is still considered established by the other, then any data received by the host that still believes the connection to be active will cause the half-open connection to be discovered. When a half-open connection is detected, the receiving peer sends a packet with the RST flag and a sequence number derived from the incoming packet to signify that the connection is no longer in existence.

Sequence Variables

Each TCP connection maintains a large set of variables in the TCP control block. The information stored in the control block includes the connection state, timers, options and flags, a queue that holds data received out of order, and several sequence-number variables. The sequence-variables define the send and receive sequence space, including the current window for each. The window is the range of data sequence numbers that are currently allowed to be sent, from the first byte of data not yet acknowledged, up to the end of the range that has been offered in

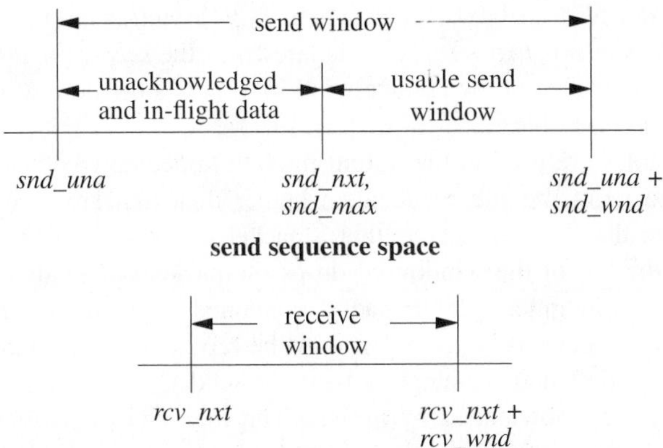

Figure 14.4 TCP sequence space.

the window advertisement. The variables defining the windows in FreeBSD are a superset of those used in the protocol specification [Postel, 1981]. The send and receive windows are shown in Figure 14.4. The meanings of the sequence variables are listed in Table 14.2.

The area between *snd_una* and *snd_una* + *snd_wnd* is known as the ***send window***. Data for the range *snd_una* to *snd_max* have been sent but not yet acknowledged and are kept in the socket send buffer along with data not yet transmitted. The *snd_nxt* field indicates the next sequence number to be sent and is incremented as data are transmitted. The area from *snd_nxt* to *snd_una* + *snd_wnd* is the remaining usable portion of the window, and its size determines whether additional data may be sent. The *snd_nxt* and *snd_max* values are

Table 14.2 TCP sequence variables.

Variable	Description
snd_una	lowest send sequence number not yet acknowledged
snd_nxt	next data sequence to be sent
snd_wnd	number of data octets peer will receive, starting with *snd_una*
snd_max	highest sequence number sent
rcv_nxt	next receive sequence number expected
rcv_wnd	number of octets past *rcv_nxt* that may be accepted
rcv_adv	last octet of receive window advertised to peer
ts_recent	most recent timestamp received from peer
ts_recent_age	time when *ts_recent* was received

normally maintained together except when TCP is retransmitting. The area between *rcv_nxt* and *rcv_nxt* + *rcv_wnd* is known as the ***receive window***. Whenever TCP updates the size of the receive window, it stores the new advertised window in the *rcv_adv* variable.

These variables are used in the output module to decide whether data can be sent, and in the input module to decide whether data that are received can be accepted. When the receiver detects that a packet is not acceptable because the data are all to the left of the window, it drops the packet but sends a copy of its most recent acknowledgment. If the packet contained old data, the first acknowledgment may have been lost, and thus it must be repeated. The acknowledgment also includes a window update, synchronizing the sender's state with the receiver's state. As data are acknowledged by the receiver, the values contained in all the variables increase, moving to the right in Figure 14.4.

If the TCP timestamp option is in use for the connection, the tests to see whether an incoming packet is acceptable are augmented with checks on the timestamp. Each time that an incoming packet is accepted as the next expected packet, its timestamp is recorded in the *ts_recent* field in the TCP protocol control block. If an incoming packet includes a timestamp, the timestamp is compared to the most recently received timestamp. If the timestamp is less than the previous value, the packet is discarded as being an old duplicate and a current acknowledgment is sent in response. Here, the timestamp serves as an extension to the sequence number, avoiding accidental acceptance of an old duplicate when the window is large or sequence numbers can be reused quickly. However, because of the granularity of the timestamp value, a timestamp received more than 24 days ago cannot be compared to a new value, and this test is bypassed. The current time is recorded when *ts_recent* is updated from an incoming timestamp to make this test. Of course, connections are seldom idle for longer than 24 days.

14.4 TCP Algorithms

This section examines the implementation of the TCP protocol in FreeBSD. Several aspects of the protocol implementation depend on the overall state of a connection. The state of a TCP connection depends on external events and timers. TCP processing occurs in response to one of three events:

1. A request from the user, such as sending data, removing data from the socket receive buffer, or opening or closing a connection
2. The receipt of a packet for the connection
3. The expiration of a timer

These events are handled in the routines *tcp_usr_send*(), *tcp_input*(), and a set of timer routines. Each routine processes the current event and makes any required changes in the connection state. Then, for any transition that may require sending a packet, the *tcp_output*() routine is called to do any output that is necessary.

The criteria for sending a packet with data or control information are complicated, making TCP send policy the most interesting and important part of the protocol implementation. For example, depending on the state- and flow-control parameters for a connection, any of the following may allow data to be sent that could not be sent previously:

- A user send call that places new data in the send queue
- The receipt of a window update from the peer
- The expiration of the retransmission timer
- The expiration of the window-update (persist) timer

In addition, the *tcp_output*() routine may decide to send a packet with control information, even if no data may be sent, for any of these reasons:

- A change in connection state (e.g., open request, close request)
- Receipt of data that must be acknowledged
- A change in the receive window because of removal of data from the receive queue
- A send request with urgent data
- A connection abort

The remainder of this section expands and explains these points.

Timers

Unlike a UDP socket, a TCP connection maintains significant state information and, because of that state, some operations must be done asynchronously. For example, data might not be sent immediately when a process presents them because of flow control. The requirement for reliable delivery implies that data must be retained after they are first transmitted so that they can be retransmitted if necessary. To prevent the protocol from hanging if packets are lost, each connection maintains a set of timers used to recover from losses or failures of the peer. These timers are stored in the protocol control block for a connection. The kernel provides a timer service via a set of *callout*() routines. The TCP module can register up to five timeout routines with the callout service, as shown in Table 14.3. Each routine has its own associated time at which it will be called. In earlier versions of BSD, timeouts were handled by the *tcp_slowtimo*() routine that was called every 500 milliseconds and would then perform timer processing when necessary. Using the kernel's timer service directly is more accurate since each timer can be handled independently at the interval that works best for that timer.

Two timers are used for output processing. Whenever data are sent on a connection, the ***retransmit timer*** (*tcp_rexmt*()) is started by a call to *callout_reset*(), unless it is already running. When all outstanding data are acknowledged, the

Table 14.3 TCP timer routines.

Routine	Timeout	Description
tcp_timer_2msl	60s	wait on close
tcp_timer_keep	75s	send keep alive or drop dormant connection
tcp_timer_persist	5-60s	force a connection to persist
tcp_timer_rexmt	3ticks-64s	called when retransmission is necessary
tcp_timer_delack	100ms	send a delayed acknowledgement to the peer

timer is stopped. If the timer expires, the oldest unacknowledged data are resent (at most, one full-size packet), and the timer is restarted with a longer value. The rate at which the timer value is increased (the ***timer backoff***) is determined by a table of multipliers that provides an exponential increase in timeout values up to a ceiling of 64 seconds.

The other timer used for maintaining output flow is the ***persist timer*** (*tcp_timer_persist*()). This timer protects against the other type of packet loss that could cause a connection to constipate: the loss of a window update that would allow more data to be sent. Whenever data are ready to be sent but the send window is too small to bother sending (zero, or less than a reasonable amount), and no data are already outstanding (the retransmit timer is not set), the persist timer is started. If no window update is received before the timer expires, the routine sends as large a segment as the window allows. If that size is zero, it sends a ***window probe*** (a single byte of data) and restarts the persist timer. If a window update was lost in the network, or if the receiver neglected to send a window update, the acknowledgment will contain current window information. On the other hand, if the receiver is still unable to accept additional data, it should send an acknowledgment for previous data with a still-closed window. The closed window might persist indefinitely; for example, the receiver might be a network-login client, and the user might stop terminal output and leave for lunch (or vacation).

The third timer used by TCP is a ***keepalive timer*** (*tcp_timer_keep*()) The keepalive timer has two different purposes at different phases of a connection. During connection establishment, this timer limits the time for the three-way handshake to complete. If the timer expires during connection setup, then the connection is closed. Once the connection completes, the keepalive timer monitors idle connections that might no longer exist on the peer because of a network partition or a crash. If a socket-level option, SO_KEEPALIVE, is set and the connection has been idle since the most recent keepalive timeout, the timer routine will send a ***keepalive packet*** designed to produce either an acknowledgment or a reset (RST) from the peer TCP. If a reset is received, the connection will be closed; if no response is received after several attempts, the connection will be dropped. This facility is designed so that network servers can avoid languishing forever if the client disappears without closing the connection. Keepalive packets are not an explicit feature of the TCP protocol. The packets used for this purpose by FreeBSD set the sequence number to 1 less than *snd_una*, which should elicit an acknowledgment from the peer if the connection still exists.

The fourth TCP timer is known as the ***2MSL timer*** ("twice the maximum segment lifetime"). TCP starts this timer when a connection is completed by sending an acknowledgment for a FIN (from FIN_WAIT_2) or by receiving an ACK for a FIN (from CLOSING state, where the send side is already closed). Under these circumstances, the sender does not know whether the acknowledgment was received. If the FIN is retransmitted, it is desirable that enough state remain that the acknowledgment can be repeated. Therefore, when a TCP connection enters the TIME_WAIT state, the 2MSL timer is started; when the timer expires, the control block is deleted. If a retransmitted FIN is received, another ACK is sent and the timer is restarted. To prevent this delay from blocking a process closing the connection, any process close request is returned successfully without the process waiting for the timer. Thus, a protocol control block may continue its existence even after the socket descriptor has been closed. In addition, FreeBSD starts the 2MSL timer when FIN_WAIT_2 state is entered after the user has closed; if the connection is idle until the timer expires, it will be closed. Because the user has already closed, new data cannot be accepted on such a connection in any case. This timer is set because certain other TCP implementations (incorrectly) fail to send a FIN on a receive-only connection. Connections to such hosts would remain in FIN_WAIT_2 state forever if the system did not have a timeout. The final timer is the *tcp_timer_delack*(), which processes delayed acknowledgments and is described in Section 14.6.

Estimation of Round-Trip Time

When connections must traverse slow networks that lose packets, an important decision determining connection throughput is the value used to set the retransmission timer. If this value is too large, data flow will stop on the connection for an unnecessarily long time before the dropped packet is resent. Another round-trip interval is required for the sender to receive an acknowledgment of the resent segment and a window update, allowing it to send new data. (With luck, only one segment will have been lost, and the acknowledgment will include the other segments that had been sent.) If the timeout value is too small, however, packets will be retransmitted needlessly. If the cause of the network slowness or packet loss is congestion, then unnecessary retransmission only exacerbates the problem. The traditional solution to this problem in TCP is for the sender to estimate the round-trip time (*rtt*) for the connection path by measuring the time required to receive acknowledgments for individual segments. The system maintains an estimate of the round-trip time as a smoothed moving average, *srtt* [Postel, 1981], using

$$srtt = (\alpha \times srtt) + ((1 - \alpha) \times rtt).$$

In addition to a smoothed estimate of the round-trip time, TCP keeps a smoothed variance (estimated as mean difference, to avoid square-root calculations in the kernel). It employs an α value of 0.875 for the round-trip time and a corresponding smoothing factor of 0.75 for the variance. These values were chosen in part so that the system could compute the smoothed averages using shift operations on fixed-point values instead of floating-point values because on many hardware architectures it is expensive to use floating-point arithmetic. The initial retransmission timeout is then set to the current smoothed round-trip time plus four times the smoothed variance. This algorithm is substantially more efficient on long-delay paths with little variance in delay, such as transoceanic links, because it computes the BETA factor dynamically [Jacobson, 1988].

For simplicity, the variables in the TCP protocol control block allow measurement of the round-trip time for only one sequence value at a time. This restriction prevents accurate time estimation when the window is large; only one packet per window can be timed. However, if the TCP timestamp option is supported by both peers, a timestamp is sent with each data packet and is returned with each acknowledgment. Here, estimates of round-trip time can be obtained with each new acknowledgment; the quality of the smoothed average and variance is thus improved, and the system can respond more quickly to changes in network conditions.

Connection Establishment

There are two ways in which a new TCP connection can be established. An active connection is initiated by a *connect* call, whereas a passive connection is created when a listening socket receives a connection request.

When a process creates a new TCP socket, the *tcp_attach*() routine is called. TCP creates an *inpcb* protocol control block and then creates an additional control block (a *tcpcb* structure), as shown in Figure 14.1. Some of the flow-control parameters in the *tcpcb* are initialized at this time. If the process explicitly binds an address or port number to the connection, the actions are identical to those for a UDP socket. Then, a *tcp_connect*() call initiates the actual connection. The first step is to set up the association with *in_pcbconnect*(), again identically to this step in UDP. A packet-header template is created for use in construction of each output packet. An initial sequence number is chosen using an MD5 hashing algorithm and is then advanced by a substantial amount. The purpose of the hash is to make it hard for an attacker to guess the sequence space of a connection. If parties external to the connection can guess sequence numbers, then they can disrupt communication between the two peers using the connection, for example, by injecting a packet into the data stream. The socket is then marked as *soisconnecting*(), the TCP connection state is set to TCPS_SYN_SENT, the keepalive timer is set (to 75 seconds) to limit the duration of the connection attempt, and *tcp_output*() is called for the first time.

The output-processing routine *tcp_output*() uses an array of packet control flags indexed by the connection state to determine which control flags should be sent in each state. In the TCPS_SYN_SENT state, the SYN flag is sent. Because it has a control flag to send, the system immediately sends a packet using the prototype just constructed and includes the current flow-control parameters. The packet normally contains three option fields: a maximum-segment-size option, a window-scale option, and a timestamps option (see Section 14.3). The maximum-segment-size option communicates the largest segment size that TCP is willing to accept. To compute this value, the system locates a route to the destination. If the route specifies a maximum transmission unit (MTU), the system uses that value after allowing for packet headers. If the connection is to a destination on a local network, the maximum transmission unit of the outgoing network interface is used, possibly rounding down to a multiple of the mbuf cluster size for efficiency of buffering. If the destination is not local and nothing is known about the intervening path, the default segment size (512 bytes) is used.

In earlier versions of FreeBSD, many of the important variables relating to TCP connections, such as the MTU of the path between the two endpoints, and the data used to manage the connection were contained in a set of route metrics within the route entry that described the connection. The *TCP host cache* was developed to centralize all this information in one easy-to-find place so that information gathered on one connection could be reused when a new connection was opened to the same endpoint. The data that is recorded on a connection is shown in Table 14.4. All the variables stored in a host cache entry are described in various parts of later sections of this chapter when they are relevant to the discussion of how TCP manages a connection. Notably missing from the host cache is a route-cache entry. Earlier versions of FreeBSD cached the route used for the connection. The caching of routing and forwarding information is currently in the process of being moved into the *inpcb* structure using the *inp_rt* and *inp_lle* fields, but code to exploit these fields is not written in FreeBSD 10. Hence, the route is not currently cached so every packet sent requires a routing-table lookup.

Whenever a new connection is opened, a call is made to *tcp_hc_get*() to find any information on past connections. If an entry exists in the cache for the target endpoint, TCP uses the cached information to make better-informed decisions about managing the connection. When a connection is closed, the host cache is

Table 14.4 TCP host-cache metrics.

Variable	Description
rmx_mtu	MTU for this path
rmx_ssthresh	outbound gateway buffer limit
rmx_rtt	estimated round-trip time
rmx_rttvar	estimated rtt variance
rmx_bandwidth	estimated bandwidth
rmx_cwnd	congestion window
rmx_sendpipe	outbound delay-bandwidth product
rmx_recvpipe	inbound delay-bandwidth product

updated with all the relevant information that was discovered during the connection between the two hosts. Each host-cache entry has a default lifetime of 1 hour. Anytime that the entry is accessed or updated, its lifetime is reset to 1 hour. Every 5 minutes, the *tcp_hc_purge*() routine is called to clean out any entries that have passed their expiration time. Cleaning out old entries ensures that the host cache does not grow too large and that it always has reasonably fresh data.

TCP uses ***path MTU discovery***, a process whereby the system probes the network to determine the maximum transfer unit on a particular route between two nodes [Mogul & Deering, 1990]. The discovery is done by sending packets with the IP flag *don't fragment* set on each packet. If the packet encounters a link on the path to its destination on which it would have to be fragmented, then it is dropped by the intervening router and an error is returned to the sender. The error message contains the maximum-size packet that the link will accept. This information is recorded in the TCP host cache for the appropriate endpoint and transmission is attempted with the smaller MTU. Once the connection is complete, because enough packets have made it through the network to establish a TCP connection, the revised MTU recorded in the host cache is confirmed. Packets will continue to be transmitted with the *don't fragment* flag set so that if the path to the node changes, and that path has an even smaller MTU, this new smaller MTU will be recorded. FreeBSD currently has no way of upgrading the MTU to a larger size when a route changes.

When a connection is first opened, the retransmit timer is set to the default value (3 seconds) because no round-trip time information is available yet. With a bit of luck, a responding packet will be received from the target of the connection before the retransmit timer expires. If not, the packet is retransmitted and the retransmit timer is restarted with a greater value. If no response is received before the keepalive timer expires, the connection attempt is aborted with a "Connection timed out" error. If a response is received, however, it is checked for agreement with the outgoing request. It should acknowledge the SYN that was sent and should include a SYN. If it does both, the receive sequence variables are initialized and the connection state is advanced to TCPS_ESTABLISHED. If a maximum-segment-size option is present in the response, the maximum segment size for the connection is set to the minimum of the offered size and the maximum transmission unit of the outgoing interface; if the option is not present, the default size (512 data bytes) is recorded. The flag TF_ACKNOW is set in the TCP control block before the output routine is called so that the SYN will be acknowledged immediately. The connection is now ready to transfer data.

The events that occur when a connection is created by a passive open are different from those of an active open. A socket is created and its address is bound as before. The socket is then marked by the *listen* call as willing to accept connections. When a packet arrives for a TCP socket in TCPS_LISTEN state, a new socket is created with *sonewconn*(), which calls the *tcp_usr_attach*() routine to create the protocol control blocks for the new socket. The new socket is placed on the queue of partial connections headed by the listening socket. If the packet contains a SYN and is otherwise acceptable, the association of the new socket is bound, both the send and the receive sequence numbers are initialized, and the connection state is advanced to TCPS_SYN_RECEIVED. The keepalive timer is set as before, and the output routine is called after TF_ACKNOW has been set to force the SYN to be acknowledged; an outgoing SYN is sent as well. If this SYN is acknowledged properly, the new socket is moved from the queue of partial connections to the queue of completed connections. If the owner of the listening socket is sleeping in an *accept* call or does a *select*, the socket will indicate that a new connection is available. Again, the socket is finally ready to send data. Up to one window of data may have already been received and acknowledged by the time that the *accept* call completes.

SYN Cache

One problem in previous implementations of TCP was that it was possible for a malicious program to flood a system with SYN packets, thereby preventing it from doing any useful work or servicing any real connections. This type of ***denial-of-service attack*** became common during the commercialization of the Internet in the late 1990s. To combat this attack, a syn-cache was introduced to efficiently store, and possibly discard, SYN packets that do not lead to real connections. The syn-cache handles the three-way handshake between a local server and connecting peers.

When a SYN packet is received for a socket that is in the LISTEN state, the TCP module attempts to add a new syn-cache entry for the packet using the *syncache_add*() routine. If there are any data in the received packet, they are not acknowledged at this time. Acknowledging the data would use up system resources, and an attacker could exhaust these resources by flooding the system with SYN packets that included data. If this SYN has not been seen before, a new entry is created in the hash table based on the packet's foreign address, foreign port, the local port of the socket, and a mask. The syn-cache module responds to the SYN with a SYN/ACK and sets a timer on the new entry. If the syn-cache contains an entry that matches the received packet, then it is assumed that the original SYN/ACK was not received by the peer initiating the connection, and another SYN/ACK is sent and the timer on the syn-cache entry is reset. There is no limit set on the number of SYN packets that can be sent by a connecting peer. Any limit would not follow the TCP RFCs and might impede connections over lossy networks.

SYN Cookies

SYN cache was designed to reduce the amount of kernel resources required to handle potential incoming connections by keeping a minimum amount of state for each nascent connection. The goal of SYN cookies is for the kernel not to keep any state for a connection until the three-way handshake has been completed. A SYN cookie is a cryptographically signed piece of data placed into a SYN/ACK packet sent as the second packet in the standard three-way handshake. The data encoded into the SYN cookie will allow a server to complete the setup of a TCP connection on receipt of the final ACK from the remote system. In FreeBSD, SYN cookies are generated for every received SYN packet as a way of protecting against the SYN cache overflowing. They only need to be used when the rate of incoming requests overflows the SYN cache.

Two routines, *syncookie_generate*() and *syncookie_lookup*(), are used by the kernel to generate and validate SYN cookies. When the kernel receives a SYN packet from a remote host, indicating that the remote host wishes to initiate a connection, the *syncookie_generate*() routine computes an MD5 hash that includes a secret, an index into a table of possible maximum segment sizes for the connection, as well as the local and foreign network addresses and ports for the requested connection. A table encodes the maximum-segment sizes to decrease the amount of space required to store the MSS in the cookie to three bits. The MD5 hash is placed into the initial sequence number of the SYN/ACK packet that will be sent back to the remote host. If the remote host has indicated that it supports RFC1323 timestamps, then a second MD5 hash is calculated containing the send and receive window scaling factors and a single bit indicating whether the connection supports SACK. The second hash is placed into the timestamp field of the returning SYN/ACK packet. Once the SYN/ACK packet is returned to the remote host, all the state associated with the connection is freed. When an ACK is received from a remote host it is checked to see if it contains valid syn-cookie data. A valid SYN cookie must be returned within 16 seconds of its having been generated. Packets that fall outside this 16 second boundary are discarded. The MD5 hash is again calculated over the key, the returned sequence number, and the connection information and then compared against the data received in the acknowledgment field of the ACK packet. The remote host should send an acknowledgment that is one greater than the sequence number it received. Subtracting 1 from the value in the acknowledgment and comparing it to the MD5 hash generated in the *syncookie_lookup*() routine is all that the kernel needs to do to verify that the cookie is valid. Valid ACK packets have their ISN and timestamp fields unpacked into a SYN-cache entry that is then used to set up a normal TCP connection.

Connection Shutdown

A TCP connection is symmetrical and full-duplex, so either side may initiate disconnection independently. As long as one direction of the connection can carry data, the connection remains open. A socket may indicate that it has completed sending data with the *shutdown* system call, which results in a call to the *tcp_usr_shutdown*() routine. The response to this request is that the state of the connection is advanced; from ESTABLISHED to FIN_WAIT_1. The ensuing output call will send a FIN, indicating that the connection is being closed. The receiving socket will advance to CLOSE_WAIT but may continue to send. The procedure may be different if the process simply closes the socket. In that case, a FIN is sent immediately, but if new data are received, they cannot be delivered. Normally, higher-level protocols conclude their own transactions such that both sides know when to close. If they do not, however, TCP must refuse new data. It does so by sending a packet with the RST flag set if new data are received after the user has closed the connection. If data remain in the send buffer of the socket when the *close* is done, TCP will normally attempt to deliver them. If the socket option SO_LINGER was set with a linger time of zero, the send buffer is simply flushed; otherwise, the user process is allowed to continue and the protocol waits for delivery to conclude. Under these circumstances, the socket is marked with the state bit SS_NOFDREF (no file-descriptor reference). The completion of data transfer and the final close can take place an arbitrary amount of time later. When TCP finally completes the connection (or gives up because of timeout or other failure), it calls *tcp_close*(). The protocol control blocks and other dynamically allocated structures are freed at this time. The socket also is freed if the SS_NOFDREF flag has been set. The socket remains in existence as long as either a file descriptor or a protocol control block refers to it.

14.5 TCP Input Processing

TCP input processing is considerably more complicated than UDP input handling, and the preceding sections have provided the background needed to examine the the implementation of the TCP input path. The input routine is called with parameters

```
void tcp_input(
    struct mbuf *msg,
    int off0);
```

The first few steps are similar to those of UDP:

1. Locate the TCP header in the received IP datagram. Make sure that the packet is at least as long as a minimal-size TCP header, and use *m_pullup*() if necessary to make it contiguous.

2. Compute the packet length, set up the IP pseudo-header, and checksum the TCP header and data. Discard the packet if the checksum is bad.

3. Check the TCP header length; if it is larger than a minimal header, make sure that the whole header is contiguous.

4. Locate the protocol control block for the connection with the port number specified. If none exists, send a packet containing the reset flag, RST, and drop the packet.

5. Check whether the socket is listening for connections; if it is, follow the procedure described for passive connection establishment.

6. Process any TCP options from the packet header.

7. Clear the idle time for the connection and set the keepalive timer to its normal value.

Here, the normal checks have been made and the kernel is prepared to handle data and control flags in the received packet. There are still many consistency checks that must be made during normal processing; for example, the SYN flag must be present if a connection is still being established and must not be present if the connection has been established. For simplicity, many of these checks are not described below, but the tests are important to prevent wayward packets from causing confusion and possible data corruption.

The next step in checking a TCP packet is to see whether the packet is acceptable according to the receive window. It is important that this step be done before control flags—in particular RST—are examined because old or extraneous packets should not affect the current connection unless they are clearly relevant in the current context. A segment is acceptable if the receive window has nonzero size and if at least some of the sequence space occupied by the packet falls within the receive window. Portions of the data that precede the window are trimmed, since they have already been received, and portions that exceed the window also are discarded, since they have been sent prematurely. If the receive window is closed (*rcv_wnd* is zero), then only segments with no data and with a sequence number equal to *rcv_nxt* are acceptable. If an incoming segment is not acceptable, it is dropped after an acknowledgment is sent.

The processing of incoming TCP packets must be fully general, taking into account all the possible incoming packets and possible states of receiving endpoints. However, the bulk of the packets processed falls into two general categories. Typical packets contain either the next expected data segment for an existing connection or an acknowledgment plus a window update for one or more data segments, with no additional flags or state indications. Rather than considering each incoming segment based on first principles, *tcp_input*() checks first for these common cases, an algorithm known as ***header prediction***. An incoming segment is one of two common types if it meets these five criteria:

1. It matches a connection in the ESTABLISHED state.
2. It contains the ACK flag but no other flags.
3. Its sequence number is the next value expected (and its timestamp, if any, is nondecreasing).
4. Its window field is the same as in its previous segment.
5. Its connection is not in a retransmission state.

A segment that matches these five criteria and contains no data is a pure acknowledgment with a window update. In the usual case, round-trip timing information is sampled if it is available, acknowledged data are dropped from the socket send buffer, and the sequence values are updated. The packet is discarded once the header values have been checked. The retransmit timer is canceled if all pending data have been acknowledged; otherwise, it is restarted. The socket layer is notified if any process is waiting to output data. Finally, *tcp_output*() is called because the window has moved forward and that operation completes the handling of a pure acknowledgment.

If a packet meeting the tests for header prediction contains the next expected data, and no out-of-order data are queued for the connection, and if the socket receive buffer has space for the incoming data, then this packet is a pure in-sequence data segment. The sequencing variables are updated, the packet headers are removed from the packet, and the remaining data are appended to the socket receive buffer. The socket layer is notified so that it can notify any interested thread, and the control block is marked with a flag indicating that an acknowledgment is needed. No additional processing is required for a pure data packet.

For packets that are not handled by the header-prediction algorithm, the processing steps are as follows:

1. Process the timestamp option if it is present, rejecting any packets for which the timestamp has decreased.
2. Check whether the packet begins before *rcv_nxt*. If it does, ignore any SYN in the packet and trim any data that fall before *rcv_nxt*. If no data remain, send a current acknowledgment and drop the packet. (The packet is presumed to be a duplicate transmission.)
3. If the packet still contains data after trimming, and the process that created the socket has already closed the socket, send a reset (RST) and drop the connection. This reset is necessary to abort connections that cannot complete; it typically is sent when a remote-login client disconnects while data are being received.
4. If the end of the segment falls after the window, trim any data beyond the window. If the window was closed and the packet sequence number is *rcv_nxt*, the packet is treated as a window probe; TF_ACKNOW is set to send a current acknowledgment and window update, and the remainder of the packet is processed. If SYN is set and the connection was in TIME_WAIT state, this packet is really a new connection request and the old connection is dropped; this procedure is called ***rapid connection reuse***. Otherwise, if no data remain, send an acknowledgment and drop the packet.

The remaining steps of TCP input processing check the following flags and fields, and take the appropriate actions: RST, ACK, window, URG, data, and FIN. Because the packet has already been confirmed to be acceptable, these actions can be done in a straightforward way:

5. If a timestamp option is present, and the packet includes the next sequence number expected, record the value received to be included in the next acknowledgment.
6. If RST is set, close the connection and drop the packet.
7. If ACK is not set, drop the packet.

8. If the acknowledgment-field value is higher than that of previous acknowledgments, new data have been acknowledged. If the connection was in SYN_RECEIVED state and the packet acknowledges the SYN sent for this connection, enter ESTABLISHED state. If the packet includes a timestamp option, use it to compute a round-trip time sample; otherwise, if the sequence range that was newly acknowledged includes the sequence number for which the round-trip time was measured, this packet provides a sample. Average the time sample into the smoothed round-trip time estimate for the connection. If all outstanding data have been acknowledged, stop the retransmission timer; otherwise, set it back to the current timeout value. Finally, drop the data that were acknowledged from the socket's send queue. If a FIN has been sent and was acknowledged, advance the state machine.
9. Check the window field to see whether it advances the known send window. First, check whether this packet is a new window update. If the sequence number of the packet is greater than that of the previous window update, or the sequence number is the same but the acknowledgment-field value is higher, or if both sequence and acknowledgment are the same but the window is larger, record the new window.
10. If the urgent-data flag URG is set, compare the urgent pointer in the packet to the last-received urgent pointer. If it is different, new urgent data have been sent. Use the urgent pointer to compute *so_oobmark*, the offset from the beginning of the socket receive buffer to the urgent mark (Section 14.3), and notify the socket with *sohasoutofband*(). If the urgent pointer is less than the packet length, the urgent data have all been received. TCP normally removes the final data byte sent in urgent mode (the last byte before the urgent pointer) and places that byte in the protocol control block until it is requested with a PRU_RCVOOB request. (The end of the urgent data is a subject of disagreement; the BSD interpretation follows the original TCP specification.) A socket option, SO_OOBINLINE, may request that urgent data be left in the queue with the normal data, although the mark on the data stream is still maintained.
11. Examine the data field in the received packet. If the data begin with *rcv_nxt*, then they can be placed directly into the socket receive buffer with *sbappendstream*(). The flag TF_DELACK is set in the protocol control block to indicate that an acknowledgment is needed, but should be delayed in the hope that it can be piggybacked on any packets sent soon (presumably in response to the incoming data) or combined with acknowledgment of other data received soon; see the subsection on Delayed Acknowledgments and Window Updates in Section 14.6. If no activity causes a packet to be returned before the next time that the *tcp_delack*() routine runs, it will change the flag to TF_ACKNOW and call the *tcp_output*() routine to send the acknowledgment. Acknowledgments can thus be delayed by no more than 100 milliseconds. If the data do not begin with *rcv_nxt*, the packet is retained in a per-connection queue until the intervening data arrive and an acknowledgment is sent immediately.

12. As the final step in processing a received packet, check for the FIN flag. If it is present, the connection state machine may have to be advanced, and the socket is marked with *socantrcvmore*() to convey the end-of-file indication. If the send side has already closed (a FIN was sent and acknowledged), the socket is now considered closed and it is so marked with *soisdisconnected*(). The TF_ACKNOW flag is set to force immediate acknowledgment.

Step 12 completes the actions taken when a new packet is received by *tcp_input*(). However, as noted earlier in this section, receipt of input may require new output. In particular, acknowledgment of all outstanding data or a new window update requires either new output or a state change by the output module. Also, several special conditions set the TF_ACKNOW flag. Here, *tcp_output*() is called at the conclusion of input processing.

14.6 TCP Output Processing

This section describes the implementation of the TCP send policy. A TCP packet contains an acknowledgment, a window field, and data. A single packet may be sent if any of these three fields change. A naive TCP send policy might send many more packets than necessary. Logically, three packets are sent when a user types one character to a remote-terminal connection that uses remote echo.

1. The server-side TCP receives a single-character packet.
2. It sends an immediate acknowledgment of the character.
3. Milliseconds later, the login server reads the character, removing the character from the receive buffer. TCP immediately sends a window update, noting that one additional byte of send window was available.
4. After another millisecond or so, the login server sends an echoed character back to the client, necessitating a third packet sent in response to the single character of input.

A more efficient implementation will collapse the last three responses (the acknowledgment, the window update, and the data return) into a single packet. However, if the server were not echoing input data (for example, when the user is typing his or her password), the acknowledgment cannot be withheld for too long or the client-side TCP would begin to retransmit. The algorithms used in the send policy to minimize network traffic yet maximize throughput are the most subtle part of a TCP implementation. The send policy used in FreeBSD includes several standard algorithms, as well as a few approaches suggested by the network research community. This section examines each part of the send policy.

Sending Data

The most common reason for calling the TCP output routine *tcp_output*() is that the user has written new data to the socket. Write operations are done with a call to the *tcp_usr_send*() routine. Recall that *sosend*() waits for enough space in the socket send buffer, if necessary, and then copies the user's data into a chain of mbufs that is passed to the protocol by the *tcp_usr_send*() routine. The action in *tcp_usr_send*() is simply to place the new output data in the socket's send buffer with *sbappendstream*() and to call *tcp_output*(). If flow control permits, *tcp_output*() will send the data immediately.

The actual send operation is not substantially different from that for a UDP datagram socket. The differences are that the header is more complicated and additional fields must be initialized, and the data sent are simply a copy of the user's data. However, for send operations large enough for *sosend*() to place the data in external mbuf clusters, the copy is done by creating a new reference to the data cluster. A copy must be retained in the socket's send buffer to use if retransmission is required. Also, if the number of data bytes is larger than the size of a single maximum-size segment, multiple packets will be constructed and sent in a single call.

The *tcp_output*() routine allocates an mbuf to contain the output packet header and copies the contents of the header template into that mbuf. If the data to be sent fit into the same mbuf as the header, *tcp_output*() copies them into place from the socket send buffer using the *m_copydata*() routine. Otherwise, *tcp_output*() adds the data to be sent as a separate chain of mbufs obtained with an *m_copy*() operation from the appropriate part of the send buffer. The sequence number for the packet is set from *snd_nxt* and the acknowledgment is set from *rcv_nxt*. The flags are obtained from an array containing the flags to be sent in each connection state. The window to be advertised is computed from the amount of space remaining in the socket's receive buffer; however, if that amount is small (less than one-fourth of the buffer and less than one segment), it is set to zero. The window is never allowed to end at a smaller sequence number than the one in which it ended in the previous packet. If urgent data have been sent, the urgent pointer and flag are set accordingly. One other flag must be set. The PSH flag on a packet indicates that data should be passed to the user; it is like a buffer-flush request. This flag is generally considered obsolete but is set whenever all the data in the send buffer have been sent; FreeBSD ignores this flag on input. Once the header is filled in, the packet is checksummed. The remaining parts of the IP header are initialized, including the type-of-service and time-to-live fields, and the packet is sent with *ip_output*(). The retransmission timer is started if it is not already running, and the *snd_nxt* and *snd_max* values for the connection are updated.

Avoidance of the Silly-Window Syndrome

Silly-window syndrome is the name given to a potential problem in a window-based flow-control scheme in which a system sends several small packets rather than waiting for a reasonable-size window to become available [Clark, 1982]. For example, if a network-login client program has a total receive buffer size of 4096 bytes, and the user stops terminal output during a large printout, the buffer will become nearly full as new full-size segments are received. If the remaining buffer space dropped to 10 bytes, it would not be useful for the receiver to volunteer to receive an additional 10 bytes. If the user then allowed a few characters to print and stopped output again, it still would not be useful for the receiving TCP to send a window update allowing another 14 bytes. Instead, it is desirable to wait until a reasonably large packet can be sent, since the receive buffer already contains enough data for the next several pages of output. Avoidance of the silly-window syndrome is desirable in both the receiver and the sender of a flow-controlled connection, as either end can prevent silly small windows from being used. Receiver avoidance of the silly-window syndrome is described in the previous subsection; when a packet is sent, the receive window is advertised as zero if it is less than one packet and less than one-fourth of the receive buffer. For sender avoidance of the silly-window syndrome, an output operation is delayed if at least a full packet of data is ready to be sent but less than one full packet can be sent because of the size of the send window. Instead of sending, *tcp_output*() sets the output state to persist state by starting the persist timer. If no window update has been received by the time that the timer expires, the allowable data are sent in the hope that the acknowledgment will include a larger window. If it does not, the connection stays in persist state, sending a window probe periodically until the window is opened.

An initial implementation of sender avoidance of the silly-window syndrome produced large delays and low throughput over connections to hosts using TCP implementations with tiny buffers. Unfortunately, those implementations always advertised receive windows less than the maximum segment size—a behavior that was considered silly by this implementation. As a result of this problem, the FreeBSD TCP implementation keeps a record of the largest receive window offered by a peer in the protocol-control-block variable *max_sndwnd*. When at least one-half of *max_sndwnd* may be sent, a new segment is sent. This technique improved performance when a BSD system was communicating with these limited hosts.

Avoidance of Small Packets

Network traffic exhibits a bimodal distribution of sizes. Bulk data transfers tend to use the largest possible packets for maximum throughput, whereas interactive services (such as network-login) tend to use small packets, often containing only a single data character. On a fast local-area network, the use of single-character packets generally is not a problem because the network bandwidth usually is not saturated. On long-haul networks interconnected by slow or congested links, or on wireless LANs that are both slow and lossy, it is desirable to collect input over some period and then send it in a single network packet. Various schemes have been devised for collecting input over a fixed time—usually about 50 to 100 milliseconds—and then sending it in a single packet. These schemes noticeably slow character echo times on fast networks and often save few packets on slow networks. In contrast, a simple and elegant scheme for reducing small-packet traffic (***small-packet avoidance***) was suggested by Nagle [1984]. This scheme allows the first byte output to be sent alone in a packet with no delay. Until this packet is acknowledged, however, no new small packets may be sent. If enough new data arrive to fill a maximum-size packet, another packet is sent. As soon as the outstanding data are acknowledged, the input that was queued while waiting for the first packet may be sent. Only one small packet may ever be outstanding on a connection at one time. The net result is that data from small output operations are queued during one round-trip time. If the round-trip time is less than the intercharacter arrival time, as it is in a remote-terminal session on a LAN, transmissions are never delayed and response time remains low. When a slow network intervenes, input after the first character is queued and the next packet contains the input received during the preceding round-trip time. This algorithm is attractive because of both its simplicity and its self-tuning nature.

Nagle's algorithm does not work well for certain classes of network clients that sent streams of small requests that cannot be batched. One such client is the network-based X Window System [Scheifler & Gettys, 1986], which requires immediate delivery of small messages to get real-time feedback for user interfaces such as rubber-banding to sweep out a new window. Hence, the TCP_NODELAY option was added to defeat this algorithm on a connection. This option can be set with a *setsockopt* call, which reaches TCP via the *tcp_ctloutput*() routine.

Delayed Acknowledgments and Window Updates

TCP packets must be sent for reasons other than data transmission. On a one-way connection, the receiving TCP must still send packets to acknowledge received data and to advance the sender's send window. In a bulk data transfer, the time at which window updates are sent is a determining factor for network throughput. For example, if the receiver simply set the TF_DELACK flag each time that data were received on a bulk-data connection, acknowledgments would be sent every 100 milliseconds. If 8192-byte windows were used on a 1-Gbps Ethernet, this algorithm would result in a maximum throughput of 655 Kbit/s, or less than 1 percent of the available network bandwidth. Clearly, once the sender has filled the send window that it has been given, it must stop until the receiver acknowledges the old data (allowing them to be removed from the send buffer and new data to replace them) and provides a window update (allowing the new data to be sent).

Because TCP's window-based flow control is limited by the space in the socket receive buffer, TCP has the PR_RCVD flag set in its protocol-switch entry so that the protocol will be called (via the *tcp_usr_rcvd*() routine) when the user has done a receive call that has removed data from the receive buffer. The *tcp_usr_rcvd*() routine simply calls *tcp_output*(). Whenever *tcp_output*() determines that a window update sent under the current circumstances would provide a new send window to the sender large enough to be worthwhile, it sends an acknowledgment and window update. If the receiver waited until the window was full, the sender would already have been idle for some time when it finally received a window update. Furthermore, if the send buffer on the sending system was smaller than the receiver's buffer—and thus smaller than the receiver's window—the sender would be unable to fill the receiver's window without receiving an acknowledgment. Therefore, the window-update strategy in FreeBSD is based on only the maximum segment size. Whenever a new window update would move the window forward by at least two full-size segments, the window update is sent. This window-update strategy produces a twofold reduction in acknowledgment traffic and a twofold reduction in input processing for the sender. However, updates are sent often enough to give the sender feedback on the progress of the connection and to allow the sender to continue sending additional segments.

Note that TCP is called at two different stages of processing on the receiving side of a bulk data transfer: it is called on packet reception to process input, and it is called after each receive operation removing data from the input buffer. At the first call, an acknowledgment could be sent, but no window update could be sent. After the receive operation, a window update also is possible. Thus, it is important that the algorithm runs in the second half of this cycle.

Selective Acknowledgment

A long-running TCP connection over a lossy network path will have packets dropped in flight. Once a connection has a sufficiently large transmission window open it can send several packets at once and the dropped packet may occur in the middle of the set rather than at the end. TCP normally acknowledges the last byte of the last segment that it received and which it could correctly append to any previously received data. When a segment is dropped, TCP appends any new segments that follow the dropped segment to the receive queue, but no indication is given to the sender that one or more segments were dropped, only that the last received byte is at a particular sequence number. Selective acknowledgments (SACK), are a mechanism whereby the receiver can tell the sender when one or more segments were dropped, allowing the sender to choose more efficiently the data to re-transmit [Mathis et al., 1996].

The use of SACK is negotiated at connection setup time. The inclusion of the SACK-permitted option in a packet containing a SYN, such as the initial connection request, or the SYN/ACK returned by a host receiving a connection request, indicates that the sender supports SACK. Once the connection is sending data, the receiver can send a SACK option to the sender as part of an ACK packet to indicate the data that it has already received. The receiver does not tell the sender the segments were dropped. Rather, it tells the sender the data that it has received by sending pairs of sequence numbers specifying the left and right hand sides of the received data.

SACK information is sent as an option rather than as part of the data section of the packet. The amount of information that can be sent back to the sender from the receiver is limited because the option field has a maximum size of 40 bytes. In a typical environment where other options such as timestamps are already in use, a SACK enabled receiver can only indicate three regions of data that it has received.

Figure 14.5 shows a receiver's state with four segments and two holes. Each segment contains 500 bytes. The first segment containing bytes 0 to 499 has been received and acknowledged to the sender. Three additional segments have been received but not yet acknowledged for byte ranges 1000 to 1499, 1500 to 1999,

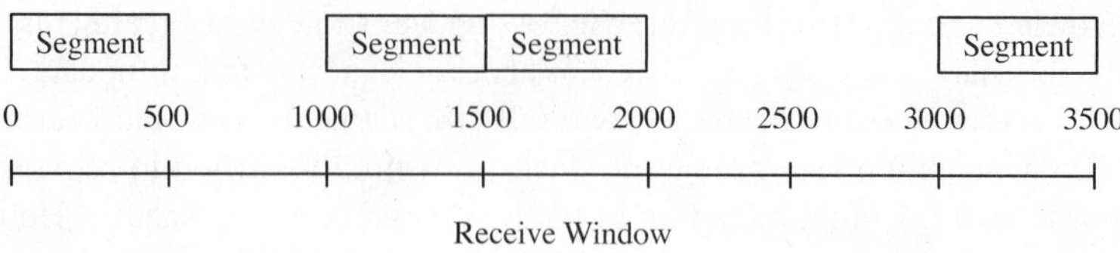

Figure 14.5 SACK receiver state.

and 3000 to 3499. Three segments are missing: those that contain bytes 500 to 999, 2000 to 2499, and 2500 to 2999. The receiver tells the sender about the segments it has successfully received, but not delivered to the application, by sending a SACK option that includes the left- and right-hand sides of up to three sections of received data, which are referred to as SACK blocks. In our current example, the receiver would send an option with the SACK blocks 1000:2000 and 3000:3500. The right hand side of the SACK block is defined to be the last received byte plus one. The SACK option has no effect on the acknowledgment field of the TCP packet sent from the receiver back to the sender. The acknowledgment field always contains the sequence value of the last correctly received byte (499 in this example). The sender does not depend on the receiver maintaining any extra state to implement SACK. It is possible that because of memory pressure, the receiving host might drop undelivered segments from its reassembly queues, thereby invalidating a previous report of data via a SACK option. The sender cannot free any data it has sent until it receives an acknowledgment for that data through an ACK with a proper acknowledgment number. The SACK option is an optimization and not a fundamental change in how TCP works.

The implementation of SACK in FreeBSD has two main data structures: One data structure for the list of SACK blocks and the other for the list of holes that the sender believes to be present in the receiver's reassembly queue. The array of SACK blocks is used differently by the sender and the receiver. On the receiver, the array of SACK blocks contains the information that the receiver will send back to the sender with the next ACK. The sender's array contains the blocks that have arrived from the the receiver. The array, *sackblks*, is contained in the TCP control block and holds a maximum of six entries because at most four sack blocks can be communicated in a single SACK option. The two extra entries in the array store blocks that the sender has received in previous updates. When a TCP connection has many packets in flight, several may be dropped due to changing network conditions, resulting in several holes appearing in the receiver's reassembly queue. Being able to store six SACK blocks per socket at the sender was deemed a reasonable compromise between memory usage and performance. Whenever a host receives data on a TCP connection, the *tcp_do_segment*() routine places the data either into the socket's receive buffer or into the reassembly queue. When data is placed into the reassembly queue, it indicates that packets were received out of order and that a hole may be present. The *tcp_update_sack_list*() routine is used by the receiver to update its list of SACK blocks. Because the receiver has had to use its reassembly queue, the TF_ACKNOW flag will be set on the TCP control block. After updating its SACK blocks, the receiver will call *tcp_output*(), which adds a SACK option containing as many SACK blocks as fit into the options field of the packet. SACK options are processed last by the *tcp_addoptions*() routine so that the maximum number of options can be stored in the 40 bytes available. A TCP connection with both timestamps and signatures enabled has space for only one SACK block, since a timestamp takes 12 bytes and a signature takes 18, leaving only 10 for SACK information. As most TCP connections do not use signatures, it is more common to have space for up to three SACK blocks. The current design of SACK does not allow space for any more SACK blocks since they can only be communicated within the limited space allowed for TCP options.

A TCP sender receives SACK blocks in the options part of a packet with the ACK flag set. The *tcp_input*() routine calls the *tcp_sack_doack*() routine to update the sender's understanding of the holes that are present in the receiver's reassembly queue. The sender maintains a scoreboard of the holes in a tail-queue structure and keeps the received SACK blocks in a per-socket array. All the received blocks are placed into the array, which is then sorted into ascending order based on the right-hand side of each block. With the SACK blocks sorted, the *tcp_sack_doack*() routine walks the list of blocks and adjusts its scoreboard. Three possible adjustments to the scoreboard can be made:

1. A SACK block may completely cover a hole, indicating that the receiver now has the data that the sender believed was missing. Here, the hole is removed from the scoreboard.

2. A block can partially cover a hole. Here, the size of the hole is reduced.

3. A block may acknowledge data within a hole, requiring that the hole be split.

Once all of the blocks have been processed, the scoreboard is again in a consistent state and can be used by the *tcp_output*() routine when it next transmits data.

The *tcp_sack_output*() routine is called when a sender wants to transmit data to a receiver and the sender has holes present in the scoreboard. If more than one hole exists, only the next hole is returned by the routine and not the complete set. The information from the scoreboard adjusts the length of the data to be sent by TCP so that the next transmission will cover as much as possible of the next hole in the scoreboard. The transmission of new data does not update the scoreboard or the array of SACK holes maintained by the sender. SACK data structures on the sender are only updated on the receipt of acknowledgments from the receiver. Once the receiver has acknowledged data past all of the holes, the sender will clear both its scoreboard and its *sackblks* array.

Retransmit State

When the retransmit timer expires while a sender is awaiting acknowledgment of transmitted data, *tcp_output*() is called to retransmit. The retransmit timer is first set to the next multiple of the round-trip time in the backoff series. The variable *snd_nxt* is moved back from its current sequence number to *snd_una*. A single packet is then sent containing the oldest data in the transmit queue. Unlike some other systems, FreeBSD does not keep copies of the packets that have been sent on a connection; it retains only the data. Thus, although only a single packet is retransmitted, that packet may contain more data than does the oldest outstanding packet. On a slow connection with small send operations, such as a remote login, this algorithm may cause a single-byte packet that is lost to be retransmitted with all the data queued since the initial byte was first transmitted.

If a single packet was lost in the network, the retransmitted packet will elicit an acknowledgment of all data transmitted thus far. If more than one packet was lost, the next acknowledgment will include the retransmitted packet and possibly some of the intervening data. It may also include a new window update. Thus, when an acknowledgment is received after a retransmit timeout, any old data that were not acknowledged will be resent as though they had not yet been sent, and some new data may be sent as well.

Slow Start

Many TCP connections traverse several networks between their source and destination. When some of the networks are slower than others, the entry router to the slowest network often is presented with more traffic than it can handle. It may buffer some input packets to avoid dropping them because of sudden changes in flow, but eventually its buffers will fill and it must begin dropping packets. When a TCP connection first starts sending data across a fast network to a router forwarding via a slower network, it may find that the router's queues are already nearly full. In the original send policy used in BSD, a bulk-data transfer would start out by sending a full window of packets once the connection was established. These packets could be sent at the full speed of the network to the bottleneck router, but that router could transmit them only at a much slower rate. As a result,

Figure 14.6 Acknowledgment clocking. There are two routers connected by a slow link between the sender and the receiver. The thickness of the links represents their speed. The width of the packets represents their time to travel down the link. Fast links are wide and the packets are narrow. Slow links are narrow and the packets are wide. In the steady state shown, the sender sends a new packet each time an acknowledgment is received from the receiver.

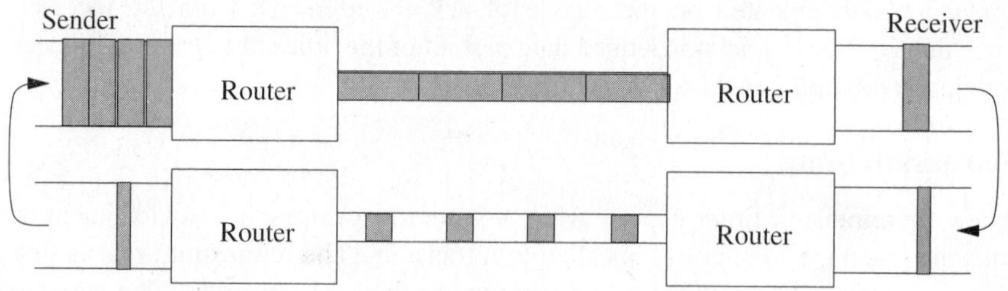

the initial burst of packets was highly likely to overflow the router's queue and some of the packets would be lost. If such a connection used an expanded window size in an attempt to gain performance—for example, when traversing a transoceanic network link with a long round-trip time—this problem would be even more severe. However, if the connection could once reach steady state, a full window of data often could be accommodated by the network if the packets were spread evenly throughout the path. At steady state, new packets would be injected into the network only when previous packets were acknowledged and the number of packets in the network would be constant. Figure 14.6 shows the desired steady state. In addition, even if packets arrived at the outgoing router in a cluster, they would be spread out when the network was traversed by at least their transmission times in the slowest network. If the receiver sent acknowledgments when each packet was received, the acknowledgments would return to the sender with approximately the correct spacing. The sender would then have a self-clocking means for transmitting at the correct rate for the network without sending bursts of packets that the bottleneck could not buffer.

An algorithm named slow start brings a TCP connection to this steady state [Jacobson, 1988]. It is called slow start because it is necessary to start data transmission slowly when traversing a slow network. Figure 14.7 shows the progress of the slow-start algorithm. The scheme is simple: A connection starts out with an initial-segment quota of one to four outstanding packets. A one-block initial-segment quota is used for a connection with a small initial window size, while a four-block initial-segment quota is used with a large initial window size. An increased initial window size takes advantage of the greater bandwidth available from fast networks [Allman et al., 2002]. Each time that an acknowledgement is received, the limit is increased by one packet. If the acknowledgement also carries a window update, two packets are sent in response. This process continues until the

Figure 14.7 The progression of the slow-start algorithm.

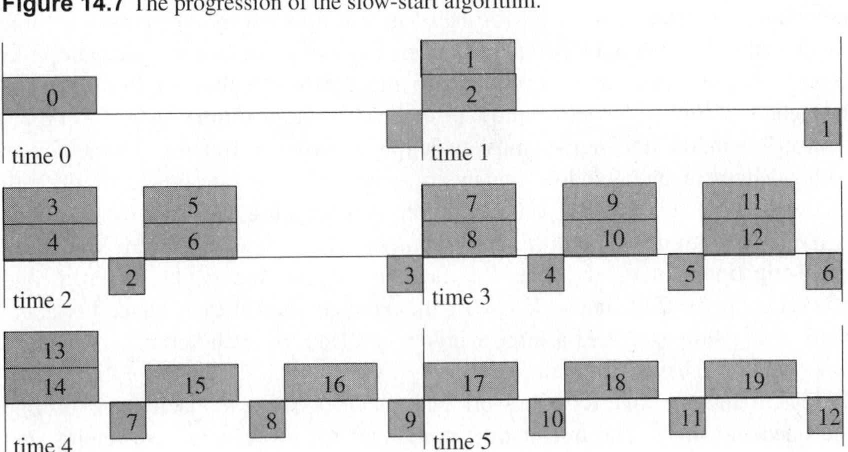

window is fully open. During the slow-start phase of the connection, if each packet was acknowledged separately, the limit would be doubled during each exchange, resulting in an exponential opening of the window. Delayed acknowledgments might cause acknowledgments to be coalesced if more than one packet could arrive at the receiver within 100 milliseconds, slowing the window opening slightly. However, the sender never sends bursts of more than two or three packets during the opening phase and sends only one or two packets at a time once the window has opened.

The implementation of the slow-start algorithm uses a second window, like the send window but maintained separately, called the congestion window (*snd_cwnd*). The congestion window is maintained according to an estimate of the data that the network is currently able to buffer for this connection. The send policy is modified so that new data are sent only if allowed by both the normal- and congestion-send windows. The congestion window is initialized to the size of the initial-segment quota, causing a connection to begin with a slow start. Whenever transmission stops, the congestion window is reset back to the same value as that used in the initial window. Otherwise, once a retransmitted packet was acknowledged, the resulting window update might allow a full window of data to be sent, which would once again overrun intervening routers. The use of slow start after a retransmission timeout prevents the sender from overrunning a congested network. The timeout may indicate that the network has become slower because of congestion, a temporary reduction of the window may help the network to recover from this condition. The connection is forced to reestablish its clock of acknowledgments after the connection has come to a halt and slow start has this effect as well. A slow start is also forced if a connection begins to transmit after an idle period of at least the current retransmission value (a function of the smoothed round-trip time and variance estimates).

Buffer and Window Sizing

The throughput of a TCP connection is limited by the bandwidth of the path that the connection must transit. Performance is also affected by the round-trip time for the path. For example, paths that traverse any of the major transoceanic links have a long intrinsic delay, even though the bandwidth may be high, but the throughput is limited to one window of data per round-trip time. After filling the receiver's window, the sender must wait for at least one round-trip time for an acknowledgment and window update to arrive. To take advantage of the full bandwidth of a path, both the sender and receiver must use buffers at least as large as the bandwidth-delay product to allow the sender to transmit during the entire round-trip time. In steady state, this buffering allows the sender, receiver, and intervening parts of the network to keep the pipeline filled at each stage. For some paths, using slow start and a large window can lead to much better performance than could be achieved previously.

The round-trip time for a network path includes two components: transit time and queueing time. The transit time comprises the propagation, switching, and forwarding time in the physical layers of the network, including the time to transmit packets bit by bit after each store-and-forward hop. Ideally, queueing time would be negligible, with packets arriving at each node of the network just in time to be sent after the preceding packet. This ideal flow is possible when a single connection using a suitable window size is synchronized with the network. However, as additional traffic is injected into the network by other sources, queues build up in routers, especially at the entrance to the slower links in the path. Although queueing delay is part of the round-trip time observed by each network connection that is using a path, it is not useful to increase the operating window size for a connection to a value larger than the product of the limiting bandwidth for the path times the transit delay. Sending additional data beyond that limit causes the additional data to be queued, which increases queueing delay without increasing throughput.

Avoidance of Congestion with Slow Start

The slow-start algorithm prevents TCP from overloading a network when packet transmission first begins, or when it resumes after a long idle period. A single connection may reasonably use a large window without flooding the entry router to the slow network on startup. As a connection opens the window during a slow start, it injects packets into the network until the network links are kept busy. During this phase, it may send packets at up to twice the rate at which the network can deliver data because of the exponential opening of the window. If the window is chosen appropriately for the path, the connection will reach steady state without flooding the network. However, with multiple connections sharing a path, the bandwidth available to each connection is reduced. If each connection uses a window equal to the bandwidth-delay product, the additional packets in transit must be queued, which increases delay. If the total offered load is too high, routers must drop packets rather than increasing the queue sizes and delay. Thus, the appropriate window size for a TCP connection depends not only on the path, but also on competing traffic. A window size large enough to provide good performance when a long-delay link is in the path will overrun the network when most of the round-trip time is in queueing delays. It is highly desirable for a TCP connection to be self-tuning, as the characteristics of the path are seldom known at the endpoints and may change with time. If a connection expands its window to a value too large for a path, or if additional load on the network collectively exceeds the capacity, router queues will build until packets must be dropped. Here, the connection will close the congestion window to the maximum segment size calculated for the link and will initiate a slow start. If the window is simply too large for the path, however, this process will repeat each time that the window is opened too far.

The connection can learn from this problem and can adjust its behavior using another algorithm associated with the slow-start algorithm. This algorithm keeps a state variable for each connection, *snd_ssthresh* (slow-start threshold), which is an estimate of the usable window for the path. When a packet is dropped, as evidenced by a retransmission timeout, this window estimate is set to a maximum of either two maximally size segments (MSS), or half of the current amount of data in flight (FlightSize):

$$ssthresh = \max(FlightSize\ /\ 2,\ 2 \times MSS)$$

Further details about the slow start algorithm are given in [Allman et al., 2009]. The current window is obviously too large at the moment, and the decrease in window utilization must be large enough that congestion will decrease rather than stabilizing. At the same time, the slow-start window (*snd_cwnd*) is set to the initial-segment quota to restart. The connection starts up as before, opening the window exponentially until it reaches the *snd_ssthresh* limit. Here, the connection is near the estimated usable window for the path. It enters steady state, sending data packets as allowed by window updates. To test for improvement in the network, it continues to expand the window slowly; as long as this expansion succeeds, the connection can continue to take advantage of reduced network load. The expansion of the window in this phase is linear, with one additional full-size segment being added to the current window for each full window of data transmitted. This slow increase allows the connection to discover when it is safe to resume use of a larger window while reducing the loss in throughput because of the wait after the loss of a packet before transmission can resume. Note that the increase in window size during this phase of the connection is linear as long as no packets are lost, but the decrease in window size when signs of congestion appear is exponential (it is divided by 2 on each timeout). With the use of this dynamic window-sizing algorithm, it is possible to use larger default window sizes for connection to all destinations without overrunning networks that cannot support them.

Fast Retransmission

Packets can be lost in the network for many reasons, two of which are congestion and corruption. TCP detects lost packets by a timeout, which causes a retransmission. When a packet is lost, the flow of packets on a connection comes to a halt while waiting for the timeout. Depending on the round-trip time and variance, this timeout can result in a substantial period during which the connection makes no progress. Once the timeout occurs, an initial-segment quota of segments is retransmitted as the first phase of a slow start and the slow-start threshold is set as shown in the previous section. If later packets are not lost, the connection goes through a slow startup to the new threshold and it then gradually opens the window to probe whether any congestion has disappeared. Each of these phases lowers the effective throughput for the connection. The result is decreased performance, even though the congestion may have been brief.

When a connection reaches steady state, it sends a continuous stream of data packets in response to a stream of acknowledgments with window updates. If a single packet is lost, the receiver sees packets arriving out of order. Most TCP receivers, including FreeBSD, respond to an out-of-order segment with a repeated acknowledgment for the in-order data. If one packet is lost while enough packets to fill the window are sent, each packet after the lost packet will provoke a duplicate acknowledgment with no data, window update, or other new information.

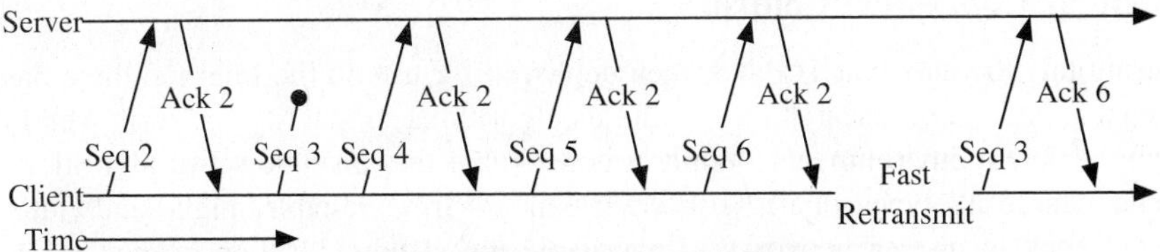

Figure 14.8 Fast retransmission. Packet with sequence number 3 is lost. Receiver returns duplicate acknowledgements for the last good packet, sequence number 2. Transmitter retransmits packet number 3 after receiving three duplicate acknowledgements.

The receiver can infer the out-of-order arrival of packets from these duplicate acknowledgments. Given enough evidence of reordering, the receiver can assume that a packet has been lost. FreeBSD TCP implements fast retransmission based on this signal. Figure 14.8 shows the sequence of packet transmissions and acknowledgments when using the fast-retransmission algorithm during the loss of a single packet. After detecting three identical acknowledgments, the *tcp_input*() function saves the current connection parameters, simulates a retransmission timeout to resend one segment of the oldest data in the send queue, and then restores the current transmit state. Because this indication of a lost packet is a congestion signal, the estimate of the network buffering limit, *snd_ssthresh*, is set to one-half of the current window. However, because the stream of acknowledgments has not stopped, a slow start is not needed. If a single packet has been lost, performing fast retransmission fills in the gap more quickly than would waiting for the retransmission timeout. An acknowledgment for the missing segment, plus all out-of-order segments queued before the retransmission, will then be received and the connection can continue normally.

Even with fast retransmission, it is likely that a TCP connection that suffers a lost segment will reach the end of the send window and be forced to stop transmission while awaiting an acknowledgment for the lost segment. However, after the fast retransmission, duplicate acknowledgments are received for each additional packet received by the peer after the lost packet. These duplicate acknowledgments imply that a packet has left the network and is now queued by the receiver. In that case, the packet does not need to be considered as within the network congestion window, possibly allowing additional data to be sent if the receiver's window is large enough. Each duplicate acknowledgment after a fast retransmission thus causes the congestion window to be moved forward artificially by the segment size. If the receiver's window is large enough, it allows the connection to make forward progress during a larger part of the time that the sender awaits an acknowledgment for the retransmitted segment. For this algorithm to have effect, the sender and receiver must have additional buffering beyond the normal bandwidth-delay product; twice that amount is needed for the algorithm to have full effect.

Modular Congestion Control

During the 30 years that TCP has been deployed for use on the Internet, there has been a great deal of research into tuning its algorithms so that they perform well in many different environments. While it is desirable that a single set of algorithms could handle all types of network environments from reliable, high-bandwidth, low-latency local-area networks to unreliable low-bandwidth high-latency wide-area networks, a single algorithm covering all of the possible combinations of network variables has proved elusive.

Ever since the release of 4.2BSD with its inclusion of TCP, the congestion-control algorithm has been periodically changed to share bandwidth more fairly and to improve overall performance. The default congestion-control algorithm in FreeBSD is referred to as New Reno because it was inherited from the final Reno release from 4.4BSD. Until the inclusion of modular congestion control in FreeBSD 7, each change to the congestion-control algorithm required a new release of the operating system [Stewart & Healy, 2007].

Modular congestion control is a system whereby any TCP or SCTP connection can choose the congestion-control algorithm that will give it the best performance. Each congestion-control algorithm, including the default, New Reno, is contained in a loadable kernel module and every TCP protocol control block contains a pointer to a *cc_algo* and *cc_var* structure. The *cc_algo* structure contains a set of function pointers that are called by TCP whenever an event occurs that indicates a change in the state of the connection related to congestion in the network. All of the variables that contain information about connection congestion are stored in the *cc_var* structure. Five congestion-control algorithms are now available in FreeBSD's TCP implementation: Hamilton Institute's delay-based congestion control [Budzisz et al., 2009], CUBIC [Ha et al., 2008], H-TCP [Leith et al., 2005], Vegas [Brakmo & Peterson, 1995], and the default New Reno [Henderson et al., 2012].

The goal of all TCP congestion-control algorithms is to prevent one or more hosts from overloading the network to the detriment of all network participants. All the algorithms provided in FreeBSD avoid congestion by controlling two variables within TCP: the congestion window *snd_cwnd* and the slow-start threshold *snd_ssthresh*. The algorithms also carefully track the round-trip time measured between the communicating hosts. These variables have already been described in the previous sections that covered the default slow start and fast retransmit behavior of FreeBSD. The following sections describe how the various congestion-control algorithms now supplied with FreeBSD treat these variables differently from the default. Each algorithm differs in how aggressively it opens the congestion window once the slow-start algorithm has completed its work, and how it reacts in the face of network congestion. All the algorithms supported by FreeBSD are encapsulated within loadable kernel modules and share a common kernel API. The *cc_algo* structure expresses the kernel API that congestion-control algorithms expose to the rest of TCP. Each of the entry points in the *cc_algo* structure, shown in Table 14.5, is used during a different part of a connection's lifetime. When a connection is first established, the *conn_init* function is called to initialize per-

Table 14.5 TCP congestion-control module methods.

Function	Description
mod_init	initialize congestion-control module state
mod_destroy	cleanup global module state on kldunload
cb_init	initialize congestion state for a new control block
cb_destroy	cleanup congetion-control state for a terminating control block
conn_init	initialize variables for a newly established connection
ack_received	called on receipt of an ACK
cong_signal	called on detection of a congestion signal
post_recovery	called after exiting congestion recovery
after_idle	called when data transfer resumes after an idle period

connection state that is privately held by the congestion-control module. Each acknowledgment received triggers a call into the *ack_received* function, which usually results in an increase in the size of *snd_cwnd*, the sender's congestion window. When congestion is discovered in the network by the receipt of a duplicate ack, the expiration of the round-trip timeout, or explicit notification by receipt of a packet with an explicit congestion-notification (ECN) flag, the *cong_signal* function is called, with the type of congestion indicated in the *type* field. Any congestion-control algorithm receiving a congestion signal is going to take action to change the size of the congestion window.

Congestion-control algorithms can be characterized by how they detect congestion in the network. The first TCP algorithms, including New Reno, detect congestion using a timeout that indicates a lost packet. More recently developed congestion-avoidance algorithms designed for high-speed high-latency networks, such as 1 Gbit per second WAN links with more than 50 milliseconds of round-trip time, detect congestion in the network by monitoring changes in the round-trip time of packets. A timing-based approach can improve TCP's ability to react to congestion since data on the connection's round-trip time is updated with each ACK received.

The Vegas Algorithm

The Vegas congestion-control algorithm is a logical extension of the Reno and New Reno work that came before it. The two main innovations of the Vegas algorithm are a new system for handling retransmissions and a novel form of congestion avoidance based on measuring the bandwidth between the two communicating endpoints. Unlike the Reno and New Reno algorithms, Vegas is more aggressive about anticipating losses in the network and therefore is more aggressive about retransmitting packets. The new retransmission mechanism was introduced to ameliorate problems inherent in the original BSD TCP implementation.

The problem was that the timers used by TCP were too coarse grained to react properly to lost packets sometimes taking over a second to realize that a retransmission was necessary. Improvements in the FreeBSD timer system and the implementation of New Reno made the changes introduced in Vegas moot, so they are not further described.

The main contribution of Vegas is a congestion-avoidance algorithm based on estimating the bandwidth between two communicating endpoints that attempts to keep a connection's bandwidth utilization within an acceptable range. Vegas defines two values, alpha and beta, that it uses to control the congestion window. Although the literature on Vegas describes its network utilization mechanism as working in terms of bandwidth, the alpha and beta values are measured in segments. In FreeBSD, the alpha and beta values are controlled via a pair of sysctl variables, *net.inet.tcp.cc.vegas.alpha* and *net.inet.tcp.cc.vegas.beta*, and are set to 1 and 3 segments respectively. Every time an ACK is received, it is processed by the module's *vegas_ack_received* function. The *vegas_ack_received* function calculates the expected and actual transmitting rate and then takes one of three actions:

1. If the difference between the expected rate and the actual rate is less than the alpha value, Vegas will increase the congestion window by one on the next round trip.
2. If the difference is greater than the beta value, Vegas will decrease the congestion window by one on the next round trip.
3. If the difference is between alpha and beta, then no action is taken.

Using alpha and beta acts as a damping function, preventing oscillations in the congestion window that could occur due to minor but noncatastrophic changes in the condition of the network.

The Cubic Algorithm

The Cubic algorithm is one of a new family of congestion-control algorithms designed to ameliorate problems with underutilization of network links. For most of the history of TCP, congestion-control algorithms operated in an environment where high bandwidth links also had low latency, such as in a local-area network. Since the late 1990s, companies commonly acquired their own private high-bandwidth links between remote locations. A typical example is a company that operates in the United States as well as Japan. It is common to have a 1-Gbit per second link between Tokyo and San Francisco with a round-trip time of about 110 milliseconds. Using the traditional methods of increasing the congestion window found in New Reno and Vegas, a single connection would take almost 10 minutes to discover the available bandwidth because the window only increases once per round trip. Trying to address the problem of underutilizing the link by simply making TCP more aggressive does not work because that leads to all the connections fighting each other over the available bandwidth, causing drops and eventually leading to congestion collapse typical in the early days of the Internet [Jacobson, 1988].

The CUBIC congestion-control algorithm works in two phases to find the correct congestion window. The names for the phases relate to the shape of the CUBIC function that has two areas, one concave and the other convex. When CUBIC is aggressively increasing the congestion window, it is in the concave region, but as the congestion window approaches the targeted maximum value it switches into the concave region so that the congestion window grows more slowly and does not accidentally overshoot the theoretical maximum size.

14.7 Stream Control Transmission Protocol (SCTP)

For most of the history of the TCP/IP protocol suite, there have been two main transport protocols. Network application designers were forced to choose between a reliable, ordered, byte-stream protocol, TCP, and an unreliable, unordered protocol with clear message boundaries, UDP. The socket API was designed to also handle a reliable message-oriented transport protocol that could be selected by supplying SOCK_SEQPACKET as the type argument to the *socket* system call. Sequential-packet protocol sockets were originally added to 4.2BSD to support the Sequenced-Packet Protocol (SPP) from the Xerox Network System [Xerox, 1981] and the *Delta-t* protocol from Lawrence Livermore National Laboratories [Watson, 1989].

The ***Stream Control Transmission Protocol*** (***SCTP***) was designed to provide a reliable message-oriented transport protocol [Stewart et al., 2000; Stewart et al., 2011]. SCTP is a direct replacement for TCP, but this section concentrates on the qualities that make it useful as a sequenced-packet protocol and also discusses some of the novel features that are not present in other transport protocols.

A sequential-packet protocol differs from a byte-stream protocol in one important way: each message is always sent and received by the application as a whole unit. A message may be broken up into smaller packets for transmission on the network. When an application sends the data, it is guaranteed that all the data passed into the *sendto* call is received at the destination in a single call to *recvfrom*, so long as the buffer passed to the *recvfrom* routine is capable of holding the entire message. When an application tries to receive a message that is larger than the buffer supplied in the *recvfrom* call, the kernel fills the buffer, discards the rest of the message, and returns without the MSG_EOR flag set. The only way to know that a message received is complete is to check for the MSG_EOR flag on return from the *recvfrom* routine.

In addition to support for a message-based protocol, SCTP has several features that are improvements on the work done in TCP including enhanced security, multihoming, multistreaming, and heartbeats that track the health of a connection.

When applications use TCP, each connection stands on its own and is unrelated to other streams of data that might be moving between the same hosts. SCTP implements ***associations*** to uniquely identify the endpoints of communication using source and destination network addresses as well as ports to differentiate one association from another. Within an association there can be multiple *streams* of data, each with its own set of performance parameters. Much like TCP, an association may contain one or more streams that are reliable ordered byte streams. The association may also contain one or more streams in which the data is ordered but has message boundaries. Each association can support up to 65,536 independent streams.

Chunks

Every SCTP packet begins with a common packet header as shown in Figure 14.9. The only information encoded in the header is the source and destination port, verification tag, and a checksum over the rest of the data contained in the packet. The header is followed by one or more chunks that are encoded as *type / length / value* tuples with an embedded set of flags, as shown in Figure 14.10. All the fields in SCTP packets are encoded so that they fall on 32-bit boundaries, making them easier to work with on commonly available 32- and 64-bit processors.

The minimum required set of the SCTP chunk types is shown in Table 14.6. Extensions to the SCTP protocol have defined new types but they are beyond the scope of this book. A more complete discussion of the SCTP protocol and extensions can be found in Stewart & Xie [2002].

Association Setup

SCTP sets up an association between two endpoints using a four-way handshake. Setting up a TCP connection only requires three packets, SYN, SYN/ACK, and ACK, but this approach has left TCP vulnerable to denial-of-service attacks, called SYN floods. A SYN attack works because TCP has no built-in mechanism for deciding whether a connection is meant to succeed or if it is meant purely to exhaust the kernel's resources. The *syn-cache* and *syn-cookies* described in Section 14.4 were designed to overcome the problems caused by using a three-way handshake. The association setup phase of SCTP is designed to foil denial-of-service attacks.

Association setup begins with a client sending a packet with an INIT chunk to a server on the network. The INIT packet contains a 32-bit random number in the verification tag that is used during the remainder of the four-way handshake.

Figure 14.9 SCTP packet header.

0 … 15	16 … 31
source port	destination port
verification tag	
CRC-32c checksum	

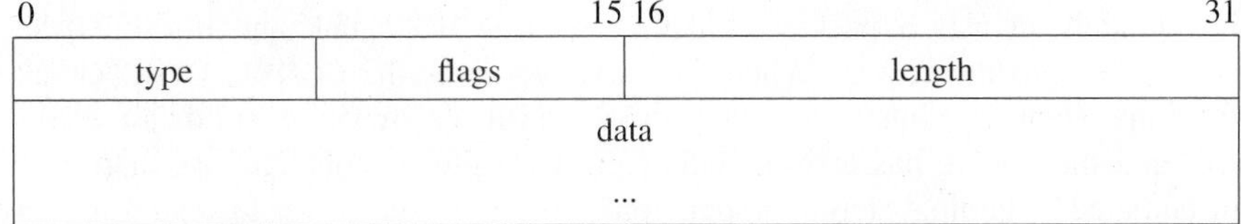

Figure 14.10 SCTP chunk.

When the server receives an INIT packet it generates its own verification tag as well as a state cookie. The state cookie contains the minimum amount of state required by a host to re-create a valid protocol control block, a timeout that limits the lifetime of the cookie, and a verification tag generated using the cookie data and a private key. The verification tag is protected using a message authentication code as described in Krawczyk et al. [1997]. The private key does not need to be shared between hosts. It is used only to verify that the cookie that was generated by the server is the same cookie that is returned by the client at the end of the association process. The server now creates a packet with an INIT-ACK chunk containing the verification tag created by the client, the new verification tag from the server, and the state cookie. When the client receives the INIT-ACK packet, it

Table 14.6 SCTP chunk types.

Type	Use
DATA	data
PADDING	padding
INITIATION	setup
INITIATION_ACK	setup
COOKIE_ECHO	setup
COOKIE_ACK	setup
OPERATION_ERROR	error indication
SELECTIVE_ACK	partial data acknowledgment
HEARTBEAT_REQUEST	connection maintenance
HEARTBEAT_ACK	connection maintenance
ECN_ECHO	congestion notification
ECN_CWR	congestion notification
ABORT	teardown
SHUTDOWN	teardown
SHUTDOWN_ACK	teardown
SHUTDOWN_COMPLETE	teardown

immediately creates a packet with a COOKIE-ECHO chunk and transmits the cookie back to the server. When the server receives the COOKIE-ECHO chunk from the client, it validates the state cookie and if the signature and data are correct and the cookie has arrived within the requisite timeout, the association is instantiated. The final step in association setup is for the server to send a packet with a COOKIE-ACK chunk back to the client. Once the client has received the packet containing the COOKIE-ACK chunk, the association is complete. To ameliorate the overhead involved in setting up an association with a four-way handshake, SCTP can transmit data in the packets that contain the COOKIE-ECHO and COOKIE-ACK chunks, thereby reducing the time between association initiation and the initial data transfer. Any host that attempts to flood another host on the network with INIT packets, similar to a SYN flood, does not cause the kernel to set up or maintain any state as no state is required until the COOKIE-ECHO is received. At the point in the handshake at which the COOKIE-ECHO has been received, the kernel has confirmed the legitimacy of the connection by decoding a packet that it cryptographically signed with its own key.

Data Transfer

Once an association has been set up between two endpoints, SCTP can start transferring data. All data transferred with SCTP are part of a distinct *stream* within the association. Each stream has a unique stream identifier. Two different sequence numbers are tracked by SCTP while transferring data. The stream sequence number tracks where data are in a particular stream and ensures the correct ordering of messages within a stream. The transmission sequence number (TSN) tracks chunks for the whole association, and is responsible for guaranteeing reliable delivery of chunks. Mechanisms such as selective acknowledgment are applied to the entire association using the TSN to track chunks and to ensure that any missing chunks are eventually retransmitted and delivered.

When an application is using SCTP as a sequenced-packet transport, the program receiving the data checks for the MSG_EOR flag to be set in the *struct msghdr* returned by the *recvmsg* routine. To provide a message-oriented service, SCTP has several functions that work together to take an arbitrary-size message and ensure that either it all arrives at the other end of the association or that an error is returned to the caller of *sendto*.

A program using TCP to send distinct records between two endpoints needs to introduce a marker into the stream of data to identify record boundaries. Even with these record markers, it is impossible to force TCP to transmit data as records because TCP does not identify the application-level boundaries. Programs using SCTP do not need to introduce record boundaries because the basic unit of data transfer is the *data chunk*. As shown in Figure 14.11, a data chunk is the abstraction used by SCTP to encapsulate application data for transmission on the network. All chunks in SCTP have a common header that includes a type, a set of flags, and a length. The length field is 16 bits. Hence, the maximum amount of data that can be described by a chunk is 64 Kbyte. The length-field's value must include the size of the header and any user data making the effective maximum size of a

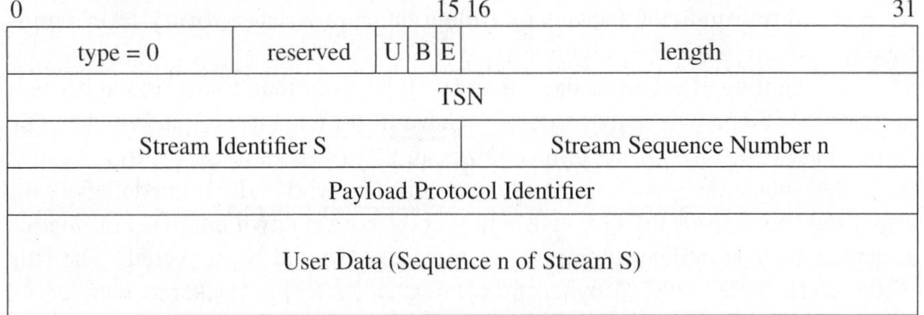

Figure 14.11 SCTP data chunk. TSN–transmission sequence number.

single chunk 64 Kbyte minus 16 bytes or 65520 bytes. Messages built from chunks can be much larger than 64 Kbyte because SCTP uses the TSN to keep all the chunks in sequence. On FreeBSD systems with the default socket buffer size, the effective size of a message passed to a single *send* call is limited to 225 Kbyte. With larger socket buffers, a single message could span several megabytes.

When a program calls the *sendto* system call on a socket opened with SOCK_SEQPACKET, the data eventually arrive in the *sctp_sosend*() routine as a *uio* structure. After a small amount of processing to extract any control data, the *uio* structure is passed to *sctp_lower_sosend*() where the real work of transmitting SCTP data begins. Data in SCTP is placed on one or more associations that are stored in the *sctp_inpcb* structure, the network-layer protocol control block for SCTP. One feature of SCTP is the ability to send a chunk of data on all the associations that are currently active for a socket. The code that handles one-to-many style of communication adds considerable complexity to the system and is not described here.

Sending data to a new unconnected address is considered an implicit send and requires the protocol to set up a new association, holding the data chunk until association setup is complete. After the the correct association is found, the data are queued for transmission by a call to *sctp_chunk_output*(). The data passed into the kernel are converted into a chunk structure by the *sctp_move_to_outputqueue*() routine. Each association has its own send-queue structure on which chunks are placed before they are transmitted. Chunks are kept in one of two queues, either the *send_queue* or the *sent_queue* queue, until they are properly acknowledged by the system receiving the data. With the chunks now correctly placed on the *send_queue*, a call is made to *sctp_med_chunk_output*() that checks to see if it is possible to send any data for the association. Like TCP, SCTP must maintain a good understanding of network conditions including any possible congestion. The *sctp_med_chunk_output*() routine is responsible for checking the congestion window before deciding whether any data may be output. If there is enough remaining space in the congestion window to send a packet, then *sctp_med_chunk_output*() creates an mbuf chain to be output by *sctp_lowlevel_chunk_output*(). It is *sctp_lowlevel_chunk_output*() that places proper IP or IPv6 headers onto the packets and transmits the packets by calling the appropriate network-layer output routine, *ip6_output*() or *ip_output*().

The handling of received packets in SCTP is easier than transmission because most of the interesting features of SCTP have to do with where packets are sent. When a network-layer protocol recognizes an SCTP packet, *sctp_input*() is called with the *mbuf* that was received from the network. It immediately calls *sctp_input_with_port*() whose task is to tear the packet down into a set of internal structures for use in determining where the packet should be delivered. The bulk of the work done by SCTP when processing an incoming packet is handled by *sctp_common_input_processing*(). This routine handles input from all the lower-layer network sources. Data chunks are handled by the code in the *sctp_process_data*() routine. Each chunk is checked to make sure that it is within the expected receive window and is then reassembled and added to a read queue by a call to the *sctp_add_to_reqdq*() routine. Once the data are on the read queue, it is the application's responsibility to retrieve it through a system call such as *recvfrom*. A call to *recvfrom* on a SEQPACKET socket will call into the *sctp_soreceive*() routine and then into the *sctp_sorecvmsg*() routine, which is the final destination of all routines that read data from an SCTP socket. If there is no data to be read when *sctp_sorecvmsg*() is called, it will block in the *sbwait* state until data arrives or the socket is closed. With data available on the read queue, the *sctp_sorecvmsg*() will copy the *mbufs* from the read queue. As data are being received from the read queue, the *sctp_user_rcvd*() routine is called to calculate whether enough space has been freed in the receiving socket to warrant signalling the sender with an ACK that more data can now be sent. Once some amount of data has been read, the call to *sctp_sorecvmsg*() will return control to the caller of the *recvfrom* system call with the data and any ancillary or control information placed into the buffers passed in by the application.

Association Shutdown

Shutting down an association is a multistep process that can be started by either of the involved hosts. When an application directs that an association is to be shut down, the sender puts the association into the SHUTDOWN_PENDING state and sets the PCB so that no more data may be sent. The sending host then waits until all the previously sent data has been acknowledged. Once all the outstanding data has been acknowledged, the client sends a packet with a SHUTDOWN chunk to the server. The host receiving the packet with the SHUTDOWN will set a flag in its own PCB that is part of the association so that user-level programs can no longer send more data. It then checks to see if it has any outstanding data to send to the client. If there are outstanding data, the server will not continue the shutdown process until all the remaining data have been acknowledged. Once all the previously sent data have been acknowledged by the client, the server will send a packet with a SHUTDOWN-ACK packet. When the client receives the packet with the SHUTDOWN-ACK chunk, it will reply with a packet with a SHUTDOWN-COMPLETE chunk. When done, the association has been shut down.

Multihoming and Heartbeats

A goal of SCTP is to provide applications with a high-availability communication channel over the Internet. Unlike a TCP connection, an SCTP association can have multiple network addresses. Should an address become unreachable because of a network partition or other failure, the association can choose to use another address to try to reach the endpoint.

Figure 14.12 shows an example of a multihomed host. A multihomed system is one that has two or more interfaces on two or more networks. Each path through the network between the two systems should be unique to provide complete protection against the loss of a single path. In the public Internet, hosts do not have control over the path that their packets traverse and so the protection from multi-homing an association is probabilistic. A corporate network, where an administrator knows the full paths of all the underlying network links has a higher probability of being able to use multi-homing effectively. Two multihomed hosts that shared the same network would be no better than two hosts each with a single interface sharing the same network. Any disruption in the shared path would break the association and the two hosts would be disconnected.

User-level code communicating over SCTP indicates to the kernel that it will use a set of addresses by calling the *sctp_bindx*() or *sctp_connectx*() (wrappers on the *bind* and *connect* system calls respectively) depending on whether the program is receiving or initiating the connection.

When a stream of data is traversing an association, problems such as network partitions are immediately obvious because the flow of acknowledgment from the other end of the association cease. An association that contains several network addresses needs a way to ensure that all of the addresses that make up the association are still reachable. SCTP maintains reachability information for every network address that is a part of an association by sending periodic heartbeat requests to any address that is part of an association but which is not the active participant in current communication. When SCTP is communicating to a foreign host, there is one primary address and one or more addresses that can be used if the primary fails. When there is no data flowing across an association, heartbeat requests are sent to all the addresses to ensure that they are all reachable. A host that receives

Figure 14.12 Multihomed hosts.

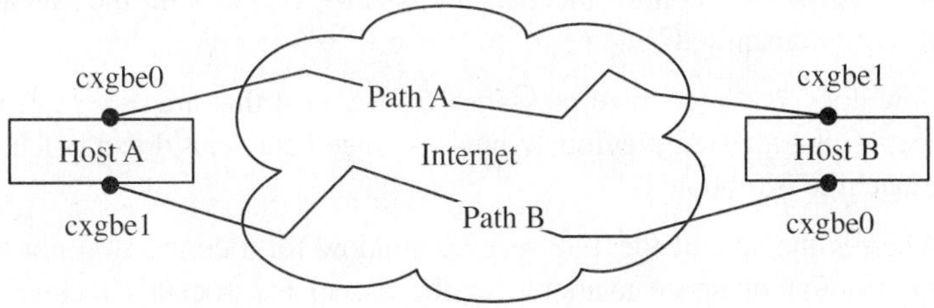

a heartbeat request immediately sends back a heartbeat response. When a host receives a heartbeat response for a previously transmitted request, the kernel updates the state of the association and then sets a timeout using the *callout* subsystem so that another heartbeat request will be sent at the next timeout interval in the future. The default timeout interval is 30 seconds plus the estimated retransmission timeout between the source and destination addresses, with a small amount of jitter added so that heartbeat packets do not become closely synchronized with each other.

The initial heartbeat timeout is set when the protocol control block is created in the *sctp_inpcb_alloc*() routine. All the timers in SCTP are handled by a centralized routine, *sctp_timer_handler*(), that calls various helper routines depending on the type of the timer that has expired. When the heartbeat timer expires, a call to *sctp_heartbeat_timer*() figures out whether a heartbeat acknowledgment has been received. If a heartbeat acknowledgment has been received, then the timer is simply re-armed and another heartbeat request is sent. When a heartbeat acknowledgment has not been received, then the address is considered to be partially failed. The kernel will continue to contact a partially failed address up to five times before that address is removed from use.

Heartbeat requests are handled directly during packet input by a call to *sctp_send_heartbeat_ack*() that immediately packs up and sends a heartbeat acknowledgment back to the sender of the request. No other processing is required on reception of a heartbeat request.

Exercises

14.1 What might cause a connection to linger forever when closing?

14.2 Is TCP a transport-, network-, or link-layer protocol?

14.3 Why are TCP and UDP protocol control blocks kept on separate lists?

14.4 Why does the output routine, rather than the socket-layer send routine (*sosend*()), check the destination address of an outgoing packet to see whether the destination address is a broadcast address?

14.5 Why does the TCP header include a header-length field even though it is always encapsulated in an IP packet that contains the length of the TCP message?

14.6 What is the flow-control mechanism used by TCP to limit the rate at which data are transmitted?

14.7 How does TCP recognize messages from a host that are directed to a connection that existed previously but has since been shut down (such as after a machine is rebooted)?

14.8 When is the size of the TCP receive window for a connection not equal to the amount of space available in the associated socket's receive buffer? Why are these values not equal at that time?

14.9 What are keepalive messages? For what does TCP use them? Why are keepalive messages implemented in the kernel rather than, say, in each application that wants this facility?

14.10 Why is calculating a smoothed round-trip time important, rather than, for example, just averaging calculated round-trip times?

14.11 Why does TCP delay acknowledgments for received data? What is the maximum time that TCP will delay an acknowledgment?

14.12 Explain what the silly-window syndrome is. Give an example in which its avoidance is important to good protocol performance. Explain how the FreeBSD TCP avoids this problem.

14.13 What is meant by "small-packet avoidance?" Why is small-packet avoidance bad for clients (e.g., the X Window System) that exhibit one-way data flow and that require low latency for good interactive performance?

14.14 Name two features that are in SCTP but are not in TCP.

14.15 What is an SCTP association?

14.16 How does the four-way handshake in SCTP defend against denial of service attacks?

*14.17 Why is the initial sequence number for a TCP connection selected at random, rather than being, say, always set to zero?

*14.18 In the TCP protocol, why do the SYN and FIN flags occupy space in the sequence-number space?

*14.19 Describe a typical TCP packet exchange during connection setup. Assume that an active client initiated the connection to a passive server. How would this scenario change if the server tried simultaneously to initiate a connection to the client?

*14.20 Sketch the TCP state transitions that would take place if a server process accepted a connection and then immediately closed that connection before receiving any data. How would this scenario be altered if FreeBSD TCP supported a mechanism where a server could refuse a connection request before the system completed the connection?

*14.21 How does UDP match the completely specified destination addresses of incoming messages to sockets with incomplete local and remote destination addresses?

*14.22 The maximum segment lifetime (MSL) is the maximum time that a message may exist in a network—that is, the maximum time that a message may be in transit on some hardware medium or queued in a gateway. What does TCP do to ensure that TCP messages have a limited MSL? What does IP do to enforce a limited MSL? See Fletcher & Watson [1978] for another approach to this issue.

*14.23 Why does TCP use the timestamp option in addition to the sequence number in detecting old duplicate packets? Under what circumstances is this detection most desirable?

**14.24 Describe a protocol for calculating a bound on the maximum segment lifetime of messages in an Internet environment. How might TCP use a bound on the MSL (see exercise 14.22) for a message to minimize the overhead associated with shutting down a TCP connection?

**14.25 Describe path MTU discovery. When the MTU of a path has suddenly increased, can FreeBSD take advantage it? Why or why not?

References

Allman et al., 2002.
M. Allman, S. Floyd, & C. Partdrige, "Increasing TCP's Initial Window," RFC 3390, available from http://www.faqs.org/rfcs/rfc3390.html, October 2002.

Allman et al., 2009.
M. Allman, V. Paxson, & E. Blanton, "TCP Congestion Control," RFC 5681, September 2009.

Bellovin, 1996.
S. Bellovin, "Defending Against Sequence Number Attacks," RFC 1948, available from http://www.faqs.org/rfcs/rfc1948.html, May 1996.

Brakmo & Peterson, 1995.
L. Brakmo & L. Peterson, "TCP Vegas: End to end congestion avoidance on a global Internet," *IEEE Journal on Selected Areas in Communications*, vol. 13, no. 8, pp. 1465–1480, August 1995.

Budzisz et al., 2009.
L. Budzisz, R. Stanojevic, R. Shorten, & F. Baker, "A strategy for fair coexistence of loss and delay-based congestion control algorithms," *IEEE Comm Lett*, vol. 13, no. 7, pp. 555–557, July 2009.

Cerf & Kahn, 1974.
V. Cerf & R. Kahn, "A Protocol for Packet Network Intercommunication," *IEEE Trans. on Communications*, vol. 22, no. 5, pp. 637–648, May 1974.

Clark, 1982.
D. D. Clark, "Window and Acknowledgment Strategy in TCP," RFC 813, available from http://www.faqs.org/rfcs/rfc813.html, July 1982.

Fletcher & Watson, 1978.
J. Fletcher & R. Watson, "Mechanisms for a Reliable Timer-Based Protocol," in *Computer Networks* 2, pp. 271–290, North-Holland, Amsterdam, The Netherlands, 1978.

Ha et al., 2008.
S. Ha, I. Rhee, & L. Xu, "CUBIC: A new TCP-friendly high-speed TCP variant," *ACM SIGOPS Operating Systems Review*, vol. 42, no. 5, pp. 64–74, July 2008.

Henderson et al., 2012.
T. Henderson, S. Floyd, A. Gurtov, & Y. Nishida, "The NewReno Modification to TCP's Fast Recovery Algorithm," RFC 6582, available from http://www.faqs.org/rfcs/rfc6582.html, April 2012.

Jacobson, 1988.
V. Jacobson, "Congestion Avoidance and Control," *Proceedings of the ACM SIGCOMM Conference*, pp. 314–329, August 1988.

Jacobson et al., 1992.
V. Jacobson, R. Braden, & D. Borman, "TCP Extensions for High Performance," RFC 1323, available from http://www.faqs.org/rfcs/rfc1323.html, May 1992.

Krawczyk et al., 1997.
H. Krawczyk, M. Bellare, & R. Canetti, "HMAC: Keyed-Hashing for Message Authentication," RFC 2104, available from http://www.faqs.org/rfcs/rfc2104.html, February 1997.

Leith et al., 2005.
D. Leith, R. Shorten, & Y. Lee, "H-TCP: A framework for congestion control in high-speed and long-distance networks," *PFLDnet Workshop*, February 2005.

Mathis et al., 1996.
M. Mathis, J. Mahdavi, S. Floyd, & A. Romanow, "TCP Selective Acknowledgment Options," RFC 2018, available from http://www.faqs.org/rfcs/rfc2018.html, October 1996.

Mogul & Deering, 1990.
J. Mogul & S. Deering, "Path MTU Discovery," RFC 1191, available from http://www.faqs.org/rfcs/rfc1191.html, November 1990.

Nagle, 1984.
J. Nagle, "Congestion Control in IP/TCP Internetworks," RFC 896, available from http://www.faqs.org/rfcs/rfc896.html, January 1984.

Postel, 1980.
J. Postel, "User Datagram Protocol," RFC 768, available from http://www.faqs.org/rfcs/rfc768.html, August 1980.

Postel, 1981.
J. Postel, "Transmission Control Protocol," RFC 793, available from http://www.faqs.org/rfcs/rfc793.html, September 1981.

Scheifler & Gettys, 1986.
R. W. Scheifler & J. Gettys, "The X Window System," *ACM Transactions on Graphics*, vol. 5, no. 2, pp. 79–109, April 1986.

Stewart & Xie, 2002.
Stewart, R & Xie, Q, *Stream Control Transmission Protocol (SCTP): A Reference Guide,* Addison-Wesley Longman, Reading, MA, 2002.

Stewart et al., 2000.
Stewart, R, Xie, Q, Morneault, K, Sharp, C, Schwarzbauer, H, Taylor, T, Rytina, I et al., M, "Stream Control Transmission Protocol," RFC 2960, available from http://www.faqs.org/rfcs/rfc2960.html, October 2000.

Stewart & Healy, 2007.

L. Stewart & J. Healy, *Light-weight modular TCP congestion control for FreeBSD 7,* available from http://caia.swin.edu.au/reports/071218A/CAIA-TR-071218A.pdf, December 2007.

Stewart et al., 2011.

R. Stewart, M. Tuexen, K. Poon, P. Lei, & V. Yasevich, "Sockets API Extensions for the Stream Control Transmission Protocol (SCTP)," RFC 6458, available from http://www.faqs.org/rfcs/rfc6458.html, December 2011.

Watson, 1989.

R. W. Watson, "The Delta-t transport protocol: features and experience," *Proceedings of the 14th Conference on Local Computer Networks*, pp. 399–407, October 1989.

Xerox, 1981.

Xerox, "An Internetwork Architecture," XSIS 028112, Xerox Corporation, Stamford, CT, December 1981.

PART V

System Operation

CHAPTER 15

System Startup and Shutdown

Most of this book focuses on the FreeBSD kernel's steady state: the invariants maintained during operation and the kernel services provided to local processes or, for network services, to remote systems. In this chapter, we describe how the kernel is bootstrapped and shut down. The details of the boot process vary significantly by hardware type and anticipated deployment but share a common structure involving the system firmware, its basic input-output system (BIOS), a variable number of stages of FreeBSD-provided boot loaders, the kernel boot, and finally userspace.

System operation begins, and often ends, with vendor-provided firmware that abstracts away low-level variations in the hardware environment. The firmware also provides information on processor, memory, bus, and peripheral device configuration to the kernel, and may provide power-management services. The interfaces to system firmware differ substantially across platforms, vendors, and deployment environments: workstations and servers have different operational models than embedded devices, all of which must be taken into account by the FreeBSD kernel. Higher-end systems often have firmware support for remote management features and network booting, over which FreeBSD layers multiple stages of scripted boot loaders, the kernel, and optionally loaded kernel modules. By contrast, embedded and small personal devices tend to have more constrained boot processes in which a simple firmware copies a statically linked kernel out of flash to main memory and then jumps to its starting address to begin execution. In lower-end environments, FreeBSD may boot from a read-only filesystem image in flash and run a single specialized application.

Kernel boot and shutdown are complex processes that depart from normal execution paths and hence require careful attention to detail. A key concern during boot is the set of dependencies between components: filesystems cannot be mounted until storage devices have been enumerated. In turn, storage device drivers depend on initialization of lower-level features such as scheduling and virtual memory. Historically, system shutdown has required somewhat less finesse: freeing each allocated piece of memory is unnecessary as the contents of memory will be lost on powerdown or reinitialized on reboot. The introduction of virtual network stacks has, however, forced increasing numbers of subsystems to provide explicit and carefully designed destructors. Dependencies remain important: user processes must be safely shut down before filesystems can be unmounted, which in turn depends on draining I/O queues to storage devices before power is turned off. The kernel defines linker-based frameworks to manage these complex dependencies: the frameworks allow components to register functions for ordered execution during the boot and shutdown processes. The frameworks also allow code to have a common structure independent of whether the code is linked into the kernel itself or loaded via a module at boot or run time.

This chapter traces the boot process starting with the firmware and boot loaders, then the kernel startup, and finally the startup and shutdown of userspace. The final section examines topics that are related to the startup procedure. These topics include configuring the kernel load image, shutting down a running system, and debugging system failures.

15.1 Firmware and BIOSes

The boot process begins with the initial hardware reset as power is turned on, but can also be triggered following a system-administrator-requested reboot, or a system crash and reset. Processors begin execution in vendor-provided firmware stored in ROM or memory-mapped flash referred to as the BIOS. The firmware performs several functions, depending on the device and vendor, including:

- Initializing low-level hardware features such as CPU caches, programmable interrupt controllers, bridges, and memory controllers.
- Running a set of boot-time diagnostics, checking CPU and memory functionality, and issuing warnings if the system may not be able to operate in production. The firmware may maintain a log of past failures—for example, a list of ECC-memory error recoveries.
- Providing pre-boot administrative services to configure RAID, remote management, and boot-device choice.
- Coordinating multiprocessor startup; a boot processor will be nominated, and other processors put in a suspended state awaiting operating-system initialization.
- Performing boot-time hardware discovery to identify and initialize devices from which an operating system may be loaded; for example, the firmware will enumerate locally attached media such as USB devices, CD-ROMs, and hard disks suitable for local booting, and it will identify Ethernet devices suitable for network booting.
- Loading and updating manufacture-time hardware descriptions based on the firmware's knowledge of the processor, chipset, and peripherals on the

integrated device. This information will be exported to the boot loader and operating system via a scheme such as the advanced configuration and power interface (ACPI) on X86 systems or Flattened Device Trees (FDT) on many embedded systems.

- Continuing, optionally, to provide run-time services via a system management mode on the main processor or an embedded management processor, even as the operating system runs. These run-time services may include features such as power management and remote-console access (e.g., serial-over-LAN).
- Providing both I/O services and device-enumeration services to support the bootstrap of standalone programs.
- Loading and executing code from the selected boot device.

After a variety of boot-time diagnostics, handling any administrative requests, and selecting a target boot device, the BIOS's next responsibility is to start bootstrapping the operating system by loading and executing the initial code. It also provides continuing early I/O and system-configuration services for the nascent operating-system loader and kernel. Firmware such as the PC BIOS, U-Boot, and Open Firmware will provide operating-system-like disk and network I/O routines until the kernel's device drivers are in operation, as well as descriptions of hardware devices that cannot be automatically enumerated, such as PCI root bridges.

In the past, PC firmware has rarely understood the filesystems of the operating systems that they must load; instead, the startup procedure read a program from a reserved area of the boot disk. The recent Unified Extensible Firmware Interface (UEFI) standard requires that new BIOSes support the FAT filesystem as an origin for later boot stages, a feature long supported in embedded and server firmware such as U-Boot and Open Firmware [Forum, 2013]. UEFI also brings security features such as cryptographically verified boot loading to X86, which will see increasing support in forthcoming FreeBSD versions.

15.2 Boot Loaders

The role of the operating-system boot-loader sequence is similar to that of the firmware: bootstrap the higher-level operating system using a restricted set of lower-level facilities. It also facilitates security, management functions, and failure recovery. Multiple stages are often used as each successive stage is able to have a larger code footprint and can rely on services and accumulated configuration state provided by the previous stage.

The first-stage boot loader on a conventional X86 system is limited to a single 512-byte sector, which is insufficient space for code that can interpret filesystems. Hence, the first-stage boot loader's only job is to determine a boot-partition and load a larger and more comprehensive boot phase from a specified sector. Later boot phases are more complete execution environments that include filesystem and networking support, allow preloading of cryptographic keys, can be scripted in a high-level language, and support an interactive menu to allow recovery from a failed upgrade.

Embedded systems trade off boot-loader size and complexity, depending on the capabilities of the physical platform and maturity of the integrated firmware. At one extreme, boot loaders from operating-system vendors are entirely avoided for reasons of space; at the other, the complete X86-like boot sequence, including scriptable loader, will be present and will offer greater flexibility.

Master Boot Record and Globally Unique Identifier Partition Table

When the X86 BIOS has selected a disk device for booting, the BIOS loads the first sector into memory at a fixed location and executes it. On most disk devices, this first sector will contain a master boot record (MBR). The 512-byte sector, illustrated in Figure 15.1, contains a fragment of boot code, disk layout information, a four-entry partition table, and a magic number (signature) that will be checked to confirm a valid boot sector is present. To continue the boot, the BIOS jumps into the operating system's boot code once it has been loaded into RAM. FreeBSD supports two different partitioning schemes on X86: *mbr*, the default prior to FreeBSD 9.0, implements the *fdisk* partitioning scheme from MS-DOS; and *pmbr*, the default in FreeBSD 9.0 and later, implements the more recent globally unique identifier partition table (GPT) scheme, which supports greater numbers of partitions and larger disk sizes.

GPT is a multisector successor to MBR that provides an additional header in sector 1, described by the *gpt_hdr* structure, and further sectors containing a variable-length table of partition entries, described by *gpt_ent* structures. FreeBSD 9.0 and later use GPT via the *pmbr* boot loader written to the first sector by the installer, although these versions continue to support optional use of **fdisk**

Figure 15.1 X86 boot-time-partition data structures: master boot record (MBR) and globally unique identifier partition table (GPT).

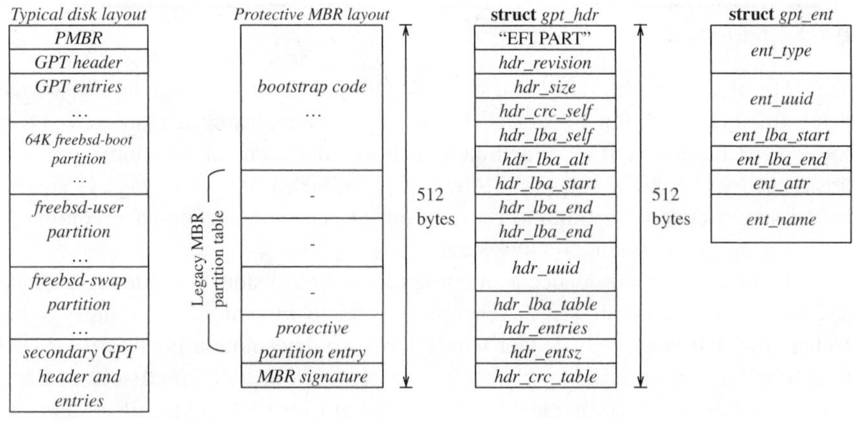

partitions if required for compatibility. When GPT is used, the boot sector contains a special variant of the MBR called a protective MBR (PMBR). The PMBR describes a single partition of the GPT type, causing *pmbr* to load the GPT and scan it for a *freebsd-boot* partition (typically sized at 64 Kbyte). If found, *pmbr* will load the first 545 Kbyte of that partition into memory, which will contain **gptboot**, the next-stage boot loader. The final action for *pmbr* is to jump into the loaded code.

The Second-Stage Boot Loader: gptboot

The second-stage boot loader, **gptboot**, can be a substantially larger multisector program as it is loaded from a partition and is not limited by the space constraints of the PMBR. This additional space allows for significantly more functionality, including support for loading configuration data and later boot code from filesystems rather than simply disk sectors. The **gptboot** boot loader has several tasks:

1. Transition to protected mode so that the boot loader can access more than the 1 Mbyte available to the 16-bit X86 MBR execution environment. This transition is done by the i386 boot extender (BTX) library against which **gptboot** is linked. BTX is a protected-mode monitor that executes the majority of the boot loader with access to a larger virtual address space, but is still able to forward requests to the BIOS by temporarily switching back to 16-bit real mode.
2. Accept a set of boot flags, which may be entered interactively on a video or serial console, or loaded from the configuration file **/boot.config**. The flags will be passed to the next boot stage via an instance of the *bootinfo* structure. Boot flags select features such as single-user mode, verbose logging, or immediate entry to the kernel debugger on start.
3. Load and start the ELF-formatted next-stage boot loader **/boot/loader** or a kernel from a filesystem in a GPT partition type of freebsd-ufs using read-only UFS support. A variation of **gptboot** named **gptzfsboot** will likewise search for a ZFS filesystem stored in a GPT partition of type freebsd-zfs; for RAIDZ, multiple partitions may be used.

The Final-Stage Boot Loader: /boot/loader

The final-stage loader, **/boot/loader**, is a scriptable, interactive boot environment that can:

- Prompt the user for input via a boot menu or command line;
- Offer a choice of kernels to load;
- Inspect and modify kernel environment variables that will be passed to the next phase of the boot;
- Preload kernel modules; and

• Preload filesystem data such as GELI keys or memory-disk images.

The **/boot/loader**'s menu-driven user interface is implemented via scripts executed by a built-in Forth interpreter, **libficl**, making more complex boot-time customization straightforward. The interpreter has access to a broad set of system APIs provided by **libstand**, a bare-metal system library. The **libstand** library implements POSIX-like APIs used by **libficl**, as well as filesystem access to UFS,

Table 15.1 **/boot/loader** user commands on X86.

Command	Description
?	list commands
autoboot	boot automatically after a delay
bcachestat	get disk-block cache stats
boot	boot a file or loaded kernel
boot-conf	load kernel and modules, then autoboot
echo	echo arguments
disable-module	disable loading of a module
enable-module	enable loading of a module
heap	show heap usage
help	detailed help
include	read commands from a file
load	load a kernel or module
load_geli	load a geli key
ls	list files
lsdev	list all devices
lsmod	list loaded modules
more	show contents of a file
pnpscan	scan for plug-and-play (PnP) devices
read	read input from the terminal
read-conf	read a configuration file
reboot	reboot the system
set	set a variable
show	show variable(s)
show-module	show module load data
smap	show BIOS SMAP
toggle-module	toggle loading of a module
try-include	try to load/interpret files
unload	unload all modules
unset	unset a variable

struct *bootinfo*

BOOTINFO_VERSION	*bi_esymtab*
bi_kernelname	*bi_kernend*
bi_nfs_diskless	*bi_modulep*
bi_n_bios_used	*bi_memdesc_version*
bi_bios_geom[]	*bi_memdesc_size*
bi_size	*bi_memmap*
bi_memsizes_valid	*bi_memmap_size*
bi_bios_dev	*bi_hcdp*
bi_basemem	*bi_fpswa*
bi_extmem	*bi_systab*
bi_symtab	

Figure 15.2 The *bootinfo* structure passed by the boot-loader to the kernel.

ZFS, CD9660, and NFS. As with **gptboot**, **/boot/loader** is linked against BTX, and so has access to BIOS services while running in protected mode.

When the loader starts, it will execute the script **/boot/loader.4th**, which will then load **/boot/kernel/kernel** and any modules enabled in **/boot/loader.conf**. The loader then presents a boot menu and begins a countdown that can be interrupted by the user. If requested by the user, the loader will drop to a command-line interpreter on the console and await input; a list of commands is shown in Table 15.1. The most commonly used commands are the "unload" command, to remove the default kernel, followed by the "load" command, to load an alternative kernel. Typically, the alternative kernel being loaded is **/boot/kernel.old/kernel**, saved by the kernel build system when installing a new kernel, in case the new kernel proves to be faulty.

The kernel is started by issuing the "boot" command, either by the user or because the countdown has reached 0. The details of the boot command are machine dependent, but for systems without a hardware-provided mapping of physical addresses into the virtual-address space, may include setting up initial memory mappings for physical memory.

As with **gptboot**, **/boot/loader** expects the next-stage binary to be an ELF file, and will pass a *bootinfo* structure pointer as an argument to the kernel, illustrated in Figure 15.2. As with **/boot/loader** before it, **gptboot** will pass on boot flags such as that for single-user mode. Unlike **gptboot**, it will also pass kernel-environment variables set during the boot, preloaded module data, memory-size information, memory-filesystem images, and ACPI table references, which will be used early in kernel boot by the virtual memory system and kernel linker.

Boot Loading on Embedded Platforms

Whereas X86 workstations and servers are resource-rich platforms intended to be maximally flexible in terms of deployment environments and workloads, embedded systems are often resource-poor environments tuned to reduce cost, size, and energy use to the minimum required for their specific function. The firmware, boot loader, and operating system may all be tuned for small size or reduced functionality, and hence vary significantly in terms of the software features present.

Very low-end devices such as network switches may have a small firmware that directly loads and begins execution of the FreeBSD kernel without any further boot-loader stages. Where the operating-system boot loaders are present, they may be stripped of features to reduce their size, compared to similar code on server-class platforms. This is the case for the ARM version of FreeBSD's **boot2**, a predecessor to **gptboot**; in contrast, the MIPS port of **boot2** is a full adaptation of the feature-rich X86 code.

Higher-end embedded devices may provide sufficiently mature and scriptable loader environments, such as U-Boot, with the result that the flexibility gained from **/boot/loader** offers little additional benefit. Other devices use both U-Boot and **ubldr**, a version of **/boot/loader** customized to run over U-Boot's firmware services. Some MIPS targets also use the **/boot/loader**. On systems where FreeBSD provides a boot loader but firmware is unable to provide I/O abstractions, the boot loader may need to incorporate device drivers [Davis et al., 2014]. Embedded environments also benefit from industry-wide reduction in size and energy use in integrated circuits, and so are becoming more capable over time. Multistage, feature-rich boot loaders will likely see increasing deployment to facilitate security, customizability, field upgrade, and recovery.

15.3 Kernel Boot

After the firmware or boot loader has started the FreeBSD kernel, the kernel must initialize both the hardware and its own data structures in preparation for the execution of application programs. The initialization process is divided into four stages. In the first stage, handcrafted assembly-language code will set up the hardware to allow more generic C-language code to operate. The second stage continues machine-dependent initialization of hardware and core data structures, but in the C language. After this stage's completion, memory size will be known, virtual addressing will be enabled, and features such as *printf*() and the kernel debugger will be available. The third stage initializes a broader set of basic kernel services such as virtual memory, scheduling, and synchronization. The fourth stage initializes higher-level services such as filesystems and the network stack, starts kernel processes, and creates the first user-level process to execute the **init** binary and user-level startup scripts.

The FreeBSD kernel attempts to rely on only limited aspects of machine state. At the point of handoff from the boot loader, the following three conditions will be in effect:

1. All interrupts are blocked.

2. The memory management unit is configured so that a range of virtual addresses corresponds directly to physical memory locations; for some

architectures, this mapping requires specific configuration actions such as the boot loader setting up suitable page tables and flushing the TLB; for others, a hardware-supported, physically mapped region provides this mapping automatically in kernel mode (e.g., MIPS).

3. The in-memory location of any firmware-provided configuration state, such as memory configuration via the X86 ACPI or FDT tables, has been identified and passed to the kernel via *bootinfo*.

The boot loader passes to the kernel the identity of the boot device, boot flags, and an initialized kernel environment consisting of name and value pairs. In addition, it will pass on information about preloaded modules including loadable kernel modules, memory images, and keying material for cryptographically protected storage.

The kernel is loaded into physical memory at a known location—for many architectures this location will be at a low physical address just above the location of interrupt-vector tables or handlers. In normal operation, the kernel image is mapped into virtual memory at an address near the top of the address space. For platforms without directly mapped regions, the kernel image may initially appear at the bottom of the virtual address space. Until the kernel is mapped to its permanent location, it requires assembly-language startup code to manually convert between its initial temporary mapping and its eventual permanent mapping. The kernel is usually loaded into contiguous physical memory, so the translation is simply a constant offset that can be saved in an index register.

An early task of the startup code is to identify the type of CPU on which the system is executing. Often, older versions of the CPU support only a subset of the complete instruction set. For these machines, the kernel must ***emulate*** the missing hardware instructions in software. For workstation and server architectures, FreeBSD can be configured such that a single kernel load image can support all the models in an architecture family. For embedded systems, it is common to have a kernel configuration tuned for each board or device, either because of space and performance limitations, or because of a lack of common conventions for an instruction set, hardware configuration, and boot-loader behavior. The early startup code may also call machine-dependent code to initialize the CPU or virtual-memory subsystem.

Assembly-Language Startup

The first steps taken during initialization are carried out by assembly-language code in **locore.S**. The goal of this code is to create a run-time environment that meets the expectations of the C code that is to follow, primarily by providing a conformant stack frame (sometimes on a fresh stack), and by initializing the register file to the C ABI that will be used by the kernel. It may also initialize low-level processor features that affect memory management and addressing, so that C code executes in a uniform and easily understood environment. Assembly code is minimized in favor of C to the greatest extent possible. The work of **locore.S** is highly machine dependent and includes the following:

- Identifying the CPU and its features
- Placing the processor into a known state; for example, by clearing the error flags on X86 and clearing or setting coprocessor-enable bits on MIPS
- Creating an initial stack or stack frame for the early boot
- Clearing the bss area (pre-zeroed C-language global variables)
- Probing the physical-memory size
- Enabling virtual addressing
- Invoking platform-specific C-language startup code
- Handing over control to machine-independent C-language startup code

In ports to more recent architectures, **locore.S** has become increasingly minimal: whereas the 32-bit X86 code is several hundred lines of assembly, the 64-bit version is less than 20. The size reduction reflects not only simplifications made by AMD in the 64-bit ISA design, but also initialization functions shifting to the boot loader or platform-specific C-language startup code.

Platform-Specific C-Language Startup

Two C-language functions are called by **locore.S**: one for platform-specific initialization and a second to proceed with the machine-independent boot (which will not return). The split allows the machine-independent boot sequence to be done in a well-defined environment. The name of the platform-specific initialization function varies by architecture; for 64-bit X86, it is *hammer_time*; for embedded architectures such as ARM and MIPS, it is typically *platform_start*. Platform-specific initialization will include most of the following steps:

- Further characterization of the CPU and configuration of its features, including caches, memory-management unit, and floating-point unit
- Initialize and enable memory-management hardware, such as virtual-address translation or caching for a hardware-supported directly mapped regions
- Set up interrupt, trap, exception vectors or handlers, and on architectures that require it, segment registers and system calls
- Process data passed from the boot loader such as the kernel environment and preloaded modules
- Tune kernel parameters—especially resource limits such as address-space and process limits—based on environment variables and compile-time defaults
- Interpret firmware-provided data such as FDT hardware descriptions
- Calculate the amount of physical memory on the machine if the architecture does not provide this information reliably via the firmware

- Set up the first kernel process and thread
- Initialize static and dynamic per-CPU storage for the boot processor
- Set up tables for multiprocessor or multithreaded operation, if necessary
- Initialize the kernel message buffer and console (enabling kernel *printf*())
- Initialize global locks such as *Giant* and the machine-dependent IPI lock
- Initialize the kernel debugger
- Invoke *pmap_bootstrap* to do early virtual-memory system initialization

Although the details of these steps vary from architecture to architecture, the broad outline described here is applicable to any machine on which FreeBSD runs.

Modular Kernel Design

The kernel is a multimillion-line C program that runs on 'bare metal,' and hence must provide its own run-time linker, memory allocator, threading model, synchronization primitives, work models, and debugging tools. Higher-level kernel services such as device drivers, filesystems, and network protocols depend on these lower-level primitives, providing facilities to one another and to user processes via the system-call interface. To manage this complexity, most kernel components are encapsulated in kernel modules that consume core-kernel primitives, register services they offer via common frameworks (such as the device-driver framework), and specify boot-order dependencies so that the kernel can ensure that any requirements are met before any code is executed.

Modules can be compiled into the kernel binary itself, or as ***loadable kernel modules*** compiled into separate ELF binaries that can be preloaded by the boot loader or loaded dynamically. Loadable modules make it possible to extend the kernel at run time as new requirements become apparent, adding significant flexibility. For example, device drivers can be loaded when a new peripheral is plugged into a USB hub, and firewall command-line tools can automatically load their corresponding kernel modules. In practice, many parts of the FreeBSD kernel source can be compiled either into the kernel or into loadable modules without source-code modification, depending on the kernel configuration used.

A key design goal in the kernel is to avoid differentiating between modules that are linked into the kernel and modules that are loaded dynamically. The same kernel programming interfaces (KPIs) declare startup and stop functions, register with kernel frameworks, and so on. This approach provides modularity without inhibiting practical deployment.

Module Initialization

In earlier versions of BSD, the kernel was brought up using handcrafted C code that implicitly (and often correctly) encoded the dependencies of each subsystem by virtue of the order in which subsystem initialization routines were invoked. An intimate understanding of the entire operating system was needed for someone to add a new service or subsystem, which slowed the evolution of the kernel and made it more difficult to customize the kernel for incorporation into larger integrated products. A significant part of the extensibility benefit of kernel modules rests on the core kernel being unaware of the specifics of modules until they are loaded. The SYSINIT framework allows modules, whether compiled into the kernel, preloaded by the boot loader, or loaded at run time, to declare a common set of ordered startup and shutdown functions. Modules register startup functions via the static SYSINIT macro, and stop functions via SYSUNINIT:

```
SYSINIT(name, subsystem, order, function, identifier)

SYSUNINIT(name, subsystem, order, function, identifier)
```

Module startup and stop functions are organized into a two-level hierarchy that determines the order in which the function should be called during boot, module load, module unload, and system shutdown. The *subsystem* argument is the first level of the hierarchy. Each subsystem is assigned a particular numeric constant that creates the first-level ordering of the modules to be loaded; an ordered list of subsystem identifiers is in the **/sys/sys/kernel.h** include file. The second level of the hierarchy is handled by the *order* argument. If two modules are in the same subsystem, the *order* determines which comes first.

The *function* argument is a pointer to the function that the kernel will invoke, and the *identifier* argument is passed to the invoked function as its sole parameter. The identifier is often a pointer to a data structure; this parameter allows a single function to be reused in multiple contexts. For example, the function *kproc_start*() is used with several SYSINITs to start kernel processes with varying names and is used for multiple subsystems.

The SYSINIT framework is implemented using linker sets: each use of one of its macros creates a static data structure describing the specific startup or stop function and its properties. The structure is tagged with a request that the compiler place its symbol in a special named section in the ELF binary indicating whether it is to be run at startup or stop. After the assembly-language startup code has completed its work, it calls the machine-independent kernel start, *mi_startup*(). The kernel binary is scanned for symbols in the startup section, whose target data structures are sorted and their function pointers called. This process will be repeated later in the boot when preloaded kernel modules are run-time linked, as modules are dynamically loaded and unloaded, and on system shutdown, using the corresponding named section.

A similar technique allows modules to declare startup and stop functions to be run each time a virtual network stack is instantiated or destroyed. Macros VNET_SYSINIT and VNET_SYSUNINIT take identical arguments, but use different ELF sections, allowing modules to easily perform per-network-stack setup and teardown.

Basic Kernel Services

Before higher-level services such as device drivers and filesystems can do any useful work, FreeBSD must set up its basic kernel services, including virtual memory, the general-purpose memory allocator, and the kernel linker. These services are shown in Table 15.2 in the order in which they are done. All these services are initialized early in the machine-independent startup sequence so that they can be used by the remainder of the kernel.

SI_SUB_TUNABLES retrieves configuration values from the boot-time kernel environment and installs them in global variables. Tunables are processed early in the boot as they override compile-time defaults. Some may be adjusted at run time via *sysctl*, such as resource limits on the number of TCP connections. Others commit the kernel to difficult-to-change resource allocation choices, such as the size of the kernel address space, and so can be set only at boot time.

Table 15.2 Basic kernel services.

Subsystem	Function
SI_SUB_TUNABLES	tune subsystem parameters from loader tunables
SI_SUB_VM	early virtual memory initialization
SI_SUB_KMEM	kernel *malloc*() initialization and dependent events
SI_SUB_HYPERVISOR	Xen HVM hypervisor detection
SI_SUB_WITNESS	configure witness lock-debugging facility
SI_SUB_MTX_POOL_DYNAMIC	initialize dynamically allocated mutex pools
SI_SUB_LOCK	initialize statically declared or allocated locks
SI_SUB_EVENTHANDLER	register statically declared event handlers
SI_SUB_VNET_PRELINK	early virtual-networking initialization
SI_SUB_KLD	initialize kernel linker and module setup
SI_SUB_CPU	initialize CPU0 properties and services (e.g., timers)
SI_SUB_RACCT	initialize kernel-resource accounting
SI_SUB_RANDOM	initialize noncryptographic random-number generator
SI_SUB_KDTRACE	initialize kernel-profiling and tracing frameworks
SI_SUB_MAC	initialize MAC framework
SI_SUB_MAC_POLICY	register MAC-policy modules
SI_SUB_MAC_LATE	end registration of static MAC-policy modules
SI_SUB_VNET	initialize virtual network-stack framework
SI_SUB_VM_CONF	complete *malloc*() initialization; tune VM limits
SI_SUB_DDB_SERVICES	initialize kernel-debugger output capture
SI_SUB_RUN_QUEUE	initialize scheduler
SI_SUB_KTRACE	initialize kernel-trace facility (ktrace)

SI_SUB_VM and SI_SUB_KMEM initialize the virtual-memory system and general-purpose kernel memory allocator. The virtual-memory system is initialized by a call to *vm_mem_init*(). Once the *vm_mem_init*() routine has completed its work, all memory allocations by the kernel or processes are for virtual addresses that are translated by the memory-management hardware into physical addresses. The kernel's *malloc*(), wrapped around the slab allocator for small allocations, and the virtual-memory system directly for larger allocations, is initialized by a call to *mallocinit*(). These subsystems are described in greater detail in Section 6.3.

SI_SUB_HYPERVISOR detects whether FreeBSD is running under Xen HVM, and if so, sets up paravirtualized features such as Xen hypercall stubs and Xen-aware virtual-memory operations, and disables emulated devices in favor of paravirtualized ones. Xen support is discussed in greater detail in Section 8.10.

SI_SUB_WITNESS initializes the optionally compiled witness deadlock-prevention facility described in Section 4.3. Witness tracks nested lock acquisitions, building a lock-order graph that will provide debugging information to the developer if the possibility of deadlock arises. The *witness_initialize*() routine allocates memory to hold lock-acquisition data used for deadlock detection, and also installs any statically declared graph edges.

SI_SUB_MTX_POOL_DYNAMIC initializes the system's pool of mutexes described in Section 4.3. Mutexes are generally allocated as global variables or embedded within data structures allocated from the heap, keeping locks close to the data they protect. The pool of mutexes is an array of mutexes looked up by hashing the pointer of an object that will return a deterministically selected leaf lock for the object. The pool of mutexes is allocated early in the boot so that it can be used by higher-level kernel subsystems.

SI_SUB_LOCK indicates the point in the boot at which it is safe for kernel modules to allocate and initialize locks; it is used both directly by module functions registered with SYSINIT, and indirectly through static-wrapper macros such as MTX_SYSINIT, RM_SYSINIT, RW_SYSINIT, and SX_SYSINIT, which as arguments will take a pointer to a global lock, its flags, and its description. Lock initialization occurs after SI_SUB_WITNESS in the boot so that storage is available to track new lock classes from inception. Initialization must also occur before any potential use of the locks in other subsystem code paths.

SI_SUB_EVENTHANDLER initializes the ***event-handler*** system, which allows the kernel and its modules to register functions to be called when events of interest occur elsewhere in the kernel. Event handlers are used to expose events such as network-interface arrival, departure, and address changes, routing changes, the creation and destruction of processes, execution of binaries, the creation and destruction of threads, system-shutdown stages, the filesystem mount and unmount events, power events, kernel-module load and unload, watchdog timeouts, and low-memory conditions. Event handlers may be declared statically using the EVENTHANDLER_REGISTER macro, which uses SYSINIT to initialize the event handler early in boot before any of the events it describes can occur.

SI_SUB_VNET_PRELINK, used only for *vnet_init_prelink*(), performs early initialization of virtual network-stack support and runs before most kernel modules have executed any code.

SI_SUB_KLD is complex as it calls many kernel functions associated with modules, linkage, and memory allocation:

1. In the first phase, the kernel prepares for the linking and initialization of kernel modules. The module registry is initialized by *module_init*() and will maintain administrative information on modules such as their reference counts and descriptions suitable for export to userspace. The kernel-linker framework is initialized, preparing lists and other data structures that will track preloaded and dynamically loaded modules. Two special memory allocators are also initialized before module events that will allocate memory: the dynamic per-CPU allocator by *dpcpu_startup*(), and the virtual-network stack allocator by *vnet_data_startup*(). The allocators have similar structures, providing frameworks for scoped global-memory allocation.

2. Next, individual linker classes will be initialized—in practice, they will consist of the ELF-specific linker code, found in *link_elf_init*(), on all systems.

3. In the next phase, the ELF linker code will search the list of modules preloaded by the boot loader for ELF kernel modules, process the symbols for each, and register them with the kernel linker for later processing and initialization.

4. In the final stage, the registration of new linker classes is halted by *linker_stop_class_add*(), and then modules linked into the kernel and those preloaded by the boot loader will be registered and initialized by *linker_init_kernel_modules*() and *linker_preload*(). This registration and initialization must sort the modules so that dependencies are taken into account when invoking the module constructors. Loadable kernel module SYSINITs with subsystems prior to SI_SUB_KLD will have those startup functions invoked only after module linking and registration have taken place. Modules are able to register optional command-line extensions to the kernel debugger, such as data-structure pretty printers. These extensions are also processed in this phase.

SI_SUB_CPU is responsible for initializing several CPU-related services, including time-counter synchronization that is required to implement kernel callouts. It is also responsible for starting execution of additional processors in multiprocessor configurations. Starting additional processors requires a blend of machine-dependent and machine-independent code performed as a series of phases:

1. The first phase is done by a set of machine-dependent *cpu_startup*() functions. Kernel virtual-memory configuration is completed by calling *vm_ksubmit_init*(), which allocates virtual address space for paging and I/O, swap, and transition *bio* storage. In general, kernel memory is not pageable,

but two pageable submaps are initialized to hold arguments to *execve* and for *pipe* storage. The buffer cache will be initialized by *bufinit*(), including data structures, current and running resource limits, and reserved memory to use in low-memory situations. Swap buffers are set up by *vm_pager_bufferinit*(). Certain machine-dependent initialization will also be done. On 64-bit X86, for example, the timestamp counter (TSC) is calibrated with wall-clock time and registered as a source of timer ticks, CPU and hyperthread information is printed, and additional CPU registers associated with floating point will also be configured. The X86 local APIC will be initialized, which allows interrupts to be configured and routed to—and between—multiple CPUs in a multiprocessor system.

2. In the second phase, the machine-independent *mp_start*() function will start additional processors using machine-dependent start functions. On many architectures, starting additional processors requires some additional interrupt configuration (e.g., setting up interrupt vectors to receive ***interprocessor interrupts*** (***IPI***s) and then sending an IPI to each additional CPU to begin execution). On other architectures, such as SPARC64, the firmware may instead provide interfaces to start the additional CPUs. After the additional CPUs are started, information about them will be printed on the console by *cpu_mp_announce*().

3. In the final phase, *callout_callwheel_init*() will configure the callout wheel for the boot CPU, making it possible to register callouts without specific CPU affinity (timers are described in Section 3.4). Additional per-CPU callout wheels will be initialized later in the boot.

Several other machine-dependent CPU-related initialization functions will also run in this phase of the boot, setting up access to the PC BIOS, allocating space for coprocessor-2 contexts for certain MIPS processors, and setting up virtual-CPU state for Xen.

SI_SUB_RACCT is responsible for initializing the kernel's resource-accounting system, used to limit and balance CPU, memory, IPC, and other resource utilization by competing processes, users, login classes, and jails. Two routines are run in this subsystem: *racct_init*(), which creates a new kernel-memory zone for accounting state, and configures *prison0*'s accounting state; and *rctl_init*(), which sets up kernel-memory zones for resource-accounting policy.

SI_SUB_RANDOM is responsible for initializing the kernel's noncryptographic pseudo-random number generator from the timestamp counter via the routine *random_init*(). It also initializes random-number generation for kernel stack protection via *__stack_chk_init*().

SI_SUB_KDTRACE initializes software-trace functions relating to two frameworks: DTrace, described in Section 3.8, and processor hardware performance monitoring counters (HWPMC), which provide access to CPU performance-sampling functions. DTrace first registers with thread- and process-creation event handlers in *init_dtrace*(), which manage storage for each thread or process that might be used with DTrace. DTrace then initializes its per-CPU debugging output buffers in *dtrace_debug_init*(). HWPMC initializes storage for "soft" events in *init_hwpmc* (), to be triggered by software sources such as locking events, page faults, and clock ticks. It accepts registrations using the macro PMC_SOFT_DEFINE via *pmc_soft_ev_register*(), which likewise uses SYSINIT. Many later-configured modules implement DTrace events, or "probes," relying on the results of this phase.

SI_SUB_MAC, SI_SUB_MAC_POLICY, and SI_SUB_MAC_LATE initialize mandatory access control (MAC), described in Section 5.10. In the first phase, implemented in *mac_init*(), data structures, locks, and kernel-memory zones are initialized. In the second phase, policy modules that have declared themselves using the MAC_POLICY_SET macro will invoke *mac_policy_register*() to attach to entry points and optionally allocate label storage. In the final phase, *mac_init_late*() sets the *mac_late* flag, which indicates to the framework that policy modules loaded after this point must be registered as "dynamic" policies requiring full synchronization when entry points are invoked. Until this point, policies that register with flags that prevent unload can be added to a linked list that does not require locks to iterate over, avoiding overhead if all policies are "static." This initialization must be completed before any operations requiring MAC authorization, such as operations involved in mounting the root filesystem as well as creation of the first process, can proceed.

SI_SUB_VNET is implemented by *vnet0_init*(), which allocates the first virtual network stack and associates it with *prison0*. This network-stack instance will be used for all processes unless further stacks are explicitly configured by the system administrator.

SI_SUB_VM_CONF completes initialization of kernel-memory zones by calling *uma_startup3*(), which starts up a callout, *uma_timeout*(), to run every 20 seconds. The timeout walks the list of kernel-memory zones performing routine activities such as updating statistics and, as required, resizing hash tables. The timeout also performs machine-dependent functions such as tuning limits on X86 local descriptor table segments.

SI_SUB_DDB_SERVICES completes initialization of the DDB in-kernel debugger by setting up its capture buffer in *db_capture_sysinit*(). The capture facility logs text output from debugger scripts to a crash partition to create textdumps, a more compact alternative to a full kernel-memory crash dump.

SI_SUB_RUN_QUEUE initializes the scheduler's run queues, CPU groups, and initial load calculations, at boot. Both the ULE and 4BSD schedulers are initialized by routines named *sched_setup*(). The system scheduler is described in greater detail in Section 4.4.

Finally, SI_SUB_KTRACE initializes the userspace kernel-trace facility, **ktrace**, by calling *ktrace_init*(), which must initialize locks and data structures, but also pre-allocate a set of trace-entry structures. These trace-entry structures will log kernel events such as system calls, data copied in and out of the user address space, signal delivery, and context switches as requested by user processes. This initialization must occur before any user process requests enabling of tracing. Section 3.8 describes **ktrace** in greater detail.

From this point onward, the bulk of basic kernel services required to support the launching of kernel threads, device-driver discovery, and the remainder of the high-level boot are now present.

Kernel-Thread Initialization

Kernel-module code enters execution in several ways—most frequently by direct function invocation from another subsystem. For example, code might be invoked as a system-call implementation by the system-call trap-handling code in user threads, as an interrupt handler in an interrupt thread, as a task function in a task thread, or as a timeout function from a per-CPU callout thread. In other cases, subsystems will start kernel threads to embody portions of their activities.

Sometimes, subsystems will create threads to provide asynchronous execution opportunities for other modules. For example, the interrupt-thread framework calls device-driver interrupt handlers in interrupt threads when it receives hardware interrupts for the corresponding device. In other cases, kernel modules create threads to allow the modules to defer blocking filesystem I/O to an asynchronous context. For example, the virtual-memory and security-audit subsystems create threads to perform disk I/O asynchronously from the process that triggered the I/O. A few threads are intrinsic to system functionality, such as idle threads required by the scheduler, as well as the first user process from which all later user processes will descend. Threads may be created on demand, as happens for iSCSI worker

Table 15.3 Kernel threads and processes started by default on X86.

Module	First Routine
SI_SUB_INTRINSIC	*proc0_init*()
SI_SUB_AUDIT	*audit_worker*()
SI_SUB_CREATE_INIT	*create_init*()
SI_SUB_SCHED_IDLE	*idle_setup*()
SI_SUB_DRIVERS	*g_event_procbody*()
SI_SUB_DRIVERS	*g_up_procbody*()
SI_SUB_DRIVERS	*g_down_procbody*()
SI_SUB_DRIVERS	*random_kthread*()
SI_SUB_KTHREAD_PAGE	*vm_pageout*()
SI_SUB_KTHREAD_VM	*vm_daemon*()
SI_SUB_KTHREAD_BUF	*buf_daemon*()
SI_SUB_KTHREAD_UPDATE	*vnlru_proc*()
SI_SUB_KTHREAD_UPDATE	*sched_sync*()
SI_SUB_KTHREAD_UPDATE	*softdep_flush*()
SI_SUB_KTHREAD_INIT	*kick_init*()

threads, which are instantiated when new sessions are configured; others are created unconditionally in boot, such as the GEOM worker threads that process upward and downward I/O requests. The modules that start kernel threads or processes during the boot are shown in Table 15.3.

SI_SUB_INTRINSIC begins the creation of the process hierarchy by executing *p0init*(). The function creates *process0*, the first process, *pgrp0*, its process group, and *thread0*, the first thread within that process. The first process is named *kernel* and its first thread is named *swapper*. Then, *p0init*() calls *pmap_pinit0*() to initialize the process's virtual-memory space and memory map. For all later processes, the kernel-memory zone allocator will automatically invoke thread- and process-creation event handlers; however, since *process0* and *thread0* are statically allocated, *p0init*() must invoke them manually. The function also charges the root user for the resources associated with this first process.

SI_SUB_AUDIT creates a kernel process and thread to support the kernel's audit subsystem, described in Section 5.11. The separate thread allows the audit process to write records to the filesystem asynchronously from the process that performed the event. The *audit_init*() function initializes the audit subsystem and then creates *audit_worker* by calling *audit_worker_init*(). The thread executes a loop that alternately awaits further events to write to the audit trail or blocks on filesystem I/O while writing records to the disk. The thread will also detect low-space conditions, which will be signalled to userspace by means of a special-device node.

SI_SUB_CREATE_INIT is responsible for forking the first userspace process, **init**. This process will execute **/sbin/init** and implement the userspace boot. The *create_init*() function uses the kernel-internal *fork1*() function to create the new process; subsystems such as MAC and audit then customize **init**'s process credential with properties that will be inherited by all other user processes. The final action of *create_init*() is to call *cpu_set_fork_handler*() to set the function that the newly created kernel thread will call to *start_init*(). The **init** process will not immediately run, as it has not yet been placed in a runnable state.

SI_SUB_SCHED_IDLE creates an idle process containing a set of per-CPU idle threads. Idle threads provide a default thread context that can always run, at the idle priority, on each CPU. This context ensures that interrupts delivered to an idle CPU always have a thread suitable to preempt and, therefore, a stack to borrow.

SI_SUB_INTR, SI_SUB_SOFTINTR, and SI_SUB_DRIVERS create a variety of kernel processes and threads in service of device drivers, including interrupt threads and GEOM's *up*, *down*, and *event* threads created by *g_init*(). Device drivers may create further threads; for example, the *random* device described in Section 5.12 creates a thread that intermittently extracts entropy harvested around the system from queues and feeds it into Yarrow. Interrupt threads serve not only devices fielding hardware interrupts, but also soft-interrupt handlers such as the callout thread and network-stack *netisr* threads.

Four subsystems initialize threads supporting virtual memory, the buffer cache, and filesystems: SI_SUB_KTHREAD_PAGE, SI_SUB_KTHREAD_VM, SI_SUB_KTHREAD_BUF, and SI_SUB_KTHREAD_UPDATE. These subsystems incorporate functions that run asynchronously from user threads, such as write-behind flushes of the buffer cache to disk, managing the vnode LRU cache, and paging activity. They also perform tasks that must occur at differing priorities. The virtual-memory subsystem and its threads are discussed in detail in Chapter 6.

SI_SUB_KTHREAD_INIT completes creation of the **init** process by calling *kick_init*(), which schedules **init**'s kernel thread. When the thread starts, it will execute *start_init*(), which performs a series of activities to bring up the filesystem and userspace environment. First, **init** calls *vfs_mountroot*() to await completion of any device initialization that may be required to mount the root filesystem. Kernel modules such as the device-driver framework, GEOM RAID storage classes, and ZFS can request that the boot process be suspended to allow device probes to continue, and higher-level storage constructs to be discovered, before the root filesystem is mounted. Each component will invoke *root_hold_token*(), which returns a reference that must later be released using *root_mount_rel*(). Once devices have settled, the kernel must now identify and mount a suitable root filesystem by means of the following four steps:

1. First, kernel environmental variables such as *vfs.root.mountfrom* and *vfs_root.mountfrom.options* are inspected to determine how root filesystem mounting should proceed. This inspection may update the *rootdevnames* array whose entries will be tried in the search for a viable mount.
2. Next, *vfs_mountroot_devfs*() mounts a *devfs* instance as the initial root filesystem. Because it requires no source device, *devfs* can be mounted before **/dev** is available. Once *devfs* is mounted, then disk-based filesystems can use the same model for root filesystems as they do for later filesystems, reducing special casing in the root mount path.
3. In the next phase, *vfs_mountroot_devfs*() will parse each device name, look up a suitable filesystem in the kernel's filesystem-module list, and attempt to mount it by calling *kernel_mount*().
4. In the final phase, *vfs_mountroot_shuffle*() will rearrange the two mounted filesystems so that the newly mounted root is available as **/**, and the earlier *devfs* mount can be found under its **/dev**.

If a failure occurs, then the next possible filesystem root will be tried. Once the root filesystem is mounted, *prison0* is updated, and the *mountroot* event handler is called to notify other kernel modules that the filesystem is now available. Creation of the userspace process is completed by *start_init*() searching for a suitable **init** binary, copying out boot-flag arguments, and issuing *execve* to load the binary. Execution will begin when the thread returns to userspace returning from *execve*.

Device-Module Initialization

With all the kernel's basic services in place, and the basic processes created, it is now possible to initialize the rest of the devices in the system including the disks, network interfaces, and clocks. Table 15.4 shows the main components used to initialize the device modules.

Table 15.4 Device modules.

Module	First Routine
SI_SUB_MBUF	*mbuf_init*()
SI_SUB_INTR	*intr_init*()
SI_SUB_SOFTINTR	*start_softintr*(), *start_netisr*()
SI_SUB_DEVFS	*devfs_init*(), *devs_set_ready*()
SI_SUB_INIT_IF	*if_init*()
SI_SUB_DRIVERS	many different routines
SI_SUB_CONFIGURE	*configure_first*()
SI_SUB_VFS	*vfsinit*()
SI_SUB_CLOCKS	*initclocks*()

Before any devices can be initialized—in particular, network interfaces—the mbuf subsystem must be set up so that the network interfaces have a set of buffers they can use for their own initialization. The mbuf subsystem initialization is handled by the SI_SUB_MBUF module and its *mbuf_init*() routine (mbufs are described in Section 12.3).

At this point in the startup sequence, hardware interrupts are not enabled on the system. The kernel now sets up all the interrupt threads that will handle interrupts when the system begins to run. The interrupts are setup by two modules: SI_SUB_INTR, which sets up the interrupt threads that handle device interrupts, and SI_SUB_SOFTINTR, which creates soft-interrupt threads. Soft-interrupt threads are used by services that handle asynchronous events that are not generated by hardware. Soft-interrupt threads provide the soft clock, which supports the *callout* subsystem. They also provide the network thread that dequeues inbound packets from the network-interface queues and moves them through the network stack.

As part of bringing up real hardware devices, the kernel first initializes the device filesystem and then readies the network stack to handle devices with a call to the *if_init*() routine. The *if_init*() routine does not initialize any network interfaces; it only sets up the data structures that will support them. Finally, the devices themselves are initialized by the SI_SUB_DRIVERS and SI_SUB_CONFIGURE modules. All devices in the system are initialized by autoconfiguration as described in Section 8.9.

Once the devices are configured, the virtual filesystem (VFS) is initialized. Bringing up the VFS is a multistage process that entails initializing the VFS itself, the vnode subsystem, and the name cache and pathname-translation subsystem that maps pathnames to vnodes.

The next systems to be set up are those relating to the real-time clock provided by the hardware. The *initclocks*() routine, which is a part of the SI_SUB_CLOCKS module, calls the architecture's specific *cpu_initclocks*() routine to initialize the hardware clock on the system and start it running. Once the hardware clock is running, other services such as support for the Network Time Protocol (NTP), *device polling*, and the *time counter* are started.

Loadable Kernel Modules

Some kernel modules can be loaded and started or shut down and unloaded while the system is running. Providing a system where kernel services can be loaded and unloaded at run time has several advantages over a system where all kernel services must be linked in at build time. For systems programmers, being able to load and unload modules at run time means that they are able to develop their code more quickly. Only those modules absolutely necessary to the system, such as the memory manager and scheduler, need to be directly linked into the kernel. A kernel module can be compiled, loaded, debugged, unloaded, modified, compiled, and loaded again without having to link it directly into the kernel or having to reboot the system. When a system is placed in the field, the use of kernel modules makes it possible to upgrade only selected parts of the system, as necessary. Upgrading in the field is absolutely necessary in embedded applications where the system may be physically unreachable, but it is also convenient in more traditional environments where many systems might have to change at the same time—for instance, in a large server farm.

Loadable kernel modules are declared in the following way:

```
DECLARE_MODULE(name, moduledata, subsystem, order)
```

Each module has a *name*, *subsystem*, and *order* that serve the same purposes here as they do in the SYSINIT macro. The key difference is the use of the *moduledata* argument, which is a data structure that is defined in the following way:

```
int (*modeventhand_t)(
        struct module *module,
        int command,
        void *argument);

typedef moduledata  = {
        const char *name;
        modeventhand_t event_handler;
        void *data;
} moduledata_t;
```

All modules have an associated version that is declared with the MODULE_VERSION macro. Without a version, it would be impossible to differentiate between different revisions of the same module, making field upgrades difficult. One last macro used by kernel modules is the SYSCALL_MODULE_HELPER that developers use to add new system calls to the kernel.

To have kernel modules that can be loaded both at boot time and at run time, two different cases must be handled. When a module is loaded at boot time, it has already been processed by the kernel's build process, which means that its system-call entry points and other data are already known to the kernel. This knowledge simplifies the loading process. All that needs to be done is to call the module's event handler with the MOD_LOAD command. At run time, the module needs to be loaded into memory, registered with the kernel, and its system calls dynamically added to the system-call table. Once all that work is done, it can be initialized by calling its event handler. All the run-time loading is handled by the *kldload* system call and the *module_register*() routine. To keep the interface that programmers use simple, all this functionality is hidden by the DECLARE_MODULE macro and the use of the single event-handler routine. When creating a kernel module, a programmer needs to be concerned only with writing the module event handler and exporting the module-handler's system calls via the macros.

A key consideration in the use of loadable kernel modules is that they are a double-edged sword with respect to security and reliability. On the one hand, loadable modules allow field upgrade of kernel components without binary patching, which can be used to correct stability defects discovered after a product is shipped. Loadable modules can likewise adapt the kernel's security model to protect against discovered vulnerabilities. On the other hand, the kernel is a critical part of the system's ***trusted computing base*** (***TCB***). Attackers that can load kernel modules can bypass the system's security policies, install subtle back doors, and mask their presence in the system by modifying the behavior of monitoring interfaces.

In practice, loadable modules have little concrete effect on the integrity of the TCB for several reasons. Integrity of the kernel depends on a secure boot process, which currently depends on correct configuration of userspace-managed protections in the filesystem. Further, userspace interfaces to system memory and I/O devices allow privileged users the ability to modify kernel memory even without an explicit loading interface. Jail and MAC policies such as Biba can be used to provide stronger integrity protection for the TCB, which includes controls on low-integrity manipulation of the kernel either by module loading or access to virtual and physical memory via **/dev** nodes.

As secure boot features such as UEFI's boot-chain signature-verification support become more widely deployed, the initial boot chain will become increasingly secure against attacks that might damage TCB integrity. A sensible future direction would be to extend these facilities into cryptographic protection of loadable kernel modules using digital signatures and other security-critical portions of the filesystem and userspace. These extensions will need to address not just kernel modules, but also configuration files and system maintenance tools. One key concern in the adoption of such techniques will be increased complexity and fragility: maintenance operations that previously required root access may now require management of cryptographic keys; similarly, administrators might be forced to choose between the performance or functionality benefits derived from kernel customization and boot-time integrity protection.

15.4 User-Level Initialization

With the start of the **init** process, the kernel is operating and functional, and userspace is in execution. There are several additional steps that must be taken before users can log in and network services are available. All these actions are driven by user-level programs that use the standard FreeBSD system-call interface that has been described in previous chapters. We shall briefly examine the steps that take place in a typical system.

/sbin/init

The **/sbin/init** program is invoked as process 1 in the final step of the kernel bootstrapping procedure. The parameters specified at the time FreeBSD was bootstrapped are passed to **init** in a machine-dependent fashion. The **init** program uses the values of these flags to determine whether it should bring up the system to single-user or to multiuser operation and whether it should check the consistency of its disks with the **fsck** program. In single-user operation, **init** forks a process that invokes the standard shell, **/bin/sh**. The standard input, output, and error descriptors of the process are directed to the system's console terminal, **/dev/console**. This shell then operates normally but with superuser privileges until it terminates.

In multiuser operation, **init** first spawns a shell to interpret the commands in the file **/etc/rc**, which is the root of a set of system startup scripts that do all the user-level initialization of the system. If the **/etc/rc** script completes successfully, **init** then forks a copy of itself for each terminal device that is marked for use in the file **/etc/ttys**. These copies of **init** invoke other system programs, such as **/usr/libexec/getty**, to manage the standard sign-on procedure. Process 1 always acts as the master coordinating process for system operation. It is responsible for spawning new processes as terminal sessions are terminated and for managing the shutdown of a running system.

System Startup Scripts

The **/etc/rc** file is mostly empty and simply serves to order and execute the various system startup scripts contained in the **/etc/rc.d** directory. It will also search for third-party startup scripts in **/usr/local/etc/rc.d**, where they may be installed by the FreeBSD ports system or package system. The **/etc/rc.conf**, **/etc/rc.conf.d**, and **/etc/defaults/rc.conf** files control which user-level services are started at boot time and some aspects of their configuration. Each of these files is loaded by the system startup scripts when they execute. The **/etc/defaults/rc.conf** file contains the default values for various shell variables that control whether a service is to be started. Administrators override the defaults by placing different values for the same shell variables into **/etc/rc.conf**. For example, to enable the use of the secure shell (**ssh**) at boot time, the following line would be placed into **/etc/rc.conf**:

```
sshd_enable="yes"
```

The heart of the rc script system is a program called **rcorder** that takes a set of shell scripts as input, works out their interdependencies, and then outputs an ordered list of names. Each startup script declares the modules that it requires as well as those it provides. The **rcorder** programs uses these REQUIRE and PROVIDE statements to determine the proper order in which to run the startup scripts.

One housekeeping task is to check the local filesystems after a system crash. If the system is not booted with the *fastboot* option, then the **/etc/rc.d/fsck** script carries out filesystem checks. In versions of BSD before FreeBSD, the filesystem checks were absolutely necessary and had to be carried out before any other work, but with the advent of soft updates and journaling in UFS (Sections 9.6 and 9.8) and ZFS (Chapter 10), that is required only if the system has shut down uncleanly (e.g., because of unexpected power loss). The program **/sbin/fsck** checks filesystem consistency and repairs damaged filesystems. Normally, **fsck** is invoked from the **/etc/rc.d/fsck** script to examine and repair each filesystem before it is mounted. When the system is initially booted, the root filesystem is mounted read-only. If the root filesystem requires repairs, FreeBSD does a variant of the *mount* system call that requests the kernel to reload all its root-filesystem data structures. Reloading ensures consistency between the data in the kernel memory and any data in the filesystem that were modified by **fsck**. Having the root filesystem mounted read-only ensures that the kernel will not have any modified data in memory that cannot be reloaded.

Following the filesystem checks, the filesystems are mounted, the root filesystem is updated to be writable, and any devices that are to be used for swapping and paging are enabled. Disk quotas are then checked and enabled, and the system starts the background processes that implement various system services. These processes include **/usr/sbin/cron**, the program that executes commands at periodic intervals; **/usr/sbin/accton**, the program that enables system accounting; **/usr/sbin/syslogd**, the system error-logging process; and **/usr/sbin/sshd**, which implements encrypted remote access to the shell. Each of these processes is started from its own startup script in **/etc/rc.d**.

/usr/libexec/getty

Historically, the **/usr/libexec/getty** program was spawned by **init** to open and initialize terminal lines—most frequently, serial terminals or modems. Today, the primary obligation of **getty** is to launch the **/usr/bin/login** sessions on the video or serial console (if any). It is sometimes used to launch X Display Manager (*xdm*) sessions to enable login via graphical user interfaces, although many systems will instead be configured to start the window system via **rc.d**. The **getty** program reads a login name and invokes the **/usr/bin/login** program to complete a login sequence.

/usr/bin/login

The **login** program is responsible for signing a user in to the system; it is usually invoked by **/usr/libexec/getty** with the name of the user who wishes to log in to the system. **Login** will then authenticate the user using the pluggable authentication modules (PAM) mechanism. PAM supports diverse authentication mechanisms including local passwords (stored in the **/etc/master.passwd** file), Kerberos distributed authentication, one-time password in everything (OPIE) one-time passwords, and a range of third-party modules supporting other distributed or hardware-token-based authentication schemes. If a secret is requested from the user—for example, a password—then **login** will disable terminal echoing. After successful authentication, **login** is responsible for performing a variety of accounting functions including adding entries to the system **lastlog** and **utmpx** files, as well as auditing the login via the audit facility described in Section 5.11.

The process credential, described in Section 5.3, must be configured to represent the user and group identifiers of the authenticated user, as well as audit properties, MAC labels, and resource limits. The **login** program must also change the current working directory to the user's home directory. The user's login name is stored in the session structure using the *setlogin* system call so that it can be obtained reliably via the *getlogin* system call by programs that want to know the login name associated with a given process. Finally, **login** uses *execve* to overlay itself with the user's shell.

The **login** program may also be invoked when a user enters the system through a network connection. For such connections, **getty** and **init** are bypassed; their functionality is subsumed by the daemon spawned when the network connection is established.

15.5 System Operation

In this section, we consider topics that are related to the system-startup procedure.

Kernel Configuration

The software that makes up a FreeBSD kernel is defined by a ***configuration file*** that is interpreted by the **/usr/sbin/config** program invoked as part of the kernel build process. The kernel build process has become considerably more complex in FreeBSD and is now controlled by a set of Makefile targets. To build a kernel, the administrator invokes **make** in the following way:

```
make buildkernel KERNCONF=<kernel_config_file>
```

The *buildkernel* argument is a Makefile target that tells **make** to build a kernel but not to install it. KERNCONF is a Makefile variable that is set to the name of the kernel configuration. Once a kernel has been properly built, it is installed by running **make** in the following way:

```
make installkernel KERNCONF=<kernel_config_file>
```

One reason for this new build process is the need to build and install the necessary kernel modules that were discussed in Section 15.3. The configuration file specifies the hardware and software components that should be supported by a kernel. The build process generates several output files, some of which are compiled and linked into the kernel's load image. It also creates a directory into which all the loadable kernel modules will be built. When the kernel is installed, its modules are installed as well. A complete description of the kernel build process is given in Hamby & Mock [2014].

System Shutdown and Autoreboot

FreeBSD provides several utility programs to halt, reboot, or power off a system, or to bring a system from multiuser to single-user operation. Safe halting, rebooting, and powering down of a system require support from the kernel. This support is provided by the *reboot* system call.

The *reboot* system call is a privileged call. A parameter specifies how the system should be shut down and rebooted. This parameter is a superset of the flags passed by the **boot** program to the system when the latter is initially bootstrapped. A system can be brought to a halt (typically by forcing it to execute an infinite loop), it can be rebooted to single-user or multiuser operation, or powered off, which causes the kernel to first halt the system and then (if supported by the architecture) request a poweroff. There are additional controls that can be used to force a crash dump before rebooting (see the next subsection for information about crash dumps) and to disable the writing to disk of data that are in the buffer cache if the information in the buffer cache is wrong.

Automatic rebooting is usually done when a catastrophic failure is recognized. The system will reboot itself automatically if it recognizes an unrecoverable failure during normal operation. Failures of this type, termed ***panics***, are all handled by the *panic*() subroutine.

When the system is shutting down, it goes through three separate phases:

- Shutdown of all services that depend on the filesystem to store data
- Shutdown of the filesystem itself
- Shutdown of services that do not depend on the filesystem

These three phases are necessary because some services will want to write some final data to the filesystem before it is turned off and may not be able to restart cleanly if they cannot do so.

Services register event handlers with the kernel to provide an orderly shutdown of the system. Each event handler is declared with the following macro:

```
EVENTHANDLER_REGISTER(name, function, argument, priority)
```

Table 15.5 lists the names of the shutdown phases. In the EVENTHANDLER_REGISTER macro, the *name* parameter identifies in which phase of the shutdown sequence the event handler's *function* will be called. The *argument* allows the module to pass itself any private data necessary for it to turn off. The

Table 15.5 Shutdown phases.

Name	Shutdown Phase
shutdown_pre_sync	before the disks are synced
shutdown_post_sync	after the disks are synced
shutdown_final	just before stopping the CPU

priority orders the shutdown routines within a phase. The *priority* serves the same purpose here as the *order* argument does in the SYSINIT macro in creating an orderly startup sequence. The *priority* is necessary to make sure that services do not go away while other services depend on them.

The kernel shutdown routine first walks the list of *shutdown_pre_sync* functions and calls each in turn, and then it shuts down the filesystems on the local disks. With the filesystems in a quiescent state, it invokes all the *shutdown_post_sync* functions. A kernel core dump is made if requested—for example, if it was called because of a kernel panic. Kernel core dumps are written directly to the swap partition and not to a normal filesystem, which is why this step can come after the filesystems have been shut down. Finally, the kernel shutdown routine invokes all the functions registered in the *shutdown_final* group. The machine then powers down if it has been directed to do so and the hardware supports software-based power-off. Otherwise, it goes into an infinite loop awaiting a reset by the user.

System Debugging

FreeBSD provides several facilities for debugging system failures. The most commonly used facility is the ***crash dump***: a copy of memory that is saved on secondary storage by the kernel when a catastrophic failure occurs. Crash dumps are created by the *doadump*() routine. They occur if a reboot system call is made in which the RB_DUMP flag is specified or if the system encounters an unrecoverable—and unexpected—error.

The *doadump*() saves the current context with a call to the *savectx*() routine and then invokes the *dumpsys*() routine to write the contents of physical memory to secondary storage. The precise location of a crash dump is configurable; most systems place the information in a primary swap partition. This operation is done by the dump entry point of the configured disk driver.

A crash dump is retrieved from its location on disk by the **/sbin/savecore** program after the system is rebooted and the filesystems have been checked. It creates a file into which the crash-dump image is copied. The system administrator can examine crash dumps with the standard FreeBSD debugging program, **kgdb**. The kernel is also set up so that a **kgdb** debugger running on one machine can attach itself across a serial line to a kernel running on another machine. Once attached, it can set breakpoints, examine and modify kernel data structures, and invoke kernel routines on the machine being debugged. This form of source-level debugging is particularly useful in developing kernel device drivers, as long as the driver being developed is not the serial-line driver itself.

Passage of Information To and From the Kernel

In 4.3BSD and earlier systems, utilities that needed to get information from the kernel would open the special device **/dev/kmem**, which gave access to the kernel's memory. Using the name list from the kernel binary, the utility would seek to the address of the desired symbol and read the value at that location. Utilities with superuser privilege could also use this technique to modify kernel variables. Although this approach worked, it had six problems:

1. Applications did not have a way to find the binary for the currently running kernel reliably. Using an incorrect binary would result in looking at the wrong location in **/dev/kmem**, resulting in wildly incorrect output. For programs that modified the kernel, using the wrong binary would usually result in crashing the system by trashing some unrelated data structure.

2. Reading and interpreting the kernel name list is time consuming. Thus, applications that had to read kernel data structures ran slowly.

3. Applications given access to the kernel memory could read the entire kernel memory. Malicious (or vulnerable) programs could snoop the terminal or network input queues looking for users who were typing sensitive information such as passwords.

4. It is desirable to provide unprivileged access to a subset of monitoring information: for example, to a user's own processes or sockets. This policy is not only difficult to enforce correctly in userspace, which does not have race-free access to kernel data structures such as the user credential, but it also violates the design goals laid out in Section 5.5 to centralize policy implementation as an aid to security extensibility. Controlling access to kernel-originated data is substantially easier within the kernel than it is when a userspace program is given access to all of kernel memory.

5. As more of the kernel data structures became dynamically allocated, it became difficult to extract the desired information reliably. For example, in 4.3BSD, the process structures were all contained in a single, statically allocated table that could be read in a single operation. In FreeBSD, process structures are allocated dynamically and are referenced through a linked list. Thus, they can be read out only one process entry at a time. Because a process entry is subdivided into many separate pieces, each of which resides in a different part of the kernel memory, every process entry takes several seeks and reads to extract through **/dev/kmem**.

6. With an increased focus on long-term binary compatibility, especially with not just individual userspace binaries but whole userspace installations running in a jail, userspace interpretation of internal kernel data structures proves

extremely fragile. A more explicit monitoring interface allows userspace monitoring tools to be more robust to internal kernel changes.

To resolve these problems, 4.4BSD introduced the *sysctl* system call. This extensible kernel interface allows controlled access to kernel data structures. The problems enumerated previously are resolved as follows:

1. Applications do not need to know which kernel binary they are running. The running kernel responds to their requests and knows where their data structures are stored. Thus, the correct data structure is always returned or modified.
2. No time is spent reading or interpreting name lists. Accessing kernel data structures takes only a few system calls.
3. Sensitive data structures cannot be accessed. The kernel controls the set of data structures that it will return. Nothing else in the kernel is accessible. The kernel can impose its own set of access restrictions on each set of data structures that it returns.
4. Kernel *sysctl* handlers are able to invoke security policies such as MAC and jails, allowing limits to be placed on monitoring processes, network connections, and so on. Each user process is limited to an appropriate view of the system.
5. The kernel can use its standard mechanisms for ensuring consistent access to distributed data structures. When requesting process entries, the kernel can acquire the appropriate locks to ensure that a coherent set of data can be returned.
6. The kernel is able to export well-defined and carefully managed versions of data structures to userspace; for example, rather than exporting the *proc* structure, which changes frequently as new kernel features are added, a separate *kinfo_proc* structure is exported from the kernel, which includes version information and padding to allow userspace to detect and adjust to changes. Userspace libraries such as **libprocstat** and **libmemstat** provide higher-level APIs used by monitoring applications such as **procstat** and **memstat**.

Additional benefits of the interface include the following:

- Values to be changed can be validated before the data structure is updated. If modification of the data structure requires exclusive access, an appropriate lock can be obtained before the update is done. Thus, an element can be added to a linked list without danger of another process traversing the list while the update is in progress.
- Information can be computed only on demand. Infrequently requested information can be computed only when it is requested, rather than being computed continually. For example, many of the virtual-memory statistics are computed only when a system-monitoring program requests them.

- The interface allows monitoring tools to run without the privilege to access kernel memory, removing them from the TCB; likewise, user processes can manipulate system settings subject to kernel policy without general write access to the kernel address space. This isolation from access to kernel memory is important for jails and virtual network stacks, in which guest superusers must be able to modify settings for their local environments, but not those of other jails or virtual stacks.

The *sysctl* system call describes the kernel namespace using a management information base (MIB). A MIB is a hierarchical namespace much like the filesystem namespace, except that each component is described with an integer value rather than with a string name. A hierarchical namespace has several benefits:

- New subtrees can be added without existing applications being affected.
- If the kernel omits support for a subsystem, the *sysctl* information for that part of the system can be omitted.
- Each kernel subsystem can define its own naming conventions. Thus, the network can be divided into protocol families. Each protocol family can be divided into protocol-specific information, and each protocol can describe its own state.
- The namespace can be divided into those parts that are machine independent and are available on every architecture, and those parts that are machine dependent and are defined on an architecture-by-architecture basis.

Since the addition of the *sysctl* system call in 4.4BSD, the number of variables it controls has been expanded to include about 3000 values that control the virtual memory system, filesystems, networking stacks, and the underlying hardware, as well as the kernel itself.

Exercises

15.1 What is the purpose of each stage in the boot-loader sequence?

15.2 What is the job of the assembly-language startup? Why is this program written in assembly language?

15.3 What processes are started when the system is booted?

15.4 How are kernel modules loaded into the system at boot time? Give an example of a kernel module.

15.5 The *reboot* system call causes the system to halt or reboot. Give two reasons why this system call is useful.

15.6 Give two reasons why loadable kernel modules are useful in developing kernel services. Give one reason not to use them.

15.7 Why is it necessary to have a particular order in which kernel services are loaded and initialized? Why is it also necessary to have a particular order in which kernel services are shut down?

*15.8 Suppose that a machine does not have a battery-backup time-of-day clock. Propose a method for determining that the time-of-day clock is incorrect. Describe a way to initialize the clock's time of day. What are the limitations of your method?

**15.9 What are the necessary macros to create a loadable kernel module? How would you test your module without linking it directly into the kernel?

References

Davis et al., 2014.
B. Davis, R. Norton, J. Woodruff, & R. Watson, "How FreeBSD Boots: a Soft-Core MIPS Perspective," *Proceedings of AsiaBSDCon 2014*, March 2014.

Forum, 2013.
Unified EFI Forum, Inc., *UEFI Specification Version 2.4,* available from http://www.uefi.org/specifications, July 2013.

Hamby & Mock, 2014.
J. Hamby & J. Mock, *FreeBSD Handbook, Chapter 9, Configuring the FreeBSD Kernel,* available from http://www.freebsd.org/doc/en_US.ISO8859-1/books/handbook/kernelconfig.html, March 2014.

Glossary

absolute pathname See *pathname*.

access control list (ACL) A form of discretionary access control that replaces the group permissions for a file with a more specific list of the users that are permitted to access the files. The ACL also includes a list of the permissions that each user is granted. These permissions include the traditional read, write, and execute permissions along with other properties such as the right to rename or delete the file. See also *discretionary access control; file permissions*.

ACL See *access control list*.

address family A collection of related address formats, as found in a single communication domain. For example, the IPv4 domain uses the Internet address family.

address-resolution protocol (ARP) A communication protocol used to map one network address to another dynamically. For example, ARP is used in FreeBSD to map Internet addresses into Ethernet addresses dynamically. See also *neighbor discovery*.

address translation A mechanism, typically implemented in hardware, that translates memory addresses supplied by a program into physical memory addresses. This facility is important in supporting multiprogramming because it allows an operating system to load programs into different areas of memory and yet have each program execute as though it were loaded at a single, fixed memory location. See also *memory-management unit*.

advisory lock A lock that is enforced only when a process explicitly requests its enforcement. An advisory lock is contrasted with a mandatory lock, which is always enforced. See also *mandatory lock*.

ambient authority Refers to the right to name objects via global namespaces such as the filesystem root or TCP/IP port namespace. Processes in Capsicum's capability mode are denied ambient authority, and hence are able to operate only on objects to which they have been delegated capabilities. See also *capability system; Capsicum; sandbox.*

ancillary data Specially interpreted data sent on a network connection. Ancillary data may include protocol-specific data, such as addressing or options.

anonymous object Represents a region of transient backing storage. Pages of an anonymous object are zero-filled on first reference and modified pages will be stored in the swap area if memory becomes tight. The object is destroyed when no references remain.

application compartmentalization Sometimes referred to as privilege separation, this technique decomposes applications into a set of sandboxed processes, each delegated narrow sets of rights necessary to perform their specific function. This technique, implemented using Capsicum in FreeBSD, helps to mitigate security vulnerabilities: successful attacks gain only limited rights in the system. See also *ambient authority; Capsicum; sandbox.*

ARP See *address-resolution protocol.*

association In the interprocess-communication facilities, a logical binding between two communication endpoints that must be established before communication can take place. Associations may be long lived, such as in stream-based communication, or short lived, such as in a datagram-based communication paradigm.

AST See *asynchronous system trap.*

asymmetric cryptography A cryptographic system that does not use the same key for decrypting data as it does for encrypting data; sometimes referred to as public-key cryptography. See also *symmetric cryptography.*

asynchronous An asynchronous thread usually has nothing to do with the currently running process. Examples are unrelated hardware interrupts.

asynchronous system trap (AST) A software-initiated interrupt to a service routine. ASTs enable a process to be notified of the occurrence of a specific event asynchronously with respect to its execution. In FreeBSD, ASTs are used to initiate thread rescheduling.

autoconfiguration The probing and identification of hardware attached to the system. Successfully identified hardware is attached to the I/O subsystem. Autoconfiguration is performed when the kernel bootstraps itself into operation and any time that a new piece of hardware is attached to the system. In a network protocol, the process by which a system discovers important information about itself and the network (such as its network address and default router) without any help from a user.

background process In job-control-oriented process-management systems, a process whose process group is different from that of its controlling terminal; thus, this process is currently blocked from most terminal access. Otherwise, a background process is one for which the command interpreter is not waiting—that is, the process was set running with the "&" operator. The opposite of a background process is a *foreground process*.

backing storage Storage that holds objects that are removed from main memory during paging and swapping operations. See also *secondary storage*.

black-hole route Used to temporarily block packets from moving through the network. A packet with a destination address that matches a black-hole route is dropped before it can be routed or forwarded.

block In the filesystem, a unit of allocation. The filesystem allocates space in block-size units or in fragments of block-size units.

block accounting The process of maintaining a count of the number of disk blocks available for the storage of new data in the fast filesystem.

block size The natural unit of space allocated to a file (filesystem block size) or the smallest unit of I/O that a character device can do (for disk devices, usually the sector size). In FreeBSD, the filesystem block size is a parameter of the filesystem that is fixed at the time that the filesystem is created.

bootstrapping The task of bringing a system up into an operational state. When a machine is first powered on, it is typically not running any program. Bootstrapping initializes the machine, loads a program from secondary storage into main memory, and sets that program running.

bottom half With regard to system operation, the collection of routines in the kernel that is invoked as a result of interrupts. These routines cannot depend on any per-process state. See also *top half*.

breakpoint fault A hardware trap that is generated when a process executes a breakpoint instruction.

broadcast A transmission to all parties. In a network, a broadcast message is transmitted to all stations attached to a common communication medium.

broadcast storm Occurs when a router is misconfigured such that it forwards all broadcast packets to its adjacent networks. A broadcast storm can be caused by a single broadcast packet being copied and transmitted multiple times throughout the network resulting in a waste of bandwidth and high levels of network congestion, degrading the overall quality of network services.

bss segment The portion of a program that is to be initialized to zero at the time the program is loaded into memory. The name *bss* is an abbreviation for "block started by symbol." See also *data segment; stack segment; text segment*.

buffer bloat A problem caused by overly large buffers present in many network routers. A network path with too much buffering can cause unnecessarily high packet delays, reducing overall network performance.

buffer cache A cache of recently used disk blocks. In FreeBSD, the buffer cache has been merged with the virtual-memory cache.

bus A standardized electrical and mechanical interconnection for components of a computer.

byte A unit of measure applied to data. A byte is almost always 8 bits.

callback In the kernel, a mechanism to notify a subsystem that an asynchronous operation has completed. In NFS, a scheme where a server keeps track of all the objects that each of its clients has cached. When a cached object is held by two or more clients and one of them modifies it, the server sends a notice to all the other clients holding that object so that they can purge it from their cache. See also *lease*.

callout queue The kernel data structure that describes waiting events. Each event in the queue is described by a structure that contains a function to be called, a pointer to be passed as an argument to the function, and the number of clock ticks until the event should occur.

canonical mode A terminal mode. Characters input from a terminal or a pseudo-terminal that is running in canonical mode are processed to provide standard line-oriented editing functions, and input is presented to a process on a line-by-line basis. When the terminal is processing in noncanonical mode, input is passed through to the reading process immediately and without interpretation. Canonical mode is also known as *cooked mode*, and noncanonical mode is also known as *raw mode*.

capability A communicable, unforgeable token of authority. In FreeBSD, capabilities are file descriptors whose permissible operations have been "refined," or limited to a specific set of operations. Capabilities are unforgeable as the kernel prevents improper modification. Capabilities are communicable as they are inherited across *fork* and *exec*, and can be delegated via local-domain sockets. See also *capability system; Capsicum; descriptor*.

capability system Permits access to underlying objects only via capabilities. Capability mode prevents processes from acquiring new capabilities via global namespaces. Applications selectively delegate capabilities to sandboxed processes to enforce access-control policies and mitigate vulnerabilities by minimizing unnecessary rights. See also *ambient authority; capability; Capsicum; sandbox*.

Capsicum A lightweight, kernel-based sandboxing framework based on the idea of a capability system. Capsicum's primary use is in limiting the impact of vulnerabilities via application compartmentalization: sandboxed processes execute without ambient authority and have access only to objects for which they have been granted capabilities. See also *ambient authority; application compartmentalization; capability; capability system; sandbox*.

caught signal A signal that, when delivered to a process, results in a signal-handler procedure being invoked. A signal handler is installed by a process with the *sigaction* system call.

central processing unit (CPU) The primary computational unit in a computer. The CPU is the processing unit that executes applications. A multiprocessor will have more than one CPU. Other processing units may be present in a computer—for example, for handling I/O.

character-at-a-time mode A mode of operation for a pseudo-terminal device whereby processes reading from the pseudo-terminal receive input immediately as it is typed. This mode differs from raw mode in that certain input processing, such as interpreting the interrupt character, is still performed by the system. See also *canonical mode*.

character device A device that provides either a character-stream-oriented I/O interface or, alternatively, an unstructured (raw) interface. All devices in FreeBSD use the character-device interface.

checksum The value of a mathematical function computed for a block of data; used to detect corruption of the data block.

child process A process that is a direct descendant of another process as a result of being created with a *fork* system call.

client ID In NFS, a client identifier uniquely identifies a client to a single server. The client ID is generated by the server and assigned to the client as part of the exchange ID operation.

client process In the client–server model of communication, a process that contacts a server process to request services. A client process is usually unrelated to a server process; the client's only association with the server is through a communication channel. See also *server process*.

cluster The logical grouping of contiguous pages of virtual memory or a file. In FreeBSD, this grouping is used by the kernel to aggregate pages when writing or reading them to or from the disk to reduce the number of I/O operations needed to move data in and out of memory.

cold start The initial phase of a bootstrap procedure. The term is derived from the fact that the software assumes nothing about the state of the machine—as though the machine had just been turned on and were cold.

communication domain An abstraction used by the interprocess-communication facilities to organize the properties of a communication network or similar facility. A communication domain includes a set of protocols, termed the *protocol family*; rules for manipulating and interpreting names; the *address family*; and, possibly, other intrinsic properties. The facilities provided by the system for interprocess communication are defined such that they are independent of the communication domains supported by the system. This design makes it possible for applications to be written in a communication-domain-independent manner.

communication protocol A set of conventions and rules used by two communicating processes. Communication protocols are most often associated with networking.

configuration file A file that contains parameters for the system-configuration program **/usr/sbin/config**. This file describes the device drivers that should be configured into the kernel and other basic kernel functionality such as the enabling of symmetric multiprocessing support.

connect request A request passed to the user-request routine of a communication-protocol module as a result of a process making a *connect* system call on a socket. The request causes the system to attempt to establish an association between a local and a remote socket.

context switching The action of interrupting the currently running thread and switching to another thread. Context switching occurs as one thread after another is scheduled for execution. An interrupted thread's context is saved in that thread's thread control block, and another thread's context is loaded.

continuation style A style of programming where two or more functions operate cooperatively by calling each other instead of returning directly at the end of execution. When the currently executing function is done with its work, it calls another function, which was passed as one of the first function's arguments, as part of its *return*() call. Programming with continuations has the effect of creating a function chain and is often used when a system wants to submit work to a hardware coprocessor but wishes to have a cleanup routine called by the hardware coprocessor when the coprocessor has completed the job.

continue signal Signal 19 (SIGCONT). A signal that, when delivered to a stopped or sleeping process, causes that process to resume execution.

controlling process The session leader that established the connection to the controlling terminal. See also *session leader.*

controlling terminal The pseudo-terminal associated with a process's session from which keyboard-related signals may be generated. The controlling terminal for a process is normally inherited from the process's parent.

control request A request passed to a communication-protocol module as a result of a process making an *ioctl* or *setsockopt* system call on a socket.

cooked mode See *canonical mode.*

copy-on-write A technique whereby multiple references to a common object are maintained until the object is modified (written). Before the object is written, a copy is made; the modification is made to the copy rather than to the original. In virtual-memory management, copy-on-write is a common scheme that the kernel uses to manage pages shared by multiple processes. All the page-table entries mapping a shared page are set such that the first write reference to the page causes a page fault. When the page fault is serviced, the faulted page is replaced with a private copy, which is writable.

core file A file (named **procname.core**) that is created by the system when certain signals are delivered to a process. The file contains a record of the state of the process at the time the signal occurred. This record includes the contents of the process's virtual address space and, on most systems, the user structure.

CPU See *central processing unit.*

crash Among computer scientists, an unexpected system failure.

crash dump A record of the state of a machine at the time of a crash. This record is usually written to a place on secondary storage that is thought to be safe so that it can be saved until the information can be recovered.

credential See *user credential.*

current working directory The directory from which relative pathnames are interpreted for a process. The current working directory for a process is set with the *chdir* or *fchdir* system call.

cylinder group In the fast filesystem, a collection of blocks on a disk drive that is grouped and managed together. The filesystem allocates inodes and data blocks on a per-cylinder-group basis. Cylinder group is a historic name from the days when the geometry of disks was known.

DAC See *discretionary access control.*

daemon A long-lived process that provides a system-related service. There are daemon processes that execute in kernel mode (e.g., the pageout daemon) and daemon processes that execute in user mode (e.g., the *routing daemon*). The Old English term *daemon* means "a deified being," as distinguished from the term *demon*, which means "an evil spirit."

DARPA Defense Advanced Research Projects Agency. An agency of the US Department of Defense that is responsible for managing defense-sponsored research in the United States.

datagram socket A type of socket supporting an unreliable message transport that preserves message boundaries.

datalink layer The network software component responsible for handling packets for a particular media protocol such as Ethernet. It normally resides above the physical layer and beneath the network layer in the ISO model of layered network protocols.

data segment The segment of a process's address space that contains the initialized and uninitialized data portions of a program. See also *bss segment; stack segment; text segment.*

decapsulation In network communication, the removal of the outermost header information from a message. See also *encapsulation.*

delegation In NFS, the process by which a server can allow a client to perform operations, such as reading and writing data, for a period of time without contacting the server. The server delegates responsibility for the reading and writing of data cached at the client.

demand paging A memory-management technique in which memory is divided into pages and the pages are provided to processes as needed—that is, on demand. See also *pure demand paging.*

demon See *daemon.*

denial-of-service attack Any attempt to overload a system such that it is unable to do work for legitimate users of the system. For example, sending a system so many packets that it runs out of mbufs and thus cannot process any other network traffic.

descriptor An integer assigned by the system when a file is referenced by the *open* system call or when a socket is created with the *socket*, *pipe*, or *socketpair* system calls. The integer uniquely identifies an access path to the file or socket from a given process or from any of that process's children. Descriptors can also be duplicated with the *dup* and *fcntl* system calls.

descriptor table A per-process table that holds references to objects on which I/O may be done. I/O descriptors are indices into this table.

device In UNIX, a peripheral connected to the CPU.

device driver A software module that is part of the kernel and supports access to a peripheral device.

device special file A file through which processes can access hardware devices on a machine. For example, a sound card is accessed through such a file.

direct memory access (DMA) A facility whereby a peripheral device can access main memory without the assistance of the CPU. DMA is typically used to transfer contiguous blocks of data between main memory and a peripheral device.

directory In UNIX, a special type of file containing entries that are references to other files. By convention, a directory contains at least two entries: dot (**.**) and dot-dot (**..**). Dot refers to the directory itself; dot-dot refers to the parent directory.

directory entry An entry that is represented by a variable-length record structure in the directory file. Each structure holds an ASCII string that represents the filename, the number of bytes of space provided for the string, the number of bytes of space provided for the entry, the type of the file referenced by the entry, and the number of the inode associated with the filename. By convention, a directory entry with a zero inode number is treated as unallocated, and the space held by the entry is available for use.

directory table The top level of a two-level hierarchy of data structures used by a forward-mapped page-table algorithm to describe the virtual address space of a process. Each entry in a directory table points to a page of page-table pages. A two-level mapping hierarchy is used on the PC architectures. See also *forward-mapped page table; page-table entry; page-table pages.*

dirty In computer systems, modified. A system usually tracks whether an object has been modified—is dirty—because it needs to save the object's contents before reusing the space held by the object. For example, in the virtual-memory system, a page in the virtual-memory cache is dirty if its contents have been modified. Dirty pages must be written to the swap area or filesystem before they are reused.

discretionary access control (DAC) Refers to forms of access-control policy in which object owners control access by other users; for example, file permissions and access control lists (ACLs). See also *access control list; file permissions; mandatory access control.*

disk partition A software scheme that divides a disk drive into one or more linear extents or partitions. Each partition is a contiguous region of a disk drive that is used as a swap area or to hold a filesystem.

distributed program A program that is partitioned among multiple processes, possibly spread across multiple machines.

DMA See *direct memory access.*

dnode A data structure used by the Zettabyte filesystem to describe objects that may change in size from tiny to huge. *Dnode*s describe filesystems, snapshots, clones, ZVOLs, space maps, property lists, and dead-block lists. When used to describe objects like files and directories, a *dnode* is embedded with a *znode.*

domain Defines a set of related network protocols. The IPv4 protocols, including TCP, UDP, SCTP, and ICMP, are all members of the Internet domain, while the IPX and SPX protocols are members of the netipx domain. The network protocols defined for IPv6 are likewise members of their own, Internet version 6, domain.

double indirect block See *indirect block.*

effective GID See *effective group identifier.*

effective group identifier (effective GID) The first entry in the groups array. The effective GID, along with the other GIDs in the groups array, is used by the filesystem to check group access permission. The effective GID is set when a set-group-identifier program is executed. See also *credential; group identifier; real group identifier; saved group identifier.*

effective UID See *effective user identifier.*

effective user identifier (effective UID) The UID that the system uses to check many user permissions. For example, the effective UID is used by the filesystem to check owner-access permission on files. The effective UID is set when a set-user-identifier program is executed. See also *credential; real user identifier; saved user identifier; user identifier.*

elevator sorting algorithm An algorithm used by the device drivers for I/O requests to move disk heads. The algorithm sorts requests into a cyclic ascending order based on the block number of the request. The name is derived from the fact that the algorithm orders disk requests in a manner similar to the way ride requests for an elevator would be handled most efficiently.

emulate FreeBSD can emulate the system-call interface of other variants of the UNIX operating system. For example, FreeBSD can run binaries compiled for Linux.

encapsulation In network communication, the procedure by which a message is created that has an existing message enclosed in it as data. A protocol normally encapsulates a message by crafting a leading protocol header that indicates the original message is to be treated as data. See also *decapsulation.*

erase character The character that is recognized by the terminal handler, when the latter is running in canonical mode, to mean "delete the last character in the line of input." Each terminal session can have a different erase character, and that erase character can be changed at any time with a *tcsetattr* system call. The terminal handler does not recognize the erase character on terminals that are in noncanonical mode. See also *kill character; word-erase character.*

errno The global variable in C programs that holds an error code indicating why a system call failed. The value to be placed in *errno* is returned by the kernel in the standard return register; it is moved from this return register to *errno* by code in the C run-time library.

event handler A function, registered with a software system, that is to be called at a later time when a particular event occurs. See also *callout queue; kqueue*.

exactly once semantics A distributed system, built in such a way that certain client operations can be serialized and can occur only once, is said to provide exactly once semantics. Remote locking operations are one instance where exactly once semantics are desirable.

extension header Message header that can be easily added and removed from a packet because it contains the header's length and some indication of where and how to begin processing the next header, if such exists.

fault rate The rate at which a process generates page faults. For a reference string, the fault rate is defined to be time independent by its being specified as the number of page faults divided by the length of the reference string.

fetch policy The policy used by a demand-paged, virtual-memory-management system in processing page faults. Fetch policies differ primarily in the way that they handle prepaging of data.

fifo file In the filesystem, a type of file that can be used for interprocess communication. Data written by one process to a fifo are read by another in the order in which they were sent. The name refers to the fact that data are transferred in a first-in, first-out fashion.

file An object in the filesystem that is treated as a linear array of bytes. A file has at least one name and the file exists until all its names are deleted explicitly.

file entry See *file structure*.

file handle A globally unique token created by an NFS server and passed back to an NFS client. The client can then use the file handle to refer to the associated file on the server. A handle is created when a file is first opened; it is passed to the server by the client in later operations, such as read and write, that reference the open file.

filename A string of ASCII characters that names an ordinary file, special file, or directory. The characters in a filename cannot include null (0) or the ASCII code for slash (/).

file offset A byte offset associated with an open file descriptor. The file offset for a file descriptor is set explicitly with the *lseek* system call, or implicitly as a result of a *read* or *write* system call.

file permissions A bitmask associated with each file or directory that limits how the owner, group, and other users in the system are able to access the object. Each can be granted read, write, or execute access; in addition, file permissions include the sticky, setuid, and setgid bits. Permissions may be managed by the file's owner, or the root user. See also *access control list; discretionary access control*.

file structure The data structure used by the kernel to hold the information associated with one or more open file descriptors that reference a file. Usually, each open file descriptor references a unique file structure. File structures may be shared, however, when open descriptors are duplicated with the *dup* and *dup2* system calls, inherited across a *fork* system call, or received in a message through the interprocess-communication facilities.

filesystem A collection of files. The UNIX filesystem is hierarchical, with files organized into directories. Filesystems include facilities for naming files and for controlling access to files. A filesystem resides on a single, logical device that may be built from part of a single disk drive or from a set of disk drives that have been aggregated together.

fill-on-demand page fault The first page fault for an individual page; it must be resolved by retrieval of data from the filesystem or by allocation of a zero-filled page.

first-level bootstrap The initial code that is executed in a multilevel bootstrapping operation. Usually, the first-level bootstrap is limited in size and does little more than bootstrap into operation a larger, more intelligent program. Typically, the first-level bootstrap loads the **/boot** program so that **/boot** can, in turn, bootstrap the kernel.

foreground process In job-control-oriented process-management systems, a process whose process group is the same as that of its controlling terminal; thus, the process is allowed to read from and to write to the terminal. Otherwise, a foreground process is one for which the command interpreter is currently waiting. The opposite of a foreground process is a *background process*.

fork file A directory containing named files for NFSv4 attributes. Each file in the directory names an attribute and each file's contents are the value associated with that attribute.

forward The direction a network packet takes through a system if it is received by a host for which it is not, ultimately, destined. See also *inbound; router*.

forward-mapped page table A large, contiguous array indexed by the virtual address that contains one element, or page-table entry, for each virtual page in the address space. This element contains the physical page to which the virtual page is mapped, as well as access permissions and status bits telling whether the page has been referenced or modified, and a bit showing whether the entry contains valid information. Most current memory-management-unit designs for architectures with 32-bit address spaces use some variant of a forward-mapped page table. See also *reverse-mapped page table; memory-management unit.*

fragment In the filesystem, a part of a block. The filesystem allocates new disk space to a file as a full block or as one or more fragments of a block. The filesystem uses fragments, rather than allocating space in only full block-size units, to reduce wasted space when the size of a full block is large.

fragment-descriptor table A data structure in the fast filesystem that describes the fragments that are free in an entry of the allocation map. The filesystem uses the fragment-descriptor table by taking a byte in the allocation map and using the byte to index into the fragment-descriptor table. The value in the fragment-descriptor table indicates how many fragments of a particular size are available in the entry of the allocation map. By doing a logical AND with the bit corresponding to the desired fragment size, the system can determine quickly whether a desired fragment is contained within the allocation-map entry.

free list In the memory-management system, the list of available pages of physical memory (also called the *memory free list*). There is a similar free list in the system for dynamically allocated kernel memory. Many kernel data structures are dynamically allocated, including vnodes, file-table entries, and disk-quota structures.

free-space reserve A percentage of space in a filesystem that is held in reserve to ensure that certain allocation algorithms used by the filesystem will work well. By default, 8 percent of the available space in the fast filesystem is held in reserve.

gateway See *router.*

generation number The number assigned to an inode each time that the latter is allocated to represent a new file. Each generation number is used only once. To make file handles harder to guess, most NFS implementations, including FreeBSD, use a random-number generator to select a new generation number.

GID See *group identifier.*

global page-replacement algorithm An algorithm that does page replacement according to systemwide criteria. A global-page-replacement strategy tends to make the most efficient use of the system memory. However, a single process can thrash the entire system by trying to use all the available memory.

group identifier (GID) An integer value that uniquely identifies a collection of users. GIDs are used in the access-control facilities provided by the filesystem. See also *credential; effective group identifier; real group identifier; saved group identifier; set-group-identifier program.*

half-open connection A connection that is open for communication in one direction between two endpoints. For example, a client may close its sending side of a stream connection because it has no more data to send but leave its receiving half of the connection open so that it can continue to receive data from the server.

handler A procedure that is invoked in response to an event such as a signal.

hard limit A limit that cannot be exceeded. See also *soft limit.*

hard link A directory entry that directly references an inode. If there are multiple hard links to a single inode and if one of the links is deleted, the remaining links still reference the inode. By contrast, a symbolic link is a file that holds a pathname referencing a file. See also *symbolic link.*

header prediction A heuristic used by TCP on incoming packets to detect two common cases: the next expected data segment for an existing connection or an acknowledgment plus a window update for one or more data segments. When one of these two cases arises, and the packet has no additional flags or state indications, the fully general TCP input processing is skipped.

heap The region of a process that can be expanded dynamically with the *sbrk* system call (or *malloc*() C library call). The name is derived from the disorderly fashion in which data are placed in the region.

high watermark An upper bound on the number of data that may be buffered. In the interprocess-communication facilities, each socket's data buffer has a high watermark that specifies the maximum number of data that may be queued in the data buffer before a request to send data will block the process (or will return an error if nonblocking I/O is being used). See also *low watermark*.

hole In a file, a region that is part of the file but has no associated data blocks. The filesystem returns zero-valued data when a process reads from a hole in a file. A hole is created in a file when a process positions the file pointer past the current end-of-file, writes some data, and then closes the file. The hole appears between the previous end-of-file and the beginning of the newly written data.

home directory The current working directory that is set for a user's shell when the user logs into a system. This directory is usually private to the user. The home directory for a user is specified in a field in the password-file entry for the user.

hop limit The number of routers through which a network packet may be forwarded before it is dropped. See also *router*.

host-unreachable message A network-layer error message indicating that the host to which a previous message was directed is unavailable because there is no known path to the desired host.

ICMP See *Internet control message protocol*.

ICV See *integrity-check value*.

idempotent An operation that can be repeated several times without changing the final result or causing an error. For example, writing the same data to the same offset in a file is idempotent because it will yield the same result whether it is done once or many times. However, trying to remove the same file more than once is nonidempotent because the file will no longer exist after the first try.

idle loop The block of code inside the kernel that is executed when there is nothing else to run. In FreeBSD, the idle loop zeros pages on the free list while it waits for a thread to be added to the run queue.

idle queue The queue where all idle threads are stored. An idle thread is run only when a CPU has nothing else to do. See also *run queue; sleep queue; turnstile queue*.

IKE See *Internet key exchange*.

inbound The direction a network packet is traveling if it has reached the system for which it is destined. An inbound network packet is delivered to an application on a system or causes an error if no appropriate application is found. See also *forward.*

indirect block In the filesystem, an auxiliary data block that holds the number of a data block. The first 12 blocks of a file are pointed to directly by the inode. Additional data blocks are described with a pointer from the inode to an indirect block; the system must first fetch the indirect block that holds the number of the data block. In FreeBSD, the kernel may have to fetch as many as three indirect blocks to locate the desired data block. An indirect block that contains data-block numbers is termed a *single indirect block*; an indirect block that contains block numbers of single indirect blocks is called a *double indirect block*; an indirect block that contains block numbers of double indirect blocks is called a *triple indirect block.*

init The first user program (**/sbin/init**) that runs when the system is booted.

initial sequence number See *sequence space.*

inode A data structure used by the filesystem to describe a file. The contents of an inode include the file's type and size, the UID of the file's owner, the GID of the directory in which it was created, and a list of the disk blocks and fragments that make up the file. Note that inodes do not have names; directory entries are used to associate a name with an inode.

input/output (I/O) The transfer of data between the computer and its peripheral devices.

integrity-check value (ICV) A value computed over a range of data by a sender that is used by a receiver to ensure that data transmitted across a network was not corrupted. See also *checksum.*

interactive program A program that must periodically obtain user input to do its work. A screen-oriented text editor is an example of an interactive program.

Internet control message protocol (ICMP) A communication protocol used for reporting errors and controlling the operation of the Internet protocols. Each of IPv4 and IPv6 includes its own version of ICMP, called ICMPv4 and ICMPv6, respectively.

Internet key exchange (IKE) A network protocol for exchanging keys used in the IPSec security protocols.

Internet protocol See *IPv4 domain.*

interpreter A program that parses and executes a descriptive language in a single step, rather than using the more common two-stage process of compiling the language and executing the resulting binary. The shell is an example of an interpreter; it parses and executes a shell script rather than first compiling it.

interprocess communication (IPC) The transfer of data between processes. Most facilities for interprocess communication are designed such that data are transferred between objects other than processes. An interprocess-communication model that is not directly process oriented is advantageous because it is possible to model scenarios in which communication endpoints are location independent and, possibly, are migrated dynamically. For example, in FreeBSD, communication is between sockets rather than between processes.

interprocessor interrupt (IPI) A special type of interrupt by which one processor may interrupt another processor in a multiprocessor system if the interrupting processor requires action from the other processor.

interrupt In computer systems, an event external to the currently executing process that causes a change in the normal flow of instruction execution. Interrupts usually are generated by hardware devices that are external to the CPU.

inverted page table See *reverse-mapped page table*.

I/O See *input/output*.

I/O redirection The redirection of an I/O stream from the default assignment. For example, all the standard shells permit users to redirect the standard output stream to a file or process. I/O redirection is implemented in the shell by first closing the descriptor associated with the I/O stream and then opening or duplicating another descriptor in its place.

I/O stream A stream of data directed to, or generated from, a process. Most I/O streams in UNIX have a single common data format that permits users to write programs in a tool-oriented fashion and to combine these programs in pipelines by directing the standard output stream of one program to the standard input stream of another.

iovec A data structure used to specify user I/O requests made to the kernel. Each structure holds the address of a data buffer and the number of bytes of data to be read or written. Arrays of such structures are passed to the kernel in *readv* and *writev* system calls. See also *scatter-gather I/O*.

I/O vector See *iovec*.

IPC See *interprocess communication*.

IPI See *interprocessor interrupt*.

IPSec The set of protocols that implement network layer security in the Internet protocols, versions 4 and 6.

IPv4 domain Version 4 of the Internet protocols. IPv4 used to be called the Internet protocols until version 6 was developed. See also *IPv6 domain*.

IPv6 domain Version 6 of the Internet protocols. The newest version of the Internet protocols with support for larger addresses, security, and autoconfiguration. See also *IPv4 domain*.

job In UNIX, a set of processes that all have the same process-group identifier. Jobs that have multiple processes are normally created with a pipeline. A job is the fundamental object that is manipulated with job control.

job control A facility for managing jobs. With job control, a job may be started, stopped, and killed, as well as moved between the foreground and the background. The terminal handler provides facilities for automatically stopping a background job that tries to access the controlling terminal and for notifying a job's controlling process when such an event occurs.

keepalive packet A type of packet used by TCP to maintain information about whether a destination host is up. Keepalive packets are sent to a remote host, which, if it is up, must respond. If a response is not received in a reasonable time to any of several keepalive packets, then the connection is terminated. Keepalive packets are used on only those TCP connections that have been created for sockets that have the SO_KEEPALIVE option set on them.

keepalive timer A timer used by the TCP protocol when using keepalive packets. The timer is set when a keepalive packet is transmitted. If a response to the packet is not received before the timer expires several times, then the connection is shut down.

kernel The central controlling program that provides basic system facilities. The FreeBSD kernel creates and manages processes, provides functions to access the filesystem, and supplies communication facilities. The FreeBSD kernel is the only part of FreeBSD that a user cannot replace.

kernel-event polling A generic method of notifying a process when an event happens or a condition holds based on the results of small pieces of kernel code termed filters. The process describes a set of events for which the process referencing the descriptor wants to be notified. Events include both dynamic transitions, such as the arrival of data to read, and state transitions, such as a rename of the file associated with the descriptor. See also *nonblocking I/O; polling I/O; signal-driven I/O.*

kernel mode The most privileged processor-access mode. The FreeBSD kernel operates in kernel mode. See also *user mode*.

kernel process A process that executes with the processor in kernel mode. The pageout daemon and *swapper* processes are examples of kernel processes.

kernel state The run-time execution state for the kernel. This state, which includes the program counter, general-purpose registers, and run-time stack, must be saved and restored on each context switch.

key In the kernel, a piece of data that uniquely identifies some resource in the system. When used by an interprocess communication system, it identifies an endpoint of communication such as a message queue or a shared facility like a region of shared memory.

kill character The character that is recognized by the terminal handler in canonical mode to mean "delete everything typed on this terminal after the most recent end-of-line character." Each terminal session can have a different kill character, and the user can change that kill character at any time with an *tcsetattr* system call. The terminal handler does not recognize the kill character on terminals that are in noncanonical mode. See also *erase character; word-erase character*.

kqueue A kernel data structure associated with a file descriptor that describes a set of events for which the process referencing the descriptor wants to be notified. Events include both dynamic transitions, such as the arrival of data to read, and state transitions, such as a rename of the file associated with the descriptor.

lease A ticket permitting an activity that is valid until a specified expiration time. In the NQNFS protocol, a client gets a lease from its server to read, write, or read and write a file. As long as the client holds a valid lease, it knows that the server will notify it if the file status changes. Once the lease has expired, the client must contact the server to request a new lease before using any data that it has cached for the file. See also *callback*.

least recently used (LRU) A policy of reuse whereby the least recently used items are reused first. For example, in the filesystem, there is a fixed number of vnodes available for accessing files. Vnodes that hold valid file data are reallocated in an LRU order, in the hope that the file referenced by the vnode may be reused by a later open request.

line discipline A processing module in the kernel that provides semantics for an asynchronous serial interface or for a software emulation of such an interface. Line disciplines are described by a procedural interface whose entry points are stored in the *linesw* data structure.

line mode See *canonical mode*.

link layer Layer 2 in the ISO Open Systems Interconnection Reference Model. In this model, the link layer is responsible for the (possibly unreliable) delivery of messages within a single physical network. The link layer corresponds most closely to the network-interface layer of the FreeBSD network subsystem. See also *network-interface layer*.

listen request A request passed to a communication-protocol module as a result of a process making a *listen* system call on a socket. This request indicates that the system should listen for requests to establish a connection to the socket. Otherwise, the system will reject any connection requests that it receives for the socket.

loadable kernel modules A collection of software that implements a kernel service but that is not statically linked into the kernel's image. Loadable kernel modules are brought into the system dynamically, possibly at run time, by actions initiated either by the system or a user. See also *permanent kernel modules*.

local domain A communication domain in the interprocess-communication facilities that supports stream- and datagram-oriented styles of communication between processes on a single machine.

locality of reference A phenomenon whereby memory references of a running program are localized within the virtual address space over short periods. Most programs tend to exhibit some degree of locality of reference. This locality of reference makes it worthwhile for the system to prefetch pages that are adjacent to a page that is faulted, reducing the fault rate of a running program.

local page-replacement algorithm An algorithm for page replacement that first chooses a process from which to replace a page and then chooses a page within that process based on per-process criteria. Usually, a process is given a fixed number of pages and must then select from them when it needs a new page.

logical block A block defined by dividing a file's linear extent by the underlying filesystem block size. Each logical block of a file is mapped into a physical block. This additional level of mapping permits physical blocks to be placed on disk without concern for the linear organization of the logical blocks in a file.

long-term-scheduling algorithm See *short-term-scheduling algorithm.*

low watermark A lower bound that specifies the minimum number of data that must be present before an action can be taken. In the interprocess-communication facilities, each socket's data buffer has a low watermark that specifies the minimum number of data that must be present in the data buffer before a reception request will be satisfied. See also *high watermark.*

LRU See *least recently used.*

MAC See *mandatory access control.*

machine check An exceptional machine condition that indicates the CPU detected an error in its operation. For example, a machine check is generated if a parity error is detected in a cache memory.

magic number The number located in the first few bytes of an executable file that indicates the file's type. Many on-disk data structures have a magic number to help verify their contents.

main memory The primary memory system on a machine.

mandatory access control (MAC) An infrastructure that allows the system administrator to impose security policies on all users in the system, in contrast to discretionary access control in which users control access to their own files. Policies include multilevel security in which labels on processes and files control access to use based on a user's clearance level and the file's confidentiality level. MAC is implemented via a reference monitor, the MAC framework. See also *discretionary access control; multilevel security; reference monitor.*

mandatory lock A lock that cannot be ignored or avoided. A mandatory lock is contrasted with an advisory lock, which is enforced only when a process explicitly requests its enforcement. See also *advisory lock.*

mapped object An object whose pages are mapped into a process address space. Processes map objects into their virtual address space using the *mmap* system call.

mapping structure The machine-dependent state required to describe the translation and access rights of a single page. See also *page-table entry.*

marshalling Preparing a set of parameters to be sent across a network. Marshalling includes replacing pointers by the data to which they point and converting binary data to the canonical network byte order. See also *remote procedure call.*

masked signal A signal blocked in a *sigprocmask* system call. When a signal is masked, its delivery is delayed until it is unmasked. In addition, in FreeBSD, the system automatically masks a caught signal while that signal is being handled.

maximum segment lifetime (MSL) The maximum time that a segment of data may exist in the network. See also *2MSL timer*.

maximum transmission unit (MTU) The largest packet that can be communicated across a network link in a single transaction.

mbuf A data structure that describes a block of data. Mbufs are used in the interprocess-communication facilities for holding network packets, as well as data that are internal to the network protocol modules. "Mbuf" is shorthand for "memory buffer."

memory address A number that specifies a memory location. Memory addresses are often categorized as physical or virtual according to whether they reference physical or virtual memory.

memory free list See *free list*.

memory-management system The part of the operating system that is responsible for the management of memory resources available on a machine.

memory-management unit (MMU) A hardware device that implements memory-management-related tasks, such as address translation and memory protection. Most contemporary memory-management units also provide support for demand-paged virtual-memory management. See also *address translation*.

message queue A local interprocess-communication mechanism that supports in-order delivery of messages. Messages are inserted at one end of the queue and removed from the other, and the kernel guarantees their ordering.

metadata In filesystems, metadata provides pointers and descriptions for linking multiple disk sectors into files and identifying those files. Metadata are the directories, inodes, and free block maps that give structure to raw storage capacity.

MLS See *multilevel security*.

MMU See *memory-management unit*.

MSL See *maximum segment lifetime*.

MTU See *maximum transmission unit*.

multilevel feedback queue A queueing scheme in which requests are partitioned into multiple prioritized subqueues, with requests moving between subqueues based on dynamically varying criteria. The FreeBSD kernel uses a multilevel-feedback-queueing scheme for scheduling the execution of threads.

multilevel security (MLS) A mandatory access control (MAC), sometimes referred to as the Bell-LaPadula policy, that controls access based on data confidentiality. In MLS, processes are labeled with clearances and objects (e.g., files) are labeled with classifications. Two rules are enforced: higher-clearance processes cannot "write down" to lower-classification objects, and lower-clearance processes cannot "read up" from higher-classification objects. See also *mandatory access control*.

multiple-root problem A problem that results from the implementation details of filesystems in non-Unix environments, such as Windows-based operating systems, in which each filesystem has its own root directory without the benefit of a single root to bind all filesystems. Directory traversal in a system with multiple root directories required changes in the NFS protocol so that users and programs could move smoothly across filesystems without the need to know about multiple root directories.

neighbor discovery The technique by which a system on a network discovers the hardware address of its neighbors, including its router, so that it can send network packets to them. The neighbor discovery protocol is used by IPv6. See also *address-resolution protocol.*

netmask A network mask defines the boundary between the host and network parts of a network address. The mask is used by various parts of the network protocol and routing systems to make decisions about whether a network address is meant for a specific node, or if it should be routed to another system in the Internet.

network byte order The order defined by a network for the transmission of protocol fields that are larger than one byte. In IPv4 and IPv6, this order is "most significant byte first."

network-interface layer The layer of software in the FreeBSD network subsystem that is responsible for transporting messages between hosts connected to a common transmission medium. This layer is mainly concerned with driving the transmission media involved and with performing any necessary link-level protocol encapsulation and decapsulation. See also *link layer.*

network layer The layer of software in the FreeBSD network subsystem that is responsible for implementing ISO layer 2 functionality. In the IPv4 domain, this functionality is implemented in the IP protocol module.

network mask See *netmask.*

newbus The device-driver infrastructure used in FreeBSD to manage the devices on the system. Newbus includes machine-independent routines and data structures for use by machine-dependent layers and provides a framework for dynamic allocation of data structures for each device. See also *autoconfiguration.*

nice A user-controllable process-scheduling parameter. The value of a process's *nice* variable is used in calculating the scheduling priority of the process's threads. Positive values of *nice* mean that the process is willing to receive less than its share of the processor. Negative values of *nice* mean that the process requests more than its share of the processor.

nonblocking I/O A mode in which a descriptor may be placed, whereby the system will return an error if any I/O operation on the descriptor would cause the process to block. For example, if a *read* system call is done on a descriptor that is in nonblocking I/O mode, and no data are available, the system will return the error code EAGAIN, rather than block the process until data arrive. See also *kernel-event polling ; polling I/O; signal-driven I/O.*

noncanonical mode See *canonical mode.*

nonlocal goto A transfer in control that circumvents the normal flow of execution in a program across routine boundaries. For example, if procedure A calls procedure B, and B calls C, then a direct transfer of control from C back to A (bypassing B) would be a nonlocal goto.

nonresident object An object that is not present in main memory. For example, a page in the virtual address space of a process may be nonresident if it has never been referenced.

nonuniform memory access (NUMA) A computer memory design with nonuniform memory access (NUMA) used in systems with multiple CPUs. Access time to the memory depends on the memory location relative to the CPU. Under NUMA, a CPU can access its own local memory faster than memory local to another CPU or shared between CPUs. See also *symmetric multiprocessing*.

NUMA See *nonuniform memory access*.

object See *virtual-memory object*.

optimal replacement policy A replacement policy that optimizes the performance of a demand-paging virtual-memory system. In this book, a policy whereby the full reference string of a program is known in advance, and pages are selected such that the number of page faults is minimized.

orphaned process group A process group in which the parent of every member is either itself a member of the group or is not a member of the group's session. Such a parent would normally be a job-control shell capable of resuming stopped child processes.

out-of-band data Data transmitted and received out of the normal flow of data. Stream sockets support a logically separate out-of-band data channel through which at least one message of at least 1 byte of data may be sent. The system immediately notifies a receiving process of the presence of out-of-band data, and out-of-band data may be retrieved from the stream out of the order in which normal data are received.

overlay In computer systems, a region of code or data that may be replaced with other such regions on demand. Overlays are usually loaded into a process's address space on demand, possibly on top of another overlay. Overlays are a commonly used scheme for programs that are too large to fit in the address space of a machine that does not support virtual memory.

page In memory management, the fixed-sized unit of measure used to divide a physical or virtual address space. See also *demand paging*.

page fault An exception generated by a process's reference to a page of that process's virtual address space that is not marked as resident in memory.

pagein An operation done by the virtual-memory system in which the contents of a page are read from secondary storage.

pageout An operation done by the virtual-memory system in which the contents of a page are written to secondary storage.

pageout daemon In FreeBSD, the kernel process that is responsible for writing parts of the address space of a process to secondary storage, to support the paging facilities of the virtual-memory system. See also *swapper.*

pager A kernel module responsible for providing the data to fill a page and for providing a place to store that page when it has been modified and the memory associated with it is needed for another purpose.

page reclaim A page fault where the page that was faulted is located in memory, usually on the inactive or cache list.

page table The data structure used by the virtual-memory system to store the mapping between virtual addresses and physical addresses. See also *page-table entry; page-table pages.*

page-table entry (PTE) The machine-dependent data structure that identifies the location and status of a page of a virtual address space. When a virtual page is in memory, the PTE contains the page-frame number that the hardware needs to map the virtual page to a physical page.

page-table pages The top level of a two-level hierarchy of data structures used by a forward-mapped page-table algorithm to describe the virtual address space of a process. On the PC, page-table pages are stored in an array called the directory table; each entry in a page-table page points to a page of bottom-level page-table entries. See also *directory table; forward-mapped page table; page-table entry; page table.*

paging The action that brings pages of an executing process into main memory when they are referenced and that removes them from memory when they are replaced. When a process executes, all its pages are said to reside in virtual memory. Only the actively used pages, however, need to reside in main memory. The remaining pages can reside on disk until they are needed.

panic In UNIX, an unrecoverable system failure detected by the kernel. FreeBSD automatically recovers from a panic by rebooting the machine, repairing any filesystem damage, and then restarting normal operation. See also *crash dump.*

parent process A process that is a direct relative of another process as a result of a *fork* system call.

partition See *disk partition.*

path MTU discovery An algorithm and set of messages used to find the largest packet that can be sent between two endpoints in the network.

pathname A null-terminated character string starting with an optional slash (/), followed by zero or more directory names separated by slashes, and optionally followed by a filename. If a pathname begins with a slash, it is said to be an *absolute pathname*, and the path search begins at the root directory. Otherwise, the pathname is said to be a *relative pathname*, and the path search begins at the current working directory of the process. A slash by itself names the root directory. A null pathname refers to the current working directory.

permanent kernel modules A collection of software that implements a kernel service that must be present at boot time and may not be removed while the system is running. See also *loadable kernel module.*

persist timer A timer used by TCP for maintaining output flow on a connection. This timer is started whenever data are ready to be sent, but the send window is too small to bother sending and no data are already outstanding. If no window update is received before the timer expires, a window probe is sent.

physical block One or more contiguous disk sectors to which the system maps a logical block.

physical mapping The software state, also referred to as the *pmap* structure, needed to manage the machine-dependent translation and access tables that are used either directly or indirectly by the memory-management hardware. This mapping state includes information about access rights, in addition to address translation.

PID See *process identifier*.

pipe An interprocess-communication facility that supports the unidirectional flow of data between related processes. Data transfer is stream oriented, reliable, and flow controlled. A pipe is specified to the shell with the "|" symbol. For example, to connect the standard output of program **a** to the standard input of program **b**, the user would type the command "a | b."

pipeline A collection of processes in which a pipe connects the standard output of one process to the standard input of the next process.

placement policy The policy used by the virtual-memory system to place pages in main memory when servicing a page fault. FreeBSD uses page coloring to optimize the placement of pages.

pmap See *physical mapping*.

pmap module The physical-mapping module manages machine-dependent translation and access tables that are used either directly or indirectly by the memory-management hardware.

polling I/O The normal mode for a descriptor whereby the system will block if a read request has no data available or a write request has no buffering available. A process can determine whether an I/O operation will block by polling the kernel using the *select* or *poll* system call. The *select* or *poll* system call can be requested to return immediately with the information or to block until at least one of the requested I/O operations can be completed. See also *kernel-event polling; nonblocking I/O; signal-driven I/O*.

POSIX The standards group for P1003, the portable operating-system interfaces established by the IEEE. Its first established standard was the kernel interface, 1003.1, which was ratified in 1988. The final POSIX standard was ratified in 1999. Since 1999, the only changes have been to keep the existing POSIX standards current.

prefetching The retrieval of data before they are needed. Many machines prefetch machine instructions so that they can overlap the time spent fetching instructions from memory with the time spent decoding instructions.

prepaging The prefetching of pages of memory. Prepaging is a technique used by virtual-memory systems to reduce the number of page faults. See also *cluster*.

priority inversion A problematic scenario in scheduling where a high-priority thread is indirectly preempted by a lower-priority thread effectively inverting the relative priorities of the two threads. This inversion violates the priority model that high-priority threads can only be prevented from running by higher-priority threads and briefly by low-priority threads that will quickly complete their use of a resource shared by the high- and low-priority threads. See also *priority propagation*.

priority propagation The propagation of the priority of a high-priority thread blocking on a mutex to a low-priority thread holding that mutex. The current owner temporarily assumes the priority of the higher-priority thread waiting on the mutex. This higher priority allows the owner to resume running if it was preempted by a mid-priority thread, and to continue running should a mid-priority thread become ready to run. When the owner releases the mutex, it drops back to its original priority. See also *priority inversion*.

private mapping When privately mapping a file in virtual memory, changes made to the memory mapping the file are not written back to the mapped file and are not visible to other processes mapping the file. See also *shared mapping*.

privilege The right to bypass normal system protections and access control. Normally, the kernel grants privilege only to processes owned by the superuser. Root users within jails have restricted privilege to prevent escape from jail. Mandatory access control may also grant or limit privilege to processes as dictated by policy. See also *mandatory access control; superuser*.

privilege separation See *application compartmentalization*.

probe The operation of checking to see whether a hardware device is present on a machine. Newer bus designs have a standardized way to identify the devices that are attached to them.

probe effect Placing data collection or debugging code in a program incurs extra execution time and a different layout of memory. These changes are referred to as the probe effect and may even cause different results.

process In operating systems, a task that contains one or more threads of execution. In UNIX, user processes are created with the *fork* system call.

process context The context of a FreeBSD process consists of user-level state, including the contents of its address space and the run-time environment, and kernel-level state, including scheduling parameters, resource controls, and identification information. The process context includes everything used by the kernel in providing services for the process. See also *process credential; thread; virtual address space*.

process credential A data structure describing the security context associated with each user process as well as cached with open files, sockets, mountpoints, and other system objects that must authorize asynchronous operations. In addition to authorizing UIDs, GIDs, security labels, and jail information, the credential contains event-auditing configuration and resource limits. See also *user credential*.

process group A collection of processes on a single machine that all have the same process-group identifier. The kernel uses this grouping to arbitrate among multiple jobs contending for the same terminal.

process-group identifier A positive integer used to identify uniquely each active process group in the system. Process-group identifiers are typically defined to be the PID of the process-group leader. Process-group identifiers are used by command interpreters in implementing job control when the command interpreter is broadcasting signals with the *killpg* system call, and when the command interpreter is altering the scheduling priority of all processes in a process group with the *setpriority* system call.

process-group leader The process in a process group whose PID is used as the process-group identifier. This process is typically the first process in a pipeline.

process identifier (PID) A nonnegative integer used to identify uniquely each active process in the system.

process model A model inherited from the Multics operating system that places userspace-program instances in separate virtual-address spaces for robustness and security. In the early 2000s, threads (encapsulating execution context such as register state) were differentiated from processes (process context containers for executing threads) to support multithreaded programming. See also *process context; thread.*

process open-file table See *descriptor table.*

processor affinity In an SMP system, a desire to run a thread on the same processor. For performance reasons, a thread should not be migrated between processors unnecessarily because of the loss of its cached working memory.

processor group A set of CPU cores on a processor supporting symmetric multithreading or a set of processors in an SMP system that is treated as a unit by the scheduler.

process priority A parameter used by the kernel to schedule the execution of the threads within a process. The priority for threads running in the timesharing class changes dynamically according to the operation of the thread. In addition, the *nice* parameter can be set for a process to weight the overall scheduling priority for its threads. See also *scheduling class; scheduling priority.*

process structure A data structure maintained by the kernel for each active process in the system. The process structure for a process is always resident in main memory. See also *thread structure.*

/proc filesystem A filesystem-based interface to active processes that provides process-debugging facilities. Each process is represented by a directory entry in a pseudo-directory named **/proc**. Applications access the virtual address space of a process by opening the file in **/proc** that is associated with the process and then using the *read* and *write* system calls as though the process were a regular file.

protocol family A collection of communication protocols, the members of which are related by being part of a single network architecture. For example, the TCP, UDP, IPv4, and ICMPv4 protocols are part of the protocol family for the IPv4 domain.

protocol-switch structure A data structure that holds all the entry points for a communication protocol supported by the kernel.

pseudo-terminal A software emulation of a hardware terminal, built from a pair of character devices: a master device and a slave device. The slave device provides a process with an interface identical to that for a hardware terminal. However, instead of having a hardware device driving it, the slave device has another process manipulating it through the master half of the pseudo-terminal. Anything written on the master device is given to the slave device as input, and anything written on the slave device is presented as input on the master device.

PTE See *page-table entry*.

public-key encryption A cryptographic system in which the keys used to encrypt data can be shared publicly, in contrast to systems that require all keys be kept secret to guarantee the security of the data.

pure demand paging Demand paging without prepaging.

push migration When the scheduler actively moves a thread from one CPU to another to balance the computational load in a system.

race condition When two or more actions for an operation occur in an undefined order. Trouble arises if there exists a possible order that results in an incorrect outcome.

rapid connection reuse A new connection that exactly duplicates the addresses and ports of a recently closed stream socket in the TIME_WAIT state.

raw-device interface The character-device interface for block-oriented devices such as disks. This interface provides raw access to the underlying device, arranging for direct I/O between a process and the device.

raw mode See *canonical mode*.

raw socket A socket that provides direct access to a communication protocol beneath the transport layer. For example, a raw socket in the IPv4 domain gives the user the ability to read and write IP packets directly without using a transport protocol such as UDP or TCP.

real GID See *real group identifier*.

real group identifier (real GID) The GID that is recorded in the accounting record when a process terminates. The real GID for a process is initially set at the time that a user logs into a system and is then inherited by child processes across later *fork* and *exec* system calls (irrespective of whether a program is set-group-identifier). See also *credential; effective group identifier; saved group identifier; set-group-identifier program.*

real UID See *real user identifier*.

real user identifier (real UID) With respect to a process, the true identity of the user that is running the process. The real UID for a process is initially set at the time a user logs into a system and is then inherited by child processes across later *fork* and *exec* system calls (irrespective of whether a program is set-user-identifier). The real UID is recorded in the accounting record when a process terminates. See also *credential; effective user identifier; saved user identifier; set-user-identifier program.*

receive window In TCP, the range of sequence numbers that defines the data the system will accept for a connection. Any data with sequence numbers outside this range that are received are dropped. See also *sliding-window scheme.*

reclaim See *page reclaim.*

reclaim from inactive A page reclaim from the inactive list. A page can be reclaimed from the inactive list if that page is freed by the page-replacement algorithm, but the page is not reassigned before a process faults on it.

red zone A read-only region of memory immediately below the last page of the per-thread, kernel-mode, run-time stack. The red zone is set up by the system so that a fault will occur if a thread overflows the space allocated for its kernel stack.

referenced page In the virtual-memory system, a page that is read or written.

reference monitor Controls access to objects in order to implement security policies such as mandatory access control. The classical definition requires that a reference monitor be tamper-proof, always invoked (non-bypassable), and small enough to subject to analysis and tests. See also *mandatory access control.*

reference string A dataset that describes the pages referenced by a process over the time of the process's execution. This description represents the memory-related behavior of the process at discrete times during that process's lifetime.

region A range of memory that is being treated in the same way. For example, the text of a program is a region that is read-only and is demand paged from the file on disk that contains it.

relative pathname See *pathname.*

relocation The copying of a program's contents from one place in an address space to another. This copying may be accompanied by modifications to the image of the program so that memory references encoded in the program remain correct after that program is copied. Code that is not bound to a particular starting memory address is said to be relocatable or position independent.

remote procedure call (RPC) A procedure call made from a client process to invoke a subroutine in a server process. Typically, the client and server processes are running on different machines. A remote procedure call operates much like a local procedure call: the client makes a procedure call, and then waits for the result while the procedure executes. See also *marshalling.*

replacement policy The policy that a demand-paged virtual-memory-management system uses to select pages for reuse when memory is otherwise unavailable.

resident object An object that is present in main memory. For example, a page in the virtual address space of a process is resident if its contents are present in main memory.

resident-set size The number of pages of physical memory held by a process. In a well-tuned system, the resident-set size of a process will be that process's working set. Usually, the precise working set cannot be calculated, so a process will have additional pages beyond that needed for its working set.

retransmit timer A timer used by TCP to trigger the retransmission of data. This timer is set each time that data are transmitted to a remote host. It is set to a value that is expected to be greater than the time it will take the receiving host to receive the data and return an acknowledgment.

reverse-mapped page table A hardware-maintained memory-resident table that contains one entry per physical page and that is indexed by physical address instead of by virtual address. An entry contains the virtual address to which the physical page is currently mapped; the entry also includes protection and status attributes. The hardware does virtual-to-physical address translation by computing a hash function on the virtual address to select an entry in the table. The hardware handles collisions by linking together table entries and making a linear search of this chain until it finds the matching virtual address. See also *forward-mapped page table*.

root directory The directory that the kernel uses in resolving absolute pathnames. Each process has a root directory that can be set with the *chroot* system call, and the system has a unique root directory, the identity of which is set at the time that the system is bootstrapped.

root filesystem The filesystem containing the root directory that is considered the root of all filesystems on a machine. The identity of a default root filesystem is compiled into a kernel, although the actual root filesystem used by a system may be set to some other filesystem at the time that a system is bootstrapped.

root user See *superuser*.

round robin In queueing, an algorithm in which each requester is serviced for a fixed time in a first-come, first-served order; requests are placed at the end of the queue if they are incomplete after service.

route In packet-switched-network communication, a route to a destination specifies the host or hosts through which data must be transmitted to reach the destination.

router A machine, also known as a gateway, that has two or more network interfaces and that forwards packets between the networks to which it is connected. Typically, a router runs a routing process that gathers information on the network topology; it uses that information to devise a set of next-hop routes that it installs in the kernel's routing table. See also *routing mechanism; routing policy*.

router solicitation A message sent by a host in an attempt, without human intervention, to discover which machine is its router. See also *autoconfiguration; neighbor discovery*.

routing daemon A process in FreeBSD that provides a routing-management service for the system. This service uses a protocol that implements a distributed database of routing information updated dynamically to reflect changes in topological connectivity.

routing mechanism The routing facilities included in the kernel that implement externally defined policies. The routing mechanism uses a lookup mechanism that provides a first-hop route (a specific network interface and immediate destination) for each destination. See also *router; routing policies.*

routing policies The routing facilities provided in a user-level process that define external policies. Routing policies include all the components that the routing daemon uses in choosing the first-hop routes, such as discovery of the local network topology, implementation of various routing protocols, and configuration information specifying local policies. See also *router; routing mechanism.*

routing redirect message A message generated by a router when the latter recognizes that a message it has received can be delivered via a more direct route.

RPC See *remote procedure call.*

run queue The queue of those threads that are ready to execute. See also *idle queue; sleep queue; turnstile queue.*

run-to-completion A model of processing in which the maximum amount of work is done on a piece of data without deferring any work until a later period. Earlier versions of network protocols repeatedly deferred work between protocol modules so that packets could be buffered and the buffers tuned to fit the application. Run-to-completion reduces per-packet overhead because important data remain in the CPU cache for as long as the processing continues, and in modern processors cache misses are a significant source of overhead.

SA See *security association.*

sandbox A restricted execution environment in which untrustworthy code can be executed without granting it the ambient authority of the user who has executed it. See also *ambient authority; application compartmentalization; Capsicum.*

saved GID See *saved group identifier.*

saved group identifier (saved GID) A mechanism that records the identity of a setgid program by copying the value of the effective GID at the time that the *exec* for the program is done. During its execution, the program may temporarily revoke its setgid privilege by setting its effective GID to its real GID. It can later recover its setgid privilege by setting its effective GID back to its saved GID. See also *credential; effective group identifier.*

saved UID See *saved user identifier.*

saved user identifier (saved UID) A mechanism that records the identity of a setuid program by copying the value of the effective UID at the time that the *exec* for the program is done. During its execution, the program may temporarily revoke its setuid privilege by setting its effective UID to its real UID. It can later recover its setuid privilege by setting its effective UID back to its saved UID. See also *credential; effective user identifier.*

scatter-gather I/O Scatter input allows a single read to be placed in several different buffers. Scatter output allows several different buffers to be written in a single atomic write. Scatter-gather I/O uses an *iovec* structure, an array of buffers and lengths, to identify the buffers to be used for the I/O. See also *iovec.*

scheduling In operating systems, the planning used to share a resource. For example, process scheduling shares the CPU and main memory.

scheduling class The FreeBSD kernel has five scheduling classes: kernel interrupts, system calls, real time, time sharing, and idle. Each process is placed into a scheduling class. Within each class, threads of the process are organized by their scheduling priority. See also *scheduling priority; process priority.*

scheduling priority A per-process parameter maintained by the kernel that specifies the priority with which the latter will schedule the execution of the threads of the process. When a thread is executing in user mode in the timesharing class, the system periodically calculates the scheduling priority using the thread priority and the *nice* parameter. See also *process priority; scheduling class.*

SCTP See *stream transmission control protocol.*

secondary storage Storage that holds data that do not fit in main memory. Secondary storage is usually located on rotating magnetic media, such as disk drives. See also *backing storage.*

sector The smallest contiguous region on a disk that can be accessed with a single I/O operation.

security association (SA) The basic channel of secure communication in IPSec. Data is secured only in one direction by a security association, which means that two security associations are required to create a fully secure channel between two hosts. See also *security-parameter index.*

security-event auditing Refers to the fine-grained logging of security-related events in the trusted computing base. The audit framework tracks security-related system calls and application events (such as user authentication) to the audit trail in the filesystem. Typical uses include post-mortem analysis following compromise and live intrusion detection. See also *trusted computing base.*

security label Additional security metadata associated with processes and objects (e.g., files and sockets) used as input to access-control polices. For example, the MAC policy MLS associates confidentiality labels with processes and objects, and the MAC policy Biba associates integrity labels with processes and objects.

security-parameter index (SPI) A 32-bit piece of data used to identify the end of a security association on a host using IPSec. The security-parameter index is used as a key when working with security associations in a system's security databases. See also *security association.*

segment A contiguous range of data defined by a base and an extent. In memory management, a segment describes a region of a process's address space. In the TCP protocol, a segment is a range of bytes within a single connection defined by starting and ending sequence numbers.

semaphores Data structures and a set of functions used for synchronizing access to a shared resource, such as an area of memory. Semaphores implement two functions: a *take* and a *give*, such that once one thread has taken a semaphore, all others that follow the first are blocked until the first thread gives the semaphore back.

send window In TCP, the range of sequence numbers that defines the data the system can transmit on a connection and be assured that the receiving party has space to hold the data on receipt. Any data with sequence numbers before the start of the send window have already been sent and acknowledged. Any data with sequence numbers after the end of the window will not be sent until the send window changes to include them. See also *sliding-window scheme*.

sense request A request passed to a communication-protocol module as a result of a process making a *stat* system call on a socket.

sequenced-packet socket A type of socket that models sequenced, reliable, unduplicated, connection-based communication that preserves message boundaries.

sequence space The range of sequence numbers that are assigned to data transmitted over a TCP connection. In TCP, sequence numbers are taken from a 32-bit circular space that starts with an arbitrary value called the *initial sequence number*.

server process A process that provides services to client processes via an interprocess-communication facility. See also *client process*.

session A collection of process groups established for job control purposes. Normally, a session is created for each login shell. All processes started by that login shell are part of its session.

session ID Defines a single conversation and set of communications parameters between an NFSv4 client and server.

session leader A process that has created a session. The session leader is the controlling process for the session and is permitted to allocate and assign the controlling terminal for the session. Normally, a session is created for each login shell. All processes started by that login shell are part of its session.

set-group-identifier program A program that runs with an additional group privilege. Set-group-identifier programs are indicated by a bit in the inode of the file. When a process specifies such a file in an *exec* system call, the GID of the file is made the effective GID of the process.

set-user-identifier program A program that runs with an UID different from that of the process that started it running. Set-user-identifier programs are indicated by a bit in the inode of the file. When a process specifies such a file in an *exec* system call, the UID of the file is made the effective UID of the process.

shadow object An anonymous object that is interposed between a process and an underlying object to prevent changes made by the process from being reflected back to the underlying object. A shadow object is used when a process makes a private mapping of a file so that changes made by the process are not reflected in the file.

shared mapping When doing a shared mapping to a file in virtual memory, changes made to the memory mapping the file are written back to the mapped file and are visible to other processes mapping the file. See also *private mapping*.

shared memory An area of memory that can be read and written by two different processes. It is the fastest way to share information between processes on the same system. See also *semaphores.*

shell A program that interprets and executes user commands. When a user logs into a UNIX system, a shell process is normally created with its standard input, standard output, and standard error descriptors directed to the terminal or pseudo-terminal on which the user logged in.

short-term-scheduling algorithm The algorithm used by the system to select the next process to run from among the set of processes that are deemed runnable. The *long-term-scheduling algorithm*, on the other hand, can influence the set of runnable processes by swapping processes in and out of main memory (and thus in and out of the set of runnable processes).

signal In UNIX, a software event. In FreeBSD, this event is modelled after a hardware interrupt.

signal-driven I/O A mode in which a descriptor can be placed, whereby the system will deliver a SIGIO signal to a process whenever I/O is possible on the descriptor. See also *kernel-event polling; nonblocking I/O; polling I/O.*

signal handler A procedure that is invoked in response to a signal.

signal post A notification to a process that a signal is pending for that process. Since most of the actions associated with a signal are done by the receiving process, a process that is posting a signal usually does little more than to record the pending signal in the receiving process's process structure and to arrange for the receiving process to be run.

signal-trampoline code A piece of code that invokes a signal handler. The signal-trampoline code contains instructions that set up parameters for calling a signal handler, perform the actual call to the signal handler, and, on return, perform a *sigreturn* system call to reset kernel state and resume execution of the process after the signal is handled.

silly-window syndrome A condition observed in window-based flow-control schemes in which a receiver sends several small (i.e., silly) window allocations rather than waiting for a reasonable-size window to become available.

single indirect block See *indirect block.*

sleep queue The queue of those threads that are blocked awaiting a long-term event such as completion of a disk read. They cannot run until the event has occurred. The name is derived from the *sleep*() routine that places threads on this queue. See also *idle queue; run queue; turnstile queue.*

sliding-window scheme A flow-control scheme in which the receiver limits the number of data that it is willing to receive. This limit is expressed as a contiguous range of sequence numbers termed the *receive window.* It is periodically communicated to the sender, who is expected to transmit only those data that are within the window. As data are received and acknowledged, the window slides forward in the sequence space. See also *receive window; send window; sequence space.*

small-packet avoidance In networking, avoiding the transmission of a packet so small that its transmission would be inefficient.

SMP See *symmetric multiprocessing*.

snapshot A filesystem snapshot is a frozen image of a filesystem at a given instant in time.

socket In the FreeBSD interprocess-communication model, an endpoint of communication. Also, the data structure that implements the socket abstraction and the system call that creates a socket.

socket address structure A generic structure for holding addresses for a socket. Many interprocess communication routines, such as *connect*() and *bind*(), need to know the network addresses of the communicating endpoints and require that a socket address structure be passed as a parameter.

soft limit A limit that may be temporarily exceeded, or exceeded a limited number of times. A soft limit is typically used with a hard limit. See also *hard limit*.

soft link See *symbolic link*.

soft updates A technique to maintain filesystem consistency. It uses delayed writes for metadata changes, tracks dependencies between updates, and enforces these dependencies at write-back time. Despite allowing blocks to be written in any order, applications always see the most current copies of metadata blocks, and the disk always sees copies that are consistent with its other contents.

software interrupt A software-initiated interrupt. It is requested with an asynchronous system trap.

software-interrupt thread A thread that is set running in response to a software interrupt. In FreeBSD, input processing for each transport-layer communication protocol is embodied in a software-interrupt thread.

special file See *device special file*.

SPI See *security-parameter index*.

spin mutex A spin mutex will not relinquish the CPU when it cannot immediately get the requested lock, but it will loop, waiting for the mutex to be released by another CPU.

stack An area of memory set aside for temporary storage or for procedure and interrupt-service linkages. A stack uses the last-in, first-out (LIFO) concept. On most architectures, the stack grows from high memory addresses to low memory addresses. As items are added to (pushed onto) the stack, the stack pointer decrements; as items are retrieved from (popped off) the stack, the stack pointer increments.

stack segment A segment that holds a stack. See also *bss segment; data segment; text segment*.

stale translation A translation or mapping that was previously true, but is no longer valid. For example, on machines that have a translation lookaside buffer, if a page-table entry in memory is changed to alter the mapping, any address translation for that page present in the translation lookaside buffer must be flushed to avoid a stale translation.

standalone device driver A device driver that is used in a standalone program. A standalone device driver usually differs from a device driver used in an operating system in that it does not have interrupt services, memory management, or full support for virtual-memory mapping. In the FreeBSD standalone I/O library, for example, a standalone device driver polls a device to decide when an operation has completed. It is also responsible for setting up its own memory mapping when doing transfers between the device and main memory.

standalone I/O library A library of software that is used in writing standalone programs. This library includes standalone device drivers that are used to perform I/O.

standalone program A program that can run without the support of an operating system.

standard error The I/O stream on which error messages are conventionally placed. This stream is usually associated with descriptor 2 in a process.

standard input The I/O stream on which input is conventionally received. This stream is usually associated with descriptor 0 in a process.

standard output The I/O stream to which output is conventionally directed. This stream is usually associated with descriptor 1 in a process.

start routine A device-driver routine that is responsible for starting a device operation after the system has acquired all the resources that are required for the operation.

stateless server A server that does not need to maintain any information about which clients it is serving or which data have been passed to them. Every request that is received by such a server must be completely self-contained, providing all information needed to fulfill it.

sticky bit The bit in an inode representing a directory that shows that an unprivileged user may not delete or rename files of other users in that directory. The sticky bit may be set by any user on a directory that the user owns or for which she has appropriate permissions. Historically, it was the bit in an inode that indicated that the text segment of the program was to be shared and kept memory or swap-space resident because of expected future use. That bit is no longer needed for this use because the virtual-memory system tracks recently used executables.

stream socket A type of socket that models a reliable, connection-based byte stream that can support out-of-band data transmission.

stream transmission control protocol (SCTP) A connection-oriented transport protocol used in the Internet. SCTP supports both stream and sequenced-packet styles of communication.

superblock A data structure in the on-disk filesystem that specifies the basic parameters of the filesystem.

superpages A capability of most hardware to allow for multiple page sizes. Larger page sizes are used to reduce pressure on the TLB. The page sizes available are dependent on the architecture. Common sizes in addition to the standard 4-Kbyte pages are 8-Kbyte, 64-Kbyte, 512-Kbyte, 2-Mbyte, and 4-Mbyte pages. See also *translation lookaside buffer*.

superuser The user whose UID is 0. Processes owned by the superuser are granted special privileges by UNIX. The superuser's login name is usually *root*. See also *privilege*.

swap area A region on secondary storage that is used for swapping and paging.

swap device A device on which a swap area resides.

swapper In FreeBSD, the name of the kernel process that implements the swapping portion of the memory-management facilities. Historically, the swapper is process 0. See also *pageout daemon*.

swapping A memory-management algorithm in which entire processes are moved to and from secondary storage when main memory is in short supply.

swap space See *swap area*.

symbolic link A file whose contents are interpreted as a pathname when it is supplied as a component of a pathname. Also called a *soft link*. See also *hard link*.

symmetric cryptography A cryptographic system that uses the same key to encrypt data as it does to decrypt data, sometimes referred to as secret key cryptography. See also *asymmetric cryptography*.

symmetric multiprocessing (SMP) A multiprocessor consists of two or more CPUs connected to a common main memory. Symmetric multiprocessing describes a kernel that can run simultaneously on all the CPUs at the same time. See also *nonuniform memory access*.

synchronous Synchronized with the currently running process. For example, in UNIX, all I/O operations appear to be synchronous: The *read* and *write* system calls do not return until the operation has been completed. (For a *write*, however, the data may not really be written to their final destination until some time later—for example, in writing to a disk file.)

system activity An entry into the kernel. System activities can be categorized according to the event or action that initiates them: system calls, hardware interrupts, hardware traps, and software-initiated traps or interrupts.

system call In operating systems, a request to the system for service; also called a system service request.

system clock The device that maintains the system's notion of time of day. On most systems, this device is an interval timer that periodically interrupts the CPU. The system uses these interrupts to maintain the current time of day and to do periodic functions such as thread scheduling.

system mode See *kernel mode*.

tag queueing Helps to coordinate I/O operations with a disk driver. Each request passed to the disk driver is assigned a unique numeric tag. After each request is finished, the tag of the completed request is returned as part of the completion interrupt. The disk driver gains efficiency by being able to reorder its I/O requests optimally. The client can ensure integrity by knowing when write requests have been saved to stable storage.

tags An extensible system for adding arbitrary data to an mbuf or mbuf cluster to communicate information between different modules in the network stack without having to modify the packet data.

TCB See *trusted computing base.*

TCP See *transmission control protocol.*

termios structure The structure used to describe terminal state. Terminal state includes special characters, such as the erase, kill, and word-erase characters; modes of operation, such as canonical or noncanonical; and hardware serial-line parameters, such as parity and baud rate.

text segment The segment of a program that holds machine instructions. The system usually makes a program's text segment read-only and shareable by multiple processes when the program image is loaded into memory. See also *bss segment; data segment; stack segment.*

thrashing A condition where requested memory utilization far exceeds the memory availability. When a machine is thrashing, it usually spends more time doing system-related tasks than executing application code in user mode.

thread The unit of execution of a process. A thread requires an address space and other resources, but it can share many of those resources with other threads. Threads sharing an address space and other resources are scheduled independently and can all do system calls simultaneously.

thread state block (TSB) A data structure used to hold thread context. The hardware-defined TSB contains the hardware portion of this context. The software TSB contains the software portion and is located in memory immediately after the hardware TSB.

thread structure A data structure maintained by the kernel for each active thread in the system. It contains the stack used when the thread is running in the kernel. Unlike the process structure, the thread structure can be moved to secondary storage if the process is swapped out. See also *process structure.*

three-way handshake A set of three messages used by a communication protocol, such as TCP, to initiate a reliable connection. Three messages is the minimum number necessary to ensure that both endpoints are aware of the connection process completing successfully.

tick An interrupt by the system clock.

time quantum In a timesharing environment, the period of time that the process scheduler gives a process to run before it preempts that process so that another process can execute. Also called a *time slice.*

timer backoff The rate at which a timer value is increased. For example, in TCP, the value of the retransmit timer is determined by a table of multipliers that provide a near-exponential increase in timeout values.

time slice See *time quantum.*

time-stable identifier An identifier that refers uniquely to some entity both while it exists and for a long time after it is deleted. A time-stable identifier allows a system to remember an identity across transient failures and to detect and report errors for attempts to access deleted entities.

TLB See *translation lookaside buffer.*

top half With regard to system operation, the routines in the kernel that are invoked synchronously as a result of a system call or trap. These routines depend on per-process state and can block by calling *sleep*(). See also *bottom half.*

trace trap A trap used by the system to implement single-stepping in program debuggers. On architectures that provide trace-bit support, the kernel sets the hardware-defined trace bit in the context of the thread being debugged and places the thread on the run queue. When the thread next runs, the trace bit causes a trap to be generated after the thread executes one instruction. This trap is fielded by the kernel, which stops the thread and returns control to the debugging process.

track In computer systems, the sectors of a disk that are accessible by one head at one of its seek positions.

track cache When the kernel is reading from a disk, memory associated with the disk that holds the data passing under the disk heads regardless of whether they have been requested explicitly. When the kernel is writing to a disk, memory associated with the disk in which data are stored until the disk heads reach the correct position for writing them.

translation lookaside buffer (TLB) A processor cache containing translations for recently used virtual addresses.

transmission control protocol (TCP) A connection-oriented transport protocol used in the Internet. TCP provides for the reliable transfer of data, as well as for the out-of-band indication of urgent data.

transport layer The layer of software in the network subsystem that is responsible for moving data between two sockets. Depending on the type of transport protocol used, the data may be delivered as a sequenced, in-order stream or as an unordered set of individual messages. See also *transmission control protocol; user datagram protocol.*

transport mode One of two modes used for secure communications in IPSec. In transport mode, only the payload of a packet is protected, whereas the network-layer protocol header is left exposed. See also *tunnel mode.*

triple indirect block See *indirect block.*

trusted computing base (TCB) The smallest subset of a system that must be secure in order for the system as a whole to be secure. In FreeBSD, this includes the kernel, key system libraries, applications running as root, and system configuration files and startup scripts.

TSB See *thread state block.*

tunnel mode One of two modes used for secure communication in IPSec. In tunnel mode, the packet to be secured is completely contained within another packet that carries the inner packet between two endpoints. The endpoints are the boundaries of the tunnel. See also *transport mode.*

turnstile Data structure used to manage threads awaiting a short-term event such as acquiring a mutex. See also *turnstile queue.*

turnstile queue The queue of those threads that are blocked awaiting a short-term event such as acquiring a mutex. They may propagate their priority to the mutex holder to speed their release of it. See also *idle queue; run queue; sleep queue.*

2MSL timer A timer used by the TCP protocol during connection shutdown. The name refers to the fact that the timer is set for twice the maximum time that a segment may exist in the network. This value is chosen to ensure that future connections will not mistakenly accept late messages from an older connection. See also *maximum segment lifetime.*

type-ahead Transmission of data to a system, usually by a user typing at a keyboard, before the data are requested by a process.

uberblock An on-disk data structure in the Zettabyte filesystem that references the root of the tree of blocks representing the storage pool.

UDP See *user datagram protocol.*

UID See *user identifier.*

uio A data structure used by the system to describe an I/O operation. This structure contains an array of *iovec* structures; the file offset at which the operation should start; the sum of the lengths of the I/O vectors; a flag showing whether the operation is a read or a write; and a flag showing whether the source and destination are both in the kernel's address space or whether the source and destination are split between user and kernel address spaces. See also *iovec.*

update dependency The required ordering of related updates to separate metadata structures to ensure recoverability in the presence of unpredictable failures. An update that must be done later has an update dependency on an earlier update because it cannot be done until the earlier update is committed to stable storage. See also *metadata.*

urgent data In TCP, data that are marked for urgent delivery.

user credential A structure that identifies a user. It contains the real, effective, and saved user and group identifiers. See also *real user identifier; real group identifier; effective user identifier; effective group identifier; saved UID; saved GID.* See also *process credential.*

user datagram protocol (UDP) A simple, unreliable datagram protocol used in the Internet protocols. UDP provide peer-to-peer, multicast and broadcast addressing, and optional data checksums. A single version of UDP works the same way on top of both IPv4 and IPv6.

user identifier (UID) A nonnegative integer that identifies a user uniquely. UIDs are used in the access-control facilities provided by the filesystem. See also *credential; effective user identifier; real user identifier; saved user identifier; set-user-identifier program.*

user mode The least-privileged processor-access mode. User processes run in user mode. See also *kernel mode.*

user-request routine A set of routines provided by each communication protocol that directly supports a socket (a protocol that indirectly supports a socket is layered underneath a protocol that directly supports a socket). These routines serve as the main interface between the layer of software that implements sockets and the communication protocol. The interprocess-communication facilities make calls to the user-request routines for most socket-related system calls. See also *connect request; control request; listen request; sense request.*

virtual address An address that references a location in a *virtual address space.*

virtual-address aliasing Two or more processes mapping the same physical page at different virtual addresses. When using an inverted page table, there can only be one virtual address mapping any given physical page at any one time. Here, the kernel must invalidate the page-table entry for the aliased page whenever it switches between the processes with the conflicting virtual addresses for that page. See also *reverse-mapped page table.*

virtual address space A contiguous range of virtual-memory locations.

virtual machine A machine whose architecture is emulated in software. The emulation may be at either the hardware level or at the operating-system level.

virtual memory A facility whereby the effective range of addressable memory locations provided to a process is independent of the size of main memory; that is, the virtual address space of a process is independent of the physical address space of the CPU.

virtual-memory object A kernel data structure that represents a repository of data—for example, a file. An object contains a pager to get and put the data from and to secondary storage, and a list of physical pages that cache pieces of the repository in memory.

virtual private network (VPN) A network that is layered on top of, or tunneled through, the public Internet using encrypted links.

vnode An extensible object-oriented interface containing generic information about a file. Each active file in the system is represented by a vnode, plus filesystem-specific information associated with the vnode by the filesystem containing the file. The kernel maintains a single systemwide table of vnodes that is always resident in main memory. Inactive entries in the table are reused on a least-recently-used basis.

VPN See *virtual private network.*

wait The system call that waits for the termination of a descendant process.

wait channel A value used to identify an event for which a thread is waiting. In most situations, a wait channel is defined as the address of a data structure related to the event for which a thread is waiting. For example, if a thread is waiting for the completion of a disk read, the wait channel is specified as the address of the buffer data structure supplied to the disk I/O system.

wildcard route A route that is used if there is no explicit route to a destination.

window probe In TCP, a message that is transmitted when data are queued for transmission, the send window is too small for TCP to bother sending data, and no message containing an update for the send window has been received in a long time. A window-probe message contains a single byte of data.

wired page Memory that is not subject to replacement by the pageout daemon. A nonpageable range of virtual addresses has physical memory assigned when the addresses are allocated. Wired pages must never cause a page fault that might result in a blocking operation. Wired pages are typically used in the kernel's address space.

word-erase character The character that is recognized by the terminal handler in canonical mode to mean "delete the most recently typed word on this terminal." By default, preceding whitespace and then a maximal sequence of nonwhitespace characters are erased. Alternatively, an alternate erase algorithm tuned to deleting pathname components may be specified. Each terminal session can have a different word-erase character, and the user can change that character at any time with a *tcsetattr* system call. The terminal handler does not recognize the word-erase character on terminals that are in noncanonical mode. See also *erase character; kill character*.

working directory See *current working directory*.

working set The set of pages in a process's virtual address space to which memory references have been made over the most recent few seconds. Most processes exhibit some locality of reference, and the size of their working set is typically less than one-half of their total virtual-memory size.

znode See *dnode*.

zombie process A process that has terminated but whose exit status has not yet been received by its parent process (or by **init**).

Index

C

D

E

F

H

I

J

K

M

N

Q

R

S

T

U

V

W

FreeBSD Kernel Internals on Video

The course is based on this book and provides a firm background of the FreeBSD kernel. It covers all the topics in this book. In addition, it covers other related topics including performance measurement, system tuning, and crash dump analysis. The class consists of fifteen lectures on the FreeBSD kernel that align with the book chapters. There are assigned readings to be completed before viewing each lecture. The first thirteen lectures have a set of exercises to be done after each video is viewed. Follow-up comments on the exercises are provided at the beginning of the lecture following the one in which they are assigned.

The planned syllabus for the the course is as follows:

1. Introduction: kernel terminology and basic kernel services
2. Processes: process structure and process management
3. Kernel-resource management: scheduling and signals
4. Security: security framework and policies, Capsicum, and jails
5. Virtual memory: virtual-memory management, paging, and swapping
6. Introduction to I/O: multiplexing I/O, support for multiple filesystems, the block I/O system (buffer cache), and stackable filesystems
7. Kernel I/O structure: special files, pseudo-terminal handling, autoconfiguration strategy, structure of a disk device driver, and machine virtualization
8. Local filesystem implementation: fast filesystem (FFS)
9. Local filesystem implementation: zettabyte filesystem (ZFS)
10. Remote filesystem implementation: network filesystem (NFS)
11. Interprocess communication: concepts and terminology, basic IPC services, system layers and interfaces, and code review of a simple application that demonstrates use of the IPC and network facilities
12. Network layer: IPv4 and IPv6 protocols, firewalls, and routing
13. Transport layer: TCP and SCTP
14. System startup: boot loaders, kernel startup, and system launch
15. System tuning: performance measurement, system tuning, and crash dump analysis

In addition to the fifteen lecture videos, you also receive a copy of the course notes containing copies of all the overhead slides used in the course, a set of weekly readings from this textbook, thirteen sets of exercises (along with answers), and a set of papers that provide supplemental reading to the text.

The course video will be produced in 2015. Until then, a course based on the first edition of this book can be purchased. Tiered pricing is available for companies, individuals, and students. On-site courses can be arranged. For up-to-date information on course availability and pricing or to place an order, see the Web page at

http://www.mckusick.com/courses/

Advanced FreeBSD Course on Video

This course provides an in-depth study of the source code of the FreeBSD kernel. It is aimed at users who already have a good understanding of the algorithms used in the FreeBSD kernel and want to learn the details of the algorithm's implementation. Students are expected to have either taken a FreeBSD Kernel Internals class (such as the one described on the previous page) or to have thoroughly read and understood this book. They are also expected to have a complete background in reading and programming in the C programming language. Students will not need to prove relationship with a source license holder, as the course is based on the non-proprietary kernel sources released by the FreeBSD project.

The class consists of fifteen lectures on the FreeBSD kernel source code. The lecture topics are:

1. Organization, overview of source layout
2. Kernel header files
3. System calls and file opening
4. Pathname translation and file creation
5. Vnode interface mechanics, writing to a local file
6. Opening, using, and closing locally connected sockets
7. User datagram protocol and routing
8. TCP algorithms
9. Fork, exit, and exec
10. Signal generation and delivery, scheduling
11. Virtual memory header files, file mapping
12. Page fault service, pageout processing
13. NFS client and server operation
14. Multiplexing with select, system startup
15. Special topics: ZFS filesystem

In addition to the fifteen lecture videos, you also receive a CD-ROM with a copy of the FreeBSD kernel source covered in the lectures and a copy of the lecture notes.

The course video will be produced in 2016. Until then a course based on FreeBSD 9.0 can be purchased. Tiered pricing is available for companies, individuals, and students. For up-to-date information on course availability and pricing or to place an order, see the Web page at

http://www.mckusick.com/courses/

FreeBSD Networking from the Bottom Up on Video

This course describes the FreeBSD networking stack. It is made up of a series of lectures derived from tutorials given by George Neville-Neil.

The class currently consists of four lectures, though additional lectures are being developed. The current lecture topics are:

1. Device Drivers: how to write and maintain network drivers in FreeBSD. By way of example it uses the Intel Gigabit Ethernet driver (*igb*). The lecture covers the basic data structures and APIs necessary to implement a network driver in FreeBSD. It is specific enough that given a device and a manual, you should be able to develop a working driver on your own.
2. The IPv6 Stack: an in-depth discussion and code walk-through of version 6 of the IP protocols, describing and dissecting the paths that packets take from the driver layer up to the socket layer of the network stack. The lecture covers the four paths packets travel through the network stack: reception, transmission, forwarding, and error handling.
3. Routing: packet forwarding and routing subsystems in FreeBSD. The routing and forwarding code are the glue that keeps the networking stack together, connecting the network protocols, such as IPv4 and IPv6, to their underlying data link layers and making sure that packets are sent to the correct next hop in the network. Topics in the lecture include the Routing Information Base (RIB), Forwarding Information Base (FIB), and the systems that interact with them. Also covered are routing sockets and the RIB/FIB APIs, the address-resolution protocol (ARP), Neighbor Discovery (ND6), the Common Address Redundancy Protocol (CARP), the IP firewall and traffic shaper control program (*ipfw*), and the packet filter interface (*pfil*).
4. Packet Processing Frameworks: The FreeBSD Kernel has several different packet processing frameworks—software that is meant to transform packets but which are not traditionally considered to be network protocols. It is these packet processing frameworks that are often the basis for new products built with FreeBSD. This lecture covers all of the packet processing frameworks, including the Berkeley Packet Filter (BPF), IP Firewall (IPFW), Dummynet, Packet Filter (PF), Netgraph, and netmap. It discusses the appropriate use of each framework and takes a walk through the relevant sections of each framework. Working examples of extensions to each framework are given so that students can see how to build new systems with and around the frameworks that are present in the kernel.

Each lecture may be purchased separately and comes with a copy of its course notes. Tiered pricing is available for companies, individuals, and students. For up-to-date information on course availability and pricing or to place an order, see the Web page at

http://www.mckusick.com/courses/

CSRG Archive CD-ROMs

Thanks to the efforts of the volunteers of the "UNIX Heritage Society" (see http://www.tuhs.org) and the willingness of Caldera to release 32/V under an open source license (see http://www.mckusick.com/csrg/calder-lic.pdf), it is now possible to make the full source archives of the University of California at Berkeley's Computer Systems Research Group (CSRG) available.

The archive contains four CD-ROMs with the following content:

CD-ROM #1—Berkeley Systems 1978–1986

1bsd	2.9pucc	4.1.snap	4.2buglist
2.10	2bsd	4.1a	4.3
2.79	3bsd	4.1c.1	VM.snapshot.1
2.8	4.0	4.1c.2	pascal.2.0
2.9	4.1	4.2	pascal.2.10

CD-ROM #2—Berkeley Systems 1987–1993

4.3reno	4.4BSD-Lite1	net.1
4.3tahoe	VM.snapshot.2	net.2

CD-ROM #3—Final Berkeley Releases

4.4	4.4BSD-Lite2

CD-ROM #4—Final /usr/src including SCCS files

Contrib	admin	games	local	sys
Makefile	bin	include	old	usr.bin
README	contrib	lib	sbin	usr.sbin
SCCS	etc	libexec	share	

The University of California at Berkeley wants you to know that these CD-ROMs contain software developed by the University of California at Berkeley and its many contributors.

The CD-ROMs are produced using standard pressing technology, *not* with write-once CD-R technology. Thus, they are expected to have a 100-year lifetime rather than the 10–20 years expected of CD-R disks. The CDs are sold only in complete sets; they are not available individually. The price for the 4-CD set is $99. The archive can be ordered from

http://www.mckusick.com/csrg/

The compilation of this archive is copyright © 1998 by Marshall Kirk McKusick. You may freely redistribute it to anyone else. However, I appreciate you buying your own copy to help cover the costs that I incurred in producing the archive.

History of UNIX at Berkeley

Learn the history of the BSD (Berkeley Software Distributions) from one of the key developers who brings the history to life, complete with anecdotes and interesting footnotes to the historical narrative.

Part I is titled "Twenty Years of Berkeley UNIX: From AT&T-Owned to Freely Redistributable." The history of UNIX development at Berkeley has been recounted in detail by Marshall Kirk McKusick in his chapter in the O'Reilly book Open Sources: *Voices from the Open Source Revolution* and is now recounted in part one of this video. It begins with the start of the BSD community at the University of California at Berkeley in the late 1970s. It relates the triumphs and defeats of the project and its releases during its heydays in the 1980s. It concludes with the tumultuous lawsuit ultimately settled in Berkeley's favor, which allowed the final release in 1992 of 4.4BSD-Lite, an open-source version of BSD.

Part II is titled "Building and Running An Open-Source Community: The FreeBSD Project." It tells the story of the independent development by the FreeBSD project starting from the open-source release from Berkeley. The FreeBSD project patterned its initial community structure on the development structure built up at Berkeley. It evolved and expanded that structure to create a self-organizing project that supports an ever growing and changing group of developers around the world. This part concludes with a description of the roles played by the thousands of volunteer developers that make up the FreeBSD Project of today.

Dr. Marshall Kirk McKusick's work with UNIX and BSD development spans over thirty years. It begins with his first paper on the implementation of Berkeley Pascal in 1979, goes on to his pioneering work in the eighties on the BSD Fast File System, the BSD virtual memory system, and the final release of 4.4BSD-Lite from the University of California Berkeley Computer Systems Research Group. Since 1993, he has been working on FreeBSD, adding soft updates, snapshots, and the second-generation Fast Filesystem to the system. A key figure in UNIX and BSD development, his experiences chronicle not only the innovative technical achievements, but also the interesting personalities and philosophical debates in UNIX since its inception in 1970.

The price for the video is $19.95. The video can be ordered from

http://www.mckusick.com/history/

Teaching a Course Using This Book

The authors have put together course material suitable for both undergraduate and graduate-level teaching using this book. An example course outline and details on obtaining the materials for your own course follow.

Systems research refers to the study of a broad range of behaviors arising from complex system design, including:

- low-level operating systems;
- resource sharing and scheduling;
- interactions between hardware and software;
- network-protocol design and implementation;
- separation of mutually distrusting parties on a common platform; and
- control of distributed-system behaviors such as concurrency and data replication.

This course:

- teaches systems-analysis methodology and practice through tracing and performance profiling experiments;
- exposes students to real-world systems artifacts such as operating-systems schedulers and network stacks, and considers their hardware-software interactions with CPUs and network-interface cards;
- develops scientific writing skills through laboratory-report exercises; and
- assigns a selection of original research papers in these areas to gain insight into potential research topics and approaches.

The teaching style blends lectures and hands-on labs that teach methodology, design principles, and practical skills. Students are taught about (and assessed via) a series of lab-report-style assignments based on in- and out-of-classroom practical work. The systems studied are real, and all wires will be live.

The materials for teaching this and other courses are available at no charge at

http://www.teachbsd.com